Water Forum '86:
World Water Issues in Evolution
Volume 1

Proceedings of the Conference sponsored by the
Hydraulics Division
Irrigation and Drainage Division
Environmental Engineering Division
Water Resources Planning and Management Division
Waterway, Port, Coastal and Ocean Division

The Committee on Hydropower Development of the Energy Division
and the Urban Water Resources Research Council of
   the Technical Council of Research
of the American Society of Civil Engineers

Host
Los Angeles Section, ASCE

Steering Committee
   Frederick L. Hotes, Chairman
   Danny L. King, Vice Chairman (Hydraulics)
   Robert H. Born (Irrigation and Drainage)
   Arthur E. Bruington (Los Angeles Section)
   Lamont W. Curtis, Jr. (Environmental Engineering)
   J. Randall Hanchey (Water Resources Planning & Management)
   Daniel Muslin (Waterway, Port, Coastal & Ocean)

Technical Program Committee
   Danny L. King, Chairman
   George R. Baumli (Irrigation & Drainage)
   William J. Brick (Hydraulics)
   Robert M. Clark (Environmental Engineering)
   Wayne G. Durough (Waterway, Port, Coastal & Ocean)
   Mohammad Karamouz (Water Resources Planning & Management)

Hyatt Regency Hotel
Long Beach, California
August 4-6, 1986

Edited by
Mohammad Karamouz, Polytechnic University, Brooklyn, New York
George R. Baumli, International Boundary and Water
   Commission, El Paso, Texas
William J. Brick, U.S. Army Engineer District,
   San Francisco, California

Published by the
American Society of Civil Engineers
345 East 47th Street
New York, New York 10017-2398

The Society is not responsible for any statements
made or opinions expressed in its publications.

PREFACE

The proceedings for WATER FORUM '86 present the results of the second conference in which the water-oriented divisions of the American Society of Civil Engineers have combined forces in a state-of-the-art forum of engineers, academics and practitioners from all over the world. The forum followed two years of planning by conference steering and program committees, members of ASCE Los Angeles Section, and staff of ASCE Headquarters in New York. More than 280 papers have been contributed to this conference. The ASCE technical water divisions of Hydraulics, Irrigation and Drainage, Environmental Engineering, Water Resources Planning and Management, and Waterways, Port, Coastal and Ocean, assisted by the Urban Water Resources Research Council and the Energy/Hydropower Division, organized the technical program. Cooperating organizations included the ASCE Mexico Section, Canadian Society for Civil Engineers, Chinese Institute of Civil and Hydraulic Engineering, Institute of Civil Engineers—Great Britain, Institution of Professional Engineers—New Zealand, Japan Society of Civil Engineers and the U.S. Committee on Irrigation and Drainage.

The conference was held at the Hyatt Regency Hotel in Long Beach, California, August 4–6, 1986. The conference format utilized 71 sessions and 8 concurrent tracks. The papers in these volumes are in the order of their presentation at the conference. Each of the papers has been reviewed and accepted for publication by the proceedings editors. All papers are eligible for discussion in the related ASCE Journals and all papers are eligible for ASCE awards.

The theme of WATER FORUM '86 was "World Water Issues in Evolution". These issues follow the recognition in our time that water must be valued as a unique natural resource. The need to efficiently use, protect, manage, and test surface and groundwater has been emphasized in papers by participants from Shanghai to Los Angeles, from Queensland to Glasgow, and from many other areas in the world. The participants of this conference have addressed many problems that people all over the world face and are working to find solutions for. We gathered here in Long Beach to renew our determination to further enhance man's ability to control and protect our natural water resources.

The Conference organizors extend their sincere appreciation to all participants, authors, moderators and to the Local Arrangements Committee, whose efforts insured the success of the Conference.

Mohammad Karamouz
Polytechnic University
Brooklyn, New York

CONTENTS

SESSION 1

Chairman: William D. Anderson

Plenary Session. . . . . *

SESSION 2, WATER POLICY TODAY

Chairman: Theodore M. Schad

A Panel Discussion of Where We Are in The Evolution
of U.S. Water Resources Policy and How Our Experience
Is Applicable to World Water Problems . . . . *

SESSION 3A, ANALYSIS OF DEBRIS, AVALANCHES, AND MUDFLOWS (I)

Chairman: James E. Slosson

Hydrodynamics of Earth Fill Dam Breach Erosion
   Vijay P. Singh, Panagiotis D. Scarlatos, John G. Collins and
   Mark R. Jourdan 1
Viscoplastic Fluid Model for Debris Flow Routing
   Cheng-lung Chen 10
Engineering Methodology for Delineating-Debris Flow Hazards in Los Angeles County
   Sree Kumar. 19
Landslide-Generated Wave Studies
   Clifford A. Pugh and Wen-Li Chiang 27

SESSION 3B, EFFECT OF CLIMATE CHANGE ON WATER RESOURCES

Chairman: Richard H. French

Sea Level Rise and Coastal Stormwater Drainage
   Chin Y. Kuo. 35
Response of Great Salt Lake to Climate Variability
   Paul A. Kay and Henry F. Diaz 43
Estimating Climate Change From Hydrologic Response
   Martin Mifflin and Jay Quade 51
Issues on Specifying Climate Forcing of Variability
   Paul A. Kay 59

*Manuscript not available at time of printing

SESSION 3C, HYDROPOWER PLANNING (I)

Chairman: Edgar T. Moore

Hydroelectric Program For Development In Mexico
Jose Antonio Maza.. 66
Cherokee Nation Power Development at a Corps Lock and Dam
Owen W. Scott.. 73
Future Hydrothermal Power of the United States
Nazeer Ahmed 81
Remote Sensing to Assess Effects of Hydroelectric Development
Stewart K. Sears, Tracey J. Ellis and David B. White.......................... 89

SESSION 3D, GROUND WATER MANAGEMENT (I)

Chairperson: Helen Joyce Peters

Saltwater Intrusion in a Highly Transmissive Unconfined Aquifer
Bradley G. Waller 97
Seawater Intrusion in Salinas Valley, California
James S. Jenks, Gerald E. Snow and Philip L. Wagner........................ 105
Studies of Long-Term Water Losses
Tiao J. Chang... 113
Subsidence by Rising and Fluctuating Ground Water
Nikola P. Prokopovich.. 121

SESSION 3E, EVOLUTION OF AGRICULTURAL DRAINAGE IN THE 1980's, (I)

Chairman: William R. Johnston

Agricultural Drainage Policy in the United States Department of Agriculture
Walter J. Ochs 129
Deferred Drainage—Prudent Policy or Tactical Folly?
Jack N. Christopher and B. K. Cummins 134
The Local Perspective on Agricultural Drainage
Stephen K. Hall 143
National Perspectives and Policy on Nonpoint Sources of Water Pollution
Carl F. Myers... 152

SESSION 3F, EXPERT SYSTEM AND ARTIFICIAL INTELLIGENCE IN WATER RESOURCES MANAGEMENT

Chairman: Mark H. Houck

An Integrated Conceptual Expert System For Flood and Water Pollution Management
William James and Alan Dunn.. 158
Intelligence Central Database System for Synchronized Distributed Processing of
Large Hydrologic Packages in Local Area Networks
Ali Unal and William James... 166

An Expert System for Snowmelt Runoff Modeling and Forecasting
 E. T. Engman, A. Rango and J. Martinec 174
Incorporating Judgement Into An Optimization Model of a Wastewater
Treatment System
 James J. Geselbracht, E. Downey Brill, Jr. and John T. Pfeffer 181
Expert Systems in Reservoir Management and Planning
 Roozbeh Kangari and Shahrokh Rouhani.................................... 187
Expert Pattern Recognition For Pollution Source Identification
 Bithin Datta and Richard C. Peralta.. 195

SESSION 4A, ANALYSIS OF DEBRIS, AVALANCHES, AND MUDFLOWS (II)

Chairman: Jeffrey B. Bradley

Flood Risk Below Steep Mountain Slopes
 L. Douglas James, David O. Pitcher, Scott Heefner, Brad R. Hall,
 Scott W. Paxman and Aaron Weston....................................... 203
Relative Landslide Susceptibility in Davis County, Utah—A Multivariate Approach
 Robert T. Pack and Loren R. Anderson 211
Debris Flows and Hyperconcentrated Streamflows
 Gerald F. Wieczorek 219
Generalized Methodology for Simulating Mudflows
 Robert C. MacArthur, David R. Schamber, Douglas L. Hamilton
 and Mary H. West... 227
Responsibility/Liability Related to Mudflows/Debris Flows
 J. E. Slosson, G. Shuirman and D. Yoakum 235

SESSION 4B, ALTERNATIVE WATER STORAGE MANAGEMENT STRATEGIES

Chairman: William P. Henry

Artificial Recharge For Managing The Great Salt Lake
 Calvin G. Clyde, Christopher J. Duffy and J. Paul Riley...................... 244
Recovery of Freshwater Stored In Saline Aquifers In Peninsular Florida
 Michael L. Merritt.. 251
Conjunctive Use and Managed Groundwater Recharge: Engineering and
Politics in Arid Lands
 Jonathon C. Goldman 261
America's National Forests, Our Ultimate Water Source
 Arne E. Rosquist, Jr... 269

SESSION 4C, HYDROPOWER PLANNING (II)

Chairman: Garith K. Grinnell

Small Hydro is Very Rarely Typical
 Stanley J. Hayes, W. R. Ivarson and V. J. Zipparro 277

Diamond Fork Hydroelectric Power Development
  Stephen J. Navin and Harvey L. Hutchinson 284
Hydropower On The Arkansas—A Non-Federal Development
  W. B. Smith and Curtis Q. Warner.. 294
Water Management of the Snowy Mountains Scheme, Australia
  Francis C. Millner 302

SESSION 4D, GROUND WATER MANAGEMENT & MODELING

Chairman: Marvin V. Damm

River Basin Network Model for Conjunctive Use of Surface and Ground Water
  John W. Labadie, Sanguan Patamatamkul and Rogelio C. Lazaro................ 310
Modeling an Alluvial Aquifer with Flood Irrigation
  Victor R. Hasfurther, Hilaire W. Peck and Steve A. Mizell.................... 320
Simultaneous Pumping from Layered Ground Water
  E. M. Laursen, S. A. A. Abed, E. Fukumori, A. Souissi and M. S. Petersen 328
Surface Water Analysis for Ground Water Simulation
  Terry L. Erlewine 336

SESSION 4E, EVOLUTION OF AGRICULTURAL DRAINAGE IN THE 1980's (II)

Chairman: Jack N. Christopher

Simple Removal and Recovery of Irrigation Drainage Salts
  George E. Wilson 344
Optimizing Drain Spacing and Depth Using Steady State Equations
  Jobaid Kabir and L. G. King... 352
Agricultural Drainage Water Treatment—Are Toxic Elements Useful?
  Rodney C. Squires and William R. Johnston 358
A GIS to Predict Non-Point Source Pollution Potential
  Wanada Baxter-Potter, Martha W. Gilliland and Michael P. Peterson.............. 366

SESSION 4F, WATER RESOURCES MODELLING USING DATABASE MANAGEMENT

Chairman: Daniel P. Loucks

Design for Compuer-Aided Water Resource Planning
  Bruce M. Chow, Sam C. White and Gary P. Rabalais........................ 374
Co-ordinated Microcomputer-based Rain Data Network and Modeling Environment
  Mark Stirrup and William James 382
Linking Database Management and Computer Models
  William F. Mancinelli 390
A Customized Database Management System for Watershed Modeling
  John C. Kaden.. 398

SESSION 5A, RESERVOIR AND AQUEDUCT SEDIMENT AND DESILTING

Chairman: Joseph B. Evelyn

An Evaluation of Sediment Resuspension Parameterizations
Keith W. Bedford 404
Gully Incision Prediction on Reclaimed Slopes
Steven R. Abt, John A. Falk, John D. Nelson and T. L. Johnson 412
Coupling Free Vortex Energy Dissipation with Sediment Control
George E. Wilson 420
Behavior of Sediment-Laden Plumes on Steep Slopes
Patrick J. Ryan.. 427

SESSION 5B, HYDROLOGY

Chairman: Constantine N. Papadakis

Stochastic Design of Wastewater Storage Ponds
Steven G. Buchberger and David R. Maidment............................. 435
Parameter Optimization of Dynamic Routing Models
D. L. Fread and J. M. Lewis.. 443
Performance of A Deterministic Storm Runoff Model
William C. Taggart, Charles L. Hardt, Terri L. Fead and Michael D. Vinson 451
Real-Time Precipitation-Snowmelt Model for the Monongahela River Basin
Daniel Hoggan, John C. Peters and Werner Loehlein 459

SESSION 5C, MAINTENANCE OF WATER INFRASTRUCTURE

Chairman: Thomas M. Walski

Making Water System Rehabilitation Decisions
Thomas M. Walski 467
Analysis of Freshwater Distribution System at the Long Beach Naval Complex
M. Michael Anderson 2181
Water Infrastructure Maintenance Needs—A Case Study
Arun K. Deb 475
The Rx for Relief from Equipment Failure
Lewis Debevec, Jr. and Thomas Smeal.................................... 484
Modernizing the Maintenance Function
James A. Noyes... 492

SESSION 5D, GROUND WATER CONTAMINATION INCLUDING FATE AND EFFECT—MONIORING AND TREATMENT (I)

Chairman: Gerald T. Orlob

An Experimental Study on the Effect of Wastewater Application in Dry Wells and
Its Impact on Ground Water
Reza M. Khanbilvardi 498

Investigating and Treating Chromium in Ground Water at a Wood Treater in California
  Wendy L. Cohen 506
Remedial Action Alternatives for Ground Water Contamination
  Jahan Tavangar, Les K. Lampe and Bruce W. Long........................... 514
Liquid Waste Pollution From a Sugar Cane Industry
  Anastasio Lopez Zavala... 524

SESSION 5E, PORT PLANNING, DEVELOPMENT, AND INLAND NAVIGATION**

Chairman: Lawrence L. Whiteneck

On the Ship's Waterways Passing through Bridges
  Kuniaki Shoji and Tomomi Wakao 530
Port Infrastructure Program in Mexico
  Luis F. Robledo and Jose San Martin 538

SESSION 5F, OPERATIONS MODELS FOR HYDROSYSTEMS

Chairman: William W-G Yeh

Central Arizona Project Startup
  Albert L. Graves and Robert S. Gooch...................................... 546
Applied Hydro Systems Operations Models
  Charles E. Abraham.. 552
Operations Models of the Columbia Reservoir System
  Gregory K. Delwiche... 557
California Water Project Operation
  Hossein Sabet and James Q. Coe... 565
Model to Maximize Release for Supplemental Generation in a Pump-Storage System
  Ricardo S. Pineda 573

SESSION 5G, INTERSTATE/INTRASTATE WATER TRANSFERS

Chairman: John W. Bird

Intrastate and Interstate Water Transfers
  Dean T. Massey... 582
Evolving Institutions for Water Transfer in the U.S.
  William E. Cox 590
Transferring Conserved Water
  D. A. Twogood 598
Interstate Agreements for Water Transfers
  John W. Bird 607

**This session was listed as session 7C in the program

SESSION 5H, REUSING TREATED WASTEWATER—
OPPORTUNITIES AND PROBLEMS

Chairman: James L. Thomas

Evaluation of Tertiary Wastewater Treatment Systems
Takashi Asano, William R. Kirkpatrick and Robert S. Jaques 612
Reusing Treated Wastewater for Irrigation of Raw-Eaten Vegetable Crops in
Monterey County, California
Bahman Sheikh, Robert C. Cooper and Robert S. Jaques...................... 620
Hydrologic Effects of Artificial Recharge Experiments with Reclaimed Water at
East Meadow, New York
Brian J. Schneider 628
Design Criteria for Mass Culturing Spirulina Algae
William M. Strachan 637

SESSION 6A, RESERVOIR AND AQUEDUCT SEDIMENT AND
DESILTING: EXAMPLES

Chairman: Howard H. Chang

Reservoir Sedimentation and Desilting in Taiwan
Chian Min Wu 645
A Proposed Desilting Reservoir System in Taiwan
Jing-San Hwang 653
Effect of African Drought on Water Resource Management in Egypt
Scot E. Smith and Keith W. Bedford 661
Sediment Penetration in Lakes asa Result of Dredged Material Disposal and
River Sediment Loads
Alaa El Zawahary and William James...................................... 667

SESSION 6B, RAINFALL RUNOFF AND FLOOD ROUTING

Chairman: Soroosh Sorooshian

Routing Comparison in Natural and Geometric Channels
Larry M. Younkin and William H. Merkel................................. 675
Rainfall-Loss Parameter Estimation for Illinois
Linda S. Weiss and Audrey L. Ishii 682
Remote Sensing Applications in the Model of Runoff Formation in Excess of Storage
Wenqiu Wei 690

SESSION 6C, HYDRAULICS AND HYDRAULIC STRUCTURES

Chairman: N. Randy Oswalt

Plunge Pool Energy Dissipators for Some Dams in Taiwan, ROC
Y. Cheng and R. L. Hsu 698
Air Slot In Tunnel Spillway of Feitsui Dam
C. L. Yen, Y. Cheng, R. L. Hsu and R. Y. Wang 706

Modeling of the Undular Jump for White Water Bypass
Mohammed A. Samad, John M. Pflaum, William C. Taggart and
Richard E. McLaughlin... 714
Toe Drain System—Barr and Milton Reservoirs, Co.
L. Stephen Schmidt.. 722
Scale Model Study Benefits Hydropower Project
Heinz G. Stefan, Karen L. C. Lindblom, Richard L. Voigt, Jr., Bruce Ainsworth
and Patrick Colgan.. 730

SESSION 6D, GROUND WATER CONTAMINATION INCLUDING
FATE AND EFFECT, MONITORING AND TREATMENT (II)

Chairman: Mohammad Karamouz

Design and Construction of TCE/PCE Removal Facilities
Shahnawaz Ahmad and Robert G. Berlien 738
Ground Water Quality Monitoring in the New York Metropolitan Area:
Statistical Alternatives
Mohammad Karamouz and Evangelos Paleologos 745

SESSION 6E, COASTAL EROSION AND SHORELINE PROTECTION

Chairman: Norman L. Arno

Estimating Probable Storm Damage On Barrier Islands
Andrew A. Dzurik, Bruce Stiftel and Anita Tallarico 754
Coastal Protection Guidelines, Orange County, CA
Craig H. Everts, Jerry Sterling, Floyd McLellen, Jim Miller and Don Cotner...... 763
Wave Height Distribution in the Coupled Harbor
Hong Sik Lee, Masafumi Kubo and Mitsuo Takezawa 771
Simplified Prediction of Storm Surge on an Open Coast Using a Microcomputer
Nenad Duplancic and Paul C. Rizzo 779

SESSION 6F, DEVELOPMENTS IN WATER RESOURCES OPERATIONS

Chairman: Duncan W. Wood

Corps of Engineers Automation of Real-Time Water Control Management
Ming T. Tseng and Earl E. Eiker 785
Application of a Stochastic Hydrology Model
Sushil K. Arora and George M. Barnes, Jr.................................. 791
Water Management of the Tenn-Tom Waterway
Edmund B. Burkett 799
Computational Enhancement to a Multidimensional Dynamic Programming Algorithm
Dennis Morrow and Bruce Loftis.. 806

SESSION 6G, LEGAL AND ENGINEERING ASPECTS OF WATER RIGHTS QUANTIFICATION

Chairman: Leonard Rice

Procedures in a Change of Water Rights
Ronald K. Blatchley 812
Factual Issues in Water Rights Changes
Leonard Rice 817

SESSION 6H, WATER REQUIREMENTS OF NATURAL VEGETATION

Chairman: Eldon L. Johns

Meadow E.T. in the Bear River Basin of Utah, Wyoming and Idaho
R. W. Hill, L. N. Allen, R. D. Burman and C. E. Brockway 823
Maximum and Actual ET from Grasses and Grass-Like Plants
R. D. Burman, L. O. Pochop 831
Water Requiremens for Range Plant Establishment
Gary W. Frasier.. 839
Phreatophyte Water Use Estimated by Eddy-Correlation Methods
Harold L. Weaver, E. P. Weeks, G. S. Campbell, D. I. Stannard and
B. D. Tanner 847
Water Use by Saltcedar in an Arid Environment
Lloyd W. Gay 855

SESSION 7A, SEDIMENT CONTROL IN CANALS

Chairman: Eugene F. Serr

Sedimentation Problems of the California Aqueduct
Jeanine Jones 863
Sedimentation Processes In Hydrosystems, Numerical-Empirical Modeling
Sam S. Y. Wang and Sergio E. Adeff 870
Sedimentation in the All-American Canal
J. P. Silva and D. A. Twogood.. 878
Sedimentation At Canal In-Line Structures
Robert I. Strand 885

SESSION 7B, FLOOD CONTROL AND STORMWATER MANAGEMENT

Chairman: John W. Labadie

Solving Stormwater Drainage Problems Through an Area Drainage Master
Study Program
Kebba Buckley... 890
Flood Reduction Efficiency of the Water-Management System in Dade County
(Miami), Florida
Bradley G. Waller 897
Emergency Flood Management Salt Lake City, Utah
Charles H. Call, Jr.. 903

Precipitation Analysis in Clark County, Nevada
  Virginia E. Bax, Les K. Lampe and Laurnal Gubler........................... 911
Stormwater Management in Kansas
  Bruce M. McEnroe 919

SESSION 7C, URBAN FLOOD CONTROL***

Chairman: Ronald L. Rossmiller

Design Storms for Urban Drainage
  UWRRC Design Storm Task Committee................................... 925
Characteristics of Intense Storms in Kansas
  Bruce M. McEnroe 933
Selecting a Stormwater Service Level for Urban Control
  Richard D. Gibney and Larry A. Roesner................................. 941
Use of Continuous Simulation Versus the Design Storm Concept for Water Quality
  Miguel A. Medina, Jr. 949
Outlet Structure Hydraulics
  Ronald L. Rossmiller... 958

SESSION 7D, ADVANCES IN PARAMETER ESTIMATION IN GROUNDWATER MODELING

Chairman: Miguel A. Mariño

Uncertainities in Groundwater Transport Modeling
  Eric W. Strecker, Wen-Sen Chu and Dennis P. Lettenmaier 966
Estimation and Inference in the Inverse Problem
  Hugo A. Loaiciga and Miguel A. Marinõo................................. 973
Mixed Solute Interactions in Groundwater Systems
  Christopher G. Uchrin, Mary Gay Heagler and Jack Katz 981

SESSION 7E, DREDGE MATERIAL DISPOSAL AND MARSH LAND DEVELOPMENT

Chairman: J. Edwin Glover

Dredge Spoil Storage Basin in the Coastal Waters Near Rotterdam—
Environmental and Coastal Engineering Aspects
  P. Vellinga, J. P. J. Nijssen, R. G. J. v. Orden and M. de Rooij 987
Land Renewal With Topsoil from Clyde Port Dredgings
  George Fleming, John Riddell and Paul Smith............................. 995
Dredged Material Disposal in the Lower Great Lakes
  Stephen M. Yaksich, John R. Adams and Richard P. Leonard 1003

***This session was listed as session 5E in the program

SESSION 7F, OPTIMIZATION OF WATER RESOURCES SYSTEMS

Chairman: Jared L. Cohon

A Robustness Constraint for the Analysis of Uncertainty
James G. Uber, E. Downey Brill, Jr. and John T. Pfeffer...................... 1011
An Optimization Approach for Locating Sediment Ponds in Stripmined Areas
Mohammad Karamouz and Reza M. Khanbilvardi............................ 1017
Optimization, Simulation and Multiobjective Analysis of Operating Rules for
Reservoir Systems
Ricardo Harboe.. 1026
Water Resources Systems Planning: Differential Dynamic Programming Models
LaDon Jones, Robert Willis and Brad A. Finney............................ 1033

SESSION 7G, WATER QUALITY

Chairman: John L. Grace, Jr.

Air-Water Oxygen Transfer at Spillways and Hydraulic Jumps
Alan J. Rindels and John S. Gulliver 1041
Improving Streamflow and Water Quality Below Dams
R. J. Ruane, C. E. Bohac, J. L. Davis, E. D. Harshbarger, R. M. Shane
and H. M. Goranflo... 1049
Gas Transfer and Secondary Currents in Open Channels
John S. Gulliver and Martin J. Halverson.................................. 1057
Oxygenation of Releases From Richard B. Russell Dam
James W. Gallagher, Jr. and Gary V. Mauldin 1065

SESSION 7H, OPERATIONS AND MAINTENANCE AND RELIABILITY ISSUES IN WASTE WATER TREATMENT

Chairman: Lewis A. Rossman

A Perspective on Performance Variability in Municipal Wastewater
Treatment Facilities
Lewis A. Rossman and John J. Convery.................................... 1073
Chlorination of Wastewater Treated by Overland Flow
T. J. Johnson and E. D. Schroeder 1081
The Reliability of Treatment Systems
Paul J. Ossenbruggen and Kenneth Constantine 1089
On-Site Microcomputer Control of a Combined Sewer Overflow Diversion Structure
William James and Mark Stirrup 1098
Computer-Aided Analysis of Treatment Plant Hydraulics
Peter J. Kolsky and Gary Friedman....................................... 1106

SESSION 8A, EROSION & SEDIMENT CONTROL IN IRRIGATION PROJECTS

Chairman: Charles E. Brockway

Water Erosion from Irrigation—An Overview
Paul K. Koluvek 1123

Effects of Erosion on Soil Productivity
  David L. Carter 1131
Erosion and Sedimentation Processes in Irrigation
  Thomas J. Trout and W. H. Neibling 1139
Management Practices for Erosion and Sediment Control in Irrigated Agriculture
  David L. Carter, C. E. Brockway, and K. K. Tanji 1147
Sediment and Erosion Control Implementation: An Overview
  Swayne F. Scott 1155
Modeling Erosion and Sedimentation in Irrigation
  Charles E. Brockway and C. W. Robison. 2189

SESSION 8B, FLOOD CONTROL AND DRAINAGE SYSTEMS (I)

Chairman: James D. Goff

The NWS Flash Flood Program: The Present and the Future
  James D. Belville and Curtis B. Barrett 1164
Real-time Monitoring and Flood Forecasting
  W. A. Evans, Jr. 1172
Regional Detention Basins as a Flood Control Solution
  David L. Brown, Steven D. Fitzgerald and Michael D. Talbott. 1179
Flood Control, Water Conservation, and Urban Change
  James L. Easton. 1187
New Developments in the H.E.C. Programs for Flood Control
  Vernon Bonner 1194
Heppner's User-Friendly Local Flood Warning System
  Vernon C. Bissel, Robert K. Hartman and John B. Halquist 1202

SESSION 8C, WATER SUPPLY INFRASTRUCTURE

Chairman: Kyle E. Schilling

Water Supply Infrastructure Needs: The Evolving Picture
  Jerome B. Gilbert. 1210
Financing Water Supply Infrastructure A Publics Works Perspective
  John P. Sullivan, Jr. 1218
Guidelines for Maintenance of Aging Water Pipes
  David H. Marks, Stefanos Andreou and Robert Clark. 1225
The United Kingdom Approach to Rehabilitation
  David Fiddes. 1232
Water Infrastructure: Research and Education Needs
  Neil S. Grigg 1240

SESSION 8D, RELIABIITY ASPECTS IN WATER DISTRIBUTION SYSTEM DESIGN

Chairman: Ian Goulter

Verification of a Supply Reliability Model
  Benjamin F. Hobbs and Gina K. Beim 1248

Drinking Water Distribution System Reliability: A Case Study
James A. Goodrich 1256
Hydraulic Reliability of Urban Water Distribution Systems
M. John Cullinane, Jr. 1264
Modeling Reliability in Water Distribution Network Design
Larry W. Mays, Ning Duan and Yu-Chun Su 1272
Model for Optimal-Risk Based Water Distribution Network Design
Yeou-Koung Tung 1280

SESSION 8E, COUPLING OF HYDRODYNAMIC AND WATER QUALITY MODELS (I)

Chairman: E. Eric Adams

Coupling of Hydrodynamic and Water Quality Models
Sandra Bird, Ross Hall and Mark Dortch 1285
The Effect of Storms on Pollution Loading Estimates
Keith W. Bedford, David Mark and Deborah Lee 1293
Lagrangian-Eulerian Approach to Modeling Contaminants
John F. Paul, Henry A. Walker and Jean A. Nocito 1301
A Unified Hydrodynamic-Water Quality Model
Alan F. Blumberg, Dominic M. Di Toro, Rita E. Vassilakis, Paul R. Paquin
and James J. Fitzpatrick 1309

SESSION 8F, RESERVOIR OPERATIONS

Chairman: Wen-Sen Chu

NID Water Supply and Hydropower Operations Model
Craig E. Crouch 1317
Multivariate Modeling of Hydrological Time Series for Generation of Reservoir
Operating Rules
Mohammad Karamouz, J. W. Delleur and M. H. Houck 1325
Reservoir System Simulation Through Network Flow Programming
Michael C. Archer and Francis I. Chung 1335
Optimal Weekly Operation of a System of Three Multipurpose Reservoirs
Alberto Rodriguez and Yun-Sheng Yu 1343

SESSION 8G, SOCIAL AND ENVIRONMENTAL CONSIDERATIONS IN WATER RESOURCE PLANNING

Chairperson: Mary A. Bergs

Facilities Planning in the Caribbean: A Case Study
Dean Slocum, Ricard Berlandy and Robert Wardwell 1351
Engineering and Policy Making: The Platte River in Nebraska
Martha W. Gilliland 1358
Modeling to Generate Alternatives: A Review
James S. Gidley and Muhammad F. Bari 1366

Community Relations on Hazardous Waste Projects: A Successful Experience
Udai P. Singh, James E. Orban and Nancy R. Tuor........................... 1374
Integrating Policy Factor in Stream-Aquifer Models
Nathan Buras 1382

SESSION 8H, IRRIGATION AROUND THE WORLD

Chairman: Michael R. Stansbury

Irrigation in Mexico
Cesar O. Ramos Valdez 1388
Irrigation Development in Alberta, Canada
Jacob W. Thiessen.. 1395
Traveling Trickler Center Pivot Design
Abdul-Mannan Turjoman and Otto J. Helweg 1403
Strategy for Ground Water Planning****
Abinash Chandra Chaturvedi.. 1407
Colorado High Mountain Aquifer Study
W. Martin Roche and William J. Steele..................................... 1413

SESSION 9A, SEDIMENTATION

Chairman: Andrew Seinkeiwich

Prediction of Sediment Yield for Southern California Watersheds
Abnish C. Amar and Elden J. Gatwood 1420
Analysis of Alluvial Fan Flooding
Desi Alvarez, Wen C. Wang and David R. Dawdy........................... 1428
Hansen Dam Sediment Modeling Study—Impact of Water Supply vs. Flood Control
Operational Modes on Sediment Deposition in the Reservoir Area
Abnish C. Amar... 1435
Annual Sediment Loads of Illinois Streams
Nani G. Bhowmik and J. Rodger Adams 1444

SESSION 9B, FLOOD CONTROL AND DRAINAGE SYSTEMS (II)

Chairman: Jerry R. Rogers

Storm Dynamics in the Lake Ontario Region
Peter Nimmrichter and William James...................................... 1425
Intense Storms and the Runoff Coefficient
W. Edward Nute 1460
Unique Flood and Drainage Problems in Los Angeles
G. J. Pederson and Iraj Nasseri 1468
Flood Control Feasibility Study for the Maumee River in Allen County, Indiana
Christopher B. Burke, S. C. L. Yin, James C. Bradley and Mark L. Strong 1476

****Originally scheduled for session 10C

SESSION 9C, EFFECTS OF IRRIGATED AGRICULTURE ON GROUND WATER QUALITY

Chairman: William F. Ritter

Irrigation and Ground Water Quality in the South
Adel Shirmohammadi and Walter G. Knisel.................................. 2206
Effects of Irrigated Agriculture on Ground Water Quality in the Corn Belt
and Lake States
W. A. Mossbarger, Jr. and R. W. Yost.................................... 1484
Effect of Irrigated Agriculture on Ground Water Quality in the Appalachian and Northeastern
States
William F. Ritter, Frank J. Humenik and R. W. Skaggs 1492
Ground Water Pollution Potential from Irrigation—Eastern U.S.*****
James N. Krider.. 1500
Impact of Irrigation on Ground Water Quality in Humid Areas
Walter G. Knisel and R. A. Leonard 1508

SESSION 9D, GROUND WATER MANAGEMENT (II)

Chairman: Irving Sherman

Interbasin Issues Related to Ground Water Management
William R. Walker... 1516
Modification of the Step Drawdown Test for Pump Selection
Otto J. Helweg.. 1524
Conjunctive Use Project in Beebe Draw, Colorado
Kenneth A. Mangelson and L. Stephen Schmidt 1528
El Paso vs. New Mexico, Ground Water or Other Options
Conrad G. Keyes, Jr. 1536
Owens Valley, California—Basin Management to Meet Both Water Resources
and Environmental Goals
Melvin L. Blevins, Gene L. Coufal, A. R. Vershel and M. R. Garcia........... 1544

SESSION 9E, COUPLING OF HYDRODYNAMIC AND WATER QUALITY MODELS (II)

Chairman: Mark S. Dortch

Management Studies of Farmington Bay, Great Salt Lake
D. George Chadwick, Jr., J. Paul Riley, Alberta J. Seierstad,
Darwin L. Sorensen and Norman E. Stauffer, Jr. 1556
A 2-D Model for the Guaiba Estuary (Brazil)
Jose A. O. De Jesus, Joel M. Branski and Luis C. H. Ferreira................. 1564
Hydrodynamic Simulation of the Upper Potomac Estuary
Raymond W. Schaffranek.. 1572
Hydraulic Modeling for Ecological Research
Misganaw Demissie, Basilis Stephanatos and Nani G. Bhowmik................ 1582

*****Originally scheduled for session 8H

xix

Water Quality and Hydrodynamics in a Shallow Lake
R. A. Luettich, Jr., L. Somlyody, D. R. F. Harleman and L. Koncsos........... 1590

SESSION 9F, WATER RESOURCES MANAGEMENT AND DEVELOPMENT

Chairman: James R. Hanchey

Organization Design of a Water Resources Institution
Jahan Tavangar and J. Paul Riley 1598
Review of Strategies for Strengthening Water Resources Management in
Taiwan, Republic of China
Chung-Yu Fung ....:.. 1608
Assessment of Drought Restriction Needs in New Jersey
Robert Dresnack, Eugene Golub and Franklin Salek 1615
The Water Problems on the Penghu Island in Taiwan
Jing-san Hwang 1622

SESSION 9G, DRINKING WATER AND SEWAGE, BIG PROBLEMS
OF BIG CITIES (I)

Chairman: Richard M. Males

Effect of Baghdad City Sewage Tretment Effluents on Dissolved Oxygen
Profiles of an Iraqi River
Qais Nuri Fattah and Faris Hammoudi Mohammad.......................... 1630
Integrated Wastewater and Sludge Treatment in a Tree Farm
Robert E. Hoffman, Martha W. Gilliland and Gary B. Keefer.................. 1639
Math Modeling of Mixing Zones in River Systems
Seok S. Park and Christopher G. Uchrin 1647

SESSION 9H, COMPUTER AIDED INNOVATIONS IN THE
WATER RESOURCES ENVIRONMENT

Chairman: Mohammad Karamouz

Computer Aided Drafting in the Water Resources Environment
Carol B. Thompson, Deborah K. Keyes and Richard H. French 1655
Computer Aided River Basin Management in the Alps
George Fleming and Sergio Fattorelli 1662
Interactive Simulation of Water Resource Systems
Daniel P. Loucks.. 1670

SESSION 10A, RIVER RESPONSE AND CHANNEL CONTROL

Chairman: Wayne G. Dorough

Response of the Citanduy River to Developments
Jerry R. Richardson and Michael A. Stevens............................... 1678
Submerged Vanes for Sediment Control in Rivers
A. Jacob Odgaard and Anita Spoljaric.................................... 1686

Classification and Behavior of Meander Migration
Edward H. Martin, Hsieh W. Shen and J. Ed Glover......................... 1694
Management Strategy for Severed Meander Bends
F. D. Shelds, Jr. and S. R. Abt 1702
Continuous Modelling of Downstream River Erosion Caused by 40 Years
of Urbanization
William James and Mark Robinson 1710

SESSION 10B, WATER DISTRIBUTION SYSTEMS

Chairman: William J. Brick

Effect of the Fluid Velocity on the Biofilm Development
Yoshihiko Hosoi and Hitoshi Murakami 1718
A New Methodology for Modelling Water Pipe Breaks
Stefanos Andreou and David H. Marks..................................... 1726
Water System Reliabiliy—Balance of Cost and Risk
John P. Velon... 1734
Grand Canyon Water Line by Directional Drilling
William C. Taggart, Christopher M. Crandell, A. William Howard and
Richard S. Carden 1743

SESSION 10C, EFFECTS OF IRRIGATED AGRICULTURE ON WATER QUALITY

Chairman: L. John Zeman

Effect of Agriculture on Groundwater Quality******
Barbara Howie 1751
A Model Relating Water and Sediment Yield to Upstream Agricultural Practices
Jurgen Garbrecht and Donn G. DeCoursey.................................. 1759
Implications of Nitrogen Transport by the Okanagan River
L. John Zeman... 1767
Converting a Mainframe Erosion Simulation Model to a Microcomputer Software
Reza M. Khanbilvardi and Andrew S. Rogowski............................. 1775

SESSION 10D, REGULATORY AND PLANNING ASPECTS OF GROUND WATER MANAGEMENT

Chairman: Karl E. Longley

Ground Water Strategy in California
Darlene E. Ruiz 1783
The Role of Local Government in Water Quality Management
Duane L. Georgeson and Marjorie G. Shovlin.............................. 1791
What About the Point-Of-Use?
George P. Hanna, Jr.. 1799

******Originally scheduled for session 9C

SESSION 10E, COUPLING OF HYDRODYNAMIC AND WATER QUALITY MODELS (III)

Chairman: William R. Waldrop

Advection Calculations Using Spline Scheme
Joel M. Branski and Edward R. Holley 1807
A Computer Model for Oil Slick Transport in Rivers
Poojitha D. Yapa and Hung Tao Shen 1815
In-Situ Microcosms for Calibrating Dynamic Models
Richard H. French 1823

SESSION 10F, INNOVATIONS IN WATER PLANNING ALTERNATIVES

Chairman: William K. Johnson

Conjunctive Water Use Planning
Robert W. Hinks and Robert A. Eichinger 1829
A New Dam in California: A Piece of Cake
William R. Everest and Robert H. Born 1837
Interaction Between the Technical and Political Processes in Solving
Flooding Problems in the Great Salt Lake, Utah
Lloyd H. Austin, J. Paul Riley and Paul C. Summers 1845
Orleans Parish Drainage Improvements
Turan Ceran 1853

SESSION 10G, DRINKING WATER AND SEWAGE, BIG PROBLEMS OF BIG CITIES (II)

Chairman: Dr. Walter M. Grayman

Water Resources Strategy—Chicago
Bill Macaitis 1860
An Optimization Model for Use in Analysis and Design of Wastewater
Treatment Systems
Chi-Chung Tang, E. Downey Brill, Jr. and John T. Pfeffer 1872
Evaluation of PCP/Oil Spill on CFT Indian Reservation Near
Nespelem, Washington
Kenneth A. Mangelson 1880
Policy Issues in Managing Nonpoint Source Pollution
William E. Cox 1890

SESSION 10H, DROUGHT FORECASTING & MANAGEMENT

Chairman: Ramachandra Rao

Simulation Models of Sequences of Dry and Wet Days
J. W. Delleur, T. J. Chang and M. L. Kavvas 1896
Use of Stochastic Hydrology in Reservoir Operation
Donald K. Frevert, M. S. Cowan and W. L. Lane 1904

Policy Screening Models for Water Supply Operation
Dean Randall, Mark H. Houck and Jeff R. Wright........................... 1912
Hale Cycle and Indian Drought and Flood Area Indices
A. Ramachandra Rao and G. H. Yu....................................... 1920
Droughts and Floods Related to Solar Sunspot Cycles
Ralph L. Chantrill 2198

SESSION 11A, RIVER HYDRAULICS AND SEDIMENTATION

Chairman: Hsieh W. Shen

Flow and Sediment Transport in Curved Channels With Nonuniform Bed Material
A. Jacob Odgaard and Sheng-Chuan Hsu 1928
A New Technique for Measuring Fine Sediment Accumulation in Gravel Bed Streams
Thomas A. Wesche, Dudley W. Reiser, Victor R. Hasfurther, Quentin D. Skinner
and Wayne A. Hubert... 1935
Development of Two- and Three-Dimensional Modeling Systems for Open Channel
Flow and Sedimentation
William H. McAnally, Joseph V. Letter and William A. Thomas............... 1943
Laboratory Model Studies of Flood Wave Propagation
Nadira Kabir and John F. Orsborn.. 1951
Sediment Intrusion Into the Substrate of Gravel Bed Streams
C. V. Alonso, C. Mendoza and G. Q. Tabio, III 1959

SESSION 11B, SEDIMENT TRANSPORT AND AQUATIC HABITAT

Chairman: Robert C. MacArthur

A Computer Program Simulation of the Effect of Upstream Agricultural
Practices on the Survival of Salmonid Embryos
J. Garbrecht and F. D. Theurer 1968
Physical Habitat Simulation and the Moveable Bed
Robert T. Milhous and Jeffrey B. Bradley 1976
Development of the Nauvoo Point Plant Beds
J. Rodger Adams, Nani G. Bhowmik, Frank S. Dillon and Richard V. Anderson .. 1984
Ecological Impacts of Sediment Transport to Tropical Reservoirs
J. E. Reuter, P. D. Vaux and C. R. Goldman.............................. 1992
An Engineer's Guide to Trout Habitat
Charles H. Call, Jr.. 2000

SESSION 11C, A BETTER WAY TO OPERATE A WATER SUPPLY PROJECT

Chairman: Roger Beieler

Taming a Pipe Network Analysis Computer Program
Terry L. Tanner.. 2009
Automated Control for Central Arizona Project Distribution Systems
Jeff Kishel... 2017
Algorithms for Automatic Control of Diversion Dams
Clark P. Buyalski... 2025

Energy Dissipation in Small Canals
A. J. Clemmens, J. A. Replogle and A. R. Dedrick.......................... 2033
Trash Busters—A Comparison of Screening Structures for Irrigation Systems
Roger W. Beieler.. 2041

SESSION 11D, DESIGN AND IMPLEMENTATION OF GROUND WATER MONITORING PROGRAMS

Chairman: Harold T. Glaser

Geohydrologic Considerations in Ground Water Modeling
Melih M. Ozbilgin... 2049
Fate of Chemical Contaminants in Soil
Sargeant J. Green... 2057
Monitoring Ground Water Quality in the Southwest
Kenneth D. Schmidt 2060

SESSION 11E, ORGANIZING FOR WORLD WATER ISSUES

Chairman: Danny L. King

North American Weather Modification Organizations
Conrad G. Keyes, Jr. 2066
Evolution of Water Organisations in England and Wales
Donald Arthur David Reeve 2074
Obstacle to Establishing An Effective Water Resources Planning Process
in Developing Countries
Steve Kadivar.. 2082

SESSION 11F, LATEST CONCEPTS IN ASSESSING MINIMUM INSTREAM FLOW REQUIREMENTS

Chairman: Les K. Lampe

Comparison of Minimum Instream Needs
Robert T. Milhous 2089
Instream Flow Needs to Protect Fishery Resources
James M. Loar, Michael J. Sale and Glenn F. Cada......................... 2098
Benefit-Cost Evaluation of Minimum Instream Flows
Les K. Lampe and Neuton V. Colston 2106

SESSION 11G, PACIFIC RIM WATER ISSUES

Chairman: W. Robert Rangeley

Technology Transfer—Consultants and Counterparts
Susan Scott-Stevens 2114
Queensland, Australia—River Diversion Schemes
John R. Lawrence 2120

Water Issues in Tropical and Sub-tropical Australia
John R. Lawrence 2128
Water Supply and Sewage Disposal: Shanghai, China
J. W. Bulkley, Chen Jiang Tao, Paul L. Freedman, Zheng Wei-Min,
Kan Chen and Wang Peibo... 2136

SESSION 11H, CANADIAN-U.S. WATER ISSUES

Chairman: George R. Baumli

Garrison Diversion Unit-An Example of United States-Canada Cooperative
Investigation
D. A. Davis, R. A. Halliday and R. D. Hofer 2143
The Changing Objectives of Garrison Diversion Unit
Darrell L. Krull 2151
Changes in Management: International Great Lakes
Leonard B. Dworsky... 2158
The Inquiry on Canadian Federal Water Policy
James W. MacLaren 2173

SESSION 12, OVERVIEW AND CRITIQUE

Chairman: Fred Hotes

Plenary Session.. *

Subject Index 2215

Author Index.. 2223

*Manuscript not available at the time of printing

HYDRODYNAMICS OF EARTH FILL DAM BREACH EROSION

Vijay P. Singh[1], M.ASCE, Papagiotis D. Scarlatos[2], A.M.ASCE,
John G. Collins[3] and Mark R. Jourdan[3]

Abstract

Mathematical description of earth fill dam breach erosion is
complicated by time-dependent, nonhomogeneous and dynamic characteristics. Processes occurring during failure of an earth dam are not
fully understood. A simplified solution can, however, be achieved by
utilizing the principles of hydraulics, hydrodynamics and sediment
transport. An analytical model is suggested in this paper. The
model is based on the continuity equation of water mass within the
reservoir, a broad-crested weir discharge formula and a velocity
power law for breach erosion. Depending on the values of certain
parameters, the resulting equations can be either linear or nonlinear. Solutions are presented for rectangular and triangular
breach cross sections.

Introduction

It has been historically documented that failure of an earth
fill dam is a process occurring over a finite period of time ranging
from a few minutes to several hours [9,11,14]. The duration of
failure can dramatically influence the shape of the released water
hydrograph which is used as an upstream boundary condition for modeling flood-wave propagation. A general approach to the dam breach
erosion problem should include hydrologic elements, hydrodynamics,
mechanics of sediment transport and geotechnical aspects. Cristofano
analytically related the water discharge from the breach to the rate
of sediment transport [4]. Brown and Rogers developed a numerical
model (DRDAM) by coupling basic hydraulic relations and the Schok-
litsch bed-load formula [2]. Fread presented a parametric model
(NSW-DAMBRK) that was of limited use since both failure duration and
terminal breach size were required as input [5]. Ponce and Tsivoglou
developed a numerical model based on the St. Venant system of equations, coupled with the Meyer-Peter and Muller sediment transport
formula [10]. Another model (BREACH), developed by Fread, was based
on basic hydraulics and the Meyer-Peter and Muller bed load formula.

---

[1]Professor, Department of Civil Engineering, Louisiana State
University, Baton Rouge, LA 70803.
[2]Water Resources Engineer, Department of Resource Planning, South
Florida Water Management District, West Palm Beach, FL 33402.
[3]Engineers, Environmental Laboratory, Waterways Experiment Station,
U.S. Army Corps of Engineers, Vicksburg, MS 39180.

The model also incorporated the effects of sloughing but under dry
soil conditions [6]. The most recent model is the BEED model [13,14]
which is a numerical model that utilizes reservoir water mass continuity, broad-crested weir hydraulics, sediment transport by the
Einstein-Brown formula and sloughing according to the contour method
[3].

The model presented in this paper is a coupled two-phase water-
sediment model based on reservoir water mass continuity, flow over a
broad-crested weir and rate of breach erosion given by a velocity
power law. Closed-form solutions are discussed for rectangular and
triangular breach cross sections.

Physical Processes and Mathematical Modeling

The reservoir water storage depletion, the breach flow hydrodynamics and the rate of breach erosion are the processes to be
modeled. Assuming that inflow, and powerhouse and spillway outflows
are negligible in comparison with breach outflow discharge, reservoir
water depletion can be approximated by the continuity relation:

$$A_s(H) \frac{dH}{dt} = - Q_b \tag{1}$$

where $A_s(H)$ is the reservoir water surface area, H is the reservoir
water depth from a reference datum, Q_b is the breach outflow discharge, and t is the time from the initiation of the erosion. For a
prismatic channel (i.e., A_s independent of H), Eq. (1) becomes linear
with respect to H. Furthermore, if the outflow is given as

$$Q_b = u \, A_b \tag{2}$$

where u is the mean breach outflow velocity and A_b is the cross
section area of the breach, then Eq. (1) yields

$$A_s \frac{dH}{dt} = - u \, A_b \tag{3}$$

Assuming that the flow over the breach can be simulated by the
hydraulics of flow over a broad-crested weir, the velocity u is

$$u = a_1 (H-Z)^{b_1} \tag{4}$$

where a_1, b_1 are empirical coefficients and Z is elevation of the
bottom of the breach from the reference datum. Because the flow over
the breach is critical, the coefficient b_1 equals 0.5. The value of
the coefficient a_1 experimentally was found to be in the range of 1.7
[1]. This coefficient drastically changes when tail-water effects
are present.

Combination of Eqs. (3) and (4) results in a single equation
with two unknowns: the water depth H, and the breach bottom elevation Z. An additional equation can be derived from the breach
erosion mechanism. The rate of erosion is a function of bed shear

stress, and can be expressed as a power function of the mean velocity, i.e.,

$$\frac{dZ}{dt} = - a_2 u^{b_2} \tag{5}$$

where a_2, b_2 are empirical coefficients. Experimental data suggested a value between 4 and 6 for b_2 [8]. The coefficient a_2 incorporates the effect of porosity, particle diameter, specific weight of the soil and water, and the longitudinal length of the breach [12]. Both coefficients in Eq. (5) should be estimated through calibration.

The system of Eqs. (3), (4) and (5) represents the basic processes of earth fill dam erosion. For completeness of the problem, initial conditions can be defined as

$$H = H_0 \text{ and } Z = Z_0 \text{ at } t = t_0 \tag{6}$$

Analytical Solutions

Historical records document the shape of the breach to be either rectangular, triangular or mostly trapezoidal [9]. Analytical solutions are presented for the first two cross sections. Both a_1 and b_1 were kept constant and equal to $((2/3)g)^{1/2}$ and $1/2$, respectively. Details of the solutions can be found in [7,14].

Rectangular Breach

It was assumed that the width b remained constant and that erosion occurred only in the vertical direction. Thus, the breach cross section is

$$A_b = b(H - Z) \tag{7}$$

For linear erosivity function, the rate of vertical expansion of the breach was explicitly related to various physical and geometrical parameters as

$$Z(t) = Z_0 + \frac{a_2 A_s}{b} \ln \left\{ \frac{a_2 A_s}{b(H_0 - Z_0) - a_2 A_s} \left\{ -1 + \lfloor (\sqrt{H_0 - Z_0} \right. \right.$$

$$\left. - \sqrt{\frac{a_2 A_s}{b}}) \exp \left(-\sqrt{\frac{2}{3} \frac{g a_2 b}{A_s}} t \right) / [\sqrt{H_0 - Z_0} + \frac{a_2 A_s}{b} \right.$$

$$\left. \left. - (\sqrt{H_0 - Z_0} - \sqrt{\frac{a_2 A_s}{b}}) \exp \left(-\sqrt{\frac{2}{3} \frac{g a_2 b}{A_s}} t \right) \rfloor \right]^2 \right\} \right\} \tag{8}$$

For the nonlinear erosivity function, the breach bottom elevation was expressed as a function of hydraulic head H–Z, i.e.,

$$\frac{b}{a_2 A_s (\frac{2}{3} g)^{1/2}} (\sqrt{H-Z} - \sqrt{H_o-Z_o}) + \ln [(1 - \frac{b}{a_2 A_s (\frac{2}{3} g)^{1/2}} (H-Z)^{1/2}) /$$

$$(1 - \frac{b}{a_2 A_s (\frac{2}{3} g)^{1/2}} (H_o-Z_o)^{1/2})] = \frac{3}{4g} (\frac{b}{a_2 A_s})^2 (Z-Z_o) \qquad (9)$$

while at the same time, the hydraulic head was given as

$$H - Z = \{a_2 A_s \sqrt{\frac{2}{3}} g(H_o - Z_o) / [\sqrt{H_o - Z_o} - (b \sqrt{H_o - Z_o}$$

$$- a_2 A_s \sqrt{\frac{2}{3}} g) \exp (- \frac{a_2 g}{3} t)]\}^2 \qquad (10)$$

Triangular Breach

The breach enlargement was assumed to occur such that the side slope remained constant. Thus, the cross section area is

$$A_b = s(H - Z)^2 \qquad (11)$$

where s is the side slope (1V:sH). For linear erosivity function ($b_1 = 1$), an implicit set of equations with respect to Z and H-Z was obtained, i.e.,

$$(\frac{s}{a_2 A_s})^{1/2} (H - Z) = \{- 1 + (\frac{s}{a_2 A_s})^{1/2} (H_o - Z_o)$$

$$+ [1 + (\frac{s}{a_2 A_s})^{1/2} (H_o - Z_o)] \exp [2 (\frac{s}{a_2 A_s})^{1/2} (Z_o - Z)]\} /$$

$$\{1 - (\frac{s}{a_2 A_s})^{1/2} (H_o - Z_o) + [1 + (\frac{s}{a_2 A_2})^{1/2} (H_o - Z_o)]$$

$$\exp [2 (\frac{s}{a_2 A_s})^{1/2} (Z_o - Z)]\} \qquad (12)$$

and

$$\ln \frac{(\frac{a_2 A_s}{s})^{1/4} - (H-Z)^{1/2}}{(\frac{a_2 A_s}{s})^{1/4} + (H-Z)^{1/2}} - 2 \tan^{-1} \frac{(H-Z)^{1/2}}{(\frac{a_2 A_s}{s})^{1/4}} = - 2 \frac{a_2^{3/4} s^{1/4}}{A_s^{1/4}} (\frac{2}{3} g)^{1/2} t$$

$$+ \ln \frac{(\frac{a_2 A_s}{s})^{1/4} - (H_o-Z_o)^{1/2}}{(\frac{a_2 A_s}{s})^{1/4} + (H_o+Z_o)^{1/2}} - 2 \tan^{-1} \frac{(H_o-Z_o)^{1/2}}{(\frac{a_2 A_s}{s})^{1/2}} \qquad (13)$$

Simultaneous solution of Eqs. (12) and (13) can yield the value of $Z(t)$. For nonlinear erosion, the variable $Z(t)$ was related to the hydraulic head as:

$$\ln \frac{1 + A_o^{1/3} h^{1/2} + A_o^{2/3} h}{(1 - A_o^{1/3} h^{1/2})^2} - 2 \cdot 3^{1/2} \tan^{-1} \frac{2 A_o^{1/3} h^{1/2} + 1}{3^{1/2}}$$

$$= 3 A_o^{2/3} (Z_o - Z) + \ln \frac{1 + A_o^{1/3} h_o^{1/2} + A_o^{2/3} h_o}{(1 - A_o^{1/3} h_o^{1/2})^2}$$

$$- 2 \cdot 3^{1/2} \tan^{-1} \frac{2 A_o^{1/3} h_o^{1/2} + 1}{3^{1/2}} \tag{14}$$

where h is the hydraulic head ($h_o = H_o - Z_o$), and

$$A_s = s / [a_2 \, A_2 \, (\tfrac{2}{3} g)^{1/2}] \tag{15}$$

At the same time, the hydraulic head was found to be given explicitly as:

$$H - Z = (H_o - Z_o) / \{\frac{s}{a_2 \, A_s \, (\tfrac{2}{3} g)^{1/2}} (H_o - Z_o)^{3/2}$$

$$+ [1 - \frac{s}{a_2 \, A_s \, (\tfrac{2}{3} g)^{1/2}} (H_o - Z_o)^{3/2}] \exp{(- a_2 \, g \, t)}\}^{2/3} \tag{16}$$

Application and Results

The equations were calibrated using the data from Teton Dam, Idaho, USA. The dam failed on June 5, 1976, and depleted 3.1×10^8 m^3 of water in approximately four hours producing a maximum discharge of 6.6×10^4 m^3/s. From the reservoir capacity curve, the surface area A_s for high water stages was found to be almost constant and equal to 4×10^6 m^2. For simulation, the water elevation H was taken 100 m, close to the original 93 m. Both A_s and H were kept constant during computations. The coefficients a_1 and b_1 were also constant and equal to $(2g/3)^{1/2}$ and 1/2 respectively. Numerical experiments were done for rectangular linear (RL) and nonlinear (RN) cases and for nonlinear triangular breach erosion (TN). The various parameters used for different runs are given in Table 1. Coefficient a_2 includes the effects of soil properties and dam geometry. By changing variable Z_o, the impact of the initial breach to subsequent dam erosion can be assessed.

Table 1. Parameter values for different
          runs.

Run	$a_2 \times 10^4$	Z_o [m]	b [m]	s
	Parameter			
RL1	7	90	100	–
RL2	7	95	100	–
RL3	7	95	80	–
RL4	9	95	80	–
RL5	5	95	80	–
RN1	0.45	99	100	–
RN2	0.45	95	100	–
RN3	0.45	99	.80	–
RN4	0.90	99	80	–
RN5	0.20	99	80	–
TN1	0.40	90	--	1
TN2	0.40	90	--	0.5
TN3	0.40	90	--	2.0
TN4	0.20	90	--	1

The simulation results for the rate of breach bottom erosion $Z(t)$ and the change of hydraulic head $h(t)$ are given in Figure 1. For rectangular breach, the dam failure time is not affected by the initial choice of width b if linear erosivity function is used. For the nonlinear function (b_2 = 1), however, $Z(t)$ depends strongly on the size of b. The erosion processes depend strongly on initial conditions, i.e., on the value of Z_o. For triangular breach, there is flexibility of choosing the side slope s because the effect of this parameter on simulation is unimportant. The value of Z_o cannot be estimated apriori with any degree of certainty. Both b and s depend on dam characteristics and can be assigned values according to historical data.

The most important parameter is the erosivity coefficient a_2. This coefficient has to be determined through calibration. For both nonlinear rectangular and triangular breach runs, the coefficient was found to be almost identical (0.4×10^{-4}). However, for the linear rectangular case, it was one order higher (7×10^{-4}). Also, solutions were very sensitive to changes in a_2. Erosivity coefficient should be evaluated through calibration.

Outflow discharge was simulated during failure of the Teton Dam as shown in Figure 2. Only the rising limb of the hydrograph is included because this is the one that is difficult to predict. The recession limb can be easily obtained by solving the reservoir water mass depletion equation. The rectangular breach solution is much better than the triangular, which gives either too high or too low

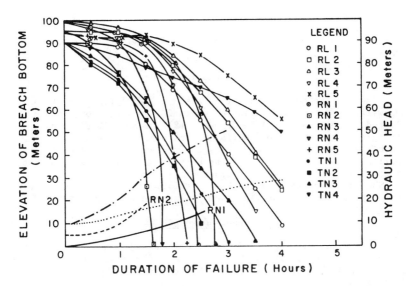

Figure 1. Rate of breach erosion and change of hydraulic head.

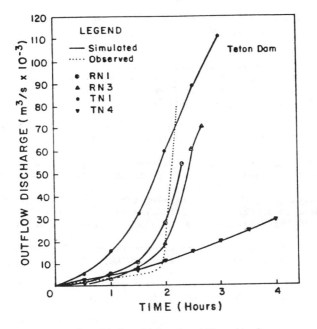

Figure 2. Rising limb of outflow discharge
during failure of Teton Dam.

discharges and longer failure time periods. Both runs RN1 and RN3
gave promising results that can be 'tuned' accordingly to match the
observed data.

Conclusions

The conclusions of this study are: (1) Analytical solutions are
a powerful tool for simulation of earth fill dam erosion, though
limited to certain simplified cases. (2) The solutions depend
strongly on the values of initial breach bottom elevation, breach
width and especially the erosivity coefficient. (3) The erosivity
coefficient was found to be of the same order of magnitude for nonlinear solutions, but was one order higher for the linear ones.
(4) The nonlinear rectangular breach solution gave promising results
when applied to the historical dam failure case of the Teton Dam.

Acknowledgements

This study was supported by Battelle Columbus Laboratories under
Contract No. DAAG29-81-D-0100, for the Environmental Laboratory, U.S.
Army Corps of Engineers, Waterways Experiment Station, Vicksburg,
Mississippi.

References

1.   Brater, E., 1959. Hydraulics, Civil Engineering Handbook.
     Urquhart, L. C., Editor, Section 4, McGraw-Hill Book Co., New
     York.

2.   Brown, R. J. and Rogers, D. C., 1977. A simulation of the
     hydraulic events during and following the Teton Dam failure.
     Proceedings of Dam-Break Flood Routing Model Workshop,
     Bethesda, Maryland, October 18-20, pp. 131-163.

3.   Chugaev, R. R., 1964. Stability Analysis of Earth Slopes.
     Israel Program for Scientific Translations, Jerusalem.

4.   Cristofano, E. A., 1965. Method of computing rate of failure of
     earth fill dams. Bureau of Reclamation, Denver, Colorado.

5.   Fread, D.L., 1977. The development and testing of a dam-break
     flood forecasting model. Proceedings of Dam-Break Flood Routing
     Model Workshop, Bethesda, Maryland, October 18-20, pp. 164-197.

6.   Fread, D. L., 1984. A breach erosion model for earthen dams.
     National Weather Service Report, NOAA, Silver Spring, MD.

7.   Gradshteyn, I. S. and Ruzic, I. M., 1983. Table of Integrals,
     Series and Products. Academic Press, New York.

8.   Laursen, E. M., 1956. The application of sediment transport
     mechanics to stable channel design. Journal of the Hydraulics
     Division, ASCE, Vol. 82, No. HY4.

9. MacDonald, T. C. and Langridge-Monopolis, J., 1984. Breaching characteristics of dam failures. Journal of Hydraulic Engineering, ASCE, Vol. 110, No. 5, pp. 567-586.

10. Ponce, V. M. and Tsivoglou, A. J., 1981. Modeling gradual dam breaches. Journal of the Hydraulics Division, ASCE, Vol. 107, No. HY7, pp. 829-838.

11. Ponce, V. M., 1982. Documented cases of earth dam breaches. San Diego State University Series No. 82149, San Diego, CA.

12. Scarlatos, P. D. and Singh, V. P., 1986. Mud flow and sediment transport problems associated with a dam-break event. Proceedings of the Third International Symposium on River Sedimentation, Jackson, MS, March 31 - April 4.

13. Singh, V. P. and Scarlatos, P. D., 1985. Modeling of gradual earth fill dam erosion. Proceedings, International Symposium on on Environmental Geotechnics and Problematic Soils and Rocks, Asian Institute of Technology, GEOTECH, Bangkok, Thailand, December 2-12.

14. Singh, V. P. and Scarlatos, P. D., 1985. Breach erosion of earth-fill dams and flood routing: BEED Model. Research Report, Battelle, Army Research Office, pp. 131.

Viscoplastic Fluid Model for Debris Flow Routing

Cheng-lung Chen,* M. ASCE

This paper describes how a generalized viscoplastic fluid model, which was developed based on non-Newtonian fluid mechanics, can be successfully applied to routing a debris flow down a channel. The one-dimensional dynamic equations developed for unsteady clear-water flow can be used for debris flow routing if the flow parameters, such as the momentum (or energy) correction factor and the resistance coefficient, can be accurately evaluated. The writer's generalized viscoplastic fluid model can be used to express such flow parameters in terms of the rheological parameters for debris flow in wide channels. Therefore, the present method can only be applied to wide channels. Three theoretical solutions of the fully-developed (no erosion or deposition) snout profile on a dry bed in wide channels are obtained based on three different assumptions on the friction slope. A preliminary analysis of the theoretical solutions reveals the importance of the flow behavior index and the so-called modified Froude number for uniformly progressive flow in snout profile modeling.

Introduction

Debris flow moves down a canyon or valley with a front armored with coarse-grained materials such as boulders. Debris flows often result from rapid hydrologic disturbances such as torrential storms, volcano eruptions, and earthquakes. The most recent catastrophic event was lahars (i.e., volcanic mudflows) triggered by the explosive eruption of Ruiz Volcano in Colombia on November 13, 1985, killing more than 20,000 people. The devastation of such debris flows is enormous, but their causes, occurrences, and mechanisms are not completely understood. To cope with such debris flow problems, the writer has made continued efforts since the 1980 eruption of Mt. St. Helens to model debris flows. Modeling debris flows, however, requires a rheological model (or constitutive equation) for sediment-water mixtures. Various rheological models, ranging from highly theoretical to very simple semi-empirical ones, have been developed or proposed for debris flow (3, 5). The writer's generalized viscoplastic fluid model that possesses both rate-independent and rate-dependent parts as well as two major rheological properties (i.e., the normal stress effect and soil yield criterion) has proven to be sufficiently accurate, yet practical, for general use in debris flow modeling (2, 3, 4, 5). This paper shows how the generalized viscoplastic fluid model can be incorporated with the one-dimensional dynamic equations to route a debris flow down a channel.

*Hydrologist, U.S. Geological Survey, Gulf Coast Hydroscience Center, NSTL, MS 39529.

Debris Flow Equations

It has been shown previously (2) that the one-dimensional unsteady flow equations for debris flow are identical to those for clear-water flow, except for different values in flow parameters, such as the momentum (or energy) correction factor and the resistance coefficient. However, the flow parameters for flow in channels with section of arbitrary geometric shape can only be determined empirically. To cast light on the roles that the flow parameters play in the debris flow process requires data on all relations among the flow parameters and the rheological properties of various sediment-water mixtures. Theoretically the flow parameters can be expressed in terms of the rheological parameters, such as the flow behavior index, the consistency index, and the yield stress index, for debris flow in wide channels, but not in narrow channels, which cause the flow to behave as three-dimensional. In the absence of the required relations between the flow parameters and the rheological parameters for three-dimensional flow, the following theoretical treatment is thus confined to the most idealized case of unidirectional plane gravity flow in wide channels.

Dynamic Equations For Debris Flow Routing.--The one-dimensional depth-averaged dynamic equations for unsteady debris flow in wide channels can be derived from the three-dimensional equations of continuity and momentum for flow of an incompressible sediment-water mixture. If one assumes no erosion and deposition of sediment in the transport process and further ignores the pressure correction factor, the equations so derived are

$$\frac{\partial h}{\partial t} + \frac{\partial (h\bar{u})}{\partial x} = 0 \qquad (1)$$

$$\frac{\partial (h\bar{u})}{\partial t} + \frac{\partial (\beta h\bar{u}^2)}{\partial x} = gh \sin \theta - gh \frac{\partial h}{\partial x} \cos \theta - \frac{\tau_o}{\rho} \qquad (2)$$

in which h = flow depth; t = time; $\bar{u}$ = depth-averaged velocity; x = space coordinate in the longitudinal direction of flow; β = momentum correction factor; g = gravitational acceleration; θ = angle of inclination of channel bed; τ_o = bed shear; and ρ = mass or bulk density of the sediment-water mixture.

The assumption of no erosion and deposition in the sediment transport process may be justified in the tip region of the snout (7), but unlikely in the remaining part of debris flow. Therefore, if the erosion and deposition of sediment are two important mechanisms in the process, Eqs. 1 and 2 should be modified by adding to them source and sink terms. However, for simplicity, the additional source-sink terms are not taken into account in the present study.

Assuming that the bed shear, τ_o, for unsteady flow is of the same magnitude as that for uniform flow with identical depth, h, and velocity, $\bar{u}$, one can then express τ_o/ρ in Eq. 2 in terms of h and $\bar{u}$, and the resistance coefficient using the uniform flow formula. For practical purposes, one of the existing uniform flow formulas, such as the Darcy-Weisbach equation and Manning's formula, may be used here. The practical usefulness of such uniform flow formulas and their

extended forms in debris flow modeling will be briefly covered later.
Setting $\sin \theta = S_o$ and $\tau_o/\rho = ghS_f$, in which S_f is called the friction
slope, and rearranging Eq. 2 with the help of Eq. 1 and assuming
$\partial\beta/\partial x = 0$ yields

$$\frac{\partial\bar{u}}{\partial t} + (2\beta - 1)\ \bar{u}\ \frac{\partial\bar{u}}{\partial x} + (\beta - 1)\ \frac{\bar{u}^2}{h} + g\cos\theta\ \frac{\partial h}{\partial x} = g\ (S_o - S_f) \qquad (3)$$

The theoretical momentum correction factor, β, for dilatant debris
flow in wide channels can be shown to be greater than that for clear-
water flow. Based on Bagnold's (1) simplified assumption of constant
concentration and consistency of the mixture over h, one can derive the
following expression of β from a generalized viscoplastic fluid model
(3, 5).

$$\beta = \frac{1 - \left(\dfrac{2\eta}{2\eta + 1} - \dfrac{\eta}{3\eta + 2}\right)\left(\dfrac{z_o}{h}\right)}{\left[1 - \dfrac{\eta}{2\eta + 1}\ \left(\dfrac{z_o}{h}\right)\right]^2} \qquad (4)$$

in which η = flow behavior index and z_q/h = yield stress index. If a
more general velocity profile developed without imposing Bagnold's
assumption (see, e.g., Ref. 4) is used in the theoretical derivation of
the β expression, the β value so determined can be shown to be much
larger than that computed from Eq. 4. However, the β expression
obtained from such a general velocity profile is more complicated than
Eq. 4. For simplicity, therefore, Eq. 4 will be used.

The friction slope, S_f, can be expressed in terms of $\bar{u}$, h, and a
resistance coefficient by means of a uniform flow formula. Use of
different uniform flow formulas results in the various expressions of
S_f. If the Darcy-Weisbach equation is used,

$$S_f = \frac{f}{8g}\ \frac{\bar{u}^2}{h} \qquad (5)$$

in which f is the Darcy-Weisbach resistance coefficient. If Manning's
formula in SI units is used,

$$S_f = n^2\ \frac{\bar{u}^2}{h^{4/3}} \qquad (6)$$

in which n is Manning's resistance coefficient.

An alternative expression of Eq. 5 in the range of laminar flow is

$$S_f = \frac{\mu_1 G}{8\rho g}\ \frac{\bar{u}^\eta}{h^{\eta+1}} \qquad (7)$$

in which μ_1 is the consistency index and G is a constant in the
theoretical expression of f for laminar flow of a viscoplastic fluid:

$$f = \frac{G}{R} \qquad (8)$$

where the generalized Reynolds number, R, and G are defined (2) as

$$R = \frac{\rho \, \bar{u}^{2-\eta} \, h^{\eta}}{\mu_1} \tag{9}$$

$$G = \frac{8}{\left(\frac{\rho*}{\rho}\right)\left(\frac{z_o}{\eta}\right)} \left[\frac{1 + \frac{1}{\eta}}{1 - \frac{\eta}{(2\eta + 1)}\left(\frac{z_o}{h}\right)}\right]^{\eta} \tag{10}$$

The bulk density modification factor, $\rho*/\rho$, in Eq. 10 is defined (5) as

$$\frac{\rho*}{\rho} = \frac{1 - (\bar{\rho}/\rho) \, \text{ctn} \, \theta \, \sin \phi}{1 + (\mu_2/\mu_1) \, \sin \phi} \tag{11}$$

in which $\bar{\rho} = C \, (\rho_s - \rho_w)$ = buoyant or submerged mass density of the sediment-water mixture (C = sediment concentration by volume; ρ_s = grain density; ρ_w = density of intergranular fluid); ϕ = static angle of internal friction; and μ_2 = cross-consistency index. Note that the range of $\rho*/\rho$, is between 0 and 1, inclusive, depending upon the slope of channel, θ, the range of which can be determined from Eq. 11 as

$$\tan^{-1} \left[(\bar{\rho}/\rho) \, \sin \phi\right] \leq \theta \leq \tan^{-1} \left[(\bar{\rho}/\rho) \, (-\mu_1/\mu_2)\right] \tag{12}$$

The concentration, C, is unknown, but Takahashi (8) estimated it from the Bagnold relation (i.e., the lower limit of θ in Eq. 12):

$$C = \frac{\rho_w}{(\rho_s - \rho_w)} \frac{\tan \theta}{(\sin \phi - \tan \theta)} \tag{13}$$

Therefore, $\bar{\rho}/\rho$ can be expressed in terms of C as

$$\frac{\bar{\rho}}{\rho} = \frac{C}{\rho_w/(\rho_s - \rho_w) + C} \tag{14}$$

Using Eq. 14, one can readily prove from Eq. 12 that the value of C determined from Eq. 13 is equal to the extreme upper limit or maximum C for fully-developed debris flow (8).

Eqs. 1 and 3 upon substitution of the β expression from Eq. 4 and the S_f expression from one of Eqs. 5-7 thus constitutes two basic working equations for debris flow routing. Usually a debris flow swells by scouring the bed after its initiation and reaches the fully-developed (or equilibrium) state before its subsidence. The fully-developed debris flow has essentially no erosivity. In the course of subsidence, the debris flow gradually deposits sediment and finally stops where it becomes the sediment gravity flow. Because Eqs. 1 and 3 do not have the source-sink terms, they cannot adequately describe the entire process of unsteady debris flow except at the fully-developed state before its subsidence. How accurately one can determine the debris flow profile at the fully-developed state, using Eqs. 1 and 3, will be addressed next.

Longitudinal Profile of Snout.--The sediment-water mixture moves in the form of waves propagating downstream in succession with a steep frontal region called the snout (or tongue) (7). The fully-developed longitudinal profile of the snout can be theoretically derived by solving Eqs. 1 and 3 with the help of one of Eqs. 5-7. The snout profile is obtained by integrating the following dynamic wave equation, which is expressed in a combined form of Eqs. 1 and 3 with the moving coordinate, ξ (= x - Ut, where U is the constant velocity of the moving coordinate system). Therefore, for uniformly progressive wavefront on a dry bed (i.e., h = 0 at ξ = 0), the snout profile is

$$\frac{1}{\tan \theta} \frac{dh}{d\xi} = \frac{1 - \dfrac{S_f}{S_o}}{1 - \dfrac{\beta(\bar{u} - U)^2}{g \, h \, \cos \theta} + \dfrac{(\beta - 1)U^2}{g \, h \, \cos \theta}} \tag{15}$$

Because this uniformly progressive snout moves on a dry bed, the so-called overrun discharge per unit width, q_o [= $(\bar{u} - U)h$, which can be transformed from Eq. 1], becomes zero and the second term in the denominator on the right-hand side of Eq. 15 disappears. The third term in the denominator on the right-hand side of Eq. 15 cannot vanish unless $\beta = 1$. Although the assumption of $\beta = 1$ will greatly simplify the integration of Eq. 15, for generality in the solution this term is retained herein. As will be shown later, this term in fact controls the shape of snout profile.

Different assumptions can be made on the expression of S_f in the integration of Eq. 15 and thus, result in various solutions of snout profiles. Use of Manning's formula (Eq. 6) in the integration of Eq. 15 is extremely difficult due mainly to the noninteger exponent (4/3) of h; therefore, only Eqs. 5 and 7 are used herein.

Use of the Darcy-Weisbach equation (Eq. 5) with the assumption of constant f is equivalent to assuming the constant bed shear, namely $\tau_o = \rho g h S_f = \rho g h_\infty S_o$ (in which h_∞ = normal depth of flow at $\xi = - \infty$, where the debris flow is essentially uniform with the normal velocity, $\bar{u}_\infty$) or

$$\frac{S_f}{S_o} = \frac{h_\infty}{h} \tag{16}$$

Substituting Eq. 16 into Eq. 15 and then normalizing the resulting equation by h_∞ yields

$$\frac{\tan \theta}{h_\infty} \xi = \int \frac{\dfrac{h}{h_\infty} + \mathbf{F}^2}{\dfrac{h}{h_\infty} - 1} \, d\left(\frac{h}{h_\infty}\right) + \text{constant} \tag{17}$$

in which $\mathbf{F} = U/\sqrt{g h_\infty \cos \theta /(\beta - 1)}$ = modified Froude number for uniformly progressive flow. Integrating Eq. 17 with the help of the boundary condition, $h/h_\infty = 0$, at the leading edge of the snout ($\xi = 0$) yields

$$\frac{\xi \tan \theta}{h_\infty} = \frac{h}{h_\infty} + (1 + \mathbf{F}^2) \ln\left(1 - \frac{h}{h_\infty}\right) \tag{18}$$

If $\mathbf{F} = 0$, Eq. 18 reduces to Takahashi's (8) solution. For Takahashi's experiment (U = $\bar{u}_\infty$ = 12.5 cm/s, h_∞ = 8 cm, θ = 18°), one can estimate $\mathbf{F}$

from its definition, provided β is known. For flow of noncohesive dilatant granules ($z_o/h = 1$ and $\eta = 2$), it follows from Eq. 4 that $\beta = 1.25$. Therefore, $\mathbf{F} = 0.0723$; this justifies Takahashi's assumption of $\mathbf{F} = 0$. Takahashi has also shown that Eq. 18 with $\mathbf{F} = 0$ agrees with his experimental result. For illustration, profiles representing Eq. 18 with various values of $\mathbf{F}^2$ are plotted in solid line (i.e., based on the assumption of constant bed shear) in Fig. 1.

If Eq. 7 is used instead of Eq. 5,

$$\frac{S_f}{S_o} = \left(\frac{h_\infty}{h}\right)^{\eta+1}$$
(19)

Substituting Eq. 19 into Eq. 15 and again normalizing the resulting equation by h_∞ yields

$$\frac{\tan\theta}{h_\infty}\,\xi = \int \frac{\left(\frac{h}{h_\infty}\right)^{\eta+1} + \mathbf{F}^2\left(\frac{h}{h_\infty}\right)^{\eta}}{\left(\frac{h}{h_\infty}\right)^{\eta+1} - 1}\,d\left(\frac{h}{h_\infty}\right) + \text{constant}$$
(20)

Integrating Eq. 20 yields

$$\frac{\xi\,\tan\theta}{h_\infty} = \frac{h}{h_\infty} - F\left(\frac{h}{h_\infty},\,\eta+1\right) + \frac{\mathbf{F}^2}{\eta+1}\ln\left[1 - \left(\frac{h}{h_\infty}\right)^{\eta+1}\right] + \text{constant}$$
(21)

in which $F(y, N)$ = varied-flow function, defined by Chow (Ref. 6, p. 254) as

$$F(y, N) = \int_0^y \frac{d\zeta}{1 - \zeta^N}$$
(22)

In the present case, $y = h/h_\infty$, $N = \eta+1$, and ζ = integration variable. Specifically, for a Bingham plastic fluid ($\eta = 1$), $N = 2$,

$$F(y, 2) = \int_0^y \frac{d\zeta}{1 - \zeta^2} = \frac{1}{2}\ln\left(\frac{1+y}{1-y}\right)$$
(23)

and for a Bagnold's dilatant fluid ($\eta = 2$), $N = 3$,

$$F(y, 3) = \int_0^y \frac{d\zeta}{1 - \zeta^3} = \frac{1}{6}\ln\left[\frac{y^2 + y + 1}{(y - 1)^2}\right] - \frac{1}{\sqrt{3}}\text{ctn}^{-1}\left(\frac{2y + 1}{\sqrt{3}}\right)$$
(24)

which was obtained by Bresse in 1860 (Ref. 6, p. 258). The constant in Eq. 21 is determined by the boundary condition at the leading edge of the snout, namely $h/h_\infty = 0$ at $\xi = 0$.

The final expressions of the snout profiles for $\eta = 1$ and 2 after taking the integration constant into account are as follows:
For $\eta = 1$,

$$\frac{\xi\,\tan\theta}{h_\infty} = \frac{h}{h_\infty} - \frac{1}{2}\ln\left(\frac{1 + h/h_\infty}{1 - h/h_\infty}\right) + \frac{\mathbf{F}^2}{2}\ln\left[1 - \left(\frac{h}{h_\infty}\right)^2\right]$$
(25)

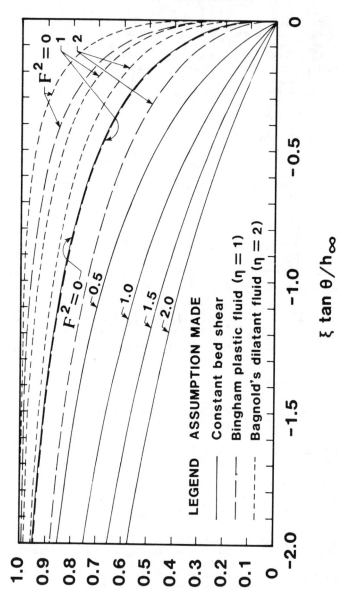

Figure 1.   Theoretical Profiles of Fully-developed Snout on a Dry Bed in Wide Channels

and for $\eta = 2$,

$$\frac{\xi \tan \theta}{h_\infty} = \frac{h}{h_\infty} - \frac{1}{6} \ln \left[\frac{(h/h_\infty)^2 + (h/h_\infty) + 1}{(1 - h/h_\infty)^2} \right]$$

$$+ \frac{1}{\sqrt{3}} \left\{ ctn^{-1} \left[\frac{2(h/h_\infty) + 1}{\sqrt{3}} \right] - \frac{\pi}{3} \right\} + \frac{F^2}{3} \ln \left[1 - \left(\frac{h}{h_\infty} \right)^3 \right] \quad (26)$$

If $F = 0$, Eqs. 25 and 26 reduce exactly to those obtained by Yamaoka (9). Yamaoka has found that Eq. 26 with $F = 0$ matches his observed profile, but Eq. 25 with $F = 0$ differs considerably from the observed one. No reasonable explanation has been given by Yamaoka, however, to attribute this agreement or disagreement between the theoretical and the experimental profiles. Because no data were reported on his experimental conditions, a reasonable estimate on the F value cannot be made. For comparison, profiles representing Eqs. 25 and 26 with various values of F^2 are also plotted in long and short broken lines, respectively, in Fig. 1.

Obviously, various assumptions made on S_f/S_o have resulted in totally different snout profiles for an identical value of F^2, as shown in Fig. 1. Nevertheless, because the definition of F contains β, which varies with η and z_o/h (see Eq. 4), it is unlikely that the value of F can be identical for different values of η. Note that Eq. 19 with $\eta = 0$ is identical to Eq. 16. Therefore, the assumption of constant Darcy-Weisbach's f or bed shear (τ_o) is equivalent to either setting $\eta = 0$ in the uniform laminar flow formula (Eq. 7) or assuming an infinitely pseudoplastic (shear-thinning) fluid as a rheological model of debris flow. It then follows from Eq. 4 that $\beta = 1$ for $\eta = 0$ and thus, $F = 0$ by virtue of the F definition. As a result, Eq. 18 with $F = 0$ represents equivalently the snout profile for $\eta = 0$. Furthermore, because Eq. 25 ($\eta = 1$) with $F = 1$ can reduce to Eq. 18 ($\eta = 0$) with $F = 0$, Eq. 18 may as well represent more than one snout profile having suitably combined values of η and F. Therefore, to select a rheological model, especially whether it is $\eta = 1$ or 2, based on the actual shape of the snout profile without taking into account the F value, as performed by Yamaoka (9), cannot be theoretically justified.

Conclusions

The one-dimensional dynamic equations developed for unsteady clear-water flow can be used to route a debris flow down a channel if the flow parameters, such as the momentum (or energy) correction factor and the flow resistance coefficient, for debris flow can be accurately evaluated. It has been shown from the writer's generalized visco-plastic fluid model that such flow parameters can be expressed in terms of the rheological parameters for debris flow in wide channels. The one-dimensional dynamic equations with the source-sink terms which account for the erosion and deposition of sediment thus constitute basic working equations in the routing of a debris flow at various stages of its process, namely from initiation to stoppage. The same equations without the source-sink terms, however, can only be used to route the debris flow at the fully-developed (no erosion or deposition)

stage. Three theoretical solutions (i.e., Eqs. 18, 25, and 26) of the
fully-developed snout profile on a dry bed in wide channels have been
derived from such dynamic equations on the basis of different
assumptions on the friction slope. It has been found that the modified
Froude number for uniformly progressive flow in addition to the flow
behavior index plays an important role in the development of the snout
profile. Although Takahashi and Yamaoka experimentally verified the
various snout profiles by ignoring the modified Froude number, the
results of their comparisons do not appear conclusive. More research
in this area is needed.

References

1. Bagnold, R. A., "Experiments on a Gravity-free Dispersion of Large
    Solid Spheres in a Newtonian Fluid under Shear," _Proceedings_, Royal
    Society of London, Ser. A, Vol. 225, 1954, pp. 49-63.

2. Chen, C. L., "Hydraulic Concepts in Debris Flow Simulation,"
    _Proceedings of the 1984 Speciality Conference on Delineation of
    Landslide, Flash Flood and Debris Flow Hazards in Utah_, Utah State
    University, Logan, Utah, 1985, pp. 236-259.

3. Chen, C. L., "Present Status of Research in Debris Flow Modeling,"
    _Proceedings of the Hydraulics Division Specialty Conference on
    Hydraulics and Hydrology in the Small Computer Age_, ASCE, Lake
    Buena Vista, Florida, 1985, pp. 733-741.

4. Chen, C. L., "Bingham Plastic or Bagnold's Dilatant Fluid as a
    Rheological Model of Debris Flow?" _Proceedings of the Third
    International Symposium on River Sedimentation_, Jackson,
    Mississippi, 1986. (in press)

5. Chen, C. L., "Comprehensive Review of Debris-Flow Modeling Concepts
    in Japan," _Proceedings of the 1984 Debris Flow Symposium_, Geologi-
    cal Society of America, Reno, Nevada, 1986. (in press)

6. Chow, V. T., _Open-Channel Hydraulics_, McGraw-Hill, New York, N.Y.,
    1959.

7. Johnson, A. M., _Physical Processes in Geology_, Freeman, San
    Francisco, California, 1970, pp. 433-534.

8. Takahashi, T., "Debris Flow on Prismatic Open Channel," _Journal
    of the Hydraulics Division_, ASCE, Vol. 106, No. HY3, Proc. Paper
    15245, Mar. 1980, pp. 381-396.

9. Yamaoka, I., "An Experimental Research on Mean Velocities of Usu
    Volcanic Ash-Pumice Mudflows in Open Channels," Experimental
    Research Report (2)485135 to the Japanese Ministry of Education
    for a Grant Aid for Scientific Research in 1979 and 1980, College
    of Engineering, Hokkaido University, Sapporo, Japan, 1981. (in
    Japanese)

Engineering Methodology for Delineating

Debris Flow Hazards in Los Angeles County

Sree Kumar *

ABSTRACT

Many urban developments in Los Angeles County are bounded by
rugged, steep-terrained, geologically active mountain ranges that are
periodically subject to wildfires. Moderate to high intensity rains
cause the watershed to become severely eroded, generating debris
flows, both mudflows and mud floods that proceed downstream into
developed areas causing considerable damage to public and private
property. Only 200 watersheds of the over 3,000 watersheds that are
susceptible to debris flows have debris control structures.
Urbanization of these hazard areas continues. Utilizing historical
and field data, elementary geomorphology and simplified hydraulics of
debris flows, a mapping strategy has been developed. The delineation
procedure includes defining the transport and deposition zone, the
flow expansion, the gradient of deposition, and quantity of debris
that is delivered to the fan. The relative likelihood of hazard
within the total fan is identified considering the influence of
adjacent canyons and the effect of improvement such as debris retention facilities, conveyances, and streets. The delineation of the
hazards below the watershed will enable development of zoning and
flood-plain management regulations.

Introduction

The unique dangers posed by debris flows, which include flood-surge
inundation, debris deposition, high impact, boulder transport and
deposition, and unpredicatable flood paths, require special attention. Flood hazard mapping using conventional hydraulic techniques
developed for clear water floods are generally not directly applicable to debris flows. Existing flood insurance maps in Los Angeles
County show areas subject to debris flows as areas of minimal hazard -
Zone C.

The traditional solution of providing mitigation measures such as
debris basins is becoming increasingly costly both for construction
and maintenance. In addition, it is not practical to provide and
manage this type of facility for the several thousands of developing
watersheds and fans. Neither can the development of the hazard be
exclusively prohibited. The compromise is flood plain regulation and
non-structural control measures, which include zoning and land-use

*Civil Engineer I, Los Angeles County Department of Public Works,
 2250 Alcazar Street, Los Angeles, CA 90033.

19

restriction, and flood-proofing to minimize the potential damage from
debris flows. The first step is flood hazard mapping.

Debris Flow Hazard Hypothesis

The term "Debris Flows", as used herein, incorporates all features
of the mudflow and mud flood phenomenon as defined by the National
Academy of Science (2). Mudflows are a specific subset of landslides
whose dominant transporting mechanism is that of a flow having sufficient viscosity to support large boulders within a matrix of smaller-
sized particles. Mud floods are a mixture of two discrete phases:
fluid (water and suspended fines) and solid (suspended load and bed
load), where sediment load may be as much as 50 percent by volume.

Debris flows in Los Angeles County are generated primarily by
(a) saturation of in-situ earth materials and subsequent gravity
induced failure, fluidization and flow (b) entrainment of sediment
stored in the steep channel by surficial flow of water. A debris
event may occur as a mudflow or mud flood or a combination of the
two. Historically it appears that the initial phase is a mudflow
which travels down as a frontal wave or pulse, carrying large boulders,
which demobilizes below the fan head. The trailing flood is a mud
flood which also deposits material in the fan and may entrain and
rework the mudflow deposits, and extend the deposition zone. The
rearmost part of the pulse is a turbulent water-flood, transporting
low to moderate quantities of sediment which in turn may entrain and
rework the mudflow and mud flood deposits, carrying debris further
down the fan. This series of flow events is repeated as successive
debris flow surges. Surges generally originate from the temporary
damming of channel by debris, damming at constrictions by vegetation
and boulders, large scale soil slips, band caving and occassionally
shallow landslides. Evidence suggests that mudflows may change to
mud floods or floods to flows depending on entrained water content.

Debris flows, in general, possess no permanent channels and are
free to pick new paths down the fan with every flooding event.
Avulsions, deposition in pre-existing channels, damming at constrictions and in natural drainageways, including hydraulic jumps at the
fan apex contribute to the unpredictability of flow direction and
inundation zones. Man made structures and development within the fan
can also influence flow direction. The combination of debris availability, steep slopes, occasional brush fires, and episodically heavy
rainfall is nearly optimal for mudflow and mud flood generation, in
Los Angeles County.

Model Formulation

Quantitative determination of the maximum debris flow hazard level
requires formulating the hydrodynamics of debris flows for unconfined
conditions. Technology in this area is still in the development stage.
For purposes of general flood plain regulation, the study focused only
on formulating mapping procedures and defining relative likelihood of
hazards within the inundation zone/deposition zone. In addition, model
development considered only unimproved, unobstructed fan area.

(I) Transport and Deposition Zones

The fan apex identifies the location at which the flow regime
changes from a transportation to a deposition mode. The fan apex
(Apex 1) is generally the intersection of the fan (deposition zone)
and the canyon slope and or location where flows leave a confined
section. The fans are generally concaved upwards in profile, but
show distinct breaks in slope i.e. segmentation. The deposition
zone, therefore, is further separated into two segments by a second
grade break (Apex 2). Uniform channel gradients are used for the
transport and deposition reaches. The transition from transportation
to deposition is assumed to be a function of channel gradient (θu),
fan gradients (θd, θf) and confinement. See Figure 1.

(II) Longitudinal Debris Deposition Profile

The cause for debris deposition is broken down into two cases:
(a) change in channel and fan gradient with or without expansion,
(b) change in channel and fan (including entrenched fan) expansion
i.e. confined to unconfined flow section with or without change in
gradient. The depth of flowing debris and deposited debris is
deepest at the apex and progressively decreases down fan. Lateral
spreading in the expanding zone and decreasing gradient are primary
reasons for reduction in depth. The debris deposition profile below
Apex 1 and Apex 2 is assumed linear and of uniform slope for each
segment. The deposition slope is assumed to be a function of fan
gradients (θd, θf) In the upstream reach, deposition is assumed horizontal or zero slope. Debris flow deposits (mudflow type) generally
have finite depths at the terminal and lateral limits. However,
since the object is to define combined hazard, mudflow and or mud
flood origins, and both primary and secondary hazard, deposition
depth at the terminus is assumed zero. Figure 1 illustrates these
features.

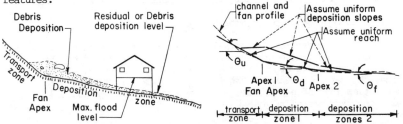

Figure 1. Transport Zone, Deposition zone, and Debris Deposition Profile

(III) Expansion Zones

Figure 2 shows three deposition areas: 1) Primary hazard zone
will represent the mudflow or mud flood, or combination deposition
area, 2) Secondary hazard zone will represent the transition of mud
flood to water flood and water flood deposition area, 3) Water flood
hazard zone where deposition is considered minimal. The modeling
procedure proposed herein considers only the primary and secondary
deposition areas.

Each canyon is assumed to posses a single zone of influence, (2βmax, Figure 2) which defines the fan area subject to debris flows, and within which the individual debris event will be contained. Each debris event will be characterized by an expansion (2β, Figure 2), assuming the fan is unobstructed i.e. unimproved or undeveloped. Topographical features, man-made structures, influence of adjacent canyons may dictate flow expansion and require multiple expansion to define the inundation area. The proposed model allows for only two succesive expansions (the second change may be convergence) and a rapid enlargement at the fan apex as illustrated in Figure 2. The direction of debris flow may be influenced by the of the canyon outlet.

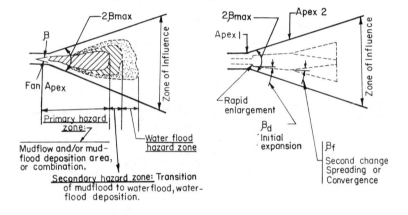

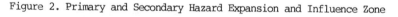

Figure 2. Primary and Secondary Hazard Expansion and Influence Zone

(IV) Cross Section Shape of Debris Deposition

The depth of debris is generally deeper in the central region and as flows diffuse the depth decreases progressively toward the lateral limit. A parabolic cross section shape has been adopted. In addition, the parabolic shape, when inverted upward would approximate deposition in confined channel, and in fans that are entrenched or with convex cross-section.

The complete deposition model is illustrated in Figure 3. The technique is to distribute a specified debris volume within a prescribed deposition pattern, considering: transport and deposition gradient, flow expansions, and debris deposition slope, to determine the debris runout length.

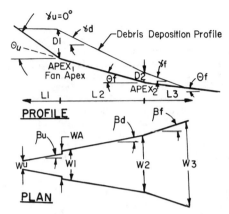

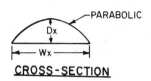

Figure 3. Debris Deposition Model

Model Criteria

The model was calibrated utilizing historical records from three major storms, the 1934 flood, 1954 flood, and the 1969 flood that occurred in different regions of Los Angeles County.

I. Transport and Deposition Gradients

Canyon and fan profiles for each contributing watershed and inundation area observed to be debris flow in origin were plotted. The fan apex was located. The reaches upstream and downstream of the fan apex (Apexl) were designated transport (θu) and deposition (θd, θ_f) zones, respectively, as shown on Figure 1. Basic statistics of the transport and deposition gradient indicated: (a) Transport slopes (θu) are greater than $6°0°$ (10.5 percent) and could be as low as $4°$ (7 percent) if well confined, (b) primary deposition slopes (θd) ranging from $3.0°$ (6.6 percent) to $8.4°$ (14.7 percent), and (c) secondary deposition slopes (θf) ranging from $2.4°$ (4.2 percent) to $5.3°$ (9.2 percent).

II. Zone of Influence and Flow Expansion

The zone of influence or maximum expansion ($2\beta max$) (Figure 2) was estimated by inspection of the flood pattern and fan cone features. Where contours of adjacent fan intersect, the locus of intersection projected toward the fan apex marks the lateral limits of the influence zone. The maximum expansion $2\beta max$ ranged from $0°$ (entrenched fan) to $90°$. Approximately 2/3 of cases ranged from $15°$ to $30°$ with mean = $29°$ and standard deviation = $11°$. Regression of maximum expansion with fan gradient, channel gradient, drainage area, relief ratio, and debris production indicated poor correlation. In addition to the topographic features, the maximum expansion may be a complex function of various geologic process active or inactive in each watershed, climatology, and influence of adjacent canyons.

The total flow expansion 2β for a single event was determined by
examining the 1934, 1954 and 1969 flood patterns. In general, the
patterns are complex with no clear definition of flow expansion, and
in many instances development and improvements have influenced the
diffusion of the debris flows. The total flow expansion (2β) ranged
from 4° to 58° including 0° for deposition in confined or channelized
reaches. On an average flow expansion 2β was 1/3 of the maximum
expansion 2βmax. Since flow expansions within a single fan may vary
from event to event and possibly for repeated events the following
cases are adopted: (1) Flow expansion (2β) = zone of influence of
2βmax. (2) Flow expansion (2β) = 1/3 zone of influence or 1/3 x
2βmax. The use of two alternate flow expansion should allow delineation of the "potential" fan area subject to debris flow hazard.
See Figure 4.

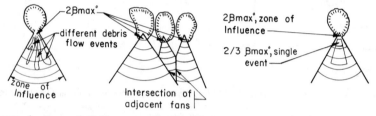

Figure 4. Zone of Influence, Single Event Expansion

III. Longitudinal Profile of Debris Deposition

The debris deposition slope is related to channel and fan gradient.
A uniform debris deposition slope and the following functional
relationship for each deposition or fan segment was adopted: Debris
deposition slope below Apex 1 (fan apex) = $\bar{Y}d = Kd * \bar{\Theta}d$ (deg), debris
deposition slope below Apex 2, = $\bar{Y}f = Kf * \bar{\Theta}f$ (deg) (Figure 3). The
deposition mechanism in either segment would be similar if subject to
the same debris flow i.e. mudflow, or mud flood, or combination.
Hence a further simplification where Kd = Kf = Kx was adopted. For
each debris flow instance, the debris runout length, the transport
and deposition gradients, the flow expansion, and the quantity of
deposition were estimated.

The debris deposition model was applied with different trails of
Kx, which in turn defines $\bar{Y}d$ and $\bar{Y}f$, to obtain debris runout lengths
which equaled (± tolerance) the observed deposition lengths. The
type of debris flow that occurred in each of the study areas and
within each study area itself could be significantly different i.e.
mudflows vs mud floods vs combinations of mudflow and mud floods.
Since the nature and type of debris flow could vary from event to
event, it is reasonable to expect different deposition limits.
Inspection of the Kx values indicate a range from 1.002 to 1.09, with
the majority of cases from 1.02 to 1.07. The lower the Kx value, the
longer the debris runout. For purpose of simulation, a low value of
Kx = 1.02 and a high value of Kx = 1.07 is adopted. The procedure
for applying this criteria is described in the following section –
Mapping Strategy.

Mapping Strategy

The debris volume which is distributed in the deposition zone is the quantity produced by a 24-hour rainfall with 50-year frequency, occurring on a saturated watershed which has recovered for a period of four years from a wildfire that completely denuded the watershed. The procedure is described in Reference 1. The mapping procedure is; plot channel and fan profile, define fan apex (Apex 1) and Apex 2, transport and deposition gradients, estimate zone of influence $2\beta max$ and single event expansion $(1/3) \cdot 2\beta max$, define deposition pattern to best fit fan micro-topography and apply the debris deposition model for various deposition slopes γd, γf. The hazard zones are classified as follows: (See Figure 5).

Undeveloped Fan: High Probability Hazard Zone as area covered for maximum expansion $2\beta max$ with debris deposition slope $\gamma d = 1.07 \times \sigma d$ and $\gamma f = 1.07 \times \sigma f$. The combination of maximum expansion and high debris slope would result in a reasonable minimum debris runout. Moderate Probability Hazard Zone as area covered beyond the High Hazard Zone for expansion of $(1/3) \cdot 2\beta max$ with debris slope $\gamma d = 1.07 \times \sigma d$ and $\gamma f = 1.07 \times \sigma f$. The runout length determined for this condition is then applied to each 1/3 segment of maximum expansion $(2\beta max)$ to extend the downstream limit across the fan. Low Probability Hazard Zone as area covered beyond the Moderate Probability Hazard Zone for the maximum expansion $2\beta max$ with debris deposition slope $\gamma d = 1.02 \times \sigma d$ and $\gamma d = 1.02 \times \sigma f$. The combination of maximum expansion and a lower debris slope would result in a reasonable upper limit of debris runout. For subsequent discussions, the hazards zone will refer to as High, Moderate and Low Hazard Zone.

Developed Fan: The above procedure for undeveloped fan is applied, i.e. assume fan is unobstructed. If the ratio of number of buildings within the High and Moderate Hazard Zone to the total hazard area is greater than 1.5, then the Low Hazard Zone is not identified. However, the degree of hazard within the High and Moderate Hazard Zone would be higher than a comparable undeveloped fan condition.

Channelized Flow Paths: If a street or channel intercepts the flow at or near the fan apex then an alternate flow path is evaluated. A uniform flow or deposition width beginning at the fan apex is adopted. Only the High and Moderate Hazard Zones are delineated where Moderate Hazard Zone is determined for the debris deposition slopes $\gamma d = 1.02 \times \sigma d$ and $\gamma f = 1.02 \times \sigma f$.

Debris Control: If a watershed has positive debris control i.e. a debris basin, then the capacity of the basin is subtracted from the total volume generated by the canyon to obtain an overflow volume. The procedure follows the undeveloped fan or developed fan case, or channelized flow, which ever is applicable, except that only overflow debris volume is distributed.

Influence of Adjacent Canyons: In general, fans from adjacent canyon coalesce some distance downstream of the fan apex. The hazard zones from individual canyons could overlap. The High, Moderate, and Low Hazard Zone from each adjacent canyon are superimposed. For each overlapping area, the higher hazard is identified. For example, when a Moderate Hazard Zone from one watershed overlaps the Low Hazard Zone of another adjacent watershed; the Moderate Hazard Zone dictates. By identifying the higher hazard zone in each overlapping area, the composite hazard zone is constructed. Figure 5 illustrates the mapping sequence and configuration.

Conclusion

The proposed methodology should allow delineation of areas subject to debris flow, and provide information to develop zoning and flood plain regulation. It also provides means to compare alternatives to structural measures versus managing the high hazard areas.

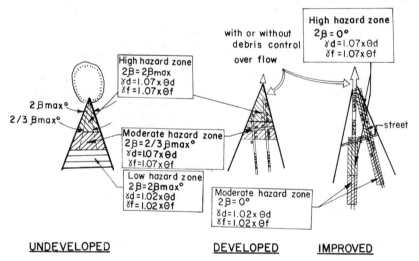

Figure 5. Definition of Hazard Zones

References

1) Los Angeles County Department of Public Works Hydrology Manual (1971)

2) National Academy of Science, Selecting a Methodology for Delineating Mudslide Hazard Areas for National Flood Insurance Program (1982)

Landslide-Generated Wave Studies

Clifford A. Pugh [1], M. ASCE
Wen-Li Chiang [2], M. ASCE

Abstract. - A serious safety of dams problem is associated with large masses of rock and debris plunging into lakes and causing damaging water waves. This concern prompted the Bureau of Reclamation to study a series of landslides in the canyon upstream from Morrow Point Dam. The problem was studied in a physical model of part of the reservoir and three of the landslides. An empirical prediction method was developed as a result of the physical model studies to predict maximum wave heights (Pugh, 1982, and Pugh and Harris, 1982). A mathematical model was also developed as a part of the studies by Tetra Tech, Inc., under contract with the Bureau of Reclamation (Chiang, et. al., 1981). This paper will briefly describe the physical model study, the empirical prediction method, and the numerical model.

Physical Model Study. - The undistorted physical model simulated 4.8 km (3 mi) of reservoir and 1.3 km (0.8 mi) of the canyon downstream from the dam at a scale of 1:250. Morrow Point Dam is a double-curvature, thin arch concrete dam constructed by the USBR on the Gunnison River 40 km (25 mi) east of Montrose, Colorado. The dam is 143 m (468 ft) high and 4 m (12 ft) thick at the crest. Figure 1 shows the reservoir, the landslides, and the model limits.

The landslide was simulated using a simple wedge shape. Simulation of the exact landslide geometry was not considered necessary since the calculated landslide velocity was less than the wave celerity. The displacement of the water is the major factor creating the wave. The potential dynamics of the landslides were computed according to a method described by Slingerland and Voight (Slingerland and Voight, 1979). The model landslide dynamics of the wedge as it enters the reservoir were designed to match the potential prototype dynamics. The model landslides were equipped with extension springs to slow them as they neared the bottom of the reservoir. The model landslide dynamics could be adjusted to simulate a variety of dynamic slide situations. The simple wedge shape made it possible to accurately measure the landslide dynamics for each test. The rate of change of displaced water and its velocity were measured incrementally for each test. Their product multiplied by water density gives the momentum flux of the water at each instant of time. Since the water waves are primarily a result of the momentum flux, the momentum vs. time relationship for the model tests was used to compare to possible prototype landslides. This method of modeling landslide dynamics

---

[1] Head, Hydraulic Equipment Section, USBR, PO Box 25007, Denver CO 80225
[2] Principal Engineer, Tetra Tech, Inc., 630 North Rosemead Boulevard, Pasadena CA 91107

also provided data to compare to results of the numerical model since
the physical model landslide dynamics were accurately known.

Wave data at 14 probe locations shown in figure 1 and landslide
dynamics were recorded continuously for each test. Data were recorded
for a total of 30 tests for landslides at locations A, B, and C.
The maximum height of a bore wave in the canyon downstream from the
dam was 7 m (23 ft). The maximum wave heights predicted at the dam
for slides A, B, and C, respectively, are 20 m (66 ft), 8.5 m (28 ft),
and 6.9 m (22.5 ft). A few examples of wave profiles measured in
the physical model study are compared with the math model predictions
in figures 2, 3, and 4. The solid circles indicate physical model
data.

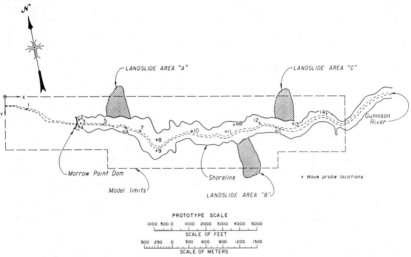

Figure 1. - Morrow Point landslide-generated wave model.

The direction of the landslide momentum was very important to the
wave height in the vicinity of the slide. Waves directly in line
with slide direction were two to three times higher than waves not
in line with the slide. Figures 2, 3, and 4 are time histories of
the water surface at probes 6A, 3, and 12, respectively, due to a
landslide at location A. The zero time is the instant the slide
releases. Waves close to the landslide are very steep and sharp.
As the wave moves away from the landslide it lengthens and smooths
out.

All electronic measurements of the landslide position, velocity,
and wave heights were taken and recorded with a microprocessor and
data acquisition system. The microprocessor had an internal clock.
The instant the slide was released the microprocessor began recording
data from the 14 wave probes, the landslide instruments, and the
clock. Twelve readings per second were taken from each of the instruments and stored on magnetic disk for later plotting and analysis.

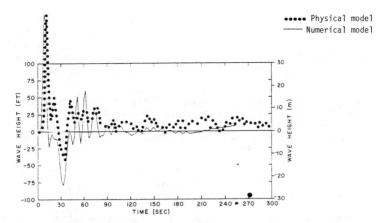

Figure 2. - Physical and numerical model wave profiles at probe No. 6A.

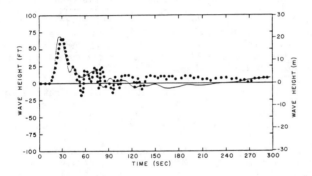

Figure 3. - Physical and numerical model wave profiles at probe No. 3.

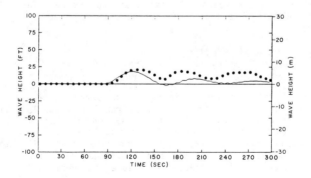

Figure 4. - Physical and numerical model wave profiles at probe No. 12.

Empirical Prediction Method. - A dimensional analysis [4] was performed on the continuity equation (2) and momentum equations (3), (4). From this analysis it was determined that the main parameters affecting the wave height and propagation are the slide Froude number, $F_r = V_S / \sqrt{gD}$, a distance parameter ℓ/D, and the time rate of change of water displacement.

A series of data plots were made relating the maximum initial wave height (η/D) to a displacement parameter (V/D^3), the slide Froude number, and the distance from the slide. For slide Froude numbers above 0.6, increases in velocity of the landslide produce only minor increases in wave heights.

An equation was fitted to the data in the original study using a logarithmic form. The wave height was found to decay with distance from the slide according to a power law.

An independent study (Huber, 1982) conducted at about the same time in Switzerland resulted in many of the same conclusions reached in this study. Huber also concluded that a displacement parameter, a slide Froude number, and a distance parameter were the primary factors influencing the wave height. The main difference between Huber's study and the Morrow Point study was the range of the displacement parameters. Historic rockfalls into Swiss lakes have displacement numbers around 0.02, while the displacement parameters for the Morrow Point study ranged from 2.0 to 4.0.

Huber developed a technique for estimating wave height based on displacement parameter, direction of propagation, slide Froude number and distance. This method was developed from a series of two-dimensional flume tests and three-dimensional wave basin tests.

It is realized that the logarithmic equation developed from the original physical model study of Morrow Point Reservoir is not valid for displacement numbers smaller than 1.0. Rockfalls into the Swiss lakes are in this range. Therefore, a power equation was developed as an alternative. The power equation still gives good estimates for the Morrow Point model waves and the Vaiont landslide case (see figure 5) and also gives reasonable estimates for smaller landslides and rockfalls. Figure 5 is a plot of the equation.

$$\frac{\eta}{D} = \frac{0.14 \ (V/D^3)^{0.50}}{10^{\frac{\ell/D}{58}}} \tag{1}$$

Equation 1 gives estimates for maximum wave heights at the dam with the wave propagating at a 90° angle to the direction of the landslide. Waves in the direction of the landslide are much higher and initially decay at about twice the rate with the distance until ℓ/D is about 20, then the decay rate stabilizes and is the same in all directions. The wave height at the dam is increased in amplitude due to the partial reflection of the dam. This increase is included in equation 1.

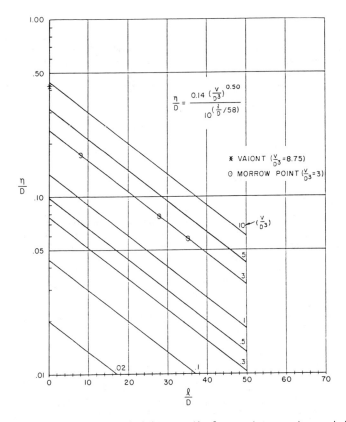

Figure 5. - Maximum wave height vs. displacement parameter and distance from the landslide.

Numerical Simulation. - A mathematical model was developed to study the generation, propagation, and dissipation of rockfall or landslide-generated water waves in bays, lakes, reservoirs, fjords, and rivers (Chiang, et. al., 1981). The mathematical model was used to simulate the laboratory tests of landslide-generated waves in Morrow Point Reservoir. The numerical results agree very well with the laboratory results. The mathematical model was also verified with several historic events and model studies reported in the literature.

The mathematical model is a set of nonlinear, depth-integrated equations to be applied to a variable depth basin. Hydrostatic pressure is assumed. Coriolis force is neglected due to the small area of application. The major forcing function is the squeeze of the water column due to the intrusion of a landslide mass. The squeeze action is represented by a change of water depth or a raise of the bottom of the basin. The lateral velocity produced by the squeeze action is simulated by the velocity due to the elevation gradient which is produced by the raise of the water column at the location of the landslide. The effects of drag due to the landslide are included in the momentum equations. The resultant set of equations is (see also Chiang and Lee, 1982, and Raney and Butler, 1975).

$$\frac{\partial \eta}{\partial t} + \frac{\partial (Hu)}{\partial x} + \frac{\partial (Hv)}{\partial y} = -\frac{\partial D}{\partial t} \tag{2}$$

$$\frac{\partial u}{\partial t} + u\frac{\partial u}{\partial x} + v\frac{\partial u}{\partial y} + g\frac{\partial \eta}{\partial x} = -F_x \tag{3}$$

$$\frac{\partial v}{\partial t} + u\frac{\partial v}{\partial x} + v\frac{\partial v}{\partial y} + g\frac{\partial \eta}{\partial y} = -F_y \tag{4}$$

The terms on the right-hand sides of momentum equations (3) and (4) include effects of bottom friction and drag due to a landslide. At a location outside of the landslide area, the resistance force is equal to that due to bottom stress:

$$F = \frac{n^2 g \ (u^2 + v^2)}{1.486^2 \ H^{4/3}} \tag{5}$$

At a location covered by the moving landslide, the resistance is represented by the drag induced by the slide [1].

$$F = -\frac{1}{2} \frac{V_r^2}{HA_s} \ (C_{Dp}A_p + C_{Dv}A_v) \ \cos \alpha \tag{6}$$

A central difference formulation is used to transform the aforementioned partial differential equations into a set of finite difference equations in an explicit form. Three kinds of boundary conditions were used in addition to the time history of the slide intrusion. At the far upstream boundary, a radiation condition allows the wave to propagate through the boundary without reflection. At the downstream boundary a dam allows overtopping if the water level is higher than the specified elevation. Other parts of the boundary are partially reflective on which part of the wave energy is dissipated.

The mathematical model was used to simulate the landslide waves generated in Morrow Point Reservoir. The model consists of 14 by 64 grid points. The grid spacing is 76 m (250 ft) in either direction. The bathymetry was obtained from the appropriate topographic maps published by the U. S. Geological Survey. Landslides at three locations (A, B, and C in figure 1) were studied.

The time history of the computed wave heights at the grid point nearby each probe is stored and plotted. Figure 2 depicts the prototype time history of the wave amplitude nearby probe No. 6A which is located in front of slide A (figure 1). The solid line represents the computed results while the solid circles indicate the laboratory data. The first peak of approximately 52 m (171 ft) prototype height is caused by the sudden push of the slide mass on the water. This peak later breaks on the south shore with part of its energy propagating both downstream and upstream. Although there appears to be a phase difference of a couple seconds (prototype), the calculated maximum height is amazingly close to the laboratory measurement. The negative wave and the reflective wave also match reasonably well. The later fluctuations due to multiple reflections and refractions in the irregular bathymetry are small and of no significant meaning.

The wave measured by probe No. 3 indicates a peak of 20 m (65 ft) in front of the dam. The results from the numerical model again show very good matching with the experimental data (figure 3).

At probe No. 12, the wave is reduced to about 6 m (21 ft) due to multiple reflection losses and dispersion effect along the path of more than 3 km (2 mi). The computed peak is slightly lower (figure 3). The phase matches with the data very well.

Conclusions. - Landslide-generated water waves were studied in Morrow Point Reservoir using a physical model. An empirical prediction method was developed from the data to estimate maximum wave height at a dam (η/D) based on a dimensionless displacement parameter (V/D^3) and the distance from the landslide (ℓ/D).

Waves are two to three times higher directly in line with a landslide than beside the landslide. For slide Froude numbers above 0.6 only minor increases in wave heights result. The wave height attenuates according to a power law with distance from the landslide.

A mathematical model was developed which accurately predicts the amplitude and phase of waves both in the vicinity of the landslide and several kilometers from the landslide. The numerical model can be used to predict waves resulting from possible landslides, rockfalls, and fault displacements in the bottom of a basin. Landslide data can be input into the model, or the model will generate an assumed landslide to produce the waves.

Acknowledgments. - The technical contributions of Dr. Henry Falvey to the physical model studies and Mr. David Divoky to the mathematical model development are greatly appreciated. Dr. David Harris was the primary coordinator for all of the studies.

Appendix 1. - References

1. Chiang, W. L., Divoky, D., Parnicky, P., and Wier, W., "Numerical Model of Landslide-Generated Waves," Report T3427, Tetra Tech, Inc., Pasadena, California, November 1981.

2. Chiang, W. L., and Lee, J. J., "Simulation of Large-Scale Circulation in Harbors," Journal of the Waterway, Port, Coastal and Ocean Division, ASCE, Vol. 108, No. WW1, Proc. Paper 16841, February 1982, pp. 17-31.

3. Huber, A., "Impulse Waves in Swiss Lakes as a Result of Rock Avalanches and Bank Slides, Experimental Results for the Prediction of the Characteristic Numbers for These Waves," Paper, Int. Comm. on Large Dams, 14th Congress, Q54, R29, Rio de Janeiro, Brazil, May 1982.

4. Pugh, C. A., "Model Studies of Landslide-Generated Water Waves, Morrow Point Reservoir," U. S. Bureau of Reclamation, REC-ERC-82-9, January 1982.

5. Pugh, C. A., and Harris, D. W., "Prediction of Landslide-Generated Water Waves," Paper, Int. Comm. on Large Dams, 14th Congress, Q54, R29, Rio de Janeiro, Brazil, May 1982.

6. Raney, D., and Butler, H. L., "A Numerical Model for Predicting the Effects of Landslide-Generated Water Waves," Research Report H751, U. S. Army Engineering Waterways Experiment Station, Vicksburg, Mississippi, February 1975.

7. Slingerland, R. L., and Voight, B., "Occurrences, Properties, and Predictive Models of Landslide Generated Waver Waves," Rockslides and Avalanches, Vol. 2, Elsevier Science Publishing, N. Y., 1979.

Appendix 2. - Notations

A_p, A_v, A_s	cross-sectional areas
C_{Dp}, C_{Dv}	pressure drag coefficient and viscous drag coefficient
D	water depth
F	resistance force
$F_r = V_s/\sqrt{gD}$	slide Froude number
F_x, F_y	total friction along x and y directions, respectively
g	gravitational acceleration
$H = \eta + D$	total water depth relative to instantaneous water surface
ℓ	distance from the landslide
ℓ/D	distance parameter
n	Manning's roughness coefficient
t	time
u, v	water velocities along x and y directions, respectively
x, y	coordinates
η	surface elevation relative to initial water surface (positive upward)
η/D	maximum initial wave height
α	angle between the instantaneous slide direction and the horizontal
V	volume of water displaced by the landslide
V/D^3	displacement parameter
V_r	horizontal landslide velocity, relative to far field water velocity
V_s	maximum landslide velocity

Sea Level Rise and Coastal Stormwater Drainage

Chin Y. Kuo*, A.M. ASCE

Global sea level rise as a result of the greenhouse effect and the past trend and future projection on the rise are discussed. Potential problems associated with coastal stormwater drainage system design and their possible solutions are presented. It is recommended that both future costs of retrofitting the system when sea level rise is realized and the cost in designing a system now against the risk of a rise are considered by planners and engineers.

The Greenhouse Effect

Earth's surface temperature is governed by the principle of heat balance among sun radiation received, reflected and heat retained. Carbon dioxide, water vapor and other gases in the atmosphere absorb some of the heat energy and therefore increase the temperature due to this heat energy trapped in the atmosphere. This phenomenon is referred to as the greenhouse warming or greenhouse effect. Hoffman (1984) has reported that CO_2 concentration in the atmosphere has increased 20% since the industrial revolution and an 8% increase during the period of 1958-82 has been observed at NOAA's Mauna Loa Observatory in Hawaii (Keeling, Bacastow and Whorf, 1982). The concentration of all greenhouse gases and vapor is expected to double by the year 2050 or sooner. In spite of the forecast uncertainties for global climate conditions, the National Academy of Sciences has issued two reports which conclude that the earth's average surface temperature would increase 1.5°-4.5°C (3-8°F) due to the doubling of greenhouse gases (Charney, 1979; Smagorinsky, 1982).

Sea Level Rise

The global warming will cause the global sea level to rise due to thermal expansion of seawater itself, snow and ice melt from mountains and polar glaciers, and ice discharges from the ice sheets in Greenland, West Antarctica and East Antarctica. In the past century, studies based upon tidal gauge measurements to determine trends have concluded that the worldwide sea level has risen 10-15 cm (4-6 inches) (Gornitz 1982). In a recent National Academy of Sciences' report, Revelle (1983) estimated that the global sea level could rise 50-150 cm (5/3 to 5 feet) by 2080. This does not take into consideration deglaciation of the antarctic ice sheet. In a separate report by the Environmental Protection Agency (Hoffman, Keyes and Titus, 1983), scenarios of future sea level rise have been projected. The estimates for low scenario are 13 cm by 2025 and 38 cm by 2075. High estimates

*Professor and Coordinator, Hydrosystems Division, Department of Civil Engineering, Virginia Polytechnic Institute and State University, Blacksburg, VA 24061.

are 55 cm by 2025 and 211 cm by 2075. Mid-range high and low are 39 cm by 2025, 137 cm by 2075; 26 cm by 2025, 91 cm by 2075. Local trends could add 1 to 2 cm per decade to the global rise along much of the Atlantic Coast and as much as 10 cm per decade in the Gulf Coast. The global warming is likely to be accompanied by significant changes in evaporation and precipitation patterns. An atmospheric doubling of greenhouse gases would cause rainfall and evaporation to increase by 11 percent worldwide (Environmental Protection Agency, 1984). Prediction model for a specific region or a specific frequency of rainfall recurrence is not currently available.

Potential Coastal Stormwater Drainage Problems

It is necessary to assess the impact of the sea level rise on coastal stormwater drainage design by identifying the potential problems associated with drainage system planning and design. The uniqueness of flooding in the coastal areas can be characterized by two key parameters: flat terrains and tidal effects (Kuo, 1984).

1. The global rise in temperature due to the greenhouse effect on the earth will increase the evaporation rate and rainfall in terms of the depth or the intensity. This phenomenon is especially pronounced in the coastal regions on a local scale basis. Tremendous heat is generated during the daytime due to extensive paved areas and many urban activities. The air temperature is high above the cities which causes the rise of the warm air mass. The relatively cold air mass above the sea will move onto the land and bring moisture with it. The landward sea breeze brings more moisture to the coastal area and thus increases the humidity and possibly generates more rainfall. This local phenomenon occurs in coastal urban areas.

2. As the sea level rises, the groundwater tables increase. At the same time, moisture content in soil increases. Surface runoff volume would increase because of the small infiltration rate. The recharge rate of the groundwater into streams will also increase and cause the increase of base flow in streams. During the storm period, the total discharge of the streamflow which is the sum of the surface runoff and base flow will increase significantly. The increase in runoff volume may add to the runoff increase caused by the urbanization process within a coastal drainage basin and aggravate the flood condition.

3. Sea level rise means the rise of tailwater for the outfall of a drainage system for both open channels and storm sewer pipes. The hydraulic gradients would decrease and reduce the velocity and the flow rate in pipes and channels. Many areas will be flooded more easily and frequently than before.

4. Increase in sea level would increase the water surface elevation of the receiving water for a pumping station. The stormwater has to be pumped against high head. Consequently, the pump will either discharge at a smaller flow rate or consume more power at a higher pumping cost than the existing sea level condition. Slow pumping rate of a pump would require a long pumping period

or frequent pumping in order to pump the runoff generated by storms to avoid flooding.

5. Due to the sea level rise, the wetland areas along the coasts, bays and estuaries will most likely increase. This translates to either the growth of more vegetation or of different species of vegetation. From the viewpoint of hydraulics, it would change the values of roughness coefficient. In the calculation of water depths in the coastal areas due to storm surge, the roughness coefficients play an important role. For example, higher water depths are expected for higher roughness coefficients. If this increase in water surface elevation is compounded with the increase of mean sea level, the resulting flood would be very significant.

6. The rise of sea level would cause the rise of water surface elevation not only in the open coastal areas, but also extended further inland in the estuaries. In other words, the impact of flooding due to sea level rise will be extended inland due to the backwater effect. The heights of floodwalls and levees need to be increased to take this effect into consideration. For future levee construction and design, the effect can be accounted for through the use of a higher factor of safety value in determining the height of the levee.

7. Decrease in conveying velocities in natural drainage channels and man-made drainage canals due to sea level rise and decrease in hydraulic gradient will slow down the transport capacity of the flow in channels and canals for sediment and debris. As a result, siltation and debris deposition take place within the drainage waterways. It would further hamper the adequacy of the drainage systems. The same phenomenon occurs for storm sewer pipes in which the deposition of the sediment and debris would reduce the pipe flow capacity.

8. Many coastal lagoons and lakes are used as stormwater detention facilities. The lakes are connected either in series or in parallel by channels which eventually lead to oceans or bays (Kuo, 1981). With sea level rise, the storage capacities of the lakes for stormwater detention would be decreased. The normal pool elevations in the lakes are high before the storms occur. Therefore, the additional storage to the normal pool storage is very little because the lakes are not deep due to flat terrains and normal pool elevations are near the ground elevations due to high groundwater tables. In addition to the decrease in lake detention capability, water quality is a problem which is caused by poor flushing as a result of sea level rise and slow flushing velocities in lake outlets (Kuo, 1980).

9. For regions such as Houston, Texas and southern California, land subsidence occurs because of excessive oil pumping underground. For the existing normal sea level, it has already posed a big problem for stormwater drainage. With the predicted sea level rise in the years to come, the drainage problems will be intensified. A similar problem of land subsidence, but due to

excessive groundwater pumping, has occurred in the coastal city of Taipei, Taiwan, Republic of China. The city is located in a basin which constantly experiences flooding problems during hurricanes and summer thunder storms. The drainage systems have been upgraded recently by replacing old pipes, re-routing flows and adding more pumping stations to take care of the internal drainage problem behind the city-wide levee system. Further improvement is necessary when sea level rises.

10. Terrebonne Parish, Louisiana is subsiding and eroding away. Physically, the parish was created several thousand years ago by the Mississippi River which brought sediment to the area forming a delta. The course of the Mississippi River changed in response to the delta formation and the river does not provide sediment to the parish. Additionally, control structures built on the river and the Gulf of Mexico further reduce the amount of freshwater and sediment reaching the area. Consequently, the parish suffers from a considerable sediment deficit, which is an important factor contributing to the loss of the barrier islands and wetlands in the parish. Terrebonne Parish, one of many parishes along the coast of the Gulf of Mexico, is a major source of seafood and fur products. The parish also has land subsidence problems due to the consolidation of old sediment deposited in the area. The existing drainage systems, consisting mainly of canals and pumping stations, are not adequate. With the predicted sea level rise, the parish will have more problems with drainage and loss of barrier islands and wetlands. The existing stormwater drainage pattern or future drainage system provides basic information to decision-making on estuary and marsh resources management. On the other hand, in order to manage the natural resources, it is necessary to alter the natural drainage ways and redesign the drainage and flood protection structures to achieve the desirable balance for ecosystems such as salinity level, water temperature, water depth and velocity in the parish (Gibbs and Kuo, 1984).

11. Canal systems are commonly seen in the deltas of major rivers for drainage, navigation, irrigation for farmlands and rice fields. For example, the Mekong River Delta in Thailand and the Yangtze River Delta in the People's Republic of China are important areas of natural resources. The entire waterway will be very sensitive in response to the sea level rise. Careful analysis and planning of canal systems requires special attention.

Possible Solutions

The following possible solutions to solve the problems associated with the drainage systems due to sea level rise are offered. This list is by no means complete. The solutions are applicable to both the existing drainage systems which need improvement to alleviate the flooding based on a predicted sea level rise and to the future drainage systems under planning which need to consider the effect of the sea level rise. Planners and engineers need to exercise their judgement in selecting an option or a combination of options to prevent the municipalities from flooding and yet provide an overall best solution which is economically, environmentally, and socially acceptable.

It should be noted that the effect of sea level rise on coastal drainage systems is more pronounced on the South Atlantic coast and the coastline of the Gulf of Mexico. There are two major reasons. First, the region has a wide coastal alluvial flat plain. Secondly, the amount of sea level rise when compared with the normal tidal range is high in terms of percent increase for the normal design tidal condition. In establishing design criteria, one should take the geographic variation in sea level rise into consideration. Specifically, individual municipalities should have their own specifications regarding drainage system design and construction based on the local conditions. The solutions to be discussed include both structural and non-structural options.

1. The local rainfall information of the rainfall intensity-duration-frequency relationship curves needs to be revised to account for the increased rainfall due to the increase in air moisture caused by the greenhouse effect.

2. The recurrence interval of the tidal height for different locations on the U.S. coastlines needs to be analyzed and the frequency curves (for example, Ho et al. 1976) need to be revised to take sea level rise into consideration.

3. For future storm sewer pipe drainage system design, the use of larger pipe sizes is expected. For the existing systems, the old pipes can be replaced by larger size pipes or a new supplemental pipe system can be installed. For old cities, a supplemental new system seems unfavorable.

4. If drainage channels are used in the drainage systems, enlargement of the existing channels, making it wider and deeper, is necessary. Sometimes, channelization to reduce the roughness coefficient would be sufficient. For future drainage sites, large easements should be provided to accommodate the large drainage channels.

5. It is most likely that in the low elevation areas the construction of floodwalls or levees is required. Locks and flap gates should be installed. The gates are closed for high tide conditions when pumps are in operation and opened when the stormwater is discharged by gravity action without the need of pumping such as items number 3 and number 4 described above.

6. When gravity flows are not available in the drainage systems, pumping is required. For future drainage sites, large size pumps should be provided to work against the high tailwaters due to sea level rise and to handle the large runoff volume which is caused by greenhouse effect. For existing drainage systems, replacement of the existing pumps with larger ones is not economically favorable. Installation of additional pumps in series or in parallel seems to be a better option. One should keep in mind that adding new pumps alone may not solve the flooding problems due to the

sea level rise if the existing storm sewer pipes leading to the pumps are not large enough to convey enough flow to the pumping stations. In this case, the pumps will discharge only the flow that the pipe system supplies. The pump won't pump the desired flow volume as one would expect to alleviate the flooding. One design method to take care of this situation is to construct a sump in the pumping station with a volume capacity large enough to supply flow to the pumps. The sump would receive flow from more than one trunk line of the storm sewer pipe system.

7. Detention basins are widely accepted as an effective means of controlling surface runoff in urban and suburban areas. The concept of detention can be applied to the drainage problem in terms of not only the detention basin, but also roof-top detention, storage trenches, porous pavement, storage in low play grounds and parking lots, underground storage in the form of groundwater recharge or construction of underground storage tanks, and in-line storage in the storm sewer pipes. With the sea level rise, the drainage capacities of storm sewer pipe systems, drainage channels and pumping facilities would all decrease. A logical alternative design method is to include detention facilities in the drainage basin, preferably located near the upstream end of the basin. From the viewpoint of hydrology, it is advantageous to have some form of detention facility installed far away from the outlet of the basin. This scheme would be able to reduce the peak discharge, delay the peak time of runoff and therefore reduce the flow loading onto the storm sewer pipes, drainage channels and pump station. After the storm has ended, the runoff volume stored in the detention facilities can then be released gradually into the drainage systems without over-burdening the system.

8. Existing buildings in the low elevation areas can be flood-proofed. Construction of basements in the future can be avoided if possible.

9. The federal and private coastal flood insurance programs need to be reviewed. Attention should be directed in particular to existing buildings and facilities.

10. For future urban developments, consideration should be given to elevating the buildings and streets while taking the sea level rise into consideration in the drainage design.

11. The frequency of occurrence of a given tidal height at a given location dictates the recurrence interval of the height of tailwater for designing a drainage canal or a storm sewer outfall. For engineering analysis, the joint probability of the frequency of the surface runoff and the tidal height can be performed based on methods available (Kuo, 1980). Also, the methods to estimate the coastal flooding caused alone by the storm surge from the sea are available (Kuo, 1980; Dept. of Housing & Urban Development, 1978). Therefore, the severe condition when extraordinary runoff occurs in conjunction with the storm surge or high spring neap tide can be analyzed and the

results should be used as design inputs to the stormwater drainage systems.

12. It is necessary to study options for drainage systems and to
    estimate costs of the project. Engineers and planners need to
    compare the costs between two cases, design of a system now
    against the risk of a rise in sea level or retrofitting the
    system in the future which is not designed for a rise. Two
    case studies were performed in Charleston, South Carolina
    (LaRoche and Webb, 1985) and in Fort Walton Beach, Florida
    (Waddell and Blaylock, 1985) to answer this question based
    upon various scenarios of sea level rise and precipitation
    increase.

Concluding Remarks

    Many engineers and planners are not aware of or do not take into
consideration the potential sea level rise in their coastal drainage
design because of the uncertainty in predicting the rise. This paper
outlines the problems associated with the impact of sea level rise on
the coastal stormwater drainage design and their possible solutions.
It is strongly recommended that any new coastal storm sewer system
design should consider, as a minimum, various sea level rise scenarios
based on Environmental Protection Agency's projection and compare
the retrofit costs and the costs of designing a system against future
sea level rise. In addition, one should keep in mind that the impact
of sea level rise is far beyond the stormwater drainage itself.
Potential problems such as shore erosion, loss of wetland, salinity
intrusion, hazardous waste disposal in coastal floodplain, etc. (Barth
and Titus, 1984) need to be considered in overall coastal stormwater
management.

References

1. Barth, M. C., and Titus, J. E., eds., Greenhouse Effect and
   Sea Level Rise: A Challenge for this Generation, Van Nostrand
   Reinhold, New York, N.Y., 1984.

2. Charney, J., Carbon Dioxide and Climate: A Scientific Assessment, National Academy of Sciences Press, Washington, D.C., 1979.

3. Gibbs, M. J., and Kuo, C. Y., "Sea Level Rise and the Master
   Drainage Plan in Terrebonne Parish, Louisiana," Report to U.S.
   Environmental Protection Agency, September, 1984.

4. Gormitz, V., Lebedeff, S., and Hansen, J., "Global Sea Level
   Trend in the Past Century," Science, Vol. 217, 1982.

5. Ho, F. P., et al., Storm Tide Frequency Analysis for the Open
   Coast of Virginia, Maryland, Delaware, NOAA TM NWS HYDRO-32,
   Department of Commerce, 1976.

6. Hoffman, J. S., Keyes, D., and Titus, J. G., Projecting Future
   Sea Level Rise, Government Printing Office, Washington, D.C.,
   1983.

7. Hoffman, J. S., "Estimates of Future Sea Level Rise," in Green-
    house Effect and Sea Level Rise: A Challenge for this Genera-
    tion, Barth and Titus, eds., Van Nostrand, New York, 1984.

8. Keeling, C. D., Bacastow, R. B., and Whorf, T. P., "Measurements
    of the Concentration of Carbon Dioxide at Mauna Loa Observatory,
    Hawaii," Carbon Dioxide Review: 1982, W. Clark, ed., Oxford
    University Press, New York, 1982.

9. Kuo, C. Y., and Price, R. W., "Culvert System to Increase
    Flushing in Lagoons and Detention Basins in Coastal Areas,"
    Proceedings of the Sixth Annual Conference on Utilization of
    Science in the Decision-Making Process, The Coastal Society,
    California, 1980.

10. Kuo, C. Y., ed., Urban Stormwater Management in Coastal Areas,
    Proceedings of the National Symposium, American Society of Civil
    Engineers, 1980.

11. Kuo, C. Y., "Methods for Stormwater Routing in Lake-Canal
    Systems," Proceedings of the Second International Conference on
    Urban Storm Drainage, Urbana, Illinois, 1981.

12. Kuo, C. Y., "Some Hydraulic Problems Related to Stormwater
    Drainage Design in Coastal Areas," Proceedings of the South-
    eastern Conference on Theoretical and Applied Mechanics, Auburn
    University, Alabama, 1984.

13. LaRoche, T. B., and Webb, M. K., "Impact of Sea Level Rise on
    Stormwater Drainage Systems in the Charleston, South Carolina
    Area," Report to U.S. Environmental Protection Agency,
    Washington, D.C., 1985.

14. Revelle, R., "Probable Future Changes in Sea Level Resulting
    from Increased Atmospheric Carbon Dioxide," in Changing
    Climate, National Academy of Sciences Press, Washington, D.C.,
    1983.

15. Smagorinsky, J., Chairman, Climate Research Board, Carbon
    Dioxide: A Second Assessment, National Academy of Sciences
    Press, Washington, D.C., 1982.

16. U.S. Department of Housing and Urban Development, Federal
    Insurance Administration, Coastal Flooding Storm Surge Model,
    Part I, Methodology, Washington, D.C., 1978.

17. U.S. Environmental Protection Agency, Potential Climatic Impacts
    of Increasing Atmospheric CO_2 with Emphasis on Water Availability
    and Hydrology in the United States, Government Printing Office,
    Washington, D.C., 1984.

18. Waddell, J. O., and Blaylock, R. A., "Impact of Sea Level Rise
    on Gap Greek Watershed in the Fort Walton Beach, Florida Area,"
    Report to U.S. Environmental Protection Agency, Washington, D.C.,
    1985.

RESPONSE OF GREAT SALT LAKE TO CLIMATE VARIABILITY

Paul A. Kay[1] and Henry F. Diaz[2]

ABSTRACT: Levels of Great Salt Lake, Utah, have fluctuated through a range of 6.2 m in the historic record since the 1840s. In water years 1983-1984, the lake rose 2.9 m in response to record precipitation in the basin. Recent (1931-1984) seasonal changes in lake volumes are regressed on seasonal temperature and precipitation in the climatic divisions from which the lake receives input. Seasonal volumetric increase is controlled by autumn, winter and spring precipitation; seasonal volumetric decrease is controlled inversely by summer precipitation. Atmospheric circulation controls of the seasonal precipitation are discussed.

INTRODUCTION

As a closed lake in a basin of interior drainage, the Great Salt Lake (GSL) of northern Utah is sensitive to climatic variability. The volume of water in GSL represents a balance between precipitation and runoff inputs and evaporation output. The surface elevation of the lake is related, non-linearly, to lake volume, so that with allowances for lags in response, lake level fluctuations are reflections of the precipitation and evaporation climatology.

The levels of GSL are known from measurements and careful interpolations since the 1840s (Arnow, 1984). Mean lake level, prior to 1982, was about 1280.5 m. The historic maximum, in 1873, was 1283.70 m, and the historic minimum, in 1963, was 1277.52 m. In water years (WY) 1983-1984, GSL experienced a historically unprecedented rise of 2.93 m to just short of the historic maximum. This rise was associated with a volumetric increase of 77% from the seasonal low at the end of summer 1982. As of spring 1986, the lake levels remained high. The unusual

---

[1] Associate Professor, Department of Geography, University of Utah, Salt Lake City, UT 84112

[2] Meteorologist, Environmental Research Laboratories, NOAA, 325 Broadway, Boulder, CO 80303

behavior was triggered by successive record wet WYs which included the wettest autumn (1982), the wettest summer (1983) and among the wettest winters on record at Salt Lake City. Karl and Young (1986) showed that the annual lake level series was well correlated with WY precipitation, and that times of rising lake levels coincided with episodes of excessive cumulative departures of precipitation. They estimated a recurrence interval of about 120 years for the WY 1983-1984 event.

The series of annual lake levels shows very strong persistence, the first order autocorrelation being about 0.98 (James et al., 1979). Annual level represents a balance between seasonal accumulation and loss, each having its own climatic characteristics; consideration of only annual data masks some of the direct relationships. Further, the relationship of lake behavior to climate is best seen when volume, rather than level, changes are considered, because the configuration of the basin is such that level is not a linear response to volume. Therefore, we have decomposed the annual series into seasonal series of volume increase and decrease.

In this paper, we examine monthly and seasonal climatic variables to find those most closely related to lake behavior in recent decades. We hypothesize that seasonal increase of GSL is primarily a function of accumulation season precipitation, and that seasonal decrease is primarily a function of summer temperature as a surrogate for evaporation. Our goal is to derive diagnostic models of seasonal climatic controls, rather than solely to achieve an efficient forecast model.

DATA

Monthly lake levels are reported in Water Supply Papers of the U.S. Geological Survey. The lake basin has experienced considerable human impact in the form of water management and withdrawals. Reconstructed pristine levels, estimated as if there had been no human impact, were calculated up to 1968 (Whitaker, 1971). Since then, it is estimated that no major additional impacts were manifest, so that an adjustment of about 1.5 m has been applied to convert actual to natural levels (Arnow, personal communication, 1985). Volumes were calculated from established stage-area-volume relationships. Seasonal increase for WY t is calculated as the maximum volume in year t less the minimum volume in year t-1, and seasonal decrease for WY t as the minimum in year t less the maximum occurring earlier the same year. The two series are independent of each other (r=-0.08). Some episodic behavior, involving runs of years of large (small) increases (decreases), may be seen (Fig. 1).

Monthly mean temperature and precipitation for the North Central (NC) and the Northern Mountains (NM) climatic divisions of Utah were obtained from NOAA's National Climatic Data Center in Asheville, NC, for 1931-1984.

These two divisions encompass the area which is the source of most of the inflow to GSL (Arnow, 1984). However, the divisions do not encompass all of the GSL basin, and NM also comprises area outside the basin. Although some misspecification in the models might occur, the number of stations in NM but outside GSL basin is small, so the bias should be minimal. We used seasonal means or sums defined as the standard four meteorological seasons. In one analysis, the divisions were treated separately, in another they were combined.

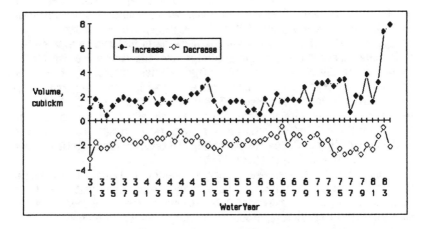

Figure 1. Seasonal volumetric changes, Great Salt Lake

METHODS

Models of seasonal controls of volumetric change were created by multiple regression analyses. Since the predictor variables in the models were interrelated, it was necessary to control for multicolinearity which might bias the regression results, leading to inefficient and misspecified models. We chose the method of all possible subsets regression to examine many likely candidates for "best" model. Our selection criterion was Mallows' Cp statistic (Draper and Smith, 1981), which is the ratio of reduction of variance by a given model to that in a theoretically correct model, adjusted for the number of variables in the model (some of which might be spurious). The chosen technique also supplied a number of diagnostic statistics for examination of residuals (Mahalanobis' and Cook's distances, pressed residuals), allowing an assessment of the influence of the extreme WYs on the model specification. Standardized regression coefficients are reported. These allow an assessment of the relative influence of each predictor on the response of the dependent variable.

MODELS OF SEASONAL CONTROL

Seasonal volume increase is best predicted by a model containing precipitation variables (Table 1). Autumn, winter and spring precipitation in NC, in that order, reproduce 60% of the variance, with a standard error of estimate of 0.89. If the lag one volume increase is included as a predictor, it becomes the most important predictor, but the relative order of the seasonal variables is unchanged. The relative influence of autumn decreases, however, to just slightly more than winter, as compared to the first model. Explained variance is 74% with a standard error of 0.72. The inclusion of NC precipitation only, when one might expect NM variables to be most closely related to stream inflows, is a result of the large multicolinearity ($r \geq 0.80$) between monthly and seasonal precipitation values in the two divisions (Kay and Diaz, 1985).

Seasonal volume decrease is poorly predicted (Table 1). A model containing summer precipitation in one division reproduces just 30% of the variance, with a standard error of 0.47. Summer temperature does not enter as a significant predictor, although the sign is as would be expeced. The relationship between volume decrease and precipitation is negative; that is, the magnitude of volume decrease is least in wet summers.

Because of the intercorrelations of precipitation between the two divisions, we decided to sum the precipitation values to represent total inflow to the lake. Temperature in NC only was used, as the lake lies mostly in that division and not at all in NM. The models were similar to those produced when the individual divisions were used (Table 2). The best model for seasonal volume increase included autumn, winter and spring precipitation. The model accounted for 55% of the variance, with a standard error of 0.95. With lag one increase included, explained variance was 70%, with a standard error of 0.78. The best model for seasonal volume decrease included only summer precipitation. Again, the relationship was inverse. The model accounted for just 29% of the variance, with a standard error of 0.47.

INCR (to 1984) = .556 NCPAUT+ .337 NCPWIN+ .266 NCPSPR
$$R^2 = .596$$
$$see = .89$$

INCR (to 1984) = .354 NCPAUT + .350 NCPSUM+ .234 NCPSPR+ .430 INCR$_{t-1}$
$$R^2 = .742$$
$$see = .72$$

INCR (to 1982) = .497 NCPAUT + .462 NCPWIN + .202 NCPSPR + .366 INCR$_{t-1}$
$$R^2 = .672$$
$$see = .49$$

DECR (1984) = .483 NMPSUM (- .178 MTTSUM)*
$$R^2 = .317$$
$$see = .47$$

Table 1. Regression models for volumetric changes as functions of seasonal and divisional data. Standardized coefficients are reported, along with explained variance (R^2) and standard error of esitmate (see). INCR=lake volume increase, DECR=lake volume decrease, NC=Northcentral division, NM=Northern Mountains division, P=precipitation, T=temperature, AUT=Sep to Nov, WIN=Dec to Feb, SPR=Mar to May, SUM=Jun to Aug. *not significant.

INCR = .365 PAUT + .284 PWIN + .210 PSPR + .440 INC$_{t-1}$
$$R^2 = .696$$
$$see = .78$$

DECR = .540 PSUM
$$R^2 = .292$$
$$see = .47$$

Table 2. Regression models for volumetric changes as functions of seasonal variables for the climatic divisions combined. Abbreviations as in Table 1.

The influence of the extreme WYs 1983-1984 on the regression models was evaluated two ways. First, models were run with data only to WY 1982, that is omitting the extreme years. The results were similar to those cited above with regards to the magnitudes of the coefficients and explained variances. Standard errors of estimates were, however, about one-half those in the other models. For example, in the model for increase (Table 1), lag one increase is less important than precipitation, and autumn is only somewhat more influential than winter. This result arises from the unusualness of the very wet autumn in 1982 that set the stage for the events of WY 1983-1984. Second, the diagnostic statistics for the models run with the full series of data indicated that although WYs 1983-1984 were indeed unusual and might be considered statistical outliers, the coefficients and residuals were not seriously affected. That is, no serious bias resulted from their inclusion in the analysis.

DISCUSSION

The hypothesis that seasonal volumetric increase is a response to accumulation season precipitation is substantiated. The order of importance of the predictor variables is of some interest. Autumn precipitation is the most effective, followed by winter then spring. It appears that early season accumulation is most effective in setting the stage for a large volume increase, perhaps by saturating the ground and establishing the snowpack, so that spring runoff is promoted. The hypothesis that seasonal volumetric decrease is a response to loss season temperature is not substantiated. It appears that precipitation, rather than temperature, is more effecitve. There is, however, a fairly strong (r=-0.6) inverse relationship between summer temperature and precipitation in NC division. A more direct measure of evaporation, taking account of sunshine, humidity and wind, might improve the model relationships.

The seasonal components of GSL behavior have been shown to respond to different seasonal precipitation variables. The controls of precipitation in the various seasons are different. In winter, precipitation is produced primarily by transient cyclones tracking eastward from the north Pacific Ocean; in spring, by cyclones that develop within the Great Basin, drawing moisture from a more southerly source; and in summer, by injections of tropical moisture associated with thunderstorm acitivity. These different mechanisms result in a regionalization of the Great Basin according to their seasonal expression and the resulting seasonality of precipitation (Kay, 1982). GSL lies on a winter boundary between very frequent (to the north) and less frequent (to the south) passage of Pacific cyclones (Mitchell, 1976). Thus, the lake should be a sensitive indicator of long-term episodes of wintertime atmospheric circulation regimes. Large seasonal volume increases should occur in episodes of southwardly displaced storm tracks during the accumulation season. The results of the models discussed above indicate that the lake may also contain a signal of less frequent but nevertheless important variations in summertime precipitation. Minimal volume decreases should occur in the episodes of enhanced northwardly extent of monsoonal flow during the evaporation season. If only annual series of lake levels were considered, it might be difficult to ascertain the climatic causes. An episode of rising lake levels might be a result of anomalous conditions in winter or in summer or in both seasons. Treating volumetric increase and decrease separately, the realtionships may be elucidated.

There is evidence in paleoclimatic proxy records that GSL has experienced episodes of lake levels as high as and higher than the present several times in the past few thousand years, perhaps as recently as within the last four hundred (Spencer et al., 1984). Tree-ring analyses, although severely limited by the absence of chronologies within the GSL basin, indicate several times of rapid lake level rise in the past three centuries (Meko and Stockton, 1985), and perhaps too regional differences in climatic fluctuations (Bingham et al., 1985). These indications might be related to fluctuations of the winter and summer climatic boundaries mentionned above. The potential appears considerable for further contributions from careful tree-ring analyses within GSL basin to questions of seasonal climatic fluctuations and lake response.

APPENDIX.—REFERENCES

Arnow, T. (1984). "Water-level and Water-quality Changes in Great Salt Lake Utah, 1847-1983," U.S. Geological Survey, Circular 913.

Bingham, G.E., Richardson, E.A., and Ashcroft, G.A. (1985). "Historical climate data of the Great Salt Lake watershed: relation to lake levels," *Problems of and Prospects for Predicting Great Salt Lake Levels*, P.A. Kay and H.F. Diaz, eds., Center for Public Affairs and Administration, University of Utah, Salt Lake City, UT, 82.

Draper, N.R., and Smith, H. (1981). *Applied Regression Analysis, second edition*, Wiley Interscience, New York, NY.

James, L.D., Bowles, D.S., James, W.R., and Canfield, R.V. (1979). "Estimation of Water Surface Elevation Probabilities and Associated Damages for the Great Salt Lake," Utah Water Research Laboratory, Utah State University, Logan, UT, Water Resources Planning Series UWRL/P79/03.

Karl, T.W., and Young, P.J. (1986). "Recent heavy precipitation in the vicinity of the Great Salt Lake: Just how unusual?" *Bulletin, American Meteorological Society* 67(1),4.

Kay, P.A. (1982). "A perspective on Great Basin paleoclimates," *Man and Environment in the Great Basin*, D.B. Madsen and J.F. O'Connell, eds., Society for American Archaeology Papers No. 2, 76.

Kay, P.A., and Diaz, H.F. (1985). "Synoptic climatological relationships bearing on lake level fluctuations," *Problems of and Prospects for Predicting Great Salt Lake Levels*, P.A. Kay and H.F. Diaz, eds., Center for Public Affairs and Administration, University of Utah, Salt Lake City, UT, 137.

Meko, D.W., and Stockton, C.W.(1985). "Tree ring inferences on levels of the Great Salt Lake, 1700 to present," *Problems of and Prospects for Predicting Great Salt Lake Levels*, P.A. Kay and H.F. Diaz, eds., Center for Public Affairs and Administration, University of Utah, Salt Lake City, UT, 63.

Mitchell, V.L. (1976). "The regionalization of climate in the western United States," *Journal of Applied Meteorology* 15(9), 920.

Spencer, R.J., Baedecker, M.J., Eugster, H.P., Forester, R.M., Goldhaber, R.M., Jones, B.F., Kelts, K., McKenzie, J., Madsen, D.B., Rettig, S.L., Rubin, M., and Bowser, C.J. (1984). "Great Salt Lake and precursor, Utah: the last 30,000 years," *Contributions to Mineralogy and Petrology* 86, 321.

Whitaker, G.L. (1971). "Changes in the elevation of Great Salt Lake caused by Man's activities in the drainage basin," U.S. Geological Survey, *Professional Paper* 750-D, D187.

Estimating Climate Change From Hydrologic Response

Martin Mifflin[1], Jay Quade[2]

In the eighty-one hydrographically closed basins within Nevada many large lakes developed during the pluvial climate of the Pleistocene. Pluvial lake area and tributary basin area have been established from the geomorphic evidence. A method is presented for estimating the climatic parameters of the lake forming pluvial climates using modern climatic relationships within the Great Basin and known hydrologic responses to varied climates. The quantitative approach could be used to estimate water supply change due to given climatic change.

Introduction

The Great Basin is composed of more than one hundred hydrographically closed basins. Eighty-one of these basins with internal drainage occur within Nevada. During the pluvial climates of the Pleistocene, the majority of the closed basins within northern and central Nevada contained stable deep-water lakes. Mifflin and Wheat (1979) mapped the detailed extent of the lakes during the late Pleistocene, and estimated the associated climates which produced the lakes. During conditions of hydrologic equilibrium (as judged by well-developed shoreline terraces and beach bars) the ratio of the lake area to the catchment basin area gives a quantitative measure of the pluvial climate hydrology.

Quantitative Approach

The size of a pluvial lake (surface area) is a quantitative measure of paleoclimate during prolonged periods of equilibrium of the pluvial lakes because it represents moisture leaving the lake:

Moisture into the lake = moisture out, or $(A_t R_t) + (A_1 P_1)$ = $A_1 E_1$, or by rearranging and factoring:

$$A_t R_t = A_1 (E_1 - P_1) \tag{1}$$

where A_t = tributary area of the basin (total basin area minus lake area), R_t = combined runoff of surface and ground water

[1]Research Professor, [2]Research Geologist, Desert Research Institute, Water Resources Center, 2505 Chandler Ave, Suite 1, Las Vegas, Nevada, 89120.

per unit area per unit of time, A_1 = maximum lake area as
indicated by the highest shore, P_1 = precipitation directly
upon the lake per unit area per unit of time, and E_1 =
evaporation of the lake per unit area per unit of time. A
useful form of Equation 1 is obtained when the runoff (R_t) is
stated in terms of climatic parameters; average basin precipitation per unit area per unit of time (P_t) minus average
tributary basin evapotranspiration per unit area per unit of
time (ET_t):

$$R_t = P_t - ET_t \tag{2}$$

By substitution of Equation 2 into Equation 1, the continuity
equation is put into terms of the product of measurable
paleohydrologic and climatic parameters:

$$A_t(P_t - ET_t) = A_1(E_1 - P_1) \tag{3}$$

It is important to differentiate between the general
character of each parameter of Equation 3. The area terms
(A_t, A_1) are directly measurable paleohydrologic parameters
preserved as physiographic features at the land surface. The
terms embodying characteristics of climate (P_t, P_1, ET_t, E_1,
R_t) are, in the paleohydrologic sense, measured only by indirect means and all may be influenced by paleotemperature;
therefore, Equations 1 and 3 are written to make this distinction by establishing a pluvial hydrologic index (Z) of the
closed basins:

$$Z = \frac{A_1}{A_t} = \frac{P_t - ET_t}{E_1 - P_1} = \frac{R_t}{E_1 - P_1} \tag{4}$$

A pluvial hydrologic index (Z) is a quantitative measure
of hydrologic response to pluvial climatic conditions, and is
quantitatively related to commonly used modern climatic indicators such as mean annual temperature, evaporation, and
precipitation.

Modern Climate and Estimation of Pluvial Climate

When a comparison is made between the modern climate and
the pluvial climate of a given basin or a given region of the
Great Basin using Equation 4, the variables of the equation
must be known. The most successful approach is to consider
the mean annual temperature, precipitation, and evaporation
as the prime variables which describe the climates.

Precipitation. - In analyzing Great Basin topographic
configurations and requirements of precipitation values in
Equation 4, about 10% of the hydrographic basin can be considered high mountain terrain and the rest is intermediate or
basin lowland. When precipitation is weighted according to
terrain altitude using the precipitation map of Nevada, it is
found that tributary basin precipitation (P_t) is usually

about 25% higher than basin floor precipitation (P_1). This, of course, will vary depending upon the particular basin and associated mountain terrain; however, a more sensitive approach is not warranted because of the estimated nature of precipitation isohyetes in the precipitation maps of Nevada.

Figure 1 has been developed for estimating precipitation with respect to mean annual temperature during the pluvial climates. The curves have been developed by plotting each 1931-1960 Weather Bureau Climatic Division value (triangles) and selected individual stations (circles) to help extend the curves. The direction of least climatic change necessary to provide more effective moisture is clearly toward lower mean annual temperatures; however, due to the spread of data represented by the upper and lower trends of the developed temperature/precipitation curves, judgement is necessary for curve selection for evaluating Equation 4. A conservative approach is to assume that the upper curve is more representative of tributary precipitation (P_t) where appropriate. The lower curve, because of the strong basin bias of the majority of the stations, seems reliable for lake precipitation (P_1) in the very arid basins. A median curve has been displayed and has been used for the less arid basins for lake precipitation. The adopted approach, using Figure 1, assumes that the modern climate interdependency of precipitation and temperature in the Great Basin also applied to pluvial climates; it permits a departure from modern climate and adjusts estimates of pluvial climate to values of known variation of temperature and precipitation within the Great Basin.

Runoff. - Runoff is a function of precipitation and evapotranspiration, however, evapotranspiration is very dependent upon subtle parameters such as terrain conditions, and distribution of precipitation in time. Thus, when evaluating climate from hydrologic conditions depicted by Equation 4, the right-hand term containing runoff is easier to use.

Runoff is a dependent variable of temperature. Figure 2, adopted and modified from Schumm (1965), clearly demonstrates just how important temperature is with respect to runoff from a given amount of annual precipitation. These curves are based on runoff throughout the United States (Langbein, et al. 1949). Mean annual runoff and precipitation is compared to weighted mean annual temperature. In Nevada, where the majority of runoff occurs during spring and early summer from snowmelt, weighted means should be close to the mean annual temperature. To aid evaluation, trends are somewhat extended beyond data supported curves into the region of low runoff and rainfall as indicated by the question marks in Figure 2.

Evaporation. - Evaporation is influenced by solar radiation, air temperature, vapor pressure, wind, and atmospheric pressure (Linsley et al. 1958). Of these variables, perhaps

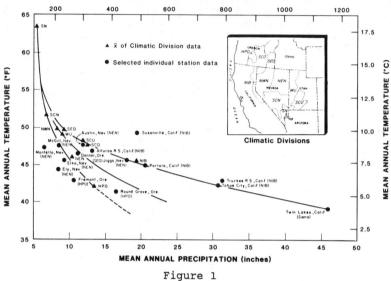

Figure 1

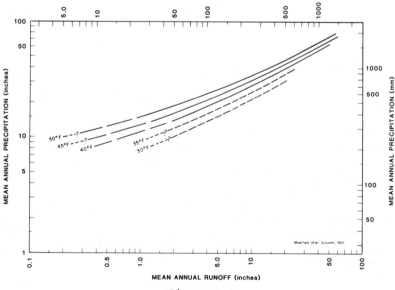

Figure 2

differences in solar radiation and air temperature are the most important factors in producing differences in evaporation from deep-water bodies in the Great Basin. All other influencing parameters are more or less similar throughout the Great Basin.

Studies in the Great Basin provide data to establish graphs for estimating evaporation rates from large lakes (Harding, 1965; Phillips and Van Denburgh, 1971; and Langbein, et al. 1949). Figure 3 demonstrates the effect of altitude (air temperature primarily) and the lesser influence of latitude (solar radiation) on lake evaporation. Data of Figure 3 suggest no more than about 183 mm (7.2 inches) of variation in evaporation within a range of 6° latitude, however, each change in altitude of 305 m (1,000 ft) generates as much as 274 mm (10.8 in) between 305 m (1,000 ft) and 610 m (2,000 ft) altitude to as little as 76 mm (3 in) of evaporation between 1830 m (6,000 ft) and 2135 m (7,000 ft) altitude.

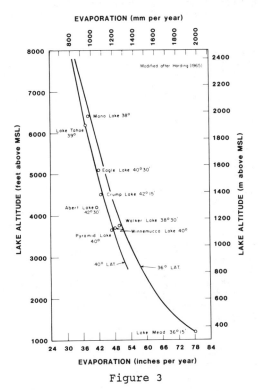

Figure 3

The pluvial lake evaporation rates can be approximated from modern rates by assuming a modern climate lapse rate of 0.638°C/100 m (3.5°F/thousand feet) and adjusting the evaporation rate according to estimated mean annual temperature drop. For example, 2.2°C, 2.8°C, and 3.3°C (4°F, 5°F, and 6°F) of lowered temperature would represent increases in altitude of 348.6 m, 435.8 m, and 522.8 m (1,143, 1,429, and 1,714 ft) respectively, and corresponding lesser rates of lake evaporation as taken from Figure 3.

Evaluation

Methods for estimating all necessary parameters of Equation 4 have been developed from either modern observations of climate and hydrology with associated extrapolations, or from the physical evidence of the pluvial lakes and their respective basins. Calculated hydrologic indices are sensitive to small differences in values of lake precipitation (P_1) and runoff (R_t) produced by assumed amounts of precipitation increase due to a temperature drop. Lake evaporation varies at a fixed rate according to a temperature drop. Adoption of a different lapse rate or different initial modern departure values could make important differences in the calculated indices.

Climatic Division means depicted in Figure 1 are believed reasonable departure points to estimate the pluvial climates of the Great Basin. It is informative to adopt a lower mean annual temperature and establish the hydrologic responses in the basins through the use of Equation 4. The magnitude of necessary mean annual temperature drop is of great interest, as suggested changes range from as little as 2.5°C (4.5°F; Antevs, 1952), to as much as 11°C (20°F; Galloway, 1970). Calculation of the indices for a given climatic zone of Nevada with Equation 4 has been performed in the following manner: 1) A mean annual temperature change is assumed and subtracted from the Climatic Division mean annual temperature of the zone of interest. 2) The corresponding increase in precipitation is established from one of the trends of Figure 1 to give either the lake precipitation (P_1) or the tributary precipitation (P_t). 3) The lake or tributary precipitation value is then calculated by adding or subtracting 25%. 4) Lake evaporation (E_1) is determined from Figure 3 by establishing lake altitude and then correcting for the temperature drop by increasing the altitude according to the modern lapse rate. 5) Runoff (R_t) is determined by using Figure 2 with the adopted mean annual temperature and the tributary precipitation already determined. 6) Computation of the pluvial index (Z) of Equation 4 is made using the derived variables of the preceding five steps.

In order to compare measured pluvial indices with calculated indices through the use of regionalized climatic parameters, the basins representing climatic zones have been grouped together to establish the mean lake elevations and the mean pluvial index $(\bar{Z})$ within each zone. The effect of this procedure is for generalized climatic relationships to be compared with generalized measured pluvial indices. Ta-

ble 1 groups the basins containing non-overflowing pluvial
lakes within the Climatic Division areas and gives the mean
altitudes and pluvial hydrologic indices for those areas
(Mifflin and Wheat, 1979).

Table 1. Mean Pluvial Lake Indices by Climatic Division

Climatic	# of Basins	Mean Lake Altitude	Mean Index $\bar{Z}$
ENWN (SCO)	3	1708 m (5600 ft)	0.68
NWN	7	1358 m (4452 ft)	0.084
NEN	18	1838 m (6025 ft)	0.295
SCN	20	1484 m (4866 ft)	0.031
SN	14	983 m (3223 ft)	0

Estimated Full Pluvial Climate

     In the four climatic regions where pluvial lakes were
present, about 2.8°C (5°F) lower mean annual temperatures
establish calculated hydrologic indices that approximated
the mean pluvial lake indices. The derived pluvial lake
precipitation (P_1) values are considerably greater than the
modern basin precipitation values (Climatic Division data).
These differences, calculated as percent increase over the
modern data, are as follows: ENWN 77%, NWN 63%, NEN 80%, and
SCN 52%. The calculated numerical increases range from 84 to
241 mm (3.3 to 9.5 in) and average 165 mm (6.5 in) of precipitation. Due to the manner in which the estimated climate
shifts were derived, the calculated increases in tributary
basin precipitation are of similar percentage, but 25%
greater in numerical magnitude. Thus, the quantitative
evaluations using Equation 4 yield, in general terms, a
statewide shift of climates to a lower mean annual temperature of about 2.8°C (5°F), with an average of 68% more precipitation. Reduction in lake evaporation averages 10%.

     Table 2 depicts the estimated pluvial climates and the
mean and extremes in annual temperature and precipitation
between 1931 and 1960 for the Climatic Divisions used in the
analysis. The largest recorded extremes in precipitation
generally approach the pluvial lake values that were estimated as necessary. With the exception of northeastern
Nevada, however, the lowest recorded temperatures are 1°C
(2°F) or more above the estimated pluvial climate temperature.

Discussion

     The analysis demonstrates that relatively small dif-
ferences in climatic parameters are sufficient to create the
marked differences in the hydrology of the Great Basin.
Changes in modern climatic parameters, if known or predicted,
can be translated into quantitative estimates of useful hy-

Table 2. Comparison of Pluvial and Modern Climates

Climate Division	Evaluated Pluvial Climate Temp/°C (°F) P_1/mm (in)		Modern Annual Temperature C° (°F) High Mean Low		Modern Annual Precipitation mm (inches) High Mean Low	
SCO (ENWN)	5.8	(42.5)	10.2	(50.4)	441	(17.38)
			8.2	(46.7)	312	(12.28)
	552	(21.75)	6.9	(44.5)	174	(6.86)
NWN	5.6	(42)	11.7	(53.0)	324	(12.75)
			9.9	(49.8)	211	(8.30)
	343	(13.5)	8.6	(47.5)	99	(3.90)
NEN	5.6	(42)	10.5	(50.9)	418	(16.45)
			7.7	(45.9)	267	(10.53)
	483	(19)	5.9	(42.6)	190	(7.47)
SCN	7.5	(45.5)	12.8	(55.0)	324	(12.77)
			10.9	(51.7)	171	(6.72)
	259	(10.2)	9.8	(49.7)	79	(3.10)
SN	14.5	(58.5)	19.6	(67.3)	289	(11.37)
			17.5	(63.5)	130	(5.10)
	203	(8)	16.6	(61.9)	36	(1.40)

drologic parameters, such as runoff, using the general approach that has been presented.

References

Antevs, E., "Cenozoic Climates of the Great Basin," Geologic Research, Vol. 40, 1952, pp. 94-108.

Galloway, R.W., "The Full-Glacial Climate in the Southwestern United States," Association of American Geography, Annuals, Vol. 60, 1970, pp. 245-256.

Harding, S.T., "Recent Variations in the Water Supply of the Western Great Basin," University of California, Water Research Center, Archive Series Report No. 16, 1965, 226 pp.

Langbein, W.B., et al., "Annual Runoff in the United States," U.S. Geological Survey, Circular 52, 1949, 13 pp.

Linsley, et al., "Hydrology for Engineers" McGraw-Hill, 1958.

Mifflin, M.D., and M.M. Wheat, "Pluvial Lakes and Estimated Pluvial Climates of Nevada," Nevada Bureau of Mines, Bulletin 94, 1979, 57 pp.

Phillips, K.N., and A.S. Van Denburgh, "Hydrology and Geochemistry of Abert, Summer, and Other Closed-Basin Lakes in South Central Oregon," U.S. Geological Survey, Professional Paper 502-B, 1971, 86 pp.

Schumm, S.A., "Quaternary Paleohydrology," The Quaternary of the United States, Wright, H.E., Jr., and Frey, D.G., eds., Princeton University Press, 1965, pp. 783-794.

Issues in Specifying Climate Forcing of Variability

Paul A. Kay[1]

ABSTRACT: Several issues arise in the specification of the role of climatic forcing of variability of water resources. The effects of human intervention must be removed so that the climate signal is clear. Physically plausible climatic variables must be identified, and their relationships to water resources response must be properly identified. Appropriate scales of space and time must be specified. These issues are illustrated by reference to studies in the Great Basin of the western U.S. and in Israel.

INTRODUCTION

The question of the effects of climate, or more exactly of climatic variability, on water resources is always acute and becomes more so under the threat of global climatic warming. The question is often approached from the viewpoint of operational hydrology, in which annual and monthly data are used to derive a deterministic or statistical model designed to provide the best predictions for the short term (one to a few years). The model is then utilized in sensitivity studies, wherein the response of a water resource system to specified changes in controlling factors is examined. For example, Revelle and Waggoner (1984) assumed a range of temperature and precipitation changes and used modern temperature-precipitation-runoff relationships to create scenarios of runoff in the western U.S. The assumption, often implicit, is that the modern interrelationships between the statistics of climate variables are invariant. For example, Nemec and Schaake (1982) used global or zonal averages of temperature and precipitation change in their case studies. In effect, this approach moves climates as invariant units across the map. It is not clear, however, that the interrelationships between variables will hold or that all variables will change proportionally for such a translocation. Future change will be considerably more idiosyncratic

---

[1] Associate Professor, Department of Geography, University of Utah, Salt Lake City, UT 84112

depending on the region's relationship to new atmospheric circulation patterns (cf. Wigley et al., 1980).

There is ample evidence in historic and paleoclimatic records that in addition to seasonal anomalies within a given climatic regime, there have been changes in the mean and variance between regimes. If we are indeed on the verge of global warming due to an enhanced greenhouse effect (Carbon Dioxide Assessment Committee, 1983), then we might anticipate changes in water reources as a response to new climatic regimes. We are in a double-bind here, regarding how best to study this problem, for although we cannot trust the modern record to provide suitable analogs for a future different climate, we cannot do other than model, statistically or deterministically, the records at hand.

A number of issues in the specification of the role of climatic forcing of water resources variability require the researcher's careful attention. There is a need to attribute causation correctly to the effects of climatic variations as distinct from the effects of human intervention. The use of a homogeneous series is imperative, and this is often easily achieved fro historic records. It is important to recognize and incorporate complex and perhaps non-linear responses to climatic control. This requires the proper specification of the controlling variables (for example, seasonal rather than annual precipitation, or lagged values), the proper specification of the form of the relationship, and the proper construction of the response model. Sophisticated multiple regression and time series techniques exist for these tasks. Most critically, scales of resolution must be correctly specified. In space, local versus regional controls and responses must be differentiated. In time, seasonal or interannual versus decadal or longer time scales must be appropriately identified. Climatic change involves changes in the means and/or variances and we should expect to find different spatial and temporal responses depending on scale; we cannot assume that all places, nor all years, will differ from the modern to a similar degree or in the same direction.

To illustrate these issues, recent work concerning Great Salt Lake, Utah, in the western U.S., and agricultural use of water in Israel are briefly discussed. In the 1980s, both regions have experienced considerable social impact due to the fluctuations of water resources in response to climatic variability, and there is some value in narrowng the range of possible future scenarios.

GREAT SALT LAKE

Great Salt Lake (GSL) occupies a semi-arid basin in northern Utah, receiving its major input of water from three river systems draining high mountains on the downwind eastern side of the lake. The behavior of GSL levels is known from measurements or estimations for over 130 years (Arnow, 1984). In that time, lake level has varied between 1283.7 m (in 1873) and 1278.3 (in 1963), and lake area between about 2600 and 6200 km². Although the lake had been rising since 1963, marked droughts in water years (WY) 1977 and 1981 stalled the rise. In response to record wet seasons in WY 1983 and 1984, the lake rose 2.9 m, more than twice the previous record two-year rise. Long-term persistence in lake levels suggests that the lake will remain at near-record levels for some years yet.

As of late winter 1986, the lake had not yet equalled historic maximum level. This suppression of level was due almost entirely to human activities within the drainage basin, for if there were no upstream withdrawals, the lake level would have been about 1285 m. The impact of human activity has, of course, not been constant nor linear through time. Thus the lake level series, as measured, is not homogeneous, and analyses based solely on it are misleading. The effects of human activity have been estimated, and series of "pristine" levels, assuming no withdrawals, have been produced (eg, Whitaker, 1971). The variability in such series may be attributed to fluctuations in climatic forcing.

Societal concerns with damage or threat to near-shore installations, public and private, dictates a focus on area of the lake; level, because it can be monitored directly, is usually the chosen variable to be predicted or modeled. However, it is clearly the volume of water entering the lake that is the response to precipitation input, and the volume of water lost that is the response to evaporation output. Thus volume or volume changes are to be preferred to levels as the dependent variable, all the more so as the stage-volume relationship is not linear (cf Currey et al., 1984). The Utah Division of Water Resources, for example, directly estimates volumes from a hydrologic model and converts them into levels utilizing the stage-volume relationship (Stauffer, 1985).

Societal concerns also dictate that the focus be on maximum level achieved each year, so many studies model either peak or end of WY levels. Karl and Young (1986) showed that the trends in peak levels correlated well with trends in excess cumulative departures of areally-averaged precipitation. James et al.'s (1979) stochastic model, based on the hyrologic model, to estimate probabilities of future peak lake levels. However, annual lake level represents an integration of seasonal input and loss, each of which is related to different atmospheric circulation mechanisms. In diagnostic models of seasonal volume changes in GSL, Kay and Diaz (1986) showed that increase and decrease in volume were related to different seasonal controls. Different combinations of changes in seasonal characteristics may be undetectable if only annual levels are considered.

Another issue regarding time concerns the length of record available for the model calibration. A record of 100 years would be judged adequate. In the case of GSL, Karl and Young (1986) showed that estimates for recurrence intervals for an event similar to the 1980s wet spell varied from 120 to 290 years, depending on whether the wet spells of the 1860s and 1980s were included or not. It is likely that judgments regarding various long-term proposals for lake management would be different if the former rather than the latter recurrence interval estimate were used. There is, then, a need to obtain records as lengthy as possible; paleoclimatic techniques such as dendroclimatology may be useful.

As regards the issue of spatial resolution, in the modern climate anomalies are not necessarily homogeneous across the study region; patterns are related to the different circulation mechanisms that operate (cf Kay, 1982). There is some evidence in proxy records of paleoclimate derived from tree rings for spatial differences in anomaly series (Bingham et al., 1985). These results are not surprising, given that GSL lies on a winter climatic boundary defined by Mitchell (1976). Depending upon shifts of that boundary, some or all of the basin will experience a given climatic anomaly, and the lake will respond to a greater or lesser degree. Thus the assumption of a single regional climatic series may be too simple.

ISRAEL

Agriculture is a major component of Israel's national economy, both for self-sufficiency and for export. Given the generally small amounts of precipitation in most of Israel, there is a great need for irrigation, especially in the dry summer season when 70% of the farmed land is irrigated. The fundamental geographical problem facing water utilization is that 85% of the resource is in the north part of the country whereas 50% of the arable land is in the south. In response, the country has achieved a highly integrated and nearly fully developed resources system, including a major redistribution infrastructure.

A theory of societal response to climatic variability states that successful societies cope with recurrent stress by adopting social and technological mechanisms that reduce the impact of successive occurences of the stress (Bowden et al., 1981). It might appear that Israel would be a good illustration in favor of the hypothesis. Agricultural activity has increased through the years and although water use has also grown, the amount of water used per unit of agricultural land has decreased. However, there might still be climatic stress on the system. WY 1986 was the third in succession of deficient precipitation, and both groundwater and surface water storage was being heavily mined. It would be useful to know how sensitive the system might yet be to climatic fluctuations.

Kay (in preparation) hypothesized that departures from the trend of water use should be related to precipitation anomalies, and that the magnitude of the departures when standardized for the degree of drought should be declining. Agricultural use of water per irrigated area was the dependent variable. This variable focused on the segment of the water use system that was thought to be directly sensitive to climatic fluctuations, and standardizes for the changes in amount of agricultural land through time. The predictor variable was an index of precipitation deficiency, calculated as the average of seasonal anomalies at a northern and a southern station. This definition was an attempt to account for both seasonal-scale and spatial differences in the precipitation regimes across the country.

The results generally confirmed the anticipated relationship of water use above expectation in years of marked negative precipitation anomaly. Quantitatively, however, the realtionship was not strong or clear. There were some water years that were dry overall in which water use was not more than expected, and some wet years in which water use was above expectation. It was possible that the chosen spatial and temporal scales were too coarse to catch the response of water use to perceived or actual deficiency. Changes in timing of precipitation events by just a few weeks at critical times of the crop cycles may affect water use to a greater degree than total amount of precipitation over a longer time span. The role of centralized regulatory control of water supplies, such as decisions to draw upon groundwater or draw down surface water reserves, must be considered to complicate the direct relationship between climate and water use.

CONCLUSIONS

The issues illustrated here regarding specification of the response of a hydrological system to climatic variation may be summarized as being issues of specification, of spatial scale, and of temporal scale. Both the response and the forcing variables need to be properly specified, to ensure that a plausible physical system is being investigated. In the case of GSL, it was suggested that seasonal changes in lake volume and seasonal climatic variables were more appropriate and promised greater understanding than lake levels and annual precipitation. In the case of Israel, an operational water need parameter might be more appropriate than the index of precipitation anomaly employed.

Misspecification of model coefficients can result if the calibration region is not homogeneous or if the model is extrapolated beyond the calibration region. For GSL, the response of the lake may be to influences accumulated over several regions, as the lake lies on a major climatic boundary that affects winter season precipitation patterns. In Israel, it might be necessary to develop a set of weights to account for differing degrees (and even signs) of water needs between the relatively well-watered north and the arid south. In both cases, single spatial series may overly simplify regional processes.

Temporal scales must be appropriate to the level of response the model is attempting to catch. In the case of GSL, seasonal scale appears appropriate; in Israel, a monthly or finer resolution might be needed. In both cases, lagged variables might be needed to adequately capture persistence. Also, estimates of recurrence interval and other statistics of the distribution and temporal behavior of hydrologic variables are sensitive to the length of record analysed. Effort to generate detailed records for the late pre-instrumental past from proxy evidence would be well rewarded with a firmer base for further analyses and modelling.

APPENDIX.--REFERENCES

Arnow, T. (1984). "Water-level and water quality changes in Great Salt Lake, Utah, 1847-1983," U.S. Geological Survey, Circular 913.

Bingham, G.E., Richardson, E.A., and Ashcroft, G.A. (1985). "Historical climate data of the Great Salt Lake watershed: Relation to lake levels," *Problems of and Prospects for Predicting Great Salt Lake Levels*, P.A. Kay and H.F. Diaz, eds., Center for Public Affairs and Administration, University of Utah, Salt Lake City, UT, 82.

Bowden, M.J., Kates, R.W., Warrick, R.A., Kay, P.A., Johnson, D.L., Riebsame, W.E., Wiener, D., and Gould, H. (1981). "The effects of climatic fluctuations on human populations: Two hypotheses," *Climate and History*, T.M.L. Wigley, D. Farmer, and M. Ingram, eds., Cambridge University Press, Cambridge, UK.

Carbon Dioxide Assessment Committee (1983). *Changing Climate*, Report of the Carbon Dioxide Assessment Committee, National Academy Press, Washington, DC.

Clark, W.C., ed. (1982). *Carbon Dioxide Review: 1982*, Oxford University Press, New York, NY.

Currey, D.R., Atwood, G., and Mabey, D.R. (1984). "Major levels of Great Salt Lake and Lake Bonneville," Utah Geological and Mineral Survey, Salt Lake City, UT, Map No. 73.

James, D.L., Bowles, D.S., James, W.R., and Canfield, R.V. (1979). "Estimation of water surface elevation probabilities and associated damages for the Great Salt Lake," UWRL/P-79/03, Utah Water Research Laboratory, Logan, UT.

Karl, T.R., and Young, P.J. (1986). "Recent heavy precipitation in the vicinity of the Great Salt Lake: Just how unusual?" *Bulletin, American Meteorological Association* 67(1), 4.

Kay, P.A. (1982). "A perspective on Great Basin paleoclimates," *Man and Environment in the Great Basin*, D.B. Madsen and J.F. O'Connell, eds., Society for American Archeology Papers 2, 76.

Kay, P.A. (in prepartion). "Climatic fluctuations and water resources in Israel".

Kay, P.A., and Diaz, H.F. (1986). "Response of Great Salt Lake to climate variability," *this volume*.

Mitchell, V.L. (1976). "The regionalization of climate in the western United States," *Journal of Applied Meteorology* 15(9), 920.

Nemec, J., and Schaake, J. (1982). "Sensitivity of water resources systems to climate variation," *Hydrological Sciences--Journal--des Sciences Hydrologiques* 27(3), 327.

Revelle, R.R., and Waggoner, P.E. (1983). "Effects of a carbon dioxide-induced climatic change on water supplies in the western United States," *Changing Climate*, Report of the Carbon Dioxide Assessment Committee, National Academy Press, Washington, DC, 419.

Stauffer, N.E., Jr. (1985). "Great Salt Lake water balance model," *Problems of and Prospects for Predicting Great Salt Lake Levels*, P.A. Kay and H.F. Diaz, eds., Center for Public Affairs and Administration, University of Utah, Salt Lake City, UT, 168.

Whitaker, G.L. (1971). "Changes in the elevation of Great Salt Lake caused by Man's activities in the drainage basin," U.S. Geological Survey, Professional Paper 750-D, D187.

Wigley, T.M.L., Jones, P.D., and Kelly, P.M. (1980). "Scenario for a warm, high-CO_2 world," *Nature* 283(5742), 17.

HYDROELECTRIC PROGRAM FOR DEVELOPMENT IN MEXICO

José Antonio Maza*, ASCE member

Abstract

This work deals with the process at present followed in México for the development of hydroelectric projects. Then, the participation of hydro electricity in the electric sector is given and, finally, the projects under study at the different planning levels.

Introduction

The purpose of this work is to give a summary of the present hydroelectric development in México and of the plans and trends for its future expansion. This task is undertaken by Comisión Federal de Electricidad (CFE), which is the government issue in charge of the planning, design, construction, operation and maintenance of the works for the generation, transmission and distribution of the electric power for public use.

With reference to the hydroelectric energy, CFE has established a process for the development of its plants which consists in the following levels:

    a. Planning   c. Construction
    b. Design and bidding   d. Operation and maintenance

At the same time, the planning level is subdivided in four levels:

    a.1 Site identification   a.3 Prefeasibility
    a.2 Site evaluation   a.4 Feasibility

The Vicemanagement of Construction is responsible for the execution of levels a, b and c, the first two through the Management of Hydroelectric Plants, and the third, through the organisms in charge of construction. Besides, the operation and maintenance are the responsibility of the Vicemanagement of Operation.

As a function of the scope and covering of the studies, the principal objectives to be achieved for each of the planning levels are:

a.1 Identification. Localization of probable sites for hydroelectric plants. National covering.

* Chief of the Unit of Civil Engineering Studies
  Comisión Federal de Electricidad. Oklahoma 85, C.P. 03810
  Col. Nápoles, México, D.F.

a.2 Evaluation. Interrelated selection of possible alternatives at the regional or basin level. Establishment of construction priorities.

a.3 Prefeasibility. Selection of the best scheme for every particular site.

a.4 Feasibility. Study and determination of the technical, economic and social feasibility of each site.

The Management of Hydroelectric Projects is in charge of the first two levels. When advancing in point a.2 and in the following levels, it is responsible for the demand prognostic of all and each region in the country, besides studying and analyzing the stability of the interconected systems. This includes all kinds of plants, regardless of their type.

To give a view of what CFE has done, is doing and plans to do, facts are presented in opposite order to the previously mentioned plan; that is to say, we will start with the centrals in operation to finish with the identified sites.

Plants in operation

In 1898, Portezuelo I entered in operation, being this the first private hydroelectric plant built in México. By 1905, the Necaxa plant began to operate; this was the first dam built for public use, even if it was English. As a whole, 46 private plants were built with a total potency of 575.5 MW, which were afterwards bought by CFE when the electric industry was nationalized in 1960. From its creation in 1937 up to 1981, CFE has built about 50 hydroelectric plants.

Between 1960 and 1980, the demand for electric energy grew in a relation of 7.5% and of 6.5% between 1980 and 1984. During the period between 1960 and 1980, hydroelectric generation was about 50% of the thermic one.

By the end of 1984, the installed capacity was of 19360 MW and the generation of 79507 GWh, of which 6532 MW and 23448 GWh corresponded, respectively, to hydroelectricity. To achieve this amount, CFE has 74 plants with 201 units and 6532 installed MW. Table 1 shows those plants with a mean annual generation of more than 100 GWh.

Table 1. HYDROELECTRIC PLANTS IN OPERATION WITH MORE THAN 100 GWh

	CAP.(MW)	GEN. (GWh)
M.Moreno T.(Chicoasén), Chis.	1500	5877
Infiernillo, Gro.	1000	3131
Malpaso, Chis.	1080	2658
B.Domínguez (La Angostura), Chis.	900	2260
J.Ma. Morelos (La Villita), Mich.	240	1162
Temascal, Oax.	154	768
Mazatepec, Pue.	215	633
P.E.Calles (El Novillo), Son.	135	603
Tingambato, Méx.	135	466
Necaxa, Pue.	109	451
Cupatitzio, Mich.	72	431

TABLE 1. Cont.

Ixtapantongo, Méx.	100	402
Santa Bárbara, Méx.	68	350
27 de Septiembre (El Fuerte), Sin.	59	277
M.M. Dieguez (Santa Rosa), Jal.	64	277
Humaya, Sin.	90	242
Tepuxtepec, Oax.	63	214
Cobano, Mich.	54	211
Patla, Pue.	34	205
Tepexic, Pue.	45	202
Tuxpango, Ver.	36	201
Colimilla, Jal.	50	196
G.A. Figueroa (La Venta), Gro.	30	140
Chilapan, Ver.	26	107
Falcón, Tamps.	31	102
Oviachic, Son.	19	101
	6309	21667

Plants in construction

From 1985, the construction of hydroelectric plants was given a new impulse. However, and due to the economic situation of the country, the construction programs have suffered great changes and adjustments.

As everywhere else, the cost of the kilowatt generated by the hydroelectric plants is lower than that generated in the thermic ones; nevertheless, these plants offer some advantages important enough under certain social and economic circumstances, which make them more attractive than the hydroelectric plants. Among others, these advantages are: their proximity to consumption centers, lower initial cost, more security during the construction stage and greater freedom when choosing its capacity. Following this trend of ideas, it is important to note that only in the Southeast part of the country there are enough hydroelectric resources, while these are generally insufficient or definitely non existing in the semiarid zones. However, the advantages of the hydroelectric plants are quite noticeable. Table 2 is a list of the plants in construction.

Table 2. HYDROELECTRIC PLANTS IN CONSTRUCTION

NAME	CAP.MW	PLANT FACTOR	GEN.GWh	OP. DATE
Caracol, Gro.	593	0.30	1534	1986
Peñitas, Chis.	420	0.52	1912	1986
Bacurato, Sin.	93	0.32	260	1986
Amistad, Coah.	67	0.56	330	1986
Aguaprieta, Jal.	480	0.22	915	1989
Comedero, Sin.	101	0.34	301	1990
	1754		5252	

Design plants

This stage includes those in schedule plus those which, being programmed for construction, have been postponed for economic reasons. Table 3 shows the list of them.

Table 3. DESIGN PLANTS. JANUARY 1, 1986

NAME	CAP.MW	GEN.GWh	PLANT FACTOR	OP. DATE
Aguamilpa, Jal.	960	2165	0.26	1992
Amp. Temascal, Ver.	250	390	0.19	1993
Itzantún, Chis.	330	723	0.25	1993
	1870	4798		

Due to the importance these projects have in the system, their closeness
to the consumption centers and the general benefits they will produce,
the construction of Aguamilpa, Itzantún and Zimapán is to be started be
fore six months. The plants listed in tables 2 and 3 are the only included in the last actualization of the Program for Works and Inversions
of the Electric Sector (POISE) of February 7, 1986.

Feasibility projects

This is the most expensive and the longest of all levels. Projects must
show their economic advantages and the social problems they can originate
while the Management of Electric Studies must approve them considering its
convenience in relation to the electric system of the country. During
this stage, the topographic, rock mechanics, geotechnic, compensation
and reaccommodation studies are done in detail, besides the technical-
economic study of the best alternative. Table 4 is a list of the projects
now at this level.

TABLE 4. PROJECTS AT THE FEASIBILITY LEVEL

NAME	CAP.MW	GEN.GWh	PLANT FACTOR
Cajón II, Jal.	608	1485	0.28
Huites, Sin.	1025	825	0.18
Cora, Nay.	184	476	0.30
Tecate, BCN	62	153	0.28
San Juan Tetelcingo, Gro.	633	1275	0.23
Zimapán, Hgo.	240	747	0.36
Copainalá, Chis.	300	950	0.36
	3052	5911	

Projects at the Prefeasibility level

By January 1986, 26 projects were studied at this level. The economic
problems which affect work design and construction have not influenced
the programs for studying projects at the Prefeasibility, Evaluation
and Identification levels. To start a project at the Prefeasibility
level, the Management of Hydroelectric Projects and that of studies
work together: the first presents a list of the existing projects at
the Evaluation level in different basins and regions, while the second
chooses the most convenient on the basis of their geographical localization and on the hypothesis of the growth demand.

Table 5 is a list of projects according to their regions and different
planning levels with their mean annual estimated generation. Among the
most important there are those of Santa Cruz, Jal., (460 and 1016);

La Múcura, Jal., (320 and 807); La Yesca, Jal., (435 and 1042); La Paro
ta, Gro., (528 and 1387); Ostutla, Gro., (240 and 752); Xuchiles, Ver.,
(298 and 652); Atexcaco, Ver., (114 and 301), Chacté, Chis., (268 and
1211); Chinin, Chis., (160 and 956), Cancuc, Chis., (81 and 532). The
numbers in parenthesis give, respectively, the potency to be installed
and the estimated mean annual generation.

TABLE 5. HYDROELECTRIC POTENTIAL

LEVEL		NORTH PACIFIC	SOUTH PACIFIC	GULF	SOUTHEAST	NORTH	TOTAL
IDENTIF.	Plants	71	100	48		11	230
	Gen.	14509	19863	8118		737	43227
EVAL.	Plants	63	19	96	90		268
	Gen.	12798	2681	20102	26675		62255
PREFEAS.	Plants	5	10	6	5		26
	Gen.	3332	4686	3868	6857		18743
FEAS.	Plants	4	1	1	1		7
	Gen.	2939	1275	747	950		5911

	Plants	Gen.
Studied potential	531	130136
Design potential	2	2888
Operation	37	22415
Suspended operation	3	269
Potential under design and construction	8	7162
	581	162870

Studies at the Evaluation level

268 sites are at this level. Table 5 shows their distribution according
to their localization and annual mean expected generation. The sites
studied are those which, once identified, present attractive topographic
and hydrological characteristics.

At this level, both the mean annual discharge and the head can be deter
mined with greater certainty. Besides, the possibilities of transferring
water from one basin to another are also studied in order to maximize
the exploitation in relation to the integral use of the system in a
region or basin. When considering the works as a whole and in cascade,
preliminary exploitation schemes are drawn for each site and evaluated
with unit cost index.

Among the most attractive basins studied there are those of the rivers
Yaqui, Son; San Pedro and Acaponeta, Sin., and Nay; affluents of the
Santiago river, Jal. and Nay; and those of the Piaxtla, Dgo., and Sin.;

the rivers Balsas, several estates; Papagayo, Gro; Verde, Oax; Pánuco,
S.L.P., and Ver; Tecolutla, Ver; Tacotalpa, Chis., and Usumacinta,
Chis. Even if the last has the greatest potential in the country, it is
too far from the consumption centers.

Studies at the Identification level

Table 5 also shows the sites at this level with their mean annual gener
ation, both total and regional. At present, there are 230 identified
sites.

This level develops completely in cabinets, with the best available
cartography, generally 1:50000. Possible outlets are identified and the
head and the mean annual discharge are evaluated. With these two
parameters and the regional plant factor given by the Management of
Studies, the mean annual generation, the potency to be installed and
the mean potency are estimated.

Equipment for already built dams

With the object of taking the best advantage of the existing hydraulic
infrastructure which is used with non hydraulic ends, a study was done
to maximize the extraction regimes and their head without affecting the
cultivated areas. The dams studied under equipment at the Identification
level are L.L. León (Granero), Chih; L. Cárdenas (Palmito), Dgo; V. Gue
rrero (Las Adjuntas), Tamps; F.I. Madero (Las Tórtolas), Dgo; B. Juárez,
Oax; Cajón de Peña, Jal; La Angostura, Son., and Trigomil, Jal.

Pumped storage projects

The North part of the country is characterized by its semiarid condition
because the hydraulic possibilities are few and of limited capacity.
Here, the greatest part of the generation is covered by thermic plants
while the peak demand by gas plants, which are very expensive to operate
and maintain.

Taking into account what has been already said, studies are followed to
localize sites for future pumped storage projects near the cities of
Monterrey, N.L; Chihuahua, Chih; Tijuana and Ensenada, B.C.N.; Cd. Juá
rez, Chih; San Luis Potosí, S.L.P; Torreón, Coah., and, finally,
Durango, Dgo.

Among these studies, the El Descanso Project in B.C.N., is the only one
now at the Prefeasibility level, with a probable potency to be installed
of 1000 MW, It is on the coast, approximately 40 km South of Tijuana
City. At present, the geological and oceanographic studies are carried
out while different schemes for the preliminary evaluation plans are
been prepared.

Final Words

The growth of the installed capacity, of the total mean annual generation and the corresponding to hydroelectricity, up to 1984, are shown
in Fig 1.

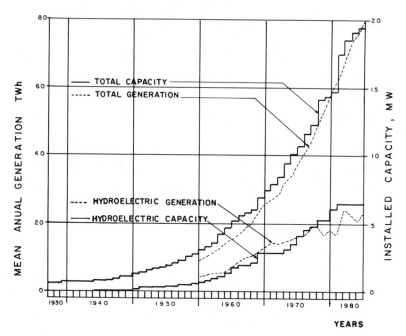

Fig 1. Growth of installed capacity and of mean annual generation

In spite of the economic difficulties México is going through, and
according to the tendencies observed, the total growth would only decrease slightly. But with reference to hydroelectric plants, the prognostic is more uncertain mainly due to the high initial investment these
works imply in relation to the thermic plants which, at present, cover
the greatest percentage of the generation. It is worth to note that dur
ing the useful life of generation plants, the operation and maintenance
of the hydroelectric ones are the least expensive.

Aknowledgement

Thank you very much to Sergio López de Lara for his great cooperation.

References

Estado Actual del Potencial Hidroeléctrico Nacional, CFE, Méx., 1985

Proceso para el Desarrollo de Proyectos Hidroeléctricos, CFE, Méx., 1981

Generaciones Históricas de Plantas Hidroeléctricas, CFE, Méx., 1983

Cherokee Nation Power Development at a Corps Lock and Dam

By Owen W. Scott, [1]M. ASCE

ABSTRACT: In a unique and unprecedented arrangement among the
Cherokee Nation of Oklahoma, the U.S. Army Corps of Engineers and
the Southwestern Power Administration, the Cherokee tribe will
finance, design and construct a powerplant of about 37.5 MW to
use the 5.5-6.1 m (18-20 ft.) head at the Corps existing W.D.
Mayo Lock and Dam on the Arkansas River in Oklahoma. The tribe
will then turn over to the Corps the completed facility, to
operate in conjunction with other Corps plants existing on the
Arkansas River and tributaries. The energy produced will be
marketed by the Southwestern Power Administration, who will pay
the Cherokee Nation a royalty of about $300,000/year for
administration costs in addition to reducing the debt on the
tribe's 20 or 30 year development bond, and about $1-3 million/
year for the remainder of the 50-year economic life assumed for
the project.

The plant will probably have three 12-1/2 MW bulb-type units.
The plans will be reviewed by the Corps, who will perform design
oversight and construction inspection for the project. A Corps
hydropower study considered development similar to the tribe's
proposal in 1980 but was not acted on, due to the Reagan
Administration's preference for non-federal power development.
The legislation is written to have the Cherokee Nation, upon
project completion and acceptance, transfer title to the facility
to the Corps.   Discussions by the tribe with the Reagan
Administration officials, the Secretary of Army and the
Southwestern Power Administration have all been favorable for the
proposed arrangement, which will enhance development in the
economically depressed area of northeastern Oklahoma, promote the
tribe's self-determination and lessen its future dependence on
federal funds for needed economic and social programs, such as
education and health. The Cherokee plan to start the design work
by mid 1986.

I.   Background

The Cherokee Nation, originally located in the Smoky Mountains of
eastern Tennessee, the western Carolinas and upper Georgia and
Alabama, was removed in 1838-39 on the "Trail of Tears" to its present
location in northeastern Oklahoma, then known as Indian Territory.

[1]Hydr. Engr., U.S. Army Corps of Engineers, North Central Div.
536 S. Clark Street, Chicago, IL 60605

The Cherokee Nation does not occupy a reservation, as such. Tribal land was allocated to the individual members in severalty just prior to the organization of the State of Oklahoma and much of it soon passed into the hands of others.

The Cherokee are one of the "Five Civilized Tribes" and have a long tradition of adapting to progress and innovation. Even before the American Revolution, they had opened diplomatic relations with England, when Attacullaculla's delegation to London in 1730 signed a treaty of friendship. (2) With the invention of Sequoyah's alphabet (or more accurately called a syllabary) in 1822, the Cherokee quickly became a highly literate people. Sequoyah (in whose honor the giant Sequoia redwood trees of California were named) is the only person in history to develop, single-handedly and without previous knowledge of writing, a new system of writing. Within a short time, the Cherokee had a written constitution, their own tribal newspaper and an extensive public school system. At the time of their removal, the Cherokee had a higher literacy rate in their own language than Whites who displaced them had in theirs. (3)

After removal to Indian Territory, the Cherokee rebuilt their progressive lifestyle in the west. Their new capital, Tahlequah, became a hub of business activity and a cultural oasis. Their bilingual newspaper and periodical became the first publications in the new territory. They strung the first telephone line west of the Mississippi River to Tahlequah. They reestablished an educational system; their 144 elementary schools and two higher education institutions rivaled all others at the time. However, Cherokee lands were gradually ceded to make room for other tribes and, ultimately, the tribal council and courts were dissolved in 1906 to make way for Oklahoma statehood in 1907.

II. Current Situation (1)

The present-day Cherokee Nation encompasses all or part of fourteen northeastern Oklahoma counties, where 28,000 of the Cherokee Nation's 61,000 tribe members reside. The highest concentration of Cherokee population is in the four counties nearest the tribal capital in Tahlequah - Cherokee, Adair, Delaware and Sequoyah. The Cherokee tribe is the largest non-reservation tribe in the United States.

Several decades after dissolution, the Cherokee Nation reorganized itself in accordance with the terms of the Indian Reorganization Act of 1934. The present Constitution of the Cherokee Nation of Oklahoma was ratified in 1975 and provides for the separation of powers between three branches of government.

Executive power is vested in the Principal Chief. A Deputy Chief presides over the 15-member Cherokee Nation Tribal Council. The three-member Judicial Appeals Tribunal consists of attorneys appointed by the Principal Chief. In the eyes of the federal government, the Cherokee Nation of Oklahoma is sovereign nation with the rights and priviliges to govern itself and create laws within the framework of the U.S. Constitution. The current Principle Chief is Ms. Wilma Mankiller, who succeeded to the office in December 1985, when the previous Chief, Mr. Ross Swimmer, accepted an appointment by President Reagan as Assistant Secretary of Interior to head the Bureau of Indian Affairs. (6)

In the past few decades the Cherokee Nation has changed from an agriculturally-based economy to an industrialized economy. The tribe led this trend through vocational education, institutional and on-the-job training, higher education grants and adult education classes.

A network of major railroad lines connects the Cherokee Nation with all U.S. cities, markets and ports. Interstate-40 and Interstate-44 and three of the state's six turnpikes traverse the Cherokee Nation. The McClellan-Kerr Navigation System on the Arkansas River, opened in 1971 by the U.S. Army Corps of Engineers, is another avenue to surrounding U.S. markets and world ports. The Port of Catoosa, at the head of navigation and serving the City of Tulsa, and the Port of Muskogee are located within the Cherokee Nation. (Legislation was recently passed to allow the Cherokee to lease the lands of the Port of Muskogee for 99 years, extending the previous 50-year limitation.) (5)

Electric generating plants operated by Oklahoma Gas and Electric, Public Service Company, the Grand River Dam Authority, the Southwestern Power Administration and several rural electric cooperatives within the Regional Electric Reliability Council area of the Southwest Power Pool (SPP) serve the area of the Cherokee Nation. The Southwestern Power Admininstration markets the power generated by Corps of Engineers dams on the Arkansas River and its tributaries.

III. Corps of Engineers Study (7)

In October 1980, the Tulsa District, Corps of Engineers, completed an interim report on the feasibility of adding hydropower facilities to the W.D. Mayo Lock and Dam 14 (Mayo L&D) in eastern Oklahoma at Arkansas River mile 375, about 15 km (9 miles) southwest of Fort Smith, Arkansas. The feasibility study was conducted under the authority of a June 30, 1979, resolution of the U.S. Senate Committee on Environment and Public Works and according to the guidelines of the "Principles and Standards for Planning Water and Related Land Resources". The degree of detail in the engineering analysis by the Tulsa District was limited to that necessary to determine economic feasibility.

The Mayo L&D is the one of a series of 17 locks and dams that comprise the McClellan-Kerr Navigation System on the Arkansas River and an essential part of the Arkansas River Basin System that was developed in general as described in the "308 Report" of 1938. The Arkansas River Basin System above Mayo L&D and below Great Bend, Kansas, consists of 28 storage reservoirs and four locks and dams on the Arkansas River and its tributaries (see Fig. 1). The system provides urban and rural flood protection and conservation water storage for navigation, water supply, water quality and the generation of electric energy. There is a total of 12.38 x 10^9 m^3 (10,043,000 acre-ft.) of

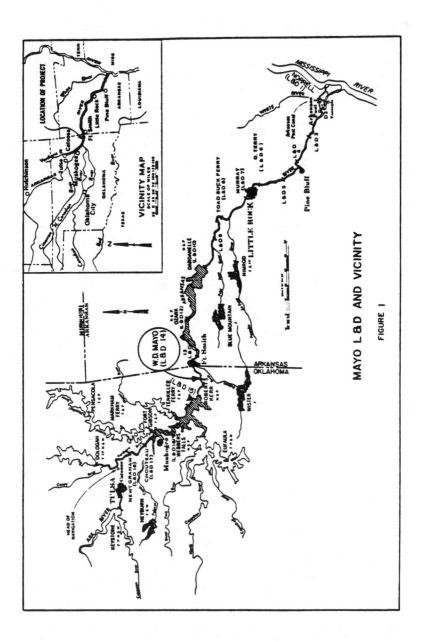

MAYO L&D AND VICINITY

FIGURE I

flood control storage in the system above Mayo L&D. The Mayo L&D and the four navigation dams above it have no flood control storage. Eight of these projects have hydropower and altogether contain 28 power units with an installed capacity of 595,400 KW. Four of the eight projects with hydropower have power storage; the other four have only limited storage and are considered run-of-river plants. The total power storage and pondage for these projects is $4.45 \times 10^9 m^3$ (3,613,000 acre-ft.).

The Mayo L&D has no power storage and would operate as a run-of-river plant in tandem with, and be remotely controlled from, the R.S. Kerr power plant which is next upstream. Therefore, the addition of hydropower facilities to the Mayo L&D would result in minimal change in the present release and flow patterns.

The existing Mayo L&D project consists of a 2,260 m (7,400 ft.) long overflow dam that includes a low concrete sill surmounted by twelve 18.3 x 6.4 m (60 x 21 ft.) tainter gates separated by 3.0 m (10 ft.) concrete piers, and the single-lift navigation lock having a 33.6 x 183.0 m (110 x 600 ft.) chamber with a normal lift of 6.1 m (20 ft.) and a maximum lift of 6.7 m (22 ft.).

Because the amount of at-site storage is small and operation of the project would very sensitive to short-time flow variations, hourly flow rates for the years 1975 and 1977 were examined to estimate the hydropower potential at Mayo L&D. These years were chosen because they reflect typical flow conditions. They were used as a basis to adjust the long-term, all-season flow-duration curves.

Alternative plans were studied in detail in three broad categories; no action, nonstructural, and structural. Several structural plans were studied, which considered the installation of one through seven 7.34 MW bulb-types units at the existing dam. The bulb turbines selected had a rated discharge of 203.9 m 3/s (7,200 cfs) and a rated head of 4.27 m (14 ft.).

The plan recommended in the Corps of Engineers' October 1980 report would have six 7.34 MW bulb generating units, for a total installed capacity of 44 MW. The installation would produce an average of 171,417,300 KWh of energy annually. The powerhouse would be constructed adjacent to the northeast end of the existing spillway and would require the removal of a part of the existing overflow embankment. It would be designed to be submersible during high flows. Approach and exit channels would be excavated to top of rock. The estimated first cost was $83.7 million in 1979 dollars and the State of Oklahoma would contribute 10 percent of that cost in cash according to the cost-sharing policy then in effect.

Participating agencies which contributed significant investigations to the Corps of Engineers study were the Federal Energy Regulatory Commission (FERC), Oklahoma Water Resources Board (OWRB), Southwestern Power Administration (SWPA) and U.S. Fish and Wildlife Service (USFWS). Views were solicited from the public, industry, organizations and governmental agencies. A public meeting was held on 4 September 1980 in Fort Smith, Arkansas.

IV. Cherokee Nation Plan

In 1970, the U.S. Supreme Court ruled that the Cherokee Nation retains
ownership of the bed and banks along a 155 km (96 mile) reach of the
Arkansas River, including the site where the Corps of Engineers owns
and operates the Mayo L&D. The Cherokee Nation is interested in
making use of this tribal resource. With the emergence of the Reagan
Administration preferance for non-federal hydropower development, the
Corps' report on the proposed development at Mayo L&D was held in the
Secretary of Army's office until March 1984, when it was forwarded to
Congress with an expression of no federal interest in implementation.
Other power entities, e.g., the Grand River Dam Authority, studied the
site but did not find its development to be feasible. The Cherokee
Nation asked, in June 1984, that the Council of Energy Resource Tribes
(CERT) study the economic feasibility of such development by the
Tribe.

In a unique and unprecedented arrangement with the Corps of Engineers
and the Southwestern Power Admininstration, and with Congressional
authorization, the Cherokee Nation will finance, design and construct
a hydropower plant of about 37.5 MW at the Corps' existing Mayo L&D on
the Arkansas River.   However, the Cherokee Nation does not wish to
become a power generating and marketing entity.   Rather, it is
interested in the power being marketed through the federal marketing
system. This requires that the project be owned and operated by the
government.   Therefore, as provided by bills currently before
Congress, the tribe will turn over to the Corps of Engineers the
completed facilities, to operate in conjunction with other existing
Corps power plants on the Arkansas River and its tributaries.   The
energy produced will be marketed by the Southwestern Power
Administration. It is expected that the power plant to be designed by
the Cherokee Nation will be essentially similar to that proposed for
the same location by the Tulsa District, Corps of Engineers, in its
Interim Feasibility Report of October 1980.

In March, 1985, the Cherokee Nation Tribal Council selected a
three-firm consortium to complete the feasibility study design,
construction management and construction of the plant. Those firms
are Benham-Holway of Tulsa, Oklahoma; Manhattan Construction of
Muskogee, Oklahoma; and Smith-Barney, a national investment company.
The Corps will perform design oversight and construction inspection,
as appropriate.   The arrangement for marketing the power with SWPA
provides that the tribe will receive a royalty of about $300,000 a
year for administration cost until the 20-30 year construction bond is
retired. Then, the royalties to the tribe could be as high as between
$1 and 3 million annually for the remainder of the assumed fifty-year
economic life of the project.   No federal funds will be used for the
project. Financing the $80-100 million will be through non tax-exempt
bonds issued by the tribe. (5)

Legislation enabling the working partnership between the Cherokee
Nation of Oklahoma and the U.S. Army Corps of Engineers has been
introduced in Congress by U.S. Senator David Boren and
Representative Mike Synar. These are amendments to HR 6 and S 1567
(Omnibus Water Bills) and S 1724 (specific to Mayo L&D). It is

reported that the entire Oklahoma Congressional delegation has been supportive of this plan to provide power for the economy of their state at no cost to taxpayers. It is also reported that former Principal Chief Swimmer held conversations on this project with Mr. Robert K. Dawson, Secretary of Army, and other Administration officials, who seem favorable to the concept. As of this writing, the plan is to have a joint enabling bill on the President's desk by mid-April and to start design work my mid 1986.

V. Conclusion

The development of hydropower at the W.D. Mayo Lock and Dam by the Cherokee Nation of Oklahoma presents several unique advantages:

1. The tribe will be able to utilize its possession of the Arkansas River bed and gain experience in working in federal and private partnerships to produce energy.

2. The Corps of Engineers will add a powerplant to the system it operates, with a minimal expenditure of its resources, and at no additional cost to the taxpayers.

3. The region, including the Cherokee Nation, will gain additional power for economic development.

4. The tribe, which now manages a $30 million annual budget, will receive income that is not dependent on federal funding to further its economic development and social programs such as health and education.

Acknowledgments:

The writer gratefully acknowledges the helpful discussions of the subject and review of this paper by John Hill and Bethel Herrold of the Tulsa District, Corps of Engineers; Larry Wise of the Cherokee Nation and Harold Aronson of the Council of Energy Resource Tribes. Also, typing and making several revisions of this paper by Lueretta Jones is greatly appreciated.

Appendix – References:

1. Cherokee Nation of Oklahoma, Nation with Promise brochure, Tahlequah, Oklahoma.

2. Cuming, A., in "Cuming's Journal" edited by Samual Cole Williams in Early Travels in the Tennessee Country, Watauga Press, Johnson City, 1928.

3. Feeling, D., in a five-part series on Three Phases of Literacy Among the Cherokee, Cherokee Advocate, Vol. IX, Nos. 4-9, May – September 1985.

4. News article, Cherokee Advocate, Vol IX, No. 10, October 1985.

5. News article, Cherokee Advocate, Vol IX, No. 11, November 1985.

6. News article, Cherokee Advocate, Vol IX, No. 12, December 1985.

7. U.S. Army Corps of Engineers, Tulsa District, <u>W.D. Mayo Lock and Dam 14</u>, Interim Feasibility Report, October, 1980.

Future Hydrothermal Power of the United States

Nazeer Ahmed[*] M. ASCE

Abstract

Public indignation toward nuclear-power expansion, and dwindling oil and gas reserves dictate the needs to look for alternative-power sources, such as coal and water. It is a prime time that use of large volumes of National coal-reserves and unlimited expansion of hydro-power with pumped storage be brought to the forefront to develop future hydrothermal-power for accelerated growth of power resources and main-stream economy of the United States. Low sales of the past, and strict environmental-laws have impeded coal production to a bare minimum, thus hampering the proper growth of electric power. To bring the Nation out of the energy slum and spur up the economic growth, it is recommended that Federal funds be made available for research and development of coal production and hydrothermal power.

Background Information

Introduction of pumped storage in design and construction of hydrothermal power-plants in the United States has proved to be an economical feature with considerable potential for future enhancement of the National power-resources. The United States abounds in hydro-power-development sites and demonstrated National-coal-reserves. At present, only one-third of hydropower potential has been developed, and includes a meager fraction of pumped-storage facilities. Similarly coal production is very low and increased coal-mining is necessary to fully capitalize the hydrothermal power-development. The present growth-rate of this type of power production is nominal due to the nonavailability of Federal funding.

Usage of a pumped-storage facility eliminates the need of large dams and substantial land-areas for water storage. Also, there is no need of running stream-waters to operate hydrothermal power-plants. In this type of design facility, the same stored-water is used over and over again. With pumped storage, a thermal power-plant can be run at full-load capacity and optimum efficiency. Presently all thermal power-plants run without pumped storage are producing electric power far below the full-load capacity and lower efficiency, thus raising the production cost enormously.

Existing coal and water resources can be economized as well as maximized to the extent that many decades of dependable electric-power can be had to improve economic growth and National properity. For the realization of such a dream, we need uniform National-policies insti-tuted by the Congress of the United States and Federal appropriations

[*]Asst. Professor, Department of Civil Engineering, Speed Scientific School, University of Louisville, Louisville, Kentucky, 40292

for research and development of coal extraction, coal burning, air-pollution abatement, efficient design-development of steam- and hydraulic-turbines, and construction of hydrothermal power-plants with pumped-storage facilities.

Economization of Hydrothermal-Power Development

The operation of hydrothermal power-plants with pumped storage combines the functions of two independent power-sources, such as water and coal. During periods of high flow in the stream, or when the upper storage-reservoir is full, the base load is carried by the hydroplant whereas the thermal plant supplies only the peaking load. This function is reversed during the night or during periods of lighter loads, when the thermal-plant units can be operated at full-load capacity to make extra power available for pumping water back to the upper reservoir. Although for pumped storage, only 66 to 78% of expendable power is recovered, this arrangement (1,13) is still very economical. The power plant is operated at its full-load capacity during each twenty-four-hour period producing power at an optimum efficiency and a much cheaper rate. This not only compensates for the power lost in filling the pumped storage, but also generates substantial profits for the utility companies. Consumer load-management can be handled more adequately and the dangers of complete blackouts or brownouts are either alleviated temporarily or eliminated completely. A hydrothermal plant with pumped storage is an economical venture and a best scheme to economize electric-power production.

Maximization of Hydropower Development

To facilitate the development and maximization of future hydro-power, five different schemes of plant layouts are shown in Fig. 1. Any of the five alternatives based on differing physiographic and geologic conditions can be adapted to a specific plant-site under consideration. In conjunction with thermal plants and pumped storage, maximization of hydropower includes usage of water discharge several times the maximum stream-discharge, development of surface-storage capacity, construction of underground reservoirs and hydroplants, increased field efficiency of hydraulic turbines, and load-management requirements. Semi-officially over 2 000 potential sites (11,12,18,19) have been recognized, where, at present, construction of underground reservoirs and hydroplants is a definite possibility. The hydropower can be maximized in the following three ways:

a.   By designing efficient hydraulic equipment.
b.   By increasing volume of water discharge.
c.   By increasing operating head.

Although hydraulic turbines have been around for some time, and every one connected with their design knows how to design efficient equipment these days, a cursory probing into this fact, however, would reveal that this may not be the case. As an example, in 1978, at the Hoover Power Plant in Nevada, the Bureau of Reclamation (16) replaced five runners, demanding from the manufacturer a guaranteed 117 MW output power under the same net head of 150 m. This provided an increase of 37% in output of the system, indicating that the design of

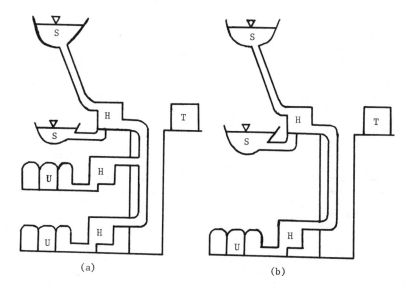

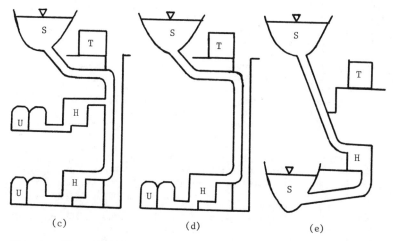

Fig. 1. Five Different Plant Layouts for the Development of Hydrothermal Power with Pumped Storage Facilities.

Legend: H – Hydroplant   S – Surface Reservoir   T – Thermal Power Plant   U – Underground Storage Reservoir

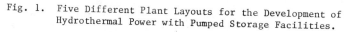

efficient hydraulic-turbines should be an objective to be achieved in
future projects. Excessive pressure drag and cavitation are, among
other things, the major causes of turbine inefficiency.

Potential-power volume of water discharge, no longer limited by
the maximum stream-discharge, can be increased as many times as
practicable through the introduction of pumped storage. This concept
elaborates the fact that production of hydropower is unlimited with
regard to the amount of discharge, and only restricted due to the
amount of available alternate-power to fill the pumped storage. Also,
once the upper reservoir is filled, then the only need which remains
to be taken care of is to replenish the losses, such as seepage and
evaporation. Bed lining can be adopted to eliminate seepage, whereas
surface covers, such as a thin layer of hydrocarbons, can be used at
the water surface to reduce evaporation.

The volume of water needed for pumped storage is a negligible
fraction of the yearly stream-flow. No large-size dams and unlimited
acreage for surface reservoirs are required. The normal stream-flow is
not interrupted at all, and water for other functional activities such
as irrigation, navigation, water supply, flood control, and recreation
can be taken care of as desired. The pumped storage need not be located at a stream.   All that is needed is a source of water to fill
the upper reservoir once, and then replenish it if some losses have
occured. One of the many interesting examples can be cited here, where
pumped storage will be used to augment the hydropower production. Salt
Spring Reservoir (15), located in California, is presently serving a
hydroplant of 9.35 MW capacity. Three storage reservoirs at a lower
elevation will be built to receive water from the Salt Spring Reservoir as the upper reservoir. This would generate total power of 17.6
MW: an unbelievable increase of hydropower as a consequence of the
introduction of pumped storage.

The run-of-river power plants, where only a certain portion of
the stream flow is used, should be eliminated from the so-called
hydraulic design criteria. Such plants simply constitute wasteful
expediture and costly production of electric power.

Another way of maximizing hydropower is to increase the head, in
particular, in the form of underground reservoirs. The underground
reservoirs (11,12,18,19) can be provided in existing mined-cavities or
newly constructed caverns. The quarried rocks have been found of high
quality and can be sold in the open market for profit. Surely such an
added incentive is worth consideration for the adoption of underground
power-plants. It is stated that there are over 1 500 hydroplants
(8,18) with a total installed capacity of more than 62 GW, many of
which are suitable for conversion to underground pumped-storage with
little or no investigative work involved. The Carters Project (4) is a
good example for underground reservoir-facilities. The quartzite is
the dominating rock in the area and provide excellent opportunities
for underground constructed caverns for storage reservoirs. The
Carters Project generates 257 MW against a net head of 105 m. Underground reservoirs can be constructed as deep as 2 000 m. However, considering a conservative estimate of 700 m deep reservoirs, additional
hydropower of 1.7 GW can be obtained easily. This shows that installation of underground power-plants is a good source of extra hydropower. However, Federal funds are a necessary prerequisite for a
systematic investigation of this monumental type of work all across

the Country to develop hydropower with underground storage-reservoirs.

The Role of Alternate Power-Source

Reliable availability of an alternate power-source is an essential requirement for hydrothermal power-development with pumped storage. This fact may be elaborated from different view points. Based on World-wide diminishing crude-oil resources, Willer (17) demonstrates through actual design analysis that development of medium-size hydroplants in the United States is very economical. He exemplifies that for a plant capacity of 200 MW with a 57% capacity factor, 1 billion kWh can be generated in one year. To produce the same power, it would take 1.5 million barrels of oil, thus providing a substantial relief for natural gas and oil inventories, and reducing pressure on home-heating oil and gasoline pumps. Now if a thermal plant and pumped storage are added to the facility, the same hydroplant not only can be run at 100% capacity factor producing power at a cheaper rate, but also can generate additional power for better load-management. Economic returns (6,7) indicate that pumped-storage projects are usually more economical if developed at sites having high heads; the Colorado Cabin Creek pumped-storage powerplant constitutes such an installation. Scherer (13) points out that pumped storage provides more uniform load, which in turn favors more base load and less or no need for peaking power-production. This way the pumped storage causes the system's overall-cost to be reduced significantly, and at the same time provides cheap excess-power for filling the storage reservoirs.

Marker (10) indicates a remarkable engineering feat in the development of small-size hydroplants. He points out that hydroplants of 0.5 to 15 MW capacity, where available heads vary only between 5 and 12 m, have been built successfully and are run at a profit. Sure enough further economy can be obtained by the addition of a thermal plant and pumped storage.

From the above narration it is clear that development of hydropower at any level is an economical venture and a profitable business. This of course also depends on the type and size of the enterprise undertaking such a business proposition. It is also apparent that a thermal plant in conjunction with a hydroplant and pumped storage would be more economical than otherwise. Large volumes of National coal deposits can be considered as reliable alternate-power-source for the development of hydrothermal power. It is strongly recommended that future hydrothermal-powerplants in the United States be designed as one unit with pumped storage toward meeting the goals of National energy independence.

Coal: The Alternate Power-Source

For a successful hydrothermal power-plant with pumped storage, a reliable alternate power-source is an essential ingredient. Due to public awareness of nuclear radiation, no nuclear plants are scheduled to be built beyond 1995. At present, only those nuclear plants are being given construction permits which were accepted before 1979. For the time being the future of nuclear power-production is bleak. Wind, tidal, and solar power are not dependable as yet. Also, crude oil and natural gas resources are on the verge of complete exhaustion and

currently have low reliability. Therefore, National coal deposits seem
to be the only alternate reliable source for the production of hydrothermal power.

Before and during World War II, coal was used for space heating
and production of steam for conversion into electric power. Coal production peaked to 688 million short tons (3,5) in 1947. From 1948 to
1973, coal production fell to lowest levels and the coal industry sustained crippling losses. Being cheaper and cleaner fuels, oil and
natural gas replaced coal usage in all sectors of industrial and
public establishments. By the 1973-74 oil embargo, coal was providing
17%, and oil and gas were meeting 77%, of the total U.S. energy needs.
Investment in the coal industry had dropped down to its lowest record.
After the oil embargo, the Nation rediscovered the usefulness of coal
power and its cheap availability.

The National coal reserves (9,14) are of the order of 1.76
trillion short tons. About 490 billion short tons of coal have been
designated as demonstrated reserve base. Based on economic studies,
245 billion short tons of coal can be mined with modern equipment and
technology. Since 1973 coal production has not shown any dramatic rise
in its mined volume as was anticipated. Rather, strict environmental
laws have discouraged its proper growth. As a consequence, industry
based on coal energy is improving only but sluggishly. Federal funding
is essential not only for the survival of coal industry but also for
the growth of National economy.

Maximization of Thermal Power Development

To obtain maximum heat energy from coal, it is necessary to have
a uniform National policy for coal extraction from both surface and
underground mines. It is mandatory that mining personnel be required
to use efficient modern-equipment whereby minimizing waste during extraction. Similarly efficient furnaces should be designed to obtain
clean coal burning. The design of thermal plants should be improved to
extract maximum heat through the steam boilers. The efficiency of
steam turbines must be improved by reducing pressure drag at the
turbine blades.

Coal-cleaning research is directed toward technology achieving
efficient and pollution-free combustion. To remove more than 75% of
impurities that degrade the environment when coal is burned, advanced
physical and chemical techniques (2,9,14) for coal cleaning are employed. Physical coal-cleaning techniques include fine grinding, froth
floatation, oil agglomeration, and high gradient magnetic separation.
Physical cleaning processes reduce ash contents of the coal and remove
90% of pyritic sulfur to yield SO_2 emissions in the range of 0.8 to
3.5 lb of sulfur per million Btu, which fall within the acceptable
limits. Chemical coal-cleaning techniques under development can remove
95 to 99% of pyritic sulfur and upto 40% of organic sulfur, making a
total sulfur-reduction in the range of 53 to 77%. Chemical processes
remove impurities and form water soluble substances that can be washed
out of the coal. Both physical and chemical processes are costly and
require Federal subsidies for coal companies to flourish and ensure
reasonable growth of hydrothermal power for National well-being.

Assessment of Future Hydrothermal Power in the United States

In 1985, 709 million short tons of coal were used for production of electricity, and 134 short tons for other uses. The present installed capacity of power plants in the U.S. (2,8) is 672 GW. Coal is providing 44.5% of the total energy as 299 GW. Similarly water is meeting 12.2% of the total energy needs as 82 GW. No nuclear power plants will be allowed to be built beyond 1995. Oil and gas power-plants have to be replaced gradually as these two resources become scarce and exhausted. Wind, solar and tidal power-development is still in its infancy and cannot be relied upon permanently. All indications are pointing toward water and coal as the dependable raw materials for future power-production.

The undeveloped run-of-river-power is of the order of 174 GW, and does not require any alternative power source as does the pumped storage. There is no limitation on the development of pumped-storage hydropower as long as an alternative power-source is available to fill the upper-storage reservoir. It is suggested that one-third of coal energy be reserved for low-load periods while two-thirds of it be used for pumping during the same time period. It is recommended that coal production be brought to a level of 6 billion short tons per year. This would generate coal power of 2 400 GW and help produce 1 600 GW of pumped-storage power. The total power-production form coal and water would be of the order of 4 250 GW, about six times the present power from all sources. The required coal-production can be brought on line in a ten-year-time period. This would provide a strong impetus for the development of new industry, manufacturing plants, increase in jobs, and economic growth.

During the official ten-year-planning period (1986 - 1995), growth in the coal extraction has been projected to be nominal -- 709 million to a little over one billion short tons. The power production is also scheduled to be on a thin scale -- maximum coal power to be added will be about 6.5 GW and minimum 1.6 GW during any given year. During the same period maximum water-power to be added will be 3.2 GW and minimum 0.005 GW. The planning of electric power-development as envisaged by the industry is not encouraging and does not anticipate any spectacular changes in economy. This indicates that Federal involvement in power production is very essential for the steering of National economy in the right direction.

Conclusions

Based on the factual information, it is concluded that the National energy-resources are not increasing at a rate commensurate with the normal growth of National productivity. As a result it is feared that there will be an energy crisis in the power industry in the near future. Wind, tidal, solar, and nuclear power-sources cannot be relied on for future power-demands. Gas and oil power-plants will be phased out gradually by the turn of the century. Only two power sources, coal and water, can be looked upon with confidence to provide the required power for consumption in the future. Hydropower can be enhanced by providing pumped-storage facilities, and coal production can be increased through Federal subsidies. Therefore, it is strongly recommended that the U.S. Congress should institute uniform policies and Federal funding for research and development of hydrothermal power plants throughout the United States.

Appendix: References

1. "An Assessment of Hydroelectric Pumped Stotage," National Hydro-electric Power Resources Study, Vol. X, Nov. 1981, The U.S. Army Eng. Inst. for Water Resources, Fort Belvoir, Virginia.

2. "Annual Energy Outlook, 1984," Energy Information Administration, Washington, D.C., Jan. 1985.

3. "Annual Outlook of U.S. Coal, 1985," Energy Information Administration, Washington, D.C., May 1985.

4. Burdin, W.W., "Design of Carters Pumped Storage Project," J. Power Div., Proc. Am. Soc. Civ. Egnrs., Vol. 96, No. PO3, June 1970, pp. 383-400.

5. "Demonstrated Reserve Base of Coal in the United States," Energy Information Administration, Washington, D.C., May 1982.

6. "Electric Power Annual," U.S. Dept. of Energy, Washington, D.C., Nov. 1982.

7. Hartman, O., and, W. Meire, "Development in High Head Pumped Storage," Water Power, Vol. 22, March 1970, pp. 102-106.

8. "Inventory of Power Plants in the United States, 1984," Energy Information Administration, Washington, D.C., July 1985.

9. Khoury, D.L., Editor, Coal Cleaning Technology, Noyes Data Corporation, Park Ridge, N.J., 1981.

10. Marker, G.A., "Socio-Economic Aspects of Small Hydro Development: A Private Development View," Hydropower: A National Energy Resource, Proc., The Engin. Foundation, March 11-16, 1979, pp. 141-154.

11. "Pumped Storage: State of the Art," By the Committee on Hydro-electric Power Project Planning and Design, J. Power Div., Proc., Am. Soc. Civ. Engrs., Vol. 97, No. PO1, July 1971, pp. 675-696.

12. Rogers, F.C., "Existing Hydroelectric Generation Enhanced by Underground Energy Storage," Pumped Storage, Engin. Foundation Conf., Am. Soc. Civ. Engrs., Aug. 18-23, 1974, pp. 415-432.

13. Scherer, C.R., "Load Management Economics with Pumped Storage," J. Energy Div., Proc., Am. Soc. Civ. Engrs., Vol. 106, No. EY1, April 1980, pp. 69-87.

14. Schmidt, R.A., Coal in America, McGraw-Hill, Inc., N.Y., 1979.

15. Stouk, J.J., "Potential Pumped Storage Projects That Would Use Existing Reservoirs," Pumped Storage, Engin. Foundation Conf., Am. Soc. Civ. Engrs., Aug. 18-23, 1974, pp. 221-252.

16. Wachter, G.F., "Modernization of Hydroelectric Units," Hydro-power: A National Energy Resource, Proc., The Engin. Foundation, March 11-16, 1979, pp. 83-96.

17. Willer, D.C., "Small Hydro Installations," Power Engineering, Vol. 84, No. 1, Jan. 1980, pp. 62-84.

18. Willett, D.C., "Underground Pumped Storage Possibilities," Pumped Storage, Engin. Foundation Conf., Am. Soc. Civ. Engrs., Aug. 18-23, 1974, pp. 433-452.

19. Willett, D.C., "Underground Pumped Storage," Hydropower: A Nat. Energy Resource, Proc., The Engin. Foundation, March 11-16, 1979, pp. 73-82.

REMOTE SENSING TO ASSESS EFFECTS OF HYDROELECTRIC DEVELOPMENT

Stewart K. Sears[x], Tracey J. Ellis[**], and David B. White[**]

Abstract

Planning for hydroelectric development of rivers in the province of Ontario, Canada requires extensive environmental evaluation and assessment. To test the feasibility of using digital analysis of remotely sensed satellite data as a means of acquiring and using environmental information to assess proposed hydroelectric development, a pilot project was conducted in 1985 using a remote Ontario river basin as a test case. The project involved mapping the 1.5 M ha Little Jackfish River drainage basin according to 14 land cover types. Three test applications were found to be useful in evaluating environmental effects of hydroelectric development, i.e., suspended sediment mapping, reservoir mapping, and wildlife habitat mapping. The technology appears to offer an extremely cost-effective means of collecting and using environmental information for the applications which were tested.

Introduction and Background

Environmental legislation in Ontario, Canada requires extensive front-end planning and environmental assessment for major public sector construction activities. Ontario Hydro, a crown corporation responsible for providing electrical power to 3 million Ontario customers, is subject to that legislation. Hence, a great deal of effort is committed to predicting and assessing potential environmental effects of constructing large generation projects. Hydroelectric development often occurs in remote regions of the province, where little up-to-date environmental information exists. Baseline data acquisition in these areas can be both time-consuming and expensive. Therefore cost-effective means of acquiring this information are highly desirable.

Ontario Hydro office studies indicated that satellite remote sensing technology can provide a useful and cost-effective tool for environmental studies (Sears, 1982) (Sears, 1983). In 1985, Ontario Hydro undertook to test these claims by conducting a pilot project with the Ontario Centre for Remote Sensing (OCRS). The project involved mapping a remote study area - the Little Jackfish River (LJR) drainage basin - according to 14 cover types, using multi-date LANDSAT satellite data (Figure 1). A series of tests were also run on a sub-area of the drainage basin to show the extent to which different types of environmental information could be extracted and interpreted

* Environmental Studies Scientist, Environmental Studies and Assessments Department, Ontario Hydro, 700 University Avenue, Toronto, Ontario, M5G 1X6

** Staff Scientist, Ontario Centre for Remote Sensing, Ministry of Natural Resources, 880 Bay Street, Toronto, Ontario, M5S 1Z8

from the original and the classified imagery. Three of those applications are summarized here.

The focus of the project was on gaining expertise, and providing information which would be useful in assessing environmental effects of hydroelectric development.

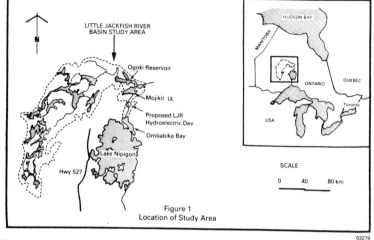

Figure 1
Location of Study Area

03279

Method

Thematic maps of generalized land cover types were produced for the LJR drainage basin through the digital analysis and visual interpretation of LANDSAT satellite data. The maps were produced using a standard supervised multispectral classification technique illustrated in Figure 2. A similar technique is documented elsewhere (Kalensky et al, 1981).

Results

The output of the LJR pilot project included eleven hard-copy map sets, at scales ranging from 1:50,000 to 1:500,000. The entire drainage basin (1.52 M ha) was mapped according to generalized land cover types using a geometrically corrected ground resolution (picture element or 'pixel' size) of 50 m x 50 m (0.5 ha).

Test applications were run on a smaller part of the basin which would be directly influenced by hydroelectric development, (i.e., the Little Jackfish River between Mojikit Lake and Ombabika Bay, (Figure 1)) in order to test the capabilities of the technology, and to obtain more information relevant to assessing environmental effects. The following outputs were obtained:

1.   1:50,000 scale map of Ombabika Bay turbidity (suspended sediments);
2.   1:50,000 and 1:100,000 scale classified (and unclassified) theme maps of Little Jackfish River, with and without elevation contours and flooded (proposed reservoir) area, including hard copies and one transparent overlay;
3.   1:50,000 scale black and white map of LJR only, with one theme (deciduous forest) highlighted in colour;

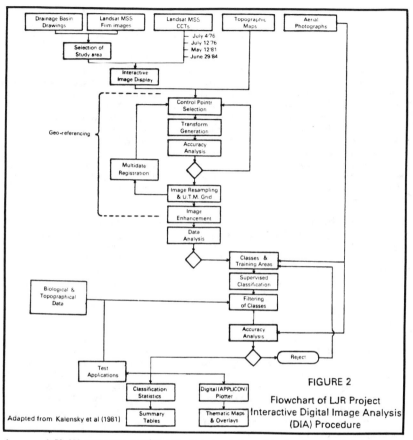

FIGURE 2

Flowchart of LJR Project
Interactive Digital Image Analysis
(DIA) Procedure

Adapted from Kalensky et al (1981)

4.   1:50,000 scale map showing only forest areas, combined and segregated into
     themes; and

5.   1:50,000 scale map showing correlated land cover types and potential moose
     habitat over a black and white background.

Three of these outputs (Nos. 1, 2 and 5, above) were found to have very good potential
for use in assessing effects of hydroelectric development, and are discussed below.
The others were considered to have good potential for use as presentation products in
scoping or information meetings with government and the public.

Suspended Sediments

Although some sub-surface water and water depth information can be interpreted from
enhanced LANDSAT imagery (Hathout, 1985), most applications of computer analyzed
satellite data are restricted to terrestrial or near-surface aquatic environments
(McKernan et al, 1985) (Hecky et al, 1984). Examples of near-surface aquatic patterns
which can be detected through satellite imagery include suspended or floating

vegetation (chlorophyl, algae), ice and snow cover, and suspended sediments. McKernan et al, (1985) and Hecky et al, (1984) found that LANDSAT imagery was valuable in monitoring changes in surface water turbidity and vegetation patterns in hydroelectric storage reservoirs.

The proposed LJR hydroelectric project has the potential to affect downstream turbidity levels due to highly erodable and unstable banks downstream of the proposed dam site. Ombabika Bay (Lake Nipigon) was therefore mapped according to five suspended sediment categories, to provide a single-date indication of pre-construction conditions. These categories represent qualitative and gross near-surface water patterns based on multi-spectral reflectance values. McKernan et al, (1985), Chagarlamudi et al. (1980), and Lillesand et al, (1983) have determined that LANDSAT reflectance values can be correlated with and validated by ground-based measurements of suspended sediment and chlorophyl-a levels from lake samples taken coincident with a LANDSAT overpass. At least two ground-satellite correlations should be performed, however, to allow for reasonably accurate corrections for illumination angle, atmospheric conditions (haze, fog), and water surface roughness and glare (McKernan et al, 1985).

The LJR test application suggested that satellite information on near-surface turbidity patterns could be very useful in monitoring changes caused by hydroelectric development when the detection of such changes by ground (boat) observations/measurements, or aerial survey are prohibitively expensive. LANDSAT imagery has the added bonus of providing a historical record of near-surface water information, plus continued repetitive monitoring (within the limits set by orbital interval and coincidental cloud cover) (Hecky et al, 1984).

Reservoir Mapping

Topographical data are necessary to produce maps or drawings of proposed reservoirs. Unfortunately LANDSAT sensors do not provide stereo imagery, hence quantitative topographical information in unavailable. The computer-based system used in the LJR project, however, is capable of accepting and superimposing digital linear information on the classified imagery. Therefore, contour lines can be manually digitized into the computer image file using contour maps or geotechnical drawings as the information source. Although this can be a time-consuming task, the LJR project indicated it could be well worthwhile in terms of ease of recall and for applications requiring different mapping scenarios (i.e., reservoirs).

Contours chosen for this application included the proposed maximum flooding elevation (327 m), and two reference contours; one above the flooded zone (350 m), and one below (300 m). They were mapped with different backgrounds, individually and collectively, to demonstrate possible uses for analysis and presentation. The contours, plus all proposed hydroelectric development structures (access roads, dams, dikes, power canal, powerhouse, construction camp) were also mapped on a transparent overlay which could be used with any 1:50,000 scale map for planning and assessment purposes. This feature was considered useful as it provided some constraint mapping capability.

Since the contour information is entered in a digital fashion, it can be used in conjunction with the classified image data to create sub-areas and associated statistical summaries. This was particularly useful in determining the area of the proposed flooding zone and the various percentages of each cover type within that zone. Very minimal computer instructions were required to generate this information.

This mapping feature gives hydroelectric planners and decision-makers the opportunity to quickly and cost-effectively assess different flooding scenarios, and the ability to assess any associated environmental or other social or technical effects.

Wildlife Habitat

Environmental assessment practitioners have recently advocated habitat evaluation procedures as a means of assessing and quantifying effects of construction activities on wildlife (Beanlands and Duinker, 1983). Hydroelectric developments often require the flooding of lands to create storage reservoirs or headponds. In the process, a variety of wildlife habitats could be lost. Since vegetative cover is the basic unit of habitat evaluation, and because LANDSAT sensors are very good at detecting surface vegetation, several researchers have used satellite imagery to map potential wildlife habitat (Lunetta et al, 1985) (Dixon et al, 1982) (Laperriere et al, 1980).

A similar effort was undertaken in the LJR project to test and demonstrate the capability to map potential moose habitat — moose being the most abundant and economically important large game species in the study area. A review of the literature on moose habitat was performed to determine if there were any correlations of habitat requirements with generalized LJR vegetation patterns. Five critical moose habitat components were identified (Ontario Ministry of Natural Resources, 1984) (Cairns et al, 1980); aquatic feeding areas, summer habitat, early winter habitat, late winter habitat, and special areas (i.e., mineral licks and calving areas). All but the latter habitat component (special areas) could be roughly correlated with certain generalized land cover types shown on the satellite images.

The resulting map appears to be of value in planning further environmental studies. For example, it indicates areas which do or do not have good potential for moose habitat. If key areas of potential habitat exist in the vicinity of a proposed project, for example, this map can indicate roughly which habitat component(s) are involved and where further studies (air photo coverage, field studies) should concentrate. Although the satellite map provides a general picture of where potential habitat exists, it gives no information on the likelihood of moose being present in any particular area, or on the actual suitability of that habitat for producing moose. The mapped information can, however, be input to Habitat Suitability Index models which quantify the capacity of a given habitat to support moose (Lunetta et al, 1985) (US Fish and Wildlife Service, 1981).

For the purpose of demonstrating the capability of satellite remote sensing technology to perform vegetation class/wildlife habitat correlations, the moose habitat map was very successful. The possibilities of future refinement and technology development in this area are extremely good.

Costs

The project was evaluated in terms of its overall costs versus benefits, based only on what it cost to produce generalized land cover maps of the entire drainage basin at 1:250,000 and 1:100,000 scales (i.e., not to perform the test applications). Based on a total study area of 15,200 km^2 (excluding Ombabika Bay), the approximate total cost to produce the maps was $40,000 or $2.67 per km^2 (CDN). Sears (1985) compared costs of other selected LANDSAT mapping projects and found that typical operational costs can be in the $1.50 to $2.50/km^2 range. The Illinois Environmental Protection Agency (1978)

compared total costs for preparing land cover inventories using satellite and other
methods:

Windshield (ground) survey: $22.96/km^2
Air-photo acquisition and interpretation: $ 7.79/km^2
LANDSAT acquisition and interpretation: $ 1.63/km^2 (1978 dollars)

Accuracy

A detailed assessment of the accuracy of the resulting classified maps (i.e.
ground-truthing) was not undertaken due to budget restrictions and due to the remoteness
of the study area. Based on previous experience with this type of mapping, OCRS has
estimated for the LJR project an accuracy of 80-95 percent for most cover types. If the
themes or cover types are consolidated into three major categories - water, forest and
open land - the accuracy of the classified imagery should be at least 90 percent.
However, the breakdown within these three categories may be less accurate.

Application to Hydroelectric Planning and Assessment

The complementary nature of LANDSAT and other data collection and analysis techniques is
illustrated in Figure 3. Classified and checked LANDSAT data can provide a general
picture of land cover patterns over a large study area. Using this information, smaller
areas worthy of more detailed (i.e., additional air-photo) study can be identified. This
information can, in turn, provide indications of which areas are worthy of ground surveys
(generalized and detailed). Each step leading up to the detailed ground surveys
represents a technique for improving the cost-effectiveness of environmental study
programs, by helping to better focus expensive field studies on geographic areas, sites,
or valued ecosystem components of most concern. This approach is particularly useful in
planning hydroelectric projects in Ontario, which are typically in remote northern
locations where access is expensive, and where up-to-date environmental information is
scarce.

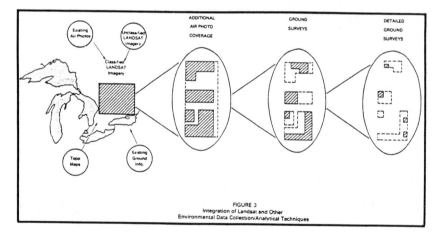

FIGURE 3
Integration of Landsat and Other
Environmental Data Collection/Analytical Techniques

Satellite imagery is ideally suited to several environmental assessment activities throughout the life cycle of a hydroelectric project; i.e., (a) Environmental planning/scoping (predicting potential consequences of various development scenarios on land/water patterns, wildlife or man, identifying environmentally sensitive areas and/or the need for more study, demonstrating to government or public proposals and plans, and performing broad-based site selection exercises), (b) Conceptual and definition phase environmental studies (i.e., vegetation mapping, modelling of ecosystems, impact predictions, identification of need for more detailed air photo or ground studies, mapping of environmentally sensitive areas, identification of existing aggregate extraction areas, water quality assessment and putting near-site environmental data within a regional or river basin context), (c) Project monitoring (i.e., monitoring construction progress, vegetation disturbance, water quality changes, urban development, snow/ice conditions, water levels, and agricultural patterns), and (d) Project follow-up/verification (i.e., provide historical records to test/verify models and predictions relating to ground-surface based changes). These, and other, applications are also discussed by Paterson (1985), McLeod (1984), and Ross et al, (1983).

Satellite data should be considered a useful part of the electric utility environmental assessment practitioner's tool-kit. In some situations, it can better direct or focus more detailed environmental studies, or it may be the only economical means of mapping a very large study area. In addition, satellite remote sensing may provide a useful environmental or project monitoring technique due to its regular, repetitive imaging characteristics. In all cases, it is important to recognize the capabilities and limitations of the technology, and to use it where it can provide timely, accurate, and cost-effective information.

Conclusion

In conclusion, the LJR satellite mapping pilot project confirmed earlier predictions of the technology which suggested that satellite remote sensing can offer a dynamic, useful and cost-effective tool for providing timely land cover information. The suspended sediment, reservoir mapping, and wildlife habitat applications were found to be very useful in helping electric utility environmental assessment practitioners better assess effects of proposed hydroelectric development. The information is useful for input to all phases of Ontario Hydro's environmental planning and assessment of proposed hydroelectric developments. Satellite remote sensing should be used to complement other environmental data collection and analysis techniques. Use of this technology will help electric utilities to better predict and assess environmental effects, and respond in a more educated fashion to environmental concerns of government and public.

References

Beanlands, G.E. and P.N. Duinker, 1983. An ecological framework for
     environmental impact assessment in Canada, Dalhousie University and Federal
     Environmental Assessment Review Office report.
Cairns, A.L. and E.S. Telfer, 1980. Habitat use by four sympatric
     ungulates in boreal mixedwood forest, J. Wildlife Management 44(4):849-857.
Chagarlamudi, P., R.E. Hecky, and J.S. Schubert, 1980. Quantitative monitoring
     of sediment levels in freshwater lakes from LANDSAT, p 115-118. In
     V.V. Salomonson, and P.D. Bhavsar (ed). The contribution of space observations
     to water resources management. Pergamon Press, New York.

Dixon, R., B. Knudson and L. Bowles, 1982. A pilot study of the
    application of LANDSAT data in the mapping of white-tailed deer habitat in
    Manitoba. In Land/Wildlife Integration No. 2, H.A. Stelfox and G.R. Ironside
    (ed), Environment Canada Ecological Classification Series No. 17.
Hathout, S., 1985. The use of enhanced LANDSAT imagery for mapping
    lake depth. Journal of Environmental Management. 20:253-261.
Hecky, R.E. and G.K. McCullough, 1984. The LANDSAT imagery of
    Southern Indian Lake: A remote perspective on impoundment and diversion,
    Canadian Technical Report of Fisheries and Aquatic Sciences No. 1266, Department
    of Fisheries and Oceans, Winnipeg, Manitoba.
Kalensky, Z.D., W.C. Moore, G.A. Campbell, D.A. Wilson and A.J. Scott,
    1981. Summary forest resource data from LANDSAT images - Final report of a
    pilot study for northern Saskatchewan, Petawawa National Forestry Institute,
    Canadian Forestry Service, Information Report PI-X-5.
Laperriere, A.J., P.C. Lent, W.C. Gassaway, and F.A. Nodler, 1980.
    Use of LANDSAT Data for moose habitat analyses in Alaska, J. Wildlife Management
    44(4):881-887.
Lillesand, T.M., W.L. Johnson, R.L. Derrell, O.M. Lindstrom and
    D.E. Meisner, 1983, Use of LANDSAT data to predict the trophic state of
    Minnesota lakes, Photogrammetric Engineering and Remote Sensing 49:2:219-229.
Lunetta, R.S., R.G. Congalton, A.M.B. Rekas, and J.K. Stoll, 1985.
    Using remotely sensed data to map vegetative cover for habitat evaluation in the
    Saginaw River basin, Presentation to American Society of Photogrammetry.
McKernan, J.M. and T.T. Alfoldi, 1985. Applications of remote sensing
    to assess limnological effects of hydro-electric development. Presentation to
    Canadian Electrical Association.
McLeod, R.G., 1984. The application of image-based information
    systems for environmental assessment, in Improving impact assessment:
    Increasing the relevance and utilization of scientific and technical
    information, S. Hart, G. Enk and W. Hornick (ed), Westview Press Boulder.
Ontario Ministry of Natural Resources 1984. Guidelines for moose
    habitat management in Ontario.
Paterson, W.M., 1985. Preliminary assessment of remote sensing
    utilization for EA planning and analysis, Ontario Hydro ES&A Department
    Technical Memorandum TM85/4.
Ross, D.I. and V. Singhroy, 1983. The application of remote sensing
    technology to the environmental assessment process, Prepared for Workshop on New
    Directions in Environmental Assessment: The Canadian Experience.
Sears, S.K., 1982. Application of remote sensing to environmental
    assessment of northern Ontario developments, Ontario Hydro ES&A Department,
    Report No. 82646.
Sears, S.K., 1983. Remote sensing resources and technology: Digital image analysis
    for design and development studies, ES&A Department, Report No. 83464.
Sears, S.K. 1985. Remote sensing pilot project technical evaluation, Ontario Hydro
    Environmental Studies and Assessments Department, Report No. 85262.
US Fish and Wildlife Service (1981). Standards for the development of
    habitat suitability in index models, Ecological Services Manual 103-ESM.

SALTWATER INTRUSION IN A HIGHLY TRANSMISSIVE UNCONFINED AQUIFER

By Bradley G. Waller*

INTRODUCTION

Early hydrologic descriptions by Munroe (1930, p. 188, 218) and Sewell (1933) indicated that pristine conditions in Dade County, Fla., were marked by high ground-water levels near the coast and in the Everglades, freshwater springs welling up through the floor of Biscayne Bay, and 50-foot (15-meter) deep wells yielding potable water by flow near the mouth of the Miami River. Dredging of the Miami Canal cut into highly permeable zones of the Biscayne aquifer (Schroeder and others, 1985), disturbed the natural balance between the fresh ground water and the saltwater of Biscayne Bay, and permitted saltwater to locally intrude the aquifer.

Saltwater intrusion is particularly dynamic in coastal Dade County because of the high permeability of the Biscayne aquifer, because of the good interconnection between canals and the aquifer, and because of the seasonal rainfall. The problem is accentuated as urban growth continues to encroach on inland wetland areas which results in lowered inland water levels. This lowering reduces the seaward freshwater hydraulic gradient and the freshwater head at the coast, both of which govern the intrusion of saltwater.

SALTWATER INTRUSION BEFORE 1946

Saltwater intrusion gained strong impetus during the 1920's and 1930's after the construction of uncontrolled primary drainage canals that extended from Lake Okeechobee across the Everglades to the coast, causing regional decline of water levels. This diversion caused water levels to decline excessively, triggering the inland movement of salt-water into the lower zones of the surficial aquifers adjacent to the coast of southeast Florida. An expanded network of drainage canals in Dade County brought about further saltwater intrusion that had advanced along a broad front as shown by the inland position of the saltwater-freshwater interface in 1946 in figure 1 (Parker and others, 1955, fig. 200).

Saltwater intruded landward along each major canal, but particularly critical was the Hialeah-Miami Springs area where some supply wells in the municipal well field had to be shut down (fig. 1). Intrusion in the south was due chiefly to below sea level ground-water levels shown on the generalized water-table contour map in figure 2 (Parker and others, 1955, fig. 45).

*Research Hydrologist, U.S. Geological Survey, Water Resources Division, P. O. Box 026052, Miami, FL 33102

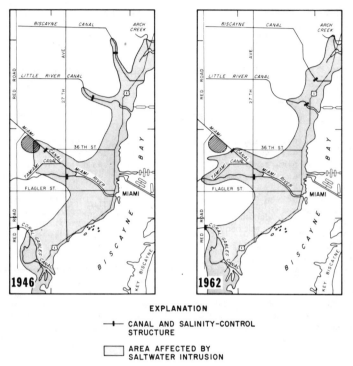

EXPLANATION

 CANAL AND SALINITY-CONTROL
STRUCTURE

☐ AREA AFFECTED BY
SALTWATER INTRUSION

▨ WELL FIELD

```
0                    5 MILES
├──┬──┬──┬──┬──┤
0          5 KILOMETERS
```

Figure 1.--Miami area showing saltwater intrusion at the base of
the Biscayne aquifer, 1946-62.

SALTWATER INTRUSION DURING 1946-62

After the record low water levels of 1945, water-supply agencies
responded to the threat of further saltwater intrusion in Dade County
by installing (in 1946) sheet-steel piling, salinity-control structures
in all primary canals as far seaward as possible. The installation and
operation of controls in primary canals were designed to control canal
flows. The interval 1946-62 could then be considered one of elemental
water control, although major flooding occurred during 1947 because
canals were not adequately designed to handle the record rainfalls from
two consecutive hurricanes. The salinity-control structures and practices halted saltwater intrusion by blocking saltwater from moving
upchannel beyond the control structures in the canals and by sustaining
high water levels near the coast during dry seasons. In some instances, after the installation of salinity-control structures, the
lobes of intruding saltwater along canals retreated seaward. The

seaward retreat was especially important along the Miami Canal because
it permitted full production again from Miami's well field adjacent to
the Miami Canal. The map of 1962 (fig. 1) shows the inland extent of
saltwater at the end of the prolonged dry season of 1962 after more
than 15 years of elemental water control and water conservation, and an
increase in well-field pumping from about 50 to 80 million gallons per
day (190 to 300 liters x 10^6 day^{-1}). The 15-year period included the
following events:

1. Record flooding, 1947-48.
2. The creation in 1949 of the Central and Southern Florida Flood
    Control District (renamed South Florida Water Management District
    in 1971). Construction and operation of a system of canals,
    control structures, levees, pumping stations, and water-storage
    areas whose functions were flood protection and water conserva-
    tion.
3. Prolonged dry seasons, 1951-52, 1955-56.
4. High water levels, 1958-60, extensive flooding in south Dade County
    after Hurricane Donna and Tropical Storm Florence, 1960.
5. Near record low water levels, 1961-62.
6. The beginning in 1961 of an extensive drainage canal network in
    south Dade County.

    Included also was the completion in 1953 of the eastern levee system
(Levees 30 and 31 in Dade County, fig. 3), and later in 1962 the completion of the southern levee (Levee 29) to enclose Water Conservation
Areas 3A and 3B. The levee system separating Conservation Areas 3A and
3B diverted (southward) part of the water that had previously flowed
from the Everglades eastward to the ocean. The enclosure of Water

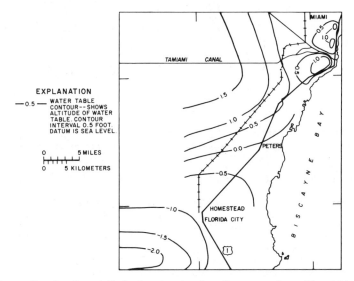

Figure 2.--Southeast Dade County showing the general configuration of
    the water table, May 19, 1945 (from Parker and others, 1955).

Conservation Areas 3A and 3B enabled the impoundment of water in Dade
County for replenishing the aquifer in coastal urban areas during dry
seasons.   The enclosure also marked the change from elemental to comprehensive water management within the region.

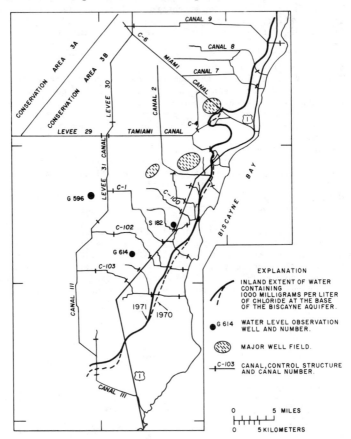

Figure 3.--East Dade County showing the inland extent of saltwater
intrusion during 1970 and 1971.

EFFECT OF SOUTH DADE COUNTY CANAL SYSTEM ON SALTWATER INTRUSION, 1963-80

     Of major significance in south Dade County was the beginning in
1961 of construction of the extensive drainage canal system, which was
designed to prevent recurrence of flood damages of the magnitude of
those caused by Hurricane Donna and Tropical Storm Florence in 1960.
The canal system in south Dade County (Canals 1, 100, 102, 103, and
the inland (northward) extension of Canal 111, fig. 5) was virtually
completed by 1967.   Unlike the canals constructed earlier, canals in
southeast Dade County were equipped with flow-regulation structures

near the coast and at sites inland (fig. 3) to step up water levels to reduce overdrainage. As designed, the canal drainage system lowered water levels during most of the 1960's and early 1970's, as shown by the long-term hydrographs of wells G-596, G-614, and S-182 in figure 4 (well locations in fig. 3). The frequency with which water levels in south Dade County approached or declined below sea level is shown in the hydrograph of well G-614. In general, annual peak water levels were lowered, and annual low levels declined further, as compared to pre-1962 levels.

The inland movement of saltwater during 1970-71 (fig. 3) represented a readvance of saltwater intrusion--a result of the record dry season in southeast Florida since completion of the south Dade County canal

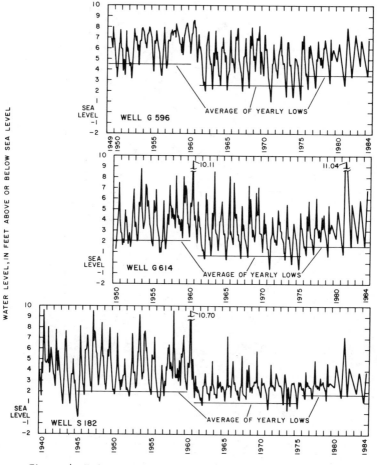

Figure 4--Hydrographs of wells G-596, G-614, and S-182 in south Dade County, 1945-83.

network. Between 1970 and 1971, the inland movement of saltwater at
the base of the aquifer was nearly 1 mile (1.6 kilometers) in the Canal
111 area and exceeded 0.5 mile (0.8 kilometer) in the Canal 103 and
Canal 1 basins. Saltwater intrusion also occurred near the Miami well
field adjacent to the Tamiami-Miami Canal basin.

Concern about the recurrent low water levels in south Dade County
provided impetus for the South Florida Water Management District and

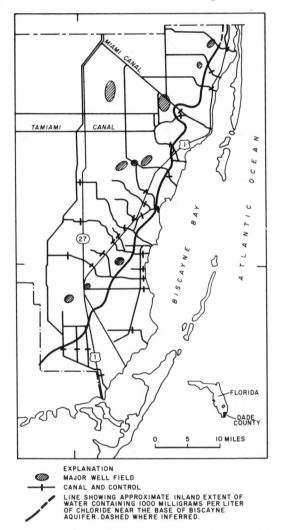

Figure 5.--Dade County showing approximate inland extent of water containing 1,000 mg/L of chloride near base of Biscayne aquifer, May 1984.

the U.S. Army Corps of Engineers to implement remedial measures to
increase the quantities of water from Water Conservation Areas 3A and
3B into south Dade County through an improved conveyance canal system.
Implementation began in 1976 and was completed before 1982. The result
was a rise of nearly 1 foot (0.3 meter) in the average of the yearly
lowest water levels in coastal areas (hydrograph of well S-182) and
rises of 1 foot (0.3 meter) in areas farther inland (hydrographs of
wells G-614, G-596, fig. 4) since 1976. A permanent 1-foot (0.3 meter)
rise in low water levels is highly important in preventing further
saltwater intrusion in south Dade County. The adjusted annual low
water levels after 1976 were approaching the annual low levels that
preceded the installation of canals (pre-1962) in much of south Dade
County.

STATUS OF SALTWATER INTRUSION, 1980-84

The approximate inland extent of saltwater containing 1,000 mg/L
(milligrams per liter) of chloride at or near the base of the Biscayne
aquifer in coastal Dade County in May 1984 is shown in figure 5. The
base of the permeable limestones in south Dade County ranges from about
60 to 100 feet below land surface and in northeast Dade County about
110 to 150 feet below. Some of the wells did not fully penetrate to
the base of the highly permeable limestone; therefore, the position
of the 1,000-mg/L line in figure 5 was estimated through a series of
interpolations of chloride concentrations. That is, the chloride
concentrations at the expected base of the aquifer were interpolated
as greater than the concentrations in the sample from the observation
well. An adjustment was then required to delineate the seaward or
landward position of the line with reference to each observation well.

Also, data obtained by Kohout (1960, fig. 3) and Kohout and Klein
(1967, figs. 3-8), describing chloride ion distribution within the zone
of diffusion between freshwater and seawater in the Biscayne aquifer of
the Silver Bluff area of Miami and the Cutler area of southeast Dade
County, were used in estimating chloride concentrations for positioning
the line seaward or landward of observation wells. At Silver Bluff,
where the zone of diffusion extended inland nearly 12,000 feet (3,700
meters), the distance between water containing 200 mg/L of chloride and
1,000 mg/L of chloride along the base of the aquifer was about 500 feet
(150 meters) in 1954. At Cutler, where the zone of diffusion extended
inland about 600 feet (180 meters), the distance between water containing 500 mg/L of chloride and 1,000 mg/L of chloride along the base of
the aquifer was less than 200 feet (61 meters) in 1958. Additional data
obtained from multidepth wells at the inland edge of the zone of diffusion indicated that the chloride concentration increased from less than
200 mg/L at a depth of 80 feet (24 meters) below sea level to greater
than 4,000 mg/L at a depth of 95 feet (29 meters) below sea level.

A comparison of the inland patterns of saltwater intrusion in 1984
(fig. 5) and 1971 (fig. 3) shows little inland saltwater migration
during the intervening period, but rather it shows a local freshening
(seaward movement) in the lower part of the aquifer in the Tamiami-
Miami Canal area as a result of the 3-mile (4.8-kilometer) downstream
relocation of the flow-regulation structure on the Tamiami Canal.

Freshening occurred despite the increase in withdrawals at the Miami-
Hialeah well field from 90 million gallons per day (340 liters x 10^6
day^{-1}) in 1971 to about 130 million gallons per day (490 liters x
10^6 day^{-1}) in 1983. Another effect of water management is that no further inland migration of saltwater has occurred since the early 1960's
in the Canal 2 basin where municipal withdrawal has increased from 70
million gallons per day (265 liters x 10^6 day^{-1}) in 1962 to nearly 130
million gallons per day (492 liters x 10^6 day^{-1}) in 1983.

The position of the 1,000-mg/L chloride line in Dade County in 1984
is the result of natural hydrologic events and man's alterations and
management practices on the hydrologic system of southeast Florida. If
saltwater intrusion is to be controlled and freshwater demands of urban
growth are to be met, continuation of adequate ground-water levels will
have to be sustained during prolonged dry periods.

Increased withdrawals from the large municipal well fields (which
represented most of the ground-water pumpage in the county) have caused
only local declines in water level and relatively minor effects on
intrusion. To satisfy demands in Dade County, locations for new well
fields were selected in inland wetlands, remote (upgradient) from
existing well fields and from heavily urbanized areas.

REFERENCES CITED

Klein, Howard, and Causaras, C. R., 1982, Biscayne aquifer, southeast
    Florida, and the contiguous surficial aquifer to the north, in
    Franks, B. J., ed., Principal aquifers in Florida: U.S. Geological
    Survey Water-Resources Investigations Open-File Report 82-255,
    4 sheets.
Kohout, F. A., 1960, Cyclic flow of saltwater in the Biscayne aquifer
    of southeastern Florida: Journal of Geophysical Research, v. 65,
    no. 7, p. 2133-2141.
Kohout, F. A., and Klein, Howard, 1967, Effect of pulse recharge on the
    zone of diffusion in the Biscayne aquifer: International
    Association of Scientific Hydrology, Publication no. 70, p. 252-270.
Kohout, F. A., and Leach, S. D., 1964, Saltwater movement caused by
    control-dam operations in the Snake Creek Canal, Miami, Florida:
    Florida Geological Survey Report of Investigations 24, part IV,
    49 p.
Leach, S. D., and Grantham, R. G., 1966, Salt-water study of the Miami
    River and its tributaries, Dade County, Florida: Florida Geo-
    logical Survey Report of Investigations 45, 36 p.
Munroe, R. M., 1930, The commodore's story: Ives Washburn Press.
Parker, G. G., Ferguson, G. E., Love, S. K., and others, 1955, Water
    resources of southeastern Florida with special reference to the
    geology and ground water of the Miami area: U.S. Geological Survey
    Water-Supply Paper 1255, 965 p.
Schroeder, M. C., Klein, Howard, and Hoy, N. D., 1958, Biscayne aquifer
    of Dade and Broward Counties, Florida: Florida Geological Survey
    Report of Investigations 17, 56 p.
Sewell, John, 1933, John Sewell's memoirs and history of Miami:
    Miami's water supply and its source: Franklin Press, Miami,
    Fla., v. 1, chap. 6.

Seawater Intrusion in Salinas Valley, California

James S. Jenks (M.ASCE)1/, Gerald E. Snow 2/, Philip L. Wagner 1/

Abstract

Seawater intrusion into two aquifers of the Salinas Valley in California has resulted in abandonment of many wells along the coast. The study described in this paper addresses the causes of seawater intrusion, its effects, and alternative methods to slow or halt the intrusion.

The rate of intrusion has been estimated to be about 19,000 acre-feet (23,400 cubic dekameters (dkm3)) per year. If no action is taken to halt the intrusion, it is projected that in the year 2000 there will be as much as 26,000 acres (10,500 ha) underlain by the contaminated 180-foot aquifer. If no action is taken the seawater intrusion will result in crop losses, job losses, losses in land value, reduced groundwater storage capacity and loss of the groundwater basin's capability to distribute water and to supply water. The cumulative cost of these losses may amount to $17.4 million per year under a low future growth scenario and $21.9 million per year for a high growth scenario.

The recommended plan is to provide an alternative water supply to the coastal area and reduce pumping in that area by a like amount. This will reduce seawater intrusion by about two-thirds. The water for the project would be provided by modifying the operation of upstream reservoirs. The project would also furnish municipal and industrial water to Fort Ord and Marina from an inland dispersed well system.

1. Leedshill-Herkenhoff, Inc., San Francisco, CA
2. Monterey County Flood Control and Water Conservation District, Salinas, CA

Rate and Extent of Seawater Intrusion

The problem of seawater intrusion into the coastal aquifers of the Salinas Valley has been recognized for many years. The intrusion front extends along the coast about 10 miles (16 km) from Moss Landing south to Fort Ord, and inland as much as 5 miles (8 km) (See Figure 1). This discussion addresses the causes of seawater intrusion, its effects, and alternative methods to slow or halt the intrusion. The study was directed by the Monterey County Flood Control and Water Conservation District and was funded in part by the State Water Resources Control Board with Section 205j grant funds from the U.S. Environmental Protection Agency.

Seawater intrusion is caused by a reversal of groundwater gradients which normally slope toward the coast. The reversal in gradients allows sea water to enter the aquifers through permeable offshore outcrops. During the irrigation season, a groundwater trough develops near Castroville that is as much as 55 feet (17 m) below sea level. There is also a year-round groundwater depression below sea level in the area north and east of Salinas. These depressions develop because the confined aquifers are not able to transmit fresh water to the coastal pumping area at a rate equal to pumping extractions.

Three aquifers have been identified in the coastal area of the Salinas Valley. These aquifers, termed the 180-foot aquifer, the 400-foot aquifer, and the deep aquifer, are all confined in the coastal area and are recharged primarily by infiltration from the Salinas River in areas 20 miles (32 km) or more from the coast. The land area now overlying the intruded 180-foot aquifer encompasses some 13,000 acres (5260 ha), plus a large area offshore formerly underlain by freshwater aquifers. About 8,000 (3240 ha) acres overlying the 400-foot aquifer have also been intruded. In recent years the seawater intrusion in the 180-foot aquifer has spread under an additional 450 acres (182 ha) each year, and in the 400-foot aquifer it has spread under an additional 275 acres (111 ha) each year. Based on a U.S. Geological survey finite element groundwater model of the Salinas Basin, the rate of intrusion is estimated to be about 19,000 acre-feet (23,400 dkm3) per year.

If no action is taken to halt the intrusion, it is projected that in the year 2000 there will be as much as 26,000 acres (10,500 ha) underlain by the contaminated 180-foot aquifer. The seawater intrusion will result in crop losses, job losses, losses in land value, reduced groundwater storage capacity and the loss of the groundwater basin to distribute water and to supply water. The cumulative cost of these losses may amount to $17.4 million per year under a low future growth scenario and $21.9 million per year for a high growth scenario.

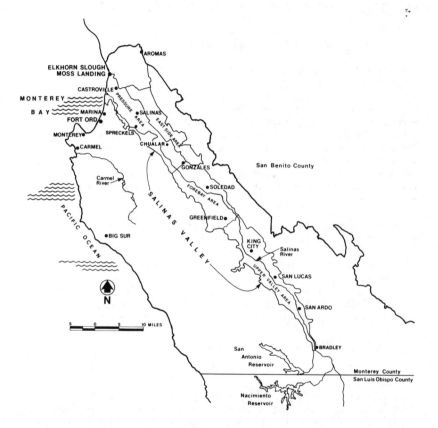

Figure 1 Salinas Valley in Monterey County, California

The U.S. Geological Survey groundwater model was used in the present study to simulate the effects of various actions that could be implemented to slow or halt seawater intrusion. The model indicates that the most effective measures are those which affect the area closest to the intrusion front. It may be that 40,000 to 50,000 acre-feet (49,300 - 61,700 dkm3) of water delivered to the coastal area could completely halt the intrusion and produce a modest seaward flow of fresh water.

Alternative Methods to Prevent Seawater Intrusion

The Salinas Valley groundwater basin in Monterey County is about 80 miles (129 km) long, extending southerly Monterey Bay to south of San Ardo. In the eastern, central and southern parts of the valley the water bearing formations are unconfined and groundwater recharge is effected mainly through percolation from the Salinas River. The natural recharge from the river is augmented by controlled releases from Nacimiento and San Antonio Reservoirs. Groundwater moves in a north-westerly direction along a fairly uniform gradient. In the vicinity of Gonzales and northward toward the coast, multiple clay layers develop, confining the aquifers, inhibiting recharge from the surface and movement of groundwater between aquifers.

Methods identified to reduce seawater intrusion involve a wide range of measures, but they can be broadly categorized as:

    1)   a reduction in groundwater pumping, primarily in the lower valley near the coast;
    2)   a redistribution of existing water supplies in the valley;
    3)   providing a supplemental water supply to the coastal area; and
    4)   construction of a seawater intrusion barrier.

Each of these methods, if fully implemented, could stop the intrusion, but each has profound economic, social and environmental implications to the valley.

Various degrees of reduction in pumping could be effected by conservation practices, imposing a moratorium on well drilling, initiating adjudication of water rights and by imposing a groundwater extraction charge. Of these measures, only adjudication has the potential to halt seawater intrusion, but the procedure would have adverse economic impacts on thousands of people in the valley. Conservation has some value in the coastal areas overlying the pressure aquifers, because excess applied water does not return to the groundwater in this area. A moratorium on drilling could prevent intrusion of the deep aquifer, but at the present time the County has no authority to limit drilling in the deep aquifer or in the shallower aquifers.

The option of redistributing existing water supplies consists of two possible types of projects. The first involves changing the timing and amounts of controlled releases from Nacimiemto and San Antonio Reservoirs such that somewhat less water would be recharged into the upper valley and flow would be maintained in the Salinas River to the vicinity of Salinas. At that point, there would be a small diversion dam that would channel water through a pumping plant to a reservoir and distribution piping serving the farmers in the coastal Castroville area. The plan, known as the Castroville Area Distribution System, has been extensively studied by the Salinas Valley Water Advisory Commission. The Salinas Valley groundwater model indicates that the project would be effective in reducing seawater intrusion by two-thirds, if coupled with a plan to supply the Marina - Fort Ord area with municipal and industrial water.

A second method of redistributing existing water supplies is to modify the pumping pattern in the valley such that pumping in the coastal area would be reduced by constructing a well field between Salinas and Chualar and conveying the water via the Salinas River to the same diversion point envisioned in the Castroville Area Irrigation Project, but costs would be higher.

Supplying supplemental water to the coastal area could be effected by other than redistribution of existing supplies. The Arroyo Seco Project was identified a number of years ago as a means to supply up to 80,000 acre-feet (98,700 dkm3) of water to the Castroville area, the area east of Salinas, the the Marina - Fort Ord and Peninsula areas, and the Pajaro and North County areas. The proposed project involves a dam on the Arroyo Seco, the main tributary of the Salinas River, and a conveyance system. The project, if implemented, could completely halt seawater intrusion if sufficient water were delivered to the coastal areas.

The deep aquifer underlying the 180-foot and 400-foot aquifers in the Pressure Area has not been extensively developed because of the high costs of wells; however, water from this aquifer is being increasingly used by irrigators whose wells in the 400-foot aquifer are being intruded. Recent preliminary studies indicate that the safe yield of the aquifer may be very low; thus, tapping it for irrigation supply in the intruded areas could result in a repetition of the intrusion that has occurred in the upper aquifers.

Reclaimed wastewater is a possible source of supplemental water. A regional plant planned in northern Monterey County could supply up to 16,000 acre-feet (19,700 dkm3) of water to farmers in the irrigation season. To do so would require tertiary treatment of the effluent to meet health requirements. Two tertiary systems are being tested - filtered effluent and the full Title-22 process - to determine their effects on the treated effluent and on various crops. The cost of tertiary treatment will be established at the conclusion of the 1986 testing period. An alternative use of the effluent is as a supply to an injection-type seawater intrusion barrier, but this requires an even greater degree of treatment at considerably greater cost.

Supplemental water could be provided by establishing an off-channel recharge project in the highly permeable Arroyo Seco Cone area, a well field along the Salinas River, and a conveyance system from the Salinas River that would deliver water to the Castroville area. The well field would induce additional recharge from the Salinas River and it would be a dependable supply. Disadvantages of such a system are the costs of pumping and conveying the water and possible lowering of groundwater levels in the vicinity of the well field.

An additional 3,700 acre-feet (4,560 dkm3) of water could be produced by raising the spillway of Nacimiento Dam. To do so would be relatively inexpensive but it would produce insufficient water to have any appreciable effect on saline intrusion. Alternatively, a project to increase the usable storage at Nacimiento by installing gates on the spillway should be considered.

A seawater intrusion barrier could be constructed along the coast to prevent intrusion. Such barriers have been operated in southern California for a number of years but all have been combination injection-pumping systems which must have an outside source of water for injection. An extraction-type barrier should be considered for the Salinas Valley since no economical imported water is available. This type of barrier is being constructed in Alameda County, but there are many technical questions that remain unanswered in order to evaluate the feasibility of such a barrier for the Salinas Valley. An extraction-type barrier would lower groundwater levels considerably, resulting in increased pumping costs, and some fresh water would be wasted by pumping to the ocean.

Recommendations and Conclusions

The recommended plan is to provide an alternative water supply to the coastal area and reduce pumping in that area by a like amount. The groundwater model indicates that delivery of 25,000 acre-feet (30,800 dkm3) to the Castroville area would reduce seawater intrusion by about two-thirds. The water for the project would be provided by modifying the operation of Nacimiento and San Antonio Reservoir. Municipal and industrial water would be furnished to Fort Ord and Marina from an inland dispersed well system withdrawing water from the deep aquifer. It is also recommended that extractions from the deep aquifer be limited.

Following implementation, the effectiveness of these measures should be assessed using data from a monitoring program and a three-dimensional groundwater flow model. If the foregoing assessment indicates that after the Castroville project is operational, seawater intrusion is still proceeding at an unacceptable rate, it is recommended that the District investigate the feasibility of an extraction type seawater intrusion barrier by conducting geologic exploration, aquifer testing, and three-dimensional computer modeling of the groundwater basin. The economical feasibility of such a barrier is established if installation and operation costs are less expensive than supplying additional supplemental water to the area. If the barrier is economically feasible, it is recommended that it be constructed and operated. If it is not feasible and the monitoring program shows continued intrusion at unacceptable rates after construction of the Castroville Distribution System, then additional supplemental supplies will be needed. Other supplemental sources include reclaimed wastewater, recharge projects with extraction wells, or additional reservoirs.

The District has the authority to implement the Castroville area distribution system and the seawater intrusion barrier, but it presently has no power to regulate pumping in the proposed project area or from the deep aquifer.

Accordingly, it is recommended that the Monterey County Flood Control and Water Conservation District act be amended to add the following:

1. Authority to restrict pumping in designated areas by
   a. limiting pumpage quantities from existing wells
   b. prohibiting new wells
2. Authority to require well registration and impose ground water extraction charges on agricultural, municipal and industrial groundwater users in designated areas.

Several possible financing methods have been identified including revenue bonds, certificates of participation, assessment bonds and interest-free loans. The recommended method of financing is a loan through the Federal Small Reclamation Projects Act (PL984) with local

costs funded through issuance of certificates. If PL984 funds are
available for the Castroville Project but not the Marina-Fort Ord
Project, $16.8 million would be funded by certificates and the total
certificate size would be $22 million. If federal funds are not uti-
lized, the total certificate size is estimated to be $44 million.
Annual debt and operating cost could be paid by water charges to Castroville landowners, water sales to Marina and Fort Ord, a groundwater
extraction charge to landowners north of Salinas and possibly District
payments resulting from revenues from the proposed Nacimiento hydroelectric project.

Preliminary estimates of the various components of a repayment program
are shown in the tabulation below, with and without a PL984 loan in
1984 price levels.

	With PL984 $/AF	Without PL984 $/AF
Agriculture Surface Water Charge	47	47
Groundwater Extraction Charge		
Urban	0	20
Agriculture	0	5
Municipal Water Charge	100	210

STUDIES OF LONG-TERM WATER LOSSES

Tiao J. Chang[*], M.ASCE

ABSTRACT: The water-loss time series are formulated for the studied watersheds in the Ohio River Basin through the use of the law of water balance to the system inputs and corresponding outputs. Stochastic processes, including the five-step procedures, are applied to test the long-term water-loss time series. The best-fit models are used to forecast probable water losses which consist of infiltration and evaporation in the region. The results are within the upper and lower bounds of their expectations based on five percent significance level.

INTRODUCTION

On a long-term basis the hydrologic cycle from the precipitation to the stream runoff in an isolated watershed can largely be represented by a black-box system, where the precipitation represents the input; the stream outflow represents the system output; the system losses mainly including infiltration and evaporation are the difference between the input and its output following the law of water balance. About two thirds of the precipitation input in the Ohio River Basin belongs to the system losses which include the portion of infiltration recharging groundwater that many water suppliers heavily depend on. Accurate estimation and forecasting of the water losses from the system is inhibited by uncertainties in weather conditions for precipitation, and uncertainties in streamflow measurements. Therefore the water supplies for the region involve risks; either risk from too much loss which results in insufficient surface water, or insufficient infiltration to recharge the groundwater. There have been attempts to quantify these existing uncertainties for better modeling to reduce the uncertainty of water supply (10,11,7,8). There is a need, however, for a comprehensive water-loss estimation and forecasting study which considers both infiltration and evaporation to eliminate the uncertainties of water supply as much as possible.

This study taking the approach to fomulate a water-loss time series for an investigated watershed through the law of mass conservation, i.e. water balance. The water balanced model is based on the Transfer Discrete autoregressive Moving Average (T-DARMA) developed by Chang (3,6) and Chang et.al. (4,5), which introduced the conceptual watershed model by using the Discrete autoregressive Moving Average (DARMA) as the system input model and a linear water-balance

---

* Assistant Professor, Department of Civil Engineering, Ohio
  University, Athens, Ohio 45701

transfer system to meet the difference between the precipitation and
the stream runoff. In the T-DARMA process the autoregressive components are conceptually interpreted as the watershed storage; while the
discrete moving average components represents the characteristics of
the system input; the losses were treated as a constant during the
corresponding season. Due to the highly uncertain evaporation and
infiltration, this is followed by application of the Autoregressive
Integrated Moving Average (ARIMA) for estimation and forecasting of
water losses through the modeling of annual water-loss time series.

Generally the time series modeling can be organized into the
following five steps, the selection of the type of model, the
identification of the form of the model, the estimation of the model
parameters, the diagnostic check of the model and the selection of the
best model. For the first step it refers to selecting the type of
model, where the ARIMA process has been taken for the annual water-
loss time series. The second step is to identify the form or the
order of the model through the use of the autocorrelation plot, which
provides the convenience of the graphical comparison. Once the form
of the model is selected, the next step is to estimate the parameters
of the identified model. The fourth step of the modeling is to do
diagnostic checking to verify the goodness of model fit to the existed
data. If several competitive models pass the diagnostic screening,
the Akaike Information Criterion (AIC) based on the principle of
parsimony is used as the final step to select the best model (1).
Results of applications of the best model to forecast annual water
losses in the Ohio River Basin are presented through the comparison
with existed data and the upper and the lower bounds with a five
percent significance level are also provided.

WATER LOSS TIME SERIES

For a studied watershed assuming that storage and all items of
inflow and outflow except evaporation and infiltration can be
measured, the volume of water is required to meet the continuity
equation, i.e. water balance or law of mass conservation. The
evaporations vary, depending on meteorological factors such as solar
radiation, vapor pressure, wind speed, and temperature, and on the
nature of evaporating surface such as vegetation, buildings, paved
streets and snow cover. On the other hand the infiltration depends on
many factors such as soil type, moisture content, organic matter,
vegetative cover, rainfall intensity, and season. While the instrument measurements for both evaporation and infiltration have been
significantly improved, a generally agreeable format for both
measurements is still far from being reached. As a result the
water-balanced computation is still justified based on the long-term
time increments. Normally the water losses including infiltration and
evaporation can be reliably computed as the difference between long-
time averages of precipitation and stream runoff, since the change in
storage over a long-time period is inconsequential.

Assuming that storage S, surface inflow I, surface outflow O,
subsurface seepage O_g, and precipitation P can be measured. It can be

obtained the evaporation E from the continuity equation:

$$E = (S_1 - S_2) + I + P - 0 - 0_g \qquad (1)$$

In a long run, storage S and surface inflow will contribute either to surface outflow or subsurface infiltration. Therefore the equation can be simplified into evaporation E, infiltration I_f, precipitation P, and surface outflow 0 as follows:

$$E = P - I_f - 0 \qquad (2)$$

To form the annual water-loss time series, a black-box system is considered for an isolated watershed, where the system input is the precipitation P, the system output is surface outflow 0; the system losses are evaporation E and infiltration I_f according to the continuity equation. The annual water loss is then taken to be the difference between the annual precipitation, which can be obtained through the Thiessen polygen method, and the corresponding watershed outflow i.e.

$$WL_t = E_t + (I_f)_t = P_t - 0_t \qquad (3)$$

where $\{WL_t\}$ is the annual water-loss time series. There are three watersheds studied in the Ohio River Basin as listed in Table 1. One annual water-loss time series from the Blue River watershed is plotted as shown in Figure 1.

ANNUAL WATER-LOSS TIME SERIES MODELING

As equ. 3 shows the annual water-loss time series are the disaggregation of annual precipitation and streamflow time series, which have been thoughtfully studied and are largely agreed to be normally distributed. The aggregation or disaggregation of normally distributed time series can be treated to have similar behavior (13). As a result the annual water-loss time series are considered to be normally distributed and the autoregressive integrated moving average (ARIMA) process is appropriate for modeling. A general ARIMA model is given as follows:

$$\prod_{i=1}^{NAR} \phi_i(B) \prod_{j=1}^{NDI} (1-B^{S_j})^{d_j}(Z_t-\mu) = \theta_0 + \prod_{i=1}^{NMA} \theta_k(B)A_k \qquad (4)$$

$$\phi_i(B) = 1-\phi_{i1}B - \phi_{i2}B^2 - \ldots - \phi_{ip_i}B^{p_i} \qquad (4a)$$

$$\theta_k(B) = 1-\theta_{k1}B-\theta_{k2}B^2 - \ldots - \theta_{kq_k}B^{q_k} \qquad (4b)$$

where NAR: autoregressive factors; NDI: difference factors; S_j: the jth differencing factor; d_j: the jth differencing factor appears d_j times; $\{Z_t\}$: time series; μ: mean value; θ_0: deterministic trend; NMA: moving average factors; A_k: random variables; B: backward operator.

The ARIMA process developed by Box and Jenkins (2) has distinctly different convariance structures among their different orders, which provide the convenience for a graphical comparison of the sample correlogram with that of the selected model. This enables the modeler to identify possible order of the model for alternative choices. The normally distributed verification allows the use of the maximum likelihood estimator for model parameter estimation. The method is based on differentiating the log-likelihood function with respect to the parameters and equating the expressions to zero. The test of goodness of fit for the annual water-loss time series is conducted by testing the assumptions of the model i.e. normality and independence. Since the normality was justified by previous researchers (9,13), the independence is checked through the Porte Manteau lack of fit test in which the autocorrelations of the residual series are taken as a whole. Then the statistic Q is determined in the following (2):

$$Q = (N-d) \sum_{k=1}^{L} r_k^2(\varepsilon) \qquad (5)$$

where $r_k(\varepsilon)$ is the kth autocorrelation coefficient of the residual series formed after the parameter estimation; L is the chosen order of the sample size N; d is the order of differencing. The statistic Q is approximately chi-square distribution with L-p-q degree of freedom, where p and q are orders of autoregressive and moving-average processes, respectively. If more than two alternative models pass the diagnostic checking, the criterion of the parsimony of parameters is applied to select the best model. The Akaike Information Criterion (AIC) is computed as follows (1):

$$AIC(p+q) = N \ln (S^2) + 2(p+q) \qquad (6)$$

where p and q are orders of autoregressive and moving average processes, N is the total number of data; S^2 is the variance of the residual series.

APPLICATIONS OF WATER-LOSS TIME SERIES MODELING

Three annual water-loss time series considered in the Ohio River Basin are based on the continuity equation in equ. 3. Due to the assumption of normality in the ARIMA modeling, a normality test is performed for each of annual series by using the following statistic:

$$R = \sum_{i=1}^{k} \frac{(N_i - N/k)^2}{N/k} \qquad (7)$$

where R is a chi-square distribution with k-2 degree of freedom; k is the total number of classes used; N_i is the number of occurrences in the ith class; N is the total number of data. Table 2 shows that two of the three time series pass the test with 5 percent significance level except the Mississinewa River watershed.

The second step of modeling is to identify possible orders of the ARIMA process. Since all three series have passed the normality test without differencing, the integrated component needs not to be considered so that only the orders of autoregressive and moving-average are identified in this stage. The data available shown in Table 1 are limited to less than 30, which discriminate higher orders of p and q. By comparison of the sample correlogram and the theoretical autocorrelation and partial autocorrelation functions, the ARIMA models with lower orders are selected.

The steps of parameter estimation and diagnostic checking are done through the uses of maximum likelihood function estimator and the test of white noise of residual series. The statistic, Q, value of each model for different watersheds is listed in Table 2 showing that the selected models are competitive. In order to select the best model among the competitive. The Akaike Information Criterion (AIC) was used (1). The AIC's values for those competing ARIMA models are listed in Table 2. Under the criterion the model which gives the minimum AIC is the one to be selected. Since the water-loss series from the Mississinewa watershed failed to pass the normality test, these data are not used for further modeling. The best model selected from the Blue River watershed based on the minimum AIC is

$$(1+0.2634B) (Z_t - 19.5280) = A_t \qquad (8)$$

and for the Whitewater River watershed,

$$Z_t - 25.4340 = (1-0.0041B) A_t \qquad (9)$$

where $\{Z_t\}$ is the annual water-loss time series; B is the backward operator; $\{A_t\}$ is the white noises.

For the purpose of water-loss forecasting, the minumum mean square error forecasting technique, developed by Box and Jenkins (2) was used. The forecasting water loss at leading time i, $Z_t(i)$ is the conditional expectation of $Z_t(i)$ at time t. Using equations 8 and 9, respectively, the results of forecasting water losses for different watersheds are shown in Figures 2 and 3, where the upper and the lower bounds of the mean square error forecasting values are also provided, with 5% significance level.

CONCLUSIONS

The annual water-loss time series formulated in this study are disaggregated process of annual precipitation and streamflow time series which are generally agreed to be normally distributed (9, 13). Statistically this would result in the normally distributed annual water-loss time series. However, one of three annual water-loss series studied in the Ohio River Basin failed to pass the normality test. It is, therefore, more appropriate to conduct

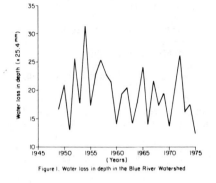

Figure 1. Water loss in depth in the Blue River Watershed

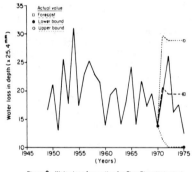

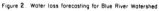

Figure 2. Water loss forecasting for Blue River Watershed

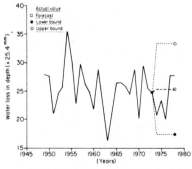

Figure 3. Water loss forecasting for Whitewater River Watershed

the normality test before the ARIMA modeling though the transformation method can possibly be used to normalize the data.

The water losses in the transfer processes between precipitation and runoff play a very significant role. The results of this research can be incorporated with or justify the watershed transfer modeling for the use of effective rainfall, which ignores the characteristics of water losses in the process. Furthermore, the forecasting results shown in Figures 2 and 3 are within the upper and lower bounds of their expectations that can provide the information for bettering the long-term water plans in the region.

Table 1 Annual water loss time series in the Ohio River Basin

Watershed Identification	Precipitation Station	Thiessen Weight	Drainage Area (sq. km)	No. of Years (data)
Blue River	Salamonia	1.000	1,194	27
Mississinewa River	Marion College Muncie Salamonia	0.357 0.109 0.634	1,766	27
Whitewater River	Cambridge Richmond	0.722 0.278	1,370	29

Table 2 Tests of annual water loss time series

Watershed Identification	Normality R**	Modeling		
		ARIMA	Q**	AIC
Blue River	25.59 <28.87	(0,0,1) (1,0,0) (1,0,1)	7.09<28.87 5.54<28.87 6.09<27.59	85.76 85.60 89.22
Whitewater River	21.34<28.87	(0,0,1) (1,0,0) (1,0,1)	6.60<28.87 7.17<28.87 7.50<27.59	82.67 83.35 86.38

*: Mississinewa watershed failed to pass the normality test.
**: Chi-square test with corresponding degree of freedom.

ACKNOWLEDGEMENTS

The author wishes to acknowledge his appreciation for the support of the Stocker Research Fund at Ohio University. He also would like to thank Pam Stettler for her assistance in typing this paper.

APPENDIX-REFERENCES

1. Akaike, H., "A New Look at the Statistical Model Identification," IEEE Trans. on Automatic Control, AS-19, 6, 1974, pp. 716-723.
2. Box, G.E.P. and G.B. Jenkins, "Time Series Analysis: Forecasting and Control," Holden-Day, San Francisco, 1976.
3. Chang, Tiao J., "Daily Precipitation and Streamflow Modeling by Discrete Autoregressive Moving Average Processes," Ph.D. Dissertation, Purdue University, 1981.
4. Chang, Tiao J., M.L. Kavvas, and J.W. Delleur, "Stochastic Daily Precipitation Modeling and Daily Streamflow Transfer Processes," Technical Report No. 146, Water Res. Research Center, Purdue University, 1982.
5. Chang, Tiao J., M.L. Kavvas, and J.M. Delleur, "Daily Precipitation Modeling by Discrete Autoregressive Moving Average Processes," Water Res. Res., Vol. 20, No. 5, 1984, pp. 565-580.
6. Chang, Tiao J., "Microcomputer Applications in Stochastic Hydrology," Proceedings of the 1985 Hydraulics Conference, ASCE 1985, pp. 371-375.
7. Clapp, R.B., G.M. Hornberger, and B.J. Cosby, "Estimating Spatial Variability in Soil Moisture with a Simplified Dynamic Model," Water Res. Res., Vol. 19, 1983, pp. 739-745.
8. Davidson, M.R., "Asymptotic Behavior of Infiltration in Soils Containing Cracks and Holes," Water Res. Res., Vol. 21, No. 9, 1985, pp. 1345-1353.
9. Delleur, J.W., P.C. Tao, and M.L. Kavvas, "An Estimation of the Practicality and Complexity of Some Rainfall and Runoff Timer Series," Water Res. Res., Vol. 12, No. 5, 1976, pp. 953-970.
10. Jensen, M.E. and J.L. Wright, "The Role of Evaporation Models in Irrigation Scheduling," Trans. ASAE, 21(1), 1978, pp. 82-87.
11. Munro, D.S., "Daytime Energy Exchange and Evaporation from a Wooded Swamp," Water Res. Res., Vol. 15, No. 5, 1979, pp. 1259-1265.
12. Salas, J.D., J.W. Delleur, V. Yevjevich, and W.L. Lane, "Applied Modeling of Hydrologic Time Series," Water Resources Publications, 1985.
13. Vecchi, A.V., J.L. Obeysekara, J.D. Salas, and D.C. Boes, "Aggregation and Estimation of Low-Order Periodic ARIMA Models," Water Res. Res., Vol. 19, No. 5, 1983, pp. 1297-1306.

Subsidence by Rising and Fluctuating
Ground Water

Nikola P. Prokopovich*

Abstract

Man-induced land subsidence, particularly subsidence due to the decline of ground-water levels in unconfined and confined aquifers, is a well-recognized, world-wide geologic hazard. Present studies by the U.S. Bureau of Reclamation in California indicate that under certain geologic conditions similar subsidence can also be caused by (1) rising ground-water levels, which creates a flotation condition, and (2) periodic fluctuation (lowering and complete recovery) of ground-water levels without an actual decline. Both types of subsidence may be present in California's Central Valley. The possibilities of subsidence generated by these conditions should be considered in the planning and design of all water developments.

Introduction

With continuing growth in world population and the steady increase of technological "know how", man-induced land subsidence has become a world-wide, well-recognized geologic hazard of great economical importance (Prokopovich, 1972). In the Central Valley of California, for example, the cost of subsidence to the Federal Central Valley Project amounted to nearly $41 million (Prokopovich and Marriott, 1983), and future subsidence in the Sacramento-San Joaquin Delta will jeopardize the $7.5 billion per year agro-industry in the San Joaquin Valley (Prokopovich, 1985b).

Much of the man-induced subsidence is related to the overdraft of ground-water aquifer systems. Numerous examples of such overdraft related subsidence have been described in America, Europe, Asia, and Africa (Anonymous, 1969(?), 1977, 1984; Donaldson and VanDomselaar, 1983; Poland, et al., 1975; Saxena, 1979).

This paper briefly describes two types of man-induced land subsidence frequently not fully recognized by geologists. They are land subsidence caused by (1) rising ground-water levels, and (2) periodic fluctuation of ground-water levels. Both types may be important, practically and theoretically, for the design, construction and operation of various canals and for the development of ground-water basins. A study of these two types of subsidence is underway by the Mid-Pacific Region of the U.S. Bureau of Reclamation.

The author is greatly indebted to Dr. L. Carbognin for valuable data on subsidence in St. Mark's Square in Venice, Italy.

*Engineering Geologist, United States Bureau of Reclamation, Mid-Pacific Region, 2800 Cottage Way, Sacramento, CA 95825-1898.

Subsidence by Rising Water Levels

    Subsidence due to rising ground-water levels is actually a form of
flotation. The best known example of flotation is "quicksand". A man
or other object standing on quicksand would become submerged--subside
into the sand. Some cases of such subsidence perhaps should be
classified as foundation compaction rather than true subsidence
(Prokopovich, 1985a). The mechanisms of flotation is diagrammatically
explained in three sketches in Figure 1. The sketches show an aquifer
system monitored by two perforated observation wells--the shallow well
"S" and the deeper well "D". No flotation will take place in the
system if (1) the ground-water level in both wells is at the same
elevation (Figure 1A) or (2) the ground-water level in the shallower
observation well is higher than the level in the deeper well (Figure
1B). In the first case there will be no pressure gradient between the
two wells. In the second case, the gradient will be oriented
downwards. Flotation will occur, however, in the case shown in Figure
1C when the ground-water level in the deeper well is higher than the
level in the shallower well. The upward pressure gradient created
under such conditions will reduce the support and increase the
effective loading of the surface material.

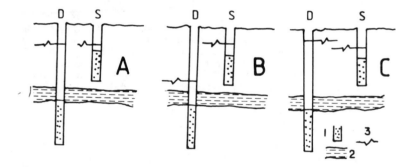

Fig. 1.   Development of flotation.   1) perforated casing;
2) semipervious layer;   3) water level.

    Examples of probable subsidence due to rising ground-water levels
are found in the collapse of rock-slab and sinking of pavement in St.
Mark's Square at St. Mark's Cathedral in Venice, Italy, currently
being studied by Italian scientists (Carbognin, 1985). The ancient,
beautiful city of Venice is built on a flat, low island traversed by
numerous canals. The island is located in a lagoon connected to the
sea and affected by tides. St. Mark's Square opens to the lagoon and
is paved by large, flat, square, heavy rock-slabs. The surface-near
surface drainage at the Cathedral is diverted, by a combination of
vertical and horizontal drains, into the lagoon where it is discharged
below normal sea level. The original surface of the square is about
70 cm (27.6") above the mean sea level, while common tides are about
63 cm (25") above this level. Water rising in the drainage system,

caused by tides, resulted in a general sinking and collapse of the
rock slab pavement in front of St. Mark's Cathedral (Figure 2).

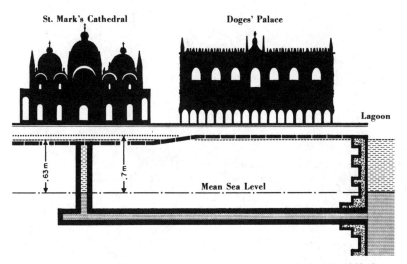

Fig. 2. Subsidence in St. Mark's Square, Venice, Italy (Modified
from drawing by Dr. P. Gatto provided by Dr. L. Carbognin).

Apparently more or less similar conditions developed locally along
the San Luis Canal in the west central part of the San Joaquin Valley
in California. The 164 km (102 mile) long concrete lined canal, with
an initial capacity of 371 m3/s (13,000 ft^3/s) extends from the
O'Neill forebay reservoir near the City of Los Banos to the vicinity
of Kettleman City (Figure 3) (Anonymous, 1981) and, as the California
Aqueduct, extends south toward the Los Angeles Metropolitan Area. The
canal is crossed by numerous concrete bridges and pipeline crossings
and has several turnout structures designed for water delivery to
surrounding agricultural land.

The canal is underlain by clayey-sandy Coast Range piedmont fluvial
alluvium deposited as major, well-defined fans of ephemeral Los
Banos, Little Panoche, Panoche, Cantua, and Los Gatos creeks. This
fan alluvium is separated by a more clayey interfan alluvium from
poorly-defined, coalescing fans of small arroyos and washes deposited
mostly as "mud flows" (Bull, 1964). The climate is dry and the
uppermost, so-called "unconfined", saline aquifer system, along the
canal prior to its construction, occurred at a depth of about 37-60 m
(120-200 feet). A ground-water body was developed, however, along the
canal after the beginning of canal operations.

Differential settlement, sagging, cracking of concrete lining, and
shearing of steel bolts was noted at several turnouts and some bridges
after a few years of canal operation (Figure 4). Some of this damage

attributed to the 1983 Coalinga earthquake, however, existed prior to the quake.

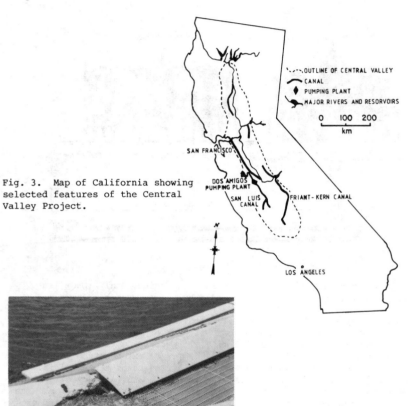

Fig. 3. Map of California showing selected features of the Central Valley Project.

Fig. 4. Structural damages at Turnout No. 3, San Luis Canal, MP.108.39.

The canal was designed and constructed prior to the present energy shortage. At the present time, due to the cost of energy, water pumplifting into the canal by the Dos Amigos Pumping Plant occurs primarily in the offpeak hours. Because of the combination of this pumplift pattern and variations in water demand and deliveries, water levels in the canal fluctuate 0.5-1 m (1.5-3 ft) (Figure 5). It is possible, therefore, that the changes in canal water levels are causing changes in the shape of the ground-water body along the canal, and a corresponding periodic development of flotation. Installation, at a typical site, of two water observation wells of differing depths is proposed for verification of this concept.

Fig. 5. Evidence of fluctuating water levels in the San Luis Canal. The arrow indicates the position of maximum water level on the bridge pier (MP.88.51).

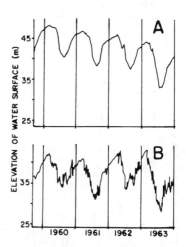

Fig. 6. Hydrographs of two wells in urban (A) and agricultural (B) areas.

Subsidence by Fluctuating Water Levels

Water-level hydrographs of undeveloped, major aquifer systems usually show relatively minor changes which reflect seasonal and long-term climatical changes in precipitation and evaporation. Conversely, water level hydrographs of developed aquifers show pronounced variations (lowering and recovery of water levels) which reflect local pumping water demand patterns (Figure 6). The

hydrographs shown in Figure 6 also show a general decline in water
levels, i.e., the existence of an overdraft.

Each lowering of water levels results in an increase in actual (for
an unconfined aquifer) or effective (for a confined aquifer) loading
(Poland & Davis, 1969; Prokopovich, 1976) which, under certain
conditions, may cause compaction of sediments and land subsidence. In
"no overdraft" cases, however, it was frequently assumed that numerous
cycles of lowering and equal recovery of water levels should cause no
subsidence (except some possible subsidence during the first
lowering).

A single laboratory consolidometer test conducted by the author
indicates, however, that such an assumption may be incorrect. In the
test, a sample of water-saturated Coast Range piedmont alluvial clay,
from the San Joaquin Valley in California, was subjected to a
prolonged consolidation (over 85 days) under a load of 6.3 kg/cm^2.
The total initial settlement of the sample at the end of this interval
was 8.8 percent. The loading was followed by a relatively prolonged,
complete unloading of the sample resulting in about 2 percent rebound.
Twelve similar loadings and unloadings of the sample were then
conducted with results graphically shown in Figure 7. The graph

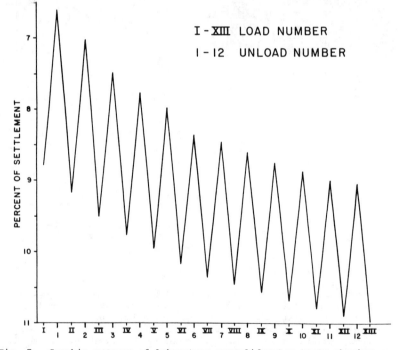

Fig. 7. Graphic summary of laboratory consolidometer tests showing
progressive compaction after several cycles of loading and unloading.

clearly indicates that continuous periodic loading-unloading, which could be caused by the lowering and recovery of ground-water levels after initial pumping, is capable of producing additional compaction-subsidence.

In California, such a process could probably explain the occurrence of land subsidence in certain reaches of the Friant-Kern Canal (Figure 3) where delivery of canal water practically arrested the decline of the ground-water table (Lofgren and Klausing, 1969).

A better understanding of these two, apparently not fully recognized, processes leading to subsidence may be of value in the design and operation of irrigation canals and associated structures. Subsidence due to the fluctuation of aquifer levels (without a general decline) should be considered in the development of all ground-water basins. The geologic framework allowing such subsidence is the absence of "previously overcompacted" deposits.

References

1. Anonymous, "Land Subsidence (Tokyo Symposium)", IAHS-Unesco Publications No. 88 and 89, International Association of Hydrological Sciences, Vol. I and II, 1969(?).
2. Anonymous, "Land Subsidence Symposium", IAHS-AISH Publication No. 121, International Association of Hydrological Sciences, 1977.
3. Anonymous, "Project Data", United States Water and Power Resources Service, Denver, CO, 1981, pp. 209-216.
4. Anonymous, "Symposium Program - Third International Symposium on Land Subsidence, Venice, Italy", International Association of Hydrogeologists, 1984.
5. Bull, W. B., "Geomorphology of Segmented Alluvial Fans in Western Fresno County, California", United States Geological Survey Professional Paper 352-E, U.S. Government Printing Office, Washington, DC, 1964, pp. 89-129.
6. Carbognin, L., Personal Communication, Institute for the Study of Dynamics of Large Masses, CNR, Venice, Italy, 1985.
7. Donaldson, E. C., and VanDomselaar, H., (editors), "Proceedings of 1982 Forum on Subsidence Due to Fluid Withdrawals, Conf.-821199", United States Department of Energy, August, 1983.
8. Lofgren, B. E., and Klausing, R. L., "Land Subsidence Due to Ground-Water Withdrawal; Tulare-Wasco Area, California", U.S. Geological Survey Professional Paper 437-B, U.S. Government Printing Office, Washington, DC, 1969, pp. B-1 to B-103.
9. Poland, J. F., and Davis, G. H., "Land Subsidence Due to Withdrawal of Fluids, in Reviews in Engineering Geology II, Geological Society of America, Boulder, CO, 1969, pp. 187-269.
10. Poland, J. F., Lofgren, B. E., Ireland, R. L., and Pugh, R. G., "Land Subsidence in the San Joaquin Valley, California, as of 1972", Geological Survey Professional Paper 437-H, U.S. Government Printing Office, Washington, DC, 1975.
11. Prokopovich, N. P., "Land Subsidence and Population Growth", Proceedings of the 24th International Geological Congress, Section 13, 1972, pp. 44-53.

12. Prokopovich, N. P., "Some Geologic Factors Determining Land Subsidence", Bulletin of the International Association of Engineering Geologists, No. 14, 1976, pp. 75-81.
13. Prokopovich, N. P., "Land Subsidence - Terminological Confusion", Bulletin of the Association of Engineering Geologists, Vol. 22, No. 1, February 1985a, pp. 106-108.
14. Prokopovich, N. P., "Subsidence of Peat in California and Florida", Bulletin of the Association of Engineering Geologists, Vol. 22, No. 4, 1985b, pp. 395-420.
15. Prokopovich, N. P., and Marriott, M. J., "Cost of Subsidence to the Central Valley Project, California", Bulletin of the Association of Engineering Geologists, Vol. 20, No. 3, 1983, pp. 325-332.
16. Saxena, S. K. (editor), Evaluation and Prediction of Subsidence, Engineering Foundation Conferences, American Society of Civil Engineers, New York, 1979.

AGRICULTURAL DRAINAGE POLICY
IN THE
UNITED STATES DEPARTMENT OF AGRICULTURE

WALTER J. OCHS, * M. ASCE

ABSTRACT

Agricultural drainage policies in the United States Department
of Agriculture (USDA) generally call for improving the root zone
environment for crop production while protecting the resource
base and avoiding harm to the environment or society. Trends in
USDA drainage policy reflect national environmental concerns and
economic problems associated with excess production. In addition,
certain advances in research and technical assistance may affect
future drainage policies. Some of these include reuse of saline
drainage water, water table control systems, computerized design
and system operation models, and drainage material improvements.

Introduction

The sustained productivity of about 30 percent of the cropland in
the United States depends to some degree on drainage. The 1977
National Resources Inventories made by SCS indicated that, of the
101 million acres of wet soil cultivated, more than 30 million
acres could benefit from improved drainage systems. This land is
fertile and general contains more organic matter and is less
erodible than drier and more sloping cropland soils.

Several USDA agencies are responsible for agricultural drainage.
The Agricultural Research Service and the Cooperative State
Research Service obviously have research responsibilities.
The Extension Service has information and technology transfer
responsibilities. The Soil Conservation Service (SCS) provides
technical assistance to farmers and groups and, in some
instances partial funding for drainage outlets. Financial
assistance for drainage has been virtially eliminated from
cost sharing programs of the Agricultural Stabilization and
Conservation Service.

The 1985 Farm Bill contains provisions for conserving wetlands.
These provisions restrict eligibility for USDA farms programs
if a farmer plans to drain, dredge, fill, level or carry out

*National Drainage Engineer, Soil Conservation Service - U.S.
Department of Agriculture - P.O. Box 2890 - Washington, D.C. 20013

practices in the wetland areas to enable the production
of an agricultural commodity. The conversion of wetlands to
croplands is expected to slow down, since many farmers will
not want to jeopardize their eligibility for USDA farm programs.
USDA drainage activity is also affected by standards and
specifications, rules related to Small Watershed and Resource
Conservation and Development Programs, and to wetland protection
policies. This paper discusses the most significant policy
matters that affect agricultural drainage.

1985 Farm Bill

The wetland conservation provision of the 1985 Farm Bill are
often referred to as the "swampbuster" provisions. Subtitle C
of the Bill describes program ineligibility, exemptions and
requirements for consultations between the Secretaries of
Agriculture and Interior. Following is the exact wording
contained in this subtitle:

Subtitle C - Wetland Conservation

PROGRAM INELIGIBILITY

SEC. 1221. ...Following the date of enactment... any
person who in any crop year produces an agricultural
commodity on converted wetland shall be ineligible for--

(1) as to any commodity produced during that crop year by
     such person --

     (A) any type of price support or payment...

     (B) a farm storage facility loan...

     (C) crop insurance...

     (D) a disaster payment... or

     (E) a loan made, insured, or guaranteed under...
         any other provision of law administered by the
         Farmers Home Administration, if the Secretary
         determines that the proceeds of such loan will
         used for a purpose that will contribute to
         conversion of wetlands (other than as provided
         in this subtitle) to produce an agricultural
         commodity; or

(2) a payment made under section 4 or 5 of the commodity
     Credit Corporation Charter Act (15 U.S.C. 714b or 714c)
     during such crop year for the storage of an agriculture
     commodity acquired by the Commodity Credit Corporation.

EXEMPTIONS

Sec. 1222. (a) No person shall become ineligible under
section 1221 for program loans, payments, and benefits
as the result of the production of a crop of an agricultural
commodity on--

(1) converted wetland if the conversion of such wetland
was commenced before the date of enactment of this Act;

(2) an artificial lake, pond, or wetland created by
excavating or diking non-wetland to collect and retain
water for purposes such as water for livestock, fish
production, irrigation (including subsurface irrigation),
a settling basin, cooling, rice production, or flood
control;

(3) a wet area created by a water delivery system,
irrigation, irrigation system, or application of water
for irrigation; or

(4) wetland on which production of an agricultural commodity
is possible as a result of a natural condition, such as
drought, and without action by the producer that destroys
a natural wetland characteristic.

(b) Section 1221 shall not apply to a loan described
in section 1221 made before the date of enactment
of this Act.

(c) The Secretary may exempt a person from section
1221... if the effect... on the hydrological and
biological aspect of wetland is minimal.

CONSULTATION WITH SECRETARY OF THE INTERIOR

Sec. 1223. The Secretary shall consult with the Secretary of
the Interior on such determinations and actions as are
necessary to carry out this subtitle...

The term "converted wetland" is defined in the Act as meaning
"wetland that has been drained, dredged, filled, leveled, or
otherwise manipulated (including any activity that results in
impairing or reducing the flow, circulation or reach of water)
for the purpose or to have the effect of making the production
of an agricultural commodity possible".

Rules and regulations for application of the wetland conservation provisions were not developed at the time this paper was
prepared.

Small Watershed Projects

Public Law 83-566, commonly called the Small Watershed Act,
was passed in 1954. Under this Act many channels have been
cost shared to provide multiple-purpose flood control and
drainage benefits. Recent policy revisions limited the
cost share rate for these types of channel systems to 50
percent of construction costs (SCS-National Watershed Manual
390-V, Project Development and Maintenance, Amend. 17, 1985).
This change is applicable to all projects authorized for planning after October 1, 1985. Before this change, many multiple-
purpose flood control and drainage channels were actually being
cost shared at about 75 percent of construction cost (100 percent
for flood control and 50 percent for drainage-- since the benefits are often inseparable the evaluations often resulted in the
75 percent cost share rate).

Technical Assistance

Soil Conservation Service policy (National Bulletin
No. 450-4-3, October 18, 1983) establishes the principal
SCS roles in technical assistance for drainage:

(1) Assist landowners in developing drainage systems, in
combination with other conservation systems, to achieve conservation objectives on the farm;

(2) Help train contractors and others in proper design and
installation of drainage systems, thus minimizing SCS time
requirements;

(3) Ensure the development and use of adequate technical
standards and materials; and

(4) To provide assistance to other Federal agencies and foreign
governments on request.

Wetland Policy

The wetland protection policy of the Soil Conservation Service
is discussed in an American Society of Agricultural Engineers
paper (Ochs et. al., 1980). The policy controls technical and
financial assistance that will result in new construction in wetlands. It requires environmental evaluations when wetlands are
involved and indicates that the evaluations must start during
the early stages of planning. These evaluations are designed
to identify the effects of proposed actions in wetland. The
primary aim of the policy is to prohibit technical or financial
assistance for practices that will alter or destroy wetland types
3 through 20 as described in Circular 39 of the U.S. Department
of Interior, Fish & Wildlife Service (USDI-FWS, 1971).

Channel Modification Guidelines

Joint guidelines on the modification of channels were prepared by SCS and the Fish and Wildlife Service. These guidelines generally provide instructions for coordination and technical evaluation of alternatives (SCS & FWS, Fed. Register, Vol. 44, No.248, Dec. 26, 1979). The guidelines facilitate coordination of field level planning and activity from the preapplication through the maintenance stages of projects.

Research

Research efforts involving drainage likely will result in policy and legislation changes in future years. Water quality concerns have accelerated research efforts in the drain water discharge area. Much research effort has also concentrated on computerized design and system operation models. This work has also facilitated the extensive research effort on water table control systems. Major drainage material improvements have been made during the past two decades and continue to be made. These technological changes and many other agricultural economy and environment changes have led to adjustments in agricultural drainage policy.

Summary and Conclusions

The 1985 Farm Bill is one of the more significant legislative items that will have a direct effect on agricultural drainage. The "swampbuster" provisions of this law should be thoroughly studied by those individuals interested in agricultural drainage policy. Other items-- such as the changes in cost sharing limit on multiple-purpose channels; potential adjustments in technical assistance, intensity or roles; and channel modification guide-lines-- could affect the application of agricultural drainage measures.

References

1. Ochs, W. J., C.H. Thomas, and K.R. Voss, Soil Conservation Service Wetland Policy, A. Soc. of Agric. Eng. Paper No. 80-2510, St. Joseph, MI, 1980.

2. United States Department of Interior. Fish & Wildlife Serv. Washington, D.C., Wetlands of the United States, Circular 39. P67, 1971.

Deferred Drainage - Prudent Policy or Tactical Folly?
J. N. Christopher[1] and B. K. Cummins[2]

Historical Perspective

Early planners of irrigation projects thought that instant success could be had by simply joining a water resource with a land resource. Projects traditionally have been planned and built with little or, at best, minimum regard for drainage requirements to maintain lands in permanent productivity. Neither the tools nor experience were available to predict and analyze needs 10 to 20 years into the future.

Early day drainage works consisted primarily of canal wasteways and some surface drainage works. As the need for subsurface drainage outlets became evident, these facilities were pressed into services as outlet drains wherever possible.

Reclamation Practices

By 1925, Congress and Reclamation began a variety of efforts to assure that water and land resources were properly matched for irrigation projects. Agronomists and soil scientists began a soil classification concept that has evolved into an effective tool for project planning. Even though drainage was a factor in the classification concept, effective analytical tools were not available for predicting future subsurface drainage requirements until the mid-1950's. By then, the precedent of waiting until drainage problems occurred before building drains was well established.

Since the 1960's, we have had the technology to analyze future requirements for drainage. But, because of tradition, economic studies, and cost efficiency in planning projects, Reclamation adopted and continues to use deferred drainage works in project development plans.

****

[1]J. N. Christopher is Chairman of Drainage Committee, ASCE. He is Chief, Drainage and Groundwater Branch, Division of Water and Land Technical Services, Engineering and Research Center, Bureau of Reclamation, Denver, Colorado

[2]B. K. Cummins is Drainage and Groundwater Technician, Drainage and Groundwater Branch, Division of Water and Land Technical Services, Engineering and Research Center, Bureau of Reclamation, Denver, Colorado.

In general, all drains on a project are planned for deferred
construction until the need is evident. This includes outlet,
suboutlet, and collector drains. Drains that are constructed along
with the delivery and distribution works generally consist of canal
and lateral wasteways needed for operation of the delivery system.
Even these are often planned for stage construction in some instances
because project development schedules indicate that full capacity may
not be needed for 10 to 15 years after the first acreages are
developed.

Investigations for planning and analysis of costs in years past tend
to support the concept of deferred drainage works. From a planning
viewpoint, early installation of drains requires significantly more
data to be gathered during planning investigations. The cost has been
generally avoided because there is little guarantee that the project
will be built. The additional planning cost has been thought
unnecessary if drains were deferred. Installation of drains not fully
used for 10 to 15 years means additional costs are included in
economic analyses for interest during construction and loss of
alternate investment opportunity. These costs are significant in
terms of formulating projects in marginally suitable areas.

Consequences of Deferred Drains

The practice of deferring drains has not always worked out as we have
planned. This is particularly true of large outlet drains such as the
San Luis Drain in the Central Valley of California and the Left Bank
Outfall Drain in Pakistan. Even smaller systems, field drains as well
as outlets, are affected by economics, but they do not have the
notoriety or involve social/environmental issues on as large a scale
as the former projects. The purpose of this paper is to explore what
some of these changes have been in the last 25 years and examine
whether "deferred drainage" is, in fact, prudent planning or a
tactical blunder in terms of assuring permanent irrigated agriculture
as required by Reclamation law.

Impacts Upon Working Definition

Perhaps the place to begin looking at the impacts of economics and
environmental concerns is with the definition of drainage.

The traditional definition of agricultural drainage has been:
"Removal of excess salts and water from the root zone." Lack of
adequate drainage as defined above has been the single greatest cause
of failure on irrigated lands.

Today, the definition of drainage must be broadened. Not only must we
consider the effects on crops, but we must also consider effects of
drainage discharge on the environment. The entire soil profile from
the ground surface to barrier must be examined under this definition.
Soils must be analyzed for occurrence and movement of trace elements,
fertilizers and pesticides, as well as soluble salts. The new
definition of drainage must include disposal of drainage effluent in

an environmentally sensitive manner. The impact of this new definition is the need to develop new analytical tools. This results in additional investigations and delays in completing projects as planned.

In 1970-1973, Reclamation combined transient-state drainage methods with a soil chemistry model and a saturated flow model to deal with return flow quantities and qualities.[1][3] The tool has been useful in estimating normal soluble salts in return flows. It does not specifically handle chemistry of trace elements, hydrocarbon compounds, or pesticides. Nevertheless, it is a tool that can be used to address the "new" or broader definition of drainage.

The broader concerns of nonagricultural interests also lead to questions regarding the traditional planning for construction of drains. For reasons stated earlier, drains are constructed when the need develops. Often, 15 to 20 years have passed since the irrigation project was authorized. In the intervening time, social goals, laws, costs, and economic criteria change. The analyses justifying project authorization may no longer apply.

Impacts of Economics on Planning and Completing Projects

The following analyses are based upon the prices paid index, prices received index, and indexing of net farm income based on information reported in Agricultural Statistics. [2, 3, 4] The procedure consists of applying the indices to estimated net farm benefits calculated for the Columbia Basin Project, Washington, in 1975 [5] and the San Luis Unit of the Central Valley Project in California in 1963 [7].

Interest rates applicable to Reclamation projects from 1960 to 1984 are shown in Table 1. The actual rates are used to determine present worth of yearly benefits and deferred costs in 1960. The procedures used in this analysis are not standard practice and are used only to show general implications of change in costs, economics, and interest rates. The 1960 base period was used out of convenience rather than a date having historical significance to either the Columbia Basin Project or the Central Valley Project.

Table 1
Interest Rates from 1960-1984

Year	Rate	Year	Rate	Year	Rate	Year	Rate	Year	Rate
1960	2.500	1965	3.125	1970	4.875	1975	5.875	1980	7.125
1961	2.625	1966	3.125	1971	5.125	1976	6.125	1981	7.375
1962	2.625	1968	3.250	1972	5.375	1977	6.375	1982	7.625
1963	2.875	1968	3.250	1973	5.500	1978	6.625	1983	7.875
1964	3.00	1979	3.940	1974	6.250	1979	6.875	1984	8.125

****

[3]Numbers in brackets refer to entries in bibliography.

Cost Trends

Everyone has felt, if not analyzed, the impacts of inflation over the last 15 to 20 years. Figure 1 shows the cost index for agricultural drains on Reclamation projects from 1960 to 1983. One dollar in 1960 is equivalent to $3.90 in 1983. The nearly four-fold increase in costs was almost an exact reflection of the index for prices paid by farmers [6].

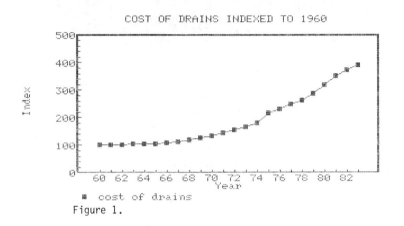

COST OF DRAINS INDEXED TO 1960

Figure 1.

The analysis of cost trends was initiated to check the notion that introduction of new technology, especially use of plastic tubing on Reclamation projects in 1969-1973, reduced drainage costs or at least slowed the inflation rate for several years. In comparing general construction cost trends with trends in drain costs, this was not evident [6]. However, in terms of constant dollars, drainage costs on Reclamation projects have decreased 39 percent since 1969 (see figure 2). The downward trend is coincidental with widespread use of plastic tubing on Reclamation projects.

Net farm income in the United States varied as shown in figure 3 between 1960 and 1982. Prices received for crops produced did not keep pace with production costs. The consequence is that a farmer's ability to repay drainage costs has greatly diminshed in the last 25 years. The following analysis quantifies these changes in simplistic terms. Benefits for lands on the Columbia Basin Project are used in this analysis. The average benefit of $116 per acre in 1975 was adjusted over the 1960-1982 period using data in Figure 3. The resulting net farm benefits are shown in Figure 4. The average benefit in 1960 was determined to be $53 per acre.

ROLLING AVERAGE COST OF DRAINS
Dollars (thousands)
30
20
10
0
60 62 64 66 68 70 72 74 76 78 80 82
Year
average cost

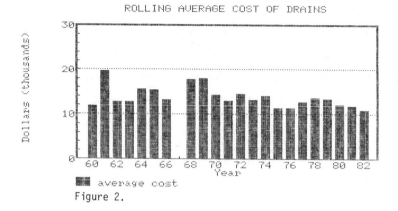

Figure 2.

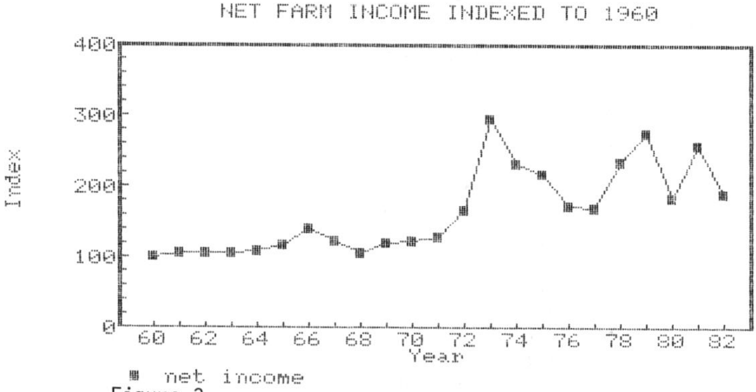

NET FARM INCOME INDEXED TO 1960
Index
400
300
200
100
0
60 62 64 66 68 70 72 74 76 78 80 82
Year
net income

Figure 3.

NET FARM BENEFITS-COLUMBIA BASIN PROJECT
Dollars/Acre
200
100
0
60 62 64 66 68 70 72 74 76 78 80 82
Year
dollars/acre

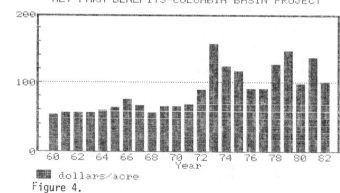

Figure 4.

In 1960, Reclamation practice was to analyze benefits over a 100-year project life. Using the 1960 Federal interest rate shown in Table 1 and assuming interest rates and net farm benefits remained constant, the present worth or allowable development costs for the project would be about $1,940 per acre at a break-even point. Performing the same computations at 8.125 percent interest (1985 Federal interest rate), the allowable cost of development would be only $650 per acre - about 34 percent of the 1960 value.

If we adjust interest rates and benefits as they actually occurred from 1960 to 1982 and use 8.125 percent interest rate for the next 77 years, the allowable cost would be $1,580 per acre. This is about 82 percent of the allowable estimated for 1960.

The average development cost, other than drainage, on Columbia Basin Project is about $550 per acre. The average drain spacing is about 600 feet. During the 23-year period of study, the following values have applied:

Cost for drainage in 1960 = $\dfrac{(43,560 \ ft^2/acre)}{(5280 \ ft/mi)} \dfrac{(\$11,862/mi)}{(600 \ ft)}$ $ 163/acre

Present worth of net benefits @ 2.5 percent $1,900/acre

Construction cost for project works $ 550/acre

                          Maximum allowable $1,350/acre

Present worth of net benefits @ variable interest rates $1,580/acre

Construction cost for project works $ 550/acre

                          Maximum allowable $1,050

By contrast, if the Columbia Basin Project were formulated today, the following values would apply:

Cost for drainage (from abstracts of bid) $ 636/acre

Present worth of net benefits @ 8.125 percent interest $ 650/acre

Construction cost for project works $ 550/acre

                          Maximum allowable $ 100/acre

The impact of economic changes would be devastating on the decision to build the Columbia Basin Project. Economics may not justify deferred drainage works. However, we have a legal obligation to maintain the productivity of the land. Using short-term economic analysis to justify individual drainage installations could create conflicts with the obligation to preserve the land resource.

Impacts of Changes in Social/Environmental Concerns

The social climate, environmental awareness, and laws have changed
along with interest rates, etc. The willingness of the general
taxpayer to subsidize or simply finance Government-authorized projects
has all but disappeared. This has resulted in a variety of changes in
economic guidelines used in analyzing projects. This has resulted in
a variety of changes in economic guidelines used in analyzing
projects. These changes are far beyond the scope of this paper.
Delays brought about by reanalysis and study because of changes in law
associated with environmental concerns are significant and will be
touched upon. The impact of simply delaying a project may not be as
devastating to completing project features as the additional costs
brought about by adding new features to a project to mitigate, avoid,
or protect something of social value.

The San Luis Drain in California is a good example of the impact. In
1963, the San Luis Drain was planned as a 188-mile facility
discharging into the lower Sacramento-San Joaquin Delta area. The
1963 cost was estimated to be about $34 million or $73 per acre.

Present worth of net benefits @ 2.5 percent interest	$5,420 acre
Construction cost for project works	$ 960/acre
Maximum allowable	$4,460/acre
1960 estimated cost of San Luis Drain	$ 70/acre
Present worth of net benefits @ 8.125 percent interest	$1,820/acre
Construction cost for project works	$ 960/acre
Maximum allowable	$ 860/acre
Present worth of net benefits @ variable interest rates	$4,420/acre
Construction cost for project works	$ 960/acre
Maximum allowable	$3,460/acre

The indexed costs for San Luis Drain in 1982 are $270 per acre. This
analysis would indicate that, no matter how we look at it, the Central
Valley Project would be justified economically.

The drain was not completed to the Delta or Bay for a variety of
reasons. Instead, Kesterson Reservoir was built as a temporary
terminal point for the San Luis Drain. The capacity of Kesterson was
planned to be sufficient until the early 1990's. The San Luis Drain
was then to be completed to a suitable disposal point when capacity at
Kesterson was reached. Concerns over toxic compounds in the return

flows caused the State to order termination of use and cleanup of
Kesterson Reservoir. A reanalysis of options for the drain is
underway. Discussion of the alternatives is beyond the scope of this
paper. Nevertheless, estimated costs of cleanup and disposal
alternatives range up to $130 million.

If the $130 million cost materializes, it represents about $33 million
in 1960 dollars. Although the total cost of $66 million would have
been justified, it represents a doubling of costs for other than
economic concerns. If the San Luis Drain had to be justified on the
basis of net benefits, the deferral of drains would not have an
impact.

Conclusions

The analyses performed in this study were highly simplistic for the
complicated issues addressed. They were intended to provide some
indication whether deferred drainage works still seemed to be an
appropriate operating policy. The study did not result in strong
evidence suggesting that deferral of drainage should be continued or
rejected.

The cost of drains has kept pace with cost of general construction and
prices paid by the farmer. Benefits from agricultural production have
risen in the last 25 years, but not at the same rate as production
costs. This has serious impacts on projects currently in the
planning stage. Justifiable expenditures are only about one-third as
much as in 1960.

Drainage costs have increased nearly four times since 1960. In terms
of constant dollars, these costs have decreased 39 percent since 1969.
This is coincidental with the use of plastic tubing in buried pipe
drains.

In the case of the Columbia Basin Project, strict application of
economic criteria would seriously impact completion of the deferred
drainage works. The decision on completion of the San Luis Drain
would appear to be tied more to politics, financing ability, and
public acceptance than to economic criteria or technical evaluation.

Serious conflicts with Reclamation's legal requirements to maintain
productivity of irrigated land in perpetuity are created in those
instances where drainage works are determined to be infeasible after
initial project development.

BIBLIOGRAPHY

1. Schaffer, Marvin J., and Ribbens, Richard W., "Generalized
   Description of Return Flow Waulity Simulation Model,"
   Environmental Protection Agency in EPA-600/2-77-179E,
   August 1977, "Prediction of Mineral Quality of Irrigation
   Return Flow, Volume V, Detailed Return Flow Salinity-Nutrient
   Simulation Model."

2. U.S. Department of Agriculture, "Agricultural Statistics," 1968.

3. U.S. Department of Agriculture, "Agricultural Statistics," 1980.

4. U.S. Department of Agriculture, "Agricultural Statistics," 1983.

5. U.S. Department of the Interior, Bureau of Reclamation, "Columbia
   Basin Project, Washington, Second Basin Siphon and Tunnel,
   State/Local/Federal Cost Sharing," August 1975.

6. U.S. Department of the Interior, Bureau of Reclamation,
   "Construction Cost Trends."

7. U.S. Department of the Interior, Bureau of Reclamation, "Definite
   Plan Report, San Luis Unit, Central Valley Project, California,
   revised February 1963.

THE LOCAL PERSPECTIVE ON AGRICULTURAL DRAINAGE

By Stephen K. Hall*

ABSTRACT -- This paper will discuss shallow, perched groundwater and resulting agricultural drainage and salt problems that have developed in the San Joaquin Valley of California over the past 30 years. The relatively recent discovery of high levels of selenium and other trace elements in the saline drainage water generated from one of the most productive agricultural areas in the world has made it difficult to develop acceptable disposal methods for this water. Politics and emotion, plus Federal and State environmental and water quality regulations, have compounded the problem. The processes used by the local water agencies in addressing this problem, and the coordination of efforts utilized with treatment and disposal plans are presented.

INTRODUCTION -- The drainage of shallow perched ground water from beneath irrigated soils is necessary in many river valleys around the world, particularly where alkaline conditions are present. The San Joaquin Valley of Central California is such a valley. It has many areas where soils are not free draining, and since much of the Valley is irrigated, drainage problems exist, particularly on the west side of the Valley.

The long term productivity of these drainage problem areas will depend upon a successfully developed system which removes this shallow perched ground water to prevent water logging of the soils and, more importantly, to provide a balance of incoming and outgoing salts in the upper soil profile.

Farmers and local water agencies in the western San Joaquin Valley have been struggling to develop such a system for a number of years. The recent discovery of the natural element, selenium, and other trace elements in the drainage water at levels which are much higher than normal has greatly complicated the implementation of any drainage solutions which might be developed.

THE SETTING -- The San Joaquin Valley is highly developed into agriculture and is crisscrossed with natural and man-made channels that are part of a water delivery system developed by Federal, State, and local agencies. The

* Executive Director, Land Preservation Association, 770 E. Shaw Ave., Suite 205, Fresno, CA 93710.

Valley is bounded by the Tehachapi Mountain Range on the South, the Sierra Mountain Range on the East, and the Coast Range on the West. A low ridge separates it from the Sacramento Valley on the North (4).

Within the San Joaquin Valley are two hydrologic basins. The San Joaquin Basin is drained by the San Joaquin River which originates in the Sierra Nevada and runs west to the trough of the Valley and then turns north and joins the Sacramento River in what is known as the San Francisco Bay-Delta estuary. The Tulare Basin, to the south of the San Joaquin Basin, is a closed basin with no natural outlet.

The climate is arid, with rainfall ranging from 5 inches (13cm.) in the south to 14 inches (36cm.) in the north (3). The soils are fertile, and a wide variety of crops can be grown; however, irrigation is necessary for virtually all crops.

Underlying much of the western Valley floor at depths of from 40-400 feet are a series of clay layers which serve to confine groundwater into distinct aquifers. Below the deepest clay layer is groundwater which is of fair to poor quality, but has historically been used for irrigation prior to the development of surface water supplies. It is still used on a limited basis where surface water supplies are not sufficient to meet irrigation demands. The top clay layer serves to prevent the downward movement of applied irrigation water and rainfall and thus contributes to the drainage problems experienced by many areas in the Valley.

THE DRAINAGE PROBLEM -- The drainage problem is really two problems. First, where water is applied to soils that are not free draining, a shallow water table develops. Since much of the Valley is underlain with shallow clay layers, perched water tables have developed above these layers as irrigation has increased. Second, much of this poorly drained soil in naturally saline. This saline condition requires that excess water be applied to prevent a buildup of salt in the upper soil profile. The excess water "leaches" the soil salts out of the upper profile; however, where a perched water table exists, this additional water causes the water table to rise. Since the water table contains high levels of dissolved salts, the water is toxic to growing crops and must be artificially drained to a depth below the crops' root zone.

The technology for draining the soil in this way is well developed; however, the high salt content of the water has made it difficult to use or dispose of it in a way that is both environmentally sound and economically feasible.

VALLEY-WIDE DRAINAGE STUDIES -- Several major studies by

VALLEY-WIDE DRAINAGE STUDIES -- Several major studies by State and Federal agencies have indicated that a Valley-wide drainage plan is needed. The last major study concluded that up to 1.1 million acres (445,200 Ha) of land in the San Joaquin Valley could ultimately require drainage (1). Virtually all of the studies completed thus far have indicated that a conveyance facility (a drain) should be built from the southern end of the Valley to a point in the western San Francisco Bay-Delta estuary.

As a part of the Congressional authorization of the Central Valley Project, San Luis Unit, the U.S. Bureau of Reclamation was directed to provide drainage service to lands within the San Luis Unit service area (7). Lands served by the San Luis Unit lie west of the San Joaquin River and much of that area has a severe drainage problem. In 1968, the Bureau of Reclamation began construction on the San Luis Drain as a part of the San Luis Unit project facilities (6).

Shortly after construction of the drain began, environmental and economic issues were raised and Congress failed to authorize sufficient funds to complete construction. As a result, the drain was never finished. Instead, Kesterson Reservoir, which had been built as a regulating reservoir, became the terminus of the drain. Kesterson Reservoir, located near Los Banos, is a 1,200 acre (486 Ha) man-made surface impoundment in the midst of a large wetlands area. With the completion of the drain stalled, it has become an evaporation basin for the drainage problem area it serves.

As of today, Kesterson Reservoir is being closed down. In 1983, the U.S. Fish and Wildlife Service discovered dead and deformed embryos in the nests of birds breeding at Kesterson Reservoir (2). Since that time, the presence of high levels of selenium have been found to have caused those reproductive problems.

Selenium is a naturally occurring element which is beneficial to animal life at trace levels, but can produce toxic and reproductive symptoms at higher levels.

Although data is still incomplete, it appears other drainage problem areas in the San Joaquin Valley may have high levels of selenium and other trace elements in their drainage water. The presence of these trace elements has not fundamentally changed the nature of the drainage problem, but their presence has greatly complicated the development of drainage water disposal options.

This is despite the fact that both the State and the Federal Governments operate large irrigation projects which serve substantial tracts of land in the San Joaquin Valley that have drainage problems.

Aside from the economic, political, and environmental problems associated with a large drain to the San Francisco Bay-Delta estuary, there are a number of other reasons why a master drainage plan has not been implemented in the Valley. Among these are:

1) Although there are many similarities in the drainage problems experienced throughout the Valley, there are a number of regional differences in the nature and severity of the problem. There are also great differences in the extent to which the physical and institutional mechanisms are in place to deal with the drainage problems in each area. These regional differences make it difficult to develop a single plan that will satisfy the needs of all Valley locations that have drainage problems.

2) It is acknowledged that some portion of the shallow water table under existing drainage problem areas comes from irrigation of upslope lands. The extent to which such upslope irrigation adds to the drainage problem is largely unknown and is probably highly variable from region to region. Irrigators in the drainage problem areas feel that upslope irrigators should pay a portion of the cost of any solutions that are developed. Upslope irrigators disagree, claiming their contribution to the problem is very slight. Such disagreements have retarded progress in developing both regional and Valley-wide solutions.

3) Unlike the sudden loss of irrigation water, which would show immediate, dramatic results, drainage problems develop over a number of years and agricultural production can continue even though yields decline as the soil gradually salinizes. Likewise, reclamation of lands through drainage takes several years to accomplish. Because of this, awareness of the problem and motivation to invest in solutions has not been great enough to result in implementation of a comprehensive plan of drainage works for the Valley.

Although progress by local, State, and Federal agencies toward an overall solution has been slow, there are two factors that may lead to action in the near future.

First, the irrigation system in the Valley has matured to the point where the drainage problem is spreading at an accelerated rate. Today, there are roughly 100,000 acres (40,500 ha) of drained land in the San Joaquin Valley generating approximately 70,000 acre-feet (86,300 dam^3) of drainage water annually. It is estimated that within ten

years up to 200,000 acres (81,000 ha) could be drained and
generating 120,000 acre-feet (148,000 dam^3)(5).

Second, with the discovery of high trace element levels
in some areas and the resulting impacts on waterfowl, the
drainage problem, which has historically been viewed as an
agricultural productivity problem, is now viewed as an
environmental problem. This shift in thinking has added an
urgency to the problem, which, in the minds of some, did
not exist before. Further, there has been a great deal of
scrutiny recently directed toward the State agencies that
have the responsibility for regulating the disposal of
agricultural drainage water. This has resulted in
increased pressure by those regulatory agencies on local
drainage problem areas to develop environmentally sound
drainage water disposal plans.

Currently, the local approach is to discharge the
drainage effluent to evaporation ponds or into surface
waters, chiefly rivers. Although these methods have been
used for some time, there are now serious water quality
questions being raised and it is believed these practices
will not be allowed to continue on a broad basis. Given
this set of circumstances, local agencies charged with
drainage water disposal responsibilities have the following
options:

1)   Develop new treatment and/or disposal
      methods for drainage water.

2)   Terminate drainage flows and allow the
      water table to rise until drainage
      problem lands go out of production.

3)   Allow drainage to continue until
      regulatory and/or legal constraints
      require action.

4)   Respond to regulatory pressure with
      interim measures while waiting for
      State and Federal agencies to develop
      longer term solutions.

Option two is not considered feasible, since allowing
land to go out of production will mean the problem will
continue to spread, resulting in catastrophic economic and
environmental impacts. Option three is not responsible and
is not being pursued by any local agency. The most likely
situation is a combination of options one and four, where
local agencies adopt interim measures to deal with the
drainage problem while working both independently and in
cooperation with State and Federal agencies to develop long
term treatment/disposal methods.

The most viable solutions involve a combination of the
following disposal methods:

Evaporation Basins - Evaporation basins are widely used
throughout the San Joaquin Valley for the disposal of
agricultural drainage water by local agencies and
individuals who have no other disposal means available.
However, where high levels of trace elements of trace
elements are present in the drainage water, there is
concern that waterfowl will use the evaporation basins as
habitat much as they used Kesterson Reservoir and the same
problems will develop. Further, as the drainage water
concentrates through evaporation, the level of selenium in
the drainage water increases to the point where it can
reach hazardous waste levels. Existing California law
prohibits the storage of hazardous wastes in impoundments
such as conventional evaporation basins. Retrofitting
evaporation basins to meet hazardous wastes disposal
facility criteria would be prohibitively expensive. That
means some form of treatment is necessary to remove trace
elements in those areas where trace element content is
high.

Deep-well Injection - Large volumes of liquid wastes are
disposed of in this state through injection into deep,
water bearing formations. This practice is very common in
oil fields and other industrial sites. Initial
investigations indicate that formations exist at 4,000 to
5,000 feet below the Valley floor which could receive
fairly large volumes of agricultural drainage water without
any serious impacts. The water quality of the existing
aquifer appears to be very poor and is overlain with a
thick layer of shale which would prevent any migration into
other aquifers. The U.S. Bureau of Reclamation is funding
studies to determine environmental and cost factors of
deep-well injection.

Selenium Removal - The removal of selenium from the
drainage water using a variety of methods has been
explored. Biological treatment and iron adsorption appear
to be the most promising at this point. Local districts
have funded two separate research projects to determine the
efficiency and cost effectiveness of these methods.
Results appear promising but are preliminary at this point.
If they prove feasible, drainage water with selenium
removed could be disposed of in evaporation or perhaps in
surface water.

Desalination - Removal of the salts from the agricultural
drainage water, perhaps in combination with selenium and
boron removal has been investigated and has the added
appeal of providing additional fresh water supplies, either
for use in the local area or for sale to other water
deficient areas in the State.

Preliminary investigations have revealed that the costs of desalination, even after the sale of produced water, would be prohibitively expensive using conventional reverse osmosis techniques. Additional research has been proposed on other techniques which could be employed at much lower cost.

PROBABLE FUTURE -- In most river valleys where salinity is a problem, it is managed by returning salts to the river system through surface and subsurface flows for export to the ocean. In the San Joaquin Valley, the political, environmental and institutional barriers that have been raised make this impossible for the foreseeable future.

Nevertheless, it will be necessary to physically isolate, either in the Valley or through export to the ocean, native and imported salt loads if agricultural productivity and environmental values are to be maintained in the San Joaquin Valley. Since the storage of salts produced by the Valley under conditions of full drainage development will probably not be practical, it is likely that there will someday be a drain or some export facility to carry that salt load to the ocean.

In the meantime, local, State and Federal agencies will continue to study near and intermediate term methods of drainage water treatment and disposal. As these methods are developed and implemented, it is likely that regional planning and operating agencies will develop to manage the growth of local systems so that they can be operated in a coordinated fashion and one day be incorporated into a Valleywide collection and disposal system, should one be developed.

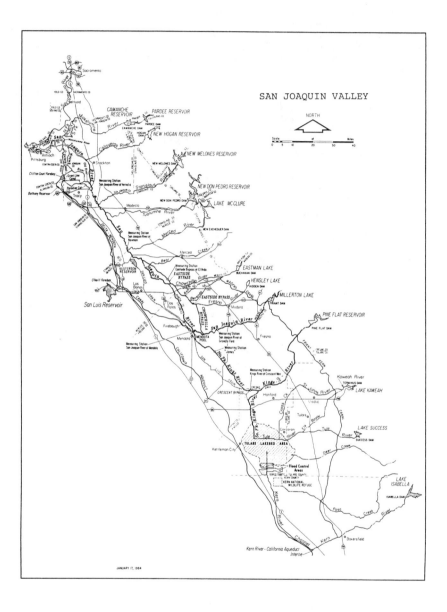

APPENDIX 1 -- REFERENCES

(1) "Agricultural Drainage and Salt Management in the San Joaquin Valley", Final Report of the San Joaquin Valley Interagency Drainage Program, U.S. Bureau of Reclamation, California Department of Water Resources, and California State Water Resources Control Board, June, 1979, pp. 162.

(2) Jones & Stokes Associates, Inc., Environmental Impact Report, Westlands Water District, "Elimination of Drainage Water Flow into the San Luis Drain", November, 1985.

(3) Nelson, Daniel G., and Johnston, William R., "San Joaquin Valley Drainage - Development and Impact," Proceedings, Irrigation and Drainage Specialty Conference, Amer. Soc. Civil Engineers, July, 1984.

(4) Price, E.P., "Agricultural Drainage Problems of the San Joaquin Valley," Proceedings, National Conference on Irrigation Return Flow Quality Mangement, Colorado State University, Fort Collins, Colorado, May, 1977.

(5) Proceedings of the San Joaquin Valley Technical Meeting on Agricultural Drainage Water Management, East Bay Municipal Utilities District Compound, Pardee Reservoir, September, 1985.

(6) Swain, Donald G., "San Joaquin Valley Drainage - A Permanent Solution, "Proceedings, Irrigation and Drainage Specialty Conference, Amer. Soc. Civil Engineers, July, 1984.

(7) U.S. Bureau of Reclamation, A Report on the Feasibility of Water Supply Development, San Luis Unit, Central Valley Project, California, May, 1955.

"National Perspectives and Policy
on Nonpoint Sources of Water Pollution"

Carl F. Myers*

EPA is very concerned about nonpoint sources (NPS) of water pollution. While we can now anticipate the end of significant conventional pollution from point sources, the end of water pollution is not nearly in sight. More than that, even when we have finished the major task of controlling toxic point sources, to which we are legally committed, the end will still not be in sight.

Over the past decade the nation has mounted an enormous effort to establish a system of industrial waste and sewage treatment facilities. We have avoided the catastrophe that threatened our waters, and revived many lakes and streams that had been thought beyond help. But there is no denying that in recent years the curve of improvement has flattened out. The 1982 Fish and Wildlife survey showed, for example, that although 67 percent of the nation's water had at least a minimum ability to support sport fish, the situation had not noticably improved during the previous five years. The 1983 ASIWPCA study showed that in the decade since 1972, of 354,000 stream miles for which there is water quality information, 13 percent had improved, three percent had gotten worse and the rest had remained unchanged.

It seems we are holding the line against water pollution. With the increases in economic activity and population in those years, this must be considered an impressive accomplishment. But the Clean Water Act doesn't tell us to just hold the line. It tells us to clean up the water so that it's fishable and swimmable. We haven't done that in an unacceptably large proportion of our waterways. And it's becoming ever more clear that much of the reason for this is our failure to adequately control nonpoint source pollution.

So while we at EPA continue to implement the major point source efforts embodied in our municipal policy and our pretreatment requirements, we must begin to place increased efforts on nonpoint controls.

Let's briefly sketch the magnitude of this problem. In the 1984 State water quality reports, we found that for assessed waters where desired uses are not being fully supported, nonpoint sources are the leading cause of this in 39 percent of rivers, 52 percent of lakes, and 48 percent of estuaries. In the 1983 Environmental Management Reports, six out of ten of the EPA regions confirmed this by naming nonpoint source pollution as the principal cause of inadequate water quality.

* Chief, Nonpoint Sources Branch, Office of Water, U.S. EPA

These figures tell us that despite the billions expended for point source control over the past 12 years by the Federal Government, State and local government, and private industry, we have accomplished much less than what we set out to do. Even when we institute secondary treatment as the law requires, even when we require clean-up beyond Best Available Technology (BAT), we will still not meet the goals of the Clean Water Act. In addition, there is increasing evidence that nonpoint pollution also represents a threat to groundwater.

We have to accept this hard reality: either we have to do better at controlling nonpoint source pollution or we have to compromise the goals of the Clean Water Act.

So let us take a serious look at nonpoint source pollution. And let's not argue about whether it's harder to control than point source. Let's agree that it surely is a different kind of job. In the first place, when we went after point sources it was at least possible to distinguish the polluters from everybody else. We had little hesitation about telling industrial facilities to clean up their waste. We understood that when cities built treatment plants they could stop polluting their own waters and those of their downstream neighbors with domestic sewage. Most important, we knew how to administer regulatory programs that require the installation of particular types of engineering.

But we can't so easily identify the nonpoint source polluters, because "they" are "us." In a sense, nonpoint source pollution is the footprint of our entire civilization, stamped on our water resources by the strength of millions of separate private and public decisions. Each of these decisions pursued some private or public good. Farmers wanted to grow more crops. Cities wanted to expand. People wanted highways between cities, and after the highways were built they found they wanted to live in suburban houses, filling up the spaces between the cities. Land development changes the pattern of water runoff. Nonpoint source pollution is the direct result of that changed pattern. It's part of the unpaid cost of development and economic growth.

It follows that significant reductions in nonpoint pollution will only come as the result of improvements in the way we manage land. That means, first of all, improving the way America's largest landowner manages land. That's the Federal Government. At EPA we intend to do all we can to help the major Federal land-holding agencies address nonpoint problems in areas under their supervision.

Outside these areas, however, we have a peculiar quandry. On the one hand, the Federal Government has, along with the States, a recognized responsibility to protect the quality of the national waters. But we now have a situation where a good part of our remaining water pollution, perhaps the bulk of it, arises from the way that private parties and local governments manage land. Thus, we see a Federal responsibility being affected in a serious way by local land management actions in which the Federal Government has for all practical purposes no direct authority.

Direct Federal regulation has never been an important factor in local land use decisions, nor in my view should it be. We have a Federal presence in air and water pollution control because these sources are correctly perceived as common, and of concern to all Americans.

Clearly, nonpoint source control cannot be handled in a traditional Federal regulatory manner. Nonpoint problems are, first of all, specific to particular sites. This means that in order to be both efficient and effective a nonpoint control effort should be targeted to put resources where the problems are. It is almost impossible to arrange national funding programs in this way. Finally, the sheer numbers of decisions that go into establishing a pattern of land use would make any attempt to direct those decisions from Washington an administrative nightmare. The kind of extensive bureaucracy you would need to run such a program would probably be opposed by nearly everyone.

Fortunately, the nonpoint problem has been recognized in many different parts of the nation, by State and local government and by the private sector. Some gratifying things are being done.

Wisconsin has a State-funded program designed to obtain increased water quality improvements in selected watersheds through the control of both urban and rural nonpoint sources. They are able to identify water quality objectives for nonpoint source control and focus on the land areas presenting the major barriers to reach those objectives. Cost-share agreements with landowners and municipalities are signed, which require the installation of best management practices within five years and maintenance by the participants thereafter.

In Vermont, close cooperation between the State and the timber industry has led to decreases in the nonpoint pollution produced by logging. The State helped to set up a system of self-policing by the industry, with a heavy emphasis on technical assistance and education. Water quality problems reported to the State are generally handled by an industry association committee, with the State moving in when voluntary efforts fail to produce results.

A particularly interesting example of a local initiative balancing interests in this area is the case of Tillamook Bay on Oregon's coast. This region is famous for both oysters and cheese, a combination that may go well during a restaurant meal, but which presents serious problems at the producer end. Coastal Oregon gets around 100 inches of rain a year, and this washes dairy cattle wastes into Tillamook Bay in such volumes that in 1977, the FDA closed the Bay to commercial harvesting because of high coliform counts in the oysters.

Since then, a grassroots effort on the part of both oystermen and dairy operators has succeeded in introducing best management practices at over half of the area's dairies. They sought and received help from the State, the soil conservation district, the Department of

Agriculture and EPA, but the main push continues to come from local citizens. The response in the Bay has been encouraging. Shellfish bed closures are much less frequent and coliform counts in the streams leading to Tillamook Bay have been significantly reduced.

I could mention many other areas in which important work has been done. There is the control of urban runoff in a developing community represented by the experience of Bellevue, Washington, helped by EPA's Nationwide Urban Runoff Program. This program has also assisted 25 other urban areas across the country to better control nonpoint sources. Or we could consider the success of the demonstration Rural Clean Water Program, on which we are cooperating with the Department of Agriculture to introduce improved best management practices in 20 agricultural watersheds facing nonpoint problems. These Federal demonstration programs have been focused on developing the knowledge base necessary to effectively control nonpoint sources.

It's a correct focus because information is the key element in nonpoint source control, almost in the same way that technology was in the case of our point source accomplishments. Our demonstration programs have taught us that successful operations in this field always have two elements present. First, they are tightly targeted on the acreage or practices that contribute the most pollution. Second, education and technical assistance are central, rather than auxiliary, features. After all, successful nonpoint control largely consists of getting a key group of people to change the way they do their usual work. The proper information is necessary to identify the essential group, and to let them know what changes are necessary.

This is in most cases best done on a local scale or a State scale, as in the examples I have mentioned. But for certain major interstate problems, some Federal involvement must continue. Our joint State-Federal projects to improve water quality in the Great Lakes, and in Chesapeake Bay and other major estuaries have nonpoint source components. These areas are the important test beds for showing what targeted Federal efforts can do to alleviate nonpoint source pollution on a larger scale.

But these examples constitute the bare beginnings of what needs to be done. The big question is where we go from here. This kind of pollution requires a different approach from the one that worked in point source controls. We must continue to redirect existing Federal, State, local and private resources onto priority nonpoint problems. To help frame this approach, EPA convened a national Nonpoint Source Task Force two years ago. In December 1984, this Task Force recommended a new national policy on nonpoint source pollution to protect surface and groundwater. Each Federal agency on the Task Force developed its own nonpoint strategy, which they are now beginning to put into effect. The Task Force strongly supported the idea that States and their local governments should play the leading role in the control of nonpoint sources, and that private sector initiatives and cooperation are essential for success.

Finally, the Task Force asked that EPA, under its existing Clean Water Act authorities, take the lead at the Federal level, to coordinate interagency management actions devoted to the control of such sources, including needed actions on Federal lands.

This is what we are doing. Coordination and refocusing of existing resources are essential if we are to have any chance at all of coping with this problem. These resources are in fact immense. When you add up the money spent on resource and environmental protection in FY 1985 by the Corps of Engineers, the Soil Conservation Service, the Forest Service, the Bureau of Land Management, and others it comes to about $10 billion. In addition, as I've noted already, the Federal government is directly responsible for managing over 650 million acres of land. In these areas, the Federal government is the "local" agency responsible for good stewardship.

We must marshall these resources and programs more effectively against what looks like a large portion of our national water pollution problem. And when I say "we" I mean the entire clean water community. States and localities have got to make it clear to the Federal presence in their neighborhoods that controlling nonpoint source pollution is vitally important. EPA will support these State and local nonpoint initiatives and work on nonpoint prolems on Federal lands, both by coordination of policy with other Federal agencies in Washington and by working directly, out of our Regional offices, on specific high-priority nonpoint projects with our Federal agency counterparts.

Interagency cooperation works. In agriculture, for example, we know from experience that where local and State agricultural agencies are able to work together and integrate water quality and erosion control objectives, a combined program can be highly successful for both ends. In situations where State agricultural agencies spend their resources exclusively for erosion control the results may not fully support water quality goals. Several States have recognized this and have adopted the approach of managing nonpoint source control on a watershed basis. This allows more targeting on the most important sources of water quality problems.

I believe the agricultural community is ready for this kind of initiative, if the message is strongly put from the right place. In May 1985, EPA co-hosted a meeting on nonpoint source pollution with the Department of Agriculture. At that time, Secretary Block said, "Where State and local officials have identified water quality to be more important than gross soil erosion -- I can assure you that we stand ready to target our resources into nonpoint source pollution from agriculture." State and local officials must rise to this challenge.

We are also going to place substantial emphasis on making better information available to States and localities. We must make sure that practical, cost-effective techniques continue to be developed and that they are disseminated to people who could use them. We also have to coordinate the major water quality and flow-based data systems at EPA and other agencies, to enable us to determine best management practices for specific water quality problems.

We hope that the net effect of this will be to increase understanding of this kind of pollution to the point where a city manager who is displeased with water quality doesn't automatically call up his sewage treatment plant and demand more steam. We hope that people will begin to comprehend how many of the things that are under the authority of localities contribute to the decline in water quality.

In short, things are going to change. The water protection professions are going to change, if they are to keep up with where the real problems are. We are going to see a lot more interdisciplinary efforts in the coming years, efforts like our Chesapeake Bay project, but at many different scales, and targeted at a variety of point and nonpoint problems. We will see changes at EPA too. For the past decade we have concentrated on major engineering programs to control sewage and industrial pollution. We must now determine the best way to tackle this different task while continuing our strong point source programs. This new challenge will be faced by us all and, based on the record achieved in this country in water pollution over the last 15 years, I'm sure it will be met.

An Integrated Conceptual Expert System
For Flood and Water Pollution Management

by

William James and Alan Dunn*

Expert Systems (ES) are presently in their infancy but development is rapid. One particularly practical role for an ES is as an interface between a complex computer model and an inexperienced user or novice. Such ES software will aid the novice by simulating the analytical skill of an expert user by using a sensitivity framework for discretization, parameter estimation, calibration, and by using an error analysis framework for evaluating the credibility of the model continuously as it executes.

The software is applied to the USEPA Storm Water Management Model (SWMM3), particularly the Runoff module in the PC implementation known as PCSWMM3. The new software conducts a sensitivity and error analysis on parameters which are not unique, or specifically known or which may be subject to variability for various reasons. Output functions considered include the peak flows, volumes of outflows, time to peak outflow, number of exceedances of a specified flow, duration of exceedance, and hydrograph shape.

First order sensitivity analysis to assess the effects of input variability are carried out by computing a large matrix of sensitivity co-efficients. The error analysis is carried out by estimation of variance and confidence ranges for the desired output. The most probable (mean) value for each parameter along with two other values for which the user is 95% sure the true value is not above or below, comprise the required input. Upper and lower boundaries are required to account for skewed distributions. (These input requirements also pressure a novice user to acquire special expertise in a hurry.)

Input variables are ranked according to sensitivity and to error. The analysis is geared to monitor those parameters which most affect the outcome. Weather episode factors (temperature and precipitation) could be used to map different patterns of rankings. By monitoring which "zone" the model conditions currently fall into, the new software could compute and rank the input parameters with greatest sensitivity and estimate their combined total error in real-time.

The resultant output hydrograph should consist of a fuzzy band of likely results as opposed to a definite value. Such graphical presentation will allow the novice to visually evaluate model uncertainty.

*Computational Hydraulics Group, McMaster University, Hamilton, Ontario, Canada, L8S 4L7

Introduction

An ES is loosely defined as "an intensive focus on knowledge" (Winston, 1984). For humans, problems are solved by considering a large background of knowledge which may concern the target problem. For an ES the same is true. This knowledge must be geared to the specific problem orientation of the system. The high degree of knowledge specific to each system is required since there does not appear to be one catchall system which can solve all problems in any problem definition.

Expert Systems (ES) are now becoming available to the average microcomputer user. While still somewhat limited, their development is rapid and their power will most likely continue to expand. A typical Expert System encodes the acquired knowledge about a specific problem into a "Knowledge Base". In the past this knowledge concerned problems outside the field of computer science. In other words the ES was developed to solve a problem which did not concern complex software as a primary target. An example of this type of ES is the program DELTA/CATS-1 which troubleshoots problems with diesel electric locomotives, (Bonissone, 1984). The user enters facts about the state of the locomotive under consideration, and the system uses rules and an inference engine to diagnose multiple problems with the locomotive and suggests repair procedures to maintenance personnel. The program is a tool used to analyse a problem outside of the program itself.

An extension to this is the creation of a program which is designed to aid a user in correctly using a complicated modelling package. In this sense, the ES is a tool to help the user utilize another tool (the complex computer model) to analyse and solve a problem. Even though the user may not distinguish between the tools, in the scope of this paper this extension is one step further removed from the original design problem than conventional ES. The overall combined package may be seen as one advanced software package to the user, however.

Hydrology and Expert Systems

There are numerous computer models available to the engineering-hydrologist. SWMM3, HEC-i, and HSP-F are a few examples of well known models in the public domain. These models provide information on urban and rural runoff, quantity and pollutant flows, sewer system routing and flood forecasting.

A conventional hydrological ES could be developed by taking an experienced hydrologist and encoding his or her decision paths and knowledge into a knowledge base. This computer-based knowledge could then be used by novice hydrologists to follow the same train of thought in solving a problem. As an example, an ES could laboriously query the user for all relevent information known to the user about a specific design problem. With this information, the ES attempts to recommend a course of action such as the use of a specific method or computer model.

However, in many cases the basic hydrology involved is familiar to

the user. In fact, most senior undergraduate engineering students with
one or two hydrology courses have mastered all hydrology basic to the
most advanced and complex packages. They are aware of the data, what it
means, and are able to enter it into a computer model. What they are
unaware of, however, is how the computer model treats this data and the
impact of uncertain data. While they are aware of the basic hydrology,
they are unaware of the effect on the computed output of the encoding
details used by the model designer. These details compounded by unreliable input parameter estimates, have an impact on the reliability and
accuracy of the model results.

Therefore, where a more typical ES may encode knowledge usually surrounding the problem, viz. knowledge of the problem environment or scenario based on the large accumulated experience of an expert hydrologist,
the extended ES envisaged in this paper encodes the knowledge of the
model designer who presumably has also acquired considerable expertise
and is another expert. The model designer's knowledge is intimately
concerned with his model sensitivity; such knowledge would help the
novice understand the importance and effect of his own data estimates on
the model performance and its relation to reality.

Sensitivity Analysis Framework

To encode the programmer's knowledge into a useful form of ES, the
actual program coding, be it in FORTRAN, ASSEMBLER, PASCAL, etc. could be
analysed. However, it is the effect that parameters and variables have
on the results that is of interest. This type of information is provided
by a sensitivity analysis which reveals to the user the parameters that
are currently sensitive to perturbation and those which are not. If a
parameter is found to be sensitive then it's estimation must be made with
care to properly model the system. Insensitive parameters on the other
hand can have a greater error range with little effect on the final
result. The principle here is that the user's uncertainty in the input
values combined with their respective sensitivity must play a part in
determining the overall confidence the user can expect in the final
computed output.

Sensitivity analysis can be carried out by a number of different
methods. The simplest form, of course, is to perturb one parameter at a
time and record the resulting change in output. If the number of parameters to be checked is relatively low then this method is acceptable.
If the number of parameters becomes large, however, individual perturbations become very time consuming. Other methods, such as the fourier
amplitude sensitivity test (FAST), variational, and direct methods exist
that are capable of handling larger quantities of parameters than single
perturbation methods (Koda et al., 1979).

Fortunately, most hydrological models have a limited number of
significantly sensitive parameters. In fact in some models the sensitivity of the environmental parameters may be insignificant compared to the
sensitivity of the driving force. As an example, the Sacramento Model
evidently produces the same error for a 1% change in rainfall input as a

10% change in its most sensitive parameter (Burnash and Ferral, 1982). The point here is that not all parameters need to undergo detailed sensitivity analysis.

In a study by James and Robinson, (1985) on sensitivity in the Hamilton urban drainage system the parameters with greatest sensitivity were ranked for both quantity and quality. The study found that for flow quantity the important parameters were percentage imperviousness, width of subcatchments, initial and final infiltration, detention storage, ground slope and percentage of impervious area with zero detention storage. For quality the list included: number of dry days, street sweeping interval, street sweeping efficiency, exponential co-efficient in the washoff equation, dust and dirt loadings, insoluble fractions due to suspended solids, availability factors, and total gutter length. This study was done for one area under a fixed set of conditions. The reader should not infer from this study that all input data sets and all weather episodes will produce the same rankings for these parameters or even the same parameters. Sensitivity should be analysed for each active environmental data set and for every weather episode applicable to the model conditions being encountered during the run.

This type of sensitivity analysis requires multiple runs and can be very time consuming. The RUNOFF module of PCSWMM3 for example takes at least 60 seconds execution time to run a simple single catchment on a personal microcomputer. For ten parameters using the expected value plus one perturbed value each, and allowing for input preparation and output interpretation, the total time spent can exceed hours.

PCSWMM3 and Automated Sensitivity Analysis

Software has been developed which forms a shell around the PCSWMM3 package. The present form of this shell is limited to the Executive (preprocessor) and Runoff modules within the model. Further, the analysis done by the system is limited to quantitative or physical parameters. The analysis has not yet been extended to include quality parameters.

TABLE 1.   PARAMETERS SUBJECT TO SENSITIVITY ANALYSIS

1. Percent of Impervious Area with zero detention storage
2. Width of subcatchment
3. Area of subcatchment
4. Percent Imperviousness of subcatchment
5. Roughness Co-efficient - Impervious Area
6. Roughness Co-efficient - Pervious Area
7. Ground Slope
8. Detention Storage - Impervious Area
9. Detention Storage - Pervious Area
10. Infiltration Rate - Maximum
11. Infiltration Rate - Minimum

The program requires the user upon entering the Auto-Sensitivity (A-S) shell to provide data for eleven parameters within the Runoff block which have been identified as probable causes of variability in the objective function. The Runoff block queries the user for up to approximately 160 variables, model parameters and control parameters. The control parameters query the user for specific methods to be used, e.g., metric or Imperial input units. The model parameters require specific knowledge on the catchment's physical attributes. For this section the Runoff block contains approximately 80 parameters. Of these, roughly 60 are quality related while the remaining 20 are quantitative. The eleven parameters considered in the A-S shell are listed in Table 1. These parameters were selected since they represented essential data which must be entered before the Runoff module is run. These values will be unique for each catchment and subcatchment in a study and their choice can have a significant effect on the output. Figure 1 shows the screen terminal prompts to the user for this information.

```
        ********************************
        *              PCSWMM3         *
        *                BY            *
        * COMPUTATIONAL HYDRAULICS INC.*
        ********************************

    ENTER JOB INITIALS (NNN)              ...  ARD

    ENTER CASE NUMBER (X)                 ...  1

    IS ARDDAT1.DAT A NEW OR OLD SWMM FILE ...  OLD

    RUN AUTO-SENSITIVITY ON ARDDAT1.DAT   (YES/NO)...  YES

    ENTER EXCEEDANCE FLOW TO BE CHECKED : 3.9
```

Figure 1a. Opening Screen.

```
                PC-SWMM3 AUTO-SENSITIVITY

     <Enter lower, then upper value for each prompt>
     1)  % OF IMP. AREA WITH 0 DET. STORAGE: 15.0 30.0
     2)  WIDTH OF SUBCATCHMENT             : 400   450
     3)  AREA OF SUBCATCHMENT              : 9.0   11.0
     4)  % IMPERVIOUSNESS OF SUBCATCHMENT  : 20.0 40.0
     5)  MANNING'S "n" - IMPERVIOUS        : 0.010 0.017
     6)  MANNING'S "n" - PERVIOUS          : 0.017 0.025
     7)  GROUND SLOPE                      : 0.01 0.05
     8)  DETENTION STORAGE - IMPERVIOUS    : 0.03 0.07
     9)  DETENTION STORAGE - PERVIOUS      : 0.10 0.30
    10)  INFILTRATION RATE - MAXIMUM       : 1.0   5.0
    11)  INFILTRATION RATE - MINIMUM       : 0.2   0.4
```

Figure 1b. Parameter Confidence Screen

For each of the eleven parameters, the user must enter two values. The first value represents the lower limit which the user feels approximately 95% certain that the true value is not beneath. Similiarly, the second value represents the upper limit which the user feels certain (95%) that the true value does not lie above. The mean value for these parameters is available in the normal input data set and is not required to be entered by the user again. The 95% certainty level corresponds to a confidence level equivalent to two standard deviations (Benjamin and Cornell, 1970). Both upper and lower bounds are considered since the distribution may be skewed. The standard deviations are used as a measure of the input uncertainty in the data set. For example, for Manning's 'n' the user might feel that the true value is say, 0.013. He/she may also feel that it is 95% likely that whatever the value of 'n' is, it is not below 0.010 nor above 0.025. Thus, although there is uncertainty both above and below the expected value, the uncertainty is skewed with greater uncertainty above than below.

The output objective function is also considered by the A-S model. Functions included are the volume of runoff, mean outflow, peak outflow, volume of runoff exceeding a specified flow rate, and length of time for the exceedance flow. By dividing the change in the output function by the change in each of the input parameters, a sensitivity co-efficient matrix can be generated (Walker, 1982). This sensitivity co-efficient matrix is derived from first order analysis and can be expressed:

$$S_{ij} = (dY_j/dX_i)(X_i/Y_j)$$

The overall uncertainty in the output is dependent on two factors: first, the input certainty associated with the user's estimates, and second, the variability of the output due to perturbations of parameters. These two factors are independent but can be combined to generate an uncertainty rating expressed as a percentage. The A-S routine calculates the total uncertainty associated with each parameter and displays this data along with the cumulative uncertainty for the model run and the relative error associated with each parameter. The relative error is perhaps the most significant data displayed when based on a single model run. Figure 2 shows a sample output from the program based on a hypothetical test catchment.

Conclusions

The output creates a listing ranked in order of sensitivity. This is typical for one run of the A-S on one catchment area under one set of weather conditions. However, these rankings and uncertainties (both input and output) may change under differing climatic conditions (temperature and percipitation). To be truly useful to the model user, sensitivity and uncertainty information needs to be compiled for various weather episodes. By placing these rankings in a matrix with temperature and percipitation on the axis, a knowledge base (KB) could be built. With this type of KB a traditional ES or conventional database application, dBASE III for example, could be used. Under this type of system the ES could extract from the user the weather conditions (generally known) and the

type of catchment under study. By comparing this data with the uncertainty matrix the model could point out parameters which should be carefully chosen and warn the user when results were unreliable due to
environmental problems or input uncertainty factors (Dunn, 1986).

```
RANKINGS FOR    TOTAL VOLUME ; LOCATION 404**********************

RANK      SENS. COEF       VARIABLE    OVERALL      % OF   TOTAL
                                       UNCERTAINTY  UNCERTAINTY

 1          419.183   %IMP OF SUB'T     21.0          29.0
 2         1790.546   MAX INFIL RATE    19.0          26.1
 3         2009.078   AREA OF SUB'T     10.0          13.8
 4         6518.561   PERV. DET STOR     6.8           9.4
 5        10665.440   MIN INFIL RATE     5.5           7.6
 6        25419.920   GROUND SLOPE       4.0           5.5
 7        13653.000   IMP. DET STOR      3.6           5.0
 8        35452.480   PERV MANNING N      .9           1.3
 9            8.057   %IMP.W/ 0 DET.      .8           1.2
10        13248.720   IMP. MANNING N      .5            .7
11            2.418   WIDTH OF SUB'T      .4            .5

CUMULATIVE UNCERTAINTY :        72.5



RANKINGS FOR      MEAN FLOW ; LOCATION 404**********************

RANK      SENS. COEF       VARIABLE    OVERALL      % OF   TOTAL
                                       UNCERTAINTY  UNCERTAINTY

 1            .028   PERV MANNING N     21.0          29.0
 2            .119   MAX INFIL RATE     19.0          26.1
 3            .134   %IMP.W/ 0 DET.     10.0          13.8
 4            .435   AREA OF SUB'T       6.8           9.4
 5            .711   %IMP OF SUB'T       5.5           7.6
 6           1.695   MIN INFIL RATE      4.0           5.5
 7            .910   PERV. DET STOR      3.6           5.0
 8           2.364   GROUND SLOPE         .9           1.3
 9            .001   WIDTH OF SUB'T       .8           1.2
10            .883   IMP. DET STOR        .5            .7
11            .000   IMP. MANNING N       .4            .5

CUMULATIVE UNCERTAINTY :        72.5
```

Figure 2.   Output Data from PCSWMM3 A-S

Acknowledgement

Parts of this paper were previously presented to a meeting on Stormwater Management Modelling held in Toronto in December 1985.

References

Benjamin, J.R. and Cornell, C.A., (1970). Probability, Statistics, and Decision For Civil Engineers, McGraw-Hill, New York, New York.

Bonissone, P., (1984). Proceedings of Conference on Expert Systems and Artificial Intelligence, L'Ecole Polytechnique, Montreal, Quebec, Unpaginated reprint.

Burnash, R.J.C., and Ferral, R.C., (1982). The Significance of Various Parameters in Fitting the Sacramento Model", presented to the Fall Meeting, A.G.U. San Francisco, December 1982, 12 pp.

Dunn, A.R., (1986). Automated Sensitivity Analysis for Stormwater Management, M.Eng. Thesis, to be submitted, McMaster University, Hamilton, Ontario.

James, William and Robinson, M., (1985). PCSWMM3.2 Executive User's Manual, Computational Hydraulics Inc., Hamilton, Ontario.

Koda, Masato, Dogrv, A.H., and Seinfeld, J., (1979). Sensitivity Analysis of Partial Differential Equations with Application to Reaction and Diffusion Processes, Journal of Computational Physics, Vol. 30, pp. 259-282.

Intelligent Central Database System for Synchronized Distributed Processing of Large Hydrologic Packages in Local Area Networks

by

Ali Unal and William James*

Continuous hydrologic modelling on personal computers with large packages like SWMM3 requires a system more sophisticated than conventional mainframe approaches. Continuous modelling applications are demanding both in processing time and input-output (I/O). A single processor executing sequentially with interruptions for manual management of I/O data is extremely inefficient.

The nodes of a local area network can be dedicated to the independent routines of a large hydrologic/hydraulic package. The server of the network can be dedicated to the control of the overall operation, if it contains an intelligent database manager which is primarily dedicated to control the time series data flow between the nodes and the central database of the system.

During a distributed data processing application, the nodes of the network should not wait for data to arrive for an unreasonable span of time. The tasks in the nodes should be synchronized ahead of time so that all processors remain operational at all times. This requires an estimate of the time a certain task is going to take as a function of the constraints in the input data file. Timing functions can be obtained for these tasks through program measurement.

To increase accuracy, such timing functions in the central controller are updated every time a routine is executed with a new input file. The intelligent central control system acknowledges each unique experience, compares with its database and makes decisions on that basis. Then the new experience is integrated into the database. Further synchronization decisions are based on the improved timing functions.

The paper describes the Computational Hydraulics Group-Hydrologic Work Group System (CHG-HWGS) which is operational in a local area network of IBM-PC compatibles. CHG-HWGS incorporates some aspects of an intelligent time series manager which has built in features for distributed processing.

*Computational Hydraulics Group, McMaster University, Hamilton, Ontario, Canada, L8S 4L7.

Introduction

The system studied here is a network of microcomputers connected to a central disk operating system functioning on a server. The system primarily relies on a data base management system (DBMS), most of which is devoted to time-series (TS) data management (James and Unal, 1983). While the server holds the network operating system, each of the nodal computers executes a separable block of logical routines to which it is dedicated. The computational routines may relate to data acquisition, precipitation analysis, runoff modelling, transport or drainage systems networks, water quality modelling, cost-benefit analysis, or statistical post-processing, as the case may be.

For a concurrent processing application, software can be written to ensure that the relevant portion of the TS output from the logically preceding block of programs (for example, the precipitation analysis), is properly completed before the logically subsequent computational procedures are allowed access to the TS (for example, the rainfall/runoff modelling). Thus a series of computational modules could access a central TS database in which the first input TS segment is analysed for storm precipitation by the rainfall module, and when complete, the output TS is made available for that segment to the rainfall/runoff module (perhaps under the control of another user). A simple example is: precipitation TS is processed for year 1979 while rainfall/runoff TS is processed up to year 1978, the transport network is processed up to 1977, the sewage treatment plant processing up to year 1976, and the dispersion of the resulting pollutants in the receiving waters up to year 1975; all of this processing occurring concurrently. This contrasts with the sequential design of USEPA Stormwater Management Model (SWMM) (Huber, et al., 1981).

Microcomputer-based distributed processing (DISP) has evolved from the traditional mainframe environment with its multi-user and multi-processing capabilities (i.e. multi-tasking). The mainframe database used by a group of engineers or scientists is also maintained on a central disk system with magnetic tape backup capabilities. Such a database could also easily be made coherent and available to every member of the research and development group with appropriate security safeguards (James and Unal, 1984b).

Identification of Solutions

Continuous modelling using a large urban storm water package like SWMM3 in a sequential time-sharing computing environment, creates two significant problems: 1) it makes manual management of I/O TS data virtually impossible and 2) it provides a non-cost-effective computing process. Solutions to these problems lie in the selected application of recent advances in computer technology to computational hydrology.

A specially adapted, applications-oriented DBMS which provides easy access to TS data, independent of details of storage can reduce the I/O data management problem. Such a TS system was developed by Johanson et

al. (1980).   The DBMS must handle variable resolution continuous TS
records efficiently (Robinson et al., 1984).

Computing efficiency can be significantly improved by replacing
sequential processing with parallel processing in which independent portions of a large package execute concurrently in a properly linked configuration of PC's.   Note that concurrent processing can also be achieved
in a mainframe environment using multi-user features, but that a PC
network is inherently more reliable (James and Unal, 1984a).

In a distributed-processing (DISP), linked configuration of single-
user microcomputers (i.e. local area networks or LAN's), the advantages
of personal computing replaces the inconvenience of a time-sharing multi-
user system.   On the other hand, DISP schemes generate further problems
such as synchronization.

For efficiency, parallel computing is of limited use if the processing in the nodes is not carefully synchronized, such that all the nodes
are computing all the time.   This of course requires a reasonably accurate estimation of execution times at any given instant for any application.   Program measurement (PM) can be applied to obtain timing relations
of computational modules (Unal and James, 1984b).

In other words, for continuous hydrologic modelling, a central
control software with TS-based data management and synchronization assistance, is an attractive alternative to sequential processing.   DISP can
be used for parallel processing in a LAN to improve computing efficiency
as well as for real-time control (RTC) applications for distributed data
gathering, management and decision making. RTC has strict time requirements.   Synchronization aspects of the central control system may allow
the system to shift between empirical (black-box) models and deterministic models which are more accurate but more time consuming.   This of
course, will improve the accuracy of the real-time decisions.

The needs of a Computational Hydraulics/Hydrology Work Group (CHWG)
are:

1.   Reliable storage, maintenance and management of a continuous
      TS-oriented hydrologic database for both query and computa-
      tional applications,

2.   Retrieval of this database for single user access (e.g. sequen-
      tial processing),

3.   Retrieval of this database for multiple user access with no
      DISP,

4.   DISP in a LAN (e.g. synchronized, parallel processing for
      continuous modelling applications to optimize computing),

5.   DISP for RTC.

Results from a simulated case study for DISP in a LAN are presented in this paper. A DISP case study for RTC requires the proper hardware and communications set-up which were not available for this study. Minimum requirements for a distributed RTC system are: microcomputer-based remote monitoring and telemetering, radio communication link, microcomputer controlled diversion structures and a central computer with the hard disk and tape drive (Haro, 1984). Nevertheless, a similar system is being used for current CHG projects. CHWGS has been constantly evolving with the expanding data management requirements of Computational Hydraulics Group (CHG) and forms a central part of our CHG's computational operations.

Query and Computational Operations of the CHG Time Series Manager (CHGTSM)

CHGTSM can be used for two different types of operations: 1) query operations and 2) computational operations (Unal, 1984). Query operations are usually intended to display the contents of CHGTSS. On the other hand, computational operations prepare input data files abstracted from the CHG Time Series Store (CHGTSS), to be utilized by computational modules. The output files from these programs are later integrated into the database. Of course, some applications may involve both query and computational operations.

Query Operations

Most of the commercially available DBMS are query-oriented. These operations present the contents of a database in an orderly manner. In any research group such as CHG, report generation constitutes the final phase of a study. Tabular as well as graphic displays of TS data such as rainfall, runoff, streamflow, pollutant loadings, wind speed, water levels, and temperature form a crucial part of a report. In the visual displays, data can be presented with different time requirements (e.g., in minutes, hours, and days). The time increments in displays may be different from the original time increments at which the data was collected. An automatic aggregation-disaggregation process is essential (Robinson et al., 1984).

Computational Operations

Computational operations require some of the query operations to extract the requested span of data. Some applications will simply require the abstracted TSS data to be prepared as input to a computational module. Other applications may demand an analysis of data during abstraction, such as statistical analysis. I/O handlers are required to input data into TSS from external sources or output data for external sources. For common external sources (e.g., CHG computational programs) the output handlers are built into CHGTSM. Input handlers are required to be written any time a new source of data is discovered.

CHGTSS

CHGTSS is a rapidly expanding database. It archives, maintains and builds the TS data which is relevant to CHG's computational operations. It currently includes rain, runoff and pollutant TS data for the City of Hamilton and rain data for the City of Toronto (Nimmrichter, 1986). Tape backup has to be an integral part of CHGTSM operations.

The Toronto database includes rain data, collected at 5 minute time steps. Data extends from 1975 for most stations to 1984 for a total of 15 stations and 141 station years.

The raw Toronto data had a size of 52.2 MBytes before being processed by CHGTSM. CHGTSM compresses the data at 2 levels: external and internal. A simple handler converted the data to the requirements of CHGTSM. Once all the data is included in CHGTSS its size is compressed to 18.4 MBytes. Total storage savings were 33.8 MBytes (88.8%). Savings for the Toronto database can be compared to theoretical expectations of 91% - 78%.

CHGTSM I/O Handlers

CHGTSM requires handlers to input data from external sources or to output data to application packages (Unal and James, 1984a). Output handlers are usually built into CHGTSM. Input handlers are used as an external utility package to link the source of data to CHGTSM.

Input Handlers

An integrated package of input handlers for CHGTSM, has recently been developed by Robinson (Robinson and James, 1984). The package was used to transfer data from CHG's data acquisition system to the Hamilton database. It is now possible to enter data directly from the Timex-Sinclair 1000 Microcomputer data acquisition system (Stirrup, 1986). Rainfall data collected by the TS1000 data logger is transferred to an IBM-PC compatible microcomputer using program TSDASUTIL (written in Sinclair BASIC) (Stirrup, 1986). This is where the handler takes over and links the data to CHGTSM. The CHGTSM handler package was also used to transform the City of Toronto database which was then entered into CHGTSS. In can translate data from AES formats. The output from external application packages (i.e. SWMM3) requires input handlers, if they are to be stored in CHGTSS. These handlers have to be built every time a new application package that is expected to produce valuable data is adapted.

Output Handlers

Currently CHGTSM can output data for PCSWMM3 computational modules functioning in continuous or event mode. Because PCSWMM3 is being used extensively in CHG, the handler (TSCONT) is transparent to the user, allowing him to prepare data with little or no inconvenience. Handlers are also available for analysis and preparation of data for the RAINPAK package (TSEVNT)(Nimmrichter, 1986). As far as query operations are concerned, CHGTSM can display data in a tabular form. A handler to link CHGTSM to a graphics package is currently being developed by Robinson.

The user is able to access any period of data of any station with full independence from the details of storage. When a year of TS data is to be analysed, CHGTSM requests the user to define the inter-event period. Assuming a definition of 60 minutes, CHGTSM isolates every span of TS data in the record which is separated by more than 60 minutes of dry weather. CHGTSM then gives the number of storms identified. At this point the user has an option to request one more year of data to be analyzed or can choose to sort the isolated storms.

Conclusions

The new database access method was developed to better serve the needs of variable resolution continuous hydrologic modelling. CHGTSM is menu driven, specialized, applications as well as query-oriented DBMS. It is specialized not only because of the unconventional access method but because it serves the needs of hydrologic applications. It has the capability to aggregate and disaggregate TS data, store variable resolution or constant time-step TS data and compress the TS data to occupy minimum physical space once it is stored in the hard disk. CHGTSM compressed a raw 52.2 Mbytes rainfall data (Toronto data) to 18.4 Mbytes, saving 88.8% in the process. CHGTSM prepares data files for event modelling applications (TSEVNT) as well as continuous modelling. TSEVNT was developed and implemented in CHGTSM as an I/O handler. It was used in the Toronto study to isolate 31466 storms from a 18.3 Mbytes (52 Mbytes before compression) database with inter-event periods defined as 60 minutes. CHGTSM ranked these storms by volume, duration and maximum intensity as well as chronologically with acceptable speed. CHGTSM isolates and ranks 120-160 storms (a typical year for Toronto database) in about 2-3 minutes of processing. For a continuous modelling application (e.g., Chedoke Creek Study) 6 months of data is aggregated/disaggregated to 5 minute time intervals (e.g., 52000 timesteps, e.g., 300 Kbytes) in about 4 minute of processing. Data was originally collected with variable time steps (e.g., 1 minute and 60 minute). All timing performances quoted are valid for the 16-bit 8088-based CORONA with 8087 coprocessor operating under MS-DOS 2.1. CHGTSM was written in FORTRAN and compiled using MS-FORTRAN 3.2 (Unal, 1985).

The computing resources of CHG are integrated by a LAN (CHGLAN). A LAN is a sufficient environment for DISP. DISP of centralized data for parallel processing of the independent modules of PCSWMM3 can be achieved through CHGTSM. The CHG Distributed Processing System (CHGDPS) was developed as a shell around DISP applications for continuous modelling, DISP was found to be 54% faster than sequential processing of the same problem. Final results could be faster if the processing is synchronized more carefully. The timing performances of the hydrologic modules used in CHG are formulated using programming measurement (PM) techniques (e.g. PMRUNOFF, PMEXTRAN, PMRAINPAK) (Unal and James, 1984b). To achieve this conventional PM techniques were adapted and enhanced for accurate timing.

The resulting timing relations are a part of CHGDPS, and could assist users with synchronization.

In selecting a computational module for a continuous hydrologic modelling problem, time and memory requirements of the computing system have to considered side by side with the physical and numerical require- ments of the mathematical model. CHGDPS as the central controller of CHWGS can be expanded to acquire the intelligence to assist the user with the choice. An alternating explicit/implicit solution method for EXTRAN is such a case. In RTC applications CHGDPS could switch between a deter- ministic and a conceptual model with no user intervention.

An upgraded intelligent data management system can manage a vast time series store which is held by hard disks and magnetic tapes, to store all the time series experience of the group in relation to urban stormwater modelling. It should ultimately give the user an option for automatic sensitivity analysis and calibration and assist with planning decisions. It should incorporate colour dislays and sophisticated graphics routines and should be adaptable to real-time control applica- tions. Its interface with the user should evolve to handle the ambigui- ties in the user's request and responses.

Clearly, programs like CHGTSM make continuous modelling more attrac- tive to engineers in a PC environment. This will hopefully result in more engineers using continuous modelling. Continuous modelling can give much better estimates of crucial environmental parameters, which will help cities plan, design and take proper precautions where necessary. The new work group scheme is cheaper, faster, more efficient and more adaptable than earlier methods. Work group co-operation that results from the new scheme improves productivity substantially.

Acknowledgements

This paper has beed abstracted from a longer recent paper by the same authors entitled "Distributed Continuous Hydrologic Processing Using Microcomputer Networks", presented to the Conference on Stormwater and Water Quality Modelling, held in Toronto, December 5-6, 1985. Funding was provided by research grants to Dr. James by the Natural Sciences and Engineering Research Council in Canada.

References

Haro, H., (1984). "Instrumentation for Rainfall Sampling", Ph.D. Thesis, McMaster University, 222 pp.

Huber, W.C., Heaney, J.P., Nix, S.J., Dickinson, R.E. and Polman, D.J., (1981). "Storm Water Management Model User's Manual Version III", Muni- cipal Environmental Research Center, USEPA, EPA-600/8-79-004, 531 pp.

James, W. and Unal, A., (1984a). "Database Management System for Urban Stormwater Modelling", 3rd International Conference on Urban Storm Drainage, Goteborg, published by Chalmers University of Technology, Sweden, pp. 1377-1386.

James, W. and Unal, A., (1984b). "CHGTSM - A Combined Hydrologic Time Series and Topographic Database Manager", Proceedings of the Stormwater and Water Quality Modelling Meeting, USEPA, Detroit, Michigan, EPA-600/9-85-003, pp. 217-232.

James, W. and Unal, A., (1983). "Computational Hydraulics System as Distributed Data Management", Recent Developments in Computer Applications in Civil Engineering, Canadian Society for Civil Engineering, 1983 Annual Conference, Ottawa, pp. 129-142.

Johanson, R.C., Imhoff, J.C. and Davis, H., Jr. (1980). "User's Manual for Hydrologic Simulation Program - FORTRAN (HSPF)". Environmental Research Laboratory, Office of Research Development, USEPA, EPA-600/2-77-064c, 678 pp.

Nimmrichter, P., (1986). "Dynamics of Storms on the Western Shore of Lake Ontario", M.Eng. Thesis, McMaster University, ca. 150 pp.

Robinson, M.A. and James, W., (1984). "Chedoke Creek Flood Storage Computed by Continuous SWMM3", CHI Report R124, to Hamilton-Wentworth Regional Engineering Department, Hamilton, ca. 150 pp.

Robinson, M.A., James, W. and Unal, A., (1984). "Continuous Variable Resolution Stormwater Modelling on a Microcomputer Using a Central Hydrologic Database Manager", Proceedings of the Canadian Hydrology Symposium, Quebec City, Quebec. Published by National Research Council of Canada, NRCC No. 24633, pp. 499-514.

Scheckenberger, R., (1983). "Dynamic Spatially Variable Rain Models for Stormwater Management", M.Eng. Thesis, McMaster University, 136 pp.

Stirrup, M., (1986). "Real-Time Microcomputer Control and Data Logging for Stormwater Diversion Structures", M.Eng. Thesis, McMaster University, 189 pp.

Unal, A., (1984). "Computational Hydraulics Group Time Series Management System - User's Manual", CHI Report R125, Hamilton, 50 pp.

Unal, A., (1986). "Centralized Time Series Management for Continuous Urban Runoff Modelling on PC's", Ph.D. Thesis, McMaster University.

Unal, A. and James, W., (1984a). "Centralized Time Series Management Programs for Continuous SWMM3 on Personal Microcomputers", Proceedings of the Stormwater and Water Quality Modelling Conference, USEPA, Burlington, Ontario, pp. 91-100.

Unal, A. and James, W., (1984b). "SWMM3 Program Measurement for Optimal Use of Personal Microcomputer Network", Proceedings of the Stormwater and Water Quality Modelling Conference, USEPA, Burlington, Ontario, pp. 101-110.

An Expert System for Snowmelt Runoff Modeling and Forecasting

E. T. Engman, A. Rango, and J. Martinec*

ABSTRACT

An expert system has been designed and is being built for predicting snowmelt runoff. The expert system mimics an experienced hydrologist by assisting the user in preparing data input, selecting parameters, and evaluating results. The expert system is built around an existing FORTRAN simulation model and is run on a LISP machine that can interpret the FORTRAN model without having to reprogram it.

INTRODUCTION

Research in the past few decades has produced a large number of complex computer models that simulate various hydrologic processes. In spite of these seemingly "better" models, practicing engineers have been reluctant to use them. One reason is that the data requirements for complex models are great and the number of parameters is usually large. For many cases the types of data are unavailable and there are few guidelines for choosing the parameters for a location different from where the model was developed. In addition, studies by Loague and Freeze (1985) and Naef (1981) demonstrated that the complex models do not necessarily yield better results. It is suspected that the people who develop the models generally have better success than others because they have a better, almost innate, sense for how to use data and select parameters.

This current status of complex hydrologic models (i.e., data intensive, many subjective decisions required by the user, and user must be a well trained expert in the area) have characteristics that appear ideal for developing an expert system. Expert systems are specific computer software processes that are capable of carrying out reasoning and analysis much like a well trained human.

An ideal application of expert systems is for solving well defined problems requiring high levels of expertise that are not always available. Typical applications involve interpretation of vast amounts of data, or interpretation of data that is very repetitive or is acquired at all hours of the day. Other applications involve problems requiring many years of experience and a large store of unusual facts associated with that experience. Thus, an expert system is based upon encoding the human expert's knowledge, along with an "inference procedure" or logical decision making process. The result

*Respectively, Research Hydrologist, and Research Leader, USDA-ARS Hydrology Laboratory, Beltsville, MD 20705; Hydrologist, Federal Institute for Snow and Avalanche Research, Weissfluhjoch/Davos, Switzerland.

is a computer program which, acting like a human expert, makes decisions based on knowledge, experience, and judgment.

In developing an expert system, the programmer programs the computer on what to do without telling it how to do it. This is a major demarkation from historic computer programming, which is typically a structured set of instructions telling the computer how to work on a set of data. This has historically resulted in a very powerful and fast analysis tool for specific problems but not a very flexible tool for handling missing data, deductive processes, or poorly defined parameters.

Recent advances in the field of Artificial Intelligence (AI), coupled with corresponding advances in speed, capacity, and reduced cost of computers, makes it practical to develop expert systems. This paper describes an expert system being developed for an existing snowmelt runoff simulation model. The expert system encodes the experience of the model developers to assist a new user in setting up the input data, selecting parameters and coefficients, and adjusting these values when simulated and measured runoff do not match. The strategy has been to use an existing simulation model that has been well documented and tested. Thus, we could concentrate on simplifying the different steps a user must take without dissecting and reprogramming the model per se. This is an important objective because, if successful, the same general approach can be used for almost any other existing simulation models. That is, an expert system can be built around the existing model, as a front end to handle input and parameter estimation, and as a rear end to evaluate the results and provide feedback to fine-tune the model.

THE SNOWMELT-RUNOFF MODEL

The snowmelt-runoff model (SRM; also referred to in the literature as the "Martinec model" or the "Martinec-Rango model") is designed to simulate and forecast daily streamflow in mountain basins where snowmelt is a major runoff factor. SRM was developed by Martinec (1975) in small European basins. With the advent of satellite snow-cover data in the 1970's, it became possible to test SRM in larger basins. Using Landsat data the model was successfully applied to various sized basins in the United States and Europe (Rango and Martinec, 1979; Rango, 1980; and Jones et al., 1981). In addition to the input of snow-cover data, SRM requires only the input of temperature and precipitation on a daily basis. Each day during the snowmelt season, the water produced from snowmelt and from rainfall is computed, superimposed on the calculated recession flow, and transformed into the daily discharge from the basin.

Model Variables and Input Data

Basin Characteristics. The basin should be divided into zones of equal elevation at intervals of about 500 m (or 1500 ft). An area-elevation curve is used for determining the zonal hypsometric mean elevation ($\bar{h}$) by a trial and error graphical procedure. The $\bar{h}$ value is used as the elevation to which base station temperatures are extrapolated for the calculation of snowmelt.

Temperature and Degree-Days. Air temperature expressed in degree-days is used in SRM as an index of the complex energy balance leading to snowmelt. The model can employ either hourly temperature input or daily maximum-minimum temperatures.

Precipitation. Measurement of representative precipitation amounts in a mountain basin is extremely difficult. Extrapolation of precipitation amounts from one or more base stations to zones in the basin must be based on user knowledge of the study area. Location of a precipitation station at each hypsometric mean elevation of the basin would be optimum.

If precipitation is determined to fall in the basin on a given day, a critical temperature, T_{CRIT}, must be examined to determine whether the precipitation is rain or snow. T_{CRIT} is usually selected to be slightly above the freezing point and may vary from basin to basin. The distinction between rain and snow is important in SRM because the rain contribution to runoff is on the same day that the rain occurs, whereas the snow contribution to runoff is delayed.

Snow Coverage. The snow-cover variable, S, of an elevation zone or basin is usually obtained from a variety of sources of snow-cover data including ground observations, aircraft photography, and satellite imagery. If the data are available, it is recommended that satellite imagery be used since it is the easiest to analyze.

Model Parameters

Degree-Day Factor and Lapse Rate. The degree-day factor is used to convert degree-days to snowmelt expressed in depth of water. In the absence of detailed temperature and snow pillow or lysimeter data, the degree-day factor can be obtained from an empirical equation developed by Martinec (1980).

The calculated degree-day values must be extrapolated from a base station to each elevation zone using a suitable lapse rate. The temperature lapse rate must be carefully determined, especially if the observation station is situated at a low altitude and the extrapolation of degree-days is made in only one direction (upwards). The lapse rate should be indicative of the mountainous region where the basin is located and based on prior climatic data.

Runoff Coefficient. The model requires a runoff coefficient, c, that is a ratio of runoff to rainfall. Because the runoff coefficient is likely to vary throughout the year as a result of changing vegetation and soil moisture conditions, the SRM computer program permits changes in c every 15 days. Usually, c is higher for snowmelt than for rainfall. Therefore, the model can handle different runoff coefficients for snow, c_S, and for rain, c_R, as determined by the user.

Recession Coefficient. The recession coefficient, k, is related exponentially to the current stream discharge. The k value must be determined by graphical procedures computed from daily discharge data for the given basin. For this determination, daily discharge values for the snowmelt season or the whole year are used. If no discharge data

are available for a basin, recession coefficients can be estimated
from empirical formulas based on basin size.

Time Lag. Snowmelt runoff is computed for a time lag between the
rise in temperature and the rise of the hydrograph of 18 hours. If
the time lag is not conveniently 18 hours, the computed discharge
values must be shifted by a certain number of hours to facilitate
comparison with published streamflow data. In large basins with
multiple elevation zones, the time lag changes during the snowmelt
season as a result of the changing spatial distribution of snow cover
with respect to the basin outlet.

The various inputs and parameters are represented schematically in
Figure 1. Selecting each of these input variables and model parameters
requires a hydrologist with considerable training and experience. The
expert system being developed at the Hydrology Laboratory is addressing
each of these so that all will become part of the expert system that
drives SRM.

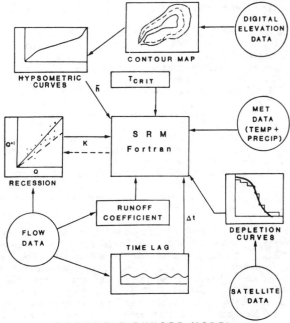

Figure 1.   Schematic of the snowmelt runoff model
and its various inputs.

COMPUTER HARDWARE AND SOFTWARE

The expert system is being developed on a SYMBOLICS* 3670 LISP machine. The 3670 is a single user minicomputer with demand-paged virtual memory (6 M bytes real memory and 474 M bytes of fixed disk storage). The machine uses a tagged architecture with a 36 bit word (4 bits for addressing). The machine uses a high resolution bit-mapped screen for a highly interactive programming environment and an integrated mouse for invoking software and graphics. Our SYMBOLICS also has a color system with a separate color monitor.

The native language for the machine is ZETA LISP. LISP is the symbolic processing language (LISt Processing) upon which many of the current AI applications are based. LISP machines are able to run LISP programs 5 to 10 times faster than conventional computers because primitive instructions have been implemented directly into the hardware.

In addition to ZETA LISP, a FORTRAN 77 tool kit enables us to use SRM (a FORTRAN model) without modification and without rewriting it in LISP. The FORTRAN tool kit effectively converts to FORTRAN code to LISP but allows us to run and interact with it as if it were FORTRAN.

We have also added an expert system tool kit, Automated Reasoning Tool (ART)*, to the SYMBOLICS. ART is a comprehensive software package that simplifies the building of full-scale expert systems. ART contains an inference engine, a knowledge base, an editor, and a monitor. The system is based on LISP but is more efficient in that each line of ART can represent several lines of LISP code.

EXPERT SYSTEM STRATEGY

The expert system being developed for the snowmelt-runoff model depends on use of high resolution graphics and a comprehensive user interface. Some of the code is written in LISP and some uses the ART language. The overall scheme is shown in Figure 2. The SRM FORTRAN model is not altered in any way. The expert system, per se, is the total of the various activities involved in data preparation and parameter selection shown exterior to SRM.

The ART program is the overall expert system manager (ES Manager) of the system. Within the ART code resides the knowledge base and the various rules that call the LISP and FORTRAN codes. The knowledge base initially consists of data and other operation-specific information, such as location of basin and weather stations. During the preparation to run phase, ART or called LISP code prepares the necessary input parameters and data. Once this has been completed, the ES Manager calls the FORTRAN model and instructs it to compute the snowmelt. As snowmelt is computed, the results are continually evaluated by the ES Manager, either by comparing simulated results to measured data or by user evaluation (judgment). If the results are not satisfactory, the user can make a series of machine-guided modifications, which generally

*The citation of particular products or companies is for the convenience of the reader and does not imply any endorsement, guarantee, or preferential treatment by the U.S. Department of Agriculture or its agents.

consist of recalculating parameters or changing coefficients according to preestablished rules. New parameters or coefficients modify the knowledge base and automatically trigger recomputation. This general process with the ES Manager is shown in Figure 2.

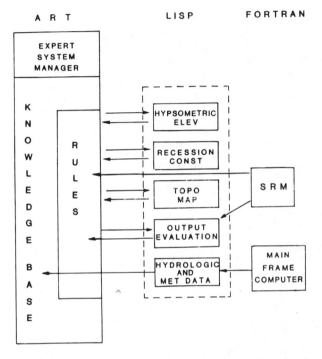

Figure 2. Schematic showing how the knowledge base and rules in the Expert System Manager interact with LISP and FORTRAN codes.

In general, we have used LISP code for reading data files from a large main-frame computer and for doing the interactive graphics. The color monitor is used for display of the basin contours and various overlays, such as the snow cover area. The interactive graphics enable one to input data to the program by mouse-tracking curves and by trial-and-error curve fitting to get satisfactory results. The user is guided by screen instructions and by menus that pop-up when decisions must be made by the user.

Graphics are also useful for the user to evaluate how well the model is predicting runoff. Graphical comparison of simulated and measured runoff will enable a user to make instant decisions as to whether or not the model is behaving satisfactorily.

One advantage to this approach is that parts of the expert system can be implemented as they are completed without affecting the model operation. Since the FORTRAN code itself is not changed, historic inputs and parameter estimation can be mixed with the expert system developed inputs and parameters. Thus, as the expert system grows and encompasses more of the model inputs, the need to do things in the "old way" will be eliminated.

Extending this thought a step further, it is hoped that the expert system will be able to "learn" from experience. The role of snowmelt forecasting is to predict runoff for a specific basin year after year. Extreme events usually cause the forecaster problems because his experience had not previously encountered such events. The expert system would behave similarly; thus, it would not be able to do better than the experienced forecaster for the unusual events. However, the expert system should be able to "remember" these events by storing them in the data base. Once remembered, it should be able to profit from this when a new event, some time in the future, has data characteristics that indicate it may be unusual.

CONCLUSIONS

The eventual destination for EXSRM, the expert system for snowmelt runoff, will be in the offices of reservoir and river basin managers. It is expected that after development is complete, the system can be installed in a smaller, less expensive single purpose expert system computer for dedicated snowmelt work. Long-range plans also include adding an image analysis expert system to help the user interpret the satellite snow cover data for input to the model.

REFERENCES

Loague, K. M. and R. A. Freeze, "A comparison of rainfall-runoff modeling techniques on small upland watersheds," Water Resources Research Vol. 21, No. 2, 1985, pp. 229-248.

Naef, F., "Can we model the rainfall-runoff process today?," Hydrologic Science Bulletin, Vol. 26, No. 3, 1981, pp. 281-289.

Jones, E. B., B. A. Shafer, A. Rango, and D. M. Frick, "Application of a snowmelt model to two drainage basins in Colorado," Proceedings of the 49th Annual Western Snow Conference, St. George, Utah, 1981, pp. 43-54.

Martinec, J., "Snowmelt-runoff model for streamflow forecasts," Nordic Hydrology, Vol. 6, No. 3, 1975, pp. 145-154.

Martinec, J., "Hydrologic basin models," In: Remote Sensing Applications in Agriculture and Hydrology, Fraysee, G., editor, A. A. Balkema, Rotterdam, 1980, pp. 447-459.

Rango, A., "Remote sensing of snow covered area for runoff modelling," Hydrological Forecasting (Proceedings of the Oxford Symposium), IAHS Publication No. 129, Oxford, U.K., 1980, pp. 291-297.

Rango, A. and J. Martinec, "Application of a snowmelt-runoff model using Landsat data," Nordic Hydrology Vol. 10, No. 4, 1979, pp. 225-238.

Incorporating Judgement Into An Optimiz
of a Wastewater Treatment Syste

by
James J. Geselbracht[1]
E. Downey Brill, Jr., M. ASCE[2]
John T. Pfeffer, M. ASCE[2]

The environmental engineer has access to a number of different tools with which to explore the nuances of complex problems. Many tools are available which allow for the efficient manipulation of models of the quantitative aspects of a problem but leave issues which are not easily quantified to the experience and judgement of the engineer. Because of this limitation, some such issues may remain unexplored. The field of artificial intelligence, and more specifically expert or rule-based systems, offers a potential means of expanding the engineer's tool kit. Rule-based systems can utilize fuzzy logic to model uncertainties in the interaction of evidence (eg. process conditions) to an outcome (eg. evaluation of design).

One application of such a tool is the evaluation of activated sludge wastewater treatment plant designs. While such plants are widely used throughout the world, an operational problem known as sludge bulking commonly occurs. Sludge bulking is a condition where the solids coming from the aeration basin settle poorly because of changes in the population of microorganisms in the sludge. If the condition is bad enough, the solids are lost over the secondary clarifier effluent weir thus violating the discharge permit.

The exact cause of sludge bulking, and the ability to predict its occurrence, has proven elusive to researchers over the years. A number of factors have been associated with the problem, but the connections are not direct. The value of several design variables (dissolved oxygen concentration, aeration tank loading, etc.) seem to affect the bulking potential of a plant. By the proper selection of the process variables, a plant can be designed to minimize the likelihood of developing problems.

----

[1]Kereomel Environmental Systems Analysts, 305 W. Washington, #1, Champaign, IL 61820; formerly Grad. Student, Univ. of Illinois at Urbana-Champaign

[2]Professor of Civil Engineering and Environmental Studies and Professor of Sanitary Engineering, respectively, Univ. of Illinois at Urbana-Champaign, 208 N. Romine, Urbana, IL 61801

...er of design guidelines exist which are meant to keep
    occurence of bulking problems in activated sludge
...ants to a minimum. These guidelines are in many cases
conflicting. In the final analysis, the designers must
utilize their judgement and past experience to make a
qualitative decision regarding the appropriate design.

Such a process of quantitative design and qualitative
evaluation can become cumbersome when the number of designs
to be evaluated is large. For example, a model of the
activated sludge process might be used to find the cost-
optimal design subject to effluent quality constraints and
a given set of design conditions (flow, influent
characteristics, local cost information, etc.) (2). If an
additional qualitative constraint is added which requires a
design with a low likelihood of experiencing bulking
problems, the optimization model loses its power. It is
unreasonable to expect the engineer to evaluate the large
number of designs which, at least implicitly, are
considered during the optimization process. The use of
design variable constraints according to textbook and state
design standards would ease the burden on the engineer, but
might cause potentially good designs to be missed and would
not capture the fuzzy interaction of design conditions
leading to bulking problems. A better approach might be to
use a rule-based system to model the qualitative evaluation
and incorporate that into the optimization model.

The rules used to model the judgement regarding bulking
problems initially were obtained from the published
research regarding the factors which various researchers
had felt might be related to the development of bulking
problems (1). Those rules were then arranged into a logic
structure which simultaneously considers the truth of those
rules and then determines the likelihood of such a design
experiencing bulking problems. An example of the rule
structure is shown in Figure 1.

Calibration

Significant problems in the modeling of the fuzzy
interaction of pieces of evidence and their association to
the overall conclusion are determining the weights of
association of the different pieces of evidence to a
hypothesis, and also determining the propositional operator
which might best describe their logical interaction. The
process of finding the weights and operators used in the
model is referred to here as its calibration.

In many cases, the model is calibrated through analysis of
historical data. The weights might be determined by
finding the conditional probability of the occurence of the
conclusion given the existence of the evidence. In the
absence of sufficient historical data, the knowledge base

might be calibrated by asking an expert for an opinion as to the proper weighting and logical arrangement of the evidence.

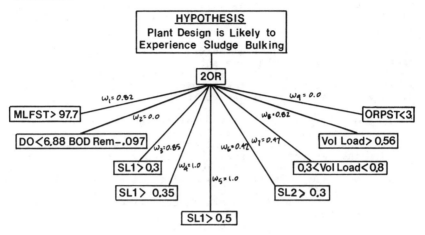

Figure 1

SAMPLE RULE BASE

Notes:
D.O.=Dissolved Oxygen Concentration, Aeration Tank (mg/L)
MLFST=Mass Loading, Final Settling Tank (kg/sq.m day)
BOD Rem= BOD_5 Removal Rate (kg BOD_5/kg MLVSS d)
ORPST=Overflow Rate, Primary Settling Tank (m/hr)
SL1=Sludge Loading, Aeration Tank (kg BOD_5/kg MLSS day)
SL2=Sludge Loading, Aeration Tank (kg BOD_5/kg MLVSS day)
VolLoad=Volumetric Sludge Loading (kg BOD_5/cu.m day)

When using fuzzy logic, several propositional operators may be used to combine evidence. The most familiar operators are AND (where the minimum branch truth value is passed to the conclusion--e.g., if one of a group of rules considered is false, then the conclusion is false) and OR (the maximum truth value is passed--e.g., if one of a group of rules being considered is true, then the conclusion is true). If the OR operator is used, the most heavily weighted piece of evidence which is satisfied would control the truth value of the conclusion no matter what the value of the other weighted branch values. Because of this limitation, the use of other possible propositional operators was explored. The XOR operator takes the weighted average of the X greatest branch truth values and passes that value on to the conclusion. Thus the X most heavily weighted pieces of

evidence which are satisfied control the truth value of the
conclusion. The use of such operators might make sense
where, for example in the case of the 2OR operator, if two
pieces of evidence were satisfied, the conclusion's truth
value is fairly certain, no matter what the other evidence
is.

The weights of the various rules, and the propositional
operator used in a rule-base such as that shown in figure 1
were needed in order that it might accurately mimic the
evaluations given by the experienced engineer. The
calibration technique was as follows:

1. A set of 15 different plant designs was given to an
    expert for his evaluation.
2. The weights of each rule were allowed to vary and
    the weight combination which gave results which
    best fit the expert's evaluation was said to be the
    best-fit model. These weights were determined for
    each of 11 rule structures and the fits of each
    structure were compared to determine the best rule-
    structure to use.
3. The consistency of both the model and the expert
    were checked with a second set of 15 designs. The
    model, using the best-fit structure and weights
    found previously, performed well in predicting the
    evaluation that the expert would give.

The calibration of the sludge bulking judgement model
showed some interesting results. First, the best fits were
obtained when the 9 rules were simultaneously combined into
the 2OR and 3OR propositional operators. Second, the
values of the weights of association of each rule to the
conclusion depended on the operator into which the rules
branched, and the other rules which were being
simultaneously considered. Third, those best-fit weight
values were not unique. Rather other, nearly optimal,
alternative weight combinations could be found.

Results such as these point to the possible danger of the
other methods of calibration. Weights found by interview
or statistical survey techniques might be valid for only
the logic structure which is presented in the interview or
survey. The addition of more rules or the use of a
different operator might require a new set of weights.

Optimization with Judgement

Once the model was calibrated, it was incorporated into the
judgement model in a straight-forward manner; each rule
became a constraint in the optimization model and the
weighted sum of each rule's satisfaction (i.e., true=1,
false=0) determined the likelihood of that design
experiencing bulking problems.

By solving the optimization model for each combination of
constraint values, an idea of the tradeoff between optimal
plant cost and the likelihood of bulking can be found.
Table 1 shows cost-optimal plant designs for five different
likelihoods of bulking. Those designs satisfy an influent
with a flow of 1500 cu.m/hr, soluble BOD_5 of 100 mg/L,
total suspended solids (TSS) of 200 mg/L, and discharge
standards of 30 mg/L for both effluent BOD_5 and TSS.
Additionally, each design uses an aeration tank dissolved
oxygen concentration of 1.5 mg/L. For that problem, the
cost-optimal solution has a rather high likelihood of
experiencing bulking problems and a design with a low
likelihood of bulking may be obtained at only about a 10%
increase over the optimal cost when bulking is not
considered.

Table 1
Cost-Optimal Designs

Likelihood	.137	.162	.374	.586	.849
Cost ($/yr)	548,662	542,696	522,494	514,210	498,227
Eff. BOD_5 (mg/L)	18.7	18.5	22.0	24.3	30.0
Eff. TSS (mg/L)	30.0	30.0	30.0	30.0	30.0
Sludge Age (days)	4.7	4.8	3.5	2.9	2.2
Recycle (%)	10	13	13	12	14
Volume A.T. (m^3)	13,390	11,430	8210	7310	5030
Area F.S.T. (m^2)	660	700	700	690	710
MLVSS (mg/L)	1000	1200	1200	1150	1230
MLSS (mg/L)	1400	1675	1675	1600	1720
BOD Rem	0.27	0.28	0.37	0.42	0.54
SL1	0.21	0.22	0.30	0.35	0.48
SL2	0.30	0.30	0.42	0.49	0.67
Vol Load	0.30	0.36	0.50	0.56	0.83
MLFST	84.8	97.7	97.7	94.3	99.6

Notes:
BOD Rem: BOD_5 Removal in Aeration Tank, kg BOD_5/ kg MLVSS d
SL1: Sludge Loading, Aeration Tank, kg BOD_5/kg MLSS day
SL2: Sludge Loading, Aeration Tank, kg BOD_5/kg MLVSS day
Vol Load: Aeration Tank Volumetric Loading, kg BOD_5/cu.m d
MLFST: Mass Loading, Final Settling Tank, kg MLSS/sq.m day

Other Applications

The use of a rule-based system for the evaluation of
activated sludge plant designs has shown promising results.
That system has been incorporated into an optimization
model so that good, cost-effective designs could be found.
While the judgement model regarding bulking problems was
fit to one experienced engineer's judgement regarding the
potential for bulking problems, that same model could be
easily calibrated for any other engineer's judgement.

There are many other potential applications of models of
judgement in the realm of wastewater engineering. One
significant area where such models might make a
contribution is in wastewater plant troubleshooting,
especially in small plants. While an experienced operator
might be able to determine the cause of a process failure,
less experienced operators might have problems. If the
judgement process of the experienced operator could be
modeled, his time could be spent in other ways while the
other operators used the model to reinforce their own
judgements or help them determine what new information to
gather in order to solve the problem. Such models could be
extremely useful in cases where one troubleshooter floats
among many plants.

In plants which are under automatic control or monitoring,
such a system could be used to warn of potential problems
as they develop (as the evidence pointing to that
conclusion becomes significant). The problem could then be
remedied before the discharge standard is violated or the
process completely fails. Such automatic decision making
would not replace the operators, but augment their
diagnostic capabilities.

New processes, which might be expected to have problems
with which the operators are not familiar, could be modeled
with the knowledge of the designer so that troubleshooting
could be relatively straightforward. The process of
determining the logic of failure for the plant would also
help the engineer determine flaws in the design before it
is built.

Probably the most important benefit of the construction of
a rule-based system is the knowledge gained by the user
being led through those rules. By interacting with the
rule-based system, experience is gained in logically
evaluating the evidence required to form an intelligent
judgement regarding the problem.

References

1.   Geselbracht, J.J., E.D. Brill, Jr., and J.T. Pfeffer,
Incorporating Judgement Into A Wastewater Treatment Plant
Design Optimization Model, Univ. of Illinois Water
Resources Center Report, May, 1986.

2.   Tang, C.C., E.D. Brill, Jr., and J.T. Pfeffer,
Mathematical Models and Optimization Techniques for Use in
Analysis and Design of Wastewater Treatment Systems,
Univ. of Illinois Water Resources Report 194, Nov., 1984.

Expert Systems in Reservoir Management and Planning

Roozbeh Kangari[1], A.M. ASCE and Shahrokh Rouhani[1], A.M. ASCE

Abstract

Reservoir planning and management procedures require a significant amount of empirical inputs from experts and specialists. This information can be denoted as empirical knowledge, which includes heuristic rules, expert opinions and inferences, and rules of thumb. Present computer-aided hydroplanning processes are primarily based on algorithmic models. The usual emphasis on algorithmic procedures has created significant constraints in model uses. Many programs have failed due to the lack of expert support for novice model users. Recent advances in artificial intelligence techniques have created a mechanism for incorporating the empirical knowledge into our algorithmic reservoir planning and management models. Our approach for the development of a prototype expert system for reservoir operation includes: identification and derivation of factual and empirical rules by interviewing field specialists; formatting the derived expert rules to be used in a knowledge engineering language (shell) program, which leads to a knowledge-based expert system. This system can be used by water resources engineers as a self-explanatory planning system, supported by a combined factual/empirical knowledge base. It can also be used by students to gain synthetic experience to organize their thought process. This expert system can be a valuable research tool for examination and validation of the empirical rules and procedures embedded in any hydroplanning process.

Introduction

Reservoir planning is a complex dynamic task, which includes many phases, such as: establishments of goals and objectives, problem identification and analysis, solution identification and impact assessment, formulation of alternatives and analysis, recommendations, decisions, implementation, operation, and management. The physiographic variations, climatic fluctuations, physical and chemical complexities, socioeconomic uncertainties and rapid population growth and urbanization all contribute further difficulties in hydroplanning processes.

These difficulties induced water resources engineers to seek for new planning tools, such as system analysis and operation research. Mathematical, statistical, and management programs were developed, which created more structured, optimal-oriented planning procedures. These programs contained causal and associative models, in

1. Assistant Professors, School of Civil Engineering, Georgia Institute of Technology, Atlanta, GA 30332.

determinstic and stochastic frameworks, with numerical and analytical
solution techniques. Optimization techniques such as linear,
non-linear, dynamic, and goal programming were also utilized.
    In spite of all these developments, as Loucks et al. (1985)
note, contemporary hydroplanning is characterized by its uncertainty,
scarcity of causal evidence on which to base a plan or policy, and
its multiobjective and multi-institutional involvements. Planners
must use considerable subjective judgement and empirical knowledge to
supplement what meager evidence might exist to help them predict even
the physical, biological, or chemical impacts of alternative
decisions. Linsley and Franzini (1979) also agree with the above and
state that there is no substitute for engineering judgement in a
project planning.
    Figure 1 shows a schematic representation of a typical reservoir

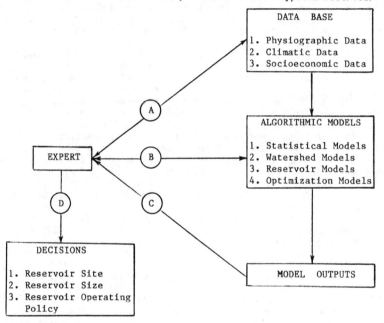

Expert's Tasks

A = Data analysis, input preparation, and alternative selection.
B = Coceptual modeling, analytical/numerical modeling, and calibration/
        validation.
C = Output analysis.
D = Policy analysis.

Figure 1. A Typical Reservoir Planning Process

planning program. As can be seen, the core of this process is the
expert. The expert can be a model maker, an experienced model user,
an expert manager, or a knowledgable hydroplanner. The data base is
usually composed of socioeconomic, physiographic and climatologic
information. The algorithmic models include statistical and
mathematical models for prediction and simulation of physical and
chemical phenomena, along with optimization procedures for evaluation
and identification of optimal plans. The model outputs may consist
of simulation and optimization results. The formalized appearance of
this process may be misleading. In fact, the successful
establishment and utilization of such a procedure requires
significant empirical inputs from the expert.

Heuristics and empirical knowledge of experts are vital parts of
any water resources planning process. These expert rules are
products of an explorative and learning process, which constitute a
valuable source of information in hydroplanning. However, these
rules rarely receive the attention that they deserve. In fact, only
a small percentage of such rules are well documented in the
literature. For example, Goodman (1984) states some of the empirical
rules and criteria for reservoir site selection. Rehak (1983) shows
an example of expert rules for estimation of surface runoff length
based on: (1) existing physically-based equations; (2) field
measurements; and (3) topological maps.

Traditionally, model makers are more concerned about the
algorithmic parts of their programs. As a result a significant gap
has been created between model users and makers. Many model users
lack the expert knowledge to analyze their data, set up algorithmic
models, and interpret and evaluate their outputs. This may lead to
the failure, or at least underutilization of many programs. Friedman
et al. (1982) indicate that some of the major constraints to
effective model use are: lack of proper training in model use and
interpretation, lack of communication between model users and
developers, and lack of required support services. In other words, a
successful model user needs the expert knowledge.

Expert knowledge is not necessarily algorithms or effective
procedures of computer sciences. In contrast to algorithmic
programs, empirical rules do not need to be complete, or unique, or
in a specific sequence (Rehak, 1983). Thus, programming of the
experts' knowledge, in an algorithmic framework, is not appropriate.
However, recent developments in artificial intelligence have created
new opportunities to deal with this critical problem. These
techniques are called heuristic programming, linguistic modeling, and
expert systems. They have been applied in different fields of
engineering for different purposes, such as data interpretation,
diagnosis, design, monitoring, system control, and training (Sriram
et al., 1984).

There are only few examples of application of these techniques
in water resources. Gasching et al. (1981) worked on a complimentary
program to aid the users of a hydrological simulation program to
select numerical values for the required input parameters. Miller et
al. (1985) suggest a system to aid hydrologic model users to simulate
single hydrologic events. Cuena (1983) suggests a conceptual
framework for an expert system to aid in the operation of flood
control and plan civil defense in flood prone areas. Rehak (1983)

also suggests some of the potential uses of expert systems in water resources.

Reservoir management has many characteristics which make it an ideal candidate for expert system studies. First, reservoir management is a process that is based on a combined set of factual and heuristic rules and models. The role of empirical rules becomes much more pronounced during extreme hydrologic conditions. Secondly, reservoir planning models are always designed by experts. In the absence of an expert, a novice model user may produce inferior or incorrect operation policies. Thirdly, recent advances in automatic hydrologic data collection indicates that reservoir operation is moving towards automation and full integration. In such a situation, the expert system can act as a repository of factual/empirical knowledge, necessary for the management of the reservoir.

The establishment of such an expert system requires the accomplishment of the following tasks: (1) identification and derivation of existing expert rules by interviewing experts in the field of reservoir management, (2) identification and establishment of factual and algorithmic rules and models used for reservoir planning, (3) integration of the derived algorithmic and heuristic rules, which leads to the organization of an expert water resources system on the basis of a combined factual/heuristic knowledge base.

Knowledge-Based Expert Systems

An expert system is a computer program that uses the expert knowledge to attain high levels of performance in a specific problem area. These programs typically represent knowledge in a symbolic manner; examine and explain their reasoning processes; and address problem areas that require years of special training and education for people to master. There are three common methods of representing knowledge: production rules, frames, and sementic nets. Our expert reservoir management and planning system is developed based on production rules. Such a rule can be defined as a pattern-invoked subprogram which is not called by other subprograms in a specific algorithmic sequence. Instead, it is activated whenever certain conditions hold. A general rule can be shown as:

"condition IMPLIES action"

The condition is usually referred to the current state of our physical system (i.e., the facts). The action in turn changes the current state of the facts. For instance at time t:

"inflow is equal to I_t, and reservoir storage is equal to S_t
IMPLIES

O_t amount of water has to be released."

Release of O_t, in turn, changes reservoir storage at the beginning of next time interval.

The above production rules (IF-THEN) operate in a cycle-wise manner. During each cycle, the conditions of each rule are matched against the current state of facts. When rules and conditions match, actions are taken. These actions affect the current state of facts, requiring new rule matchings. These rules can be classified into three general forms, as follow:

IF antecedents THEN consequence

such as:

IF   a heavy rain occurs after inflow forecast is made;

THEN   the inflow forecast may be greatly in error.
A second form of rules are:
    IF premise THEN conclusion
such as:
    IF   the storm pattern is P_t, $t_\wedge = 1,...,T$;
    THEN   the estimated inflows are $\hat{I}_t$, $t = T,...,T'$ with good
            accuracy ($\pm$ 10 percent)
The third form is:
    IF situation THEN action
An example of this rule would be:
    IF   present inflow is I_t, and present storage is S_t;
    THEN   release O_t.
All these rules are stored in a knowledge base. The expert
system, then, operates in a deductive manner. It acts as a rule
interpreter, which applies a particular set of rules for each
different case. This set of rules forms a reservoir management
inference network. This network can be extended simply by adding new
rules to its knowledge base, as more rules are provided by experts.
    Now, the user can introduce an evidence about the present
condition of the physical system. For instance, it could be:
"a storm with intensity of P_t is observed over the basin."
As the new information is received, the system decides which rules
apply. In this case the applicable rule may be:
    Rule 101: IF P_t is reported,
               THEN   estimated inflow is $\hat{I}_{t+1}$ with average accuracy.
Whenever the conditions for a rule match the state of the inference
network, the action part of that rule is exercised, as shown above.
This new state then activates another rule, such as:
    Rule 102: IF   estimated inflow is $\hat{I}_{t+1}$ with average accuracy,
               AND   storage level is S_t;
               THEN   release volume is O_{t+1}.
Again this state may cause instantiation of another rule, in which:
    Rule 103: IF   release volume is O_{t+1};
               THEN   warn local authorities of a potential flood
                      condition at a downstream location around t+2
                      hour.
    The key to the system's intelligence is that: each instantia-
tion changes the state of the inference network, causes instantiation
of other rules, and ultimately, influences the system's decisions.
In other words, a rule activation creates a chain reaction, just like
a ripple effect. This cycle of condition-action-condition continues
until a decision is reached.

Implementation
    The expert reservoir management system consists of the following
components as shown in Figure 2:
    i) Reservoir Operation Knowledge Base: It is a repository of
basic knowledge and rules about reservoir operation. The information
is divided into factual knowledge, and empirical rules. Factual
knowledge is defined as the set of explicit algorithmic models along
with physiographic, climatic, and socioeconomic data. Empirical
rules, however, are composed of expert opinions and inferences, and
rules of thumb. These information are organized in a way that can be
effectively utilized by the other components of the system.

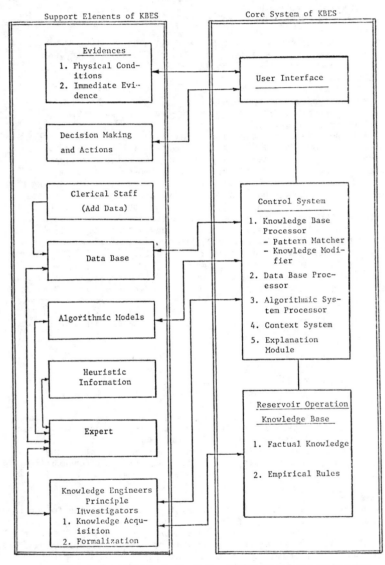

Figure 2. Architecture of Knowledge-Based Expert System
for Reservoir Management and Planning.

ii) Control System: The control system consists of three parts: knowledge base processor which utilizes the information in the knowledge base to generate intermediate outputs concerning the system's condition, which then can be used for subsequent inferences; data base and algorithmic system processors which allow the system to activate our data bases and algorithmic models, when needed; context system that allows the user to provide the system with information about condition of reservoir system at any stage of operation; and explanation module which provides the system with the capability of explaining its reasoning and strategy to the user.

iii) User Interface: The user interface provides the capability for the user to monitor the performance of the system. It also provides input concerning physical and immediate conditions of the system (i.e., evidence), and redirects the problem solving approach.

The two key tasks in the development of a knowledge-based expert system are the acquisition and the formalization of knowledge. The knowledge in an expert system is originated from many sources, such as data bases, case studies, empirical data, reports, investigators' experiences, and most important of all, the field experts. Our experience shows that work with the experts must be done in the context of solving particular problems. It is seldom effective to ask an expert directly about his/her rules for solving a specific type of problem. In fact, they usually have a great difficulty to express their rules. They have a tendency to state their conclusions, and the reasoning behind them, in general terms. Such statements are too broad for modeling purposes.

To extract knowledge from an expert, the following steps can be taken. Observing the expert to solve realistic problems, without interrupting him or her with questions. Step two is to select a set of representative problems, and informally discussing them with the expert. Step three is to ask expert to describe the basis of his or her judgements and empirical rules, which leads to a hierarchical organization of the knowledge base. Step four is to ask expert to solve a series of problems. The expert should be asked to determine the rationale behind his or her reasonings. This approach allows focus on specific aspects of decision making at every level of the solution process. Step five is to solve a range of easy to fairly complex problems using the concepts, formalisms, and rules acquired from the expert. Next step is to examine and criticize each rule to evaluate the control strategies. This includes verifying the accuracy of each rule and its justification. Afterward, the system should be presented to other specialists to compare strategies of different experts to identify the important points of disagreement.

At the knowledge formalization stage the key concepts, sub-problems, and control features that are derived in the knowledge acquisition phase should be mapped into more formal representations. This process consists of three important parts. In part one, the acquired concepts are formalized to determine how they may be linked to each other. Part two consists of understanding the underlying models used in the process. Part three consists of understanding the nature of data, whether the data can be explained in terms of certain hypotheses. The formalized knowledge will form a partial specification for organizing the knowledge base.

Conclusions

Implementation of the reservoir management and planning expert system has many benefits. It can act as a repository of empirical knowledge, provided by field specialists. This repository can be a valuable tool for future hydroplanners. It can also be used as a teaching or a training tool. For instance, its explanation module can describe why a rule has been activated, or why an action has been suggested. It can also help students to organize their thought processes. Furthermore, it will be an ideal research tool, allowing us to test and to improve our acquired empirical knowledge. This may lead to more efficient and successful hydroplanning.

References

1. Cuena, J., The Use of Simulation Models and Human Advice to Build an Expert System for the Defense and Control of River Floods, Proc. Eighth IJCAI, pp. 246-249, 1983.

2. Friedman, R.M., et al., Use of Models for Water Resources Management, Planning and Policy, Office of Technology Assessment, U.S. Congress, Washington, D.C., 1982.

3. Gasching, J., et al., Development of a Knowledge-Based Expert System for Water Resources Problems, Tech. Report SRI Project 1619, SRI International, August 1981.

4. Goodman, A.S., Principles of Water Resources Planning, Prentice-Hall, Inc., NJ, 1984.

5. Linsley, R.K. & J.B. Franzini, Water Resources Engineering, McGraw-Hill Book Co., NY, 1979.

6. Loucks, D.P. et al., Interactive Water Resources Modeling and Model Use: An Overview, WRR, Vol. 21, No. 2, 1985.

7. Miller, S.W., V.P. Singh, and S.S. Iyengar, Design of a consultation system for hydrologic modeling, presented at the Vth World Congress on Water Resources, Brussels, June 9-15, 1985.

8. Rehak, D., Expert Systems in Water Resources Management, Proc. ASCE Conference on Emerging Techniques in Storm Water Flood Management, Oct., 1983.

9. Sriram, D., A Bibliography on Knowledge-Based Expert Systems in Engineering, CECRL, Carnegie-Mellon University, SIGART, July 1984.

EXPERT PATTERN RECOGNITION FOR POLLUTION SOURCE IDENTIFICATION

Bithin Datta[1], A.M. ASCE and Richard C. Peralta[2], A.M. ASCE

This paper presents an approach for developing an Expert System to aid the identification of locations and magnitudes of a finite number of groundwater pollution sources. A pattern recognition algorithm is used as a secondary knowledge base. The finite sequential recognition algorithm is accessed from within the knowledge base. The expected risk in the pattern classification decision and a heuristic confidence threshold is compared to decide on the acceptability of the source identification.

INTRODUCTION

Identification of groundwater pollutant source locations and magnitude of pollutant fluxes is a difficult task, even for a system with well defined boundary conditions and known hydraulic parameter values. This paper presents an approach for developing an Expert System to aid the identification of the locations and magnitudes of a finite number of such sources. The types of pollutant sources can include: a leaking effluent pipe line, leaking storage tanks, or an unidentified geologic formation.

CHARACTERISTICS OF AN EXPERT SYSTEM

An Expert System is a man-machine system that can effectively elucidate and reproduce the knowledge base (including facts and rules) of human experts, in a particular professional domain. Therefore, the main emphasis in Expert System research is on knowledge engineering. Knowledge engineering involves the extraction, articulation, and computerization of the expert's knowledge in a specific area of interest (Hayes-Roth et. al., 1983). It can be viewed as a process of compiling human expertise in a machine usable form.

The two major components of an Expert System are the inference engine and a set of production rules. Domain-specific knowledge is represented in terms of the production rules. The inference engine is a processing element that employs a control strategy to access and manipulate the data base, and utilize solution heuristics for a goal directed inference. As noted in Johnston (1985), an Expert System differs from other traditional data processing approaches in its utilization of symbolic representation, symbolic inference, and heuristic search methods. Detailed discussion of these topics can be found in Palmer (1985) and Stefik et. al., (1983).

---

[1] Dept. of Civil Engineering, Univ. of California, Davis, CA, 95616.
[2] Dept. of Agricultural Engineering, Univ. of Arkansas, Fayetteville, AR, 72701.

OBJECTIVES

Our objective is to examine the potential use of an Expert System with the following characteristics. The goal of the system is to identify groundwater pollution source locations, from limited pollution concentration data and few measurement sites. The knowledge base is composed of a set of production rules that can optionally access and activate one or more separate programs. One of the programs the knowledge base can access is an optimal sequential pattern classification algorithm.

The pattern recognition algorithm plays the role of a secondary knowledge base. The pattern classifier is used for making a statistical inference of the locations and magnitudes of pollutant sources. The inference is based on the matching of discretized numerical feature measurements (of concentrations at measurement sites) with the features obtained from simulation of concentrations for various combinations of potential locations and magnitudes of entering pollutants. The matching process is accomplished by a finite sequential pattern recognition technique.

The final role of the knowledge base is to specify the criteria for accepting or rejecting the inferences of the pattern classifier. The knowledge base provides the heuristics for such decisions in the form of threshold values for confidence or certainty factors. These threshold values are based on subjective evaluation of uncertainties associated with the simulation and measurement of aquifer concentrations. The risk of making a terminal classification (obtained from the pattern recognition routine) is compared with the knowledge base confidence thresholds to select one of the options: a) make a terminal inference; b) reinitiate the process after obtaining additional measurements.

BACKGROUND

Gorelick et. al. (1983) addressed the problem of identifying groundwater pollution source location and magnitude by using traditional computational methods, including multiple linear regression and mathematical programming. Their approach included both steady state and transient transport. For the steady state case, the mixed integer programming model was successful in identifying locations and magnitudes of the sources, while the stepwise multiple regression model failed to provide sufficiently accurate identifications. For the transient case, both the linear programming model and the regression model were successful in locating the sources, but appreciable errors were detected in the prediction of the magnitude of the pollutant sources. However, these models (Gorelick et. al., 1983) can serve as useful screening tools for initially identifying possible locations and magnitudes of pollutant sources. Our goal is to present an alternative approach to solving this identification problem by using an Expert System. For illustrative purposes we will confine our discussion to transient transport.

THE HYPOTHETICAL PROBLEM

Figure 1 shows a hypothetical system of cells (4.8 km x 4.8 km), and steady state potentiometric head contours. Zero flow boundary condition exists along the periphery of this cell system. A pipe conveying effluent (containing chlorides) is passing through the center of the cells (5,1); (5,2); (5,3); (5,4); and (5,5). For simplicity we assumed that the only concentration measurement site is located at the center of cell (3,3). Measurements taken at regular time intervals indicate potential leakage from the effluent pipe. Without any prior information these leakages may be located at any one or all cells through which this pipe is passing. However, a screening model has identified two possible locations, cells (5,2) and (5,4). The magnitudes of leakages are estimated to be within 100.0 to 200.0 litres/day. The concentration of chloride in the effluent is 1000.0 mg/l.

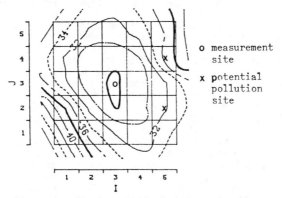

o measurement
   site

x potential
   pollution
   site

Figure 1. The hypothetical system of cells

SIMULATION OF CONCENTRATION AT MEASUREMENT SITE

The concentration measurements are taken at discrete times t, t+1, etc., corresponding to the time interval used in a groundwater solute transport model. The following procedure can be used to simulate the solute concentrations at the measurement sites (Chankong et. al., 1985):

a) simulate unit step response in concentration at a given site, due to a unit input solute flux at a potential source using the Konikow and Bredehoeft (1978) solute transport model;
b) find impulse response of the system at a given location at the end of a given time interval;
c) convolute the impulse response with the solute flux magnitudes at all possible sources to simulate the concentration of contaminant, Cn(t) at a measurement site at discrete time t.

The above procedure is based on the assumption that "the flow and transport equations describing the groundwater models can adequately be treated as linear constant-coefficient partial differential or difference equations" (Chankong et. al., 1985). One advantage of this procedure is, that only the step responses need to be stored in the data base, and the necessary computations can be performed through the inference engine. This will eliminate the necessity of running the entire solute transport model time after time.

SEQUENTIAL PATTERN RECOGNITION USING DYNAMIC PROGRAMMING

The main objective of a pattern recognition technique is the classification of input patterns based on measurements or feature extractions from input patterns. Let us assume, there are N features that can be measured for each of the input patterns. w_1, w_2, ..., w_m are the m possible pattern classes to be recognized. Each set of N features are designated as the vector X (X_1, X_2, X_n, ..., X_N) which is a particular point in the N dimensional feature space 0_χ. The pattern recognition problem is to assign each feature vector X, or a particular point in the feature space to a particular pattern class w_j.

In our illustration, the extracted features are the concentration of pollutants at the measurement sites of the aquifer, at a discrete time t, t + 1, etc. The extracted features from the observed patterns are the concentrations resulting from discretized amounts of leakage at one or all possible combination of potential sites. The function of the pattern classifier is to recognize the magnitude and location of the leakage sites corresponding to a given set of measured concentrations. The option available to the classifier is to terminate the recognition process at a stage, n, so that the expected risk of making the terminal decision is less than the risk of continuing the sequential process to the next stage. The heuristic role of the Expert System is to decide whether this risk is acceptable (less than a threshold value), or to recommend another set of measurements at time t + 1. Another role of the Expert System includes the initial screening of potential leakage sites. This can be accomplished through the use of a screening model such as the one described in Gorelick et. al. (1983). This option can drastically reduce the number of pattern classes needed to be matched in order to arrive at a terminal classification.

At a given time a finite number of concentration measurements are available. Therefore, a finite sequential recognition process using dynamic programming is adopted in designing the finite sequential classifier.

Using sufficient statistics to reduce the dimensionality of the sequential recognition system, the basic functional equation governing the sequence of expected risk is given by (Fu, 1968):

$$Q_{N-1}(k_1, k_2, ..., K_r)$$

$$= Min \begin{bmatrix} \text{Continue: } C(K_1, K_2, ..., K_r) \\ + \sum_{i=1}^{m} P(w_i) \sum_{j=1}^{r} P_{ij} Q_{n+1}(K_1, ... K_j+1, ... K_r) \\ \text{Stop: } \underset{i}{Min} R(K_1, K_2, ... K_r; d_i) \end{bmatrix} \qquad (1)$$

At the Nth stage (N feature measurements are available) when a terminal decision is made,

$$Q_N(K_1, K_2, ..., K_r) = \frac{Min}{i} R(K_1, K_2, ..., K_r;d_i) \qquad (2)$$

where,

$Q_N(K_1, K_2, ..., K_r)$ = the minimum expected risk of the entire decision process, having observed the joint event $(K_1, K_2, ..., K_r)$

K_j = the number of occurrences of E_j, j=1, ..., r
E_j = quantiles of the feature space, j=1, ..., r
r = total number of quantizations of each feature measurement
$C(K_1, K_2, ..., K_r)$ = cost of continuing the sequential process at the nth stage
$P(w_i)$ = a priori probability of class w_i occurring
P_{ij} = probability of occurrence of E_j for class w_i
d_i = decision that the ith pattern class is acceptable

$$R (K_1, K_2, ..., K_r;d_i) = \sum_{i=1}^{m} P(w_i)L(w_i,d_j)P(K_1, K_2, ..., K_r/w_i) \qquad (3)$$

= the expected risk of making a decision that pattern belongs to class i, having observed the joint event $(K_1, K_2, ..., K_r)$
$L (w_i, d_j)$ = loss incurred by making a terminal decision d_j when the input pattern is from class w_i

$$P(K_1, K_2, ..., K /w_i) = \frac{n!}{K_1!K_2!...K_r!} \prod_{j=1}^{r} (P_{ij})^{K_j} \quad n = 1,2,...,N \qquad (4)$$

It is therefore possible to determine Q_N using equations 2 and 3, for a given N. Subsequently we can determine the optimal stopping rule, using the functional equation 1. There are other possible refinements such as the assumption of Markovian dependence structure amongst the feature measurements. For the puspose of illustration we confined ourselves to the above procedure.

APPLICATION TO THE POLLUTION SOURCE IDENTIFICATION PROBLEM

We start with the initial screening of potential leakage sites for the hypothetical problem. Accordingly, there are two potential leakage sites, cells (5,2) and (5,4). Therefore, there are 3 possible combinations of leakage sites ($_2C_2 + _2C_1 = 3$), either one of them or both. To accomodate possible magnitudes of leakages, the ranges of solute flux amounts are also obtained. (The concentrations of input flux is known from the concentration of the effluent in the pipe.) This range (to be estimated from the screening model) is assumed to be 100-200 l/d. This range is discretized into 10 identical quantiles, E_j, j=1, 2, ..., 10. Therefore, the identification of the magnitudes and locations is a 120 (10+10+100) pattern class problem. The following values must also be computed.
1. The unit step response in concentration at the measurement site, using a solute transport model.
2. Concentration $C_n(t)$ at time t, for all combinations of source locations and magnitudes (median values of all quantiles) of input solute fluxes, using the step response values.

3. Values of P_{ij} for all values of i and j.
    In order to accomplish this particular computation any of the
    following two methods can be adopted.
    a) assume a random error term in the simulated concentration at
        the measurement site, so that

$$C_n(t) = \overline{C}_n(t) + e_t \qquad (5)$$

$C_n(t)$ = actual concentration at time t at the measurement site
  e_t = an error term with a specified distribution function so
        that the parameters of the distribution function reflect
        the amount of uncertainty in the measurements
$\overline{C}_n(t)$ = simulated concentration at the measurement site

Monte Carlo simulation techniques can be used to obtain the
distribution $C_n(t)$.
  b) The distribution function of $C_n(t)$ is obtained by adding ran-
      domized error terms to the predicted aquifer parameter values
      while simulating $C_n(t)$ directly from a solute transport model.

Once the distribution functions $C_n(t)$ are obtained for all possible pattern classes w_i (i=1,..., m), the following computations are
needed. For each discrete quantile (E_j), find P_{ij} using the distribution functions. For example, if F_2 = (110.0, 119.9) and E_3 = (120.0,
129.9), P_{23} = $F_2(129.9)-F_2(119.99)$, where $F_2(X)$ denotes the probability (Prob.$(C_n(t) \leq X)$ for a particular pattern class w_2. In order to
be able to use the functional equations, 1,2, and 3, the following
values are also needed. Example values are given below.
    i)   prior probabilities $P(w_i)$ = (1/m)
    ii) measurement cost = 0.03/measurement for all measurements
    iii) loss function $L(w_i,d_j)$ = 0 if I = j (correct recognition)
                                  = A (a constant) i≠j
It is now possible to employ the finite sequential pattern recognition
algorithm.

THE EXPERT SYSTEM

The basic requirement in building an Expert System to solve a
domain specific problem is the development of a knowledge base, a goal
driven inference engine, and a run time environment. The heart of the
system is the structured knowledge base and the inference engine to
execute the knowledge base objectives. The solution heuristics are a
part of the inference engine. A number of softwares are available for
knowledge and information processing, and for goal driven inferences.
In our judgement the INSIGHT 2 software (Level Five Research, Inc.)
has a number of features suitable for the specific problem addressed
here. Its most important characteristics are:
    i)   capability to initialize and execute external programs during
         the execution of a knowledge base,
    ii) options for using both a backward chaining or forward chaining
         inference engine,
    iii) a simple knowledge representation language (Production Rule
         Language, PRL). A sample basic knowledge representation can
         be described as:

```
IF      Condition 1
AND     Condition 2
AND     CALL PRG
SEND    V1
SEND    V2
RETURN  C1
AND     C1 < = 0.1
THEN    (Event 1) is possible CF 85
ELSE    (Event 2) CF 65
```

This rule specifies that if conditions 1 and 2 exist, a Pascal program 'PRG' provided with the variable values V_1 and V_2, returns the output value of C1. If C1 $<$ 0.1, the Event 1 is a possibility with confidence 85. If not, Event 2 is likely with confidence 65. It should be noted here that decisions with certainty implies either that the decision is true, or false. However, for decisions involving uncertain reasoning or information, it is necessary to return a subjective confidence in a decision. The confidence statement (CF) enables the system to evaluate degree of certainty in fuzzy reasoning, or to reject a user specified information, if the confidence level is lower than the knowledge base threshold.

In our illustrative example of developing a sample Expert System to identify the magnitude and location of aquifer contaminant sources, a similar production rule can be described as the simplest building block, for a more elaborate system.

```
IF:     Condition 1  (pollutant detected at measurement sites)
IF:     Condition 2  (a set of potential sites and the range of
                      input concentration magnitudes detected
                      through a screening model)
AND:    Call PATTERN (The pattern recognition program)
SEND:   (Numerical identification of potential sites, magnitude
        of solute flux sources, set of neumerically represented
        pattern classes)
RETURN: (Decisions regarding pattern classifications i.e.,
        magnitude and locations of sources as determined by the
        sequential recognition routine, and the risk associated
        with the terminal decision)
AND:    R(the risk of classification decision) < = 0.1
THEN:   (Accept the decision or pattern classification) CF 90
ELSE:   (Take new measurements at the next discrete time, t+1,
        and repeat the process with the new data)
```

This sequence of production rules are presented only as a sample. Further refinements and expansions are necessary to deal with various situations in an actual application.

SUMMARY AND CONCLUSIONS

This paper proposes an approach to the development of an Expert System that can accomplish the goal of identifying the locations and magnitudes of pollutant sources in an aquifer. Especially for transient solute transport conditions, conventional optimization methods have not proven to be adequately successful. Therefore, an alternative approach is proposed. The advantage of this approach is the

potential for utilizing highly developed pattern recognition tools and
stochastic methods to solve this identification problem.

The Expert System knowledge base utilizes a pattern recognition
technique to make decisions. The heuristics of the search and decision process are provided in the form of threshold values of confidence or certainty factors. Since most Expert Systems are
implemented on microcomputers with limited memory, the reduction in
the dimensionality of goal directed search is important. The approach
proposed here requires access to an internally activated program, from
within the knowledge base. This option may require at least 500 k
bytes of RAM and a hard disk drive. the dimensionality of the goals
to be selected is, however, drastically reduced by using an initial
screening model. We believe this approach of coupling pattern
recognition techniques with the knowledge base and the inference
engine will be useful in many other applications of Expert Systems.

ACKNOWLEDGEMENT

The first author is grateful to Professor Mark Houck of Purdue
University for introducing him to the concept of Expert Systems, and
to Professor Richard Palmer of the University of Washington, Seattle,
for his suggestions regarding the choice of softwares.

APPENDIX 1 - REFERENCES

1. Chankong, V. Y.Y. Haimes, and C. Du, 1985. Risk Assessment for
    Groundwater Contamination: II, Proceedings of the ASCE Speciality
    Conference on Computer Application in Water Resources, Buffalo,
    New York.
2. Fu, K.S., 1968. Sequential Methods in Pattern Recognition and
    Machine Learning, Academic Press, New York, 228 p.
3. Gorelick, S.M., B. Evans, and I. Remson, 1983. Identifying
    Sources of Groundwater Pollution: An Optimization Approach, Water
    Resources Research, 19(3), 779-790.
4. Hayes-Roth, F., Waterman, D.A., and Lenat, D. B., 1983. An
    Overview of Expert Systems, in Building Expert Systems, F.
    Hayes-Roth, D.A. Waterman, and D.B. Lenat eds., Addison-Welsley
    Publishing, Reading, Mass.
5. Johnston, D., 1985. Diagnosis of Wastewater Treatment Processes,
    Proceedings of the ASCE Specialty Conference on Computer
    Applications in Water Resources, Buffalo, New York.
6. Konikow, L.F., and Bredehoeft, J.D., 1978. Computer Models for
    Two-Dimensional solute Transport in Ground Water, U.S.G.S.,
    Techniques of Water Resources Investigations, 7.
7. Palmer, R.N., 1985. A Review of Artificial Intelligence,
    Proceedings of the ASCE Specialty Conference on Computer
    Applications in Water Resources, Buffalo, New York.
8. Stefik, M. et. al., 1983. Basic Concepts for Building Expert
    Systems, in Building Expert Systems, F. Hayes-Roth, D.A. Waterman,
    and D.B. Lenat eds., Addison-Welsley Publishing, Reading, Mass.

FLOOD RISK BELOW STEEP MOUNTAIN SLOPES

L. Douglas James[1], David O. Pitcher[2],
Scott Heefner[3], Brad R. Hall[4],
Scott W. Paxman[5], and Aaron Weston[6]

Introduction

In the Intermountain West, mountains rise steeply above the desert lowlands. Alluvial fans spread at approximately the critical hydraulic slope below apexes at canyon mouths. People pay a premium price for high residential sites on these fans for the panoramic overview below and closeness to the mountains above. Periodic torrents that rage out of the canyons are devastating at the apex and have diminishing effects downstream. This paper addresses that hazard. The torrents are of two types. Floods obey open channel flow and sediment transport equations and leave deposits graded from coarse to fine as the flow slows. Debris flows move as water-lubricated masses that destroy by churning action and leave giant tongues of well mixed materials where water loss makes them too viscous to move further (Johnson and Rodine 1984). This paper addresses flood risk but considers the effect of debris flows in catchment headwaters.

The primary flood loss on alluvial fans is property damage, largely to streets and utilities, making local government a major loser. The amount depends on water depth, velocity, duration, and sediment content. Depth, the principal variable used to estimate urban flood damages, determines water contact and static forces. Velocity adds impact forces, scours soil, transports loose objects, and increases drownings (James and Hall 1986). Duration prolongs deterioration and lost occupancy. Sediment scours, penetrates, and adds to the cost of clean up. Information on these four flood properties can be used by the private sector in deciding whether site amenities justify the potential loss and in designing flood proofed buildings to reduce damage when floods occur. It also helps communities design adequate debris basins, storm water conveyance systems, and floodplain management programs.

Flood Hazard Definition on Alluvial Fans

Riverine flood hazard is delineated by estimating peak flows, computing backwater curves, and plotting water surface profiles on a topographic map (Thomas and Lindskov 1983). Economic loss is estimated by integrating a stage-damage relationship over a range of frequencies The method gives   notoriously poor results on alluvial fans (James et al. 1980) because of:

[1]Director, Utah Water Research Laboratory, Utah State University, Logan, UT 84322.
[2]Engineer, Division of Water Resources, Bountiful, UT 84010.
[3]Engineer, Post, Buckley, Schuh & Jernigan, Atlanta, GA 30327-2878.
[4]Hydraulic Engineer, U.S. Army Corps of Engineers, Seattle District, Seattle, WA 98124.
[5]Engineer, Division of Water Resources, Bountiful, UT 84010.
[6]Engineer, Brewer Assoc., Durango, CO 81301.

1. Snowmelt-rain interactions. Intense rainfalls produce flash
floods that are larger from mountainsides left wet by melting winter
snows. Snowmelt floods have a volume determined by the winter snowpack
accumulation, a peak determined by the rate of spring warming and are
larger after mountain soils have been saturated by fall rains. Floods
emerging from a canyon may be augmented by intense showers on paved
urban areas.

2. Water-soil interactions. Decades may pass when no years have
sufficient snowmelt infiltration to cause landslides, rainfall
intensities for surface erosion, or streamflow for bank cutting.

3. Canyon sediment storage. Flash floods do not last long enough
to carry all the dislodged soil from the mountain heights to the
alluvial fan. Alluvium accumulates in the canyons until scoured out
by large-volume snowmelt floods (or debris flows) that can be a major
flood sediment source (Jeppson and Farmer 1986).

4. Rarity of damaging events. Most years have minor flood losses.
Over a 139-year history, about 75% of the flood damages in Utah resulted
from rapid snowmelt in 1952, 1983, and 1984 (James et al. 1980, Tempest
1984). Consequently, a)critical combinations in the above runoff and
sediment production processes are too rare to have good observational
data and b)residents have little experience in coping with historical
episodes.

5. Channel capacities determined by sedimentation. Channels on the
fans are enlarged by erosion and bank sloughing and obstructed by
sediment deposition, particularly at culverts. The larger the flood,
the further the channel regime change from erosion to deposition is
moved downstream. Both flow and sediment hydrographs must be used to
design debris basins and conveyance channels.

6. Prolonged inundation. Sediment deposition (geologically and
during individual events) aggrades channels to elevations higher than
the surrounding land. Flat snowmelt hydrographs can overflow into urban
areas for extended periods.

7. Hydraulic separation. The overflow becomes hydraulically
disconnected from the natural watercourse and must be analyzed
separately by flow path.

8. Anthropocentric flow patterns. Flow depths match street curb
heights, and rates fall within normal hydraulic capacities (McGinn
1980). Consequently, streets determine flood patterns. Also irrigation
canals can intercept flood runoff and be overtopped outside normal
floodplains. Approximate hazard mapping methods based on uniform
flooding opposite channel reaches (Magura and Wood 1980) or random
spreading over a uniform fan (Dawdy 1979) are inadequate.

9. Disposal by infiltration. In nature, flood waters often
entirely infiltrate coarse deposits over short distances below canyon
mouths. When urban development covers natural spreading areas or
channelization conveys flows quickly past them, floods travel into
downstream areas that previously had no problem.

10. Multidimensional stage-damage functions. Conventional
relationships estimate building damage from short periods of clear water
flooding. They do not cover high velocity, sediment laden flows that
continue for weeks or urban landscaping, streets, and utilities where
most alluvial fan loss occurs.

Hazard Delineation by Simulation

The above analysis shows that alluvial fan flood hazard mapping requires water and sediment hydrograph formation and routing through a distributary network tracking depth, velocity, duration, and sediment content. The processes are rare, interactive, and unmeasured. Each output has a different frequency distribution. There is no one 100-year storm. Simulation is a promising approach for analyzing complicated systems. One can model the physical system, calibrate on recent events, and input multiple sequences and combinations of precipitation, temperature, and evaporation within known correlation structures and distributions to examine many flood conditions and extrapolate to extreme events.

The continuous hydrologic simulation model developed and calibrated from local intermittent records for flood hazard mapping in Davis County, Utah, combined five submodels. A Runoff and Sediment Yield Model developed from the Stanford (Kentucky) Watershed Model (Ross 1970) simulates runoff and average water storages. The annual maximum soil water content and its date are supplied to a Landslide Prediction Model to estimate landslide timings, locations, and volumes. The first model is then used to simulate runoff and surface erosion from both natural and disturbed areas. The runoff and sediment hydrographs are routed to the mouth of the canyon by a Steep Channel Routing Model and there used by a Sediment Deposition and Culvert Blockage Model to simulate overflows. Finally, a Multiple Path Flood Routing Model routes the flows through the streets to locate and characterize the inundation. Important gaps require research, but we have a structure guiding future theoretical refinement and data gathering.

Runoff and Sediment Yield Model (Pitcher 1986)

A catchment is divided into three elevation and two aspect zones to account for variation in precipitation and temperature on mountain slopes. As shown in Figure 1, water balance accounting tracks zonal

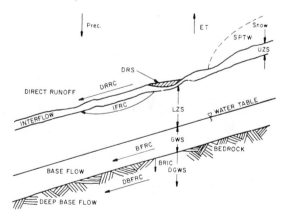

Figure 1. Soil moisture storages and flow components for the UMRSM.

water storage totals in the snowpack (SPTW), on the ground surface (DRS), in the phreatic zone (LZS), in a perched water table (GWS), and within the bedrock (DGWS).   Water can reach the stream (after progressively longer residence times) as direct runoff over the ground surface, interflow through the phreatic zone, baseflow from the perched water table, and deep baseflow from the bedrock.

Mountain storage gage data were used to estimate the storm precipitation increase with elevation.   Annual average lapse rates were used, represent winter conditions poorly (Barry and Chorley 1976, p. 77) but are reasonable during spring runoff.   Average zonal temperature and radiation are used to estimate evapotranspiration (Hargraves and Samani 1982) and to distinguish rain from snow.   The model uses published data (List 1968) to vary solar radiation on a level surface over the year. Incoming radiation was varied with elevation and aspect from information by Bagley et al. (1966) and shadows (Aurestah 1983) cast by ridges into canyons.   The simulations generally matched snow course data and melt hydrographs.

The Modified Universal Soil Loss Equation (MUSLE), was used to simulate sediment yield from surface erosion.   Parameter estimates was based on Wischmeier and Smith (1978).   The runoff erosivity factor developed by Williams (1975) was used to link erosion to the peak runoff rate, and the volume of direct runoff, summed to the present over a storm period.   Landslides alter runoff and erosion.   Hydrologically, they reduce soil storage and infiltration rates to the lower values of underlying horizons.   Erosion wise, they eliminate vegetative cover but may expose a more resistant soil.   The simulated overall effect was to increase erosion rates by about 50.   Records from small catchments gaged in Davis County (DeByle and Hookano 1973) were used to calibrate the model by aspect and zone.   Typical results are in Figure 2.   Multiple-zone catchments were simulated by areal weighting and summing.

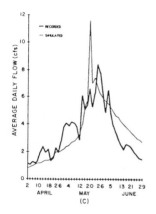

Figure 2.   Comparisons of simulated to recorded monthly flow volumes and daily flows in Halfway Creek watershed, 1957.

Landslide Prediction Model (Weston 1986)

Landslips occur where water ponds within a soil on a steep slope. Conditions are most favorable where snowpacks remain deep until melted by rapid warming in late spring. Infiltration rates exceeding soil hydraulic conductivity temporarily saturate soil layers (Jeppson and Farmer 1985) and may be joined by seepage from out of the bedrock. Water adds weight and seepage forces. It reduces a soil's cohesive strength as the normal forces between grains move to pore pressures in the water. As the water content increases, the added force and reduced resistance favor landslips. With sufficient thickness the soil depth (Johnson and Rodine 1984), the slide becomes a flow. The critical factors of soil depth and permeability are estimated by zone in hydrologic model calibration. Soil moisture is tracked in runoff simulation. Worst conditions are specified by a ratio of the maximum point value to a zonal average calibrated to match observed landslides. These data were used in a probabilistic "infinite slope" (Graham 1984) analysis to model landslips, and flows followed if the soil depth exceeded the critical value. For modeling landslides in Steed Canyon, the catchment (Figure 3) of 2.54 sq mi was divided into 263 grid cells. Maps and aerial photos gave cell ground cover, slope, elevation, and soil classification (used to estimate soil cohesion and internal friction angles). Cover gave root cohesion.

Steep Channel Routing Model (Paxman 1986)

For routing in Steed Canyon, the streams were divided into 15 reaches. Subcatchment runoffs were combined at mapped confluences and translated by kinematic routing based on regional channel geometry (Phillips and Harlin 1984) calibrated to local cross sections and an assumed of a fixed bed channel. The flow depths and velocities,

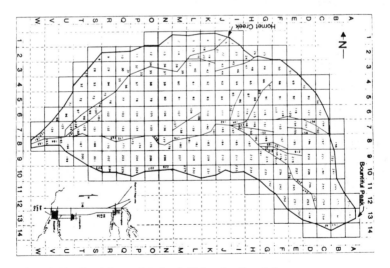

Figure 3.   Cell, Used to model landslides in Steed Canyon.

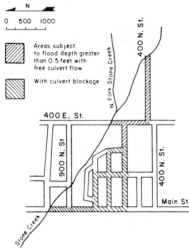

Figure 4.   Sediment-laden flow, streets flooded to a depth $\geq$ 0.5 feet,
Stone Creek, Bountiful City, Utah.

slightly supercritical, were then used in sediment transport equations
for steep mountain streams (Smart 1984) to route sedigraphs. A sediment
balance was applied to each reach to model aggradation and scouring.
Debris flows were assumed to block the stream with natural dams. The
model fills the temporary reservoir with water and soil, collapses the
dam on overtopping (Fread 1984), and erodes the material as limited by
stream transport capacity.

Sediment Deposition and Culvert Blockage Model (Hall 1985)

     Once the flow emerges onto the fan, it begins to deposit sediment.
Inlet control was assumed at the culvert entrance. Friction slopes were
calculated for water moving through the pool and used to estimate
sediment transport capacity (Meyer-Peter and Muller 1948).   Sediment
deposition restricts the opening. Filled ponds overtop by weir flow
into the crossing street. The water may cross the embankment but often
flows down the street. Sediment passing a culvert moves downstream for
the routing to be repeated. The model was calibrated with flows,
sediment properties, and culvert blockages observed in Stone Creek in
1983 and 1984. The effect of a blockage is shown on Figure 4.

Multiple Path Flood Routing Model (Heefner 1983)

     Street flow is supplemented by local rainfall and depleted as flows
overtop curbs and infiltrate. Grade changes, such as at flat intersections, cause flows to fluctuate between supercritical and
subcritical, favoring kinematic routing as a robust method for Froude
numbers near unity. Energy and momentum relationships are used to model
flow divisions at intersections.   The streets subject to overflow
flooding from Mill Creek were subdivided into segments and described by
field geometric data for routing to determine depths, velocities, and
areas inundated.

Conclusions

The model outlined above can be used directly to estimate the sediment deposition and area flooded by velocity and depth by precipitation and temperature sequences, given the calibration for the gaged mountain tributaries of Farmington Creek. Probabilistic risk can be estimated by running with an extended meteorological record or synthesized event sequences. Frequency analysis of the results can be used for flood hazard mapping and structural and nonstructural design. The modeling promises a framework for quantifying flows and hazards to encourage an optimal balance between flood risk and land use on alluvial fans.

References

Aurestah, Reza. 1983. Irrigation water conservation in an urbanized area of the western United States. PhD thesis, Dept. of Civil and Environmental Engineering, Utah State University, Logan, Utah.

Bagley, Jay M., Duane G. Chadwick, and J. Paul Riley. 1966. Application of electronic analog computer to solution of hydrologic and river-basin-planning problems: Utah simulation model II. Report PRWG 32-1, Utah Water Research Lab, Utah State University, Logan, Utah. 129 p.

Barry, R. G., and R. J. Chorley. 1976. Atmosphere, weather and climate. Atmospheric composition and energy. Methuen & Co. Ltd., New York, N.Y.

Dawdy, David R. 1979. Flood frequency estimates on alluvial fans. American Society of Civil Engineers, Journal of the Hydraulics Division 105(HY11):1407-1413.

DeByle, N. V., and Ezra Hookano. 1973. Research related to the Davis County experimental watershed: An annotated bibliography. General Technical Report INT-4, U.S. Department of Agriculture, Forest Service, Ogden, Utah.

Fread, D. L. 1984. A breach erosion model for earthen dams. Hydrologic Research Laboratory, National Weather Service, Silver Spring, Maryland. 30 p.

Graham, J. 1984. Chapter 6, Methods of stability analysis. In: Slope Instability. Brunsden, Denys, and David B. Prior (Eds.). John Wiley & Sons, New York, N.Y.

Hall, Brad R. 1985. Aggravation of snowmelt floods by sediment deposition at culverts. M.S. thesis, Dept. of Civil and Environmental Engineering, Utah State University, Logan, Utah.

Hargraves, G. H., and Z. A. Samani. 1982. Estimating potential evapotranspiration. American Society of Civil Engineers, Journal of the Irrigation and Drainage Division 108(IR3):225-230.

Heefner, Scott N. 1983. Analysis of flood characteristics on an urbanized alluvial fan: Mill Creek drainage basin, Bountiful, Utah. M.S. thesis, Dept. of Civil and Environmental Engineering, Utah State University, Logan, Utah. 191 p.

James, L. D., and Brad Hall. Accepted for 1986 publication. Risk Information for Floodplain Management. Journal of Water Resources Planning and Management Division. American Society of Civil Engineers.

James, L. D., D. T. Larson, D. H. Hoggan, and T. F. Glover. 1980. Floodplain management needs peculiar to arid climates. Water Resources Bulletin, 16(6):1020-1029. December.

Jeppson, Roland W., and Eugene E. Farmer. 1986. Mechanics associated
    with Utah's 1983 slides and debris flows. USDA Forest Service,
    Intermountain Forest and Range Experiment Station, Ogden, Utah.
    106 p.
Johnson, A. M., and J. R. Rodine. 1984. Debris flow, p. 257-361. In:
    Slope instability. Denys Brunsden and David B. Pior (Eds.). John
    Wiley & Sons, Inc., New York, New York.
List, R. J. 1968. Smithsonian meteorological tables. Smithsonian
    Institute Press, City of Washington, D.C., 114:501.
Magura, Lawrence M., and Darrel E. Wood. 1980. Flood hazard
    identification and flood plain management on alluvial fans. Water
    Resources Bulletin 16(1):56-62.
McGinn, R. A. 1980. Discussion: Flood frequency estimates on alluvial
    fans by David R. Dawdy. American Society of Civil Engineers,
    Journal of the Hydraulics Division 106(HY10):1718-1720.
Meyer-Peter, E., and R. Muller. 1948. Formulas for bed load transport.
    International Association of Hydraulics Research, 2nd meeting,
    Stockholm, Sweden. (original not seen; abstracted in Graf (1971)).
Paxman, Scott William. 1986. The routing of water and sediment down
    steep natural channels. M.S. thesis, Dept. of Civil and
    Environmental Engineering, Utah State University, Logan, Utah.
Phillips, P. J., and J. M. Harlin. 1984. Spatial dependency of
    hydraulic geometry exponents in a subalpine stream. Journal of
    Hydrology 71:277-283.
Pitcher, David O. 1986. Parametric surface erosion modeling of
    mountain watersheds in Utah. M.S. thesis, Dept. of Civil and
    Environmental Engineering, Utah State University, Logan, Utah.
Ross, G. A. 1970. The Stanford Watershed Model: The correlation of
    parameter values selected by a computerized procedure with physical
    characteristics of the watershed. Research Report No. 35,
    University of Kentucky Water Resources Research Institute,
    Lexington, Kentucky.
Smart, G. M. 1984. Sediment transport formula for steep channels.
    Proceedings of the Hydraulics Division, ASCE 110(HY3).
Tempest, L. 1984. Current events update, oral presentation at
    Specialty Conference on Delineation of Landslide, Flash Flood and
    Debris Flow Hazards in Utah, June 14-15, Utah State University,
    Logan, UT.
Thomas, B. E., and K. L. Lindskov. 1983. Methods for estimating peak
    discharges and flood boundaries of streams in Utah. U.S.
    Geological Survey, Water Resources Investigations Report 83-14129.
Weston, Aaron. 1985. Sediment yield from landslips in steep mountain
    watersheds in Utah. M.S. thesis, Dept. of Civil and Environmental
    Engineering, Utah State University, Logan, Utah.
Williams, J. R. 1975. Sediment-yield prediction with universal
    equation using runoff energy factor. In Present and prospective
    technology for predicting sediment yields and sources. ARS-S-40.
    U.S. Department of Agriculture.
Wischmeier, W. H., and D. D. Smith. 1978. Predicting rainfall erosion
    losses--a guide to conservation planning. U.S. Department of
    Agriculture, Agricultural Handbook No. 537.

Relative Landslide Susceptibility in Davis County, Utah
- A Multivariate Approach

Robert T. Pack*
Loren R. Anderson**

Introduction

A rare combination of climatic variables including (1) sustained above normal precipitation beginning in 1981 and continuing through the spring of 1984, (2) cool temperatures throughout the spring periods of 1983 and 1984, and (3) a dramatic rise in mean daily temperatures in May led to numerous landslides in Davis County, Utah in both 1983 and 1984. Though landslides had been triggered by heavy rainfall in previous years (Marsell, 1971), the spring periods of 1983 and 1984 had the first occurrences of snowmelt triggered landslides in Utah's recorded history.

In 1984, the geographic distribution of debris slides was similar to that observed in 1983. In some cases, slides occurred in the headwall areas adjacent to 1983 slides. The majority, however, occurred in virgin areas where no previous signs of instability were observed. In an area where over 100 slides occurred in 1983, about 40 occurred in 1984.

The complex distribution of soil properties makes prediction of slope stability extremely difficult in these mountain watersheds. Using inductive soil mechanics methods, it would have been virtually impossible to predict the distribution of Davis County debris slides prior to their occurrence. The need to assess these watersheds for their susceptibility to possible future landslide activity led to the adoption of a deductive statistical method of evaluation based on external variables, i.e. geomorphology, vegetation, etc., rather than internal variables, i.e. soil shear strength, porewater pressure, etc. This paper presents the results of an analysis of relative landslide susceptibility in Davis County, Utah which uses a statistical method based on discrete discriminant analysis.

Landslide Susceptibility Defined

Total risk is a measure which all land-use planners and managers would ideally like to discover in any landslide study. Factors which contribute to landslide risk can be subdivided into those which have to do with (1) the triggering event, (2) the resulting failure, (3) the exposure at the time of failure, and (4) the resulting consequence.

*Thurber Consultants, Ltd., Victoria, British Columbia.
**Department of Civil and Environmental Engineering, Utah State University, Logan, Utah 84322-4110.

A complete risk analysis involves the evaluation of probabilities
associated with each of the four categories for all possible combinations of scenarios. Then, depending on which factors contribute
most to the overall risk, aversion measures are employed to reduce
risk to acceptable levels. Figure 1 is a diagram of a suggested
risk-based method for establishing priorities for alternative actions
which would reduce landslide risk. This diagram shows a few of the
many factors which contribute to risk, the probabilities P(*) of
which need to be evaluated.

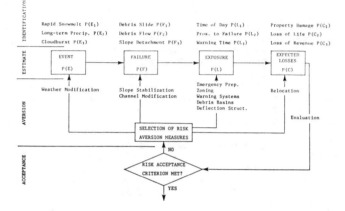

Figure 1,   Diagram of risk-based analysis for mitigating landslide risk.

        It is rarely possible to evaluate all probabilities required in
a complete risk analysis. When the probability of the triggering event
P(E) and the probability of a failure given the trigger P(F:E) are both
evaluated, the study is termed a 'landslide hazard analysis'. The
results of such a study are usually presented in terms of magnitude
frequency charts and hazard maps. However, in many cases, it is
difficult to determine return periods for relatively infrequent
landslide triggering events such as an unusually heavy snowmelt
which occurred in Davis County. In such cases, the probability of
failure is evaluated relative to known past triggering events. This
kind of study is termed a 'relative susceptibility analysis' where
the probability of the triggering event P(F) is not determined. The
probability of failure given a known past triggering event P(F:E=past
event) is evaluated for geographic areas and presented in terms of a
landslide susceptibility map. This kind of probability has no time-
dependence; therefore, no recurrence intervals can be presented.

        This study evaluates relative landslide susceptibility in Davis
County relative to snowmelt triggering events during the springs of
1983 and 1984. The goal is to determine where on the watershed slopes
debris slides are most likely to occur in the future.

Landslide-Related Variables in Davis County

A detailed study of individual landslide sites identified several important debris slide-related variables which have affected the behavior and distribution of slides in Davis County. In mapping relative susceptibility over a large area, it is important to identify variables which are easily measured at sites which have not failed but which also directly relate to slope instability. Table 1 is a list of external variables which have been found to affect landslide distribution in other studies as well as in Davis County. Included in the table is the variable type, measurability, and the internal variable most likely influenced by the external variable. Of these variables, nine were chosen for detailed statistical analysis mostly on the basis of measurability. They include (1) ACROSS - across-slope shape (swales vs. ridges); (2) DOWN - down-slope shape (benches and other breaks in slope); (3) TERRA - geomorphological unit; (4) VEGET - vegetative unit; (5) SLOPE - slope gradient; (6) ASPECT - topographic aspect; (7) ELEV - elevation; (8) DISTLS - distance to nearest landslide; and (9) DISTRT - distance to upslope ridge.

EXTERNAL VALUE	TYPE	INTERNAL VARIABLE AFFECTED	IDENTIFIED IN DAVIS CO.	IDENTIFIED IN OTHER	MEASURABILITY	CHOSEN VARIABLES
Rainfall Rate	TEMPORAL	u	O	X	FAIR	O
Snowmelt Rate	TEMPORAL	u	X	X	FAIR	O
Long-Term Precipitation	TEMPORAL	u	X	X	FAIR	O
Fire	TEMPORAL	C_r,u	O	X	GOOD	O
Earthquake	TEMPORAL	all	O	X	POOR	O
Slope Gradient	SPATIAL	β	X	X	GOOD	X
Elevation	SPATIAL	u,ϕ,c	X	X	GOOD	X
Aspect	SPATIAL	u,ϕ,c	?	X	GOOD	X
Distance to Channel	SPATIAL	M	X	X	GOOD	O
Distance to upslope Ridge	SPATIAL	u	X	X	GOOD	X
Distance to Previous Landslide	SPATIAL	all	X	X	GOOD	X
Across-Slope Shape (swales)	SPATIAL	u,ϕ,c,M	X	X	GOOD	X
Down-Slope Shape (benches)	SPATIAL	u,ϕ,c,M	X	X	GOOD	X
Geomorphological Unit (Soil Type and Thickness)	SPATIAL	ϕ,c,u,M,H	X	X	FAIR	X
Vegetative Unit	SPATIAL	C_r,Y,s,u	X	X	GOOD	X
Critical Weak Zone	SPATIAL	all	X	X	POOR	O
Bedrock Lithology	SPATIAL	ϕ,c,u	X	X	FAIR	O
Bedrock Structure	SPATIAL	β,ϕ,c,u	X	X	POOR	O
Existence of Soil Pipes	SPATIAL	u	X	X	POOR	O
Percent Fines in Soil	SPATIAL	ϕ,c	X	X	FAIR	O

Definitions: u - porewater pressure   H - soil thickness ϕ - soil friction angle
c - soil cohesion C_r- root cohesion   s - surcharge load
Y - soil density β - slope of failure   M - soil mobility index
X - yes   surface
0 - no

Table 1.   External variables which effect landslide distribution.

Data on these nine variables were collected for 299 sites distributed across 39 watersheds in Davis County. These sites can be subdivided into five subgroups including thirty pre-1983 landslide sites, eighty-five 1983 landslide sites, forty-five 1984 landslide sites, twenty-four sites which showed ground cracking in 1984, and

one-hundred fifteen randomly chosen unfailed sites. The 115 landslides
which occurred prior to or during 1983 were first compared to the
115 unfailed sites in the initial part of this study which was
conducted prior to the 1984 events. Each of the nine variables were
first analyzed separately for the 230 sites to determine which were
best able to discriminate between failed and unfailed sites. This
univariate analysis is described below.

Univariate Analysis

This analysis employs a statistical model which uses discrete
variables to discriminate between classes, i.e. between the landslide
class w_1 and the unfailed class w_2. It is based on the multinomial
model as described by Goldstein and Dillon (1978).

The variable ACROSS was broken down into 5 discrete categories
including (1) sharply concave contour shape or V-notch gully, (2)
concave contour shape or swale, (3) straight or uniform contour shape,
(4) convex contour shape or rounded ridge, and (5) strongly convex
contour shape or sharp ridgecrest. In statistical terms, this random
variable x_1 has 5 states. The discriminating ability of this variable
is measured in terms of the state probability $P_s(w1|x)$ that a site of
unknown class is in fact an unstable site given a particular state such
as 'concave contour shape' is identified at the site. This probability
is used synonymously with the probability of failure $P(F)$ in relative
susceptibility mapping. A non-parametric estimate of $P(F)$ for the
specific case with equal numbers of failed and unfailed sites in given
by $n_1(x)/n(x)$ where $n_1(x)$ is the number of landslide sites in a given
state and $n(x)$ is the total number of sites in a given state. The
relative landslide susceptibility for each category is above average
if the calculated value of $P(F)$ is above the a priori probability of
0.5 and below average if $P(F)$ is less than 0.5. The more discriminating
a variable is, the closer $P(F)$ values for each state are to either
1.0 or 0.

The variable ACROSS was found to have $P(F)$ values of 0.68, 0.67,
0.60, 0.15, and 0.0, respectively, for each of the categories described
above. As has been found in other regions, concave to uniform slopes
are more susceptible to landsliding than convex slopes. Explanations
for this behavior include the formation of elevated porewater pressures
due to the concentration of laterally flowing groundwater in swales,
lower strength properties of soils weathering in these areas, the
steeper slopes associated with gullies, and the fact that convex slopes
often have shallower soils. If this variable were used in a simple
univariate classification model, the decision rule would be to
assign a site to a high landslide susceptibility rating if it has a
concave to uniform slope (i.e. where $P(F)>0.5$) and to assign it to a
low susceptibility rating if it lies on a convex slope (i.e. where
$P(F)<0.5$). Using this procedure, 69 of the 230 sites would be
misclassified which is equivalent to a success rate of 70%. This
success rate is actually optimistic as the model is tested on the
same data from which it is derived.

Each of the other eight variables were also analyzed for their ability to act as univariate classifiers. It was necessary to divide the variables SLOPE, ASPECT, ELEVATION, DISTLS, and DISTRT into discrete categories for use in the multinomial model. This was accomplished by plotting approximated normal distributions for both failed and unfailed sites. Classes were then split so as to produce values of P(F) close to 1.0 or 0.0. It was found that any attempt to subdivide ASPECT into discrete categories resulted in values of P(F) very close to 0.5 for 5 categories or less. Due to its poor discriminating power, this variable was never considered further in the analysis. The other variables have some degree of discriminating power. As univariate classifiers, the following success rates result for these variables:

$$
\begin{array}{ll}
\text{TERRA} & \ldots \ldots 73\% \\
\text{DISTLS} & \ldots 73\% \\
\text{ACROSS} & \ldots 70\% \\
\text{SLOPE} & \ldots \ldots 70\% \\
\text{VEGET} & \ldots \ldots 69\% \\
\text{DISTRT} & \ldots 66\% \\
\text{DOWN} & \ldots \ldots 65\% \\
\text{ELEV} & \ldots \ldots 63\%
\end{array}
$$

It is interesting to note that the top four variables in the list include TERRA, DISTLS, and SLOPE which have been the most commonly employed variables in past relative landslide susceptibility studies. The variable ACROSS is also one of the most important landslide-related variables mentioned in the literature on debris slides which mobilize into debris flows.

Relative Landslide Susceptibility Using Multivariate Analysis

As seen above, no one variable alone constitutes an adequate classifier for relative landslide susceptibility mapping. By combining variables into a multivariate classification, performance can usually be increased. In the case of a bivariate analysis, the two discrete variables x_1 and x_2 can be combined to produce classification cells each defined by the intersection of particular categories of each variable. Each cell is similar to a state or category used in the univariate analysis. Values of P(F) are calculated in a similar fashion except $n_1(\bar{x})$ and $n(\bar{x})$ are calculated for each classification cell represented by the vector $\bar{x}$ instead of for each category x of a single variable. Similarly, the analysis can be expanded to include several variables with classification cells represented in n-dimensional variable space.

This classification model has intuitive appeal. However, several difficulties exist. The first, and perhaps most obvious problem, is the proliferation of classification cells where several variables with several possible categories are used. For example, if 4 variables are used with 5 possible values each, 625 classification cells result. If state probabilities are estimated for each cell, a large sample must be taken in order to fill each cell with enough samples for the probabilities to be estimated with reliability. The goal then is to minimize the number of variables and categories within each variable while maximizing the success rate of the classification model.

A bivariate analysis of independence reveals that the four best univariate classifiers TERRA, DISTLS, SLOPE, and ACROSS are mutually independent for the given data. Cochran (1962) argues that if all variables are independent, then the best set of k variables consists of the k best single variables. Moreover, the categories of each variable with $P(F)<0.5$ can be combined along with categories with $P(F)>0.5$ to form dichotomous variables without any loss of classifier performance. Assuming these four variables are in fact independent and can be dichotomized, the resulting 16-cell classification model is optimal. It can be argued that no other four-dimensional multinomial model can surpass its performance using the same variables. Increasing the dimensionality of the classifier by adding the next-best variable VEGET causes two problems: (1) VEGET is dependent on TERRA, and (2) the minimum of 32 classification cells necessary in a 5-D model would require more data than presently available in order to produce $P(F)$ values with reasonably narrow confidence intervals.

Having selected the classification model, it is important to evaluate its effectiveness in discriminating between landslide and unfailed sites. The first learning sample consists of 66 sites chosen at random from the 115 sites which failed in and before 1983. The second learning sample consists of 65 sites chosen from the 115 unfailed sites. These two learning samples are used in calculating classification cell probabilities. The a priori probability is therefore $66/131=0.504$. The remaining samples on which the classification is tested include the following five subgroups: (1) 50 unfailed sites, (2) 20 1983 landslide sites, (3) 45 1984 landslide sites, (4) 29 pre-1983 landslide sites, and (5) 24 sites which only showed signs of ground cracking in 1984.

Classification cell probabilities are again calculated using the formula $P(F)=n_1(x)/n(x)$ as in the one-dimensional case described above. The resulting cell probabilities for the 16 cells based on the learning sample are shown in Figure 2. The figure also shows the number of samples used in estimating each $P(F)$ in the upper right-hand corner of each cell. Those three cells within which the classification rule specifies that sites be classified as landslide sites, i.e. $P(F)>0.504$, are shaded in the figure. This classification was then used to classify the five groups of test samples described above. The following success rates resulted:

UNFAILED SITES 86%
1983 LANDSLIDES 95%
1984 LANDSLIDES 89%
1984 CRACKING 67%
PRE-1983 LANDSLIDES . . 79%

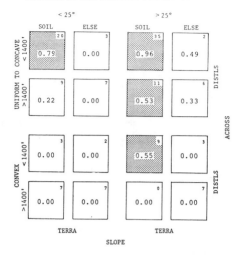

Figure 2. Landslide classification cells.

Due to the amazing similarity of climatic events which lead to landsliding in both 1983 and 1984, the factors affecting the spatial distribution of landslides appear to have been quite similar during both years. Thus, the classifier based on 1983 landslide data does a good job (89%) of classifying 1984 landslide sites. Such performance gives confidence in the classification being able to correctly identify areas which are likely to be susceptible to debris slides in the future if a similar combination of climatic variables recurs. If another type of mechanism, such as a heavy cloudburst, triggers landslides, the present model may not perform nearly as well.

The discrimination between failed and unfailed sites is conservative. In other words, the percentage of failed sites classified as stable (5% for 1983 and 11% for 1984) is lower than the percentage of stable sites classified as unstable (14%).

The relatively poor success rate for sites showing ground cracking in 1984 is not surprising. Field studies in 1984 revealed that these sites generally exhibited temporal and spatial behavior quite distinct from that of debris slides and debris flows. Because of this, the variables which affect their spatial distributions are likely to have been different. The pre-1983 landslides were also poorly classified due to different temporal factors which had lead to their occurrence in the past. Many of these past landslides may have been initiated by heavy rainfall or by stream undercutting. Again, the variables which affected spatial distributions are likely to have been quite different. Because this study focuses on debris slides which initiate debris

flows, no attempt was made to improve the ability of the classifier
to correctly classify pre-1983 landslides and 1984 ground cracking.

Conclusions

    The multinomial classification model developed in this study was
able to classify 299 sites of known stability with an average 88%
accuracy. The discrete dichotomous variables used in the analysis are
well adapted to computer-aided landslide susceptibility mapping. Maps
showing only two map units can be developed for each of the four
variables and then digitized into the computer using a gridded cell
format. The computer can then combine the map information, calculate
probabilities, and then assign susceptibility classes to each map cell
according to the classification model. The results can then be
output in the form of a landslide susceptibility map of use to land
use planners, property owners, government agencies and other concerned
individuals.

    The validity of this specific classification model is limited to
the delineation of debris slide susceptibility in the Wasatch Mountains
of Davis County. Susceptibility delineations are also limited to
landslide events triggered by sustained above normal precipitation and
rapid snowmelt. If other combinations of triggering events were to
occur, the correlation of landslide locations with various landslide
related variables might differ. Despite these limitations, the
statistical methods demonstrated in this study could be used in
other areas where similar types of landslide data are available for
analysis.

References

Cochran, W.G. 1962. On the performance of the linear discriminant
    function (report on a discussion of a paper by W.G. Cochran).
    Bulletin of the International Statistical Institute 35:157-158.

Goldstein, M. and Dillon, W.R. 1978. Discrete discriminant analysis.
    John Wiley and Sons, New York, New York.

Marsell, R.E. 1971. Cloudburst and snowmelt floods, p. N1-N18. In
    Environmental Geology of the Wasatch Front. Utah Geological
    Association Publication (1).

Pack, R.T. 1985. Multivariate analysis of relative landslide
    susceptibility in Davis County, Utah. Unpublished Ph.D.
    Dissertation, Utah State University, Logan, Utah.

DEBRIS FLOWS AND HYPERCONCENTRATED STREAMFLOWS

By Gerald F. Wieczorek*, M. ASCE

Examination of recent debris-flow and hyperconcentrated-streamflow events in the western United States reveals (1) the topographic, geologic, hydrologic, and vegetative conditions that affect initiation of debris flows and (2) the wide ranging climatic conditions that can trigger debris flows. Recognition of these physiographic and climatic conditions has aided development of preliminary methods for hazard evaluation. Recent developments in the application of electronic data gathering, transmitting, and processing systems shows potential for real-time hazard warning.

INTRODUCTION

During the past decade, several regions of the western United States experienced episodes of debris avalanches, mudflows, and hyperconcentrated streamflows that resulted in loss of life and extensive property damage. These sediment-water flows are distinguished from normal streamflow according to the classification system (Fig. 1) from Pierson and Costa (1984). Subsequently in this paper the term debris flow will be used to collectively refer to mudflow, and debris avalanche. Because debris flows have been inadequately understood, hazard evaluation, land use regulation, and engineering design of storm runoff systems have not taken into account their nonstandard hydraulic aspects. Little was known about physiographic conditions that favor flows, as well as climatologic factors such as rainfall intensity or the rate of snowmelt necessary for triggering flows. Recently developed methods of hazard recognition and evaluation based on available physiographic and climatic information are especially important in the establishment of real-time warning systems.

Episodes of debris flows and hyperconcentrated streamflows in California, Nevada, and Utah illustrate a wide variety of climatic triggering events and differences in physiographic conditions where these occur. This paper presents information on these events and conditions and discusses recent developments in hazard recognition, evaluation, and warning.

CASE HISTORIES

Southern California.-In the Los Angeles area, the problem of debris-flow occurrence in areas stripped by wildfires has been long recognized. Shortly after midnight on January 1, 1934, an intense downpour after more than 12 hours of rainfall brought debris flows down several canyons into the La Cañada Valley, causing significant

*Civil Engineer, U.S. Geological Survey, 345 Middlefield Rd., MS 998, Menlo Park, CA, 94025

property damage and loss of life. As described in Troxell and
Peterson (1937, p. 82-83), "the water surface at the peak of the flood
[was] .... greatly raised in the center of the cross section" and "a
wall of water came down the stream channel ... with boulders riding
along the top of the wave...the mixture compared to concrete with
boulders." The debris-producing drainages had been burned in November
of 1933, allowing sediment from erosion of small rivulets and gullies
and from stream-channel deposits to be mobilized into debris flows by
the intense runoff.

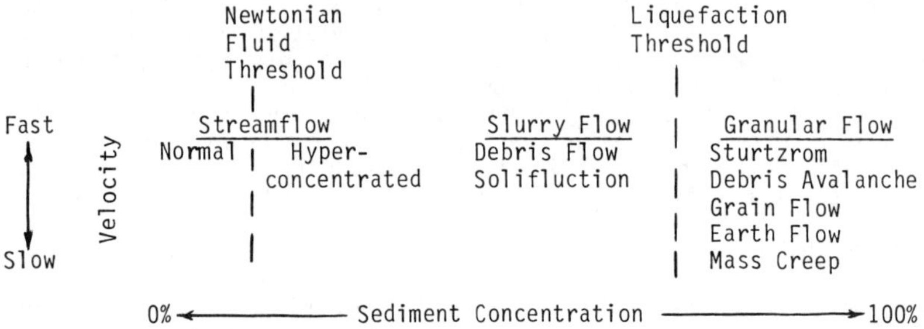

```
                    Newtonian                    Liquefaction
                    Fluid                        Threshold
                    Threshold
                        |                            |
Fast          ⌄      Streamflow         Slurry Flow  |   Granular Flow
 ▲            ⁺⁼⁼     Normal |  Hyper-   Debris Flow  |   Sturtzrom
 |            ⁻⁻              |  concentrated  Solifluction  |   Debris Avalanche
 |            ⁰⁻                         |                |   Grain Flow
 ▼            ⁻▪                         |                |   Earth Flow
Slow          ⌄                         |                |   Mass Creep

        0% ◀──────────── Sediment Concentration ────────────▶ 100%
```

Figure 1. Classification of Sediment-Water Flows (modified from
Pierson and Costa, 1984).

        Southern California has experienced many episodes of brush fire
followed by periods of high sediment production and debris flow. Dry
ravel of soil and organics during and immediately after fire carries
much loose debris into channels which can be easily mobilized in flows
during high runoff. Rill formation and development of rill networks
in addition to the formation of a layer of water-repellent soil, a few
millimeters below the soil surface, formed during fire is another
major process contributing to the production of abundant debris after
a fire (Wells & Brown 1981). The abundant debris, both on slopes and
in channels, and the rapid concentration of runoff from denuded
watersheds with water-repellent soil accentuates the debris-flow
problem.
        Debris flows commonly occur also in nonburned areas; however,
there they are initiated principally as shallow landslides on steep
slopes of colluvial soil and ravine fill. Moreover, in nonburned
areas, specific meteorologic conditions, primarily antecedent rainfall
and peak storm intensity, are necessary for initiating debris flows;
peak storm intensity is more strongly associated with debris-flow
initiation than is actual storm size (Campbell 1975). Because
rainfall in southern California is predominantly orographic, intense
rainfall and subsequent debris-flow activity may be generally confined
to certain areas.

Northern California.-The January 3-5, 1982, storm in the San Francisco
Bay region dropped as much as half the mean annual precipitation in a
period of about 32 hours, causing widespread landsliding and
flooding. Thousands of slides induced by the storm transformed into
debris flows that swept down hillslopes or drainages, causing

significant property damage and loss of life (Brown et al. 1984). Before the storm, debris flows had been recognized in the San Francisco region, but their potential had not been fully appreciated, in part because they had occurred only locally in the years since population had spread into susceptible steep terrain.

Antecedent rainfall, as well as storm intensity and duration, were significant factors in debris-flow distribution. Seasonal rainfall, as well as rainfall during the month preceding the storm, had been unusually heavy, leaving the hillside soils with high moisture content at the beginning of the storm. A threshold of storm intensity and duration for abundant debris flows was determined based on a study of storms in the region (Cannon & Ellen 1985).

Debris flows in the January 1982 storm occurred predominantly in colluvial soils located in swales. These swales concentrated ground water in the soils over bedrock resulting in high pore-water pressures and initiation of debris flows (Reneau et al. 1984). To generate high pore-water pressures in these soils, rainfall must be of moderate to high intensity and long duration.

Human modification of hillslopes and channels was directly responsible for some debris flows in the January 1982 storm. Culverts which generally would have been able to handle the flow of clear water plugged with debris, particularly trees, brush, and boulders. These blockages typically collapsed as ponded water levels rose behind the road embankments, sending surges of water and debris down the channel as debris flows or hyperconcentrated streamflows.

Basin and Range.-The arid portions of the western United States are subject to "flash floods" that range from clear-water floods to debris flows. Although there have been few witnesses to these events in the sparsely populated areas, the abundance of alluvial fans, consisting of debris-flow and stream gravel deposits in varying proportions (Blackwelder 1928), attest to a long and pervasive debris-flow history.

On September 14, 1974, an intense thunderstorm passed over Eldorado Canyon near Lake Mojave, Nevada. The duration of rainfall was short, generally less than an hour, but intensities were very high--from 3 to 6 in/h (7.6-15.2 cm/h) for 30 minutes. The intense rain eroded shallow soils, leaving rills on some of the sparsely vegetated hillsides, and the high runoff scoured unconsolidated alluvium from the larger stream channels. The initial surge was described as heavily laden with sediment and having a consistency generally equivalent to freshly mixed concrete. Descriptions characterized the first surge as a debris flow with subsequent surges of hyperconcentrated streamflow (Glancy & Harmsen 1975).

Wasatch Range.-In spring of 1983, rapid snowmelt in the Wasatch Range of northern Utah triggered numerous debris flows and hyperconcentrated streamflows that affected populated areas near the mouths of canyons north of Salt Lake City. Debris flows originated as landslides that incorporated large amounts of additional loose material from channel sides and bottoms as they surged down the canyons. Flooding was exacerbated by sediment deposited in the channels by landslides and debris flows.

Several climatic conditions in the winter of 1982 and spring of

1983 were responsible for causing these events. These conditions included (1) saturated soil mantle at the start of winter resulting from heavy, late autumn rains; (2) heavy winter snowpack; (3) low temperatures during late winter and early spring, permitting retention of the deep snow cover; and (4) sustained high temperatures once melting started. The cool weather in 1983 continued until about the middle of May when a sustained hot spell commenced, resulting in a very rapid melting of the above-normal snowpack. Subsequent high runoff resulted in flooding (Lindskov 1984) and rapid infiltration, causing temporary high ground-water levels. Such conditions triggered landslides, many of which were mobilized into debris flows. Of the many debris flows that occurred, only a few reached or extended beyond the mouths of canyons into developed areas (Wieczorek et al. 1983).

DEBRIS-FLOW HAZARD EVALUATION

The preceding examples illustrate some common physiographic settings and climatic triggering mechanisms for flows in mountainous regions of the western United States. The physiographic settings reflect the varying geologic, hydrologic, topographic, and vegetative conditions under which flows can be initiated. These examples also show the common sources of debris--landslides, rill erosion, dry ravel, channel bank collapse, and scour of stream channel deposits. Table 1 shows the general physiographic and climatic conditions for debris flows in the western United States.

To identify areas subject to debris flows and to plan and design for their occurrence it is necessary to (1) determine where they are likely to occur, (2) determine when they are likely to occur, and (3) determine where and how far they are likely to travel. Although the characteristics in Table 1 are descriptive of areas prone to debris flows, they are not criteria for evaluating susceptibility or runout distance, factors that vary widely with specific site characteristics.

Within the San Francisco Bay region a method for mapping debris-flow susceptibility was developed and subsequently evaluated against distribution of flows in the January 1982 storm within a small sample area (Smith 1986). Almost all (98%) flows originated in areas previously designated as most susceptible to debris-flow initiation. In the Wasatch Range of Utah, Pack (1985) used an analysis of geology, vegetation, slope gradient, and slope shape to classify 88% of the 1983 debris-flow sites as highly prone to failure. Whether these locally successful methods have widespread applicability is unknown.

The problem of forecasting the path and runout of debris flows has been addressed using several approaches: (1) historic or prehistoric evidence of flows, (2) empirical methods, and (3) mathematical models. Based on historic and prehistoric debris-flow deposits, Glancy and Katzer (1977) mapped the debris flow hazard level for an area south of Reno, Nevada. Their evaluation predicted the general area inundated by a hyperconcentrated streamflow in May of 1983, but failed to predict the exact boundary of the affected area because the peak flow rate of water and debris was much greater than anticipated (Glancy 1985). The difficulty of properly estimating volume and flow rate of potential debris flows or hyperconcentrated streamflows seriously affects the accuracy of evaluating routing or runout. Likewise runout and routing are affected by human construction or channel alteration.

Methods of estimating debris-flow runout have been based on empirical relationships between runout and other parameters, such as potential energy. For debris flows in Utah, Vandre (1985) proposed that runout on a 10% or flatter gradient was proportional to the elevation difference between debris-flow scarp and fan. Wieczorek and others (1983) evaluated the potential for debris-flow runout beyond a canyon mouth by calculating the volume of a landslide that mobilized and flowed to a canyon mouth and used that standard for comparison with semidetached landslides that had not yet mobilized. These various methods are site specific and cannot be extended to other regions without further analysis; therefore, their wider applicability is unclear.

Mathematical models for determining debris-flow paths require difficult-to-obtain, field-measured values. Wigmosta (1983) used fluid mechanics theory to calculate velocity, discharge of peak flow, and other flow parameters at locations along the channels of several large debris flows from the May 1980 eruption of Mount St. Helens, Washington. Jeppson (1985) used computer models to simulate debris flows from a canyon that experienced a debris flow in Utah during 1983. Chen (1985) developed one-dimensional equations for debris

TABLE 1. - Conditions for Debris Flows in Western United States

Physiographic Setting	Characteristics of Climatic-Triggering Event(s)	Principal Source(s) of Debris
Los Angeles Ranges of Pacific Border Province[*]		
Loose thin soils over bedrock on sparsely vegetated steep hillsides. Following a wildfire, a very shallow water-repellent soil layer is created. Wildfire removes vegetation, reducing soil restraining effect of roots.	Antecedent rainfall is important except in burned areas. Although storms may last several days, short-term peak intensity is most important. Following a wildfire, the first several storms are the most important. Orographic rainfall can be significant.	Shallow translational landslides; following a wildfire, dry ravel, rill erosion, and gully erosion.
California Coast Ranges of Pacific Border Province		
Moderate to thick colluvial soils in swales on steep slopes. Slopes may be thinly or thickly vegetated. Locations of ground-water concentration are important.	Antecedent rainfall is important. Both storm intensity and duration are important. Continuous moderate to high intensity lasting many hours is an important factor.	Rotational and translational landslides. Organic debris can constitute a major component of flows and cause blockages of culverts and bridges.
Basin and Range Province		
Loose thin soil on steep hillslopes. With sparce vegetation, runoff during storms is quickly concentrated.	High-intensity, short duration rainfall during convective storms on naturally barren hillslopes or where vegetation has been removed.	Rill erosion on hillsides; stream bank collapse and scour of stream channel deposits.
Middle Rocky Mountain Province		
Moderate to thick colluvial soils in locations of groundwater concentration on steep hillsides.	Rapid melting of heavy snowpack from sudden warm spell.	Rotational and translational landslides with significant contribution from scour of channel banks and deposits.

[*]Physical divisions of the United States from Fenneman (1946).

flows down a narrow valley, but points out that these equations do not apply on an alluvial fan, where debris flows can expand laterally, and for which a two-dimensional model is needed. Measurements of the rheologic properties of debris flows are relatively few, so at least for now the results from such models are largely theoretical.

HAZARD WARNING

Recognition of debris-flow triggering events and analyses to identify thresholds critical for the triggering of debris flows provide the possibility of issuing hazard warnings. The National Weather Service and the U.S. Geological Survey jointly issued a debris-flow advisory in the San Francisco Bay region in radio bulletins during the storm of January 26, 1983, based on rainfall comparisons to the January 1982 storm. Although scattered debris flows were observed following this warning, they were not so abundant as in January of 1982 because rainfall totals in the 1983 storm fell far short of forecasts and amounts in the 1982 storm.

Since 1983, an Automated Local Evaluation in Real Time (ALERT) system (Clark et al. 1983) of telemetry rain gauges has been installed in the San Francisco Bay region under coordination of the National Weather Service. This system is similar to one previously established in Ventura County, California, which provided data for flood peak analyses and allowed preventative measures to avoid a flood disaster in February of 1980 (Bartfeld & Taylor 1982). One of the ALERT stations in the San Francisco Bay region is outfitted by the U.S. Geological Survey with devices to monitor ground-water level fluctuation in shallow soils on steep slopes where debris flows are likely to be initiated (Alger, Mark & Wieczorek 1985). These data, along with rainfall measurements, are intended to provide real-time monitoring of hillside processes during storms. In the San Francisco Bay region, with the ALERT network, those responsible for the public welfare are in a much better position than ever before to issue flood and debris-flow warnings.

In Utah and other western states telemetered data on snowpack water equivalent, total precipitation, and air temperature are collected under the SNOTEL acquisition system (Crook 1983) to monitor the accumulation of the snowpack as well as the onset of rapid melting. This provides an indicator of regional hillside conditions, which is useful for hazard evaluation and warning. Following the events of 1983 along the Wasatch Front of Utah, several landslide sites were instrumented to measure temperature, precipitation, and hillside movement. In the spring of 1984 alarms triggered by landslide movement gave advance warning of debris flows (McCarter & Kaliser 1985).

SUMMARY AND CONCLUSIONS

Both on a site-specific and regional scale, advances in electronic data monitoring and transmission have made debris-flow hazard warning feasible in real time. However, judicious warnings depend upon an understanding of the debris-flow-initiation process in a particular physiographic setting, and development of historic thresholds or models upon which warnings can be reliably based.

APPENDIX 1. - REFERENCES

Alger, C. S., Mark, R. K., and Wieczorek, G. F. (1985). "Hydraulic Monitoring at a Debris-flow Site," EOS, Transactions of American Geophysical Union, Vol. 66, No. 46, 911.

Bartfeld, I., and Taylor, D. B. (1982). "A Case Study of a Real-time Flood Warning System on Sespe Creek, Ventura County, California," Proceedings on the Symposium on Storms, Floods and Debris Flows in Southern California and Arizona 1978 and 1980, National Academy Press, Washington, D.C., 165-176.

Blackwelder, E. (1928). "Mudflow as a Geologic Agent in Semiarid Mountains," Geological Society of America Bulletin, Vol. 39, 465-484.

Brown, W. M., III, Sitar, N., Saarinen, T. F., and Blair, M. L. (1984). "Debris Flows, Landslides, and Floods in the San Francisco Bay Region, January, 1982--Overview and Summary," National Academy Press, Washington, D.C.

Campbell, R. H. (1975). "Soil Slips, Debris Flows and Rainstorms in the Santa Monica Mountains and Vicinity, Southern California," U.S. Geological Survey Professional Paper 851.

Cannon, S. H., and Ellen, S. (1985). "Rainfall Conditions for Abundant Debris Avalanches in the San Francisco Bay Region, California," California Geology, Vol. 38, no. 12, 267-272.

Chen, C. L. (1985). "Hydraulic Concepts in Debris Flow Simulation," Proceedings of a Specialty Conference on Delineation of Landslide, Flash Flood, and Debris Flow Hazards in Utah, Utah State University, 236-259.

Clark, R. A., Burnash, R. J. C., and Bartfeld, I. (1983). "Alert, a National Weather Service Program for a Locally-Operated, Real-time Hydrologic Telemetry and Warning System," Proceedings of the International Technical Conference on Mitigation of Natural Hazards Through Real-Time Data Collection Systems and Hydrologic Forecasting, World Meteorological Organization, U.S. National Oceanic and Atmospheric Administration, and California Department of Water Resources, 51.

Crook, A. G. (1983). "The SNOTEL Data Acquisition System, and its Use in Mitigation of Natural Hazards," Proceedings of the International Technical Conference on Mitigation of Natural Hazards Through Real-Time Data Collection Systems and Hydrologic Forecasting, World Meteorological Organization, U.S. National Oceanic and Atmospheric Administration, and California Department of Water Resources, 83.

Fenneman, N. M. (1946). Physical Divisions of the United States, U.S. Geological Survey, Washington, D.C., scale 1:7,000,000.

Glancy, P. A. (1985). "The Ophir Creek Debris Flood of May 30, 1983--A Real Test of Geohydrologic Hazard Mapping," Proceedings of a Specialty Conference on Delineation of Landslide, Flash Flood, and Debris Flow Hazards in Utah, Utah State University, 195.

Glancy, P. A., and Harmsen, L. (1975) "A Hydrologic Assessment of the September 14, 1974, Flood in Eldorado Canyon, Nevada," U.S. Geological Survey Professional Paper 930.

Glancy, P. A., and Katzer, T. L. (1977). "Flood and Related Debris Flow Hazards Map, Washoe Lake Area, Nevada," Environmental Series, Nevada Bureau of Mines and Geology.

Jeppson, R. W. (1985). "Mechanisms Associated with Utah's 1983 Slides and Debris Flows," Proceedings of a Specialty Conference on Delineation of Landslide, Flash Flood, and Debris Flow Hazards in Utah, Utah State University, 197-234.

Lindskov, K. L. (1984). "Floods of May to June 1983 Along the Northern Wasatch Front, Salt Lake City to North Ogden," Water Resources Bulletin 24, Utah Geological and Mineral Survey.

McCarter, M. K., and Kaliser, B. N. (1985). "Prototype Instrumentation and Monitoring Programs for Measuring Surface Deformation Associated with Landslide Processes," Proceedings of a Specialty Conference on Delineation of Landslide, Flash Flood, and Debris Flow Hazards in Utah, Utah State University, 30-49.

Pack, R. T. (1985). "Multivariate Analysis of Landslide-Related Variables in Davis County, Utah," Proceedings of a Specialty Conference on Delineation of Landslide, Flash Flood, and Debris Flow Hazards in Utah, Utah State University, 50-65.

Pierson, T. C. and Costa, J. E. (1984). "A Rheologic Classification of Subaerial Sediment-water Flows," Abstracts with Programs, Geological Society of America, Vol. 16, No. 6, 623.

Reneau, S. L., Dietrich, W. E., Wilson, C. J., and Rogers, J. D. (1984). "Colluvial Deposits and Associated Landslides in the Northern San Francisco Bay Area, California, USA," Proceedings of IV International Symposium on Landslides, Canadian Geotechnical Society Vol. 1, 425-430.

Smith, T. C. (1986). "A Method for Mapping Relative Susceptibility to Debris Avalanches with an Example From San Mateo County, California," Special Publication, California Division of Mines and Geology, Sacramento, Calif.

Troxell, H. C., and Peterson, J. Q. (1937). "Flood in La Cañada Valley, California January 1, 1934," U.S. Geological Survey Water-Supply Paper 796-C, 53-98.

Vandre, B. C. (1985). "Rudd Creek Debris Flow," Proceedings of a Specialty Conference on Delineation of Landslide, Flash Flood, and Debris Flow Hazards in Utah, Utah State University, 1985, 117-131.

Wells, W. G. II, and Brown, W. M. III (1981). "Effects of Fire on Sedimentation Processes," Sediment Management for Southern California Mountains, Coastal Plains and Shoreline, Report No. 17-D, Environmental Quality Laboratory, California Institute of Technology, Pasadena, 83-122.

Wieczorek, G. F., Ellen, S., Lips, E. W., Cannon, S. H., and Short, D. N. (1983). "Potential for Debris Flow and Debris Flood Along the Wasatch Front Between Salt Lake City and Willard, Utah, and Measures for Their Mitigation," U.S. Geological Survey Open-file Report 83-635.

Wigmosta, M. S. (1983). "Rheology and Flow Dynamics of the Toutle Debris Flows From Mt. St. Helens," thesis presented to the University of Washington, at Seattle, in partial fulfillment of the requirements for the degree of Doctor of Philosophy.

Generalized Methodology for Simulating Mudflows

Robert C. MacArthur[1], A.M. ASCE, David R. Schamber[2], A.M. ASCE,
Douglas L. Hamilton[3], A.M. ASCE, and Mary H. West[4]

In this paper, a one-dimensional dynamic flood-routing model, for
non-Newtonian fluid properties, is described and applied to two different mudflow events: Holbrook Canyon, Utah, and Mount St. Helens,
Washington.

Introduction

In the spring of 1983, widespread landslides and debris flows
caused an estimated $250 million in damage in the State of Utah.
Extensive landslides sent torrents of mud and debris down onto residential areas situated at the mouths of steep canyons. Many of these
events are described by Figure 1. In Region A, a mudflow is initiated by a landslide or soil slip, which is preceded by saturated
ground conditions, rapid snowmelt, and/or excessive rainfall. The
mudflow material then travels in a confining channel from Region A to
B, where the flow is essentially one-dimensional. At point B, the
fluid emerges onto an unbounded plane or fan, and spreads out in the
streamwise and transverse directions. Here the flow is two-
dimensional.

On May 18, 1980, Mount St. Helens, in southwestern Washington,
erupted violently, setting off a chain of devastating mudflow events.
Mudflows occurred in the South Fork of the Toutle River, and in the
Lewis River tributaries of Smith Creek, Muddy River, and Pine Creek.
A massive mudflow on the North Fork of the Toutle River originating
from the debris avalanche deposit near the mountain caused widespread
destruction as it moved downstream through the lower Toutle and
Cowlitz Rivers. Unlike the Utah mudflows, this mudflow was initiated
by rapid snow- and ice-melt resulting from the volcanic eruption.

---

[1] Vice President, Simons, Li & Associates, Inc., 3555 Stanford Road,
P.O. Box 1816, Fort Collins, Colorado 80522, USA.

[2] Associate Professor, Civil Engineering Department, University of
Utah, Salt Lake City, Utah 84112, USA.

[3] Civil Engineer, Simons, Li & Associates, Inc., 3901 Westerly Place,
Suite 101, Newport Beach, California 92660, USA.

[4] Graduate Student, Civil Engineering Department, University of Utah,
Salt Lake City, Utah 84112, USA.

In most hydraulic problems, flows are turbulent and obey the laws of Newtonian fluids. Jeyapalan et al. (1983) and Pierson (1984) conclude that mudflows are often laminar in nature. Figure 2 shows the behavior of various types of fluid when a shear stress is applied to them. Mudflow materials often behave as Bingham plastic fluids having an initial shear strength. Once shearing stresses exceed this critical shear strength the material flows and behaves like a very viscous Newtonian fluid.

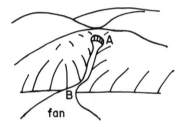

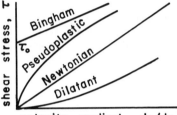

Figure 1. Mudflow Event   Figure 2. Behavior of Various Fluids

This paper will present the generalized methodology for simulating the dynamic behavior of mudflows occurring in confined channels. The general formulation of the transient one-dimensional mudflow model is presented along with results from applications of the model to Holbrook Canyon, Utah, and Mount St. Helens, Washington.

Governing Equations

The dynamics of one-dimensional, transient mudflows are governed by the equations of mass and momentum conservation. Mathematically, these equations can be written as follows:

$$A \frac{\partial V}{\partial x} + VB \frac{\partial y}{\partial x} + B \frac{\partial y}{\partial t} + VA_x^y = 0 \tag{1}$$

$$\frac{\partial V}{\partial t} + V \frac{\partial V}{\partial x} + g \frac{\partial y}{\partial x} = g(S_0 - S_f) \tag{2}$$

In Equations 1 and 2, x = distance along the canyon; t = time; A = cross-sectional area of flow; B = top width; V = flow velocity in the x-direction; y = flow depth; A_x^y = rate of change of area with respect to x holding y fixed; g = gravitational constant; S_0 = bottom slope; and S_f = frictional resistance term produced by boundary shear.

The resistance term is related to the mud properties and flow variables by assuming a Bingham type fluid (Jeyapalan, et al., 1983). Mathematically,

$$S_f = \frac{2\eta V}{\gamma R^2} + \frac{\tau_y}{\gamma R} \tag{3}$$

in which η = fluid viscosity; γ = unit weight of the fluid; τ_y = yield stress of the fluid; and R = hydraulic radius i.e. area divided by the wetted perimeter.

The governing flow Equations 1 and 2, are hyperbolic in nature and can be readily transformed into characteristic form. Mathematically,

$$\frac{d}{dt}(V \cdot \underline{+} \omega) = g(S_0 - S_f) \underline{+} \frac{c}{A} VA_x^y \underline{+} (V \underline{+} c) \int_0^y \frac{g}{c^2} \frac{\partial c}{\partial x} d\eta \tag{4}$$

$$\frac{dx}{dt} = V \underline{+} c \tag{5}$$

in which c = celerity of an elementary gravity wave is given by

$$c = (\frac{gA}{B})^{1/2} \tag{6}$$

and ω = Escoffier stage variable is given by

$$\omega = \int_0^y \frac{g}{c} d\eta \tag{7}$$

Four ordinary differential equations are defined by Equations 4 and 5. The so-called forward characteristic equations are defined by the upper sign e.g., $(V + \omega)$ and $(V + c)$, while the backward characteristic equations are defined by the lower sign e.g., $(V - \omega)$ and $(V - c)$. The simultaneous solution of these four equations yields depth and velocity surfaces in $x - t$ space.

Top width and area are represented by a power law expression. Mathematically,

$$B = (k_L + k_R) y^m \tag{8}$$

$$A = (\frac{k_L + k_R}{m + 1}) y^{m+1} \tag{9}$$

in which k_L and k_R define the left and right hand widths respectively for a given depth. The exponent m defines the shape of the cross section i.e., $m = 0$ for a rectangular section, $m = 1/2$ for a parabolic section, and $m = 1$ for a triangular section. In general, k_L, K_R, and m can be specified functions of distance, x, to capture the nonprismatic nature of a particular canyon or valley. In practice, this may be very difficult to achieve for all but simple expansions and contractions (Franz, 1976). Using Equations 8 and 9, the wave celerity and stage variable reduce to

$$c = (\frac{gy}{m + 1})^{1/2} \tag{10}$$

$$\omega = 2 [g(m + 1)y]^{1/2} \tag{11}$$

If the exponent m is independent of distance, x, the last term in Equation 4 vanishes and the numerical solution is simplified.

Numerical Solution

The numerical solution of the characteristic equations is developed by employing a finite difference approximation in the x-t plane. Figure 3 depicts the solution domain with time lines t_i and t_{i+1}. Each time line is divided into n node points i.e., x_k for $k = 1$, $2, \ldots, n$. The points can be evenly spaced or irregularly spaced depending on the variation of depth and velocity. In Figure 3 the solution is known at time t_i and it is desired to determine the solution along t_{i+1}. The characteristic curves in Figure 3, c^- and c^+, are approximated by straight lines or parabolas depending on the order of the differencing scheme. The finite difference approximation of Equations 4 and 5 becomes

$$\frac{x_p - x_L}{\delta t} = \lambda_L (V_L + c_L) + \lambda_p (V_p + c_p) \tag{12}$$

$$\frac{x_p - x_R}{\delta t} = \lambda_R (V_R - c_R) + \lambda_p (V_p - c_p) \tag{13}$$

$$\frac{(V_p + \omega_p) - (V_L + \omega_L)}{\delta t} = \lambda_L F_L^+ + \lambda_p F_p^+ \tag{14}$$

$$\frac{(V_p - \omega_p) - (V_R - \omega_R)}{\delta t} = \lambda_R F_R^- + \lambda_p F_p^- \tag{15}$$

in which

$$F^{\pm} = g(S_0 - S_f) \mp \frac{c}{A} VA_x^y \mp (V \pm c) \int_0^y \frac{g}{c^2} \frac{\partial c}{\partial x} d\eta \tag{16}$$

and $\delta t = t_{i+1} - t_i$. The unknowns in Equations 12-15 are x_L, x_R, y_p, and V_p i.e. the locations of the intersection of c^- and c^+ on the t_i time line and the depth and velocity at node P. For $\lambda_L = \lambda_R = 1$ and $\lambda_p = 0$ the scheme is first-order, explicit and the characteristics are approximated by straight lines. For $\lambda_L = \lambda_R = \lambda_p = 1/2$, the scheme is second-order, implicit and the characteristics are approximated by parabolic curves. The program can be executed using either the first order or second order scheme to generate the solution. The first order computation is explicit and relatively fast, but requires a small δt.

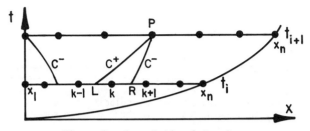

Figure 3. Computational Domain

Selection of the second order scheme requires the simultaneous solution of four nonlinear equations (12 - 15). The linear scheme is used to initialize this method and the equations are solved iteratively by Newton's method. Generally, 1 to 2 iterations are required for convergence at each computational point.

In the first order scheme, linear interpolation for y and V is used at points x_L and x_R. In the second order scheme, parabolic interpolation for y and V is used at points x_L and x_R. For both cases, a simple search procedure assures that the interpolation nodes (e.g., x_{k-1}, x_k, x_{k+1} for a parabola) always straddle the points x_L and x_R so that extrapolation is avoided. Near the advancing front of the wave the mud depth increases rapidly from zero to a finite value a short distance behind the nose. In this region, linear or parabolic interpolation of depth can produce inaccurate results, which may eventually pollute the entire wave profile and abort the computer run. In order to avoid this situation, the depth is interpolated between nodes x_{n-1} and x_n using a rigid plug approximation. In this region, the wave moves essentially undeformed, while the water surface slope becomes very steep as $y \rightarrow 0$ and $S_f \rightarrow \infty$. Equation 2 can then be expressed as a simple balance between free surface slope and S_f near the wave tip. If the τ_y term in Equation 3 is neglected, and furthermore if $R \sim y$, then the resulting ordinary differential equation can be integrated to give a 1/3 power law variation of y with x for $x_{n-1} \leq x \leq x_n$. This expression is used for interpolation of depth at the advancing front.

Initial and Boundary Conditions

During the early stages of flooding, the entire wave is treated as a rigid plug and various terms in Equation 2 are neglected. This leads to a closed-form, integrated solution which serves as an appropriate initial condition.

At the left-most boundary, $x = 0$ in Figure 3, a mudflow discharge hydrograph, Q_0, is specified as a known function of time. The shape, duration, peak discharge, time to peak discharge, and total volume for a particular mudflow event can be specified with this hydrograph. For subcritical flow at $x = 0$, the known discharge equation, $Q_0 = V_p A_p$, is solved simultaneously with a backward characteristic emanating from point 1 on time line t_{i+1} and intersecting the line of known values along t_i. If the flow is supercritical at x = 0, the assumption of normal depth coupled with Q_0 provides values of depth and velocity at the left boundary. The program monitors the local value of Froude number in order to select the appropriate condition.

At the wave front the depth is zero, and the advance trajectory is determined by using the Whitham assumption i.e., $V_n = V_{n-1}$. Once $V(n-1, t_j)$ and $V(n-1, t_{j+1})$ are determined, the wave advance speed is computed as a simple average of the two velocities and the wave front displacement is then the product of δt and the wave speed.

Holbrook Canyon Application

In the spring of 1983 several communities north of Salt Lake City, Utah, at the base of the Wasatch Range, were inundated with mud produced by rapid melting of a record snowpack. Holbrook Canyon, near the Town of Bountiful, Utah, produced a mudflow on the order of two million cubic feet. The computer model presented herein is used to simulate this mudflow. The canyon geometry is approximated as prismatic with m = 0.75 and $k_L = k_R = 2.5$ (c.f. Equations 8 and 9) and $S_0 = 0.12$. Upstream, at x = 0, a discharge hydrograph is specified as shown in Figure 4. This hydrograph has a total volume of 2.6 million cubic feet, and the peak discharge and time to peak discharge are commensurate with actual measurements taken on Rudd Creek Canyon, which is approximately 7 miles north of Holbrook Canyon. The length of the canyon is approximately 14,600 feet. Fluid properties for this simulation are γ = 125 lb/ft^3, n = 10 lb·sec/ft^2, and τ_y = 20 lb/ft^2. These values were determined from data taken by Pierson (1984) on Rudd Creek. Discharge hydrographs obtained from the numerical solution at x = 7,000 and x = 14,600 are shown in Figure 5. The advance trajectory of the leading edge of the wave and surface profiles at various times are also shown in Figures 6 and 7.

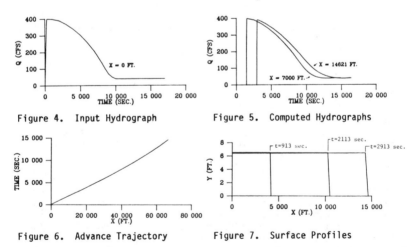

Figure 4. Input Hydrograph

Figure 5. Computed Hydrographs

Figure 6. Advance Trajectory

Figure 7. Surface Profiles

Mount St. Helens Case Study

Since the 1980 eruption of Mount St. Helens, several mudflows have occurred along the North Fork of the Toutle River. These mudflows have transported millions of cubic yards of sediment down to the Cowlitz and Colombia Rivers. To minimize the need for dredging, the Portland District of the U.S. Army Corps of Engineers proposed the construction of a sediment retention structure. To aid in the general design and spillway sizing, the one-dimensional mudflow model is applied to predict routed mudflow characteristics at the proposed site (The Hydrologic Engineering Center, 1985). The study reach is about 7.5 miles in length, 1,000 feet wide on the average, and has an average slope of 0.0093. Estimated ranges of mudflow properties are available from Major (1984). Table I shows the combinations of fluid properties used for the sensitivity analysis as well as the results from the one-dimensional mudflow model. Figure 8 shows an example plot of routed mudflow hydrographs with constant viscosity and unit weight but with varying yield strength.

Table I. Sensitivity Analysis - Mt. St. Helens

Run No.[1]	VIS[2]	YST[3]	WT[4]	T_A[5]	T_p[6]	Q_p[7]	Y_p[8]	V_p[9]
1	6	8	125	42.3	47.3	228000	16.4	13.9
2	6	21	125	57.8	66.8	188000	22.2	8.4
3	6	31	125	76.7	92.7	145000	28.2	5.1
4	27	8	125	61.2	69.2	203000	24.2	8.4
5	27	21	125	74.9	91.9	170000	28.9	5.9
6	27	31	125	90.7	108.7	137000	32.3	4.2
7	100	8	125	88.8	102.8	171000	34.2	5.0
8	100	21	125	103.4	122.4	145000	37.2	3.9
9	100	31	125	117.7	141.7	121000	39.7	3.0
10	6	8	100	46.0	51.0	221000	18.0	12.3
11	6	21	100	68.6	82.6	166000	26.1	6.3
12	6	31	100	97.5	117.5	111000	32.5	3.4
13	27	8	100	67.1	76.1	194000	26.2	7.4
14	27	21	100	86.1	102.1	152000	31.6	4.8
15	27	31	100	111.2	134.2	108000	36.1	3.0
16	100	8	100	97.8	112.8	161000	36.5	4.4
17	100	21	100	116.9	139.9	128000	40.2	3.2
18	100	31	100	138.9	166.9	96000	42.4	2.3

Fluid Properties / Routed Flow Properties at the Proposed Dam Location

[1] Channel characteristics for simulations—
Upstream Station Location: 0.0', Elev.: 1118.00'
Dam Site Location: 32,300', Elev.: 820.00'

[2] Viscosity in lb·sec/ft^2

[3] Yield Strength in lb/ft^2

[4] Unit Weight in lb/ft^3

[5] Travel time in min. for wave front to reach damsite

[6] Travel time in min. for peak discharge to reach damsite

[7] Peak discharge at damsite in cfs

[8] Depth of flow at peak discharge at damsite in ft

[9] Average velocity of peak flow at damsite (Q_p/1000 Y_p) in fps

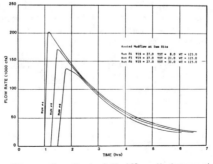

Figure 8. Routed Mudflow Hydrograph

Summary

The one-dimensional mudflow model has been successfully applied to a range of problems. The Holbrook Canyon study tests the model's ability to simulate flows in steep canyons (12% slope in this case). The Mount Saint Helen's study uses a channel slope of about 1% but with a much longer routing reach. A current on-going study involves routing a mudflow through Rudd Creek Canyon which has an average slope of 31 percent. In the future, a two-dimensional mudflow model will be used to analyze flooding on alluvial fans. The hydrograph determined from the one-dimensional model will serve as the input to the two-dimensional model. The one-dimensional mudflow model has been verified by a limited amount of experimental data (Schamber and MacArthur, 1985), however, further, extensive laboratory experiments are required to validate and improve the existing models.

Acknowledgements

This research was sponsored by the U.S. Army Corps of Engineers, Portland District, Omaha District and Hydrologic Engineering Center, and by the Federal Emergency Management Agency. Their technical and financial assistance is gratefully acknowledged. The results and opinions presented herein are solely those of the authors and not necessarily those of the Corps of Engineers or FEMA.

References

Franz, Delbert D., 1976. Discussion of "Dimensionless Solution of Dam-Break Flood Waves," Journal of the Hydraulics Division, ASCE, Dec., pp. 1782-1784.

Hydrologic Engineering Center, 1985. "Toutle River Mudflow Investigation," report prepared for Portland District, U.S. Army Corps of Engineers Special Projects Report No. 85-3, July, 45 pp.

Jeyapalan, J.K., J.M. Duncan, and H.B. Seed, 1983. "Analysis of Flow Failures of Mine Tailings Dams," Journal of Geotechnical Engineering, ASCE, Vol. 109, No. 2, Feb., pp. 150-171.

Major, Jon J., 1984. "Geologic and Rheologic Characteristics of the May 18, 1980 Southwest Flank Lahars at Mount St. Helens, Washington," thesis presented to The Pennsylvania State University in partial fulfillment of the requirements for the degree of Master of Science.

Pierson, Thomas, C., 1984. "Effects of Slurry Composition on Debris Flow Dynamics, Rudd Canyon, Utah:" in Delineation of Landslide, Flash Flood, and Debris Flow Hazards in Utah, Proceeding of Specialty Conference, Utah State University, Logan, June 14-15, pp. 132-152.

Schamber, D.R., and R.C. MacArthur, 1985. "One-Dimensional Model for Mudflows," Hydraulics and Hydrology in the Small Computer Age, Proceedings of the Specialty Conference, ed. W.R. Waldrop, ASCE, Vol. 2, August, pp. 1334-1339.

RESPONSIBILITY/ LIABILITY RELATED TO MUDFLOWS/DEBRIS FLOWS

J. E. Slosson[1], G. Shuirman[2], and D. Yoakum[3]

Introduction

Recent court decisions have shown a tendency to hold the professionals involved in planning, construction and maintenance of engineered facilities, as well as government, liable for losses and damages.

In previous decades, most cases filed against government entities were dismissed by the courts because of immunities established by legislation. This sovereign immunity was based upon English law which prescribed that no one could file an action against the king or government. Court decisions during the past three decades have slowly stripped government of some of these prescribed immunities. Possibly, the most significant of these cases was Albers v. Los Angeles County (1965) where both the trial court and the appelate court found Los Angeles County responsible for damages resulting from reactivation of the ancient Portuguese Bend Landslide. Subsequently, plaintiffs' attorneys have been able to slowly strip other protective immunities from governmental entities and government employees.

Numerous cases filed against government during the past few years have claimed that government: (1) failed to take action to prevent the damage even though having knowledge of the potential for damage and/or losses (Ablieter, et al. v. Allstate); (2) failed to properly or adequately design and construct (Woolrich, et al. v. City of San Diego); and (3) was a contributing factor because of work accomplished by government (Albers v. County of Los Angeles). Recent cases filed in Los Angeles Superior Courts have seen both government and government employees being charged with dereliction of duty, failure to recognize hazards, and failure to provide adequate review and field inspection. To date, no lawsuits have prevailed against government employees, but data presented in court related to failure of employees to properly perform their functions have been used against government and have assisted the plaintiffs' attorney(s) in winning.

The Ablieter v. Allstate case involved back-up of storm water from a culvert under U.S. Highway 101 in Woodland Hills and consequent inundation of about 30 residential properties. Plaintiff property owners alleged that California Department of Transportation (CalTrans), was aware the culvert was undersized, yet continued to postpone remedial

[1] Slosson and Associates, 14046 Oxnard Street, Van Nuys, CA 91401
[2] Civil Engineer, 15928 Ventura Boulevard #225, Encino, CA 91436
[3] GeoSoils, Inc., 5650 Van Nuys Boulevard, Van Nuys, CA 91401

action. Both CalTrans and the County of Los Angeles settled prior to
trial. California law now holds government responsible for loss of
life, injury, and property damage if government was aware of the hazard
and took no action to mitigate. Other litigation against government
during the past 10 to 20 years has seen decisions going against government much more frequently. The City of San Diego (Wood, et al. v. City
of San Diego, 1985) was recently held responsible to homeowners for
grading related to construction of a public street and adjacent undeveloped property. Structures were later built on this undeveloped land
with subsequent settlement of the fill. In another case, (Woolrich
et al. v. City of San Diego) the City of San Diego was found
responsible because of an undersized culvert under the San Diego/Tijuana
Trolley road base fill. In 1980 and 1983, flooding occurred damaging
residential structures adjacent to the flood control channel and upstream of the undersized culvert.

Numerous cases have been, and are being, filed naming as defendants
the developer, developer's consultants and/or the carriers of the homeowners insurance. In most situations, the developer is named because
of the strict liability rule for the manufacturer of a product. In
some cases, the insurance company is often named via the third-party
involvement rule for the concurrent proximate cause of damage. In
almost every case, the developer and/or insurance carrier will file a
cross-complaint against the consultants. These complaints are often
successful in such cases where the work of the professionals did not
meet prudent practices. A 1985 California Supreme Court ruling
(Tech-Bilt, Inc. v. Woodward-Clyde & Associates) stripped the 10-year
statute of limitations from consultants for cross-complaints. This
allows the developer and/or insurance carrier to reach back with no
time limitation on professional work completed.

Consequently, professional consultants (civil engineer, engineering
geologist, geotechnical engineer, structural engineer, et cetera) are
targets in the original complaint as well as targets of cross-complaints
filed by the developer and/or insurance carrier if either or both
should lose in the first round. It behooves professional consultants
to perform in a judicious manner and not rely on poorly written and
poorly enforced local government codes or what other professionals may
be doing. As an example, recognition of mudflow/debris flow hazards
and their mitigation is seldom or adequately addressed in the codes
(one exception noted is the City of Los Angeles). This does not
relieve the consultants of the professional responsibility to recognize
and analyze this natural hazard and to recommend appropriate
mitigation. There are sufficient data available to preclude the often-
heard excuse "It was not mentioned in the code and I haven't given any
thought to that problem". Dozens of case histories from the past two
decades are available with good background references in the professional journals. Some consultants have been heard to state that they
had read some of the journal articles, but since local government did
not require reference, they have ignored referencing these hazards in
spite of known high property losses and loss of life.

The combined experiences of the authors during the past few decades
indicate that many of the problems and losses related to damage from
floods, landslides, mud/debris flows, and water-related subsidence are

directly or indirectly attributable to the inability and/or failure of
government (local, state, and sometimes federal) to adequately enforce
existing policies, codes, or regulations. For example -- flood damage,
debris flow, and landslide damage along the western front of the
Wasatch Mountains in 1983 caused serious damage to homes and public
facilities with significant monetary loss. Most of these losses were
attributable to failure by government to properly enforce floodplain
management regulations. A portion of the losses can be attributed to
lack of technical knowledge and scientific/engineering experience.
Another portion is due to failure to appropriately utilize the limited
expertise available. However, the greatest portion appears to be due
to failure of state and local governments to adopt codes and/or failure
to enforce the existing codes and regulations. Data suggest that > 50%
of the 1983 Utah flood/debris flow/landslide damages and losses could
have been prevented without adversely impacting construction and/or
economic growth.

Land subsidence, landslides, and surficial slope and/or slump problems that have plagued some cities and counties in California are also
due, in part, to failure of affected cities to adequately enforce
existing grading codes and regulations at the permit stage (the City of
Los Angeles and the County of Los Angeles being the exception to this
generalization). Furthermore, they have often failed to utilize some
form of inspection by their personnel and/or to insist on certification
of the work done by the professionals to assure quality control.

The construction of housing and public facilities in portions of the
foothill areas of the western states have revealed and created hazardous conditions related to mudflows and debris flows. Failure to
recognize the cause of mudflows and debris flows, whether natural or
man-made, has been a prime excuse as well as a major contributor to
extensive damages and losses which have occurred in California, Arizona,
Nevada, Utah, Colorado, and other western states. A few of the patent
case histories are: the 1983 Wasatch Front, Utah floods and debris
flows; the 1980 floods, debris flows, and/or landslides which
occurred in the San Francisco, San Diego, and Los Angeles areas; and
similar events in the San Francisco Bay area in 1982.

Investigations conducted following many of these disastrous events
strongly suggest that sites of mudflows and debris flows can be
recognized prior to the event. The effects of natural and/or man-made
conditions, controls, and causes are predictable. Geomorphic analyses
indicate that similar geologic events, whether historic or recent, have
often preceded the disasters which the authors have studied. Since the
locations of past mudflows and debris flows can be recognized and
locations of future such events can be predicted with reasonable
accuracy (the only unknown being the timing), it is logical to conclude
that proper utilization of the geological sciences, meteorology,
hydrology, and civil engineering could reduce damage and losses by an
estimated 90%. Failure to prudently incorporate known technological
capabilities into investigations will result in future losses at a
much greater dollar cost than the cost of appropriate design and
mitigation measures. Recent studies suggest that the benefit/cost
ratio favoring prudent engineering design may be as high as 100:1 or in
some cases over 1000:1.

In reviewing the history of recent catastrophies, it is evident
that timing of predictable catastrophic events is predicated upon
saturation of soil, alluvium, colluvium, and slopewash and the
resultant conversion of dry, loose, porous, solid mass into a fluid
mass capable of rapid downslope motion. Saturated earth material
conditions usually result from periods of prolonged high intensity
rainfall (i.e., Utah, 1982-83 and California, 1980), moisture from
abnormally high snow-melt conditions, and/or leakage of water from
reservoirs, water lines, onsite septic systems, excessive landscape
watering, et cetera. Another significant contributing condition, often
related to very destructive debris flows, is abnormally high runoff of
water and sediment transport resulting from a fire-flood sequence.
This phenomenon is associated with wildfire burns followed within one
to three years by above-average to record-breaking rainfall.

The following quotes relative to the subject have previously been
included in the public record:

● The San Diego Union, September 19, 1982

    In response to questions by the San Diego Union regarding what the
    City of San Diego has done to reduce the losses from landslides,
    one of the authors stated "Local government in San Diego has done
    very little to correct the potential problems"; "...the city does
    not adequately enforce many of the minimum standards set by the
    State of California"; "Local government in San Diego is very
    limply, weakly utilizing state required codes"; "...the city
    should be a prime target in years to come if homeowners whose
    houses are ruined by a landslide decide to blame local government
    for allowing construction in an unstable area that would threaten
    public safety".

● In the winter of 1981-82, the San Francisco Bay area suffered
    damages from landslides, mudflows, and floods estimated to have
    been in the excess of $300 million. The California State Board
    of Registration for Geologists and Geophysicists, as a regular
    function, conducted hearings and field trips related to these
    geologic hazards. Following the hearings and field trips, the
    Board, at its next monthly meeting, passed the following
    resolution: "...the responsibility for the damages and losses
    from the January mudslides should be placed at the door of many
    of the local governments for: (1) failure to adequately enforce
    Chapter 70 of the Uniform Building Code; and (2) failure to have
    licensed certified engineering geologists on staff available via
    contract to review all geologic reports submitted to local
    government and to inspect geologic conditions periodically
    during grading and construction, in order to assure that the codes
    and standards are properly complied with."

    The Board was also critical of the State of California, Department
    of Housing and Community Development for failure to police local
    government. In addition, the Board was informed by legal staff
    that "recent decisions by the courts have recognized the liability
    of local government for failure to enforce established statutes,
    codes, and ordinances". Again, government was found, in part,

responsible for the losses because of its failure to provide inspection to assure quality control.

● In the June 1985 issue of Civil Engineering, a letter to the editor by Jerry Haimoqitz, Consulting Engineer, Neshomic, New Jersey, stated:

"Engineers sell their services to repeat customers who are experts at beating down prices in a market flooded with too many licensed engineers. Owners are asking engineers to bid for the privilege of playing chicken; to see who can do the least work and still get by.

"Market forces are making engineers choose between playing chicken and bankruptcy. This clash of corporate titans is causing a problem in the lower ranks of all organizations involved in the project. Construction contractors have no pride; the craftsman is gone."

The authors' exposure to the applied technology field over the past 25 years supports the quote by Haimoqitz. Thus, if the client is applying pressure on the consultant, and if the client, consultant, and politicians are all applying pressure on government employees, it appears that most governmental entities will allow the standard of practice and professional work to drop to a standard desired by the client.

The most often used excuse or rationale is that "we met the code" or "we did everything required by the city or county of ...", or "the city or county accepted it". Thus, government becomes the excuse as well as the cause - at least, partially. Some of the most successful plaintiffs' attorneys in California have been including local government as a defendant when damage due to poor quality engineering, geology, or construction generates losses. Some have even made local government the prime defendant; local governments have lost a few such cases and are currently facing many more suits at much higher dollar factors. The attorneys representing the aggrieved homeowners on the Big Rock Mesa landslide in Malibu, California have filed cases in excess of $500 million, and the possibility exists that filings, including those related to neighboring landslides, may exceed $1 billion. Many jurisdictions, including the federal government, some state government, and local governments, are now in court (or will be in the near future) presenting defense arguments related to "failure to perform a duty". An example of such is the aforementioned Big Rock Mesa landslide litigation naming the County of Los Angeles and the State of California as defendants. The attorney for some of the homeowners on Big Rock Mesa made the following statement: "... agencies, by projects, acts, or omissions caused the landslide" and "We believe that what the county did might be likened to a failure to respond to a ticking time bomb".

As a case in point relative to reluctance to enforce is that within the City and County of San Diego, the rationale for not adequately enforcing has been: (1) "It never rains in San Diego" - so there is no reason to worry about subdrains, surface drains, or the quality of

compaction, or (2) "We are enforcing the code and/or applying specifications that the consultants have told us are adequate". The first
statement is ludicrous and the second makes no sense if one assumes the
quality of professional work will drop to the lowest level allowed by
government.

In California, similar cases, but with lesser dollar values, have
been filed against the City of San Diego, County of San Diego, City of
San Clemente, City of Los Angeles, City of Pacifica, County of Los
Angeles, County of Marin, County of San Mateo, City of San Jose, City
of Santa Clara, and other local governments. Similar cases have been
filed against governments in other states.

Current Legislation Enacted and Proposed

Legislative bills were introduced in 1984 and 1985 in California to
help cities, counties, the state and private firms cope with the
onslaught of "deep pockets" court rulings. Two of these bills partially
survived the effect lobbying by the trial attorneys only to be stalled
until the 1986 legislative sessions. Currently under the doctrine of
"joint and several liability", a defendant who is found only partially
responsible (including 1 percent to 10 percent) for injuries, damages,
and/or losses sustained by a plaintiff can be ordered to pay the
entire judgement if the chief defendant(s) is insolvent and unable to
pay the judgement amount.

The problem is not unique to California, but the risk of the "joint
and several liability" factor seems to be heavily emphasized in that
state. Increased liability insurance rates have been nationwide with
premiums for governmental agencies sky-rocketing as high as 700 percent
forcing some of the larger agencies and governments to operate under the
"go bare" policy (self-insure). Geotechnical consultants also are facing a similar dilemma. This is not a viable option for smaller
municipalities or private companies which could virtually be eliminated
by a single judgement. Nine states including Arkansas, Florida,
Texas, and Michigan have entered into a risk pool for expansive
coverage. Other states are attempting to legislate relief for the
interests that complain the most, such as California's $250,000 cap on
medical malpractice. States such as Pennsylvania and New York are
investigating "tort reform" - basically wholesale revision of rules for
dealing with civil-damage cases. A result of the crisis is
reciprocal assignment of guilt by the chief characters in the drama,
each accusing the other of being the culprit - the trial lawyers, the
insurance companies, the insured. The insured, up to now, have been
regarded as the least able to produce a voice loud enough to compete
with the strength of the lawyers and insurers,--but the problem has
become so acute that a common cause has evolved and we see a banding
together to exchange ideas and approaches to gain control of an
unwieldy problem. When small business, large corporations, small
municipalities and big government simultaneously face the enormity of
premium increase in the ranges from 75 percent to 700 percent in one
year, curtailment of services, increases in cost to consumers of
products, increased unemployment due to layoffs and the closing of
businesses, it is inevitable that drastic changes must take place and
quickly. Only a united approach under a vast umbrella can bring

about meaningful change. We, as professionals, must combine our
efforts with others to stress legislative changes as one link in the
chain. The ripple effect must be slowed, and legislation is a step in
the right direction provided the voices can be heard.

One of the bills authored by State Senator John Foran (D-San Francisco) would limit the amount of court judgements against private and
public defendants that are only partially responsible. In effect, this
bill would limit judgements against any one of the defendants to that
percentage of responsibility that was assigned specifically to that
individual defendant. Current law allows the courts to require a
defendant who contributed only a small percentage, but has "deep
pockets", to pay the entire judgement. This current interpretation
of the law has caused insurance companies to cancel liability insurance
for both public and private entities or to raise their premiums to
staggering figures.

Legislative changes in process in California that are of interest to
the licensed professionals are:

- SB 1488 (1985) which became law in January of 1986 requires, in
  addition to a declaration signed by a professional licensed in
  architecture, engineering, and land survey for the original
  complaint, declarations for each cross-complaint also be signed
  by the appropriate licensed professional.

- SB 453 (1985) which became law in 1986 provides that insurers
  who provide professional liability insurance for real estate
  licenses shall not exclude coverage for liability from breach
  of duty to conduct reasonable/diligent inspections and research.
  The 1984 appellate court decision of Easton v. Strassburger
  found the realtor responsible to disclose recognizable
  geologic/geotechnic defects. This bill requires that insurers
  continue to provide liability coverage.

- AB 1636 (1985) became law in 1986 and provides for the
  licensing and policing of insurance adjustors. This is an
  attempt to legislate responsibility.

How to Avoid Litigation

One of the authors has for 25 years relied on advice given him by a
talented criminal attorney (and not an attorney specializing in product or professional liability). His advice was straight forward and
elementary - "Do the best professional job possible and conscientiously
try to avoid errors or omissions". This philosophy has created an
environment whereby only three claims or cases have been filed in that
time space and all three were dismissed as frivolous.

Another bit of advice to consider is that a professional should not
lower his or her professional standards to meet the standard adhered to
by the competitors. An often-heard comment is "You really can't blame
us for that failure. Remember, if it were not for the low professional
standards of the competition, we would certainly have met higher
standards and would have avoided these failures, but we must be

competitive because we have just invested in a new building, have a
very generous profit sharing program, and have been adding staff as we
expand" or "We have to be competitive, so don't blame us for what
society has caused" or "You know that we would like to do a more
complete analysis, but if we didn't agree to take the contract, someone
else would have. You have to do what the client wants and for what the
client is willing to pay or a competitor will take the contract from
you". You should either do what you, as a professional, believe is
correct and complete or refuse to do the work. We have seen
professionals grudgingly agree to a sub-standard effort for a low to
inadequate budget. Some have been sued and have had judgements against
them in the tens to hundreds of thousands of dollars for projects where
their billing (and professional effort) was scaled down to a few
hundred dollars or a thousand or two. The client gets a cheap job and
a defacto insurance policy (or warranty) and the professional loses.
We have heard the client say "We are gambling and you have to take some
of the risk with us or we will get another consultant".

Another recommendation is not lower your professional effort
because "the city of .... does not require a detailed analysis and
they seldom, if ever, inspect the project and/or review the reports and
design. They only look to see if a licensed engineer, geologist, et
cetera has signed the report and design".

When failure occurs, both the involved professional and local
government will be sued. Since statewide good practices and standards
are often considered standard by the judge, the professionals are dead
in the water, so to speak. Court after court is holding the professionals responsible for the good standards practice utilized in jurisdictions such as the City of Los Angeles. If one lowers standards to that
of a local jurisdiction which has no professional or staff and does not
require good prudent practices, one most likely will be found
responsible for each and every loss where there is a failure to
discuss or no recognition of the hazard and/or recommendation for
mitigation. The obvious solution is: refusal to do substandard
professional work.

Some professionals, for various reasons, most of which are economic,
are reluctant to utilize assistance from others who may possess a
special expertise or knowledge factor. When necessary, use the services
of outside talent.

Most professional societies (such as ASCE) have published guidelines
for certain types of professionals. Avoid clients who state that
guidelines are un-American and they will not pay for what they claimed
was unnecessary work. Failure to meet the minimum criteria of
professional society guidelines is often considered incompetence or
substandard professional behavior by the Courts. We recommend that you
make use of such guidelines, produce a good professional document
and/or set of drawings and thus avoid failures and the courtroom.

APPENDIX. - LEGAL CASES CITED

1. Albers v. County of Los Angeles
   (62 Cal 2d, 250, 1965)

2. Ablieter, et al v. Allstate
   (a group of seventeen cases which were settled out of court, 1984)

3. Easton v. Strassburger
   (152 Cal App 3d, 90, 1984)

4. Tech-Bilt, Inc. v. Woodward-Clyde Associates
   (213 Cal. Rptr. 256, 1985)

5. Wood, et al v. City of San Diego
   (settled during trial, 1985)

6. Woolrich, et al v. City of San Diego
   (settled prior to trial, 1983)

ARTIFICIAL RECHARGE FOR MANAGING THE GREAT SALT LAKE

by

Calvin G. Clyde, F.ASCE, Christopher J. Duffy, M.ASCE,
and J. Paul Riley, M.ASCE*

Abstract

The Great Salt Lake occupies the lowest point in a drainage basin of approximately 22,000 mi^2 (57,000 km^2). Inflows to the lake occur as surface runoff, groundwater flows, and precipitation directly on the lake surface. The only outflow from the lake is through the evaporation process. Because it is a so-called terminal water body, lake volumes are very sensitive to prevailing climatological conditions. Since the beginning of the historic period of record in 1847, wide cyclic variations have occurred in the lake level. Periods of wet weather increase inflows and reduce evaporation losses, and thus cause increases in the lake volume. During sustained dry periods, the reverse occurs and lake levels decline.

The unique features of the Great Salt Lake make it very important to the State of Utah. Its mineral rich water and interesting shores appeal to both industry and vacationers. Until recently, some of the great waterfowl sanctuaries in the U. S. existed along the easterly and northerly shores of the lake. However, during the past three years, precipitation amounts throughout the drainage basin have significantly exceeded normal values. The resulting record breaking inflow volumes and lower than normal evaporation rates have caused an unprecedented rate of rise in the lake surface which attained an elevation of nearly 4210 ft (1283.2 m) above mean sea level (amsl) in May 1985. The rising waters already have caused extensive damages to both public and private properties, including roads, highways, railroads, hunting club facilities, mineral extraction facilities, waterfowl areas, homes, water treatment facilities, and agricultural lands.

In order to reduce future damages from the rising waters of the lake, various alternative flood control possibilities are being considered. Among these is a plan to use groundwater aquifers in the basin to store water during periods of above average runoff for extraction during periods of below average flows. The conjunctive management of surface and groundwater supplies within the drainage basin of the Great Salt Lake offers potential for reducing the magnitude of the fluctuations in the lake surface.

*Department of Civil and Environmental Engineering, Utah State University, Logan, UT 84322

The Great Salt Lake (see Figure 1) is the remnant of a large inland body of water known in geological terms as Lake Bonneville. Because there are no surface outflows from the basin, the Great Salt Lake is referred to as a terminal body of water, the volume of which at any particular time is determined by the difference between inflows and outflows. Inputs to the lake are mainly from three rivers, namely, the Bear, Weber, and Jordan Rivers, other relatively small surface streams, groundwater, and direct precipitation on the lake itself. The only significant water loss from the lake is through evaporation from the water surface. In any one period of time (for example, one year) inflows to the lake might differ significantly from evaporation losses, with the difference being made up by a change of water storage within the lake. Because there is a direct and positive relationship between change in lake storage and surface area (and thus between total evaporation from the lake), the lake level tends to be self regulating (that is, there is a positive feed-back mechanism). However, weather factors involved in long-term trends in climate patterns usually work together to contribute to changes in the lake level. For example, during periods of higher than normal precipitation, inflows to the lake are increased, while these same weather conditions tend to reduce evaporation rates. The lake level in the long term also is affected by man-induced changes in inflow such as diversions which increase consumptive use and inter-basin transfers (either to or from the Salt Lake drainage basin).

Since the arrival of the Morman pioneers in the Salt Lake valley in 1846 much human development has occurred in the area immediately adjacent to the lake. Most of these developments lie within the basic use categories of transportation, lake brine industries, wildlife, and recreation. Because the level of the lake surface impacts these lakeside developments, records of the level have been kept since 1847. The average level of the lake surface over this period of time is 4201.10 feet (1280.49 m) above sea level. Extreme levels of record range from a high in the early 1870's of 4211.50 feet (1283.67 m) above sea level to a low in the early 1960's of 4191.3 feet (1277.51 m) above sea level. Corresponding surface areas for the lake area are approximately 2500 square miles (6475 km^2) and 1000 square miles (2590 km^2), respectively. High water extremes of the lake surface level adversely affect each of the four use categories listed above. Low water extremes also tend to negatively impact all categories except, perhaps, transportation.

Following the high water of 1872, the lake surface gradually declined until it reached a low in 1905 of about 4196 feet (1278.94 m) above sea level. From 1905 until 1980 lake level fluctuations remained within a relatively narrow range between a minimum in 1963 of about 4191 feet (1277.42 m) and a maximum in 1924 of 4205 feet (1281.68 m). In September 1982 the lake level stood at 4199.8 feet (1280.10 m) above sea level. However, at that time the lake seemed to be following a rising trend, and by May 1985 the lake had reached a stage of 4209.95 feet (1283.19 m) above sea level, an increase of more than 10 feet (3.05 m) in less than three years, and the rising trend is projected to continue with the 1986 spring runoff. This rapid rise, coupled with an increase in the lake surface area, has caused

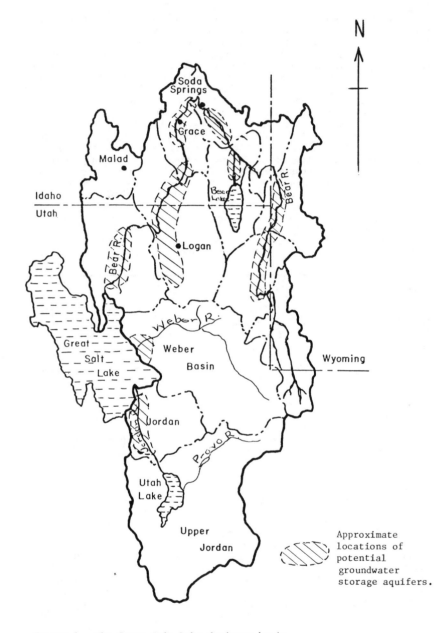

Figure 1.   The Great Salt Lake drainage basin.

damage to roads, railroads, wildlife-management areas, recreational facilities, agricultural land and buildings, and industrial (mineral extraction) installations which had been established near the previous lake surface.

It was not until the late 1970's when lake levels seemed to be trending upward that serious consideration was given to management procedures for controlling the levels of the lake. Lake level control depends upon regulating either inflows or evaporation or both. The increasing seriousness of the threat of floods from the lake has caused several possible management alternatives to be investigated. One of these possibilities is the use of groundwater aquifers in the basin to store water during periods of above average runoff for use during periods of below average flow. With sufficient capacity, this form of storage would effectively damp wide storage (and thus surface level) fluctuations in the lake itself.

The amounts of storage required for various degrees of lake level regulation have been investigated by means of a stochastic model for the lake level surfaces. For example, if the lake level were to have been kept at or below elevation 4202 feet (1280.77 m) for the high water period of the 1860's and 1870's, it is estimated that a total of about 12.6 million acre-feet (15.54 x 10^9 m^3) of off-lake storage would have been required. For the low water period of the 1960's an estimated 2.4 million acre-feet (2.96 x 10^9 m^3) would need to have been released to the lake to hold a minimum level of 4195 feet (1278.64 m) above sea level. Thus, in this case, if, in fact, 12.6 million acre feet (15.54 x 10^9 m^3) were stored during the wet period, 10.2 million acre-feet (12.58 x 10^9 m^3) would be available for consumptive use (such as additional irrigation) during a subsequent dry period, leaving the remaining 2.4 million acre-feet (2.96 x 10^9 m^3) available for lake level control. These numbers are, of course, cited for illustrative purposes only, and would vary depending upon the manner in which the groundwater storage was utilized in terms of the lake management objectives. If, for example, a primary objective were to control maximum lake levels below a specific elevation, the groundwater reservoirs would need to be drawn down as quickly as possible during dry periods to ensure that storage space was available for the next high-water period.

Water stored in the aquifers would be withdrawn during dry periods and the aquifers would be artificially recharged using excess surface supplies during wet periods. Thus, conjunctive management of surface water supplies and groundwater storage would relieve flooding at the lake during wet periods and conserve water for lake control, and for agriculture and other uses during dry periods. It is noted that from the point of view of agriculture and many other uses, the lake itself (even in the absence of high water damages), because of its very high mineral content, does not constitute a viable freshwater storage location.

Stated briefly, the management procedure described above has the potential for achieving the following:

1. Reducing water surface fluctuations of the Great Salt Lake, and thus of reducing damages resulting from both high and low water surface stages.

2. Reducing both actual and the perceived levels of risk for lakeshore developments.

3. Providing sufficient storage within the basin for adequate control of the lake level fluctuations. Remaining in-basin surface storage sites would provide relatively little storage, have low benefit-cost ratios (usually less than unity), and generally would involve serious environmental considerations.

4. Fostering additional agricultural development and other related activities within the general area. The reliability would be increased of fresh-water supplies during dry periods.

5. Enhancing the economic potential of some wet and low-lying lands within the drainage basin by lowering water tables, particularly during dry periods.

6. Reducing the potential for fresh water losses by evaporation. Evaporation losses under artificial recharge management conditions usually are significantly less than those from surface reservoirs which store corresponding water quantities.

7. Increasing base flows in the rivers during dry periods, and thus enhancing (a) hydroelectric power generation from existing facilities and (b) various in-stream uses, such as aquatic and wetland environments, aesthetic environment, and recreation.

8. Replenishing aquifers in areas where water tables are dropping due to pumping.

9. Providing lake level control with a relatively high benefit/cost ratio. It is cautioned, however, that costs associated with the proposed artificial recharge have not yet been investigated.

Several aquifers exist within the Great Salt Lake drainage basin which seem to have potential for being incorporated into a system of managed groundwater reservoirs. As indicated by Figure 1, these lie within the drainage basins of the Bear, Weber, and Jordan Rivers. However, before a management plan of this nature could be initiated extensive investigations are needed involving such topics as aquifer characteristics, the availability of recharge water at specific locations, the recharge potential at specific locations, the recharge potential of the various aquifers, the environmental aspects, and the institutional and legal aspects. For all drainage basins subject to both short and long-term fluctuations in the supply or input rate, increasing the availability of water supplies for a broad spectrum of purposes, including flood control, requires increasing the water storage potential. The conjunctive management of surface water supplies and groundwater storage offers this possibility for the drainage basin of the Great Salt Lake.

Bibliography

Allen, M. E., Ronald K. Christensen, J. Paul Riley. 1983. Some lake level control alternatives for the Great Salt Lake. Utah Water Research Laborartory, Report No. UWRL/P-83/01. Utah State University, Logan, Utah.

Arnow, Ted. 1978. Water budget and water-surface fluctuations, Great Salt Lake, Utah. Open File Report 78-912. U. S. Geological Survey, Salt Lake City, Utah. 21 p.

Bjorkland, L. J. and L. J. McGreevy. 1971. Ground-water resources of Cache Valley, Utah and Idaho. Technical Publication No. 36. Utah Department of National Resources, Salt Lake City, Utah.

Bjorkland, L. J. and L. J. McGreevy. 1974. Ground-water resources of the lower Bear River drainage basin, Box Elder County, Utah. Technical Publication No. 44, State of Utah, Dept. of Natural Resources.

Feth, J. H., D. A. Barker, L. G. Moore, R. J. Brown, and C. E. Verirs. 1966. Lake Bonneville: Geology and hydrology of the Weber Delta District, including Ogden, Utah. Geological Survey Professional Paper 518, U. S. Government Printing Office, Washington, D. C.

Harza Engineering Company. 1976. Preliminary assessment of alternatives for flood damage abatement: Great Salt Lake. Prepared for N. L. Industries, Salt Lake City, Utah.

Haws, F. W. 1969. Water related land use in the Bear River drainage area, Utah, Study Unit No. 2. Utah Water Research Laboratory, Utah State University, Logan, Utah.

Haws, F. W. and T. C. Hughes. 1973. Hydrologic inventory of the Bear River study unit. Utah Water Research Laboratory, College of Engineering, Utah State University, Logan, Utah.

Holmes, W. F. et al. 1982. Developing a state water plan: Ground-water conditions in Utah, Spring of 1982. Cooperative Investigations Report Number 22. Utah Division of Water Resources and U.S. Geological Survey. Utah Department of Natural Resources, Salt Lake City, Utah. 85 p.

James, L. D., D. S. Bowles, W. R. James, and R. V. Canfield. Estimation of water surface elevation probabilities and associated damages for the Great Salt Lake. Water Resources Planning Series UWRL/P-79/03. Utah Water Research Laboratory, Utah State University, Logan, Utah.

Mower, R. W. 1968. Ground-water discharge toward Great Salt Lake through Valley Fill in the Jordan Valley, Utah. U.S. Geological Survey Professional Paper 600-D. pp. D71-D74.

Schlotthauer, W. E., B. W. Nance, and J. D. Olds. 1981. Identifi-
    cation and characteristics of aquifers in Utah. Utah Division of
    Water Rights, Salt Lake City, Utah.

U.S. Department of Agriculture. 1978. Summary report - Bear River
    Basin cooperative study, water and land resources. Soil
    Conservation Service, Economics, Statistics and Cooperative
    Service, Forest Service in cooperation with Idaho, Utah, and
    Wyoming.

U.S. Department of the Interior. 1970 Bear River investigations:
    Status report. Bureau of Reclamation, Salt Lake City, Utah.

Utah Department of Natural Resources and Energy and Division of State
    Lands and Forestry. 1983. Recommendations for a Great Salt Lake
    contingency plan for influencing high and low levels of Great
    Salt Lake. Salt Lake City, Utah.

Utah Division of Water Resources. 1976. Multiobjective interagency
    study of the Bear River Basin water and related land resources.
    Utah Department of Natural Resources, Salt Lake City, Utah. 160
    p.

Willett, Hurd C. 1976. The prediction of future water levels of
    Great Salt Lake, Utah on the basis of solar climatic cycles.
    Final Report for Great Salt Lake Division, State of Utah
    Department of Conservation, Salt Lake City, Utah.

RECOVERY OF FRESHWATER STORED IN SALINE AQUIFERS IN PENINSULAR FLORIDA

By·Michael L. Merritt[1]/

ABSTRACT

Subsurface freshwater storage has been operationally tested at
seven sites in central and south Florida. Injection was into a high
chloride water aquifer at six sites, and into a high sulfate water
aquifer at the seventh. Recovery efficiency has ranged from 0 to 75
percent in high chloride water aquifers, and has exceeded 100 percent
in the high sulfate water aquifer. Computer modeling techniques were
used to examine the geohydrologic, design, and management factors governing the recovery efficiency of subsurface freshwater storage. The
modeling approach permitted many combinations of geohydrologic and
operational conditions to be studied at relatively low cost. The model
study showed that processes that significantly reduce recovery efficiency are hydrodynamic dispersion, buoyancy stratification, and background hydraulic gradients. High permeability combined with high native aquifer water salinity promotes buoyancy stratification. Recovery
efficiency tends to improve in successive cycles.

INTRODUCTION

Injection of surplus freshwater into saline water aquifers for
later recovery and use during periods of water scarcity is a concept
of particular significance for regions where the natural freshwater
supply tends to shift seasonally between surplus and deficit relative
to public supply requirements. South Florida provides a typical example of such a hydrologic regime. During wet seasons, large quantities
of surplus freshwater are flushed to the ocean through a system of
canals. Near the end of wet seasons, canal flows are regulated to
retain water in reservoirs that are both natural (Lake Okeechobee)
and manmade (water-conservation areas). Nevertheless, periodic water
deficits still occur in many parts of the 11-county study area shown
in Figure 1. Lowered water levels near the end of dry seasons have
caused the migration of saltwater toward coastal municipal well fields
and temporary restrictions on water use by the public.

The problem reveals the need for water-conservation measures
to further reduce losses to the ocean and atmosphere. A traditional
method of water conservation is to increase the volumes of water impounded in reservoirs during periods of abundance. The flat topography
of south Florida and high cost of land inhibit enlargement of the
surface reservoir system, but subsurface reservoirs, in the form of
artesian carbonate aquifers that contain nonpotable saline water, occur
within 1,500 feet (450 meters) of land surface throughout most of the

---

[1]/ Hydrologist, U.S. Geological Survey, Miami, Fla.

study area. Where these aquifers contain water of low to moderate
salinity (500 to 2,000 mg/L chloride), they would be suitable for the
temporary storage of amounts of water equivalent to part of the freshwater that is presently released to the ocean during wet seasons.
Various aspects of this water-conservation technique related to south
Florida are discussed by Merritt and others (1983) and Merritt (1985).
This paper is a brief summary of the findings reported in the earlier
papers for presentation to attendees of the Water Forum 86 Conference
sponsored by the American Society of Civil Engineers.

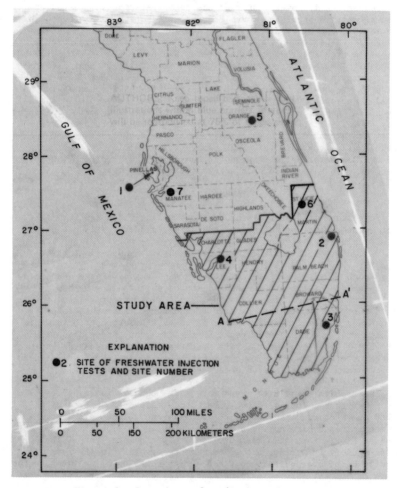

Figure 1.--Locations of recharge-recovery tests.

RECHARGE-RECOVERY TESTS IN PENINSULAR FLORIDA

Operational freshwater storage projects in central and south Florida (sites 1 to 7, Fig. 1) have injected water into formations above the horizon of water of seawater salinity (Fig. 2). These include the Oligocene Suwannee Limestone, and the Eocene Ocala Limestone and Avon Park Formation of the Upper Floridan aquifer and the Miocene Hawthorn Formation within the intermediate aquifer system separating the Upper Floridan aquifer from the surficial aquifer system. The principal receiving zones are discrete intervals of secondary-porosity limestone. Results of the seven series of tests are shown in Table 1. At sites 1 to 6, low chloride water was injected into higher chloride water aquifers. At site 7, low sulfate water was injected into a high sulfate water aquifer. At sites 1 to 6, recovery took place until the chloride concentration of recovered water reached 250 mg/L. The volume recovered, expressed as a percentage of the volume injected, is termed "recovery efficiency."

The first injection and recovery tests in peninsular Florida known to the author were performed in Orange County (site 5, Fig. 1) in east-central Florida (Tibbals and Frazee, 1976). Injection was into a 250-foot (76-meter) interval of the Ocala Limestone and underlying Avon Park Formation beneath a confining layer of clay or clayey sand. The main receiving zone was believed to be a 5-foot (1.5-meter) cavity near the bottom of the well. Five injection periods were each followed almost immediately by recovery. The success of the tests is attributable to the low salinity (650 mg/L) of the receiving zone, so that appreciable buoyancy stratification did not occur. These tests illustrated that recovery efficiency tends to improve appreciably in successive similar cycles. The decrease in cycle 4 has been attributed to the destruction of the zone of dispersion by the higher volume of injectant (Tibbals and Frazee, 1976). The 75-percent recovery efficiency of the last cycle was the highest observed to date (1986) in tests in high-chloride water aquifers in south Florida.

Tests at site 1 (Fig. 1) in Pinellas County in west-central Florida (Black, Crow, and Eidsness, Inc., 1974) were performed in a well open to a highly permeable and highly saline (19,700 mg/L chloride) part of the Avon Park Formation. The total uncased zone was 254 feet (77 meters) thick, of which a 40-foot (12-meter) interval was the main receiving zone. Fair recovery efficiencies (43 to 46 percent) were obtained in the first two tests in which recovery immediately followed the injection phase, and also (39 percent) in the third test in which a 10-hour storage period separated the injection and recovery phases. However, less than 1 percent was recovered after the fifth and sixth cycles, which included storage periods of at least 16 hours. The poor results of the last three tests suggested that injected freshwater rapidly migrated upward due to buoyancy, allowing saline water to enter the lower part of the uncased section of the well. This ended the recovery of usable water.

Results of the tests in Palm Beach County (site 2, Fig. 1) in southeastern Florida conducted by the Florida Department of Natural Resources (J. J. Plappert, written commun., 1977) were more encouraging,

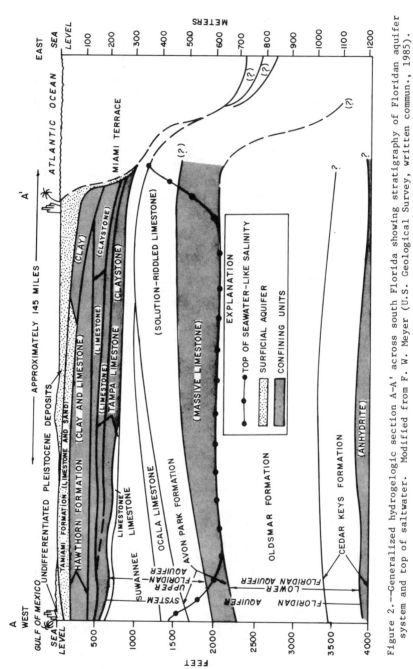

Figure 2.--Generalized hydrogeologic section A-A' across south Florida showing stratigraphy of Floridan aquifer system and top of saltwater. Modified from F. W. Meyer (U.S. Geological Survey, written commun., 1985).

Table 1.—Results of injection, storage, and recovery tests at seven sites in central and south Florida[1]

Site No.	Aquifer transmissivity (ft2/d)	Chloride concentration		Quantities injected (gal x 10⁶)	Storage period (days)	Recovery efficiency (percent)
		Injection water (mg/L)	Aquifer water (mg/L)			
1	800,000	24	19,700	0.046	0	43.5
				.110	0.03	45.5
				.906	.41	38.6
				3.960	.96	0
				1.730	.65	0.29
				4.900	.78	0.09
2	[2]/10,000 - 20,000	65	1,980	20.5	15	0
				100.0	30	4.7
				306.0	30	18.0
				102.0	120	35.2
3	10,950	65	1,200	41.9	2	32.9
				85.0	54	47.8
				208.0	181	38.5
4	700 - 800	60	550	.571	0	38.7
		150 - 350		6.831	47	9.7
		80 - 100		29.026	99	30.4
5	100,000 - 200,000	20	650	11.2	0	33.9
				11.0	0	51.8
				11.6	0	66.4
				33.0	0	43.5
				28.5	0	75.1
6	6,000	200	1,000	1.488	37.5	2.8
7	38,000 - 40,000	3/34 - 66	3/130 - 162	10.054	5	101.0
				12.215	5	100.0
				11.128	5	100.0
				10.067	28	103.0
				26.037	28	101.0
				29.764	28	101.0
				2.043	.01	93.0

1/ ft2/d = 0.0929 m2/d; 1 gallon = 3.785 liters
2/ Not measured, but estimated by F. W. Meyer, (written commun., 1985).
3/ Sulfate concentrations.

perhaps because the lower salinity of the native aquifer water (2,000 mg/L chloride) was not a condition that would cause an appreciable degree of buoyancy stratification to occur. The injection well was open to 290 feet (88 meters) of permeable Avon Park Formation, but a 5-foot (1.51-meter) interval appeared to be the principal receiving zone. Recovery was by natural artesian flow. The recovery efficiency increased with successive cycles until 35 percent efficiency was reported in the fourth cycle. The test results showed that recovery efficiency increases with greater volumes and also with successive cycles.

At site 6 (Fig. 1) in St. Lucie County in southeastern Florida (Wedderburn and Knapp, 1983), injection was chiefly into three distinct water-bearing zones of the Ocala Limestone and Avon Park Formation associated with zones of dissolution near formation contacts and containing water of about 1,000 mg/L chloride. The study involved one injection-storage-recovery cycle for which the recovery efficiency was only 2.76 percent. The low percent was due to the high chloride concentration (200 mg/L) of the injectant and to the low volume injected.

Freshwater injection tests were conducted by the U.S. Geological Survey (F. W. Meyer, written commun., 1985) in Dade County in southeastern Florida (site 3, Fig. 1). The injection well was open to 150 feet (46 meters) in the Tampa and Suwannee Limestones and the Avon Park Formation. Injection was chiefly into a 12-foot (3.7-meter) thick highly permeable zone within the Suwannee Limestone. Results of three injection, storage, and recovery tests (Table 1) indicate that significant amounts of freshwater could be recovered successfully after months of residence in the aquifer. A decline in recovery efficiency was recorded for the third cycle, which probably was related to the migration of injected water downgradient from the injection-recovery well during the 181 days of storage. Plugging of the wellbore was a serious problem, but was remedied by periodic backflushes of the well lasting from 1 to 3 hours.

In Manatee County in west-central Florida (site 7, Fig. 1), low sulfate water was injected into a section of the Suwannee Limestone containing water low in chloride but high in hydrogen sulfide and sulfate concentrations (CH_2M HILL, 1984). Two recharge-recovery wells were of similar construction and open to 300 feet (91 meters) of the Tampa and Suwannee Limestones. Two principal receiving zones in the Suwannee were identified. The first six recovery cycles were terminated when over 100 percent of the injected volumes were recovered. The quality of the water recovered in cycles 1 to 4 improved in succeeding cycles, each of which had nearly the same volume of recharge. The end-of-cycle sulfate concentration decreased from 142 to 116 mg/L. The volume of recharge increased in cycles 5 and 6, and the end-of-cycle sulfate concentration decreased to 112 mg/L. There was an increase in the sulfate concentration of the injectant in the low-volume cycle 7, and higher sulfate concentrations were present in recovered water. The recovery efficiency was only 93 percent.

Freshwater storage tests were conducted by the U.S. Geological Survey (Fitzpatrick, 1986) in northeastern Lee County in southwestern

Florida (site 4, Fig. 1). The injection well was constructed with
153 feet (47 meters) of open hole in limestone of the Hawthorn Formation. Two principal receiving zones were indicated within a 60-foot
(18-meter) interval. A 39-percent recovery efficiency was obtained
from the low-volume first cycle, in which water for injection was
obtained from the nearby Caloosahatchee River and filtered. Injection
and recovery rates diminished sharply during the first cycle due to
plugging, but rates improved significantly after the well was acidized.
The observed 9.7-percent recovery efficiency in the second cycle was
low because of the high chloride concentration of the injectant. The
third cycle began with the injection of treated and filtered river
water followed by injection of raw water from the river. Following a
99-day storage period, a recovery efficiency of about 30 percent was
obtained. During injection of the untreated river water, there was a
steady increase of wellhead pressure due to plugging, which was not
mitigated by periodic backflushing.

MODELING THE RECOVERY OF INJECTED FRESHWATER

A three-dimensional, finite-difference solute and thermal transport model (INTERCOMP, 1976; INTERA, 1979) was used to assess the
relation of recovery efficiency to hydrogeologic and operational
conditions (Merritt, 1985). Injection and recovery in a hypothetical
aquifer was simulated, and recovery efficiency was computed. Sensitivity analyses were performed to determine how recovery efficiency varies
when hydrogeologic or management parameters were varied. A description
of the design of the hypothetical aquifer and selected results of the
model analyses follow.

Design of a Hypothetical Aquifer for Model Analyses

A hypothetical aquifer was designed that was considered representative of a brackish artesian limestone aquifer. The hydraulic
characteristics were based upon those estimated from aquifer tests
and geophysical logging of the injection zone at site 3 (Fig. 1). The
150-foot (46-meter) open-hole interval, shown in Figure 3, is divided
into five hydraulically distinct, vertically uniform layers. The outer
layers are relatively impermeable and act as confining layers receiving
very little flow from the injection wells. The 12-foot (3.66-meter)
middle layer is the most permeable, receiving 65 percent of the injected water. Various dispersion models (choices of longitudinal dispersivity coefficient) were used. Setting the transverse dispersivity
coefficient to zero assumed no transverse dispersion ("interlayer
dispersion" when flow is predominantly in the lateral direction).

Results of Sensitivity Analyses

Native-water density was shown to be an important factor affecting
the degree of buoyancy stratification. Results indicated that for a
given native-water density there seems to be a certain range of permeability in which virtually no stratification occurs during time periods
comparable to those of the simulation. This permeability range is
lower for higher values of native-water density. As simulated permeability values increase beyond this range for each density value, an

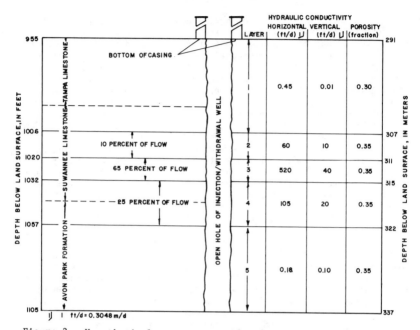

Figure 3.--Hypothetical prototype aquifer designed for model analyses.

increasing degree of stratification occurs, apparently because of a
decrease in the frictional retarding force opposing upward (buoyant)
flow for the prevailing density contrast and opposing outward flow in
upper layers.

When the upper limit of the concentration of constituents considered acceptable in recovered water is less than half the average of the
concentrations in the injected and native aquifer waters, hydrodynamic
dispersion is a deleterious process that reduces recovery efficiency.
Model runs in which longitudinal dispersivity varied verified that
recovery efficiency decreased when dispersivity increased. If the
upper limit is greater than the average, hydrodynamic dispersion works
to the benefit of the injector, and recovery efficiencies greater than
100 percent can be realized.

The length of a storage period can be a significant factor if
natural or manmade background hydraulic gradients move the injected
freshwater downgradient from the injection well. After recovering only
part of the potable water, further pumping would then draw native saline water from the upgradient direction while appreciable amounts of
injected freshwater remain in the downgradient direction. In a single-
layer Cartesian representation of the most permeable layer at site 3,
background flow caused by a natural hydraulic gradient in the aquifer
was assumed to be 44 ft/yr (13.4 m/yr) along the x-axis of the grid,
and was simulated by compatible initial and boundary pressure specifications. Results showed a slight decrease of recovery efficiency after

6 months of residence in the aquifer and a major decrease of recovery efficiency after 5 years, when the injected freshwater body had moved an appreciable distance downgradient. Generalization of these results requires a knowledge of aquifer thickness, porosity, and downgradient pore velocity, and an estimate of the volume to be injected and likely storage period.

Results of model analyses show that there is a large increase of recovery efficiency with increasing volume of injected water for small volumes, but that the rate of increase is small at large volumes. Zero recovery efficiency would occur for a sufficiently small injection volume because of the effect of hydrodynamic dispersion. Consequently, operational tests performed with small injection volumes cannot be expected to yield encouraging results.

The recovery efficiency of the first cycle of injection and recovery is not a good indicator of the potential of the system, as recovery efficiency tends to improve in subsequent cycles. With each successive injection, the zone of dispersion progressively increases in volume from accretion of residual freshwater from previous injections, leading to a progressive increase in recovery efficiency even if the volumes of injected freshwater do not increase. Model analysis results for various dispersion models indicated major improvement in the first several cycles. Improvement continued at a reduced rate in later cycles. When longitudinal dispersivity was specified to be 20 feet, first-cycle recovery efficiency was 30 percent. After 12 cycles, it improved to 84 percent.

CONCLUSIONS

The results of seven operational freshwater storage and recovery tests in peninsular Florida have ranged from disappointing to promising. Recovery efficiencies in high-chloride water aquifers have ranged from 0 to 75 percent, demonstrating the dependence of recoverability upon geohydrologic conditions, the design of the system, and various operating parameters.

Generally, the model study shows that a loss of recovery efficiency resulted from: (1) processes causing mixing of injected freshwater with native saline water (hydrodynamic dispersion); and (2) processes or conditions causing the irreversible displacement of the injected freshwater with respect to the well (buoyancy stratification and background hydraulic gradients). A significant result is the theoretical demonstration that recovery efficiency should improve considerably in initial successive cycles, provided that each recovery phase ends when the chloride concentration of withdrawn water increases to some prescribed value less than that of the more saline native water. Other results show that a high degree of aquifer permeability or high salinity of the native water, or a combination of these factors, would permit rapid buoyancy stratification and bring about a substantial loss of recovery efficiency.

REFERENCES CITED

Black, Crow, and Eidsness, Inc., 1974, Results of drilling and testing of the stormwater injection well for the City of St. Petersburg, Florida, Project no. 412-72-01(4), July 1974.

CH₂M HILL, 1984, Final report—Recharge-recovery at Lake Manatee: Phase II: FC16398.A0, March 1984.

Fitzpatrick, D. J., 1986, Tests for injecting, storing, and recovering freshwater in a saline artesian aquifer, Lee County, Florida: U.S. Geological Water-Resources Investigations Report 85-4249 (in press).

INTERA Environmental Consultants, Inc., 1979, Revision of the documentation for a model for calculating effects of liquid waste disposal in deep saline aquifers: U.S. Geological Survey Water-Resources Investigations 79-96, 73 p.

INTERCOMP Resource Development and Engineering, Inc., 1976, A model for calculating effects of liquid waste disposal in deep saline aquifers, Part 1—Development, Part 2—Documentation: U.S. Geological Survey Water-Resources Investigations Report 76-61, 253 p.

Merritt, M. L., 1985, Subsurface storage of freshwater in south Florida: A digital model analysis of recoverability: U.S. Geological Survey Water- Supply Paper 2261, 44 p.

Merritt, M. L., Meyer, F. W., Sonntag, W. H., and Fitzpatrick, D. J., 1983, Subsurface storage of freshwater in south Florida: A prospectus: U.S. Geological Survey Water-Resources Investigations Report 83-4214, 69 p.

Tibbals, C. H., and Frazee, J. M., Jr., 1976, Ground-water hydrology of the Cocoa well-field area, Orange County, Florida: U.S. Geological Survey Open-File Report 76-676, 67 p.

Wedderburn, L. E., and Knapp, M. S., 1983, Field investigation into the feasibility of storing freshwater in saline portions of the Floridan aquifer system, St. Lucie County, Florida: South Florida Water Management District Technical Publication no. 83-7, 71 p.

Conjunctive Use and Managed Groundwater Recharge:
Engineering and Politics in Arid Lands

Jonathon C. Goldman, A.M. ASCE*

Abstract

In regions with alluvial groundwater basins, increasing consumer
demands for water, irregular surface water flows, and high evapotranspiration rates, managed recharge and long-term conjunctive water use
may provide quantitative, qualitative and energy economies when compared with conventional water management alternatives. The practice of
conjunctive management encompasses these resource development and operation strategies. Quantitative savings are achievable when underground
formation losses are less than reservoir surface evapotranspiration
over duration of storage. Water quality improvements are possible
using soil filtration of surface waters and evapotranspiration suppression. Energy savings can be realized with an off-peak electric rate,
conjunctive-use operating strategy.

Techniques for successful siting and operation of groundwater storage installations can benefit from recent developments in, and applications of, computer-based operation of surface water storage and conveyance networks. Despite technical and economic feasibility, obstacles
to construction and operation of conjunctive management facilities are
often legal and institutional, including the separation of surface
water law from that of groundwater.

Recognition of benefits, problems and potential costs helps to
identify suitable sites for physical demonstration of conjunctive
management feasibility. Physically demonstrated technical and economic
feasibility can be used as leverage in clearing the legal and institutional barriers to such water management.

Introduction

Efficiency in water resource use is demanded worldwide. As a
result, sophisticated tools of hydrologic and operations analysis have
been developed to aid in design and operation of reservoirs, well-
fields, and crop irrigation systems. But integrated systems, including
the conjunctive management of surface and groundwater, for example, are
rare. Conjunctive use refers to a dual-source water supply system
capable of storing, extracting, treating and delivering an engineered
balance of both surface and groundwater to users. Conjunctive use is

*Project Geohydrologist, Kennedy/Jenks/Chilton, Inc., 657 Howard
Street, San Francisco, CA 94105; formerly with Morrison-Knudsen
Engineers, Inc., San Francisco, CA, whose support is also acknowledged.

enhanced by the practice of managed groundwater recharge[22] which utilizes the underground for long-term storage of surplus surface water
such that it may subsequently be efficiently extracted as groundwater.
Probably, the rarity of such integrated, conjunctively managed systems
reflects the complexity of the task. However, the potential benefits
of conjunctive management in arid and semiarid environments make the
investigation of such water resources systems attractive;[10] and by
physically demonstrating the technical and economic feasibility of
these systems, legal and institutional obstacles to their widespread
practice may be removed.

The Need for Conjunctive Management

An arid or semiarid environment is often characterized by substantial variability in streamflow volume and frequency.[27] As an example,
Rincon Creek in southern Arizona has a mean annual flow of approximately 1100 cfs (31 m^3/s) but a standard deviation of 900 cfs
(25 m^3/s).[25] Variability of this sort, under pressure from demand for
water, encourages the development of groundwater resources which do not
suffer from high-frequency supply variability. Unfortunately, with
demand exceeding safe-yield (a term subject to controversial definition[13]), water tables drop and the cost of energy used to lift water
from underground directly limits the use of pumped water.[28]

An alternative to groundwater resource development is surface water
impoundment. In general, this is the traditional technology when
streamflows and topography are adequate to justify dams and reservoirs. A fundamental economic drawback to continued application of
such strategies is the extensive evaporation losses endured by reservoirs in arid areas. Evaporative loss is doubly damaging in that not
only is a significant depth of water removed, but the undesirable
constituents dissolved or suspended in impounded waters are concentrated by evaporation. Thus, the quality of water not evaporated is
degraded by the evaporation process.

In addition, surface water available in an arid area may be of poor
quality when compared with that underground. Flow events on ephemeral
streams often consist of floods which may be high in suspended sediments, or in perennial streams, flows which are high in dissolved
solids concentrations. The end result is that the average annual
benefit derivable from a surface water source in an arid or semiarid
area is less than that achievable in a humid environment with smaller
streamflow variability.

The Tools for Conjunctive Management

A management system to resolve some of the needs described above
can be conceptualized as an optimization of multiple water resources
and water qualities for use. The objective is to maximize net economic
benefits utilizing a surface water source and a managed groundwater
recharge facility. In periods of bountiful surface water supply
(record flows on the Colorado River system in 1984, for example), water
is diverted from the river and allowed to recharge groundwater basins.
Soil filtration using managed recharge in conjunction with the qualita-

tive benefits of evaporation suppression improve water quality.[10]   In
times of drought, groundwater is extracted during off-peak power demand
periods and conveyed to short-term reservoir storage and use.[7,20]
Operations and control theory necessary for such systems have been
applied in resource management. Computer models have been used to
screen feasible development and control scenarios from inefficient
schemes,[17,6] to determine resilience of proposed strategies under
simulated (including stochastic) operating stresses,[24,16,18] and to
provide control algorithms for optimal operations in real-time.[5,4,18]

Managed recharge has also been applied in a variety of situations.
Most commonly, treated municipal wastewater is used to recharge the
groundwater in water-scarce regions like the Dan Region in Israel;[12] El
Paso, Texas;[15] Nassau County, New York;[23] and Wroclaw, Poland.[14]
Secondary benefits, like prevention of seawater intrusion, further
justify managed recharge in Orange County, California.[1]

From the point of view of an engineer, the tools for conjunctive
management are off-the-shelf hard- and software. If a water conveyance
system as complex as the 3000 cfs (85 m^3/s), 1.4 million acre-feet per
year, \$3.5 billion Central Arizona Project (CAP) can be digitally con-
trolled,[5] and water and wastewater systems can be fully automated,[4]
then certainly the technical needs of a conjunctively managed water
resource system can be met with existing technology. The problem is
that existing tools have not been combined into an integrated system.

Obstacles to Conjunctive Management

Efficient operation of a conjunctively managed water resource
system on a large scale would be expensive and complex. But the
fundamental obstacle to conjunctive management and managed groundwater
recharge is institutional--the laws and regulations of local, state and
federal entities with authority over water.[3,13,26] Of specific concern are three primary issues. First, law and custom regarding rivers
and streams are traditionally separated from those regarding water
underground.[9,19] Second, law and custom regarding water quality are
separate from that of water quantity, which makes management for water
quality difficult. And third, there is a traditional lack of regard
for third-party impacts--the "tragedy of the commons"[11] which discourages economic efficiency in fully-allocated resource markets.[3]

Arizona's example is an educational illustration of obstacles to
conjunctive management and recharge.[20,21,2] Specifically, the feasibility of utilizing Butler Valley, Arizona to store water from the CAP
aqueduct underground in water-rich years for subsequent extraction in
times of low flow on the Colorado River was investigated on behalf of
the Central Arizona Water Conservation District.[21] Problem issues
identified included conflicting jurisdictional authorities, lack of
legal protection for water to be recharged (is recharge a beneficial
use?) and lack of protection for water stored underground.[21] In addition, because of market constraints in water resources,[3] analysis of
the economic feasibility of conjunctive management and recharge is not
easily determined. The true value of water, like information, cannot
be realized unless it can be freely exchanged.

In summary, institutional and legal obstacles to integrated water management can conspire to limit the demonstration of technical and economic efficiency. Physical and economic demonstrations are required which transcend these obstacles and provide the information and communication necessary for justification, design and implementation of conjunctively managed facilities through institutional and legal adjustments.

Demonstrating the Feasibility of Conjunctive Management

Throughout the American Southwest and other arid and semiarid parts of the world, special entities have historically had authority to manage water resources for the public good.[19] Though often managers of irrigation water, such organizations begin to supply water to municipalities as farmlands are developed as residential and industrial areas. An excellent example of such transformation is central Arizona's Salt River Project, which conjunctively uses surface and groundwater to supply both arable lands in the Salt River Valley and some of the municipal and industrial needs of Tempe and Mesa, Arizona. Maass and Anderson[19] (1978) observe that such institutions which are successful operate with a foundation of conflict resolution, equity, distribution of income and local control as objectives. Recently, changes imposed by judicial or legislative action have provided the opportunity for creation of such entities, especially among American Indian communities.[8] Because of the unified authority that these organizations represent, contradictory or ambiguous laws and institutions may be more effectively ignored in such communities and thus the obstacles to demonstration of conjunctive management may be lessened compared with less-consolidated regulatory environments. For example, the situation facing the Papago Tribe of southern Arizona represents a significant union of authority with respect to water management and planning.[8] The Papago Tribe was awarded groundwater, wastewater effluent and a Central Arizona Project (CAP) allotment by the U.S. Congress in 1982 in settlement of a lawsuit brought against water users in the Tucson groundwater basin.[8] In contrast, the Butler Valley project discussed by Marsh, Herndon and Rusinek[21] (1984) on behalf of the water district responsible for CAP water distribution, is handcuffed by the involvement of distinct authorities of the U.S. Bureau of Reclamation (USBR), the Arizona Department of Water Resources (DWR), the Central Arizona Water Conservation District, the Arizona Groundwater Management Act, and others. In general, centralized authority over surface and groundwater is necessary for conjunctive management.

In order that central authority is retained, it is necessary that the catalysis for implementation of such a demonstration come from within that organization.[29] In order that the technology for such a demonstration be made available, the management authority must have access not only to an appropriate location for demonstration, but to the capital and expertise necessary for its design, implementation, operation, and interpretation of results.

Conclusions

Because of their advantages in overcoming legal and institutional constraints to innovative systems, large, centralized water management organizations are in a strong position to investigate the technical and economic feasibility of large scale conjunctive management of water resources. By demonstrating the feasibility of such management, savings in water quantity, quality and storage operation costs may be realized in arid and semiarid environments worldwide. Only by investigating this feasibility can the obstacles to widespread conjunctive management be justified or replaced.

Therefore, it is crucial to the public interest that opportunities for such investigations be identified, encouraged and implemented.

Appendix I - References

1. Argo, D.G. and Cline, N.M., "Groundwater Recharge Operations at Water Factory 21, Orange County, California," Artificial Recharge of Groundwater, T. Asano, ed., Butterworth Publishers, Boston, MA, 1985, pp. 359-395.

2. "Arizona Lawmakers Debate Groundwater Recharge Bill," U.S. Water News, Vol. 1, No. 8, February, 1985.

3. Bagley, J.M., Kimball, K.R., and Kapaloski, L., "Water Banking--A Concept Whose Time Has Come," Proceedings of the Specialty Conference of Water-Related Divisions Water Forum '81, American Society of Civil Engineers, August 10-14, 1981, pp. 1019-1027.

4. Bishop, D.F., and Schuk, W., "Water and Wastewater: Time to Automate?" Civil Engineering, Vol. 56, No. 1, January 1986, pp. 56-58.

5. "CAP: The Canal with Cruise Control," Engineering News Record, Vol. 214, No. 11, March 14, 1985, pp. 34-35.

6. Chaturvedi, M.C., and Srivastava, D.K., "Study of a Complex Water Resources System with Screening and Simulation Models," Water Resources Research, Vol. 17, No. 4, August 1981, pp. 783-794.

7. Cluff, C.B., "Statement on Recharge of CAP," Press Release, Tucson, AZ, January, 1985, pp. 1-6.

8. Goldman, J.C., "Before the Water Comes: A Short-Range Plan for Papago Water Resource Development," thesis presented to the Massachussetts Institute of Technology, at Cambridge, Massachussetts, in 1984, in partial fulfillment of the requirements for the degree of Master of Science.

9. Gunnison, R.B., "Controversial Water Deal in Imperial Valley," San Francisco Chronicle, Monday, November 25, 1985, p. 12.

10. Hall, C.W., Piwoni, M.D., and Pettyjohn, W.A., "Research for Groundwater Quality Management," Artificial Recharge of Groundwater, T. Asano, ed., Butterworth Publishers, Boston, MA, 1985, pp. 719-747.

11. Hardin, G., "The Tragedy of the Commons," Science, December 1968.

12. Idelovitch, E. and Michail, M., "Role of Groundwater Recharge in the Wastewater Reuse in the Dan Region Project: Summary of Five-Year Experience, 1977-1981," Artificial Recharge of Groundwater, T. Asano, ed., Butterworth Publishers, Boston, MA, 1985, pp. 481-507.

13. Keith, S.J., "Stream Channel Recharge in the Tucson Basin and its Implications for Ground-Water Management," thesis presented to the University of Arizona, at Tucson, Arizona, in 1981, in partial fulfillment of the requirements for the degree of Master of Science.

14. Kempa, E.S. and Cebula, J., "Role of Groundwater Recharge in the Water Resource Management in Poland," Artificial Recharge of Groundwater, T. Asano, ed., Butterworth Publishers, Boston, MA, 1985, pp. 541-564.

15. Knorr, D.B. and Cliett, T., "Proposed Groundwater Recharge at El Paso, Texas," Artificial Recharge of Groundwater, T. Asano, ed., Butterworth Publishers, Boston, MA, 1985, pp. 425-480.

16. Krzysztofowicz, R., "Bayesian Models of Forecasted Time Series," Water Resources Bulletin, Vol. 21, No. 5, October 1985, pp. 805-814.

17. Loucks, D.P., Stedinger, J.R., and Haith, D.A., "Deterministic River Basin Modeling," Water Resource Systems Planning and Analysis, Prentice-Hall, Englewood Cliffs, NJ, 1981, pp. 267-268.

18. Loucks, D.P., Stedinger, J.R., and Haith, D.A., "Water Resources Planning Under Uncertainty," Water Resource Systems Planning and Analysis, Prentice-Hall, Englewood Cliffs, NJ, 1981, pp. 122-129.

19. Maass, A. and Anderson, R.L., ...and the Desert Shall Rejoice: Conflict, Growth, and Justice in Arid Environments, M.I.T. Press, Cambridge, MA, 1978.

20. Marsh, F., "Recharge Potential of Southwest Alluvial Basins in Proximity to the Central Arizona Project Aqueduct," Water Resources Research Center, University of Arizona, Tucson, AZ, for U.S. Bureau of Reclamation, Boulder City, NV, September 1984, pp. 1-8.

21. Marsh, F., Herndon, R., Rusinek, W., "Preliminary Investigations to Evaluate Feasibility of Conjunctive Water Management in Butler Valley, Arizona," Water Resources Research Center, University of Arizona, Tucson, AZ, for Central Arizona Water Conservation District, Phoenix, AZ, Aug. 1984, pp. 1-9.

22. Morel-Seytoux, H.J., "Conjunctive Use of Surface and Ground Waters," Artificial Recharge of Groundwater, T. Asano, ed., Butterworth Publishers, Boston, MA, 1985, pp. 35-67.

23. Oliva, J.A., "Operations at the Cedar Creek Wastewater Reclamation-Recharge Facilities, Nassau County, New York," Artificial Recharge of Groundwater, T. Asano, ed., Butterworth Publishers, Boston, MA, 1985, pp. 397-424.

24. Peralta, A.W., Peralta, R.C., and Asghari, K., "Evaluating Water
    Policy Options by Simulation," Proceedings of the Specialty
    Conference on Computer Applications in Water Resources, Water
    Resources Planning and Management Division and the Buffalo
    Section, American Society of Civil Engineers, June 1985,
    pp. 1411-1420.

25. Reich, B.M., "Magnitude and Frequency of Floods," CRC Reviews in
    Environmental Control, Vol. 1, Chemical Rubber Company,
    Cleveland, OH, 1976, p. 308.

26. Schneider, A.J., "Groundwater Recharge with Reclaimed Wastewater:
    Legal Questions in California," Artificial Recharge of Ground-
    water, T. Asano, ed., Butterworth Publishers, Boston, MA, 1985,
    pp. 683-702.

27. Slayter, R.O., and Mabbutt, J.A., "Surface Drainage in Arid and
    Semiarid Regions," Handbook of Applied Hydrology, V.T. Chow,
    ed., McGraw-Hill Inc., New York, NY, 1964, p. 24-22.

28. Vaux, Jr., H.J., "Economic Aspects of Groundwater Recharge,"
    Artificial Recharge of Groundwater, T. Asano, ed., Butterworth
    Publishers, Boston, MA, 1985, pp. 703-718.

29. Wiener, A., The Role of Water in Development, McGraw-Hill, Inc.,
    New York, NY, 1972.

AMERICA'S NATIONAL FORESTS

OUR ULTIMATE WATER SOURCE

Arne E. Rosquist, Jr.*

Abstract

National Forest System lands in the western United States make up 21 percent of the total land area but yield over 55 percent of the region's streamflow and provide more than 90 percent of the West's usable water supply. As they struggle to resolve the almost universally recognized "coming water supply crisis," these facts seem lost to water and land management planners outside the Forest Service, the agency charged with administering the National Forests. Water resource planners must become aware of the value of these National Forest watersheds and take steps to become involved in the planning of their management and development.

Introduction

"Water is essential to life and prosperity. And yet, this most vital resource is the most mismanaged, abused, polluted, and disputed of all resources. The evolution of laws and vested rights controlling the use and allocation of a 'free' commodity has resulted in overlapping and often conflicting jurisdictions. So many levels of government and agencies are involved that in fact no institution, no effective process, is capable of addressing the broad and essential issues relating to water quality and quantity.

The institutional problems are so complex and deeply ingrained that effective solutions will also be complex and highly controversial. Passage of time, however, will add complexity and controversy. Resolution is needed before scarcity and contamination force the issue." (1)

This excerpt from a 1980 American Forestry Association report on renewable natural resources is a concise yet complete expression of the state of this country's water resource management. In the 6 years since its publication little progress has been made--while reports of water shortages, contamination, and conflicts have increased. Newspaper articles, news magazines, and journals of business and professional organizations regularly document a growing public and media concern for the state of this country's water resources (Figure 1).

* Forest Hydrologist, Lolo National Forest, Bldg. 24, Fort Missoula, Missoula, Montana 59801.

In a 1983 survey (6), state governors and their staffs reported that they expected natural resources to be the source of their most pressing problems in the next several years. The issue within the natural resource area most cited was water. In fact, not only was water the most mentioned future problem area by the governors, but it was classed as the top future issue to be addressed by nearly 10 percent of the survey's respondents.

Figure 1.   National News Coverage Dramatizes Public
Concern for Water Supplies.

The plague of water resources, and a long-held feeling by water resource professionals, is that something has to be done, but nothing is ever satisfactorily completed. Ten years ago the National Water Commission spent $5 million to prepare a report entitled, "Water Policies for the Future," (10). This report, still considered one of the finest government reports on national water problems, states:

> "To increase efficiency in water use and to
> protect and improve its quality, and to do these
> things at least cost and with equity to all parts
> of the country will require changes in present
> water policies and programs."

More than a decade after this call for action, the Water Information News Service (9) finds that copies of the report now gather dust on many library shelves, covers torn, pages dog eared, and sections highlighted but largely forgotten. A reoccurring theme in the Commission's report is the recommended "shift in national priorities away from development of water resources to restoration and enhancement of water quality." In spite of that recommendation, the emphasis in water-resource management continues to be development.

National Forest Water Yield

While the great body of professional and popular literature details examples and signs of the coming water crisis and calls for quick action to head off disaster, none of the material ever addresses the source of our "most precious national resource"--our watersheds.

Whether water is used for municipal, industrial, or agricultural purposes, and regardless if it is pumped from a surface stream or from beneath the ground, virtually every molecule of water used in this country originates in some headwater basin in the form of rain or snow.

For the most part, particularly in the west, these headwater basins are in public ownership and managed as National Forests. The great rivers of the west (the Columbia, Missouri, Colorado, Platte, and Rio Grande) all have their headwaters in National Forests (Figure 2). Twenty National Forests straddle the Continental Divide between Canada and Mexico and another 2 dozen lie along the slopes of the Cascade and Sierra Nevada Mountain Ranges. While more than one-half of the land mass of the 11 western states has an annual runoff of 1 inch or less, the 21 percent of the land area occupied by National Forests has annual runoff of nearly 15 inches (Figure 3) (3, 4, 10). The western National Forests yield over 55 percent of the regions streamflow and more than 90 percent of the west's usable water (4, 10).

Considering that virtually every drop of water that is used runs off National Forest lands, the National Forests are truly this country's watersheds. Ground water reservoirs are also sustained or recharged by National Forests. The Snake Plain Aquifer in southern Idaho for example is recharged by 6.5 million acre-feet of water per year from the Targee, Caribou, Challis, and Salmon National Forests (7). On a broader scale, cities and farms in Nebraska, Kansas, and Oklahoma (hundreds of miles from a National Forest) draw their water from wells drilled into the Ogalala or High Plains Aquifer, which is recharged (though inadequately to keep up with demand) through the National Forests on the east slopes of the Rockies from Wyoming to New Mexico. The headwaters of the Columbia and Missouri River systems, rising on the National Forests of Montana, produce over 28 million acre-feet of water per year (5). In many respects, this water may be the most important product derived from National Forests. However, it is cash flow and employment that are considered the main Forest benefits. And while the debate over Forest management objectives in Montana centers on the timber products industry, downstream states are making plans to use this National Forest runoff for their own economic benefit.

Need for Integrated Watershed Planning

Competing demands for water in all parts of the country make it absolutely necessary to examine both National and local water needs and explore alternatives that can be taken to meet present and future

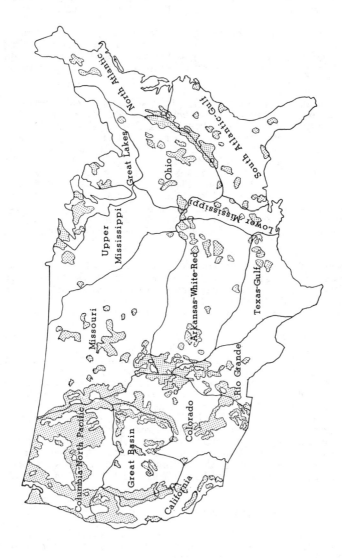

Figure 2. National Forest Lands within the Major U.S. River Basins

demand. This involves consideration of not only the physical management of the water and watershed resources but also the existing system of legal, political, legislative, and administrative management of these resources.

The conflict and competition among state and federal agencies for budget and authority is as fierce as the battles over the water itself though, and the powerful development oriented agencies easily out-compete the resource management oriented Forest Service. The Senate appropriations committee recommended nearly $2 billion in FY 1984 for construction activities of the Army Corps of Engineers, Bureau of Reclamation, and Tennessee Valley Authority (8). This $2 billion is 100 times the $20 million recommended for all watershed management activities on the 89 National Forests in the 11 western states. This imbalance may be a result of misplaced support considering that pro-tection of the source is one of the oldest and highest traditions of water and watershed management.

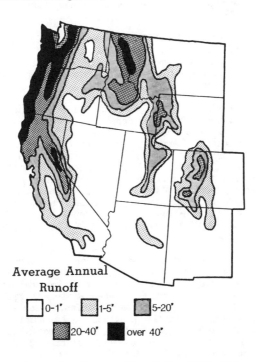

Average Annual Runoff

☐ 0-1"   ▨ 1-5"   ▨ 5-20"
▨ 20-40"   ■ over 40"

Figure 3.   Average Annual Runoff in the
Western United States (4).

In 1897, the National Forest System was created with the dual objectives of maintaining favorable conditions of water flow for downstream uses and providing for a sustained yield of timber. Burnett, et al. (5) suggest that water may be the most important product yielded by these lands, but today this aspect of National Forest management receives virtually no consideration by individuals or organizations outside the Forest Service.

The National Water Commission noted:

> "A practical potential exists for increasing or otherwise improving water supplies by application of appropriate land-management techniques." (10)

In addition, the Commission specifically recommended:

> "The Congress and the President should direct Federal agencies having land management responsibilities to give adequate consideration to water yield as an objective of multi-objective land-management plans." (10)

In response to the National Forest Management Act of 1976, the Forest Service prepared, and is now issuing, the first round of Forest Plans. These comprehensive land- and resource-management plans have been written to guide the management of individual National Forests for the next 10 to 15 years.

Forest plans on each National Forest were developed in response to the most urgent public issues and management concerns expressed to Forest managers. The competing special interests of the timber industry and the environmental community, however, resulted in the Forest planning process concentrating heavily on balancing timber supply demands with sufficient amounts of land designated for wilderness. No organization outside the agency requested that water yield or water supply be a planning consideration. While many Forest Plans provide detailed management requirements to safeguard water quality, the opportunity to implement the specific recommendation of the National Water Commission to consider water yield as a land-management objective has been missed.

Resource managers throughout the west face a dilemma caused by increasing water demands for energy, agricultural production, domestic and industrial needs, and instream flows. Resolving this dilemma will be further complicated by the number of agencies and special interests involved and the diversity of their authorities. Lack of knowledge about how much water is legally available with which to plan is another significant problem faced by managers. Compounding all these problems is the fact that many of the most controversial aspects of water use are influenced by longstanding social customs and local biases not appropriate to resolving regional issues.

Recommendations

Water resource planners and specialists have recommended several fundamental actions that must be taken now to resolve this country's critical water problems. The top priority actions frequently mentioned are to:

1. Recall the 1973 recommendations of the National Water Commission and shift national priorities away from development (construction) of water resources to the restoration and enhancement of water quality and the conservation of water use.

2. Recognize that the very first step in assuring safe and plentiful water supplies is protecting its source. Existing sources in their natural state (free from pollution due to man's activities) must be given the highest priority and the best practical standard of protection. These sources, the headwaters of the major river systems in this country, are managed within the National Forest System for multiple-use objectives.

3. Conduct a thorough evaluation of existing State, Regional, and National water-related objectives to identify areas of compatibility and incompatibility.

4. Review existing State and Federal laws to resolve their nonuniformity which hinders establishing or achieving compatible State, Regional, and National water-resource goals.

5. Assess the legal availability of water at key locations and identify needed actions to resolve conflicts regarding:

   a. Indian reserved water rights;
   b. Federal reserved water rights;
   c. State water rights;
   d. unused water rights;
   e. unadjudicated water, and;
   f. actual water use.

Unless these and other crucial water issues are addressed seriously, objectively, and promptly, conflicts will escalate the water crisis to the level where resolution by water resource professionals becomes impossible but must be imposed by political action at the National level.

Appendix - References

1. American Forestry Association. 1980. Renewable Natural Resources, Key to the Future. Report on the National Conference on Renewable Natural Resources. Washington, D.C. 56 p.

2. Anderson, Henry W., Marion D. Hoover, Kenneth G. Reinhart. 1976. Forests and Water: Effects of Forest Management on Floods, Sedimentation and Water Supply. USDA Forest Service General Technical Report PSW-18/1976. Pacific Southwest Forest and Range Experiment Station. Berkeley, CA. 115 p.

3. Beattie, Byron. 1967. Harvesting the National Forest Water Crop. U.S. Department of Agriculture, Forest Service, Division of Watershed Management. Washington, D.C. 14 p.

4. Bureau of Reclamation. 1971. Western U.S. Water Plan, 1971 Progress Report. Department of the Interior. Washington, D.C. 34 p.

5. Burnett, G. Wesley, David G. Conklin, Paul R. Saunders. 1981. Montana Forests: A Synthesis. Western Wildlands, Vol. 7 No. 4. Montana Forest and Conservation Experiment Station. Missoula, MT. pp 32-37.

6. National Governors Association. Governors Priorities: 1983. Office of Public Affairs. Washington, D.C. 44 p.

7. Robertson, J.B., Robert Schoen, J.T. Barraclough. 1974. The Influence of Liquid Waste Disposal on the Geochemistry of Water at the National Reactor Testing Station, Idaho: 1952-1970. Open-File Report IDO-22053. U.S. Geological Survey, Water Resources Division. Idaho Falls, Idaho. 231 p.

8. Senate Committee Reports Appropriations Bill. In: Water Information News Service, Vol. VII, No. IV. Information News Service, Inc. Washington, D.C. June 21, 1983. 10 p.

9. Water Commission Celebrates Tenth. In: Water Information News Service, Vol. VII, No. IV. Information News Service, Inc. Washington, D.C. June 21, 1983. 10 p.

10. Water Policies for the Future. Final Report to the President and to the Congress of the United States by the National Water Commission. U.S. Government Printing Office. Washington, D.C. June 1973. 579 p.

Small Hydro is Very Rarely Typical

Stanley J. Hayes*
W.R. Ivarson, Member, ASCE**
V.J. Zipparro, Member, ASCE**

Abstract

Engineering design of a small hydro project is often considered to be straightforward. Many potential developers assume that the engineering effort can be reduced to "typical" designs which do not require specific expertise. However, as will be shown, each potential project is unique and requires unique design features and specialized engineering capabilities. There is no such thing as a "typical" small hydro project.

Introduction

Development and redevelopment of small hydroelectric projects has increased dramatically recently, driven by increased energy prices, Federal tax incentives, and the Public Utility Regulatory Policies Act which requires utilities to buy energy from small power producers at the avoided cost of generating it themselves. Although falling oil prices and the uncertain future of tax incentives will slow this activity somewhat, Federal energy policy and increasing electricity rates in certain markets will provide the impetus for continued strong activity in this area.

Small hydro development generally consists of the use of "standardized" generating equipment which can be purchased at a much lower cost than equipment custom designed for a specific site. Since the equipment is standardized and the projects often utilize existing dams, many developers assume that the overall project design can be accomplished by "typical" designs and that only a minimal engineering effort and, therefore, minimal engineering cost is required. However, each project has unique features and constraints which pose unique challenges to the engineer and which, in many instances,

*   Senior Mechanical Engineer, Harza Engineering Company, 150 So. Wacker Drive, Chicago, Illinois 60606
**   Head, Small Hydro Facilities Section, Harza Engineering Co.
***   Head, Hydroelectric and Pumped Storage Department, Harza Engineering Co.

require innovative and creative solutions to achieve feasible designs.
Achieving these designs may sometimes require what would seem to be
disproportionate expenditures for engineering. However, without this
effort, some projects would have been prematurely judged infeasible
and never built. The following describes the authors' recent experiences on five small hydro projects. These experiences demonstrate
that virtually no small hydro project is "typical," and that having
the resource of experienced and specialized hydro designers is essential in development of a feasible design.

Barton and Superior Hydroelectric Projects

The Barton and Superior Projects were developed simultaneously by the
city of Ann Arbor, Michigan. Both projects are low head, run-of-river
installations. The project economics were such that the Superior
project was marginal as a "stand-alone" project but the two projects
developed together constituted a viable and attractive opportunity for
the City.

The Barton dam with integral powerhouse is located on the Huron River
near Ann Arbor, Michigan and was built by Detroit Edison in 1913. The
powerhouse originally housed two vertical Francis units in an open
flume intake; the generating equipment was removed in 1962 and the
dam, powerhouse, and associated property were sold to the City of Ann
Arbor in 1963.

Based on feasibility studies, the most logical and economical
redevelopment appeared to consist of utilizing the two unit bays and
draft tubes in the existing powerhouse and installing one 600 kW and
one 300 kW unit, either Francis or fixed-blade propeller. However,
when the generating equipment was bid, the most attractive offer,
based on equipment cost and energy generation, actually consisted of a
single vertical Kaplan (adjustable-blade) unit with a rated output of
910 kW under 23.5 ft (7.16 m) net head. This alternative required
construction of a new draft tube to maximize energy production from
the proposed unit. The unit began commercial operation in February
1986.

The Superior dam and powerhouse are also located on the Huron River
near Ann Arbor, Michigan, and were built by Detroit Edison in 1919.
the generating equipment was removed in 1962 and the dam and associated property sold to the City of Ann Arbor in 1963. In 1972 the
dam underwent major repairs and the original powerhouse was
demolished.

Since the normal maximum gross head at the site is only 16 ft
(4.88 m), which limited the energy available for hydroelectric
redevelopment, determining the least costly project design was crucial
to the feasibility of redevelopment. Disturbing the existing dam to
construct a new intake was determined to be infeasible due to dam
stability, seepage, and economic considerations. The final solution
consisted of constructing a 7 ft. (2.13 m) penstock over the top of
the existing dam. A vacuum system was provided to establish and
maintain a siphon to draw the water over the top of the dam and to the

unit. The siphon arrangement offers the potential for economic hydroelectric development at many small dams, but is limited to sites where the "lift" over the dam is 1/2 to 2/3 the actual atmospheric head at the site.

As at Barton Dam, feasibility studies indicated that the optimal redevelopment would consist of installation of two units (385 kW and 180 kW) but the most economical solution (from the bids received) was a single double-regulated (adjustable wicket gates and runner blades) tubular unit with a rated output of 575 kW under 14 ft. (4.27 m) net head. To minimize powerhouse costs, the unit was designed and installed with the main shaft axis inclined 45 degrees. Interestingly, while economics was the overriding concern during project design, the owner's serious concerns regarding potential vandalism at the site led to selection of reinforced concrete penstock and powerhouse in lieu of a less costly fiberglass penstock and prefabricated metal or wood frame powerhouse. The unit is scheduled to begin commercial operation in April 1986. Overall project layout is shown in Figure 1.

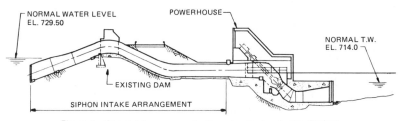

Figure 1. General Arrangement - Superior Hydroelectric Project

Hinckley Dam Hydroelectric Project

The Hinckley hydroelectric project is owned and operated by the New York Power Authority (NYPA). The project is located on the West Canada Creek near Rome, New York. The dam was built about 1914 to supply water to the Erie Canal; in addition, the reservoir supplies water for the City of Utica. The dam was owned and operated by the New York Department of Transportation until recently when NYPA was granted a perpetual easement and rights to develop the hydroelectric power potential. The energy potential developed consists of capturing the energy from releases made at the dam to meet the needs of two hydroelectric projects downstream of Hinckley dam.

As at Superior dam, the project required an intake at the existing dam. At Hinckley dam, the least costly and most readily constructed option was to install the penstock in the existing concrete non-overflow dam section. This option required tunneling through approximately 57 feet (17 m) of concrete, which was done behind a steel intake bulkhead installed on the upstream face of the dam. The bulkhead frame was installed using underwater construction techniques and also serves as the permanent supporting frame for the trashracks.

The trashracks can be removed and the bulkheads reinstalled for inspection and maintenance operations. This arrangement avoided the
costly alternative of constructing a 50 foot cofferdam for the construction of the intake. The intake was constructed at the low-level
outlet works of the dam; a portion of the outlet works was retained to
provide bypass releases during construction and when the plant is
shutdown, and the remainder of the outlet works was removed or
plugged.

The powerhouse is located approximately 200 ft (61 m) downstream of
the dam. The water conductor consists of a single 15 ft (4.57 m)
diameter penstock which bifurcates into two 10.5 ft (3.2 m) diameter
penstocks supplying each unit. The powerhouse contains two double-
regulated tubular units, each rated at 3.5 MW under 50 ft (15.24 m)
net head. The plant began commercial operation in January 1986.
Overall project layout is shown in Figure 2.

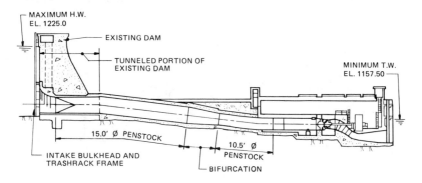

Figure 2. General Arrangement - Hinckley Hydroelectric Project

Dillon Dam Hydropower Project

The Dillon Dam Hydropower Project, located near the town of Dillon,
Colorado, will utilize the existing Dillon Dam and Outlet Works. The
existing project was built by the Denver Water Department in the early
1960's to store water for diversion to the east side of the continental divide and for use through the Denver Municipal Water System. The
outlet works controls releases to the Blue River which would otherwise
be blocked by the dam. The outlet works consists of an intake, 15 ft
(4.57 m) diameter concrete pressure tunnel, a control gate structure,
and 15 ft (4.57 m) diameter free-flow tunnel which connects to a
stilling basin at the toe of the dam. A morning-glory type spillway
also connects to the free-flow tunnel downstream of the control gate
chambers.

The hydroelectric project was made feasible by the dam safety need for
a permanent free discharge tunnel bypass. This bypass would allow for
maintenance on the free discharge tunnel while maintaining required

flow releases to the Blue River. Bypasses to the Blue River are made
in accordance with conditions granted to the Denver Water Department
by the Department of the Interior. A minimum release of 50 cfs or
inflow to reservoir, whichever is less, must be continually
maintained. The use of the bypass pipeline would double as a
penstock.

In order to construct the penstock, a temporary bypass system was
constructed in order to dewater the existing outlet works and enable
construction of the penstock and modifications to the control gate
chamber. The system consisted of 3 submersible pumps which pump the
required releases over the top of the dam and down to a multi-jet
sleeve valve located in a stilling chamber constructed adjacent to the
existing stilling basin. Two main pumps maintain the required 50 cfs
release and a third small pump is used to fill the system or for
operation by a diesel generator to maintain a low level release during
power outages. When the penstock construction is finished, the sleeve
valve will be connected to the penstock to provide additional operational flexibility for releases. General layout of the temporary
bypass system is shown in Figure 3.

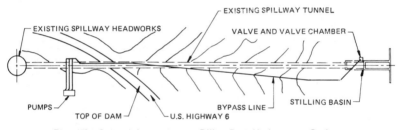

Figure 3. General Arrangement - Dillon Dam Hydropower Project
Temporary Bypass System

The hydroelectric development will consist of an adaptor on the center
control gate which transitions to a 4 ft (1.22 m) diameter steel
penstock encased in concrete below the existing free-flow tunnel. The
penstock will run directly below the tunnel from the gate chamber to
immediately upstream of the stilling basin, where it will angle over
to a powerhouse to be constructed adjacent to the stilling basin. The
powerhouse will house a single horizontal Francis unit, with a rated
output of 1.73 MW under a net head of 223 ft (67.97 m). The powerhouse will also contain a 2.5 ft (0.76 m) diameter Howell-Bunger type
free discharge valve (with conical plug guard valve) to provide
releases beyond the generating unit's hydraulic capacity or when the
unit is shut down. The unit is scheduled to enter commercial operation in July 1987. A general layout of the installation is shown in
Figure 4.

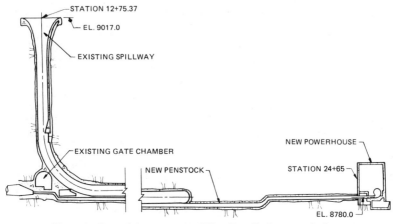

Figure 4. General Arrangement - Dillon Dam Hydropower Project

Moose River Hydroelectric Project

The Moose River Project is being developed by Long Lake Energy
Corporation, a private developer. The project is located on the Moose
River near Lyonsdale, New York, and will not use any existing dam or
structures. A low rubble masonry weir will be constructed to stabilize the project headwaters. Water will be continually spilled over
the weir to maintain the fish habitat between the dam and powerhouse
and for recreational use. River flow will be diverted to a new intake
structure and through a 15 foot diameter unlined rock tunnel 5070 feet
(1545 m) in length, excavated by a tunnel boring machine (TBM). The
powerhouse will contain a single vertical Kaplan unit, with a rated
output of 12.2 MW under 123 ft (37.5 m) net head. The unit will
operate in a run-of-river mode under headwater level control.

In order to reduce hydraulic transients in the long penstock to acceptable levels, some means of surge suppression is required. The
project topography and economics precluded the use of a conventional
surge tank. The solution adopted will consist of an airtight reinforced concrete compressed air surge chamber, with a system of
compressors and pressure and level controls to establish and maintain
a cushion of air in the chamber and suppress hydraulic transients in
the penstock. The project is currently under final design and is
scheduled to begin commercial operation by December 1987. The overall
project layout is shown in Figure 5.

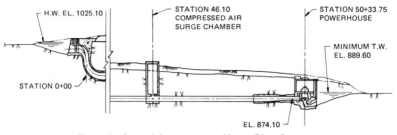

Figure 5. General Arrangement - Moose River Project

Summary and Conclusions

As can be seen from the above examples, each small hydro project offers unique challenges to the engineer. Developers and engineers should not approach projects under the assumption that "small hydro" implies a minimal or reduced engineering effort. Design features such as siphon intakes, tunneling through existing dams without expensive cofferdam schemes, and compressed air surge chambers cannot be considered "typical" and can determine the feasibility of a project and ultimately determine whether or not the project will be built. The engineer must take a creative and flexible approach to each project, and ensure that each project receives the attention and effort necessary to provide the best hydroelectric development at each site. This effort requires all the resources and capabilities of an experienced hydroelectric engineer, and may sometimes appear disproportionate to the development. However, it is this effort that can ultimately result in the project becoming a reality rather than another abandoned study.

Acknowledgements

The authors wish to acknowledge the employees of the Small Hydro Facilities Section of Harza Engineering Company for their assistance in preparation of this paper.

Diamond Fork
Hydroelectric Power Development

Stephen J. Navin, M. ASCE[1] and Harvey L. Hutchinson[2]

Abstract

The Strawberry Valley Project was conceived in the early
1990s as an irrigation project to supply a maximum of
635 cfs of water from the Strawberry Reservoir through a
3.8-mile-long tunnel to the Diamond Fork Drainage of the
Spanish Fork River for summer irrigation at the south end
of Utah Lake.

The tunnel was constructed between 1906 and 1912 through a
sequence of sandstone, limestone, and shale of the Wasatch
Mountain Range. The tunnel has a concrete arch section
with inside dimensions of 7-ft wide x 8.5-ft high.

The original timber support has long since decayed leaving
voids behind the tunnel lining. Visual inspection and
limited diamond drilling of the lining in 1974 indicated
that the major reaches of the tunnel are in good shape.

The impulse radar mapping and a detailed visual mapping
program pinpointed the reaches of the tunnel needing
repair. This has greatly reduced the risk associated with
rehabilitation of the tunnel.

Rehabilitation methods proposed for the tunnel include an
extensive contact grouting program using foamed cement/fly
ash backfill grout placed from pumping plants up to
9,000 ft away and a new reinforced concrete lining.

The Diamond Fork Hydroelectric Power Development Project
is an example of how private enterprise can develop the
unique solution to engineering problems and make an
80-year-old dream become a reality.

---

[1]Chief Engineer - Mining & Metallurgical Division, The
Ralph M. Parsons Company, 100 West Walnut Street,
Pasadena, CA 91124.
[2]Manager, Engineering-Science, Inc., 242 South Main
Street, Alpine, UT 84003.

Introduction

The Diamond Fork Power Development Project will use the irrigation water of the Strawberry Valley Reclamation Project and take advantage of the 2,600-ft elevation difference to develop 80 MW of hydroelectric power. The original project was conceived in the early 1900s to supply a maximum of 635 cfs of water from the Strawberry Reservoir. This water is transported through a 3.8-mile-long tunnel to the Diamond Fork Drainage of the Spanish Fork River for summer irrigation of 42,000 acres located at the south end of Utah Lake. The tunnel was one of the first to be constructed and funded by the Reclamation Act of 1902, and it has been in continuous use since its completion in 1916. It is noteworthy that the Strawberry Valley Project, which includes the tunnel, was the first reclamation project to pay back its entire construction cost to the Federal Government.

Description

The tunnel is within the Uinta Formation and Green River Formation, which were deposited during Eocene time. The Uinta Formation represents a regressive phase of deposits from the last stage of ancient Lake Uinta. The formation in this area consists of interbedded sandstone, siltstone, and shale. The sandstone is tan to gray, fine-grained, calcareous, soft to hard, and interbedded with thin shale beds. The siltstone is also tan to gray, locally sandy, calcareous, soft to hard, and generally well indurated. The shale is gray to dark gray, well compacted, calcareous, and soft to moderately hard.

The rock formations in the vicinity of Strawberry Tunnel have been subjected to a minor degree of faulting, folding, and fracturing; the primary tectonic activity has been mild uplifting and warping during the Wasatch Mountain building era.

Unconfined compressive strengths of intact samples tested from 930 to 14,276 psi.

TUNNEL HISTORY

Strawberry Tunnel is located approximately 30 miles southeast of Provo, Utah, in the Wasatch Mountain Range. The tunnel conveys water from the Strawberry Reservoir (Soldier Creek Dam), in the Colorado River Basin, to the west side of the range in the Diamond Fork and Spanish Fork Rivers of the Bonneville Basin (Figure 1).

The historical documents indicated that the original design of the tunnel allowed for three classes of rock condition:

Class I   No timber support, concrete tight to the rock.

Class II   Timber set on 4-ft to 6-ft spacing, tight lagging over crown, concrete to rock, and lagging.

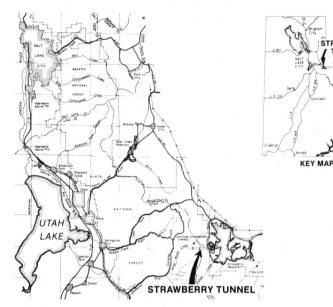

Figure 1. Map of Tunnel Area

Class III   Timber set on close spacing with tight lagging all
             around, invert struts, and rubble fill behind
             lagging concrete to lagging.

These are sections of the tunnel where the overbreak was 4 ft
beyond the timber set. These areas were packed tight with split
lagging to transfer the rock load to the timber set. Figure 2 shows
the use of heavy timber packing and rubble fill, and the original
Class II design.

The concrete lining was not designed for rock support of
backfilling behind the timber support system. Its purpose was to
prevent erosion and slaking of the bedrock and to provide an adequate
conduit for the transmission of water.

INSPECTION OF TUNNEL

There are only a few historic documents available, and these are
in many diverse places. The Utah Historical Society has photographs
and some site drawings. The old documents referred to advance rates
that could be translated into rock stability or groundwater
encountered. The condition of the tunnel lining was reported in
"Examination of Strawberry Tunnel, 1918," which proved to be a useful
document in locating geological contacts.

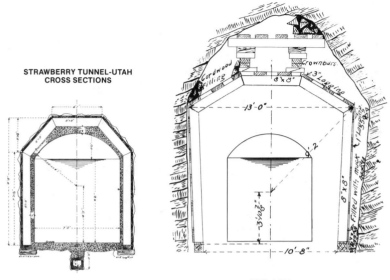

STRAWBERRY TUNNEL-UTAH
CROSS SECTIONS

DESIGN   INPLACE

Figure 2. Heavy Timber Packing, Rubble Fill,
and Class II Design

A recent visual inspection of the tunnel identified the
following potential problems:

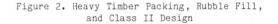

- Cracked concrete
- Stress relief cracking
- Sulfate attack
- Water inflow

Figure 3 identifies the major water inflow and stress relief
areas. Water inflow rates were estimated during the inspection. It
can also be seen that the water and stress relief zones are
associated with those geologic areas in which the rock type changes
at suspected contact zones. The extensive shale zone from Station
119+00 to 154+00 also exhibits stress relief and water inflow.

The areas where drain holes were placed in the original concrete
lining allowed for estimates of lining thickness, depth of void, and
inspection of the wall rock. As part of the detailed tunnel
inspection program, a test procedure had to be found that could
quantify concrete thickness, voids, buried timber, and rock. The
method chosen was impulse radar.

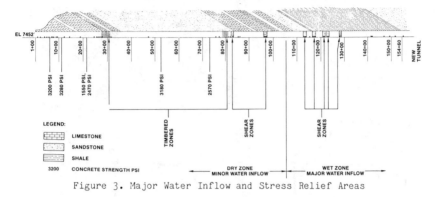

Figure 3. Major Water Inflow and Stress Relief Areas

The typical radar record illustrated in Figure 4 shows the important parts of the reflected signal. The surface of the concrete is the top horizontal line in the graph. The horizontal scale is dependent upon the rate of travel of the transducer over the ground. The vertical scale is in nanoseconds, which can be converted to a depth scale, provided the velocity of propagation is known; in this case, the speed is 2.5 nanoseconds/ft of concrete.

The main feature of the data is that the display of dark bands typically occur on multiples and are the reflections caused by oscillations or reverberations in the reflection of the pulse. These reverberations vary in intensity with the degree of the dielectric contrast of the materials being probed. This oscillation can limit the ability of the system to discriminate closely spaced interfaces, but usually does not impede the detection and location of the features of interest; in this case, wood sets and voids.

Results of the Tunnel Inspections

The general condition of the concrete is good to very good for 80% of the tunnel's length. The areas that exhibit visual signs of concrete failure due to stress were also areas indicating heavy timber concentration on the impulse radar scan. The radar scans indicated that timber sets were used for the entire length of tunnel investigation. Set spacing was 6 ft in good ground and down to an estimated 3-ft spacing in areas of suspected heavy ground.

Repair Alternatives

Free Air Tunnel - This is the simplest of the repair alternatives. The program would be limited to repair to the lining where major failures are present, replacement when necessary, and then low-pressure grouting. The lining reconstruction would be limited to rock bolting and a concrete reinforcing program. Rock bolts would tie the concrete shell to the rock and epoxy grouts would be used to glue the cracked concrete together. The grouting program

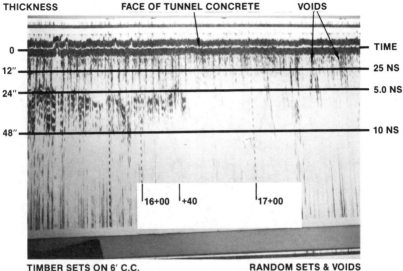

Figure 4. Typical Radar Record

would use cement grout to fill the extensive voids that have been located by the impulse radar survey. The outlet structure would be replaced, as would the first 500 ft of the west portal.

Pressure Tunnel - To get all of the available energy out of the Strawberry system, the tunnel must be a pressure conduit capable of the full hydrostatic head produced by a full reservoir; this pressure is 150 ft of water.

It is proposed to improve the resistance of the material surrounding the tunnel by means of pressure grouting. This will fill all open voids and also consolidate the soft residue from the rotted timber, as well as the loose muck that was backfilled behind the timber.

The difficulties of grouting an unreinforced lining to 100 psi causes field problems that would make the program prohibitively expensive. The alternative was to design a reinforced concrete liner to be placed within the existing tunnel. Figure 5 shows the proposed reinforced tunnel liner. The invert will be excavated 1.5 ft by a road header mining machine. The concrete lining will be reinforced with tension #8 bar on 6-in. centers and longitudinal #4 bar at 18-in. First concrete placement will be at the invert, than the arch. The final phase of the work will be a two-pass grouting program. The first pass will be a low-pressure (50 psi) bulkfilling operation; the second will be a high-pressure (150 psi) pass. The last 1,000 ft downstream will, in addition to the new concrete liner, require a steel liner.

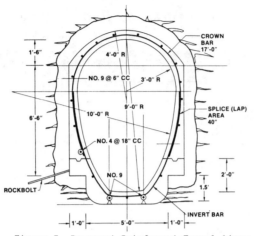

Figure 5. Proposed Reinforced Tunnel Liner

Power Generation Alternatives

The Bureau of Reclamation's alternative (Figure 6) shows the Syar Tunnel, the flow-through Syar Power Plant, the Syar Dam and reregulation reservoir, Corona Aqueduct, a peaking power plant located at Sixth Water, Sixth Water Dam and a reregulating reservoir, Dyne Aqueduct, Dyne Powerplant used for peaking purposes, Monks Hollow Dam and Reservoir, Monks Hollow power plant, and Diamond Fork pipeline and power plant.

Strawberry-Parsons alternative (Figure 7) consists of the upgraded Strawberry Tunnel, with a normal flow of 450 cfs and four power systems. Power System No. 1 would consist of an 84-in. pipeline and penstock that would carry an average of 450 cfs ft of water during periods of drought. The power plant would have an installed capacity of about 35 MW. It is assumed that water deliveries to this power plant as well as to other power plants would be on a steady-flow basis and that the flows would not vary except between the summer and winter months. Power System No. 2 would include an inlet structure consisting of a small diversion structure to regulate the flows in and out of Sixth Water Creek and optimize the fishery sections. The water from the tailrace of Power Plant No. 1 would pass through the inlet structure and be transported in an 84-in. pipeline to Power Plant No. 3 located at the upstream end of Hayes Reservoir. Hayes Reservoir would be capable of holding about 45,000 AF of water. The Hayes Power Plant would have an installed capacity of approximately 6 MW.

Cost comparisons of the two alternatives are presented in Table 1.

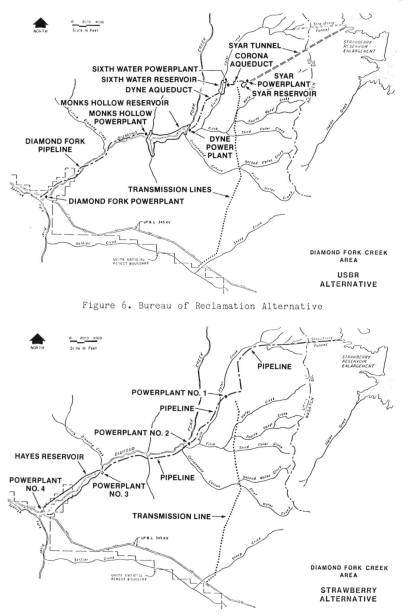

Figure 6. Bureau of Reclamation Alternative

Figure 7. Strawberry - Parsons Alternative

Table 1. Preliminary Cost Comparisons

$ Million	USBR 1984	Strawberry- Parsons 1985
Total Construction Cost	538.0	166.3
Total Nonfederal Construction Cost	270.6	166.3
Annual Cost		
Interest and Principal (11%, 24 yr)	32.4	19.9
Operation and Maintenance and Replacement (1% of total construction cost)	2.7	1.7
Total Annual Cost	35.1	21.6
Installed Plant Capacity (MW)	166.0	80.0
Average Annual Generation (million kWh)	362.0	428.00
Unit Cost of Power (mills/kWh)	97.0	50.0
Cost Increase in DRSP Power Rates (mills/kWh)	4-7	0-1.1
Additional Costs to be paid by Strawberry Water Users ($ million), Includes Tunnel Rehabilitation or Syar Tunnel, Reregulating Reservoir, Diamond Fork Pipeline	150-169	-0-

Economic and Economic Comparisons

The assumptions governing analysis include:

1. The Diamond Fork Power System and related water supply and deliveries would be operated so as to:

   - Preserve irrigation, municipal, and industrial water rights; manage flood control; enhance fish and wildlife habitats; and produce other benefits identified in the September 1984 Report Supplement.

   - Enhance power production and power benefits to the extent feasible consistent with preservation of their benefits, as mentioned above.

2. Project costs and federal expenditures would be reduced in an amount equal to the costs of facilities covered by nonfederal participants, with costs of facilities as estimated in the Bureau of Reclamation Report Supplement (January 1984 prices).

3. Contracts would be made so as to identify and preserve the interest and benefits of all participants.

4. Refinements in the analysis that would follow execution or agreements covering power and associated facilities, project water operations, power sales and deliveries, and other items, as necessary, would be made later.

5. Singlepurpose alternatives, separable costs, and project benefits (other than power) would remain the same as identified in the Bureau of Reclamation September 1984 Report Supplement.

Conclusions

The overall assessment that the tunnel condition was good, was confirmed by the impulse radar survey. The proposed repair methods are feasible and have been successfully applied to other tunnels.

The Strawberry-Parsons alternative of utilizing the Strawberry Tunnel with private financing is the most cost-effective project.

References

1. Profile of Strawberry Tunnel, United States Reclamation Service, 1915.

2. Study of Wood Lagging Behind Tunnel Lining, an evaluation of 70 Year Old Wood Lagging in Strawberry Tunnel, Utah, Water and Power Resources Services, March 1981.

3. Continuous Subsurface Profiling by Impulse Radar, Geoscan, Weare, New Hampshire, 1984.

HYDROPOWER ON THE ARKANSAS - A NON-FEDERAL DEVELOPMENT

W. B. SMITH[1] AND CURTIS Q. WARNER[2]

ABSTRACT

Development of the hydropower potential on the Arkansas River Navigation System has been considered since the early planning phases of the navigation project. However, only two of the eleven navigation locks and dams in Arkansas were initially constructed with hydropower facilities. In 1980, Arkansas Electric Cooperative Corporation (AECC) filed preliminary permit applications with the Federal Energy Regulatory Commission for developing the hydropower potential at the nine remaining locks and dams in Arkansas operated by the U.S. Army Corps of Engineers. The sites traverse the state from Fort Smith at the western border of Arkansas to the Mississippi River confluence at the eastern border.

AECC was issued preliminary permits to study seven of the nine undeveloped sites (two permits were issued under preference provisions to local municipals). Two phases of feasibility studies were then performed by Benham-Holway Power Group; these studies resulted in the preparation of applications for seven major licenses. From these, three sites were surrendered by AECC for economic reasons, but in the fall of 1983 four major licenses were issued to AECC by FERC. The projects will involve construction of low head run-of-river hydropower facilities beside U.S. Army Corps of Engineers' dams. The hydropower facilities will utilize multiple-unit, horizontal-axis Kaplan turbines.

In mid-1984, the AECC Board of Directors authorized initiation of engineering to develop the first hydropower facility at Lock and Dam No. 13 near Fort Smith, Arkansas. The Board authorized construction of the first plant, a 33-MW open-pit configuration, to begin construction in October 1985, with scheduled completion on or before December 1988.

This paper describes the history of project development from initial conception through receipt of construction proposals. It also describes the unique engineering features of the equipment and construction requirements, coordination of design with the U.S. Army Corps of Engineers for non-federal development on a river system, a review of future power requirements in the area, and a summary of the innovative methods of financing that are being examined by Arkansas' generation and transmission cooperative.

---

[1] W. B. Smith, P.E. - Vice President/Hydropower; Benham-Holway Power Group, 5314 South Yale Avenue, Tulsa, Oklahoma 74135. Registered Professional Engineer in Oklahoma, Arkansas, Missouri, Kansas, Utah, and Colorado. B.S. in Civil Engineering from University of Missouri-Rolla, 1974. Field of Interest - Hydropower.

[2] Curtis Q. Warner - Engineer/Arkansas Electric Cooperative Corporation, 8000 Scott Hamilton Drive, Little Rock, Arkansas 72219. B.S. in Mechanical Engineering from Memphis State University, 1979. Field of Interest - Power plants.

A. HISTORY OF DEVELOPMENT

The majority of rural Arkansas is provided electric service by seventeen rural electric distribution cooperatives. Arkansas Electric Cooperative Corporation (AECC) is the statewide generation and transmission cooperative responsible for supplying its seventeen member co-ops wholesale power and energy. AECC's facilities include 1407 megawatts of coal-fired capacity and 315 megawatts of oil- or gas-fired capacity.

The U. S. Army Corps of Engineers began construction of the McClellan-Kerr Arkansas River Navigation System during 1957, and the navigation system was opened to traffic in 1971.[1] The Arkansas River Navigation System provides worldwide access for goods to and from the mid-section of the United States. The navigation system links the Port of Catoosa near Tulsa, Oklahoma, with the Mississippi River.

When the Corps constructed the locks and dams they evaluated the hydropower potential of the man-made "drops" which replaced the descending natural slope of the Arkansas River.[2] The original decision of the Corps resulted in construction of hydropower at only four sites, Dardenelle Lock and Dam and Ozark Lock and Dam in Arkansas, and Robert S. Kerr Lock and Dam and Webbers Falls Lock and Dam in Oklahoma. The remaining fourteen locks and dams' which traverse the states of Oklahoma and Arkansas were constructed without hydropower facilities, due primarily to the relative abundance of inexpensive oil and gas available at the time. The water which flows through the spillway gates of the fourteen undeveloped sites was considered energy which could not be economically recovered.

But in 1978, with a considerably different fuel supply situation, the managers of Riceland, C&L, and Arkansas Valley Electric Cooperatives decided the time had come to re-examine the economics of the unconstructed hydropower sites, many of which were within or adjoining their service territories. They, along with the fourteen other cooperatives which comprise AECC, began further studies of the sites in Arkansas.

1. Feasibility Studies

In November 1980, Arkansas Electric Cooperative Corporation retained the Benham-Holway Power Group (BHPG), a nationwide consulting firm experienced in hydropower development, to develop the first technical and economic evaluation of the potential benefits available to AECC's consumers. BHPG was the design engineer and construction manager for the Lawrence Hydroelectric Project, the first all-American low-head hydropower development in the United States. Using the experience of the design for the Lawrence Project, BHPG developed a concept for evaluating low-head hydropower potential at each of the following sites which the Federal Energy Regulatory Commission issued preliminary permits; Dam No. 2, Locks and Dams No. 3, 4, 5, 6, 9, and 13.[3]

After conferring with major suppliers of turbines and generators worldwide, the preliminary feasibility report was developed.[4] The results established a basis of long-term benefits to AECC customers and a potential additional source of generation for AECC, using a renewable resource to supplement their existing oil fired units and partial ownership of five coal-fired generating stations.

The AECC staff then requested that detailed studies be performed on each of the seven sites for which AECC held preliminary permits. BHPG began detailed discussions with representatives of the Little Rock District Corps of Engineers to obtain available data for this study. The preliminary concepts were re-examined and found to remain valid. BHPG further defined the parameters which might be utilized in a future design and prepared detailed cost estimates and began initial consultations with the environmental agencies that would be involved in the projects. BHPG compared the benefits of each hydropower project with the comparable energy costs of AECC's alternatives, another coal-fired plant, or a lignite plant. The results of this phase of feasibility study for each plant and for various combinations are shown in Table 1 and Figure 1[5].

TABLE 1

| Parameter | Lock and Dam | | | | | | |
	2	3	4	5	David D. Terry (No. 6)	9	13
Type of Turbine	Bulb	Bulb	Bulb	Bulb	Bulb	Bulb	Bulb
Size (Meters)	7.0	5.8	5.8	5.8	5.8	5.8	6.7
No. of Units	3	4	4	4	4	4	2
Capacity (Kilowatts)	120,000	48,000	27,200	36,000	39,600	42,600	33,200
Design Flow Per Unit (CFS)	12,000	8,000	7,000	7,700	8,100	8,200	11,300
Nominal Gross Head (Feet)	38	18	12	15	16	17	19
Estimated 1982 Cost (Million $)	142	102	101	96	101	85	59

After extensive consultations with the AECC staff and a detailed presentation to AECC's Board of Directors, the preparation of license applications for each of the seven sites was authorized in January 1982.

2. FERC Licensing

BHPG began a re-evaluation of each project during the preparation of each license application. The turbine and generator manufacturers were provided more detailed hydrological and power head data and were requested to "re-evaluate" their energy projection and cost quotations. Coordination continued throughout the licensing process with FERC and the Corps. AECC made a presentation at the White House to outline the administration policies which AECC was following "Non-Federal Development at Federal Sites". This would utilize private funds to develop hydropower at federal projects and help maximize the development of America's natural resources.

During the preparation of the license application, AECC had modified its status from a non-taxable entity to a taxable non-profit entity. AECC had determined that the use of leverage lease provisions in the tax laws would provide considerable benefits in the financing of their latest coal-fired unit. If built soon enough, at least one of the hydropower sites might also qualify for a leverage lease and the energy tax benefits.

Due to a re-negotiated coal transportation contract and its resulting reduction in energy costs for equivalent coal-fired generation, AECC determined that the projects at Locks and Dams 4, 5, and 6, which had been marginally feasible, were now no longer feasible. Those three sites and their preliminary permits were released by AECC. The Federal Energy Regulatory Commission (FERC) issued licenses for the four remaining sites in the fall of 1983.[6]

3. Preliminary Engineering

In late 1984, BHPG recommended a plan for proceeding with development of the four licensed projects. This included the collection of data to proceed with initial design, detailed technical discussions with FERC and the Corps, and initiation of model studies.

The Alden Research Laboratory had the only recent experience in modeling low-head hydropower projects at existing Corps of Engineers navigation locks and dams - Racine on the Ohio River and Demopolis on the Tom Bigbee River. Detail proposals and final negotiations commenced with Alden and the Corps.

It was agreed to initially perform two studies. The Phase A - Fixed Bed Model Study, studied the effects of the project on navigation. This model, at a scale of 1:120, covers a river reach of approximately 8,000 feet upstream from the dam and approximately 5,500 feet downstream from the dam. The model encompasses the entire overbank area north of the river to the existing levee and to elev. 395 on the south side of the river. This model area was approximately the same magnitude which the Corps has previously modeled at the Waterways Experiment Station (WES)[7] at Vicksburg for the original navigation model in 1970. The second model, required by BHPG to finalize project design, was a Phase B - Detailed Powerhouse Model, at a scale of 1:60.

Extensive modeling has been performed during the past nine months with additional scope of work being required by the Corps. Some of the methods and procedures proposed by Alden were required to be modified to conform to the Corps procedures in order for the data to quality for review. The final results obtained in July 1985 show that the installation of the hydropower facility has no major hydraulic effects on the existing Corps structure. Specific results of interest included:

No measurable changes in water surface elevations for the upstream pool by placement of the earth construction cofferdam in the floodplain.

The head loss across the structure was actually reduced, partly by the removal of a portion of a constricting downstream revetment and partly by the addition of length to the overflow embankment.

The Corps has required that a Phase C - Movable Bed Model be performed to study the effects of possible sedimentation changes, since the headrace and tailrace channels cut through existing diked revetments.

4.   Detailed Engineering

With the development of the Lock and Dam No. 13 Hydropower Project critically linked to the existing tax laws, a schedule and development philosophy were finalized in September 1984. The project is required to be completed on or before December 31, 1988, in order to maximize the benefits from the energy tax credit. To meet this schedule of completion date and the start of construction date of October 17, 1985, set out in the FERC license, BHPG was authorized to proceed with detailed engineering in October 1984. It was determined that, although preferred, the conventional, individual construction packages were not an applicable approach. As a result, the philosophy of three construction contracts was developed:

    Contract 1 - Turbines, Generators, and Accessories
                 (Equipment Purchase)

    Contract 2 - Generator Step-Up Transformers
                 (Equipment Purchase)

    Contract 3 - Project Construction and Equipment Installation
                 (Development of construction drawings, project
                 construction, and installation of equipment
                 purchased in Contracts 1 and 2

    BHPG is responsible for developing, procuring selected bidders, negotiating, and assisting AECC in award of each contract.

    The Contract 1 documents provided each of the manufacturers an opportunity to submit alternate proposals, based on the operational river conditions of the Arkansas River, in addition to the required base bid.

    This contract was awarded and executed in May 1985[8], and detailed engineering and turbine model tests are in progress. The final selection of equipment for Contract 1 followed the open-pit concept. Each unit consists of a 5.8-meter diameter Kaplan runner, a high-speed generator, and a two-stage epicyclic-speed increaser in the pit area. The gear will transform the 78.4 rpm rotation of the runner to the 900 rpm generator speed. The high speed synchronous generator is considered more reliable and stable than the typical lower speed generator.

    This concept presented the opportunity for AECC to develop the project within the limited time constraints by minimizing the installation period using smaller, more standardized equipment. The open-pit is expected to provide more accessibility for AECC maintenance for each of the three approximately 10-MW units in the future.

    The Contract 2 documents are currently scheduled for bidding in November 1985.

    Contract 3 is an "all inclusive" contract. The general contractors, with their supporting engineers, are required to finalize the design concepts set out in the proposal documents for review by BHPG. With this method, site construction can begin in accordance with the FERC requirements, while final detailing of the powerhouse is in progress. The owner, the engineer, the manufacturers, and the contractor with his engineer, must work together in close cooperation to complete this project in the scheduled time period.

5.   Construction

    Construction is scheduled to begin on October 1, 1985. The specific FERC requirements to satisfy the terms of this license for start of construction are that "clearing and grubbing of the project area are completed, with start of construction on either the seepage barrier or earth embankment of the construction cofferdam in progress, and that a satisfactory

schedule for completion of the cofferdam and project has been submitted."
The FERC definition of "start of construction" has evolved to a commitment,
by AECC, of genuinely pursuing the construction completion of any of their
licensed projects as quickly as possible.

B. DEVELOPMENT OF A RIVER SYSTEM

1. Similarity of Sites

Six of the seven undeveloped sites on the Arkansas River in Arkansas,
which AECC had originally held preliminary permits for, could have been
developed using identical turbine runners. The rating of the generators
would have been only slightly different due to the differences in available
power head at each site, but the general powerhouse arrangements could have
been identical.

As AECC considers developing the three remaining sites for which they
hold FERC licenses, the cost effectiveness of similarity will continue to be
examined closely. Cost savings could possibly result from negotiating with
the turbine manufacturer who is preparing the design and is initiating
fabrication for the units on the first project - Lock and Dam No. 13.
Project design engineering could be reduced for two of the three remaining
projects, as was experienced by BHPG during the feasibility study and
licensing phases of the seven projects. The AECC preventive maintenance
program could also be streamlined by the use of interchangable equipment at
each site. The specific benefits can be speculated on the Arkansas River
projects, but standardization is always a design goal for AECC.

2. Corps of Engineers Involvement

The Corps of Engineers has been continually involved in the non-federal
development of the Arkansas River projects. During the feasibility study
phase, the Corps, at initial coordination meetings, provided data and
general development guidelines for initial considerations. During the
licensing phase, the Corps became more involved with specific design
requirements for those portions of the projects which could affect the
structural integrity or operation of the existing navigation locks and dams.
At the design stage of the Lock and Dam No. 13 Project, many in-depth
meetings have occurred to review the design submittals by BHPG. As a result
of these recent activities over the past six months, the most significant
recommendations that can be expressed to non-federal developers at a federal
dam are as follows:

> "Begin initial discussions early with the Corps, maintain open
> communication continuously, and provide sufficient time in the
> project schedule for review and approval of design submittals."

The Corps of Engineers is well versed in their own standards for
developing hydropower projects. The economic development of the private
sector, however, often requires more innovative methods of development.

C. ECONOMICS AND FUTURE POWER REQUIREMENTS

The development of the Arkansas River projects is contingent upon two
vital factors, demand for energy and cost of development to the AECC member
ratepayers.

1.   Alternative Financing Considerations

With the current administrative policy of using private money to develop
projects, the availability of funding through the Rural Electrification
Administration (REA) has diminished.   An REA representative stated at a
recent AECC Board Meeting that federal loans for this project are "not
available."

As a result of this statement and recent successes by AECC with
alternative methods of long-term financing, other financing options were
evaluated for the Lock and Dam No. 13 project and will be examined as the
remaining sites are considered for final approval of development.

AECC is in the final stages of establishing the construction and
long-term financing arrangements for the Lock and Dam No. 13 Hydropower
Project.   Converting the construction loan into the permanent long-term
financing scheme using a leverage lease financing scheme is an experience
with which AECC is familiar. This will provide AECC the opportunity to sell
the financing portion of the project to investors who will benefit from the
tax credits available; energy tax credit, investment tax credit, and
accelerated depreciation.

The resulting benefits to AECC member ratepayers include a reduction of
the debt service payment to a point where a rate increase may not be required
when the project comes on line. As shown on Figure 2, the projected rates
to the member co-ops with the development of a coal or lignite plant in the
early 1990's escalate at a significantly higher rate than the hydropower
project at Lock and Dam No. 13 since the fossil units are so labor
intensive.

2.   Future Power Requirements

Although AECC currently has some "excess" capacity, the predicted load
growth of 4 to 5% per year will require the addition of about 300-MW of
baseload (lignite) capacity in the late 1990's.   The four run-of-river
hydropower sites do provide some capacity benefit, but they can only be
expected to provide about one-half of their nameplate capability in the
summer months due to expected river flow conditions. Despite the fact that
AECC is a summer peaking cooperative, the savings in displaced fuel costs
year-round tip the economic scales in favor of the hydropower projects. The
energy from the Lock and Dam No. 13 site would have met 3.3% of AECC's 1984
energy sales; not a big percentage, but enough to displace $3.2 million in
fuel costs.

3.   Basis of Feasibility

Each owner or developer has a unique definition of feasibility.   For
AECC, the term feasible project was evaluated with many considerations. The
members of the Board of Directors and the more experienced members of AECC's
staff realized they would probably not see a positive cash flow from any of
the Arkansas River projects, but they see the potential savings to future
generations of rural Arkansas families by developing the hydropower projects.
Each hydropower project is evaluated on its own merit and is compared with an
equivalent amount of energy from a future coal or a future lignite plant.
Though dependable capacity was considered, the benefits for capacity were
negligible when compared with the benefits from energy production. To AECC,
these projects are feasible.

D. __CONCLUSIONS__

The development of hydropower on the Arkansas River is progressing, but numerous hurdles still remain. The benefits derived from developing the full potential on the Arkansas will take more than the cumulative years of construction to realize but the economy of the state is expected to benefit and the member ratepayers of AECC will be the ultimate winners through reduced rates for their future generations.

REFERENCES

1. Department of the Army, Little Rock District, Corps of Engineers, McClellan-Kerr Arkansas River Navigation System.

2. Department of the Army, Little Rock District, Corps of Engineers, November 1981, Arkansas River and Tributaries, Hydropower and Other Purposes, Arkansas and Oklahoma.

3. Federal Energy Regulatory Commission, Preliminary Permits issued: Dam No. 2 - 3033 (9-18-80); Lock and Dam No. 3 - 3034 (9-19-80); Lock and Dam No. 4 - 3032 (11-19-80); Lock and Dam No. 5 - 3042 (11-20-80); David D. Terry Lock and Dam No. 6 - 3045 (11-20-80); Lock and Dam No. 9 - 3044 (11-20-80); and Lock and Dam No. 13 - 3043 (9-19-80).

4. Benham-Holway Power Group, March 1981, Preliminary Evaluation of Hydroelectric Power at Seven Arkansas River Locks and Dams.

5. Benham-Holway Power Group, December 1981, Executive Summary of Hydropower Development.

6. Federal Energy Regulatory Commission, FERC Major Licenses - Existing Dam issued: Dam No. 2 - 3033-001 (8-10-83); Lock and Dam No. 3 - 3034-001 (8-10-83); Lock and Dam No. 9 - 3044-001 (7-20-83); and Lock and Dam No. 3 - 3043-002 (10-18-83).

7. U. S. Army Engineer Waterways Experiment Station, July 1970, Technical Report H-70-8, Hydraulic Model Investigation, Lock and Dam No. 13 Arkansas River Navigation Project.

8. Contract 1 - Turbines, Generators, and Accessories, awarded to Voest-Alpine International Corporation, May 6, 1985.

Water Management of the
Snowy Mountains Scheme
Australia

Francis C Millner*
(Member Institution of Engineers, Australia)

Abstract

The Snowy Mountains Scheme in south-eastern Australia provides a
classic example of Water Resources Planning and Management on a
National scale. The Scheme provides mainly peak electricity for the
states of New South Wales and Victoria and the Australian Capital
Territory and enables the interbasin transfer of water from a coastal
to an inland river system where it is utilised for irrigation and
urban water supply by three States. The paper describes the main
features of the Scheme and the management of its operation. Comment
is made on political and legal aspects, system analysis, environmental
aspects and the performance of the Scheme.

The Scheme

The Snowy Mountains Area is the source of the River Murray,
Australia's main, (catchment 1 060 000 km^2 - 660 000 square miles) but
poorly fed, (average annual runoff 17 000 x 10^{6}m^3 - 13 800 000 acre-
feet) inland river system. The area contains Australia's highest
mountain (elev. 2 228 m - 7 310 feet) where snow lies permanently on
the ground during winter months and which forms part of a Dividing
Range which broadly parallels the eastern coastline some 100 km (60
miles) inland. Precipitation in the area is some four times the average for the dry Australian continent.

The Snowy Mountains Scheme impounds the coastward flowing waters
of the Snowy River and its tributary, the Eucumbene, at high elevations and diverts them inland to the Murray and Murrumbidgee Rivers,
through two tunnel systems driven through the Snowy Mountains. The
Scheme also involves the utilisation of the headwaters of the Murray
and Murrumbidgee Rivers and as a consequence of the topography of the
area the regulation of the Tooma River, a tributary of the Murray, by
transmountain diversion to the Tumut River and the upper Murrumbidgee
by transmountain diversion to the Eucumbene Catchment.

These waters generate mainly peak load electricity to compliment
the predominantly coal-fired systems in New South Wales and Victoria
as they pass through the power stations to downstream storages for reregulation for irrigation purposes. The provision of additional downstream storage was an integral part of the Scheme and enables

*Operations Planning Engineer, Snowy Mountains Authority, P O Box 322,
Cooma, New South Wales 2630, Australia.

good flexibility for electricity production during winter months. The Scheme reached its designed capacity of 3 740 MW in 1974 after twenty-five years of construction.

Features of the Scheme

- Sixteen large dams, 80 km (50 miles) of aqueducts and over 145 km (90 miles) of tunnels
- Five surface and two underground power stations

Broadly, the Scheme falls into two sections: the northern, Snowy-Tumut Development and the southern, Snowy-Murray Development. Both developments are connected by tunnels to the Scheme's main regulating storage, Lake Eucumbene. Separate accounts are kept of the water in Lake Eucumbene belonging to each Development in order to achieve the agreed division of water between the Murray and Murrumbidgee valleys. Figure 1 shows a plan of the diversions of the Scheme.

Snowy-Tumut Development

The Snowy-Tumut Development provides for the diversion of the Upper Murrumbidgee, the Eucumbene and the Tooma Rivers to the Tumut River, and for the combined waters of these four rivers to generate electricity in four power stations in their fall of 800 m (2 625 feet). The transmountain tunnel system includes the Eucumbene-Tumut Tunnel, connecting Lake Eucumbene with Tumut Pond Reservoir. The normal function of the tunnel is to divert water through the Dividing Range from Lake Eucumbene to the Tumut River, but during periods of high flow, water in excess of that required for operating the power stations is diverted in a reverse direction to Lake Eucumbene for storage.

The Tumut 1 and 2 Power Stations have a total capacity of 600 MW and are normally operated in tandem. The Tumut 3 Power Station has a capacity of 1 500 MW housing six 250 MW units three of which have undercoupled pumps each 200 MW for pumped storage operation. This section of the Scheme provides additional water to the Blowering Reservoir (1 630 x 10^{6}m^3 storage capacity - 1 320 000 acre-feet) which was constructed by the State of New South Wales for regulation of releases for irrigation in the Murrumbidgee Valley and contains Blowering Power Station of 80 MW capacity.

Snowy-Murray Development

The Snowy-Murray Development involves the diversion of the Snowy River, by a transmountain tunnel system, to the Geehi River, the waters again falling some 800 m (2 625 feet) and generating up to 1 500 MW in Murray 1 and Murray 2 Power Stations. Additional power is generated in the 60 MW Guthega Power Station which makes use of the waters in the Snowy River above the tunnel system.

An essential part of this Development is the two-way Eucumbene-Snowy Tunnel which connects the Snowy River with Lake Eucumbene. When

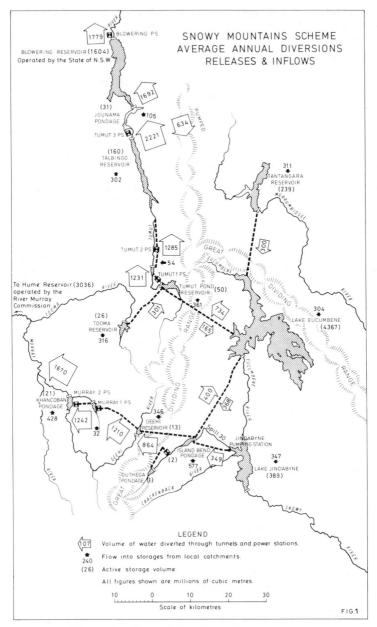

Figure 1 - Plan of the Diversions of the Scheme

the flows in the Snowy and Geehi Rivers exceed the needs of the Murray power stations, water from the Snowy River at Island Bend is diverted through this Tunnel for storage in Lake Eucumbene. Low flows in the Snowy and Geehi Rivers are supplemented by diverting the stored water from Lake Eucumbene back through the same tunnel to the Murray power stations. Additional water is supplied to the transmountain tunnel system near Island Bend by the Jindabyne project which pumps, from Lake Jindabyne, the run-off from the Snowy catchment downstream of Island Bend.

Below Murray 2 Power Station, Khancoban Dam was constructed to re-regulate the diurnal fluctuations of releases associated with peak electricity operation and thereby prevent erosion effects on down-stream river banks. The Snowy-Murray Development provides additional water to the Hume Reservoir which is under control of the River Murray Commission and was increased in capacity by $620 \times 10^6 m^3$ (500 000 acre-feet) to $3\ 100 \times 10^6 m^3$ (2 500 000 acre-feet) to regulate releases from the Scheme for irrigation.

Regulation of Water

The regulation achieved by the reservoirs coupled with the two-way tunnel diversions makes possible firm uniform monthly releases for electricity production almost regardless of inflow conditions. Lake Eucumbene of $4\ 367 \times 10^6 m^3$ (3 500 000 acre-feet) capacity is the main storage of the Scheme and provides long-term regulation of water for both the Snowy-Murray and Snowy-Tumut Developments.

While the construction of the Scheme enabled the inland diversion of an annual average quantity of $1\ 130 \times 10^6 m^3$ (920 000 acre-feet) of even greater significance is the high degree of long-term regulation of all waters of the Scheme. This ensures that over the worst recorded drought period the output from the Scheme will not be less than 85% of average. A firm release of just over $1\ 000 \times 10^6 m^3$ (810 000 acre-feet) is available from each of the developments during droughts.

Political Arrangements and Legal Aspects

In Australia it has long been accepted that the management of water resources is the responsibility of the States, except that in the case of the Australian Capital Territory and the Northern Territory, the Federal Government exercises all power over water supply and water resources management. Where rivers form the border between two States, such as the Murray between New South Wales and Victoria and the Darling between New South Wales and Queensland, agreements have been negotiated between the particular States to resolve any possible disputes over rights to the water of these rivers. For example, the distribution of the waters of the River Murray between New South Wales, Victoria and South Australia is laid down in an agreement originally reached in 1914 between the Commonwealth, New South Wales, Victoria and South Australia. This Agreement was amended later to allow for water diverted from the Snowy

Mountains Scheme. Any attempt to develop the water resources of the
Snowy Mountains area obviously involved both New South Wales and
Victoria, the Australian Capital Territory under the seat of Govern-
ment Act, and, indirectly, South Australia through the earlier River
Murray Waters Agreement.

The Snowy Mountains Authority was established by Federal legislation and the Federal Government sought consititutional power for the
legislation through its powers of defence and of generating and
supplying electricity to the Australian Capital Territory. Opinions
differ as to whether the Snowy Mountains Scheme actually lay within
the constitutional powers of the Federal Government. These differing
opinions were never resolved, but rather, the federal legislation
setting up the Snowy Mountains Authority was under-pinned by an Agreement between the Federal Government and the Governments of New South
Wales and Victoria and joint legislation enacted between these
parties. The Snowy Mountains Agreement was not finalised, however,
until January 1959, by which time work on the Scheme was well advanced
with some US $ 200 million already invested in the works. This Agree-
ment between the Commonwealth and the States of New South Wales and
Victoria authorised the Snowy Mountains Authority to construct the
Snowy Mountains Scheme and set out the basis for:

The control, sharing and diversion of waters.
The protection of catchment areas.
The charges to be made for electricity.
The rights of the Commonwealth to reserve electricity for the
Australian Capital Territory from the output of the Scheme.
Responsibilities regarding operation and maintenance of the
Scheme.
The constitution and role of the Snowy Mountains Council.

Operation and Maintenance

Under the terms of the 'Agreement', the Snowy Mountains Council
was established. One of the main duties of the Council is to direct
and control the operation and maintenance of the permanent works of
the Authority for the control of water and production of electricity.
The Council consists of eight members representing the Commonwealth,
the Snowy Mountains Authority and the State of New South Wales and
Victoria. Directions by the Council are carried out by an Operations
Engineer nominated by the Authority and Assistant Operations Engineers
nominated by each of the Electricity Commissions of New South Wales
and Victoria.

Operation of the Scheme with appropriate provision for maintenance
is co-ordinated through a series of interlocking operating plans with
the objective of optimising the use of water for irrigation and
electricity production within legal and physical characteristics of
the Scheme. The plans are prepared by officers of the Authority and
the Electricity and Water Commissions for consideration by Council.
Long-term studies are carried out in relation to future developments
and requirements of the electricity and irrigation systems. Each year

an annual plan is prepared that provides the broad limits of operation for the ensuing twelve months, as well as drawing attention to specific operating constraints that could arise during the period. Within the limits provided by the Annual Plan, more detailed co-ordination is carried out at monthly and three-monthly intervals in conjunction with electricity and irrigation interests using estimates of monthly requirements. A computer program is used to simulate the operation of the Scheme for a period of 12 months in advance to provide continuity. Separate studies are made for low, median and high inflow sequences combined with most probable, maximum or minimum estimates of electricity requirements as well as irrigation requirements.

Through the provision of the downstream regulating storages at Hume and Blowering, day to day operation does not normally need to consider irrigation requirements. In providing for peak electricity requirements operations need to be extremely flexible and weekly and daily programs are prepared within the framework of the monthly programs. The weekly programs serve as a basis to arrange diversions, pumping and other releases that need to consider a weekly cycle of operation. On a daily basis, operation is only restricted by physical limits or by standing instructions that affect capability.

Environmental Aspects

The major works of the Scheme were constructed at a time when the question of the effect of public works on the environment was not such a public issue as it is today. It is clear that under present conditions, where major environmental impact statements would be required, progress on such a Scheme as the Snowy Mountains could have been considerably delayed while some of the possible issues were resolved. This is not to say, however, that environmental aspects were not considered during the design and construction of the Scheme. As most of the Snowy Mountains Scheme is located within a National Park, a number of provisions were included in the Snowy Mountains Agreement for the protection of the natural assets of this area.(1).

Although flows in the rivers from which the water has been div-erted have been practically reduced to zero below the respective dams, downstream tributaries feed these rivers after some 50 km. During periods of low flows, however, it is necessary to make releases for riparian purposes. Further, the upstream regulations on these rivers has considerably reduced flooding, and because these storages spill only on an average of about once in every 10 years special arrange-ments are necessary on such occasions to warn downstream landowners. One of the major problems associated with the inland diversion of water is the limited capacity of the river channels for some 80 km immediately below the main outlets of the Scheme before the river channels join the major inland river systems. A considerable amount of work was carried out to improve these river channel capacities. In some cases, it was necessary to purchase floodaffected properties or to pay compensation for flooding or rises in ground-water levels adjacent to the river that affected the agricultural use of adjacent floodplain land.

System Analysis

During the investigation and design of the Snowy Mountains Scheme, system simulation studies were carried out to determine the optimum sizes of the numerous storages, tunnels, aqueducts, pipelines and power stations involved. The measurement of direct benefits being directly related to the cost of providing electricity by alternative means. The main basis of such studies was the use of historical and correlated records of flows. Precipitation records in the area were few and scattered and were considered unreliable on account of the then difficulty in measuring precipitations in the form of snow. At the time of establishment of the Snowy Mountains Authority in 1949, about 45 years of stream flow records were available from base stations on the main streams leaving the Snowy Mountains area. However, few records were available from the smaller streams in the mountains, and it was initially necessary to rely on estimates of run-off at the higher altitudes until adequate correlations were established with the gauging stations the Snowy Mountains Authority constructed in the area. The earlier estimates of run-off in the mountains have subsequently proved to have been extremely well made.

Performance of the Scheme to Date

In the formative years of the Scheme, there were critics of its long-term economic viability in view of projected reductions in the cost of production from thermal plant as a consequence of increases in thermal efficiencies and the construction of large thermal plants adjacent to coalfields. As events have proved, the investment in the Scheme for hydro-electricity generation alone which repays the entire cost of the Scheme has been of great value. In 1984-85, the average cost of energy production by the Scheme was 2.1 cents per kilowatt hour, being less than half the cost of electricity sold to bulk consumers by the Electricity Commission of New South Wales and Victoria in that year.(2).

The connection of the Scheme since 1959 by 330 kV transmission lines to the electricity systems of New South Wales and Victoria has also been of significant economic advantage. This has enabled sharing of reserves and the interchange of electricity between New South Wales and Victoria to their mutual advantage in optimising system costs. Extensive use has also been made of the power and pumping stations of the Scheme to provide spinning and fast reserve for both States from interrupting pumping, partially loaded units, changeover from synchronous condenser operation and the ability to start hydro units quickly with consequent savings in fuel costs of thermal plants.

When the Scheme reached its designed capacity of 3 740 MW in 1974, this figure represented 33% of the capacity of the combined New South Wales, Victoria and Snowy systems, and during shortages of thermal generating plant the Scheme has been called upon to operate at the limit of the diversion capacity available. The Scheme was designed to produce peak electricity, and good flexibility exists on a short-term basis, however, it is not able to replace base load generation for

prolonged periods. Some increase in the diversion capacity of the
Scheme may have been of advantage, however, a limit to prolonged
operation at high discharges is the channel capacity of the rivers
below the outlets of the Scheme as well as irrigation considerations.

Since generation from the Scheme commenced, energy production has
been 101% of the quantities originally notified available. The period
of operation has included two severe drought periods in 1967-68 and
1982-83 as well as a very wet period in 1974-75 when storage in the
Scheme reached 99% of total capacity. The regulation of water
provided by the Scheme played an important part to mitigate the effect
of very severe droughts in 1967-68 and in 1982-83 in the irrigation
areas of south-eastern Australia. In 1982-83, the storage in the
Scheme was reduced to 18% of capacity and natural inflows to some
irrigation catchments were described as being substantially below
those previously recorded over some 100 years of available records.

The Scheme, however, has not been without its problems, the most
significant of which was a collapse of an unlined section of the
Eucumbene-Snowy Tunnel in 1970. Major electrical and mechanical
plants have performed well, particularly with the stress of peak
operations but as some of this equipment has been in operation for 30
years, the time has come where replacements can be necessary. This
also applies to communication and control systems where arrangements
are in hand for replacement with high technology systems now
available.

The adverse environmental effects have been minimal and are far
outweighed by the beneficial aspects. The construction of the Scheme
has also brought new skills to Australia and greatly enhanced the
recreation potential of the area.

Acknowledgement

The Author thanks the Snowy Mountains Authority for permission to
publish this paper.

References

1. Johnson K E and Millner F C 'Mass transfer of water into the
inland of Australia for irrigation and power by the Snowy Mountains
Hydro-electric Scheme'. International Commission on Irrigation and
Drainage - R6 Special Session, Athens 1978.

2. Annual Reports and Official Publications of the Authorities
involved.

RIVER BASIN NETWORK MODEL FOR CONJUNCTIVE USE OF
SURFACE AND GROUNDWATER
by

John W. Labadie, M. ASCE[1], Sanguan Patamatamkul[2]
and Rogelio C. Lazaro[3]

ABSTRACT

A generalized river basin computer model called CONSIM is
presented for management of the conjunctive use of surface and
subsurface storage in an interconnected stream-aquifer system. The
model simulates the hydrologic system and optimizes water allocation
period by period based on costs, benefits, or water right priorities.
The water resource system is configured as a least-cost flow network of
nodes and links and solved by the out-of-kilter algorithm on a
microcomputer. A user-interfaced management system is available for
easily inputing, organizing, and editing data for any river basin to be
simulated using CONSIM. In order to demonstrate the usefulness of the
model, a case study section of the South Platte River basin in eastern
Colorado was selected for examing the potential for artificial recharge
of excess spring runoff and increased pumping during dry periods to
avoid demand shortages.

INTRODUCTION

Three of the most challenging aspects of the optimal management
of river basin water resources are: (1) modeling transient
interactions between surface water and groundwater with reasonable
accuracy, but at affordable computer cost; (2) including legal and
institutional structures governing direct flow water rights, storage
rights, exchanges and interstate compacts, as well as surface reservoir
operating policies and plans for augmentation; and (3) generalizing
model input structure to form a user-interfaced management system
(UIMS) that can be easily applied to a wide variety of river basin
conditions using commonly available computing equipment such as
microcomputers. Few models are available which meet all three of these
challenges.

[1]Prof., Dept. of Civil Engrg., Colorado State Univ., Ft. Collins, Colo.
[2]Prof., Ofc. of Water Resources Develop., Fac. of Engrg., Khon Kaen
Univ., Khon Kaen, Thailand.
[3]Water Mngmt. Specialist, International Agric. Develop. Service, Dhaka,
Bangladesh.

310

Optimization has been successfully linked with stream-aquifer simulation models for river basin management purposes, including the work of Young and Bredehoeft (1972) and Labadie and Khan (1979) which involved sequential solution of separate stream-aquifer simulation and optimization models. Complete finite difference numerical models were employed in these studies for accurately simulating groundwater flow and stream-aquifer interaction. Daubert and Young (1982) used the discrete kernel as influence function approach to stream-aquifer modeling for direct incorporation into a linear programming model, with consideration of economic and institutional factors governing water allocation. Danskin and Gorelick (1985) developed a similar methodology, but with use of mixed integer programming. Though other researchers have attempted to directly incorporate finite difference or finite element models into optimization models, it appears that the influence function approach holds the most promise for complex, large-scale management problems in connected stream-aquifer systems. Most of these modeling studies rely on use of the revised simplex method within the algorithm, such as branch and bound methods in integer programming and successive linearization methods in nonlinear programming. However, investigators such as Glover and Klingman (1981) have shown that modern network flow optimization algorithms require roughly an order of magnitude less computer core storage and up to two orders of magnitude less computer time than comparable revised simplex code. Since network algorithms are so efficient, it becomes feasible to perform numerous iterations and adjustments so as to consider certain nonlinear or dynamic system aspects. Integer-valued flows can be easily computed and network algorithms such as the "out-of-kilter" method (OKM), which is used in this study, do not require initial feasible solutions. These are valuable features for microcomputer applications.

Most of the applications of network flow optimization models to river basin management have been confined to surface-water only. An exception is the model of Hamdan and Meredith (1975), although groundwater is treated in a simplistic, lumped fashion without consideration of stream-aquifer hydraulic interchange. What follows is a presentation of a comprehensive network flow optimization model, based on a surface water network model developed by the Texas Water Development Board (1972) and its extensions (Shafer, 1979), which considers stream-aquifer hydraulics through an analytically-based influence function or discrete kernel method. It is designed for application under complex legal and institutional factors governing water allocation, can be executed on a 16 bit microprocessor, and has a generalized user-friendly data input and editing structure.

FEATURES OF PROGRAM CONSIM

Overview

The basic concept of CONSIM is that any physical surface water and groundwater system can be conceptualized as a capacitated network of nodes and links (Figure 1). Any complex, interconnected system of river reaches, tributaries, reservoirs, diversions, pipelines, canals, well fields, aquifers , and irrigated areas and municipal/industrial demands can be considered in this fashion. Surface reservoirs and

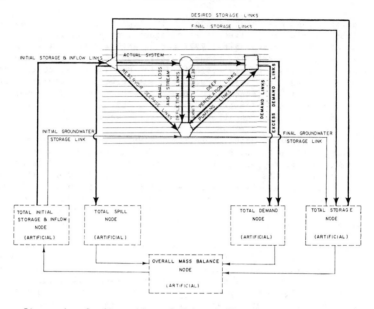

Figure 1.   Configuration of Network Flow Problem in CONSIM.

groundwater basins are represented as storage nodes. Non-storage nodes
would be points of surface water diversion, river intersection,
irrigation demand areas, or other types of demands.   A link is
analogous to a river reach, canal, closed conduit or stream-aquifer
interchange with a specified direction of flow and maximum and minimum
capacities. Losses or gains to a stream are assumed to accumulate at a
downstream node rather than being distributed over a link. Higher
orders of accuracy in defining distributed gains or losses can be
obtained by simply defining more nodes. Each link has associated with
it a unit "cost" of transferring one unit of flow from one node to
another.   The link cost term may be an actual cost, such as pumping
cost for a pipeline, or a fictitious cost representing a relative
priority for flow in that link, perhaps based on water rights. It may
also be a negative cost, which represents a benefit or other quantity
which should be maximized rather than minimized, such as hydropower.

Network Optimization Problem

     The river basin network is constructed in a fully "circulating"
manner by adding certain artificial nodes and links to the actual
network system.   This guarantees that mass balance is satisfied at all
nodes throughout the entire network, as shown in Figure 1. Details on
construction of these artificial nodes and links are given in Labadie,
et al (1983).   It should be noted that the model user only supplies the
actual system nodes and links in CONSIM. The artificial nodes and
links are automatically added by the model.

With a selected time interval and a given operational or management horizon, a network flow optimization problem of the following form is solved period by period:

$$\min \sum_{i=1}^{N} \sum_{j=1}^{N} w_{ij} Q_{ij} \tag{1}$$

subject to:

$$\sum_{i=1}^{N} Q_{ij} - \sum_{i=1}^{N} Q_{ji} = 0; \quad j=1,\ldots,N \tag{2}$$

$$LO_{ij} \leqslant Q_{ij} \leqslant HI_{ij}; \quad i,j=1,\ldots,N \tag{3}$$

where Q_{ij} is the flow in link (i,j) defined by initial node i and terminal node j; LO_{ij} is the lower bound on flow; HI_{ij} is the upper bound; and w_{ij} are costs, benefits (or negative costs), or priority factors related to flow in link (i,j). Definitions of the link bounds is given in Table 1. Computation of the hydrologic data used to define these link bounds is given in the following section. It should be noted that iterative procedures requiring repetitive solution of the network problem are needed for computing channel losses, reservoir evaporation, irrigation return flows and stream depletion due to pumping (see Labadie, et al, 1983).

If water is to be allocated according to priorities rather than according economic factors, then the w_{ij} are computed as follows:

for reservoirs: $w_{ij} = -(1000 - OPRP_i \times 10)$
(for link connecting reservoir i to artificial total storage node j)

for demands: $w_{ij} = -(1000 - DEMR_i \times 10)$
(for link connecting demand i to artificial total demand node j)

where $OPRP_i$ and $DEMR_i$ are integer ranking factors between 1 and 100 specified by the user, where a lower number means a higher ranking. Groundwater pumping is assumed to be used only if surface water is insufficient to meet demands.

Model Components

Reservoir operation: CONSIM utilizes reservoir target storage levels or guide curves for all reservoirs as specified by the user. The first option is for users to input specific target levels for each reservoir and each period. This is particularly useful for calibration purposes when observed historical storages are input to check if the model can match these, as well as computed downstream flows, to observed data. As an alternative, an operating rule can be specified that conditions target end-of-period storages on up to three levels of the current "hydrologic state" of the system; wet, average, or dry as defined by the user. The hydrologic state is defined as the current water in storage in a selected subsystem of reservoirs plus expected inflows during the period. Reservoirs with higher priorities are filled to their target storage levels first. Water is stored above these levels only to prevent unnecessary spillage or wasted outflows. Hydropower can also be computed with input of turbine characteristics and area-capacity-head tables.

Table 1.   Link Types and Their Corresponding Lower and Upper Bounds.

Link Type	Lower Bound, LO	Upper Bound, HI
Physical system link a. river reach link b. canal link	Minimum river capacity* (U)[1] Minimum canal capacity (U)	Maximum river capacity (U) Maximum canal capacity (U)
Initial storage and inflow link	Previous end-of-month storage plus current monthly or weekly inflow, plus current monthly or weekly return flows (B)	Same as LO (B)[2]
Final desired storage link	Reservoir minimum pool plus minimum estimated seepage (U)	Percent of maximum capacity desired (monthly or weekly operating rule) plus maximum estimated seepage (U)
Final storage balance link	Zero (B)	Zero (B)
Demand link	Zero (B)	Demand at node (U)
Excess demand link	Zero (B)	Amount required for artificial recharge (U), or canal capacity and demand link difference
Spill link	Zero (B)	Total of all surface water reservoir capacities multiplied by ten (B)
Mass balance links a. total initial storage plus inflow links b. total final storage links	Σ initial storage plus initial groundwater storage (B) Σ final desired storage (B)	Same as LO (B) All surface water reservoir capacities plus their maximum evaporation and seepages plus HI of groundwater final storage (B)
c. total demand link d. total spill link	Zero (B) Zero (B)	Σ Demands (B) Σ Spills (B)
Node to groundwater links** a. reservoir seepage link b. deep percolation link	Zero (B) Zero (B)	Actual seepage (B) Actual deep percolation at node (demand node in particular) (B)
c. river depletion link	Zero (B)	Actual river depletion at depletion node (B)
d. channel loss link e. initial groundwater storage link	Zero (B) Initial groundwater storage (B)	Actual channel loss (B) Same as LO (B)
Groundwater to node links a. return flow links b. pumping links c. groundwater final storage links	Zero (B) Zero (B) Zero (B)	Actual return flows (B) Pumping capacities (B) Σ upper bounds of links in No. 9 plus initial groundwater storage (B)

* Should be zero unless minimum flow is required. However, a minimum flow requirement may cause infeasible solutions.

** The river depletion and channel loss may flow through the same link. In this case, the upper bound is the summation of both flow.

[1] U is for user supplied parameters.

[2] B is for program default parameters.

Demands: The river basin is divided into a number of subareas which are represented in the model as nodes. A node may simply be (1) an undeveloped area, (2) an irrigated area supplied by a canal and/or pumped groundwater, or (3) a municipal or industrial area. Water demands for developed areas may be historical, forecasted, based on water right decrees, or computed from evapotranspiration models. Water that flows through instream or "flow-through" demand nodes remains in the network and is not consumed. Therefore, demands for streamflows to maintain fisheries or control pollution can be prioritized much like any other demand. Specifying a flow-through demand downstream of a reservoir and conditioning the demand on the hydrologic state of the system is a way of developing operating rules for the reservoir based on release rather than target storage levels.

Channel losses: Program CONSIM computes river reach and diversion canal losses for any link over period k, as specified by user input of channel loss coefficients cc_{ij} representing the fraction of the inflow rate at node i at the head of the reach or section which is lost to seepage. Channel losses are accumulated at node j, the terminus of the link. Channel losses can return to groundwater storage in CONSIM. If a channel or unlined canal receives groundwater return flow, it must be regarded as a river reach in the model.

Potential evapotranspiration: The modified Blaney-Criddle method for predicting monthly crop requirements is included in CONSIM. If this is considered unsatisfactory, or a smaller time interval is being used, other methods can be used outside the model with the demands then entered directly. The modified Penman method is a good choice, but requires considerably more data. For the modified Blaney-Criddle method, the user supplies, for each demand area and time period, crop coefficients based on growth stage, mean air temperatures and percentage of daylight hours. SCS Technical Release No. 21 (1970) can be consulted for much of this information. For nonirrigated areas, the potential evapotranspiration is calculated by first treating the area as being irrigated and then multiplying the consumptive use by an empirical coefficient ce_i with value between zero and one.

Surface runoff: Unregulated inflows to the system at various node points can either be specified by the user or computed by the model using precipitation data. The user can input weighting factors based on a Thiessen network or other methods to translate gaged precipitation records to a particular area. For demand i during time period k, effective precipitation PR_{ik} over the entire area is calculated using a user input effective precipitation coefficient cp_{ik}. User defined threshold precipitation levels $AVPR_{ik}$, above which runoff is expected to occur, are then used to compute surface runoff RO_{ik}. Selection of various levels of $AVPR_{ik}$ becomes a means of taking into account varying soil moisture conditions over each period. One unique river node must be specified for each demand area for receiving surface runoff from that area. If more than one node is needed for better accuracy, then the demand area must be divided into subareas.

Groundwater recharge and storage: For irrigation demand node i during time period k, the total applied water for irrigation is

$$A_{ik} = (Q_{ik} - C_{ik}) + PR_{ik} + P_{ik} \qquad (4)$$

where Q_{ik} is the total canal flow diverted to area i, C_{ik} is the channel loss, and P_{ik} local groundwater pumpage. This water is assumed by uniformly applied over the demand area.

Groundwater recharge I_{ik} is then computed by CONSIM as

$$I_{ik} = (1 - ct_i)A_{ik}RF_{ik} \qquad (5)$$

where ct_i is an empirical tailwater coefficient and RF_{ik} is recharge fraction computed using the method employed by Konikow and Bredehoeft (1974). This method requires user specification of an empirical recharge parameter c which is used to define the relationship between RF and the ratio of applied water to potential evapotranspiration. Note that recharge is assumed to reach the water table during the time period considered. The tailwater from excess irrigation is then added to surface runoff. An accounting of groundwater storage in various aquifer sections is maintained, as well as temporary streambank storage due to river stage fluctuations.

Return flows: CONSIM computes return flows from canal losses, reservoir seepages, groundwater recharge from irrigation and precipitation. Recharge over a particular demand area is assumed to be uniformly distributed.

For demand node i and any current time period considered, the total return flow from previous and current time periods due to groundwater recharge from applied water is:

$$IRF_{ik} = \sum_{\tau=1}^{k} I_{i\tau} \, \delta_{i,k-\tau+1}; \text{ where } \delta_{i,k-\tau+1} = 0 \text{ for } k-\tau+1 > N \qquad (6)$$

where response $\delta_{i,k-\tau+1}$ is essentially a discrete kernel or influence function representing the return flow in period k due to a unit recharge in period τ, or $k-\tau+1$ periods previous to k. It is computed using an analogy to a parallel drain system, as originally developed by Maasland (1959).

As shown in Figure 2, one dimensional flow to an effluent stream reach is assumed in CONSIM for all return flow calculations.

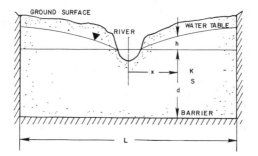

Figure 2.   Idealization of Stream-Aquifer System (from Glover, 1974).

By assuming that h is small compared to d, the linearized form of the one dimensional groundwater flow equation is

$$\alpha \frac{\partial^2 h}{\partial x^2} = \frac{\partial h}{\partial t} \qquad (7)$$

where α = T/S, T = transmissivity, which is equal to Kd; S = specific yield; h = height of the water table measured from the assumed original stable water table level.

For CONSIM, α is regarded as a "surrogate" parameter which is adjusted from actual S and T values to represent nonideal boundary conditions. Maasland (1959) obtained the solution to this equation from which the discrete kernels are calculated (see Labadie, et al (1983) for details).

Discrete kernel functions are similarly computed for return flows from canal loss using the one dimensional line source solution (McWhorter, 1972). Again, nonideal conditions are accounted for by calibration adjustments in "surrogate" parameter K. An average distance of the canal from the river is assumed. Discrete kernels for return flows from reservoir seepage are computed using the point source solution of the governing one-dimensional groundwater flow equations as obtained by Glover (1974).

Stream depletion due to pumping: The total stream depletion due to pumping is

$$PSD_{ik} = \sum_{\tau=1}^{k} P_{i\tau}\alpha_{i,k-\tau+1}; \text{ where } \alpha_{i,k-\tau+1} = 0 \text{ for } k-\tau+1 > N \qquad (8)$$

where in the case of groundwater withdrawal, the same principles described above are applicable. Here, however, it is river depletion that is considered rather than return flows to the river.

CASE STUDY

A case study area was selected for demonstrating the usefulness of CONSIM for a portion of the South Platte River basin in eastern Colorado from the diversion to North Sterling Reservoir near Brush, Colorado to Julesburg near the Nebraska border; a length of approximately 90 miles (144.8 km) and a drainage area of about 500 sq mi. (1295 km2). Precipitation averages from 12 to 16 in. (305 to 406 mm) per year over the area. The river is fed by a large alluvial aquifer which is important for supplying water to the river in summer and fall, since flows from mountain snow melt occur mainly in the spring.

The study area was divided into subareas or demand nodes primarily based on areas supplied by a single diversion canal, though areas receiving only groundwater are also included (Figure 3). Groundwater pumpage is important to many of these demand areas for meeting late season irrigation demands, but is often curtailed because stream depletions due to pumping may cause injury to higher priority surface water diversion rights. The purpose of this study was to determine if optimum decisions on increased artificial recharge of

excess spring runoff can support late season pumping to meet all
demands, while guaranteeing that surface water diversion rights are
satisfied and the aquifer is not mined. A critical dry period in the
early to mid 1950's, that created severe demand shortages, was selected
for providing monthly hydrologic input.

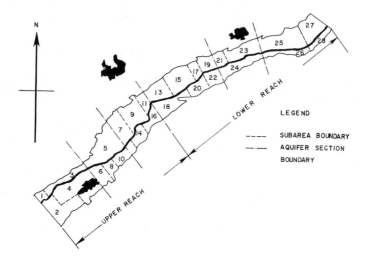

Figure 3. Approximate Spatial Decomposition of the Case Study Area

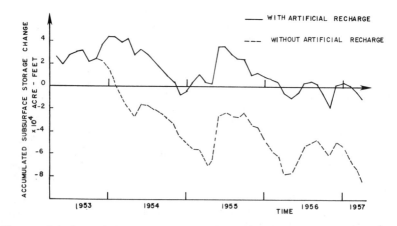

Figure 4. Comparision of Subsurface Storage Changes: With and Without
Artificial Recharge.

Considerable calibration work was required, which is detailed in Labadie et al (1983). In general the model performed well for dry and average years, but was less satisfactory for wet years due to lack of data on local runoff. The model results showed that with optimal management of artificial recharge, reservoir operations, and groundwater pumping, all demands could be met. The effect on the groundwater basin of pumping with and without artificial recharge is shown in Figure 4.

REFERENCES

Danskin, W. R. and S. M. Gorelick, "A Policy Evaluation Tool: Management of a Multiaquifer System Using Controlled Stream Recharge," Water Resources Research, 21(11), pp. 1731-1747, 1985.

Daubert, J. T. and R. A. Young, "Ground-Water Development in Western River Basins: Large Economic Gains With Unseen costs," Ground Water, 20(1), pp. 80-85, 1982.

Glover, F. and D. Klingman, "The Simplex SON Algorithm for LP/Embedded Network Problems," Mathematical Programming Study, 15, pp. 148-176, 1981.

Glover, R. E., "Transient Groundwater Hydraulics," Dept. of Civil Engrg., Colo. State Univ., Ft. Collins, Colo., 1974.

Hamdan, A. S. and D. D. Meredith, "Screening Model for Conjunctive-Use Water Systems," Journal of the Hydraulics Div., ASCE, 101(HY10), pp. 1343-1355, Oct. 1975.

Konikow, L. F. and J. D. Bredehoeft, "Modeling Flow and Chemical Quality Changes in an Irrigated Stream-Aquifer System," Water Resources Research, 10(3), pp. 546-562, 1974.

Labadie, J. W. and I. Khan, "River Basin Salinity Management via the ASTRAN Method: (2) Case Study," Journal of Hydrology, 42, pp. 323-345, July 1979.

Labadie, J. W., S. Phamwon, and R. C. Lazaro, "A River Basin Network Model for Conjunctive Use of Surface and Groundwater: Program CONSIM," Completion Report No. 125, Colo. Water Resources Research Inst., Colo. State Univ., Ft. Collins, Colo., June 1983.

Maasland, M., "Water Table Fluctuations Induced by Intermittant Recharge," Journal of Geophysical Research, 64(5), pp. 549-559, 1959.

McWhorter, D. B., et al., "Analytical Model of Stream-Aquifer Systems with Pumping and Recharge," Completion Report, Colo. State Univ., Ft. Collins, Colo., 1972.

Shafer, J. M., "An Interactive River Basin Water Management Model: Synthesis and Application," Tech. Report No. 18, Colo. Water Resources Research Inst., Colo. State Univ., Ft. Collins, Colo., Aug. 1979.

Texas Water Development Board, "Economic Optimization and Simulation Techniques for Management of Regional Water Resource Systems: River Basin Model SIMYLD II -- Program Description," Systems Engineering Division, Austin, Texas, July 1972.

U.S. Dept. of Agric., "Irrigation Water Requirement," U.S. Soil Conservation Service, Enginering Div., Tech. Release No. 21, 1970.

Young, R. A. and J. D. Bredehoeft, "Digital Computer Simulation for Solving Management Problems of Conjunctive Groundwater and Surface Water Systems," Water Resources Research, 8(3), pp. 533-556, 1972.

Modeling an Alluvial Aquifer
with Flood Irrigation

Victor R. Hasfurther[1], M.ASCE, Hilaire W. Peck[2], Steve A. Mizell[3]

Abstract

Interaction between an unconfined alluvial aquifer, recharged by
flood irrigation, and the associated stream system in a glacial
outwash area of Wyoming was studied. The United States Geological
Survey model entitled, "A Modular Three-Dimensional Finite-Difference
Ground-Water Flow Model," was chosen as the model best suited for
simulating the stream-aquifer system. The methodology used for
calibrating the USGS model and the methodology used in performing a
sensitivity analysis on selected model parameters are based on a
comparison to actual data collected on a 30 square mile area. Results
obtained from the operation of the model were return flows to the
stream, change in storage of the aquifer, and groundwater inflow minus
groundwater outflow to the aquifer.

Introduction

Water is an important resource in the State of Wyoming, and the
proper allocation, use, and development of this resource will affect
many aspects of life as well as the economy of the State. Ranching
and farming, two of our oldest and most important industries in the
State of Wyoming, depend heavily on water for their maintenance and
continued development. One important area of concern at present is
the evaluation of the irrigation water requirements for farm and
ranch operations and the effect that diversion of water has upon
stream systems. The effects of stream diversion and the importance of
return flows due to these diversions is of prime importance to the
dynamics of the stream system and the proper and beneficial use of the
waters within that system by the water rights appropriated for use.

Alluvial aquifers recharged primarily through flood irrigation
diversions result in water being consumptively used and an interaction
resulting between the aquifer and the stream system in terms of return
flows. In general, only a portion of the water diverted for flood
irrigation is consumptively used. The rest can be looked upon as
being stored in an underground reservoir. However, no expenditure for
dam construction is required as is the case with a surface reservoir.

[1]Professor of Civil Engineering and Acting Director, Wyoming Water
 Research Center, University of Wyoming, Laramie, Wyoming   82071.
[2]Engineer, Bureau of Reclamation, Denver, Colorado   80225.
[3]Hydrogeologist, Wyoming Water Research Center and Assistant
 Professor, Department of Geology/Geophysics, University of Wyoming,
 Laramie, Wyoming   82071.

The water is less susceptible to loss through evaporation, and the
land surface can still be put to productive uses. The main benefits
derived from this underground reservoir are an increased likelihood of
maintaining instream flow and a steadier more reliable source of water
downstream through the resulting return flow pattern of the stream-
aquifer system.

This paper presents a study on an alluvial aquifer in Wyoming
which is high on the watershed of a large stream system. The aquifer
is recharged due to flood irrigation and as a result the stream has
developed into a highly regulated semi-flood free drainage system.
The study of the interaction of the stream-aquifer system over time
and how it acts as a groundwater reservoir for maintaining instream
flows and release of water for downstream uses through return flows
was the main purpose of the study.

Model Selection

Since the 1960's, when high-speed digital computers became widely
available, numerical techniques have been used to treat mathematical
surface-groundwater system modeling (Wang and Anderson, 1982). The
ability of numerical models to simulate complex surface-groundwater
systems much more readily than analytical models using either finite-
element or finite-difference techniques on the partial differential
equations of flow is well documented (Faust and Mercer, 1980; Freeze
and Cherry, 1979). Finite-element and finite-difference groundwater
models each have advantages and disadvantages. Faust and Mercer
(1980) in a series of groundwater modeling papers concluded that for
most groundwater flow problems, finite-difference models were
generally adequate.

For this study, a model that would simulate an unconfined water
table aquifer with direct stream interaction was needed. Two
three-dimensional finite-difference models were found that satisfied
this requirement. Rovey (1978) developed a finite difference model
which was used to simulate the stream-aquifer system of the Arkansas
River in Colorado. McDonald and Harbaugh (1984) of the United States
Geological Survey (USGS) developed a modular three-dimensional finite-
difference groundwater flow model which handles stream-aquifer
interaction also. The USGS model was chosen for use because of its
extensive documentation and modular units which allowed for ease of
change in subroutines where necessary.

Peck (1985) detailed the ways in which both models handled the
necessary flow equations for and between each cell of the grid system,
boundaries and stream-aquifer system and compared the two models.
Special subroutines are available for handling river seepage for both
saturated and unsaturated flow situations, recharge, pumping wells,
evapotranspiration and drains in the USGS model.

The USGS model deals in terms of a stress period which is a time
interval during which all external stresses are constant. The length
of each stress period and each time step is specified by the user.
The results of a given stress period are cumulative volume of water
added to storage and released-from storage from the various sources

(i.e., river leakage, recharge, evapotranspiration, etc.) along with
individual amounts from each source.

Methodology

   The study is based on a comparison to actual data collected on an
alluvial glacial outwash area of 30 square miles in west-central
Wyoming. There is one major stream that flows through the study area
and a secondary stream of significance. Surface-groundwater interaction occurs between the uppermost aquifer (unconfined) and the
streams. The upper aquifer varies in thickness across and through the
valley with depths to bedrock in the deeper sections of 30 to 40 feet.
A layer of fine grained material separates the alluvial aquifer from
the underlying regional aquifer and it is assumed that no significant
interchange of water occurs between the aquifers. There is a surface
elevation drop of 270 feet in approximately 9 miles through the study
area.

   Ranchers within the study area boundaries practice flood
irrigation. When there is sufficient water available, their method of
irrigation is to recharge the unconfined alluvial aquifer until it is
approximately full. The aquifer is kept this way until approximately
two weeks before haying is to begin. At this time all irrigation is
stopped and the water level in the aquifer is allowed to drop. After
haying is completed, irrigation is resumed on a much less intense
scale. This later period of irrigation lasts until the onset of
cooler weather, and generally keeps the water table from dropping
rapidly during the fall months.

   To help in the evaluation of the model, a large monitoring system
was installed on the study area to allow a water budget analysis to be
performed. Streamgages, groundwater monitoring wells, precipitation
gages, lysimeters and staff gages were placed throughout the study
area. The water budget analysis gives numbers that can be compared
with model results in a quantitative manner.

   A network of 32 seasonal continuous recording streamgages were
established along the major and secondary streams and on a large
number of the major diversion ditches throughout the study area.
Rating curves were developed for all streamgages. A full year
operational gage exists at the lower end of the study area. Diversion
records are used to determine the amount of recharge to be applied in
the model over different parts of the study area. Evapotranspiration
estimates are made from actual lysimeter data taken at a nearby site
(10 miles west of the study area) with exactly the same type of
vegetative material as in the study area. One precipitation gage was
installed in the central part of the study area to be used in
connection with Weather Service stations located at the top and near
the bottom of the study area. The precipitation is applied to the
study area using the Thiessen Polygon method.

   A network of 25 alluvial aquifer water table wells were installed
throughout the study area to monitor water levels in an effort to
determine storage and timing characteristics of the aquifer. Well
levels were measured once per week during the entire spring, summer

and fall periods on the same day of each week. During the winter
period, well levels were measured approximately monthly. Weekly and
monthly plots of the water table contours are produced for use in
analysis of groundwater gradients and storage. Storage and transmissivity or permeability values were either determined from pump tests
or well logs of the material for different sections of the aquifer.

Figure 1 shows the finite difference grid used with the USGS
model. The x's indicated on Figure 1 are the outline of the study
area. The grided area is 8 miles long by 5 miles wide on Figure 1.
The calibration procedure required the following quantities be
estimated as input to all or some of the grids of the model. These
quantities were: starting water level elevations, specific yield,
hydraulic conductivity, aquifer bottom elevation, river stage, riverbed conductance, riverbed elevation, recharge rate, water level
elevations at constant head boundaries and conductance of the interface between the aquifer and constant head boundaries. These values
were either measured in the field or estimated from the field data
collected. Starting water level elevations were obtained directly
from a plot of the actual water table contours produced from well
level measurements. Specific yield and hydraulic conductivity values
were estimated from well tests and well logs for the area and were
variable over the area. Estimates of aquifer bottom elevation were
made from the well logs. Staff gages read once per week were set at
intervals along all major stream sections and were used to obtain
river stage and riverbed elevation. Recharge rate was determined by
subtracting the evapotranspiration from diversion records of a given

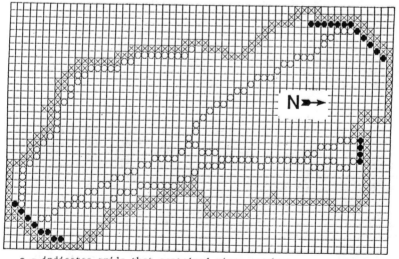

o - indicates grids that contained river reaches
• - indicates grids that were treated as general head broundaries

Figure 1. Finite-Difference Grid for the Study Area.

area and then spreading the remaining volume over that area and
letting it infiltrate. Riverbed conductance was estimated by the
authors from visual inspection and suggested values given in the USGS
model documentation.

The time period for which the model was calibrated was selected
(July 30, 1984 to September 3, 1984) when recharge was approximately
zero. Since hydraulic conductivity and riverbed conductance were felt
by the authors to be the least reliable estimates for values input to
the model, the procedure used in calibration was to vary hydraulic
conductivity and riverbed conductance in blocks over the study area.
These values for each block of the study area were adjusted until
water level elevations predicted by the model in grids containing
field observation wells were within one foot of the water level
elevation actually measured at the end of the calibration time period.

Once the model was calibrated, the model was used to simulate the
entire period of record over which data had been collected. This
resulted in four different stress periods being used and covered the
period from June 4, 1984 through January 2, 1985. Independent
estimates of some of the quantities produced by the model were
obtained from a water budget analysis for comparison. Details of all
the above procedures are given in Peck (1985).

A sensitivity analysis was performed on several of the model
input parameters so that data collected during 1985 and 1986 would
produce more reliable actual values of those parameters to enable more
accurate calibration of the model over the entire time period of the
study. Those parameters selected for sensitivity analysis were
specific yield, hydraulic conductivity, river stage, riverbed
conductance and riverbed elevation. These particular parameters were
selected because they were quantities on which field testing or
measurement could be performed to improve the accuracy of the value.
The parameters selected for sensitivity analysis were varied over a
range of values which would actually be reasonably possible for the
study area.

Results

One of the results of the groundwater model simulation was the
production of water level elevation values at all grid cells through
time from an initial set of starting heads (June 4, 1984). Figure 2
indicates the results due to model simulation and those actually
measured for July 16, 1984. Actual and model predicted values for
other days indicated similar results.

An important component of this study was the determination of
return flows to the main stream system and the timing of the return
flows for purposes indicated in the introduction. Return flow is
divided into two components in this study; overland return flow and
flow returned via the groundwater system. The overland return flow is
that water diverted for flood irrigation not consumptively used by the
vegetation or infiltrated to the alluvial aquifer during the
irrigation season. The study area does not have overland return flow
collection channels but field observations resulted in visual

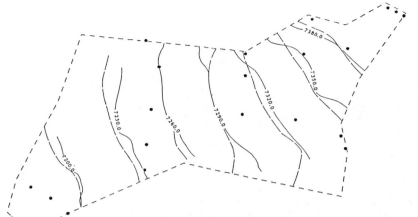

● - indicates observation wells

Broken lines indicate contours
obtained using water table
elevations from model results

Solid lines indicate contours obtained
using observation well data

Figure 15. Comparison of Model Water Table Contours
With Observed Water Table Contours.

observation of such flows. Therefore, a water budget analysis was
made in which overland return flow was equated to the amount of
diversion plus precipitation per stress period minus the areally
distributed recharge applied to the model and evapotranspiration.
For the entire irrigation period, it was determined that 13 percent of
the volume diverted during this period was overland return flow. At
non-irrigation or low irrigation times, no overland return flow was
assumed to occur.

    Shown in Table 1 are model results for total return flow. The
model was run so that output included a cumulative volumetric budget
each week on the day well readings were taken. The values in Table 1
indicate the monthly values. Included in the volumetric budget are
river leakage into and from the aquifer into the stream system. River
leakage into the aquifer is subtracted from aquifer leakage into the
stream system to obtain the volumes of groundwater return flow shown
in Table 1.

    The values in the fifth column of Table 1 are obtained by
dividing the accumulated return flow from the model results by the
accumulated diversions obtained from flow records. The percent
returned increases with time because the amount diverted decreases
with time much faster than does return flow. Similar results for
return flows resulted from a water budget analysis.

Table 1. Results of Model Return Flow.

1984 Dates	Model* Groundwater Return Flow (ac-ft)	Accumulated Model Return Flow (ac-ft)	Accumulated Diversion (ac-ft)	Cumulative Percent Returned of Total Diversions
6/4/-7/1	13,782	13,782	24,596	55
7/2-7/29	13,235	27,017	40,900	66
7/30-8/26	6,130	33,147	41,730	79
8/27-9/28	3,921	37,068	43,111	86
9/29-10/26	1,951	39,019	45,129	86
10/27-11/14	964	39,983	45,129	89
11/15-1/2/85	1,691	41,674	45,129	92

*Model groundwater return flow was determined by the difference
between total inflow minus total outflow over river reach during the
indicated time period plus overland return flow.

The aquifer was very nearly recharged by the time the first well
measurements were taken on June 4. This earlier recharge was due
mainly to snowmelt within the study area and snowmelt runoff from
surrounding higher areas. Because no earlier well measurements were
available, an estimate of snowmelt recharge could not be made. The
return flows calculated by the model, therefore, include recharge due
to snowmelt. The percent returned of total diversions would therefore
be less than those shown in Table 1 for an entire year.

From the results indicated in Table 2, it is evident that the
stream-aquifer interaction in the study area is fairly rapid during
the irrigation season or high water table times and decreases as the
water table drops in the non-irrigation season. Considering the data
in Table 2, it appears that through the winter approximately 20
percent of the flow in the study area is due to return flows. A
portion of the return flows are due to snowmelt as discussed
previously. The effect of snowmelt on return flows would decrease
rapidly with time because of the fast response time of the aquifer.
Information contained in Table 1 also indicates that the alluvial
aquifer is acting as a large storage reservoir buffering over 40,000
acre-feet of return flows over the year. The model also gave changes
in storage within the aquifer over time. Comparison of model results
to actual measurements of storage represented an overall difference of
approximately 3 inches in water table elevation (approximately 4,000
acre-feet).

The sensitivity analysis on certain model parameters indicated
that specific yield and riverbed elevation did not cause significant
changes in model results for variations of 75 percent in the specific
yield value and six feet elevation change in the riverbed. However,
hydraulic conductivity, river stage and riverbed conductance were all
found to have a significant effect on model results for an order of
magnitude increase and/or decrease in the values from the original
model values used.

Table 2. Percent of Flow Leaving Study Area
Due to Return Flows

1984 Dates	Model* Groundwater Return Flow (ac-ft)	Surface Flow Leaving Study Area (ac-ft)	Percent of Flow Leaving Study Area Due to Return Flow
6/4/-7/1	13,782	20,205	68
7/2-7/29	13,235	19,023	70
7/30-8/26	6,130	8,259	74
8/27-9/28	3,921	6,660	59
9/29-10/26	1,951	4,764	41
10/27-11/14	964	3,534	27
11/15-1/2/85	1,691	7,317	23

Conclusions

A complex alluvial unconfined aquifer was successfully modeled using a three-dimensional flow model (USGS) with surface-groundwater interaction. Evaluation of the effects of flood irrigation and the resultant return flow of the system indicated that this glacial outwash alluvial system responds fairly rapidly between the surface stream system and the aquifer.

Acknowledgments

This research was supported by the Wyoming Water Development Commission and the Wyoming Water Research Center.

References

Faust, C.R. and J.W. Mercer, "Ground-Water Modeling: Numerical Models," Ground Water, 1980, Vol. 18, No. 4, pp. 395-403.

Freeze, R.A. and J. A. Cherry, Groundwater, Englewood Cliffs, New Jersey: Prentice-Hall, Inc., 1979, 61 pp.

McDonald, M.G. and A. W. Harbaugh, "A Modular Three-Dimensional Finite-Difference Ground-Water Flow Model," U.S. Geological Survey Publication, 1984.

Peck, Hilaire W., "A Model for an Alluvial Aquifer Receiving Recharge from Flood Irrigation," M.S. Thesis, University of Wyoming, Laramie, 1985, 107 pp.

Rovey, C.E., "Numerical Model of Flow in a Stream-Aquifer System," Ph.D. Dissertation, Colorado State University, Fort Collins, 1978, 73 pp.

Wang, F.W. and M.P. Anderson, Introduction to Goundwater Modeling, San Francisco, California: W.H. Freeman and Company, 1982, pp. 1-3.

SIMULTANEOUS PUMPING FROM LAYERED GROUND WATER

E.M. Laursen[1], S.A.A. Abed[2], E. Fukumori[3], A. Souissi[4] & M.S. Petersen[5]

Laboratory experiments with a Hele-Shaw model and a sand model, and an approximate mathematical analysis using finite elements and the computer, have demonstrated that fresh water can be pumped from a layer on top of salt water by pumping from both layers simultaneously. The investigation has indicated that at least ten times as much fresh water can be pumped as with a single ordinary well in the fresh water zone; how much more will depend on the quality of water required.

The configuration of the wells will depend on the site: depth to fresh water, depth to interface, thickness of transition zone, drawdown, aquifer characteristics. Some examples can be suggested, but many other variations are undoubtedly possible.

The concept was thought of in connection with the problem of obtaining drinking water in coastal aquifers, but it should be possible to extend the idea to multiple simultaneous pumping in layered, polluted ground water.

Introduction

Coastal areas in desert regions often have a thin layer of fresh water overlying a salt-water intrusion. This layer is slowly seeping to the sea, and near the sea may be very brackish because of the mixing induced by the tidal range. Pumping of any amount of fresh water is impossible because the interface between the fresh and salt layers upcones (rises) forty times as much as the drawdown of the fresh-water table. The definition of thin, then, becomes a fresh-water layer, so thin that the amount of water needed cannot be pumped.

The concept of simultaneous pumping from imaged wells -- one in the fresh water, the other in the salt water -- has been investigated in

[1]Professor Emeritus, Department of Civil Engineering and Engineering Mechanics, University of Arizona, Tucson, Arizona.
[2]Ministry of Municipal and Rural Affairs in Jeddah, Saudi Arabia.
[3]State University of New York-Buffalo, Buffalo, New York.
[4]Ecole Supeireud d' equipement, Medjez Elbab, Republic of Tunisia.
[5]Visiting Associate Professor, Department of Civil Engineering and Engineering Mechanics, University of Arizona, Tucson, Arizona.

three M.S. theses. Each of them demonstrated that ten times as much fresh water could be pumped by also pumping salt water as could be pumped by pumping fresh water alone. There is a cost to be paid to accomplish this end, but there is a benefit -- more fresh water. Moreover, the salt water does not necessarily have to be a valueless by-product. The obvious uses of the salt water are to obtain salt through evaporation, and to obtain food through aquaculture.

The successful separate, simultaneous pumping of fresh and salt water does not depend on the difference in density of the two fluids, but on the flow to the two sinks being potential with a bounding stream surface separating the flow toward one sink (well) or the other. Therefore, the concept should be applicable to multiple, simultaneous pumping from several layers. The situation of interest being a layer of polluted water. It should be advantageous to extract the polluted water without diluting it with unpolluted water.

The Research and the Results

The first research project was conducted by Abed (1982) who used a Hele-Shaw model 4 x 8 ft (1.2 x 2.4 meters) with a spacing of 2 mm (0.079 inches), tap water and an artificial, dyed sea water, both at room temperature. As shown in Fig. 1, the interface upconed if only the fresh-water well was operated; downconed if only the salt-water well was operated, and the interface stayed horizontal if both wells were operated at the correct pumpage rate. The correct pumpage rate was approxiamtely 10% higher for the salt water than for the fresh water. The rate of pumping fresh water when salt water was also pumped was ten times the rate of pumping when only fresh water was being pumped before the presence of salt water contamination could be detected.

(a) Upconing   (b) Downconing   (c) Horizontal

Fig. 1 The salt-water, fresh-water interface

The second research project was conducted by Fukumori (1982) who used a potential flow, finite-element computer model. He duplicated Abed's work to compare the two approaches, and in general the comparison was good. The mathematical model showed upconing, downconing and the horizontal interface; a wavy interface (as did

Abed's Hele-Shaw model) when the wells were not the same distance from the interface. Fukumori's approximate mathematical model also indicated that it should be possible to pump ten times as much fresh water by also pumping salt water. A difference was that the mathematical model indicated that the salt water pumpage should be slightly less, instead of more, than the fresh water pumpage. This difference has not been resolved; it may be due to the velocity distribution between the parallel plates of the Hele-Shaw model. The difference is not considered to be important because of the results of the third study.

The third research project was conducted by Souissi (1984) who used a sand model 4 x 8 ft (1.2 x 2.4 meters with a spacing of 2 inches (50 mm), glass beads 0.58 mm (0.023 inches), tap water and artificial, dyed sea water. Souissi's experimental set up essentially duplicated that of Abed and Fukumori, Again, the same general results were obtained: upconing, downconing and much more water pumped. However, the amount of salt water that had to be pumped increased with the thickenss of the brackish-water layer between the fresh and salt water. The salt-water pumpage had to be 20% more than the fresh-water pumpage -- possibly more. On the other hand, with a thick brackish layer, it was not possible to pump fresh water, only except for a short time, while the interface rose into its upconed position. How much fresh-water could be pumped depended on the thickness of the brackish-water layer, the distance of the well from the interface, and the salt-water contamination which was considered tolerable. By pumping from the two wells simultaneously, it was possible to pump just fresh water out of the upper well and the amount could be much more than ten times -- depending on what contamination was accepted. It is readily apparent that a third well in the brackish layer would result in three waters of different quality; possibly the brackish water would have a use in irrigating special crops.

All three approaches to the problem concurred in demonstrating that it was possible to pump fresh water and salt water simultaneously with the interface a dividing stream surface. Abed's Hele-Shaw model was the most dramatic approach in that the two fluids could be seen. Fukumori's mathematical model was the most promising approach in that it should be possible to solve ever more complex geometric situations. Souissi's sand model was the most realistic approach in that it could demonstrate the effect of a brackish (mixed) zone between the fresh and salt water. Each model had its place in the investigation of the concept.

Previous Work

During the investigation, library research brought to light several papers and reports of more-or-less the same idea. Fader (1957) was

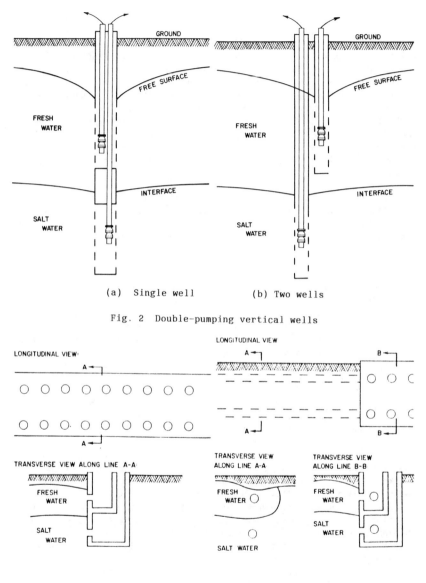

(a) Single well   (b) Two wells

Fig. 2 Double-pumping vertical wells

(a) Trench   (b) Trench and horizontal wells

Fig. 3 Double-pumping horizontal systems

concerned with salt-water intrusion in leaky aquifers in Louisiana, and
suggested it might be controlled by pumping both fresh and salt waters
from separate, nearby wells. Long (1965) later conducted field tests
which showed that the idea did work. Underhill and Atherton (1964)
suggested double pumping of stagnant, fresh water off the top of the
intruded salt water in the Libyan coastal desert, but there is no
record of its having been tried. Wickersham (1977) reported on Jacobs
doublet well which was patented in 1965, and added a variation of a
high pressure injection pipe. Bardelli (1960) may have anticipated
Jacobs and Wickersham with a similar device. None of the doublet wells
have been tried as far as is known. A doublet in a uniform flow forms
a sphere with the fluid inside the sphere staying separate from the
fluid outside the sphere; it seems logical the doublet flow of salt
water would perform similarly except for mixing at the interface and,
in effect, create an impermeable, distorted spheroidal mass at the end
of the well. Iwasa and Takeuchi (1969) studied the axisymetric case,
both analytically and experimentally. Both approaches demonstrated
that the fresh and salt water could be pumped separately.

Applications

It would seem that the time for some field installations has come.
Theoretically, the concept should work; practically, it has worked in
the laboratory with the mixing that occurs in flow through porous
media. The porous media of the real world is more complex; moreover,
with its nonhomogeneity and non-isotrophy, real world geometries are
likely to constrain possible solutions. Therefore, in the first field
trials, an effort should be made to have the installation flexible and
to monitor the discharge.

A possible installation is shown in Fig. 2, with two pumps in a
single-well and packers to isolate the different portions of the well.
The drawdown and position of the interface should be estimated; and
monitored with an observation well near the installation. If the
quality of water is not as expected, the rate of pumping should be
adjusted and, if necessary, the position of the packers and pumps. A
blocked off area between the inflows to the two pumps might make the
performance less sensitive to the position of the interface. A
two-well system, as shown in Fig. 2, should perform almost the same;
the closer the two wells, the more they should act as a single, double-
pumping well. To build in flexibility, the wells could be longer than
estimated to be necessary with the excess length closed off by packers.

If the layer of fresh water is very thin so that the drawdown of an
axisymetric well is excesive, two dimensional well systems, such as
shown in Fig. 3, might be used. If the water table is very shallow, a
long trench might be the easiest construction. If the water table is
not that shallow, a pair of pipes (one above the other) between short

trenches, or pits, might be a better solution. For even deeper water tables with thin layers of fresh wter, an adaptation of the Rainey well system, as shown in Fig. 4, has possiblities.

Usually, the first question or objection to the double-pumping concept is, "What about the salt water? What do you do with it?" The simplistic, unhelpful answer is, "Anything you want to." The salt water costs something for operation and maintenance and for amortization of the capital, even though these costs can be written off as part of the cost of being able to pump the fresh water.

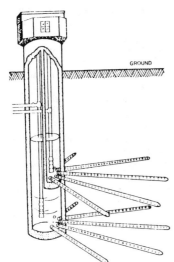

GROUND

In addition, the salt water cannot be discharged with reckless abandon lest it do harm in some way, or adversely affect the drawing off of the fresh water. If the sea is near, an obvious solution is to return the salt water to the sea through a channel or pipeline. If the sea is far, it should be sufficient to dispose of the salt water at some goodly distance toward the sea; hopefully, far enough away so the salt-water table is not appreciably raised. However, it would be prudent to consider the salt water a by-product which can have value,

Fig. 4 A Modified
Ranney well system

and to seek beneficial uses for it. Plain salt has value, and can be obtained by the use of evaporation ponds. Aquaculture has proven to be an economic enterprise; fish, shrimp, lobster are in demand, although canning or freezing equipment may be required if there is not a market nearby. If the brackish layer is also extracted by a third pump, it may be useable for irrigation of salt-resistant varieties of grains and grasses.

Summary and Conclusions

Theoretically and experimentally, it has been established that it is possible to pump much more fresh water by also pumping salt water when the fresh water overlies the salt water, as much as ten times as much as can be pumped as with a single fresh-water well.

There are areas in the world, especially in arid coastal areas, where fresh water is wasting to the sea, in which fresh water is a limiting resource. In these areas, there may be a thin layer of fresh water and the problem is one of how to obtain this needed water. Standard single well technology is often not sufficient because the interface upcones forty times the drawdown with the result that the water pumped is brackish and is potable only because there is no other choice.

The operational definition of a thin layer is a layer of fresh water on top of salt water which is so thin that the amount of fresh water desired cannot be pumped. Of course, more fresh water can be pumped by installing two wells, or ten wells, but the costs rise and much of the fresh water is lost to the sea. More wells, however, is always an option that can be considered.

The concept of the imaged well presented here holds great promise for better utilization of the scarce fresh water available in arid coastal areas. There will undoubtedly be problems which will become evident in the first field installations of the imaged well system, but it should be possible to overcome those problems by monitoring, adjusting and, if necessary, going back to the laboratory or computer for further research. Instead of further research based on the questions of researchers, better that it be based on the problems of users.

It is worth noting that the density difference between fresh and sea water is only a minor factor in the imaged well concept. Therefore, simultaneous pumping from two (or more) wells should also be applicable to layered polluted waters. If the relatively concentrated polluted layer can be extracted, its disposal should be simpler and less costly.

Acknowledgements

The figures in this paper are from the Proceedings of two conferences where the concept was presented in an effort to find someone interested in trying the concept in a field installation. The first conference was sponsored by the National Water Well Assocation on Practical Applications of Ground Water Models; the second conference was sponsored by the King of Morocco on Drought Water Management and Food Production. The research was accomplished by the middle authors under the guidance of the first and last author.

APPENDIX A

References

Abed, S.A.A. 1982. Wells Imaged About an Interface: Hele-Shaw Model, M.S. Thesis, University of Arizona, Tucson, Arizona.

Bardelli, U. 1960. New System of Pumping Underground Fresh Water Afloat Upon Sea Water in Porous Formation. International Association of Scientific Hydrology, V. 2, pp. 442-451.

Fader, S. W. 1957. An Analysis of Contour Maps of 1955 Water Levels, with a Discussion of Salt Water Problems in Southwestern Louisiana. Louisiana Geological Survey and Louisiana Department of Public Works, Water Resources Pamphlet No. 4, pp. 16-21.

Fukumori, E. 1982. Wells Imaged About an Interface: Mathematical Model. M.S. Thesis, University of Arizona, Tucson, Arizona.

Iwasa, Y. and H. Takeuchi. 1969. Control of Sea Water Level in Coastal Porous Media by Means of Double Pumping. Thirteenth Congress of the International Association for Hydraulic Research, V. 4, pp. 391-400.

Laursen, E. M. A Technique for the Capture of Fresh Water Wasting to the Sea. Proceedings of Conference on Drought, Water Management and Food Production. Agadir, Morocco, Nov. 21-24, 1985.

Laursen, E. M., S.A.A. Abed, E. Fukumori, A. Souissi, and M.S. Petersen. Wells Imaged About an Interface. Practical Applications of Ground Water Models. National Water Well Association, August 19-20, 1985.

Long, R. A. 1965. Feasibility of a Scavenger Well System as a Solution of the Problem of Vertical Salt-Water Encroachment. Department of Public Works, Water Resources Pamphlet No. 15, pp. 1-22.

Soussi, A. 1984. Wells Imaged About an Interface: A Sand Model. M.S. Thesis, University of Arizona, Tucson, Arizona.

Underhill, H. W. and M. J. Atherton. 1964. A Coastal Ground Water Study in Libya and a Discussion of a Double Pumping Technique. Journal of Hydrology, V. 2, pp. 52-64.

Wickersham, G. 1977. Review of C.E. Jacob's Doublet Well. Ground Water, V. 16, No. 5, pp. 344-347.

Surface Water Analysis for Ground Water Simulation

Terry L. Erlewine*
Associate Member, ASCE

Abstract

The California Department of Water Resources (DWR) has applied a hydrologic-economic modeling (HEM) system to the analysis of ground water use in the San Joaquin Valley. An important component of this modeling system is the surface water allocation model (SWAM) which estimates ground water pumpage and recharge in the Valley. The SWAM additionally provides a cataloging of surface flows in the Valley and estimates amounts of water use and supply. The SWAM has been used in conjunction with other models in the HEM to calibrate a ground water model and to project future ground water conditions in the Valley.

Introduction

The San Joaquin Valley, a semiarid inland valley in California, is one of the United States' most productive agricultural regions. Because of the Valley's natural aridity, irrigation water supplies and ground water pumping are crucial to the viability of agriculture. In 1980, total water applications in the Valley were estimated to be 20.4 million acre-feet, of which approximately 8.9 million acre-feet was supplied by ground water pumpage (2). Overuse of ground water in the Valley, as reflected in the 1.5-million-acre-foot annual overdraft, is a major concern of water managers. To analyze problems associated with ground water use, the California Department of Water Resources (DWR) has applied a combined hydrologic-economic modeling (HEM) system to simulate water supply and water use in the Valley.

The HEM is made up of four computer models that simulate physical and economic aspects of the San Joaquin Valley. Two of the models -- the surface water allocation model (SWAM) and the ground water model (GWM) -- simulate the physical processes of surface and subsurface water movement in the Valley. The SWAM accounts for surface water supply and use; the GWM simulates ground water levels. Besides the SWAM and the GWM, two economic models in the HEM simulate the economic effects of ground water use. The San Joaquin Valley positive production model (SJVPPM) is a mathematical programming model that projects farmers' cropping patterns and income. The linear quadratic control model (LQCM) is an optimal control model that integrates the results of each of the individual models and projects optimal water use in the Valley (1).

This paper explains how DWR uses the SWAM to facilitate Valley ground water simulations. Described first is the SWAM and its solution procedure; second, the GWM and its interactions with the SWAM; and last, the application of the SWAM to various ground water simulations.

*Associate Engineer with the State of California Department of Water Resources, 3374 East Shields Avenue, Fresno, California 93726.

SWAM Description

The SWAM is a versatile computer model developed for DWR by Resource
Management Associates (RMA) to simulate the impacts of alternative
management policies on valley water use (4). The SWAM consists of two
general parts -- a network accounting of surface water movement in the
Valley and a general simulation of water supply and use to the bottom
of the crop rooting zone of the Valley's 33 subareas. These subareas,
called detailed analysis units (DAUs), were identified by DWR on the
basis of water use and water supply characteristics.

SWAM Surface Network. The SWAM surface network is a flexible system
of junctions and channels. The surface water network has been defined
in the San Joaquin Valley considering the availability of existing data
collection efforts. A schematic representation of a portion of the
SWAM network is shown on Figure 1. On this figure, SWAM junctions
correspond to intersections of physical stream channels, points of
diversion from the Valley's rivers, or DAUs where water is ultimately
used. Upstream junctions are represented on Figure 1 as triangles, and
ordinary junctions appear as small circles. DAUs are called demand
junctions by the SWAM and are represented by ellipses.

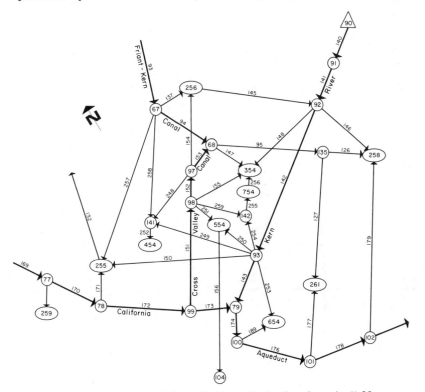

Figure 1. SWAM Network in a Portion of the San Joaquin Valley

SWAM channels represent natural stream channel segments or canal systems and appear on Figure 1 as the lines connecting the network junctions. The SWAM "solves" a system of flows beginning at upstream channels where rivers or canal systems enter the Valley. Working its way downstream, the SWAM maintains water budgets for each channel that consider upstream and downstream flows, stream evaporation, ground water losses or gains, and phreatophyte use. In the cases of stream evaporation and ground water losses, the SWAM allows the user to either specify these parameters or estimates them itself based on unit rates for channel lengths or upstream flow.

Besides this channel water budgeting, the SWAM maintains junction water budgets by balancing combined channel inflows with outflows at any junction point. At junctions with diversion channel outflows, the amount of flow diverted may either be provided directly to the SWAM as input or estimated by the SWAM based on a diversion curve which computes diversions based on some key upstream flow. The final output of the SWAM's network portion is a listing of flows, evaporation rates, and ground water recharge rates in each channel in each time period of a simulation run. Flows in key downstream channels are especially useful for validation of program input since they integrate the effects of all channel flows.

DAU Water Budgets. Demand junctions correponding to the Valley's DAUs where water use occurs are also specified for the SWAM. In these DAUs, a complex water budget is maintained to balance water use with the water supplies available from precipitation, surface water diversion, and ground water pumpage. This water budget is shown schematically on Figure 2. Surface water diversions to any demand junction are computed by totaling the flows in individual surface

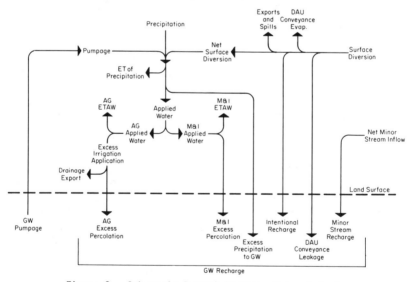

Figure 2.   Schematic Demand Junction Water Budget

diversion channels. The amount of diverted water that reaches farmers is computed by subtracting the amount of spills, conveyance evaporation, conveyance seepage, and intentional recharge. The SWAM also routes precipitation through the upper soil layer on either a monthly or yearly basis to determine the amounts of evapotranspiration (ET) and precipitation recharge to ground water.

Agricultural consumptive use, the main component of water use in the Valley, is computed by the SWAM on the basis of unit crop water use rates and crop acreages. Numerous options are available for the annual adjustment of unit crop water use rates -- options which consider variations in total ET and effective precipitation. Crop acreages may be specified to the SWAM for up to six different years and are linearly interpolated for missing years. Evapotranspiration of applied water (ETAW) for municipal and industrial (M&I) purposes can be either specified directly to the SWAM or estimated in the program based on population and per capita water use rates. Once the agricultural and M&I ETAW have been determined, the amount of applied water is estimated by the SWAM based on irrigation efficiency values.

The final computation made by the SWAM demand junction budget determines both ground water pumpage and recharge. Ground water recharge is determined by summing the quantities of the individual items of ground water recharge determined earlier in the analysis. Ground water pumpage is estimated as the last unknown in the water balance, being computed as the total applied water demand less the amount of surface water deliveries to San Joaquin Valley water users. Once derived, the annual estimates of pumpage and recharge are written onto computer files for later use by the GWM and the SJVPPM.

GWM Description

The HEM model most intimately associated with the SWAM is the GWM. The GWM's primary purpose is to predict changes in ground water levels by simulating storage changes and ground water movement in the Valley. The GWM depicts flow in two aquifer layers -- an unconfined layer where the water level is free at its surface and a confined, artesian aquifer bounded at its top by a thick, relatively impermeable clay layer (5).

Ground water heads are simulated in the GWM by a finite element algorithm that requires division of the ground water basin into three- or four-sided elements. Hydrologic stresses on the ground water basin (pumpage and recharge) and geologic parameters (specific yield, storativity, and hydraulic conductivity) are assumed to be uniform within each element. The GWM additionally requires definition of nodes at the intersections of element boundaries and at element boundary midpoints. The GWM solves a system of nonlinear equations that projects initial ground water levels at nodes forward at semiannual time steps for the length of a simulation.

An important consideration in the definition of the GWM network was its relationship with the SWAM. As previously discussed, DAUs are the smallest areal unit in the SWAM for which pumpage and recharge are computed. To correspond to this DAU level of aggregation, the GWM network was defined so that each DAU could be represented by an integral number of elements. By default, the GWM uses a uniform distribution of the SWAM pumpage and recharge within the elements that make up a DAU. In DAUs where pumpage and recharge are not uniformly

distributed, the GWM allows the user to override this assumption and
supply the model with an allocation of pumpage and recharge.

SWAM Use in Calibration

   Before a ground water model can be used with confidence, it must be
calibrated for some historical time period. Calibration requires use
of both the SWAM and the GWM. Ideally, the actual water supply during
this calibration period should be close to the long-term average water
supply of an area. Additionally, the calibration period should ideally
be preceded by, and end with, a dry year so that the amount of water in
transit in the unsaturated zone will be similar. In the San Joaquin
Valley, the period 1970 to 1977 was originally selected for GWM
calibration. Recently this calibration period was extended to include
the years 1978 through 1982 (3).

   In the calibration period, measured ground water levels were
collected and analyzed to determine what aquifer conditions they
represented. Water levels that represented known aquifer conditions
were used in the calibration process; many well measurements were not
used to calibrate the model because little was known about the
construction of the wells where the measurements were made or because
the measurements themselves appeared to be irregular. The selected
well measurements were then processed using kriging, a statistical
estimation procedure that estimates confined and unconfined water
levels at GWM nodes based on the set of ground water level
measurements.

   Calibration of the GWM in the San Joaquin Valley involved the
comparison of simulated ground water levels with the kriged water
levels based on measurements. Initial conditions were provided to the
GWM for the first time period of the calibration (spring 1970), and
pumpage and recharge were estimated for subsequent time periods using
the SWAM. For the calibration runs, the SWAM network served largely as
a data base management system. During the calibration period, data
were available for nearly all flows into the Valley as well as surface
water diversions and imports. Wherever these measurements were
available, they were input into the SWAM as annual values. Seepage
losses from streams to ground water, and ground water accretions to
streams, were also provided to the SWAM. SWAM-computed downstream
flows provided useful checks on the completeness and accuracy of the
surface-flow figures input into the SWAM channels.

   Ground water pumpage was one of the largest unknowns during
calibration. In the SWAM, such pumpage is computed by subtracting
surface water deliveries from applied water estimates. During
calibration, agricultural applied water in the SWAM was based primarily
on three items: irrigated crop acreage, unit crop ETAW, and irrigation
efficiency. Estimates of these items are subject to some uncertainty.
Irrigated crop acreages were interpolated linearly between crop surveys
conducted by DWR at approximately seven-year intervals. Unit crop ETAW
was initially left unchanged from year to year, but pumpage estimated
in this manner appeared to be unrealistic. DWR later added a procedure
to the SWAM that uses monthly pan evaporation and precipitation
measurements to annually adjust unit crop ETAW. This added procedure
improved pumpage estimates considerably. Irrigation efficiencies are
largely unmeasured and are subject to a relatively large degree of
uncertainty.

U. S. Geological Survey (USGS) pumpage estimates provided DWR
with one source with which to crosscheck SWAM-estimated ground water
pumpage (6). These USGS estimates are based on an analysis of power
consumption records and unit power consumption determined in pump
tests, and they provide an independent estimate of ground water
pumpage. Unfortunately, USGS estimates for the entire Valley were
available only for the years 1970 and 1971, and similar estimates for
portions of the Valley were available only for the years 1975 through
1977. Despite these limitations, the USGS estimates provided an
indication of the reasonableness of the SWAM estimates.

Normally, the parameters calibrated in a ground water model are
geologic values such as specific yield, storativity, and hydraulic
conductivity. In the Valley, however, calibration was expanded through
use of the SWAM to include uncertainties in the hydrologic system.
Geologic parameters were calibrated, based on a comparison of simulated
and observed ground water levels, but in many cases hydrologic
estimates also proved susceptible to adjustments. Frequently, apparent
errors in simulated ground water levels could be traced to the SWAM,
and suspicious and erroneous values in it could be adjusted.

SWAM Use in Projections

The San Joaquin Valley HEM can produce several different types of
ground water level projections depending on which combination of models
are used. Recently, DWR used three of the HEM models to project the
ground water levels that would result from different levels of imports
from the proposed Mid-Valley Canal. The canal was proposed in the
mid-1970s as a possible interim measure to alleviate overdraft problems
in the Valley. Recently, the canal, or a similarly located conveyance
facility, has come under renewed study as possible means to transport
U. S. Bureau of Reclamation Central Valley Project water to the
overdrafted areas of the Valley.

In projecting the future ground water levels for comparing
Mid-Valley Canal imports, several scenarios were defined with the help
of the SWAM, the GWM, and the SJVPPM. The scenarios projected were a
"base case" of current levels of water supplies and three alternative
levels of Mid-Valley Canal imports (250,000, 550,000, and 800,000 acre-
feet.) The water supply for each of these scenarios was assumed to be
uniform each year. The quantity of this supply was based on the
average of a 1922-1978 long-term period since year-to-year hydrologic
variations were not as important to this analysis as the long-term
trends of ground water levels.

The Mid-Valley Canal projections each began in the year 1983 and
ground water levels were forecasted to the year 2010. The projection
procedure itself consisted of an iterative process involving the
SJVPPM, the GWM and the SWAM. Iteration was required because of
the interrelationships between ground water pumping costs and crop
acreages. The SJVPPM, the economic model, can predict crop acreages
based on surface and ground water costs. The GWM can predict future
ground water levels and pumping costs, but to do so it requires data on
future ground water pumping based on crop acreages. The SWAM links the
two other models by using SJVPPM-projected crop acreages to estimate
ground water pumpage for the GWM.

The iterative process begins with an initial estimate of crop acreages in the SWAM to predict future ground water pumpage and recharge for use in a GWM projection. The GWM then provides ground water pumping costs to the SJVPPM, allowing the SJVPPM to predict future crop acreages. These predicted crop acreages are in turn used in the SWAM and the GWM to evaluate the impact of land use changes on ground water levels. This process can continue through many cycles but ultimately stops when the change in ground water pumping costs from one cycle to the next is negligible. Results from the hydrologic and economic models are then consistent, and the projection run is completed.

The results of the projection runs showed that additional surface water imports considerably benefited the ground water basin. Ground water levels were higher with additional imports, but in all cases the rise in ground water levels was somewhat mitigated by the additional water use resulting from increased crop acreage. The increase in crop acreage was projected by the SJVPPM based on an increase in ground water levels and a corresponding decrease in ground water pumping costs caused by additional surface imports. Thus, additional surface water imports did not reduce ground water overdraft on a one-to-one basis. For example, increasing surface imports by 250,000 acre-feet resulted in a projected year 2000 overdraft reduction of 190,100 acre-feet.

Another interesting aspect of the Mid-Valley Canal projection results was that the unit benefits of imported ground water decreased with greater levels of imports. The primary benefits of additional surface imports were decreases in ground water pumpage costs. The imports of additional surface water had two general effects on total ground water pumpage costs: they directly replaced a certain amount of ground water pumpage, and they reduced pumping lifts by raising ground water levels. To some extent, these two effects cancel each other out. The first increment of additional surface water has a large marginal benefit because it reduces ground water pumping costs for a large amount of ground water pumping. Subsequent increments of surface water raise the ground water level more, but the total amount of ground water pumpage is reduced at the same time.

Summary

The SWAM has proven to be a valuable tool for water resources planning in the San Joaquin Valley. Originally designed as one component of an overall hydrologic-economic model, the SWAM has proved to be useful in its own right by providing a convenient reference source for hydrologic data. In the future, only slight modifications are expected to be made on the SWAM for its use in the San Joaquin Valley. Statewide, however, the model is in the first stages of application to the Sacramento Valley and may be applied to California's central coastal region in the near future. In these applications, additional modifications may possibly be made to enhance the program's versatility and adaptableness to different hydrologic situations.

Appendix I. References

1. California Department of Water Resources, "The Hydrologic-Economic
    Model of the San Joaquin Valley", Bulletin 214, December 1982.
2. California Department of Water Resources, "The California Water
    Plan", Bulletin 160-83, December 1983.
3. California Department of Water Resources, "Ground Water Study,
    San Joaquin Valley: Third Progress Report", September 1985.
4. McLaughlin, D., "Hydrologic Modeling Task Report for the San
    Joaquin Valley Groundwater Study", November 1982.
5. McLaughlin, D., "User's Manual for the San Joaquin Groundwater
    Model (GWM)", November 1982.
6. U. S. Geological Survey, "A Summary of Ground-Water Pumpage in
    the Central Valley, California, 1961-77", Water Resources
    Investigations Report 83-4037, October 1983.

Appendix II. Notation

    The U. S. Customary-International Unit conversion for acre-feet is
as follows: 1 acre-foot = 1,233.482 cubic metres.

Simple Removal and Recovery of Irrigation Drainage Salts

George E. Wilson*

Introduction and Problem Statement

Management of salinity in irrigation waters is of major
importance in agricultural and water resource activities. Water
supply sources for these activities are frequently sinks for
irrigation return (drainage) waters containing high salt loads
(10,14). Reservoirs used for water flow management can also result
in salt concentration increases due to evaporative water losses
(8,11). Irrigation drainage water salt loads account for most of the
salinity increase.

Irrigation drainage waters are a necessary complement to
agricultural irrigation (10). Salt concentrations around the plant
root zone must be maintained below certain levels to prevent
reduction in crop productivity. This is normally accomplished by
applying water quantities in excess of those required by the plant.
The net excess, or drainage water, leaves the root zone with much of
the applied salt load plus the additional salts leached from the
soil. The salt load in the drainage water will depend on the salt
content of the applied water, the quantity of excess water applied,
and the leachable salt content of the soil (14).

Salinity increases in water supply sources have major economic
impacts. It has been estimated that the cost of salinity increases
in the Colorado River basin amount to 25 ¢/acre-ft-mg/l in 1974
dollars (5,16). This amounts to a current cost of $460/ton. This
cost can be compared with the estimated current cost of $70/ton for
desalination of return water not including cost for final collection,
storage and disposal of the removed salt (17).

The California San Joaquin Valley has a major drainage and salt
management program underway (2,3,12,13). By 2005 drainage water
quantities are estimated to be 424,000 acre-ft/yr or a daily
equalized flow of 380 mgd. Total annual salt loads are estimated at
2.74 million tons, or 3.13 million cubic yards of crystallized salt.
Desalting of these waters has been investigated for several years
(2,13). The recommended plan chose the more economical alternative
of flow management, partial salt concentration through evaporation
ponds and marshes, and final disposal to the Pacific Ocean via Suisun
and San Francisco Bay (3). It appeared much simpler to dispose of
these vast quantities of salt as concentrated solutions to the ocean
rather than manage them in a major materials handling project.

*President, EUTEK SYSTEMS, 1509 Kingsford Dr., Carmichael, CA. 95608

The first reservoir in the flow management system was Kesterson, a name now known nationally. Selenium was concentrated in this reservoir and marsh and was exposed to fish and waterfowl at toxic concentrations. Numerous alternatives have and are being considered to resolve this critical problem. Desalination with careful materials handling procedures is one possibility. However, costs and complexity make it of questionable practicality. Another alternative is to prohibit the practice of irrigated agriculture in land areas from which the selenium is leached. The implementation of this alternative is politically and economically unattractive.

A Simple On Farm Management Alternative

This paper reports on preliminary tests of an alternative for simple removal and recovery of irrigation drainage salt. Because of its simplicity it should lend itself to on farm application. Using a novel system for evaporating waters from capillary surfaces, salts are concentrated and crystallized away from the water body. Stored water does not experience the salt concentrating effect of final impoundments (8,11). Thus, storage facilities would not require lining and other measures to prevent infiltration. Evaporation rates from the capillary surfaces have been measured as more than twice those of plain water surfaces. Area requirements would therefore be substantially less.

The economics of this alternative appear to be very attractive. The process represents a total solution with dry crystallized salt as the only end product. The cost per ton of totally recovered salt is estimated to be less than that required to obtain a concentrated brine using conventional desalination technology (2,13,17).

Description of Test System and Procedures

A bench scale reservoir system with simulated wind movement and radiation heating was constructed as shown on Figure 1. Measurements included:

1. Net water evaporated per unit time.

2. Accumulated crystallized salt zone versus time.

3. Wind flow rate and velocity across the surface.

4. Net radiation absorbed on the surface and its distribution over the surface.

5. Conductivity of the feed and reservoir water versus time.

6. Relative humidity of air over surface.

7. Temperature distributions in reservoir and capillary surface waters and in the overlying air layers.

In order to evaluate the relative evaporative efficiency of capillary versus plain water surfaces it was necessary to conduct

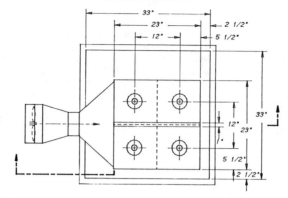

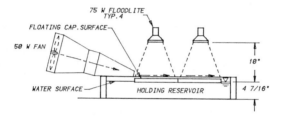

FIG.1 TEST APPARATUS

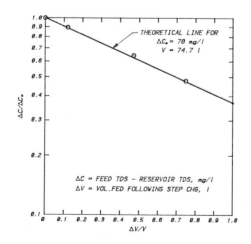

FIG.2 RESPONSE TO STEP CHANGE IN FEED SALINITY

control tests with the plain water surface. Traditional procedures
for estimating evaporation from water surfaces have failed to take
into account the relative contributions of sensible and radiant heat
inputs and losses (1,4,6). Careful examination of estimated
evaporation rates using these procedures revealed major discrepancies
which could not be resolved with established heat and mass transfer
data for humidification processes (7,9,15). Radiant heat absorption
and the relative contribution due to convective heat transfer assumed
by these procedures were significantly different than those measured
in these tests. This necessitated abandonment of these estimating
procedures as a means of comparing evaporative efficiencies.

Each test run was conducted over several diurnal periods to
ascertain the influence of the uncontrolled environmental variables
on the evaporative process. Measured heat and mass transfer
coefficients were compared with standard correlations (7,9,15) and
found to be of reasonable magnitudes.

Preliminary Test Results

Salt Capture

A step increase in feed water conductivity relative to initial
reservoir conductivity was made to measure the efficiency of salt
capture. The results have been plotted on Figure 2. There was no
significance difference between the measured results and the
theoretical line representing 100 percent capture of salt on the
capillary surface. Since all evaporation occurs from the capillary
surface covering the holding reservoir, this means that waters held
in the holding reservoir do not experience the increase in salinity
which occurs in open reservoirs.

Salt Crystallization

Crystallization of salts began to occur immediately at the sink
point on the capillary surface as shown on Figure 3. Some water
continued to diffuse through the crystal deposits and evaporate,
however, most of the crystallization occurred at the periphery of the
deposit area. Density of the deposited material was approximately
1/4 lb/sq ft-layer. Increased depths of crystallized material were
achieved by vertically layering the capillary material.

Evaporation Efficiency

All other factors equal, the rate of evaporation from the
capillary surface was significantly greater than from the plain water
surface. In the absence of wind but with radiant heating the
capillary surface unit area evaporation rate was more than twice that
measured for plain water surfaces.

Wind proved to be the most energy efficient means of enhancing
evaporation rates from the capillary surface. At a surface wind
velocity of 9 ft/sec the unit area evaporation rate was 27 times that
measured in the absence of wind. This compares with only a sevenfold
increase measured (in the absence of waves) over plain water surfaces

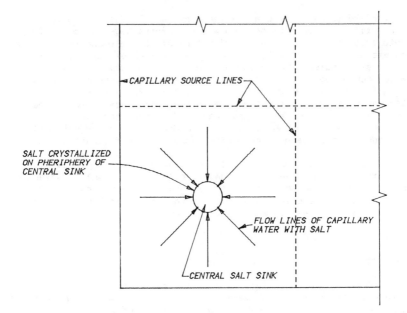

FIG.3   CAPILLARY FLOW & SALT DEPOSITION PATTERNS

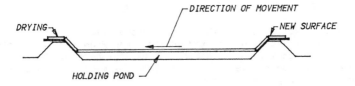

FIG.4   ON FARM CAPILLARY EVAPORATION SYSTEM
        FOR SALT REMOVAL AND RECOVERY

(4). Waves on water surfaces were noted to decrease unit area
evaporation rates. Thus, a further advantage of evaporation from
capillary surfaces is the absence of waves.

The efficiency results can be used to estimate the relative area
requirements of capillary surfaces versus plain water surfaces. A
minimum twofold reduction in area would occur under stagnant, no wind
conditions. Further reductions will occur depending on the magnitude
of winds and the potential for waves over plain surfaces. Assuming
no waves and wind speeds of 10 ft/sec capillary surfaces should
require only 1/8th the area of plain evaporation ponds achieving the
same rate of evaporation.

Practicality

The preliminary test results were used together with published
information on the San Joaquin Valley irrigation drainage water
characteristics to obtain estimates of the practicality of capillary
surface evaporation for salt removal and recovery. Drainage water
amounts to approximately one foot per year over the entire drained
area with TDS averaging 5000 mg/l (13). Plain surface evaporation
rates have been assumed to be 4 ft/yr (3).

Assuming capillary surface evaporation rates 8 times plain
surface rates, area requirements for capillary systems would be
1/32nd acre/acre drained or approximately 3 percent of the total
drained area. This is much more attractive than the 25 percent area
requirement for plain surface ponds.

The one acre-ft/yr-acre drained of drainage containing 5000 mg/l
TDS would yield 13,590 lbs of salt annually. At 1/4 lb salt/sq ft of
capillary surface, 54,360 sq ft of surface material would be required
annually to remove and recover this material. As this recovery would
occur on 1/32nd acre/acre drained, or 1361 sq ft/acre drained, the
capillary material would have an average life of (1361x365)/54360 =
9.1 days. This seems quite practical and manageable for on farm
implementation. On Figure 4 is shown an arrangement for such an
application.

Economics

A 1000 acre drained farm would require a 31 acre capillary
surface evaporation system which would generate 6,800 tons (7,750 cu
yd) of crystallized salt annually. This salt would be incorporated
in 1,250 acres of capillary surface material costing $100/acre. The
annual cost per ton of salt removed and recovered would be
(100x1,250)/6,800 = $18.40. Labor requirements would be minimal.
Total material volume is within the material handling capability of
this size of farming operation and would require no specialized
equipment.

Comparison of this cost with the $460/ton cost for increased
salinity impacts (5,16) makes clear the cost effectiveness of this
alternative. Furthermore, through on farm implementation this

alternative would eliminate the need for a costly valley wide
drainage water collection and flow management system.

Perhaps the most important feature of on farm drainage water
control regards irrigation management. In this approach the results
of irrigation management practice are observable on farm. Their
effectiveness can be assessed and immediate remedial action taken by
farm managers to meet irrigation management objectives.

Conclusions

Preliminary test results comparing evaporation from capillary
surfaces with plain water surfaces have shown:

1. area requirements substantially less, all other factors
   equal.

2. total salt capture on capillary surface materials without
   salinity increases in ponded waters.

3. salt capture capacity of approximately 5.45 tons/acre of
   capillary material.

4. simple operation requiring minimal attention which could be
   easily integrated into on farm operations.

5. less costly than conventional salt removal and recovery
   alternatives.

6. substantially less costly than the cost impacts of salinity
   increases were no salinity control implemented.

Appendix I - References

1. Babbitt,H.E., Doland,J.J. Water Supply Engineering, 5th Ed,
   McGraw-Hill, N.Y., 1955, pp 102-108
2. Brice,D.B., Smith,B.E., "Desalting of Agricultural Drainage
   Water for Reuse", Proceedings, Water Reuse Symposium II, Aug
   23-28, 1981, Wash, D.C., pp 997-1006
3. Dept.of Water Resources, State of Calif., Agricultural Drainage
   and Salt Management in the San Joaquin Valley, Final Report,
   June 1979
4. Easterbrook,C.C., "A Study of the Effects of Waves on
   Evaporation from Free Water Surfaces", Water REsources Tech
   Publication, Research Report No. 18, BuRec, USDI, 1969
5. Kleinman,A.P., Brown,F.B., "Colorado River Salinity - Economic
   Impacts on Agricultural, Municipal, and Industrial Uses", Engr.
   & Res. Ctr., BuRec, USDI, Denver, Colorado, Dec. 1980
6. Linsley,R.K., et al, Hydrology for Engineers, McGraw-Hill, N.Y.,
   1958, pp 90-109
7. McCabe,W.L., Smith,J.C., Unit Operations of Chemical
   Engineering, 2nd Ed, McGraw-Hill, N.Y., 1967, pp 678-706
8. Meron,A., Eren,J., "Effect of Salinity on Agricultural
   Reclamation", Proceedings, Water Reuse Symposium III, Aug 26-31,
   1984, San Diego, CA, pp 543-553

9. Perry,R.H., Green,D., Eds, Perry's Chemical Engineers Handbook, 6th Ed, McGraw-Hill, N.Y., 1984, pp 12-3 - 12-13, 12-22 - 12-24
10. Pettygrove,G.S., Asano,T., Eds, Irrigation with Reclaimed Municipal Wastewater, Report No. 84-1 wr, Calif SWRCB, Sacramento, CA, July, 1984, pp 7-6 - 7-12
11. Pionke,H.B., Workman,O.D., "Effect of Two Impoundments on the Salinity and Quantity of Stored Waters", W.R. Bul.v 10, No. 1, Ag. Res. Serv., S. Grt. Plains Watershed Res. Ctr., Chickasha, OK., 1974, pp 66-80
12. Price,E.P., "Agricultural Drainage Problems of the San Joaquin Valley", Proceedings of National Conference on Irrigation Return Flow Quality Management, May 16-19, 1977, Dept.of Ag. and Chem. Engineering, Colorado State Univ., Ft. Collins, CO, pp 283-287
13. Smith,B.E., Brice,D.B., "Treatment of Agricultural Drainage Water for Reuse", Proceedings ASCE Water Forum '81, Aug 10-14, 1981, San Francisco, CA
14. Tanji,K.K., et al, "Evaluation of Surface Irrigation Return Flows in the Central Valley of California", Proceedings of National Conference on Irrigation Return Flow Quality Management, May 16-19, 1977, Dept.of Ag. and Chem. Engr., Colorado State Univ., Ft. Collins, CO., pp 167-173
15. Treybal,R.E., Mass Transfer Operations, 2nd Ed, McGraw-Hill, 1968, pp 176-219
16. Valantine,V.E., "Impacts of Colorado River Salinity", ASCE JIDD, 100, No.IR4, 1974, pp 495-510
17. Walker,W.R., "Combining Agricultural Improvements and Desalting of Return Flows to Optimize Local Salinity Control Policies", Proceedings of National Conference on Irrigation Return Flow Quality Management, May 16-19, 1977, Dept.of Ag. and Chem. Engr., Colorado State Univ., Ft. Collins, CO., pp 203-213

OPTIMIZING DRAIN SPACING AND DEPTH
USING STEADY STATE EQUATIONS

By J. Kabir[1], A.M. ASCE and L.G. King[2]

ABSTRACT

A method is developed for minimizing the total cost of establishing relief drains by choosing appropriate depth and spacing of the drains. Solution graphs are presented for a wide range of input variables. A simple procedure has also been developed for computing the Hooghoudt's drain spacing using the optimal design. Use of the technique shows that total cost is relatively insensitive to the drain spacing.

INTRODUCTION

The cost of establishing a drainage system for an irrigated land depends on the cost of pipe, envelope material, and the cost of excavation required to install the drains. Spacing of the drain is a function of depth from the soil surface. In general, drain spacing increases with the increase in depth, but the length of drain, and thus the cost of pipe, decreases with the increase in drain spacing. Using this interrelationship between drain spacing, depth of drain, and cost of pipe, one can design the optimal combination of drain spacing and depth to minimize the total cost of establishing a drainage system. This paper presents a technique which can be used when designing drain spacing to best meet drainage requirements and to minimize cost.

In this analysis the total cost of establishing a drainage system has been divided in two parts: a) cost of pipe and envelope material, and b) cost of excavation. It does not include placement cost and other construction costs, but it is possible to include these costs in this analysis if they can be evaluated in terms of per unit length of drain such that they can be combined with the cost of pipe and envelope materials.

PROBLEM ANALYSIS

Drain Spacing

The steady-state drain spacing formula generally used in the United States is the Donnan formula (2)

$$S_D^2 = (4K/Q_d)(b^2 - a^2) \tag{1}$$

---
[1] Hydraulic Engineer, Austin Research Engineers Inc, 2600 Dellana Lane, Austin, Texas 78746.
[2] Professor and Chairman, Agricultural Engineering Department, Washington State University, Pullman, Washington 99164.

in which S_D = Donnan drain spacing; K = saturated
conductivity; a = depth of the impermeable barrier measur
drain; b = depth of maximum allowable water table bet
measured from the impermeable barrier; Q_d = steady-state re⌐⌐⌐⌐⌐⌐ ⌐⌐⌐⌐,
as shown in Figure 1. In designing a drainage system, one has to

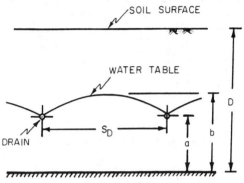

Figure 1. Definition Sketch

compute the drain spacing, S_D, and the depth of the impermeable barrier
measured from the drain, a. Other parameters in Eq 1 are determined by
the given soil profile and the crop under consideration. Now, Eq 1 may
be written as

$$(Q_d/4K) = (b^2-a^2)/S_D^2 \qquad (2)$$

The quantity in the left side of Eq 2 may be denoted as drain capacity.
The objective of the designer is to select values of a and S_D such that
the cost is minimal for a given value of drain capacity.

<u>Drain Cost</u>

The total cost of establishing drain per unit area is given by

$$C = C_e (D - a) L + C_p L \qquad (3)$$

in which C_e = cost of excavation per unit length of drain per unit
depth; D = depth of the impermeable layer measured from the soil
surface; L = length of drain per unit area; and C_p = cost of drain and
surrounding envelope materials per unit length of pipe. Other costs
which can be expressed in terms of length can be added to C_p value.
For a spacing of S_D, length per unit area L = $1/S_D$. So Eq 3 may be
written as

$$C = C_e(D-a)/S_D + C_p/S_D \qquad (4)$$

The objective of the designer is to minimize the cost C in Eq 4 to
obtain a given value of drain capacity $Q_d/4K$ of Eq 2.

OPTIMIZATION METHOD

In designing a drainage system to have a minimum total cost of
excavation, pipe and envelope materials Eq 2 has to be solved such that

the cost function of Eq 3 is minimized. This can be achieved by following the classical microeconomic theory of minimizing production cost by choosing certain combination of labor cost and capital investment (1). The solution technique involves selecting the drain spacing and drain depth such that the ratio of marginal capacity of the system equals the marginal cost. For drain spacing design the term on the left side of Eq 2 may be used as drain capacity. One can write,

$$(\partial/\partial a) \ (Q_d/4K)/(\partial/\partial S_D) \ (Q_d/4K) = (\partial C/\partial a) \ (\partial C/\partial S_D) \qquad (5)$$

in which the cost function C is defined by Eq 4.

Substituting Eqs 2 and 4 in Eq 5, taking the partial derivatives and rearranging, one can write

$$a = b^2/(D + C_p/C_e). \qquad (6)$$

Substituting the value of a from Eq 6 in Eq 1, the drain spacing is given by

$$S_D = [\ (4Kb^2/Q_d) \ \{1 - b^2/(D + C_p/C_e)^2\}]^{1/2} \qquad (7)$$

Drain depth and spacing computed by Eqs 6 and 7, respectively, would result in a minimum total cost for a given value of C_p and C_e. Total cost per unit area can be obtained by using Eq 3.

Graphical Solution

Dimensionless graphical solutions of Eqs 6 and 7 are shown in Figures 2 and 3, respectively, for wide ranges of input variables. These figures can be used for a quick and illustrative determination of drain depth and spacing of minimum costs. The curved lines in the log-log plot in Figure 2 are solutions of Eq 6 for different values of depth of impermeable layer, D. The straight lines of Figure 3 are solutions of Eq 7 for different values of a/b ratio. These figures are set such that they can be used for any system of units.

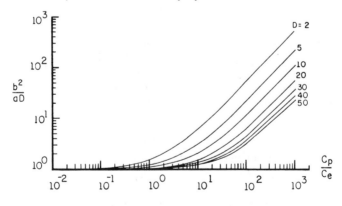

Figure 2. Dimensionless Graphical Solution of Eq 6

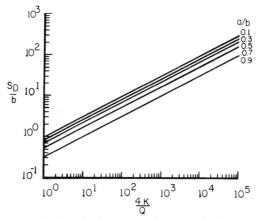

Figure 3. Dimensionless Graphical Solution of Eq 7

COMPARISON WITH HOOGHOUDT'S DRAIN SPACING

Although the steady-state drain spacing formula generally used in the irrigated areas of the United States is the Donnan formula (2), some designer prefers Hooghoudt's equation for computing drain spacing. Hooghoudt's drain spacing for isotropic soil is given by

$$S_H = [(4K/Q_d)(b - a)^2 + 2 (b - a)a']^{\frac{1}{2}} \qquad (8)$$

in which the equivalent depth a' is given by

$$a' = a \ [1 + (a/S_H)(2.546 \ln(a/r) - \alpha \ )]^{-1} \qquad 0 \leqslant (a/S_H) \leqslant 0.3 \quad (9)$$
$$= S \ (2.546 \ln (S_H/r) - 2.928)^{-1} \qquad (a/S_H) > 0.3 \quad (10)$$

where $\alpha = 3.55 - 1.6 \ (a/S) + 2 \ (a/S)^2$ and r = drain radius.

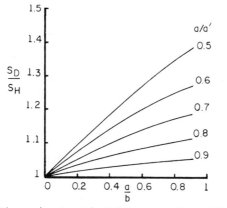

Figure 4. Graphical Representation of Eq 9

Combining Eqs 1 and 8, one can obtain

$$S_D/S_H = [\{(b/a) + 1\}/\{(b/a) + (a'/a) - 1\}]^{1/2} \qquad (11)$$

Fig. 4 shows a graphical representation of Eq 11 for different values of a'/a.

EXAMPLE OF OPTIMAL DESIGN

A drainage system is to be designed for the following conditions so that the total cost is minimal. Saturated hydraulic conductivity K = 10 ft/day (3.048m), steady-state recharge rate Q_d = 0.0059 ft/day (1.798 x 10^{-3}m/day), depth of impermeable barrier from ground surface D = 30 ft (9.144m), depth of water table is to be no closer than 4 ft (1.219m). Assume C_p/C_e = 1.0 (0.3048).

Using Figure 2, for C_p/C_e = 1 ft (0.3048m), D = 30 ft (9.144m) one can find b^2/aD = 1.033. Again b = 26 ft (7.925m). So a = 21.81 ft (6.648m). This value of a can also be computed by using Eq 6. Now using Figure 2, for a/b = 0.839, $4K/Q_d$ = 6780 one can find S_D/b = 44.82. So S_D = 1165 ft (355m). This value of S_D can also be computed by Eq 7. So the drain should be placed 21.81 ft above the barrier at an spacing of 1165 ft (355m).

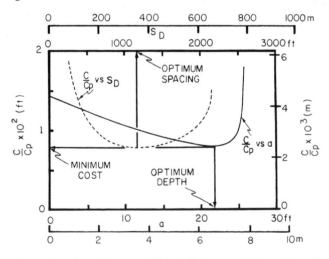

Figure 5. Sensitivity of Total Cost on Depth and Spacing

Total cost per unit area can be obtained by using Eq 4. Since C_p/C_e = 1 ft (0.3048m), from Eq 4 total cost per unit area C = $0.00789 C_p ($0.0259 C_p). Figure 5 shows the sensitivity of the total cost on the values of a and S_D. This figure also shows that the optimal design indeed produces a design at minimum cost.

If it is desired to have Hooghoudt's drain spacing one has to compute the value of a' by iterative procedure using Eqs 9 or 10, depending on the value of a/S_H. Assuming a drain radius $r = 1$ ft (0.305m), iterative computation will give $a' = 20.12$ ft (6.133m). Using Fig 6 for $a/b = 0.839$, $a'/a = 0.92$ one can obtain $S_D/S_H = 1.04$. So the Hoogoudt's drain spacing $S_H = 1120$ ft (341m). This value can also be computed using Eq 11. It may be noted here that, if S_H is used as the drain spacing, the total cost should be computed by using this value in Eq 4. From Fig 5 it may be noted that the increase in total cost due to the change in spacing from $S_D = 1165$ ft (355m) to $S_H = 1120$ ft (341m) is very small.

SUMMARY AND CONCLUSIONS

A least cost design for steady-state relief drain spacing and depth has been developed, based on Donnan formula and microeconomic theory. A simple technique has also been developed to compute Hooghoudt's drain spacing using the optimal valves. Sensitivity analysis showed that the procedure indeed minimized total cost. An example of the application of the method to the design of drain spacing and depth is presented. The example problem shows that a moderate deviation from the optimal drain spacing causes a small change in the total costs.

APPENDIX I - REFERENCE

1. Henderson, J.M. and Quandt, R.E., Microeconomic Theory: A Mathematical Approach, McGraw-Hill Book Company, 1980.

2. U.S. Dept. of Interior, Bureau of Reclamation, Drainage Manual, A Water Resources Technical Publication, 1st Ed., 1978.

APPENDIX II - NOTATION

a_l = depth of impermeable barrier measured from the drain;
a' = Hooghoudt's equivalent depth;
b = depth of maximum allowable water table between the drains measured from the impermeable barrier;
C = total cost per unit area;
C_e = cost of excavation per unit length of drain per unit depth;
C_p = cost of drain and envelope materials per unit length;
D = depth of impermeable layer measured from the ground surface;
K = saturated hydraulic conductivity;
L = length of drain per unit area;
Q_d = steady state recharge rate;
r = drain radius;
S_D = drain spacing using Donnan formula; and
S_H = drain spacing using Hooghoudt's equation.

AGRICULTURAL DRAINAGE WATER TREATMENT-ARE TOXIC ELEMENTS USEFUL?

Rodney C. Squires and William R. Johnston, M. ASCE [1]

ABSTRACT: The problems pertaining to disposing of agricultural drainage water in the San Joaquin Valley are explained. Details are
presented on a pilot plant which is pretreating the drainage water for
the selective removal of toxic elements. Data collected to date
suggests that the toxic elements might be recovered and sold as useful
materials.

INTRODUCTION

Irrigated agriculture on the westside of California's San Joaquin
Valley began in the 1880's with water diverted from the San Joaquin
River and was augmented with groundwater pumping from the late 1920's
through the 1960's. Additional water was imported to the area with the
completion of the Federal Delta-Mendota Canal in 1950 and the San Luis
Canal in 1968. Irrigation has led to a severe saline agricultural
drainage water problem (14) which today threatens up to 1,000,000 acres
(400,000 ha) of agricultural land. Moves to alleviate the drainage
problem began in the early 1900's with the installation of open drains
followed in the early 1950's by tile drainage facilities designed to
control saline subsurface water tables. In 1960 Congress mandated, as
part of the San Luis Unit, the construction of Federal drainage
facilities (19) to transfer subsurface drainage water to a discharge
point near Chipps Island into the Sacramento-San Joaquin Delta-San
Francisco Bay Estuary. In 1968, the U. S. Bureau of Reclamation (USBR)
began construction of the San Luis Drain, a concrete-lined drainage
canal, and Kesterson Regulating Reservoir, a 1,200 acre (480 ha)
containment intended to regulate the northward flow of drainage water.
However, the various Federal, State and local agencies involved with
drainage problems, with water quality issues and with the protection of
fish and wildlife all developed different views on the management of
agricultural drainage water and a great deal has been written on all
aspects of this issue.(5-10)(13)(16-17)(20-21).

In the late 1970's part of a regional subsurface drainage collector
system was constructed in Westlands Water District (WWD). Subsurface
agricultural drainage water is collected and conveyed in the collector
drains to the San Luis Drain through which the drainage water flows
northward into Kesterson Reservoir. Flows started in 1978 and
gradually increased until, by 1981, the inflow to Kesterson consisted
entirely of subsurface agricultural drainage water when the annual input
had reached the reservoir capacity to manage the water.

[1] Partner, Binnie & Partners-EPOC AG. Corp., 1314 E. Shaw Ave.,
Fresno, CA 93710, and Assistant Manager-Chief of Operations,
Westlands Water District, P. O. Box 6056, Fresno, CA 93703.

The discovery of problems related to the accumulation of the trace element selenium in the drainage water flowing into Kesterson attracted extensive public attention starting in 1982 (12). Because of this, the USBR suspended its efforts to obtain permits from the State Water Resources Control Board (SWRCB) to discharge agricultural drainage water into the Sacramento-San Joaquin Delta estuary. Therefore, the San Luis Drain was not extended beyond Kesterson. In early 1985, the SWRCB adopted an order requiring the USBR to either close Kesterson as a drainage facility or bring it into compliance with State environmental protection laws and regulations (5). The emergence of the selenium-related problems also focused attention on the Grasslands Water District (GWD), which historically has used agricultural drainage water from some 18 irrigation districts or entities as part of its water supply for wildfowl habitat, and the SWRCB also directed GWD to formulate and implement a program to reduce the amount of selenium intake to the wetlands area. A Task Force was organized to develop such a program.

Subsequent to the SWRCB order, the Department of Interior (DOI) decided to close Kesterson as a drainage facility because of possible violations of the Migratory Bird Treaty Act. As a result, WWD has implemented an intensive water conservation and management program, a voluntary, grower-managed subsurface drainage water recycling program and a subsurface drain plugging program to reduce and stop the flow of drainage water going from the WWD collector system to Kesterson - approximately 7,000 ac. ft. per year (8827 Ml/y) (6.5 mgd). Flows of drainage water to Kesterson Reservoir must be eliminated by June 30, 1986, so that the USBR will have several options available to it and time to comply with the SWRCB order by February 1988.

DISCUSSION

A specialized treatment process has been developed and is being used to operate a pilot level plant to treat the subsurface agricultural drainage waters for removal of the potentially toxic elements in the water in such a way that they might become useful by-products.

Table I is a summary of the water quality parameters of the drainage water which leaves the 42,000 acre (17,000 ha) part of the WWD via collector underdrains flows into the San Luis Drain. The data in Table I show that the drainage water is brackish, has a high sulphate concentration, carries high selenium and boron concentrations and contains a range of heavy metals. Two problems exist, one of salts and the other of potentially toxic elements. Even though many undesirable elements and compounds are present in the drainage water, difficulties with its disposal may not have been observed had the water not been retained and evaporated in the Kesterson Reservoir. As the water evaporates, the concentrations of the toxic elements increased to a level where they became potentially harmful to wildlife.

Since legal and political constraints are preventing Valley subsurface agricultural drainage water from flowing into Kesterson, and beyond to the Bay and ocean, farmers, local agencies and others, along with State and Federal agencies are investigating a variety of alternatives for its disposal. Containment in evaporation ponds is receiving close

WATER QUALITY SUMMARY

TABLE I

Parameter	Unit(ppm)	SAN LUIS DRAIN AT MENDOTA DWR & USBR Analyses Range		MURRIETA FARM Pilot Plant Site
Sodium as Na		2190	2700	1850
Potassium as K		7	10	9
Calcium as Ca		555	710	600
Magnesium as Mg		270	300	225
Akalinity as CaCo3		195	220	218
Sulphate as SO4		4650	5600	3250
Chloride as Cl		1550	2000	1800
Nitrate as NO3		48	60	109
Ammonia as N		.01	.06	.1
Silica as SiO2		37	42	40
TDS		9850	11600	7210
Suspended solids		10	20	
TOC		9.5	16	
COD		30	52	
BOD		3	5.8	
Boron		15	19	10.6
Selenium		.23	.35	.36
Strontium		6.4	7.2	5.7
Iron		.15	.5	.14
Aluminum		0	0	.1
Arsenic		0	0	.005
Cadmium		.001	.02	.013
Chromium (Total)		.02	.036	.06
Copper		.01	.02	.03
Lead		.001	.006	.14
Manganese		.01	.02	.02
Mercury		.0001	.0002	.0005
Nickel		.02	.06	.07
Silver		.001	.001	.02
Zinc		.01	.02	.03

Parameter	Unit			
Temperature	deg C.	18	29	
pH		8.2	8.7	7.36
Conductivity	Mmmho/cm	-	-	8600
Turbidity	F.T.U.			1.2

NOTES
1. Maximum values reported from 1981 to 1984
2. Data is averaged from figures given by the California Department of Water Resources and the USBR. Water samples drawn from the San Luis Drain at or near Bass Avenue, Mendota.

attention, but this results in the salts and toxic elements concentrating as the water evaporates. Specific elements such as selenium and other heavy metals concentrate and pose a threat to wildlife and other beneficial uses of the Valley water supply. Therefore, extensive and expensive measures appear to be necessary in order to manage the drainage water.

It is clear that if the drainage waters are pretreated to remove the toxic compounds, the resulting salty water could be more readily managed for disposal or reuse. The water could be placed in evaporation ponds which would not need to be designed or managed for handling potentially toxic liquids.

TREATMENT PROCESSES

Physical water treatment processes, such as desalination by reverse osmosis, have been tested as a method of separating the toxic elements from the water. However, these processes are expensive to purchase and operate because extensive pretreatment is necessary to render the drainage water suitable for desalination. Sulphate scaling and other fouling of the membranes must be avoided. A further disadvantage of these processes is that they produce a concentrated solution which is a concentrated admixture of all the contaminants (18).

Biological processes, however, can be used to remove the toxic elements sequentially thereby permitting their recovery as by-products, creating a viable treatment process for those waters. Any revenue from the sale of these elements would therefore help to defray the costs of treatment.

DESCRIPTION OF THE BIOLOGICAL TREATMENT PROCESS

Fig. 1 shows a schematic diagram of the treatment process installed at Murrieta Farms, on Westlands Water District near Mendota, California. Subsurface drainage water is pumped from the WWD collector drain sump (P1) to the biological reactor tanks (R1 and R2) through which the water passes in series. In these reactor tanks the dissolved inorganic selenate in the water is converted to an organo-selenium complex and is insolubilized so that, after being pumped (P3), it is filtered in the crossflow microfiltration unit (XF1). The selenium concentrate is collected and the water passing the crossflow microfiltration unit is pumped (P4) into the next Reactor (R3) which operates anaerobically to destroy the sulphates and to convert the heavy metals to insoluble sulphides for collection in the second crossflow filter (XF2).

The permeate from the crossflow filter (XF2) passes via the collection tank and pump (P6) moves the permeate to the Ion exchange unit for boron removal.

The pilot plant has shown that selenium can be reduced from a feed concentration of between 350 and 500 ppb (ug/l) to between 3 & 5 ppb (ug/l). Heavy metals such as molybdenum, chrome and cadmium have been shown to be reduced to a few ppb. Sulphates destroyed in reactor (R3) generate hydrogen sulphide gas which when passed into a photosynthetic

reactor (R4) can be converted to elemental sulphur (11). The pilot
plant has reached 33% sulphate removal and further work is in hand to
demonstrate that 70% removal should be possible.

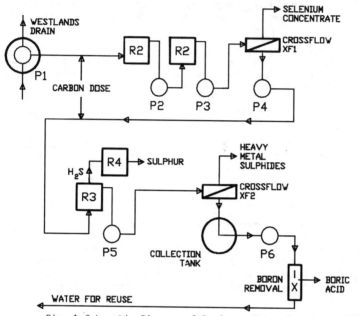

Fig. 1 Schematic Diagram of Drainage Water Treatment Plant

BY-PRODUCTS AND THEIR USES

(a) Sulphur. The drainage water generally contains about 5.8 tons of
sulphur per million gallons. (1.39 kgs/m3). At an overall conversion
efficiency and removal of sulphate at 70%, 4 tons (3.64 tonnes) of
elemental sulphur can potentially be produced per day for each mgd (3785
m3). The amount which could be produced from the 6.5 Mgd of drainage
water presently collected by the WWD collector drains amounts to 9,500
tons (8636 tonnes) sulphur per year. At least four times this amount of
sulphur could potentially be produced if WWD continued to install
drainage facilities.

Table II shows the amount of sulphur used in the San Joaquin Valley
and in the WWD as a dusting fungicide. (22) (3). It can be seen that a
ready market would exist at the present cost of sulphur at $140 per ton.
($154/tonne). The value of the sulphur recovered equates to $186 per
acre ft. (14.74¢/m3) of drainage water treated.

(b) Selenium. The selenium which is presently being recovered would
amount to 3.3 lbs per mgd (0.39 g/m3). This amounts to 3.95 tons (3.59
tonnes) selenium per year from the 6.5 mgd (24.6 Ml/d) currently

discharged by the WWD. The animal feed industry consumes sodium selenite or selenate in a concentration of 200 ppm mixed with a limestone base valued at 10 cts/lb or $200/t ($220/tonne) and higher quality selenium-methionine compounds are valued at $200,000 per ton ($220/tonne). (1) (15). Selenium is quoted at about $30/lb ($66/kg) giving a potential revenue of $33 per acre ft (2.61¢/m3).

(c) Boron. Boric acid is recovered as crystals which precipitate in the acid regeneration solution of the ion-exchange plant. About 8 ppm (mg/l) of boron is removed at about 72 tons per year (65.4 tonnes/yr) Boric acid is valued at about $1,000/ton ($1,100/tonne), thus the revenue from recovery of boron could approach $10/acre ft. (0.79¢/m3).

TABLE II

SULPHUR USE AND COST

Crop	Sulphur Use lbs/ac.	SAN JOAQUIN VALLEY * Use Ac.	t/yr.	Cost $mil./yr.	WESTLANDS WATER DISTRICT** Use Ac.	t/yr.	Cost $mil./yr.
Cotton	80	1436000	57440	8.04	297174	11887	1.66
Grapes	100	539000	26950	3.77	6767	338	0.05
Sugar Beets	60	105000	3150	0.44	5699	171	0.02
Tomatoes	30	98000	1470	0.20	57937	869	0.12
TOTALS		2178000	89010	12.45	367577	13265	1.85

Note: * San Joaquin Valley (3)
     ** Westlands Water District (22)

ECONOMICS

The overall capital and running costs of a drainage water treatment plant are estimated as follows, allowing capital charges at 5% interest over 20 years:

		$/ac. ft.	cts/m3
A.	Capital		
	Boron & Se removal	55	4.36
	SO4 removal	60	4.75
B.	Running costs		
	Boron & Se removal	44	3.49
	SO4 removal	40	3.17
	Subtotal	199	15.77
C.	Potential revenues		
	Sulphur	186	14.74
	Selenium	33	2.61
	Boron	10	0.79
	Profit	$30	2.37

CONCLUSION

Based on the data presented in this paper it appears that the treatment of subsurface agricultural drainage water in the San Joaquin Valley
of California may produce useful toxic elements.

Some aspects of the treatment proposals obviously require further
testing to confirm the results and estimates of by-product values.

However, the preliminary economic evaluations reveal that the
treatment of the drainage water could produce useful materials. Once
the toxic elements and the sulphates have been removed it is also
possible that the treated water could more readily be desalted using
reverse osmosis which would provide reusable water, or discharged safely
to either evaporation ponds or a saltwater sink.

APPENDIX 1 --- REFERENCES

1. Anderson, M. S., Lakin, H.W., Beeson, K. C., Smith, Floyd F., and
    Thaker, Edward, "Selenium in Agriculture," Agricultural Handbook,
    No. 200, U. S. Dept. of Agriculture.

2. Binnie & Partners, Executive Summary Report to Westlands Water
    District, Dec. 1985.

3. California Department of Water Resources, "Water Conservation in
    California," California Bulletin 198-84, July 1984.

4. California State Water Resources Control Board, "Plan for
    Assessing the Effects of Pollutants in the San Francisco Bay- Delta
    Estuary,"Publication No. 82-7SP, October 1982.

5. California State Water Resources Control Board. "Decision 85-1,"
    February 1985.

6. Daniel, Dick A., "San Joaquin Valley Drainage and Marsh Manage
    ment," Proceedings Irrigation and Drainage Specialty Conference,
    Amer. Soc. Civil Engineers, July 1984, Flagstaff Arizona, pp. 445-
    450.

7. Johns, Gerald E. "San Joaquin Valley Drainage Water Quality and
    Disposal," Proceedings Irrigation and Drainage Specialty
    Conference, Amer. Soc. Civil Engineers, July 1984, Flagstaff,
    Arizona, pp. 433-444.

8. Johnston, William R., Drainage Problems and the Proposed Solution
    for a Large Irrigated Area in the San Joaquin Valley of California
    USA), International Commission on Irrigation and Drainage, Seventh
    Congress, Apr. 1969, pp. 26.247-26.262.

9. Johnston, William R., Steinert, Byron C. and Stroh, Craig M.,
    "Benefits from the Drainage of Heavy Irrigated Soils," Proceedings
    Fourth National Drainage Symposium, American Society of Agricul-
    tural Engineers, Dec. 1982, pp. 171-177.

10. Jones and Stokes, "An Evaluation of the Feasibility of Utilizing Agricultural Tile Drainage Water for Marsh Management in the San Joaquin Valley, California," for the U.S. Fish and Wildlife Service and U.S. Bureau of Reclamation by Jones and Stokes Associates, Inc., 1977.

11. Maree, J. P., and Strydon, Wilma F., "Biological Sulphate Removal in an Upflow Packed Bed Reactor," Water Res., Vol. 19, No. 9, 1985.

12. McKevitt, Jim, U. S. Fish & Wildlife Service Memorandum, Sacramento, CA, Dec. 23, 1982.

13. Meixner, G. Donald, "Status of San Joaquin Valley Drainage Problems," California Department of Water Resources, Bul. 127-74. Dec. 1974, pp. 66.

14. Nelson, Daniel G., Johnston, William R., "San Joaquin Valley Drainage - Development and Impact," Proceedings Irrigation and Drainage Specialty Conference, Amer. Soc. of Civil Engineers, July 1984, pp. 424-432.

15. Private communications with various animal feed compounders.

16. Swain, Donald G. "San Joaquin Valley Drainage - A Permanent Solution," Proceedings Irrigation and Drainage Specialty Conference, Amer. Soc. Civil Engineers, July 1984, Flagstaff, Arizona, pp. 451-461.

17. U. S. Bureau of Reclamation, California Department of Water Resources, and California State Water Resources Control Board,"Agricultural Drainage and Salt Management in the San Joaquin Valley. Final Report of the San Joaquin Valley Interagency Drainage Program, June 1979, pp. 162.

18. U. S. Bureau of Reclamation, "Reverse Osmosis, Desalting of the San Luis Drain - Conceptual Level Study," Sept. 1985.

19. U.S. Congress, "San Luis Unit Authorization Act," PL 86-188, 74 Stat. 156, June 1960.

20. U. S. Dept. of Interior, Bureau of Reclamation, "San Luis Unit," Feasibility Report, May 1955, pp. 156.

21. U. S. Dept. of Interior, Federal Water Pollution Control Administration,"Effects of the San Joaquin Master Drain on Water Quality of the San Francisco Bay and Delta," Central Pacific Basins Comprehensive Water Pollution Control Project Report, Jan. 1967, pp. 101.

22. Westlands Water District, Facts and Figures, 1985.

A GIS to Predict Non-Point Source Pollution Potential

Wanada Baxter-Potter*, associate member ASCE
Martha W. Gilliland*, member ASCE
Michael P. Peterson**

Abstract

The non-point pollution potential of agricultural lands was analyzed using a geographic, computer based system. Bacterial pollution received special emphasis. The system accepts digitally mapped information on soil type, topography, and land use; calculates characteristics such as slope, and slope length; and relates these characteristics to soils and land use parameters in order to produce three dimensional maps of runoff potential, sediment pollution potential, and bacterial pollution potential. While validation in other river basins is needed, the system can improve our ability to allocate resources for non-point source pollution control more efficiently. It can also promote better communication between researchers and decision makers.

Introduction

Non-point sources are now the major sources of criteria pollutants in surface waters. Gianessi and Peskin (1981) have pointed out that non-point sources contribute significant percentages of such pollutants as BOD (57%), nutrients (87% of phosphorus and 88% of nitrogen), total suspended solids (98%), and bacteria, and that sediment and sediment-attached pollutants have been recognized in particular as "...the most widespread source of pollutants discharged into the nations's surface waters." Agricultural sources, particularly cropland, pastureland, and rangeland, produce almost 64% of the sediment discharged to surface waters (Gianessi and Peskin, 1981). In Nebraska, the most prominent pollutant which precludes the attainment of "swimmable-fishable" national water quality goals, as set forth in the 1977 Clean Water Act, is coliform bacteria (Nebraska Department of Environmental Control, 1982).

Non-point source pollution from agricultural sources originates on the land, and different parcels of land exhibit different potentials for pollution production. Non-point source pollution potential is typically a function of the use and management of land by people, of the physical properties of the land, and of the hydrologic and meteor-ologic properties of the area. Non-point source pollution models typically represent these factors with several parameters, most of which are geographic in character. Yet, during modeling, that geographic character is frequently lost. For example, soil character-istics, topographic parameters, vegetative cover, and information on erosion control practice are often taken from maps, aerial photos, and/or satelite data. In the process of transferring such information into a mathematical model, the geographic character is stripped from the information.

*Department of Civil Engineering, University of Nebraska-Lincoln, Omaha, Nebraska 68182 **Department of Geography-Geology, University of Nebraska-Omaha, Omaha, Nebraska 68182

The goal of this study was to develop a geographically based tool
for analyzing and communicating non-point source pollution potential,
with special emphasis on bacterial pollution. Such a tool would allow
the geographic character of information to be retained, could deal with
diverse parcels of land, and would be responsive to the bacterial
pollution problem in Nebraska.

The geographic information system (GIS) model developed utilizes a
raster format and is somewhat unique in that it is modular, transportable, and expandable. For each cell, a set of parameter values are
input and manipulated according to three equations that deal with
distinct aspects of non-point source pollution. The output is
three-dimensional maps runoff and pollution potential useful for
analysis, communication, and planning.

The study area is located in eastern Nebraska in the lower Elkhorn
River Basin. Fecal coliform (FC) bacteria standards are violated
regularly in this river. Possible sources of the bacteria are
municipal sewage treatment plants, feedlots, and grazing livestock.
Feedlots number in the thousands in the Basin, and livestock grazing is
extensive and commonly associated with small streams. Three small
watersheds within the 2.59 km^2 (one square mile) study area were
studied. Each represented a distinct land use: a large feedlot, a
pasture, and a corn field.

Methods

This section describes the GIS used, the three accepted predicitive formulae used and their implementation in the GIS, the data base
developed, and calibration procedures used.

The GIS used in this study was the Raster Geographic Information
System for Mapping (RGISM) developed in the Remote Sensing Applications
Laboratory at the University of Nebraska at Omaha. In developing the
design philosophy for RGISM, Peterson and Long (1984) identified three
goals; the system was to be: (1) modular rather than monolithic, (2)
transportable, and (3) flexible and expandable. These goals led to a
unique system design that utilizes the standard operating system file
structure of the host processor rather than an internal filing system.
A significant amount of programming, common in more monolithic GIS's,
is eliminated. RGISM is organized as a family of free standing program
modules written in standard Fortran 77. Each module performs a
specific process on, or manipulation of, data files. This approach is
distinctly different from the conventional organization of monolithic
GIS's which compile all manipulation programming in one large program.
The module approach eliminates the necessity of loading unused programming into the host processor's core memory and in general makes more
efficient use of system resources. Other GIS's may use a chained
modular approach, but often they rely on non-standard programming and
so are very system specific; they are not transportable. RGISM
requires only that the host processor be equipped with a Fortran 77
compiler and virtual memory.

To meet the goal of flexibility and expandability, user specified
operations were added to the list of available map manipulations. To
add an operation to RGISM the user need only write a program module to
perform that operation. Due to the free-standing structure of RGISM,
editing and debugging a monolithic master GIS program is not required
in order to incorporate the new operation. To aid the user in the

development of a new program module, a library of subroutines and
functions has been developed. Most of these library operations are I/O
operations. However, there are also library operations which read and
display comments from input files, and insert comments into output
files. These library functions can be called by the user from within
the new program module. The only programming burden which is left to
the user is the Fortran description of the new manipulation to be
performed, frequently less than ten lines of programming.

Three accepted predictive formulae were implemented as RGISM
program modules: (1) the Soil Conservation Service Curve Number
technique (SCSCN) for the prediction of potential runoff; (2) the
Universal Soil Loss Equation for the prediction of potential erosion;
and (3) a simple loading function for the prediction of bacterial
densities in runoff.

Application of the SCSCN technique requires the assessment of:
(1) antecedent soil moisture conditions; (2) soil hydrologic type; and
(3) land use and treatment class. Both hydrologic soil type, and land
use and treatment class are geographic in nature and may vary spatially
within a small watershed.

RUNOFF is the module implementing the SCSCN technique. The module
prompts the user to enter the 24-hour precipitation. Then, on a cell
by cell basis, the module (1) consults the soils map and interprets
hydrologic soil group, (2) consults the land use map and interprets
land use and treatment class, (3) calculates the runoff potential for
that cell, and (4) stores the predicted runoff potential in the
appropriate location in an output map file. The consult/calculate
process is repeated for each cell until the runoff potential map is
complete. Output is a map of storm runoff potential.

The Universal Soil Loss Equation is an empirical equation designed
to compute long time average soil losses due to sheet and rill erosion.
The equation ignores sediment yields from gully, streambank, or streambed erosion. Erosion losses are expressed as the product of five
factors. The factors are: (1) rainfall erosive potential, (2) soil
erodibility, (3) a terrain factor which considers slope length and
steepness, (4) a cover and management factor, and (5) a support or
erosion control practice factor. With the exception of the rainfall
factor all of these may vary spatially within a small watershed and are
geographic in nature.

USLE is the module implementing the Universal Soil Loss Equation
to predict erosion potential. This module also prompts the user to
enter the 24-hour precipitation. The rainfall erosive potential factor
is calculated from daily precipitation. Then, on a cell by cell basis
the module executes the following five steps. (1) It consults a slope
map and a slope length map and calculates the terrain factor. The
slope and slope length maps must have been created earlier using a
RGISM program module called SLOPE. (2) The module consults the soils
map and assigns a soil erodibility factor based on soil type. (3) The
land use map is consulted and a cover factor is assigned. (4) A
practice factor is assigned on the basis of land use class and slope.
Finally, (5) the predicted erosion potential is stored in the
appropriate location in an output map file. This consult/calculate
process is repeated for each cell until the erosion potential map is
complete. Output is a map of erosion potential.

Certain bacteria have been identified as indicator organisms for
assessing the of probability fecal contamination in surface waters.

Total coliform (TC) concentrations in the Elkhorn River are commonly over 100,000 organisms/100 ml, well in excess of water quality criteria. Stocking rates, age and type of fecal deposits, antecedent conditions, temperature, season, and rainfall intensity are some of the factors which affect bacterial densities in runoff. The relationships of these factors to bacterial densities are not well defined and are not quantified in a predicitive fashion. McElroy (1976) has suggested that bacterial densities in runoff from feedlots might be approximated with typical density values from the literature. This approach, used here, is clearly a simplication since it ignores factors (other than land use) that can cause extreme variations in bacterial density.

GERMS is the module that predicts bacterial densities in runoff. This module simply consults the land use map and, on a cell by cell basis, assigns a typical TC and FC density for each land use class. Two potential bacterial density maps are produced, one for TC densities and one for FC densities.

The data base for this analysis consists of four maps: a land use map, a soils map, an elevation map, and a base map. The land use map was compiled from aerial photographs and field scouted information. The soils map is a digitized version of the SCS Soil Survey map. The digital elevation model was produced using the ELEVMOD program to interpret a compilation of: contour information from a US Geological Survey 7.5' quadrangle, additional estimated elevation data obtained from field observation, and surveyed elevation data for critical areas. The base map is an outline of the 2.59 km^2 study area and contains locations of match points used to align and rescale other digitized maps before converting them to raster format.

All three of the predictive equations utilized contain some type of land use related factor. However, implementation of each of the predictive equations requires a slightly different land use classification system. In order to avoid the necessity of compiling and digitizing three separate land use maps, a full purpose land use classification system was devised; the SCSCN "cover" classes (U.S. Soil Conservation Service, 1972) were harmonized with Universal Soil Loss Equation classes (Wischmeier and Smith, 1978 and Novotny and Chesters, 1981) and with land use distinctions which affect bacterial densities in runoff. The final full purpose classification system contained 46 land use classes.

A similar approach was used for inputing soils information related to soils characteristics. A single soils map is consulted by both the RUNOFF program module and the USLE program module. In the case of both the data base land use map and the data base soils map, the basic map necessarily contains more information and detail than any one of the program modules might require.

In order to provide some calibration, field data were gathered during one spring and fall season. Runoff samples were collected from each of the three distinct agricultural land uses found in the study area. These samples were analyzed for bacterial densities and for suspended solids. The bacterial density data were used to supplement typical density data from the literature and to confirm the applicability of data from the literature to other settings. The suspended solids data were used to calibrate the model. Calibration was based on the assumption that the measured suspended solids concentration in runoff from a watershed should equal the total predicted erosion from that watershed divided by the total predicted runoff volume. In order to calculate total predicted runoff and erosion, the boundries of the small watersheds from which field samples were taken were mapped and digitized. Then a program module was developed which consults the watershed map, the runoff potential map and the erosion potential map to calculate total runoff volume, total erosion, and predicted suspended solids concentrations for each watershed. These predicted concentrations were then compared with measured concentrations for these watersheds.

Results

The study area, with land uses and sampling sites noted, is shown in Fig. 1. Within the 2.59 km^2 area, three types of land use predominate. A large feedlot (capacity 13,000 head) occupies most of the northeast quadrant; the southeast corner is occupied by a seasonally grazed pasture; and most of the remaining land (shaded area) is used for corn production. Figs. 2 and 3 are examples of the three-dimensional output from the GIS. They are oriented as though viewed from the southwest. The feedlot is in the uppermost (northeast) corner and the pasture is in the lower front (southwest) corner.

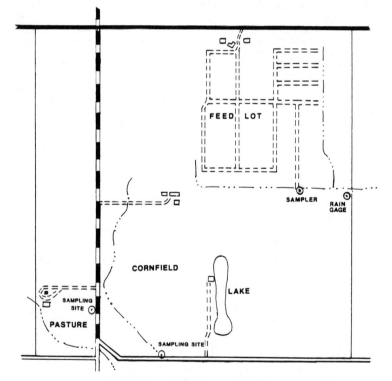

Figure 1. Study Area Site Map

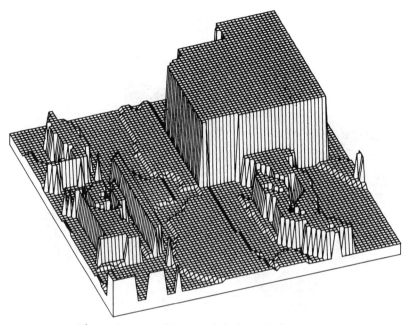

Figure 2. Runoff Potential for a 1.4 cm Storm
(maximum Runoff = 0.58 cm)

Fig. 2 is a three-dimensional representation of runoff potential
within the study area when subjected to 1.37 cm (0.55 in.) of precipitation in a 24 hour period. Runoff potential ranges from 0.57 cm (0.23
in.) from the feedlot to 0.0 cm. The variation of runoff potential
within the corn field reflects the effect of soil type on runoff
potential. The more highly permeable soils in the southeastern
extremes of the corn field yield less runoff than the less permeable
soils which flank the lake and adjoin the western boundry of the
feedlot. Within the pasture soil type variations are overshadowed by
land use; runoff potential is uniform.
    Fig. 3 is a three-dimensional representation of erosion potential
within the study area when subjected to a 3.29 cm storm. The influence
of several factors in USLE is evident. First, erosion from the feedlot
is virtually zero. This primarily reflects the low erodibility factor
associated with feedlots. Since the erodibility factor for feedlots

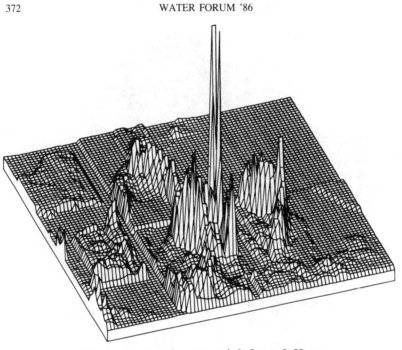

Figure 3.   Erosion Potential for a 3.29 cm
Storm (Maximum Erosion = 7.79 mt/ha)

is assigned on the basis of land use rather than soil type, no soil
type patterns are reflected in the feedlot erosion potential. Second,
land use distinctions (which are reflected in the cover and management
factor) are evident, particularly in the SW 1/4 of the SW 1/4 of the
study area where the erosion potential for the pasture is distinctly
lower than that for the surrounding areas. Roads are also clearly
discernible because of their low erosion potential. The low cover and
management factors for the pasture and paved roads dominate the USLE
equation, minimizing the effects of soil type and topography. Third,
in the corn fields the interplay of the soil erodibility and the
terrain factors is apparent. For example, in the E 1/2 of the SE 1/4 a
swath of loamy fine sands is distinct from its neighboring soils (silt
loams and fine sandy loams) due to its lower erodibility. But elsewhere in the corn fields the most striking influence is that of the
terrain factor. The steep slopes surrounding the lake reflect the
highest erosion potential in the study area.

     These three dimensional maps are useful tools for analysis,
planning, and particularly for communication. For example, the results
of a proposed pollution mitigation measure can be "viewed" before it is
implemented. Similarly, a land owner can examine a picture (literally)
of the relative significance of the non-point source pollution that
might arise from different parcels of his/her land.

Appendix: References

Gianessi, L.P., Peskin, H.M., and Young, G.K., 1981, Analysis of
    National Water Pollution Control Policies, part 1: A National
    Network Model: Water Resources Research, v.17, no.4, 7 p.
McElroy, A.D., ed. 1976, Loading Functions for Assessment of Water
    Pollution from Non-Point Sources: Environmental Protection Agency,
    Office of Research and Development, Washington, D.C.,
    (EPA/600/2-76/151), 444 p. (Su. Doc. No. EP 1.23/2:600/2-76-151)
Nebraska Dept. of Environmental Control, 1982, 1982 Nebraska Water
    Quality Report: Department of Environmental Control, Lincoln,
    Nebraska.
Novotny, P.E., and Chesters, G., 1981, Handbook of Nonpoint Pollution:
    Sources and Management: Van Nostrand Reinhold Co., New York,
    555 p.
Peterson, M.P., and Long, M.D., 1984, personal communication, Asst.
    Professor and RSAL Computer Co-ordinator (respectively), Dept. of
    Geography-Geology, University of Nebraska-Omaha, Omaha, Nebraska.
U.S. Soil Conservation Service, 1972, SCS National Engineering
    Handbook, Sec. 4, Hydrology, 548 p. (Su. Doc. No. A57.6/2: En
    3/sec. 4/rev. 2)
Wischmeier, W.H., and Smith, D.D., 1978, Predicting Rainfall Erosion
    Losses - A Guide to Conservation Planning: U.S. Dept. of
    Agriculture, Agricultural Handbook No. 537, 58 p. (Su. Doc. No.
    Al.76:537)

Acknowledgments

Some of this work was funded through a grant from the Jane Layman
Fund of the University of Nebraska-Lincoln. RGISM was developed at the
Remote Sensing Applications Laboratory at the University of Nebraska-
Omaha.

DESIGN FOR COMPUTER-AIDED WATER RESOURCE PLANNING

Bruce M. Chow[1] , Sam C. White[2] , and Gary P. Rabalais[3]

INTRODUCTION

This paper discusses an integrated approach to computerizing the major functions of regulatory agencies involved in water resource planning and water quality protection. This integrated approach consists of studying the individual agency responsibilities to understand how they fit together as a system. Likewise, it relies on the various software packages being able to work together as a unit. This paper is based on an actual project with the Department of Environmental Quality (DEQ) of the State of Louisiana.

FUNCTIONS AND PROJECT GOALS

Water resources planning and water quality protection responsibilities fall into three general categories:

1. Administering and allocating grant money for water resources projects (waste treatment plants, dams, waterway maintenance, etc.)

2. Maintaining waste discharge permits

3. Monitoring water quality for planning, reporting, and standards enforcement

With the purchase of a Digital Equipment Corporation (DEC) VAX 11/780 and 11/750, DEQ sought to computerize the record keeping and reporting functions of the above responsibilities. The computer system would serve to streamline access to and use of the information previously stored on paper records.

The specific goals for the computerization project emphasized the concept of integration where independent and separate pieces of the system could work together as a unit. This concept applied to both the database structure and the related software. Integration provided a more cost-effective approach by minimizing the total amount of custom

---

1   Supervising Engineer, James M. Montgomery, Consulting Engineers, Inc., P.O. Box 7009, Pasadena, CA 91109-7009.
2   Project Manager/Senior Engineer, CRS Sirrine, 216 South Pleasantburge Dr, Greenville, South Carolina 29606.
3   Engineer, James M. Montgomery, Consulting Engineers, Inc., 3200 Ridgelake Drive, Suite 400, Metaire, LA 70002.

software that had to be developed.   Therefore, the integration
objective translated to following goals:

1. All databases must work together.

2. Use existing software wherever possible.

3. Take advantage of software layering (built-in interaction
    between software products).

IMPLEMENTING INTEGRATION GOALS

Implementing an integrated system requires understanding both the
individual parts of the system as well as how they must work together.
This applies to database structure as well as software design.
Database integration provides a stategic balance between using highly
specialized and disjointed databases and trying to contain all possible
information in a single but inefficient database. In contrast, in an
integrated system, individual databases with specific functions are
kept separate, yet a means to make the databases work together, when
necessary, is provided.   Finding this means to link the databases
requires a full understanding of how information from each database
would be used. Therefore, it was necessary to take time early in the
project to study the uses for each of the potential databases.

Software design and construction also embraced the integration concept.
Both the use of existing software wherever possible and taking
advantage of software layering are means to make a system of software
packages work together.   They also minimize the cost of the project
since customization can require large amounts of time devoted to design
and debugging. Making the software work together required a thorough
understanding of how the DEQ existing software and the DEC packaged
software worked both individually and together.

The Systems Approach to Databases

One must understand how all of the individual parts of the system will
work in order to make them work together as an integrated system. With
DEQ, an initial requirements study identified four separate database
categories:

o   Water quality monitoring data

o   Discharge permits

o   Construction grants data

o   Stream segment prioritization

Water quality data resulted from routine monitoring and special
sampling programs.   This data was used for studying water quality
trends and for determining whether water quality in a given stream
segment was meeting goals for designated water resource use (recreation
-- no body contact, recreation -- body contact, etc.).   Stream segments
are geographic areas analogous to either watersheds or water districts.

A map of the 130 stream segments in the state of Louisiana is shown in
Figure 1. Water quality data had the unique characteristics of
requiring the flexibility to add new types of water quality analyses
and new sampling locations as they become available. In addition to
DEQ's need to interpret their water quality data, results of the
routine water quality monitoring in these stream segments were also
submitted to the EPA STORET system, a database for water quality data
collected nationwide. Therefore, the database software had to provide
a means to submit data electronically to the STORET system in a
compatible format.

Discharge permits embodied three related activities. The first was
keeping records on the location, address, telephone, and person to
contact at a facility discharging into any given water body in the
state. The second activity was keeping a list of permitted discharge
(pounds BOD or COD per day, temperature limits, etc.) for each
facility. Finally, the third was to calculate the annual permit fee
and to print a letter to the facility notifying them that the fee was
due. For efficient data storage, the discharger information and the
allowable discharges were kept in separate databases. The permit fees
database was also kept separate because access to it would be different
than to the other two databases.

The construction grants database was used to set a priority for funding
construction projects such as wastewater treatment plants. Project
priorities were determined by severity of need, potential benefits, and
number of people affected.

Whereas the construction grants database focused on individual
projects, the stream segments prioritization database focused on an
entire stream segment (or region). The stream segments prioritization
database provided a means to rationally determine which stream segments
were most in need of attention for planning potential water quality
improvement projects. The calculation was based on numerous indices
calculated from water quality data. The indices can be thought of as
analogous to the familiar Langelier Index which uses pH, temperature,
total dissolved solids, alkalinity, and calcuim concentration to arrive
at a single number indicative of calcium carbonate saturation. The
indices provided a way to account for many water quality parameters,
essentially assigning them a relative importance. The system for
calculating the indices had already been programmed on the PDP-11, but
in order to adapt it to the new database system, it had to be re-
written to allow greater flexibility in the types of mathematical
functions used and to provide an easier method to document the formulas
used.

The common element in each of the individual databases was that they
all referred to stream segments. Water quality data was taken at
specific sampling points within a given stream segment. Dischargers
were located by stream segment in addition to their street address.
Water reclamation projects were located by stream segment and the need
for them was partially determined by the water quality in the stream
segment. Finally, the water quality indices were designed for use with
stream segments. Therefore, it became apparent in the conceptual
design portion of the project that all of the databases could be linked
through a common field containing the stream segment number as
diagrammed in Figure 2. In addition, the stream segment link provided

FIGURE 1

LOUISIANA STREAM SEGMENTS

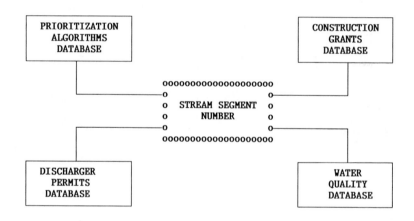

FIGURE 2.

DATABASE CONFIGURATION

a means to add databases in future software projects which could use
the same basic software.

Using Existing Software

A large amount of useful existing software consisted of subroutines
written in Fortran on a DEQ-owned PDP-11 computer running a Cal-Comp
plotter. The subroutines were built to draw a map of the previous 115
stream segments and color code them based on the value of the
particular water quality index in question. Because DEC software has a
good reputation for being upwardly compatible (that is, software built
for the PDP-11 should run on a VAX with minimal changes), the most
cost-effective approach was to adapt existing software to the new
database system. Fortunately, this consisted of two simple tasks:

o   Formatting the necessary input files

o   Revising array sizes for 130 stream segments in place of 115

The existing plotting software required a formatted input file
specifying each stream segment and the water quality index value for
it. This file could be created within Datatrieve (the database query
language chosen for the project) using new software and passed to the
existing plotting software. The map coordinates defining the new 130
stream segments were digitized by a subcontractor and loaded into two
other input files used by the plotting software. Adjusting the array
sizes required minimal effort.

The Layered Software Approach

The database system built for DEQ required the following capabilities:

o   File management

o   Data access (search, sort, print, graph)

o   Screen formatting

o   Computations and data manipulations

File management is the basic undergirding for the entire database
system. In brief, it provides the basic record access, file
management, and key structuring utilities necessary for the database.
The Record Management Services (RMS) software, which was associated
with the Virtual Memory System (VMS) operating system, provided these
utilities. RMS also serves to standardize these processes so that all
DEC software can access the same files.

Data access required that the users need only tell the computer what
they wanted while the software determined how to get it. The

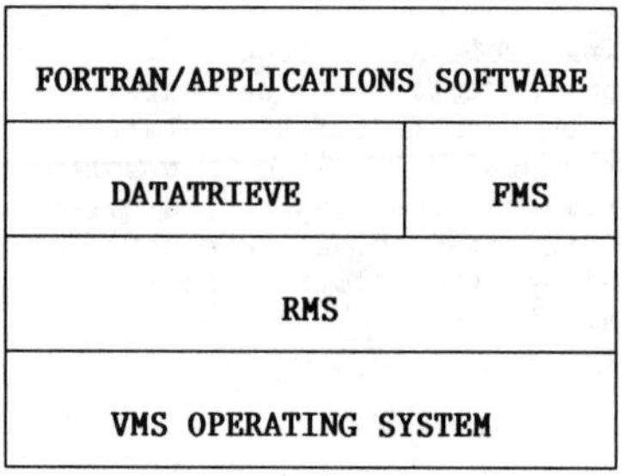

FORTRAN/APPLICATIONS SOFTWARE	
DATATRIEVE	FMS
RMS	
VMS OPERATING SYSTEM	

FIGURE 3.

SOFTWARE LAYERING

Datatrieve software package was used for that purpose. A typical command would be

FIND GROUP IN RESULTS WITH DATE BETWEEN "1-JAN-1983" AND "30-DEC-1983"

where "GROUP" is a temporary subset of data called up for use from the database called "RESULTS". Notice that the user does not have to understand the mechanics behind retrieving data from a file on harddisk. Likewise sorting is as follows:

SORT GROUP BY ASCENDING VALUE

Again, the user does not need to know the complex algorithms for sorting data. He simply commands that it be done. The same applies to printing and plotting data.

Complex calculations or data formatting (e.g. for sending data to STORET) are not possible with standard Datatrieve, but they are possible with Fortran. Example calculations were those used to compute the various water quality indices used in the stream segment prioritization process. Single calculations often required data from many records at once. In addition, they sometimes included Boolian equations (IF-THEN-ELSE decisions) in addition to arithmetic formulas. Datatrieve was good at finding the necessary records, but had difficulty placing all of the retrieved data together into a single equation. Therefore, the Datatrieve Call Interface was used which allowed programmers to write Fortran routines which issued commands to Datatrieve or which could take over processing when it came time to run the calculations or special data formatting.

Screen formatting provided a means to set up terminal screens so that they resembled a paper data sheet. They were also used to build options menus for the calculations and Calcomp plotting subroutines. The DEC software package used for these purposes was FMS.

The result of using the layered approach, illustrated in Figure 3, was a customized software package which combined the functionalities and advantages of each individual software products and minimized the individual weaknesses. For this project users and programmers linked screen formatting software to Datatrieve and controlled Datatrieve from a fortran program. Fortran provided the overall program control, Calcomp plotting subroutines, and calculation capabilities; Datatrieve provided data query and screen plotting; FMS provided formatted screens for data entry and menus.

CONCLUSION

Integration concepts apply to both database structure and software development. Implementation requires a time investment into studying how the databases will be used and how the software could be used to take advantage of their individual strengths yet cause them to work together. However, the resulting database system is well worth the time spent.

Co-ordinated Microcomputer-Based Rain Data Network and Modelling Environment

Mark Stirrup and William James, Member ASCE*

A co-ordinated microcomputer controlled rainfall collection network has been designed which includes drop counting precipitation sensors, tipping bucket raingauges, Z80-A microprocessor based data loggers which communicate with 16-bit 8086 based microcomputers, and data base management software for archiving data.

The data collection instrumentation and the data base software were developed at McMaster University. Various versions of the data aquisition system (DAS) exist. The latest version is based on the Timex/Sinclair 1000 (TS1000) microcomputer. It also contains the capability of controlling diversion structures in combined sewer networks.

All data loggers can be connected to drop counting precipitation sensors or standard tipping bucket raingauges. The Timex/Sinclair based system has two channels so both can be connected. The drop counters were designed to provide increased resolution over that of the tipping buckets. A drop has a volume of approximately 0.05 ml while a tip usually measures about 10 ml.

Data is stored on audio cassette tapes in the field. The data can be transmitted to IBM-PC compatible microcomputers through their serial ports and archived in a central data base by a time series manager. The data is then easily retrievable for computer modelling. The U.S.EPA's Stormwater Management Model Version III (SWMM3) has been adapted to run on IBM-PC compatibles. The program PCSWMM3 was adapted to exploit this data environment.

Data Acquisition System

A complete package was recently developed at McMaster University by Haro (1984), for sensing rainfall intensity at a fine time and space resolution. It comprises a drop counter precipitation sensor, (DCPS) a microcomputer based data acquisition system (DAS), and an intelligent data decoder.

Two models were designed for use with the DCPS : the first is a high-power version (HPDAS) which uses stand-by batteries, powered by a 110 volt source; the second is a low-power model (LPDAS), based on CMOS components, that runs solely by 9 volt batteries. These DAS can be modified to collect information from other sensors, such as tipping bucket raingauges, wet/dry precipitation collectors, etc.

*Computational Hydraulics Group, McMaster University, Hamilton, Ontario.

The DAS units count the number of drops collected by the DCPS over a programmable time interval, usually one minute, process the time series and store them on audio cassette magnetic tape. The cassettes are removed and transported to a central site for processing.

TS1000-Based Data Acquisition System

A low-cost DAS has been developed based on the Timex/Sinclair 1000 microcomputer. This system was developed as part of another study which investigated the feasibility of implementing local real-time operation of a combined sewer overflow regulator, using inexpensive 8-bit microcomputers (Stirrup, 1986). A brief overview of this system is included in this paper. A complete description is included in the original thesis.

The TS1000 microcomputer features a Z80-A microprocessor supplied with Sinclair BASIC in 8k ROM and 2k RAM, expandable to 64k RAM. Interfacing the external world with the TS1000 is a straight forward task; peripherals simply fit over the card via the edge connector. A circuit published recently (Anon., 1983) was modified by the present authors to meet the needs of a DAS. The input/output (I/O) interface handles all incoming rainfall data. Two channels are provided for rain data input: one for high resolution DCPS data and the other for lower resolution data from a tipping bucket raingauge (TBRG). The TS1000 and input/output (I/O) interface (which together are called the TSDAS) perform the task of data acquisition, while the TS1000 and an RS-232 interface serve as a data decoder. The board was wirewrapped by the writers and enclosed in a black plastic case, approximately 7.5 x 1.5 x 4.5 inches. The unit weighs about 12 ounces.

Drop Counter Precipitation Sensors

During rainfall, the DCPS collects rain water in a funnel which channels it through a stainless steel tube. The water is released from the tube in the form of drops, which are of almost constant volume. The falling drops close an electric circuit resulting in the drops being counted. Given the drop volume and the number of drops counted during a certain time interval, the rate of rainfall can be determined. A complete description of the sensor can be found in the PhD thesis by Haro (1984). Technical details for the DCPS are:

Collection area:	9998.03 sq. mm
Mean drop size:	0.0047 mm of rain
Maximum rainfall rate:	approx. 150 mm/hr
Water retention (from dry state):	0.05 mm of rain
Sensor dimensions: Height:	375.00 mm
Inside diam.:	112.83 mm

Limitations of the DCPS are as follows:

1) Formed drops are of almost constant size (0.047 ml) at low rainfall rates. However, recent tests have shown that at higher intensities, drop volumes decrease to a minimum (0.029 ml) just before the streaming point (Stirrup and James, 1985). At low rates drop size may be assumed constant without losing much

accuracy. However, at high rates a calibration curve which
relates drop volume to rainfall rate must be constructed from a
series of DCPS tests.

2) For very high intensity rainfall the flow changes from drops to
    a continuous jet.   Tests show that, for the tube provided,
    continuous jet flow commences only well above 150 mm. of rain
    per hour, which is a rare event. Jet flow, when it does occur,
    usually lasts only one or two minutes. During this short period
    no drops are counted, creating a shortfall in the computed
    rainfall total. Some simple guidelines have been developed to
    allocate these shortfalls to individual events.

3) When the sensor is operated from the dry state, some water must
    be collected before water will pass through the stainless steel
    tube. Also, once the sensor is wet, some water must build up at
    the top of the tube to overcome the surface tension and then
    pass through the tube.   The amount of water required from the
    dry state is approximately 0.05 mm of rain and the amount
    required to overcome the surface tension is approximately 0.01
    mm of rain.   These amounts are considered negligible in most
    measurements,   but   may cause some analytical problems in
    disciplines other than Civil Engineering Flood Hydrology.

4) The stainless steel tube may be blocked by foreign particles.
    Regular maintenance will help to eliminate such occurrences.

5) The tube may also be blocked by air bubbles which form above the
    inlet. This increases the amount of rain needed to overcome the
    surface tension above the tube. The amount varies with the size
    and position of the bubble.   This problem generally occurs at
    the beginning of a storm after long dry periods. A breather
    aperture was added to the fine mesh screen, above the drop tube,
    to remove these bubbles.

We found that TBRG still provided useful information for the larger
storms, i.e. those above the DCPS streaming rate, but the higher
resolution data provided by the DCPS was more desirable where attainable.
The difference in the resolution of the two gauges is illustrated by
Figure 1. The figure shows two hyetographs, one each for a DCPS and TBRG,
at a one-minute timestep. The storm was recorded by a DCPS with a drop
volume of 0.05 ml (or 0.005 mm of rain). The same event, recorded by a
TBRG with a bucket volume of 10 ml (or 0.2 mm of rain) would appear as
shown in Figure 1. Note how the poorer resolution of the TBRG affects the
shape of the hyetograph, especially at lower rainfall rates.

Data Acquisition Software

The software which controls the operation of the DAS units is written in
assembly language.   Operation of the TSDAS is handled in BASIC for
simplicity, but could also be acheived using a Z80-A machine code
program. This paper concentrates on the TS1000 based system.   The
controlling software package (TSDASUTIL) is menu-driven and includes the
following attributes:

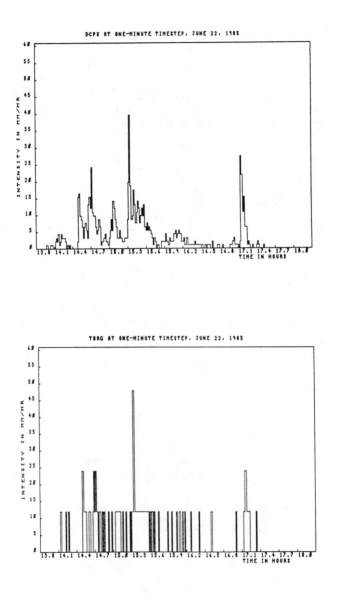

Figure 1: Rainfall Hyetographs from DCPS and TBRG

1) collects rainfall data,
2) saves program and data,
3) retrieves and/or plots data,
4) updates data base through a communications link.

Generally, the 16k RAMpack will log more than one month of rainfall data. Since only non-zero values are stored, the amount of memory used will depend on how wet the collection period is. A 64k RAMpack lengthens the collection period. The TS1000 uses mains power. The I/O interface is powered by the 9 volt supply on the TS1000 and thus needs no external power. The 64k RAMpack which we chose for our system also provides six hours of battery backup in case of mains power outages. During each site visit, the program and collected data should be saved on cassette tape for later processing at the central site. Once the program is interrupted by the proper command, it will automatically be saved by TSDASUTIL. The tape can be removed for decoding and data processing at the central site while the program continues to run at the diversion structure. The program/data tape is not needed to run the program since TSDASUTIL resides in RAM after LOADing. A blank tape is brought to the site when data is retrieved. A monitor and recorder are taken into the field and connected to the TS1000. They should thus be battery operated and easily portable.

In order to process and plot the collected information, TSDASUTIL and the data stored within it must be reloaded onto a TS1000, usually at the central site. This TS1000 should have at least 16k of RAM. The rainfall record is reconstructed as a time series of drop (or tip) count/time pairs, ready for processing by the plotting or data communication routines. Simple processing of the data may also be carried out in the field, and plots may be obtained. Included in TSDASUTIL is a low resolution graphics routine for the presentation of rainfall hyetographs on a television screen and/or TS2040 parallel printer.

Data Transmittal

The TS1000 is not suitable for storing large quantities of time series data. Long time series can be more readily stored on a more powerful 16-bit microcomputer, preferably with a hard disk, and operating with the use of some type of data base management system (DBMS). The data is then easily accessible to anyone for any number of applications, including data processing, high resolution graphics, report generation, and hydrologic modelling.

Data collected by the DAS and TSDAS is stored on audio cassette tapes in the field. The data is then transferred to IBM-PC compatible microcomputers through their serial ports.

Tapes from the DAS are played through a microcomputer-based data decoder (DD), which reads the data from the tape, verifies it, and communicates the rainfall time series to the microcomputer for further processing. The DD software is written in assembly language.

Software written in BASIC is included in TSDASUTIL which communicates the collected data to the host computer (IBM-PC compatible) via an RS-232 serial interface. The RS-232 interface transmits data at

600 baud to the host, however, the limiting factor in the speed of the communications is the BASIC routine which sends the data. The routine was written in BASIC for simplicity, allowing use of the LPRINT command to output data via the RS-232 interface. A machine code routine would speed up the transfer of information.

Software, written in BASIC, reads the data transmitted to the host computer's serial port, from the DD or TSDAS, 120 characters at a time, and writes the data to a disk file. This program, called TSDASDECOD, also performs some preliminary data processing, creating a data file compatible with a variety of programs developed by the Computational Hydraulics Group (CHG). This facilitates further processing of the data and archiving in our data base.

Time Series Management

The CHG data base resides on an IBM-PC compatible machine with a 52Mbyte hard disk drive and 9-track magnetic tape drive. This machine also acts as the file server for our local area network (LAN). Additional IBM-PC compatibles, each with 512kbytes of RAM, 8087 math co-processors, and two floppy disk drives are connected to the LAN. All machines can access the hard drive's 52Mbytes, where the data base resides. Large hydrometerological data bases, such as those maintained by government agencies, usually reside on mainframes. The 9-track tape drive permits easy access to these records for long-term continuous modelling studies.

The Computational Hydraulics Group Time Series Manager (CHGTSM) was developed to provide easy access to time series data, independent of details of storage. The data base contains all rainfall, streamflow, and pollutant loading data collected by the CHG in Hamilton, Ontario for the period 1980 to 1984 as well as rainfall data from a larger network in Toronto, Ontario for the period 1975 to 1984. The CHGTSM handles variable resolution continuous time series records, and has the capability to aggregate and disaggregate time series data (Unal and James, 1985). Such a system is a minimum requirement for the manipulation of the long time series required (and produced) by continuous hydrologic modelling.

PCSWMM3

Continuous precipitation records, retrieved from the CHGTSM can be transformed into meaningful continuous water quantity and quality time series by a deterministic model such as the U.S. EPA's Stormwater Management Model Version III (Huber et al., 1981). The CHG has adapted the program for use on IBM-PC compatibles (PCSWMM3) (James and Robinson, 1984). Used with hard disk storage, PCSWMM3 provides for cost-effective long-term continuous simulation. A LAN extends this capability to multiple users. Figure 2. illustrates schematically the hydrologic computing environment discussed in this paper.

Conclusions

Our complete data acquisition system, including the DCPS, DAS, TSDAS, CHGTSM, LAN, and other associated software have provided us with an efficient environment for hydrologic modelling. Continuous rainfall data for input to models such as PCSWMM3 are made available to us more

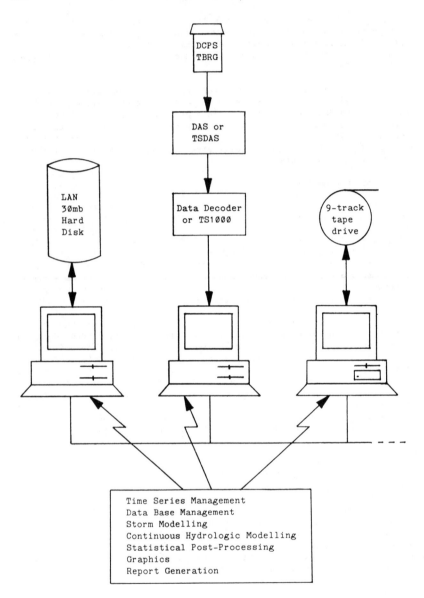

Figure 2: Hydrologic Computing Environment

quickly and easily than in the past. Additionally, with less expensive, higher resolution precipitation sensors and loggers, gauging networks can become denser, providing more representative rainfall data. The end result will be more accurate hydrologic modelling.

Ongoing research by the CHG includes the development and testing of a combined DCPS-TBRG, the design of a better backup power system for the TSDAS, and the modification of the I/O interface, and control software to other inexpensive microcomputers or hand-held calculators. Additionally, the PCSWMM3 package continues to be regularly updated and supported.

Acknowledgements

Portions of this paper have been abstracted from two presentations:

James, W. and Stirrup, D.M., (1986). Microcomputer-Based Precipitation Instrumentation, to be presented at the International Symposium on Comparison of Urban Drainage Models with Real Catchment Data, Dubrovnik, Yugoslavia, 12 pp.

Stirrup, D.M. and James, W., (1986). Microcomputer Data Acquisition Control and Modelling of a Combined Sewer Diversion Structure, to be presented at the International Conference on Water and Data Processing, Paris, France, 10 pp.

References

Anon., (1983). ZX Interface Board, Electronics Today International, April issue, pp. 46-51.

Haro, H., (1984). Instrumentation for Rainfall Sampling, Ph.D. Thesis, McMaster University, Hamilton, Ontario, 222 pp.

Huber, W.C., Heaney, J.P., Nix, S.J., Dickinson, R.E. and Polmann, D.J., (1981). Storm Water Management Model User's Manual Version III, Office of Research and Development, Municipal Environmental Research Laboratory, USEPA, 531 pp.

James, W. and Robinson, M.A., (1984). PCSWMM3 - Version III of the Executive, RUNOFF and Extended Transport Blocks Adapted for the IBM-PC, Proceedings of the Conference on Stormwater and Water Quality Management Modelling, USEPA, Burlington, Ontario, pp. 39-51.

Stirrup, D.M., (1986). Use of Low-cost Microcomputers for Distributed Data Acquisition and Real-Time Control of Combined Sewer Overflows, M.Eng. Thesis, McMaster University, Hamilton, Ontario, 190 pp.

Stirrup, D.M. and James, W., (1985). Drop Counter Precipitation Manual, Version II, Computational Hydraulics Inc. Report R136, 23 pp.

Unal, A. and James, W., (1985). Distributed Continuous Hydrologic Processing Using Microcomputer Networks, Proceedings of the Conference on Stormwater and Water Quality Management Modeling, USEPA and Ontario MOE, Toronto, Ontario, pp. 169-179.

LINKING DATA BASE MANAGEMENT AND COMPUTER MODELS

William F. Mancinelli*

ABSTRACT

Current economics has forced many organizations to optimize operations. With recent advances in technology, analysis of complex systems through computerized models is being more commonly used to this end. On moderate-to-large models, a large amount of data is required and an even greater volume of output is produced. Selecting the right information and manually organizing it in the desired format is very time consuming. Storing, tabulating, and graphing large volumes of data, not usually a strong point of a computer model, is more appropriate for a data base management system. A blend of these two technologies, data base management and scientific analysis, allows a "best of both worlds" approach. The most appropriate analysis tool can be used without concern for data storing and handling capability. At the same time, the data base management software with the best graphics, tabulation, sort, and ad hoc query abilities can be selected to support that analysis program.

BACKGROUND

This paper does not address the development of an analysis model, but rather how to get the best use of an existing model. The traditional approach to computer analysis is briefly described and several problems and potential solutions are noted. The majority of the paper deals with specific requirements and situations, using the Hydraulic Simulation Model (HSM) of the Metropolitan Water District of Southern California (Metropolitan) as a case study.

Proper ongoing modelling analysis traditionally requires several steps. The data must be set up in the precise format required by the modelling program and where possible, manually checked for errors. The data is "merged" with the program and the analysis is run, with the results printed out, giving rise to "another large slab" of computer paper. Considerable sifting and tabulating is needed to get the final results in presentable form. A typical analysis may require only a few minutes of actual computation time, but will demand hours (even days) of setup and interpretation.

---

* Engineer, Operations Division, The Metropolitan Water District of Southern California, Box 54153, Los Angeles, California 90054

There are other problems as well. Visually checking input data is tedious and unreliable. Bad data can cause the program to abort and waste valuable time, or worse yet, can result in what appears to be a good run when in fact the results are in error.

The majority of models do not readily produce graphics, nor do they easily link with a graphics generator. Often, graphics are produced manually from a tabulation of computer results, a difficult and time consuming task.

Inconsistent results are troublesome. Using the same elementary model, some very different values can result if there are small differences in input data. Such differences are hard to detect, especially in large volumes of data. Data is not normally shared by the different users. In some cases, this is the result of hardware or operating system configuration; however, the primary reason is lack of a data manager to provide organization and security.

Adaptability to input and output format changes is a problem. Users may vary in approach, background, interest, and discipline. Normally, each must adjust to the program's format requirements. Invariably, these are not the way the user prefers them, but tailoring a model to individual needs is a very large problem.

Probably the biggest problem is anticipating requests for new information, different output reports, or special tabulations. Modifications for such special requests usually require considerable time. In some cases, requirements are not met at all. In fact, the time spent modifying the program can take longer than the user is willing to wait, and the information is obsolete by the time the revision is complete.

POSSIBLE SOLUTIONS

There are several ways to address these problems and three such potential solutions are briefly discussed here. The first approach tacks additional logic onto the original program. "User-friendly" software may be added to input data in a format the user prefers. An input validation and verification routine can be added. Graphics and statistics routines can be added as well as a large number of output report routines. Selective input and/or output is often accomplished through "flags", but this adds another layer of complexity.

More and more added program code soon creates a "monster", heavily overburdened, inefficient, awkward, and ultimately unusable. Execution time slows and computer resource usage increases, sometimes requiring a larger piece of hardware or sophisticated chaining techniques. Modifications become more difficult due to the growing complexity of the logic.

As an alternative, independent programs can be created, each with a special function such as input, error checking, or graphics. This reduces the overburdening of the analysis program, but requires an

additional level of software to control the flow of work. A change
in one program may unknowingly impact another. Although this is a
vast improvement over the "monster", the resulting "mix and match"
technique can cause confusion.

Using a data base management system (DBMS) to complement the analysis
program is yet another approach. Graphics, tabulations, error checking, and report generation are functions best performed by a DBMS,
while analysis is best handled by scientific programming languages
such as FORTRAN or BASIC. In many cases, packaged or modifiable
versions of each can be readily purchased but a combined version is
very rare.

Depending upon hardware, software, staffing, time constraints, and
personnel backgrounds, any of these and other approaches may be
appropriate. The later method is being used by Metropolitan in
conjunction with HSM.

METROPOLITAN'S APPROACH

Metropolitan is a wholesaler of water for domestic, municipal,
agricultural, and groundwater replenishment uses serving an area of
5,100 square miles with a population of over 13 million people in
the Los Angeles and San Diego urban areas. The system includes 14
in-line hydroelectric plants, eight reservoirs, five filtration
plants, and numerous flow control facilities.

Recently, Metropolitan began development of a very large hydraulic
simulation model to represent its entire supply and distribution
system. The program produces hydraulic gradeline and flow information concurrently for both open channel and pressure flow portions
of the system. A pseudo time-series analysis is performed by analyzing sequential, time-varied "snapshots" of the system under assumed
steady-state conditions. A total of 24 time periods, each of
variable duration, is allowed. Transitional flows are not modelled.

At this time, a prototype of the eastern portion of the system has
been completed and is undergoing calibration and overall testing.
The entire model, when completed, will consist of approximately 600
nodes and pipes. A typical run will encompass 12 time periods and
produce values of pressure, flow, water surface elevation, valve
status, demand, and other information for each node/pipe and for
each time period. The result is a printout ranging from 400 to 500
pages. Change the input slightly, rerun the analysis, and produce
another 500 pages. The problem becomes obvious very quickly.

In planning and designing the HSM, Metropolitan wanted a model that
could handle such large volumes of information in a relatively
easy-to-use format and be used for a variety of reasons by planners,
engineers, operators, and managers alike. To avoid inconsistencies,
a "central" model and a shared data base was considered essential.

Metropolitan's corporate DBMS is intended to provide online, central
data access for large business applications such as payroll,

personnel, and inventory. Relative to the total volume of information in the data base, the HSM data is small and has little impact on the system; however, all of the data handling and graphic features of the "big system" are available.

Metropolitan's data base software is ADABAS and the programming language to access it is NATURAL, a fourth generation language (6). Both are products of Software AG of North America. The analysis program, written in VS FORTRAN (FORTRAN 77), is an enhanced version of the University of Kentucky modelling program developed by Professor Donald Wood (3, 5). The modelling program and the data base management software are currently running on an IBM 4381/Model 3 computer using CMS in a VM/SP-HPO operating system.

DATA BASE STRUCTURE

To better understand the HSM data base, envision the entire Metropolitan corporate data base as a large group of file cabinets (see Figure 1). In just one drawer of one of the cabinets, all of the input and output data for all HSM analyses is stored. That drawer is filled with file folders in which all the input and output data for a particular run is organized. Inside each folder are many sheets of paper representing records in the data base.

All information for a particular node or pipe for all time periods is contained in one record (i.e., one sheet of paper). Each sheet contains system data, input data, and output data. System information, or "housekeeping" data, includes folder name, facility name, type, description, node number, pipe number, and miscellaneous codes. The input data includes elapsed times, valve status, demand, operating water surface elevation, and similar data. Finally, the output data, which was placed in the record as the result of a successful analysis run, contains the hydraulic gradeline elevation, flow rate, available head, and computed water surface elevation.

Because all the data for a facility or location is contained on one record, data can be sorted, compared, tabulated, and graphed fairly easily. Comparisons between records for the same location under different run conditions (sheets in different folders) are also relatively easy.

NATURAL is used to set up friendly input screens, validate the data, store it, and send a copy of it to the analysis program (see Figure 2). When analysis is complete, NATURAL brings the output back to the data base (2). The data base can be searched as often as required, in as many ways as desired. The folder stays in the system until the owner, the one who originally set it up, deletes it. Under this system, input data and results are always together, eliminating confusion as to what data was used to produce the results in question.

Any authorized person can review and use the input and output data. Changes can only be made by the owner and only during the active analysis period. A number of "original" or "basic" folders are maintained on the system, protected from change by anyone. These

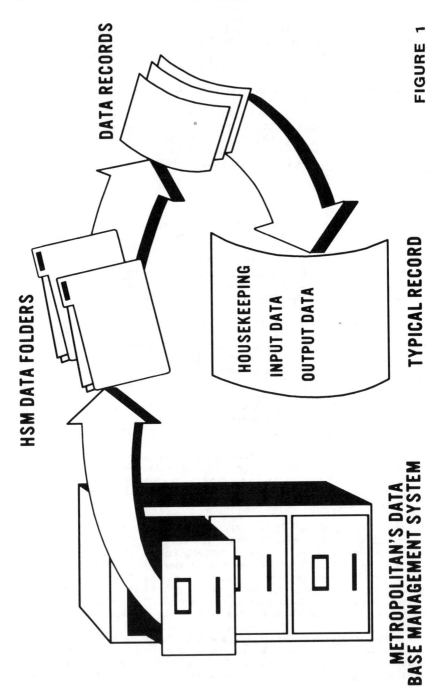

FIGURE 1

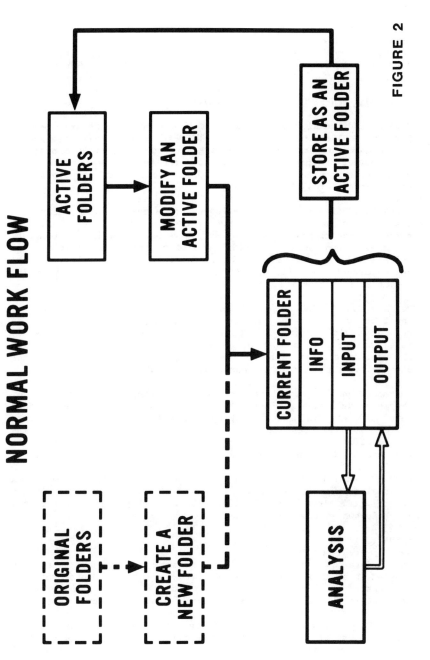

NORMAL WORK FLOW

FIGURE 2

folders represent certain basic scenarios, such as high demand
conditions, low demand conditions, minimal storage situations, and
others. They may be copied, modified, and saved in modified form,
but the original remains unchanged as a base from which to start
again.

ADDITIONAL BENEFITS AND SPECIAL FEATURES

Several additional benefits have resulted from the combined use of a
DBMS and FORTRAN analysis program. NATURAL allows a modular approach
to input/output screens with each generated by a separate program.
Using predefined program function keys (PF keys), the user has free
movement forward and backward through the screens and can bypass the
normal progression if so desired.

ADABAS/NATURAL also allows development of access logs to record all
transactions to every record and to every program module. Several
paths for changing and reviewing data have been provided and monitoring their usage determines which should be made more efficient and
which should be deleted. In-house development of a help facility,
geared specifically for the HSM system and for those employing it,
is yet another benefit.

Being modular, the system allows the user to temporarily exit any
input or output screen, type in notes, messages, and comments, then
return to the original position in the input or output sequence.
Notes are stored in whatever folder has been designated, allowing
the user to document (online) the assumptions and the reasoning for
changes. The documentation stays with the data.

The model can be used for new operator training, refresher training,
emergency drills, and other similar uses. Without the ease of data
entry and retrieval supplied by ADABAS/NATURAL, the setup and output
review would be much too tedious, and although the accurate in its
portrayal of the system's responses, the model would not simulate a
real working environment for the operator.

A final benefit is the ability to down-load analysis results to a
personal computer (PC) for use in spread-sheets or any other similar
PC software. Those more familiar with PC packages can use the data
in their own environment.

SUMMARY

Using data base management to complement a scientific analysis
program has considerable reward. The setup and interpretation
portions of the analysis work now take minutes rather than hours and
are more in line with the time involved for actual calculations.

The link has resulted in less frustration, fewer bad runs, a more
efficient use of time and equipment, and a greater utilization of a
very important model that might otherwise receive only occasional
use due to its complexity.

APPENDIX I--REFERENCES

1) MANCINELLI, W. F., "Utilizing Data Base Management Techniques to Organize Hydraulic Model Results", Proceedings of the American Water Works Association Distribution System Symposium, in Seattle, WA, September 8-11, 1985, pp. 127-133.

2) MANCINELLI, W. F., "Using ADABAS/NATURAL to Organize Computer Model Results", Proceedings of the International Software AG Users' Conference, in San Diego, CA, May 12-16, 1986, pp. __ - __

3) TANNER, T. L., "Adapting a Pipe Network Analysis Computer Program", Proceedings of the ASCE Specialty Conference on Computer Applications in Water Resources, in Buffalo, NY, June 10-12, 1985, pp. 430-437.

4) TANNER, T. L., "Taming a Pipe Network Analysis Computer Program", Proceedings of the ASCE Water Forum '86 Conference, in Long Beach, CA, August 4-6, 1986, pp. __ - __.

5) WOOD, D. J., User's Manual -- Computer Analysis of Flow in Pipe Networks Including Extended Period Simulations, Office of Continuing Education/Engineering, 223 Transportation Research Building, University of Kentucky, Lexington, KY, 40506-0043, 1980.

6) _____, NATURAL User's Manual Version 1.2, Software AG of North America, Inc., 11800 Sunrise Valley Drive, Reston, VA 22091, August 1982.

A Customized Database Management System
for Watershed Modeling

John C. Kaden[*]

Most watershed models require a considerable amount of input
data. This data needs to be collected, managed and formatted for
input to the model. When large watershed areas are being studied
and continuously monitored, it is desirable to create a database
management system (DBMS) that provides the necessary capability to
build and maintain a database and is fairly easy to use. This paper
will describe a DBMS which was developed to manage large amounts of
watershed data for use in MULTSED, a water and sediment yield model
developed by Colorado State University. The DBMS was developed
using Microrim's R:base 4000 and MS DOS. Before describing the
DBMS any further, a brief overview of MULTSED will be given.

MULTSED routes water and sediment across a watershed and
through the channel system. The model requires a variety of input
data, such as soil parameters, vegetative cover, watershed and
channel geometry, rainfall parameters and various flow and
resistance coefficients. A typical watershed is divided into a
sequence of plane and subwatershed units that are homogeneous in
parameter composition. Water and sediment delivery is analyzed for
each of these subunits, and results are linked together to determine
total delivery through the stream system. Consequently, each
subunit has a corresponding set of data for all the parameter groups
mentioned above. Once this information is available, the user can
select and combine various units for a simulation scenario. This is
done by creating computational sequence files for the units
selected. All the necessary input files are then ready for model
analysis and output.

The data described above is organized in the DBMS by
subwatershed, plane and channel units. Data for each type of unit
is stored in a separate R:base relation, shown pictorially in Figure
1 below. An R:base relation is composed of rows and columns, where
each row represents a set of data, and each column represents an
attribute or parameter. A relation may have as many as 256 columns
and practically an unlimited number (2.5 billion) of rows. There
may be as many as forty relations in a single database. Figure 2
shows how data is organized in a relation for plane units. This
particular arrangement of data is the basis for all operations
discussed, henceforth.

[*]Systems Programmer, US Army Construction Engineering Research
Laboratory, P.O. Box 4005, Champaign, IL 61820-1305.

256 attributes

2.5 billion
rows
-------->

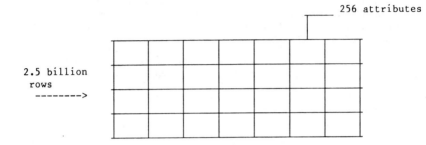

Figure 1.

plane unit #1

plane unit #2
.
.
.
.
plane unit #n

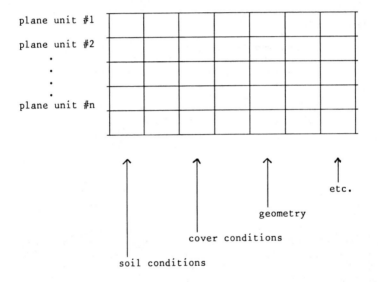

etc.

geometry

cover conditions

soil conditions

Figure 2

The DBMS is a collection of command files that are linked together into a menu system, providing the capability to perform various tasks by choosing from a list of options. It begins with the batch file command GO, which generates the initial menu shown in Figure 3 below. This menu allows the user to manage the MULTSED database, format data for model input, run MULTSED and perform basic file maintenance operations.

1) Access database
2) Format MULTSED input
3) Run MULTSED
4) Remove MULTSED files
5) Quit

Figure 3

Selecting option 1 yields the following R:base menu shown in Figure 4. This main menu allows the user access to type of watershed unit and sequence file, an edit screen and reloading the database. (The reload option is necessary from time to time, because R:base does not restore space from deleted information automatically. Reload will rewrite the database, restoring all unused space from deleted information).

1) Manage data for planes
2) Manage data for subwatersheds
3) Construct a computational sequence
   for planes and subwatersheds
4) Manage data for channels
5) Manage data for reservoirs
6) Construct a computational sequence
   for channels and reservoirs
7) Manage data for parcels
8) Help using edit screens
9) Reload database and exit
10) Quit

Figure 4

Selecting options 1-7 in Figure 4 will yield another menu with options for inquiring, adding, modifying or selecting input data for MULTSED. For example, if option 2 is selected, the following menu will appear as shown in Figure 5. This menu's functions are demonstrated pictorially in Figures 5a and 5b below. For any of the operations inquire, add or modify a forms screen will appear for

data manipulation shown in Figure 6. Each data field is highlighted
as the carriage return is used, prompting the user to add or modify
data values.

1- Add data	9- Select range of rows for MULTSED input
Inquire or modify parameters for:	10- Show previous range selected for MULTSED
2- Identification	
3- Soil	
4- Cover	
5- Geometry	11- Return to main menu
6- Other	12- Quit
7- Rainfall	
8- Sediment	

Figure 5

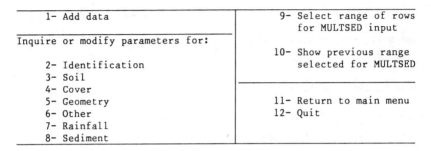

add a new
row of data

modify a sub-
group of data

Figure 5a

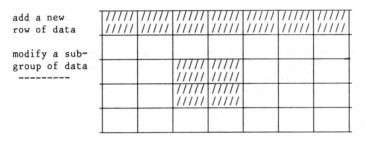

subject range
of rows for
MULTSED

Figure 5b

Soil Parameters

Code:_____
Title:_____

                                        Left Plane   Right Plane

Hydraulic conductivity (in/hr):   _____   _____

Porosity: _____   _____

Initial soil moisture: _____   _____

Final soil moisture: _____   _____

Average capillary suction (in):   _____   _____

Plasticity index (percent):   _____   _____

Erosion rate constant (lb/ft 2-sec):   _____   _____

Figure 6.   Soil parameters forms screen

Referring back to the startup menu in Figure 3, selecting
option 2 yields the format menu shown in Figure 7. This menu
provides options for formatting selected input data form the various
types of watershed units or computational sequence files. An R:base
supplementary package called Extended Report Writer takes the
selected input data and formats it according to the model's input
specifications.

                f1)   Planes
                f2)   Subwatersheds
                f3)   Computational sequence for planes
                      and subwatersheds
                f4)   Channels
                f5)   Reservoirs
                f6)   Computational sequence for channels
                      and reservoirs
                f7)   Parcels
                f8)   Return to main menu
                f9)   Quit

                        Figure 7

Option 3 in Figure 3 is selected to run MULTSED. A menu of options is given for choosing what type of watershed unit is to be analyzed. After MULTSED is finished another menu is provided for saving output files. These menus are shown in Figures 8 and 9, respectively.

ml) Execute msed1 - planes and subwatersheds
m2) Execute msed1 - planes only
m3) Execute msed1 - subwatersheds only
m4) Execute msed2 - reformat files
m5) Execute msed3 - channels and reservoirs
m6) Execute msed3 - channels only
m7) Execute msed3 - reservoirs only
m8) Return to main menu
m9) Quit

Figure 8

s1) Save msed1 output
s2) Save msed3 output
s3) Return to MULTSED menu
s4) Return to main menu
s5) Quit

Figure 9

The last option in Figure 3 is used to remove all input and output files used for and generated by MULTSED. The user is cautioned to save any important output before using this option. To look at any output files that have been saved the user must exit the system and display the files with the DOS command TYPE.

An Evaluation of Sediment
Resuspension Parameterizations

Keith W. Bedford*

Introduction and Definitions

The recent attention to managing surface water toxic substances has resulted in a number of modeling approaches, all of which to a great or lesser extent require accurate treatment of the rates and types of sediment transport. Many of these models make predictions for inland waters and therefore must deal with not only sands but cohesive sediments, i.e., clays and silts, and predictions which account for the alternate resuspension and deposition of sediment. The problem of specifying or parameterizing the entrainment of these sediments is quite difficult and a number of recommended procedures have been published. It is primarily the intent of this paper to try and organize these methods into several categories or approaches and secondarily, to evaluate the limits of each approach particularly as regards the ability to make the field measurements required by each. In anticipation of the conclusion, this author believes that many of the approaches are severely limited in that they cannot be fully validated in-situ and that either new instruments or new theoretical developments are necessary. Before proceeding to this evaluation, it is necessary to list some important definitions which by and large have been extracted from reviews of near-bottom hydrodynamic and sediment transport works by Grant et al. (1986), Nowell and Hollister (1985), Bedford and Abdelrhman (1986a,b) and Lumley (1978).

If a near bottom coordinate system is adopted with x being the horizontal/streamwise coordinate and z being the coordinate perpendicular to x and positive up, then the following differential equation for a sediment grain size class is written as:

$$\frac{D\bar{c}}{Dt} = \frac{\partial \bar{c}}{\partial t} + \frac{\partial \overline{Nx}}{\partial x} + \frac{\partial \overline{Ny}}{\partial z} = \bar{S} \tag{1}$$

where
$$\overline{Nx} = \bar{u}\,\bar{c} + \overline{u'c'} - D\frac{\partial \bar{c}}{\partial x} \tag{2}$$

$$\overline{Nz} = \bar{w}\,\bar{c} + \overline{w'c'} - \bar{w}_s\,\bar{c} - D\frac{\partial \bar{c}}{\partial z} \tag{3}$$

and $\bar{S}$ = a source sink term.

Nx and Nz are termed the horizontal and vertical flux, respectively, with Nzo being equal to Nz(z=0); w_s is the settling velocity for the grain size class; u and w are the horizontal and vertical velo-

---

Professor, Department of Civil Engineering, The Ohio State University, 2070 Neil Avenue, Columbus, Ohio 43210

cities, respectively responsible for the advection of the sediment particles and D is the molecular diffusion. The source sink term (Lumley, 1978) could account for the creation or destruction of class size grains by aggregation or disaggregation as well as certain bed entrainment representations. If spatial or temporal averaging is performed, as indicated by the overbar on the variables, then remnants of the averaging procedure appear as cross correlations between the fluctuating components and must be related to the averaged variables. It is also traditional to assume that molecular diffusion is relatively unimportant in the averaged equations. It is the position of this author that the net vertical particle concentration flux, consists of resuspension, a flux away from the bottom, and deposition, a flux towards the wall. As it is a vector, horizontal flux, Nx, does not play a role in the resuspension or deposition flux, Nz.

Analysis Methods - A Summary

Methods for measuring or parameterizing Nzo, the bottom vertical flux are quite analogous to the problem of determining τo, the bottom shear, and therefore a similarly overlapping and confusing segmentation of classification procedures are available. In keeping with a traditional transport phenomena approach, three general categories are identified; the empirical approach which also encompasses empirical source sink approaches, a continuum approach, and a control volume approach. Tables 1, 2, and 3 have been prepared to summarize the procedures.

Empirical Procedures

Through a variety of Buckingham π arguments and exploratory or correlation procedures, entrainment and deposition are quantified by a variety of parameters, some of which represent extremely complicated molecular scale processes. Table 1 lists the entrainment and deposition forms as source sink terms rather than direct fluxes, the distinctions between either form are for the empirical approaches blurred. The references cited are among the first to suggest such parameterizations and only a few of the many variables used in these models have been listed in the Table. A welter of empirical coefficients is found in these formulations, suggesting that a very site specific reliance upon field data will be required for calibration and use. These formulations are principally found in numerical models.

Continuum Approaches

At the heart of the continuum approach is the use of a theoretical treatment to either substantiate field measurements or in some cases directly calculate a missing piece of data with which to make a speculative calculation for Nzo. We list in Table 2 the empirical approach from Table 1 to again demonstrate that the empirical procedure crosses many categories. Method number 2, the direct measurement of Nzo, is at this point but speculation as no such instrument for direct measurements exists. Rather, using a

Table 1   Empirical Approaches to Nzo

Type	Applica-cation	Equation Form	Formulae or Distri-butions Assumed	Valuables To Be Measured	Ref.
1.) Purely Empiric-al	Noncohe-sive	$N_{zo} = f(\tau_o)$	u_* calculated τ_o from measured log boundary	τ_o	Shields (Vanoni, 1975)
2.) Source/ Sink	Cohesive/ Noncohes-ive	$\frac{Dc}{Dt} = SE + SD$ SE = Entrain-ment source SD = Deposi-tion Source	variously a.) Bed shear b.) Settling velo-city for par-	variously a.) Grain Size distribution b.) Critical Shear Stress c.) Moisture Con-'tent material d.) Time delay after deposi-tion e.) Brownnian Col-lision rates f.) Viscosity g.) Critical Stress Deposition h.) Flocculation Concentration i.) hindered Set-ling Concen-tration	Krone et al. (1977) Hayter and Mehta (1982) Scarlatos (1982) W. Lick (1985) W. Lick (1982) Uchrin and Weber (1980) Onishi (1984)

Table 3   Control Volume Method for Nzo

Type	Application	Equation Form	Distribution or Formulae Assumed	Measured Variables	References
1. Direct Flux Needed	Cohesive/ Noncohesive	$Nzo = (\overline{w'c'} - \overline{w_s c})\big|_{z=0}$ $= dI/dt - \{(\overline{w'c'} + \overline{w_s c})\big|_{z=\alpha}\}$ $I = \int_{z=0}^{z=\alpha} cdz$	1. Advection flux, N_x, is unimportant over small time periods 2. W_s – calculable or measurable	1.) A vertical profile of c 2.) Grain size distribu-tion 3.) w measured at z = α.	Bedford et al., (1986)

Table 2 Continuum Approaches to Nzo

(Definition $N_z = \bar{w}\,\bar{c} + \overline{w'c'} - \bar{w}_s\bar{c} - D\frac{\partial c}{\partial z}$)
(Note:

$\quad\quad$ (1) $\quad$ (2) $\quad$ (3) $\quad$ (4) $\quad$ (5)

Type	Application	Equation form	Formulae or Distributions Assumed	Variables to be Measured	Reference [*]
1.) Empirical (Sec. I.2)					
2.) Direct Measurement	Cohesive/ Noncohesive	None	None	N_{zo}	Not Possible at this time
3.) Quasi Direct Measurement	Cohesive Noncohesive	$Nzo = (\overline{w'c'} - \bar{w}_s\bar{c})\vert\; z=0$	a.) Assume/Calculate value for w b.) $\bar{w} = 0$ c.) $D\frac{\partial c}{\partial x} = 0$ d.) $\overline{w'c'} = K\partial c/\partial z$ e.) K from formulae	a.) $\bar{c}$ (z=0) b.) $\partial c/\partial z$ or c.) $\overline{w'c'}$ d.) grain size distribution	Not performed to date in field Nakato et al. (1978)
4.) Equilibrium Flux:		$Nzo= 0 = (\overline{w'c'} - \bar{w}_s\bar{c})$	a.) No net flux b.) Can be integrated to give profile c.) Steady equilibrium boundary layer flow		Rouse (1937)
5.) Boundary Layer Approach a. Implicit Form	Cohesive/ Noncohesive	a.) Boundary Layer Solution for various forcing Functions b.) By assuming the Exact Solution is valid the N_{zo} variables are calculated/ interpolated with the one or two point data c. Nzo = f{(\overline{w'c'} - \bar{w}_s\bar{c}) \vert z=z^* \vert d. z^* = height where values are measured for interpolation of N_{zo}	a.) Exact Profile solution b.) Calculate ws c.) $\bar{w} = 0$ d.) $D\frac{\partial c}{\partial z} = 0$ e.) $\overline{w'c'} = k^{\partial c/\partial z}$	a.) Concentration and vertical velocity at one or two points in. concentration profile b.) grain size distribution	Analogous To Momentum Procedure; Bedford et al. (1996) Boundary Layer Typical Solution a. Grant and Madsen (1986)
b. Measured Form	cohesive	a.) Nzo = f{(\overline{w'c'} - \bar{w}_s\bar{c}) \vert z=z^* \vert b.) Function f is measured from field data and used to interpolate N_{zo}	a.) ws is calculated	a.) Value of C measured at least 3 and preferably 4 pts in profile; or b.) A profile of concentration c.) Measured values of w' at the same 3 or 4 pts. d.) gram size distribution	Bedford et al., (1986)

variety of more readily measured data and some knowledge of the
anticipated sediment profile, a net vertical flux can be inferred.
Such is the basis for Nos. 3, 4, and 5a. Solution 5a invokes the
well known boundary layer approach wherein the equations of motion
and transport are integrated under simplified forcing function
conditions to determine a profile, $C(z)$. This profile can then be
assumed to exist and therefore only one or two points in the
"profile" need be sampled in order to interpolate near bottom fluxes.

Instead of assuming a profile, method 5b directly measures the
profile and uses these direct measurements to interpolate the near
bottom flux behavior. Method 5b, by making no presumption about
anticipated profiles, would appear an attractive procedure.

Control Volume Method

This method developed by this author and his graduate assistants
(Bedford et al., 1986) is possible due to newly developed ultrasonic
acoustic procedures for measuring very detailed concentration
profiles. A control volume is assumed to exist from the bottom to
the top-most current meter near the top of the insonified volume and
using typical boundary layer assumptions (e.g., Grant and Madsen,
1986), the concentration equation is vertically integrated. In so
doing a flux balance is achieved involving only terms than are
measureable. Nzo is then directly calculable without any
preconceived or anticipated behaviors. This procedure is newly
developed and just being intercompared with methods II5a and II5b.

Summary Evaluation and Conclusions

While it is helpful to perhaps review each method in detail, it
is felt that a more useful approach is to first identify comments
which apply to all Nzo calculation procedures then discuss
individual procedures as necessary.

First, it is apparent that many of the formulae, especially
those in the empirical section, require data that is difficult if not
impossible to measure. This is especially the case when measuring
variables that control flocculation and the various measures of shear
in the water column. Recent instrumentation advances (see for
example the BASS instruments in Grant et al., 1984) now permit a
boundary layer shear measurement to be made, but many, if not most,
of the other variables must be estimated and predicted, not directly
measured. This being the case, it is hard, if not impossible, to
construct an experiment which could directly measure the data
required for parameterization validation.

Secondly, it is also apparent that the instrumentation required
for the simplest measurements of concentration and velocity are only
now being developed. Such is the case with the BASS instruments
which now fully resolve the 3D velocity field with enough precision
required to identify the streamwise velocity component required by
the boundary layer formulae (Grant and Madsen, 1986). Such attention
to particle measurements needs to be developed. Direct concentration

measurements are now being made either optically or acoustically; the acoustic systems giving a very dense and therefore more desirable profile than the point optical systems. Current acoustic systems (e.g., Hess and Bedford, 1985) yield up to 110 concentration points in a one meter vertical column as compared to the four or so point measurements usually taken optically. The instrument deficiencies are most severe, however, in the area of in-situ grain size analysis. This critical piece of information is required in all the Nzo procedures and can't be measured in-situ. Short of grab samples, pumped samples, or long period settling devices, it is not possible to determine ws with any precision in-situ. When dealing with flocculating particles, small changes in conditions cause large changes in settling characteristics (Lick, 1986) and it is difficult to know what changes in ws occur during transport back to the laboratory.

Third, the use of procedures which assume a sediment boundary layer to exist is very suspect and should be abandoned for now. The existence of even the simplest in-situ boundary layer is only now being measured or confirmed (Grant et al., 1986, Bedford et al., 1986) and these are for only the very simplest forcing functions, i.e., steady flow or as possibly modified by a monochromatic wave. Experiments in more realistic in-situ settings, marked by ripples, dunes, worms, stratification, internal waves, random wave fields, etc., are only being planned and not near execution; therefore, since the average theoretical profiles haven't been validated, it is hard to justify an Nzo method that uses results from a presumed concentration profile to measure Nzo.

In summary, then, methods II5b and III1 appear at this point to require the fewest assumptions about the anticipated behavior of C(z) and provides estimates of Nzo from data that can be measured. Therefore, at this time, II5.b and III.1 appear optimal approaches to parameterization. Improved devices for measuring C(z) on Nzo directly will, of course, dramatically change this summary and hopefully will be developed quickly. Finally, the ability to make rapid in-situ estimates of ws appears to be a major instrument deficiency requiring immediate remedy.

Acknowledgment

This work was made possible by the author's current research on sediment resuspension and transport including ONR N00014-83-K-0003, EPA No. R005852-01, and NOAA-Ohio Sea Grant No. NA84AA-D-0079 R/EM-4. Their support is appreciated.

References

1.) Bedford, K. and M. Abdelrhman, "Improved Acoustic and Analysis Methods for Parameterrizing Resuspension in Monroe Harbor/Raisin River: Pt I, A Review of Near Bottom Transport Processes of Importance to Lake Erie and the Great Lakes," Final Rept. US. EPA Large Lakes Res Station, 92 pgs, Feb, 1986.

2.) Bedford, K. and M. Abdelrhman, "Analytical and Experimental Studies of the Benthic Boundary Layer and Their Applicability To Near-Bottom Transport in Lake Erie," To Appear: Int Assoc. for Great Lakes Res Lake Erie Synthesis Volume, 1986.

3.) Bedford, K., C. Libicki, O. Wai, M. Abdelrhman, and R. Van Evra, "The Structure of the Bottom Sediment Boundary Layer in Central Long Island Sound," Proc. Physical Processes in Estuaries: From Conf. of Same Name Delft Hydraulics Laboratory, September, 1986.

4.) Grant, W. and O. Madsen, "The Continental-Shelf Bottom Boundary Layer," in Ann. Rev. of Fluid Mech., M. Van Dyke, ed., Vol 18, pp. 265-306, 1986.

5.) Grant, W., and R. Williams, and S. Glenn, "Bottom Stress Estimates and Their Prediction on the Northern California Continental Shelf during CODE-1: The Importance of Wave-Current Interaction," J. Phy. Oceanography, Vol. 14, pp. 506-527, 1984.

6.) Hayter, E. and A. Mehta, "Modeling of Estuarial Fine Sediment Transport for Tracking Pollutant Movement," Report No. UFL/COEL-82/009, U.S. Environmental Protection Agency, December 1982.

7.) Hess, F. and K. Bedford, "Acoustic Backscatter System (ABSS): The Instrument and Some Preliminary Results," in Deep Ocean Sediment Transport, R. Nowell and C. Hollister, ed., pp. 357-380, 1985.

8.) Krone, R., R. Ariathuri, and R. MacArthur, "Mathematical Model of Estuarial Sediment Transport," Technical Report D-77-12, U.S. Army Corps of Engineers, 1977.

9.) Lick, W., "Entrainment, Deposition, and Transport of Fine-grained Sediments in Lakes," Hydrobiologia, No. 91, pp. 31-40, 1982.

10.) Lick, W., Personal Communication, unpublished, September, 1985.

11.) Lick, W., "Cohesive Sediment Resuspension in Lake Erie," Int. Assoc. for Great Lakes Research Lake Erie Synthesis Volume, 1986.

12.) Lumley, J., "Two-Phase and Non Newtonian Flows," Topics in Applied Physics, P. Bradshaw, ed., Springer Verlag Publ, pp. 289-324, 1978.

13.) Nakato, T., et al., "Wave Entrainment of Sediment from Rippled Bed," Journ. of Wat., Port, Coastal, and Ocean Division, ASCE, Vol 103, No. WW1, 1977.

14.) Nowell, A. and C. Hollister, Deep Ocean Sediment Transport, Elsevier Pub. Co., 1985.

15.) Onishi, Y. and F. Thompson, "Mathematical Simulation of Sediment and Radionuclide Transport in Coastal Waters," Report No. NUREG/CR-2424, U.S. Nuclear Regulatory Commission, Vol. 1, May, 1984.

16.) Rouse, H., "Modern Conceptions of the Mechanics of Fluid Turbulence," Transactions ASCE, Vol. 102, No. 1965, pp. 463-543, 1937.

17.) Scarlatos, P., "On the Numerical Modeling of Cohesive Sediment Transport," Journal of Hydraulic Research, Vol. 19, No. 7, pp. 61-67, 1981.

18.) Sheng, Y., "Mathematical Modeling of Three Dimensional Coastal Currents and Sediment Dispersion," Report No. CERC-83-2, U.S. Army Corps of Engineers, September, 1983.

19.) Uchrin, C. G. and W. Weber, "Modeling of Transport Processes for Suspended Solids and Associated Pollutants," in Fate and Transport Case Studies, Modeling, Toxicity, R. Baker, ed., Ann Arbor Science Publishers, Inc., pp. 407-423, 1980.

20.) Vanoni, V., ed., Sedimentation Engineering, ASCE pub., 1975.

GULLY INCISION PREDICTION ON RECLAIMED SLOPES

by

Steven R. Abt,[1] M. ASCE, John A. Falk,[2]
John D. Nelson,[3] M. ASCE and T. L. Johnson,[4] M. ASCE

Abstract

An investigation was conducted to estimate the potential of gully intrusion into reclaimed waste impoundments. A series of eight reclaimed impoundments exhibiting gully intrusions were surveyed. An empirical analysis was performed to correlate drainage area, precipitation, embankment slope, cover soil properties and time to the maximum depth of gully incision.

The results indicated that the number of rainfall events that cause runoff, the tributary area to the gully, the soil median grain diameter and the initial slope of the reclaimed impoundment were related to the average vertical rate of gully incision. An expression was also presented for estimating the long-term stable slope through the reclamation area and for estimating the rate of decay of the slope in the gully as a function of time.

Introduction

The protection of the public health and the environment from the potential hazards of waste materials has stimulated the assessment of waste stabilization procedures and methods. Current waste stabilization methods concentrate and cap the materials with an earthen cover. Reclamation standards require that waste impoundments be designed and constructed to insure the long-term stabilization for periods of 200 to 1000 years.

One mechanism which may endanger the integrity and stability of the reclaimed waste impoundment is gully erosion. Gully erosion is the development of deep incisions into the soil surface by the dislodging and transporting of soil particles from concentrated flows. Reclaimed embankments and impoundments are particularly susceptible to erosive forces on immature surfaces. Impoundment covers are generally comprised

[1]Assoc. Prof., Dept. of Civil Engrg., Colo. State Univ., Fort Collins, Colo. 80523.
[2]Grad. Res. Asst., Dept. of Civil Engrg., Colo. State Univ., Fort Collins, Colo. 80523.
[3]Prof. and Ldr. of Geo. Engrg., Dept. of Civil Engrg., Colo. State Univ., Fort Collins, Colo. 80523.
[4]Hydraulic Engrg., Nuclear Regulatory Comm., Silver Spring, Md. 20910.

of locally derived materials which were stockpiled or removed from an adjacent site. The newly placed material is considered more vulnerable to intrusion than an in situ material with similar soil and site conditions. Therefore, it is imperative that the erosive potential be delineated to protect the reclaimed slopes from cover degradation due to gully development.

The objective of this investigation was to empirically derive a procedure to predict the maximum depth of gully incision that could potentially occur on a reclaimed waste impoundment slope as a function of time. It is anticipated that the results shall provide a basis from which an evaluation and design criteria can be formulated.

Assumptions

Several assumptions were made to facilitate data acquisition and analysis. These assumptions are summarized as follows:

● The rate of gully advancement and valley slope degradation will decrease with time while the cover material is assumed to remain relatively homogeneous with time.

● Should a watershed develop upstream of and be tributary to a gully, the watershed area shall remain relatively unchanged throughout the study period.

● The effects of differential settlement on the long-term rates of gully incision are considered negligible.

● The effects of vegetative cover on erosion do not significantly impact the gully formation potential for sites with vegetation cover of less than 50 percent.

● The location and elevation of the toe of the reclaimed slope shall remain relatively constant.

Study Region

Eight study areas were investigated near Casper, Rawlins, Riverton and Rock Springs, Wyoming. The primary considerations in the selection of the individual sites were the proximity to reclaimed waste disposal areas exhibiting gully erosion and the willingness of the organizations to permit access. The distinction between locations was based upon proximity and the availability of continuous climatological data. Sites were categorized according to age, reclamation status and location. The study sites exhibited gully erosion with variable depths, widths, lengths and shapes. The two to three most pronounced gullies at each site were identified and included in the study. The site age is the period of time since reclamation in which there has been little or no maintenance. Undisturbed study sites ranging from 7 to 19 years were included in the study.

Each reclaimed site consisted of stripmined overburden rock and soil with a highly variable grain size distribution. The material had been graded into a uniform slope. A thin, 3-6 inch layer of stockpiled native topsoil was applied to the material and reseeded. However, one reclaimed site composed of uniform, fine-grained mill tailings was armored with a cobble cover.

Data collection and site documentation included the gathering of field information at each reclaimed impoundment, the laboratory analysis of soil samples, a search of available rainfall records and photographic documentation. The field data encompassed taking physical measurements of established gullies on existing reclaimed impoundments. The gully dimensions of length, maximum depth, gully width at the point of maximum depth, embankment slope and embankment height were obtained. Also, the tributary drainage area to each gully was estimated. Vegetative cover was approximated for the impoundment cap and embankment. A summary of the field measurements is presented for each site in Table 1.

Table 1.   Summary of Field Measurements

Site	Drainage Area (Sq ft)	Initial Slope	Gully Length (ft)	Slope Length (ft)	Maximum Gully Depth (ft)	Width at Dmax (ft)	Location of Dmax Relative to Toe	Vegetative Cover (%)
A	840	0.230	210	217	2.87	3.12	0.3013	35
B	819	0.212	181	189	1.25	2.40	0.2492	30
C	35,048	0.167	174	183	3.50	3.97	0.3970	5
F	4,032	0.287	203	219	1.20	2.60	0.5251	40
I	1,021	0.152	191	192	0.60	1.86	0.3612	10
L	530	0.285	49	56	2.25	5.77	0.7678	5
N	390,000	0.166	815	826	2.90	3.40	0.5557	15
O	637	0.293	128	134	0.40	0.85	0.2510	15

Soil samples were obtained from each site for laboratory analysis. Samples were extracted from the middle of the embankment slope at an approximate depth of one foot below the surface from the top bank of the most prominent gully at each site. All samples from each site were combined, mixed and quartered prior to testing and are considered disturbed samples. An Atterberg limit and a grain size analysis were conducted on each soil sample. The soil samples are generally classified as poorly graded to well graded sand and silty sand. The low value of the Plasticity Index (PI) combined with the small percentage passing the No. 200 sieve suggests that the soils are noncohesive in behavior although variable from site to site.

The rainfall data were derived from the U.S. Weather Service Weather Stations located in Casper, Rawlins, Riverton and Rock Springs, Wyoming. The climate, temperature variations, amounts and patterns of precipitation, and elevation were similar in the four regions. Thirty years of continuous climatological record were obtained for each of the four weather stations. The rainfall data were reduced by determining the number of 24-hour storm events that annually occurred in which precipitation depths of 0.5 inches, or greater, were recorded.

The incipient value of 0.5 inches of rainfall was selected based upon an analysis of when runoff generally occurs for sites with SCS curve numbers of approximately 80. In accordance with the rainfall-runoff relationships presented by the U.S. Department of Agriculture (2), incipient runoff will initiate at a rainfall depth of approximately 0.5 inches. Since gullying cannot initiate and develop without runoff, the number of precipitation events having depths of 0.5 inches or greater were determined.

Results and Discussion

Field observations and physical measurements were qualitatively and quantitatively analyzed by Falk (1) with the objective of describing the intrusion potential of a gully. Although the age of the reclaimed study impoundment ranged from 7 to 19 years, several trends and similarities were identified in gully development.

The shape of the gullies in cross section varied considerably from the point of channel initiation to the base of the slope. The maximum gully depth was most often found to occur in the middle one-half of the slope. The gully shape at the toe of the slope usually resembled a wide, braided alluvial fan. The gully changed from a distinct incised channel into many shallow rivulets at the base of the slope. The shape of the gully at the maximum depth of incision was V-shaped for the recently formed gullies and U-shaped for the mature gullies where the bottom width was approximately equal to or slightly less than the top width.

Gully Factor

An expression was sought to correlate the annual rate of gully degradation to the site specific parameters influencing gully development. Therefore, the maximum gully depth measured on each of the reclaimed slopes was divided by the age of the reclaimed impoundment to obtain an average annual rate of incision. The average annual rate of incision was correlated graphically to the area tributary to the gully (A), the number of precipitation events of 0.5 inches or greater (P), the initial embankment slope (S_i), and the soil median grain diameter (D_{50}). The rate of maximum gully incision can be expressed as

$$D_{max/t} = \frac{(A) \, P \, (S_i)}{(1 + D_{50})} \tag{1}$$

The right side of Eq. 1 shall be referred to as the Gully Factor (GF).

The gully measurements were averaged for each site as plotted and presented in Fig. 1. One point, A, shown on Fig. 1, remains apart from the general trend exhibited for reclaimed slopes. The difference in the observed outlier and the remaining points was due to the composition of the impoundment material. Flyash from a coal-powered generation plant was mixed and layered with stripmined overburden and top soil prior to reclamation. Furthermore, large, unassimilated pockets of ash were observed in the zones of gully activity. The average annual rate of gully incision for point A is, in part, attributed to the rapid erosion of flyash concentrations located within the reclaimed slope. Therefore point A was excluded from the analysis in deriving Eq. 1.

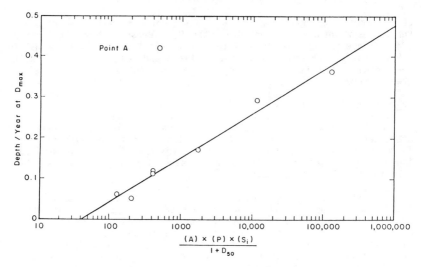

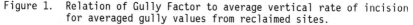

Figure 1. Relation of Gully Factor to average vertical rate of incision for averaged gully values from reclaimed sites.

Stable Slope

Gully erosion does not occur at a constant, unchanging rate, but will continue until equilibrium conditions are achieved (3). Usually, the slope is gradually reduced by erosion and approaches a threshold value, or stable slope, that is compatible with the site specific flow conditions. Since it was assumed that the drainage area, median particle size of the cover material and the potential for runoff (rainfall) will remain essentially unchanged during the active periods of the gully, the remaining variable in the Gully Factor is the gully slope angle. The effects of erosion through time will reduce the initial gradient until the gully will no longer maintain a migrating headcut. The gully will reach its equilibrium and the slope will stabilize.

It is observed in Fig. 1 that the x-intercept is the graphical point at which erosive degradation ceases. The value of this intercept on a semi-logarithmic plot corresponds to a Gully Factor of 41.2. The stable slope, S_s, for an existing gully on a reclaimed pile or embankment can be estimated as:

$$S_s = \frac{(41.2)(1 + D_{50})}{(A)(P)} \qquad (2)$$

where A is the drainage area, P is the number of precipitation events sufficient to cause runoff, and D_{50} is the median grain size of the slope material.

Time-Dependent Slope

Since the development of the stable slope does not occur at a constant rate, a long-term approach and analysis will temper the yearly variations in the rate of gully incision. The degradation is expected to decrease as the initial slope angle is reduced by the effects of erosion. The effects of time on the rate of incision into the embankment can be expressed in the form:

$$\frac{dy}{y} = k \, dt \tag{3}$$

where k is a constant and y is the incision depth which is a function of the time t. Rearranging Eq. 3, integrating, solving for y and applying the law of exponents

$$e^{kt + C} = e^{kt} \cdot e^{C} \tag{4}$$

If the symbol B is used for the constant of integration, e^{C}, a more convenient form of Eq. 4 can be expressed as:

$$y = Be^{kt} \tag{5}$$

The value of y reflects exponential growth when k is positive. When k is negative, y represents exponential decay.

The initial slope angle, S_i, of the reclaimed embankment exists only at the time of construction (t = 0) as presented in Fig. 2. The slope angle, or transition slope at the time of the field measurement, S_t, is a function of the vertical height from the base or toe elevation of the reclaimed embankment to the lowermost point of deepest gully incision, D_{max}, the horizontal slope distance, X, the slope length, L, and the distance from the toe to D_{max}, L_D. The transitional slope can be expressed as:

$$S_t = S_i - \frac{D_{max}}{(\frac{L_D}{L})(X)} \tag{6}$$

The ratio of the time-dependent slope and the initial design slope, S_t/S_i, represents the relative change in the slope angle between the initial conditions (t = 0) and the field measurements. The exponential decay equation is a means to determine the slope ratio for any

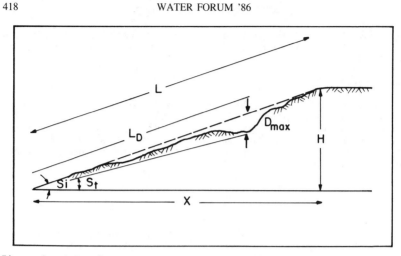

Figure 2. Lateral cross section of a typical reclaimed slope showing
gully and associated headcut.

interval of time. Therefore, the transitional slope can be expressed as
a function of the initial slope and time in the form

$$S_t = (S_i)Be^{-kt} \tag{7}$$

The initial slope angle equals the transitional slope angle only at the
time of construction, $t = 0$. When $t = 0$, the value of B in Eq. 7 is
unity. The value of the constant k was selected to comply with the
observed maximum gully depths and the occurrence of D_{max}
expressed as a fraction of the measured gully length. Since k is site
specific, a means of determining a k value applicable to any site was
warranted. A relationship was determined between the stable slope, S_s,
for each site and a calibration value. The product of the stable slope,
S_s, and the value G equals the constant k.

$$k = (S_s)(G) \tag{8}$$

Substituting unity for B and expressing the k in terms of S_s and
G, the transitional slope is expressed as:

$$S_t = (S_s)e^{-(GS_st)} \tag{9}$$

Equation 9 estimates the erosional slope angle for any point in
time. However, it is recommended that an upper time limit of 200 years
be used in applying Eq. 9. The transitional slope, S_t, is steeper than
the stable slope and less than the initial slope of construction. The
transitional slope should decrease at a decreasing rate.

Conclusions

An empirical investigation was conducted to formulate numerical guidelines for predicting the potential for gully incisions into a reclaimed waste impoundment. The following conclusions result from this investigation.

1) The contributing drainage area, the initial slope angle, the annual number of storm events greater than one-half inch precipitation, and the median grain diameter were determined to most significantly affect the rate of gully development and incision.

2) The variables of drainage area, initial impoundment slope angle, number of runoff events and the median grain diameter were correlated to the average annual maximum depth of gully incision on reclaimed slopes. The parameter encompassing these four variables, as presented in Eq. 1, is defined as the Gully Factor.

3) A means of estimating the long-term stable slope, S_s, for a reclaimed waste impoundment was formulated as a function of the Gully Factor.

Acknowledgments

The authors express their appreciation to the U.S. Nuclear Regulatory Commission for supporting the project reported herein under contract number 19X-077326 ORNL. Also, Oak Ridge National Laboratory is acknowledged for their contract administration assistance and support in this endeavor. Mr. David LaGrone and Mr. Ron Uhle are acknowledged for assistance in the data collection and analysis.

Disclaimer

The opinions expressed in this paper are those of the authors and do not necessarily represent the official policy of the Nuclear Regulatory Commission.

References

1. Falk, J. A., 1985. Prediction of Gully Incision on Reclaimed Slopes. M.S. Thesis, Colorado State University, Fort Collins, Colorado, p. 76.

2. Harvey, M. D., C. C. Watson, and S. A. Schumm, 1985. Gully Erosion. U.S. Department of Interior, Bureau of Land Management, Technical Note 366, 181 pp.

3. USDA Soil Conservation Service, 1964. Hydrology Guide for Use in Watershed Planning. National Engineering Handbook, Section 4, Supplement A.

Coupling Free Vortex Energy Dissipation with Sediment Control

George E. Wilson*

Introduction

The use of free vortex energy dissipation in water transport systems has been long practiced. Like the hydraulic jump used for energy dissipation in open channel flow, vortex generators in conduit flow mix high velocity with low velocity waters to dissipate the kinetic energy as viscous heat.

Traditionally, sediment control in water transport systems has relied on some type of gravity settling system, usually located off a sediment ejector.(5) These systems are typically designed to settle sands larger than 100 micron. There remains those abrasive sands between 30 and 100 micron.

A recent discovery now makes possible and practical simultaneous free vortex energy dissipation and sediment control down to a 30 micron sand sphere (7,8,9). The technology can also be applied to remove abrasive sediments from pump suction waters. Area requirements for 30 micron sand removal systems are less than 5 percent those of equivalent gravity settling basins.

Principles of Free Vortex Energy Dissipation

As applied for simultaneous energy dissipation and sediment control a vortex generator is called a centrifugal solids classifier. Its general shape and location are shown on Figure 1. Flow is introduced tangentially to an enclosed cylindrical chamber to maintain a rotating body of fluid. Unlike a paddle stirred vessel (forced vortex), the resulting free vortex is irrotational (6).

The ideal free vortex is characterized by constant angular momentum, U_r*r = constant. Consequently the tangential velocity, U_r, becomes very large as the radius r is decreased from the wall (R) to the exit discharge cylinder (r_e). The kinetic energy associated with this tangential velocity, K.E. = $U_r^2/2g$, is dissipated as the swirling effluent discharges into the outflow stream. As shown on Figure 2., of all the headlosses through the unit, that associated with the free vortex (h_v) is the major one.

*President, EUTEK SYSTEMS, 1509 Kingsford Dr., Carmichael, CA. 95608

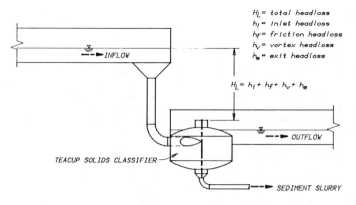

H_L = total headloss
h_I = inlet headloss
h_f = friction headloss
h_v = vortex headloss
h_e = exit headloss

$H_L = h_I + h_f + h_v + h_e$

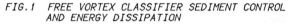

**FIG.1   FREE VORTEX CLASSIFIER SEDIMENT CONTROL
AND ENERGY DISSIPATION**

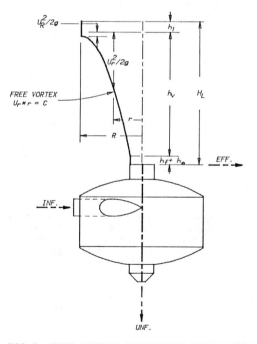

FIG.2   FREE VORTEX CLASSIFIER HEADLOSSES

Liquid/Particle Separation Efficiency of the Free Vortex Classifier

Liquid/particle separation occurs within the free vortex classifier (Teacup) as a consequent of centrifugal forces exceeding fluid drag forces carrying particles through the system. In water transport systems, sediment is typically dilute. Discrete particle settling laws apply (5). The acceleration of gravity, g, is replaced with a centrifugal acceleration term, $a = U_r^2/r$. If the particle is being held in a circular path of constant radius, r, the velocity of the fluid relative to the particle will be $Q/2\pi rh$ where Q represents the net outflow and h is the height of the cylinder at radius r.

The critical or cut point particle separation occurs at the classifier's discharge cylinder, $r = r_e$. The forces on the particle at this position have been shown on Figure 3. The centrifugal force, F_a, tends to keep the particle from exiting with the outflow. It operates as a consequence of the particle's positive mass in water, m $= (\rho_s - \rho_1)V_p$. The drag force, F_D, is a consequence of the outflow velocity flux through the discharge cylinder defined above. The drag coefficient, C_D, is a function of the particle Reynolds Number (6). The cross sectional area of the particle normal to the outflow velocity flux, A_p, is normally assumed to be that of a sphere.

Liquid/particle separation occurring in the Teacup solids classifier in water transport systems is quite different than that occurring in hydrocylones (4). The latter are normally applied to solid slurry streams in which discrete particle separation laws do not apply. Inlet velocities are much higher in hydrocyclones, resulting in a higher percentage of inlet headloss, h_i, and a free vortex that no longer exhibits conservation of angular momentum. Taken together, these differences result in quite different particle removal efficiencies and headlosses for a given flow and cut point particle size.

Collection and Classification of Separated Sediment

Rotating a cylinder of liquid over a flat base results in a radially inward velocity component within the viscous boundary layer (3). The magnitude of this component is approximately 1/6th that of the overlying tangential velocity. A cutaway of this boundary layer is shown on Figure 4.

Particles eventually settle by gravity into the boundary layer. The radial velocities within the layer tend to drag the particle toward the center of the base. This phenomenon can be observed in a teacup containing leaves after it has been vigorously stirred. Thus, the name Teacup solids classifier.

Classification or separation of particles according to specific gravity occurs within the boundary layer of a free vortex due to the acceleration of liquid with reduction of radius. It can be shown that two particles with equal settling velocity in a constant (gravity) acceleration field will describe different paths within the free vortex boundary layer if they have different specific gravities. This is due to the greater influence of the drag force on

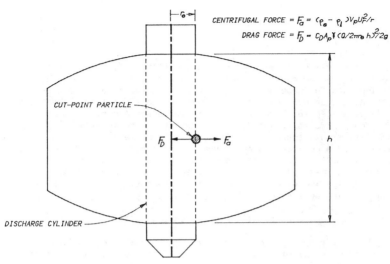

CENTRIFUGAL FORCE $= F_a = (\rho_s - \rho_l) V_p U_F^2 / r$

DRAG FORCE $= F_D = C_D A_p \gamma (Q/2\pi r_e h)^2 / 2g$

FIG.3   CUT POINT PARTICLE FORCES

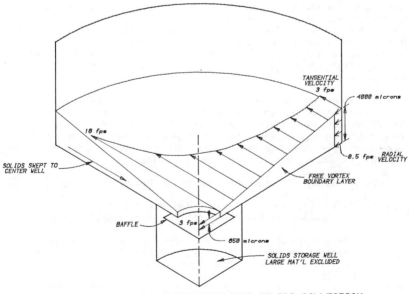

FIG.4   FREE VORTEX BOUNDARY LAYER SOLIDS COLLECTION
AND CLASSIFICATION

larger particles in a field of increasing acceleration. A forced
vortex boundary layer does not exhibit this classification property
because of the absence of this field.

Teacup solids classifiers spin at substantially lower tangential
velocities than do hydrocyclones. This is in order that particles
settling into the base boundary layer will be swept to the center
well. At higher cyclonic velocities the centrifugal forces on these
particles exceed the boundary layer radial drag forces. The
separated particles remain "pinned" against the outer wall and
accumulate within the unit. A Froude Number criteria was discovered
that assured a positive sweep of separated particles to the unit's
center well (7). The simultaneous application of this criteria with
the cut point particle centrifugal separation criteria results in a
unique combination of dimensions to meet separation, collection, and
classification requirements (8).

Case Study: Dual Purpose Wastewater Treatment (2)

This study was conducted to determine if the Teacup solids
classifier would be effective in removing abrasive sediments entering
a wastewater treatment plant. Because of the high concentration of
organic solids in the influent it was essential that removed sediment
be classified and free of organic material so that it could be
disposed of simply.

The study was conducted as part of the graduate engineering
program at California State University at Sacramento. The study was
carried out at the Sacramento City Main WWTP having an average dry
weather flow of 45 mgd. A one mgd Teacup solids classifier took its
inflow from the well mixed influent channel immediately downstream of
the flow measurement structure. The cut point particle size of the
classifier was 65 micron. This compared with the nominal 200 micron
particle design of the gravity settling basins used in the plant for
sediment control.

The study was conducted over a two week period. Sediment
volumes and masses per unit volume of flow were compared for the
Teacup and the gravity settling basins. Sediment carryover was also
compared. The organic content of the dewatered separated sediment
was carefully measured to determine the practicality of sediment
removal to such a small cut point particle size.

Following are the major conclusions reached by the study:

1. A 12-fold greater mass of sediment per unit volume
    throughput was removed by the free vortex solids classifier.

2. Percentage of organics contained in the classifier's
    removed sediment was less than one half that of sediment
    removed by the gravity settling basins.

3. The classifier removed 73% of the total entering inorganic
    solids (sediment and colloidal). This compared with only
    6% removed by the gravity settling basins.

4. The head requirements to operate the classifier and its
    absence of moving parts make it an ideal flow distribution
    device ahead of the treatment plant, protecting the plant
    from hydraulic overload.

Case Study: Control of Combined Sewer Overflows (1)

This case study of the Teacup solids classifier followed the
previous study and was conducted at the same location. Data were
only taken during periods of excess wet weather flows based on 24
hour totals. Previous experience at the plant showed no increase in
sediment removed per unit volume of throughflow with excess flow
conditions.

A total of 15 excess flow events were measured with paralleled
comparisons of sediment removed per unit volume throughflow for the
Teacup solids classifier versus gravity settling basins. Following
were the major conclusions:

1. Gravity settling basins showed no increase in sediment
    removed per unit volume throughflow under excess flow
    conditions. This was attributed to hydraulic washout and
    resuspension and loss of fine sediment in the mechanical
    collection, washing and dewatering steps.

2. Free vortex classifier removal of sediment increased 5-fold
    with a 25% increase in total daily plant flow over average
    dry weather. Removed quantities per unit volume
    throughflow were steeply increasing at this point and were
    projected to reach 10-fold with a 30% increase.

3. Organic content of removed sediments paralleled those
    measured in the previous case study.

4. 90% of the total annual sediment load to the plant was
    projected to enter during the 30 peak flow days of the year.

5. The study established the feasibility and benefit of
    applying the no-moving-parts free vortex classifier
    technology for flow regulation upstream of flow sensitive
    treatment facilities. Because of the headloss through the
    unit, bypassed flows could be discharged to elevated
    temporary storage basins and then returned by gravity and
    treated under low flow conditions.

Conclusions

1. Water transport systems benefit through sediment control
    due to:

    a. reduced sediment deposits.
    b. reduced abrasive wear on mechanical elements.

2. Water transport systems make good use of energy dissipation
    to:

a. achieve sudden drops in transport system energy grade
    lines.
b. regulate and distribute flows hydraulically without
    mechanical elements.
c. protect flow sensitive downstream processes/uses.

3. Sediment control down to the abrasive limit of 30 micron
    sand and energy dissipation can be achieved simultaneously
    with a Teacup free vortex solids classifier.

4. Case studies have demonstrated that sediment removed by the
    Teacup is easily disposed of due to excellent
    classification from organic solids.

5. Peak sediment control occurs at peak flow conditions in the
    Teacup when sediment loads per unit volume throughflow are
    greatest.

Appendix I.- References

1. Huang, L.C., "Control and Regulation of Combined Sewer Overflows
    with the Stormwater Teacup", Thesis Submitted in Partial
    Satisfaction of the Requirements for the Degree of Master of
    Science, 1979, California State University, Sacramento.
2. Jones, D.W., "Evaluation of the Stormwater Teacup as a Dual
    Purpose Wastewater Treatment Process", Thesis Submitted in
    Partial Satisfaction of the Requirements for the Degree of
    Master of Science, 1979, California State University, Sacramento.
3. Schlichting, H., Boundary Layer Theory, 6th Ed., McGraw-Hill,
    N.Y., N.Y., 1968, pp. 213-218.
4. Trawinski, H., "Hydrocyclones", in Solids/Liquid Separation
    Equipment Scale-Up, Purchas, D.B., Ed., Uplands Press, London,
    1977, p. 241.
5. Vanoni, V.A., Ed., Sedimentation Engineering, ASCE - Manuals &
    Reports on Engineering Practice - No. 54, 1975, pp. 576-587.
6. Vennard, J.K., Street, R.L., Elementary Fluid Mechanics, 5th
    Ed., John Wiley & Sons, 1976, pp. 602-604.
7. Wilson, G.E., "Apparatus and Method of Classifying Solids and
    Liquids", U.S. Patent No. 4,146,468, 1979.
8. Wilson, G.E., "Teacup Pretreatment of Wastewaters", Proceedings
    of the National Conference on Environmental Engineering, ASCE,
    Jul 8-10, 1980, pp. 651-656.
9. Wilson, G.E., "Is There Grit In Your Sludge?", Civil
    Engineering, April, 1985.

BEHAVIOR OF SEDIMENT-LADEN PLUMES ON STEEP SLOPES

Patrick J. Ryan*

ABSTRACT

The near field behavior of dense, sediment-laden flows on steep slopes was investigated as part of a study of mine tailings disposal. A literature review was performed which indicated that field and laboratory data were very limited and that no validated models existed covering this type of behavior. Simple analytical models and limited laboratory data were used to generate dilution vs. distance curves. These models assumed no deposition in the immediate vicinity of the outfall, and indicated relatively high levels of dilution that were strongly dependent on the bed slope. Later, physical model studies were performed at a 1:50 scale, and the effect of parameters such as bed slope, outfall diameter and velocity, and effluent density was investigated. Contrary to the assumptions used in developing the simple analytical models there was a large amount of near-outfall deposition, which resulted in significant changes to the plume behavior.

The basic assumptions used in the analytical studies will be discussed, and the results obtained will be compared with the behavior observed during the physical model studies.

INTRODUCTION

The Quartz Hill Molybdenum Project proposes to discharge 36,350-72,700 metric tons of tailings solids per day into a fjord in southeast Alaska for a period of approximately 55 years. The tailings will be discharged in the form of a dense slurry on the side of the fjord at a depth of approximately 50 meters. Just prior to discharge, the tailings slurry, a mixture of solids and freshwater, will be premixed with seawater. An extensive field data collection and modelling program was undertaken to predict the behavior of the tailings during and after deposition. The objectives of the modelling program were to define the characteristics of the mixing zone near the outfall, to predict the deposition pattern of the tailings and to investigate the possibility and distribution of suspended fines in the fjord water column. The overall program was designed to focus on each of the above program objectives in turn, and then to combine the results so as to produce a clear understanding of tailings behavior.

This paper focuses on the studies performed to define the behavior of the plume near the outfall, i.e. in the mixing zone or near field region. This region is defined as the zone near the outfall where the tailings plume behavior is dominated by outfall and effluent

*Chief Hydrologic Engineer, Bechtel, Inc., San Francisco, CA 94119

characteristics, typically a distance of approximately 100 outfall diameters from the discharge point.

Outfall and Effluent Characteristics

For the purpose of this study the following effluent and outfall characteristics were assumed:

o Discharge rate (solids)   36,350-72,700 tonnes/day
o Solids concentration   50% by weight
o Fresh water flow   36,350-72,700 m³/day
o Premixing ratio (seawater:slurry)   1 - 4 (by weight)
o Discharge Velocity (V)   2 - 4 m/s
o Outfall Diameter (D)   0.7 - 2.5m
o Mean particle diameter   30 μ

Side slopes in the fjord in the region of the outfall were in the range of 5°-35°. Typical excess densities ratios ($\Delta\rho/\rho$) of the tailings freshwater-seawater mixture with respect to the seawater were in the range of 0.05 - 0.4, and hence both the excess densities and slopes were very large compared to values for typical outfalls. Outfall densimetric Froude Numbers ($V/\sqrt{gD \,\Delta\rho/\rho}$) were typically in the range of 1-4.

Approach

The near field studies were performed in three steps, a literature review, modifications to existing analytical models, and a physical model study.

Literature Review

A literature search was performed to determine the existence of field data, laboratory data and/or validated models for predicting the behavior of dense plumes on steep slopes. Literature on outfalls for tailings, sewage, heated water, brine and drilling mud was investigated. Despite the enormous amount of literature on outfall behavior, it was concluded that the specific problem of three-dimensional, steady-state, dense flows on steep slopes was essentially virgin territory. No field data were available giving average or centerline plume concentrations in the immediate vicinity of an outfall, no validated models existed, and laboratory data were very limited. The limited laboratory data were reported by Fietz and Wood (1967), and showed that dense plume behavior on a slope was totally different from that of standard axisymmetric bouyant plumes. The dense plume spread very rapidly after leaving the outfall, and resulted in a very wide, thin plume within 5-10 outfall diameters. The only theoretical work was that of Nielsen (1971), but this work was not verified against either field or laboratory data, and resulted in very high dilution predictions. In addition, the Nielsen model was developed for a slot-type outlet, with a width much greater than the depth, in contrast to the typical circular outlet for tailings discharges.

Analytical Models

The second step involved modifying existing jet/plume models
and/or schematizing the outfall in such a way as to minimize the
differences between the actual characteristics of the tailings
outfall, and the model characteristics. The major problem in applying existing
plume models to the tailings plume is that the models do not account
for the effect of the bottom boundary, which both eliminates
entrainment across part of the plume boundary, and modifies the effect
of gravity and the entrainment rate. These effects were included in
the modified model by replacing the gravity term (g) in the standard
expression for vertical buoyant plumes by (g sin θ), and the neutral
entrainment coefficient E_0 by E_0 sin θ, which is in line with Ellison
and Turner (1959) and Britter and Linden (1980). The above approach
results in dilution being proportional to (sin θ)$^{4/3}$, similar to the
slope dependence derived by Nielsen. In the momentum dominated region
in the immediate vicinity of the outfall, the effect of slope will be
minimal, and the approach here was to treat the outfall as a surface
jet, using the standard EPA approach (Shirazi and Davis, 1974). This
approach already includes the boundary effect, with the implied
assumption that bottom friction is not important, and therefore the jet
in contact with the bottom will act in a similar manner to a surface
jet. Using the above approach, curves of dilution versus distance were
developed for a range of premixing, bottom slopes and exit velocities.
Figure 1 shows an example of the dilution versus distance curves
developed for a premixing of 1 and a discharge rate of 54,500
tonnes/day.

Several other approaches were also developed, including
calibrating the Nielsen model against the data from Fietz and Wood
(1967), and similar curves were developed to those shown in Figure 1.
Comparison of the various approaches showed relatively good agreement
for the low velocity, high density, low Froude No. discharge, but quite
poor agreement for the high velocity, low excess density discharge on
relatively flat slopes (<10ᵛ).

Based on the dilution/discharge curves it was concluded that:

o   The major effect on dilution was due to bottom slope, i.e. the
    slope of the side of the fjord, with dilution increasing with
    slope.
o   With the exception of the high velocity, low slope
    combinations, premixing and exit velocity had no effect on the
    plume beyond approximately 100m from the outfall.
o   For slopes in the range of 10ᵛ-20ᵛ, total dilution (premixing
    plus outfall dilution) at 100 meters from the outfall ranged
    from 30-80.

A major assumption in the above analysis was that no significant
deposition would take place in the near field and, hence, the tailings
jet/plume would move down a flat plane. As will be discussed later,
this assumption was not valid.

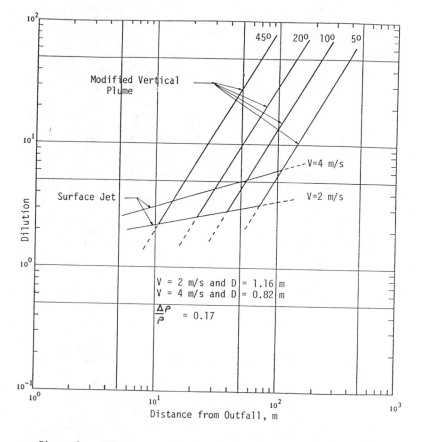

Figure 1   Dilution vs. distance from outfall. Surface jet/
            modified vertical plume approach.

Physical Model Study

Due to the lack of data and validated models for dense plumes on steep slopes, a physical model study was performed at the Iowa Institute of Hydraulic Research, (Jain and Kennedy, 1984). A scale of 1:50 was selected resulting in outfall diameters in the model of 2-4 cm. The tests were performed in a glass-sided tank with a working section 12m long, 3m wide and 2.3m deep. The sloping bed was modeled by a 5m long, 3m wide plywood ramp, hinged at one end to allow adjustment of the bed slope. Temperature and sediment concentration measurements were taken using a rack of moveable probes which allowed 3-dimensional measurements to be made in the plume.

The tests were run using actual tailings from the pilot plant tests. These tailings were screened so as to satisfy the model scale requirements which were based on the particle fall velocity, and resulted in $d_r=(L_r)^{1/4}$ where d_r and L_r are the ratios of the particle diameters and length scales in the model and prototype, respectively.

The tests were generally run in fresh water, with the density difference between the carrier fluid, a mixture of freshwater and seawater, and the seawater receiving fluid being simulated by heating the tailings slurry. This meant that temperature could be used as a tracer, and considerably simplified the measurement of dilution. A limited number of runs were performed using saltwater to ensure that using freshwater did not cause any significant change in plume behavior.

A total of 49 test runs, involving over 4 tonnes of tailings, were performed. The temperature and sediment concentrations inside the plume, and the configuration of the bottom deposits, were measured for:

o   Three levels of premixing (ratio of mass of seawater to mass of tailings slurry); 1:1, 1:2, and 1:4.
o   three slopes; 5˘, 12.5˘, and 25˘.
o   three outfall velocities; 1.1 m/s, 2.5 m/s, and 4.5 m/s.

Discussion of Results

Key observations from the model study were as follows:

o   The tailings plume was always observed to be a coherent, bottom attached, shallow plume, with the tailings confined to a thin layer, typically less than 5m thick (prototype) near the bottom.

o   The plume behavior was unsteady and significantly influenced by the configuration of the bottom deposits. Three types of flow configurations were identified; jet flow, sheet flow, and channel flow. Jet flow occurred in the initial tests, prior to deposition of large quantities of tailings near the outfall. In this regime the flow spread very rapidly and formed a wide shallow plume within a short distance from the outfall. This type of flow persisted for about 5 hours (model time) during which the fan shaped bottom deposits continued to

aggrade, finally forming a scoop shaped region near the
outfall. After this stage the effluent spilled over the rim
of the scoop, and appeared to be draped over the tailings
deposits. This type of flow was called sheet flow, and
persisted for approximately three hours, with the bed
configuration remaining relatively stable. At the end of this
period the flow suddenly began to erode the bottom sediments,
and a deep channel appeared in the deposits, with virtually
the total flow being confined to the channel. After several
more hours, the channel suddenly filled in, and sheet flow was
re-initiated. Finally, the flow reverted to the channel flow
configuration.

o The amount of dilution achieved varied with the type of flow.
   The ranges of the minimum dilutions at 100 m from the outfall
   for the jet flows, sheet flows, and channelized flows was 20
   to 42, 9 to 16, and 5 to 9, respectively (See Figure 2). The
   values for total bulk dilution (including premixing) are at
   least a factor of three larger than the above values.

o The effect on dilution of the premixing ratio, outfall
   velocity, and outlet diameter was found to be insignificant.

o The effect on dilution of the bottom slope for both jet and
   sheet flows was found to be significant. The dilution
   increased with increasing slope. Channelized flows were less
   affected by the slope.

o The configuration of the deposits was also affected by the
   bottom slope. For small values of bottom slope, the outlet
   was buried under the deposited sediment in a relatively short
   period. However, the model outfall continued to operate, and
   since the shear strength of the tailings material in the model
   was not scaled, the burial of the outlet in the model does not
   necessarily indicate similar behavior in the field.

o The predictions of the modified plume model discussed above
   were in reasonable agreement with the model results for jet
   flows (see Figure 2), where the effect of already deposited
   sediment on the tailings plume was not significant. However,
   once significant deposition occurred, and the flow was
   channelized, dilution decreased markedly, resulting in a more
   coherent plume.

o The use of fresh water instead of seawater did not cause any
   change in plume behavior.

Conclusions

1. Sediment-laden plumes on steep slopes behave as shallow, coherent
   flows, restrained laterally by levees of deposited material. In
   the initial stages prior to deposition of a large amount of
   material, the flow tends to spread rapidly and dilution is
   relatively high. After a relatively short period (of the order

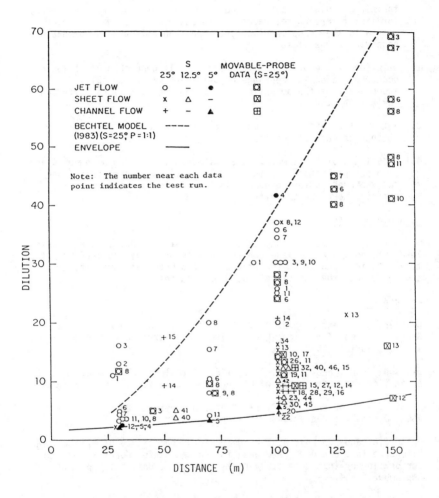

Figure 2   Variation of dilution versus distance from the outfall   (Jain and Kennedy, 1984)

of days in the prototype) the nature of the flow changes, and it appears to drape over the deposited material and dilution drops markedly. This period also has a relatively short duration before the plume fluidizes some of the deposited material, cuts a channel for itself through the deposits and channelized flow takes over, with a further drop in dilution. The channelized behavior has been observed in the field.

2. Dilution of the plume was relatively small once channelization had occurred, being in the range of 5-10, and was essentially independent of the amount of premixing, the outfall velocity and outlet diameter.

3. Bottom slope affected dilution, but the dependence was not very strong for channelized flow.

4. Existing analytical models are not adequate for computing dilution or other parameters for these types of flows, except in the very early stages, prior to deposition of significant amounts of material near the outfall.

Acknowledgements

Acknowledgements are due to Dr. S. C. Jain and Dr. John F. Kennedy, Institute of Hydraulic Research, University of Iowa, who performed the model studies, and to United States Borax & Chemical Corporation, who sponsored both the analytical and model studies.

References

Britter, R.E., and Linden, P.F., 1980 "The Motion of a Front of a Gravity Current Travelling Down an Incline", Journal of Fluid Mechanics, Vol. 99, Part 3, 1980.

Ellison, T. H., and Turner, J.S., 1959 "Turbulent Entrainment in Stratified Flows," Journal of Fluid Mechanics", Vol. 6, Part 3, 1959.

Fietz, T.R., and Wood, I., 1967, "Three Dimensional Density Current", ASCE, Journal of Hydraulics Division, November, 1967.

Jain, S.C. and Kennedy, J. F., "Near Field Model Study of Mine Tailings Discharge Into a Fjord", Prepared for United States Borax & Chemical Corporation by Institute of Hydraulic Research, University of Iowa, September, 1984.

Nielsen, J. H., 1971, "The Three Dimensional, Steady Spread of a Density Current Down on Inclined Plane," Basic Research Report No. 22, Hydraulic Laboratory, Tech. University of Denmark, 1971.

Shirazi, M. A., and Davis, L. R., 1974, "Workbook of Thermal Plume Prediction - Vol. 2 - Surface Discharges", EPA-R2-72-0056, Environmental Protection Technology Series, U. S. Environmental Protection Agency, Corvallis, Oregon, 1974

Stochastic Design of Wastewater Storage Ponds

Steven G. Buchberger, A.M. ASCE and David R. Maidment, M. ASCE[*]

Abstract

The performance of wastewater storage facilities at land treatment sites depends on the mean levels of the inflow and outflow, facility capacity, climatic variability and project duration. We combine the principle of mass conservation with basic ideas from probability theory and then apply Monte Carlo simulation techniques to develop a family of design charts called storage performance functions (SPF). The SPF is a graph of the cumulative probability distribution of annual storage levels versus a storage index calculated from wastewater inflow and outflow rates, facility size, climatic variability and project duration. Results show that, to meet a specified level of storage reliability, the required capacity of a wastewater pond is larger for regions where climatic variability is high than for regions where climatic variability is low. An example illustrates how the SPF can be used to size a wastewater storage pond to meet a given performance standard.

Introduction

Three major land treatment processes are used to dispose of municipal wastewater (EPA, 1981): (1) slow rate irrigation, (2) rapid infiltration and (3) overland flow. Figure 1 illustrates these processes at a land application site where a storage pond of capacity, C, receives wastewater inflows, Q, and makes releases, R, to an adjacent treatment field where wastewater is disposed by plant evapotranspiration, ET, deep infiltration, I, and surface discharge, D. The distinction between the three major land treatment alternatives depends on which component dominates the disposal process. A "slow rate" (irrigation) process relies on ET; a "rapid infiltration" process relies on I; an "overland flow" process relies on D. If regulated releases to the field are not permitted (R=0), the land treatment system is a complete retention evaporation pond where the natural release from storage is governed by the rate of net potential evaporation, N, computed as the difference between potential evaporation, E, and precipitation, P.

The primary purpose of the pond is to provide storage during times when the inflow exceeds the outflow. The capacity of the pond depends on two parameters: (1) surface area and (2) embankment height.

[*]Research Assistant and Associate Professor, respectively.
Department of Civil Engineering, The University of Texas at Austin, Austin, Texas 78712

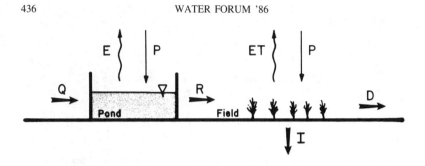

Figure 1.   Definition sketch for land treatment system.

Most conventional methods for sizing wastewater storage ponds use a
two step process, each step based on the principle of continuity
(USBR, 1970; Clements and Otis, 1980; EPA, 1981; Middlebrooks et al.,
1983; Texas Water Commission, 1983). In the first step, the pond
surface area is obtained from a rate balance representing the ratio of
the mean annual wastewater inflow to the average annual outflow per
unit area. The embankment height is then estimated with a monthly
average mass balance using the area obtained from the rate balance.
Because this procedure inherently implies that the annual net inflow
(inflow minus outflow) is zero every year, it does not explicitly
account for annual climatic variability, carryover storage, or project
duration. Consequently, the combined rate and mass balance approach
provides no way to measure long-term reliability of the storage pond.

A second approach to estimate wastewater storage requirements uses
frequency analysis of annual storage days based on a daily climatic
criteria (Whiting, 1976). This method recognizes the variability of
annual outflows but tacitly assumes that the storage levels return to
the empty state each year. This assumption is difficult to justify
unless the mean annual level of the outflow greatly exceeds that of
the inflow, a condition which is not likely to exist at land
application sites where the area of the treatment field is determined
from an average rate balance (EPA, 1981).

The problem of determining wastewater storage requirements is
analogous to design of a water supply reservoir except that the pond
inflow is deterministic, outflow is stochastic and the facility is
successful when its storage is nearly empty rather than full. We
have exploited this analogy in a previous investigation of the
performance of complete retention ponds (Buchberger and Maidment,
1985). In this paper, we extend this work and present a reliability
based method for determining wastewater storage requirements at land
application sites. Our analysis is geared toward treatment processes
which are driven by the variability of annual net potential
evaporation (irrigation systems and complete retention ponds) but the
basic principles apply to any land treatment system or other storage
process where the distribution of the net input can be estimated.

Problem Formulation

It is assumed that the storage pond has vertical sides and an impermeable floor of area, A_p. The adjacent field is used to irrigate an area, A_f. Then the annual net inflow to the pond is

$$X = Q - (N + a_r L)A_p \qquad (1)$$

where $a_r = A_f/A_p$, ratio of field to pond areas,
$L = R/A_f$, annual hydraulic loading rate, and
Q, N, R were defined previously.

From the mass conservation principle, pond storage at time t is

$$S_t = S_{t-1} + X_t \qquad (2)$$

from which the the cumulative distribution function (CDF) of S_t is

$$H(s) = G(0)F(s) + \int_{0^+}^{C^-} F(s-u)g(u)du + [1-G(C^-)]F(s-C) \qquad (3)$$

in which $H(s)$ = CDF of S_t, $G(s)$ = CDF of S_{t-1}, $F(x)$ = CDF of X, and and $g(s) = G'(s)$, $t = 1,2,3...$ and $0 \leq s \leq C$.

The first and third terms on the right hand side of (3) are the probability mass of storage at the lower boundary (empty pond, $s=0$) and upper boundary (full pond, $s=C$), respectively. The convolution integral represents the distribution of storage between the pond's boundaries. Solutions of equation (3) for $t>0$, provide reliability based estimates of storage requirements. To proceed, assume that X is serially independent and normally distributed with mean, μ, and variance, σ^2, and consider, for the moment, a wastewater storage pond without boundaries, the so-called "infinite reservoir." Under these ideal conditions, with $S=0$ at $t=0$, we have

$$S_t \sim N(\mu t, t\sigma^2) \qquad (4)$$

from which it follows that the solution to (3) is

$$H(s) = \Phi[(s-\mu t)/(\sigma t^{1/2})] \qquad (5)$$

in which $\Phi[z]$ is the CDF of the standard normal variate, z. To generalize this result, define the standardizing transformations

$$k = s/\sigma \qquad (6)$$

$$\varepsilon = \mu/\sigma \qquad (7)$$

where k is a standardized reservoir variate with dimensions of time and ε is the dimensionless mean net inflow also known as "reservoir drift" (Pegram, 1980). For the special case when the numerator in (6) equals the reservoir capacity, C, the variate, k, is denoted k_* and called the "standard reservoir." A positive drift implies that the reservoir tends to accumulate storage over time. Conversely, a

negative drift means that the reservoir tends to deplete storage.
When the drift is zero, the mean levels of the inflow and outflow are
balanced so that the equilibrium distribution of storage is uniform
throughout the reservoir. Note that the zero drift condition is the
basis of conventional rate and mass balance procedures for sizing
wastewater storage ponds. Substituting (6) and (7) into (5) yields

$$H(s) = \Phi[\Psi(k,\varepsilon,t)] \tag{8}$$

where we call $\Psi(k,\varepsilon,t)$ the "storage index" which is given by

$$\Psi(k,\varepsilon,t) = (k-\varepsilon t)/(t^{1/2}). \tag{9}$$

The storage index is a fundamental parameter that embodies the key
factors affecting reservoir performance, namely storage size (k),
project duration (t), and the mean and variance of the net inflow (ε).
In the following sections we show how $\Psi(k,\varepsilon,t)$ can be used to design
wastewater storage facilities at land application sites.

Problem Solution

Returning now to a finite reservoir, solutions of (3) are estimated
using Monte Carlo data generation techniques to simulate operation of
a wastewater storage pond. The experimental procedure is as follows.
A standardized pond capacity is chosen and divided into 22 intervals,
20 interior states between 2 boundaries. Initial storage is set to
zero. Synthetic traces of the net inflow are generated simultaneously
for a vector of annual reservoir drift values. Storage fluctuations
are monitored and the ending storage levels are recorded for selected
project durations. The simulation is carried out for many trials so
that the observed discrete relative frequencies of wastewater levels
approximate the continuous CDF of pond storage. The process is
repeated for different standardized pond capacities. Results are
plotted on a family of graphs called storage performance functions
(SPF) such as those presented in Figure 2 which shows the CDF of k at
time t, $J_t(k)$, versus $\Psi(k,\varepsilon,t)$ for a standardized pond capacity,
$k^* = 2$ years, and project durations of t = 1, 5, and 25 years.

In Figure 2, when t>1 year, the lines for $k=0^+$ and for $k=2^-$
delineate the storage distribution between the lower and upper
boundaries of the pond, respectively. All intermediate storage levels
lie in the shaded region between these limiting cases. In contrast,
when t=1 year, the SPF collapses to a single line. Here all storage
levels are distinguished only by their unique storage index value.
The probability that the pond is empty or full at time t is

$$\Pr[\text{pond is empty at time } t] = \Pr[k \leq 0] = J_t(0^+) \tag{10}$$

$$\Pr[\text{pond is full at time } t] = \Pr[k \geq 2] = 1 - J_t(2^-) \tag{11}$$

There are many measures to describe storage reliability. In the
context of a wastewater storage pond, we define annual performance
reliability at time t, $\alpha(t)$, as the probability that the pond does
not spill during the interval (t-1,t) or

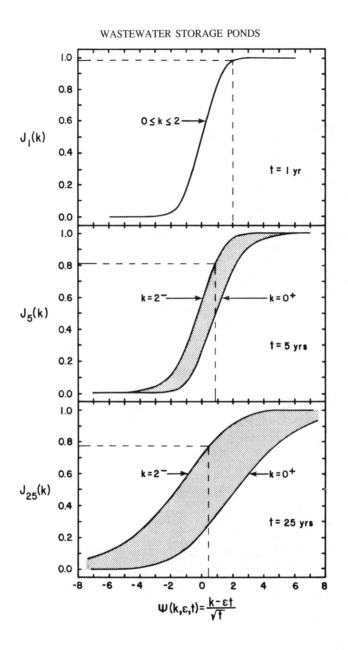

Figure 2. Storage performance functions for standardized pond of size
$k^* = 2$ yrs, initially empty with normal independent annual
net inflows. Dashed lines are used in design example.

$$\alpha(t) = J_t(k^{*-}) \tag{12}$$

where $J_t(k^{*-}) = Pr[k \leq k^{*-}] = Pr[k < k^*]$. The SPFs in Figure 2 show that for a given time, the reliability of the pond improves as the storage index increases. Equation (9) indicates that the storage index is greater with a negative drift than with a positive drift condition. This reiterates our previous observation that positive drift implies storage accumulation while negative drift implies storage depletion.

Design Example Using the SPF

The most direct way to demonstrate the utility of the storage performance function is with a design example. For the sake of illustration, assume that the annual net potential evaporation rate, N, and the annual hydraulic loading rate, L, have a common positive coefficient of variation, γ, and correlation coefficient, ρ. The coefficient of variation measures local climatic variability; the correlation coefficient measures the linear dependence between N and L. It is reasonable to expect that ρ is positive since the climatic conditions which encourage or suppress net evaporation at the pond are likely to have the same effect on plant consumptive use in the field. To consolidate the following calculations, it is convenient to use the mean, λ_1, and variance, $(\gamma\lambda_2)^2$, of the total wastewater disposal rate (N+L) per unit area where λ_1 and λ_2 are given by

$$\lambda_1 = E[N] + a_r E[L] \tag{13}$$

$$\lambda_2 = \{(E[N])^2 + (a_r E[L])^2 + 2\rho a_r E[N]E[L]\}^{1/2} \tag{14}$$

in which $E[]$ is the expectation operator. Assuming that the annual wastewater inflow, Q, is constant, the mean, μ, and the variance, σ^2, of the annual net inflow to the pond, X, are

$$\mu = Q - \lambda_1 A_p \tag{15}$$

$$\sigma^2 = (\gamma\lambda_2 A_p)^2. \tag{16}$$

The required floor area of the pond is found by substituting (15) and (16) into (7) and solving for A_p

$$A_p = Q/[\lambda_1 + (\varepsilon\gamma\lambda_2)]. \tag{17}$$

Consider the following values of the design parameters:

Q=120 af/yr	(148,000 m³/yr),	ρ=0.70,
E[N]=3 ft/yr	(0.9 m/yr),	γ=0.30,
E[L]=2 ft/yr	(0.6 m/yr),	a_r=6.00.

Then equations (13) and (14) give

λ_1=15.0 ft/yr (4.6 m/yr) and
λ_2=14.3 ft/yr (4.4 m/yr).

As a starting point, apply the conventional rate balance method which implies a zero drift condition (ε=0) so that (17) yields

$A_p = Q/\lambda_1 = 120/15 = 8.0$ ac (3.2 ha),

and the corresponding required area of the irrigation field is

$A_f = a_r A_p = (6.0)(8.0) = 48.0$ ac (19.4 ha).

The standard deviation of the net inflow is from (16)

$\sigma = \gamma\lambda_2 A_p = (0.30)(14.3)(8.0) = 34.3$ af/yr (42,300 m³/yr).

Assuming that the standardized pond capacity, $k^* = 2.0$ yr, the storage capacity, C, and the depth (embankment height), h, of the pond are

$C = k^*\sigma = (2.0)(34.3) = 68.6$ af (84,600 m³) and,
$h = C/A_p = k\gamma\lambda_2 = 68.6/8.0 = 8.6$ ft (2.6 m).

How reliable is this pond? With equation (9) we compute

$\Psi(2^-,0,1) = 2.00,$
$\Psi(2^-,0,5) = 0.89,$
$\Psi(2^-,0,25) = 0.40.$

Entering these values on the abscissa of Figure 2, we find the following time dependent reliabilities (refer to the dashed lines in Figure 2) from the appropriate ordinate scale:

$\alpha(1) = J_1(2^-) = 98\%,$
$\alpha(5) = J_5(2^-) = 81\%,$
$\alpha(25) = J_{25}(2^-) = 77\%,$

which indicate there is a 2%, 19%, and 23% risk that the pond will spill during years 1, 5, and 25, respectively. In a similar manner, additional estimates of the risk of spill can be obtained using SPFs developed for other standard reservoir capacities.

In contrast to the conventional rate balance procedure, consider a reliability based design approach in which, for purposes of this example, regulatory standards require that the risk of a spill during year 5 not exceed 5%. Then Figure 2 gives $\Psi(2^-,\varepsilon,5) = 1.80$. Substituting this value of the storage index into (9) and solving for the drift yields

$\varepsilon = [k-\Psi(k,\varepsilon,t)(t^{1/2})]/(t) = [2.0-(1.8)(2.23)]/5 = -0.40.$

Again using (17), the new estimates of the pond and field areas become

$A_p = 120/[15+(-0.40)(0.30)(14.3)] = 9.0$ ac (3.6 ha) and
$A_f = (6.0)(9.0) = 54.0$ ac (21.9 ha).

In order to meet the stricter performance standard, the areas of the storage pond and the irrigation field must be increased about 13%. Because, in this example, the standardized pond capacity is fixed at $k^* = 2.0$ yrs, the embankment height remains unchanged. Note, however, that if the coefficient of variation of N and L were increased from 0.30 to 0.60, the embankment height would likewise double.

Summary and Conclusions

Conventional methods for estimating wastewater storage requirements at land application sites do not explicitly consider annual climatic variability, carryover storage, or project duration. These methods provide no measure of annual storage reliability. Using techniques from stochastic reservoir theory, we develop families of storage performance functions that show the CDF over time of wastewater storage levels versus a fundamental storage index. An example using an irrigation treatment system illustrates how the storage performance function can be used to complement current design practice for sizing wastewater storage facilities.

References

Buchberger, S.G. and D.R. Maidment (1985) "Performance of Evaporation Ponds Under Stochastic Conditions," in Proc of Fourth Internatinal Hydrology Symposium, Multivariate Analysis of Hydrologic Processes ed by H.W. Shen, Colorado State University, Fort Collins, CO.

Clements, E.V. and R.J. Otis (1980) "Design Manual--Onsite Wastewater Treatment and Disposal Systems," EPA-625/1-80-012.

Environmental Protection Agency (1981) "Process Design Manual for Land Treatment of Municipal Wastewater," EPA-625/1-81-013.

Middlebrooks, E.J., et al. (1983) "Design Manual--Municipal Wastewater Stabilization Ponds," EPA-625/1-83-015.

Pegram, G.G.S. (1980) "On Reservoir Reliability," Journal of Hydrology, 47:269-296.

Texas Water Commission (1983) "Design Criteria for Sewerage Systems, Appendix B--Land Disposal of Sewage Effluent."

U.S. Bureau of Reclamation (1970) "Brine Disposal Pond Manual."

Whiting, D.M. (1976) "Use of Climatic Data in Estimating Storage Days for Soils Treatment Systems," EPA-600/2-76-250.

Parameter Optimization of Dynamic Routing Models

D.L. Fread and J.M. Lewis*

Abstract - A methodology has been developed for determining the optimal parameters of dynamic routing models thereby eliminating costly and time-consuming preparation of detailed cross-sectional data. The methodology utilizes (1) approximate cross-sectional properties represented by separate power functions for channel and floodplain, and (2) a very efficient optimization algorithm for determining the Manning n as a function of either stage or discharge. Essential data required for implementing the methodology are stage hydrographs at both ends of each routing reach and a discharge hydrograph at the upstream end of each river. The methodology is applicable to multiple routing reaches along main-stem rivers and their tributaries. Optimal n values may be constrained to fall within a specified min-max range for each routing reach. Specific cross-sectional properties at key locations, e.g., bridges, dams, unusual constrictions, also can be utilized within the optimization methodology. The methodology was tested on 1275 miles (2051 km) of major rivers and their principal tributaries in the U.S. with promising results; the average root-mean-square error was 0.44 ft (0.13 m) or 2.9 percent of the change in stage.

Introduction

Flood routing is an essential tool for flood forecasting and engineering design or analysis of hydraulic structures. Of the many flood routing methods that have been developed, dynamic flood routing based on a four-point implicit finite difference solution of the one-dimensional equations of unsteady flow (Saint-Venant equations) has generally been accepted as the most powerful with feasible computational requirements. Dynamic routing enables the prediction of water elevations (h) and discharges (Q) along a single waterway or a network of interactive waterways. Complex hydraulic phenomena such as reverse flows, backwater effects from tributary inflows and hydraulic structures, flow accelerations, levee overtopping, etc. may be properly accounted for in dynamic routing. However, such phenomena are neglected by the simple hydrologic routing techniques, and yet these are sometimes selected for such applications because data for optimizing their parameters is more readily available than for dynamic routing.

Dynamic routing has been applied when there was a substantial amount of cross-sectional data available to characterize the cross-sectional area (A) and top width (B) as known functions of h. This required the existence of detailed hydrographic survey information and topographical maps, as well as considerable time consuming effort by

*Senior Res. Hydrologist & Res. Hydrologist, National Weather Service Hydrologic Res. Laboratory, 8060 13th St., Silver Spring, MD 20910.

hydrologists to reduce the basic cross-sectional information to the form of A and B as specified tabular functions of h. In order to eliminate the necessity for using such costly and often unavailable detailed data, a very powerful and computationally efficient parameter optimization methodology which utilizes minimal cross-sectional information was developed for application by the National Weather Service hydrologists for flood forecasting. Also, this methodology could be used advantageously by hydrologists/engineers concerned with unsteady flow prediction in waterways of many developing countries where detailed cross-sectional data is prohibitively expensive to obtain because of the remote locations of the waterways and the relative magnitude of the effort required for a single engineering study.

Theory and Background

The Saint-Venant equations of unsteady flow consist of a conservation of mass equation, i.e.

$$\partial Q/\partial x + \partial(A + A_o)/\partial t - q = 0 \tag{1}$$

and a conservation of momentum equation, i.e.,

$$\partial Q/\partial t + \partial(Q^2/A)/\partial x + gA(\partial h/\partial x + S_f) - qv_x = 0 \tag{2}$$

where:

$$S_f = n^2 \, |Q|Q/(2.21 \, A^2 \, R^{4/3}) \tag{3}$$

in which x is the distance along the longitudinal axis of the waterway, t is time, Q is discharge, A is active cross-sectional area, A_o is inactive (off-channel storage) area, q is lateral inflow (positive) or outflow (negative), g is the gravity acceleration constant, h is water surface elevation or stage, v_x is the velocity of the lateral flow in the x-direction, S_f is the friction slope computed by Manning's equation, n is the Manning coefficient, and R is the hydraulic radius.

In this paper, a dynamic routing model, FLDWAV, based on Eqs (1) and (2) which are solved by an implicit 4-point nonlinear finite difference technique described elsewhere (Fread, 1985; Fread and Smith, 1978) is used to implement and test the optimization methodology.

Data normally required to calibrate a dynamic routing model are: 1) cross-sectional area (A) and width (B) as a function of water surface elevation (h) for sections representative of the routing reach, 2) the Manning n which may vary with either elevation or discharge throughout the routing reach, 3) observed discharge and stage hydrographs at the upstream end of the routing reach, and either a stage or discharge hydrograph at the downstream extremity of the routing reach.

To avoid the costly and time-consuming tasks of gathering detailed cross-section data and then reducing the data into tables of top width (B) and water elevation (h), simple approximations are used to represent an average cross-section within each routing reach. A power function, $B_c = k_c Y_c^{m_c}$, is used for the channel and another

power function, $B_f = k_f Y_f^{m_f}$, is used for the floodplain. The

parameters k_c, m_c, k_f,m_f are estimated from 1) topographical maps,
2) visual inspection of a few easily accessible cross-sections, and/or
3) a few available cross-sections of the river. The shape parameter
(m_c) can be easily computed, i.e.,

$$m_c = (\log B_2 - \log B_1)/(\log Y_2 - \log Y_1) \qquad (4)$$

in which B_2 and Y_2 are the estimated bank-full width and depth and B_1
and Y_1 are estimates of an intermediate width and depth. The scaling
parameter (k_c) is computed from the basic power function, i.e.,
$k_c = B/Y^{m_c}$. Similarly the shape and scaling parameters for the floodplain can be computed from estimates of the floodplain widths and
depths. Sometimes it is appropriate simply to estimate the shape
parameter, i.e., rectangular-shape (m=0), parabolic shape (m=0.5),
triangular shape (m=1.0) or ⋏-shapes (m>1). The parameter optimization methodology which has been programmed as an integral option
within the FLDWAV routing model allows the k and m parameters to be
specified directly or to be computed by the program from the specified
B and Y values for each routing reach.

When unusual cross-sections exist in a routing reach, e.g., at a
bridge, dam, or some natural constriction, those cross-sections' top
width and elevation tables may be specified; they each remain distinct
from the average section described by the two power functions.

A parameter optimization algorithm within FLDWAV iteratively
determines the best value for the Manning n which is allowed to vary
with h or Q for each reach of waterway bounded by water level recorders. An objective function defined as the difference between the
computed and observed upstream stage hydrographs for several ranges of
flow is minimized by a Newton-Raphson technique (Fread and Smith,
1978; Fread, 1985). A numerical derivative is used in lieu of the
analytical derivative for the rate of change of the objective function
with respect to the change in the Manning n. With starting values for
n based on an assumption of steady flow or simply using a reasonable
estimate, convergence to an optimal set of values is obtained in three
to four iterations, i.e., the optimal n relation with h or Q for the
reach of water bounded by known stage hydrographs can be obtained
within three to four evaluations of the objective function; an evaluation consists of routing the flood hydrograph through the reach and
comparing computed and observed upstream stage values. An option in
FLDWAV allows the hydrologist to estimate a range of minimum and maximum n values within which the optimal n values must reside. When the
optimal values are outside the specified min-max range, the cross
section is automatically reduced or increased sufficiently to allow
the next optimization to yield n values within the allowable range.

The optimization algorithm can be applied to multiple routing
reaches, commencing with the most upstream reach and progressing
reach-by-reach in the downstream direction. An observed discharge
hydrograph is used as an upstream boundary condition for the most upstream reach. Then, the discharges computed at the downstream boundary using the optimal n values are stored internally by the program and
used as the upstream boundary condition for the next downstream
reach. Dendritic river systems are automatically decomposed into a

series of multiple-reach rivers. Tributaries are optimized before the
main-stem river and their flows are added to the main stem as lateral
inflow(s).

This parameter optimization methodology offers several advantages
over one described by Wormleaton and Karmegam (1984) which required 26
iterations to find the optimal parameters. It was restricted to a
trapezoidal shaped cross-section with a constant n value and was for a
single routing reach bounded by gaging stations with observed stage
and discharge hydrographs from a previous flood.

The optimal n values obtained via the parameter optimization
methodology presented herein is limited to expected applications where
the maximum discharges do not greatly exceed those used in the optimization. Also, the methodology is best suited for applications where
flood predictions are primarily required at locations along the waterway where level recorders exist. Unless detailed cross-sectional
information at significant constriction or expansions is utilized in
the optimization methodology, the cross sections throughout each routing reach should be generally uniform.

Applications

The new parameter optimization methodology has been tested on the
following four river systems:

Lower Mississippi. This is a 292 mi (470 km) reach of the Lower
Mississippi River consisting of eight water level recorders. The discharge is known at the most upstream station. This reach of the Lower
Mississippi is contained within levees for most of its length. The
average channel slope is an extremely mild 0.0000064. The discharge
varies from low flows of about 100,000 cfs (2,832 m/s) to flood discharges of over 1,200,000 cfs (33,985 m/s). A total of 25 cross
sections located at unequal intervals including the locations of the
level recorders were used in the computations. The results of the
parameter optimization are shown in Table 1. The effectiveness of the
optimization is represented by the root-mean-square (rms) error
between the computed and observed stage hydrographs at each level
recorder. The average rms value is 0.37 ft (0.11 m). Also, this is
presented as a percentage of the total change in water elevation which
is only 2.4 percent. The average number of iterations or times that
the flood is routed through each reach is three. Although the n
values vary with discharge, the average value is shown for each reach.

Ohio-Mississippi. This is a dendritic river system consisting of 393
miles (633 km) of the Mississippi, Ohio, Cumberland, and Tennessee
Rivers with a total of 16 water level recorders and discharge measurements at the most upstream stations on each of the four rivers. The
channel bottom slope is mild, varying from about 0.000047 to 0.000095.
Each branch of the river system is influenced by backwater from downstream branches. Total discharge through the system varies from about
120,000 cfs (3,398 cms) to flood flows of 1,700,000 cfs (48,145 cms).
A total of 45 cross-sections located at unequal intervals were used in
the computations. The results of the parameter optimization are shown
in Table 1. The average rms error is 0.62 ft. (0.19 m) representing

Table 1. Optimization Results for Four Major River Systems

RIVER SYSTEM River	Station	Root-Mean-Square Error ft (m)	Percent	Iterations	n_{avg}
L. MISSISSIPPI					
L. Mississippi	Red River Ldg.	0.11 (.03)	0.5	3	.025
"	Baton Rouge	0.16 (.05)	0.7	3	.018
"	Donaldsonville	0.16 (.05)	0.9	3	.015
"	Carrollton	0.27 (.08)	2.5	2	.014
"	Pt. Hache	0.27 (.08)	4.7	3	.015
		Avg 0.19 (.06)	Avg 1.9	Avg 3	
OHIO-MISSISSIPPI					
Ohio	Shawneetown	0.65 (.20)	2.3	3	.018
"	Golconda	0.67 (.20)	2.4	4	.021
"	Paducah	0.68 (.21)	2.7	3	.023
"	Metropolis	0.59 (.18)	2.8	4	.020
"	Cairo	1.04 (.32)	4.8	6	.026
Cumberland	Berkley Dam T.W.	0.77 (.23)	2.8	4	.016
Tennessee	Kentucky Dam T.W.	0.85 (.26)	3.4	4	.036
U. Mississippi	Chester	0.34 (.10)	1.4	3	.026
"	Grand Tower	0.47 (.14)	2.0	3	.032
"	Cape Girardeau	0.51 (.15)	2.2	2	.024
L. Mississippi	New Madrid	0.72 (.22)	3.8	3	.022
		0.66 (.20)	2.8	3	
ILLINOIS-MISSISSIPPI-MISSOURI					
Illinois	Morris	0.30 (.09)	2.2	2	.025
"	La Salle	0.21 (.06)	1.2	4	.030
"	Henry	0.30 (.09)	2.8	4	.020
"	Peoria	0.21 (.06)	1.6	5	.046
"	Havana	0.63 (.19)	3.3	3	.038
"	Beardstown	0.50 (.15)	2.7	3	.033
"	Meredosia	0.15 (.05)	0.6	3	.022
"	Harding	0.54 (.16)	2.8	3	.017
Mississippi	L&D No. 24 T.W.	0.38 (.12)	1.8	3	.028
"	L&D No. 25 T.W.	0.41 (.13)	1.8	2	.039
"	Dixon Ldg.	0.35 (.11)	1.7	4	.033
"	Alton	0.18 (.05)	0.6	3	.023
"	St. Louis	0.47 (.14)	1.1	4	.024
Missouri	Hermann	0.68 (.21)	2.7	4	.034
		0.38 (.12)	1.9	3	
COLUMBIA					
Columbia	Bonneville	0.22 (.07)	2.4	4	.040
"	Washougal	0.27 (.08)	4.5	3	.032
"	Vancouver	0.31 (.09)	6.2	4	.024
"	Columbia	0.40 (.12)	8.3	4	.016
"	Wauna	0.74 (.23)	11.4	3	.022
Willamette	Portland	0.30 (.09)	5.0	3	.024
		0.37 (.11)	6.3	4	

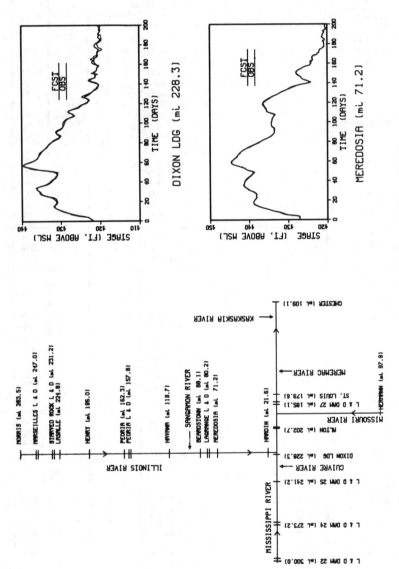

Fig. 1 -- Illinois-Mississippi-Missouri River System

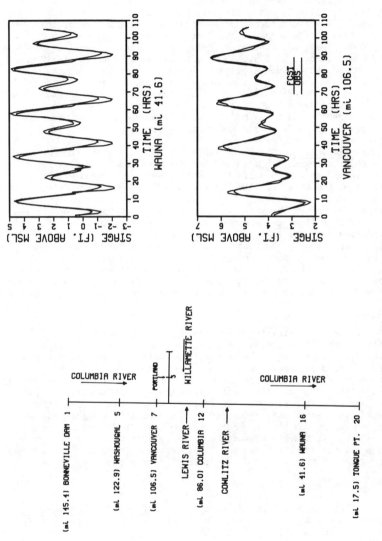

Fig. 2 -- Columbia River System

2.5 percent of the change in water elevation during the flood. An
average of only three iterations were required.

<u>Illinois-Mississippi-Missouri</u>. A schematic of this dendritic river
system is shown in Figure 1. It consists of 463 miles (741 km) of the
Mississippi, Illinois, and Missouri Rivers with a total of 9 lock and
dams and 18 level recorders. Discharges are known at the upstream end
of each river. The channel bottom slope is mild, varying from 0.00002
to 0.0002. The total discharge through the system varied from
3,600 cfs (102 cms) to 885,000 cfs (25,064 cms). A total of 117 cross
sections located at unequal intervals were used in the computations.
Results of the parameter optimization are shown in Table 1. The
average rms error was 0.38 ft (0.12 m) representing 1.9 percent of the
change in water elevation during the flood. About three iterations
were required for each reach. Comparisons of computed and observed
water elevation at Meredosia and Dixon Landing are shown in Figure 1.

<u>Columbia-Willamette</u>. The lower 128 miles (206 km) of the Columbia
River and the lower 24.4 mile (32 km) reach of the Willamette River
have a very flat bottom slope (0.000011), and the flows are quite
affected by the tide from the Pacific Ocean. A schematic of the
reaches modeled are shown in Figure 2. The tidal effect extends as
far upstream as the tailwater of Bonneville Dam during periods of low
flow. Reverse flows can occur as far upstream as Vancouver. A total
of 25 cross sections located at unequal distance intervals were used
in the computations. Results of parameter optimization for a 3-day
low flow period are shown in Table 1. The average rms error was 0.37
ft. (0.11 m) or 6.9 percent of the change in water elevation. An
average of four iterations were required. Comparisons of computed and
observed water elevations at Wauna and Vancouver are shown in Figure 2.

Summary

A parameter optimization methodology for dynamic flood routing
models has been developed which for some applications can eliminate
the need for costly and time-consuming detailed cross-sectional information. The cross sections within a reach are approximated by separate power functions for the channel and the floodplain. A very efficient optimization algorithm determines the optimal Manning n values
which may vary with either water elevation or discharge. Minimum-
maximum constraints can be imposed on the optimal n values. One or
more cross sections within a reach may be specified in detail by a
table of top widths and elevations. The methodology has been tested
with promising results on several large river systems; the average rms
error was 0.44 ft (0.13 m) or 2.9 percent of the change in stage.

Appendix - References

Fread, D.L., "Channel Routing," Chapter 14, <u>Hydrological Forecasting</u>,
    (Ed: M.G. Anderson and T.P. Burt) John Wiley, 1985, pp. 437-503.
Fread, D.L. and Smith, G.F., "Calibration Technique for 1-D Unsteady
    Flow Models," <u>ASCE</u>, 104(7), Paper 13892, Jul 1978, pp. 1027-1044.
Wormleaton, P.R. and Karmegam, M.,"Parameter Optimization in Flood
    Routing," <u>ASCE</u>, 110(12), Paper 19352, Dec. 1984, pp. 1799-1814.

PERFORMANCE OF A DETERMINISTIC
STORM RUNOFF MODEL

William C. Taggart, M, 1,
Charles L. Hardt 2, Terri L. Fead, A.M., 3, Michael D. Vinson 4

Proponents of deterministic modeling in urban hydrology maintain that surface conditions, overland flow hydraulics and channel hydraulics will be continually changing; therefore, mathematical models which represent the pertinent physical processes and have the capability to test proposed modifications should be used. Proponents of the more Stochastic/Statistical approaches contend that these mathematical representations are not well enough founded, are unsupported and that a better approach is to calibrate a model with numerous measurable parameters analyzed across many basins and characteristics so that one can transfer them to other basins or future conditions.

The arguments for one model versus another are often inaccurate because most models combine both methodologies. For example, the MITCAT model (Ref. 1), often categorized as deterministic, uses primarily kinematic wave "deterministic" overland flow and channel routing components which are often combined with a variety of infiltration methods. The infiltration methods (SCS, Holtan, Horton, Antecedent) are statistically and empirically based, and more deterministic methods (Green and Ampt) are more difficult to use or to obtain data for. Current literature demonstrates the effective use of Kinematic Wave Models to prototype performance for a variety of land uses, particularly for rainfall events which cause significant flows and flood hazard. These techniques are not to be used for base or continuous flow modeling, at least not without considerable modification for the radically different regime of flow.

Tulsa Case Study

A Master Plan was being prepared for 3 basins: Coal Creek, Dirty Butter Creek and Flat Rock Creek Basins (a 35 square mile area). These basins cover the Northwest Quadrant of Tulsa, Oklahoma (see Figure 1). There were no stream gauge records; rainfall data was recorded for a few events, and only limited stage data (of questionable quality) for a couple of storms was available. Previous flood plain mapping had been completed based on unit hydrograph theory with coefficients derived with data mainly from Oklahoma City for urbanized areas and other locations in Central and Northeastern Oklahoma. Coefficient curves are presented in terms of "Percent Urbanized", and thus a very lumped parameter approach was taken. Selection of the coefficient is controversial and varies from user to user.

Figure 2 illustrates comparative peak unit discharges for several studies in the Tulsa area. The discharges shown for the Coal Creek Basin for the Unit Hydro-

1. Principal; 2. Principal; 3. Project Engineer; and 4. Project Engineer, McLaughlin Water Engineers, Ltd., 2420 Alcott Street, Denver, Colorado 80211.

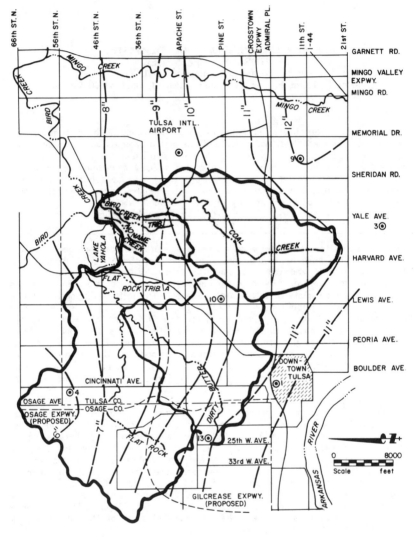

LEGEND

▬▬▬▬ STUDY BASIN BOUNDARY

—8"— ISOHYETALS MAY 27, 1984 EVENT

⊙ RAIN GAGE

STUDY AREA
GENERAL LOCATION MAP
FIGURE 1

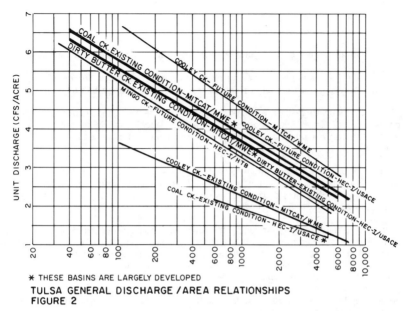

* THESE BASINS ARE LARGELY DEVELOPED

TULSA GENERAL DISCHARGE / AREA RELATIONSHIPS
FIGURE 2

graph Models are lower than other basins due to discrepancies in tributary area, timing coefficients and infiltration parameters. The Coal Creek and Dirty Butter Basin's "existing development" is largely built out, whereas the Cooley Basin is only partially developed at its lower end.

Hydraulic Network Sensitivity

Much of the watershed area involved has storm sewers which connect into very large trunk lines that replace open streams until line capacities are exceeded. When this occurs, two streams exist which have different hydraulic characteristics, timing patterns and routing effects. Sensitivity tests were performed which demonstrated the importance of modeling this situation, because large errors were possible. It was important to model the many small "inadvertent" storages, at certain locations including freeways and certain arterials, as some of these reduce flows downstream.

Modeling strategies were explored, four of which were modeled in detail because of the extremes in range of simplification.

The cases were:

1. A simple surface stream conveyance network (omitting the storm sewer system).

2. A simple storm sewer conveyance network (omitting the surface overflow stream during major floods).

3BB. A dual stream system having pipe and surface streams for overflow.

3BC. A dual stream system having pipe and surface streams for overflow, with a more detailed model reflecting the pipe size change in the upper reach.

The most accurate test case is 3BC. Although Case 3BB used similar conveyance combinations, Case 3BC accounts for a significant pipe size change in the upper reach by modeling 2 subbasins with combined pipe and overland flow systems.

Discharge is routed to points where total flow is compared to existing storm sewer capacity. These capacities were determined by weighing the length and capacity of each storm sewer size along a stream segment. Excess discharge is routed to the overland flow element.

Figure 3 illustrates 5-year and 100-year downstream hydrographs. General differences in peak are correlated to the contrasting characteristics between overland streamflow and pipe conveyance. Inspection shows that Case 2 peaks occur sooner, higher and sharper than in Case 1 which might be anticipated due to the higher velocities possible in the storm sewers. However, with the 100-year rainfall, these differences are less evident because overland flow velocities have increased with the higher discharges. Where storage exists, these differences are also dampened.

While Case 3BB is similar to Case 1 (all overland flow) for the 100-year event, it tends towards Case 2 (all storm sewer) for the 5-year event. This is logical when considering the capacity of the storm sewer and suggests adoption of the more refined model (3BB) to accommodate the frequency range. There was little difference between the hydrographs from Cases 3BB and 3BC; thus, it was concluded that techniques employed for Case 3BB were adequate.

May 27, 1984 Flood
The Memorial Day storm of 1984 occurred after most of the work was completed. This allowed cumulative testing of the hydrology and hydraulic models. Isolated testing of the hydrology model was not possible since calibrated stream gauges did not exist. Figure 4 illustrates rain gauge data for the event, along with the 100-year design rainfall used. The rain gauge locations and the isohyetal map for the storm are depicted in Figure 1.

Immediately following the 1984 flood, high-water marks were located and surveyed. The rainfall records were input into the MITCAT runoff model. Rainfall data from a given gauge was input to adjacent subbasins, and other subbasins were given rainfall from the Theisen Polygon Method. This combined method provided the realistic simulation of rainfall peaks. The total rainfall volume generated was checked to agree with volumes calculated from the isohyetal map. This procedure accounts for the intensities of rainfall in different areas and the total volume of rainfall at key locations in the basin. MITCAT-generated discharges were reduced for storm sewer capacity and input into the HEC-2 model. The resultant HEC-2 water surface elevations were plotted on the profiles and compared to the high-water marks.

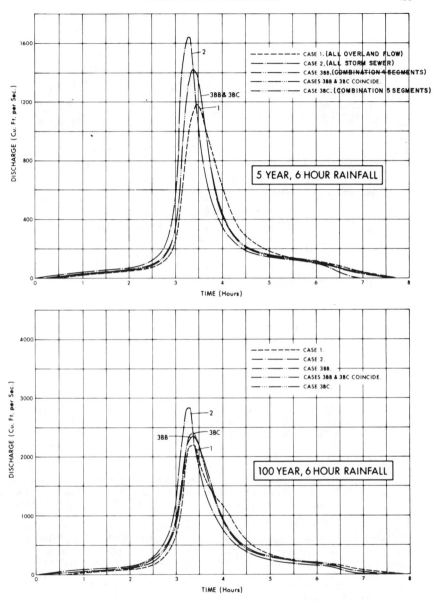

TEST CASE HYDROGRAPH COMPARISON
FIGURE 3.

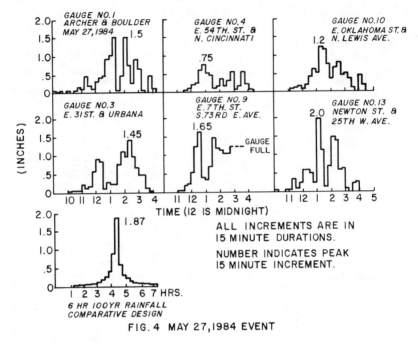

FIG. 4 MAY 27, 1984 EVENT

No general trend (higher or lower) was evident in an overall comparison of high-water marks to HEC-2 generated elevations (Figure 5). This indicates that the MITCAT model is adequately representing the hydrology of the basins. At points of discrepancy, the HEC-2 model was scrutinized and necessary adjustments were made. If the HEC-2 modifications did not bring the water surface close to the high-water marks, then discharges were checked by storm sewer capacity and by unit discharge comparisons. When high-water marks appeared questionable because of unknown survey ties or complicated hydraulic situations, they were not used, especially if the HEC-2 modeling appeared reasonable.

The high-water marks primarily served as a verification of HEC-2 modeling and discharge profile adjustment. In a number of locations, HEC-2 cross sections were adjusted to reflect hydraulic conditions that occurred during the flood. Cross sections were also modified to reflect ground conditions observed in the field. A number of changes were made in 'n' values and bridge modeling techniques. Following the high-water mark calibration, the 100-year design discharges were input to the HEC-2 model and water surface elevations, profiles, and flood plains were revised.

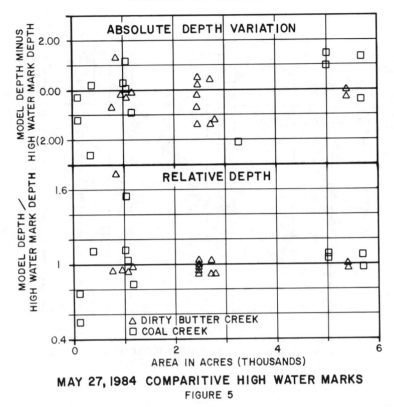

MAY 27, 1984 COMPARITIVE HIGH WATER MARKS
FIGURE 5

It was noted that the 100-year flood plain maps (completed prior to May 27, 1984 as part of this modeling effort) were quite similar to the flooding which occurred. This was also true when comparing MITCAT 100-year model and the May 27, 1984 model results (Figure 6). This only reaffirms that the May 27, 1984 event resulted in a flood plain that was similar to the predicted 100-year flood, particularly for the larger tributary areas.

Based on the area discharge comparisons in Figure 2, one can draw the conclusion that the Unit Hydrograph Models utilized would have predicted lower discharges than MITCAT, and that resultant water surface elevations using that particular Unit Hydrograph approach would have been generally lower than the actual high water marks.

Conclusion
The modeling effort reproduced results comparable to the flooding that occurred. All changes made as a result of examining the high water marks led to changes in the hydraulic model and did not effect the discharges modeled.

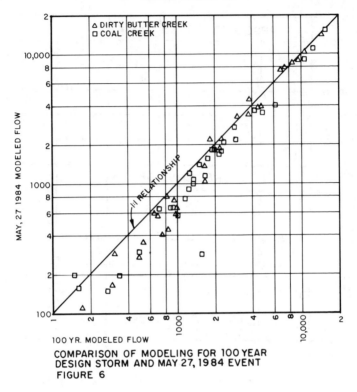

100 YR. MODELED FLOW

**COMPARISON OF MODELING FOR 100 YEAR
DESIGN STORM AND MAY 27,1984 EVENT
FIGURE 6**

From Figure 2 it can be seen that discharges predicted with a regional unit hydrograph approach would have been lower than those produced by MITCAT. The higher discharges from MITCAT are a function of the detailed overland flow and stream routing efforts. The actual flood event (May 27, 1984) illustrates that the "deterministic" model gave more realistic results. In areas where substantial hydraulic complexities exist and investigation of more detailed hydraulic options are desired, the data presented here support use of the "deterministic" modeling approach. However, far more effort is needed in the area of practical infiltration models, design storm approaches, and the use of synthetic rainfall records and runoff models to generate true runoff statistics rather than assuming that a given statistical rainfall will result in the corresponding flood frequency.

APPENDIX 1. Reference
1.   Camp Dresser & McKee, MITCAT, A Hydrologic Simulation Model Users
     Manual, (March 1980).

Real-Time Precipitation-Snowmelt Model
for the Monongahela River Basin

By Daniel H. Hoggan[1], John C. Peters[2], and Werner Loehlein[3]

Introduction

The Pittsburgh District, U.S. Army Corps of Engineers, is responsible
for operating two multipurpose reservoirs in the 7400 square mile
Monongahela Basin, which is located in Pennsylvania, West Virginia and
Maryland. Operation of a third reservoir, which is presently under
construction, will soon be required. The real time forecasting of runoff
for operational purposes requires simulation of snow accumulation and
snowmelt throughout the Basin. This paper describes capabilities of a
recently developed model, SNOSIM, for performing such simulation. The
application of this model as part of a comprehensive system of water
control software, and some initial simulation results, are presented.

Basin and Reservoir System Characteristics

The Monongahela Basin is situated in the unglaciated Allegheny
Plateau and is characterized with rugged, high rolling hills. The Basin
is long and narrow with a total length of 144 miles and an average width
of 51 miles. Elevations range from about 4800 feet at the southern
divide to 710 feet at Pittsburgh.

Two existing reservoirs, Tygart and Youghiogheny, and a reservoir
presently being constructed, Stonewall Jackson, comprise a system for
which the primary purpose is flood control. However, the reservoirs are
also used for to store water for navigation, pollution abatement and
water supply. The winter season flood control capacities for the Tygart,
Youghiogheny and Stonewall Jackson reservoirs are 278,000., 151,000. and
38,550. acre feet, respectively. Flood control reservations for the
summer are somewhat less.

---

[1]Prof., Civil and Environmental Engrg., Utah State University, Logan,
Utah.
[2]Hydr. Engr., The Hydrologic Engrg. Center, Davis, Calif. 95616.
[3]Hydr. Engr.,U.S. Army Engr. Dist., Pittsburgh, PA, 15222.

A real-time data collection network for water control is presently based on 52 self-timed data collection platforms (DCP's) which report via satellite telemetry. The DCP's report stages and elevations measured at 33 stream and reservoir sites, and precipitation at 28 sites. Precipitation data from an additional 14 sites outside the Basin are used for making estimates of subbasin-average precipitation. The Basin is divided into 40 subbasins for purposes of runoff simulation.

Computer Program SNOSIM

The SNOSIM program simulates snow accumulation, ripening, and melt processes to determine snowmelt contributions to runoff, and computes rainfall attenuation and lag caused by snow on the ground. Rain which passes through the snowpack is added to snowmelt to obtain rainfall equivalent.

SNOSIM is a component of an on-line software system that includes capability for data acquisition and processing, precipitation analysis, streamflow forecasting, reservoir system analysis, and graphical display of data and simulation results (Pabst and Peters, 1983). A Data Storage System (DSS) provides a means for storage and retrieval of measured data and simulation results. An interactive executive program facilitates use of the software system. Alternative future precipitation and temperature scenarios, or alternative operational constraints, can be readily specified with the program.

Data Requirements

Data requirements for SNOSIM are subbasin averages of maximum and minimum temperatures, snow depths, and precipitation. Aperiodic point density data at scattered locations are needed for an updating capability of the simulation program. In addition to the streamflow and precipitation data available from the network described earlier, daily measurements of temperature (30 stations) and snow depth (50 stations) are available, and aperiodic measurements of snow density are taken at three stations.

Snow depths ordinarily reach a maximum of three to four feet at the highest elevations in the basin, and all of the snow may melt within a few days from the influence of abnormally high temperatures. The time interval of computations, which may be selected from a range of one to several hours, should be set relatively short (e.g.,3 hours) to effectively simulate these conditions. Daily maximum and minimum temperatures are converted to simulation time interval averages according to a diurnal temperature distribution curve. Daily snow depths are interpolated linearly. Observed snow depths also are adjusted upward slightly with a linear relationship developed by the Pittsburgh District from snow survey experience.

Model Components

The code for SNOSIM may be divided into four major components:

```
 _____
|                                                  |
|      INTERACTION WITH OPERATIONAL PROGRAMS       |
|            AND DATA STORAGE SYSTEM               |
|_____|
|                                                  |
|            DIVISION OF PRECIPITATION             |
|              INTO RAIN OR SNOW                   |
|_____|
|                                                  |
|      SNOWPACK WATER EQUIVALENT AND DENSITY       |
|        ACCOUNTING AND MELT COMPUTATIONS          |
|_____|
|                                                  |
|   COMPUTING OF LAG AND COMBINING  OF RAIN WITH   |
|     SNOWMELT TO PRODUCE EQUIVALENT RAINFALL      |
|_____|
```

Computational Logic

Precipitation is divided into rain or snow according to a freezing temperature index. Rain, thus obtained, is treated in one of three ways: 1) if there is no snow on the ground, it adds directly to equivalent rainfall, 2) if snowpack exists, but is not ripe (snow density is less than threshold melt density), the rain is attenuated, 3) if the snow is ripe, the rain is lagged before being added to equivalent rainfall.

Tracking of snowpack density is essential in the simulation to determine when melt will be triggered. Density accounting is accomplished by additions and subtractions to water equivalent. Precipitation, whether rain or snow, is added. Snowmelt and sublimation are subtracted.

Snow ripening and melt processes are divided into two stages -- from the beginning of the period of simulation until the time of forecast, and from the time of forecast until the end of the period of simulation.

In the first stage, subbasin averages of observed precipitation, temperature, and snow depth and an estimated or observed initial value of snow density are used to compute a regular time series of water equivalent, snowmelt, and snow density values. This series of computations may be updated with an interactively assigned value of snow density for any time interval in the simulation.

When snow density is less than the threshold melt density and
precipitation occurs, water equivalent in the current time interval is
equal to water equivalent in the previous time interval plus
precipitation. When there is no precipitation, the water equivalent of
the previous period is reduced by a small sublimation loss. If the snow
is ripe and the air temperature is above freezing, snowmelt is occurring,
and water equivalent from the previous period is reduced by the amount of
melt. Although rainfall also may be occurring, the rain is in transit
through the snowpack and does not add to the water equivalent of the
snow. The rain is accounted for separately and added to melt later in the
process after adjustment for lag. Rain does, however, accelerate snowmelt
slightly, so the melt rate is increased by an amount proportional to the
intensity of the rainfall (US Army Corps of Engineers, 1960).

In the second stage of simulation, which occurs after the time of
forecast, forecasts of precipitation and temperature are used, and the
computations are essentially the same as in the preceding stage except
that no snow depths (either forecast or observed) are available. They
must be computed. Snow depths during the forecast period are computed in
four different ways depending on temperature and snow density conditions.
In the first case, when snow density is equal to or above the threshold
melt density and air temperature is greater than freezing, melt is
occurring and the density can be expected to remain fairly constant.
Snow depth under these conditions is computed by dividing water
equivalent by density.

In the second case, when snow density is less than melt density and
air temperature is greater than freezing, snow depth is reduced slightly
by consolidation of the snowpack. Although no melt is occurring in the
usual sense of water leaving the snowpack, liquid water from melt
occurring at the snow surface is moving to lower levels and increasing
snowpack density (Corps of Engineers, 1956). For shallow snowpacks it is
assumed that the reduction in snow depth under these conditions is
directly proportional to the amount of melt occurring at the surface
based on air temperature and inversely proportional to the average
density of the snowpack.

In the third case, when air temperature is below freezing and snow
density is greater than zero, snow depth in the current period is equal
to snow depth in the previous period reduced by sublimation and increased
by snowfall, if any has occurred. Average density of new snow in the
United States has been found to be approximately 10 percent (American
Society of Agricultural Engineers, 1982), and this value is adopted for
computing the depth of new snow.

In the fourth case, when air temperature is less than freezing and
there is no snow on the ground for the previous period, snow depth is
equal to any new snowfall which occurs during the period divided by the

density of new snow.

Snow density for each time interval during the forecast period is computed by dividing water equivalent by snow depth.

The lagging of rain and snowmelt through the snowpack is computed with a lag factor which has the effect of imposing minutes of lag per inch of snow depth. US Army Corps of Engineers (1960) indicates 3 to 4 hours of lag for moderate depths of snow. The Pittsburgh District has used 4 to 6 hours of lag in its computations. Based on this information, 30 minutes of lag per inch of depth is probably reasonable for vertical drainage. In regions of mild to flat slopes, the delay to runoff caused by snowpack may be much longer than for vertical transit of water through the pack alone (US Army Corps of Engineers, 1960). Thus, a much greater lag factor may be needed to adequately model areas of low relief.

As a final step, after rain and snowmelt are adjusted for lag, lagged amounts of each occurring in the same time interval are added and these are combined with any unlagged rainfall occurring during snow-free time intervals to produce an equivalent rainfall hyetograph for the entire period of simulation.

Input and Output

Much of the input required, aside from the climatological data to be processed, is generated with the interactive executive program which links SNOSIM with data storage and other software. Forecast date and time, starting and ending time of simulation, and computational time interval are set. Zone-specified future precipitation and maximum and minimum temperature departures from normal may be entered. Five simulation parameters may be set: 1) coefficient of lag, 2) freezing temperature, 3) threshold melt density, 4) snowmelt coefficient, and 5) sublimation factor. Snow density data for updating can be specified either zonally or for individual subbasins and by specified amount or percentage change to existing values.

Since the model has zonal assignment capabilities, a basin zone file is required, which assigns subbasins to common zones for temperature, density, precipitation, and other variables. Similarly, since departures from normal daily temperatures are used in forecasting, and normal daily temperatures also are used to fill in missing data, a file of normal daily temperatures for each temperature station is required.

Output from the model consists of two tables for each subbasin listing observed and computed values of key variables for all time intervals in the simulation, and a summary table consisting of one line for each subbasin presenting totals and other comparative data.

Procedure for Real Time Forecasting

    The following sequence of steps is followed in a real-time
application of SNOSIM:

    (1) Precipitation, streamflow, maximum daily temperature, minimum
daily temperature and daily snow depth measurements reside in a 'master'
data base (a DSS file). These are retrieved for use in a program that
performs spatial weighting of point data to obtain subbasin-average
values. The program is designed to search for the nearest reporting
gages so that missing data does not have to be filled in prior to
developing the spatial estimates. The subbasin-average values are
written to a DSS file.

    (2) Computer program SNOSIM retrieves the subbasin values for
precipitation, temperatures and snow depth, as well as values for future
precipitation and temperature. Snow accumulation and melt are
calculated, and values for rainfall equivalent, as well as other
simulated quantities for each subbasin, are stored for subsequent use.

    (3) Computer program HEC1F retrieves the rainfall equivalent values
and calculates discharge hydrographs for the subbasins. Hydrographs are
routed and combined throughout the Basin to provide forecasted
hydrographs of inflow to the reservoirs and hydrographs at downstream
control points. HEC1F makes use of observed streamflow data wherever it
is available in the process of tracking flood wave movement through the
stream network. Capability also exists to optimize runoff parameters for
gaged headwater subbasins (Peters and Ely, 1985).

    (4) Computer program HEC-5 retrieves the hydrographs calculated with
HEC1F, as well as reservoir storages, and performs a simulation to
determine optimal reservoir releases. Reservoir releases are determined
in accordance with constraints at downstream control points while keeping
the system "in balance". A wide variety of factors that affect release
decisions can be accommodated, including channel capacities at downstream
control points, emergency conditions requiring prereleases, minimum-flow
requirements, etc. Output such as hydrographs of discharge, reservoir
stage and storage are written to a DSS file for subsequent display and
analysis.

    (5) Additional iterations of steps (2), (3) and (4) are made as
required to enable evaluation of alternative future
precipitation/temperature conditions or operations constraints.

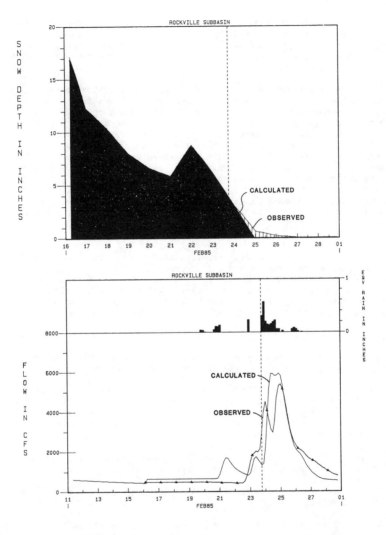

FIGURE 1. Observed and Forecasted Snow Depths
and Hydrographs at Rockville, West, Virginia.
Time of Forecast is 1800 on February 23, 1985

Example Application

     A snowmelt flood event of February 1985 was used for testing SNOSIM.
A build up of snowpack by mid February followed by a period of relatively
high temperatures produced high runoff that lasted about one week and
peaked around February 24. All snow at the gaging stations was melted in
the course of the event.

     The model was applied to the fifteen headwater subbasins in the
Monongahela River Basin. The fit of computed with observed hydrographs
was quite good in a few cases without any adjustment of parameters other
than the assumption of zero loss rates, which is consistent with winter
conditions. Comparative hydrographs for one of these subbasins is shown
in Figure 1. In other cases, the timing of hydrograph peaks was
significantly off. Further analysis revealed that this problem might
largely be attributed to the averaging process used to arrive at subbasin
average temperatures and snow depths from station data. By adjusting the
weights of the subbasin nodes relative to the contributing stations,
significant improvement in fit of computed with observed hydrographs was
possible with little or no adjustment of the snow simulation parameters.

Acknowledgements

     The writers wish to express appreciation to Dr. Arthur Pabst of HEC
for helpful suggestions in developing procedures and designing the
program. Dennis Huff of HEC was particularly helpful in assisting with
data processing and program development. William Silesky and Robert Yue
of the Corps of Engineers Pittsburgh District provided valuable
assistance in assembling data and providing other information.

Appendix 1.--References

     Haan, C. T., Johnson, H.P., and Brakensiek, D.L., 1982. Ed. Hydro-
logic Modeling of Small Watersheds. American Society of Agri. Engr.

     Pabst, A. F. and Peters, J.C., 1983. "A Software System to Aid in Making
Real-Time Water Control Decisions." Paper presented at the Technical Conference on Mitigation of Natural Hazards Through Real-Time Data Collection and Hydrological Forecasting." (Also available as Technical Paper
No. 89 from the Hydrologic Engineering Center, Davis, California.)

     Peters, J. C. and Ely, P.B., 1985. "Flood-Runoff Forecasting with
HEC1F." Water Resources Bulletin. Paper No. 84141. February.

     U.S. Army Corps of Engineers, 1956. Snow Hydrology. North Pacific
Division, Portland, Oregon.

     U. S. Army Corps of Engineers. 1960. Runoff from Snowmelt. EM
1110-2-1406.

Making Water System Rehabilitation Decisions

Thomas M. Walski, M. ASCE*

Abstract

This paper presents a framework for making economically justifiable decisions concerning water distribution system rehabilitation.

Background

As a water system ages there are numerous approaches to maintaining and upgrading the system. These range from doing nothing to cleaning or cathodically protecting pipes to completely replacing large portions of the system.

At present, decisions to rehabilitate portions of water distribution systems involve a great deal of judgment and sometimes guesswork. Decision making is difficult due to the complexity of alternative solutions and the difficulty in quantifying many of the benefits and costs.

Shamir and Howard (1979), the US Army Corps of Engineers, New York District (1980, 1984), US Army Corps of Engineers, Buffalo District (1981), Walski and Pelliccia (1982), O'Day (1982) and the City of Philadelphia (Weiss et al. 1985) have all proposed models for making pipe replacement decisions based on pipe break history. O'Day (1983, 1986) and Elhaj (1985) have described processes for gathering the data for making these decisions.

Boyle Engineering (1982), Moyer et al. (1983) and Walski (1984) have described decision making with regard to leak detection and repair. Walski (1982, 1985a) described the decision making process for pipe cleaning and lining and developed cost data for water system rehabilitation work (Walski 1985b). Gessler and Walski (1985) incorporated pipe cleaning as an alternative in a pipe sizing optimization model.

The East Bay Municipal Utility District (Ramos 1985) has the most comprehensive method for quantifying benefits and costs for system rehabilitation work. One can easily quibble with the numerical values they use to quantify such things as fire protection and public relations, but their quantification of benefits makes decision making easier.

Maddaus et al. (US Dept of Housing and Urban Development 1984) recommended using life cycle economic evaluation for infrastructure

*Research Civil Engineer, US Army Corps of Engineers Waterways Experiment Station, Vicksburg, MS 39180, USA.

rehabilitation decision making but could only give a cursory description because of the broad scope of that work.

In spite of all of the above work, decision making for water system
rehabilitation remains difficult because of the nature of the problem.
This paper will present an economic framework for making water system
rehabilitation decisions. First, it will be necessary to discuss the
problems faced by old water mains and the types of solutions. The
remainder of the paper will describe ways of evaluating the benefits
and costs of alternatives to reach a decision.

Problems and Solutions

Making decisions about rehabilitation of old water mains is difficult because there are so many types of problems and therefore many
types of solutions. Before getting into decision making, the utility
needs to quantify to the extent possible the costs and benefits of the
various alternatives. The costs of old water mains are realized by the
utility and its customers in numerous ways which are often concealed
within the utility's operating and maintenance budget or indirectly
borne by customers in the form of poor fire flows, low pressure, outages or red water. These costs need to be identified.

The costs of old water mains include: 1. costs associated with
pipe breaks, 2. the value of water lost through leaks, 3. the cost of
detecting and repairing small breaks, 4. cost of replacing broken
valves, or extra time and larger areas left without service because of
broken valves during maintenance work, 5. extra energy cost for pumping through old pipes, 6. cost resulting from low pressure during peak
use periods, 7. additional damages or increased insurance rates due to
lower fire flows, 8. damages due to water quality deterioration in
mains, and 9. the present worth of eventually replacing the main.
Ideally, one could simply add up all of these costs for each rehabilitation alternative and select the alternative with the least cost. The
problem with this, however, is that it is virtually impossible to quantify many of the above costs.

The solutions that can be considered are just as broad as the problems and include: 1. main replacement, 2. pipe cleaning or pigging,
3. pipe lining with cement mortar, slip liners or flexible sock
liners, 4. paralleling old mains with new ones, 5. valve exercising
with replacement of broken valves, 6. line flushing, 7. adding corrosion inhibitor chemicals or water stabilization, 8. installing additional pumping, 9. installing additional storage to cut down on peak
flows, 10. internal reconstruction of joints or 11. cathodic
protection.

Table 1 shows the relationship between the types of problems occurring in water mains and the types of solutions to address those problems. Note that there is not a one-to-one correspondence between the
cost given above and the problems that cause those costs to be
realized. This increases the difficulty in decision making.

Table 1
Overview of Distribution System
Rehabilitation Techniques

Solution	Physical Integrity				Carrying Capacity			Other		
	Breakage	Lost Water	Leak Detection	Inoperative Valves	High Energy Use	Low Pressures	Low Fire Flows	Red Water	Bacterial Regrowth	Reliability
Replacement	X	X	X	X	X	X	X	X	X	O
Parallel Mains					X	X	X			X
Cleaning					X	X	X			
Cement Mortar Lining		O			X	X	X	X	X	
Slip Lining	O	X	X		X	X	X	X	X	
Sock Liners		O	O		O	O	O	X	X	
Valve Replacement				X						O
Internal Seals		X	X							
Pump Upgrade					O	X	X			O
Additional Storage					X	X	X			X
Cathodic Protection	X									
Corrosion Inhibitor/Stabilization					O	O	O	X		
Chlorine Booster									X	
Flushing								X	O	
Joint Restraints	X	X								

X = Significant Effect, O = Marginal Effect.

To simplify the discussion, the problems resulting from old water mains can be grouped into three categories: 1. physical integrity, 2. carrying capacity and 3. water quality and reliability. The above categories are not an arbitrary breakdown but rather point the way to a procedure for making better pipe rehabilitation decisions as presented below.

Cost and Benefits

The existence of several different types of problems suggests that any procedure to select rehabilitation alternatives will need to be a multistep procedure. Such a procedure is presented below. It consists of: 1. identifying pipes that need to be replaced due to their poor physical integrity; 2. selecting some combination of: a. pipes to be cleaned, b. the diameter of pipes parallel to old pipes c. diameters of replacement pipes or d. installation of additional pumping and storage capacity, to meet fire flow and pressure requirements, and quantifying the cost of each clearly defined alternative; and 3. making a qualitative assessment of effects of each alternative that cannot be monitized, i.e. stated in units of cost. Dividing the evaluation into three steps can help the engineer compare costs and benefits in a more organized manner.

Many of the costs described above, especially those under the category of "physical integrity" can be quantified. Using the type of approach presented first by Shamir and Howard (1979), Walski (1986) has developed a procedure for identifying when to replace water mains due to their loss of physical integrity. This procedure is based on determining the costs of pipe maintenance activities on a dollar per mile per year basis and projecting those costs into the future to find the optimal year for replacement. It considers not only pipe breakage but also water loss due to leakage, leak detection and repair, and inoperative valves. This procedure can be used to identify which pipes need to be replaced in the near future because they simply leak and break too much. If the only problem with the physical integrity of pipes is joint leakage, it may be economical on large mains to reconstruct the joints from the inside (Hayre 1985).

Once pipes to be replaced have been identified, the engineer must decide how to meet pressure and fire flow requirements through the planning horizon. This means that the engineer must select the diameter of pipes to be replaced, the pipes which need to be cleaned and lined, and the pipes which need to be paralleled. If only the large diameter trunk mains are considered in this analysis, it may be possible to select the optimal strategy using manual calculations (Walski 1984). In complicated grid systems, however, use of some type of pipe network model is essential for this step. This can be done with a traditional trial-and-error approach, or a model to optimally select pipe sizes or identify which pipes need to be cleaned (Gessler and Walski 1985) can be used.

The engineer must also consider increasing pumping capacity or placing additional elevated storage near locations with high peak demands as alternatives to new pipes or pipe rehabilitation. In most older systems, both pumping and storage are usually adequate and only come into consideration when either is old and needing replacement in itself.

The engineer should insure that loss of carrying capacity in the mains is indeed due to internal pipe roughness and not due to erroneously closed or partly closed valves in the system. Several loss of head tests and fire flow tests need to be conducted as part of any rehabilitation study, and if possible sections of old pipe should be excavated and visually inspected.

Once several good alternatives (e.g. cleaning only, new pipes instead of cleaning) have been identified, it is necessary to calculate the present worth of costs of each. This can be stated as

Cost = Present Worth [Replacement - Decrease in energy + New

parallel pipe + Pipe cleaning (and lining)

- Decrease in breaks - Decrease in water loss - Decrease in

valve maintenance - Decrease in leak detection]   (1)

The above equation may seem almost impossible to evaluate. However, the engineer should remember that decrease in breaks, water loss, valve maintenance and leak detection will probably be the same for all alternatives and can therefore be ignored. This simplification is due to the fact that the bad pipes in the system have been marked for removal in the first step of the procedures. If flow demands become large before the pipe is scheduled for replacement, it may be necessary to move the date for replacement of those pipes forward but otherwise, the only consideration is the size of the replacement pipe which is determined by carrying capacity and not physical integrity considerations.

If the only "physical integrity" problem is that of numerous inoperative valves, then valve replacement can be made part of a pipe cleaning project.

Another simplification is the fact that, except for large trunk mains, the change in energy costs due to paralleling or cleaning pipes is negligible. In the large force mains from pumping stations, it is best to consider the head, flow, efficiency and fraction of time for each pump operating point and sum the savings over all operating points (i.e. combinations of pumps) as shown below.

$$\text{Energy Cost (\$/yr)} = 11.41 \ (P/e_m) \sum_{i=1}^{n} f_i Q_i h_i / e_i \qquad (2)$$

where

Q_i = flow rate at operating point i, mgd
f_i = fraction of time at operating point i
h_i = head at operating point i, ft
e_i = efficiency of pump at operating point i, fraction
P = price of energy, cent/kw-hr
n = number of different pump combinations (operating points)
e_m = efficiency of motor, fraction.

The engineer should not necessarily select the alternative with the lowest total cost from equation 1 above. One of the alternatives may have a slightly higher cost but have greater reliability or, in meeting minimum fire flows at all locations, provide much greater fire flows at some locations. Similarly, one alternative (e.g. cement mortar lining) may significantly reduce red water problems. Only after considering all factors should a final decision be reached.

Nature of the Solutions

There are no simple rules for solving pipe rehabilitation problems. As Table 1 demonstrates, there are numerous technologies for rehabilitating water systems and most solve several problems. The only way to solve all of the problems is by complete replacement, but this is in general the most expensive alternative.

Nevertheless, it is possible to make some general observations based on this author's experience. First, if the system's problems are primarily due to loss of the pipe's physical integrity, replacement will usually be the best solution. On the other hand, if the problems are primarily loss of carrying capacity, then cleaning or paralleling will be the most economical.

Second, for systems with fire flow and pressure problems, pipe cleaning will be most economical if future demands will not increase dramatically. Parallel mains will be needed if water demands are expected to grow significantly. This is due to the fact that there is an upper limit to the amount the carrying capacity can be increased by cleaning.

Third, it will usually be more economical to replace small pipes while it will be economical to rehabilitate large pipes. This results from the fact that the cost of new pipe increases dramatically as a function of diameter while the function relating cost of rehabilitation techniques and diameter is not as steep. Another reason is that small pipes tend to have higher breakage rates since they are more susceptible to beam breaks.

Fourth, water loss reduction will tend to be a significant factor in decision making only when the utility is running out of its source, treatment or pumping capacity. In these instances, loss reduction will result in savings in capacity expansion costs, while in most other instances, loss reduction only results in savings in pumping energy and treatment chemicals. Loss reduction may also be important for utilities that purchase their water from others.

While the above observations provide some quantitative guidance for decision making, each utility must do its best to quantify all costs since such factors as cost and breakage rates will vary widely from one utility to another or even from one neighborhood to another.

Summary

Making decisions regarding water distribution systems has always involved a great deal of judgment due to the complexity of the decisions involved. This paper presents a framework for approaching the problem in an organized manner to develop economically justifiable solutions. The key is to break decision making into three steps: 1. analyze the need for replacement based on physical integrity, 2. find the least cost solution to meet pressure and flow requirements, and 3. assess the water quality and reliability consequences.

References

Boyle Engineering, 1982, "Municipal Leak Detection Program Loss Reduction-Research and Analysis," California Dept of Natural Resources.

Elhaj, R., 1985, "Information System for Improving Management of Water Supply Mains," Ph.D. Dissertation, Colorado State University, Ft. Collins, CO.

Gessler, J. and T. M. Walski, 1985, "Water Distribution System Optimization," TR EL-85-11, US Army Engineer Waterways Experiment Station, Vicksburg, MS.

Hayre, J., 1985, "Weko-Seal Internal Sealing System," AWWA National Convention, p. 43.

Moyer, et al, 1983, "The Economics of Leak Detection," J AWWA, 75-1, p 28.

O'Day, D. K., 1982, "Organizing and Analyzing Leak and Break Data for Making Main Replacement Decisions," J AWWA, 74-11, p. 588.

O'Day, D. K., 1983, "Geoprocessing-A Water Distribution Management Tool," Public Works, 114-1, p. 41.

O'Day, D. K., 1986, "A Computerized Infrastructure Management Program," Public Works, 117-2, p. 65.

Ramos, W. L., 1985, "Benefit/Cost Analysis Procedure for Determining Water Main Replacement," AWWA Nat. Conf., p. 1.

Shamir, U. and C. D. D. Howard, 1979, "An Analytical Approach to Scheduling Pipe Replacement," J AWWA, 71-5, p. 248.

US Army Corps of Engineers, Buffalo District, 1981, Urban Water Study, Buffalo, NY.

US Army Corps of Engineers, New York District, 1980, New York City Infrastructure Study, Vol 1, Manhattan.

US Army Corps of Engineers, New York District, 1984, New York Water Supply Infrastructure Study, Vol 2, Brooklyn.

US Department of Housing and Urban Development, 1984, "Utility Infrastructure Rehabilitation."

Walski, T. M., 1982, "Economic Analysis of Rehabilitation of Water Mains," J WRPM, 108-3, p 296.

Walski, T. M., 1984, Analysis of Water Distribution Systems, Van Nostrand Reinhold, New York, NY.

Walski, T. M., 1985a, "Cleaning and Lining versus Parallel Mains," J WRPM, 111-1, p. 43.

Walski, T. M., 1985b, "Cost of Water Distribution System Infrastructure Rehabilitation, Repair and Replacement," TR EL-85-5, US Army Engineer Waterways Experiment Station, Vicksburg, MS.

Walski, 1986, "Replacement Rules for Pipes with Breaks and Leaks," submitted to J AWWA, (copies available from author).

Walski, T. M. and A. Pelliccia, 1982, "Economic Analysis of Water Main Breaks," J AWWA, 74-3, p 140.

Weiss, R. A. et al., 1985, "Water Supply Infrastructure Study," Philadelphia, Pa.

Acknowledgment

This paper was prepared under the Water System Operation, Maintenance and Rehabilitation work unit of the Water Supply and Conservation Research Program at the US Army Corps of Engineers Waterways Experiment Station (WES). Permission to publish was granted by the Chief of Engineers. Helpful comments on the first draft were provided by F. Doug Shields of WES.

Water Infrastructure Maintenance Needs -
A Case Study

Arun K. Deb, F. ASCE*

Introduction

Water systems in many cities, particularly in the Northeastern
section of the United States, are very old. Some of the distribution
system pipelines are more than 100 years old. With lack of proper and
timely maintenance of the distribution network systems, the incidence
of main breaks is increasing at high rates in many cities.
Unaccounted for water in many large cities is very high, ranging from
25 to 50 percent of pumped water. Due to this large amount of
unaccounted for water, water utilities are losing large amounts of
revenues per year. Adoption of measures to prevent loss of water in
many cases is cost-effective. In order to illustrate the magnitude of
infrastructure problems of large cities, a test case infrastructure
study for the City of Buffalo water system has been conducted.

The objectives of the study are to evaluate the Buffalo water
system, to identify the problem areas, to suggest possible alternative
solutions, to estimate costs to rehabilitate the system and to make a
financial and institutional analysis to determine the magnitude of
shortfall.

System Description

The water distribution system in the City of Buffalo is typical
of many older cities in the Northeastern United States. Buffalo's
Division of Water began its operations in 1868.

Water demand in Buffalo has been declining since the mid 1950's
when the average demand was 136 million gallons-per-day. The 1980
average daily, maximum daily, and peak hourly water demands for the
City of Buffalo are 101 mgd, 140 mgd, and 172 mgd respectively. The
estimated average daily demand in the year 2010 will be 130 mgd.

The Buffalo distribution system consists of 783 miles of pipes,
four pumping stations and four reservoirs. The two large pumping
stations are more than 50 years old. About fifty percent of the
distribution pipes were laid before the year 1900. In the present
system, only thirty percent of the production is metered, while most
of the residential services (about 80,000) are charged on a flat rate
basis.

*Vice President, Roy F. Weston, Inc., West Chester, PA 19380

475

The piping system averages 80 years of age, is composed primarily of unlined cast iron. These pipes are pitted, corroded and tuberculated. These conditions present a substantial hydraulic constraint on the system's ability to deliver water at sufficient pressure and to have desired levels of fire protection.

The City of Buffalo Water Division maintains a good record of all main breaks and leaks. This study analyzed main break data from 1975 to 1980 and found an annually averaged 255 main and joint breaks or 326 breaks per 1000 miles of distribution mains.

The Hazen-Williams Coefficient (C-value) of selected pipes of the Buffalo Distribution system have been measured in 1945, 1955, and again in 1980. Using these field data, a set of regression equations has been developed relating C-values with age for different sizes of pipes. Most of the C-values for transmission mains have been found to be in the range of 40 to 80, indicating a deteriorated pipe condition. This is probably due to internal corrosion, tuberculation and sedimentation. The unaccounted for water for the Buffalo water system was estimated to be about 30 percent.

Water Conservation

In this study, the feasibility of various water conservation measures in the Buffalo Water System is analyzed and the financial impact is evaluated. Three water conservation measures, metering, unaccounted water management and home water conservation are analyzed.

The Buffalo Water System has about 80,000 unmetered flat rate residential customers. The residential water consumption is estimated to be as high as 125.4 gallons per capita per day. This is very high in comparison with a national average of 64 gpd. By complete metering of the water system, it is expected that a water savings of 32.4 gallons per capita per day can be achieved resulting in a total savings of 11.4 mgd. A preliminary cost analysis shows that by complete metering of the system, the Division of Water will have an additional yearly cost of $1.6 million and an additional yearly income of $1.8 million. Therefore, complete metering of the Buffalo Water System has been found to be cost effective.

Unaccounted water loss for the Buffalo Water System is estimated to be between 26.5 and 32.4 percent of water pumpage. A considerable portion of this water is believed to be lost by leakage and breakage of watermains. By adopting an unaccounted water management program, including a regular leak detection program, it is possible to reduce this loss of water to 15 percent and achieve a water conservation of 11.4 percent or 11.7 mgd. This option of water conservation has been found to be cost-effective.

Water demand projections up to the year 2010 with various conservation options are developed and plotted in Figure 1. Figure 1 also shows the projection of revenue producing water.

Adoption of voluntary home conservation option would reduce water pumpage by only 3.3 percent, with the reduction of revenue producing water by the same amount. This option is considered marginal at best and, as such, deserves a lower priority than the previous two options for future considerations.

Adoption of all three conservation measures analyzed in this study, i.e., metering, unaccounted water management and home conservation, will provide a savings of 26 percent of water in the year 2010 over the no conservation option.

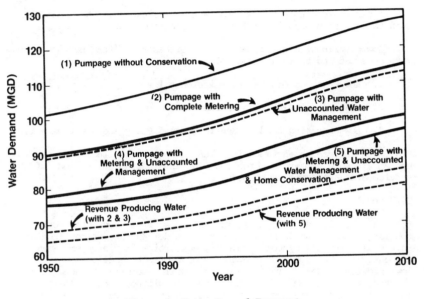

Figure 1   Water Demand Forecast
with Various
Conservation Measures

Distribution System Analysis

The methodology used in this study is a systems analysis approach of the entire pipe network of the Buffalo Water system. A skeletonized Buffalo water distribution pipe network has been simulated under various conditions of water demands using a computer model developed by the University of Kentucky. The skeletonization is accomplished without sacrificing the accuracy of the results. The simulated pipe network consists of 155 miles represented by 302 pipes of sizes ranging from 10 inches to 60 inches, 182 nodes, four storage reservoirs and three pumping stations.

To ensure that the hydraulic behavior of the Distribution System is accurately simulated, the computer model was calibrated using three independent sets of field data. These data are flow and pressure measurements taken throughout the distribution network during various water demands. Throughout the calibration, model input variables were adjusted until the calculated quantities matched the field measured quantities. Further assurance of the model's capability to simulate the water system was attained through verification of the model under a different set of field conditions. This step verified that the model indeed predicts the flow and pressure values measured in the field.

After satisfactory calibration and verification, the model was used to predict hydraulic conditions of the pipe system.

Low distribution pressures in the northeast of the service area were observed and these are due to:

1. Low C-values of the transmission mains

2. High ground elevation in the area

3. Low operating head of Kensington and Ferry storage reservoirs

With the continued deterioration of the existing distribution system, severe pressure problems in the northeast region of the service area are expected to occur.

Cell Model

In general, adequate water is available from hydrants connected to large transmission mains to meet fire demands at various locations in the distribution system. However, acute fire flow problems will be encountered when drawn from hydrants connected to smaller mains in the low pressure area. This condition will steadily worsen if no substantial improvement is made to the piping system. These small main situations could not be analyzed using the calibrated Buffalo Water Distribution System Model. A special cell model simulating details of a typical small diameter loop or cell of the network has been developed to identify the fire flow problem areas supplied from smaller mains.

A typical representative pipe network cell bounded by transmission mains (Figure 2) consists of smaller distribution mains with diameter sizes ranging from 4 inches to 12 inches. The cell model was then rigorously tested for various fire flows on 6, 8, 10 and 12 inch mains by varying the transmission pressure from 25 psi to 95 psi and the distances from the transmission mains from 500 to 1000 feet. Table 1 shows the computer results in terms of minimum pressure in the transmission mains required in order to have 1000 gallons per minute of fire flow from each main size at a specified distance from transmission mains at 20 psi residential pressure. From this result, it appears that sufficient fire flow water will not be available from smaller mains bounded by transmission mains with low pressures. On the basis of this cell model study, estimation of lengths of various smaller mains to be cleaned and relined has been made and is shown in Table 2.

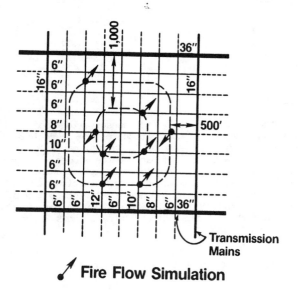

Fire Flow Simulation

Figure 2   Typical Distribution
Grid Cell

Table 1
Fire Flow Adequacy of Distribution Mains

Fire Flow from Main Size Inches	(psi) of Transmission Main Minimum Pressure at which a Minimum 1000 gpm Flow will be Available	
	500 Feet from Transmission	1000 Feet from Transmission
12	25	35
10	35	35
8	35	65
6	75	90

Table 2
Lengths of Smaller Mains to be
Cleaned and Relined

Size (Inches)	Length (Miles)
12	32.88
10	31.74
8	39.34
6	151.53
Total	255.49

Improvement Analysis

From pipe network analysis, water conservation analysis, main break analysis and physical examination of the conditions of water intakes, treatment, pumping and storage, a 30-year capital improvement plan for the Buffalo Water System has been developed. In this plan, it is recommended to clean and reline 103 miles of transmission mains (16 inches to 60 inches) and 255 miles of distribution mains (4 inches to 12 inches); to install about 80,000 new meters for household uses; and to rehabilitate and retrofit intake structures pumping stations, filtration plant and storage facilities. Table 3 shows a summary of capital costs for improvements.

Table 3
Summary of Capital Costs for Improvements

Improvement Measures	Lower Range	Upper Range
	Million Dollars	
Rehabilitation to Retrofit of Pumping and Treatment	55.0	69.4
Distribution System	96.0	222.6
Metering	20.0	20.0
Total	171.0	312.0

Financial Analysis

In order to implement the capital improvement program developed in this study, a preliminary financial analysis has been made using a financial analysis model. The model was used to calculate revenues, expenditures and annual deficits/surpluses associated with the upper and lower range of the possible capital costs required to undertake system improvements. The financial shortfall was calculated for each limit of the range. Existing water use rates and fees provided the basis for projected revenues.

Approach

Expenditures were based on capital costs and and operations and maintenance costs. All capital costs were financed during the year incurred at 8.6 percent over a 15-year term.

Accumulated deficits and surpluses were calculated. The accumulated totals are expressed in 1980 dollars. However, with inflation, the accumulated totals represent the sum of annual deficits or surpluses which are each separately affected by inflation.

The following assumptions are made in this analysis:

1. The study period for the analysis has been assumed to be 30 years beginning in 1981.

2. All capital expenditures would be met by current means of loans of bonds of 8.6 percent over 15 years.

3. The capital construction programs have not been limited to the $2 to $4 million per year that has been available to the Division of Water.

Analysis

Shortfall was calculated under two different sets of assumed conditions for analysis purposes. These conditions are:

1. Without inflation, using current revenues from user charges, operation and maintenance and capital costs.

2. With user charges doubled (without inflation).

Tables 4 and 5 show the result of shortfall analysis under various conditions of user charges. Under existing user charges (Table 4), the City of Buffalo Water Division will have significant shortfall.

Cases were also analyzed for the sensitivity of shortfall to a 100 percent increase in user charges. The resulting affect on shortfall was then measured by using the financial analysis model. The summary analysis of results is shown in Table 5. Due to the substantial increase in revenues associated with the doubling of the user charges, annual shortfalls are reduced substantially and produce accumulated surpluses.

Table 4
Shortfall Under No-Inflation and Current User Charge

	Peak Annual Shortfall ($1000)	Accumulated Shortfall ($1000)	Year of Peak Shortfall
Lower Range	13,583	190,748	1994
Upper Range	26,368	429,164	1995

Table 5
Shortfall Under No Inflation and User Charges Doubled

	Peak Annual Shortfall ($1000)	Accumulated Shortfall ($1000)	Year of Peak Shortfall
Lower Range	No Shortfall	-297,329	--
Upper Range	10,708	- 58,913	1995

Summary and Conclusions

The City of Buffalo has recognized a significant problem in funding and raising capital to support the infrastructure needs of its community. Buffalo, like other older urban centers, has experienced the opposing forces of population decline and loss of industry and employment; while the need to replace, rehabilitate and modernize its housing stock and infrastructure are met by inflation and increased demand for services.

Problems and rehabilitation needs of Buffalo Water systems have been identified.

This study examines a number of alternatives for upgrading the City of Buffalo Water Distribution System and estimates a range of capital costs between $171 million and $312 million in 1980 dollars. A financial analysis was performed assuming that the improvements would be phased throughout a 30-year planning period and financed with 15-year bonds at current rates.

This study makes some very significant observations about a typical urban water system of northeastern United States such as the decline of population in recent years, deteriorated main conditions with high main break rates and lower C-values. With the decline of population and water revenue, many older cities are also facing significant shortfalls in capital in order to implement a proper rehabilitation plan of water systems

Acknowledgements

This study was funded by the New York Department of Environmental Conservation and was conducted under the supervision of the Army Corps of Engineers, Buffalo District.

THE Rx FOR RELIEF FROM EQUIPMENT FAILURE

Lewis Debevec, Jr.*, M.ASCE, and Thomas Smeal**

Abstract: A predictive maintenance program was developed for a treatment plant with a large number of pieces of critical mechanical equipment. The predictive maintenance program was based on the fact that an operating piece of equipment is constantly providing vibration data. Using an inexpensive, portable vibration meter, data was accumulated to monitor the changing mechanical condition of critical pieces of equipment. The large amount of historical data generated required an efficient method of recording, retrieving, analyzing and graphing the data. Using a computer and database software, an information handling system for the predictive maintenance program was developed. Each piece of critical mechanical equipment in the predictive maintenance program had a dedicated file. Each file had a record containing the date of the vibration reading and the actual vibration readings. From the stored data, statistical and graphical capabilities of the software were used to analyze and graph the data to provide the facts for planning maintenance based on prediction. Utilizing this system, a decision could be made as to when equipment was to be repaired before a critical failure occurred.

Introduction

The Northeast Ohio Regional Sewer District's (NEORSD) newest treatment facility, the Westerly Water Pollution Control Center (WPCC), is situated on a 14-acre site on the northwest side of Cleveland on the shore of Lake Erie. The Westerly WPCC consists of an Advanced Waste water Treatment Facility (AWTF) and a Combined Sewer Overflow Treatment Facility (CSOTF).

The AWTF consists of a physical/chemical plant that has a design treatment capacity of 2.2 m^3/s (50 mgd), with an average flow of 1.83 m^3/s (41.7 mgd) for the year 1985. The AWTF was designed to treat a peak flow of 4.4 m^3/s (100 mgd). The treatment process train consists of control valves which divert excess flow to CSOTF, bar screens, comminutors and aerated grit chambers. The removal of suspended solids and phosphorus is accomplished by chemical precipitation and sedimentation. Lime is added in flash-mix tanks to raise the pH to the desired set point. The flow then enters the flocculator/clarifiers where the solids coagulate and settle. After

*Assistant Chief of Operations, Northeast Ohio Regional Sewer District, 3826 Euclid Avenue, Cleveland, Ohio 44115
**Maintenance Planner, Northeast Ohio Regional Sewer District, 5800 W. Memorial Shoreway, Cleveland, Ohio 44102

clarification, carbon dioxide addition lowers the pH to the desired
set point. The flow is ozonated and pumped through horizontal,
tri-media, pressure filters. The effluent from the pressure filters
is collected in a common header and then flows down through granular,
activated-carbon columns where the remaining organic material is
adsorbed from the wastewater. Chlorine disinfection completes the
liquid treatment train.

Sludge removed from the clarifiers is gravity thickened and
centrifuged into a cake that is incinerated in a multi-purpose,
multi-hearth incinerator where the calcium carbonate in the sludge is
converted to lime. The lime is reused and the remaining ash is
landfilled. Spent carbon is regenerated on site and returned to the
carbon columns.

The CSOTF provides coarse screening and primary settling to 13.2
m³/s (300 mgd) of combined sewer overflow and coarse screening for
additional flows up to 79.2 m³/s (1800 mgd). In the event of rain,
flow that is not discharged from the facility is stored and pumped
back to the AWTF when the high flow has subsided. The solids that
have collected in the CSOTF are pumped to the AWTF headworks for
processing. Besides serving as a treatment facility for combined
sewer overflow, the facility receives backwash water from the
pressure filters and carbon columns and serves as an equalization
tank from which this flow is returned to the AWTF at a uniform rate.

Maintenance Concept

The plant has eighteen pumps, ranging from 25 to 1,700
horsepower, that are critical for continuous plant operation. These
include grit pumps, lime slurry pumps, clarifier sludge pumps,
thickened sludge pumps, main pumps and backwash pumps. In most
cases, there is only one pump on standby. For example, there are
three clarifier sludge pumps; and, two pumps are required to keep
four clarifiers in service. The failure of a clarifier sludge pump
requires immediate repair so that the standby unit will be available.

The plant has ten fans or blowers, ranging from 30 to 1,000
horsepower, that are necessary for satisfactory plant performance.
These include grit channel blowers, carbon dioxide blowers, induced
draft fans, combustion air fans and ozone recycle blowers. In most
cases, a fan or blower has a backup, but in the case of the
combustion air fan, the backup exists as a second incinerator.
Therefore, it is critical that plant maintenance personnel have a
knowledge of the condition of the fans or blowers at all times.

Each piece of equipment provides valuable data that can be used
to determine the mechanical condition of the equipment. The typical
data provided may include pressure, temperature, flow, torque, motor
current draw, revolutions and vibration. Vibration, a mechanical
action, when converted to an electrical signal, is the most important
indicator of a machine's mechanical condition. During normal
operation, a piece of rotating equipment emits a specific vibration

signal. When this signal changes, it indicates that something is
going wrong with the piece of equipment.

When the Westerly Plant was placed in operation, maintenance on
the equipment was performed on a "breakdown" basis. It was soon
evident that this method would result in the plant violating its
National Pollutant Discharge Elimination System (NPDES) Permit on a
regular basis. Critical equipment was identified and plans for
monitoring the equipment were begun. It was decided that the best
method for monitoring the equipment was by utilizing vibration
analysis. A review of the vibration equipment available showed that
low cost vibration analyzers could be used to perform the job.

Vibration Analysis

The use of vibration analysis as a tool requires an understanding
of the characteristics of vibration. The characteristics of
vibration can be defined by amplitude and frequency.

Amplitude is defined as the amount of vibration. There are three
ways to measure the amount of vibration:

The first, displacement, is a measure of the actual physical
movement of the vibrating surface. Displacement is usually measured
in mils where one mil is equivalent to one one-thousandth (1/1,000)
of an inch.

The second way that amplitude can be measured is velocity.
Velocity relates to the speed of vibration. Velocity is defined as
the rate of change of displacement with respect to time. Velocity
measurements are usually made in inches per second.

The third way of measuring vibration amplitude is acceleration.
Acceleration is a measure of the forces imparted on the vibrating
object as it changes velocity. Acceleration is defined as the rate
of change of velocity with respect to time. Acceleration is usually
measured in terms of gravity, or G.

The other characteristic of vibration, frequency, is defined as
the number of vibration cycles in a given period of time. Frequency
is usually measured in cycles per minute or cycles per second.

Predictive maintenance is a science based on the fact that
deterioration of an operating piece of equipment can be identified
early enough to prevent the equipment from failing. The backbone of
a predictive maintenance program is vibration measurement and
analysis because they provide a quick and relatively inexpensive
method of detecting and identifying minor mechanical problems before
they become so serious that they cause an unscheduled shutdown of the
equipment. To assist the plant personnel in the determination of the
specific changes, a chart was developed that predicted the causes of
vibration. Table I lists the common causes of vibration and tells
how they can be identified.

FREQUENCY/RELATIVE TO SHAFT SPEED	VIBRATION CAUSE
Lower than shaft rpm	Oil whip
1 times rpm	Unbalance
2 times rpm	Looseness
1 or 2 times rpm	Bent shaft
1 to 5 times rpm	Faulty belts
20 to 50 times rpm	Antifriction bearing
Number of teeth times rpm	Worn gears

Table I. Causes and identification of vibration source

Monitoring

To begin the monitoring, a portable vibration meter with an accelerometer pickup was purchased. The meter made it possible to measure the amplitude of vibration in displacement, velocity and acceleration. After the purchase of the portable vibration meter, a route was developed that the maintenance mechanic would be able to follow one day a week. Vibration reading locations were painted on each piece of equipment to be monitored and data sheets were printed to be used to record the readings that were obtained. After the data was collected, it was returned to maintenance to be entered into the record for each piece of equipment.

Computer Application

A large amount of data was generated with this type of activity, and since all the information was necessary, an efficient method of filing, retrieving and analyzing the data was needed in order that the data provide meaningful information. Hand filing all the data could have sufficed, but an inordinate amount of time and effort would have been expended to properly maintain the files. Analyzing the collected data would have been difficult because it was not easily ordered in any kind of format unless additional time was invested. By using a personal computer with a 16/24 bit 80286 microprocessor and a fully integrated information management system, an electronic filing and analyzing program was easily designed to handle the task.

The first task in constructing the database was to define a unique file for each piece of equipment. Each file was given a separate and distinct file name which, in most cases, was the same as the plant identification name. Then, a custom-designed record form was developed for each file. The record form was the repository of the data collected in the field and contained such information as the

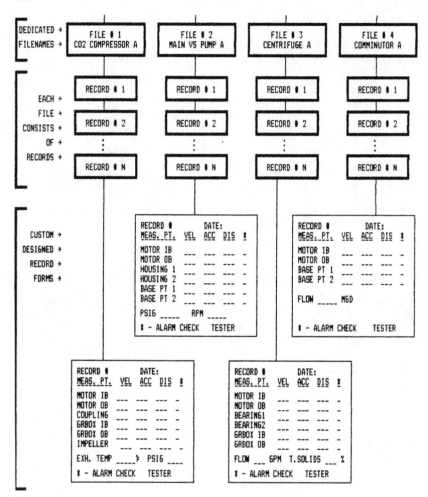

Figure 1. Predictive maintenance database structure

record number, the data, the location of the readings and the readings for the displacement, velocity and acceleration of each point to be recorded. Figure 1 illustrates the Predictive maintenance database structure.

The next item was to develop a template or form that would provide blanks on the screen so that data could be entered into the form directly from the keyboard. Figure 2 is a typical screen display for an entry of readings from the Carbon Dioxide Compressor. The first column on the template corresponds to the numbered measuring point on the equipment. The next column is the description of the measuring point. The next three columns show the recorded value for displacement in mils, the recorded values for velocity in inches per second, and the values obtained from the piece of equipment for acceleration in G. The letters "T" or "F" in the columns marked with an asterisk are not entered by the person entering the data. They are added by the computer after the data is compared to a limit value. Each entry is checked, and if it is higher than the limit, an "F" is placed in the column next to the reading. This technique serves to alert the person entering the data that a measuring point is out of limits. This allows the person entering the data to immediately alert maintenance that a mistake may have occurred in the reading.

EQUIPMENT DESCRIPTION		TAG NUMBER			DATE	
CO_2 COMPRESSOR A		CM-312-A			06/07/85	

MEAS. PT.#	MEASURING POINT DESCRIPTION	: DISP. : MILS	:*: :*:	VELOC. IPS	:*: :*:	ACCEL. G	:*: :*:
1	MOTOR INBOARD	: 0.250	:T:	0.155	:T:	0.22	:T:
2	MOTOR OUTBOARD	: 0.255	:T:	0.155	:T:	0.23	:T:
3	COUPLING	: 0.300	:T:	0.195	:T:	0.35	:T:
4	GEARBOX INBOARD	: 0.275	:T:	0.175	:T:	0.30	:T:
5	GEARBOX OUTBOARD	: 0.566	:T:	0.388	:T:	0.62	:T:
6	IMPELLER HOUSING	: 0.430	:T:	0.210	:T:	0.56	:T:

DISCHARGE TEMPERATURE: 188F   PRESSURE: 22 PSIG   TESTER: T. JONES

Figure 2. Computer screen display for CO_2 compressor

The design of the data entry form was easily accomplished using the database program, "Forms Design Utility". The form can be changed at any time to enhance the reporting of data. This form was also printed with the data areas blank. The form was then used by the person taking the vibration readings so that when the data was copied into the computer, there was less chance of error. It is true that the data is handled twice, once when the data is obtained in the field, and then again when it is copied into the computer. But, this redundancy is more than compensated for by the quality of the final product.

The next task involved the development of standard reports. The most important part of any integrated information management system is the statistical and graphing capabilities. A fully integrated database program does not restrict what the user wants from the data stored in the equipment files. Primarily, it was desirable to be able to see as much historical data as possible so a true trend could be established. The database program that was chosen allowed automatic generation of these statistics: average, minimum, maximum, variance and standard deviation. Reports are easily generated that show data sorted by data and provide the desired statistics. For example, Figure 3 is a report of nine observations of data showing the average, variance, standard deviation, minimum and maximum values for the nine observations. Since just about any mathematical computation can be performed within the database program, data integrity can even be tested mathematically.

DATE	PT1A	PT1D	PT1V	
09/01/85	0.290	0.800	0.550	
09/08/85	0.290	0.800	0.500	
09/15/85	0.295	0.880	0.550	
09/22/85	0.295	0.950	0.600	
09/29/85	0.315	0.950	0.650	
10/04/85	0.333	0.950	0.650	
10/11/85	0.333	1.100	0.650	
10/18/85	0.333	1.100	0.650	
10/25/85	0.330	1.100	0.650	
	0.313	0.959	0.606	Ave
	0.000	0.015	0.003	Var
	0.020	0.121	0.058	Sdv
09/01/85	0.290	0.800	0.500	Min
10/25/85	0.333	1.100	0.650	Max

Number of Observations: 9

Figure 3. Statistical analysis of vibration measurements

The graphing function of the software provides the ability to print a line graph of the vibration readings plotted against time. Data stored in the database allows the printing out of a line graph of up to the last thirty readings. Figure 4 is a graph showing a comparison of the acceleration measurements made on the CO_2 Compressor A for two months. This allows maintenance to view graphically what changes have taken place in the last nine acceleration readings.

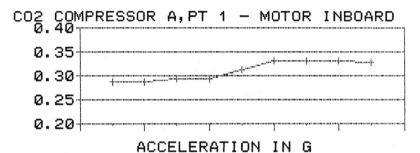

CO2 COMPRESSOR A, PT 1 - MOTOR INBOARD

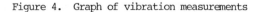

ACCELERATION IN G

Figure 4. Graph of vibration measurements

Conclusion

The task of keeping a treatment plant with equipment critical to
continuous plant operation on "line" or on "ready standby" requires
the ability to predict equipment failure. An inexpensive vibration
meter, a personal computer with a printer, a fully integrated
information management system, a maintenance mechanic, and training
was used to detect equipment vibration problems. The program can
provide a quick and inexpensive method of predicting an impending
failure. This advanced knowledge allows the operation and
maintenance forces to prepare to work on a piece of equipment in an
orderly manner instead of having to react to a disastrous failure.

MODERNIZING THE MAINTENANCE FUNCTION

James A. Noyes*

Large-scale multibillion dollar water resource projects, such as the Central Arizona Project, receive significant media coverage and win awards thereby catching the eye of the public. What goes unseen and unrealized is the cost to operate and maintain these systems once the ribbon-cutting ceremony is a vague memory. In this era of Proposition 13 and Gramm-Rudman budgets, it becomes increasingly clear that the maintenance dollar must be stretched to the point of maximum productivity. One way to reach this goal is to replace the "this is the way we've always done it" approach with one that examines the maintenance function from a systems viewpoint and uses modern data processing tools.

The Los Angeles County Department of Public Works maintains one of the largest and most complex flood control and water conservation systems in the world. The system includes 14 flood-regulating dams, 150 debris dams and basins, 31 storm water pumping stations, 2,200 acres of water percolation basins, and several thousand miles of channels and storm drains. The rapid urbanization of the Los Angeles metropolitan area after World War II was accompanied by an equivalent expansion in this infrastructure as well as in the demand for funds to operate and maintain it. In the early 1970's, the Department recognized that if the historic rate of expenditures continued, the day would come when all discretionary funds would be required for maintenance. A system study of the maintenance function was conducted with the goal of creating a new system that provides for structural and operational integrity and be cost effective. A new Maintenance Management System was developed, and initial implementation occurred in 1976. This system is not yet complete but continues to evolve based on experience.

The system is based on three key, but simple concepts. The first of these is the establishment of criteria or standards for maintenance which provide benchmark positions to be used in determining the frequency and extent of maintenance work. Without standards, the performance of maintenance work becomes subjective and can easily lead to excessive expenditures or to under-maintenance which increases the chance for failure or more costly reconstruction.

*Assistant Deputy Director, Road Maintenance Division, Los Angeles County Department of Public Works, 1540 Alcazar Street, Los Angeles, CA 90033.

The development of standards removes the subjective part of the analysis. The standards are known and resources are not wasted when the standards indicate that work does not need to be performed. There are two types of standards (Figure 1). The first of these is the Maintenance Standard, and it represents the ideal condition or the desired state after work is done. The Acceptable Maintenance Condition (AMC) is a lesser condition and defines the condition at which maintenance work becomes necessary. At any point in between the Maintenance Standard and the AMC, no work is performed. It is only when the AMC is reached or exceeded that work becomes necessary. The Department has defined 39 flood control and water conservation facilities or appurtenances thereto, such as catch basins, channel inverts, and fencing, for which Maintenance Standards and AMC's have been formulated. These standards serve three functions. They provide management with a tool to establish, control, and adjust service levels, especially in the face of budgetary limitations, by redefining them. They allow for impartial and objective decision making as opposed to a subjective approach that will vary among field supervisors and will guarantee consistency throughout the maintenance organization. Finally, they form the basis for designing a unit of work called a routine.

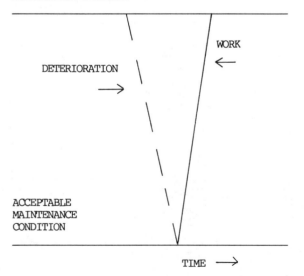

Figure 1

A routine describes a maintenance job that is preplanned, pre-
estimated, prescheduled, and preapproved by management (Figure 2).
The basis for preparing routines is that a majority of maintenance
work is repetitive. It is known that certain types of work have to
be done. A routine is a plan for execution of work prepared in
accordance with the Maintenance Standard and AMC. The resources
necessary to execute the routine are estimates based on industrial
engineering standards. Routines are prescheduled based on knowing
approximately when the AMC point will be reached. After the plannng,
estimating, and scheduling are done, the routine is administratively
approved and becomes a contract between management and the work force
responsible for its execution. As routine work is completed, a
history is built and the resource estimates and schedules can be
adjusted based on actual practice. Currently, there are
approximately 7,000 routines that have been in a stored computer file
system.

ROUTINE NO. 220-0

Description: Clean 214 catch basins. See addendum
              for exact location.

Resource requirements:

		Number	Total Est. Hours
Personnel	Foreman	1	4
	Truck Driver	1	16
	Laborer	1	16
Equipment	Vacuum Truck	1	16
	Pickup Truck	1	4
Material	N/A		

Schedule: August

Figure 2

The advantages to having a roster of routines are in scheduling,
budgeting, and management. Simulation of the routine workload
provides management with a picture, for any specified time period, of
the needs for personnel, equipment, and material resources.
Workloads can be adjusted to eliminate resource constraints and
seasonal weather interferences. Budgets can be prepared using as a
basis the financial requirements to do the preventive maintenance
identified by the routines.

Although a majority of work performed originates from the routines, the system provides for nonroutine work which cannot be prescheduled or pre-estimated. These jobs undergo a planning and estimating process, are assigned a priority, are approved and then stored in the computer in a job file with the routines. They are scheduled for execution in accordance with their priority and in combination with other routine and nonroutine jobs in resource optimization packages.

The final component is the development of a comprehensive, computer-based management information system to assist managers in the performance of their duties. This Maintenance Management Reporting System (MMRS) was two years in developing and went into operation in July 1983. Its features were changed several times during the course of development. This system basically performs four functions. It produces information and reports, stores data on thousands of jobs, and provides on-line screens to view this information, allows for on-line data entry to it and the cost accounting system, and produces work authorization forms, called job orders, and records for payroll purposes.

MMRS produces 37 different reports. The frequency of these reports varies from annually to an as-needed basis. The reports cover four major areas: scheduling, cost, performance, and routine file information. One scheduling report provides information on individual jobs that are current, meaning approved but not yet completed. This report provides a means to optimize the scheduling of manpower and equipment, and it can also aid in the acquisition of materials. Other scheduling reports are at the program level and are for management perspective. There are 10 cost reports which report on expenditures in various fashions. These reports are at the individual job level and at program levels. They are used to audit performance versus the budget and to help improve estimating techniques. The performance reports allow measurement of the production of individual supervisors and crews on individual jobs against predetermined job estimates. The reports help to measure the accuracy of estimates and to assist in evaluation of job execution. The routine file reports shows various slices of summary information based on the individual routines. These routines can be used in such diverse ways as preparing budget estimates and assisting in the scheduling of work.

MMRS is an on-line system which allows for the entry of data and the ability to view data. Data on any routine or nonroutine job that has been entered into the system is stored in the system and can be viewed on the screen. This includes, for jobs that are in progress, a very accurate approximation of their current cost. There is a one-day lag in the costing mechanism, so for example, the cost of jobs through Tuesday is available Thursday morning, assuming that all pertinent information was entered on Wednesday. Labor hours of personnel and working hours for equipment are entered through on-line terminals, and this data is processed through the cost accouting system to yield job costs. This method of data entry has been a cost savings because it replaced a more time-consuming keypunch operation.

The terminals are also used to enter all information on new routines and nonroutine job orders.

MMRS also produces job orders for all routine jobs. The individual responsible for work scheduling uses the terminal to order the routine job orders for the next work period, and the computer searches the routine file for this period and prints the job orders. Because of the relationship between MMRS and the cost accounting system, MMRS also produces employee records which feed the payroll system.

The evolution of a new maintenance system that meets the desired goals of operational integrity and efficiency is not an easy task. A well thought out plan is mandatory as is the attention and interest of the organization's management. In particular, there are two thoughts to keep in mind as the process unfolds. First, the definition of exactly what the maintenance program is to do must be established. This is done by analyzing current practices and identifying their shortcomings or deficiencies and by investigating the methods of similar organizations. This analysis will result in the development of requirements for a maintenance system. A requirement is a broad, policy-like statement which sets the general framework for the organization. For example, a requirement might be, all levels of management will have the information necessary to properly execute their jobs in accordance with the organizational structure and their defined responsibilities. These requirements form the basis for designing a new system. A common trap that engineers fall into and must be avoided is designing the system before the requirements are agreed upon. Using the above requirement, the design process would include identifying the information necessary and defining job descriptions and responsibilities and how the information would be used. Second, there must be sensitivity to all participants in the system from the Department head to the laborer in the field. Each plays a role in the maintenance system and each must be consulted in order for the new system to be accepted.

A similar process is necessary in developing a computer-based system. First, determine what the system is to do before assessing hardware and software needs. It is common to see a computer or program demonstrated and decide that it is the right one. Resist this temptation and determine the agency's needs and then evaluate hardware and software against it. Second, make a thorough initial determination of the types of information that the system should provide and then decide the who, what, when, where, and why for these. Everyone in the organization should know what the system is going to do for them and why. Once this has been done and equipment purchased, tested, and debugged, then be prepared to make changes. It is inevitable that regardless of the amount of testing that is done, users will want to add, delete, and change portions of the system after it has become operational. Go into the process with the attitude that after the initial operational period, changes will occur. Third, start small. In designing a management information system, there is a temptation to provide too much information, to ask for every conceivable type of report. The result is that an overwhelming amount of information is produced and it is too much for anyone to digest. It is always easier to work from a good solid base and add refinements or additional information to it then it is to start with a large mass of information and then attempt to reduce it. Each managerial level should initially be provided with one or two key reports that they need and once they become familiar with them, others can be added.

An Experimental Study on the Effect of Wastewater
Application in Dry Wells and Its Impact on Groundwater

by

Reza M. Khanbilvardi[*]

Abstract

    A study was conducted in order to gather accurate
information on the effectiveness of dry wells for use in
wastewater disposal and the effect of such disposal practice
on groundwater. To determine this effect, accurate information on the variation in the quality of wastewater during
percolation through soil was obtained in a laboratory test.
The results of the study indicated that wastewater can be
renovated to some degree in limestone soil media. Ca and Mg
hardness and ammonia nitrogen concentrations increased with
increaseing soil depth. While, pH and alkalinity were
essentially unchanged during the percolation process at
depths beyond two feet of soil.

Introduction

    On-site wastewater disposal is considered to be one of
the most widely used methodology not only in United States
but in different parts of the world as well. However, use
of this method may cause some problems in the groundwater.
This is, especially, crucial for those communities where
groundwater is the only source of domestic water supply.

    In addition to soil type, several geological parameters
affect the use of on-site wastewater disposal systems. Of
these, impermeable soil layers, high groundwater table, and
shallow depth to bed rock are the most important ones. Other
factors affecting the change in quality of wastewater in the
soil media are hydraulic conductivity, permeability, porosity, and particle size of the soil media.

    This study was directed toward gathering information
regarding the use of on-site disposal of wastewater on the

* Assistant Professor, Department of Civil Engineering, The
City College of The City University of New York,Convent Ave.
New York, N.Y. 10031.

quality of groundwater in Pennsylvania. To achieve this, an experiment was conducted to find the effect of a typical and predominant soil type in Central Pennsylvania on wastewater renovation. Renovation is defined as the removal or transformation of the chemical or biological contaminants.

The disposal of wastewater onto the land for the purposes of renovation and recycling in Pennsylvania has been the subject of extensive studies since 1960's. Willman(7) used limestone, sandstone, and shale sands combined with 0, 3, 6, and 12 percent clay for renovations of septic tank effluent. Coilkosz et al.(2) studied the effects of acid mine drainage on Pennsylvania soil. They used Rayne(fine loamy, mixed soil developed from acid shales) and Guernsey (fine, mixed soil developed from limestone and shale)soil material after the acid mine water had passed through it. Delong(3) used soil columns to study the movement of sewage effluent through soil media.

Methodology

A laboratory set-up was designed(Fig. 1) to investigate the effect of a limestone based soil (predominant in Central PA.)on wastewater renovation. Table 1 shows the soil properties. Four cylinders used in this study had 4-inch internal diameter and were constructed from 1/4" thich plexiglass. A plexiglass plate, 6.5 inches on a side was fastened to the bottom of each cylinder. A 5/8" hole was drilled into the center of each bottom plate and a 1/2" diameter galvanized pipe, two inches in length, was screwed into each base plate. In order to prevent loss of the soil material fromthe cylinders,four layers of window screen with a layer of glass wool in between the layers of screen were placed immediately over the outlet from the cylinders. Soil depths used in the cylinders were 1, 2, 4, and 6 feet.

One gallon plastic containers with tapered nozzles were placed filled with primary clarifier effluent obtained from

Table 1. Soil Properties

% Passing Seive				Permea-bility in/hr	Moist. Capcit. in/in	Max Dry Density lb/cu. ft.
No.4	No.10	No.40	No.200			
80-100	80-100	65-90	10-35	2.0-6.3	.02-.06	118-125

The Pennsylvania State University Wastewater Treatment Plant The rate of wastewater applied to the soil columns was set at 1 gal/day. This resulted in a soil loading rate of

11.5 gpd/sq.ft.A complete description of the laboratory set-
up was reported by Khanbilvardi and Long(4). The parameters
used to monitor the wastewater quality are shown in Table 2.
Raw wastewater was applied to each soil column every day and
samples were taken from the oulets of each cylinder daily.
Settled raw sewage and effluent samples from each soil
column were stored and measured at room temperature(23°C)
on the same day. Analyses were conducted according to a
five day schedule(one cycle). The experiment was run for a
total of 20 cycles of five day each.

Table 2. Testing Schedule for One Cycle (5 days)
          and Method of Measurements.

Day	Parameter(s) Measured	Method
1	pH	pH meter,
	Hardness	EDTA titrimetric,
	Alkalinity	Potentiometric titration to end point pH (1)
2	Chemical Oxygen Demand (COD)	University of CA Short Method(5).
3	Kjeldahl Nitrogen	Standard Method(1).
	Ammonia Nitrogen	Acidimetric Method(1).
4	Nitrate Nitrogen	Chromotropic Acid(1).
5	Nitrate+Nitrite Nitrogen	Nitrite Conversion & Chromotropic Acid Method(1).

Results

The average pH values for each depth of soil are shown
in Fig.2. The data indicated that the average pH values did
not change significantly with respect to time and depth
specially after the 8th cycle. Since dry soil was used,soil
conditions were not stable during the first 8 cycles.

Figure 3 shows the increase in calcium and magnesium
hardness as well as total hardness with increase in soil
depth. This bahavior was expected (7) because limestone
based soil contains calcium and magnesium carbonate which
contributed to increased hardness with increasing depth after
an adjustment period of 8 cycle.

The COD data, presented in Fig. 4 indicate that reduction
in COD did occur as the wastewater percolated through the
soil profile. Values shown in Fig.4 obtained by taking the

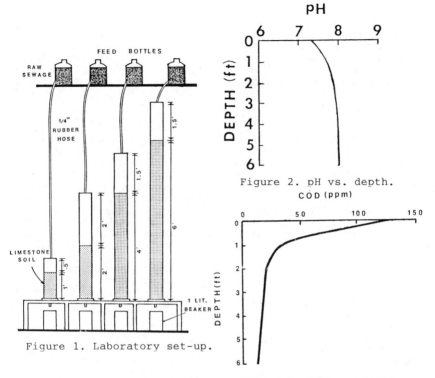

Figure 1. Laboratory set-up.

Figure 2. pH vs. depth.

Figure 4. COD vs. depth.

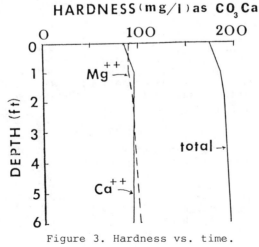

Figure 3. Hardness vs. time.

the average of the data values after the initial adjustment
period(lag period) which lasted up to the 7th cycle. During
this period, the organic suspended solids in the applied
wastewater were removed by detention in the voids, or physical
adsorption on the dry soil particles. Starting 8th cycle,the
population of soil bacteria, although no bacterial data were
collected, was believed to increase significantly.Decomposition
of organic wastes by these "heterotrophic Bacteria" resulted
in COD reduction.

Because of microbiological activity in the soil, changes
in most of observed nitrogen forms are significantly dependent
on time. Therefore,plotting average values for different soil
depth was felt to be inaccurate. As the result, Fig. 5 thru
9 were plotted to show time dependency of these parameters.
Figure 5 indicates that reduction in Total Kjeldahl Nitrogen
(TKN) was significant after the 6th cycle (lag period). The
reduction of TKN in the early part of the lag period was due
to a filtering out of the suspended solids and organic wastes
than to biological transformations. This figure also shows
that significant reduction occurred in 1st foot of soil .

Organic nitrogen variation in time for different soil
depth is shown in Fig. 6. The significant removal of organic
nitrogen , after the initial lag period, was due to two mechanisms: (I)decomposition of organic compounds by the heterophic
bacteria, and (II) from conversion of org.-N to ammonia-N
by saprophytic bacteria in either aerobic or anaerobic media
(6). Figure 7 shows ammonia-N data in influent and columns
effluent. Due to the range of pH values observed in this test
(about neutral), all available ammonia-N is considered to be
predominantly in the form of ammonium ion(NH_4^+)(6). Then, in
aerobic condition, ammonia can be oxidized to nitrite-N and
ultimately to nitrate nitrogen. This process can take place
only under aerobic conditions and only first foot of soil is
expected to have aerobic conditions. Therefore, the above
conversion was completed within the 1st foot of soil. After
the 1st foot, the condition in the soil columns would turn to
anaerobic and consequently the present nitrate-N would be
denitrified to nitrogen gas. Nitrogen gas tends to scape the
media. However, during this process some of the gas was converted to organic-N (nitrogen fixation). Organic nitrogen in
anaerobic conditions was, ultimately, transformed to ammonia
nitrogen by;

$$HNO_3 + 4\ H_3 \longrightarrow NH_3 + 3\ H_2O \ \ \dots\dots\dots\dots(1)$$

Hence, the greater the depth of soil, the greater was the
conversion of nitrogen gas to ammonia nitrogen.

The amount of nitrate nitrogen in the settled raw sewage
was very small and there was an insignificant amount of nitrite-N in the original settled raw sewage. The data in Fig.
8 show the changes which occurred in nitrate-N during the
percolation period. This figure shows that the amount of

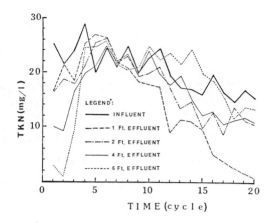

Figure 5. Total Kjeldahl-N vs. time.

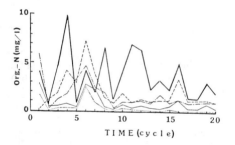

Figure 6. Organic-N vs. time.

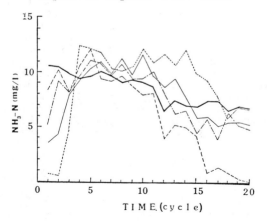

Figure 7. Ammonia-N vs. time.

nitrate in the effluent from the columns before the 12th cycle was very small due to the small amount of nitrate in the influent. After this point, population of autotrophic bacteria had increased significantly enough for nitrification of ammonia to occur as can be concluded from the observed increase in nitrate concentration in the effluent from 1 foot soil column. Because of the anaerobic conditions which existed in the soil columns after the first foot of depth, denitrification resulted in almost no trace of nitrate in after the first foot of soil(Fig. 8). Therefore, ammonia-N can be oxidized to nitrate-N by nitrifying bacteria. The energy required for growth of nitrifying organisms is obtained from this reaction. Therefore, in the carbonic acid system or aqueous phase the overall oxidation reaction would be:

$$NH_4^+ + 3/2\ O_2 + 2\ HCO_3^- \xrightarrow{\text{bacteria}} NO_2^- + 2H_2CO_3 + H_2O \quad ....(2)$$

$$NO_2^- + 1/2\ O_2 \xrightarrow{\text{bacteria}} NO_3^- \quad ....(3)$$

This indicates that alkalinity would be decreased by oxidation of ammonia-N. This decrease is shown in Fig. 9. Also, the overall reaction for denitrification process is:

$$NO_3^- + 0.833CH_3OH + 0.167H_2CO_3 \longrightarrow 0.5N_2 + 1.33H_2O + HCO_3^- \quad ...(4)$$

This equation shows that H_2CO_3 would be reducted and alkalinity(HCO_3^-)would be increased in denitrification process. The increase in alkalinity as the result of denitrification process in 2, 4, and 6 foot columns are shown in Fig. 9.

Summary

The primary purpose of this soil column study was to show the effects of soil depth and time on the variation in wastewater quality(pH, hardness, COD, nitrogen forms, and alkalinity)in a soil system. This was accomplished by using four different columns containing 1,2,4,and 6 feet depths of limestone-based soil. The results indicated that: (a) while changes in pH and alkalinity were observed, they were not sufficient to significantly affect groundwater quality,(2) the Ca^{++} and Mg^{++} hardness of percolated wastewater increased with increasing limestone soil depth, (3)almost complete reduction in COD, org.-N, Nitrite-N, and nitrate-N occurred in the first two feet of limestone soil, (4)the amount of ammonia nitrogen in the percolated wastewater remained unchanged at the end of six feet of limestone soil although some transformation of ammonia-N did take place.

References

1. American Public Health Association, 1975. Standard Methods for the Examination of Water and Wastewater. 14th Ed. Washington D.C.
2. Coilkosz, E.J., L.T. Kardos, and W.F. Beers,1978. "The Effect of Acid Mine Drainage Water on Top Pennsylvania Soil",Soil Science,Vol.127, No. 2, pp. 102-107.
3. Delong, E., 1978. "The movement of Sewage Effluent Through

Soil Columns", Jour. of Env. Quality,Vol.7,No.1,pp.133-136.
4. Khanbilvardi,R.M. and D.A.Long,1985."Effect of Soil Depth
   on Wastewater Renovation". Journal of Env. Health. Vol.47,
   No. 4, pp. 184-188.
5. University of California Sanitary Engineering Research
   Laboratory, 1960. News Quarterly, 10:5.,1301 S. 46th
   Street , Richmond, CA 44804.
6. U.S. Environmental Protection Agency, 1975. Process Design
   Manual for Nitrogen Control, Technology Transfer. Government Printing Office, Washington,D.C.
7. Willman, B.P., 1979. Renovation of Septic Tank Effluent
   in Sand-Clay Mixture. Master of Science Thesis, The
   Pennsylvania State University, University Park, PA.

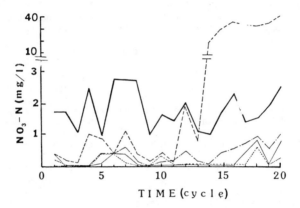

Figure 8. Nitrate-N vs. time.

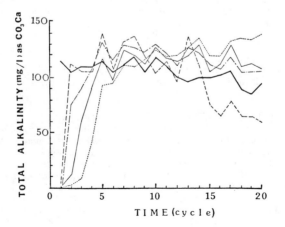

Figure 9. Alkalinity vs. time.

Investigating and Treating Chromium in
Ground Water at a Wood Treater in California

by Wendy L. Cohen, P.E.*
Member, ASCE

Abstract

A wood treating facility, operating for more than five years without required permits, contaminated soil and ground water on and offsite. The company moved slowly in response to enforcement orders and never completely defined the extent of contamination. Ground water treatment occurred sporadically and did not prevent the plume from spreading. Litigation against the company by the State of California is ongoing in Superior Court.

Introduction

In the fall of 1973, Valley Wood Preserving, Inc. (Valley Wood) began operating a wood treating and preserving facility in Turlock, California (see Figure 1). The plant consisted of two pressure treatment cylinders, each with a pump and railroad track, an asphalt drip pad, and tanks for chemical storage and mixing of wood preservative solution. The treatment fluid was a water-based, copper-chromate-arsenic solution in the relative proportions of 18.1% copper (CuO), 65.5% chromate (CrO_3), and 16.4% arsenic (As_2O_5) (2).

Lumber was pushed on a treatment train into a steel pressure cylinder which was evacuated to a vacuum to remove air and moisture from the wood cells and then filled with preservative solution. The vacuum was then released to force the treatment fluid into the wood. Treated lumber was stacked on the asphalt pad to drip dry, and most of the treatment fluid was recycled to two sumps (actually asphalt depressions) for reuse. There was no berm around the drip pad or treatment area to contain runoff and no clear drainage pattern to the sumps. In fact, the sumps did overflow periodically as evidenced by contaminated soil offsite on three sides of Valley Wood's property. After drip drying, the treated wood was stored on bare ground to dry further. Between 1973 and 1978, the paved area was expanded four times to accommodate increased production. Thus, areas of bare ground used previously for treated wood storage were paved over. In addition, areas around the treatment cylinders and mixing and storage tanks were not paved during the first two years of operation (2).

In August 1973, the California Regional Water Quality Control Board (Regional Board) sent a letter to Valley Wood requesting a Report of Waste Discharge for the new plant in Turlock. This report was supposed to include details of the proposed facilities for containment of process wastewater even though a "closed system" was planned. The report was never filed and wood treating operations continued for more than five years without a reported waste discharge or Regional Board permit, and without knowledge of Board staff (2).

* Associate Water Resource Control Engineer, California Regional Water Quality Control Board, Central Valley Region, 3201 S Street, Sacramento, CA 95816.

Problem Discovery and Regulatory Response

After complaints by neighbors to the Stanislaus County Health Department, a Valley Wood representative contacted the Regional Board in February 1979. Regional Board staff conducted an inspection of the facility in March and found 67 mg/l of chromium in water ponded on soils on the property. Soil samples collected during another inspection in May 1979 contained up to 3,100 milligrams chromium per kilograms soil (mg/kg). The drinking water standard for chromium is 0.05 mg/l, and the shallow ground water is used locally for domestic supply. In letters in April and May, Regional Board staff requested that Valley Wood submit a Report of Waste Discharge and a technical report indicating measures they would take to prevent toxic chemicals from entering unpaved areas. In a letter in June, staff requested additional soil sampling to define the extent of soil contamination (2).

Valley Wood submitted a Report of Water Discharge in June 1979. The report showed that chromium concentrations in storm runoff from a paved storage area onto soils reached 130 mg/l, twice the concentration of chromium in the treatment solution. Information in the report also showed that treated lumber stored on unpaved areas will form "salt crystals" of treatment solution on the wood surface during humid conditions which will then dissolve and be washed off during rainfall (2).

The Regional Board adopted Waste Discharge Requirements in July 1979 which included a time schedule to attain complete containment of all toxic wastewater and runoff. Valley Wood submitted two reports which were found to be inadequate to show compliance with the requirements. In August 1979, the Regional Board issued a Cleanup and Abatement Order (C&A) to Valley Wood requiring cleanup of contaminated soils and abatement of the discharge of wastes to soils (2).

In the fall of 1979, Valley Wood removed and disposed of approximately 1,500 cubic yards of contaminated soils from on and offsite. However, substantial chromium contamination (up to 380 mg/kg) remained, especially in deeper soil layers (below 9 feet) where ground water was encountered. Chromium was first found in the ground water in November 1979 at almost 8 mg/l in a shallow onsite monitoring well which had been installed in August of that year (Well 1, see Figure 2). After pumping, this well contained 131 mg/l. Detectable levels of copper and arsenic also were found but below drinking water standards. Regional Board staff wrote another letter requesting additional soil sampling and an investigation to assess the extent of ground water contamination. Also in November 1979, Stanislaus County permanently revoked Valley Wood's use permit, and the plant ceased operation. Homeowners adjacent

FIGURE 1

Location Map

San Francisco

Turlock

Los Angeles

CALIFORNIA

to the site were concerned about potential contamination of their water wells and had petitioned the county in the spring to revoke the permit (2).

The Regional Board issued a second C&A in April 1980 to require investigation and cleanup of ground water. Valley Wood's violation of this order was referred to the State Attorney General (AG) in May 1980, and a complaint was filed in Stanislaus County Superior Court in June for injunctive relief. After the referral, Valley Wood installed new monitoring wells, began treating ground water, and retained various consultants to perform the required investigations (see following sections). In July 1980, they auctioned off all remaining inventory and equipment. However, Valley Wood never submitted a technical report of a ground water investigation as required by the 1980 C&A (2).

In June 1983 when Valley Wood stopped treating ground water and declared that it was out of funds to continue cleanup, the AG filed a motion for injunction in the lawsuit. This motion was not filed earlier because Valley Wood was working towards cleanup during the previous three years. In September 1983, the court issued a preliminary injunction requiring compliance with the Regional Board's C&A. However, Valley Wood told the court it could not comply with the C&A due to a lack of money, although the company never declared bankruptcy. A contempt hearing was held in early 1984, but the court found Valley Wood not in contempt because it was unable, not unwilling, to comply (5).

In January 1984 the Regional Board asked the AG to seek civil monetary remedies against Valley Wood. At the same time, the Board issued a C&A to the president of the corporation who also owned the land on which Valley Wood operated until August 1980 when he transferred the deed to Valley Wood. A complaint was filed in the civil liability suit against Valley Wood in March 1984. The complaint was amended in May to add nine more individual and corporate defendants including the six shareholders in Valley Wood and three other companies in which they also own shares. Valley Wood's attorney filed a motion for summary judgment in September 1985 asking the court to dismiss the case outright without a trial. At the court hearing in November, the State argued that the motion should be denied because factual matters are in dispute and triable issues exist. The judge had not yet issued a decision on the motion by the end of February 1986 (3).

Meanwhile the State continues to build its case against Valley Wood and the other defendants emphasizing that there is such unity of interest and ownership that the separate personalities of the corporation and the individual shareholders no longer exist. Thus, the individuals should be held personally liable for the acts of the corporation. A complaint has also been filed against the president and former property owner for violation of his C&A; this suit may be pursued at a later date (5).

Investigations

Between late 1979 and 1983, Valley Wood hired several consultants to investigate soil and ground water contamination. CH2M Hill was retained in December 1979 to conduct a ground water pollution study and soil sampling program. They sampled soil beneath the asphalt in 12 locations and at four depths (down to 42 inches) at each location. Samples were tested for total chromium with results up to 2,000 mg/kg (or parts per million, ppm) six inches below the surface. Half of the surface samples contained more than 50 mg/kg and

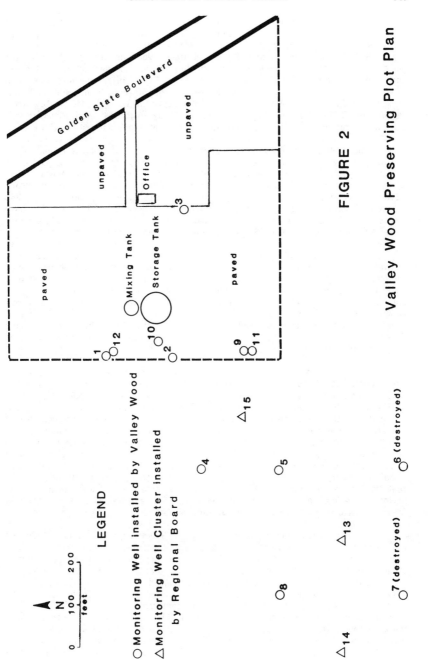

FIGURE 2

Valley Wood Preserving Plot Plan

levels up to 375 mg/kg were measured between 36 and 42 inches. The highest levels were found around the mixing tank and treatment cylinders with lower levels in most of the storage areas. CH2M Hill also installed a second monitoring well (Well 2, see Figure 2) in February 1980 and performed a 24-hour pump test. The chromium concentration in Well 2 was 115 mg/l (at 63 feet deep) and in Well 1 was 129 mg/l (at 20 feet deep). CH2M Hill recommended removal of all soils with chromium levels in excess of 50 ppm and additional soil sampling at 29 locations down to a maximum depth of 12 feet (1). Valley Wood terminated CH2M Hill's services in March 1980 saying it was nearly bankrupt, so the consulting firm never completed the ground water pollution study (3).

Valley Wood installed additional monitoring wells at various times during the next few years in response to Regional Board requests or orders. Before a scheduled court hearing in July 1980, Valley Wood installed Well 3 onsite and Wells 4 and 5 offsite (see Figure 2). In November of that year another onsite well was added (Well 10). Three more offsite wells were installed in July 1981 (Wells 6, 7, and 8), and onsite Well 9 was added in November 1981. The last two onsite wells (11 and 12) were installed around June 1982. Offsite Wells 6 and 7 were destroyed sometime in 1983 when they were run over by a tractor (2).

In May 1982, Valley Wood told Regional Board staff that Dewante and Stowell would conduct the required ground water pollution study but never submitted a report of this investigation. In the fall of 1983, Valley Wood's insurance company authorized J.H. Kleinfelder and Associates to develop a work plan for a ground water investigation. The work plan was to include a soil contamination assessment and a recommended plan for soil removal in conjunction with ground water treatment as required by the September 1983 Superior Court injunction. Kleinfelder prepared the work plan but was not given authorization by the insurance company to proceed with the study (2).

In the summer of 1984, the Regional Board hired Dames and Moore Consultants (D&M) to conduct a ground water pollution and soil contamination study at Valley Wood. The purpose of the study was to define the hydrogeology of the site, determine the horizontal and vertical extent of ground water and soil contamination, and describe a conceptual design of remedial actions. During the study, D&M characterized the physiography, geology, and hydrology of the site and inventoried wells in the vicinity. The initial field program included sampling, chemical analysis, and electrical logging of the ten existing on and offsite wells and an electrical resistivity survey. Three new sets of wells were installed downgradient in clusters of three at depths of about 20, 40, and 60 feet to locate the edge of the plume. Soil samples were taken onsite in ten borings to a maximum depth of eleven feet. Soil samples also were obtained from six perimeter and two background borings (4).

Results of the initial sampling and analysis completed in late 1984 for the existing wells showed total chromium concentrations ranging from 0.05 mg/l in offsite Well 8 to 15.8 mg/l in Well 2 onsite. The measured values indicated an increase in concentration over the previous year for most wells. Chromium concentrations in the new well clusters, installed in April 1985, ranged from 0.003 mg/l in Cluster 14 (furthest from the site) to 51 mg/l in Cluster 15 (closest to the site). Results indicate the contaminant plume is 800 to 1,000 feet in length and migrating to the southwest. The contamination extends to at least 60 feet in depth but has no consistent pattern of vertical distribution. The width of the plume is not well defined. Total chromium measured in soil samples ranged from 2.6 to 270 mg/kg with the highest levels generally occurring from the ground surface to about five feet deep. The study showed that widespread soil contamination remains beneath asphalted areas. D&M concluded that the potential exists for further ground water contamination by leaching from the soil over time. They recommended a more extensive soil sampling program, a standard pump test, and additional wells to define the lateral extent of the plume (4).

Ground Water Treatment

Valley Wood began pumping from Well 1, the first shallow monitoring well onsite, in January 1980 in an attempt to contain the pollution. The well was pumped around the clock at 2 gallons per minute (gpm), and contaminated ground water was placed in a newly-completed 660,000-gallon storm water storage tank (see Figure 2). Pumping from the deeper Well 2 was begun in February; this well could produce 30 gpm. Beginning in March, stored water was pumped from the tank and sprayed on the two asphalt depressions onsite for evaporation. CH2M Hill completed a water balance which determined the elevation to which these ponds could be filled and still safely contain all normal seasonal rainfall (1). More than 300,000 gallons of polluted ground water were pumped and evaporated in this manner. Residue left after evaporation was swept up and supposed to be taken to a hazardous waste disposal facility, but there is no information on whether this was done. During windy periods, blowing spray and dust created a nuisance for neighboring residents, and Valley Wood soon discontinued the evaporation (3).

In July 1980 Valley Wood started treating ground water by chemical precipitation. In this procedure, contaminated water is first acidified with sulfuric acid to reduce hexavalent to trivalent chromium and form chromic sulfate in solution. Sodium bisulfide is then mixed in, and the reaction forms chromium sulfide and sodium sulfate. After a certain retention time, the mixture is transferred to another tank where the pH is neutralized by lime addition, thus allowing the chromium sulfide to precipitate out and settle by gravity. Hallanger Engineers tested the process in July with a batch treatment of 7,000 gallons of polluted ground water, reducing chromium levels from almost 55 ppm to less than 1 ppm, better than 90% removal. A two-week test period in July again showed chromium removal to less than 1 mg/l. Chemical treatment had the advantage of high chromium removal but the disadvantage of increasing the sulfate concentration in treated water (3).

Full-scale chemical treatment began in August 1980. Ground water was first pumped to a mixing tank where the chemicals were added, and then to the storm water storage tank for clarification and neutralization. Valley Wood requested and received conditional approval to discharge treated water to unpaved areas onsite north and south of the driveway for percolation (see Figure 2). The conditions set on the discharge were designed to prevent sulfate contamination of ground water and required Valley Wood to 1) retain treated ground water onsite, 2) use the asphalt-lined ponds to obtain maximum evaporation, 3) maintain the chromium level in treated water at less than 1 mg/l, 4) blend treated water with another source of water to maintain sulfates below 400 mg/l, and 5) cease discharge if sulfates in Well 2 exceed 250 mg/l. Over 2.5 million gallons of ground water were chemically treated between July and September 1980. Treatment operations were shut down by Stanislaus County in October due to concern from neighbors about sulfate contamination (3).

In another attempt to comply with the Board's C&A, Valley Wood began treating ground water again in July 1981, this time by a electrochemical process. The electrochemical cell is composed of two carbon steel plates through which direct current is passed. Ferrous ion produced at the anode reduces hexavalent to trivalent chromium which then reacts with hydroxide ion evolved at the cathode to precipitate ferric and chromium hydroxide. Contaminated ground water was run through the electrochemical unit, pumped to the storage tank for settling, and then discharged to the unpaved areas for percolation. The unit was able to reduce hexavalent chromium concentrations to less than 0.05 ppm running at 150 gpm and with an influent chromium level of 9 ppm. If the influent contained higher levels, the unit had to run at a lower rate to achieve the same removal. Removal rates measured in July, September, and October 1981 were 95-98% (3).

For almost a year, Valley Wood pumped ground water from several wells both on and offsite for electrochemical treatment. A second treatment unit was added in April 1982, and pumping and treatment continued with both units operating until 1 December 1982. Both units were then shut down because Valley Wood said the insurance company failed to commit to pay for their operation. (Another insurance company carrying excess liability coverage continues to pay for Valley Wood's defense against the State's lawsuit, however). One unit was put back into operation in late December and run until 27 June 1983 when it was shut down, and no further ground water treatment occurred. Some 70 million gallons were treated electrochemically between July 1981 and June 1983. During both chemical and electrochemical treatment operations, chromium levels in Well 2 dropped from 115 mg/l in February 1980 to about 9 mg/l in June 1982 at which level it stayed until treatment ceased. No mass balance was ever done on the quantity of chromium removed from or remaining in the ground water and soil (3).

Six alternative ground water treatment technologies were evaluated in the Regional Board investigation by Dames and Moore. As a subcontractor in the study, Kennedy Jenks Engineers considered only those treatment alternatives which use known proven technology for removing chromium and for which equipment is available. The alternatives considered were granular activated carbon (GAC), electrochemical reduction, ion exchange, chemical reduction, reverse osmosis, and electrodialysis. Kennedy Jenks recommended that GAC, electrochemical reduction, and chemical reduction be considered in greater detail. This recommendation was based on available reliability and performance data, potential for high chromium removal efficiencies, operational requirements, and relative costs (4).

Summary and Conclusion

In summary, Valley Wood Preserving operated a wood treating facility using improper waste disposal methods which contaminated soil and ground water both on and offsite. Valley Wood operated for more than five years without obtaining the required water quality control permits and then moved slowly and incompletely in response to enforcement orders issued by the Regional Water Quality Control Board. Valley Wood never completed a comprehensive study to define the extent of contamination. Ground water treatment operations were sporadic and did not prevent the contaminant plume from spreading. The site is on California's Superfund list, and litigation against the company by the State is ongoing in Superior Court.

Although seven years have passed since discovery of contamination at

Valley Wood and the State has invested extensive administrative and legal efforts, the problem has not yet been resolved. Contaminated soils continue to leach chromium to the ground water, and the contaminant plume continues to travel towards domestic water supplies. The Regional Board's general policy is to work cooperatively with dischargers as long as possible before beginning legal proceedings which are time-consuming and cumbersome. In this case, the company's partial actions to comply with the Board's orders delayed the State's pursuit of legal remedies.

In the past, despite legal remedies available to the State, a recalcitrant polluter could postpone required cleanup expenditures for a long time, if not forever. State legislation passed in 1984 now allows the Board to impose administrative fines without going to court for failure to comply with enforcement orders or technical reporting requirements. This powerful new tool is being used with increasing frequency throughout California and is resulting in compliance and action from otherwise resistant dischargers. Further use of administrative fines should help bring about more remedial actions at existing contaminated facilities and deter new facilities from operating in a manner harmful to the environment.

References

1. CH2M Hill, Letter reports to Valley Wood Preserving, January-February 1980.

2. California Regional Water Quality Control Board, Central Valley Region, Agenda, Special Hearing, Valley Wood Preserving, Inc., Stanislaus County - Consideration of Referral to the Attorney General for Civil Monetary Remedies, 19 January 1984.

3. California Regional Water Quality Control Board, Central Valley Region, Case Files, Valley Wood Preserving, 1973-1986.

4. Dames and Moore Consultants, Hydrogeologic Investigation and Remedial Technology Assessment, Valley Wood Preserving, Inc., Turlock, California, October 1985.

5. Gnekow, Kathleen E., Deputy Attorney General, State of California, personal communication, January-March 1986.

REMEDIAL ACTION ALTERNATIVES FOR GROUNDWATER CONTAMINATION

by
Jahan Tavangar[1], Les K. Lampe[2], and Bruce W. Long[3]

ABSTRACT

Preliminary remedial action alternatives are formulated for a site contaminated by heavy metals. The results of soils and hydrogeologic investigations are summarized and three corrective alternatives are developed and economically evaluated. All alternatives include groundwater extraction, chemical treatment, and soil leaching processes. This paper presents only the conceptualization of remedial action alternatives and does not cover the groundwater modeling that will be done before finalizing the design.

BACKGROUND

The site is a manufacturing facility which has been operating since 1952. The manufacturing process used a solution of inorganic salts consisting of sodium dichromate $(Na_2Cr_2O_7 \cdot 2H_2O)$, copper sulfate $(CuSO_4 \cdot 5H_2O)$, and arsenic acid $(AsH_3O_4 \cdot 1/2H_2O)$. Since 1965, an acidic solution of sodium dichromate and copper sulfate has been used instead. The principal components of the plant are two wasterwater disposal facilities, a paved product storage area, and a storm water collection system. Figure 1 is a plan view of the site showing its principal features. Soils and groundwater have been contaminated by the metals, copper, arsenic, and chromium. The principal sources of contamination appear to be the disposal facilities.

SITE INVESTIGATION

Field investigations were conducted to characterize the soils and hydrogeologic conditions, as well as to determine the extent of contamination. The following paragraphs summarize the findings of these studies.

---

[1] Groundwater Hydrologist, Black & Veatch Engineers-Architects, P.O. Box 8405, Kansas City, Missouri 64114, (913) 339-2000.

[2] Head of Water Resources Department, Black & Veatch Engineers-Architects, Kansas City, MO.

[3] Chemical Engineer, Black & Veatch Engineers-Architects, Kansas City, MO.

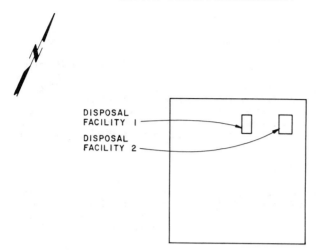

FIGURE I - PLAN VIEW OF THE SITE

SOILS INVESTIGATION

The soils investigation had the following objectives:

o   To characterize the lithology of soils underlying the site to a depth of 40 feet (i.e. unsaturated zone).

o   To obtain soil chemical data in order to determine the extent of unsaturated zone contamination by heavy metals.

o   To investigate the nature and extent of soil contamination under and around the disposal facilities giving special attention to relationships between soils, vadose moisture, and groundwater contamination in these areas.

Cores were drilled and sampled at 40 locations including off-site background samples. Soil samples were taken from the continuous cores at depths of 1, 2, and 5 feet and at subsequent 5-foot intervals. In addition to the core samples, seven lysimeter nests were installed around the disposal facilities. Samples of soil moisture were analyzed to characterize the movement of contaminated water to the saturated zone.

Since the elements of concern, i.e., arsenic, copper, and chromium are naturally present in the soils of the area, two off-site borings were drilled and sampled in order to establish the background levels of these elements. As a result of the soils investigation, it became apparent that near-surface (within 5 feet) soils contamination exists in the vicinity of the disposal facilities. However, the contamination of soils deeper than 5 feet is limited to the disposal facility 1. Furthermore, with the exception of the disposal facility 1, copper and arsenic levels in the soils were within background levels. Therefore, chromium is the main contaminant affecting the site. Figure 2 shows the location of the borings, lysimeters, and monitoring wells.

HYDROGEOLOGIC INVESTIGATIONS

A hydrogeologic investigation was conducted to characterize the local geology, groundwater conditions, and the vertical and horizontal extent of the groundwater contamination plume. The following paragraphs summarize the findings of this investigation.

LOCAL GEOLOGY

Two exploratory boreholes were drilled to define the lithology and thickness of the subsurface material. The information obtained from these boreholes was also used in designing 23 monitoring wells. The drill cutting samples were examined along with geophysical logs of the boreholes to define the local geologic conditions.

The subsurface materials underlying the site consist of heterogeneous and lenticular alluvial sediments characterized by discontinuous lenses of sand, gravelly sand, silty sand, sandy silt, clayey silt, and silty clay. Lithologic information suggests that the alluvial deposits become coarser with depth. Several hydrogeologic cross sections of the site were developed to better define the subsurface material.

GROUNDWATER CONDITIONS

Twenty three monitoring wells and 11 piezometers were installed to assess the hydraulic characteristics of the underlying aquifer as well as the quality of the groundwater. Fourteen of the monitoring wells penetrated the aquifer approximately 100 feet and the remaining 8 wells were drilled to about 180 feet below land surface. The aquifer underlying the site was found to be unconfined, with a water table about 45 feet deep. Water levels observed suggested that the direction of flow is toward south, with a hydraulic gradient of about 0.0017.

Short-term pumping tests were performed on the monitoring wells to estimate the transmissivity of the aquifer. The results of tests performed in the shallow monitoring wells suggest transmissivities on the order of 5,000 to 20,000 gpd/ft in the upper 40 feet of the aquifer as opposed to a range of 25,000 to 50,000 gpd/ft for the interval between 120 and 180 feet below land surface. As was found during the geologic investigation, subsurface materials become coarser with depth, resulting in increasing transmissivities with depth. Figure 3 shows water level contours in the vicinity of the site.

Groundwater samples collected from the monitoring wells were analyzed for common ions, arsenic, copper, hexavalent chromium and total chromium. The only groundwater contaminant was found to be hexavalent chromium. Figures 4 and 5 show contours of equal concentration of chromium found in shallow and deep monitoring wells.

FORMULATION OF REMEDIAL ACTION ALTERNATIVES

Three preliminary alternatives have been conceptualized for the cleanup of soils and groundwater that have been contaminated by hexavalent chromium. All alternatives involve soil leaching systems and groundwater extraction and treatment processes. In all cases, the disposal facilities will be capped to prevent further infiltration of contaminated water. Furthermore, the entire site will be paved and storm water will be collected and conveyed to an on-site treatement plant.

Soil leaching is done to mobilize and flush out hexavalent chromium from the unsaturated zone. This is done by building berms around the highly contaminated areas and ponding water in the resulting leaching basin.

The contaminated groundwater must be extracted and treated. Therefore, a treatment plant will be constructed on-site to remove the chromium before disposing of the water.

ALTERNATIVE 1

This remedial action alternative utilizes a number of wells located within the contamination plume to extract the polluted groundwater and prevent further migration of the plume. As is seen in Figures 4 and 5, the plume is deeper in the middle and becomes shallower toward its periphery. Consequently, extraction wells will be screened corresponding to the vertical extent of the plume. Recovered contaminated groundwater is conveyed to the treatment plant and eventually discharged into a nearby canal. A portion of the treated water is diverted into the leaching basin to maintain its water level. Two deep wells will be used, each pumping at about 240 gpm to create drawdowns of about 25 feet with radii of influence of about 420 feet. Furthermore, four shallow extraction wells will be installed, each pumping at about 160 gpm to create radii of influence of about 340 feet. Figure 6 shows the plan view of this alternative.

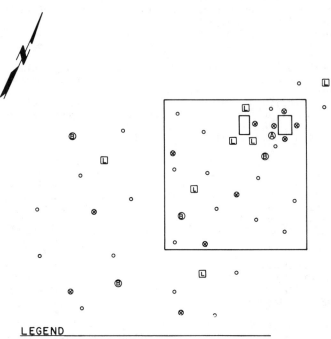

LEGEND

○   MONITORING WELL
⊗   PIEZOMETER WITH CONTINUOUS SOIL SAMPLE
Ⓑ   BORE HOLE
Ⓐ   ANGLE BORE HOLE
🄻   LYSIMETER NEST

FIGURE 2 - LOCATION OF PIEZOMETERS, BORE HOLES,
AND MONITORING WELLS.

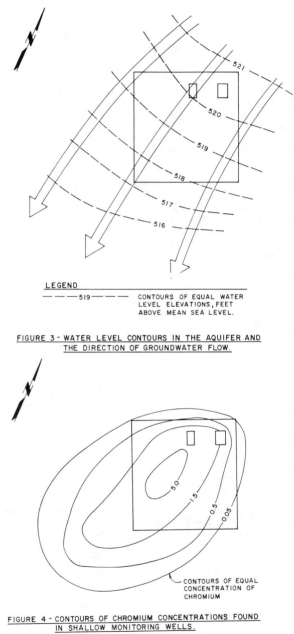

LEGEND

— — —519— — — CONTOURS OF EQUAL WATER
LEVEL ELEVATIONS, FEET
ABOVE MEAN SEA LEVEL.

FIGURE 3 - WATER LEVEL CONTOURS IN THE AQUIFER AND
THE DIRECTION OF GROUNDWATER FLOW.

CONTOURS OF EQUAL
CONCENTRATION OF
CHROMIUM

FIGURE 4 - CONTOURS OF CHROMIUM CONCENTRATIONS FOUND
IN SHALLOW MONITORING WELLS.

The process of pumping, treating, and discharging would be continued until chromium concentrations in recovered water and in monitoring wells have been reduced to acceptable levels. This is estimated to take about five years.

ALTERNATIVE 2

The second alternative considered for the cleanup of contaminated soils and groundwater utilizes two shallow and one deep extraction wells located downgradient from the contamination plume. The deep well will be pumped at about 250 gpm and each of the shallow wells at 150 gpm, to create the appropriate drawdowns and radii of influence and thereby containing the plume.

Extracted groundwater will be treated in an on-site treatment plant, after which a portion of the treated water will be diverted to the leaching basin and the rest will be discharged into a rockfilled recharge trench located upgradient from the contaminant plume. This closed-loop process would be continued until chromium concentrations in the extracted water and in monitoring wells drop to satisfactory levels. This is estimated to take approximately fifteen years. Figure 7 shows the plan view of this alternative.

ALTERNATIVE 3

The third alternative incorporates the use of a slurry wall downgradient from the contaminant plume to prevent further migration. Extraction wells will be constructed upgradient from the slurry wall to lower the rising water level. The extracted contaminated water will then be treated and injected back into the aquifer downgradient from the slurry wall.

Slurry walls work best in geological settings where an impervious layer exists within 100 feet from ground surface. This condition is not satisfied in the deep alluvial deposits underlying the site, with no impervious layer within 300 feet from surface. In this situation, a slurry wall will not be effective in preventing the migration of the plume because of excessive leaks under the wall. Therefore, this alternative is not appropriate in this situation and will not be considered any further.

EVALUATION OF ALTERNATIVES

The two feasible alternatives, i.e., Alternatives 1 and 2, are evaluated on the basis of their capital and operation and maintenance costs and the lowest cost alternative will be selected.

From Table 1, it is concluded that Alternative 1 is preferred on the basis of cost. It also requires one-third of the time needed by Alternative 2, to cleanup the contaminated soils and groundwater.

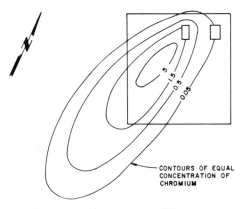

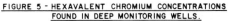

CONTOURS OF EQUAL
CONCENTRATION OF
CHROMIUM

FIGURE 5 - HEXAVALENT CHROMIUM CONCENTRATIONS
FOUND IN DEEP MONITORING WELLS.

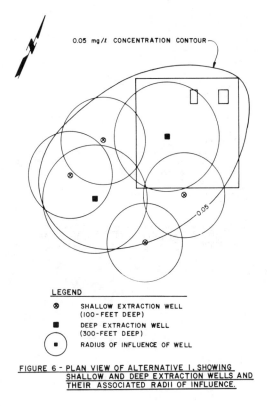

0.05 mg/ℓ CONCENTRATION CONTOUR

LEGEND

⊗ SHALLOW EXTRACTION WELL
   (100-FEET DEEP)

■ DEEP EXTRACTION WELL
   (300-FEET DEEP)

(•) RADIUS OF INFLUENCE OF WELL

FIGURE 6 - PLAN VIEW OF ALTERNATIVE 1, SHOWING
SHALLOW AND DEEP EXTRACTION WELLS AND
THEIR ASSOCIATED RADII OF INFLUENCE.

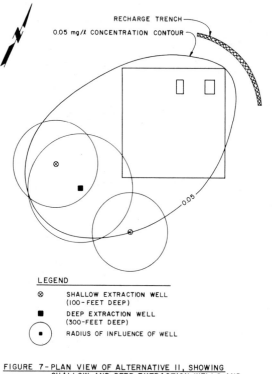

LEGEND

⊗ SHALLOW EXTRACTION WELL
    (100-FEET DEEP)

■ DEEP EXTRACTION WELL
    (300-FEET DEEP)

● RADIUS OF INFLUENCE OF WELL

FIGURE 7-PLAN VIEW OF ALTERNATIVE II, SHOWING
         SHALLOW AND DEEP EXTRACTION WELLS AND
         THEIR ASSOCIATED RADII OF INFLUENCE.

Therefore, environmental and health risks are also less for the prefered alternative.

COST EVALUATION

Table 1 summarizes the costs of Alternatives 1 and 2. Both the initial costs and the operation and maintenance costs are considered.

Table 1. Estimated present worth of the costs of Alternatives and 2.

ITEM	COST	
	ALTERNATIVE 1	ALTERNATIVE 2
	$	$
Well construction (including pumps)	240,000	120,000
Pipeline from wells to treatment plant	40,000	38,000
Treatment plant construction	2,000,000	1,500,000
Recharge trench construction	--	60,000
Leaching basin construction	15,000	15,000
Groundwater monitoring	10,000	25,000
Pumping cost	213,000	450,000
Treatment plant operation	900,000	1,220,000
Maintenance cost	190,000	250,000
TOTAL COST	$3,608,000	$3,678,000

LIQUID WASTE POLLUTION FROM A SUGAR CANE INDUSTRY

Anastasio Lopez Zavala* M. ASCE

Abstract

The water pollution survey as performed in this study, indicates that all liquid wastes from the mill are segregated. The chemical waste sewerage systems supposedly conveys these wastes to a stabilization lagoon currently out of order. The grease and oil wastes pass through a grease separator tank. The sewage flow from toilets and bathrooms in the mill pass through a septic tank system, and its effluent joins the influent to a sewage treatment plant which serves the personnel and workers housing facilities outside the plant. The runoff from the plant site is collected by a storm channel in adjacent circulation streets.

All wastes are combined through an open channel and after 1.75 miles (3 km), the channel discharges to an "absorption well" where flooding and ground water pollution occur. The study recommends practical measures to cope with these problems.

I. Background

The Federal Government in Mexico owns about 55 sugar cane mills out of 65 in the country with a net sugar production of about 3 million metric tons a year (1984-1985). At the present time there is a water pollution control program enforced by the Secretaria de Desarrollo Urbano y Ecologia (Urban Development and Ecology Secretariat) and this program is currently being applied to the Mexican sugar cane industry.

The present study was performed from June through December 1984 in a sugar cane mill located in southern Mexico.

II. Objectives

An environmental diagnosis in regard to water usage and water pollution problem was performed at the mill during June 1984 (end of sugar cane crop 1983-1984) and during December 1984 (middle of crop 1984-1985) with the following objectives:

*Research Professor. Atmospheric Sciences Center, National Autonomous University of Mexico. Mexico, Mexico, D.F.

a) To determine water flow diagram and mass balance along the different processes in the mill.
b) To determine the present status regarding wastewater treatment.
c) To determine wastewater segregations.
d) To make recommendations on basis of current Mexican regulations and enforcing water reclamation criteria.
e) Cost determination of proposed recommendations.

III. Water Survey

The water supply source for the entire mill plus offices is a 3 deep well system with a total net pumping capacity of 3800 g.p.m. (240 l.p.s.) for the 1984-1985 crop. For the previous season, 1983-1984 crop, the net pumping was 2,927 g.p.m. (185 l.p.s.). This pumping excess in the order of 873 g.p.m. (55 l.p.s.) indicates a higher water consumption for the mill processes.

With respect to water recycled, during the 1983-1984 crop the value was of 53,500 g.p.m. (3,376 l.p.s.) and for the 1984-1985 crop this value was 42,000 g.p.m. (2,650 l.p.s.) which indicates a decrease in water recycle efficiency.

From the cooling towers a total of 11,700 g.p.m. (738 l.p.s.) goes to turbo-generators cooling and fire protection systems: 11,400 g.p.m. (719 l.p.s.) to each of sugar evaporators "A", "C", and "R" cooling; and 7,600 g.p.m. (480 l.p.s.) to sugar evaporator "B", making a total of 53,500 g.p.m. (3,376 l.p.s.) of water recycle flow. The mill is supplied with water from a reservoir about 90 feet (30 m) higher than the mill.

There is a water recycle ratio of 18.2 which may be improved since the segregated wastes, as will be seen later, accounts for a 30% of total well pumping value.

IV. Wastewater Survey

The mill wastewater is made up as follows: chemical wastes from evaporatos washings. These washings contain scale-removings with alkaline chemicals which are sent directly to a neutralizing tank. Once this operation is done, a muriatic acid washing follows which is also conveyed to the neutralizing tank. Once all these washings are neutralized, the product is discharged to the main drain in the form of a trapezoidal open channel. This operation from evaporator washings is performed every two weeks. Another chemical waste is that from the softening and rinse in the ion exchange units with a flow of 903 g.p.m. (57 l.p.s.) and carried on only at the beginning of the crop. Other chemical wastes are filter washings; carbon column rinses; polluted water from condensates (recycled); steam boiler bottom flushings, and floor washings. All these wastes are collected through a grating protected open channel interior system which discharges to a peripherial open channel, which connects downstream into a trapezoidal open channel. Another waste is rather small leaks of grease and oil in valve stuffing box and packings. This is sent directly by a 6 inch (15 cm) diameter pipe to a gravity separator tank. The segregated oil in this tank is removed and stored in drums and used later on to burn bagasse in steam boilers as oil make up. The effluent from the gravity separator tank discharges to the trapezoidal open channel.

Another waste is that from the septic tanks which serve all toilets from the administrative office and the mill. The effluent from the septic tanks is combined with the influent to the sewage treatment plant which provides service to the personnel and workers housing facility (400 people) nearby the mill site. The storm sewerage is located outside the plant and starts as an earthen channel. Inside the plant area, the storm channels are concrete lined and grated.

The storm channel on one side out of the plant site area receives all chemical wastes from clarifiers, evaporators, centrifuges, refineries and molasses tanks, floor washings and finally receives the neutralizing tank and gravity separator effluents and flowing south connects to the trapezoidal open channel.

After approximately 0.50 miles (800 m), this channel receives the housing facilities sewage treatment plant effluent and later on about 1.25 miles (2 km) flows into an absorption well. The mill has been in operation for 9 years and it seems apparent by visual observation that the absorption well no longer has absorption capacity since the area is flooded probably due to the fact that the soil pores in the well are clogged. The well dimensions are 11.5-foot diameter and 16.4-foot depth (3.50 X 5.0 m). This fact was observed in December 1984, when the rainy season was over. The total dry weather flow in the channel is 1.28 MGD (56 l.p.s.) while the total wet weather flow, in the rainy season, is 35.5 MGD (1,550 l.p.s.). The sewage treatment plant effluent flow is 0.11 MGD (5 l.p.s.). The main constituent in the soil is clay.

V. Wastewater Analyses

Wastewater samples in the trapezoidal channel taken just after the joining with the housing facilities sewage treatment plant effluent, indicate that in June 1984 the BOD_5 was 4775 mg/l and the suspended solids were 2382 mg/l, while in December 1984, BOD_5 was 372 and suspended solids 600 mg/l. The pH and grease and oil values are 7.5 and 20 mg/l respectively at all times.

Samples taken in the sewage treatment plant effluent indicates a water of high quality with a turbidity value of 0 as may be observed in the following Tables I and II.

TABLE I

ANALYSES OF A WATER SAMPLE TAKEN AT THE HOUSING
FACILITIES SEWAGE TREATMENT PLANT (STP)

Parameter	Influent	Effluent
Date	June 15, 1984	June 15, 1984
Hour	12	12
BOD_5 @ 20°C, mg/l	110	22
Total solids, mg/l	1180	736
Total volatile solids, mg/l	224	108
Total fixed solids, mg/l	756	628
Total suspended solids, mg/l	14	8
Volatile suspended solids, mg/l	8	5
Fixed suspended solids, mg/l	6	3
Total dissolved solids, mg/l	1166	728
Volatile dissolved solids, mg/l	216	103
Fixed dissolved solids, mg/l	950	625
Settleable Imhoff solids, ml/l	0.04	0.01
Air temperature °C	32	32
Water temperature °C	29	29
Grease and oil, mg/l	8	0
Total phosphate, mg/l	1.8	2
pH	7.5	7.5
Total coliforms MPN/100 ml	1×10^6	460
Fecal coliforms MPN/100 ml	8758	132

In Decmeber 1984 the results of analyses on the sewage treatment plant effluent were as indicated in Table II

TABLE II

Parameter	Effluent
Date	Dec. 18, 1984
Hour	12:40
BOD_5 @ 20°C, mg/l	62
COD, mg/l	122
Total coliforms, MPN/100 ml	300
Fecal coliforms, MPN/100 ml	62
Turbidity, JTU	0

VI. Discussion

From the above analyses of both the effluent from the mill and the effluent from the housing facilities sewage treatment plant, it may be observed that the effluent has a poor quality because actually there is no treatment at all, since the stabilization lagoon is full of bagasse and a supposedly existing clarifier unit is also full of bagasse, despite the fact that there is a good removal in the gravity separator tank and a good neutralizing effect in the corresponding tank. On the other hand, the sewage treatment plant effluent is of good quality, but unfortunately it is combined with the mill effluent which negates the treatment process.

With respect to the well absorption flooding, probably this might
be due to the fact that the suspended solids value is very high
(between 600 and 2382 mg/l) for that soil constituent, mainly clay,
and also that the wet weather flow discharges directly in that place.

It is also observed from the field surveys, that all chemical
wastes from the mill are connected to the outside channel which
conveys the storm runoff. This practice was probably recommended at
the start or operations back in 1975 for the dilution effect would
lower the BOD_5 and S.S. values to acceptable limits. After
performing some computations we realize that the BOD_5 value cannot
go lower than 240 mg/l, and the net result is the ground water
pollution. The clogging of soil pores, even with a low value of 110
mg/l in S.S. due to the dilution effect, is a speedy process because
of the soil natural constituent, mainly clay.

VII. Proposed Modifications and Recommendations

Due to the presence of bagasse in the interior mill yards, the
storm sewerage system is easily clogged during the rainy season and it
may be avoided by keeping a good cleaning operation at all times.

The existing stabilization lagoon and the clarifier unit should
both be cleaned of bagasse and debris. The sample range in BOD_5 and
S.S. values (4775 to 372 and 2382 to 600 mg/l, respectively) on a
preliminary assumption, and after more analyses be performed during a
period of 20 weeks on a weekly basis, suggests the installation of an
equalizing tank at the lagoon. This lagoon can be subdivided in such
a way as to have a primary section for this equalizing tank, a
secondary or middle section for aeration tank, with corresponding
return sludge pipe and a third section serving as final clarifier.
The existing circular clarifier may be converted to an aerobic
digestion tank.

It will be necessary, however, to install a small sand filter as
tertiary treatment in order to accomplish a minimum of 20 mg/l in both
BOD and S.S. over all effluent quality. A chlorinator will also be
required.

To avoid the wastewater discharge from floor washings, steam
boilers and condensers flushings to the peripheral channel as
currently is practiced, it is recommended to install an 8 inch (20 cm)
diameter asbesto-cement pipe connected to the proposed industrial
waste treatment plant equalizing tank influent.

In view of the risk that the flooded area at the absorption well
reaches the housing facilities boundary, it is suggested that the
following modifications be made: Once the proposed industrial waste
treatment plant is in operation, its effluent should be separated from
the storm runoff and should be conveyed through a pressure 12-inch (30
cm) diameter steel pipe to the recycle pipe going into the cooling
tower in the mill. This recommendation is important in order to
immediately stop the present practice of discharging the whole plant
effluent into the absorption well flooded area. Along with this

recommendation, it will be possible to save a 23% of total water supply from the well by using the industrial treated effluent as reclamation water for processes purpose.

On the other hand, the storm runoff discharge to the channel should be stopped, 35.4 MGD (1550 lps), since this flow goes finally into the flooded area. It should be now concentrated in an equalizing lake in the neighborhood of the housing facilities through a new earth channel for 35.4 MGD capacity. The equalizing pond shall have 196 x 164 x 4.9 ft. (60 x 50 x 1.5 m) with 3.28 (1.0 m) freeboard. The discharge from the equalizing pond shall be to an open channel into the nearby crop land assuming a runoff impervious coefficient of 0.20 for the entire 17.8 acre (8 ha) mill area.

It is also recommended that the present housing facilities sewage treatment plant effluent be incorporated into the new industrial waste treatment plant effluent and both conveyed to the cooling towers for reclamation purposes.

VIII. Conclusions

The present situation in this Mexican sugar cane mill regarding water pollution aspects is that the wastewater segregation systems need improvements to really separate chemical wastes from storm runoff. Besides, it is required that chemical wastes, other than grease and oil and acid and basic liquid wastes, receive an optimum treatment by rehabilitating some existing treatment units and installing some additional treatment units in order to have an efficient new tertiary treatment to comply with the stringent effluent quality discharge conditions currently enforced in Mexico. The problem of ground water pollution in the absorption well may be alleviated by following recommendations as set forth in this paper.

On the Ship's Waterways Passing through Bridges

Kuniaki Shoji*, Tomomi Wakao**

ABSTRACT

In this paper authors studied about the waterway passing through the bridge in view of the analysis on the ship collision accident. For the purpose of this study, cases of ship collision accidents were collected and investigated.

Authors conclude that the probability of ship collision is increased in case that the main span is less than 2 or 3 times the ship length and in case that the straightaway is less than 8 times the ship length from this study. These results are very similar to the figures of the ship avoidance area in marine traffic engineering.

INTRODUCTION

Recently, owing to the increase of marine traffic and bridge piers in navigable waters, ship collision accidents with bridges have been increasing. The accidents of the Tasman Bridge of Australia in 1975, the Tjörn Bridge of Sweden in 1980 and the Sunshine Skyway Bridge of U.S.A. in 1980 were brought about by ship collision. In 1983, the IABSE (International Association for Bridge and Structural Engineering) Colloquium about ship collision with bridges and offshore structures was held in Copenhagen. In Japan, it is also an important issue to keep the safety of bridges against ship collision, because Honshu-Shikoku Connecting Bridges and Tokyo Bay Crossing Bridge-Tunnel which span ship's navigating waterways are being constructed partly and planned now.

In this paper authors collected the cases of ship collision accidents with bridges from the report of Japan Association for Preventing Marine Accidents. From these data initially the causes of ship collision accidents were listed. From causes of the accidents, the process of the ship collision accidents was presumed.

Next, the main span of the bridge, the horizontal clearance, the straightaway (the distance between the bridge and the turning point) were investigated from these accident data. These are important design items of the waterways passing through the bridge, because NTSB in U.S.A.

* Associate Professor, Tokyo University of Mercantile Marine, 2-1-6 Etchujima Koto-ku, Tokyo 135, Japan
** Manager of the Marine Traffic Research Department, Japan Association for Preventing Marine Accidents, Yuseigojokai-Build., 1-14-1 Toranomon Minato-ku, Tokyo 105, Japan

recommended a study of hazards of lift-span bridges with narrow openings,
deep water supports and curved channel, after the accident of the Sidney
Lanier Bridge in 1957.

NUMBER OF SHIP COLLISION ACCIDENTS WITH BRIDGES

   Fig.1 shows the number of accidents in 1980 and 1981. From Fig.1, it
is seen that the number of accidents is about 10 per a year. This figure
is about 10 times the number of serious accidents investigated by A.G.
Frandsen (1982). It is considered that the data include small accidents
and the effect of the month or the season is scarcely regarded from Fig.1.

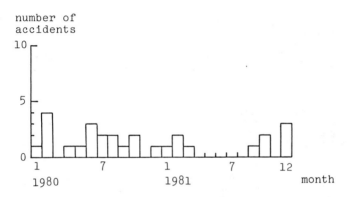

Fig.1 Ship Collision Accidents with Bridges in 1980-1981

CAUSES OF SHIP COLLISION ACCIDENTS WITH BRIDGES

   The causes of ship collision accidents were collected from the report
of Japan Association for Preventing Marine Accidents. Those are listed
as follows.
 1. indirect causes
    weather conditions (strong wind, dense fog, storm and so on)
    sea conditions (strong current, existance of ice and so on)
    waterways (curved channel, narrow opening and so on)
 2. direct causes
    fault in steering gear or main engine
    broken mooring line or towline
    unmanned drifting
    operator's negligence, mishandling

   The ship collision accident with the bridge is related to these causes
as Fig.2. Serious accidents of the Tasman Bridge in 1975, the Tjörn
Bridge in 1980 and the Sunshine Skyway Bridge in 1980 were brought by
navigating vessels.

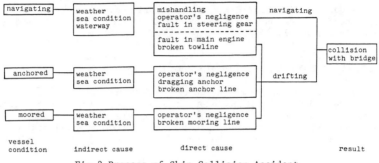

Fig.2 Process of Ship Collision Accident

DEFINITION ABOUT WATERWAY, BRIDGE AND SHIP

In this paper, authors especially investigate about the waterway which was one of the indirect causes. For the purpose of the analysis, the notations among the waterway, the bridge and the ship are defined in Fig.3.

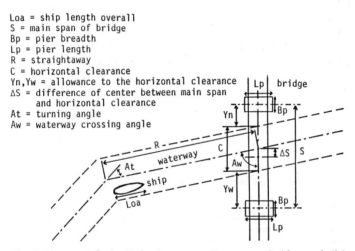

Loa = ship length overall
S = main span of bridge
Bp = pier breadth
Lp = pier length
R = straightaway
C = horizontal clearance
Yn,Yw = allowance to the horizontal clearance
ΔS = difference of center between main span and horizontal clearance
At = turning angle
Aw = waterway crossing angle

Fig.3 Diagram of the Relation among Waterway, Bridge and Ship

ON THE MAIN SPAN OF BRIDGE

Fig.4 shows the relation between colliding ship's size (Loa) and main span of bridge (S). From Fig.4, it is seen that the probability of ship collision is increased in case that the main span (S) is less than 2 or 3 times the ship length (Loa). The cases of the accident of the bridge which has a narrow span are as follows.
1963. 9 Sørsund Bridge (Norway) S=100m, Loa=108m

1972.11 Sidney Lanier Bridge (U.S.A.) S=75m, Loa=174m
1975.12 Fraser Bridge (Canada) S=117m, Loa=200m
1977. 2 Benjamin Harrison Memorial Bridge (U.S.A) S=72m, Loa=187m
1977. 7 Tromsø Bridge (Norway) S=80m, Loa=41m
1979.10 Second Narrows Railway Bridge (Canada) S=152m, Loa=175m
1980. 1 Tjörn Bridge (Sweden) S=278m, Loa=172m
1980. 5 Sunshine Skyway Bridge (U.S.A.) S=263m, Loa=186m
1981.10 Jordfallet Bridge (Sweden) S=44m, Loa=48m

length overall
    Loa(m)

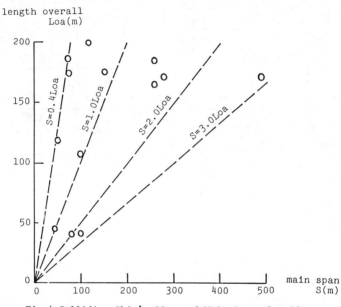

Fig.4 Colliding Ship's Size and Main Span of Bridge

ON THE HORIZONTAL CLEARANCE AND ALLOWANCE

The relation between the main span (S) and the horizontal clearance
(C) is

$$S = C + Yn + Yw$$

where Yn and Yw are allowance to the horizontal clearance. These are
larger than a half pier breadth (0.5Bp). From the consideration about
the wind and current effect near the bridge pier by Iwai et al. (1976
and 1979), narrow side allowance (Yn) had better be kept more than 2 or
3 times the pier breadth (Bp).

Table 1 shows the relations among main span, horizontal clearance and
allowance on several bridges in Japan. The horizontal clearance (C) has
mostly about 50% of the main span (S). And the allowance (Yn) is mostly
more than 2 or 3 times the pier breadth (Bp). Speaking from a mental
point of view, the center line of the waterway had better coincide with

the center of the main span. However, there are instances where this
does not apply according to the geographical condition and so on. The
difference of the center between the main span and the horizontal clearance is shown in Table 2. The difference is less than 10-15% of the main
span in Japanese bridges.

Table 1 Horizontal Clearance and Allowance

bridge name (prefecture)	S:m	C:m	Bp:m	Yn:m	C/S	Yn/S	Yn/Bp
SHIMOTSUISETO BRIDGE (OKAYAMA,KAGAWA)	940	420	36	120	0.447	0.128	3.33
OHNARUTO BRIDGE (TOKUSHIMA,HYOGO)	876	369	25.5	190	0.421	0.217	7.45
IWAGUROJIMA BRIDGE (KAGAWA)	420	275	25	70	0.655	0.167	2.80
HITSUISHIJIMA BRIDGE (KAGAWA)	420	180	25	85	0.429	0.202	3.40
WAKATO BRIDGE (FUKUOKA)	367	254	17	56.4	0.693	0.154	3.32
OHSHIMA BRIDGE (YAMAGUCHI)	325	260	23	32.5	0.800	0.100	1.41
KURONOSETO BRIDGE (KAGOSHIMA)	300	100	10	100	0.333	0.333	10.00
HIROSHIMA BRIDGE (HIROSHIMA)	150	120	10	15	0.800	0.100	1.50

Table 2 Difference of Center between Main Span and Horizontal Clearance

bridge name (prefecture)	S:m	ΔS:m	ΔS/S
KANMON BRIDGE (FUKUOKA,YAMAGUCHI)	712	25.0	0.035
HAKUCHO BRIDGE (HOKKAIDO) plan	720	58.6	0.081
SHIMOTSUISETO BRIDGE (OKAYAMA,KAGAWA)	940	140.0	0.149
NORTH BISANSETO BRIDGE (KAGAWA)	990	50.0	0.051
AKASHIKAIKYO BRIDGE (HYOGO) plan	1780	95.0	0.053

ON THE STRAIGHTAWAY

Fig.5 shows the relation between colliding ship's size (Loa) and the

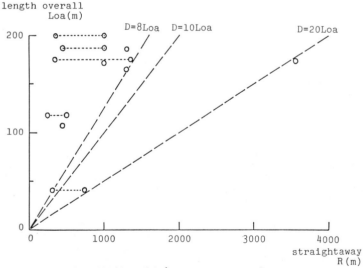

Fig.5 Colliding Ship's Size and Straightaway

straightaway (R). In Fig.5, a pair of o mark which connected by horizontal broken line is the accident case that the entering course of ship is unknown. From Fig.5, it is concluded that the probability of ship collision is increased in case that the straightaway (R) is less than 8 times the ship length (Loa). The cases of the accident of the bridge which has a short straightaway (curved channel) are as follows.

1963. 9 Sørsund Bridge (Norway) R=450m, Loa=108m
1975.12 Fraser Bridge (Canada) R=1000or370m, Loa=200m
1979.10 Second Narrows Railway Bridge (Canada) R=1350or350m, Loa=175m
1980. 5 Sunshine Skyway Bridge (U.S.A.) R=1300m, Loa=186m
1981. 2 Newport Bridge (U.S.A.) R=1000m, Loa=171m

ON THE WATERWAY CROSSING ANGLE

Speaking from a mental point of view, the waterway had better be at right angles to the main span of the bridge. However, there are instances where this does not apply according to the geographical condition and so on. The waterway crossing angle (Aw) is shown in Table 3. The minimum crossing angle is 65° in Table 3.

SEVERAL BRIDGES IN JAPAN

Several bridges which span the waterways are shown in Fig.6 (a), (b), and (c). These bridges have some factors among the short straightaway (R), the difference of center line (ΔS) and the waterway crossing angle (Aw). Fig.6 (a) and (b) are the bridges which belong to the Honshu-Shikoku Connecting Bridges.

CONCLUSION

In this paper, authors investigated about the waterway passing through the bridge. Those are the main span, the horizontal clearance, the difference of the center between the waterway and the main span, the straightaway and the waterway crossing angle.

Table 3 Waterway Crossing Angle

bridge name (prefecture)	Aw:deg	S:m
WAKATO BRIDGE (FUKUOKA)	69°	367
KANMON BRIDGE (FUKUOKA,YAMAGUCHI)	84°	712
HIRADO BRIDGE (NAGASAKI)	82°	465
NORTH BISANSETO BRIDGE (KAGAWA)	65°-88°	990
SOUTH BISANSETO BRIDGE (KAGAWA)	65°-80°	1100
INNOSHIMA BRIDGE (HIROSHIMA)	67°	770
HAKUCHO BRIDGE (HOKKAIDO) plan	82°-86°	720

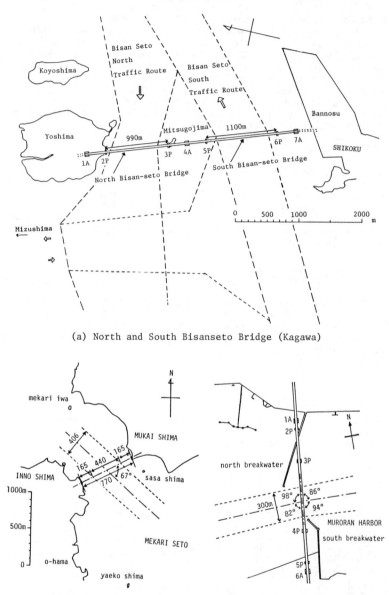

(a) North and South Bisanseto Bridge (Kagawa)

(b) Innoshima Bridge (Hiroshima)   (c) Hakucho Bridge (Hokkaido) plan

Fig.6 Examples of the Bridges which Span the Waterway in Japan

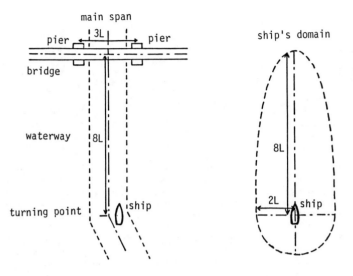

Fig.7 Waterway Passing through Bridge and Ship's Domain

Especially, the results on the main span and the straightaway are as follows.

(1) The probability of ship collision is increased in case the main span is less than 2 or 3 times the ship length.

(2) The probability of ship collision is increased in case the straightaway is less than 8 times the ship length.

These results are very similar to the figures of the ship avoidance area (ship's domain) in marine traffic engineering as shown in Fig.7.

REFERENCES

Frandsen,A.G., 1982,Accidents Involving Bridges, IABSE Reports Vol.41, pp.11-26.

Iwai,A. and Shoji,K., 1976, On the Effect of Wind around the Pier upon the Coursekeeping of Ship, The Journal of Japan Institute of Navigation No.55, pp.77-86.

Iwai,A. and Shoji,K., 1979, On the Effect of Current around the Pier upon the Course - Keeping of Ship (in Japanese), The Journal of Japan Institute of Navigation No.61, pp.163-172.

Port Infrastructure Program in Mexico

Luis F. Robledo *
Jose San Martin **

Abstract

The high degree of interdependency which occurs between transport and
all the other sectors that determine the economical development system of
the nation, creates the need for a global scope planning, which must in-
tegrally cover the short, medium and long perspective terms of development. In this way, a proper equilibrium of goals can then be established.

In Mexico the policies, guidelines, goals and methodologies refering
to transport, are the responsibility of the "Secretaria de Comunicacio-
nes y Transportes" (Ministry of Transport and Communications).

In the present paper a planning and programming system for port infra
structure development is presented, where the interrelations between the
different elements which form the transport system as a whole, are analysed and a mechanism of coordination and integration for the port system
is proposed to fit within the National Transport Structure.

Introduction

The means and mediums of transport are widely linked with the develop
ment of the various world cultures and directly connected with commerce,
which little by little has transformed itself, actually becoming a highly
complex activity.

The majority of the developing countries have to confront a formidable
collection of political, economical and social problems in order to increase the level of their economy and to improve the quality of life of
its population. Reliable systems of transport are within the essential
pre-requisites for the development of the mentioned countries.

Although the main purpose of a transport system is to transfer people
and goods from one location to another, it also propitiates common interest ties and unity within the individuals of a nation and is an integra
ting and structuring factor as well as an orientator for the territorial
development possibilities. That is to say, that the country's transport
system contributes to the realization of national objetives, favouring
the development of economy and social integration.

 * General Director of Port Projects of the Ministry of Transport and
   Communications in Mexico, Insurgentes Sur 664, 6o. Piso, C.P. 03100
   Mexico, D.F.
** Subdirector of Port Planning and Programming, same address.

Concretely, a country's transport system permits the commerce of goods, the transport of people and contributes to the economical expansion of the nation, interconnecting production centers with consumer centers, thus, incorporating existent markets with new ones, finally favouring social cohesion and political stability, effects which are considered "non economical" and "of qualitative" nature.

The Necessity of Integral Planning for the National Transport System.

Mexico has become a complex country with a diversity of economical, political and social problems. Planning is being used as a basic instrument in seeking solutions to these problems.

The high degree of transport interdependency with nearly all other sectors of the nation (industry, commerce, agriculture, etc.) demands that its planning be realized with and integral, interdisciplinary and global scope in the short, medium and long perspective terms. This is done in order to maintain the equilibrium of transport growth with the other sectors and to help to realize their objetives. The ports (as an element of the transport system), for their optimal planning must be included within this integral scope.

The Ports and the National Development.

It is essential to identify the role which the ports and their infrastructure should play within the Integral Transport System and within the social, economical and political development of the country, in order to count with a solid base for the realization of an efficient planning. To accomplish this it is necessary to have a clear idea of how these two levels (National Development and the Integral Transport System) are conducted and related to one another and in this way be able to situate the ports within the mentioned reference frames (see figure 1).

The first national level is conformed by different variables such as the national gross product, oil prices, raw material prices, interest rates (external debt), politics (internal and external), inflation and the balance of trade among others, as the most significant variables. These interacting variables determine a large part of the actual situation and set the pattern to elaborate the general development guidelines needed to be followed by the country.

In this first large frame of reference (national level), the different sectors of the country operate (commerce, industry, agriculture, etc.). The transport sector interacts and assists the above mentioned sectors. It is composed of highways, rural roads, railways, airports and the ports in all their types (commercial, touristic, industrial, fishing and oil ports).

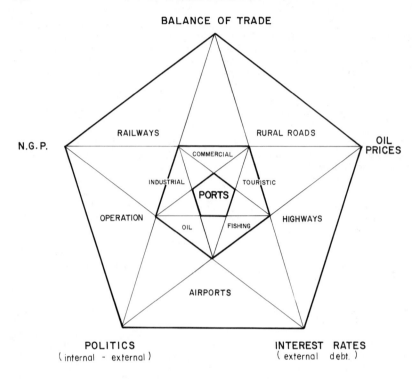

FIGURE I. THE PORTS WITHIN THE NATIONAL DEVELOPMENT SYSTEM.

The Integral Transport System and its Organizational Structure.

For the first time in the history of the Mexican Transport Sector, all of its subsectors are found grouped within the same structure, unified by the same general politics, guidelines, objetives, methodologies and subjected to the same process of decision making. This is how it is sought to implement an Integral Transport System with two subsystems: the Infrastructural Subsystem and the Operational Subsystem, as shown in figure 2.

The elements of the Infrastructural Subsystem are the Ministerial Departments of: Port Projects, Highway Projects, Rural Road Projects, Railroad Projects, Road Maintenance and Conservation Projects and Airport Projects.

The elements of the Operational Subsystem are the Ministerial Departments of: Port Development and Operation, Merchant Marine, National Railways, Federal Auto Transport, Civil Aeronautics and Tariffs. The Operational Subsystem operates the infrastructure built by the Infrastructural Subsystem departments.

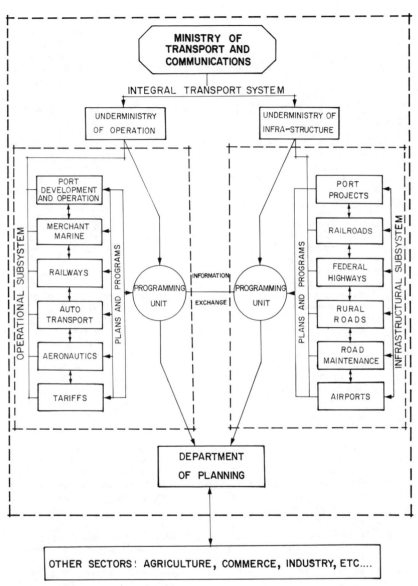

FIGURE 2. THE ORGANIZATIONAL STRUCTURE OF THE INTEGRAL TRANSPORT SYSTEM.

This structure of the Ministry of Transport and Communications permits the integration of the responsibility of construction and conservation of the transport infrastructure together with the regulation and coordination of the operation, allowing the satisfaction of the increasing demand not only through the expantion of the infrastructure but also through the increase of efficiency.

The Functional (Decision - Making) Structure of the Integral Transport System.

The Department of Planning (D.P.) of the Ministry of Transport and Communications is the coordinator of the transport sector's development. The responsibility of the D.P. is to implement the planning process for the structuring of the Integral Transport System, whose principle objective is to achieve an optimal combination and equilibrium within the different means of transport.

In order to accomplish this the D.P. has to dictate the politics and lineaments and supply the methodology and unified information for all the subsectors of transport, so that these in turn elaborate their plans and programs with an integral approach (see figure 3). During this process, the D.P. coordinates, analyses, evaluates, selects and decides which plans and programs are of priority for transport development, structuring this way the National Program of Transport and Communications; all this in tight coordination with the Ministry of Programming and Budgeting.

Subsequently, the same D.P. evaluates the results derived from the execution of the programs of each subsector, realizing an analysis of variation, through which the deviations with respect to the established goals are detected. This is done in order to feedback and correct the plans and programs of the different subsectors and the National Program of Transport and Communications.

The National Program of Port Infrastructure Development (NPPID).

The main objective of the NPPID is to define the role which the port-maritime subsystem should play within the Integral Transport System, in order to contribute to an optimal combination and equilibrium of the means of transport. For this purpose a planning methodology was designed, whose most important results are to determine and assign the functions that each national port must realize.

The planning conceptual model of expansion and development of commer cial and industrial ports is shown in figure 4 (the fishing and touristic ports follow slightly different models, which won't be explained in the present paper). First, the general economical and social development guidelines are determined by the National Development Plan (NDP), which is the ruling document for the planning of national life. From this, the transport politics and objetives are derived and placed in the National Transport and Communications Program (NTCP), which in turn defines the maritime transport and the port development strategies. On the other hand, from the probable national development scenarios, the global port traffic

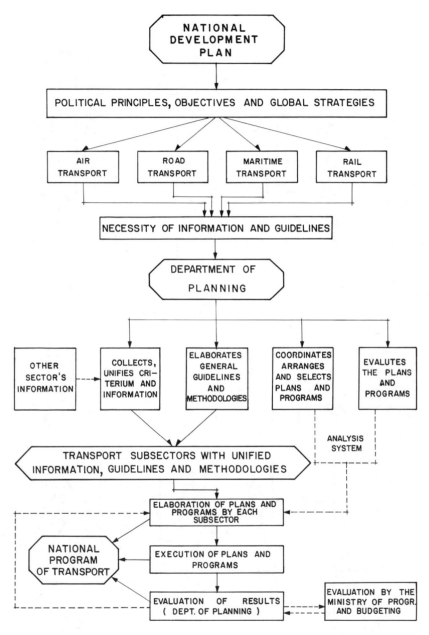

FIGURE 3. THE FUNCTIONAL STRUCTURE OF THE INTEGRAL TRANSPORT SYSTEM

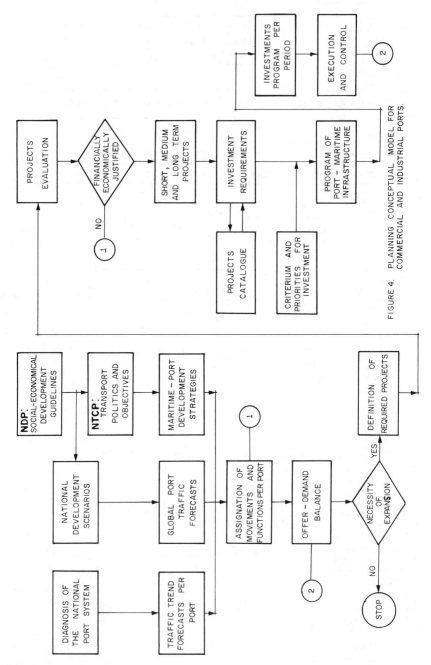

FIGURE 4. PLANNING CONCEPTUAL MODEL FOR COMMERCIAL AND INDUSTRIAL PORTS.

forecasts are obtained and through an analysis and diagnosis of the national port system's actual situation, a traffic trend forecast for each port is elaborated. From the port development strategies and the global and trend forecasts of port traffic, the assignation of movements and functions to be realized by each port is determined.

Next, the balance between the offer of the existent port infrastructure and the demand required for the efficient cargo transfer is stated. If the necessity of expanding the infrastructure is detected, the required projects are defined (in order to realize such growth) and a financial, economical and social evaluation of each project is accomplished. If the mentioned projects cannot economically, financially and socially be justified, the process is set back to the revision of the port movements assignation. If they are justified, the short, medium and long term projects are defined, the investment requirements are calculated and a catalogue of projects is elaborated.

Once that the necessary projects for the expansion and development are identified, the criterium and the analysis process for the selection of the investments to be realized are implemented. Through this process, the program of port-maritime infrastructure projects and the investments program per period (per year) is obtained. Finally, a financial and economical evaluation for each project in both programs is completed for its subsequent approval, execution and control.

CENTRAL ARIZONA PROJECT
STARTUP

By Albert L. Graves [1], Robert S. Gooch, A.M. ASCE [2]

INTRODUCTION

In its second year of operation, the Central Arizona Project is heading towards an automated operation that will be one of the most sophisticated in the world. This sophisticated operation will use software developed through the structured programming approach which leads to software modules that each have individual functions. The repackaging of the modules for different canal systems on other projects can easily be accomplished. It is anticipated that the development of transportable, modular CAP control software will allow other projects with remote or supervisory control systems to implement CAP type control with minimal effort.

The Central Arizona Project is a water conveyance scheme, lifting and conveying Colorado River water from Lake Havasu on the Colorado River 190 miles (300 km) to Phoenix and another 150 miles (240 km) to Tucson. The completed project will have 14 pumping plants with over 100 pump units, 37 dual gate check structures, and over 40 turnout structures. The remote pumping plants, check structures, and turnouts will be unmanned except for daytime maintenance crews. The operation of the entire system is controlled by a Programmable Master Supervisory Control System (PMSC) (Gooch & Graves, 1985) which consist of a dual computer master station and intelligent remote computers at the field sites.

The PMSC has the capability to work simply as a remote control device or to act as a sophisticated supervisory system, developing control actions in the master station and downloading them to the remote terminal units (RTU) at the field sites. The RTUs have the capability to be programmed with stand alone strategy, take direct instructions from the master computer, or accept schedules for future operation. It is the latter mode that will be employed on the CAP using the newly developed control software in the master station to develop schedules. The hardware required for this type of system is state of the art, but the overall cost is relatively low compared to much less capable systems of the past.

---

1. Chief, Water Systems Branch, U.S. Bureau of Reclamation, Arizona Projects Office, P.O. Box 9980, Phoenix, Arizona 85068

2. Civil Engineer, U.S. Bureau of Reclamation, Arizona Projects Office, P.O. Box 9980, Phoenix, Arizona 85068

PHILOSOPHY OF OPERATION

The two overriding objectives in CAP operation are constant volume in canal pools and minimal starts on pump units. The constant volume operation allows for rapid response to user demand and minimizes the fluctuations experienced in traditional upstream or downstream control schemes. Minimizing pump starts (and stops) with fluctuating user demands and attempting to maintain constant pool volume requires the use of scheduling software to take all variables into account and follow a logical operation path.

The original scheduling software described elsewhere as Aqueduct Control Software (ACS)(Gooch & Graves, 1985), used multiple models to develop pump and gate schedules. The schedules were then reviewed by operators and approved for transmittal each hour to the RTUs. The ACS models used a constant volume approach for pump operation and a gate stroking (Falvey & Luning, 1979) approach for checkgate operation. The models could be run for one hour or for as long as 24 hours to develop 1 to 24 hours of schedules.

SHORTCOMINGS OF THE FIRST GENERATION

The original ACS, or ACS I as it is now called, could control the CAP canal system and could develop schedules to meet the constant volume objectives, but it had some shortcomings. The major problems were the length of time required to perform the calculations, the lack of sophistication relative to input data, and the disregard of the minimal pump start criteria. The long run times were directly attributable to the unsteady state solution set required in the gate stroking solution, and the disregard of the pump start criteria was due in part to the modeling concept.

To be fully functional, it was soon discovered that the scheduling software must be able to contend with a lack of data from some sites due to equipment outages. It was also discovered that the software must also be cognizant of planned outages of equipment so that maintenance schedules did not contend with operation schedules.

SECOND GENERATION AQUEDUCT CONTROL SOFTWARE

The second generation of ACS, or ACS II, has two separate executable tasks: PDRIVR, which schedules the pumps, and GDRIVR, which schedules the radial gate movements.

PDRIVR is automatically executed each hour at 15 minutes after the hour. A pump schedule is generated for the next 160 hours and is stored in a file waiting approval to be downloaded to the pumping plant RTUs. The existing schedule and its effect on the canal, and the newly generated schedule and its effect on the canal, are compared graphically on CRT dislays. The judgment and the experience of the operator is then called upon to decide whether to use the existing schedule or the newly generated schedule. This manual intervention in the control process loop provides a balance in the sometimes

conflicting goals of minimizing pump starts and maintaining a constant
volume of water in the canal. In general, if the operator chooses the
new schedule, he will achieve the goal of constant volume. If he
chooses to stay with the existing schedule, he will achieve the goal
of minimizing pump starts.

GDRIVR is automatically executed each hour at 15 minutes before the
hour. A gate opening is determined for each gate in the aqueduct each
hour of the day enabling the use of the latest telemetry in the data
base. The objective of GDRIVR is to maintain a constant volume of
water between each set of checkgates. The gate openings are
downloaded to the checkgate RTUs without review by the operators, and
the changes automatically take place on the hour.

PROGRAM STRUCTURE

As previously stated, ACS II has a modular structure. There are two
executable tasks, PDRIVR and GDRIVR, each containing a number of
modules that perform specific functions. There are 24 modules used in
these two tasks, many of which are used by both tasks. At the next
level down are another 19 modules that perform functions that are
common to more than one module in the first level.

Each module is linked to the tasks in only two places. There is a
COMMON block that contains constants such as the geometry of the canal
and telemetry from the data base. Any variables that the module needs
to perform its function, and any variables that result from its
function, are passed as formal parameters. Therefore, as long as the
module contains these two connection points, it can act as a "black
box", i.e. the other modules are not at all effected by the procedures
within the module.

The only criteria for a module are the function it performs and the
required connection to the other modules via the COMMON block and the
formal parameters. Each module may vary in size or may be written in
a different language as long as it meets the criteria. Each module
contains complete documentation in the form of abstracts, input/output
lists, "Pseudo-code" -- a hybrid of english and computer language,
lists of abstract data structures and variable names, and comments
within the code itself.

GATE SETTING

A major difference between the first and second generations of ACS is
the use of a steady state gate setting module in place of the more
accurate but much less efficient unsteady state method. The steady
state calculations are based on linearized hydraulic equations
developed by others (Becker, et al, 1981).

The use of a less accurate method was justified by thorough comparative testing of the two methods. The testing of these methods
involved generating flow and depth schedules from turnout schedules
that ranged in character from fairly steady to wildly varying using a

control volume algorithm. Both methods of gate setting then used
these results to calculate gate openings for a 24 hour period. These
gate openings, along with the initial conditions and turnout schedule,
were then run through an unsteady state simulation model and the
resulting water surfaces, volumes delivered, and flows were compared.
The results can be summarized as follows:

1. The unsteady state model stays closer to the desired flow
    schedule.

2. The steady state method results in a calmer water surface
    during drastic changes in flow.

3. The difference in volume delivered through the gates due to
    the difference in methods was between 0.03% and 0.2% of the
    total volume delivered over the entire 24 hour period.

4. The largest difference in depth in a pool at the end of 24
    hours due to the difference in methods was approximately 0.1
    foot.

5. The maximum discrepancy in the volume delivered over any one
    hour, in the worst case, only caused a difference in depth of
    approximately 0.08 foot.

Since the actual condition is unsteady, the steady state method would
be expected to generate a flow schedule that is not as close to the
desired schedule as the unsteady state method. This is shown to be
true in Figure 1. However, the flows resulting from the steady state
method are not different enough from the desired flow schedules to

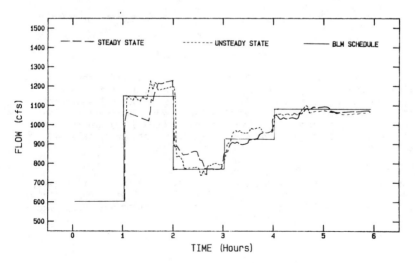

Figure 1 - Comparative Flows

warrant discarding the method. The largest discrepancy in change in
pool volumes over a 24 hour period resulted in a net difference in
depth of approximately 0.1 foot, which is the minimum increment of
depth that can be detected by telemetry.

It is also interesting to note that the steady state method results in
a calmer water surface after drastic flow changes are made (Figure 2).
The reason this occurs is that the steady state method does not track
the transients like the unsteady state method and therefore does not
react to them. In addition, the unsteady state method uses a smaller
time increment which allows a quicker reaction which, in turn, makes
it more likely that transients will have an effect on gate setting.

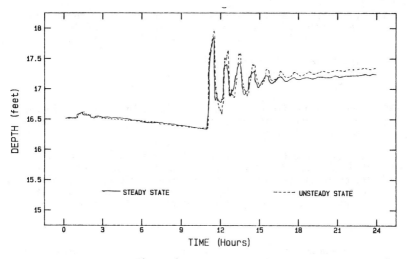

Figure 2 - Depth Comparison

The tests were run using a fifteen minute time increment for the
steady state method of gate setting. In ACS II, as mentioned
previously, only one gate setting is made in an hour. The difference
in water surface as a result of this larger time increment is minor.
The largest difference in any of the test schedules due to the
difference in time increment was a mere 0.03 foot, practically
undetectable.

The steady state method runs hundreds of times faster than the
unsteady state method. Because of this advantage in execution time,
the calmer water surface, and the relatively small difference in flows
and depths, the steady state method for gate setting was chosen for
use in the Aqueduct Control Software.

SUMMARY

The second generation of ACS is in general a more workable, more practical, software package than the original. The major changes are an increased tolerance for bad field data, a more important role for the minimizing of pump starts, a faster execution time, and an improved structure.

In addition   to being more workable for the CAP, the increased tolerance for bad or questionable values from the data base and its modular structure make the scheduling models transferable to other aqueduct systems. The faster execution time allows for more runs at shorter increments to take advantage of more current telemetry. And finally, by working in the more important role for minimizing pump starts by using the operator in the decision loop, the software allows more flexibility in the overall operational philosophy of an aqueduct system.

BIBLIOGRAPHY

Becker, L., Graves, A.L., and Yeh, W.W-G., 1981, "Central Arizona Project Operation," Proceedings of the International Symposium on Rainfall-Runoff Modeling, Water Resources Publications, Littleton, Colorado.

Falvey, H.T., and Luning, P.C., 1979, "Gate Stroking," Internal Report, Engineering and Research Center, Bureau of Reclamation, Denver, Colorado.

Gooch, R.S., and Graves, A.L., 1985, "Central Arizona Project Supervisory Control System," Proceedings of Computerized Decision Support Systems for Water Resource Managers: Case Studies of Large Systems, ASCE Spring Convention, Denver, Colorado.

APPLIED HYDRO SYSTEM OPERATIONS MODELS

*Charles E. Abraham

An extensive information network is required to manage the operations of large hydro systems. Information of reservoir conditions, power operations, and hydromet conditions are necessary to update projected individual and system operations. Long-term statistical information on these various elements is needed for comparison and risk analysis. The manager of large systems must continually assess such current and long-term conditions in order to best achieve the project purposes.

The decision-making process for operations of large hydro systems includes many influences other than technical. Political, social, public safety, and other undefinable issues can often cause unplanned changes to the overall operations plan. The manager must rely on a number of tools for background in assessing effects on project objectives.

This paper focuses on one of these applications considered to be a "bread and butter" tool, the computer simulation of system operations. Computer programs that simulate operations through future time periods on hourly, daily or monthly time periods are routinely used to guide operations in achieving objectives and assessing the effects of various scenarios. Major physical elements needed to describe reservoir, river, power, and other functions are modeled tying the system of reservoirs together so that their simulated performance can be assessed, both individually and as a system.

Early computer modeling were site specific performing simple functions with little concern for automation to improve the outcome. High speed computers and good data base management systems combined with optimization considerations have resulted in highly sophisticated models. Some are sight specific, whereas others have been developed for general applications. The development and adaptation of general applications programs and site specific programs used in modeling large hydro systems (Columbia River, Missouri River, and Central Valley Project hydro systems) are reviewed. The additional needs and potential improvements of models used in large hydro system operations from an operations manager's view are discussed.

*Chief, Central Valley Operations Coordinating Office, U. S. Bureau of Reclamation, Mid-Pacific Region, 2800 Cottage Way, Sacramento, California 95825.

INTRODUCTION

It's a hot summer afternoon capping off a week of dry hot days. Water and power demands are up and the hot weather is taking its toll on water quality. Additional water releases are required, but which reservoirs and river systems should provide the needed water. Maximum flexibility in power and water supplies must be maintained to support continuing needs and efficiencies.

This is only one of many situations that routinely confront a water operations manager. Good decisions can be made only when enough information is available on alternatives, risks, and sensitivity. Computerized water and power management systems that can track vital information and analyze various operational scenarios are helping managers do the job. However, we have barely scratched the surface in the implementation of such tools that are now available. Decisions are arrived at from technical information, as well as the recognition of political or social concerns, and it is these latter concerns, that especially dictate the need for technical background for guidance and determination of physical risks.

APPLICATIONS

Some of the early computerized applications were simply large input/output systems whereby raw data were processed following existing manual procedures and output was in the form of formatted bulletins. Such information was not always available in the form and time needed for guidance in deciding a course of action. As technology became available, sophistication was included to provide sequential river and reservoir routing models, whereby, information based on the simulation of forecasted conditions, could be available in a timely manner. Still others have developed highly sophisticated optimization models. All of these applications are important pieces to the overall needs but, if applied independently, require a large amount of data transcription and manipulation.

Probably the most important element in an automated system is a workable data base and associated management system that can efficiently manage the real-time hydro system information. It should possess the capability to store and access long-term data from which statistics of the various elements can be drawn. It must possess the capability to store and access short-time interval data and, above all, it should be automated so that raw data from field reporting stations can be obtained and basic processing performed with little or no manual intervention. Basic to all of this is near instantaneous response for the user. Time delays only tend to discourage full use of the system, thereby, perhaps bypassing some useful sensitivity analyses.

No situation seems to be the same as the last and we often find that physical, biological, political, social, and other unexpected conditions cause significant concerns in the course of action. Unexpected requirements must be considered and a risk analysis is often in order. However, many of todays simulation models and optimization processes do not provide for such considerations.

DISCUSSION

It is mind boggling to consider an all inclusive program to answer the many different concerns in a large hydro system. Specialized programs dealing with specific elements or areas in a hydro system are very useful which suggests a package of programs that readily communicate with the data base. For example, time dependent simulation procedures might include a separate program or source for precipitation and/or snowpack to develop a runoff forecast or an array defining probabilistic runoff amounts, whereas another model would deal with the simulation of streamflow and reservoir operations. Depending on the control (water quality, water supply, fishery, power, flood, etc.), the simulation of various elements may be broken down even further. Underlying all of this is the need to assess the unexpected condition that suddenly arises and must be dealt with quickly. These various models should reflect the concerns for optimizing guidelines, an element not well understood in real-time operations.

Realistic objectives should be set and avoid dealing with more technical detail than necessary for the intended purpose. In real-time, information may be missing or unavailable within the needed time frame and may at best be a gross estimate. Concerns should focus on the major elements that would be available effecting results for the operational decision-making process. For example, time and spatial distribution of forecasted precipitation may be of little significance or misguiding considering the unreliability of the product. On the other hand, probabilistic scenarios may better provide the needed perspective. Long-term operational planning models may, by necessity, be more involved with detail such as power commitments, detailed power heads, and optimizing considerations. Again, this lends support to a network of specialized programs, all communicating to a common data base.

Programming logic to provide for automatic reservoir release simulations can be difficult and complex and may be of little value for short term analysis. Interactive features for simulating operations can recognize any one of a number of particular and unexpected conditions such as special operational needs caused by a drowning, construction, streamflow measurement, water quality or fishery needs, water supply, power, etc. Taken as a whole, engineer interaction with the computer through the "what if" process is very effective in developing a final product.

There have been attempts to apply large generalized programs to real-time hydro system use. Benefits for quick and easy applications seem obvious. However, experience in the Columbia, Missouri and Central Valley Basins has proven this practice to be a formidable task meeting with limited success in application. Programs experiencing the most use in real-time applications are those programs that were developed in and for the particular area and element of concern. Though there are a number of commonalities from one basin or area to another, there are many extremely important unique features that cause difficulty in the application of generalized programs. General application programs are, from necessity, large and very complex, to reflect so many different conditions but this feature makes it difficult to modify logic without involving extensive repairs and training. Therefore, rather than an all inclusive program, logic should concentrate on common, routinely accepted engineering procedures such as reservoir accounting, streamflow routing, and combining, etc., allowing for differences in sophisticated control logic. Each particular system application would require specific programming and training support. In most cases, the final product would probably experience greater success than attempting to alter complex programs. This also allows for easier adaptation of new procedures in basic programs. The adaptation of new research from the academic community takes too long, especially in real-time applications.

Finally, more involvement by the academic community in real-time water applications is needed. The National Workshop on Reservoir Systems Operations[1]/ provided an excellent forum to bridge the gap between the practicing engineers and the academic community. However, it has been seven years since that workshop and many new practicing engineers are not even aware of that workshop. Such workshops should occur more often and be focused on more localized concerns. Perhaps, universities could take a lead through their Extension Services. The Operations Management Technical Committee of the Water Resources Planning and Management Division in ASCE has sponsored workshops and sessions in various conferences promoting technical information transfer. Also, various agencies maintain specialized expertise for training and research to recognize and implement state-of-the-art procedures. Therefore, it would seem that there is adequate organization and institutional facilities in place. Better and more effective use should be made of them focusing on real-time water and power operations.

CONCLUSIONS

Our existing water resources projects face new and additional objectives than they did when planned and constructed. This brings on additional challenges to the water operations manager. He finds

himself with less flexibility in alternatives to meet authorized
purposes along with additional environmental needs. Therefore,
there is a pressing need to implement state-of-the-art technology to
better arm the manager with appropriate information to be used in
the decision-making process. We have made good strides but there is
much to be accomplished in the application of technological
procedures to real-time water and power system operations.

APPENDIX A

REFERENCES

1/ Dr. Gerrit H. Toebes and Alice A. Shepherd, "Proceedings of the
National Workshop on Reservoir Systems Operations," ASCE (1979)

OPERATIONS MODELS OF THE COLUMBIA RESERVOIR SYSTEM

Gregory K. Delwiche[1]

ABSTRACT

The Columbia River, with a drainage basin of 259,000 square miles, is the fourth largest river in North America. The river basin has been extensively developed for flood control, power, navigation, irrigation, fishery, recreation and other purposes. Several of the computer models used in management of the basin's reservoir system will be described. Among the models discussed are the Streamflow Synthesis and Reservoir Regulation Model (SSARR), the Hydro System Seasonal Regulation Model (HYSSR), the GASPILL and FISHPASS models and various water supply forecast procedures. Emphasis will be placed on the use of these models as tools in the water management decision-making process and not on the actual mechanics of the models. In addition, the performance of the SSARR model and the water supply models during a period of unseasonably warm and wet weather in February 1986 will be briefly described.

INTRODUCTION

Management of the Columbia River reservoir system to meet the needs of all its diverse users is an extremely complex task even without the uncertainty of hydrologic events. During February 1986 several meteorological events occurred triggering rapid and unpredictable rises in streamflow throughout the basin. Often times, events of this type expose the limits of the computer models which river managers are so dependent upon for planning as well as real-time operation. This paper discusses several of the models used in managing Columbia River system reservoirs and touches upon both the performance of these models and their shortcomings during February's events.

---

[1] Reservoir Control Center, US Army Corps of Engineers, North Pacific Division, Portland, OR.

BASIN DESCRIPTION

The Columbia River, with a drainage basin of 259,000 square miles (671,000 sq km), is the fourth largest river in North America. The river drains much of southeastern British Columbia, as well as western Montana, and most of Idaho, Oregon and Washington (see Figure 1). About seventy percent of the basin runoff occurs between April and August as the winter snowpack of the northern Rocky Mountains melts. This hydrologic pattern, along with the basin's geographic character, has allowed particularly harmonious and extensive multipurpose water resources development. Since the early 1900s at least 100 federal dams and 135 non-federal dams have been built for flood control, power, navigation, irrigation and other multiple purpose benefits. Basin-wide storage capacity is about 50 million acre-feet (maf) (61,500 cu hm), or twenty five percent of the average annual runoff of 200 maf (245,000 cu hm). Total installed hydropower capacity is over 30,0000 megawatts, of which about two-thirds is federally operated.

THE COLUMBIA/SNAKE DRAINAGE SYSTEM

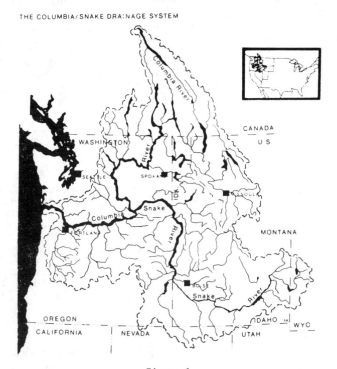

Figure 1

RESERVOIR SYSTEM MODELS 559

OPERATION OF THE RESERVOIR SYSTEM

The four major types of reservoirs in the basin are headwater storage projects, run-of-river projects, pondage projects and lakes with dams to regulate their outflow. Springtime snowmelt runoff is stored in the headwater storage reservoirs and released during the autumn and winter months when natural flows are low and power demands high. This type of operation provides flood control while also increasing the marketable firm energy capability of the river. Each of the major storage reservoirs is drawn down to a variable minimum level which is dependent upon mountain snowpack and water supply forecasts.

Because of the diversity of both project owners and reservoir uses, management of the reservoir system does not occur in one centralized location or by one entity. At the operational level, a series of legislative acts, contracts and agreements has set up an interagency framework for river management. Among the cornerstone agreements which govern river operations are the Columbia River Treaty with Canada, the Pacific Northwest Coordination Agreement, the Northwest Power Planning Council's Fish and Wildlife Program, and the legislative acts which set the missions for the Corps of Engineers, Bureau of Reclamation and the Bonneville Power Administration which is the agency that markets energy generated at Federally-owned dams.

The North Pacific Division (NPD) of the Corps of Engineers plays an important role in the management of the reservoir system. NPD's Reservoir Control Center (RCC) directs the daily operation of the reservoir system during the snowmelt season. During the remainder of the year RCC schedules the daily operation of the Corps' headwater storage projects and sets up a framework for operation of the Corps' run-of-river projects within multiple purpose constraints.

OPERATIONAL COMPUTER MODELS

The Corps' North Pacific Division has developed several highly sophisticated computer models to simulate different aspects of reservoir system operation. Among these models are the Streamflow Synthesis and Reservoir Regulation Model (SSARR), the Hydro System Seasonal Regulation Model (HYSSR), and the FISHPASS and GASPILL Models. Also important in Columbia River operations are various interagency water supply forecasting models.

The SSARR model is used in the Reservoir Control Center as a tool in making real-time regulation decisions, to make long-term runoff forecasts and to evaluate operational strategies for different long-term runoff patterns. The model is actually run by an interagency team of river forecasting specialists from the National Weather Service's

Northwest River Forecast Center (NWRFC) and hydraulic engineers from NPD's Water Management Branch. Short-term and
long-term streamflow forecasts generated by the SSARR model
are officially issued by NWRFC to the public. Since these
forecasts are dependent on river regulation decisions this
interagency arrangement for forecasting not only prevents
duplication of effort in manpower and computer facilities
but is beneficial in enhancing forecast accuracy.

SSARR is a mathematical, hydrologic model whereby
streamflow is first synthesized by evaluating the entire
hydrologic process from snowmelt and rainfall runoff and
then routed through a system of rivers and reservoirs. The
model is comprised of a generalized hydrologic watershed
model, a river system model and a reservoir regulation
model. Several versions of the model are run seasonally,
depending on the dominant hydrologic processes, forecast
duration requirements and operational planning needs.

During the winter, streamflow east of the Cascade Mountains is relatively constant and near baseflow level.
Consequently, the watershed model is generally not run and
unregulated flows are synthesized using correlations between
observed flows, average flows and water supply forecasts.
In the winter, the model is used primarily as an aid for
making longer term reservoir regulation decisions so that
flood control drawdown requirements can be met with a smooth
river regulation and within the constraints of other project
purposes. Most winter SSARR runs are made for a thirty day
period although longer term runs are occasionally made if
needed.

Immediately before and during the snowmelt season the
full model is run and streamflow is synthesized for periods
up to 90 days. Runoff scenarios are assessed by applying
different weather sequences to the snowmelt process so that
various regulation strategies can tested. Since the maximum
available basin-wide flood control space is less than half
of the average spring runoff volume, judicious use of this
space is required to maximize flood control success, power
sales and still refill reservoirs. After the snowmelt
season is over and reservoirs are full, the watershed model
is no longer run and thirty day runs using the river system
and reservoir regulation portion of the model are resumed.

Occasionally during the fall, winter and early spring
months, warm weather often accompanied by heavy precipitation occurs throughout the Columbia basin. Streamflows
usually change rapidly in response to these conditions and
detailed short-term streamflow predictions are necessary for
both reservoir regulation and to issue river stage forecasts
to the public. When these situations arise, three day SSARR
runs with six hour forecast intervals are made using the
watershed model for portions of the basin where needed.
During February 1986 an extended series of warm wet storms
hit the Columbia basin and the three day model was extensively used. The performance of model during this weather
sequence will be discussed later in this paper.

The HYSSR model is used for seasonal hydropower system regulation studies. The model is presently used to evaluate the impacts of non-power constraints on the system's firm energy capability. A fifty year sequence of historical flows is analyzed to determine the extent that changes in operating requirements affect the system's ability to meet a predetermined firm energy capability. In other words, constraints are modeled to evaluate their effects on firm energy if the driest period in the fifty year historical record were to reoccur. The model is also used to make fifty one-year studies of the system's ability to refill if the selected amount of firm energy is generated in each of the fifty years.

Water supply models are also an important aspect of Columbia system regulation. Water supply forecasts are first made in mid-December for the January through August forecast period. These forecasts are primarily derived using regression-based relationships. Snowpack measurements, precipitation indices and observed streamflow are used in the models. All forecast procedures assume that median precipitation will occur during the remainder of the forecast period. Thus, as would be expected, forecast uncertainty decreases with time. For the entire Columbia drainage, 171 different sub-basin forecasts are made. Cross-correlations are checked to assure that forecast differences between adjacent drainages are reasonable.

The FISHPASS model, which is currently being developed, will be used to evaluate different operational strategies for improving juvenile fish passage conditions in the mainstem Columbia and Snake Rivers. The effects of spill, structural improvements in passage facilities and various river flow conditions can all be analyzed. Observed fish passage indices are used in the model to quantify existing passage conditions and evaluate the effects of changes in operational strategies.

The GASSPILL model is used as a tool in distributing spill among mainstem Columbia and Snake River projects. During periods of heavy spill in the system, nitrogen supersaturation often causes gas bubble disease in both outmigrating juvenile fish and returning adults. By shifting spill to areas of the river with lower dissolved gas concentrations and controlling maximum amounts of spill in areas of high supersaturation, the incidence of gas bubble disease can be controlled. The GASPILL model is used to test the mitigative effects of various spill patterns, spill amounts and spill distribution throughout the basin.

PERFORMANCE OF SSARR IN FEBRUARY 1986 FLOODS

Between mid-February and early March 1986 a series of unseasonably warm and wet weather systems caused rapid rises in streamflow throughout the Columbia basin. The Snake River and lower Columbia tributary basins, as well as all

basins draining the western slopes of the Cascades, were hit
particularly hard by this weather pattern.
   Before this sequence began, water supply and snowpack
throughout the basin was well below average. Cumulative
precipitation indices for the water year through mid-
February were 81 percent of normal for both the Snake River
above its mouth and the Columbia River above The Dalles,
Oregon. Precipitation was generally near average in
October, November and January but was at record low levels
in many places during December. The weather changed
abruptly in mid-February when the first of a series of moist
and warm systems hit the Pacific Northwest. By the end of
February, monthly precipitation indices were as high as 400
percent of normal for parts of the Snake basin, 250 percent
of normal for the entire Snake basin and 185 percent for the
Columbia above The Dalles. Cumulative indices for the water
year through February were 108 and 99 percent of normal at
the latter two sites. Figure 2 illustrates the changes in
precipitation indices for both the Clearwater basin, which
is a major tributary to the Snake River, and the entire
Snake basin. Various water supply forecasts which were
issued for Dworshak reservoir (on the North Fork Clearwater
River) through early March are also shown.
   The SSARR model was used extensively during this wet
period to make short-term streamflow predictions. The entire watershed-to-reservoir model was run for essentially
all tributary basins of the Columbia River. Streamflow was
synthesized based on forecasted rainfall and freezing levels
after being intialized with observed conditions. Thus,
streamflow forecasts were dependent to a large degree on
forecasted weather.

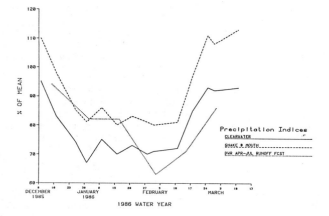

Figure 2

Figure 3 shows forecasted versus observed precipitation
at the Eugene, Oregon airport. This figure indicates the
general trend of forecasted rainfall being lower than observed rainfall throughout much of the Columbia basin during
this weather sequence. Since SSARR's streamflow predictions
are so dependent on weather forecasts, synthesized flows
were generally less than observed. This trend was especially apparent for headwater streams since these watersheds
generally receive more precipitation. This pattern made it
risky to base decisions for regulation of headwater reservoirs on forecasted inflows. Interestingly, observed
streamflow at important downstream control points such as
the Snake River at its mouth and the Columbia River at
Vancouver, Washington was relatively close to the forecasted
levels. This was probably because forecasts for these control points are primarily based on the routing of streamflow
which has already been observed upstream. Consequently, although the SSARR forecasts were extremely useful in issuing
reliable streamflow forecasts at downstream control points,
the model's reliability in predicting headwater flows was
only as good as the weather forecasts used as input. Thus,
for river regulation, especially in the headwater areas, the
model was used primarily as a tool to indicate the potential
order of magnitude for headwater flows. Regulation during
this event became a real-time operation in which decisions
were made in response to observed conditions. Forecasts were
used primarily as guidance to assure that regulation changes
due to immediate needs did not sacrifice the ability to control future potential streamflow.

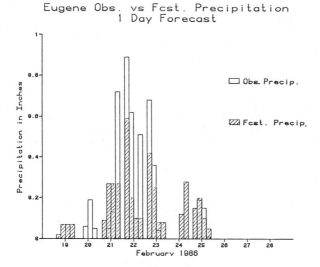

Eugene Obs. vs Fcst. Precipitation
1 Day Forecast

Figure 3

Since this weather sequence produced considerable valley and mid-elevation snowmelt, a major and difficult-to-
forecast change in water supply occurred. Most low-
elevation snow throughout the basin was gone, but high
elevation snowpack increased significantly. Snowcourse
data, which is incorporated into most of the water supply
models, should have accurately reflected this change in
conditions, but precipitation indices are also an important
part of the water supply forecast procedure. These indices
generally are an indirect measure of snowpack because most
precipitation east of the Cascades falls as snow during the
winter. But during mid- and late-February much of the basin
precipation fell as rain. Thus, February's extremely high
precipitation indices may produce an inflated indication of
water supply. It can also be argued, however, that snowcourse data, if representative of the entire basin, may dam-
pen the effects of the high precipitation indices.
Hindsight studies after the snowmelt season will be necessary to evaluate the validity of water supply forecasts
issued immediately after this wet period.

CONCLUSION

Operations models for predicting runoff and water
supply are an important tool used in regulation of the
Columbia reservoir system. The SSARR model has annually
demonstrated its usefulness as both a planning and regulation tool during the spring snowmelt period. But
reliability of the model for making short-term streamflow
forecasts during warm and wet weather periods is only as
good as the reliability of weather forecasts for these
sequences. The accuracy of regression-based water supply
models may also be hindered by unusual weather sequences.
Extended Streamflow Prediction (ESP) procedures are currently being evaluated for use in long-term streamflow
forecasting in the Pacific Northwest. This approach will at
least give an indication of the probability for streamflows
that could occur throughout an extended forecast period.
This could especially improve the accuracy of late-season
forecasts, but there is still too much uncertainity to expect much improvement in forecast reliability early in the
winter when critical reservoir drawdown decisions often have
to be made.

CALIFORNIA WATER PROJECT OPERATION

M. Hossein Sabet, A. M. ASCE and James Q. Coe[1]

ABSTRACT

The California State Water Project (SWP) is operated and managed using state-of-the-art operations research and optimization techniques.

Medium- and long-range studies for the operation of the SWP are performed using a simulation/optimization model called NEOSYS. NEOSYS simulates and optimizes the operation of five main SWP reservoirs and produces reports with monthly detail. The optimization is performed by a dynamic programming optimization model which minimizes power costs using reservoir storages as state variables. NEOSYS is capable of performing studies of up to 50 years duration. It has been used for operation studies, preliminary and final allocation of power costs, and feasibility of expanding project facilities since 1980.

The electrical schedules for operation of the pumping and generating plants for power sales and purchases are determined using a network flow programming optimization model. Hydraulic feasibility of the hourly electrical schedules produced by this model is checked by a number of hydraulic simulation models. These models have been used in this way since April 1, 1983.

A comprehensive large-scale optimization model has been developed to replace the network model and the hydraulic simulation models presently used for operations scheduling. It can also be used for long-range yearly studies and preliminary scheduling of water and power. It operates on weekly and daily bases and can provide hydraulic and electrical schedules with hourly detail. It consists of hydraulic network components to meet storage objectives of all the reservoirs, a linear programming component to determine the schedules at pumping and generating plants, and a network programming component to balance electrical loads and resources within the SWP. The model is scheduled for use in July 1986. It will initially be used for determining preliminary operations. After the model is fully tested, it will be used for determining actual hourly schedules.

INTRODUCTION

California State Water Project.-The SWP commences in the Upper Feather River region with three small lakes which provide water for recreation, irrigation, and domestic use (5). Downstream from these lakes is the

---

[1] Respectively; Associate Electrical Utilities Engineer, and Chief of Modeling Support Section, Department of Water Resources, Sacramento, California, 95082.

Oroville Complex which includes Lake Oroville (the Project's principal reservoir), and Hyatt and Thermalito Pumping/Generating Plants with 900 megawatts (MW) generation capacity (1). Releases from Oroville flow through natural channels of the Feather and Sacramento Rivers to the Sacramento-San Joaquin Delta. In the south Delta, the Banks Pumping Plant lifts water from the Delta at Clifton Court Forebay into Bethany Reservoir. From this reservoir water is lifted to the South Bay Aqueduct which serves the southern San Francisco Bay area. Most of the water from Bethany Reservoir flows into the Edmund G. Brown California Aqueduct which is the primary conveyance feature of the SWP for delivery of water to Central and Southern California. San Luis, a 2.04 million acre-foot (2,510 million cubic meters) reservoir, owned jointly by the California Department of Water Resources (DWR) and the U.S. Bureau of Reclamation, is a major offstream storage facility which

Fig. 1 - The California State Water Project

receives water from O'Neill Forebay. From O'Neill Forebay water also flows through the Aqueduct and is raised 969 feet (295 meters) by four pumping plants before reaching the foot of the Tehachapi Mountains. The A. D. Edmonston Pumping Plant lifts the water 1,926 feet (587 meters) in a single lift to enter ten miles of tunnels and siphons to Tehachapi Afterbay. The East Branch carries water to Lake Perris, the southernmost terminus of the Project, 444 miles (715 kilometers) from the Delta where the Aqueduct begins. Water in the West Branch is carried to Pyramid Lake in Los Angeles County then to Castaic Lake, terminus of the West Branch.

Operation Objectives.-The fundamental operation objective of the SWP is to provide water service in accordance with the existing contracts. In the early 1960s, DWR entered into 75-year water contracts with 31 local agencies serving areas throughout California. Under the contracts, the Department promises to make all reasonable efforts to most economically operate the facilities and to make deliveries within contractual entitlements. The contractors promise to pay their respective shares of the costs the Department incurs for such efforts.

Until March 31, 1983, energy required for SWP operation in excess of that generated by power recovery plants on the aqueduct system was purchased by DWR from major California utilities. At that time, the contract for supply of the required energy expired and DWR began balancing its loads and resources and buying and selling energy on the general market, like an electric utility.

MODELS

NEOSYS.-NEOSYS is a comprehensive simulation/optimization system for performing medium- and long-range studies of the operations of the SWP from the Delta to the Project termini at Lake Perris and Castaic Lake (see Fig. 1). NEOSYS contains three models, together with supporting functions for data handling. The three models are a simulation model, an optimization model, and a model which generates initial solutions for the optimization model. It operates for one to fifty years in increments of a year with a time step of one month.

The NEOSYS simulation model consists of several spatially-oriented components. The first begins at the terminus of each branch and works upstream, using water demands, beginning storages, storage changes, and constraints to calculate total flow volumes at each point in the SWP system in accordance with hydraulic continuity. The other components are identified collectively as "peaking" algorithms, which means that they distribute volumes of pumped or released water to periods of high or low electrical demand within the month. These periods are identified as "on-peak" (8:00 a.m. to 10:00 p.m. on weekdays) and "off-peak" (all other times). The algorithms for the Coastal Branch, North Bay Aqueduct, and South Bay Aqueduct (Fig. 1) distribute the volumes uniformly. For Delta Pumping Plant, San Luis Pumping-Generating Plant, and Devil Canyon and Castaic Generating Plants, on-peak generation and off-peak pumping are maximized to the limit of the physical constraints. The remaining facilities are identified as the "core system", bounded by O'Neill Forebay, Lake Silverwood, and Pyramid

Lake.   The core system includes seven pumping plants and two generating plants.

In general, the core system is peaked to maximize on-peak generation and off-peak pumping.   This is done considering the position and relative production/consumption rates (Table 1) of the pumping and generating plants.   The entire system is first peaked toward maximum off-peak volume to minimize on-peak power consumption at Edmonston Pumping Plant.   Then the schedule is held from O'Neill Forebay through Edmonston and at Pearblossom Pumping Plant while the West Branch is recalculated to maximize on-peak flow at Warne Generating Plant. Finally, Edmonston, Pearblossom and Warne are held and off-peak volume at Oso Pumping Plant is maximized, thereby also maximizing on-peak volume at Alamo Generating Plant.   Constraints considered are flow capacity of the aqueduct and the immediate upstream plant and capacity of the aqueduct to accept storage volume changes.   The results are flows at every point in the system and energy consumption or production at the plants.

Table 1.-Energy Consumption/Production for SWP Plants

Plant	Kilowatt-hours per Acre-foot	
	Consumption	Production
Edmonston	2,239	
All core plants except Edmonston	1,779	
All plants, Dos Amigos to Edmonston	3,727	
Oso plus Warne minus Alamo		194
Oso minus Alamo	387	

The NEOSYS optimization uses an Incremental Dynamic Programming (IDP) model in which the state variables are the reservoir storages at San Luis Reservoir, Lake Silverwood, Lake Perris, Pyramid Lake, and Castaic Lake and the stages are months (2, 6).   The objective is to minimize the total cost of weighted on-peak power, which is defined as the sum of the monthly weighted net power consumption rates.   Individual weighting factors can be applied to each month of a run.   The input data are the same as for the simulation model plus data for controlling the IDP.

The model selects the least-cost combination from a discrete set of reservoir storages provided by establishing an "initial trajectory", or a known satisfactory solution, and defining a "restrictive corridor", consisting of two additional storages for selected reservoirs, both in the vicinity of the initial trajectory.   For each stage, there are from 1 to 3^5 = 243 combinations of storage at the beginning and also at the end of the stage, thus providing up to 59,049 potential solutions to be considered.   The IDP uses a version of the simulation model to calculate energy quantities for these solutions.   The result is the set of storages providing the least-cost solution.   The entire process is iterated until the improvement for an iteration is a satisfactorily small amount.   The program user may control the number of iterations, the spacing of storage values about the initial trajectory, and the choice of reservoirs to be used.   For the first iteration, the monthly storages for the initial trajectory are provided by the solution-generating model (described below). For succeeding iterations, the initial trajectory is the best solution found in the previous iteration.

The solution-generating model is a network flow programming (NFP) model of the facilities of the SWP from the Delta to Lake Perris and Castaic Lake. In a NFP, the system being modeled is transformed into a capacitated network flow problem consisting of nodes and links, which is solved by the "out-of-kilter" method or a modification of it (3). The solution-generating NFP is solved monthly and is arranged to maximize the storages in San Luis Reservoir, Lake Silverwood, Lake Perris, Pyramid Lake, and Castaic Lake. It requires the same input data as the simulation model except that ending storages are not required. The output is a set of storages for the five reservoirs above which provides an appropriate initial trajectory for the IDP model.

Electrical Scheduling Model.-Scheduling of electrical features of the SWP is performed by a simulation/optimization model referred to here as the electrical scheduling optimization model. It determines the hourly schedules at pumping and generating plants and provides schedules for electrical energy sales to and purchases from other electric utility companies in the State.

The model consists of a NFP component called the Power Allocation Network (PAN), and several hydraulic simulation components. PAN represents the contractual agreements between DWR and other electric utilities, the pumping plants (power loads), the generating plants (power resources), and the transmission lines used by the SWP. It is designed for daily use and has 24 periods representing the hours of the day. These periods are tied together by total energy quantities for the day.

The input data to the model includes capacities of pumping and generating plants, capacities of transmission lines, contracted energy available and required, energy demands at pumping plants, and energy available at generating plants. The data is input by the users at the DWR Project Operations Control Center. To minimize the time required for data input, the files which contain input data of the previous day are updated with new data and re-used. Screen editing programs are highly efficient and user friendly. After the data are read, the constraints which control the arcs of the network are updated (see Fig. 2). To reduce time used for determining the solution to the network, an initial feasible solution is computed. The PAN is then solved using an improved version of the "out-of-kilter" algorithm (8). The transmission losses are provided by the network solution. These losses are applied to the network and it is solved once again. This process is repeated until an accurate estimate of losses is obtained. The final solution provides hourly electrical schedules.

The hydraulic feasibility of the hourly schedules at the Oroville hydro-generation plants is determined by the Oroville Hydraulics Simulation Model. The electrical schedules at Hyatt and Thermalito plants are simulated for each hour of the day. The plant schedules are constrained to be within the maximum and minimum operating level or be

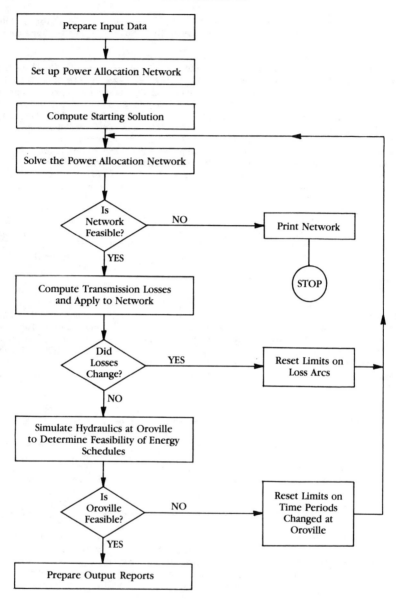

Fig. 2 - Flow Chart For The Electrical Scheduling Model.

idle. The storages at Lake Oroville, Thermalito Forebay, and Thermalito Afterbay are constrained to be within their minimum and maximum limits. If these constraints cannot be met, the schedule is modified for the infeasible hours and the PAN is solved with new limits. This procedure continues until a feasible solution for Oroville complex is obtained.

Hydraulic simulation models are then used to obtain detailed operating schedules at facilities which do not directly use or generate electricity. These are reservoir storages and elevations, pool storages, and check structure flows.

Hydraulic and Electrical Optimization Model.-A comprehensive large-scale optimization model has been developed to provide schedules for operation of water and power for the SWP. The model is designed to provide hourly schedules for water and power operation, prescheduling estimation of power use and needs, weekly schedules, and annual operation studies. It is designed to minimize on-peak energy use and maximize on-peak energy production. As a result of this peaking, most of the pumping is done during off-peak hours when energy can be purchased inexpensively and most of the generation is done during on-peak hours when energy can be sold at a higher rate.

The hydraulic optimization part of the model provides water schedules at pumping and generating plants in the system. The hydraulic optimization begins with simple simulation of flows for the North Bay Aqueduct, South Bay Aqueduct, and the Coastal Branch. A NFP component is solved for the Oroville Complex. This component provides the outflow available for export considering the objective storages at Oroville and time lag. The water demand downstream of Clifton Court Forebay is computed by solving a hydraulic NFP component. If this demand is more than water available from Oroville for export, an attempt is made to increase the Oroville outflow by modifying objective storages at Oroville. If the demand is still more than the available supply, the demand NFP component is solved with limited supply at Clifton Court Forebay. The solution provides total flow at pumping and generating plants for the day or the week under consideration. These flows are peaked using a linear programming (4) optimization component solved for the core system (7) and several hydraulic simulation components for the other portions of the SWP.

To ensure that O'Neill Forebay storage stays within its operation limits after the peaking is performed, a NFP component which starts at Banks Pumping Plant and ends at Buena Vista Pumping Plant is solved. The network modifies schedules at the Banks, San Luis, and Dos Amigos plants to bring O'Neill Forebay within its limits. The electrical loads and resources are computed from the schedules at pumping and generating plants for use in the electrical computation which follows.

The electrical computation provides schedules for sales and purchases using the loads and resources provided by the hydraulic models and by energy contracts. The electrical computations are carried out by PAN, the same NFP component used in the electrical scheduling optimization model. This implementation of PAN calculates initial electrical

schedules at Warne and   Oroville without regard to the hydraulic
consequences. Then the hydraulic feasibility of the schedules is
checked by a hydraulic simulation component at Oroville and a hydraulic
NFP component at Warne. In case of hydraulic infeasibility the PAN is
solved again with new bounds, and the process continues until a
compatible electrical and hydraulic solution is found.

The output of the model provides schedules of sales and purchases of
electrical energy, energy and hydraulic schedules at pumping plants
and generating plants, flows at check structures, and storages at
reservoir and aqueduct pools.

STATUS

NEOSYS has been used for medium- and long-range operation studies, such
as pre-1985 power purchase determination, preliminary and final
allocation of power cost, and feasibility of expanding SWP facilities
since 1980. The hourly schedules for operation of pumping and
generating plants and for sales and purchases of electrical energy have
been determined by the simulation/optimization model since April 1983.
The comprehensive large-scalemodel developed for operation of water and
power in the State has been fully tested for weekly and is being tested
for daily operation. This model is scheduled for use in July 1986. It
will initially be used for determining preliminary schedules. After it
is fully tested, it will be used for hourly operation.

APPENDIX I.-REFERENCES

1. "Basic Facts Booklet, California Water Project", Division of
    Operations and Maintenance, Department of Water Resources, the
    Resources Agency, State of California.

2. Bellman, R. and Dreyfus, S., Applied Dynamic Programming, Princeton
    University Press, Princeton, New Jersey, 1962.

3. Ford, L. R., Jr., and Fulkerson, D., Flows in Networks, Princeton
    University Press, Princeton, N. J., 1976

4. Hadley, G., Linear Programming, Addison-Wesley Publishing Company,
    Inc., Reading, Mass., 1962.

5. Kahrl, W. L., The California Water Atlas, Department of Water
    Resources, State of California, 1978-1979.

6. Larson, R. E., State Increment Dynamic Programming, American
    Elsevier Publishing Co., Inc., New York, 1968.

7. Sabet, M. H. et al, "Optimal Operation of California Aqueduct",
    Journal of the Water Resources Planning and Management Division,
    ASCE, Vol. III, No. 2, April, 1985, pp. 222-237.

8. Texas Water Development Board, Economic Optimization and Simulation
    Techniques for Management of Regional Water Resources Systems,
    July, 1972, pp. 83-106.

Model to Maximize Releases For
Supplemental Generation in a Pump-Storage System

Ricardo S. Pineda, P.E.*

Abstract

An optimization model has been developed to maximize releases for supplemental power generation in a pump-storage system. The model was
developed to aid in the scheduling of pump-storage operations at two
facilities of the California State Water Project (SWP). These facilities, the San Luis Pump-Generating Plant and the Hyatt-Thermalito Pump-
Generating Plants and their accompanying reservoirs, play key roles in
the SWP's mandate to provide a firm supply of water and reliable sources
of energy needed to meet contractual demands of water in the San Joaquin
Valley and Southern California in the most economical way possible.

The model allows a base operation of pumping and/or generating to be
scheduled at the plant for a given study length (e.g., a week). This
study is then broken down into on-peak/off-peak time periods. Electrical energy during an on-peak time period has a higher economic value
for potential sale or exchange than does electrical energy during off-
peak time periods. The model optimizes the distribution of releases
and return pumping (pumpback) during the time periods so as to maximize
the volume of releases to be used for supplemental power generation
during the on-peak time periods. At the end of the study, the pumpback
volume and the supplemental generation volume are equal. The maximum
and minimum storage constraints in the two reservoirs of the pump-
storage system and the plant capacity constraints are maintained in
each time period.

To determine the maximum quantity and optimal distribution of releases
for supplemental power generation, the model represents the pump-
storage system as a flow network to be solved using a network flow
programming algorithm. A flow network is a collection of flow-carrying
arcs and continuity points referred to as nodes. Arcs come together at
nodes and continuity of flow is maintained at each node. Given a unit
cost for the flow in each arc, the network flow algorithm determines
the flow in each arc so as to minimize the total flow cost in the
network. The arc flows can then be translated into a hydraulically
feasible schedule of operations for the pump-storage system. The
network flow problem is solved using a method referred to as the "Out-
of-Kilter" algorithm. Once formulated, the network flow problem is
rapidly solved using a digital computer. The model is written in ASCII
Fortran V and does not require a large amount of computer memory nor
any proprietary computer programs.

* Associate Water Resources Engineer, California State Department of
Water Resources, P. O. Box 942836, Sacramento, CA 94236-0001

The pump-storage optimization problem can also be formulated as a
linear programming (LP) problem. The LP problem for a typical 12-time-
period week would contain 24 decision variables and 73 constraint
equations. The comparable flow network consists of 68 arcs and 24
nodes, which is comparatively a very small network.

The model is a low-cost, easy to use, and highly effective means of
determining an optimal schedule of releases and return pumping in a
pump-storage system, in order to maximize the amount of releases for
supplemental power generation. System operators can use the output of
the model to schedule a hydraulically feasible pump-storage operation
with little difficulty. The model has been tested on the San Luis and
Hyatt-Thermalito pump-storage facilities of the California State Water
Project and the results indicate that the model has the potential of
being highly beneficial as an aid in the operation of the SWP as an
interconnected bulk energy dealer.

Description of Model

The optimization model was developed to maximize releases for
supplemental power generation in a pump-storage system. A
representation of a typical pump-storage system is shown in Figure 1.
In a typical pump-storage system there are two reservoirs and one pump-
generating plant. For the pump-storage system shown in Figure 1, water
flows from Reservoir A to Reservoir B under pumping mode and from
Reservoir B to Reservoir A under generating mode. Unit volume energy
factors vary with the head on the pump-generating plant but for a given
volume of water, more energy is used in pumping than is recovered in
generation. Some pump-storage systems operate on a cyclical pump-
generating basis. In these systems, water is released to the
downstream reservoir (Reservoir A) during the day when energy demands
are high and electrical peaking capacity is required. The water that
has been released for generation is pumped back into the upstream
reservoir (Reservoir B) when energy demands are low and excess
electrical capacity is available.

A second type of system is one in which the pump-storage operation is
done in addition to a main (base) operation of pumping and/or
generating.In a system such as this, pumping and/or generating is
scheduled during the time periods and a secondary pump-storage operation
is scheduled in addition to the base operation in order to obtain energy
to meet peak energy demand loads. In both systems, the amount of water
released for supplemental power generation is equal to the amount of
water returned to storage through pumpback pumping. This ensures a net
change in reservoir storage equal to zero at the end of the study.

The model was developed to optimize the pump-storage operations at the
Hyatt-Thermalito Pump-Generating Plants and the San Luis Pump-
generating Plant. Both are facilities of the California State Water
Project and both operate with a base operation of pumping and/or
Generating. By specifying a base pumping and/or generating operation
equal to zero, the model can maximize the volume of releases for power
generation in a system that operates entirely as a cyclical pump-
storage system with no base operation.

FIGURE 1:
REPRESENTATION OF PUMP-STORAGE SYSTEM.

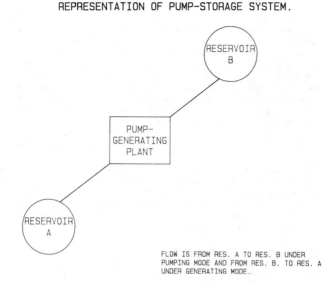

FLOW IS FROM RES. A TO RES. B UNDER
PUMPING MODE AND FROM RES. B. TO RES. A
UNDER GENERATING MODE.

FIGURE 2:
NETWORK REPRESENTATION OF PUMP-STORAGE
SYSTEM FOR A THREE-TIME-PERIOD ANALYSIS.

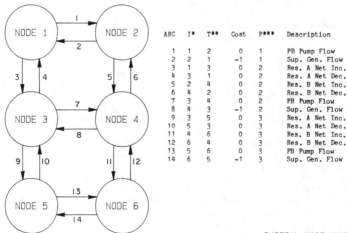

ARC	I*	T**	Cost	P***	Description
1	1	2	0	1	PB Pump Flow
2	2	1	-1	1	Sup. Gen. Flow
3	1	3	0	2	Res. A Net Inc.
4	3	1	0	2	Res. A Net Dec.
5	2	4	0	2	Res. B Net Inc.
6	4	2	0	2	Res. B Net Dec.
7	3	4	0	2	PB Pump Flow
8	4	3	-1	2	Sup. Gen. Flow
9	3	5	0	3	Res. A Net Inc.
10	5	3	0	3	Res. A Net Dec.
11	4	6	0	3	Res. B Net Inc.
12	6	4	0	3	Res. B Net Dec.
13	5	6	0	3	PB Pump Flow
14	6	5	-1	3	Sup. Gen. Flow

 * INITIAL NODE NUMBER.
 ** TERMINAL NODE NUMBER.
 *** TIME PERIOD NUMBER.

To determine the schedule of maximum releases for supplemental power
generation, the model divides the study into time periods referred to
as on-peak and off-peak periods. The model maximizes releases for
supplemental power generation during the on-peak periods because the
generated energy has its highest economic value during these periods.
In the given example, no scheme was established to rank in order of
importance the supplemental generation in the on-peak periods or the
pumpback pumping in the off-peak periods. All on-peak and off-peak
periods were given equal weight for the determination of the schedule
of releases for supplemental power generation in the system. However,
if desired, a weighting scheme for ranking the supplemental generation
and pumpback pumping in the on-peak and off-peak periods, respectively,
could be established by adjusting the unit flow cost for each arc in
the network representing supplemental generation and pumpback pumping.

The mathematical assumptions from which the flow network is devised are
stated in the equations in Appendix A. These equations are used to
formulate the model as a linear programming (LP) problem. For a weekly
analysis using the LP format, the problem would consist of 24 decision
variables and 73 constraint equations. This is a formidable problem
that could be solved more easily using the flow network technique.

The flow network shown in Figure 2 is a three-time-period
representation of the pump-storage system shown in Figure 1. In this
network, there are six nodes and 14 arcs. Each node acts as a
continuity point and each arc acts as a directional link between two
nodes. The flow on the arcs are the decision variables of the problem
and are determined by the network flow algorithm referred to as the
"Out-of-Kilter" algorithm (OKA). The OKA determines the flow on each
arc based upon minimizing the total cost of flow in the network. The
total cost of flow in the network is equal to the sum of the products
of the flow on each arc and the unit flow cost for that arc, for each
arc in the network. The flow on each arc is controlled by upper and
lower bounds on flow and by a unit flow cost. To maximize the amount
of releases for supplemental power generation in the pump-storage
system, a unit flow cost equal to -1 is assigned to the arcs
representing supplemental generation in each on-peak period. The unit
flow costs for all other arcs in the network are set to zero. The unit
flow cost for each arc is generally set to zero unless it is desired to
induce or inhibit flow on the arc. Flow on an arc is inhibited by
assigning a positive unit flow cost to the arc, where flow on an arc is
induced by assigning a negative unit flow cost to the arc.

For the sample network shown in Figure 2, nodes 1, 3, and 5 represent
continuity points for Reservoir A in time periods 1, 2, and 3,
respectively. Time periods 1 and 3 are on-peak periods and time period
2 is an off-peak period. Nodes 2, 4, and 6 represent continuity points
for Reservoir B. Arcs 1, 7, and 3 represent pumpback pumping in
periods 1, 2, and 3, respectively. Similarly, arcs 2, 8, and 14
represent the supplemental generation in each period. To prevent
generation in an off-peak period, the upper and lower bound on flow for
each arc representing supplemental generation in the off-peak periods

are set to zero. To prevent pumping in an on-peak period, the upper and lower bound on flow for each arc representing pumpback pumping in the on-peak periods are set to zero. Arcs 3 and 9 represent the net increase in storage in Reservoir A for periods 1 and 2, respectively. Similarly, arcs 5 and 6 represent the net increase in storage to Reservoir B. Arcs 4 and 10 represent the net decrease in storage in Reservoir A, and arcs 6 and 12 the net decrease in storage in Reservoir B. There are no increase or decrease arcs for period 3 since it is required that the net change in reservoir storage in the last time period be equal to zero. This ensures that the total pumpback pumping volume will be equal to the total release for supplemental generation for the study.

The model was verified through test runs using data from the Hyatt-Thermalito Pump-Generating complex and the San Luis Pump-Generating complex, both facilities of the SWP. The results of one such test are shown in Table 1 and Figures 3 and 4. In this example, the study length is equal to a week and the week is broken down into 12 on-peak and off-peak time periods. Oroville Reservoir is the upstream reservoir and Thermalito Afterbay is the downstream reservoir. Hyatt and Thermalito Pump-Generating Plants are located between the two reservoirs. There is a third reservoir that lies between the two plants but it is neglected in this analysis since pumpback flows are assumed to be equal through both plants. The test showed that a total of 13,883 MWH could be generated in the on-peak periods above the base generating schedule at each plant and that a total of 18,193 MWH of off-peak energy is required to return the water associated with this generation back into Oroville Reservoir. It is not shown in the data, but in each off-peak time period the maximum pumping capacity was utilized. If more pumping capacity was available, the network flow algorithm would have increased the amount of pumpback pumping and supplemental generation in the off-peak and on-peak time periods, respectively.

TABLE 1 : SUMMARY OF HYATT-THERMALITO PUMP-STORAGE OPERATIONS

PERIOD NUMBER	1	2	3	4	5	6	7	8	9	10	11	12	TOTAL
PERIOD LENGTH (HRS.)	14	10	14	10	14	10	14	10	14	10	14	34	168
PB PUMPING VOL.	0	1.728	0	1.728	0	1.728	0	2.81	0	2.81	0	16.706	27.51
PB GENERATING VOL.	12.761	0	12.753	0	1.996	0	0	0	0	0	0	0	27.51
ORVILLE END STOR.	4080.546	4076.698	4058.322	4054.496	4046.872	4042.843	4037.142	4036.409	4031.448	4030.714	4025.752	4043.261	
THERMALITO AFTERBAY END STOR.	38.69	38.945	52.408	52.693	55.355	54.188	54.188	51.378	51.378	48.568	48.568	21.34	
HYATT GENERATION E.	5608	0	5605	0	877	0	0	0	0	0	0	0	12090
THERMALITO GENERATION E.	832	0	831	0	130	0	0	0	0	0	0	0	1793
TOTAL GENERATION E.	6440	0	6436	0	1007	0	0	0	0	0	0	0	13883
HYATT PUMPING E.	0	975	0	975	0	975	0	1586	0	1586	0	9428	15525
THERMALITO PUMPING E.	0	168	0	168	0	168	0	272	0	272	0	1620	2668
TOTAL PUMPING E.	0	1143	0	1143	0	1143	0	1858	0	1858	0	11048	18193
HYATT BASE OPER. VOL.	7.803	7.141	7.811	7.12	7.818	7.32	7.89	5.108	7.151	5.108	7.151	4.513	81.934
THERMALITO BASE OPER. VOL.	11.364	9.684	11.372	9.663	11.379	8.211	10.712	7.651	10.711	7.651	10.712	15.553	124.663
ORVILLE BASE END STOR.	4093.307	4087.73	4082.108	4076.553	4070.925	4065.168	4059.467	4055.924	4047.411	4047.419	4042.457	4043.261	
THERMALITO AFTERBAY BASE END STOR.	25.929	27.962	28.622	30.635	31.301	31.862	31.862	31.862	31.862	31.862	31.862	21.34	

ALL VOLUMES IN CUBIC HM.
ALL ENERGY (E.) IS IN MWH.
AND IS A RESULT OF PUMPBACK
(PB.) OPERATIONS.

HYATT AND THERMALITO BASE OPERATIONS
+ GENERATING, - PUMPING.

FIGURE 3:
OROVILLE RESERVOIR ENDING STORAGE
VS. TIME

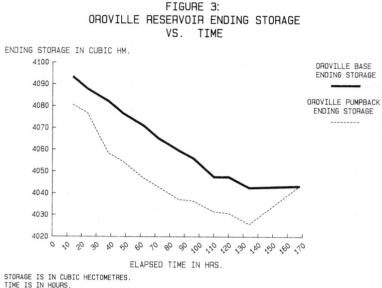

ENDING STORAGE IN CUBIC HM.

OROVILLE BASE
ENDING STORAGE

OROVILLE PUMPBACK
ENDING STORAGE

ELAPSED TIME IN HRS.

STORAGE IS IN CUBIC HECTOMETRES.
TIME IS IN HOURS.

FIGURE 4:
THERMALITO AFTERBAY ENDING STORAGE
VS. TIME

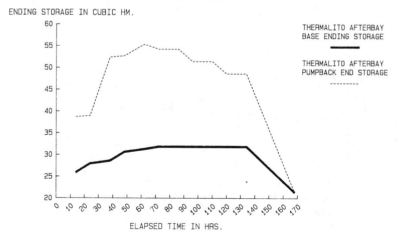

ENDING STORAGE IN CUBIC HM.

THERMALITO AFTERBAY
BASE ENDING STORAGE

THERMALITO AFTERBAY
PUMPBACK END STORAGE

ELAPSED TIME IN HRS.

STORAGE IS IN CUBIC HECTOMETRES.
TIME IS IN HOURS.

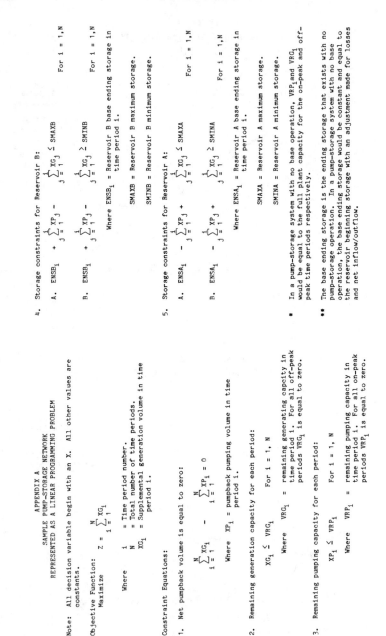

APPENDIX A
SAMPLE PUMP-STORAGE NETWORK
REPRESENTED AS A LINEAR PROGRAMMING PROBLEM

Note: All decision variable begin with an X. All other values are constants.

Objective Function:

Maximize $Z = \sum_{i=1}^{N} XG_i$

Where i = Time period number.
        N = Total number of time periods.
        XG_i = Supplemental generation volume in time period i.

Constraint Equations:

1. Net pumpback volume is equal to zero:

   $$\sum_{i=1}^{N} XG_i - \sum_{i=1}^{N} XP_i = 0$$

   Where XP_i = pumpback pumping volume in time period i.

2. Remaining generation capacity for each period:

   $$XG_i \leq VRG_i \qquad \text{For } i = 1, N$$

   Where VRG_i = remaining generating capacity in time period i. For all off-peak periods VRG_i is equal to zero.

3. Remaining pumping capacity for each period:

   $$XP_i \leq VRP_i \qquad \text{For } i = 1, N$$

   Where VRP_i = remaining pumping capacity in time period i. For all on-peak periods VRP_i is equal to zero.

4. Storage constraints for Reservoir B:

   A. $ENSB_i + \sum_{j=1}^{i} XP_j - \sum_{j=1}^{i} XG_j \leq SMAXB \qquad \text{For } i = 1,N$

   B. $ENSB_i + \sum_{j=1}^{i} XP_j - \sum_{j=1}^{i} XG_j \geq SMINB \qquad \text{For } i = 1,N$

   Where $ENSB_i$ = Reservoir B base ending storage in time period i.

   $SMAXB$ = Reservoir B maximum storage.

   $SMINB$ = Reservoir B minimum storage.

5. Storage constraints for Reservoir A:

   A. $ENSA_i - \sum_{j=1}^{i} XP_j + \sum_{j=1}^{i} XG_j \leq SMAXA \qquad \text{For } i = 1,N$

   B. $ENSA_i - \sum_{j=1}^{i} XP_j + \sum_{j=1}^{i} XG_j \geq SMINA \qquad \text{For } i = 1,N$

   Where $ENSA_i$ = Reservoir A base ending storage in time period i.

   $SMAXA$ = Reservoir A maximum storage.

   $SMINA$ = Reservoir A minimum storage.

* In a pump-storage system with no base operation, VRP_i and VRG_i would be equal to the full plant capacity for the on-peak and off-peak time periods respectively.

** The base ending storage is the ending storage that exists with no pump-storage operation. In a pump-storage system with no base operation, the base ending storage would be constant and equal to the reservoir beginning storage with an adjustment made for losses and net inflow/outflow.

APPENDIX B
REFERENCES

Durbin, E. P., and Kroehke, D. M., The Out-Of-Kilter Algorithm A Primer, RM-5472-PR, The Rand Corporation, December 1967.

Ford, L. R., Jr., and Fulkerson, D., Flow in Networks, Princeton University Press, Princton, N. J., 1962.

Jensen, Paul A., and Barnes, J. Wesley, Network Flow Programming, John Wiley and Sons, Inc., New York 1980.

Martin, Quenten, Optimal Operation of Surface Water Resources Systems for Water Supply and Hydroelectric Power Generation, Texas Department of Water Resources Austin, Texas, November 1980.

Rosenthal, Richard E., A Nonlinear Network Flow Algorithm for Maximization of Benefits in a Hydroelectric Power system, Management Science Program The University of Tennessee, Knoxville, Tennessee, August 1979.

Taha, H. A., Operations Research, MacMillan Publishing Co. Inc., New York, 1976.

Texas Water Development Board, Economic Optimization and Simulation Techniques for Management of Regional Water Resources Systems, Texas, July 1972.

Woolsey, Robert E. D. and Swanson, Hunington S., Operations Research for Immediate Application, Harper and Row Publishers, New York, 1975.

INTRASTATE AND INTERSTATE WATER TRANSFERS

Dean T. Massey[*]

ABSTRACT: Water transfers may be affected by either or both federal or state law. Riparian states generally do not permit transfers of water outside the watershed of origin, while the opposite is true in the appropriation states provided there is no harm to existing appropriators. Statutes prohibiting the export of water may be an unconstitutional burden on interstate commerce. The test is one of reasonableness in light of competing state and federal interests. The three mechanisms utilized to apportion interstate water are interstate compacts approved by Congress, judicial allocation and legislative allocation. Interstate litigation results when states have failed to negotiate an apportionment among themselves. Courts use a judicial decree to allocate the disputed interstate water among contesting states by applying the "equitable apportionment" doctrine. Congressional apportionment has been used once, to apportion water in the lower Colorado River basin. The federal government may preempt existing state control over water rights for matters concerning interstate commerce, navigation and the development of federal projects.

INTRODUCTION

Transfers of water in the United States may be affected by either or both federal or state law under our dual form of government depending upon the origin of the water for the transfer, whether the transfer is intrastate or interstate and the type of water used for the transfer. The division between powers delegated to the federal government under the U.S. Constitution to regulate water and those reserved to the states in its 10th amendment is not always clear and sharp. Water within state boundaries is generally managed and allocated according to state and local laws unless Congress chooses to exercise a constitutional based power that requires water.

Sources of water for transfers may be from watercourses or lakes located wholly within a single state or from interstate watercourses or lakes. Transfers may involve intrastate transfers of intrastate and interstate water, interstate transfers of intrastate water or interstate transfers of interstate water. Interstate water may also involve boundary waters between two or more states that must be allocated among them. Different state laws may be applicable to the transfer of surface or ground water. State water laws governing transfers, particularly for intrastate transfers, may also differ depending upon whether the state adheres to the riparian or prior

[*]Attorney, Law School, University of Wisconsin, Madison, Wis. 53706

appropriation doctrines or to a hybrid system that respects both doctrines. Either the "absolute ownership" or "reasonable use" rule is used to allocate groundwater in the riparian states and some of the appropriation states. Some appropriation states also use the "correlative rights" or "prior appropriation" rules.

This article deals with federal and state laws governing transfers of water, whether such transfers are intrastate or interstate. Most of the article is devoted to an analysis of the laws relating to intrastate water transfers, interstate transfers of intrastate water and transfers of interstate water. The article then analyzes the federal powers relating to water transfers.

INTRASTATE TRANSFERS OF WATER

Intrastate transfers of either intrastate or interstate water may depend upon which doctrine the state adheres to, if the transfer is to a watershed other than the one where the water supply originated and if the water rights are attached to or separate from the land where first applied. Different laws apply to transfers of water to another parcel of land within the watershed of its origin than to transfers of water to a parcel of land outside the watershed. If water rights are attached to the land, a transfer depends upon whether they are severable from the land and the conditions upon which they are severable.

The use of water under the riparian doctrine is generally restricted to riparian lands and to the watershed of the water source. Water use on land not adjoining the water body, even though owned by the riparian and within the same watershed, may be prohibited regardless of actual harm to others under the "natural flow" rule. The "reasonable use" rule requires proof of actual harm from a riparian's use of water on nonriparian land within the same watershed. Generally any use of water on land outside the watershed, even though the land is a part of a tract adjoining a stream, is unreasonable per se and prohibited even if it does not cause injury. A few states will now permit a transfer of water to nonriparian land outside the watershed if others are not harmed (Getches, 1984; Laitos, 1985).

Riparians ordinarily transfer riparian rights when they sell the land. However, rights to use the water may be expressly reserved by riparian landowners when they sell parts of their riparian land to others. A different situation arises if a riparian landowner seeks to transfer riparian rights to a nonriparian within the same watershed without selling a portion of the riparian land. The general rule is that a transfer of riparian rights by a riparian landowner to a nonriparian is binding between the parties. A riparian landowner gives up the right to divert or use any water for which the rights have been transferred to another. However, a majority of the states hold that transfers of riparian rights separate from the sale of any portion of the riparian land held by the seller are invalid as to other riparians. Thus, a nonriparian who purchases the water rights cannot object to other riparians' conduct even if the conduct would have been considered unreasonable to the original riparian transferrer of the water rights (Cox, 1982; Getches, 1984).

All appropriation doctrine states allow appropriators to transfer
water rights separately from the land to another parcel of land by
sale or lease subject to certain statutory restrictions. Statutes
permit water rights to be severed from the land under conditions that
protect other users. When a severance has been effected, the water
right becomes attached to the new land without loss of priority of
appropriation. A transfer of water rights may not exceed the quantity
of water under the rights held by the transferrer. Transferring water
from one watershed to another is permitted under the appropriation
doctrine provided it causes no harm to existing appropriators in the
watershed of origin. Unappropriated water, however, may be transferred as needed. Some appropriation states permit the establishment
of special management districts or control areas where severe groundwater shortages exist and allow them to adopt very restrictive rules
regarding transfers (Laitos, 1985; Massey, 1983).

INTERSTATE TRANSFERS OF INTRASTATE WATER

Several states, more particularly those in the West, have statutes that forbid or limit the transfer of intrastate water for use out
of the state. These anti-export statutes fall into three generalized
but distinct categories. The first endeavors to create an absolute
prohibition of the interstate transfer of intrastate surface or ground
water or both. The second allows the exportation of intrastate water
only if receiving state reciprocates in allowing exports. Under the
third category, the legislature, governor or state agency must approve
all exports or at least those in excess of a certain quantity. The
purported purpose of these statutes is to preserve scarce water
resources by limiting nonresident access to local supplies (Clyde,
1982).

Anti-export statutes may be challenged in federal courts as being
an unconstitutional burden on interstate commerce. Congress has
authority under the Commerce Clause of the Constitution to regulate
commerce among the several states. The Commerce Clause forbids states
from adopting statutes that discriminate against or unreasonably
burden interstate commerce, even though Congress has not legislated in
the affected area. Statutes that are protectionist in nature and
discriminate on their face or in their application will be held
invalid (Clyde, 1982; Massey, 1983).

Water has been held to be an article of commerce and as such
subject to the Commerce Clause; therefore, its transfer cannot be
restricted in any way that discriminates against interstate commerce
(Sporhase, 1982). The validity of anti-export statutes is dependent
upon the type of water exportation restrictions that are imposed by
the statutes and if those restrictions impose an impermissible burden
on interstate commerce in violation of the Commerce Clause. The test
to evaluate the validity of anti-export statutes considers: (1) an
evaluation to see if legitimate state or local interests for keeping
the water within the state are present; (2) the evanhandedness of the
statute by comparing it with statutes on intrastate transfers to see
if the state discriminates against nonresidents; (3) the balancing of
state or local benefits and the burden on interstate commerce to see

if state or local interests outweigh any competing national interest;
and (4) assuming a legitimate state or local interest does exist,
whether the purpose could be better achieved by alternatives with less
discrimination against interstate commerce (Massey, 1983).

Essentially, the four-part test is one of reasonableness in light
of competing state and federal interests. Consideration is given to
whether a state has a strong interest in protecting its own resources
and has regulations to do so. The federal interest in free trade,
along with other federal interests, will be weighed against such state
interests. A finding that a statute is discriminatory does not in
itself make it unconstitutional if the burden is reasonable and a less
burdensome regulatory alternative does not exist. This may involve a
complex inquiry into the way a state's water allocation system might
be operated, short of embargo legislation, to conserve water effectively. An obvious alternative might be to impose intrastate
restrictions on water use (Abrams, 1983; Getches, 1984).

Absolute embargoes prohibiting interstate transfers are unconstitutional except in extreme circumstances. In order for the court
to find that there is no alternative less burdensome upon commerce
than an embargo, a state would have to prove water scarcity and
maximum efforts to deal with the problem by in-state conservation
measures. Reciprocal embargoes are improper because they are not
based on factors that justify state restrictions for conservation
purposes, but upon the legislative choices of the sister state.
Embargo statutes that prove objectionable may be replaced by statutes
imposing various discriminatory conditions upon out-of-state uses.
Statutes requiring legislative or administrative approval of exports
are supported by a state interest in dealing with a variety of water
users (Abrams, 1983; Massey, 1983).

TRANSFERS OF INTERSTATE WATER

Rivers, groundwater and lakes often do not respect state boundaries, thus producing disputes between states. States have an
interest not only in receiving their fair share of interstate water,
but also in protecting their citizens from upstream activities that
affect the quantity and quality of water. An upstream state may
attempt to divert excessive amounts of water or build a dam on an
interstate river, thereby diminishing the amount of water available to
downstream states or alter or degrade the quality of the downstream
water by discharging pollutants in the river. One state's water
rights system cannot allocate rights to water with complete disregard
for water needs of other states along the interstate waterway.

Because traditional state control of water ends at a state's
boundaries, interstate allocative mechanisms must be employed both to
resolve and avoid interstate disputes. The three basic mechanisms
utilized to apportion interstate water are interstate compacts,
judicial allocation by interstate litigation and legislative allocation by congressional apportionment (Getches, 1984; Laitos, 1985).

Interstate Compacts

By far the most common and effective allocative mechanism is the
interstate compact, where states within a basin negotiate an apportionment of water among themselves. Over 20 compacts allocating
interstate water resources have been negotiated by states and approved
by Congress. Allocation of water among states can be in terms of a
specific number of acre-feet, percentage of total stream flow or a more
general allocation based on "equitable apportionment" principles. A
compact also allows states to allocate unappropriated water for future
use (Laitos, 1985).

Interstate compacts may adversely affect public or private water
rights established by state law and may restrict diversions for all
types of intrastate transfers. Delivery of certain quantities of water
pursuant to a compact become the most senior water commitment in the
river system. Thus, all surface and ground water diversions by state
water rights holders are subject to regulation to the extent necessary
to deliver the amount of water required by the compact terms. State
legislation that conflicts with the terms of an interstate compact
cannot prevent enforcement of the compact, and a water rights decree
under state law cannot confer water rights in excess of the state's
share of water. Apportionment of water by a compact is binding upon
the citizens of the compacting states whether or not citizens were
parties to the negotiation (Getches, 1984).

Judicial Allocation

When states have made no effort to negotiate water rights, or have
been unable to agree upon apportionment of them for their citizens,
interstate litigation results for a judicial adjudication of those
rights. Interstate litigation may involve disputes between private
citizens of two different states, a private citizen of one state
against another state or two different states against each other. In
many instances a state may become involved on behalf of its citizens by
suing another state to prevent harm to its citizens by actions of
private citizens in the other state.

Typically, private litigation over water rights occurs when a
downstream water user sues an upstream water user in another state
because the upstream water user has interfered or threatens to
interfere with the downstream user's asserted rights. Actions may be
brought in federal courts by private citizens if there is a diversity
of citizenship, the financial amount of the controversy is sufficient
and a federal question is involved (Getches, 1984). Federal courts have
long established their jurisdiction over interstate water disputes
(Kansas, 1907).

If states disagree over the apportionment of water from interstate
streams, the dispute may be adjudicated in the U.S. Supreme Court. The
Constitution grants that Court original jurisdiction in all cases in
which a state is a party. Statutes provide that in controversies
between two or more states the Supreme Court's jurisdiction is
exclusive (Getches, 1984; Laitos, 1985).

The Supreme Court uses a judicial decree to allocate the disputed interstate water among the contesting states by applying the "equitable apportionment" doctrine. A basic tenet of the doctrine is that "equity of right," coupled with a balancing of equities that will establish justice between the states, and not equality of amounts apportioned, should govern. Each state is awarded a quantity of water from the interstate stream that is distributed by the state's allocation system (Kansas, 1907). The Court in making an equitable apportionment considers existing uses, new uses, efficiency of uses and maximum value of the water (Colorado, 1982). The decree in an adjudication between states is binding on all claimants to the water, whether or not they were parties to the suit (Getches, 1984).

Legislative Allocation

Another procedure to resolve disputes relating to interstate water is by an act of Congress. Congressional apportionment has been used only once, and that was by the Boulder Canyon Project Act of 1928 concerning water in the Colorado River. The act apportioned interstate water in the lower Colorado River basin between Arizona and California (Laitos, 1985).

FEDERAL POWERS OVER WATER TRANSFERS

State law generally controls the creation and nature of water rights; however, it is subject to preemption by the federal government for matters concerning interstate commerce and navigation, development of federal water projects, federal water quality protection statutes, international treaty obligations and the need to carry out programs and policies on public lands. The federal government has built dams for flood control, licensed hydroelectric generation facilities, improved navigability of watercourses, authorized a network of irrigation projects and imposed protections on certain rivers and streams for wildlife preservation and recreation. Congress has powers to regulate navigation under the Commerce Clause, to manage federal property under the Property Clause, to tax and spend funds for the general welfare of the people and to provide for the defense of the nation. When these powers are properly asserted, they override conflicting state laws under the Supremacy Clause (Ellis, 1970).

The most important source of federal authority over water is its power under the Commerce Clause to regulate commerce among the several states. As navigation has been held to be a function of commerce, commerce on all waters that are interstate and navigable is subject to regulation by Congress (Gibbons, 1824). Under the current federal test of navigability, a watercourse is navigable if it is navigable in fact, could be navigable with reasonable improvements or was once navigable (Getches, 1984). The power to control navigable waters may include the power to protect the navigable capacity of a watercourse by preventing diversions of the water itself or of the water in nonnavigable tributaries that affect navigability or by preventing obstructions, such as the construction of flood control structures or hydroelectric generation projects, that affect stream flow. It may also include the power to destroy the navigable capacity of the watercourse and prevent navigation by permitting diversions and the construction of obstructions (Laitos, 1985).

Federal powers over navigable waters may be exercised affirma-
tively, negatively and permissively. The federal government may take
affirmative action by improving navigation channels and harbors and
constructing protective works. Negatively, the federal government may
prohibit interference with the navigable capacity of water over which
it exercises jurisdiction under the Commerce Clause. Permissively, the
federal government may license that which it may prevent or delegate to
others that which it may itself do (Ellis, 1970).

Congress's interest in the nation's water resources also includes
the authorization to divert water to irrigate arid lands in the West.
The Reclamation Act of 1902 was passed to bring these lands into
agricultural production by the construction of federal irrigation
projects for the benefit of public and privately-owned lands.
Congressional reclamation authority was first based on the Property
Clause, under which Congress may pass laws for the management of
federal property, but the power to tax and spend funds to promote the
general welfare provided a later basis (Getches, 1984; Laitos, 1985).

SUMMARY AND CONCLUSIONS

Intrastate transfers of water may depend upon whether the state
adheres to the riparian or appropriation doctrine, the transfer is to a
watershed other than the one where the water supply originated, the
water rights are attached to or separate from the land where first
applied and the water is surface or ground. Different laws apply to
transfers of water to another parcel of land within the watershed of
its origin than to transfers of water to a parcel of land outside the
watershed. The use of water under the riparian doctrine is generally
restricted to riparian land and to the watershed of its origin. All
appropriation doctrine states allow appropriators to transfer water
rights separately from the land to another parcel of land by sale or
lease subject to certain statutory restrictions regardless of whether
the water is transferred within or without the watershed.

Anti-export statutes forbidding or limiting the transfer of water
out-of-state may be challenged as being an unconstitutional burden on
interstate commerce. The validity of these statutes is dependent upon
the type of restrictions imposed and whether they impose an impermissible burden on interstate commerce. Essentially, the test is one
of reasonableness in light of the competing state and federal
interests. A state may not discriminate against nonresidents by
imposing stricter requirements on out-of-state transfers than on
in-state transfers.

The three basic mechanisms used to apportion interstate water are
interstate compacts, judicial allocation and legislative allocation.
Delivery of certain quantities of water pursuant to a compact becomes
the most senior water commitment in the river system. If states
disagree over the apportionment of water, federal courts use a judicial
decree to allocate the disputed water among the contesting states by
applying the "equitable apportionment" doctrine. Local law of the
states bordering the stream is used as the basis for apportioning the

stream's flow. Legislative allocation of interstate water by
congressional act has been used once to apportion water in the lower
Colorado River basin.

Congress relies on a number of constitutional powers to oversee
the nation's water resources in preempting state laws controlling water
rights. These include powers to regulate navigation, manage federal
property and tax and spend funds for the general welfare. The most
important source of federal jurisdiction is its power to regulate
navigation among the states. This power to regulate extends to
removing obstructions that interfere with navigation and constructing
structures that destroy navigation, such as flood control and hydroelectric generation projects. It may also include the power to protect
watercourses by preventing diversions of the water itself. Congress
has the authority under its spending and property powers to develop
projects to supply irrigation water for arid lands.

APPENDIX -- REFERENCES

1. Abrams, R.H., "Interbasin Transfers in a Riparian Jurisdiction,"
    William & Mary Law Review, Vol. 24, No. 4, 1983, pp. 591,
    608-621.

2. Clyde, S.E., "State Prohibitions on the Interstate Exportation of
    Scarce Water Resources," University of Colorado Law Review, Vol.
    53, No. 3, 1982, pp. 529-540.

3. Colorado vs. New Mexico, 459 U.S. 176, 103 Sup. Ct. 539 (1982).

4. Cox, W.E., "Establishment and Maintenance of Water Rights in the
    Eastern United States," Agricultural Law Journal, Vol. 4, No. 1,
    Callaghan & Co., Wilmette, Ill., 1982, pp. 53, 58-63.

5. Ellis, H.H., Beuscher, J.H., Howard, C.D., & DeBraal, J.P.,
    Water-Use Law and Administration in Wisconsin, University of
    Wisconsin Press, Madison, Wis., 1970, Chap. 17, pp. 472-523.

6. Getches, D.H., Water Law in a Nutshell, West Publishing Co., St.
    Paul, Minn., 1984.

7. Gibbons vs. Ogden, 22 U.S. 1 (1824).

8. Kansas vs. Colorado, 206 U.S. 46, 27 Sup. Ct. 655 (1907).

9. Laitos, J.G., Natural Resources Law, West Publishing Co., St.
    Paul, Minn., 1985, Chap. 7, pp. 472-639.

10. Massey, D.T., Hong, A.C., & Szilagyi, A., "Interstate Transfer of
    Colorado Water for San Marco Coal Slurry Pipeline," Oklahoma Law
    Review, Vol. 36, No. 1, 1983, pp. 1, 16-29, 41-56.

11. Sporhase vs. Nebraska, 458 U.S. 941, 102 Sup. Ct. 3456 (1982).

Evolving Institutions For Water Transfer in the U.S.

William C. Cox,* M.ASCE

Abstract

   Water transfer has been a basic water management tool during
development of the United States. Water transfers have always been
controversial, and the institutional framework within which transfer
must be implemented imposes several constraints. A major source of
constraint is state water allocation law, which defines rights for
water use and development, including in some cases restrictions on
place of use that limit transfer. Powers of state governments to
control water transfer to locations outside the state of origin are
restricted by the powers of the federal government regarding
interstate commerce. The federal role also encompasses direct
participation in water development activities, including projects
involving significant water transfers. The federal government also
regulates water development by others. The existing institutional
framework is necessarily complex, but excessive complexity should be
controlled. Need for water transfer will continue to arise, and
efficient resolution of associated conflict will continue to be an
important function of water management institutions.

Introduction

   Transfer of water has been a basic management tool for balancing
water supply and demand during the history of the United States.
Interbasin transfers in some cases have been implemented to provide
water to areas of limited local supplies from other areas, sometimes
at considerable distances, where water is relatively abundant.
Transfers have also occurred in humid regions, illustrating that
concentrations of population and socio-economic development
activities can create demands that exceed local supplies even where
such supplies are relatively abundant.

   Water transfer has always been a controversial activity. An area
identified as the source of water to be transferred can be expected
to be concerned about potential impacts on current and future
activities dependent on water. The traditional concern focusing on
impacts on productive activities has been expanded to include impacts
on environmental attributes of water in its natural state. Concern

*Associate Professor, Civil Engineering Department, Virginia Tech,
Blacksburg, VA 24061

over impacts, both real and imagined, is generally translated into
active opposition to transfer proposals.

Water transfer opposition can be expressed in a variety of ways
within the institutional framework for water management decisions.
A primary control is state water allocation law that defines legal
rights for water use. These rights, together with supplemental state
regulation for environmental protection and other purposes, are an
important institutional factor in any water development proposal. A
basic consequence of state definition of water rights is the tendency
for state boundaries to serve as obstacles to water transfer since
states may attempt to restrict export of water. Since states generally delegate some of their authority to lower levels of government,
local political boundaries can also serve as obstacles to water
transfer.

Attempts by states to prohibit or limit interstate water transfer
are subject to federal powers as defined by the U.S. Constitution.
Federal powers include several water management activities, with
regulation of interstate commerce the most significant authority
relative to water transfer. This authority establishes constraints
on state powers to control interstate transfers and can also be
exerted in other ways that impact state management activities.

This brief institutional overview identifies three issues in need
of more detailed analysis. First, the provisions of state water
allocation law need consideration as they relate to the transfer
issue. Second, attention needs to be given to the extent to which
various political boundaries serve as obstacles to transfer,
including an assessment of the authority of the federal government to
override state attempts to constrain interstate transfer. Third,
additional powers of the federal government that either facilitate or
constrain transfer require analysis.

Status of Transfer Under State Water Allocation Law

Water allocation law has evolved independently within the
individual states, but the states traditionally have been grouped
into two categories on the basis of similarity of applicable laws:
the western states that accept the doctrine of prior appropriation
and the eastern states that accept the riparian doctrine. These
categories remain valid, but a third category should be added to
include states that have adopted administrative water allocation
systems not based on either of the two traditional doctrines.

Appropriation doctrine states. The central principle of the
appropriation doctrine is that the right to use water from a natural
source should be assigned to water users on the basis of the demonstrated ability to apply water to a beneficial use. Although establishment of an appropriation now generally requires administrative
approvals as well, application of water to a beneficial use continues
to serve as a fundamental component of the appropriation process.
The doctrine protects those who develop water first by imposing a
hierarchy on water rights wherein standing is determined on the basis

of date of initiation of water use (or date on which related construction commenced). Each water right is of superior standing to those
initiated at later dates and inferior to all initiated at earlier
dates (Clark, 1967-1984).

In keeping with its applicability in areas of general water
scarcity, the traditional appropriation doctrine contains no constraints on the transfer of newly appropriated water. Use of water
on land adjacent to a stream is given no preference relative to use
on land removed from the stream in question, and use within the
watershed is not preferred over use outside the watershed.

Transfer of water in the appropriation states is not always
without constraint, however. Certain states have supplemented the
basic concepts of the appropriation doctrine with measures to protect
areas where water originates from detrimental export. Such protection is likely to include reservation of water for future development
of the area of origin and for maintenance of natural environmental
conditions (Robie and Kletzing, 1979).

A second form of constraint exists where transfers involve previously appropriated water. Initiation of new water uses through
acquisition of previously appropriated water is generally feasible
since appropriative rights are transferable among water uses, users,
and locations of use. Such transfers are subject to governmental
supervision, however, and constraints are imposed to prevent adverse
impacts on other parties. Protection of return flows on which other
water rights are based is a major focus when rights transfers are
proposed. Where existing appropriations are being acquired for
transfer, protection of other water users will likely require limitation of the water that can be transferred to the amount consumed in
the previous use (Trelease and Lee, 1966; Williams, 1973).

Riparian doctrine states. The water right under the riparian
doctrine is defined as a component of ownership of land bordering a
natural watercourse. As a component of real property, riparian
rights do not have to be exercised to be given legal recognition but
can exist indefinitely in a dormant state. Under the generally
accepted form of the doctrine at present, the riparian right includes
the right to make a reasonable use of water on riparian land.
Reasonableness is a relative matter dependent on the circumstances of
the individual case; therefore the riparian right, unlike the
appropriative right is not fixed in magnitude but can vary over time
with changing water availability and water-use activities.

Transfer of water under the riparian doctrine is subject to the
inherent limitation that water must be used on riparian land. The
basic requirement for land to be considered riparian to a particular
stream is physical contact. The maximum extent of riparian land is
the boundary of a stream's watershed, and any portion of a tract of
land extending outside the water shed is excluded from riparian
status (Farnham, 1972). This restriction is a theoretical prohibition of interbasin transfer. The prohibition is, however, subject to
an important qualification: its enforcement requires a lawsuit by an

injured riparian landowner. Where surplus water exists, transfers
may lawfully be implemented, and interbasin transfers are relatively
common in riparian jurisdictions.

Nevertheless, the riparian doctrine's prohibition of interbasin
transfer continues to be a major factor whenever transfers are
proposed in riparian jurisdictions. Determining whether the
prohibition will apply is complicated by the difficulty of
identifying surplus water not needed for satisfaction of riparian
rights. Opponents of a proposed transfer will invariably claim that
the transfer is prohibited by the riparian doctrine, and the potential transferrer will confront substantial uncertainty regarding the
legal validity of the transfer. Uncertainty associated with the
riparian doctrine generally must be resolved through a court
proceedings (Cox and Shabman, 1984).

States With Other Administrative Allocation Programs. Several
states in recent years have replaced traditional allocation systems
with alternative allocation programs implemented through administrative permitting programs. Since these programs are based on
detailed legislation, they differ from one another in certain
provisions, but they share basic characteristics. They generally
have one feature in common with the appropriative doctrine: existing
water uses are protected by prohibition or restriction of new water
uses. They differ from appropriation in that permitted water uses
usually have equal standing rather than a hierarchal order. In times
of shortage, permit holders may be subjected to restrictions that
apply uniformly to all uses or to designated categories of use (see,
e.g., Fla. Stat. Ann. secs. 373.013 et seq.).

Allocation programs in this category generally do not prohibit
transfer of water. Removal of constraints on the efficient use of
water (such as the riparian doctrine's limitation of water use to
riparian land) is one reason for development of alternative
allocation systems. The desirability of a proposed use generally is
evaluated in terms of a wide range of considerations, with location
of use viewed as one factor among several.

State Controls Supplemental to Water Allocation Law. Water
transfer is likely to be subject to other state control measures that
operate simultaneously with the allocation system. These
supplemental controls generally focus on construction of water
development facilities. They are designed to achieve a variety of
objectives, one of the most fundamental of which is protection of
natural environmental conditions. Individual controls provide
protection for such components of the environment as scenic rivers,
historical sites, fish and wildlife, and wetlands (Cox and Shabman,
1983). Construction activities inconsistent with the objectives of
these controls may be restricted or completely prohibited, in some
cases after the water-rights issues associated with the activity have
been resolved.

Political Boundaries as Obstacles to Transfer

Political entities tend to view activities within their boundaries differently than they do similar activities outside their boundaries. In the case of application of water to a productive use, a political body is likely to favor water use within its boundaries and may attempt to restrain or prohibit water export.

Local Governmental Boundaries. Local powers generally do not include direct water allocation authority, but local influence over water transfer can be asserted whenever local governments are given authority over water resource development. In some cases, local authority can be substantial. In the State of Virginia, for example, a local government desiring to develop a water supply within the boundaries of a second jurisdiction must obtain permission from that jurisdiction. Such authority to approve or disapprove is not absolute, however. If approval is denied, an appeal to a specifically constituted court is authorized (Va. Code Ann. sec. 15.1-37). In some cases, a state itself may use local political boundaries as constraints in water transfer. For example, the state of California has focused on county boundaries in certain area-of-origin protection legislation (Cal. Water Code sec. 10505).

State Boundaries. State boundaries have frequently posed an obstacle to water transfer. One of the common forms taken by constraints on interstate water movement has been state reciprocity legislation prohibiting export to any state not allowing transfer of water in the opposition direction between the two states. State-imposed constraints on interstate water transport are limited by federal authority to regulate interstate commerce.

The 1982 U.S. Supreme Court case of Sporhase v. Nebraska (458 U.S. 941, 1982) involved use of water pumped from a well on Nebraska land to irrigate land in Colorado. No permit for the groundwater use had been requested and would not have been available since Nebraska law on export of water required reciprocity from the other state involved, a condition not satisfied by Colorado law. The U.S. Supreme Court held that a reciprocity requirement not tailored to a legitimate state resource conservation issue is inconsistent with federal authority over interstate commerce.

Sporhase limits state power to control interstate transport of water, but certain power is recognized. First, the Supreme Court suggested that the power to restrict export of water during times of severe shortage, a condition not demonstrated in the Sporhase case, would likely be upheld. Second, the Court indicated that restrictions on export generally would be valid if closely related to legitimate water conservation efforts. The court suggested that, with proper evidence, a total ban on exportation may be justified by consideration of legitimate conservation needs. Thus, the Sporhase decision, while holding that state laws categorically discriminating against out-of-state water users are invalid, has preserved substantial flexibility for restricting export where such action is closely related to valid water management objectives.

Additional Federal Involvement in Water Transfer

The federal role in water transfer is substantially broader than
exercise of its power to limit state constraints on interstate
commerce. These additional functions include both direct
participation in transfer projects as well as imposition of its own
constraints on transfer by other parties.

Federal Participation in Transfer Projects. The federal government traditionally has been a major water resources developer. The
original focus of attention was enhancement of navigation by improvement of navigable waters, an activity authorized by the power of
national government to regulate interstate and foreign commerce.
Subsequent to this origin associated with improvement of navigation,
water development activities of the federal government have grown to
encompass most of the major objectives of water management, including
significant water transfer.

Federal participation in water transfer projects raises the
question of the extent to which such action can override state water
allocation law. Federal power to carry out or approve transfers
without regard to state law appears clear where navigable waters are
involved. Extensive powers were recognized by the U.S. Supreme court
in the 1963 case of Arizona v. California (373 U.S. 546, 1963). The
Court found that legislative approval for the Hoover Dam project on
the Colorado River and actions of the Secretary of Interior in
forming contracts for project water, including contracts for
interbasin transfer, constituted an allocation of the water not
constrained by state law. A recent Supreme Court decision
(California v. United States, 438 U.S. 645, 1978) acknowledged the
right of the states to impose conditions on certain federal water
projects in some situations, but federal powers are extensive.

Although constitutional authority may exist, the potential for the
national government to implement projects for the transfer of water
from one region of the country to another is limited by other
considerations. Exercise of national powers involves the interaction
of opposing interests within the political process, and the
representatives of potential areas of origin for water transfer often
are successful in obstructing implementation of proposals for major
transfers.

Federal Restriction of Water Transfers. Federal control of
navigable waters also includes restriction of water transfer or other
development adverse to federal interests. The power to prohibit
interference with navigability was upheld by the U.S. Supreme Court
as early as 1899 in a case involving proposed construction of dams
and diversion of water from the Rio Grande River in the territory
later to become the State of New Mexico (United States v. Rio Grande
Dam and Irrigation Co., 174 U.S. 690, 1899). Since its first
application to protect navigability, the power to regulate water
resources development has expanded to include environmental
protection.

Control over water development is exerted through regulatory
programs under three principal federal laws: the Rivers and Harbors
Act of 1899 (33 U.S.C.A. secs. 401 et seq.), the Federal Power Act
(16 U.S.C.A. sec 791a et seq.), and section 404 of the Clean Water
Act (33 U.S.C.A. secs. 1251 et seq.). Issuance of permits under
these three permitting programs is constrained by other legislation
intended to ensure consideration of various interests in the
regulatory process and to provide a degree of protection for such
interests (these constraints also generally apply to activities
undertaken or funded by federal agencies). The broadest of these
measures is the National Environmental Policy Act (42 U.S.C.A. secs.
4321 et seq.), but a variety of other constraints exist (see Cox and
Shabman, 1983).

Conclusion

The institutional framework for water transfer in the United
States is complex. Because of the inherent tendency of transfer
proposal to be controversial, this institutional complexity
essentially ensures lengthy conflict whenever transfer proposals are
developed. Comprehensive review of transfer proposals is desirable
because of the potential of certain transfers to create harmful
effects in excess of benefits. However, excessive institutional
complexity can lead to undesirable results. Protracted conflict
leads to unnecessary delays and costs in reaching decisions and in
some cases may lead to inappropriate choices of water supply
strategies. For example, the inability to resolve conflict may
frustrate implementation of socially desirable transfers and lead to
selection of more costly solutions to water supply problems.

More effective management of water transfer may require modification of existing institutions. Two types of changes appear to have
promise. First, some consolidation of the numerous independent
decision processes appears desirable. This approach has the greatest
potential application within the boundaries of individual states. In
states with significant degree of local governmental control and
relatively weak or decentralized state controls (e.g., a riparian
doctrine state), consolidation to achieve a more centralized approach
may provide better management of the transfer issue. Such consolidation could take the form of comprehensive state controls over water
use. However, more selective measures such as control of certain
types of water transfer may be an appropriate solution where overall
water conflict is relatively infrequent. Consolidation of decision
processes is less feasible for water transfer across state boundaries
although interstate institutional mechanisms are appropriate in some
cases.

Second, expanded use of compensation within related decision
processes has potential to improve resolution of transfer-related
conflict. The inability of the area of origin to receive compensation for transfer of surplus water is a major source of opposition to
water transfer. The prospect of compensation would reduce opposition
to transfer of water objectively determined to be in excess of
reasonable economic and environmental needs of the area of origin.

Such compensation should be paid by the water transferrer, with the amount of compensation to be calculated as a portion of transfer benefits determined by comparing the costs of water transfer to the costs of the next best alternative source of supply.

Efforts to improve decision-making processes associated with water transfer are important because the need for transfer will continue to arise. The incorporation of demand management into water-supply planning will reduce development of new supplies, but continued growth in population and human activity will require some measure of continued supply development. This additional development in some cases will involve proposals for water transfer, and even short-distance transfer may be institutional complex. Timely and efficient resolution of the resulting conflict will continue to be a major function of water management institutions.

Appendix - References

1. Clark, R.E. (Ed.) (1967-1984). Waters and Water Rights, 7 Vols. The Allen Smith Col, Indianapolis.

2. Cox, W.E., and Shabman, L.A. (1983), "Institutional Issues Affecting Water Supply Development: Illustrations from Southeastern Virginia" (VWRRC Bulletin 138). Virginia Water Resources Research Center, Blacksburg, Virginia.

3. Cox, W.F., and Shabman, L.A. (1984). "Virginia's Water Law: Resolving the Interjusrisdicational Transfer Issue." Va. J. Nat. Res. L., Vol. 2, 181-234.

4. Farnham, W.H. (1972). "The Permissible Extent of Riparian Land." Land and Water L. Rev., Vol. 7, 31-61.

5. Robie, R.B., and Kletzing, R.R. (1979). "Area of Origin Statutes - The California Experience." Id. L. Rev., Vol. 15, 419-441.

6. Trelease, F.J., and Lee, D.W. (1966). "Priority and Progress—Case Studies in the Transfer of Water Rights." Land and Water L. Rev., Vol. 1, 1-76.

7. Williams, S.F. (1973). "Optimizing Water Use: The Return Flow Issue." Univ. of Colo. L. Rev., Vol. 44, 301-321.

Transferring Conserved Water

D. A. Twogood, M.ASCE[1/]

ABSTRACT

The transfer of water from areas of surplus to areas of need is not uncommon. However, the proposal to transfer water salvaged by water conservation programs from one area to another is a new concept, which is described in this paper.

Imperial Irrigation District (District), located in the southeast portion of California, diverts from the Colorado River at Imperial Dam. The Metropolitan Water District (MWD) serves the Southern California coastal area which continues to experience rapid growth in population and water needs, yet has limited water resources. The District's water right to the Colorado River has a higher priority than that of the MWD.

The District has made improvements in its water system during the past thirty years which have increased efficiency and conserved water. However, additional programs have been identified which can conserve several hundred thousand acre-feet of additional water. The MWD Colorado River Aqueduct has capacity for a possible transfer of water between the District and MWD. The cost of the necessary water conservation programs are greater than the practical ability for Imperial Valley farmers to pay. However, such costs appear to be well within the ability of MWD to pay. Furthermore, most new sources of water, including expansion of the State Water Project, are greater than the estimated unit water costs for conservation programs in Imperial Valley.

An Agreement between the two parties can and must be mutually beneficial. MWD would acquire a new water supply at a reasonable cost. The District would gain an improved system at no cost to its water users with probable reduced operation and maintenance costs.

INTRODUCTION

Many examples of the concept of transferring water from areas of surplus to areas of need exist in California and the arid west. However, the proposal to transfer water salvaged by water conservation projects and programs is a new concept, which is being explored by the District and MWD. The Southern California area served by water from the Colorado River is shown in Figure 1.

1/ Executive Officer, Imperial Irrigation District, El Centro, CA.

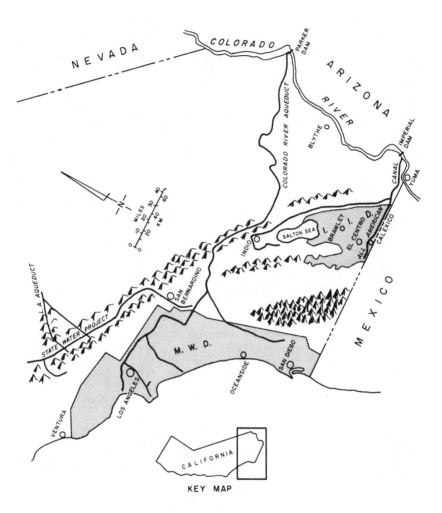

Figure I. Colorado River Service Area in California

The District diverts water from the Colorado River at Imperial Dam and delivers about 2.8 million acre-feet (MAF) (3.5 million dam^3) annually to one-half million acres (202,000 ha) of land within Imperial Valley for agricultural, domestic, industrial, and other beneficial uses.[5] This supply, conveyed through the All-American Canal, is the sole source of water for the Valley. Rainfall and runoff are infrequent and insufficient, and groundwater is not usable because of its low quality and permeability.

The MWD also diverts water from the Colorado River, through its Colorado River Aqueduct originating at Parker Dam, to supplement local supplies and its share of water from the State Water Project originating in Northern California. In 1985, MWD diverted nearly 1.3 MAF (1.6 million dam^3) from the Colorado River.

IMPERIAL IRRIGATION DISTRICT

Water was first diverted from the Colorado River to Imperial Valley in 1901 by the California Development Company, based upon a series of water appropriation filings between 1895 and 1899. Diverted water was conveyed through the Imperial Canal, also known as the Alamo Canal, which ran through Mexico about 40 miles (64 km) before crossing into the United States east of present-day Calexico, California, to serve about 1500 acres (607 ha) that year. Diversions and irrigated acreage gradually increased during the next three years, although silting of the headworks and canal caused severe difficulties.

During the next several years, physical, financial, international complications and legal problems plagued the project, and Imperial Irrigation District was formed in 1911 for the purpose of acquiring properties of the California Development Company, including its water rights.

An extensive drainage system was constructed by the District, beginning in 1923, and on-farm tile drainage systems have been installed by landowners since 1929. During this period of construction, the District operated and maintained the canal and open-drain systems as necessary to provide continuous service to water users. Removal of silt and weed control were constant maintenance problems.

In 1932, the District executed the "Contract for Construction of Diversion Dam, Main Canal and Appurtenant Structures and for Delivery of Water" with the United States. During the decade of the thirties while Hoover Dam, Imperial Dam and the All-American Canal were being constructed, the District struggled with severe financial difficulties, during which the District's canal and drainage systems deteriorated, and it took several more years to rehabilitate them. In 1942, the first water was delivered through the All-American Canal.[3]

The District has gradually improved the water system by replacing timber and rubble structures with concrete, replacing timber bridges and corrugated-iron culverts with reinforced-concrete pipe, concrete-lining over one-half of the lateral canal system, installing remote and automatic controls on major structures, and constructing four regulating reservoirs to conserve water and provide more flexible service. These programs gradually improved the efficiency of the District's system and have resulted in conserving water that was previously lost to seepage or operational discharge (spills).

Today, Imperial Irrigation District operates and maintains Imperial Dam, the All-American Canal having a capacity at the head of 15,155 cfs (429 m³/s), 1625 miles (2615 km) of main canals and distribution laterals, 1451 miles (2335 km) of drains, 113 miles (182 km) of which have been placed in underground pipe; and over 13,000 appurtenant structures (such as checks, headings, deliveries, culverts and bridges).

METROPOLITAN WATER DISTRICT OF SOUTHERN CALIFORNIA

The MWD, serving the major cities and urban areas of the Southern California coastal plain, was formed in 1928 to build an aqueduct from the Colorado River and distribute water to its member cities. Construction started in 1932, and the aqueduct began delivering Colorado River water to several MWD member cities in June 1941.

The Colorado River Aqueduct, beginning at the intake pumping plant on the western shore of Lake Havasu, carries Colorado River water 242 miles (389 km) to Lake Mathews, its terminal reservoir near Riverside, California, where it connects to the distribution network. The aqueduct was designed for a capacity of 1,605 ft³/s (45 m³/s).

Water for the south coastal area of California served by MWD and the city of Los Angeles comes from (1) local water supplies, (2) the Los Angeles Aqueduct supply from the Mono Basin-Owens Valley, (3) Colorado River and (4) State Water Project. During the past decade MWD imported about one-half of the water used by about 13 million consumers. The MWD wholesales this water to 27 member agencies which, along with 130 cities and other agencies deliver it to homes, businesses and a few farms in the 5100 square mile (1.3 million ha) service area.

COLORADO RIVER WATER RIGHTS

The Imperial Irrigation District has rights to the use of Colorado River water by virtue of appropriations and permits from the State of California, a contract with the United States of America authorized by the Boulder Canyon Project Act, and a Decree of the United States Supreme Court in the case of Arizona v. California. These rights are held by the District for the benefit of lands within its boundaries, and are not quantified precisely except in the Supreme Court Decree which provides that the District has a present perfected right to water required to irrigate 424,145 acres (172,000 ha) or 2.6 million acre-feet (MAF) (3.2 million dam³) per annum, whichever is less, with a priority date of 1901.

The 1929 California Limitation Act limited California's annual
consumptive usage to 4.4 MAF (5.4 million dam^3), plus not more than
one-half of any excess or surplus water unapportioned by the Colorado
River Compact of 1922.

Under the California Seven-Party Agreement, dated August 18, 1931,
the District is entitled to its share of the first 3.85 MAF
(4.7 million dam^3) of California's allocation. In priority order,
Palo Verde Irrigation District, the Yuma Project, Imperial Irrigation
District and lands in Imperial and Coachella Valleys to be served by
the All American Canal, and 16,000 acres (6,500 ha) of Mesa lands in
the Palo Verde Irrigation District are entitled to 3.85 MAF
(4.7 million dam^3) annually. Priority 4 allocates 550,000 acre-feet
(AF) (678,000 dam^3) annually to Metropolitan Water District. These
first four California priorities total 4.4 MAF (5.4 million dam^3) and
that quantity is accorded a priority over the Central Arizona
Project. Accordingly, during periods of normal river flow, the first
four priorities will be protected even if the Central Arizona Project
takes its 2.8 MAF (3.4 million dam^3) entitlement and Nevada takes its
300,000 AF (370,000 dam^3). At the same time, MWD and others will
suffer the shortages. Figure 2 shows the annual flow of the Colorado
River at Lee Ferry (Compact point) for the period 1964 through 1983,
in relation to the Lower Basin Compact apportionment and California
entitlements.

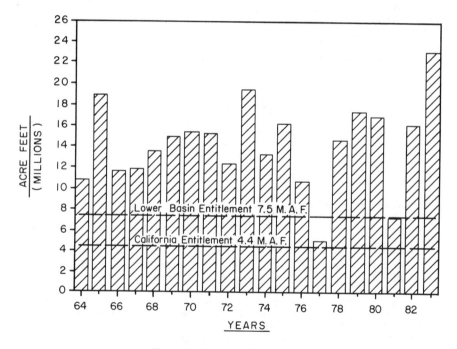

Figure 2 Colorado River at Lee Ferry

The 1932 All American Canal Contract provided, among other things that "The United States shall, from storage available in the reservoir created by Hoover Dam, deliver to the District each year at a point in the Colorado River immediately above Imperial Dam, so much water as may be necessary to supply the District a total quantity, including all other waters diverted for use within the District from the Colorado River, in the amounts and with priorities in accordance with the recommendation of the Chief of the Division of Water Resources of the State of California... (Subject to availability thereof for use in California under the Colorado River River Compact and the Boulder Canyon Project Act)...." (Article 17).

In times of shortage, present perfected rights must be satisfied first in order of their priority dates. Of the California users described in the Seven-Party Agreement, only the Palo Verde Irrigation District, Imperial Irrigation District, and the Reservation Division, Yuma Project California Division (non-Indian portion), have present perfected rights.

The Colorado River water rights held by MWD are based upon the Seven-Party Agreement and its 1930 Water Delivery Contract with the Department of the Interior. The MWD is entitled to its fourth priority quantity plus its share of any surplus, as provided by the "Law of the River," as the series of legal documents has been described.

Conserved or surplus water, which is a portion of District water appropriated pursuant to state law may be transferred and used outside of the District boundaries if the District's Board of Directors finds it to be for the best interest of the District (California Water Code Sections 22259, 109, 1011, and 1244).

WATER CONSERVATION

The need for water conservation has become apparent in recent years for several reasons. As the population of California and other western states increases, the problems of providing water to meet the resulting requirements become more difficult due to economic and environmental concerns. Using existing supplies more efficiently appears to be part of the solution.[1]

The District has a firm, relatively large water supply, adequate to meet current and future needs, since the major development of Imperial Valley has been accomplished. The District's water distribution system, built during the first three decades of this century, is a gravity system and includes several hundred miles of unlined canals and laterals. Losses from such a system are to be expected, and when on-farm losses are included fall into three categories: (1) seepage and evaporation (2) operational discharge, and (3) tailwater runoff from irrigated fields.

The District's gravity drainage system collects and conveys these losses plus leach water and natural drainage to the Salton Sea, long recognized as a repository for drainage waters. Since the Sea has no

natural outlet, the level of the Sea fluctuates as the result of
inflow from the 8,360 square mile (2.2 million ha) drainage area,
offset only by evaporation. In recent years, total inflow has
exceeded evaporation and the level of the Sea has continued to rise,
resulting in flooding of private properties adjacent to the Sea.
The District recently lost a major lawsuit, settled another and
paid out several million dollars in damages because of this flooding.
Other claims and suits are pending. Although the District has had a
significant water conservation program for over thirty years,
resulting in concrete-lining over one-half of its canal and lateral
system, construction of four regulating reservoirs, installing remote
control at more than twenty major structures, building seepage
recovery systems, making improvements to farm irrigation systems, and
improving operation and management of the total system, significant
losses still occur.

Table 1 shows District average diversion, use and losses for the
five-year period 1981 through 1985. The three categories of losses,
which include those targeted to be reduced (seepage, operational
discharge and tailwater), amount to 533,000 AF (657,500 dam^3) per
year.

TABLE 1 - DIVERSION, USE AND LOSSES

	1981 - 1985 Average Amounts[a]	
	1,000 AF	(1,000 dam^3)
Inflow to District (AAC @ Drop 1)	2,593*	(3,198)
Canal losses (seepage, evaporation)	161	(198)
Operational discharge	102	(126)
Delivered to Users	2,330*	(2,874)
Consumptive Use	1,780	(2,196)
Farm, urban runoff:		
(Tailwater, sewage effluent)	270	(333)
Agricultural leaching	280	(345)
Natural runoff	75	(93)
Discharge to Salton Sea from Imperial Valley[b]	888*	(1,095)

[a] All figures are estimated except those marked *.
[b] Sum of losses, leaching, and natural runoff.

The District completed a Water Conservation Plan in 1985, which
identified the most feasible programs to be implemented.[2]   The
Plan identified potential water savings in the total annual amount of
325,000 AF (400 dam^3), as shown in Table 2.

TABLE 2 - ESTIMATED POTENTIAL WATER SAVINGS

	Average Annual Amounts	
	1,000 AF	(1,000 dam^3)
Potential reduction in:		
Canal seepage	100	(123)
System operational discharge	100	(123)
Tailwater	125	(154)
Totals	325	(400)

The District subsequently retained Parsons Water Resources, Inc. (Parsons) to make further studies and reports to implement the District's Water Conservation Plan, including preparation of an Environmental Impact Report. Parsons has completed two reports entitled "Water Requirements and Availability Study" and "Water Transfer Study."[4] In the first report, Parsons estimated that past conservation programs have reduced annual losses by more than 100,000 AF (123,000 dam^3). The latter report identifies MWD as being the logical transferee for water conserved by the District.

Parsons has delineated projects which, together with other measures, would develop potential savings of 358,000 AF (441,000 dam^3) per year, and has estimated the capital cost of these projects and measures to be $233 million as shown in Table 3. Annual operation, maintenance, replacement, and mitigation of environmental impacts would be added, and have not been estimated.

TABLE 3 - ESTIMATED COST OF CONSERVATION PROGRAMS

	Estimated Cost[a] ($1,000)
Canal Lining:	
(3 main canals, 350 miles (563 km) of laterals)	$ 89,000
Reservoirs	18,000
System Improvements	12,000
System Automation	21,000
On-farm Improvements	21,000
Sub-total	161,000
Power Offset Facilities	40,000
Miscellaneous and Reserves	32,000
Total Project Capital Cost	$233,000

[a] Parsons Water Resources[4]

DISTRICT/MWD NEGOTIATIONS

The District and MWD met several times during 1985 to discuss a water transfer arrangement. The MWD expressed an interest to acquire up to 250,000 AF (308,000 dam^3) of water per year from the District, and indicated a willingness to pay for conservation measures to accomplish water savings of this magnitude. These negotiations resulted in a draft Memorandum of Understanding (MOU) being developed for presentation to the respective boards, as a first step in achieving a long-term transfer arrangement. The MOU provided, among other things, that MWD would pay the District $10 million per year in exchange for its making available for MWD an annual diversion at Parker Dam of 100,000 AF (123,000 dam^3), saved by the District's water conservation improvements and measures.

Public hearings on the MOU were held throughout the District's service area, at which concerns about the proposal were expressed by water users and other citizens. At a following board meeting, the District directors voted against the MOU as written, but agreed to continue negotiations to resolve concerns of constituents. Since that time, several meetings have been held. Both parties seem optimistic that an agreement can be reached within a reasonable time.

CONCLUSIONS

Transfer of conserved water which is surplus to the requirements of the District, to help MWD meet its future water needs, on the condition that MWD pay for the necessary conservation measures, is a concept that is mutually beneficial. The District will benefit from an improved system with probable reduced operation and maintenance costs, and its water rights would not be diminished. The MWD would receive, through existing conveyance facilities, a needed new water supply at a reasonable cost, which cost would be comparable or lower than alternative sources.

REFERENCES

1. Environmental Defense Fund, 1983, Trading Conservation Investments for Water, Berkeley, California.

2. Imperial Irrigation District, 1985, Water Conservation Plan.

3. Imperial Irrigation District, 1982, Welcome to the Imperial Irrigation District, Imperial, California.

4. Parsons Water Resources, 1985, Water Requirements and Availability Study for Imperial Irrigation District, November.

5. Twogood, D. A., 1985, Proposal for Funding Water Conservation Programs, Proceedings of the Specialty Conference, Irrigation and Drainage Division ASCE, San Antonio, Texas, July.

INTERSTATE AGREEMENTS FOR WATER TRANSFERS

John W. Bird,[1] F.A.S.C.E.

ABSTRACT

Any state is typically subjected to opposing forces that wish to 1) preserve limited water resources for future in-state uses or 2) to export that resource for out-of-state use. Statutes to prevent the export of water from the state of origin to another state have usually been held to be unconstitutional and, as such, are invalid. If states are to protect their water resources, it appears that they must enter into interstate agreements to define the conditions under which water may be taken from one state to another. Such interstate agreements (with federal consent) can normally withstand attacks of unconstitutionality. This would appear to be the most favorable method available to a state to protect its water resource.

INTRODUCTION

The western states characteristically are termed as water-short or arid states. To meet legal restrictions and water supply needs, most of them have adopted the appropriation doctrine for the acquisition and distribution of water. Along with timber, coal, and other resources, water is commonly considered to be a natural resource of a state, which often has a special interest in its natural resources and often has legislation for the conservation and preservation or development of the resource. In a number of states, for example, "The water of all sources of water supply within the boundaries of the state, whether above or beneath the surface of the ground, belongs to the public" (8). The regulation of such a resource commonly favors in-state consumption. In planning for future growth and needs, states commonly attempt to preserve some of the natural resource for future use. To meet these goals, some states have had statutes either prohibiting the export of water for use in another state (3) or permitting it only if the receiving state reciprocates (6).

While the U.S. Geological Survey reported in the "National Water Summary 1983 - Hydrologic Events and Issues" that the United States does not expect to have a national water supply problem, there are serious problems with water distribution and quantity in some areas of the United States. As a result, there have been demands to take water

---

[1] Professor, Civil Engineering Department, University of Nevada, Reno, Nevada 89557

from one state (of supply) to another state (of use) with no consideration of (supply) state planning or needs. Sporhase is an example
of the type of problem which may occur in almost any state where there
is less water available than is in demand.

SPORHASE

The lands near the Colorado-Nebraska border are fairly dry and
require irrigation to successfully grow crops. Sporhase applied for a
permit in Colorado to appropriate groundwater for use on lands in
Colorado, and that permit was denied. He then pumped groundwater from
an existing well on land he owned in Nebraska and used it on the
Colorado land. This action was in violation of Nebraska law, which
provided that no one may export groundwater from Nebraska unless: 1)
"The withdrawal of the groundwater requested is reasonable, is not
contrary to the conservation and use of groundwater, and is not otherwise detrimental to the public welfare;" and 2) "The state in which
the water is to be used grants reciprocal rights to withdraw and
transport groundwater from that state for use in the State of
Nebraska" (6). Since Colorado did not allow export of its groundwater
(3), the second condition could not have been satisfied even if
Sporhase et al. applied for a permit. In suit by Nebraska against
Sporhase over this action, the defense relied upon the Commerce Clause
of the U.S. Constitution (10) which provides that "the Congress shall
have power ... to regulate commerce ... among the several states."
Nebraska premised its claim to limit export of water on its public
ownership of groundwater and upon the fact that Nebraska water law
generally did not permit landowners to buy or sell groundwater.
Nebraska argued that, since individuals could not trade in groundwater, the State should be regarded as the resource's owner. Upon
appeal, the U.S. Supreme Court ruled (7) that the first part of the
statute was constitutional but that the second half would have to have
been carefully tailored to the State's legitimate conservation and
preservation interests to survive the challenge under the Commerce
Clause. While Nebraska required conservation measures such as the
installation of flow meters, well spacing requirements, and groundwater quotas, there was no evidence relating the statute to legitimate
conservation and preservation interest since it applied whether there
was a water surplus or shortage; and, so, the statute failed this
test. The Court said that it would be reluctant to condemn export
restrictions exacted in times of "extreme shortage," and a "legitimate
conservation and preservation interest" would be valid if it were
narrowly constructed. These two expressions will probably be subject
to future conflicts and definitions.

The Sporhase decision raised other questions relating to state
embargoes upon interstate transfers of water during periods of "short
supply" or if there is a "legitimate conservation and preservation
interest." For example, may a water supply be preserved under the
Wild Rivers Act or a state equivalent?

In another region, New Mexico enacted a permit system for controlling groundwater exports after its export ban was struck down in

El Paso (2). There, the court held that economic activities could be distinquished from the health and safety of the public. Further, the State's interest in protecting economic enterprise was insufficient to justify a discriminatory export restriction; and New Mexico's statute for embargo was invalid. In new legislation, the New Mexico State engineer is required to consider the supplies of water available to an applicant in his home state. This part of the statute raises the question of the power of a state regarding the possibility of justifying an export restriction if there are wasteful practices in the importing state or if an actual water surplus exists in the importing state (9). Neither Sporhase nor El Paso gave consideration to conditions of water availability or conservation practices in the importing state. The recent court decisions suggest that, if the importing state is wasteful in its use of water and practices little or no conservation measures, an embargo may be allowable. But, if it appears that the state is attempting to hoard its water resource for some future speculative use, an embargo restricting water export would not be allowable. If a state is to successfully prevent the appropriation of its waters for use out of state, it is going to have to tailor its laws carefully. The courts recognize the need of the state to limit appropriations and determine priorities for appropriations.

An area of potential contention is associated with the loss of a water right. For example, if El Paso does not use its New Mexico based water for a period of time, can it lose its right under the forfeiture provision? It is apparent that legislators are going to need to carefully rewrite their anti-export statutes or enter into interstate agreements regarding interstate transfers of water. There is some consideration that interstate agreements are superior to court decisions in meeting state needs.

INTERSTATE TRANSFERS OF WATER

The expressions in El Paso and Sporhase indicate that interstate transfers of water are viewed as critical in some of the western states. There is some consideration that such transfers amount to the piracy of a valuable resource. While the states have the major responsibility of initiating intrastate transfers, suits permitting interstate transfers are typically beyond their control or planning process. One method of approaching the problem of interstate water transfer is the interstate agreement or compact. The authority for states to formally contract or agree between themselves is contained in the Compact Clause (11) of the U.S. Constitution. The federal government is usually included as a necessary participant in any interstate compact relating to water; and the terms of such a compact, once negotiated and ratified by participating states and the federal government, are binding upon all parties involved. While it may take years to develop an interstate compact, it is generally felt that the time is well spent, especially when the results of an uncertain or potential suit are considered. Such a suit could change water resource use plans for a state, while a compact could provide a base for state planning. The stability of a compact is that a compact cannot be amended by one party without the consent of all parties. A

subsequent state statute which conflicts with such a compact can be,
and has been declared, ineffective by the courts (4). Court decisions
on interpretations of such interstate agreements may be sought from
federal courts. Because the compact is both federal and state law, it
provides a viable mechanism for reducing conflicts among states.
Water allocation compacts are designed to equitably apportion the
waters of a state (usually interstate rivers at this time) in order to
avoid conflicts over the distribution and use of the waters involved
and to promote interstate cooperation. Interstate compacts are
usually viewed by the courts and water resource interests as superior
devices over separate or federal legislation in resolving interstate
water disputes.

     Two recent court decisions raise the question as to whether a
compact could prevent diversions of groundwater beyond the boundaries
of compacting states to meet out-of-basin (state) needs. Sporhase and
El Paso are cases that suggest that interstate compacts should be
considered to limit or define interstate transfers of groundwater.
Presently, for example, New Mexico is considering the viability of its
new State legislation to prevent or reduce the possibility of out-of-
state groundwater diversions. It is to be expected that an interstate
compact between New Mexico and its neighbors would be faster and surer
than reliance on state law.

     This is demonstrated in a recent case involving a challenge to an
interstate compact restricting transfers of water from a basin. A
water company sought a declaratory judgment against Article X of the
Yellowstone River Compact. Article X expressly precludes the transfer
of water out of the Yellowstone River Basin without the consent of
Montana, North Dakota, and Wyoming. The plaintiff claimed that
Article X was unconstitutional because it impermissibly burdened
interstate commerce and denied equal protection under law. The court
dismissed the plaintiff's (Intake Water Company) challenge of Article
X on the grounds that, since the compact was ratified by Congress, it
must be viewed as federal legislation immunized from attack on the
grounds cited in Sporhase (5). In one sense, Sporhase and El Paso
present warnings of the perils of individual state actions, while
Intake stands as testimony of the potential benefits of collective
action to regulate the transfer of water under a federal-state interstate compact.

COMMENTS AND CONCLUSIONS

     For those involved in water resource planning, there are a number
of problems. Sporhase and El Paso have resulted in a number of
questions that may end with the loss to out-of-state users of water
planned for in-state uses. While it is possible for a state to
narrowly tailor a statute for the conservation of the water resource,
it is quite probable that a court will invalidate that statute as
violating the Commerce Clause. Any such statute must be careful to
not discriminate against out-of-state residents. It is expected that
conservation efforts by the state alone would not be sufficient;
there would have to be a widespread conservation interest in the state

to convince a court that the interest was sufficient to prevail over Commerce Clause requirements. Many states have a problem agreeing with their neighbors, but it would probably be advantageous to the states to begin negotiating on interstate compacts regarding water resources. The problems are far from simple. Texas, for example, is a water exporter to Oklahoma (1) and a water importer from New Mexico.

Recent concerns relating to either surface or groundwater (Ogallala aquifer, for example) needs could be addressed either individually or collectively in negotiations that would necessarily include the federal government. Since neither Sporhase nor El Paso considered the problem of groundwater mining, this is an area open to both legislation and interstate agreements. States, such as Texas, New Mexico, and Colorado, have the choice of negotiating compacts to equitably divide the available water resource; or they can pass statutes of questionable value to preserve their resource. In the second case, the possibility that their statute(s) may be nullified must be considered as real under conditions not foreseen by the legislature. It would appear that the interstate compact is the preferred choice for protecting a state's water resource.

REFERENCES

1. Altus v. Carr, 385 U.S. 35 (1966).

2. City of El Paso v. Reynolds, No. 80-730HB (DNM Jan. 17, 1983).

3. Colorado Revised Statute sec. 37-90-136 (1973).

4. Hinderlider v. La Plata River and Cherry Creek Ditch Company, 304 U.S. 92 (1938).

5. Intake Water Company v. Yellowstone River Compact Commission, Civil No. 1184, D.C. Montana, (1983).

6. Nebraska Revised Statutes, sec. 46-613.01 (1978).

7. Nebraska v. Sporhase, 329 NW 2d 855 (1983).

8. Nevada Revised Statutes 533.025 (1971).

9. New Mexico Statutes Annotated, sec. 72-12 (1983).

10. United States Constitution, Article 1, sec. 8, Cl. 3.

11. United States Constitution, Article 1, sec. 10, Cl. 3.

EVALUATION OF TERTIARY WASTEWATER TREATMENT SYSTEMS

Takashi Asano*, William R. Kirkpatrick**, and Robert S. Jaques***

Introduction

The recent trend toward the use of reclaimed municipal wastewater for purposes such as landscape and food crop irrigation, groundwater recharge, and recreational impoundment often requires tertiary or advanced wastewater treatment. Principal treatment processes and operations for tertiary treatment of municipal wastewater for reuse and treatment of surface water for potable water are similar; both normally include chemical coagulation followed by flocculation, sedimentation, filtration, and disinfection. Alternatively, direct filtration with lower chemical doses and without sedimentation is used. It is known that both bacterial pathogens and viruses are removed in these processes in varying degrees. The high degree of pathogen removal achieved by a properly operated treatment system ensures the safe use of the reclaimed wastewater.

The purpose of this paper is to evaluate factors affecting the optimum operations of coagulation-flocculation and filtration processes in municipal wastewater reclamation and reuse. Special reference is made to the recently completed five-year study at Castroville, California, the "Monterey Wastewater Reclamation Study for Agriculture" (MWRSA), where pertinent data, collected at the Castroville Wastewater Treatment Plant, are used to assess design and operational variations of the above treatment processes.

Factors Affecting the Wastewater Reclamation Systems

Contaminants of interest in municipal wastewater vary in size by several orders of magnitude, from a few Angstroms of soluble substances to a few micrometers for suspended and settleable matter (Levine et al., 1985). The removal of a large proportion of these contaminants in wastewater is accomplished by gravity sedimentation. However, because many of the contaminants are too small for gravitational settling alone

*Water Reclamation Specialist, California State Water Resources Control Board, P.O. Box 100, Sacramento, California 95801, and Adjunct Professor, Department of Civil Engineering, University of California, Davis, California 95616
**Sanitary Engineer, Engineering-Science, 600 Bancroft Way, Berkeley, California 94710
***Agency Engineer, Monterey Regional Water Pollution Control Agency, 220 Country Club Gate, Pacific Grove, California 93940

in an economical time frame, and these contaminant particles host bacteria and viruses, the aggregation of these particles into larger, more readily settleable or filterable solids is essential for successful separation by sedimentation and/or filtration. Fine particulate matter is thus removed from wastewater by addition of inorganic or organic chemicals that accelerate the aggregation of suspended matter into larger aggregates. This process is often referred to as chemical coagulation and flocculation. In addition, to inactivate bacteria and viruses effectively, a disinfection step must follow filtration to ensure the safety of the reclaimed wastewater (Sanitation Districts of Los Angeles County, 1977; Asano, et al., 1985).

Removal of suspended and colloidal particles in secondary effluents can be accomplished effectively in a "complete" treatment system consisting of coagulation, flocculation, sedimentation and filtration. Wastewater particles can also be effectively removed without the sedimentation step by removing all of the solids in the filter. This direct filtration may include coagulation and flocculation or the flocculation step may be bypassed and the effluent applied directly to the filters (in-line flocculation). The complete treatment system is quite effective with respect to solids and virus removal; however, both the capital and operational costs of the system are high (Sanitation Districts of Los Angeles, 1977; Dryden, F.D., et al., 1979). The major applications of direct filtration in wastewater reclamation and reuse are: (1) direct filtration of secondary effluent, (2) filtration of chemically coagulated effluent, and (3) filtration of chemically coagulated and flocculated effluent using relatively low chemical doses.

Castroville Wastewater Treatment Plant

The Castroville Wastewater Treatment Plant in California consists of primary sedimentation and a complete mix activated sludge basin which uses three mechanical surface aerators. Mixed liquor from the aeration basin is continuously recirculated over a shallow redwood lath roughing tower. The biologically oxidized flow then passes from the aeration basin into two ten-foot deep secondary clarifiers. Clarified effluent that is not pumped to the tertiary plant is discharged to a regional ocean outfall. Primary and waste secondary sludges undergo anaerobic digestion with the resultant residuals dried on sand drying beds.

The tertiary treatment plant consist of two parallel treatment process trains. One is chemically coagulated direct filtration and the other is a set of linked unit processes that fulfill the complete treatment requirements of the California Wastewater Reclamation Criteria: chemical coagulation, clarification, and filtration. Both flow streams are followed by the required disinfection process. Since this latter process meets all treatment requirements of California Administrative Code, Title 22, it is referred to in this paper as the Title-22 or T-22 process. The chemically coagulated direct filtration process is referred to as the Filtered Effluent (FE) process.

In the filtered effluent (FE) process, alum and polymer are added as filter aids, mechanical turbine rapid mix and flocculation chambers provide mixing and flocculation development time, the effluent is

filtered by a dual media gravity filter, and, finally, chlorine is added
to the effluent before storage. The Title-22 (T-22) process, is more
complex. Higher doses of alum and polymer are used than in the FE
flowstream. Flocculation is followed by sedimentation before filtration
through a dual-media gravity filter and chlorination.

Treatment Plant Performance Evaluation

The performance of the Castroville Wastewater Treatment Plant is
evaluated primarily in terms of the concentrations of 5-day biochemical
oxygen demand (BOD_5), total suspended solids (TSS), turbidity, and
coliform bacteria in the effluent at various stages of treatment. Table
1 summarizes the concentrations of BOD_5, TSS, and turbidity of the
secondary effluent, filtered effluent, and Title-22 effluent from May
1984 to April 1985. The data are presented in terms of a log-normal
probability distribution which describes the value in terms of the
probability of occurrence of a given concentration.

TABLE 1. BOD_5, TSS, and Turbidity in the Castroville Treatment Plant
Effluents.

Parameter	No. Samples	Percent Chance of Parameter Value Being Less Than or Equal to That Listed Below						Maximum Value
		50	80	90	96	98	99	
BOD_5[a] (SE)	74	14.3	22.3	28.0	35.9	42.1	48.6	53
Total Suspended Solids[a]								
SE	302	13.4	19.5	23.7	29.2	33.4	37.7	38
FE	286	1.6	3.1	4.3	6.3	8.0	10.0	17
FC	275	4.4	7.6	10.1	13.8	16.8	20.2	59
T-22	273	0.8	1.5	2.1	3.0	3.8	4.7	12
Turbidity[b]								
SE	288	3.8	5.5	6.7	8.2	9.3	10.5	12.0
FE	282	1.1	1.7	2.2	2.9	3.4	4.0	9.4
T-22	262	0.6	0.9	1.1	1.5	1.7	2.0	3.4

[a] Expressed in mg/L.
[b] Nephelometric Turbidity Units (NTU).
Key: SE = secondary effluent; FE = filtered effluent with flocculator
installed; FC = flocculator-clarifier effluent; T-22 = Title-22 effluent

Performance of the Tertiary Systems

Turbidity and Suspended Solids

Upon review of Table 1, a consistent ratio of about 2:1 can be
observed in the performance of the two tertiary treatment trains (FE and

T-22) in terms of their respective total suspended solids and turbidity removal. The T-22 process scheme nearly always met the turbidity standard of 2 NTU while the FE flow stream achieved 85 percent compliance. It is believed that this difference is due to the high dose of chemicals and the sedimentation process in the T-22 scheme and the resultant difference in particle filterability. Though this ratio may not hold for all similar tertiary plants, the abundance of data consistently following this pattern over five years at Castroville allows the conclusion that a similar ratio would be found in the performance of these two treatment trains elsewhere. Therefore, treatment equivalency in absolute terms between these two different tertiary trains is not likely possible. However, if equivalency is defined as meeting a pre-designated standard for a fixed percentage of the time (such as 90 percent), then establishing performance equivalency is quite possible for regulatory purposes.

Bacteria

Total coliform (most probable number per 100 mL, American Public Health Assn., et al., 1985) is used at Castroville to evaluate bacterial removal. As shown in Table 2, coliform compliance was met the majority of the time by both tertiary treatment trains with the T-22 system being more reliable. The table represents 14 daily samples taken each month for one year. These data are representative of a total combined chlorine residual of 5 mg/L after a 90-minute theoretical contact time.

TABLE 2. 7-Day Running Median Coliform Level Compliance by Month

Month	FE	Percent Compliance[a] T-22	Month	FE	T-22
May 84	100	100	Nov 84	100	100
Jun 84	84	100	Dec 84	0	100
Jul 84	53	100	Jan 85	0	100
Aug 84	100	100	Feb 85	43	83
Sep 84	100	100	Mar 85	81	93
Oct 84	100	100	Apr 85	100	100

[a]Compliance with 2.2 MPN/100 mL after chlorination (California Administrative Code, 1978).

It should be noted that during all five years of study, tests for the presence of natural virus, salmonella, shigella, Ascaris lumbricoides, Entamoeba histolytica, and miscellaneous parasites in both tertiary effluents were all negative whereas natural virus were found in the unchlorinated secondary effluent samples 80 percent of the time.

Tertiary Treatment Optimization Studies

FE Process Optimization

To enhance chemical coagulation and flocculation, a baffled serpentine flocculation chamber was constructed ahead of the FE filters. Mixing speed, flocculation time and energy, and alum/polymer dosage were systematically varied to sixteen separate settings. Each test was run for at least ten days of "normal" plant operation which is defined as no unusual event in either the secondary plant or the FE process train.

Based on the statistical analyses of the data, the following conclusions were reached:

1. The relationships between chemical dose and effluent turbidity and suspended solids indicate that the various alum and polymer dose rates had little effect on the turbidity or suspended solids.

2. A possible relationship exists, between effluent quality and flocculation time and energy. The flocculation time and energy ranged from 2 to 14 minutes and 10 to 60 sec^{-1} (G), respectively. For both turbidity and suspended solids, the 14-minute flocculation time resulted in the poorest FE quality. The two-minute flocculation time resulted in about average values whilst the series that used three to six passes (6 to 12 minutes) resulted in the best FE water quality. The previously noted 2:1 ratio between the FE and T-22 process trains was reduced to a range of 1.0 to 1.5 for the three to six pass test series.

3. Relationships between secondary effluent turbidity and suspended solids with FE effluent quality data were developed; however, they resulted in poor statistical correlations.

4. For the ongoing operations, the following operating conditions were selected:
   ° Rapid mixer tip speed and energy, 360 ft/min and 150 sec^{-1};
   ° Flocculation theoretical detention time and energy (G), eight minutes and 35 sec^{-1}; and
   ° Chemical dose: 5 mg/L alum (as $Al_2(SO_4)_3 \cdot 14H_2O$) and 0.06 mg/L anionic polymer (Dow 825).

Title-22 Process Optimization

As a condition of comparison for the FE and T-22 processes, it is necessary that the coagulant dose be optimized for the T-22 treatment train. Seventy-five data were collected for this purpose with the alum dosages of 50, 130, 210, 285, and 570 mg/L (as $Al_2(SO_4)_3 \cdot 14H_2O$).

It is likely that the coagulation-flocculation and sedimentation process with high alum dose ahead of filtration act as a damper to any large fluctuations in secondary effluent turbidity and suspended solids and thus allows the filtration process to "polish" the effluent reliably and consistently. However, it is not likely that the chemical dose has any significant effect on the final turbidity when it is in the lower range, say less than about 2 NTU. Optimizing the T-22 process with high chemical dose for lowest final turbidity is difficult to achieve because the influence of SE turbidity is obviously present and statistically significant. Use of the lowest chemical dose that achieves the effluent objective reliably is, therefore, a rational operational approach.

Chlorination

Several observations on the chlorine disinfection process at Castroville were made in conjunction with the evaluation of tertiary treatment systems and summarized below:

1. There was little correlation between the chlorine dosage level and the chlorine contact tank.

2. There was little correlation between the effluent chlorine residual and the effluent coliform density except at high doses where excellent removals were consistently obtained.

3. It was virturally impossible to maintain a steady chlorine residual in the effluent even though frequent chlorine dose adjustments were made on the basis of residual chlorine measurements immediately (about 2 minutes) downstream of the chlorine injection point.

These observations were particularly puzzling because the Castroville plant provides tertiary treatment under constant flow rate, 24 hours per day. It was anticipated, therefore, that the high quality of the tertiary effluent, coupled with a steady flow, would result in ideal conditions for chlorine disinfection, i.e., a textbook situation. Such was not the case. Frequently, the immediate chlorine residual was lower than the effluent chlorine residual after 90 minutes. Furthermore, the difference between the two residual levels fluctuated widely and rapidly. Dye tracer studies showed that the modal residence time is different at different times of the day and short-circuiting occurred despite well baffled plug-flow design for the chlorine contact tank. At certain times the dye entering the chlorine contact tank followed the surface zone, whereas at other times it followed the tank bottom, prior to becoming well dispersed. Temperature profile of the chlorine contact tank showed 1 to 2° F variation from bottom to top of the tank potentially creating a density current.

Summary and Conclusions

To achieve efficient bacteria and virus removal, often necessary in wastewater reuse applications, two important criteria for the operation of tertiary treatment are: (1) the filtered effluent should be low in suspended solids and turbidity prior to disinfection to reduce shielding of viruses and thus the chlorine demand, and (2) sufficient chlorine must be applied to the wastewater for an adequate time duration.

To evaluate factors affecting the optimization of chemical coagulation and filtration in municipal wastewater reclamation and reuse, the pilot tertiary treatment plant was constructed in conjunction with the Monterey Wastewater Reclamation Study for Agriculture. Two parallel tertiary treatment trains consisting of direct filtration of secondary effluent and a complete treatment train (T-22) were investigated to assess performance and optimization. Total suspended solids, turbidity, and coliform bacteria were used for the treatment plant performance analyses. In addition, tertiary treatment optimization studies were conducted with respect to alum and polymer doses, mixing energy and flocculation time, and reliability of operation.

Consistently higher removal in the ratio of about 2 to 1 was observed in the performance of the complete treatment (T-22) train and direct filtration (FE) trains in terms of total suspended solids and turbidity. The T-22 treatment train nearly always achieved the turbidity standard of 2 NTU whereas the FE process achieved about 85 percent compliance. However, the health significance of an extremely small probability of virus contamination and differences in turbidity measurement due to these two different treatment trains has not been established. Because of uncertainties associated with risk assessent of viruses in reclaimed wastewater, improvements in wastewater treatment technology and operation of both conventional and tertiary wastewater treatment plants are warranted. Specific observations and concerns are:

1. In secondary treated wastewater which is partially nitrified and subject to the presence of other oxidizable constituents, accurate prediction of the chlorine residual concentration as a function of applied chlorine dose is erratic at best.

2. Chlorine residual control with knowledge of chlorine species appears to be a key factor in consistently achieving bacterial and virus removal criteria. This also appears to be the findings at several tertiary filtration plants operated by the County Sanitation Districts of Los Angeles County, California (Chen, 1985). Thus, continuous and accurate measurement of chlorine residual species is important.

3. In reviewing the results from other tertiary treatment plants at several locations, the residual chlorine concentration varies at each plant with the objective being to meet the coliform standard of 2.2 MPN/100 mL. At Castroville, the target range of 7 to 10 mg/L total combined residual appears adequate, although the flow proportioned dose required to achieve it is quite variable and unpredictable.

Acknowledgement

A large number of agencies and individuals participated in the Monterey Wastewater Reclamation Study for Agriculture. Special thanks are due to R. C. Cooper, E. Anderson, B. Sheikh, E. Kundidzora, and R. Cort in collecting and analyzing the data used in developing this paper.

References

American Public Health Association, American Water Works Association, Water Pollution Control Federation (1985). Standard methods for the examination of water and wastewater, Sixteenth edition.

American Water Works Association (1981). Preceedings of AWWA Seminar on Coagulation and Filtration: Back to the Basics, Amitharajah, St. Louis, Missouri, June 7.

Asano, T., Tchobanoglous, G., and Cooper, R.C. (1985). Significance of coagulation-flocculation and filtration operations in wastewater reclamation and reuse. Proceedings Water Reuse Symposium III - The Future of Water Reuse, American Water Works Association, Denver, Colorado.

California Administrative Code (1978). Wastewater reclamation criteria. Administrative Code, Title 22, Division 4, Chapter 3.

Chen, C.L. (1985). County Sanitation Districts of Los Angeles County. Personal communication.

Dryden, F.D., Chen, C.L., and Selna, M.W. (1979). Virus removal in advanced wastewater treatment systems. Journal Water Pollution Control Federation, 51, 8, 2098-2109.

Levine, A.D., Tchobanoglous, G., and Asano, T (1985). Characterization of the size distribution of contaminants in wastewater: treatment and reuse implication. Journal Water Pollution Control Federation, Vol. 57, No. 7, 805-816, July

O'Melia, C.R. (1972). Coagulation and flocculation, in Physicochemical Processes for Water Quality Control. (W.J. Weber, Jr.), Wiley-Interscience.

Sanitation Districts of Los Angeles County (1977). Pomona Virus Study - Final Report. Prepared for California State Water Resources Control Board, Sacramento, California.

REUSING TREATED WASTEWATER FOR IRRIGATION OF
RAW-EATEN VEGETABLE CROPS IN MONTEREY COUNTY, CALIFORNIA

Bahman Sheikh,* Robert C. Cooper,** Robert S. Jaques***

Introduction

Crops which are eaten raw, such as lettuce, celery, and cauliflower present a special situation insofar as the use of reclaimed water for their irrigation is concerned. The potential for direct transmission of pathogenic microorganisms and/or contamination of kitchen environments has led regulatory agencies to adopt the most strict guidelines for such reuse. In the State of California, these guidelines are contained in the California Administrative Code, Title 22.

Water shortage, seawater intrusion in local aquifers, and a recognized need for a regional wastewater management system combined to make the concept of using reclaimed effluent for irrigation of locally grown vegetables attractive. However, local farmers and public health officials wanted to be shown, with a pilot project, that the concept was safe, economical and did not hurt their yields, sales, or public image.

Overview

The demonstration project was entitled the Monterey Wastewater Reclamation Study for Agriculture (MWRSA). It was principally a field trial study of the feasibility of irrigating food crops which may be consumed raw with reclaimed municipal wastewater effluent.

The MWRSA field operations site was located on a farm in Castroville, California (about 200 km south of San Francisco) and consisted of 1.2 ha (3 acres) of experimental plots and 6 ha (15 acres) of demonstration fields.

The experimental plots consisted of 96 subplots irrigated with three different water types, fertilized at four different rates, and cultivated with six different crops over five years. The three water types being compared were (1) filtered secondary effluent (Filtered Effluent); (2) coagulated, flocculated, settled, and filtered secondary

*Bahman Sheikh, Senior Associate Engineering-Science, 600 Bancroft Way, Berkeley, California 94710
**Robert C. Cooper, Professor University of California, Berkeley, California 94720
***Robert S. Jaques, Agency Engineer, Monterey Regional Water Pollution Control Agency, 220 County Club Gate, Suite 34, Pacific Grove, CA 93950

effluent (Title-22 water[a]); and (3) local well water as a control. The four fertilizer rates were zero, one third, two thirds, and the full fertilizer rate commonly used in the area. Each combination of water type and fertilizer rate was replicated four times in the experimental plots. The purpose of the experimental plots was to generate reliable statistical data on the separate effects of the water types and fertilizer rates on the various crops and the soil.

Soils, plant tissues, and irrigation waters in the experimental plots were frequently sampled and extensively analyzed for chemical, physical, and microbiological characteristics, including viral contamination. Statistical tests were applied to the data to determine if there were significant differences between the characteristics of soils and plants receiving different water types under different fertilization regimes.

Materials and Methods

Split Plot Design

The experimental plots were the most prominent component of MWRSA. From these plots, quantitative, statistically analyzable data are obtained to test the hypothesis that "reclamation is safe and acceptable for irrigation of food crops that are eaten raw." The experimental design was patterned closely after standard agricultural experimentation techniques.

Six crops common in the north Monterey County area were grown over the five-year period of the experiment. One half of the plots were continuously planted with artichokes, and the other half were planted with a succession of different vegetables: celery, broccoli, head lettuce, romaine lettuce, and cauliflower.

Sampling Program

During and after each growing season, samples of plant tissues, plant residues, surface and deep soils, and irrigation and runoff waters were collected and analyzed for viruses, bacteria, pathogens, metals, and a host of other chemical and physical parameters. The results of these tests were then subjected to analysis of variance (ANOVA) to separate the effects of the various water types and fertilizer rates from random variations due to chance.

Treatment Plant

To provide the two tertiary streams of reclaimed water to the experimental and demonstration plots, the then existing Castroville secondary treatment plant was extensively modified and expanded. Prior

---

[a]This name was chosen because the water conforms strictly to the specified treatment process steps contained in the California Administrative Code, Title 22, Division 4 for direct reuse of food crops eaten raw (non-processed food crops).

to modification, the secondary plant provided conventional activated sludge treatment. (Plant flows averaged 0.18 m3/s (0.4 MGD)). Two small tertiary process flowstreams were added following the secondary treatment processes. One process stream consisted simply of filtration followed by chlorine disinfection and dechlorination. It was called the Filtered Effluent flowstream. The other process stream consisted of chemical coagulation, flocculation, settling, filtration, chlorine disinfection, and dechlorination. Since this latter flowstream included all of the processes specified in Title 22 of the California Administrative Code, it is referred to as the Title-22 flowstream.

Virology

The use of reclaimed water for the irrigation of food crops poses a potential health risk due to infectious diseases. Health authorities have voiced a particular interest in enteric virus disease. The virus study included: (1) development and evaluation of methods for the recovery of animal viruses from irrigation waters, irrigated plants and irrigated soils; (2) determination of characteristics of virus survival on plants and soils; (3) on-site monitoring of irrigation waters, plants, and soils; and (4) determination of treatment plant effectiveness in virus inactiviation through extensively repeated virus seeding. The developmental studies (1) and (2) above were conducted using vaccine strain poliovirus.

The assay of vegetables and soils for the presence of virus involved the elution of viruses from plant surfaces or from soil by suspending the material in pH 9.0 three percent beef extract. The resultant extract was precipitated at pH 3.5 and centrifuged. In the case of soil, the beef extract-soil mixture was centrifuged prior to, as well as after, acidification. The resultant solids were treated and assayed for virus.

Analysis of Variance

Analysis of variance (ANOVA) is the primary statistical technique used to determine if significant differences exist between the characteristics of the soils and plants receiving different water types and fertilization treatments.

ANOVA tests whether the differences in the various measured parameters (including soil and plant heavy metals and chemicals) are attributable to the different water and fertilizer treatments, or whether apparent differences simply reflect natural random variations or errors in sampling. ANOVA tests the probability of significant differences at generally accepted (but arbitrarily defined) error rates of either 5 percent or 1 percent.

Results

Five years of field data have been collected and analyzed. The hypothesis that there are no significant differences in crops irrigated with tertiary effluents and those irrigated with well water has been upheld.

No viruses have been detected in any of the tertiary effluent samples. Total and fecal coliform counts in the reclaimed irrigation waters were consistently higher than levels found in well water due to regrowth following dechlorination, mainly during storage. However, these differences were generally not reflected in significant differences in the coliform counts in the soil or plant tissue samples. To determine the effects of dechlorination on regrowth, dechlorination was discontinued in the third year with no ill effects on the produce.

Heavy metal content in all of the irrigation waters was low; in many cases below detection levels. Both reclaimed water types met agricultural and drinking water standards for metals. Even though copper levels in edible cauliflower tissue were significantly higher in plants irrigated with reclaimed water than in plants irrigated with well water, those levels were lower than copper levels in commercially-grown cauliflower from other nearby fields.

The reclaimed waters used for irrigation contained considerably higher levels of certain chemicals, including nutrients, than did the well water. This is believed to have caused the consistently higher levels of sodium and chloride in the soils in the subplots irrigated with reclaimed water. These effects were more pronounced at the 30-cm soil depth than in the deeper soils. In addition, the higher nutrient content in the reclaimed waters was believed responsible for the higher nutrient content in the associated plant tissues. The higher yields noted for the crops irrigated with reclaimed water are also believed to be due to the added nutrient value of the reclaimed waters.

There were no appreciable differences between the observed quality of vegetables grown with well water and those grown with either of the reclaimed waters.

As expected, many factors correlated with fertilizer rate, including several soil heavy metals and chemicals, several plant metals, and yield. Fertilizer appeared to contribute far more nutrients and metals to the soil and the plant tissue than did the reclaimed waters.

Virus Survival

The results of four tests of virus survival on artichokes and two types of lettuce are shown on Figure 1. There was an obvious decrease, with time, in the average number of viruses recovered from the plants exposed to local conditions. Virus decay apears to be log linear with time. There seemed to be no significant relationship between the number of viruses recovered from a plant and the weight of the plant.

Results indicate that the average T99[b] value for artichokes was 5.4 days, and the T99 values for romaine and butter lettuce were 5.9 and 7.8 days, respectively. These values can be compared to the T99 values

---

[b] The T99 values represent the number of days for a 99 percent (two orders of magnitude) reduction in poliovirus on plants in the test plots at Site D.

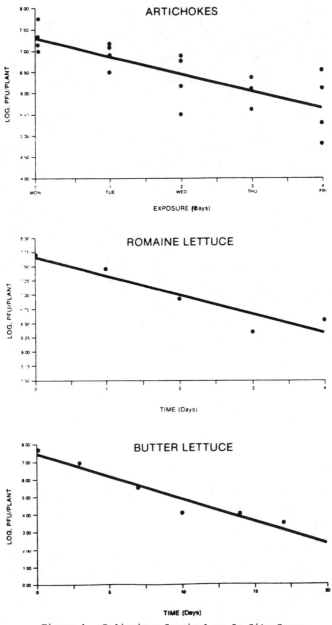

Figure 1. Poliovirus Survival on In Situ Crops

determined in the environmental chamber studies conducted in 1980 at the beginning of MWRSA; the T99 values for poliovirus decay were determined to be 8.6 days for artichokes and 15.1 days for romaine lettuce. The in situ T99 values determined during Year Four are shorter than those previously reported. This may reflect that field conditions with variability in temperature and humidity are more hostile to viruses than the steady conditions of an environmental chamber.

Heavy Metals

Because no heavy metals were being detected in any of the water samples, analytical techniques were refined during the third year to improve detection levels. Even with these refinements, concentrations of cadmium, zinc, iron, manganese, copper, nickel, cobalt, chromium, and lead were generally close to or below the lower detection limit for all three water types. For all three water types, median heavy metal concentrations were well below irrigation water quality maximums for continous use on all soils. The average heavy metal content in reclaimed irrigation waters even met the California State safe drinking water standards.

Soil Characteristics

Soil samples from the experimental plots were collected from three depths: 30-cm (1 ft), 100-cm (3 ft) and 200-cm (6 ft). Samples were analyzed for microbiological content, heavy metals, other chemicals, and physical properties.

Surface soils were sampled for microbiological content, which includes analysis for total and fecal coliform. Any samples with fecal coliform counts above the detection limit were tested for presence of the pathogens Salmonella and Shigellae. All soils were analyzed for parasites - Ascaris lumbriocoides, Entamoeba histolytica and miscellaneous parasites and none were found positive.

Fifteen soil chemical parameters were measured on all soils sampled from the experimental plots: pH, electrical conductivity, calcium, magnesium, sodium, potassium, carbonate, bicarbonate, total Kjeldahl nitrogen (TKN), nitrate, ammonia, phosphorus, chloride, sulfate, and boron. In addition, the sodium adsorption ratio (SAR) and adjusted SAR were calculated on the soil saturation extracts. Nine heavy metals were analyzed on all soil samples at three depths. An example for zinc is shown on Figure 2.

Plant Tissue Characteristics

As in the case of the soil samples it was found that in many instances the fertilizer application rate had a much greater effect on plant tissue parameters levels than did the type of irrigation water used. Total and fecal coliform levels and heavy metal levels on plants in the neighboring fields were measured. No relationships between the levels of any of these parameters and distance from the project site were evident. Thus, there appeared to be no transmission of harmful aerosols from the project site.

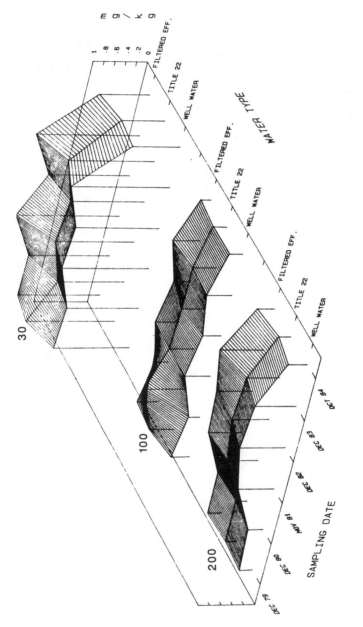

Figure 2. Zinc in Artichoke Soil, 1979–1984.

30=30 CM DEPTH   100=100 CM DEPTH   200=200 CM DEPTH

Yield

Statistically significant yield differences due to water type have been observed in the lettuce, celery, and broccoli crops. In these cases, yields were significantly higher in the crops irrigated with the reclaimed waters. The Filtered Effluent irrigated crop yields were usually slightly higher than the Title-22 irrigated crop yields. Typical yield data, are exemplified in Figure 3.

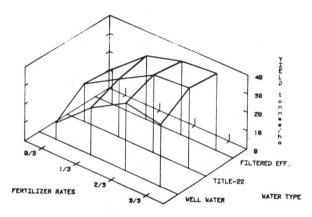

Figure 3.   Leaf Lettuce Yield, July 1983

Quality and Shelf Life

Samples of each crop harvested were boxed and placed in cold storage warehouses for varying time periods of up to four weeks following harvest. The produce was examined at weekly intervals during the storage period for signs of pithiness, flaccidity, black heart, outside tissue breakdown, discolorations, decay and other signs of spoilage. In general, all of the produce was of excellent quality and showed no unexpected deterioration over time. The quality and shelf life of all produce grown with the two reclaimed waters was as good as, and in some instances superior to, the produce grown with well water.

Conclusions

Through the five years of conduct of the farming phase of MWRSA, all the data obtained indicate that use of reclaimed water for food crop irrigation will be acceptable. No health-related adverse impacts have been found, and no drawbacks in terms of soil or groundwater quality degradation have been observed. Conventional farming practices have thus far proven adequate, and the marketability of the produce does not appear to pose any obstacles.

EFFECTS OF ARTIFICIAL RECHARGE ON GROUND-WATER QUALITY,
LONG ISLAND, NEW YORK

Brian J. Schneider, Henry F. H. Ku, and Edward T. Oaksford*

ABSTRACT

Artificial-recharge experiments were conducted at East Meadow in
central Nassau County, Long Island, N.Y., from October 1982 through
January 1984, to evaluate the degree of ground-water mounding and
chemical effects of artificially replenishing the ground-water system
with tertiary-treated wastewater. More than 3×10^6 m^3 of treated
effluent was returned to the upper glacial aquifer through recharge
basins and injection wells in the 15-month period.

Reclaimed water was provided by the Cedar Creek wastewater-
treatment plant in Wantagh, 10 km to the south. The chlorinated
effluent was pumped to the recharge facility, where it was fed to
basins by gravity flow and pumped to injection wells. An observation-
well network was installed at the facility to monitor physical and
chemical effects of reclaimed water on the ground-water system.

Recharge with reclaimed water increased the concentration of
sodium and chloride in ground water but lowered the concentrations of
total nitrogen (nitrate plus nitrite) and some low-molecular-weight
hydrocarbons. Reclaimed water was well within the New York State
effluent standards for ground-water recharge. Specific-conductance
measurements and Stiff diagrams of chemical analyses were used to help
define the extent and shape of the plume formed by reclaimed water.

INTRODUCTION

Several human activities on Long Island, New York, have affected
the ground-water system. Excessive ground-water pumping has caused
aquifer depletion, loss of streamflow, and intrusion of saltwater into
nearshore aquifer systems. Waste-disposal systems have caused
widespread contamination of the shallow ground-water system, and
sewering in Nassau County has led to an increase in consumptive loss.
All of these effects could be partly mitigated through artificial
recharge of ground water.

Reclamation and reuse of water are being practiced throughout the
world for a variety of purposes and in a variety of ways; some of the
most significant artificial-recharge studies in the eastern United
States have occurred on Long Island.

*Hydrologists, U.S. Geological Survey, 5 Aerial Way, Syosset, NY 11791

The U.S. Geological Survey, in cooperation with Nassau and Suffolk
Counties, has conducted artificial-recharge experiments at three sites
on Long Island. A demonstration tertiary-treatment facility at the Bay
Park sewage-treatment plant in southern Nassau County (fig. 1) purified
about 2.27×10^3 m^3 of wastewater per day for reuse during 1968-73; the
reclaimed water met all New York State drinking-water standards except
for nitrogen. The water was injected through a 146.3-m-deep injection
well near the plant. A pilot research project near the village of
Medford in Suffolk County (fig. 1) investigated the use of recharge
basins for artificial recharge with reclaimed water from 1975-78, with
emphasis on processes within the unsaturated zone and their effect on
recharge rates and on the quality of reclaimed water as it percolates
downward.

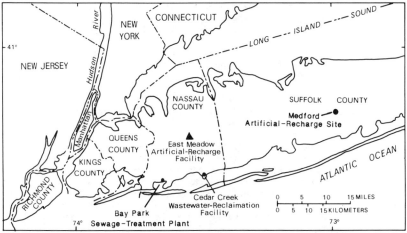

Figure 1.--Location of East Meadow artificial-recharge facility,
Cedar Creek wastewater-reclamation facility, and two
other artificial-recharge sites in Nassau and Suffolk
Counties, N.Y. (From Schneider and Oaksford, 1986.)

The most recent artificial-recharge studies on Long Island, and
the subject of this report, were done during 1982-83 at East Meadow in
central Nassau County (fig. 1), in cooperation with the Nassau County
Department of Public Works. Tertiary-treated wastewater (reclaimed
water) from the Cedar Creek wastewater-treatment plant 10 km to the
south (fig. 1) was piped into shallow basins and injection wells to
replenish the water-table aquifer. The 1982-83 studies were designed
to evaluate the hydrologic and chemical effects of artificially
replenishing the ground-water system with reclaimed water. This paper
discusses the operation of the artificial-recharge facilities and also
characterizes water quality beneath the study area before recharge.
Changes in water quality caused by the introduction of reclaimed water
and several tools to monitor those changes are also presented.

ARTIFICIAL-RECHARGE FACILITIES AND OPERATIONS

Reclaimed water was supplied by the advanced wastewater-treatment facilities at the Cedar Creek wastewater-treatment plant in Wantagh--a conventional activated-sludge facility designed to treat 1.7×10^5 to 1.89×10^5 m^3/d of domestic sewage. Approximately 1.89×10^4 m^3/d of influent sewage is diverted to the advanced wastewater-treatment plant after screening and grit removal; the remaining 1.5×10^5 to 1.7×10^5 m^3/d undergoes secondary treatment and is discharged to the ocean. The advanced wastewater-treatment process consists of four steps:

1. chemically aided primary treatment to improve the removal of phosphorus, biochemical oxygen demand (BOD), suspended solids, and heavy metals;

2. A two-stage biological treatment system consisting of a nitrification-denitrification process to promote biological nitrogen removal in combination with oxidation of remaining carbonaceous material and secondary clarification;

3. rapid sand filtration and activated-carbon treatment to reduce concentrations of suspended and dissolved organic compounds in the effluent to a few parts per billion; and

4. chlorination to disinfect and storage of the effluent to enable continuous delivery of 1.5×10^4 m^3/d to the injection wells and basins at the recharge site.

The East Meadow artificial-recharge site occupies a 1.41×10^5-m^2 area in the Town of Hempstead (fig. 1). The site contains an operations building, 11 recharge basins, and 5 injection wells (fig. 2). Eight of the basins were built for artificial-recharge experiments; the other three were built earlier for stormwater retention. The wells were built to inject reclaimed water directly into the water-table aquifer. The site also contains an old sewage-treatment plant, which was shut down in 1979.

A ground-water-monitoring network, which consists of 96 observation wells, was established within a 2.6-km^2 area encompassing the recharge site. Each well site contains either one, two, or three wells with 50.8-, 76.2-, 101.6-, or 152-mm (2-, 3-, 4-, or 6-inch) inside diameter screened at various depths.

The recharge operation began on October 6, 1982, and ceased on January 9, 1984. Within that 460-day period, more than 3.03×10^6 m^3 of reclaimed water was returned to the ground-water system. About 2.72 $\times 10^6$ m^3 (89 percent) was applied to the recharge basins, and 3.3×10^5 m^3 (11 percent) was injected through wells. An average of 8.9×10^3 m^3/d was applied in 338 days through basins and 50 days through injection wells.

Testing at basins 1, 4, 5, 6, and 7 (fig. 2) consisted of releasing reclaimed water at desired flow rates into each basin and (1) monitoring the onset and possible causes of clogging; (2) calculating

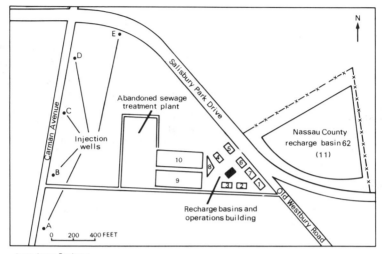

Base from Beckman
and Avendt, 1973
Figure 2.--Plan view of recharge facility showing location of recharge
basins and injection wells.   (From Schneider and Oaksford,
1986.)

infiltration rates in relation to test duration; (3) monitoring local
water-level fluctuations in response to recharge; (4) measuring and
mapping the extent and height of ground-water mounding; and (5)
collecting and analyzing water samples from beneath the facility to
detect changes in local ground-water quality. Testing was done at
basins 2 and 3 in the summer and fall of 1983 to monitor the effect of
the unsaturated zone on percolating reclaimed water.

All five injection wells were used in the fall and winter of 1983.
A 1-day injection test was done at two wells in early October 1983 to
evaluate the injection wells and monitoring equipment. A 50-day test
followed, with no more than four wells in operation at one time, to
evaluate the operation of the injection wells and the response of the
aquifer system to long-term injection of reclaimed water.

More than 200 analyses for selected organic and inorganic constituents from 48 observation wells screened in the upper glacial and
Magothy aquifers were used to characterize background water quality
beneath the recharge facility before recharge operations. Previous
data reported by Katz and Mallard (1981) indicate that ground water
beneath the site contains elevated concentrations of nitrate, chloride,
sulfate, and ammonium ions, although the concentrations generally
decrease with depth. The presence of these ions is caused by nonpoint
sources, which include effluent from cesspools, septic tanks, stormwater discharge sumps, and sewers; salts for road deicing; fertilizers
used on lawns and in agriculture; and chemicals used in industry.
Precipitation and stormwater runoff are the principal agents in moving
substances from these sources through the ground to the water table.

Low-molecular-weight halogenated hydrocarbons, such as trichloroethylene, chloroform, 1,1,1-trichloroethane, and tetrachloroethylene,
also have been detected in wells that tap the water-table and underlying aquifers in the study area. The chemical quality of ground water
at the study site before recharge began is summarized in table 1.

The reclaimed water received at the recharge site met the requirements of the "State Pollutant Discharge Elimination Systems" (SPDES)
permit set by the New York State Department of Environmental
Conservation for discharge of reclaimed wastewater into the upper
glacial aquifer. More than 100 physical, chemical, and biological
constituents were monitored daily to ensure compliance with these
requirements. These constituents included major cations and anions,
nutrients, selected metals, low-molecular-weight halogenated hydrocarbons, organochlorine, organophosphorus insecticides, chlorinated
phenoxy, acid herbicides, and polychlorinated biphenyls (PCBs).

Table 1.--Ground-water quality in upper glacial and Magothy aquifers
in study area, 1977-82, before recharge began

[From Schneider and others, 1986]

Constituent	Median	Minimum	Maximum	Number of samples
Temperature (°C)	14.0	12.0	18.5	181
Specific conductance (μS/cm)	300	26.5	545	174
Nitrogen, dissolved (mg/L as N)	9.10	.35	22.0	65
Nitrogen, NO_2 + NO_3 dissolved (mg/L as N)	9.20	.08	25.0	204
Carbon, organic total (mg/L as C)	.80	.20	12.0	74
Calcium, dissolved (mg/L as Ca)	18.0	.80	55.0	205
Magnesium, dissolved (mg/L as Mg)	3.40	.30	9.30	205
Sodium, dissolved (mg/L as Na)	24.0	3.00	71.0	205
Potassium, dissolved (mg/L as K)	3.70	.20	10.0	203
Chloride, dissolved (mg/L as Cl)	28.0	1.80	100	207
Chromium, total recoverable (μg/L as Cr)	10.0	1.00	100	199
Sulfate, dissolved (mg/L as SO_4)	39.0	.20	150	176
Lead, total recoverable (μg/L as Pb)	.00	.00	450	203
Nickel, total recoverable (μg/L as Ni)	.00	.00	30.0	105
Zinc, total recoverable (μg/L as Zn)	30.0	10.0	860	172
Dichlorobromomethane (μg/L)	.20	<3	1.00	84
Carbon tetrachloride (μg/L)	.20	<3	1.00	84
1,2-Dichloroethane (μg/L)	.20	<3	130	53
Bromoform (μg/L)	.70	<3	8.00	84
Chloroform (μg/L)	1.00	<3	33.0	84
Toluene (μg/L)	1.00	<3	3.00	80
Benzene (μg/L)	1.00	<3	30.0	80
Tetrachloroethylene (μg/L)	5.10	<3	1,320	84

(continued)

Table 1.--Ground-water quality in upper glacial and Magothy aquifers
in study area, 1977-82, before recharge began (continued)

[From Schneider and others, 1986]

Constituent	Median	Minimum	Maximum	Number of samples
1,1-Dichloroethane (μg/L)	6.00	<3	300	84
1,1,1-Trichloroethane (μg/L)	7.95	<3	217	84
Chloroethylene (μg/L)	4.00	<3	500	84
Trichloroethylene (μg/L)	7.65	<3	260	84
Aldrin (μg/L	< .01	< .01	.01	175
Lindane (μg/L)	< .01	< .01	.01	175
Chlordane (μg/L)	< .10	< .10	1.00	175
DDD (μg/L)	< .01	< .01	.01	175
DDE (μg/L)	< .01	< .01	.01	174
DDT (μg/L)	< .01	< .01	.01	175
Dieldrin (μg/L)	.01	< .01	1.40	175
Endosulfan (μg/L)	< .01	< .01	.01	173
Endrin (μg/L)	< .01	< .01	.02	175
Heptachlor (μg/L)	< .01	< .01	.01	175
Heptachlor epoxide (μg/L)	< .01	< .01	.06	175
PCB (μg/L)	< .1	< .1	.60	175
Mirex (μg/L)	< .01	< .01	.01	170
Silvex (μg/L)	< .01	< .01	.21	143
Total dissolved solids (mg/L)	187	19.0	343	31

EFFECTS OF RECHARGE ON WATER QUALITY

Water samples were collected periodically from the observation-well network and analyzed for inorganic compounds, nutrients, and trace organic constituents to determine (1) alterations in ground-water quality through comparison with the background data, and (2) areal distribution of reclaimed water at and near the injection site.

Results show that ground water affected by reclaimed water differs substantially from ambient ground water in some respects. Concentrations of sodium and chloride, for example, were four to five times higher than ambient levels although they were well within New York State drinking-water and SPDES permit limits. Other constituents, such as total nitrogen (nitrate plus nitrite as N), insecticides, and PCB's, were lower in plume water than in ambient water. For example, the median concentration of total nitrogen in ambient water was 9.1 mg/L, with a range of 0.08 to 25 mg/L, whereas the median value from 54 samples of plume water was only 1.8 mg/L. Similarly, the median concentration of 1,1,1-trichloroethane in 84 ambient water samples was 7.95 μg/L, with a range of <3 to 217 μg/L, whereas the median concentration of 60 samples of plume water was 1.0 μg/L.

Specific-conductance measurements were useful in defining the approximate extent and shape of the plume formed by reclaimed water. The median specific-conductance of ground water before recharge was 300

μS/cm, and the median value in pure reclaimed water was 850 μS/cm.
Field measurements of specific conductance permitted a relatively
reliable and immediate confirmation of plume location.

Another method used to compare plume water with ambient water was
the use of Stiff diagrams, in which the concentrations of cations and
anions are plotted on individual horizontal lines, and the data points
are connected to form an irregular polygon (fig. 3). The width of the
pattern is an indication of total ionic content (Stiff, 1951).

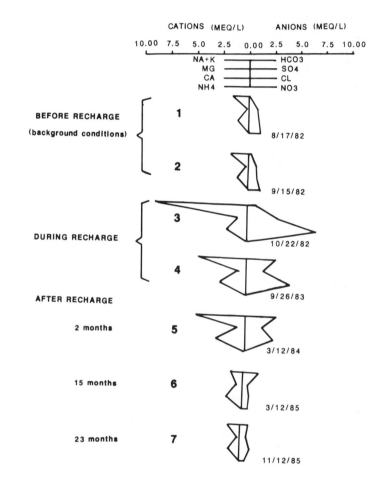

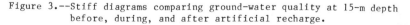

Figure 3.--Stiff diagrams comparing ground-water quality at 15-m depth
        before, during, and after artificial recharge.

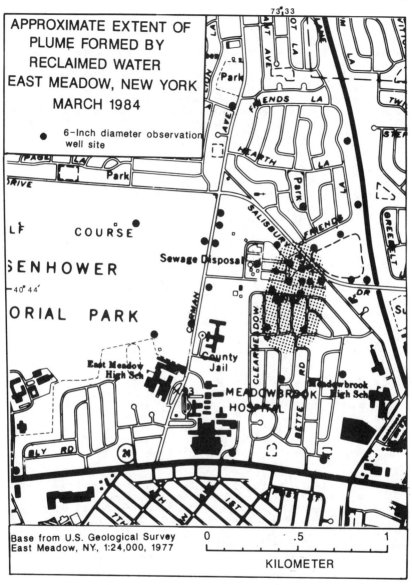

APPROXIMATE EXTENT OF
PLUME FORMED BY
RECLAIMED WATER
EAST MEADOW, NEW YORK
MARCH 1984

• 6-Inch diameter observation
well site

Base from U.S. Geological Survey
East Meadow, NY., 1:24,000, 1977

0   .5   1

KILOMETER

Figure 4.--Map showing approximate location and extent of plume formed
by reclaimed water at 15- to 20-m depth interval as of March
1984.

A set of Stiff diagrams for one well 15 m deep and 18 m
downgradient from a recharge source (fig. 3) depicts the water-quality
history before, during, and after the recharge tests. Mixing,
dilution, and dispersion are the mechanisms of concentration changes.
The composition of the most recent sample (no. 7) is similar to those
collected before recharge, which suggests that water in the shallow
aquifer near the recharge source has returned to former conditions.
Other parts of the aquifer will be affected, however, as the
reclaimed-water plume moves downgradient and deeper. The approximate
extent of the plume formed by reclaimed water as of March 1984 at the
15-to 20-m depth is shown in figure 4.

Plotting the chemical results in this manner is useful in defining
the shape and extent of the plume and is being used in the current
phase of the study, which includes analysis of the transport of
ground-water solutes in the upper glacial aquifer.

REFERENCES CITED

Beckman, W. J., and Advendt, R. J., 1973, Correlation of advanced
    wastewater treatment and ground-water recharge: Chicago,
    Illinois, Consoer, Townsend, and Associates, 430 p.

Franke, O. L., and McClymonds, N. E., 1972, Summary of the hydrologic
    situation on Long Island, New York, as a guide to water-management
    alternatives: U.S. Geological Survey Professional Paper 627-F,
    59 p.

Katz, B. G., and Mallard, G. E., 1981, Chemical and microbiological
    monitoring of a sole-source aquifer intended for artificial
    recharge, Nassau County, New York, in Cooper, W.J., (ed.),
    Chemistry in water reuse: Ann Arbor Science, v. 1, p. 165-183.

Schneider, B. J., Oaksford, E. T., 1986, Design and monitoring
    capability of an experimental artificial-recharge facility at East
    Meadow, Long Island, New York: U.S. Geological Survey Water-
    Resources Investigations Report 84-4321, 41 p.

Schneider, B. J., Ku, H. F. H., and Oaksford, E. T., Hydrologic effects
    of artificial-recharge experiments with reclaimed water at East
    Meadow, Long Island, New York: U.S. Geological Survey Water-
    Resources Investigations Report 85-4323 (in press).

Stiff, H. A., Jr., 1951, The interpretation of chemical water analysis
    by means of patterns: Journal of Petroleum Technology, v. 3, no.
    10, p. 15-17.

Design Criteria For Mass Culturing Spirulina Algae

William M. Strachan*
M. ASCE

ABSTRACT

Certain species of Spirulina, a blue-green alga, are the only
single cell protein (SCP) organisms being profitably cultured for
human consumption on a mass scale. Having a greater digestible
protein content that any other food, Spirulina is one of nature's
highest yielding foods per unit area cultivated (10 kg/day/1000m^2). A
traditional food in Africa and Mexico, where this microalgae thrives
in warm, alkaline lakes, recent experience with human consumption has
confirmed it to be completely non-toxic. One extract of Spirulina,
developed by Dr. Christopher Hills has been used as a nutrient for
cell cultures and contains a growth factor called Spirulina Growth
Factor (SGF). Another extract of 17 of Spirulina's carotenoids has
recently been investigated by Harvard University for the regression
of cancer tumors. A patent on this product, called Phycotene, has
been applied for.
    A major expansion of the sales of this nutritious microalgae in
the commercial marketplace occurred in 1981 when $50 million was sold
in the U.S. and $10 million was sold in Japan. A major portion of
world production then came from Lake Texcoco in Mexico where
fertilizer is added to enhance the growth of the indigenous
Spirulina. The development of production in man-made ponds has been
necessary to meet the exponential demand for high grade Spirulina
products for human consumption. The largest of these facilities has
120,000 m^2 of pond area and is designed to produce over 1200 kg/day
of high grade product.
    Ironically, three large rift lakes in Ethiopia, totalling over
1,500,000 m^2 in harvestable area, are not being harvested despite the
hunger situation in that country. Lake Bogoria (29,000,000 m^2), in
Kenya, has the potential for feeding almost ten million people if
harvested. A $30 million investment would be needed to sustain this
level of output.
    Numerous experiments have been conducted using wastewater as a
nutrient source for animal grade Spirulina but so far no production
facilities for this purpose have been constructed. This method of
culture also holds promise for development of self-supporting
ecosystems in space colonies.

*Project Engineer, R. D. Zande & Associates, Limited
1237 Dublin Road, Columbus, OH 43215

THE NUTRITIONAL COMPOSITION OF SPIRULINA

Thousands of people use Spirulina as a nutritional supplement. In some experiments people have survived for over four months on an exclusive diet of Spirulina and water without any ill effects. This experience is due to the fact that Spirulina is nature's highest protein staple.

PROTEIN COMPARISON OF FOODS
(Nakamura 1982)

FOOD TYPE	PERCENTAGE OF PROTEIN
Beef	18-20%
Eggs	18%
Wheat	6-10%
Rice	7%
Soybeans	29%
Spirulina	64.2-72.6%

The protein in Spirulina is also highly digestible with a net protein utilization ratio of between 51 to 61% (Hills 1980). Spirulina contains the eight essential amino acids plus ten of the non-essential amino acids, normally found in a well balanced ratio. However, as a prime consideration in the design of systems for mass culturing Spirulina, this balance may be altered by controlling pH and nutrient supply.

Spirulina is rich in essential vitamins and minerals including vitamin A, vitamin B-12 and other essential B vitamins, calcium, iron, zinc, and selenium. Medical researchers at Harvard have recently completed research into the cancer preventative properties of the carotenoids in Spirulina through Dr. Hills sponsorship. Medical uses of Spirulina, documented in the book The Secrets of Spirulina (Hills 1980), which include weight control, detoxification of the liver, and treatment of cataracts have been studied in Japan. Because of strict FDA regulations, however, no specific claims about the therapeutic benefits or effects of Spirulina can be made in the United States. Tests have shown Spirulina to be completely non-toxic but more testing, being conducted following FDA guidelines and under FDA supervision, must be completed before Spirulina can obtain FDA approval for medical uses.

The therapeutic effect of Spirulina is attributed in part to its 17 carotenoids and amino acid assimilation, especially from the amino acid L-Glutamine (Hills 1980). In addition the porphyrin bile pigments in Spirulina are believed to enhance carbohydrate metabolism and cell respiration (Hills 1980). This seems to be supported by the fact that an extract of Spirulina has been used successfully in providing nutrients to cell cultures.

SPIRULINA'S NATURAL OCCURRENCE AND ANCIENT USE

Varieties of Spirulina have a ubiquitous occurrence in natural waters and are presented as a polluted water algae in the Standard Methods (Rand, Greenburg, Taras, and Franson 1976) algae plates. The freshwater varieties of Spirulina and many of the saltwater and brackish water varieties are too small to harvest. The larger, harvestable varieties are found in nature in the warm, alkaline

inland lakes of Africa, and South and Central America. Some examples
follow:

SOME HARVESTABLE LAKES WHERE SPIRULINA OCCURS NATURALLY (Fryer and Iles 1972, Nakamura 1982)		
NAME AND LOCATION	HARVESTABLE AREA	pH
Bogoria, Kenya AF	29,000,000 m²	10
Buccacina, Peru SA	10,000 m²	9
Chad, Chad AF	25,000,000 m²	7.1-8.3
Chiltu, Ethiopia AF	900,000 m²	9.7
Aranguadi, Ethiopia AF	550,000 m²	11.0
Tanganyika, Tanzania AF	34,000 km²	8.6-9.2
Texcoco, Mexico NA	400,000 m²	*
Rudolph, Kenya AF	8547 km²	9.4-10.0
AF-Africa NA-North America		
SA-South America	*Artificially Controlled	

The realization that Spirulina is suitable as a foodstuff has come
from its use by the natives of Chad. There "dihe" cakes, made with
Spirulina harvested from Lake Chad, have been a traditional food for
thousands of years (Nakamura 1982). The native pre-Columbian peoples
of Mexico used Spirulina as a staple. The Aztecs, who called
Spirulina "Tecuitlatl", enhanced its cultivation in the alkaline
lakes of the Valley of Mexico with nutrient inputs from their
wastewater collection systems. Sattellite photography has revealed an
extensive system of canals in Belize and Guatemala that were likely
used for the cultivation of Spirulina by the native Mayans (Hills
1980). This would explain how the Mayan civilization may have fed a
population of over two million people that flourished for over 1,000
years.

CELL STRUCTURE, GENETIC ENGINEERING POSSIBILITIES AND PHYLOGENY

Blue-green algae are very interesting organisms in that they are
procaryotic, having a cell structure like a bacterium, but also
contain chlorophyll-a like a plant. Unlike most procaryotic organisms
however, the blue-green algae, including the filamentous, multi-
cellular Spirulina, lack a distinct nuclear membrane. A unique
property of the Spirulina cell is it's lack of a thick cell wall,
which contributes to it's digestibility. These latter two facts put
together make the organism very amenable to genetic engineering
techniques. Cell lysis and genetic recombination may occur in nature,
aided by the natural alkaline environment, and does occur via
cyanophages. This explains why some species of Spirulina are found to
mutate easily.

One genetic engineering avenue that holds promise for Spirulina
would be to increase the CO_2 utilization efficiency of the organism
by manipulating the sequence used for carboxylation and oxygenation
to reduce oxygenase activity (von Wettstein 1983). Another very
promising possibility would be to impart the ability to fix
atmospheric nitrogen to the Spirulina organism. This could be done by
transferring this trait from other blue-green algae that do fix
nitrogen or by transferring this trait from nitrogen fixing bacteria

such as Klebsiella for which nitrogen fixation genetics and cloning
techniques have been well characterized (Metting 1985).

Phylogenically Spirulina is classified as follows: Phylum-
Cyanophyta, Order-Nostocales, Family-Oscillatoriaceae (Desikachary
1959), Genus-Spirulina, Tribes-Arthrospira and Euspirulina (Nakamura
1982). Confusion arises out of this last division of the Spirulina
genus into septate (Arthrospira) and non-septate (Euspirulina) forms.
In many species considered non-septate, a membrane or parts of a
membrane delineating separate cells within a filament can sometimes
be discerned. The only species which has been judged with certainty
to be unicellular is Spirulina abbreviata (Nakamura 1982). More
research is needed to establish with certainty what criteria are to
be used to further subdivide the species.

An important consideration in the harvesting of Spirulina is the
size range of the species to be isolated for culturing. The following
is a table of species whose size make them suitable for mass
production:

SPECIES SUITABLE FOR MASS PRODUCTION
(NAKAMURA 1982)

Species	Where Found
Arthrospira maxima Geitler	North America
Arthrospira jenneri Geitler	Worldwide Dist.
Arthrospira platensis Geitler	Africa, Mexico, Argentina
Spirulina flavorirens Wislouch	Lake Zerinayen
Spirulina laxissima G.S. West	Lake Tanganyika
Spirulina major Kutz	Worldwide Dist.
Spirulina gigantea Schmidle	Africa, India
Spirulina princeps Wet. G.S. West	Africa, Brazil, Ceylon

NUTRIENT REQUIREMENTS FOR CULTURING

The basic requirements to be considered for culturing Spirulina
are salinity, alkalinity, carbon, nitrogen, and trace elements. From
an economic standpoint the use of natural alkaline water from a lake
or well and treated seawater would be the best choices. The salinity
of the medium affects the buoyancy of the organism and the purity of
the culture. A higher salinity helps the organism to float and
inhibits bacterial contamination. Nakamura (1982) found the optimum
salinity for the medium to be in the range of 0.05-2.0%, the optimum
pH to be between 8.5-10.0, and the optimum temperature range to be 32-
42°C.

Spirulina may use CO_2 or bicarbonate as inorganic carbon sources.
Organic sources of carbon could be used to produce a high yield but
this would be expensive. More research into the possibilities of
mixotropic culturing is needed. The most economical source of carbon
for culturing is bicarbonate occuring in the natural water being used
for culturing. Waste CO_2 gasses from combustion or from the
purification of anaerobic digester gas are also economical carbon
sources.

The input of nitrogen into the culturing system may come from the
ammonia fertilizers commonly used in agriculture. Since ammonia in
the form of nitrate is easily utilized by Spirulina, wastewater can
be used as a source of this important nutrient. Several successful
experiments in the use of wastewater for cultivating Spirulina are

documented in the literature. Saxena, Ahmad, Shyam, and Amala (1982) successfully cultivated Spirulina platensis for use as a poultry feed using raw domestic wastewater in an integrated pisciculture and water reclamation system. Kosaric, Nguyen, and Bergougnou (1974), in some of the first experiments involving the artificial cultivation of Spirulina, grew Spirulina maxima using the secondary effluent from the London municipal wastewater treatment plant as a nitrogen source and combustion gasses as a carbon source. Oron, Shelef, and Levi (1979) cultured Spirulina maxima in outdoor ponds using cow manure as a nutrient source hypothesizing that the Spirulina protien could be dried, sterilized, and fed back to the cows.

LARGE SCALE SEMI-NATURAL CULTURE

Spirulina growing in Lake Texcoco in the Valley of Mexico was eaten by the Aztecs who enhanced its growth by channelling wastewater into the lake. In modern times the Sosa Texcoco, SA company has used the lake for extraction of caustic soda and the production of Spirulina. This company has added fertilizers to the lake as documented by Santillan (1982) to increase the production. This facility presently obtains a yield of over 4000 kg./day. A schematic flow diagram for the semi-natural culturing and harvesting method is presented in Figure 1.

Although Lake Texcoco is presently the only natural lake being enhanced for mass culturing, this method seems to hold the most promise for development both from an economic and production standpoint. At the time of this writing Dr. Hills of Microalgae International is working diligently to make arrangements with the Kenyan government for harvesting one of the lakes in this country. Unfortunately, a permanent solution to the African hunger problem lies dormant as large quantities of Spirulina are left to rot.

A possible variation of semi-natural culture would be to inoculate alkaline lakes in which no harvestable Spirulina grows with seed cultures of a harvestable variety. Likewise artificial inland lakes could be created, either along the coastline with treated seawater, or inland using alkaline water from wells. A technique for treating seawater for Spirulina culture by precipitating calcium and magnesium has been investigated by Faucher, Coupal, and Leduy (1979). A schematic diagram of a system of this type using treated seawater is presented in Figure 2.

MASS CULTURE IN MAN-MADE PONDS AND RACEWAYS

Many investigators have experimented with pilot plants for culturing Spirulina but the cost of scaling up is high. The need for pond liners and artificially created nutrient media can make this method prohibitively expensive for mass production. Microalgae International has privately financed the construction of three demonstration man-made pond facilities. The Israeli government, seeing the potential for Spirulina as a food, has given a grant to one of these facilities which is located in the Port of Eliat. This 90,000 m^2 facility was constructed with an investment of \$4.5 million. A 120,000 m^2 facilcty, called Green Gold Farms, has been constructed by Microalgae International on the outskirts of Desert Hot Springs, California for an investment of \$5.3 million. This facility is presented as the state of the art in man-made pond culturing techniques. As shown in the accompanying picture this facility obtains it's culturing liquid from a well which produces 63 l/s of 32°C water. The water is stored in a reservoir before it is enhanced with nutrients and salts and fed into raceways. Spirulina inoculum is grown out in a series of progressively bigger ponds before being introduced into sixteen large production ponds. A unique aspect of the Desert Hot Springs Facility is a hot air solar collector totalling 4000 m^2 in area which is used to power the spray dryer. The drying of the concentrated Spirulina slurry is the most costly aspect of any harvesting operation because of the energy input required.

Advantages of culturing Spirulina in man-made ponds include a better control over nutrient inputs and culture purity. This contributes to a greater possible harvest per unit area. A harvest of 10-15 $g/m^2/day$ is typical for semi-natural culture whereas a harvest of upwards of 30 $g/m^2/day$ is possible with culturing in man-made ponds. An advantage of culturing in man-made raceways that has not yet been tried on a large scale is the ability to cover the ponds. By covering, incoming light energy can be reduced to the optimum of 4000-5000 lux and the potential for contamination from wind blown material can be eliminated.

POSSIBILITIES FOR ADVANCED SYMBIOTIC SYSTEMS

As the acceptance and use of Spirulina increases, the possibilities for advanved man-made systems will become economical. An ideal system would use treated saltwater or available alkaline water for its culture medium. Nutrients would be supplied from wastewater and CO_2 waste gasses. Pumps would be wind driven turbines and dryers would be solar powered. The symbiotic system would be integrated with animal husbandry or pisciculture. A hypothetical process flow schematic for such an advanced system is presented in Figure 3. Possibilities for improvement in raceway design include the air supported tube, patented by Dr. Hills, and systems conceived by the author which allow for the production of desalinated water as a process byproduct. The latter is proposed as a method for fighting the worldwide trend of desertification caused by the destruction of the tropical rainforests and increasing CO_2 levels from the burning of fossil fuels. If this present trend continues the cultivation of Spirulina on an extensive scale may be neccessary to feed an overpopulated planet as well as to restore a natural balance of atmospheric gasses.

Green Gold Farms, supply pump and reservoir.

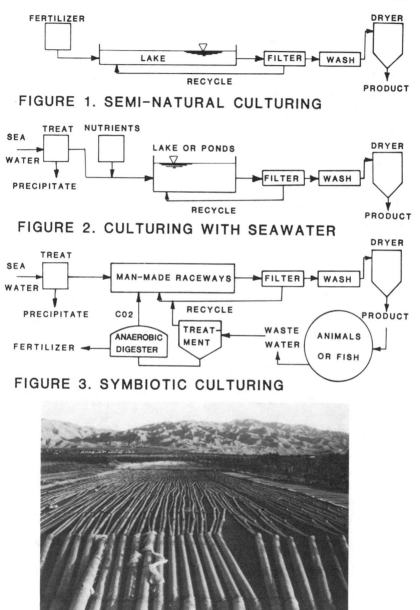

FIGURE 1. SEMI-NATURAL CULTURING

FIGURE 2. CULTURING WITH SEAWATER

FIGURE 3. SYMBIOTIC CULTURING

Green Gold Farms, solar collector.

REFERENCES

1. Desikachary, T.V., Cyanophyta, Academic Press, New York, NY, 1959, pp. 187-197.

2. Faucher, O., Coupal, B., and Leduy, A., "Utilization of Seawater-Urea as a Culture Medium for Spirulina maxima," Can. J. Microbiol., Vol. 25, 1979, pp. 752-759.

3. Fryer, G. and Iles, T., The Cichlid Fishes of the Great Lakes of Africa, t.f.h. Publications, Neptune, NJ, 1972, pp. 8-9.

4. Hills, C., "The Role of Amino Acid Metabolism in the Synthesis of Hormones and Brain Chemicals, with Special Reference to the Ingestion of the Vegetable Plankton Spirulina", J. Nutrirional Microbiol., Vol. 1, No. 8, 1980, pp. 3-12.

5. Hills, C., "Spirulina - the Maya's Secret", J. Nutritional Microbiol., Vol. 1, No. 9, 1980, pp. 3-10.

6. Hills, C., "Spirulina as an Aid in Cell Respiration", J. Nutritional Microbiol., Vol. 1, No. 10, 1980, pp. 5-16.

7. Hills, C., ed., The Secrets of Spirulina, University of the Trees Press, Boulder Creek, CA, 1980.

8. Kosaric, N., Nguyen, H., and Bergougnou, M., "Growth of Spirulina maxima Algae in Effluents from Secondary Wastewater Treatment Plants", Biotech. and Bioeng., XVI, 1974, pp. 881-896.

9. Metting, B., "Soil Microbiology and Soil Technology", Biotechnology: Applications and Research, Technomic Publishing Co., Inc., Lancaster, PA, 1985.

10. Nakamura, H., Spirulina: Food For A Hungry World, Univ. of the Trees Press, Boulder Creek, CA, 1982.

11. Oron, G., Shelef, G., and Levi, A., "Growth of Spirulina maxima on Cow Manure Wastes", Biotech. and Bioeng., XXI, 1979, pp. 2169-2173.

12. Rand, M., et. al., ed., Standard Methods for the Examination of Water and Wastewater, 14th edition, American Public Health Association, Washington, D.C., 1976.

13. Santillan, C., "Mass Production of Spirulina", Experientia, Vol. 38, No. 1, 1982, pp. 40-43.

14. Saxena, P., Ahmad, M., Shyam, R., and Amala, D., "Cultivation of Spirulina in Sewage for Poultry Feed", Experientia, Vol. 39, No. 10, 1983, pp. 1077-1083.

15. Wettstein, D. von, "Genetic Engineering in the Adaptation of Plants to Evolving Human Needs", Experientia, Vol. 39, No. 7, 1983, pp. 687-713.

Reservoir Sedimentation and
Desilting in Taiwan

Chian Min Wu*, AM. ASCE

Abstract

     This paper presents a brief review of the recent data
about reservoir sedimentation in Taiwan. The island of
Taiwan is infested with numerous flashy streams with steep
slopes and huge sediment loads, thus, the major reservoirs
have experienced heavy sediment deposit. The encroachment
on the live storage capacity is often found to be of a
serious magnitude, and several reservoirs have been even
declared to be abandoned. Recently, however, two control
measures, sluicing by desilting tunnel at Gen-Shan-Pei
Reservoir and evacuation of sediment by dredging at Shihmen Reservoir have demonstrated to have sufficient economic
value. Both of them show the successful applications of
hyper-concentrated flow for reservoir desilting either by
gravity or mechanical means.

Introduction

     For many years, the major reservoir systems in the
world are subject to some degree of sedimentation. The
loss of storage capacity is a worldwide concern. In an
age that has progressed to the landing of human beings on
the moon, it is possible that in time either the reservoirs
of today will no longer be needed or that more effective
methods of retaining their capacity will be developed.
However, until then, one must continue the struggles so
that the reservoirs will continue functioning.

     Located in weak, fractured and deeply weathered
geological area, rivers in Taiwan are characterized by
their short, steep valleys with heavy sediment transport.
The conditions are further aggravated by earthquakes which
damage the stability of the valley slopes. Thus, the
major reservoir systems in Taiwan have experienced heavy
sediment deposit. In spite of a comprehensive sediment
control program presenting various implications to
individuals working in different fields, the damage
created by sediment is still varied and extensive.
Several reservoirs have been declared to be abandoned.

---

* Chief Engineer, Water Resources Planning Commission,
  Ministry of Economic Affairs; 2 Ningpo E. St., Taipei
  10767 Taiwan, ROC.

However, recently two control meansures, sluicing by
desilting tunnel at Gen-Shan-Pei Reservoir and Evacuation
of sediment by dredging at Shih-men Reservoir have demonstrated to have sufficient economic value to justify the
removal of the sediments from the reservoir. Both of them
show the successful applications of hyper-concentrated
flow for reservoir desilting either by gravity or mechanical
means. In this paper reservoir sedimentation in Taiwan
is briefed and studies made in desilting reservoir sedimentation are summarized.

Reservoir Sedimentation in Taiwan

        Taiwan, being a province of the Republic of China,
is located approximately 150 kilometers off the coast of
the mainland China. Embracing an area of 36,000 square
kilometers, it has a population of 19 million by mid-1984.
To support this population, many dams have been built for
irrigation, water supply, power generation, flood mitigation, and water pollution control.

        Preliminary register of dams in Taiwan prepared for
the International Commission on Large Dams (1983) shows
that there are more than 56 dams in Taiwan, which are
higher than 3.6 meters (11.8 feet) in height. The
statistics also show that 55 percent are of the concrete
type and other 45 the rockfill or earth type. Of this
number 45 are higher than 15 meters (50 feet). The highest dam is Tachien (Teh-Kee) Dam, an arch concrete dam
with a height of 180.0 meters (590 feet), a length of
290.0 meters, a concrete volume of 430,000 cubic meters
and a gross reservoir capacity of 232×10^6 cubic meters
(193,253 acre-ft). Tseng Wen Dam, the second highest, is
an embankment dam with a height of 147.0 meters (482.2
feet), a length of 470.0 meters, a volume of 12.9×10^6 m^3
and gross reservoir capacity of 712.7×10^6 cubic meters.
The statistics indicate that there are 5 high dams over
100 meters in height. However, because of the steep
river slope the reservoir pockets are limited resulting
in relatively small reservoir capacities. The total
reservoir capacity for all dams added during 1921 to 1984
is $1,998 \times 10^6$ m^3. In 1985 the annual yield of reservoir
flow was $6,082 \times 10^6$ m^3, of which $3,216 \times 10^6$ m^3 was for
consumptive use, and because of multipurpose operation
$5,160 \times 10^6$ m^3 went to non-consumptive use. The total
reservoir yield ($6,082 \times 10^6$ m^3) was about 33% of the total
annual water utilization in Taiwan. Other water resources
include the run-off river flow and ground water flow.

        Unfortunately, reservoir resurvey shows that the
total reservoir capacity was decreasing at a rate of
1.67×10^6 m^3 per year. The average siltation rate varies
from 16,300 m^3/km^2/yr. (1.63 cm/year) to 30 m^3/km^2/yr.
(0.003 cm/yr.) of the catchment area. A wide variation
in this rate has been observed. Table 1 gives the data

Table 1   Sedimentation Data of Taiwan Reservoir

S. No.	Name of Reservoir	Catchment area(km)	Reservoir Capacity($10^6 m^3$)	Rate of Sedimentation ($m^3/km^2/yr.$)
1	Shihmen	763.4	309.1	2,700
2	Ten-Kee	592.0	255.4	1,900
3	Wu Sheh	219.0	150.0	4,900
4	Tsengwen	481.0	712.7	8,800
5	Pai ho	26.5	25.1	14,300
6	Gen Shan Pei	10.6	6.9	9,400
7	A-Kung-Tien	31.9	36.3	16,300
8	Lu-Liao	7.5	3.8	30
9	Tapu	104.0	9.0	2,200
10	Ku Kuan	707.8	17.1	600

for some typical big and small reservoirs in Taiwan. These reservoirs are distributed over the length and breadth of the country and include both hilly as well as plain regions. Due to high sedimentation rate, special attention has been given to the economic problem associated with the loss of reservoir life. An estimate of reservoir life shows that out of the 45 major reservoirs there are only 2 reservoirs with reservoir lives of over 200 years, 5 over 100 years, 6 over 50 years with a total average reservoir life of only 65 years. At least 4 reservoirs were declared to be abandoned in the past 20 years.

The above reservoir life is estimated for the ultimate life. Studies of the sediment distribution show that the Borland-Miller type-curves are, in general, also applicable to Taiwan but the empirical constants should be modified. If the proportion of the deposits in dead and live storages are taken into consideration, the effective lives of the reservoirs will be shorter than the said values. These reservoirs all have larger sediment accumulations, and replacement storage, if available at all, can no longer be provided at low costs because of the growing construction costs and, more importantly, disappearance of low-cost dam sites.

Sedimentation Arresting Measures

In order to compare the reservoir lives of reservoirs in Taiwan with those of other countries, empirical reservoir life equation was proposed. An analysis of existing survey data from 13 major reservoirs showed that the sedimentation rate could be expressed as

$$r_s = K_1 (C/A)^{n1} \qquad\qquad (1)$$

or

$$r_s = K_2 (C/I)^{n2} \qquad\qquad (2)$$

where r_s is the annual deposit rate in percentage and its reciprocal is the reservoir life in years C is the reservoir capacity in m^3 , A is the catchment area in m^2 , and I is the annual inflow in m^3 . Studies of worldwide data show $n_1 = -0.42$ wherease $n_2 = -0.47$. Comparison of k_1 from worldwide data shows that the mean value is 0.14, whereas from Taiwan data it is 1.80. This means under same C/A condition, the reservoir life in Taiwan is one-tenth of the worldwide average. Comparison of K_2 shows that it is 0.85 and 0.21 for Taiwan and worldwide average, respectively.

In order to prolong the reservoir life, it has been proved that engineering measures, such as check dams and debris basins, are effective. However, they cease to function after one or two flood seasons. Non-engineering measures such as soil conservation program are also comprehensively taken. However, the drive for them is not always vigorous and sustained.

Conventionally, studies of the site condition in Taiwan showed that offset reservoir with effective intake control is the only solution to the problem. Two offset reservoirs are representative of this kind of engineering measure, of which the Sun-Moon Lake is comparatively free from sediment problem because of its high settlement efficiency in the intake area.

In order to alleviate the sediment problem of the Sun-Moon Lake, an intake dam named Wu-Chieh Dam, a concrete gravity dam 58-meter high with dead storage of 18×10^6 m^3, was built. Water is diverted to the Sun-Moon Lake to form an offset reservoir. In 1941, after 6 years of operation, the dead storage of Wu-Chieh Dam was completely silted up. Since then, the dam has been subject to devastating forces of both water and sediments of all sizes. Spillways were severely eroded. Thus, the benefit of the offset reservoir is built at the expense of the diversion intake works.

In spite of a comprehensive sediment control program presenting various implications to individuals working in different fields, the damage created by sediment is still varied and extensive. Recently, however, two control measures, sluicing by desilting tunnel at Gen-Shan-Pei Reservoir and evacuation of sediment by dredging at Shihmen Reservoir have demonstrated to have sufficient economic value to justify the removal of sediments from the reservoir.

Dredging At Shihmen Reservoir

Desilting is an expensive and frustrating operation that involves sluicing and subsequent removal from downstream works or mechanical excavation and disposal. At Shihmen Reservoir the site condition is favorable to dredging.

The Shihmen Dam is of an embankment type, 133 meters
in height, 360 meters in length, forming a reservoir whose
total capacity is 316x10^6 cubic meters. The dam was put
into operation in May 1963. However, when the first
flood brought about by typhoon Gloria hit the reservoir,
the maximum inflow was reported 10,200 cms, almost equivalent to the design spillway capacity of 10,900 cms. In
that single flood 10.5x10^6 m^3 of sediment was trapped in
the reservoir. Succeeding surveys show that the annual
rate of siltation has been more than three times as high
as that estimated at the time of project design. Afterwards,
the intake tower was reconstructed, hundreds of check dam
were installed and three upstream dams were constructed,
of which the highest one, Jonghua Dam, is 81 meters high
with reservoir capacity of 12.4x10^6 m^3. In spite of
these expensive investments, the silting rate still
remained as high as 2.1x10^6 m^3/year. The effect of the
sediment deposit was so serious that it even affected the
daily operation of the intake tower. Finally, a mechanical
excavation and disposal plan was set.

Hydraulic dredger was utilized to remove the deposited
materials as deep as 80 meters. A submersible dredge
pump with pumping capacity of 900 m^3/hr, a suction head of
25 m, and power of 170kwx10px60HZ was used to draw the
sand. The suction head was enhanced with water jetting
nozzles of 3.2 m^3/min flow, 150 m head, and as a result
of the powerful ejecting effect, earth and sand dredged by
jetted water were effectively sucked into the suction pipe.
The mixture was then pumped ashore by a boost dredge pump
with 560kwx4px60HZ power. The dredging was conducted from
the seriously affected downstream intake part. Because of
the sorting action of the reservoir, the materials deposited
in this part were mainly fine materials. With the vertical
suction method, high degradation degree was possible and
the mud containing rate could be up to 30%. This makes
the unfeasible reservoir sediment removal by dredging
changing economically justified. The main features of the
dredger are as follows:

```
Carrier Vessel : Legth    : 48.0  m
                 Breadth  : 8.0   m
                 Depth    : 2.25  m
                 Draft    : 1.15  m

Dredger   :     Dredging capacity : 200 - 220 m3/hr.
                (sediment)
                hauling distance  : 1500 - 3000 m.
                pumping capacity  : 900 m3/hr.
```

The economic life of the dredging facilities is
estimated at 10 years and it is planned to evacuate 300,000 ~
600,000 m^3 each year. The dredging commenced in March

1985 and at the end of 1985 a total of 680,000 m^3 was
desilted. Though it has only a year of record, it has
been proved to be very powerful in clearing the deposit
near the intake, resulting in a great reduction of the
burden for reservoir operation.

Sluicing at Gen-Shan Pei Reservoir

The Gen-Shah Pei Dam, constructed in 1938, is an
earth dam 30.0 meters (98.4 feet) high, 256 meters long,
with original reservoir capacity of 6.98x10^6 m^3. During
its initial stage after the completion of the construction,
the reservoir functioned mainly as water storage, which
resulted in serious deposit of sediments. The spillway
was heightened by 0.9 meter in 1943 to increase the storage
capacity to 7.7x10^6 m^3. Afterwards, the intake tower was
reconstructed several times. However, those alone were
not sufficient enough to solve the sediment problem in the
reservoir. In 1957 resurvey, the remaining capacity
amounted only to 2.73x10^6 m^3, i.e., losing 60% of its
original capacity. In 1955 the sediment-flushing facility-
a desilting tunnel - was constructed. The invert elevation
of the desilting tunnel is roughly equal to the elevation
of the original river bed. It is 203 meters in length,
1.5 meters in diameter and 9.28 cms at maximum capacity.
After the completion of the tunnel 3 years of prototype
experiments were followed. Inflow and outflow rates, as
well as the drawdown rate, were varied to establish
sediment outflow from the reservoir under various conditions. Studies of field data were made to estimate the
efficiency and length of life that can be expected from
future reservoir drawdowns with respect to removing sediment
from the reservoir. As a result of this series of experiment, the operation method has been altered, draining
water during the first period of the rainy season and
storing water during the last period. When necessary, the
controlled discharge operation method was employed.

The past 28 years, desilting operation verified that
the desilting efficiency was quite high. Data were
collected to determine sediment movement and redistribution
of substantial sediment deposits within the reservoir area.
Results indicate that controlled reservoir inflow, i.e.,
clear water under storage condition, does not significantly
improve the carrying capacity of the sediment, and hence
has no flushing effect. The relative efficiency of sediment withdrawal by reservoir drawdown has varied considerably
with fluctuation of reservoir storage and redistribution
of sediment within the reservoir. Sediment desilting is
greatest at empty reservoir storage and will be limited if
a storage cushion is required at the bottom for supply
purpose. Hyperconcentrated flow of as high as 45% content
can be expected. Increased concentrations of sediment
withdrawn from the reservoir can be obtained by increased
inflow at empty storage. A stable channel gradient

will ultimately prevail through the reservoir, and combined with some continued channel widening, will provide sufficient sediments for desilting if reservoir storage can be kept empty and inflows can be fluctuated. From 1955 to 1980 a total of 8.5×10^6 m^3 of silt was desilted through the desilting tunnel with an annual average desilting capacity of 328,800 m^3. The average desilting sediment content by volume was as high as 8.94%, namely, there was an average flow of 3.67×10^6 m^3 of flow during the desilting period of May to August. The desilting flow is roughly equal to 38% of the annual runoff, and the average period of desilting operation per year is 53 days. As the desilting quantity is roughly equal to the average silting rate in the reservoir, the Gen-San-Pei reservoir is free from its severe sediment problem. Thus, the sediment deposit in reservoir has been greatly reduced, and in general, equilibrium has been achieved in the reservoir area. Concentrated discharge, fine particle size and steep slope - all these factors favor the transport of hyperconcentrated flow and consequently give a high desilting efficiency of the reservoir sedimentation. Hence, desilting period can be altered to achieve the capacity equilibrium.

Laboratory studies of the desilting flow show that the settling velocity of particles in desilting muddy flow decreases with concentration increasing. Rheological measurements of reservoir sediment also show that the viscosity of muddy water increases with the concentration increasing. All these contribute to the carrying capacity of the desilting flow, thus the flow can transport very high concentration under a relatively small flow. The water-sediment mixture behaves as a Bingham fluid. The behavior of Bingham fluid is characterized by

$$\tau = \tau\beta + \mu \, \frac{du}{dy} \qquad \text{for } \tau \rangle \tau\beta \quad \text{———————} \quad (3)$$

in which τ=the shear stress; μ=the plastic viscosity; u=the local velocity; and y=a coordinate perpendicular to the flow direction. A rotating viscosimeter was used to study the property of the desilting flow. It was found that the yield stress, $\tau\beta$, increased with concentration, Cw, according to the relation

$$\tau\beta = 0.94 \times 10^{-10} \, C_w^3 \quad , \quad r = 0.94 \quad \text{———————} \quad (4)$$

where $\tau\beta$ is in g/cm^2, Cw in kg/m^3. The viscosity, μ varied as

$$\mu = -0.00153 + 0.46 \times 10^{-8} \, C_w^{1.68} \qquad r = 0.82 \quad \text{———} \quad (5)$$

where μ is measured in g-sec/cm^2.

The existence of $\mu\beta$ and the increase of $\mu\beta$ make particles in muddy flow settle more slowly than in clear water.

The effect of reduced settling velocity also can be revealed by the tendency of the sediment-laden capacity curve. From desilting data, an empirical equation of commonly used parameters is obtained as

$$Cw = 847.07 \left(\frac{U^3}{ghw}\right)^{-0.49} , \quad r = -0.82 \quad \text{————} \quad (6)$$

where Cw is the sediment content in kg/m^3, h is the depth of flow in meter, U and w are the velocity of flow and the settling velocity of particle in m/sec, respectively. Plotting of the tested and field data shows that the desilting data turns to left as the concentration is higher than 100 kg/m^3. This means that if the sediment size is kept unchanged and consequently w is constant, then flow can carry higher concentration under smaller flow intensity.

Alternatively, a similar empirical equation can be obtained as

$$Cw = 369.3 \left(\frac{VS_f}{w}\right)^{-0.69} , \quad r = -0.93 \quad \text{————} \quad (7)$$

where s_f is the slope of the energy gradient (m/m). As these equations are dimensionless in form, they can be used to predict the desilting capacity of a similar structure. Other forms of transport equation, such as using critical tractive force, critical flow discharge and critical slope are possible, yet the correlation is not preferable.

Conclusion

The experience gained in the last four decades in Taiwan has been valuable and has cleared many of the misconceptions about the reservoir sedimentation problem. It is now possible to have a more realistic assessment of the sedimentation problem for many reservoirs. However, one must still continue the struggles so that the reservoirs will continue functioning.

APPENDIX - References

1. Kira, H "Hydraulic Studies on the Sedimentation in Reservoirs". Memoris of Faculty of Agr. Kagawa University. No.12, 1963.

2. Wu, Chian Min, "Sedimentation Damage of Hydraulic Structures in Taiwan", Proc. Int. Symp. on River Mechanics, IAHR, Vol.1. Jan. 1973, pp. A14-1 ~ A14-12.

A Proposed Desilting Reservoir System in Taiwan

Jing-San Hwang*

ABSTRACT

Owing to the urgent need of water for municipal and industrial uses in Southern Taiwan where there is rapid urbanization and industrialization, the construction of reservoirs for collecting abundant water during the wet season is considered an effective measure of water resource management. The Nanhwa reservoir is proposed to be completed in 1991 for the purpose of supplementing the water supply for Southern Taiwan, especially for the Tainan and Kao-hsiung Municipal Districts in order to meet the demands by 21st century.

The desilting system is designed somewhat unique in that the reservoir is divided into two bays; water flows into the forebay for sedimentation and then over flows into the afterbay for storage and operation. The sediments carried by the inflow water will nearly all deposit in the forebay to be removed by periodic flushing. According to the flow routing, including water and sediment, the trap efficiency can be predicted and the forebay of the Nanhwa reservoir will function as a settling basin and will contain almost no permanent sediments.

This paper presents the planning and current status of the project; physical (including hydrologic and geological) and economical evaluations are included. At the moment, the project is under review for its feasibility and is expected to be approved in the near future, but the decision maker is still reluctant to accept this concept.

Introduction

Owing to the increasing demands for water resources by municipal and industrial users in Southern Taiwan as a consequence of rapid urbanization and industrialization in this region, the construction of reservoirs to impound run-off water during the wet season is an effective measure for water resources management. The Nanhwa reservoir is proposed to be completed in 1991 to supplement the water supply for Southern Taiwan, especially for the Tainan and Kao-hsiung Municipal Districts in order to meet the demand by the 21st century.

The proposed reservoir is to be located upstream of Hoku Creek, a tributary of the Tsengwen River at the township of Nanhwa in Tainan County. It will be operated after its completion in conjunction with

* Chief, Planning Team, Taiwan Provincial Water Conservancy Bureau, 37-8 Liming Road, Nantwen District, Taichung City, Taiwan, R.O.C.

the water collected from its own watershed and water diverted from Chishan Creek, a neighbouring larger river, to provide approximately
29,200 ha-m of raw water a year for municipal and industrial usage in
the area.

Figure 1 shows the schematics of the general layout of the Nanhwa
reservoir system. This system is somewhat unique in that the reservoir
is divided into two bays; water flows into the forebay for sedimentation and then over flows into the afterbay of the reservoir for storage and operation. The sediment carried by the inflow water will nearly
all be deposited in the forebay to be removed by periodic flushing.
There will be a flushing tunnel of 5.5 meters diameter and 1,500 meters
long provided. It is designed to be built at the low point of the forebay.

According to the flow routing, including water and sediment, the
trap effeciency can be predicted. The forebay of the Nanhwa reservoir
will function as a settling basin and will therefore contain almost no
permanent deposition. The probable life of the afterbay of the Nanhwa
reservoir is also estimated to be prolonged from 110 years without any
desilting scheme to 470 years using the special operational arrangement
(1985, Hwang).

Figure 2 shows the water supply scheme for the Tainan and Kao-hsiung Districts. In conjunction with the water that could be diverted
from the lower reach of the Kaopin River, a total of 88,840 ha-m of raw
water will be provided for these Districts to meet requirements by the
year 2001.

Climate and Hydrology

Because the Tropic of Cancer passes through the middle south of
Taiwan, a little bit north of the basin, its climate is semitropical
with high precipitation between May and September and relatively dry
during the rest of the year. The average annual rainfall of the watershed above the damsite is 3,300 mm. It is abundant, though very unevenly distributed.

During the wet season, about 92 % of the annual rainfall occurs
intensively and results in serious watershed erosion. A great deal of
heavily sediment-laden flow runs off in a short period of time and
rapidly empties itself into the ocean. Only 8 % of the annual rainfall
is attributed to the dry season from October to the following April.

Almost all the streams in Taiwan are nearly dry in the dry season
and Hoku Creek is no exception. The average annual runoff water collected from the watershed is 21,900 ha-m estimated from the historical
flow records since 1959 at the gauging station of Yietien, some 15 km
downstream of the damsite. The maximum recorded runoff is 39,500 ha-m
(1977) while the minimum is 10,600 ha-m (1970).

The effective capacity of the Nanhwa reservoir will be 15,000 ha-m.
As the water collected from its own watershed is not enough for the

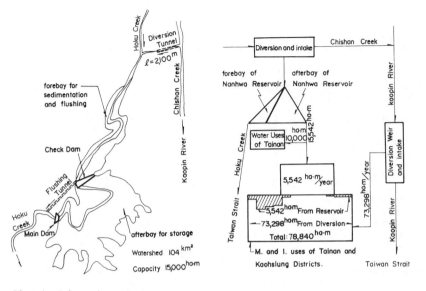

Fig. 1. Schematics of the General
Layout of Nanhwa Reservoir

Fig. 2. Water Supply Scheme for Tainan and Kao-hsiung Districts

reservoir operation, additional supplemental water has to be diverted
from the neighbouring larger river, Chishan Creek, to meet the requirement. Table 1 indicates the hydrological conditions of the watershed
above the Nanhwa damsite and at Chishan Diversion, including the catchment area and the run-off records.

The water sources both collected from its own watershed and diverted
from Chishan Creek will all flow into the Nanhwa reservoir to be used
together to yield approximately 29,200 ha-m a year for the area of demand. The historic data for the reservoir system reveals that the water
is not only unevenly distributed seasonally, but the long term variation is significant too.

Table 1. Hydrologic Condition of Water sources

Streams:	Watershed(km^2)	Run-off Records (ha-m)		
		Mean	Maximum	Minimum
Hoku Creek	104	21,900	39,500	10,600
Chishan Creek	304	79,600	128,600	43,200
		48,000*	98,000*	15,400*

* Available water for diversion.

In both Hoku Creek and Chishan Creek, the minimum annual records are only 30 % of the maximum annual records. Consequently, only 15,000 ha-m of raw water may be provided by the reservoir system, about a half of the annual requirement for users, if no risk of water shortage is to result (1985, TPWCB).

Geology and Sedimentation

The Hoku Creek is a tributary of the Tsengwen River; its watershed is located between the catchments of Chishan Creek in the southeast and Tapu Creek in the northwest. The highest point of the basin is at the northwest about 1,000 meters above the mean sea level. The damsite is the lowest point of the basin that is about 100 meters above the mean sea level located at the southwest of the basin. The watershed is oblong in shap and 104 km² in size, located in the Western Foothills which is one of the three major geologic provinces on Taiwan.

The Western Foothills Province is mostly composed of Pliocene rocks. The rocks are mainly alternations of sandstone and shale with locally interspersed limestone and tuff lenses. The total thickness is 8,000 meters or more. This is the best-known geologic province on Taiwan because of the extensive mineral exploration and other human activities in this area. The formation in the reservoir area and near the damsite largely belongs to Cholan Formation.

The Cholan Formation was named by Torri, 1935 (1975, Ho), after the township of Cholan in the southern part of Miaoli County. This formation is composed of 1,500 to 2,500 meters of sandstone, siltstone, mudstone and shale in a monotonous alternating sequence. Based on a preliminary surface investigation including an overview of geologic observation and a geologic environmental investigation, a surface mapping and a preliminary report have been completed, respectively.

The rocks around the damsite are closely classified as silty sandstone or sandy siltstone. The strength of the rocks is moderate around 100 to 400 kg/cm² acquired by the uniaxial compression tests on the rock cores. The geologic study has concluded that either a concrete gravity dam or an embankment dam will fulfill safely requirements on the foundation of the Nanhwa damsite.

The watertightness of the reservoir basin is quite adequate because of the silty sandstone and sandy siltstone alternations. The dam type, concrete dam or embankment dam, will be determined on the basis of the availability of natural material for its construction and the cost of the construction. After a study of the above mentioned items, an embankment dam was chosen to be the dam type.

So far, 202 meters of adits have been excavated on both banks of the Nanhwa damsite and 65 holes have been drilled with a total depth of 2,598 meters, which all are located around the damsite and the foundation of the ancillary structures. As the result of the exploration by adits and borings, the local geological condition has already been determined as a monotonous structure of homogeneous formation for the area concerned (Aug. 1985 TPWCB).

All of the rocks in the watershed of the Nanhwa reservoir are relatively fresh in age, Miocene to Pleitocene, and generally weak, resulting in serious erosion of the watershed. The higher the erosion rate
of the watershed the larger the depletion rate of the reservoir. The
probable life of a reservoir depends primarily upon the available capacity for sedimentation and the sediment yield from a watershed to the
reservoir. The sediment yield for the Nanhwa reservoir is estimated to
be 15 mm a year over the whole watershed (1985, Hwang and Yen). In order to prevent the rapid depletion of the reservoir storage capacity
after its completion, a reservoir operational pattern has been formulated based on a detailed operation study including sediment and water.
The general layout of the whole engineering system is also arranged
according to the operational pattern for water.

Alternatives and Their Evaluation

The annual water demands for the objective area is estimated to be
around 29,200 ha-m by the year 2001. Several alternatives have been conceived to provide water to meet the demand, including: (1) the Nanhwa
reservoir constructed only to regulate the stream flow of the Hoku
Creek; (2) water is diverted over basin from Chishan Creek without any
reservoir regulation; (3) water is diverted from Chishan Creek into the
Tsengwen reservoir, the biggest reservoir existing in Taiwan, to
increase the inflow water for its operation; and (4) water is diverted
from Chishan Creek in conjunction with the construction of the Nanhwa
reservoir (1985, Sinotech).

The first case could only provide approximately 19,000 ha-m a year
even if the dam is constructed to a height of 100 meters. The second
case could not evenly provide the water demanded owing to the long dry
season when the creeks are almost dry from October to the following April.
The third case could only increase 10,400 ha-m of reservoir yield for
use. The remaining capacity of the Tsengwen reservoir for the operation
of diversion water from Chishan Creek is only 15 years, because 420 ha-m
of sediment is deposited annually in the reservoir.

Based on the evaluation of the above mentioned alternatives, the
proposed scheme is the construction of the Nanhwa reservoir in conjunction with the over basin diversion from Chishan Creek. There are three
major components of the engineering system; first the diversion weir
and tunnel and their ancillary structures, second the Nanhwa dam and its
ancillary structures, and third the check dam and flushing tunnel.

Evaluation of the Desilting System

The uniform annual series factor can be applied to an equal cash
flow in each year. But in a reservoir project with sediment deposition,
the cash flow will not be equal. The simplest pattern of the uniformly
increasing gradient series, a series in which the cash flow increase/
decrease by some constant amount between each pair of years, can be

applied for the economical evaluation of a depleting reservoir project
(1971, James and Lee).

The present-worth method can also be combined and used to figure
out the present value of reservoir yield in an economical life as the
computation of the following equation:

$$Py = (Si \times \frac{P}{A} - \frac{Si}{Lp} \times \frac{P}{G}) \cdot r \text{ --------------------------} (1)$$

where Si = initial storage capacity (ha-m)

$$\frac{P}{A} = \frac{(1+i)^N - 1}{i(1+i)^N} = (\frac{P}{A} , i \%, N)$$

Lp = Probable life (years)
i = Discount rate (%)
N = Economical life (years)

$$\frac{P}{G} = \frac{(1+i)^{N+1} - (1+Ni+i)}{i^2(1+i)^N} = (\frac{P}{G} , i \%, N)$$

r = Reservoir operational ratio

Figure 3 indicates the effects of the reservoir desilting on the
Nanhwa reservoir. Although the probable life can be estimated to be
prolonged from 110 years to 470 years with desilting and the total yield
of the whole reservoir life with desilting is three times larger than
that without desilting, the economical evaluation with a 50-year economical life and a 6 % discount rate reveals that the cost of a unit of
raw water is 25 % more expensive than that without desilting.

Accordingly, the economical evaluation seems not to be reasonable
for a long term view point because the adverse effects of the deposited
reservoir on a water resource system are not taking into account in the
evaluation. Based on the economical view point with a short term, say
50 years, people are reluctant to accept a reservoir with a desilting
system instead of a conventional one, in spite of the benefit for future
generations.

In a small island environment, such as Taiwan, the rivers are all
relatively short and steep, and the sites for dam and reservoirs are
not easily or plentifully available. In economical analysis of a reservoir project at the moment, only the total reservoir yield during the
economical life is considered. The adversities of the deposited sediment in the water resources system will be severe but have not been
accounted. According to the long term view point, this is very important because there will be not so many dam-reservoir sites available for
future generations, unless large amounts of sea water can be desalted
economically.

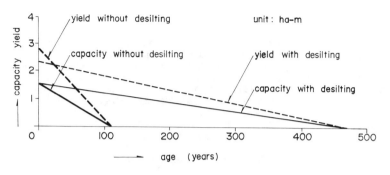

Fig. 3. Illustration of the Effects of Reservoir Desilting of Nanhwa.

Conclusions

The proposed project including the Nanhwa reservoir and the over basin diversion system has been investigated and studied over the last three years. A feasibility report has been prepared and presented to the government for approval.

The Taiwan Water Supply Corporation (TWSC) intends to construct the proposed system to provide water to meet the increasing urgent demands of the next decade. The project was reviewed by the Provincial Government last year, and then submitted further to the National Government for approval.

After review and discussion in the Council for Economical Planning and Development, the project was approved conditionally upon the proviso the reservoir can be implemented from the next fiscal year, 1987, but the efficiency and the economical evaluation of the desilting system should be carefully studied again considering the adversities of the reservoir sedimentation.

Based on the concluding comments of the project approval, the efficiency of the Nanhwa reservoir desilting scheme is now under further study using hydraulic models and mathematical analysis that is expected to achieve a reasonable result this year. If it is justified, it could then be suggested that the facilities of the desilting system, the check dam and flushing tunnel, can be implemented in conjunction with the reservoir and its appurtenances.

References

1. Ho, C.S.: *An Introduction to the Geology of Taiwan explanatory Text of the Geologic Map of Taiwan, published by the Ministry of Economic Affairs, R.O.C., December 1975.*
2. Hwang, J.S.: *The Study and Planning of Reservoir Desilting in Taiwan, Water International 10 (1985) 7-13.*
3. Hwang, J.S. and W.S. Yen,: *Prediction of the Sediment Yield on the Watershed to Nanhwa Reservoir, Journal of Chinese Agricultural Engineering Vol. 31, No.2 pp. 20-25, June 1, 1985 (in Chinese).*
4. James, L.D. and R.R. Lee,: *Economics of Water resources Planning, McGraw-Hill, New York, 1971.*
5. *A Report of Review Study on the Nanhwa Reservoir Project, 2. A study of Water Supply Capability and Alternatives Evaluation, Planning team, Taiwan Provincial Water Conservancy Bureau, R.O.C., October 1985 (in Chinese).*
6. *A Report of Review Study on the Nanhwa Reservoir Project, 14. Preliminary Design and Evaluation of Dam and its Appurtenances, prepared by Sinotech Engineering Consultants, Inc., for TPWCB, December 1985 (in Chinese).*
7. *A Report of Review Study on the Nanhwa Reservoir Project, 15. A Report of Boring, Adit Exploration and Geological Investigation, Planning Team, Taiwan Provincial Water Conservancy Bureau, R.O.C., August 1985 (in Chinese).*

Effect of African Drought on Water Resource Management in Egypt

Scot E. Smith
Keith W. Bedford[*]

Introduction

The precarious drought conditions that until recently prevailed
in Africa is the subject of this present investigation. The region
was close to utter devastation until the drought was mitigated by
naturally occurring rainfall in the spring of 1985.

1980 marked the beginning of the worst drought to hit the Sahel
and east Africa in 70 years. The consequences of the drought were
compounded by inappropriate farming methods, bureaucratic
insensitivity and inaction, over-exploitation of land by a country
that is overpopulated, and the basic infertility of the soil.

In this paper we shall look at the ways in which Egypt was
affected by the drought in terms of the availability of water and the
constructive measures that should be implemented to insure the very
survival of the people and country in the event of a new drought.

Nile Hydrology

The present drought was the result of the failure of rain clouds
to reach the edge of the African monsoon envelope which lies 15
degrees north and south of the equator (1). Rainfall was literally
non-existent in the Ethiopian Highlands since 1928.

The drought that had affected Egypt in recent years had not
reduced the discharge of White Nile water and it may be presumed that
it was a constant factor that proved of great benefit. The Blue Nile,
by contrast, has always shown great seasonal periodicity.

Major Impoundment Projects on the Nile

Six major impoundments line the Nile between Uganda and Egypt.
They range in size from 1 billion cubic meters of the Sennar Reservoir
to over 168 billion cubic meters for the Aswan High Dam Reservoir.

The High Dam at Aswan is the latest, but probably not the last,
major impoundment project on the Nile. Built under a storm cloud of

[*]Assistant Professor and Professor, respectively, Department of Civil
Engineering, 2070 Neil Avenue, The Ohio State University, Columbus,
Ohio, 43210

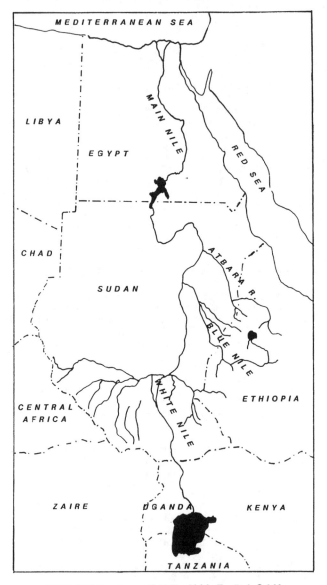

FIGURE 1 : THE NILE BASIN

political and environmental controversy in the 1960's, the dam has performed its intended purpose by providing Egypt with the essential edge against both flood and drought.

A high percentage of the Nile's water is permanently lost to downstream users due to naturally occurring swamps and marshes. The largest of these swamps, known as the Sudd, is located in central Sudan. In an attempt to reduce the loss of water to evaporation in the Sudd, a bypass canal (Jonglei Canal) is being constructed. It is estimated that over 14 percent of the annual discharge of the Nile evaporates in the Sudd (3).

Despite the enormous amount of water lost to the atmosphere and through seepage, the Nile discharges an average of 84 billion cubic meters of water annually during a normal year (6). Of that amount, about 55 million cubic meters reach Egypt at the head of the Aswan Reservoir. Approximately 12% of that quantity is lost from evaporation and seepage leaving less than 50 billion cubic meters of water in the live storage of the reservoir. During the past six years, however, the average annual inflow to Aswan has been 43 billion cubic meters, according to the Egyptian Ministry of Irrigation (4). There has, therefore, been no net addition of water to the Aswan Reservoir since 1978 and withdrawals have been exceeding inflow for every year thereafter.

Effect of the Drought on Egypt

Despite the fact that the Aswan Reservoir was at its lowest level in 10 years in August 1985 and stored less than half its capacity, there were few obvious manifestations of drought in Egypt. The government had not instituted water conservation measures and continued to start new land reclamation projects in the desert.

The Minister of Irrigation, Mr. Essam Radi, addressed the problem of a continued drought early in 1985 (4). His manipulation of statistics created an ill-founded optimism about the country's water resources. While it is true that there was an inflow of 59.5 cubic meters to the Aswan reservoir in 1985, he did not take into account the steady decline of amounts and withdrawals in previous years that were never made up for. So pronounced was the inability of the Nile to replenish the water levels during the drought years, that simple calculations revealed ultimately a shortfall condition would obtain.

Recent rains indicate the end of this drought cycle. The Aswan Reservoir level is so low, however, that water conservation must still be practiced by Egypt at least until the flood in 1986 to prevent shortfalls.

The live storage capacity of the reservoir on August 1, 1985 was 16.0 billion cubic meters of water. If this figure is accurate, a prediction of the live storage in the reservoir may be made for the period August 1, 1985 to July 31, 1986. Assumptions on losses through withdrawal, evaporation and seepage were based on averages reported by the Egyptian Ministry of Irrigation (4). The results of the simulation are given in Table 1.

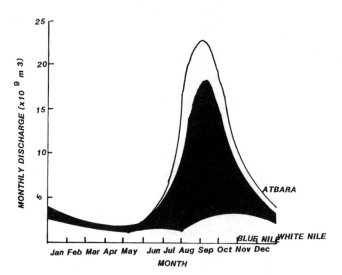

FIGURE 2 : RELATIVE CONTRIBUTION
FROM THE BLUE NILE AND ATBARA RIVERS

TABLE 1. - MONTHLY SIMULATION OF THE ASWAN RESERVOIR FOR 1985/86
(all volumes in billions of cubic meters)

Month	Inflow	Sudanese Withdrawal	Evaporation & Seepage	Release from High Dam	Live Storage (month end)
Aug.	9.1	1.25	0.58	5.60	17.67
Sept.	17.08	1.02	0.64	3.80	29.29
Oct.	10.56	1.00	0.68	3.80	34.37
Nov.	5.77	1.78	0.69	3.70	33.97
Dec.	3.96	1.81	0.65	3.60	31.87
Jan.	2.41	1.64	0.55	3.60	28.49
Feb.	1.61	1.51	0.50	3.90	24.19
Mar.	1.50	1.22	0.44	4.60	19.43
Apr.	1.33	0.84	0.55	4.40	14.97
May	1.40	0.41	0.64	5.10	10.22
Jun.	1.37	0.45	0.58	6.50	4.06
Jul.	2.81	0.95	0.51	6.90	-1.49

The results of the simulation imply that some draft reduction from the High Dam will have to occur in 1985/86 in order to prevent water shortfalls. The government of Egypt is attempting to reduce water consumption by three percent (4). That would represent approximately 1.67 billion cubic meters of water which would be barely sufficient to cover the live storage requirement.

Water Conservation Measures

The Ministry of Irrigation is attempting to reduce water consumption by the following means:

- Reduction of withdrawal from the High Dam for hydroelectirc power production. The anticipated savings would total about 1.0 billion cubic meters of waters.
- Reuse of agricultural drainage water. If all of the water were recycled, nearly 5.0 billion cubic meters of water would be saved (6). Recycled water contains a higher concentration of dissolved salts, however, which would lower soil fertility.
- Require farmers to irrigate only at night and so reduce evapotranspirative loss.
- Clean canals of aquatic vegetation and so reduce loss of water through evapotranspiration.

In addition to these actions, it is imperative that a number of other steps be taken to mitigate another drought. They include:

- Modify cropping patterns to low water demanding crops. Farmers could be encouraged through government incentive programs to grow plants that require less water. Currently many high water requirement plants are grown because they are used for hard currency exchange (cash crops).

- Use of groundwater in Delta aquifers. Wells could be dug to tap existing groundwater reserves. The wells would be used only in the event of a shortage due to the potential problem of salt water intrusion from the Mediterranean.
- Reduction of evaporation from the Aswan Reservoir. Wind breaks on the northwestern side of the reservoir would significantly reduce evaporation which accounts for nearly 12 percent of the total inflow to the reservoir.
- Complete a number of projects with the Sudan and Uganda on the upper Nile to capture more runoff and reduce evaporation. An example would be the Jonglei Canal which is about two-third complete.

To conclude, one needs to urge Egypt to implement measures to reduce its water consumption and increase its supply. The nation's population is increasing at an unprecedented rate which will result in higher demands for water in the future (5). The limits of the Aswan Reservoir have been tested by the recent drought, and clearly they could not withstand another drought of comparable severity.

References

1. Bell, Barbara, "The Dark Ages in Ancient History", Journal of Archaelogy, Vol. 75, No. 3, 1971, pp. 1-26.

2. Berry, L., "Assessment of Desertification in the Sudano-Sahelian Region: 1981-1984, UNEP, Nairobi, XVIII, 146pp.

3. Moghraby, A., "The Jonglei Canal-Needed Development or Potential Ecodisaster?" Environmental Conservation, Vol. 9, No. 2, 1982.

4. Radi, M.A., "Government Efforts to Conserve Water", Al Ahram, (Egyptian National Newspaper), March 26, 1985 p. 1 (translated from Arabic).

5. Rauth, Robert, "Preventing Famine in Africa", San Francisco Chronicle, June 23, 1985, p. 4.

6. Waterbury, John (1979) Hydropolitics of the Nile Valley, Syracuse University Press, 1979.

Sediment Penetration in Lakes as a Result of
Dredged Material Disposal and River Sediment Loads

by

Alaa El Zawahary and William James*

Dredging and dumping of dredge spoil is one of the most serious and frequent of the problematic activities which take place in coastal waters. Nearly all dredge spoil disposal sites in U.S. coastal waters are in the nearshore areas, in water less than 30 m deep. At the dredge site there is also much turbulence and resuspension of sediment. If the sediments are polluted, resuspension can greatly increase the toxic materials concentration in the surrounding area. Despite this, the affected area is relatively confined. On the other hand the plume that develops during spoil dumping may have a wide-spread effect.

Currents in the nearshore region differ markedly from those in the offshore regions. Stratification, nonlinear accelerations, bottom topography and friction may all be of great importance in the coastal boundary layer. To resolve the small time and length scales of the coastal zone eddies, a fine numerical grid size is required. To resolve the entire lake or ocean using such a fine grid may be very expensive in terms of computer resources. Pollutant transport within the coastal boundary layer is highly sensitive to the vertical current structure and to the magnitude of the vertical current, especially during upwelling and downwelling episodes.

To generate coastal currents, including the vertical structure of the currents, a rigid-lid channel-type model, with fine grid in the coastal zone, was modified to include the non-linear acceleration terms, and two different forms of the vertical eddy viscosity were added, representing two different hypotheses concerning the vertical transfer of momentum. The model is called ERCH herein.

A computer program called SEDTRAN was developed to predict the sediment concentration distribution within the coastal boundary layer. The program solves the three dimensional time-dependent mass balance equation including the settling term, and the sediment transport equation using a forward time difference, central finite difference for the diffusion terms and upwind finite difference with flux-corrected transport technique for the advection and settling terms. The model was partially validated using the limited suspended sediment measurements collected by the Heidelberg College water quality laboratory in Lake Erie, and data

*Computational Hydraulics Group, McMaster University, Hamilton, Ontario, Canada, L8S 4L7.

published by the U.S. Geological Survey (USGS) in 1979.

To investigate the effect of coastal currents on the suspended sediment plume and patch, and the extent of suspended sediment in both coastal and offshore waters, several types of sediment-related activities
were studied: (a) continuous dredging using side-caster dredge; (b)
dumping of sediment spoils; and (c) river sediment loads.

The simulated results were used to define: (1) a representative
zone influenced by a nearshore source of pollution and (2) the sediment
grain size distribution across the coastal boundary layer.

One-Layer Model "ONELAY"

A model developed by Simons and Lam (1982) assumed that the basin is
relatively well-mixed vertically. The model computes the vertically
integrated current and the free surface elevation for a given wind and
given inflow and outflow. The non-linear acceleration terms are dropped,
the Coriolis term is included, and either linear or nonlinear bottom
friction can be modelled.

Since the Simon and Lam model used constant wind stress, the model
was modified by the authors to include hourly average wind speed and
direction time series for the wind stress calculations. The modified
model is called ONELAY (ONE LAYER) herein.

SEDTRAN

The general goal of a water quality model is to predict the concentration of a contaminant over space and time, starting from the boundary
conditions, the initial flow structure and the initial contaminant concentration distribution. The contaminant concentration is highly sensitive to the mean current and turbulent fluxes. Truly predictive water
quality models necessarily include the prediction of the current and
turbulent fluxes as well as the concentration. But it is useful in many
cases to use sophisticated water quality models without simultaneously
predicting the current and turbulent fluxes. In this case the hydrodynamic model is run first, the appropriate data are stored and then used to
run the mass transport model. In the less difficult situations, where
the current and turbulent fluxes are known from observations, the mass
transport model only is run.

In the present study the hydrodynamic models are run first to generate the current field, the current field is stored and then used as
input to the mass transport model. The field observations are used to
verify, calibrate and validate the hydrodynamic models and to estimate
the turbulent fluxes by means of the diffusion coefficient calculations.

To study the effect of the different flow regimes on the sediment
distribution within the coastal boundary layer, both the detailed vertical structure of the horizontal flow and the vertical velocity have to be
incorporated in the mass transport model. Thus, a three-dimensional time

dependent mass transport model is required.

Sediment transport and deposition in the coastal zone can be divided
into two major topics according to the sediment source: (i) sediment
discharge from a land source (sewers, industrial outfalls and runoff),
and (ii) sediment load generated by erosion and resuspension of the lake
shore and bottom.

Sediment resuspension calculations require measurements of a
reference concentration for each time step of the simulation period, to
construct the logarithmic-suspended load concentration profile. It is
very difficult, if not impossible, to establish a reference concentration
for each time step. The other alternative is to relate the reference
concentration to the shear velocity and the bed load discharge (Einstein,
1950). For more details refer to a previous study (Elzawahry, 1981).
Bed load calculations require relating the sediment characteristics to
the flow properties through some empirical constants in an iterative
procedure. It is not an easy task to develop three-dimensional time
dependent sediment transport models capable of computing the sediment bed
load, the sediment resuspension distribution and the inflow sediment
distribution. Such models are expected to be very costly and the results
are expected to be difficult to interpret. When Chen (1971) formulated a
longitudinal dispersion equation for suspended sediment with a moving
bed, the work involved many simplifications and formulations. Moreover,
the sediment resuspension is highly influenced by thermal stratification.
The thermocline behaves as a diffusive floor preventing the bed sediment
from resuspension in the epilimnion.

SEDTRAN was developed to predict the inflow sediment concentration
distribution within the coastal boundary layer. The program solves the
three dimensional time dependent mass balance equation including the
settling term, and the sediment transport equation using a forward time
difference, central finite difference for the diffusion terms and upwind
finite difference with flux-corrected transport technique for the advection and settling terms.

The ability of the numerical model to simulate efficiently one, two
or three space variables was tested by many numerical test examples. The
model was partially validated using the limited suspended sediment measurements collected by the water quality laboratory at Heidelberg College. Part of the data published by the U.S. Geological Survey (USGS) in
1979, were also used in the validation.

The sediment concentration is assumed to be a function of the three
space coordinates and time. The three velocity components in the alongshore, the cross-shore and the vertical directions previously computed by
ERCH are input to SEDTRAN which generates a three dimensional sediment
plume/patch. The three velocity components are assumed to vary only in
the alongshore and the cross-shore directions. The horizontal diffusivi-
ties are assumed to be constants or functions of time, the values being
obtained from a statistical analysis. The vertical eddy diffusivity is
assumed to be a function of time, wind stress, water temperature and

water depth. The settling velocity is calculated for each grain size
using Stokes law for Reynolds numbers less than 0.1 and the relation
reported by Simons and Sentruk (1977) for Reynolds numbers larger than
0.1. SEDTRAN simulates up to 10 sources of sediment with variable locations. The source concentrations can be constant or time dependent. The
model simulates a continuous source to generate a plume and a pulse to
generate a patch; bottom topography is also accomodated.

Application to Sediment Disposal

To investigate the effect of coastal currents on the suspended sediment plume and patch, and the extent of suspended sediment in both coastal and offshore waters, several types of sediment-related activities
were studied. The cases, simulated by running both ERCH and SEDTRAN,
were equivalent to: (a) continuous dredging, e.g. using side-caster
dredge; (b) dumping of sediment spoils; and (c) river sediment loads.

Point Source

For the case of dredging the harbour entrance or constructing a
nearshore structure using suction dredging, a continuous surface point
source 1 km offshore was simulated. For disposal of heavy particles, a
surface source is the worst case, since the entire water column is polluted. This case was simulated for the period July 1 to 5, 1979 when a
strong shore parallel current persisted. The currents computed by ERCH
were input to SEDTRAN using $dx = dy = 500$ m, $dz = 2.5$ m, $dt = 300$ sec, K_x
$= 2.6 \times 10^4$ cm^2/sec and $K_y = 6 \times 10^3$ cm^2/sec. The computed results
showed that, for the flow profiles at 12:00 hours on July 1, a near-
surface onshore component was accompanied by return flow at 5 m depth,
strong nearshore north-east flow with return flow at about 9 km offshore,
and a downward nearshore current. For the computed sediment plume at
18:00 hours on July 1, the plume was directed toward the north-east,
occupying a narrow width at surface and wider at depth. At the surface
the plume extended about 10 km and 2 km along and across the shore
respectively. At 10 m depth the plume also extended 10 km but 5 km
across the shore.

The flow profiles were computed for the period July 1 to 5, 1979,
and show several current direction combinations for u, v and w with
different magnitude between weak and strong currents. The computed
sediment plumes also show different shapes at different directions with
increasing shoreline concentrations with time. The concentrations decreased as a function of distance from the source as is to be expected.
The computed plume shapes and dimensions were not always similar for all
depths. During the five day simulation the plume extended about 18 km
and the 10% concentration about 8 km and 2 km along and across the shore
respectively. The maximum shoreline concentration was about 54% of the
source concentration and covered about 250 m of the shore.

To study the effect of the source location across the coastal boundary layer, a surface point source located 3 km offshore was used. The
flow profiles for August 24 were computed. At 18:00 hours, due to the

relative remoteness of the shore from the source, the plume was elongated in the horizontal mean current direction, and relatively wide. The plume extended about 10 km and 5 km along and across the shoreline respectively. The maximum shoreline was about 1% of the source concentration.

As mentioned earlier the most critical parameter is the sediment grain size. So two additional cases, representing fine sand and very fine silt, were studied. In the case of the fine sand range (particle size 0.1 mm), at 18:00 hours the plume covered a relatively smaller area at all depths, while the 0% concentration did not reach the shoreline. The plume extended to about 4 km and 3 km along and across the shore, respectively. The concentrations computed at lower depths were relatively high, having a maximum value of 80% and 70% at 5 m and 10 m, respectively.

The plume computed using the very fine silt range (0.005 mm) was sensitive to the horizontal current. At the surface the plume covered about 18 km and 5 km along and across the shore, respectively. The maximum shoreline concentration was about 2% of the source concentration. The concentrations at lower depths were relatively small, having a maximum value of about 17% and 3% at 5 m and 10 m depths, respectively.

Dredging and dumping of dredge spoil is one of the most serious and frequent of the problematic activities which take place in coastal waters. Nearly all dredge spoil disposal sites in U.S. coastal waters are in the near shore areas, in water less than 30 m deep (Bishop, 1983). At the dredge site there is much turbulence and resuspension of sediment. If the sediments are polluted, resuspension can greatly increase the toxic materials concentration in the surrounding area. Despite this, the affected area is relatively confined. On the other hand the plume that develops during spoil dumping may have a more wide spread effect. These results may be interpreted to represent the impact zone of a side-caster dredge for three grain sizes that could be expected in dredge spoil.

Sediment Patch

The transport of sediment particles dumped in the coastal zone was investigated by again assuming a surface instantaneous source located 3 km offshore. The sediment patch was simulated using the August 24 currents and the parameters for the particle size ranges given earlier. The computed sediment patch at 1:00 hours on August 24 for a particle size of 0.1 mm, showed that, due to the high settling velocity (0.5 cm/sec), no sediment was found in the upper 5 m. Sediment was found below the 5 m depth with increasing concentrations downward. At the 5 m depth the patch extended about 2 km along and across the shore with maximum concentrations of 1% of the original dumped sediment concentration. At 10 m depth, the patch extended about 4 km along and across the shore respectively with maximum concentration of 9%. The centre of the gravity of the patch hardly moved at all, the flow being dominated by vertical advection (the settling term). One hour later, no sediment was found in the entire water column.

At 9:00 hours on August 24, no sediments were found in the water
column for a particle size of 0.02, and the 0.005 mm patch reached the
shoreline at the surface with concentrations less than 0.04%. It is
important to note that, though concentrations computed for the patch were
much less than those of the plume, the initial patch concentration is
usually much higher than that achieved by the continuous source concentration.

Vertical Line Source

Major sources of coastal water pollution are rivers, where runoff,
industrial and waste loads are emitted. The annual average suspended
sediment load from the Cuyahoga river is about 2×10^5 tons/year. Close
to the river mouth the suspended sediment transport is influenced more by
the river inertia than coastal currents. Rivers flow into the lake as a
turbulent jet such that inertia decreases rapidly at distances about 16-
20 times the river width. A vertical line source of 100 mg/l located 500
m offshore was used to simulate the river. The plume was computed using
the August 24 currents for the three particle sizes given earlier.

The sediment plume at 18:00 hours on August 24 for a particle size
of 0.005 mm was computed. At the surface the plume extended about 14 km
and 1.5 km along and across the shore, respectively, with a maximum shoreline concentration of 65%. Similar plume shapes were found at lower
depths but with decreased plume length and increased plume width.

Neutral Density Tracer

A surface point source located 1 km offshore was simulated using the
August 24 currents and a zero fall velocity. This case may represent any
conservative neutral density pollutant, for example Chloride. For the
computed plume at 18:00 hours on August 24, the plume extended about 14
km and 3 km along and across the shore, respectively, at the surface. The
maximum concentrations at the 5 m and 10 m depths were about 9% and 4% of
the source concentration.

The Influence Zone of a Nearshore Source

Based on the results for all the simulated cases and for some other
cases not reported here (such as June 1-6), as well as a sensitivity
analysis, an "influence zone" of a nearshore source (located up to 3 km
offshore) was plotted. The lines of constant percentage of source concentration represent the zone of effective pollution, for example in the
region between the 10% line and the shoreline, the 10% concentration may
be found for any flow regime and for any conservative (neutral or heavier
density) substance. The same results were used again to find the spatial
distribution of the sediment particle sizes across the coastal boundary
layer. Figure 1 shows the settling areas of three particle sizes. The
results are in agreement with the distribution of percent-size fraction
in surficial sediment in Lake Erie (Thomas et al., 1976) where the surficial sediment grain size distribution is about 80% sand and 20% silt up
to 7 km off Cleveland and more than 60% clay beyond 15 km offshore.

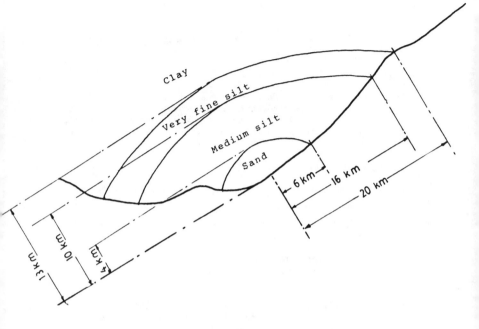

Figure 1.   Spatial distribution of sediment grain sizes within the
coastal boundary layer off Cleveland.

Conclusions

Several typical sediment-related activities which may take place in
the coastal boundary layer were simulated using ERCH and SEDTRAN (river
flow into the coastal zone, continuous dredging and instantaneous sediment dumping). All the cases were simulated in the nearshore area (less
than 3 km from the shore). The suspended sediment concentration to a
minimum value of 0.1% of the source concentration was tracked. The
simulation included combinations for the three typical sediment grain
sizes: very fine silt, medium silt and fine sand. The results showed
that, in most cases, concentrations of more than 10% of the source concentration extended only to about $1/2$ of the total plume length or width.
The plume shape and dimensions were not constant at all depths, due to
the vertical variability of the currents. The maximum distance of travel
in the alongshore direction was at the surface, and was caused by the
maximum near-surface shore-parallel current. The maximum penetration
across the coastal zone was not always at the surface, especially in the

cases of downwelling, where the offshore component takes place at depth.
The maximum shore concentrations were due to the river sources. Figure 1
should prove useful for the design of offshore or nearshore activities
such as a water treatment plant, recreation areas, harbour maintenance
and nearshore dredging or dumping.

Acknowledgements

This work was made possible by a small grant through the Inland
Waters Directorate of Environment Canada and by the interest of T.J.
Simons, F. Boyce, and R. Murthy of that organization. The paper was
abstracted from a longer paper presented to the CSCE Annual Conference in
Toronto in 1986.

References

Bishop, P.L., (1983). "Marine Pollution and Its Control", McGraw-Hill
Book Company.

Chen, C.L., (1971). "Sediment Dispersion in Flow with Moving Boundaries", J. Hydraulics Div., ASCE, Vol. 97, No. HY8, pp. 1181-1201.

Einstein, H.A., (1950). "The Bed-load Function for Sediment Transportation in Open Channel Flows", U.S. Dept. Agric., Soil Conserv. Serv., T.B.
No. 1026.

Elzawahry, A.E., (1981). "Transient Sediment Deposition and Resuspension
in One-dimensional Zone Between an Outfall and a Receiving Water", M.Eng.
Thesis, McMaster University, Hamilton, Ontario, Canada, 146 p.

Simons, D.B. and F. Sentruk, (1977). "Sediment Transport Technology",
Water Resources Publications, Colorado, USA.

Simons, T.J., and D.C.L. Lam, (1982). "Documentation of a Two-dimensional x-y Model Package for Computing Circulation and Pollutant Transport", Lecture notes of course CE754, McMaster University, Hamilton,
Ontario.

Thomas, R.L., J.-M. Maquer and A.L.W. Kemp, (1976). "Surficial Sediment
of Lake Erie", J. Fish. Res. Board Can. 33:385-403.

ROUTING COMPARISONS IN NATURAL AND GEOMETRIC CHANNELS

Larry M. Younkin[1], M.ASCE, and William H. Merkel[2]

ABSTRACT

A method of establishing composite geometric cross section shapes hydraulically similar to natural cross sections with flood plains is proposed. The method is based on the nondimensionalized St. Venant equations. The concept was tested by comparison of flood routing results for a range of conditions in twelve natural and their similar geometric cross sections. Average errors for area and discharge were found to be less than one percent for most of the 205 test pairs.

INTRODUCTION

The Soil Conservation Service is conducting a study to identify an improved, simplified flood routing method for inclusion in their TR-20 computer program. The method must be applicable over the wide range of conditions for which the program is used including routing in natural channels with flood plains. The infinite variety of conditions dictate a need for a nondimensional basis to assist the organization and to reduce the number of tests required for the study. To derive this basis the one-dimensional St. Venant equations for discharge and area were nondimensionalized(2) yielding the forms for the continuity equation:

$$\frac{\partial Q\star}{\partial X\star} + \frac{\partial A\star}{\partial t\star} = 0$$

and for the equation of motion - momentum:

$$F_0\star^2 \left[\frac{\partial Q\star}{\partial t\star} + \frac{\partial}{\partial x\star} \left(\frac{Q\star^2}{A\star}\right) \right] + \frac{A\star}{T\star} \frac{\partial A\star}{\partial x\star} - A\star\left[1 - \frac{1}{P_0\star^{4/3}} \left(\frac{Q\star}{K\star}\right)^2\right] = 0$$

where (terms with star superscripts are nondimensional variables while those with a subscript of zero are reference constants)

---

[1] Department of Civil Engineering, Bucknell University, Lewisburg, PA.
[2] USDA - Soil Conservation Service, Hydrology Unit, Engineering Division, Washington, DC.

$Q^* = Q/Q_0$, dependent discharge

$A^* = A/A_0$, dependent flow area

$x^* = x/x_0$, independent longitudinal distance

$t^* = t/t_0$, independent time

$F_0^* = (\dfrac{Q_0^2}{gA_0^{5/2}})^{1/2}$, a Froude number

$T^* = T/A_0^{1/2}$, the top width

$P_0^* = P_0/A_0^{1/2}$, the wetted perimeter

$K^* = \displaystyle\sum_{i=1}^{m} \dfrac{A_i^{*5/3}}{n_i^* P_0^{*2/3}}$, the conveyance

$A_i^* = A_i/A_0$, the area of the ith segment

$P_i^* = P_i/A_0^{1/2}$, the wetted perimeter of the ith segment

$n_i^* = n_i/n_{c_0}$, the Manning's roughness coefficient for the ith segment

m - number of segments in a cross section

and

Q_0 - reference discharge usually selected as the peak of the inflow hydrograph

A_0 - uniform flow area for Q_0 discharge

$x_0 = A_0^{1/2}/S_0$, a longitudinal length

$t_0 = x_0 A_0/Q_0$, time

n_{c_0} - composite Manning's n at Q_0 - A_0 uniform flow

S_0 - channel bed slope.

Thus, assuming a one-dimensional analysis of the reach routing is applicable, two channels with the same A^* - T^* and A^* - K^* relationships; F_0^*; P_0^*; nondimensional initial, upstream boundary, and downstream boundary conditions, and nondimensional reach length, L^*, will yield the same routing results.

Based on this concept, an attempt was made to validate the simulation of natural cross sections by composite trapezoidal shapes representing a main channel and symmetrical flood plains. This representation should improve the ability to evaluate the effect of variable shapes and hopefully may lead to the identification of groups of hydraulically similar channels permitting a reduction in the number of tests required. Twelve cross sections from six watersheds in six states were selected from SCS projects. They represented various shapes: flat flood plains at the same elevation, flat flood plains at different elevations (shown in Figure 1), terrace and single flood plain, levee sections, and others that are best described as compound and complex (one example is shown in Figure 2). The simplified

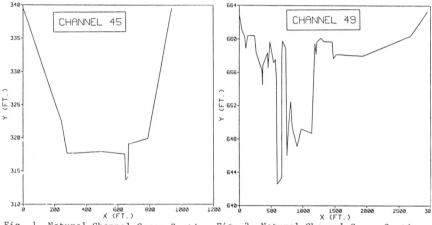

Fig. 1. Natural Channel Cross Section   Fig. 2. Natural Channel Cross Section

composite shapes are defined by the nondimensional: channel bottom, top of bank, extent of flood plain, and top of valley wall widths; top of bank, extent of flood plain, and top of valley wall elevations; and channel roughness n (shown in Figure 3).

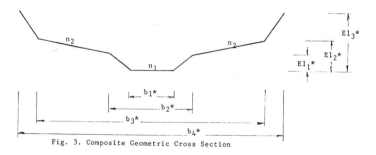

Fig. 3. Composite Geometric Cross Section

DETERMINATION OF THE COMPOSITE GEOMETRIC SECTIONS

The values of these nondimensional terms for the representation of a particular natural flood plain section were found from the nondimensional area vs. top width (A* - T*) and area vs. conveyance (A* - K*) relationships for the natural shape (shown for the cross sections of Figures 1 and 2 in Figures 4 and 5 respectively). The geometric terms

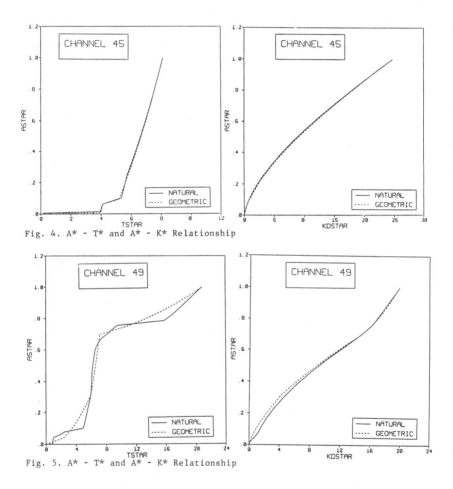

Fig. 4. A* - T* and A* - K* Relationship

Fig. 5. A* - T* and A* - K* Relationship

values were found from the A* - T* curve with the channel bottom, top of bank, and top of valley wall widths and elevations generally being placed on the curve and the extent of flood plain point located from minimum error of fit. Roughness values were found by setting the

conveyances at top of bank equal. The goodness of fit of the composite
A* - T* curve varied with the complexity of the natural cross section.
The composite A* - K* curve generally approximated the natural cross
section curve very closely (for example, see Figures 4 and 5). The
geometric terms values for deep flood plain flow conditions in the
twelve natural cross sections are listed in Table 1.

TABLE 1. NONDIMENSIONAL GEOMETRIC CROSS SECTIONS

Cross Section	b_1^*	b_2^*	b_3^*	b_4^*	El_3^*	El_2^*	El_3^*	n_1^*	Error
43	1.25	1.90	2.90	4.28	0.090	0.092	0.330	1.07	0.27
44	0.54	0.71	6.80	7.51	0.073	0.077	0.208	0.86	0.20
45	3.96	4.12	5.20	8.14	0.016	0.022	0.158	0.95	1.12
46	0.38	0.40	12.60	14.22	0.005	0.112	0.135	0.49	0.44
47	0.21	2.32	9.90	13.75	0.074	0.127	0.176	0.62	0.49
48	1.84	2.13	7.00	13.79	0.070	0.213	0.233	1.11	0.57
49	0.88	5.99	7.20	20.83	0.092	0.150	0.172	1.57	1.21
50	0.26	2.66	22.50	26.38	0.107	0.113	0.144	0.81	0.46
U53	0.00	3.15	10.90	16.13	0.058	0.060	0.126	0.92	-
52	0.33	22.10	30.60	32.02	0.014	0.032	0.044	0.92	4.13
035	0.40	1.00	14.80	15.12	0.138	0.202	0.228	0.94	0.84
100	1.44	2.14	3.10	5.53	0.245	0.257	0.380	1.10	0.30

ROUTING TEST PLAN

A weighted, four point implicit finite difference method of solving
the full dynamic model(1) was used for routing in a single prismatic
reach with each natural cross section and its similar composite section.
The upstream boundary condition for all tests was a gamma-shaped
discharge hydrograph. Three peak discharges were tested in each channel
pair, one resulting in deep flood plain flow, one for bank full flow,
and one resulting in shallow flood plain flow. An equal number of tests
for uniform flow, critical flow, and fixed stage downstream boundary
conditions were conducted. Initial conditions were always the steady
base flow discharge. Test parameter values are shown in Table 2. For
the inflow hydrograph, the ratio of peak to base flow was set equal to
20 and the skew was set at 1.2 for all tests. A nondimensional reach
length of 0.6 was used.

TABLE 2. TEST PARAMETER VALUES

Test Condition	Relative Flow Depth	F_o* Min.	Max.	tp*	Downstream Boundary Cond.
1	Deep Flood Plain			2.0	Uniform
2	Deep			2.0	Critical
3	Deep	0.005	0.231	2.0	Fixed Stage
4	Deep			0.2	Uniform
5	Deep			0.2	Critical
6	Deep			0.2	Fixed Stage
7	Bank Full			2.0	Uniform
8	B.F.			2.0	Critical
9	B.F.	0.041	0.234	2.0	Fixed Stage
10	B.F.			0.2	Uniform
11	B.F.			0.2	Critical
12	B.F.			0.2	Fixed Stage
13	Shallow Flood Plain			2.0	Uniform
14	Shallow			2.0	Critical
15	Shallow	0.0036	0.254	2.0	Fixed Stage
16	Shallow			0.2	Uniform
17	Shallow			0.2	Critical
18	Shallow			0.2	Fixed Stage

RESULTS

The combination of 18 test conditions in 12 single prismatic reaches with different cross sections means that 216 pairs of tests were attempted. Of these, 205 pairs of tests were successfully completed permitting comparison of reach routing results in natural and hydraulically similar composite geometric channels. Comparisons of results were made for area at the upstream end, and at one-third and two-thirds of the distance along the reach. Discharge comparisons were made at the one-third and two-thirds reach length sections and at the downstream end.

For the 105 tests with nondimensional time to peak of 2.0, the average error, based on natural cross section test results, for area comparisons was less than 0.2 percent with a standard deviation of error less than 1.0 percent. For the same set of tests, the discharge comparisons yielded an average error of less than 0.1 percent with a standard deviation of error less than 0.5 percent.

The test conditions with nondimensional time to peak of 0.2 resulted in higher errors. The average error for area comparisons from those 100 pairs of tests was less than 0.6 percent with a standard deviation less than 4 percent. For the discharge comparisons, the average error was less than 1.25 percent with a standard deviation of error less than 4.0 percent. Even these error results are exaggerated by an apparent poor fit of Channel 47. Errors for several of the tests in that channel ranged from 10 to 20 percent.

Errors in timing comparisons closely followed those for area and discharge.

CONCLUSIONS

Natural channels with flood plains can be adequately represented by hydraulically similar composite geometric cross sections for purposes of flood routing studies. A four-point minimum error fit of the natural cross section A*-T* relationship and one point on the A*-K* relationship establishes the similar geometric cross section.

ACKNOWLEDGEMENTS

For the past year, funding for Mr. Younkin's involvement in this continuing study has been through a Cooperative Agreement with the USDA-Agricultural Research Service.

REFERENCES

1. Fread, D. L., "Theoretical Development of Implicit Dynamic Routing Model," Dynamic Routing Seminar, Lower Mississippi Forecast Center, Slidell, LA, Dec. 1976.

2. Katopodes, N. D., and Strelkoff, T., "Dimensionless Solutions of Border Irrigation Advance," Journal of The Irrigation and Drainage Division, ASCE, Vol. 103, No. IR4, Proc. Paper 13400, Dec. 1977, pp. 401-417.

RAINFALL-LOSS PARAMETER ESTIMATION FOR ILLINOIS

Linda S. Weiss[1], P.E., A.M. ASCE and Audrey L. Ishii[1], S.M. ASCE

ABSTRACT

The U.S. Geological Survey is currently conducting an investigation to estimate values of parameters for two rainfall-loss computation methods used in a commonly used flood-hydrograph model. Estimates of six rainfall-loss parameters are required: four for the Exponential Loss-Rate method and two for the Initial and Uniform Loss-Rate method. Multiple regression analyses on calibrated data from 616 storms at 98 gaged basins are being used to develop parameter-estimating techniques for these six parameters at ungaged basins in Illinois.

Parameter-estimating techniques are being verified using data from a total of 105 storms at 35 uncalibrated gaged basins. Computed discharge hydrograph characteristics (total volume of flow, peak discharge, time to peak discharge) are being compared with characteristics of observed discharge hydrographs.

INTRODUCTION

Water-resources managers often need to estimate peak discharge, volume of runoff, and time distribution of runoff from rainfall. Values for unit-hydrograph and rainfall-loss function parameters associated with the U.S. Army Corps of Engineers Hydrologic Engineering Center flood-hydrograph model (HEC-1) (1981) are needed to estimate discharge hydrographs for ungaged basins. The U.S. Geological Survey has developed a technique for estimating the unit-hydrograph parameters for ungaged basins in Illinois (Graf and others, 1982b). Estimating techniques or guidelines for selecting parameter values of the rainfall-loss function are also needed and are not presently available.

An investigation is being conducted by the U.S. Geological Survey in cooperation with the Illinois Department of Transportation, Division of Water Resources. The purpose of the investigation is to develop techniques or guidelines for estimating parameters of two rainfall-loss computation methods used in the HEC-1 model, and to verify the parameter-estimating techniques using data from uncalibrated gaged basins. This paper describes the methodology, progress, and preliminary findings of the investigation.

[1]Hydrologist, U.S. Geological Survey, WRD, Urbana, Illinois 61801

The HEC-1 flood-hydrograph model was used to calculate two unit-hydrograph parameters for 98 gaged basins in Illinois (fig. 1) -- TC, time of concentration, and R, storage coefficient. A total of 621 storms occurring from February through November were used for model calibration. The unit-hydrograph parameters and a technique for estimating their values for ungaged basins have been published (Graf and others, 1982a and 1982b).

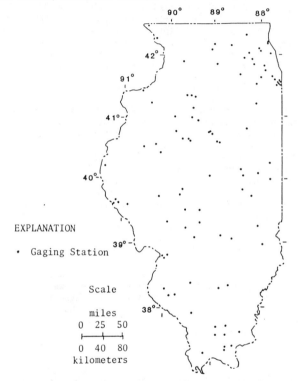

Fig. 1.--Study Area.

As part of their investigation, Graf and others (1982a) cali-brated the model for the 98 gaged basins using a four-parameter function to compute rainfall loss due to interception, evapotrans-piration, depression storage, and infiltration. The Exponential Loss-Rate method relates rainfall loss rate to rainfall intensity and accumulated losses (U.S. Army Corps of Engineers, 1981). The four loss-rate parameters in the HEC-1 model that can be adjusted are ERAIN, RTIOL, STRKR and DLTKR. ERAIN is the exponent of precip-itation in the function; RTIOL is the rate of exponential decrease of the loss-rate coefficient with accumulated loss; STRKR is the value of the loss-rate coefficient at the start of rainfall; DLTKR is the amount of initial accumulated rainfall loss during which the decrease in loss-rate coefficient is parabolic.

A second model calibration was performed for 32 of the 98 gaged
basins using a different function to compute rainfall losses (George
Garklavs and K. A. Oberg, U.S. Geological Survey, written commun.,
1986). A total of 209 storms were used for model calibration. The
Initial and Uniform Loss-Rate method has two adjustable parameters,
STRTL and CNSTL. STRTL is the initial volume of rainfall used to
satisfy antecedent soil-moisture deficiency. Thereafter, rainfall is
lost at a constant rate, CNSTL. The Initial and Uniform Loss-Rate
method is similar to methods using an infiltration index, defined as
that rate of rainfall above which the rainfall volume equals the
runoff volume (Linsley and others, 1975). Garklavs and Oberg (U.S.
Geological Survey, written commun., 1986) found that there is no
significant difference in the accuracy of modeled hydrographs computed using the two methods for estimating rainfall excess in the
HEC-1 model.

Unit-hydrograph (TC, R) and loss-rate parameter values may be
computed using a nonlinear optimization technique in the HEC-1 model.
This technique minimizes an objective function, which is the square
root of the weighted-squared differences between observed and computed discharge. The parameters ERAIN, RTIOL, STRKR, and CNSTL were
optimized to basin-average values, while the parameters DLTKR and
STRTL were optimized to individual storm values. The reader is
referred to the HEC-1 users manual for a more detailed explanation
of the two rainfall-loss functions and optimization techniques (U.S.
Army Corps of Engineers, 1981).

METHOD OF STUDY

Three phases are being used in the development of rainfall-loss
parameter-estimating techniques: model calibration on the remaining
66 gaged basins using the Initial and Uniform Loss-Rate method;
development of estimating techniques using statistical methods; and
verification of estimating techniques using discharge hydrograph
characteristics from 35 additional gaged basins.

Model Calibration

The model was calibrated for the remaining 66 gaged basins using
the Initial and Uniform Loss-Rate method. The five February and
November storms were discarded, since there were not enough values in
those months for statistical significance, leaving a total of 616
storms that occurred in the months from March through October. Thus,
98 optimized values of the variables ERAIN, RTIOL, STRKR, and CNSTL,
and 616 optimized values of the variables DLTKR and STRTL were
available for analysis. Table 1 shows a statistical summary of the
computed loss-rate parameter values.

Table 1.--Statistical summary of computed loss-rate parameter values

	ERAIN	RTIOL	STRKR (in/h)	DLTKR (in.)	CNSTL (in/h)	STRTL (in.)
Number of observations	98	98	98	616	98	616
Mean or average	0.495	2.935	0.239	1.614	.0713	1.013
Standard deviation	.0477	1.324	.142	1.414	.0365	.833
Minimum	.34	1.12	.02	.00	.00	.00
Maximum	.64	7.45	.85	7.30	.18	5.23
Range	.30	6.33	.83	7.30	.18	5.23
Standard error of the mean	.00482	.1337	.0143	.0568	.00368	.0334

Development of Loss-Rate Parameter-Estimating Techniques

Techniques for estimating values for parameters used in the two loss-rate methods are being developed using statistical methods. Rainfall-loss parameter values obtained from calibration of data from the 98 gaged basins could be related to basin characteristics which have little or no regional trend (drainage area, channel length, slope), or to those that may have regional trends (topography, rainfall distribution, land use, geology). Values of rainfall-loss parameters that vary from storm to storm could be related to climatological characteristics such as air temperature, evapotranspiration, and antecedent soil moisture.

Regional trends in loss-rate parameters are identified using polynomial trend analysis (O'Leary and others, 1966). Multiple regression models are formed from polynomials of successively higher degree. This multiple regression technique uses map coordinates as independent variables, and the parameter for which the regional trend is being investigated as the dependent variable. Each regression model defines a surface, a first-degree model defining a planar surface, a second-degree model defining a parabolic surface, and successively higher-degree models describing surfaces of increasing complexity. First and second-degree models, respectively, are represented by equations of the form:

$$z = b_0 + b_1 x + b_2 y \tag{1}$$

$$z = b_0 + b_1 x + b_2 y + b_3 x^2 + b_4 xy + b_5 y^2 \tag{2}$$

where x and y are map coordinates, z is the estimated value of the
dependent variable, and b_0 through b_5 are regression coefficients
computed by the least squares method. Successively higher degree
models can be tested for significance and the model that best
represents the data selected. As in other regression models, the
goal is to identify systematic trends and to separate those trends
from random variation.

The relation of parameters to drainage area, slope, and length
is being investigated. Storm-dependent loss-rate parameters (DLTKR,
STRTL) are also related to mean monthly precipitation, evapotranspiration, and air temperature. Groups are defined by nominal data
including hydrologic region (Mitchell, 1954), rural or urban drainage
basin (urban is defined as greater than about 7-percent impervious
area) (Graf and others, 1982b), the presence of strip-mined land, and
month (March through October). Additional variables under consideration are surface storage area, percent forest cover, and latitude and
longitude.

Verification of Estimating Techniques

Thirty-five uncalibrated gaged basins with an average of three
storms each (105 storms) are being used for verification of the
parameter-estimating techniques. Basins are selected to provide a
range in drainage areas similar to those of the original 98 gaged
basins. Drainage areas ranged from 0.45 to 362 square miles, with a
mean of 73.9 square miles.

Parameter-estimating techniques are verified using three computed discharge hydrograph characteristics: V, total volume of flow;
Q, peak discharge; and T, time to peak discharge. The three sets of
V, Q, and T available for comparison are: one set for the 105
observed hydrographs; one set for the computed hydrographs obtained
when rainfall-loss parameters are estimated for the Exponential Loss-
Rate method, and unit-hydrograph parameters are estimated according
to methods presented in Graf and others (1982b); and one set for the
computed hydrographs obtained when rainfall-loss parameters are estimated for the Initial and Uniform Loss-Rate method, and unit-
hydrograph parameters are estimated according to methods presented
in Graf and others (1982b). The techniques are verified using the
computed hydrograph percent differences, hereafter referred to as
errors, in V, Q, and T with the equation:

$$PD(Y) = [(Y_0 - Y_x) / Y_0] \times 100 \qquad (3)$$

where PD(Y) is the error for the hydrograph characteristics V, Q, or
T; Y_0 is the value of V, Q, or T for the observed hydrograph; and Y_x
is the value of V, Q, or T for the hydrograph computed when parameters are estimated using either method of calculating rainfall
excess. The mean and standard deviation of the errors in V, Q, and T
are computed for all storms modeled at each basin. This provides a
measure of the overall accuracy with which estimating techniques for
all rainfall-loss and unit-hydrograph parameters reproduce observed
hydrographs.

PRELIMINARY RESULTS

Estimating techniques for the parameters of the Initial and Uniform Loss-Rate method follow. The reader is cautioned that at this stage of the project, the techniques are unverified and may change.

a. STRTL values were separated into eight monthly data sets. Mean monthly values and 95-percent confidence intervals for STRTL were computed and are shown in table 2.

Table 2.--Mean monthly values and confidence intervals for STRTL (the initial-volume loss-rate parameter used in the Initial and Uniform Loss-Rate method)

[STRTL, in inches]

Month	Number of observa- tions	Mean monthly STRTL	One standard deviation	95-Percent Confidence Interval for STRTL	
				minimum	maximum
March	56	0.40	0.51	0.27	0.54
April	106	.72	.62	.60	.84
May	116	.72	.59	.61	.83
June	156	1.03	.73	.92	1.15
July	76	1.46	.87	1.26	1.66
August	56	1.59	.85	1.36	1.81
September	31	1.61	1.02	1.24	1.99
October	18	1.70	1.31	1.05	2.35

b. CNSTL has a significant first-degree regional trend when tested at the 5-percent significance level. The analysis of variance of that trend analysis is given in table 3. The first-degree surface has a standard deviation of 0.03 and explains 19 percent of the variation in the data. The first-degree trend surface was contoured and is presented in figure 2.

Table 3.--Analysis of variance of CNSTL (the constant loss-rate
         parameter used in the Initial and Uniform Loss-Rate method)
         trend analysis data

         [Only first-order terms of polynomial trend analysis are
         significant at the 5-percent level. Number of values is
         98, CNSTL in inches per hour]

Source	Sum of squares	Degrees of freedom	Mean square	Value of the f-statistic
Linear surface	0.025	2	0.013	
				11.53
Deviations from linear	.104	95	.001	

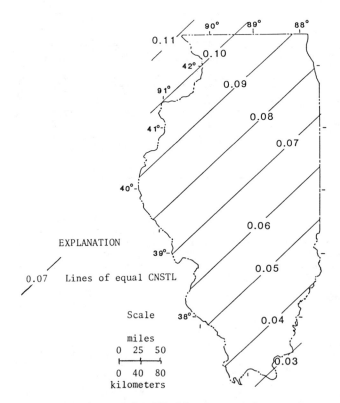

Fig. 2.--Values of CNSTL (the constant loss-rate parameter used
         in the Initial and Uniform Loss-Rate method).

SUMMARY

Estimating techniques for selection of values of parameters for two rainfall-loss functions associated with the HEC-1 flood-hydrograph model are being developed. Parameter values from 616 storms at 98 gaged basins in Illinois were obtained by calibration of the HEC-1 model. The calibrated parameter values are related to basin and climatological characteristics using multiple regression analyses. Rainfall-loss parameter values necessary for input to the model may be estimated for ungaged basins in Illinois. Data from 105 storms at 35 uncalibrated gaged basins are being used for evaluation of the parameter-estimating techniques. Estimating techniques are being verified using the hydrograph characteristics of total volume of flow, peak discharge, and time to peak discharge.

REFERENCES CITED

Graf, J. B., Garklavs, George, and Oberg, K. A., "Time of Concentration and Storage Coefficient Values for Illinois Streams," U.S. Geological Survey Water-Resources Investigations 82-13, 1982a, 35 pp.

Graf, J. B., Garklavs, George, and Oberg, K. A., "A Technique for Estimating Time of Concentration and Storage Coefficient Values for Illinois Streams," U.S. Geological Survey Water-Resources Investigations 82-22, 1982b, 16 pp.

Linsley, R. K., Jr., Kohler, M. A., and Paulhus, J. L. H., Hydrology for Engineers, McGraw-Hill Co., New York, N.Y., 1975, 482 pp.

Mitchell, W. D., "Floods in Illinois: Magnitude and Frequency," Illinois Department of Public Works and Buildings, Division of Waterways, 1954, 386 pp.

O'Leary, Mont, Lippert, R. H., and Spitz, O. T., "Fortran IV and Map Program for Computation and Plotting of Trend Surfaces for Degrees 1 through 6," Kansas Geological Survey Computer Contribution, v. 3, 1966, 48 pp.

U.S. Army Corps of Engineers, Hydrologic Engineering Center, Davis, Ca., "HEC-1 Flood Hydrograph Package Users Manual," 1981.

REMOTE SENSING APPLICATIONS IN THE
MODEL OF RUNOFF FORMATION IN EXCESS OF STORAGE

Wenqiu Wei[*]

ABSTRACT

The model of runoff formation in excess of storage applied in
some humid regions of China is revised in this paper, so that the
model can adopt the information provided by Landsat remote sensing.
Soil available storage capacity and initial moisture content in a
watershed are two important parameters. The parameters of original
model are determined by means of statistical and optimum seeking
methods, and are only an index of a fictitious mass. The parameters
of the revised model are determined by using the information provided by Landsat remote sensing, and have clear physical meaning
and reflect actual soil storage in the watershed. It bases yield
calculation on reliability. The model proposed provides reliable
basis for flood calculation and forecasting.

Key words: remote sensing; hydrologic simulation; soil moisture;
soil storage; infiltration; runoff; rainfall; soil type; grid cell;
model.

INTRODUCTION

Catchment hydrologic simulation is a new technique in the last
20 -30 years. It plays an important role in determining practical
hydrologic problems and researching hydrologic law. Since America
launched ERTS-1 (later renamed Landsat-1) in July of 1972,catchment
hydrologic simulation is combined with the technique of Landsat remote sensing. Undoubtedly, the development of technique of Landsat
remote sensing will move catchment hydrologic simulation towards a
new stage.

Landsat photograph or computer compatible tape (CCT) provided
by Landsat remote sensing is used in this paper, so that the soil
type in all parts of the catchment is recognized, and the corresponding soil storage capacity and final constant infiltration rate
are determined. They are two important parameters in the model. At
the same time, we recognize soil moisture content, i.e.the initial
soil storage in the model. According to the principle of runoff
formation in excess of storage, we can calculate runoff amount formed in all parts of the catchment, and then compute the runoff
amount formed in entire catchment by means of the arithmetic mean
or the weighted average method.

*Wenqiu Wei, Lecturer on hydrology, Wuhan Institute of Hydraulic
and Electric Engineering, Wuhan, Hubei Province, People's Republic
of China.

I. FLOWCHART OF THE MODEL OF RUNOFF

FORMATION IN EXCESS OF STORAGE

For simplicity, we don't consider vertical distribution of soil
type and soil moisture content. If evaporation occurring during a
rainfall, vegetation interception and depression storage are
neglected, the calculated formula of runoff formed by the rainfall
can be expressed as

$$R = P - (W_m - W_o)$$

Where P is precipitation of the rainfall; R is the runoff amount
formed by the rainfall; W_m is the soil storage capacity,in field
capacity; W_o is the initial soil moisture content (or initial soil
storage). The unit of above symbols is in millimeters.

The runoff R includes two parts: surface runoff RS and groundwater runoff RG, Which can be calculated by

RS = R - TFC

RG = TFC

Where TFC is the final constant infiltration volume, it depends
on the final constant infiltration rate FC, rainfall intensity and
duration of the final constant infiltration.

Obviously, the distribution of W_m, FC and W_o are heterogeneous
in all parts of a basin. The model of runoff formation in excess of
storage provided in past   mainly considered how to settle the
question of heterogeneous distribution of above parameters (East
China college of Hydraulic Engineering,1977; W.Wei and R·ᴍ·Ragan,
October,1983). Using Landsat photograph or CCT provided by Landsat
remote sensing, the information of heterogeneous distribution of
W_m, FC and W_o in all parts of the basin can be obtained. First,
the basin is divided into a number of grid cell, the area of every
grid cell can be controled enough to make the distribution of W_m,
FC and W_o in a rather homogeneous level. Next, we recognize soil
type and W_o in every grid cell by means of Landsat photograph or
CCT, and determine corresponding W_m and FC according to the soil
type in every grid cell. Finally, we compute the runoff amount
formed in the area of every grid cell, and then compute the runoff
amount in the area of entire basin by using arithmetic mean method.
The flowchart for using remotely sensed technique in the model of
runoff formation in excess of storage is shown in Figure 1.

II.CLASSIFICATION OF SOIL TYPE

Soil textual classification is adopted to distinguish different
soil type. According to the relative proportions of clay, silt and
sand particles present in a mass of soil, soil type is divided into
a number of classes. This paper adapts the classification in

"Hydrological Maps" published by UNESCO,1977. Table 1 lists the soil type and their relative proportions of clay, silt and sand particles. Soil moisture indices for various soil type are given in table 2. After we recognize the soil type and their distribution in a basin by using information provided by Landsat photograph or CCT, the corresponding distribution of W_m and FC in all parts of the basin in accordance with table 2 can be determined.

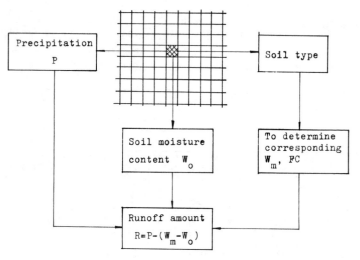

Figure 1. The flowchart for using remotely sensed technique in the model of runoff formation in excess of storage.

Table 1. Particles component of various soil texture

Soil type	Soil particle content (%)		
	Sand (2-0.02mm)	Silt (0.02-0.002mm)	Clay (<0.002mm)
Sandy	>85		<15
Sandy loam	55-85	<45	<15
Loam	>30	>40	<30
Clay loam	<30	<40	>30
Silt clay	<20	<40	>30
Clay	<20	<40	>40

Table 2. Moisture-holding and infiltration indices

Soil type	Moisture at field capacity (volume %)	Moisture at wilting point (volume %)	Final constant infiltration rate (mm/hr.)
Sandy	9-22	3-11	7.8-11.4
Sandy loam	14-29	6-13	3.6-7.8
Loam	24-39	11-18	3.6-7.8
Clay loam	30-43	14-21	1.2-3.6
Silt clay	34-47	16-23	1.2-3.6
Clay	37-57	18-25	0-1.2

III. RECOGNITION OF SOIL MOISTURE CONTENT

According to spectral characteristics of soil moisture, we can directly measure soil moisture content by using reflected solar, thermal infrared and microwave technique (E.T.Edwin,1981; T.J. Schmugge, T.J.Jackson and H.L.Mckim,1979). Fig.2 shows isoline map of soil moisture content in the range of the surface layer (0-5cm).

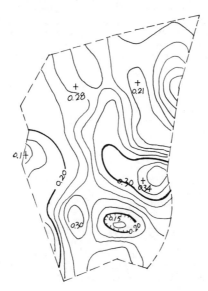

Fig.2. Soil moisture isoline map in Rangeland
watershed near Chickasha, Oklahoa,
May 10, 1978.

But, they seem to be sensing the moisture content in a layer 5-10 cm thick at the surface. This limitation implied that remote sensing approaches will not be able to satisfy the requirement in the available depth of the soil layer storing moisture. Usually, the available depth of the soil layer storing moisture is approximately 50 cm (W.Wei and R.M.Ragan,1983). For this reason, we have to establish a soil moisture profile model to indirectly determine the soil moisture content, or to directly substitute the soil moisture content of the surface layer 5-10 cm for that of the available depth of the soil layer storing moisture (E.T.Edwin,1981).

IV. CALCULATION OF RUNOFF YIELD

The runoff formed by a rainfall in a basin is first computed in the area of every grid cell, and then is computed in entire basin.

1. Calculation of yield in the area of every grid cell

Although soil type of every grid cell is rather identical, sand content of same soil type has a variational range, so that the distribution of available storage capacity in the area of every grid cell probably is heterogeneous. In order to consider the heterogeity, usually the curve of the available storage capacity is established. The entire area of the grid cell is divided into several subareas according to the magnitude of the available storage capacity, and these available storage capacity are arranged in ascending order of magnitude, a curve relating storage capacity and corresponding area can be plotted. We will define this curve as the curve of the available storage capacity in the area of the grid cell. An example is shown as Figure 3 (W.Wei and R.M.Ragan,1983).

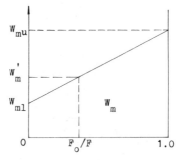

Fig.3. The curve of the available storage
capacity over the area of a grid cell

In Figure 3,the ordinate W_m' expresses available storage capacity at any point in the grid cell in millimeters; the abscissa F_o/F is percentage, in which the numerator F_o denotes the area with available storage capacity at any point less or equal to W_m', and the demoninator F is entire area of the grid cell; W_{mu} is the maximum of W_m', and W_{ml} is the minimum of W_m', i.e. upper limit and lower limit of the available storage capacity; W_m expresses average storage capacity over the area of entire grid cell. For reducing calculation, the curve of the available storage capacity is expressed as a straight line.

It is convenient to compute runoff in the area of a grid cell by means of the curve of the available storage capacity. Assume average precipitation over the area in the grid cell in a computation period is P, and initail soil moisture content (initail soil storage) is W_o, when evaporation occuring during the rainfall, vegetation interception and depression storage are insignificant, runoff amount R formed by the rainfall is computed in the following two cases.

In first case, if $W_o \leqslant W_{ml}$, the ordinate P_o corresponding to W_o at the curve of the available storage capacity can be computed as follows:

$$P_o = W_o$$

Calculation of R is shown in Fig.4.

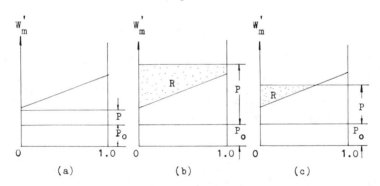

Fig.4. Diagram for determining runoff yield R in $W_o \leqslant W_{ml}$ case.

If $P+P_o \leqslant W_{ml}$, R=0, as shown in Fig.4 (a).

If $P+P_o \geqslant W_{mu}$, R= P-(W_m-W_o), as shown in Fig.4 (b).

If $W_{mu} > P+P_o > W_{ml}$, R=$(P+P_o-W_{ml})^2/2(W_{mu}-W_{ml})$, as shown in Figure 4(c).

In second case, if $W_o > W_{ml}$, the ordinate P_o corresponding to W_o at the curve of the available storage capacity can be computed as follows:

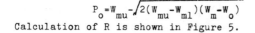

$$P_o = W_{mu} - \sqrt{2(W_{mu} - W_{ml})(W_m - W_o)}$$

Calculation of R is shown in Figure 5.

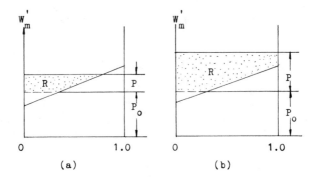

$$(a) \qquad\qquad\qquad (b)$$

Figure 5. Diagram for determining runoff
yield R in $W_o > W_{ml}$ case.

If $P + P_o \leqslant W_{mu}$, $R = P(P + 2P_o - 2W_{ml})/2(W_{mu} - W_{ml})$, as shown in Figure 5 (a).

If $P + P_o > W_{mu}$, $R = P - (W_m - W_o)$, as shown in Figure 5 (b).

After runoff yield R in some period is computed, we can further determine surface runoff RS and groundwater runoff RG according to comparison rainfall intensity with final constant infiltration rate. Final constant infiltration rate has a variable range, upper limit is expressed as FC_u, and lower limit FC_l. If length of period is expressed as $\triangle t$, then RS and RG is computed in the following three cases.

In first case, if $R/\triangle t < FC_l$, RG=R, RS=0.

In second case, if $R/\triangle t \geqslant FC_u$, RG=$\frac{1}{2}(FC_u + FC_l)\triangle t$, RS=R-RG.

In third case, if $FC_u > R/\triangle t > FC_l$, RG=$\frac{1}{2}(R + FC_l \triangle t)$, RS=R-RG.

Total runoff amount formed by this rainfall is equal to the sum of the runoff amounts formed in all periods.

2. Calculation of runoff amount formed in entire basin

After the runoff amount formed in the area of every grid cell is determined, the runoff amount formed in entire basin can be computed by using arithmetic mean method. For reducing computation, we first determine the area of every soil type, and then compute runoff amount formed in the area, and finally compute runoff amount formed in entire basin by means of the weighted average method.

V. CONCLUSIONS

In order to evaluate proposed model, runoff amount R_c formed by three rainfall events occuring in Taohe river basin, China, is computed respectively. At meanwhile observed runoff amount R_a corresponding to above three rainfalls is computed. The results listed in table 3 shows that R_c approaches to R_a. The proposed model accords with the actual situation of runoff formed by the basin.

Table 3. Comparison of computing and observing
runoff at Taohe river basin

Rainfall date	R_c (mm)	R_a (mm)
July 14,1979	24.7	24.7
Sept.14,1979	32.5	32.6
Aug. 23,1980	30.4	30.5

Soil classification and corresponding moisture-holding capacity and infiltration capacity, the depth of the available storage and the curve of the available storage are determined according to practical case and experiment data, some of which require to research further.

REFERENCES

Edwin,E.T. 1981. Remote sensing application in water modeling: Applied modeling in catchment hydrology. Water resources publications.

East China college of hydraulic engineering, 1977. Flood forecasting method for humid regions of China. Nanking, China.

Schmugge,T.J., Jackson,T.J. and Mckim,H.L. 1979. Survey of In-situ and remote sensing methods for soil moisture determination. Satellite hydrology. AWRA.

Studies and report in hydrology 20, 1977. Hydrological maps.UNESCO WMO.

Swain,P.H. and Davis,S.M. 1978. Remote sensing: The quantitative approach. McGraw-Hill, New York.

Wei,W. and Ragan,R.M. October,1983. A model of runoff formation in excess of storage based on Landsat remote sensing. University of Maryland, Civil engineering research series.

Wei,W. and Ragan,R.M. October,1983. A simplified storm-flood forecasting model. University of Maryland, Civil engineering research series.

Plunge Pool Energy Dissipators
for Some Dams in Taiwan, ROC

Y. Cheng*, M. ASCE & R. L. Hsu**

This paper presents a brief description of the characteristics of
the plunge pool type energy dissipators, including design considerations, hydraulic model tests, as well as the results of prototype
operation, for some dams in Taiwan, ROC.

INTRODUCTION

To cope with the great increase of water demand due to rapid
economic development in Taiwan, a number of reservoirs have been constructed over the past thirty years. Taiwan is a narrow island and most
of its rivers originated from the Center Mountain Range are short and
steep. The longest river is no more than 190 km in length and the river
gradient ranges from 1:50 to 1:100 at the dam areas. Furthermore, typhoons usually hit the island during the period of June through October,
bringing heavy downpours. The specific discharge can be as high as
20-35 cms per km^2 for a catchment area of 500-1,000 km^2. Annual
sediment production ranges from 2-17 mm per km^2, depending on the
vegetative coverage and geological conditions of the sites. In view of
the factors such as the huge flood, supercritical flows and heavy
sediments in the river channel, the authors and their colleagues at the
Sinotech Engineering Consultants, Inc. have conceived that plunge pools
are the most economic and suitable means for the energy dissipation,
instead of the long and deep stilling basins which are more costly to
construct.

SHIHMEN SPILLWAY

General Description - The Shihmen Reservoir is the first multipurpose
water resources development project implemented in Taiwan for irrigation, power generation, water supply and flood control. The
133-meter high Shihmen embankment dam impounds, at the normal high
reservoir water level of 245 m, a gross storage of 316 x 10^6 m^3. An
open-chute spillway with a design discharge of 10,000 cms is provided on
the right ridge of the dam. The spillway crest has a total width of 100
m and a net width of 80 m, and converges downward to 60 m at the middle
of the chute. Then, the same width is kept down to the flip bucket end.
The flip bucket has a lip angle of 35°, a radius of 15 m and an invert
elevation of 148.42 m. Fig. 1 shows the plan and profile of the
spillway.

To maintain a constant release for downstream irrigation use, an afterbay weir is constructed at 1,300 m downstream of the flip bucket to
creat an afterbay to regulate the tailwater of peak power generation.
With a capacity of 2 x10^6 m^3, the afterbay is 270 m wide at the toe of
the dam and has a normal water depth of 8 m. A plan of the afterbay and
the adjacent permanent structures is given in Fig. 2.

*President, Sinotech Engineering Consultants, Inc., Taipei, Taiwan, ROC
**Manager of Hydraulic Engineering Department, Sinotech Engineering
Consultants, Inc., Taipei, Taiwan, ROC

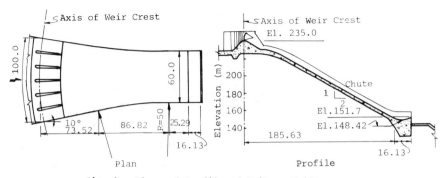

Fig. 1. Plan and Profile of Shihmen Spillway

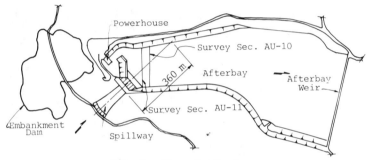

Fig. 2. Plan of Afterbay

Design Considerations - For energy dissipation, consideration was made to utilize the afterbay as a plunge pool in view of the availability of a projected length of 360 m from the bucket lip to the left bank of the pool along the spillway center line and an 8 m water cushion depth in the pool. The spillway alignment was designed to project the impact zone of the water jet away from the foundation of the dam, the spillway and other permanent structures. With this design, though some scouring was expected in the pool due to insufficient cushion depth, it would not creat any dam safety problem. Therefore, for economic and practical considerations, the pool depth was not deepened and the afterbay weir was not heightened, nor was it necessary to protect the impact zone with reinforced concrete pavement.

To understand the scour condition of the pool bottom, a 1:60 hydraulic model test with movable bed was conducted. The test showed that: 1) Of the two bucket lip angles, 35° and 15°, tested, the former was found to cause shallower scour depth and the scour holes were also located farther away from the bucket. (See Table 1). The lip angle of 35° was therefore adopted in the design. Table 1 also shows the relation between scour patterns and discharges based on the bed material of 19 to 37 mm gravel sizes; and 2) Effects on scour depths and locations of

scour holes by different gravel sizes for bed material are as shown in
Table 2.(4) The resultant scour patterns concluded that under the
design discharges, the extents of scour holes were within allowable
limits, and it was confirmed that the design considerations were
reasonable.

	Bucket Lip Angle	Discharge (cms)	Distance of Scour Hole Center to Bucket Lip (m)	Scour Depth (m)
Table 1. Test Results for Bucket Lip Angles of 35° and 15°, Shihmen Spillway		3,000	168	14.0
	35°	6,000	188	16.5
		10,000	208	21.0
		3,000	138	17.0
	15°	10,000	148	23.0

	Discharge (cms)	Mean Dia. of Gravel (mm)	Bottom Elev. of Scour Hole (m)
		25	112.5
	3,000	50	118.0
		100	123.0
		125	(no scour)
Table 2. Test Results for Different Bed Material, Shihmen Plunge Pool		25	110.0
	6,000	50	116.5
		100	122.0
		150	(no scour)
		25	104.0
	10,000	50	109.8
		100	114.5
		150	(no scour)

Actual Operation - The Shihmen reservoir has been in operation for 23
years since the final closure of the diversion tunnel in May 1963.
Table 3 gives a list of the major typhoons occurred and the corresponding flood operation during this period. It was noted that only four
months after the reservoir had been impounded Typhoon Gloria brought a
world record-breaking rainfall and resulted in a spillway discharge of
9,600 cms, which was nearly the same as the design discharge. The
reservoir water level reached an elevation of 249 m, while the water
level of the afterbay was 141 m (the afterbay weir was only partly completed). After the passage of the flood, the afterbay was dewatered for
continuation of the construction work of the afterbay weir and it was
found out that a large scour hole had developed near the middle of the
afterbay. However, no adverse influence to the dam structure was observed. Investigation of the scour hole revealed that the bed rock
formation consists of alternating mudstone and sandstone intercalated by
carbonaceous clay, and an important fault passed right through the scour
hole. Thereafter, the scour hole was cleaned out and the cross-sections
of the plunge pool surveyed. Fig. 3 shows two of the cross-sections,
AU-10 and AU-11, surveyed in October 1963, as well as those surveyed by
the Shihmen Reservoir Bureau in 1967, 1978 and 1980, as represented by
Line 1, 2, 3 and 4, respectively. The solid line, Line 1, indicates
that the deepest scour occurred near cross-section AU-10, at a distance
of 210 m from the bucket. After Typhoon Gloria and until 1967, three

releases were made. However, the discharges were all less than 1,000 cms, and the scour hole was somewhat backfilled, as shown by Line 2. Subsequently, three discharges ranging from 4,000 to 5,000 cms and ten smaller discharges all less than 1,000 cms were made from 1967 through 1978, which caused new scouring as shown by Line 3, and it appears that the scour hole has moved upstream, i.e. to the neighborhood of cross-section AU-11, or about 160 m from the bucket. Then, from 1978 to 1980, the discharges were all less than 1,000 cms, the cross-section measurements afterward are indicated by Line 4, which shows no significant change from Line 3. The scour hole has not changed much since 1980.

By employing the resultant pool depth after the scouring, the ratio of cushion depth h to energy head H at the bucket lip was calculated to be about 1/3. This value may serve as reference for similar design in the future.

Table 3. Major Typhoons and Flood Operation of Shihmen Spillway

Date	Typhoon	Maximum Discharge (cms)	Date	Typhoon	Maximum Discharge (cms)
Sept.1963	Gloria	9,600	Sept.1971	Bess	3,960
Sept.1969	(Tropical Depression)	1,050	Aug. 1972	Betty	4,980
Sept.1969	(Tropical Depression)	1,630	Aug. 1984	Holly	1,860
Sept.1969	Elsie	4,220	Aug. 1985	Nelson	4,490
Oct. 1969	Flossie	1,550	Oct. 1985	Brenda	1,580
Sept.1971	Fran	1,460			

Remarks: Flood operations for discharges < 1,000 cms are as follows:
Oct.1963–Aug. 1967 : 3 times. Sept.1967–Apr.1978 : 10 times.
May 1978–Mar. 1980 : 2 times. Apr. 1980–Oct.1985 : 10 times.

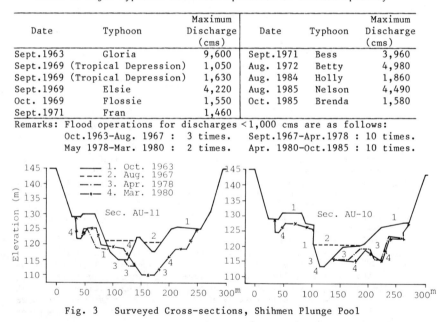

Fig. 3   Surveyed Cross-sections, Shihmen Plunge Pool

TSENGWEN SPILLWAY

General Description - The multi-purpose Tsengwen Reservoir is also designed for irrigation, power generation, water supply and flood control. Its embankment dam is 133 m high and at the normal high reservoir water level of 225 m the reservoir is impounded to a gross storage of 708 x10^6 m^3, which is the largest in Taiwan. An open-chute spillway with a design discharge of 9,470 cms is located on the right bank of the dam. The parallel chute has a total width of 52 m and a net width of

48.9 m at both the spillway crest and the flip bucket ends. In order to adapt to the existing ground and rock surface conditions and to save construction cost, the chute and bucket were divided by two training walls into three channels of equal width. Similarly, the bucket invert elevations were set, from right to left, at 132, 136, and 140 m respectively, with the corresponding lip angles of 36°, 33° and 30°, while the bucket radiuses are all 25 m. Through this arrangement, the three water jets could impinge together into the pre-excavated plunge pool that follows the bucket. The plan and profile of Tsengwen spillway are shown in Fig. 4.

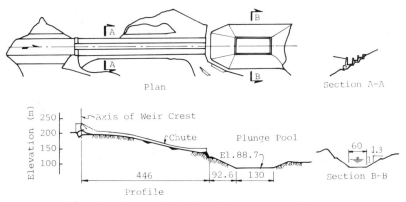

Fig. 4. Plan and Profile of Tsengwen Spillway

Design Considerations – Since the capacity of the irrigation intake at 5 km downstream of the dam is adequate enough to regulate the tailwater of peak power generation, there was no need to provide an afterbay. Furthermore, due to the steep slope of downstream river channel, the low depth of tailwater, and the limited chute width designed to save excavation cost, the unit discharge of the spillway is quite large. Studies made during the design stage led to the conclusion that if a stilling basin was adopted for energy dissipation, a long apron would be required which would greatly increase the construction cost. But if a pre-excavated plunge pool was adopted, since the pool would be located on sound rock foundation, and taking the experiences of design and operation of the Shihmen spillway as references, the pool only needed to be excavated for 26 m (to El. 88.7 m) to comply with the requirement of h/H = 1/3, and at the same time most of the excavated material could be used as structural backfill to save the construction cost. Based on these considerations, the plunge pool type was adopted.

To confirm the above design considerations, a 1:60 hydraulic model of the spillway and plunge pool was constructed and tested under the design discharge and the maximum recorded discharge of 5,550 cms (equivalent to 100-year return period) conditions. The tests revealed that when the pool floor elevation was lowered from 88.7 m to 85 m, the hydrodynamic pressure showed almost no difference, clearly indicated that the elevation of 88.7 m could meet the design requirement.(3) As a result of the test, the plunge pool was set with a floor width of 60 m and length of 130 m, while the slopes of its side banks and the downstream side were 1 on 1.3 and 1 on 2.5, respectively.

Meanwhile, to understand the scour pattern in the plunge pool, a movable bed hydraulic model test using gravels of 5 mm mean diameter was also conducted. Table 4 gives the resultant locations and depths of the scour holes. From the table, it is seen that a scour depth of 5.8 m could be developed under a spillway discharge of 5,550 cms. However, in actuality, the pool foundation is of sound bed rock, and by inferring from the case of Shihmen spillway, it was concluded that no scouring would occur in the prototype under the above discharge. And under larger discharges, only the downstream side of the plunge pool might be scoured. In view of the lower possiblity for larger floods to occur, it was decided that to repair after scour would be more economical than to provide a larger pre-excavated pool, and the design for the plunge pool was confirmed.

Table 4. Results of Movable Bed Test for Tseng- wen Plunge Pool (Bed Material= 5 mm Diameter Gravels)	Discharge (cms)	Dist. of Scour Hole Center to Bucket(m)	Scour Depth(m)
	5,550	151	5.8
	9,470	189	14.8

Actual Operation - It has been more than 13 years since completion of the Tsengwen reservoir in October 1973. Table 5 lists the flood operation record during this period. From observation of the pool floor after each operation, no scouring has been found. Evidently, the design of the plunge pool has met the economic and safety requirements.

Table 5. Flood Releases (>1,000 cms) of Tsengwen Spillway	Date	Typhoon	Maximum Discharge (cms)
	Sept.1974	(Storm)	1,208
	Aug. 1975	Nina	2,250
Remarks: From Aug. 1975 to	Aug. 1975	(Storm)	3,750
Sept. 1981, there were	July 1977	Thelma	1,500
14 operations with all	July 1977	Vera	1,500
discharges smaller	Aug. 1977	Irma	1,500
than 1,000 cms.	Sept.1981	Clare	5,300

PALING SPILLWAY

General Description - The 38-meter high Paling Dam, which functions as a check dam for the Shihmen Reservoir, is a buttress type gravity dam located 37 km upstream of the Shihmen Dam. The dam is built with a 80.4-meter long free overfall type crest spillway, with a design discharge of 6,100 cms, for plunging into a pre-excavated pool. Because of the shallow overburden on the left side of the plunge pool, and for the purpose of not disturbing the stability of the left bank through excessive excavation, the spillway crest was so arranged that the left side is not only set at 1 m higher than the right side but also provided with a super-elevated flow surface. This arrangement not only causes the normal overflow to fall entirely into the pool, but also eliminates the impact of flood discharge on the left slope of the pool. The 27-meter long plunge pool has a width similar to that of the spillway and was excavated to the bed rock with its floor placed with a 1.5-meter thick reinforced concrete pavement. At the downstream end of the pool, a secondary dam was formed by excavating the river bed material having a slope of 1 on 1.25 on the upstream side and covered with a 1.5-meter

thick reinforced concrete pavement. To ensure its stability a row of
deep caissons at the downstream side of the secondary dam was constructed and anchored into the bed rock. And similar to the spillway
crest, the left portion of the secondary dam was also elevated to 1 m
higher to improve the hydraulic performance of the plunge pool. The
plan and the profile along the center line of the spillway and the
plunge pool are shown in Fig. 5.

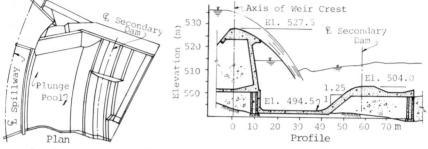

Fig. 5. Plan and Profile of the Paling Spillway and Plunge Pool

Design Consideration - Design considerations for the Paling plunge
pool include: 1) water jet falling from the spillway should be entirely
confined within the plunge pool; 2) the secondary dam should have a
sufficient height to prevent occurrence of free jump inside the pool;
and 3) no negative pressure is allowed on the surfaces of the secondary
dam. The preliminary layout of the plunge pool was designed by referring to <u>Section 211: Free Overfall Spillway with Impact Block</u> of the
"Design of Small Dams", USBR.(2) Since the depth of the pool was set to
reach the bed rock, decision of the invert elevation of the pool was
firstly made. Then the length and the cushion depth required were
calculated to make possible the subsequent determination of the location
and the height of the secondary dam. For confirmation of the
suitability and reliability of the preliminary design, a 1:60 hydraulic
model test was carried out.(1) Under the discharges of 4,000 and 6,100
cms, three alternative layouts of the plunge pool by varying the
upstream side slope of the secondary dam and the pool length were
investigated. It was discovered that under Alternative I, the resultant
cushion depth was insufficient and there was negative pressure on the
secondary dam. Under Alternative II, some improvements of the hydraulic
performance in the pool were observed. However, the negative pressure
was still detected. Finally, Alternative III was tested and found to
have the best energy dissipation effect and to be able at the same time
to satisfy the above-mentioned design considerations. Consequently, it
was selected as the definite design layout. A summary of the test
results of these three alternatives is presented in Table 6.

Actual Operation - Since its completion in June 1977, there have been
constant normal discharges into the plunge pool. And during the 9 years
of its operation, the spillway has also accommodated the passage of 16
flood discharges all in excess of 500 cms, with the largest discharge
being 3,350 cms. Repeated observations indicate that the plunge pool
has performed satisfactorily, and investigation into the plunge pool
structures also shows that they are in good condition.

Table 6. Test Results for Layout of Paling Plunge Pool

Alternative Layout	Invert Elevation (m)	Length of Pool(m)	U/S Slope of Secondary Dam	6,100 cms h (m)	*Min. Press.	4,000 cms h (m)	*Min. Press.
I	494.50	29	1 : 0.75	13	-7.7	11	-3.6
II	494.50	27	1 : 1.0	14	-1.5	12	0
III	494.50	27	1 : 1.25	17	1.5	13	1.4

*Minimum pressure measured on the secondary dam, in meters.

SUMMARY

From the foregoing description of the spillway energy dissipators, the following indications are observed:

1. The operation data and scouring condition of the Shihmen and Tsengwen spillways indicate that for the ski-jump type spillway, if the plunge pool is located on rock foundation, the ratio of cushion depth h to energy head at the bucket lip H could be reasonably assumed to be equal to or greater than 1/3.

2. For the open-chute type spillway with flip bucket and plunge pool, energy dissipation can best be achieved by setting the bucket lip to approximately 35°.

3. Based on the actual scouring data of the Shihmen plunge pool, it could be inferred that if the pool is located on weak bed rock, the extent of scour hole might be represented by the result of a 1:60 hydraulic model test using 50 mm size gravels as the movable bed material.

4. For the ski-jump type spillway, the plunge pool needs not be pre-excavated to the depth required to accommodate the probable maximum flood. Since the water jet from the flip bucket can be located far away from the dam foundation, and even though the pool floor may be scoured to some extent by rarely happened large floods, it would not affect the safety of the structures and could be easily repaired. Based on the same reasoning, the pool floor also needs not be paved.

5. For free overfall type spillway, the water jet will have an impact on the plunge pool which is adjacent to the dam, and reinforce concrete pavement on the pool floor to ensure safety is advisable.

6. The fact that the hydraulic model test results of the three spillways conform reasonably well with the actual operation indicates that it is advisable to conduct the tests to obtain the required information during the design stage.

References

1. Bureau of Reclamation, "Hydraulic Model Studies for Morrow Point Dam", Engineering Monograph No. 37, 1967

2. Bureau of Reclamation, "Design of Small Dams", 2nd Edition, 1973

3. Bureau of Reclamation, "Impinging Jet", REC-ERC-80-8, Oct. 1980

4. Johnson, P. L., "Hydraulic Model Studies of Plunge Basin for Jet Flow", REC-ERC-74-9, Bureau of Reclamation, 1974

AIR SLOT IN TUNNEL SPILLWAY OF FEITSUI DAM

C.L. Yen[1], M. ASCE, Y. Cheng[2], M. ASCE

R.L. Hsu[3], and R.Y. Wang[4]

ABSTRACT

The tunnel spillway of the Feitsui Reservoir Project near Taipei has a head drop of more than 110 m, and maximum discharge of 1,500 cms. For prevention of cavitation in the tunnel, an air slot is installed at the upstream end of the elbow section of the tunnel. Hydraulic model of 1:60 ratio for four different designs of the air slot have been tested. On the basis of their hydraulic performances, the final design selected from the four tested is of 120 cm deep by 73.5 cm wide and has an upstream ramp 21 cm high and a downstream recess of 15 cm. Pressures and water surface profile were measured in the model of the final design. Numerical simulation was carried out to further confirm the results of model tests.

INTRODUCTION

In Taiwan, favorable dam sites are increasingly difficult to find as the demand for water grows. New reservoirs often require water releasing facilities with high head drops. The Feitsui Reservoir Project, now under construction and scheduled for completion in 1987, is a case in point. The project, located at about 30 km southeast of Taipei City, is designed to meet the demand for public water supply which is expected to rise to 3.3 million tons per day by the year 2,030.

The water releasing facilities of the project include a crest spillway, three sluiceways, a tunnel spillway and a river outlet. The crest spillway is comprised of eight bays with crest elevation at 161 m and its overflow falls into a plunge pool. The design capacity for the crest spillway is 7,670 cms. The three sluiceways provide a discharge capacity of 700 cms. The sill of sluiceway intake is at elevation 100 m which is 70 meters below normal high water level. The functions of the sluiceways are to release flood, to flush sediment and to evacuate reservoir water in case of emergency. The river outlet has a design capacity of 47 cms and its sill is at elevation 85 m. The function of the river outlet is to release water reqiured for the downstream area

1. Professor, Civil Engineering, National Taiwan University, Taipei, Taiwan, ROC.
2. President, Sinotech Engineering Consultants, Inc., Taipei, Taiwan, ROC.
3. Manager, Department of Hydraulic Engineering, Sinotech Engineering Consultants, Inc., Taipei, Taiwan, ROC.
4. Professor & Chairman, Agricultural Engineering, National Taiwan University, Taipei, Taiwan, ROC.

when the operation of power generation is suspended.

The tunnel spillway, located at the right abutment of the dam, is connected with the diversion tunnel through the addition of an inclined tunnel (see Fig.1). It has a design capacity of 1,500 cms. The main functions of the tunnel spillway are to help release floods that are larger than the combined capacity of the crest spillway and the sluiceways, and evacuate reservoir water in case of emergency. The intake of the tunnel spillway is divided by a pier into two bays, each of which is provided with a fixed-wheel gate to control the release. It is designed for hydraulically free flow, with the flow area not to exceed 75% the entire cross-section of the tunnel. For prevention of cavitation (Colgate, 1971; Quintela, 1980; Pinto et al, 1982), an air slot is installed at the upstream end of the elbow section of the tunnel spillway.

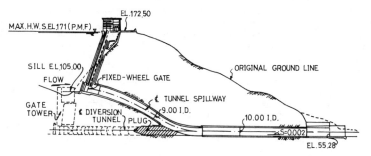

Fig .1 Profile of Diversion Tunnel and Tunnel Spillway

The intake sill of the tunnel spillway is located at elevation 105 m. Its entrance is of two bays, each varying from 4 m × 9 m to 4 m × 6m in a length of 16.49 m. This portion, under pressure flow at the design discharge, is then followed by free flow with a two-bay section, each of 4 m × 9.04 m with an arch on top. The two-bay section ends at Sta. 0 + 044.23 and then transformed gradually into circular shape of 9 m in diameter at Sta. 0 + 084.03. From there on the same diameter is maintained to Sta. 0 + 128.36 whose bottom elevation is at 65.11 m. This is then followed by a vertical bend expanding gradually to 10 m in diameter to connect the diversion tunnel at Sta. 0 + 167.86. The bottom elevation there is 55.57 m. The diversion tunnel has a diameter of 10 m and a bottom slope of 0.002. The total length of tunnel spillway from entrance to the exit is 386 m. The design of the tunnel spillway and its associated air slot was carried out by Sinotech Engineering Consultants, Inc.

LABORTORY STUDY

In the design of air slot, it was considered essential for protection of the tunnel surface of the vertical bend. The air slot is required to furnish sufficient air to the flowing water for all discharges up to the design maximum of 1,500 cms. In addition, the configuration of the slot and all adjacent areas would necessarily be such

that the flow should be hydraulically acceptable for all discharges. A
series of model tests for the design of air slot has been conducted at
the Hydraulic Research Laboratory of National Taiwan University. The
scale ratio of the model is 1:60. Four Different designs of air slot were
tested, from which the final design was chosen. During these studies no
attempt was made to measure the quantity of air entrained in the water.
Neither pressure distributions nor water surface profiles were measured,
except for the case of recommended air slot.

Preliminary Design - The preliminary air slot at Sta. 0 + 95.40 was a
uniform offset of the wetted portion of tunnel circumference. Although
air was entrained in the flowing water, the edges of the jet near the
water surface impinged on the downstream tunnel surface created large
disturbances in the upper portion of the cross-section, which was supposed to be left free. As the discharge increased, greater amounts of
water was spouted up to occupy the upper portion. At the discharge
over 1,400 cms almost the entire cross-section of the tunnel was filled.
This then resulted in very serious oscillatory water surface in the downstream tunnel. This situation was not hydraulically acceptable. Therefore the preliminary design was abandoned.

Air Slot No.1 - In an attempt to prevent water from surging up to occupy
the free area of the tunnel cross-section, an air slot of 73.3 cm × 6.1
cm was designed. This slot was with a ramp at its upstream end and a
recess at the downstream end. The ramp lift varied from 6.1 cm at the
invert to zero at 3.05 cm above the springline. An air entrance portal
was also provided at each end of the air slot. The details of the air
slot are given in Fig.2 and their dimensions are shown in Table 1.

    The results of model tests indicated that although at low dis-
charges air was entrained in the jet, water entered the slot from the
spillway water surface for all discharges. For small discharges, water

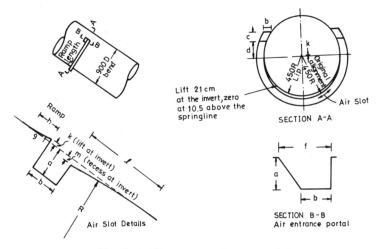

Fig. 2 Configuration of Air Slot

drained down the slot and was carried away by the jet at the invert.
However, as the spillway discharge increased, the water surface in the
slot rose to higher level and eventually reached the same elevation as
the spillway water surface. At that point no air was entrained into the
jet through the slot. Thus, the purpose of the air slot is totally
defeated. Further increase in spillway discharge forced the water with
sufficiently high head, into the slot to cause the formation of spouts
and surges above spillway water surface. This again resulted in oscil-
lating water surface along the tunnel downstream. It was concluded that
this design was not hydraulically acceptable either.

Table 1 Dimensions* of Air Slots

Design	a	b	c	d	f	h	k	ℓ	m	R
No.1	73.3	73.3	97.8	183.3	128.3	55.0	6.1	211.3	12.2	1833.2
No.2	135.4	73.5	98.0	242.0	175.1	189.0	21.0	210.0	25.4	1477.5
Recom-mended	120.0	73.5	98.0	242.0	163.5	189.0	21.0	210.0	15.0	880.8

* All dimensions are in centimeters

Air Slot No.2 - On the basis of the testing results of Air Slot #1, the
ramp height was raised to 21 cm and the downstream edge was further
depressed to 25.4 cm. The depth of the slot was increased to 135.4 cm.
Other dimensions are listed in Table 1. The tests for this design
showed that there was quite an improvement over Air Slot #1 in that the
jet jumped over the slot far enough to avoid water from entering the
slot from the water surface of the spillway discharge. However, some
filling was still taking place. Most of the filling was from the back-
flow due to impingement of the jet against the tunnel surfaces immediately downstream from the slot at some distance below the level of
springline. This was attributed to the larger depression downstream of
slot edge. The water in the slot was swept away by the jet near the
tunnel invert. The phenonena of spouts and surges were also observed
but with much smaller magnitudes. Although this Air Slot #2 was hydraulically much better than #1, some modifications were still desirable.

Recommended Air Slot - The Air Slot #2 mentioned above was modified by
reducing the magnitude of downstream depression to 15 cm (see Table 1).
The recommended design consisted of a slot of 120 cm deep by 73.5 cm
wide (Fig.2) at Sta. 0 + 121.59, a ramp of 189 cm long in the direction
of flow and a recess of 210 cm long. The upstream face of the slot was
lifted by 21 cm at the tunnel invert. The intersection of the ramp and
upstream face of the air slot was of the same radius as the tunnel, with
a 21 cm eccentricity in the plane normal to the centerline of the tunnel.
Thus, the lift varied from 21 cm at the invert to zero at a point 10.5 cm
above the tunnel springline.

The ramp lifted the jet away from the tunnel surface and over the
air slot. The jet remained clearly free for some distance downstream
before impinging on the tunnel surface. The distance to the point of
jet impingement, called cavity length, appeared to reach maximum at the

tunnel invert. The cavity length decreased as discharge was decreased.
This type of impingement will not damage smooth concrete surfaces. The
impingement of the jet on the tunnel surface downstream also caused side
fins to form at lower discharges. The fins at lower discharges did not
reach the top of the tunnel and was not objectionable. At larger discharges, the fins disappeared as the ramp lift diminished near the
springline of the tunnel and the jet was subjected to less contraction
at higher portion of the tunnel cross-section. In the meantime the fins
that were generated at the lower portion was suppressed by the upper
portion of the jet.

The air slot remained practically free of water, and air was drawn
into the jet for all discharges. Air was visible in the model jet
starting at the air slot and continued downstream well beyond the P.T.
of the bend. An estimation indicated that there would be sufficient air
remaining in the water to prevent cavitation for the rest of tunnel.

NUMERICAL SIMULATION

In order to further check the results of hydraulic model test, a
numerical simulation has also been carried out by employing computer
model developed on the basis of a three-dimensional finite element
method.

Governing Equations - As this analysis is only intended to be a check of
the experimental results, steady incompressible irrotational flow is
considered here for simplicity of analysis. Laplace equation of
velocity potential can be employed to describe the flow:

$$\nabla^2 \phi = 0$$

where ϕ = velocity potential funation. The velocity and pressure distributions in the flow field can be obtained from velocity potential
function:

$$u_i = \frac{\partial \phi}{\partial x_i} \tag{1}$$

and the Bernoulli equation

$$\frac{p}{\gamma} + \frac{\Sigma u_i^2}{2g} + z = H \tag{2}$$

In the equations above, u_i = x_i-component of velocity; p = pressure; γ =
specific weight of water; z = elevation and H = total energy head.

Boundary Conditions - To solve for the flow field, boundary conditions
are necessary. They are described as follows(also see Fig.3):

1. On Γ_1: Uniform flow is considered. The derivative of ϕ with
   respect to the normal is equal to the negative of uniform velocity
   at this section.
2. On Γ_2: The pressure is atmospheric and normal velocity must be
   zero. Since the free surface itself is a streamline, the velocity
   potential satisfying the latter must also satisfy the require-

ment that the velocity is tangential to the free surface.
3. On Γ_3: The section taken is far enough from the air slot so that its potential is constant across the surface.
4. On Γ_4: This is a cavity subject to a subatmospheric pressure within the range of $-1.0 \text{ m} \leq p/\gamma \leq 0$.
5. On Γ_5: The normal velocity component is zero on the boundary. Since the tunnel is symmetrical with respect to the vertical plane through the tunnel invert, only one-half of the tunnel is considered in the problem. Therefore, the boundary Γ_5 includes the surface along the wetted perimeter and the vertical plane of symmetry.

Solution Technique - Assuming that the velocity potential in Eq.(1) can be approximated within a finite element in the following form (Segerlind, 1976),

$$\phi = N_j \, \phi_j \tag{3}$$

then Eq(1) can be expressed as (Chung, 1978)

$$\int_\Omega N(\nabla^2 \phi) \, d\Omega = 0 \tag{4}$$

In the equations above, $j = 1,2,\ldots.M$, where M is the total number of nodes in an element; N_j = interpolation function; ϕ_j = nodal values of ϕ; and Ω = domain of analysis.

By use of Green-Gauss theorem and Gaussian quadrature integration method Eq.(4) can be transformed into the following form:

$$|A_{ji}| \, (\phi_j) = |B_j| \tag{5}$$

where $|A_{ji}|$ and $|B_j|$, respectively, are coefficient matrix and flux vector which are functions of coordinates and weighting coefficients. The velocity components at a nodal point is given by

$$u_i = \frac{1}{D} \sum_{k=1}^{D} \left(\sum_{j=1}^{M} \frac{\partial N_j}{\partial x_i} \, \phi_j \right) \tag{6}$$

in which D is the total number of elements for node j to connect with; and M is the total number of nodes in each element.

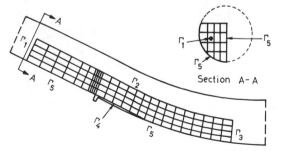

Fig. 3 Finite Elements of Flow Field

To simplify handling of input data, calculation of nodal coordinates and division of flow field into isoparametric elements has been excuted in computer. Coons' patch method (Coons, 1967) has been employed to subdivide each section into a number of elements (Fig.3).

It is extremely difficult to determine the exact location of the two free surfaces, Γ_2 and Γ_4, that satisfy the boundary conditions as described previously. Approximation becomes necessary. The lower surface of the nappe trajectory is determined by assuming a two-dimensional free jet issuing from the vertex of the ramp, with p = 0 on Γ_2 and a subatmospheric pressure head of -0.3 on Γ_4 (Wei & DeFazio, 1982). The distance between the ramp and the intercept of the free jet at the tunnel invert is called cavity length. The intercept is considered as the reattachment point. The bounding surfaces Γ_4 and Γ_5 are then regarded as a fixed boundary. It is further assumed that the lower free surface is shaped in such a way that it intersects with any vertical plane, parallel to that containing the tunnel invert. This assumption is also checked in laboratory tests to be approximately true.

Simulated Results - The flow characteristics around the air slot in the tunnel spillway of the Feitsui Reservoir have been simulated by the numerical method just described above for the design discharge of 1,500 cms. The water surface profiles obtained in the numerical simulation and model tests are in close agreement, except in the vicinity of the air slot where the measured water surface profile is higher and the cavity length is shorter than that of the simulated (Yen & Wang, 1983).

The pressure distribution along the tunnel invert is shown in Fig.4(a). Again, the simulated results are in reasonably good agreement with that of the model tests. However, at the ramp vertex the simulated pressures are higher than the measured ones. Similar situation can also be said for the pressure at the reattachment point. This is at least partially due to the fact that the effects of fluid viscosity is not included in the simulation. The observed cavity length is somewhat shorter than the simulated one. This may be attributed to the fact that

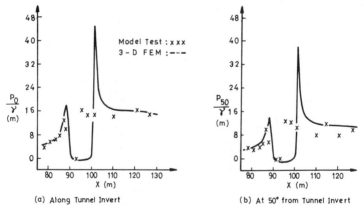

Fig. 4 Pressure Distribution Around Air Slot

the assumed pressure in the cavity is lower than the actual pressure in addition to the omission of viscous effects.

In Fig.4(b) is also shown the pressure distribution along a longitudinal section making an angle of 50° with the vertical plane through the invert. The simulated results shown in this figure also exibit the same general features as those in Fig.4(a).

SUMMARY

(1) For a tunnel spillway with high head drop such as the one for the Feitsui Reservoir, the aeration device by uniform offset of tunnel boundary can not function well because the impingement on the downstream tunnel surface creates   spouts and surges.

(2) For the Feitsui Tunnel Spillway with design maximum discharge of 1,500 cms and head drop of more than 110 m, the air slot of 120 cm by 73.5 cm, having upstream ramp lift of 21 cm and downstream recess of 15 cm at the tunnel invert, and diminishing to zero at 10.5 cm above the springline, is an appropriate design to keep air entrained freely by the jet. Thus, the air slot can function properly as a device for prevention of cavitation.

(3) Numerical simulation by using three-dimensional finite element method to solve the Laplace equation for potential flow, subject to appropriate boundary conditions, shows that the pressure distributions and water surface profiles measured in model tests are generally in good agreement with the simulated results. Thus, the reliability of model tests for the recommended air slot is confirmed.

REFRENCES

Chung, T.J. (1978), Finite Element Analysis in Fluid Dynamics, McGraw-Hill Book Co., pp. 79-205.
Colgate, D.M. (1971), "Hydraulic Model Studies of Aeration Devices for Yellowtail Dam Spillway Tunnel, Pick-Sloan Missouri Basin Program, Montana," Engineering and Research Center, USBR, REC-ERC-71-47.
Coons, S.A. (1967), "Surfaces for Computer-Aided Design of Space Forms," M.I.T. Project MAC, MAC-TR-41.
Pinto, N.L. de S., Neidert, S.H. and Ota, J.J. (1982), "Aeration at High Velocity Flows," Water Power & Dam Construction, February, pp. 34-38, and March, pp. 42-44.
Quintela, A.C. (1980), "Flow Aeration to Prevent Cavitation Erosion," Water Power & Dam Construction, January, pp. 17-22.
Segerlind, L.J. (1976), Applied Finite Element Analysis, East Lansing, Michigan, pp. 323-333.
Wei, C.Y. and DeFazio, F.G. (1982), "Simulation of Free Jet Trajectories for the Design of Aeration Devices on Hydraulic Structures," Proceedings, 4th International Conference on Finite Elements in Water Resources, Hannover, F.R.G.
Yen, C.L. and Wang, R.Y. (1983), "Hydraulic Model Studies of Feitsui Reseavoir Project," Research Report No.66, Hydraulic Research Laboratory, National Taiwan University, Taipei, Taiwan, ROC.

MODELING OF THE UNDULAR JUMP FOR WHITE WATER BYPASS

Mohammed A. Samad, Ph.D.; John M. Pflaum, M
William C. Taggart, M, Richard E. McLaughlin

Abstract

Two of the authors have reported previously (Ref. 2) on the hazard that a conventional hydraulic jump with a uniform reverse surface roller presents to white water boaters. There are a number of concepts which can be utilized to create bypasses around dams. These can involve flat gradients, small drops with constrictions and movable or adjustable chutes. The theory of the hydraulic jump at an abrupt drop has been utilized by the authors on several projects. Typically, several chutes and pools are used to break up the total fall. The intent is to create a hydraulic jump that is safe for boaters. This is accomplished by maintaining a horizontal supercritical discharge at the surface, thus eliminating dangerous reverse (or upstream) surface currents. Because numerous flow conditions are typically considered, the analysis technique has been computerized. Two projects of McLaughlin Water Engineers, Ltd., have involved modeling efforts that were very useful, both in academic terms to confirm theory, and to refine the design to achieve good initial prototype performance. Results of a modeling effort for the design of a white water bypass at a grade control structure on the Arkansas River in Pueblo, Colorado are presented herein.

Introduction

The analysis and physical modeling of a hydraulic jump at an abrupt drop were conducted in connection with the design of a river bed grade control structure and white water boat chute on the Arkansas River in Pueblo, Colorado. The design of a grade control structure was necessitated by ongoing degradation of the present river bed which threatened existing sewer lines, bridge foundations and an upstream levee lining. To fulfill the Pueblo Conservancy District's intention of making the structure navigable for boats, a white water bypass was developed to allow for recreational boating access. The principal project features are presented in Figure 1. A series of chutes and pools were designed to break up the total drop of 11 feet (3.35 m) at the structure. Each of the four 2-foot drop (0.61 m) reinforced concrete chutes is followed by 4 foot (1.22 m) deep (nominal) rock-lined stilling pools. A fifth chute and pool, to be constructed of boulders and large rock, provide the remaining transition to the river bed downstream. Each chute is trapezoidal in section with a bottom width that tapers from the upstream crest to the downstream end.

The white water bypass was modeled by using two tail water conditions, one for the present condition of the river bed and one for the future degraded bed.

The above named Authors are Engineers with McLaughlin Water Engineers, Ltd.
2420 Alcott Street, Denver, CO 80211

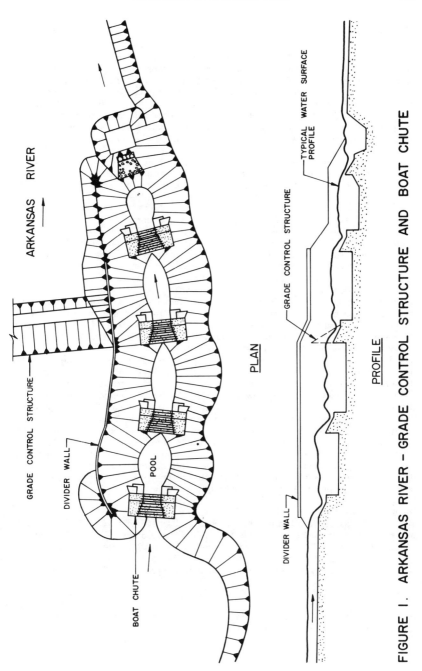

PLAN

PROFILE

FIGURE 1. ARKANSAS RIVER – GRADE CONTROL STRUCTURE AND BOAT CHUTE

Hydraulic Design
The design of the boat chute was treated as a hydraulic jump at an abrupt drop, which refers to the drop at the channel invert at the stilling pool downstream of the chute. The flow behavior at an abrupt drop is illustrated in Figure 2. For a given approaching Froude number, the downstream depth at a drop may fall in any of the five regions as shown in Figure 2. The lower limit of region 1 is the depth at which the jump will begin to travel upstream. The upper limit of region 5 is the depth at which the jump will begin to travel downstream. The drop does not control the jump in these two regions. The jump is stable in regions 2 and 4. The intermediate region 3 represents an undular state of flow without a breaking point.

Equations have been developed for occurrence of hydraulic jump for region 2 and region 4 by Hsu (Ref. 1) for unit width rectangular section. Basically, continuity and momentum equations have been applied to arrive at these equations.

By applying the same principle, equations can be derived for different types of channel geometry. However, because the chute is wide, the premise was that the hydraulic conditions in the center of the chute would correlate better to the jump form rather than the average hydraulics of the entire section. Therefore, a unit width analysis was utilized. The upstream energy grade was calculated using the critical energy of the entire inlet section. A unit width flow was obtained using the average energy of the section. A supercritical profile (incorporating frictional losses) was then computed down the chute to the abrupt drop. At this section the equations for region 2 and region 4 as developed by Hsu (Ref. 1) were applied. A computer program was developed to solve these equations to compute the tail water needed to create the desired jump form between these two regions. This created a target band width for the tail water. The tail water was assumed to be controlled by the crest of the next downstream chute. Therefore, it was expected that the actual tail water would occur somewhere between the energy grade and the critical depth of the entire section of the downstream crest. From previous chute projects, it was known that this tail water elevation was not only difficult to predict, but hard to define. The tail water elevation in the pool varies substantially with location in the pool. The tail water in each pool is a function of the horizontal jet entering the pool because pools were not long enough to allow this jet to fully expand to the area of each pool. This implies that the tail water is also a function of the shape and fall in the upstream chute. Since the tail water at the chute drop is a function of the many independent variables, the need for a physical model is apparent.

Model Description
The model was constructed and tested in the 20 foot (6.1 m) by 100 foot (30.48 m) river mechanics flume in the Hydraulics Laboratory of the Engineering Research Center of Colorado State University in Fort Collins, Colorado. The model length scale ratio was 1 to 12, and the relationships for other flow variables were derived from model similitude based on the Froude number.

Construction of the model was completed by utilizing the site grading plan prepared by the authors. The first four chutes were made of wood with cement side slopes to simulate reinforced concrete, while the fifth chute was constructed of roughened cement to simulate a prototype construction of grouted boulders. The pools downstream of the chutes were constructed of rock cemented together

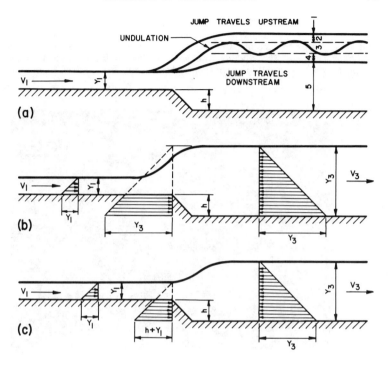

REGION 2:

$$\mathbf{F}^2 = \frac{1}{2} \frac{y_2/y_1}{1 - y_2/y_1} \left[1 - \left(\frac{y_2}{y_1} - \frac{h}{y_1} \right)^2 \right]$$

REGION 4:

$$\mathbf{F}^2 = \frac{1}{2} \frac{y_2/y_1}{1 - y_2/y_1} \left[\left(\frac{h}{y_1} + 1 \right)^2 - \left(\frac{y_2}{y_1} \right)^2 \right]$$

FIGURE 2. FLOW BEHAVIOR AT AN ABRUPT DROP

to form a rigid bed. The remaining topography was covered with cement
mortar. Half round strips were placed across the horizontal surfaces of the
first four chutes to simulate the 6-inch (15.24 cm) diameter roughness elements
in the prototype. The divider wall was fabricated from plywood to simulate
the prototype sheet piling. The completed model is shown in Figure 3.

FIGURE 3. MODEL OF WHITE WATER BYPASS

Water was supplied by a lift pump to a head box and diffuser located upstream
of the model. The tail water elevation below the last downstream chute was
regulated by a series of stop logs at the downstream end of the river flume.
The flow conditions in the model simulated the flow rates and depths of the
prototype. By controlling the upstream and downstream water surface levels,
the corresponding flow rates through the chutes were established. The model
flow conditions were established by first regulating the control valves in the
supply piping to set a constant upstream river water surface elevation. The
downstream river tail water elevation was then calculated from the prototype
river stage relationships. Adjustments in tail water elevation were made by
regulating the stop logs in the model. For each upstream river water surface
elevation, a minimum and maximum tail water elevation was used. The maximum
tail water represented water surface elevations just after the construction of
the prototype, while the minimum tail water represented the effect of
anticipated prototype erosion of 3 feet (0.91 m) to the river bed downstream.

Modeling Results
The theoretical water surface elevation, obtained by running supercritical water
surface profile along the first 3 chutes, and the measured water surface
elevations are shown in Figure 4. Mannings 'n' value was assumed to be .03.
A plan and profile view of the chute configuration which produced the undular

LOCATION	FLOW cfs(m³/s)	Y₁ ft(m)	DEPTH ft(m)	REGION 2 ft(m)	REGION 4 ft(m)	CALCULATION BASIS
CALCULATED	220(6.2)	0.7(0.2)	5.8(1.8)*	6.2(1.9)	5.1(1.6)	UNIT WIDTH
		1.0(0.3)	5.8(1.8)*	6.6(2.0)	5.5(1.7)	AVE. DEPTH
	500(14.2)	1.2(0.4)	7.0(2.1)*	7.5(2.3)	6.1(1.9)	UNIT WIDTH
		1.6(0.5)	7.0(2.1)*	7.8(2.4)	6.5(2.0)	AVE. DEPTH
CHUTE 1	220(6.2)	1.3(0.4)	5.4(1.7)	*LEVEL OF ENERGY AT POOL		
	500(14.2)	2.1(0.6)	6.0(1.8)			
CHUTE 2	220(6.2)	1.0(0.3)	5.4(1.7)			
	500(14.2)	1.9(0.6)	6.1(1.9)			
CHUTE 3	220(6.2)	0.9(0.3)	5.4(1.7)			
	500(14.2)	2.3(0.7)	6.2(1.9)			

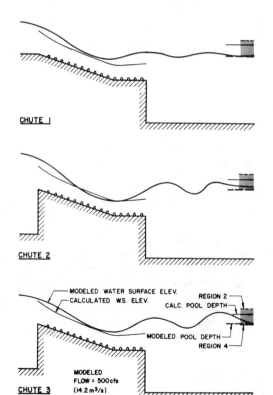

CHUTE 1

CHUTE 2

MODELED WATER SURFACE ELEV.
CALCULATED W.S. ELEV.
REGION 2
CALC. POOL DEPTH
MODELED POOL DEPTH
REGION 4
MODELED FLOW = 500cfs (14.2 m³/s)
CHUTE 3

FIGURE 4. PROFILE AT FIRST THREE BOAT CHUTES

jump is shown in Figure 1. Shown in Figure 4 are the computed and measured water surface profiles. When the results of simplified hydraulic analysis and the observed data are compared, differences are noted. The depth at the outlet of the chute is greater than expected. This may be explained by several reasons. The width of the chute contracts and the supercritical flow distribution varies along the chute. Since unit width equations were utilized, the depth at the outlet of the chute would be greater than that expected with the unit width analysis. Also, cross waves created by the contraction of the chute may affect the wave form and, consequently, the outlet depth of the chute. Another apparent difference is the expected and predicted tail water elevation. The primary purpose of this model was to create an undular jump with proper tail water depth. For most flows tested, 100 cfs - 5000 cfs prototype, the mean pool tail water was above the critical depth of the downstream crest. For the flow shown in Figure 4, the tail water depth is close to critical depth in all three chutes. However, other flows did not demonstrate this close correlation with critical depth. The pool velocities varied as expected with location in the pool as shown in Figure 5. The center jet expanded very little, while eddy currents existed on both sides of the jet. It was apparent that this had a significant effect on both the tail water depth and the jump form.

The computed average depth at the chute outlet is higher than the depth obtained by unit width analysis. The corresponding calculated depths for region 2 and region 4 did not relate well with the observed depths in the pool.

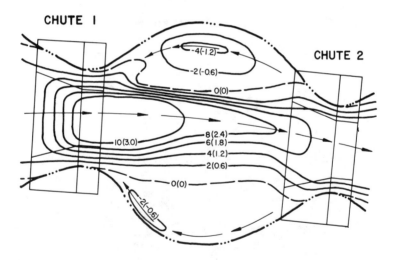

FIGURE 5. MEASURED SURFACE VELOCITIES IN POOL (PROTOTYPE CONDITIONS) IN fps(m/s) FOR 500 cfs (14.2 m³/s)

CONCLUSION

Unit width hydraulic analysis was an effective tool for analyzing the boat chutes and pools for size and configuration tested. Unit width analysis appears to be a better basis for determining region 2 and 4 based on the comparison between the model and predicted result. Its limitations stem from the three dimensional flow pattern found in the chutes and in the pools. Research in the areas of cross waves created in the chute, expansion of the horizontal jet in the pool and varying tail water conditions would provide more accurate predictions for an undular hydraulic jump. The analysis and the model indicated that a configuration could be arrived at which created a favorable undular hydraulic jump at the range of flows tested.

References

1. Hsu, En-Yun: "Discussion on Control of the Hydraulic Jump by Sills," by John W. Forster and Raymond A. Skrinde, Transactions, American Society of Civil Engineers, Vol. 115, pp. 988-991, (1950).

2. Taggart, William C. et al, "Modifications of Dams for Recreational Boating", Proceedings, American Society of Civil Engineers, Hydraulics Division, Water for Resource Development Conference, pp. 781-785, (August, 1984).

TOE DRAIN SYSTEM - BARR AND MILTON RESERVOIRS, CO.

by L. Stephen Schmidt, P.E., A.M. ASCE[*]

Abstract:

The purpose of this paper is to describe the design and construction of toe drains in difficult soil conditions for two 70+ year old dams in Colorado using a unique toe drain installation procedure. The dams are sand on sand foundation, thus presenting significant problems for toe drain construction because the drains must be installed in cohesionless material below the water table. Toe drain construction was made practical and economical through employment of a specialized machine. The machine excavates for the drain, installs the filter gravel zone, and installs the drain pipe in one continuous operation while maintaining design line and grade. The installation process does not require dewatering, trench shoring/bracing, or excavations standing open for any length of time. A unique solution was employed to provide a surface discharge point for two of the drains at an elevation lower than the surrounding ground and water table, eliminating the need for pump systems. A convenient flow measuring device for each drain was designed and constructed.

Introduction

The purpose of this paper is to describe the design and installation of toe drains in difficult soil conditions using a unique toe drain installation procedure. The procedure incorporated a machine which excavates for the drain, installs the filter gravel zone, and installs the drain pipe in one continuous operation while maintaining design line and grade. The installation process does not require dewatering, trench shoring/bracing, or excavations standing open for any length of time. Use of this specialized machine to install drains in cohesionless sands below the water table is described for two projects in Colorado.

Project Description

Barr Lake and Milton Reservoirs are located in the Beebe Draw, northeast of the Denver metropolitan area (Figure 1). Each reservoir impounds in excess of 37 million cubic meters (30,000 acre-feet) of water for agricultural irrigation use in Beebe Draw, and small portions of the Box Elder Creek and South Platte River valleys. The reservoirs are normally filled during the period from October through April, with the water being imported via feeder canals from the South Platte River.

* Project Manager, Rocky Mountain Consultants, Inc., 8301 E. Prentice Avenue, Suite 101, Englewood, Colorado 80111.

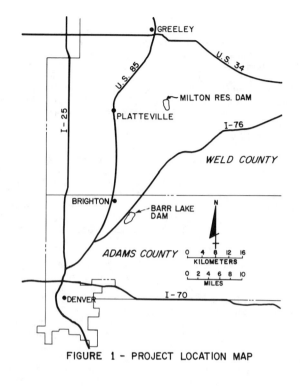

FIGURE 1 - PROJECT LOCATION MAP

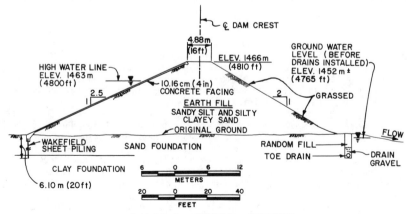

FIGURE 2 - TYPICAL SECTION

Both reservoirs were constructed during the period from 1909 to 1912, reportedly including a limited toe drain system. By 1980 the toe drains either could not be located or were in poor condition where located. Design and construction of toe drain systems for the Milton and Barr Lake Dams were authorized as part of the Farmers Reservoir and Irrigation Company's (owner of the reservoirs) program to upgrade and rehabilitate these reservoir facilities. In this paper will be described the new toe drain systems ultimately constructed at these two dams, and the procedure used to construct the drains.

Geotechnical Conditions

The geotechnical conditions at each dam are quite similar. The dams are constructed of fine to medium sands, silty sand, and clayey sand. The foundations of each dam consist of a stratum of sands of the same description as used to construct the dams. Underlying the sand foundation is a stratum of clay, sometimes sandy. Below the clay are alluvial gravel deposits which overlie shale bedrock and extend the length of Beebe Draw. A typical dam cross-section is shown on Figure 2.

The "impermeable" barrier of each dam consists of two components. First, the upstream face is surfaced with a 10.16 to 15.24 cm (4 to 6 inches) thick concrete slab. Second, at the upstream toe of the concrete facing and tied to the facing is a wooden sheet pile cut-off wall extending the length of the dam and founded in the clay stratum. Old records indicate that in some areas at the Milton Dam, the piling did not completely penetrate the sand stratum and reach into the clay stratum. Pilings exposed during other maintenance activity, were found to be in acceptable condition except in areas at the piling/facing interface where erosion of the sand foundation had exposed the top of the piling, allowing alternate wetting and drying. (As a matter of interest, the piling is triple lapped untreated Oregon Fir and long leaf Yellow Pine (from the New Orleans, Louisiana area).

Seepage Conditions

The concrete facing, which contained numerous cracks and joints, and the sheet pile cut-off provide varying degrees of water tightness. Although the phreatic surface within the embankments was rather low because of the pervious nature of the embankment and foundation materials, the phreatic surface was quite high in the foundation immediately downstream of the dam.

At Barr Lake Dam, the ground water table was within .46 to .61 m (1.5 to 2.0 feet) of the ground surface. Numerous springs and seeps appeared along the banks of an irrigation ditch running parallel to the dam axis at a distance of 46 to 61 m (150 to 200 feet) from the downstream toe of the dam. The ditch was originally constructed to collect seepage appearing at the ground surface downstream of the dam.

At Milton Dam, the water table was at the surface within 4.6 to 15.2 m (15 to 50 feet) of the downstream toe of the dam. In addition, numerous seeps and springs were present within 91 m (300 feet) of the downstream toe of the dam. The lower portions of Beebe Draw are marshy areas for a distance of 3.22 km (2 miles) downstream of the dam.

These seeps, springs, and marshy areas have been in existence for many years and were not in themselves cause for alarm or emergency action. Nevertheless, the high water table has a detrimental effect on overall embankment stability; other things being equal, a lower water table would increase the factor of safety in a stability analysis. The existing conditions were undesirable because the collection and discharge of seepage was uncontrolled. Any number of conditions could change, increasing discharge, causing sand boils, or leading to piping of foundation material. No measurement of seepage quantity to detect changing conditions was practicable.

The existing open joint 15.24 cm (6 inch) clay tile drains were of limited extent, could not be located, or were in poor condition. A new toe drain system was desirable to enhance overall embankment stability, and to control and monitor seepage.

Design Considerations

The primary design consideration was to determine a practical construction method for the new drain system. Open trenching was impractical due to the high water table and essentially cohesionless soils. Trenching with shields or shoring, while perhaps possible, presented difficulty in dewatering. Any open trench presented the danger of sand boils in the floor of the excavation and possibly embankment instability at the toe of the dam. Even if a dry year occurred when the reservoir was near empty and water levels downstream of the dam might be low, favorable conditions for open trenching would only be available for a few weeks, if at all.

During the design process, the engineer became aware of a pipe drain installation machine used to construct drains for agricultural land. This machine had also been successfully utilized for emergency installation of toe drains at Lower Latham Reservoir, located a few kilometers north of Milton Reservoir. The machine is basically a modified track mounted chain belt trenching machine (Figures 3 and 4).

The modification to the trenching machine consists of a trench shield mounted immediately behind the excavating chain. The shield is only open at the top and at the lower rear where the opening corresponds to the dimensions of the gravel envelope to be installed. A curved steel pipe serves as an installation guide for the flexible drain pipe. As the machine moves along, the shield is maintained full of filter gravel as flexible pipe is fed into the pipe guide. The toe drain (i.e., perforated pipe and gravel envelope) issues forth from the rear of the shield as the trencher progresses. The drain is kept on grade by sensors on the machine which track a laser beam. The sensors control the hydraulic system of the machine which regulates the elevation of the shield. The trench (above the drain gravel envelope) is immediately backfilled behind the shield. The only such machines known to be available in the region are owned and operated by Loloff Construction Company, Kersey, Colorado.

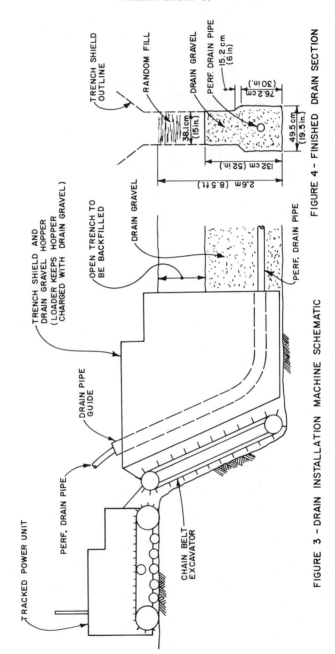

TRENCH SHIELD OUTLINE

RANDOM FILL

DRAIN GRAVEL

PERF. DRAIN PIPE

15.2 cm (6 in.)

76.2 cm (30 in.)

38.1cm (15 in.)

49.5 cm (19.5 in.)

132 cm (52 in.)

2.6 m (8.5 ft.)

FIGURE 4 - FINISHED DRAIN SECTION

TRENCH SHIELD AND DRAIN GRAVEL HOPPER (LOADER KEEPS HOPPER CHARGED WITH DRAIN GRAVEL.)

OPEN TRENCH TO BE BACKFILLED

DRAIN GRAVEL

PERF. DRAIN PIPE

DRAIN PIPE GUIDE

PERF. DRAIN PIPE

TRACKED POWER UNIT

CHAIN BELT EXCAVATOR

FIGURE 3 - DRAIN INSTALLATION MACHINE SCHEMATIC

Once the construction method was established, that method dictated many details of the design. The drain pipe used was flexible 20.32 cm (8 inch) diameter perforated polyethylene per ASTM F-405. At the time the work was done this was the largest such pipe known to be readily available and compatible with the machine. The length of each drain was then formulated such that the pipe would flow 1/3 to 1/2 full providing a substantial factor of safety on capacity. The machine available can set the pipe at a depth of 2.44 to 2.59 m (8.0 to 8.5 feet) on a continuous basis with 2.90 m (9.5 feet) possible for short distances.

Outfalls

The ditching operation starts at the discharge end of the drain at a suitable low area on grade with the drain. The trencher then works into the bank of a ditch (at Barr Lake for example) or gradually works deeper into the ground as it moves away from the low area toward the toe of the dam (at Milton for example).

Some difficulty in establishing a suitable point of discharge for two of the drains at Milton was experienced. The problem was that these two drains were lower in elevation than any of the surrounding land and drainage ways. The only area at an elevation lower than the drain was the invert of the canal which distributes the water released from Milton Reservoir. If the canal was carrying water, no reduction in phreatic surface would be provided by these two drains because no head differential to the flowing canal would be present.

Use of sumps and pumps was not desirable because of the capital cost of electrical service to the site, pump systems and construction, and the continuing cost of operation and maintenance. Fortuitously, the arrangement of the outlet works and stilling basin provided a low cost solution.

The outlet works for the reservoir consists of twin 1.22 m (48 inch) diameter conduits with 1.22 m (48 inch) gate valves on the downstream end of the conduits at the stilling basin. Despite the fact that gate valves are not desirable for throttling applications, these valves are in good condition after 70+ years of service to throttle (control) discharge from the reservoir. When the valves are closed, water in the stilling basin drains out to the canal. When the valves are open, the stilling basin and canal contain water to a depth of 0.91 to 1.52 m (3 to 5 feet); however, due to the jet of water from the valves, the area upstream of the valves remains dewatered. Any water appearing in the stilling basin upstream of the valves is swept-out by the jetting action which occurs.

The two aforementioned drains were routed to a manhole set near the stilling basin. A measuring weir was installed in the manhole to monitor toe drain discharge. From the manhole, the toe drain water was conveyed in a solid pipe to a point behind the gate valves and about 30.48 cm (12 inches) above the stilling basin floor (Figure 5). When water is being released from the reservoir, the toe drain discharge is swept away by the jet from the valves in a manner similar

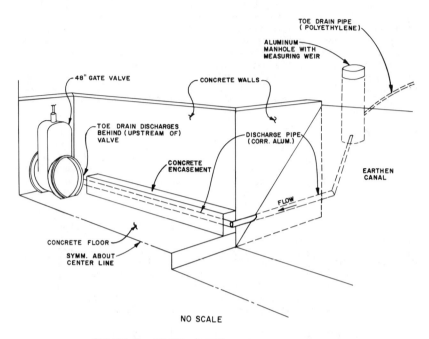

NO SCALE

FIGURE 5 - DRAIN OUTFALL IN STILLING BASIN

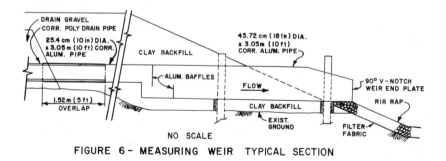

NO SCALE

FIGURE 6 - MEASURING WEIR TYPICAL SECTION

to a jet pump. When the gate valves are closed, the toe drain
discharge simply drains out of the stilling basin and down the canal.

Results

The toe drains were installed in two phases at Barr Lake Dam
(1981 and 1983) and at Milton Dam in 1984. The results of the
installations were in some cases sudden and dramatic as seeps and
springs ceased to flow as the trencher/installer passed between the
seep and the toe of the dam.

The discharge of each toe drain is measured on a regular basis
using the V-notch weir assembly shown on Figure 6. The engineer has
found this assembly to offer the following advantages:

° Fabricated from readily available components at reasonable
  cost.

° Corrosion resistant.

° Provides proper stilling ahead of the weir.

° Discourages or prevents animals from entering the drain.

° Provides opportunity to observe whether the drains produce
  sediment while excluding entry of surface soil.

° Can be easily cleaned.

To date the drains are operating satisfactorily with total drain discharges varying in a normal pattern with changes in the water surface
elevation of the reservoir.

Summary

A new toe drain system was designed and constructed at each of
two 70+ year old dams. The dams are sand on sand foundation, thus presenting significant construction problems for standard toe drain
construction procedures. The toe drain construction was made practical and economical through employment of a specialized machine
which combines the trenching and drain installation into one continuous operation. A unique solution was employed to provide a surface discharge point for two of the drains at an elevation lower than
the surrounding ground and water table without the need for sumps and
pumping systems. A convenient flow measuring device for each drain
was designed and constructed.

Scale Model Study Benefits Hydropower Project

Heinz G. Stefan,[1] Karen L. C. Lindblom,[2] Richard L. Voigt, Jr.[3]

Bruce Ainsworth[4] and Patrick Colgan[5]

The Jim Falls Project on the Chippewa River in Central Wisconsin deals with the replacement of an aged 11 MW run-of-river hydropower plant by a 48 MW peaking plant. A hydraulic model built to a scale of 1:60 at the St. Anthony Falls Hydraulic Laboratory, University of Minnesota, was used extensively to test and develop suitable hydraulic design geometries for several elements of the project. Numerous experiments were conducted on the configuration of the headrace and the diffuser at the end of the tailrace. The addition of a stilling basin and its non-symmetrical geometry were accepted on the basis of model experiments. The flow around the piers of a proposed bridge downstream from the power station was studied in the model. The criteria used for design selection were satisfactory hydraulic performance and construction cost reduction. Construction costs were reduced by shortening the tailrace channel and by placement of excavated rock (fill) in the headwater pool instead of off-site disposal. The model study produced a design which was hydraulically more satisfactory than the original design, allowed personnel from regulatory agencies a 3-D view of the project, permitted plant operators to view hydraulic performance, and produced enough savings in project construction cost to cover the expense for the model study. A description will be given of the main project elements highlighting the role of the model study.

Introduction

The Jim Falls Hydro Redevelopment Project is located on the Chippewa River at the town of Jim Falls, Wisconsin. It includes a two unit powerhouse for 353 m^3/s (12,000 cfs) design flow and approximately 15 m (50 ft) head, a new headwater pool with pilot channel, tailrace channel and an auxiliary spillway next to the powerhouse (Fig. 1). The new spillway has three tainter gates 8.7 m (29 ft) wide and 9.6 m (32 ft) high, topped with flaps 7 m (23 ft) wide and 2.7 m (9 ft) high for debris sluicing. The auxiliary spillway design flow is 1825 m^3/s (65,000 cfs). The existing main spillway, about 1500 m (1 mi) upstream from the site, will be refurbished and used in normal flow passing

---

[1]Associate Director, [2],[3]Research Fellows, St. Anthony Falls Hydraulic Laboratory, Department of Civil and Mineral Engineering, University of Minnesota, Minneapolis, MN 55414.
[4]Project Engineer, Black & Veatch, Kansas City, MO 64114.
[5]Project Engineer, Northern States Power Company, Minneapolis, MN 55401.

operations. The proposed headwater pool includes a portion of the existing power canal. The 1/2 PMF (probable maximum flood) is 4635 m³/s (165,000 cfs). An undistorted 1:60 scale model was constructed and operated at Froude similarity. The model extended from approximately 750 m (2500 ft) upstream to approximately 600 m (2000 ft) downstream of the powerhouse. See Ref. 1 for details of the hydraulic model study.

Spillway Orientation

Initial model tests with the auxiliary spillway at a 35° angle to the powerhouse showed a large counterclockwise surface eddy upstream of the powerhouse. Floating debris collected in this eddy and could not be successfully sluiced over the tainter gate flaps because flow was moving away from the spillway. The surface eddy also generated cross-flow velocities of several feet per second at the upstream face of the powerhouse.

Discharge through the auxiliary spillway at the 35° orientation and with a short apron and endsill produced a supercritical, jet-like discharge across the river bed to the opposite river bank. The run-up on that opposite bank, the potential for bed scour, and the effect on the proposed downstream bridge piers were of extreme concern. It was concluded that a stilling basin was needed. To place that basin within a cofferdam, a re-orientation of the entire spillway structure was required. The spillway was therefore placed parallel to the powerhouse as shown in Fig. 1.

Headrace Design

Debris sluicing and vorticity

After the spillway relocation (zero degree orientation), surface flow patterns were nearly identical to those with the 35° orientation. To improve removal of floating debris over the flap gates, the surface eddy had to be eliminated or reversed. This could be accomplished through changes in headrace topography. Several options were considered (Regions A through D, Fig. 1). It appeared that the very non-uniform depth of the headrace upstream from the powerhouse had much to do with the eddy formation. Filling in a deep trough on the right side (Region D, Fig. 1) reduced the strength of the eddy appreciably, but did not reverse it. Water moving in from the left side of the headrace contributed to the sense of rotation of the surface eddy. High cross-flow velocities from left to right were generated at the surface downstream from Region B, Fig. 1, by the strong convergence of the headrace upstream from the power station and shallow depths in Region B. As a tentative remedial action, an auxiliary channel was cut (Region A, Fig. 1) but even then the model experiments produced a large counterclockwise surface eddy which rendered trash sluicing ineffective. The surface eddy was finally reversed by increasing the depth in region B, Fig. 1, and debris sluicing through the flap gates became very effective (see Ref. 1).

It was observed that the opening (Region C in Fig. 1) to the right of the large upstream island created a "jet" which caused instability in the flow patterns in front of the powerhouse. The "jet" also contributed to intermittent vortex formation in front of the rightmost

turbine intake. Closing the gap between the island and the right
embankment stopped the "jet," stabilized the flow patterns in front of
the powerhouse, and reduced the frequency of intake vortex formation.

On its left side, the approach flow to the powerhouse was limited
by a high vertical retaining wall (see Fig. 1). The shear on this wall
produced a boundary layer flow. The flow separated at the break in the
wall; this enhanced vortex formation on the left side of the powerhouse
intake. Several alternative wall configurations were tested. A 3 m
(10 ft) deep "shelf" on top of the retaining wall (Fig. 2) prevented
the vortex formation. The effectiveness of the shelf is an interesting
feature of the Jim Falls design. The "shelf" allows the circulation to
be distributed over a large area, and thereby reduces the probability
of vortex formation. The shelf also provides a region for the circulation to dissipate some of its energy. The most suitable shelf
geometry was determined through experimentation.

Effectiveness of the shelf design was measured in terms of the
fractional time during which dye core vortices were observed. Ideally
there would be no vortex formation at all; however, this was not fully
achievable. Dye core vortices occurred intermittently 5 percent of the
time near the right turbine intake. Further improvements are described
in a following section.

Cellular wall

To save on construction cost Black and Veatch proposed to replace
the right retaining wall in the headrace with a cellular wall shown in
Fig. 1. Model tests showed that the proposed cell alignment allowed
too much space for the clockwise eddy in front of the spillway. This
increased the eddy velocity and intermittency. This undesirable effect
was corrected by realigning the cells.

Rockfill placement in headwater pool

As the project design progressed, it became apparent that excess
rock material from excavation in the areas of the tailrace, powerhouse,
spillway, stilling basin, and pilot channel would be available. Offsite disposal was one option. Another was to use the rockfill material
to aid in stabilization of the flow conditions in the headwater pool.

Options for the placement of rockfill on either side of the pilot
channel were investigated in the model. Fill was placed in those areas
where flow velocities had been small, in order to maintain the total
conveyance of the system. Flow towards the powerhouse responded
strongly to the rockfill placement. Eight different rockfill configurations were tested in the model at a flow rate of 450 m^3/s (16,000
cfs) through the powerhouse. This flow rate was chosen because it
accentuated the flow patterns compared to the 335 m^3/s (12,000 cfs)
turbine design flow. Configuration No. 8 produced the best results
(Fig. 3). When the discharge was reduced to the design flow of 335
m^3/s (12,000 cfs), frequency of dye core vortex formation near the
turbine intakes decreased to less than 0.5 percent of the time. At a
combined flow of 385 m^3/s (13,600 cfs) through the powerhouse and 740
m^3/s (26,400 cfs) over the auxiliary spillway, no dye core vortices
were observed in front of the powerhouse intakes. Surface dimples were
swept away by high cross-flow velocities at the powerhouse face. The
powerhouse and auxiliary spillway can, therefore, be operated

simultaneously without excessive vortex formation in front of the turbine intakes. The rockfill forced more flow down the pilot channel and allowed flow from the old headwater canal to spread out over a larger area, thus reducing cross-flow velocities.

Velocities were measured with a micropropeller meter at cross sections just upstream of the powerhouse. Velocity profiles with the rockfill in place were slightly more uniform over depth than before.

Rockfill placement according to Fig. 3 was recommended for construction because it decreased the frequency of dye core vortex formation at the powerhouse intakes and improved the approach flow to the turbines, besides allowing for easy disposal of excess rock material. There remains concern that the flow will wash finer material out of the rockfill and into the turbine intakes. It was recommended that further consideration be given to this potential problem after size distributions from blasting become known.

Tailrace Design

The tailrace is to be blasted out of the rock of the riverbed. Water depth in the tailrace will be approximately 7.5 m (25 ft). At 325 m^3/s (12,000 cfs), the flow in the tailrace looked good in the model. No separated flow regions were seen in the bend or at the diffuser outlet. The back pressure created by the 1:10 bottom slope of the diffuser (Fig. 4) was sufficient to allow widening of the diffuser angle. This was desirable because it produces a greater width across the diffuser outlet, which in turn reduces discharge velocities.

To reduce excavation cost, it was also desirable to move the diffuser as far upstream as possible. The beginning of the ramp was therefore moved 33 m (110 ft) upstream from its original location.

The modified diffuser and the original diffuser design are shown in Fig. 4. The diffuser angle was expanded more on the left than on the right because of river bed topography. This expansion also enhanced a natural flow tendency toward the left and facilitated a more uniform flow distribution in the river.

Stilling Basin

A stilling basin became necessary for hydraulic reasons and because of poor (heterogeneous) rock quality at the foot of the auxiliary spillway. The original design showed a deep symmetrical basin, with vertical sidewalls flaring at 10° in the downstream half.

During experiments with discharge rates up to 1825 m^3/s (65,000 cfs), a submerged hydraulic jump formed in the basin, indicating excessive basin depth. The flow over the left rim of the stilling basin created transverse velocities and standing waves which caused tailwater fluctuations at the powerhouse on the order of .3 to .6 m (1 to 2 ft). The symmetrical basin design had a fairly well-rounded bottom configuration. The plunging flow from the spillway would therefore run along the bottom and up onto the downstream 1:4 ramp where it caused a boil (upwelling). It appeared desirable to make better use of the upstream part of the basin for energy dissipation and to improve the flow-away conditions along the rim of the basin. When a short 1:4 downward sloping ramp between the spillway face and the stilling basin was removed, the nappe of the spillway flow entered the basin at a steeper angle than before, and the distance to the boil was shortened.

Consequently, the flow across the rim of the stilling basin was somewhat smoothened.

There were two concerns about the rock wall separating the
stilling basin and the tailrace: a) disturbance of the tailrace flow
by water spilling from the stilling basin, and b) structural stability.
It was decided to build a straight constant width, vertical concrete
wall separating the stilling basin from the tailrace. The height of
the wall was investigated later in the testing program. The original
symmetry of the basin was abandoned. To compensate for the loss of rim
length, and to direct the stilling basin effluent more towards the
existing river bed, an entirely asymmetrical basin was designed (Fig.
5). The basin's right wall was given a 45° flare. In order to match
the topography of the riverbed, the far right corner of the basin was
1.5 m (5 ft) lower than the left corner. This was intended to move
more water to the right into the riverbed. The low point at the
stilling basin outlet also aided in the passage of sluiced debris from
the stilling basin at low flows.

Without any baffle blocks, a large clockwise eddy formed in the
right portion of the stilling basin. However, at design flows the
hydraulic jump was contained in the basin. A single row of baffle
blocks, 2.3 m (7.5 ft) high, 2.3 m (7.5 ft) wide, and 1.8 m (6 ft)
long, oriented 15° counterclockwise to the flow, provided good energy
dissipation and reduced size and strength of the clockwise eddy. To
reduce the disturbance in the tailrace, the leftmost baffle block was
removed, leaving six blocks on the floor of the stilling basin. Model
tests also provided information on the required height of the wall between the stilling basin and the tailrace. The original criterion was
that a spillway flow of 365 m^3/s (13,000 cfs) be fully contained in
the basin while allowing 335 m^3/s (12,000 cfs) through the turbines.
For this case a wall elevation of 272 m (908 ft) was sufficient.
However, a wall only .6 m (2 ft) higher (El. 273 m, 910 ft) was able to
contain an auxiliary spillway flow of 700 m^3/s (25,000 cfs), with minimal disturbance in the tailrace. This wall height was chosen for
construction. The final design of the stilling basin is shown in
Figs. 5 and 6. The basin floor is 3 m (10 ft) higher than in the original design, as a result of geologic exploration and for hydraulic
reasons. Flows across the basin rim were uniform yet supercritical.
Because of the minimal tailwater elevations in the very steep river
bed, this could not be avoided.

A very simplified description of the asymmetrical stilling basin
hydraulics is as follows. The baffle blocks (Figs. 5 and 6) deflect
the water to the right. The highest water surface elevation occurs at
the corner where the expansion begins. Water flows away from the
"boil," outward towards the stilling basin rim and inward towards the
spillway face. The elevation of the right wall of the stilling basin
eliminates the return flow of water into the basin from the river.

Conclusions

The 1:60 scale hydraulic model of the Jim Falls Hydropower
Redevelopment Project was used to determine the hydraulic performance
of a large number of alternative designs, to delete undesirable
designs, and to improve acceptable ones.

Project cost savings were achieved by reducing the length of the
tailrace canal and by finding suitable on-site placement areas for

excess rock material. Debris sluicing was made feasible by modification of the headwater canal. Intermittent vortex formation at the turbine intake was minimized by excess rock placement in the headrace. A
stilling basin which minimizes the impact of flood flows on power
generation, river bed scouring, and the downstream bridge piers was
developed. The hydraulic performance of the recommended design was
found satisfactory. The project is now under construction.

Acknowledgements

     The design contributions by Craig Johnson, and David Guyot of
Black and Veatch, and by engineers from Motor Columbus Baden,
Switzerland, are gratefully acknowledged.   Mr. Charles Brown of
Northern States Power Company is project manager.

Reference

1. Stefan, H., Lindblom, K.L.C., Voigt, R. L., and Garver, R. J.,
   "Jim Falls Hydropower Model Study," Project Report No. 238, St.
   Anthony Falls Hydraulic Laboratory, University of Minnesota,
   Minneapolis, MN 55414, Aug., 1985, 108 pp.

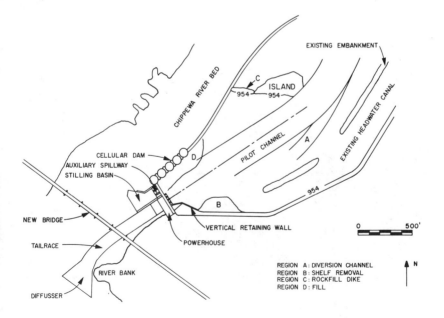

Fig. 1. Project layout and locations of principal headwater
         pool modifications (A through E).

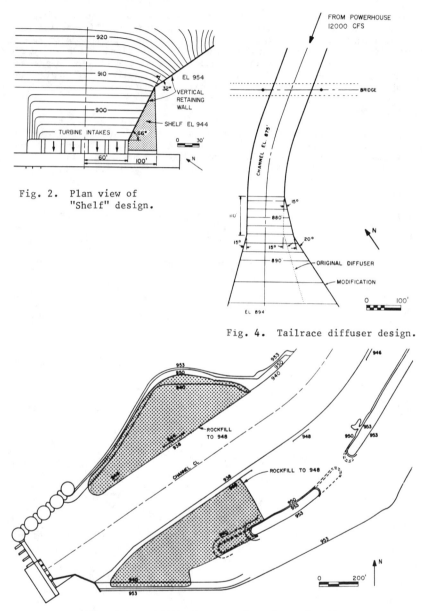

Fig. 2. Plan view of "Shelf" design.

Fig. 4. Tailrace diffuser design.

Fig. 3. Rockfill placement (configuration 8).

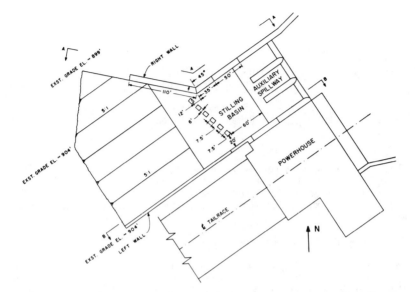

Fig. 5. Stilling basin design: Plan view.

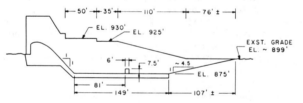

SECTION A-A: RIGHT STILLING BASIN WALL

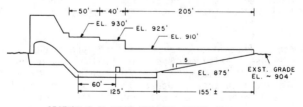

SECTION B-B: LEFT STILLING BASIN WALL

Fig. 6. Stilling basin design, sectional views.

DESIGN AND CONSTRUCTION OF
TCE/PCE REMOVAL FACILITIES

Shahnawaz Ahmad[1]
Robert G. Berlien[2]

This paper presents a review of the design and construction of a facility in Arcadia, California, to remove trichloroethylene (TCE) and tetrachlorethylene (PCE) from groundwater. The City of Arcadia is located in Southern California, approximately 15 miles east of Los Angeles.

Occurrence of TCE/PCE in Groundwater

In general, TCE, PCE, and related compounds are volatile, nonflammable in air, and have poor solubility in water. These characteristics make them useful solvents; they are widely used in industries and households for cleaning and degreasing.

Possible sources for TCE/PCE contaminants appearing in the groundwater include industrial discharges (by means of spreading on the land or improper disposal at dumps), landfill leachates, septic tank degreasers and similar products from individual households, sewer leaks, accidental spills, cleaning and rinsing agents used on tanks and machinery, and leaking storage tanks. Organic solvents from improper pump lubricants or from well drilling aids are also potential sources.

These volatile organic compounds (VOC's) are heavier than water and therefore travel down through the aquifers at a faster rate. They are not readily soluble and do not adhere well to soil particles. They have been classified as suspected carcinogens. However, more testing and research data is required before the actual cancer risks are known.

The Environmental Protection Agency has developed SNARLS, (Suggested No Adverse Response Levels) now known as "Health Advisories" for certain VOC's. From these documents, the California Department of Health Services had adopted an Interim Operating Plan for Los Angeles County water utilities with organic solvent contamination. This plan establishes "Action Levels" of 5 ug/l for TCE and 4 ug/l for PCE.

---

[1] Senior Associate, ASL Consulting Engineers, Pasadena, California
[2] Water Manager/Assistant City Engineer, City of Arcadia, California

TCE/PCE Removal Alternatives

The following alternatives were considered for removal and/ or reduction of TCE/PCE from Arcadia's drinking water supply:

1. Drill new wells.

2. Blending of high and low TCE/PCE well waters

3. Purchase imported water through the Metropolitan Water District of Southern California (MWD)

4. Adsorption:

   o Granular or powdered activated carbon
   o Synthetic resins

5. Aeration:

   o Diffused aeration
   o Spray aeration
   o Tray aeration
   o Packed tower

New wells were not considered because of the expense and because of unknown water quality problems at the available sites.

Blending of high and low TCE/PCE well water was also eliminated due to lack of wells in the area with low TCE/PCE concentrations. Sufficient reductions of TCE/PCE concentrations would not have been achieved.

Utilization of MWD water was eliminated because of the high cost. In addition, this water has a higher dissolved mineral content than Arcadia's well water. It is also heavily chlorinated and occasionally has color, taste, and odor problems; therefore, the City may receive customer complaints about taste and odor during the months the connection is used.

Adsorption using GAC or synthetic resins is another possible effective method for removing volatile organics. However, capital costs and annual maintenance and regeneration costs made this alternative prohibitive for Arcadia.

Spray and tray aerators have been utilized in water treatment for carbon dioxide removal; however, these designs are less efficient than packed tower and do not provide maximum efficiency for volatile organic removal. They are mainly used when precipitation or sedimentation is anticipated that would cause the media in a packed tower to become clogged.

For the diffused air process, the existing reservoir at Arcadia to receive the treated water could not be used without substantial modifications, thereby significantly increasing the cost.

It was therefore decided to operate a pilot plant test study using a packed tower aerator.

Theory of Packed Tower Design

Packed tower aerator designs for removal of volatile organics are influenced by several factors, such as:

o Air : water ratio

o Contact time or packing height

o Hydraulic loading rate

o Type of packing material

o Air and water temperatures

o Type of contaminant

The first four factors can be controlled in the design of an air stripping unit, while the remaining two factors vary with the water supply.

Although experimental results have indicated high removal efficiencies (greater than 99 percent) through the optimum design of packed column systems, pilot-scale testing is necessary prior to final design for a specific application.

Pilot Plant Operation

A 21-inch by 21-inch packed tower aerator was constructed by General Filter Company of Ames, Iowa. The plant was operated for a series of tests using different water flow rates and packing depths.

Air to water ratios were maintained at 15:1 minimum and 30:1 maximum. Air to water ratios in excess of 30:1 have a lessening effect on the efficiency of the removal process. Each test was performed first with a packing depth of 10 feet and then repeated with a packing depth of 7.5 feet to determine the affect of different packing depths.

Packing media comes in several different designs, sizes, materials, and shapes. Normally the smaller sizes are more expensive. The small packing sizes provide greater surface area but also increase the air head losses thereby increasing blower size requirements. If precipitation or sedimentation is a problem, the smaller sizes are also more susceptible to clogging. Generally speaking, media made from plastic is less costly than those made of metal or other materials. For this test, it was decided to use a 3-1/2" media which provided a good balance between water surface area and air passages.

FIGURE 1
PILOT PLANT

Tests were run at loading rates of 33, 25, 20, and 10 gpm per square foot of packing material. Since the pilot plant had a cross sectional area of approximately three square feet, these loading rates translated into 100, 75, 60, and 30 gpm, respectively. At each flow rate, water samples were taken of the influent and effluent and sent to a lab for analysis. Removal efficiencies obtained for TCE and PCE were 90-95%. The data thus accummulated was then extrapolated to determine the size requirement for a full scale plant. The data obtained in the field pilot plant study provided good correlation with theoretical design models developed in the General Filter Company laboratories.

Design Criteria

The TCE/PCE Removal Facilities at Arcadia was based on the following design parameters:

1. Maximum TCE and PCE influent levels at 50 and 10 ug/l, respectively.

2. Maximum TCE and PCE effluent levels less than 4.5 and 4 ug/l, respectively.

3. The treatment facilities must be capable of obtaining the above effluent requirements at flow rates up to 5000 gpm.

The desired removal efficiency can be achieved at the required flow by using two 9-feet x 9-feet aeration towers. The aerators are approximately 25.5 feet high, each one equipped with a single 5 h.p. blower, and mounted on individual steel platform towers, approximately 8.5 feet high.

Water can be pumped from either or both wells to either or both packed towers. The packed towers are mounted above the higher water line of the reservoir in order to allow the effluent from the air stripping towers to flow by gravity into the reservoir thereby eliminating expensive repumping costs.

Air Quality

The Southern California Air Quality Management District (SCAQMD) has the permit authority over any installation of equipment which would cause air pollution. The SCAQMD has no ambient air quality standards for TCE, but has recommended allowable limits of 52 parts per trillion (ppt) for TCE and 13 ppt for PCE. Based on Gaussian dispersion modeling of emissions from the two air stripping towers, the maximum annual average concentrations of TCE and PCE were 42 and 6 ppt respectively. These concentrations were not objectionable and a permit to construct the TCE/PCE removal facilities was issued by the SCAQMD.

FIGURE 2
TCE/PCE REMOVAL FACILITIES

Costs

The design and construction costs for the TCE/PCE Removal Facilities at Arcadia were approximately $220,000. Annual operation and maintenance costs are estimated to be $5,000. The cost of removing TCE/PCE, including amortized capital costs, was estimated to be approximately 3 cents/1000 gallons or $10/acre-foot.

GROUNDWATER QUALITY MONITORING IN THE NEW YORK
METROPOLITAN AREA: STATISTICAL ALTERNATIVES

Mohammad Karamouz*, M. ASCE and Evangelos Paleologos*

Abstract

The need for development of groundwater monitoring
strategies for the New York metropolitan area with emphasis
on statistical analysis has been investigated in this
study. Statistical methods including Bayesian decision
theory and analysis of error and uncertainty in groundwater
monitoring and sampling frequency are discussed. It is
demonstrated that Bayesian decision theory is of
significant value to groundwater monitoring because of its
flexibility to incorporate new information and to evaluate
the financial implications of decisions.

Introduction

Groundwater contamination in New York State has
resulted from a long period of commercial, industrial,
agricultural and residential development particularly in
the dense development which characterizes much of Long
Island. During the past decade growing concern for point
and non-point pollution sources has led to monitoring
programs to detect the contaminants. Also, improved
sampling and analytical techniques and equipment have been
developed. There is, however, a growing need for the
development of analytical guidelines to help decision
makers and regulatory agencies to consider the stochastic
nature and the value and cost of the data which have to be
collected.

This paper presents some initiatives from a broader
research project that is underway at Polytechnic
University. This part of the study is oriented towards
providing a basis for a more thorough approach to managing,
evaluating and eventually optimizing regulatory monitoring.
The emphasis has been given to an overview of sampling
frequency and the application of Bayesian decision theory
to groundwater quality monitoring. Bayesian decision theory
is of great value to groundwater monitoring because of the
generally high cost of establishing sampling stations. With
Bayesian decision theory, a utility function is used to
compare possible alternatives, which incorporates
evaluations of both risk and cost in the analysis.

* Assistant Professor and Graduate student respectively,
Dept. of Civil & Environmental Engineering, Polytechnic
University, Brooklyn, New York 11201.

Groundwater Contamination in the New York Metropolitan Area

Long Island has a total population of seven million, of which over three million depend on groundwater as the only source of drinking water. Other uses include industrial processes, agricultural irrigation and cooling. Of the four major political subdivisions, Nassau County and Suffolk County are totally dependent on groundwater for any use. A part of Queens similarly depends on groundwater. The rest of Queens and Brooklyn are connected to the New York City surface supply system. Long Island consists of layers of unconsolidated material underlined by bedrock; the major geological formations are the Upper Glacial, the Jameco, the Magothy and the Lloyd. Because of the extensive contamination of some parts of the Upper Glacial, the last two deeper aquifers are the primary sources of public water supply. In 1977, E.P.A. designated the Long Island aquifers as "Sole Source" of drinking water.

The highest priority threat to the Long Island groundwater is posed by synthetic organic chemicals. The guidelines developed by NYSDOH (New York State Department of Health) in 1977 set a limit of 50 ppb for any single organic and some have even lower limits. The total concentration should not exceed 100 ppb.

The three major categories of synthetic organics are:

a) Solvents and degreasers: used in a variety of commercial (laundries, rug cleaners, and auto cleaner solvents) and industrial processes (food plants, metal processing plants, etc.); also used for cleaning sewer lines and cesspools. These solvents find their way to the groundwater by leaks, spills, etc. Trichloroethylene 1,1,1-trichloroethane and tetrachoroethylene are particulary threatening because they can penetrate deeper into the aquifer.

b) Gasolene and petroleum: are regulated by NYSDOH and NYSDEC (New York State Department of Environmental Conservation). Benzene, xylene and toluene were the cause for the closure of two wells. Contamination occurs from leaks (gas station storage tanks and pipelines), spills and stormwater runoff.

c) Pesticides and herbicides: especially used in the agricultural areas of eastern Suffolk. The highly permeable soils help even the non- persistent pesticides to contaminate groundwater. The use of aldicarb was banned in 1979 due to widespread detection in groundwater.

The U.S.Council on Environmental Quality (1981) has rated New York State among the four states having the highest concentration of many toxic organic chemicals in drinking water wells.

Groundwater Monitoring

Since the passage of the Safe Drinking Water Act of 1974 (PL 93-523) there has been considerable activity in ground water quality monitoring. Groundwater monitoring programs are designed to provide continuing measurement, observation, and evaluation of groundwater resources against pollution.

Monitoring can be considered as a system for which a network is designed to provide a specific type of information with a specific degree of accuracy and precision. The major considerations for the design of the network are the locations of the sampling stations, the water quality parameters to be monitored and the frequency of the sampling. After the samples are collected and tested in the laboratory, a statistical analysis can be performed. The final stage is to utilize the information from the analysis to make decisions which affect the water quality or the operation of the network.

In recent years, attention has been shifting from collecting numerous data (usually never utilized) to the statistical analysis of data. The need for a more rational allocation of resources to optimize the activities for a given purpose, and the need to use the analytical tools, has been stressed and recommendations have been made (see Ward and Loftis, 1983).

In an ideal situation, the water quality variables should be specified first so that their variation in time and space can be considered when designing the monitoring network. In most actual cases, however, the network is defined first and then an attempt is made to identify what should be monitored. The sampling station locations are a sample representation in space and sampling frequencies are a sample representation in time. There is a great need for basic statistics that agencies can use to determine compliance with regulatory standards and for more complex statistics to study special problems like interdependency of water quality parameters, spatial and temporal correlation of the data, etc. One way of classifying regulatory monitoring purposes is to differentiate between the need to obtain trends (means) in water quality for certain management functions (e.g. planning) and the need to obtain extremes in water quality for other functions(e.g. enforcement of water quality standards).

In planning for groundwater monitoring, it may be very useful to recognize various deficiencies in surface water monitoring and to not repeat the same mistakes. The most important lesson from surface water quality monitoring has been stated by Ward (1981): "to perform water quality monitoring to meet the letter of the law (regulations), without being concerned about developing a scientific understanding of the hydrological process involved, often results in data that will yield very little useful information."

There are pronounced differences in the characteristics of surface water and groundwater that should be fully understood before trying to implement past experiences learned from surface water monitoring. For example, the ready access of surface water contrasts with the need for a well to access ground water, and the rapidly changing surface water quality contrasts with the relatively slow occuring changes in groundwater quality.

The EPA has defined four main types of monitoring (Todd et al., 1976).

- Ambient-trend monitoring: measures quality that reflects temporal and spatial trends in groundwater area.
- Source monitoring: measures effluent quality and quantity from pollution sources which could affect groundwater.
- Case-preparation monitoring: to accumulate data for enforcement actions.
- Research monitoring: for studies of groundwater quality and pollution occurence and movement.

Groundwater monitoring on a routine basis has received little attention compared to the importance given it under P.L. 93-523. As of 1980 the USEPA and state agencies have been trying to organize a national groundwater quality monitoring system. A systems viewpoint of regulatory monitoring based upon a subjective classification of monitoring purposes and activities should provide the basis for optimizing the regulatory water quality monitoring system.

Sampling Frequency

Water quality monitoring by definition is a statistical sampling operation. It is highly desirable that the monitoring purpose be carefully defined in terms of the statistical precision and confidence sought and the essential use of the results.

Sampling depends on the type of parameters sampled to establish water quality. Some of these parameters need to be sampled as often as daily or weekly and others are sampled once a year. The New York State Department of Environmental Conservation (NYSDEC) recommends quarterly sampling for groundwater monitoring wells at landfill sites. The New York State Department of Health (NYSDOH) required sampling of public water supply wells on an annual basis.

A basic level of statistic used in the literature has emphasized practicality. This involves making some simplifying assumptions. The first one is that the data for every water-quality parameter being sampled follows a normal distribution. Several researchers have shown that most water-quality parameters can be described by either the normal or log-normal distribution. The second assumption is that the sample statistics can be treated as population statistics. Thus, for each station the sample variance is assumed to be the variance of the whole statistical population at the station. This assumption implies that there will be no significant change of the parameter in the future.

One way to determine the effectiveness of a certain level of sampling is to compute the precision of the estimate (see EPA (1978)).

$$\text{Precision} = \frac{Z\,\sigma_i}{\sqrt{n_i}}$$

where Z is a confidence coefficient that depends upon the desired level of confidence (i.e. $Z= 1.96$ for 95% confidence level), σ_i is the population variance, and n_i is the number of samples taken per year at station i.

A small value of precision corresponds to a narrow confidence interval and leads to a strong conclusion on a parameter's average quality. Thus the stations with small variation in water quality have high precision and those with large variation have a low precision.

The need for a rational criterion for the determination of the sampling frequency was addressed by Sanders and Adrian (1978). Sampling frequency is a function of the magnitude of half the confidence interval of the mean of annual concentration.

$$n = [\ t_{\alpha/2}\, S/R\ ]$$

where R is half the expected confidence interval of the mean. S is the sample standard deviation of water quality concentration, and $t_{\alpha/2}$ is the value of Students' t associated with the level of significance α.

The EPA requires sampling for three sets of parameters. The first set is characteristic of the drinking water suitability (Safe Drinking Water Act). The second is a basis for the quality of groundwater for non-drinking uses. The third set consists of pH, specific conductance, total organic carbon (TOC), total organic halogen (TOX) which are indicators of groundwater contamination.

The requirement for the owner of a disposal facility is to sample quarterly and analyze all three sets of

parameters for the first year, so that seasonal effects can
be incorporated.   After the first year, the contamination
indicators (pH, etc.) should be sampled semi-annually and
the rest at least annually.

Bayesian Decision Theory

In general, Bayesian decision theory is based on the
posterior probability of the state of nature.   Namely, the
prior distribution $P[a_i]$ of the state of nature a_i can be
combined with sample likelihood $P[A / a_j]$ through Bayes
theorem:

$$P [a_i | A] = \frac{P [A | a_i] P [a_i]}{\sum_j P[A | a_j] P[a_j]}$$

Where A is a sample characteristic. Refer to DeGroot (1970)
for a discussion on optimal (Bayesian) statistical decision
theory.

In Bayesian decision theory, the prior probabilities
are incorporated into the decision process by the basic
theorem of Bayes.   The opinion and judgment of the analyst
in the interpretation of probability can be included as
well.   For example, the statistical data from the previous
years can be used to formulate a prior probability
distribution, which can be updated every year.   The sample
frequency can be reevaluated each year giving weight to the
latest data available and also including the latest
analyst's opinion regarding a suitable sampling frequency.

The process to be followed in a groundwater
monitoring program determines the way of implementing
decision theory. Decision variables, states of nature, and
an action space should be defined and gains or losses
associated with the decisions should be determined.
Examples of decision variables to be considered are: the
groundwater flow direction;   the travel time for the
contaminants to penetrate the aquifer; and the
concentration of an indicator (nitrate, total organic
carbon (TOC), total organic halogen (TOX), etc.).

The prior probability distribution of the decision
variables can be based on either historical data, the
opinion of engineers acquainted with the area or both
whenever there is not much information. Alternatives to be
investigated are the feasible solutions, consisting of a
series of upstream and/or downsteam wells or some other
means of detection (i.e. electrical resistivity survey).

A loss function can be used to compare possible
alternatives and to incorporate the risk in the analysis.
Once a realistic loss function has been developed, the
optimal solution can be found by minimizing the loss

function. (See Davis et al. 1972).

In general the loss function should include four categories of costs (Todd et al., 1976): a) damage costs associated directly with the pollution; b) avoidance costs in order to avoid or reduce the damage; c) abatement costs related to the reduction of pollution and d) transaction costs, the cost of monitoring a network and enforcing a policy. The loss associated with the presence of contamination may be expressed as in Figure 1.

This is a typical loss function similar to the loss function used by Grosser (1984). Below a minimum concentration (standard) the loss associated with contamination is zero. After that, the loss function first increases linearly and then exponentially as the concentration of contaminants increases.

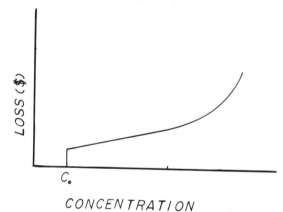

Figure 1 - Loss Function

Grosser (1984) applied Bayesian decision theory to determine an optimal sampling frequency for chlorides in a public water supply well in Long Island. Both discrete and continuous probability distributions were used in his study. He also presented real and hypothetical applications of Bayesian decision theory to New York groundwater problems and concluded that the Bayesian approach is a flexible method that can be used in the design of groundwater monitoring systems.

Duckstein and Kisiel (1971) discussed the relationship between the Type I and II errors and Bayesian decision theory. A null hypothesis can be defined assuming that the population means of contamination upgradient and

downgradient of a disposal site, estimated by sample means,
are equal. Type I error is the chance of rejecting the null
hypothesis when ,in fact, it is true, and the Type II error
is the likelihood of accepting null hypothesis when, in
fact, it is false. The implication of Type I and II errors
in connection with a t test has also been demonstrated in
a recent report by the Environemntal Institute of Water
Management Studies, University of Alabama (1985). The
nature of type I and II errors suggest the implication of
posterior probability using Bayesian decision theory,
specially, when several downgradient wells exist.

The use of Bayesian decision theory may prove to be
useful in the procedure recommended in EPA (1985). In
this procedure a t distribution is used to compare the
average value of a water quality parameter obtained from a
network of upgradient wells with the average value from
each downgradient well. An interesting discussion on the
validity of the statistical method employed and the
correlation of the indicators can be found in the Open File
Report No. 7 published by the University of Alabama (see
references). In the recommended procedure by EPA the
formulation of a typical Bayesian problem can be
established with the action space divided into at least
two regions (a1 : stay in detection monitoring phase, a2 :
assessment monitoring should be initiated). Type I and II
errors can also be employed in the analysis specially in
the cases where various alternatives with different
confidence intervals are compared.

Summary and Conclusion

Some problems associated with groundwater monitoring
have been addressed in this paper. Emphasis has been given
to the pollutants regulated in the New York metropolitan
area. The statistical alternatives to improve the decision
making and to incorporate uncertainty in the analysis have
also been discussed. The use of Bayesian decision theory
and some of its applications to groundwater monitoring have
been demonstrated. Further research is needed to justify
some of the initiatives addressed in this paper and to
reach the long term objectives of developing and optimizing
systems and strategies for monitoring groundwater
pollutants.

Acknowledgement

The authors wish to thank Professor Alvin S. Goodman
for his constructive comments throughout the preparation of
this manuscript.

References

Council on Environmental Quality (1981), "Contamination of Ground Water by Toxic Organic Chemicals," prepared by D.E. Burnmaster.

Davis, D.R., Kisiel, C.C., and Duckstein, L., "Bayesian Decision Theory Applied to Design in Hydrology," Water Resources Res., 8(1), pp 33-41, Feb. 1972.

DeGroot, M.H., "Optimal Statistical Decisions," McGraw Hill, N.Y. 1970.

Duckstein, L., and Kisiel, C.C., "Efficiency of Hydrologic Data Collection Systems: Role of Type I and II Errors," Water Resources Bul., 7(3), pp 592-604, June 1971.

Environmental Institute for Water Management Studies, Univ. of Alabama, "Statistical Approaches to Groundwater Monitoring. Open File Report No. 7, Dec. 1985.

Environmental Protection Agency, "Evaluating the Sampling Frequencies of Water Quality Monitoring Networks," EPA - 600/7-78-169, Interagency Energy-Environment Research and Development Program Report, Aug. 1978.

Environmental Protection Agency, "RCRA Groundwater Monitoring Enforcement Guidance," Office of Solids Waste and Emergency Response, Aug. 1985.

Grosser, P.W., "Application of Bayesian Decision Theory to Groundwater Monitoring," Ph.D. dissertation, Dept. of Civil Engineering, Polytechnic Institute of New York, Jan. 1984.

Sanders, G.I., and Adrian, D.D., "Sampling Frequency of River Quality Monitoring," Water Resources Res., 14(4), pp569-576, 1978.

Todd, D.K., Tinlen, R.M., Schmidt, K.D., and Everett, L.G., "Monitoring Groundwater Quality: Monitoring Methodology," Environmental Protection Agency Report No. EPA-600/4-6-026, 1976.

Ward, R.C., "Groundwater Quality Monitoring - What Information Is To Be Obtained?", Groundwater, Vol. 19(2), pp130-132, March 1981.

Ward, R.C., and Loftis, J.C., "Incorporating the Stochastic Nature of Water Quality Into Management," Journal WPCF, Vol. 55(4), pp408-414, April 1983.

ESTIMATING PROBABLE STORM DAMAGE ON BARRIER ISLANDS

Andrew A. Dzurik[1] M.ASCE; Bruce Stiftel[2], Anita Tallarico[3]

ABSTRACT

This paper demonstrates a methodology for estimating probable property damage losses from hurricanes on barrier islands. Using the case study of Gasparilla Island, Florida, it estimates value of structures over the next 20 years based on current appraisals and land use plans, and applies damage functions based on storm surge, wind, and waves. The probability of different categories of hurricanes are applied for each year of the 20 year period, and alternative development scenarios are considered.

INTRODUCTION

Problem identification, Florida's barrier islands have experienced extraordinary population growth and urbanization over the past several decades in spite of the fact that they are vulnerable to extensive damage from severe storms. The probability of hurricanes is high in Florida, and barrier islands suffer the severest storm damage from storm surge, wind action, and flooding (Dolan, 1980; Frank, 1979; and Sharma, 1981). Almost 4,000 people have died in Florida since 1900 from hurricanes and associated floods, and billions of dollars in damages have occurred (Fernald, 1981). The urbanized land area of barrier islands has increased over 200 percent from 1955 to 1975, and population has more than doubled. These trends will likely continue in spite of governmental efforts to purchase land or restrict development, as under the federal Coastal Barriers Resources Act of 1983, the Coastal Zone Management Act of 1972, and the National Flood Insurance Program. The continued pace of coastal development is of increasing concern and Florida is particularly significant because of its large number of barrier islands and the increasing levels of development (Lins, 1980). Currently, twenty-three percent of all policies in the National Flood Insurance Program (NFIP) are for properties in Florida, and a large portion of them are on barrier islands.

1   Associate Professor, Dept. of Civil Engineering, FAMU/FSU College of Engineering, Tallahassee, FL 32306.

2   Assistant Professor, 3 Graduate Research Assistant, Dept. of Urban and Regional Planning, Florida State University, Tallahassee, FL 32306.

A number of damage cost curves and estimates of structures at risk have been done for riverine flood zones, but studies of coastal damages are limited. Two studies have been done to date with regard to potential hurricane damage along the lower Gulf Coast (TBRPC, 1983; SWFRPC, 1982). Among the few studies on coastal damage assessments, one looked at the benefits and costs of raising structures to the wave crest level associated with 100-year storm surges (Sheaffer and Roland, Inc., 1980). Several earlier studies called attention to problems of flood insurance on barrier islands (Miller, 1976) and methods of accounting for storm surge and wave action (Miller, et al. 1977).

A strong need exists for analysis of property at risk on barrier islands, and more particularly, for systematic evaluation for likely development management alternatives to reduce property at risk. This study addresses that need by way of a case study.

Setting. The study focuses on the Lee County portion of Gasparilla Island on South Florida's Gulf Coast as an example of a rapidly developing barrier island in a hurricane-prone region. The relevant planning agencies with respect to the study area are the Lee County Planning Department and Department of Emergency Operations, and the Southwest Florida Regional Planning Council. The planning agencies fall under the planning requirements of the State of Florida as administered by the Department of Community Affairs.

Hurricane probabilities along this portion of the Gulf Coast is substantial. In the past year, several hurricanes passed by the region and caused flooding and erosion, but none of them made landfall in the region. Just the same, it is only a question of time before a major hurricane strikes Lee County and Gasparilla Island.

OBJECTIVES

The overall study goal is to develop a procedure to determine the probable damages to public and private investments on Florida's barrier islands and to evaluate alternative development management tools in terms of probable hurricane storm damage to structures and public infrastructure. Underlying this goal is the intent to improve information available to state and local governments about the effectiveness of selected development management tools in reducing probable hurricane damages on Florida's barrier islands. This is accomplished by determining probable storm-related losses on a developing barrier island, projecting future probable land uses under current trends and land use plans for island, designing alternative development management practices, and estimating future losses under these alternative practices.

To accomplish these goals, the following objectives were established:

o   Select a rapidly urbanizing barrier island representative of developing on barrier islands as a case study.

o   Inventory land uses and structures on the barrier island
     in order to estimate current damage potential.

o   Project future land use and development patterns expected
     to result from the existing land use plans.

o   Identify alternative future land use and construction
     patterns under selected development management scenarios.

o   Estimate probable losses to development under the current
     plans and under alternative development scenarios.

o   Evaluate the effectiveness of development management tools
     with respect to reducing probable storm-related losses.

METHODOLOGY

     The strategy for conducting this research follows a logical and
straightforward procedure with several important increments: (1)
site selection, (2) storm surge estimate, (3) structure survey, (4)
structure valuation, and (5) damage estimates. The last three steps
of this process are then repeated using forecasts of probable build-
out to the year 2005 from local comprehensive plans. The combined
estimates of probable damage to existing and planned structures give
aggregate probable property damage losses to the year 2005 using
joint probability linear damage functions.

     Site selection. The purpose of the island selection process
was to choose a barrier island for study that would allow us to
analyze hurricane phenomena and land use conditions pertinent to the
project objective. The criteria for island selection centered on
several factors. The island must be a developing coastal barrier
with infrastructure in place to support development, but with
substantial vacant land suitable for development still available.
In addition, hurricane storm surge data must be available and the
island must be subject to a relatively high probability of hurricane
storm wants. Finally, the responsible local planning agency must
indicate a willingness to support the study.

     A letter with the above criteria was sent to 25 local, state and
federal planning or planning-related offices around the state. The
list obtained in response identified 19 islands that agencies
thought were suitable for study. The list was reduced to eight
islands by considering hurricane probability, hurricane modeling
adequacy and availability, percentage of island developed, total
island acreage, land use plan adequacy and availability, and
accessibility of the island.

     Refined criteria were established to use in the final
selection, including:

-    structure count for actual inventory
-    uncommitted developable land

- pressure to develop
- size of uncommitted developable parcels
- agency cooperation and ease of data access
- availability of current and future land use data
- property appraisal data, including value of structures
- extent of island in V-zone

The site selected was the Lee County portion of Gasparilla Island on the Gulf Coast in South Florida because it satisfied the refined criteria in such a way to satisfy time and budget constraints.

Surge estimate. The major damage caused by hurricanes is from storm surge inundation. Hurricanes bring extremely low atmospheric pressure and build-up of water across vast reaches of the sea. Thus, storm surge can easily exceed 10 feet above mean sea level with waves added to the top of this.

The SLOSH model (Sea, Lake and Overland Surges from Hurricanes) was selected as the most appropriate and readily available technique for estimating storm surge levels (Jelesnianski, 1974). A number of coastal locations have already been analyzed with the SLOSH model to give still-water flood inundation (surge) at given grid locations under various storm conditions. (NHC, 1985; U.S. Congress, 1983; Florida Division of Emergency Management, 1985). This information is essential to determining stage-damage relationships.

SLOSH provides a variety of data. It gives estimates of still-water surge heights for hurricanes of varying intensities, directions, and speeds based on polar grid patterns for coastal communities. Once adjusted to this polar grid, a land use map with elevations can be superimposed on the SLOSH grid which varies from 0.5 to 1.5 mi.^{2} landward and seaward. SLOSH provides a maximum and minimum estimate of surge per grid cell varying with the given hurricane category (Safir-Simpson classification).

Structure survey. Collecting elevations per structure of the first inhabitable floor in the study area is a prerequisite to designating the stage-damage relationship. Each structure was surveyed to determine the elevation of the first inhabitable floor above MSL (see Sheaffer and Roland, 1984).

The result of the extensive field survey was data on first floor elevations for all 694 commercial, light industrial and residential units in the Lee County portion of Gasparilla Island. The actual structure count and recorded elevations produced 508 records. The mean elevation for structures built under FIA codes is 14.63 ft. MSL. The mean elevation for the structures built pre FIA is 7.67 ft. MSL. Additional information was also obtained during the survey on structure type, estimated age, number of floors, and use of the structure.

Structure valuation. Estimating structure values is another prerequisite to forming the stage-damage relationship. In estimating damages to structures the primary concern is loss of structural value. We have chosen the replacement value as our measure of structure valuation.

A replacement cost is the total cost of construction required to replace the entire structure at current prices (Applebaum 1984). The Lee County property appraiser's data was a reliable source because the replacement value is based on the structure alone, not the land or market value. The data is also updated annually accounting for depreciation and inflation variables. Hence we feel we have accounted for the common criticisms of assessing structure value. The mean building replacement value for all residential, commercial, and light residential units at the end of 1985 was $83 160.

Damage estimates. Storm surge is the event when the coastal water level rises above mean sea level independent of diurnal tide action (Petak & Atkinson, 1982). This landward moving raised sea level is independent of the possibility of winds and shore bottom characteristics creating waves on top of the surge. This is a non-velocity characteristic of storm flooding.

The depth-damage percentage, indicating the percent of damage from non-velocity flooding is a function of structure use and size (Corps of Engineers, 1985; Berke, 1985). This is simply because different building uses (residential commercial, industrial) are structurally different, and irreparable damage occurs at different elevations.

The SLOSH estimates are the base data needed for the non-v-zones and v-zones as defined by the Federal Insurance Administration (FIA). This estimate does not include tidal variations, but we add to the SLOSH surge estimate to account for varying waves as discussed further in the surge-damage and wave-damage methodologies. The SLOSH estimate of surge is based on the MSL so all landward elevations must be subtracted from the land based elevation above MSL to determine where inundation begins. Finally, SLOSH also provides wind intensities per hurricane category.

The depth-damage percentage figures employed originated from the FIA in 1970. They were revised in 1974 to exclude residences with basements. (In 1974 FIA denied insurance to residences with basements). In addition, the Corps of Engineers has added to these computations, through historical data, a variety of commercial and industrial uses, specific to use. These are the depth-damage percentages used to estimate damages in nonvelocity zones, but with one modification. Non-velocity zones are those subject to still-water inundation, or surge. Along with other authors (WFRPC, TBRPC, Ruch, FIA), we add 2.1 to the maximum surge elevation derived from SLOSH estimates to account for the inevitability of waves superimposed on the surge in these non-velocity zones. The 2.1' represents a maximum possible breaking-wave of 3' in these non-velocity zones (National Academy of Sciences; 1977). The damages from the total surge estimate is then derived from non-velocity damage curves (Corps of Engineers, 1985). Contrastingly, the velocity zone has variable sizes of waves and employs a separate set of depth-damage curves. The waves in the v-zone are calculated as a function of surge depth (National Academy of Sciences 1977). Then the damages are derived utilizing Rich's "Damage in Percent from Total Value (V-zones)" estimates, (1984).

To determine wind damage different methodologies were combined. These methodologies can be divided into two major steps, determining maximum and minimum peak gust velocities, and estimating wind damages by land use for each hurricane category.

The base data for step one is the SLOSH polarized grid printout of maximum and minimum diminishing winds left and right of the eye. These estimates are one minute sustained winds. To determine the decrease in winds inland (from friction loss of Gulf warm water as generator) Malkin's factor was applied (Goldman and Ushijima, 1974). This factor applies .05 for every mile inland. To determine the peak gusting wind, multiply 1.43, 1.31 or 1.11 by the maximum and minimum estimates and add that to the 1' sustained wind. These factors account for terrains of water, grassland and woodlands or urban areas, respectively (Australian Tropical Forecasting Manual, October 1977).

Damages from peak gusting winds were estimate by Freidman's "most likely percentage of value lost estimates" (Friedman, 1974). These value-lost estimates are categoried by single family residential, multi-family residential, and non-residential.

Total probable damages for the study period (1985-2005) were estimated by applying the above damage-estimating techniques to the probable storm events for each year. Thus, the probable loss in any given year is based on storm surge and wind calculated for each of five storm categories. The storm categories and probabilities for Gasparilla Island are shown in Table 1.

Table 1. Estimates Hurricane Probabilities at Gasparialla Island

Storm Category*	Probability** (annual)	Wind (mph)	Central Pressure (millibars) (inches)		Surge (feet)	Damage
1	.275	74-95	980	28.94	4-5	minimal
2	.123	96-110	965-979	28.50-28.94	6-8	moderate
3	.062	111-130	945-964	27.89-28.49	9-12	extensive
4	.029	131-155	920-944	27.17-27.88	13-18	extreme
5	.020	155+	920	27.17	19+	catastrophic

* Safir-Simpson Scale

** Probability of hurricane entering, or existing, or parallel along Lee County in any one year.

For each year we take the mean value of wind speed for each storm category U_i (i = storm category 1,2,3,4,5) and calculate the storm surge, wave, and wind damage as described above. Damages, D_{ijt} are then estimated based on value of structures, V_{it} projected to be in place for that year (j = land use type, 1,2,3; t, year 1,2,....20). Probable damage for any given year is the sum of damages estimated for each storm category times the probability of the event. Although the same probabilities are used for each of the next 20 years (1986-2005), the value of structures increases as new construction takes place according to a build-out schedule estimated from the land use plan. The probable damage estimate, for any year t may be given by:

$$D_t = \sum_{i=1}^{5} \sum_{j=1}^{3} P_i\, D_{ijt}$$

where $D_{ijt} = f(\overline{U}_i,\, V_{ijt})$

The total probable damage over the 20 year study period is the sum of damages in each year:

$$D = \sum_{t=1}^{20} D_t$$

With all meteorological, structural, and land use data entered and stored in a computer file, the methodology provides estimated total probable damages over the next 20 years.

CONCLUSIONS

The study shows that we can estimate probable storm damage over the next twenty years by combining meteorological data with structural and land use data. The results are still preliminary for the next stage is to estimate infrastructure damage and to compare probable damages under alternative development scenarios. These comparisons will help to demonstrate the effects of different development management strategies.

Several research needs became evident in the course of the study. There has been little work done on estimating damages from wave energy (as opposed to flooding from still water levels). The question of land damage losses also needs to be addressed; i.e., what is the damage if land becomes permanently submerged via erosion, but a structure remains in the water. Another gap in our knowledge of damage estimates are the long term effects of corrosion from salt water saturation of wood and metal. Current damage estimates only deal with immediate effects.

REFERENCES

Berke, P. 1985. "Application of a Computer System for Hurricane Emergency Response and Land Use Planning". Journal of Environmental Management. 21,000-000.

Dolan, Robert et. al. 1980. "Barrier Islands." American Scientist. 68.

Fernald, Edward A., ed. 1981. Atlas of Florida. Tallahassee: Florida State University Foundation.

Florida Department of Community Affairs, Division of Emergency management. 1985. Personal Communication, Tallahassee, Florida.

Frank, R.A. 1979. "Living With Coastal Storms: Seeking an Accomodation." Orlando, FL: National Conference on Hurricanes and Coastal Storms.

Friedman, Don G., 1974. "Computer Simulation in Natural Hazard Assessment." Hartford, Ct: The Travelers Insurance Company.

Goldman, J.L. and Ushijuma, T. 1974. Decrease in hurricane winds after landfall. Journal of Structural Division, ASCE.

Jelesnianski, C. 1985. Draft: "SLOSH" (Sea Lake and Overland Surge From Surges) Silver Spring, Maryland: U.S. Department of Commerce, Natinal Oceanic and Atmospheric Administration.

Lins, Harry F., Jr. 1980. Patterns and Trends of Land Use and Land Cover on Atlantic and Gulf Coast Barrier Islands. U.S.G.S. Professional Paper No. 1156. Washington, DC: U.S. Department of the Interior, Geological Survey.

Malkin, W. 1959. "Filling and Intensity Changes in Hurricanes Overland." National Hurrican Research Project. Vol. 34.

Miller, H. Crane. 1976. "Barrier Islands, Barrier Beaches, and the National Flood Insurance Program: Some Problems and a Rationale for Special Attention," Barrier Islands Conference. Annapolis, MD; Conservation Foundation.

Miller, Crane et al. 1977. "Methodology for Calculating Wave Action Effects Associate with Storm Surges," National Academy of Sciences, National Reserach Council.

Miami Hurricane Center, Brian Jarvinen. 1985. Personal Communication. Coral Gales, Florida.

National Academy of Sciences 1977. "Methodology for Calculating Wave Action Effects with Storm Surges." Washington, D.C.: National Academy of Sciences.

Petak, W.J. and Atkinson, A.A. 1982. Natural Hazard Risk Assessment and Public Policy. New York: Springer-Verlag.

Ruch, Carlton. 1984. "Hurricane Vulnerability Analysis for Aransas,
    Kenedy, Kleberg, Nueces, Refugio, and San Patricio Counties."
    College Station: Research Division of College of Architecture and
    Environmental Design, Texas A & M University.

Sharma, Dinesh. 1981. Barrier Islands - Man Influenced Systems.
    Washington, DC: Barrier Islands Coalition.

Sheaffer and Roland, Inc. 1984. "Surveying Buildings for Flood Hazard
    Mitigation." Local Assistance Series 3A. Chicago: Illinois
    Department of Transportation, Division of Water Resoruces.

Southwest Florida Regional Planning Council. 1982. Southwest Florida
    Hurricane Loss Study. Ft. Myers, FL.

Tampa Bay Regional Planning Council. 1983. Tampa Bay Region Hurricane
    Loss and Contingency Planning Study. St. Petersburg, FL.

United States Army Corps of Engineers. 1985. John K. Graham, Mobile
    District. Personal Communication. Mobile, Alabama.

United States Federal Emergency Management Agency. Federal Insurance
    Administration. 1984. "Flood Insurance Rate Map" Community Panel
    125124, for County of Lee, Florida (unincorporated areas).

United States Federal Emergency Management Agency. Federal Insurance
    Administration. 1984. Flood Insurance Study for County of Lee,
    Florida, (unincorporated areas).

COASTAL PROTECTION GUIDELINES, ORANGE COUNTY, CA

Craig H. Everts, M. ASCE[1]
Jerry Sterling, M. ASCE[2]
Floyd McLellen, F. ASCE[2]
Jim Miller, A.M. ASCE[2]
Don Cotner, M. ASCE[2]

ABSTRACT

As a result of coastal storms in the past several years the County of Orange (California) incurred large and unanticipated costs in providing emergency protection for private shorefront dwellings. Many of those dwellings were badly damaged because of inadequate design to counter ocean wave forces. In 1984, the County initiated a study to provide objective coastal design data and to establish uniform minimum design standards for protective devices such as seawalls and revetments, and for pile-supported dwellings. Coastal property owners and regulatory officials benefit by the availability of the data and guidelines for use in the design of new coastal protective devices and structures, and in evaluating the adequacy of existing devices and structures.

INTRODUCTION

Emergency protection costs and property losses resulting from wave storms were extraordinarily high in Orange County, California, in 1983. Inadequately designed and constructed coastal protective devices (CPD's), such as vertical walls and revetments, failed with subsequent damage to structures behind them. In addition, many structures, mostly private residences, were built in regions where beach scour and wave forces were active, but were not protected by CPD's.

---

[1]Moffatt & Nichol, Engineers, 250 W. Wardlow Road, Long Beach, CA 90807

[2]Environmental Management Agency, County of Orange, P.O. Box 4048, Santa Ana, CA 92702-4048

To reduce private property losses and costs involved in providing
emergency assistance, Orange County recently: (1) designated the
zone within which ocean wave phenomena must be considered; (2)
established a set of site-specific guidelines and site-specific
data for the design of CPD's and structures in that zone, and (3)
established a permitting review and analysis procedure based on
those guidelines. The guidelines and permitting review and
analysis procedure is available in manual form (County of Orange,
1985). The primary users are County plan-checkers who must
approve proposed construction in the ocean wave zone along five
shoreline reaches under County jurisdiction, and engineers to
verify their design meets minimum requirements. Coastal data and
guidelines can be used by property owners designing new CPD's and
structures, and in evaluating the adequacy of existing devices
and structures. The contents of the manual are also intended as
a technical design supplement to zoning, land use, specific
plans, and Local Coastal Programs.

Criteria and considerations for the technical design of CPD's and
structures are not absolute requirements for design methodology.
Site-specific design reports and studies prepared by qualified
professionals, possibly using more rigorous methodologies for
addressing uncommon design circumstances, may be appropriate.

Guidelines and design data are keyed to five coastal reaches in
Orange County. Design objectives are:

- to protect structures from wave impact damage,
- to protect structures from erosion of underlying soils,
- to protect structures from ballistic damage by floating and
  other wave-transported debris,
- to protect structures from flood damage caused by ocean
  phenomena, and
- to minimize adverse impacts on adjoining
  property/structures resulting from construction of a
  protective device or a structure.

Ecological concerns and design appearance on the beach are
addressed at the Local Coastal Program level.

This report briefly describes the steps involved in the plan
check procedure.

PLAN CHECK PROCEDURE

The plan check procedure shown in Figure 1 is based on an
evaluation of the level of protection a structure or protective
device provides against design wave conditions. Without a
special design, wave forces above the underside of a structure or

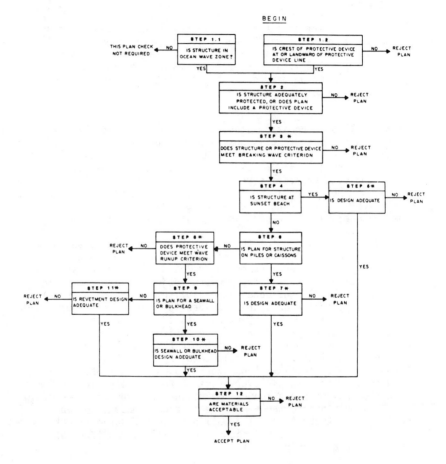

BEGIN

Figure 1. Plan check procedure for coastal protective devices and dwellings in the ocean wave zone of Orange County, California.

over the crest of a protective device are considered
unacceptable. Overtopping without wave forces, the most common
circumstance, is acceptable, but structures behind CPD's may
require floodproofing. Steps that require design data are
identified by asterisk in Figure 1. STEP 3 addresses breaking
waves and STEP 8 addresses wave runup. When followed through in
its entirety, all appropriate design objectives will be
addressed.

STEP 1. A determination is made in this step whether a proposed
structure is within the designated ocean wave zone (STEP 1.1)
and/or a proposed CPD is landward of the designated protective
device line (STEP 1.2). The protective device line is that
geographic location beyond which a protective device may not
encroach on the beach.

STEP 2. This a condition step. If a proposed structure is
supported on piles or caissons without a protective device, or if
it is a protective device, the plan-checker goes to STEP 3. If a
proposed structure is located in the ocean wave zone but is not
protected by a protective device, and if it is not on piles or
caissons, the design is conditionally unacceptable because of its
susceptability to breaking wave forces, flooding, loss of sand as
the beach erodes and other ocean-related phenomena.

STEP 3. The elevation of the design breaking wave is addressed
in this step. Design water surface elevation and beach scour
elevation (lowest level expected during design life of structure
or protective device) at the protective device line are primary
data that must be considered in establishing design water depth.
These site-specific data are provided in a series of figures and
tables with a method to determine changes that may occur over the
life of the structure or protective device. The design breaking
wave elevation, adapted from the SHORE PROTECTION MANUAL (Corps
of Engineers, 1984), is established using a depth-limiting
assumption. If the lowest horizontal supporting member of a
structure or the crest elevation of a protective device is lower
than the maximum elevation of the design breaking wave the design
is considered unacceptable. While it can be made acceptable,
costs to construct a private dwelling, cabana, garage, deck or
restroom for direct wave-impact forces will, in most cases,
preclude such a design.

STEP 4. This is a condition step. If a proposed structure is
located in Sunset Beach, the plan-checker goes to STEP 5 which
addresses conditions at Sunset Beach. If not, the plan-checker
goes to STEP 6.

STEP 5. In special cases such as Sunset Beach, flooding caused by ocean water flowing over or through gaps in the artificial dune is the only design consideration. Design guidelines are based on the assumption that the beach will be artificially maintained with a width of at least 150 ft (46m) from the ocean-facing private property line. Should the beach retreat to less than that width, storm erosion and breaking wave activity at the structures may occur. Structures at Sunset Beach are required to be supported on piles or caissons with a minimum pile or caisson length of 20 ft (6m). This requirement is made to prevent a rapid loss of structures in the event beach nourishment is terminated or delayed. The minimum vertical distance between the ground elevation and the underside of the structure is based upon wave run-up estimates, the elevation of the beach or artificial dune in front of the structure, and the ground elevation beneath the structure. Landward drainage of flow during flooding events is required (the grade decreases landward).

STEP 6. This is another conditional step directing the plan-checker to go to STEP 7 if the plan is for a structure, and STEP 8 if it is for a protective device.

STEP 7. A structure on pilings or caissons requires foundation conditions be evaluated by a qualified geotechnical professional. A procedure is given to calculate (conservatively) wave forces on individual piles and on the entire pile group. Site specific data are used to obtain total force per unit width of the pile based on the vertical distance from the design water surface elevation to the design scour elevation. Requirements for protection of the landward end of a structure are also given when wave runup on the beach will extend underneath the structure. This factor is important, especially where the shoreline is retreating and maximum runup height and potential uplift pressures at the landward end of the structure will increase during its design life.

STEP 8. Wave runup and overtopping of a protective device is considered acceptable under specified conditions. This step designates the minimum distance a structure must be set back from the crest of the protective device. When runup elevation exceeds the elevation of the protective device, damage to glass, decking, and possibly the exterior surface of the ocean-facing wall of a structure may occur.

Damage may be prevented or mitigated by locating the ocean-facing wall of the structure landward of the crest of the protective device. This distance is defined herein as the runup setback distance based on the assumption that runup flow will be carried

toward the structure by: (1) the horizontal component of runup
flow on a sloping protective device, and (2) onshore winds. The
horizontal distance traversed by the tip of the uprush watermass
is assumed equal to the vertical uprush limit above the top of
the protective device.

STEP 9. This is another conditional step directing the plan-
checker to STEP 10 if the protective device is a seawall or
bulkhead, and STEP 11 if it is a revetment.

STEP 10. A seawall or bulkhead is designed to support, stabilize
and protect the property and any structures behind the device.
Because many types of seawalls and bulkheads, including gravity
walls, cantilever walls, anchored walls, double walls, and
composite walls, may provide adequate protection, and because the
designs vary so greatly, general design considerations adequate
for plan check purposes only are presented in this step. Actual
design requires a more detailed analysis.

Considerations in the plan-check procedure of this step include:
(1) lateral loads caused by earth, water and surcharge on the
landward side of the device, (2) soil retention behind the
device, (3) wave forces on the device, and (4) requirements for
wing walls. Most seawall and bulkhead failures during the 1983
wave storms in Orange County occurred because backfill material
was lost and the wall failed in shear or inward-bending moment.
Seawall failures are less likely to occur where backfill is
properly placed, compacted and retained. Another mode of failure
is due to scour at the toe of a cantilever or tieback wall, and
to inadequate tieback design.

Recommendations are provided to minimize the potential adverse
effects of protective devices on adjacent property:

●   Seawalls, bulkheads and revetments should be constructed in
     line with adjacent protective devices to eliminate the
     possibility of reflected waves from wing walls.

●   Seawalls, bulkheads and revetments should be tied to
     adjacent protective devices whenever possible to prevent
     the loss of backfill and to present a relatively uniform
     face to breaking waves.

●   A toe revetment should be provided to a distance of at
     least 5 ft (1.5m) above the natural design scour depth to
     reduce some wave reflection and decrease scour in front of
     the device.

●   If wing walls are used, toe revetments are recommended,
     where possible, in situations where adjacent property is

not fronted by a protective device, i.e., the adjacent structure is on piles.

STEP 11. Rock is the most common type of revetment material used in southern California. A rock revetment can adjust and settle somewhat after construction without causing structural failure. It also allows for relief of hydrostatic uplift pressure generated by wave action. An underlying filter allows for pressure relief over the entire foundation area. Required design considerations are: (1) revetment slope (slopes steeper than 1:1.5 are not allowed) , (2) cover layer design (stone weight), (3) thickness of cover layer (a two-unit armor layer thickness is recommended), (4) underlayer and filter design (the most common design today is a geotechnical fabric filter overlain by either armor stone or an underlayer stone and then armor stone; another design is several graded layers of stone successively larger in size that properly transitions between the in-situ soils and the armor layers; both are acceptable), (5) revetment toe (a basic principle is to design the toe to be deep enough as to have an apron that can settle into a scour pocket to prevent the revetment from being undermined), and (6) prevention of soil loss behind revetment.

STEP 12. Materials are considered in this step. The most commonly used materials in construction in the ocean wave zone of Orange County are wood, concrete, steel and stone. Synthetic fabrics are commonly used as a filter material. Guidelines are provided to assist in evaluating the materials used for the foundation of structures, seawalls and bulkheads, and revetments.

MANUAL APPLICATION AND REVISION

The manual is now is use in Orange County. It makes the County's job of evaluating plans easier and more uniform, and will reduce damages and the need for expensive County emergency measures in the future.

Periodic revision of the manual is required. Coastal design data are referenced to 1984 conditions and must be updated because changes occur with time. These include net shoreline position changes and sea level changes with respect to land. Design wave height and water surface elevation data, including El Nino-Southern Oscillation effects, can be improved as the existing data set is lengthened. Site specific data such as scour depths, bedrock elevations, and net shoreline position changes will be updated through direct efforts by the County. In addition to improvements in the coastal design data section, the section on coastal design criteria will be updated as new experimental and theoretical results became available.

Two specific conditions were not addressed in the investigation, but should be included in a revision. Pressure venting guidelines are needed for structures on piles at Sunset Beach. The surface gradient at Sunset Beach is away from the ocean. Only the case of a beach slope toward the ocean is presently considered in the manual. In certain locations, the protective device line was located at the base of a bluff. Guidance is required at those sites where a CPD is needed to prevent bluff recession.

REFERENCES

County of Orange, "Coastal Flood Plain Development, Orange County Coastline", Environmental Management Agency, County of Orange, Santa Ana, California, Jan 1985, 137p.

U.S. Coastal Engineering Research Center, "Shore Protection Manual", Waterways Experiment Station, Corps of Engineers, Vicksburg, Mississippi, 4th Ed., 1984.

Wave Height Distribution in the Coupled Harbor

Hong Sik Lee[1] Masafumi Kubo[2] Mitsuo Takezawa[3],M.JSCE

Abstract

The wave height in the harbor sheltered by the breakwater is carried out by the numerical simulation and the experiment. In the result,the coupled harbor by setting up double arms breakwater was adopted as the extension method,and the effective harbor entrances were found as $G1/L=1.0$ and $G2/L=1.0$.

Introduction

In this study,two kinds of harbor planning for setting up breakwater from a rectangular harbor are assumed. The one is the model interrupted by horizontal straight breakwater at where separated with the distance of $1.0L$(L;wave length)from the harbor entrance,the other is the harbor model extended by double arms breakwater at two edges of original rectangular harbor(see Model No.10 of Table 1).

First of all,the numerical simulation by adopting diffraction theory and hydraulic model test were carried out in order to compare with wave height distribution in harbors with respect to these models for layout of breakwater. As the result of comparison with two models by the numerical simulation and the experiment,it is found that the former model interrupted by offshore breakwater shows the strong mutual interference between coastal revetment and breakwater tips,and the high reflection wave that would be harmful to moored small ships at the backwall of the harbor(Lee,Kubo & Takezawa 1985).

Therefore,the latter was selected as the harbor model supposed to be effective for utilizing the new wide water facilities,the deepening water depth and preventing deposition due to sediment transport at the harbor entrance. As the latter model of the study,the extended harbor is divided into two regions of the inner and the outer harbor,and furthermore two entrance gaps are simultaneously with five kinds of width (a half of wave length;0.5L).

From the result obtained by the numerical simulation and the experiment,the relation between harbor entrance and wave height due to diffraction in·a harbor is discussed in order to obtain effective entrance gaps for coupled harbor.

Harbor Model

The sketches of harbor models adopted by this study as the first step are presented in Fig.1(A),(B). The width of the outer and the inner gap G1,G2 is respectively defined in the Table 1. Two entrance gaps are enlarged regularly with the breadth of 0.5L,and harbor models

1.Gr.Stud.,2.Prof Emeritus,3.Prof.,Department of Civil Engineering, College of Science & Technology,Nihon University,1-8 Kanda Surugadai, Chiyoda-Ku,Tokyo,101,Japan

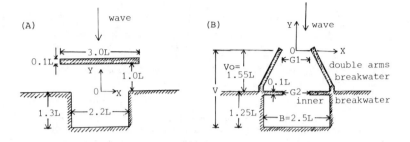

Figure 1(A),(B). Sketches of harbor models

will be composed of the coupled harbor.   However,in cases of the inner
gap G2=2.5L,they are not become the coupled harbor.
    Though the former model is one case as shown in Fig.1(A),all the
latter models are twenty-five cases of assembled condition which varies
the inner and the outer gap with the interval of 0.5L.
    All the harbor models were made of concrete block of the length 240
cm(7.874 ft),the width 20cm(7.874 in)and the height 30cm(11.811 in).

Table 1.Harbor models and their entrance gap

Model No.	G1/L	G2/L	Model No.	G1/L	G2/L
1	0.5	0.5	16	2.0	0.5
2	"	1.0	17	"	1.0
3	"	1.5	18	"	1.5
4	"	2.0	19	"	2.0
5	"	2.5*	20	"	2.5*
6	1.0	0.5	21	2.5	0.5
7	"	1.0	22	"	1.0
8	"	1.5	23	"	1.5
9	"	2.0	24	"	2.0
10	"	2.5*	25	"	2.5*
11	1.5	0.5			
12	"	1.0	* inner breakwater		
13	"	1.5	is not exist		
14	"	2.0			
15	"	2.5*			

Experiment Work

    For the purpose of comparing with the   numerical   simulation result,
the experiment was carried out in a rectangular basin of the length 19m
(62.336 ft),the width 7m(22.966 ft)and the depth 1.5m(4.921 ft)as shown
in Fig.2.   Wave absorber was installed at the one side vertical wall of
the basin with 3m X 7m(9.843 ft X 22.966 ft),and wave paddle of flap
type wave generator was installed at the opposite end of the basin.
    The actual size of the basin used for experimental work is 14m X 7m
(45.931 ft X 22.966 ft)in order to minimize the reflection effect from
the wall.

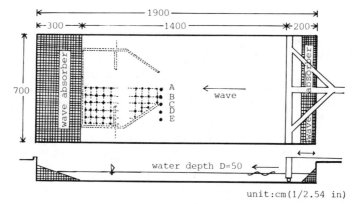

unit:cm(1/2.54 in)

Figure 2.Experimental Apparatus

The generated wave is the regular wave of which the height Hi=3.33cm (1.311 in),the period T=1.2sec and the water depth D=50cm(1.64 ft).
The wave length L is obtained as 200cm(6.562 ft)by the small amplitude wave theory.

The incident wave height was measured by five quantity type wave gages simultaneously at the incident wave location near the harbor entrance before the model was set up. The incident wave height was obtained as the averaged value measured by five gages at the points(A)∿(E).

Six quantity type wave gages were used for measuring each meshes of 50cm(1.64 ft)interval in models. The wave height was recorded in analogue recorder through amplifiers. The number of measuring points in a harbor model was 61∿72,and effective wave height in a model was the value averaged from fifth to eighth wave.

The harbor model was mounded vertically on the basin bottom by superposing two blocks of which the height should be 60cm(1.969 ft),so that the incident wave height Hi=3.33cm(1.311 in)is propagated in the constant water depth of 50cm(1.64 ft)to vertical block of height 60cm (1.969 ft).

Method of the Numerical Simulation

Wave diffraction may be treated in general as the sum of the incident and the scattering components in the sheltered region by structure(see St.Isaacson 1978;Harms 1979;Lee 1985). The authors tried to apply that diffraction problem to the waves in the coupled harbor formed by double arms breakwater and inner breakwater.

In the numerical simulation of this study,wave reflection from back wall of the inner harbor and the front face of inner breakwater is assumed simply,and it is added to the sum of two components.

Therefore,waves in the coupled harbor were assumed as the sum of the three components of incident,scattering and reflection. With respect to the theoretical expansion of this assumption,the outline of the method will be mentioned briefly.

Let us consider a train of regular wave of period T,wave length L and unit wave height propagated to the harbor entrance,and take an original point at the center of the harbor entrance. It will be defined that X axis is the right direction of coastal revetment,Y axis to the offshore and Z axis is considered to the vertical direction from the water surface where water depth D is constant.

Assuming that the fluid is inviscid,irrotational,incompressible,it can be defined that there exists a velocity potential which satisfies the Laplace's equation.

$$\nabla^2\Phi=0 \qquad\qquad ------------------(1)$$

The velocity potential by the linear simple harmonic wave motion can be sought in the equation(5)which satisfies the boundary conditions(2)∿ (4).

$$\partial\Phi/\partial Z-(\sigma^2/g)\Phi=0 \qquad \text{at } Z=0 \quad -----(2)$$

$$\partial\Phi/\partial Z=0 \qquad \text{at } Z=-D \quad -----(3)$$

$$\partial\Phi/\partial n=0 \qquad \text{fixed condition} ---(4)$$

$$\phi(X,Y,Z)=\frac{Hi\cdot g}{2\sigma} f(X,Y) \frac{\cosh k(Z+D)}{\cosh kD} \quad -----(5)$$

where: g=gravitational acceleration,Hi=incident wave height,k=wave number, σ=angular frequency and f(X,Y)=wave function.

The wave function which satisfies the variation of incident wave angle in any direction may be divided as the sum of three components by the assumption of this study,so that it may be obtained the following equation :

$$f(X,Y)=fi(X,Y)+fs(X,Y)+fr(X,Y) \qquad ---------(6)$$

The incident wave profile may be described as the equation(7),and reflection wave in here will be assumed as the equation(8).

$$fi(X,Y)=-i\exp\{-ik(X\cos\theta+Y\sin\theta)\} \qquad ---------(7)$$

$$fr(X,Y)=-i\exp\{-ik(X\cos\theta-\acute{Y}\sin\theta)\} \qquad ---------(8)$$

where: $\begin{cases} \acute{Y}=2V-|Y| \; ; (|X|<\frac{G2}{2}) \text{ or } (|X|\geqq\frac{G2}{2} \text{ and } |Y|>Vo) \\ \acute{Y}=2Vo-|Y| \; ; (|X|\geqq\frac{G2}{2} \text{ and } |Y|\leqq Vo) \end{cases}$

The scattering wave function which satisfies the Helmholtz's equation will be determined as the function which satisfies the radiation condition.   It is well known that it can be approximated to the boundary integral equation by the Green's theorem(e.g.,Hwang & Tuck 1970;Lee J.J. 1971)as shown in the equation(9).

$$fs(X,Y)=-\frac{i}{2}\int_S \{fs(Xi,Yi)\frac{\partial}{\partial n}(H_0^1(kR))-$$
$$H_0^1(kR)\frac{\partial}{\partial n}(fs(Xi,Yi))\}ds ----(9)$$

Hereby the diffraction coefficient KD in the harbor are obtained as the ratio divided by incident wave height.

$$KD=H/Hi=|f(X,Y)| \qquad ------(10)$$

Comparison and Analysis

From the comparison of the numerical simulation and the experiment, they have comparatively good agreement though some values obtained by the numerical simulation are larger than those of the experiment(see Lee & Takezawa 1985). There is a tendency which the numerical simulation results are extremely large when the diffraction coefficient KD of the experiment result is appeared large. However,the numerical simulation result is well coped with the experimental result.

A reason that the numerical result appeared to be larger than that of the experiment may be the wave reflection problem which is assumed for perfect reflection. As an example among the whole models,Fig.3 is presented for two results in case of the model No. 7.

Comparing two results at any position of interval 0.5L from the original point of the harbor entrance,they have good agreement.

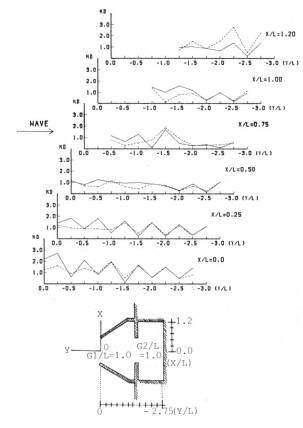

Figure 3.Comparison of two results
(———by numerical, ···········by experimental)

Discussion for Selecting Harbor Model

    Let us discuss internal assessment due to mean values obtained in
all measured points for five models which has no inner breakwater for
selecting the harbor entrance.
    The mean values of KD are increasing gradually with the harbor ent-
rance is widening as shown in Fig.4.   In here,it may be concerned with
the following equation(11),but it is not always satisfied for the prediction in all areas in a harbor.

$$KD = 0.20 \times G1/L + 0.75 \qquad \text{------}(11)$$

    The mean value of KD at Y/L=-1.5 and Y/L=-1.55 were found approxima-
tely 0.5 and 1.0 as shown in Fig.5,so that the position of Y/L=-1.55 for
the front face of inner breakwater is considered avoidable.

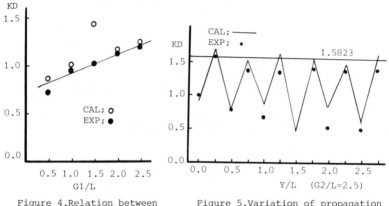

Figure 4.Relation between   Figure 5.Variation of propagation
Mean KD and G1/L   (in case of no inner breakwater)

    In contrast,the relation between the harbor entrance gap G1/L and
inner harbor's KD at the near of the backwall where Y/L=-2.5,Y/L=-2.75
is given by the following equations(12),(13)as shown in Fig.6.

$$KD = 0.167 \times G1/L + 0.265 \qquad \text{-----}(12)$$
$$KD = 0.45 \times G1/L + 0.775 \qquad \text{-----}(13)$$

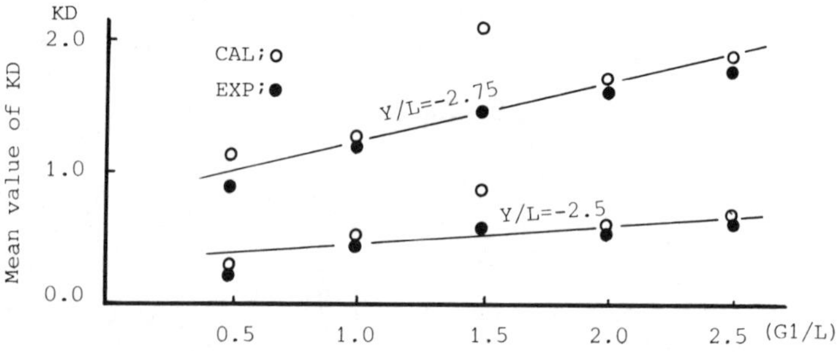

Figure 6. Mean KD at the near the backwall

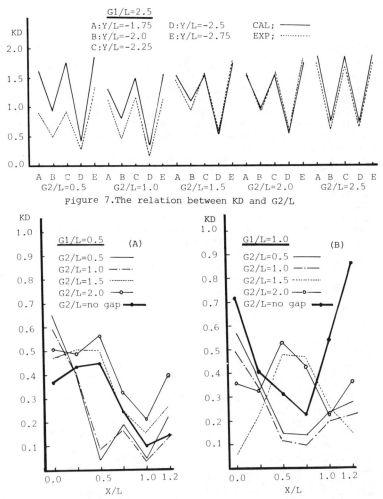

Figure 7.The relation between KD and G2/L

Figure 8(A),(B). KD in cases of G1/L=0.5,1.0 at the Y/L=-2.5

From these facts,KD at the position Y/L=-2.75 is shown to be larger than that of Y/L=-2.5 and also position near to backwall is being influenced with ease by the width of the harbor entrance G1/L(Lee In Press).

To discuss the relation between KD in the inner harbor and G2/L, their values of the inner harbor's region for Y/L=-1.75(A)∿Y/L=-2.75(E) under the condition of G1/L=2.5,G2/L=0.5∿2.5 are presented in Fig.7.

In this extent the model of G2/L=1.0 had the lowest KD in the whole models in Fig.7.   To summarize synthetic review from the discussion as have been mentioned above,the problem for choice of the harbor entrance gap is compressed whether G1/L=0.5 or G1/L=1.0,so that the comparison on the both entrance gaps will be conducted at the Y/L=-2.5 as shown in Fig.

8(A),(B).   As the above result,the model No.6,7 were found the effect
of lower than the other models.

Conclusion

   To summarize the analysis and the discussion as some items,it may be
refered as follow.
   1.The result of the numerical simulation due to this study can be corre-
     sponded well with the experiment work.
   2.The harbor interrupted by a horizontal straight offshore breakwater
     confronted some problems in comparison with the harbor extended by
     double arms breakwater on navigation,sedimentation,harbor calmness,etc.
   3.In case of the entrance gap G1/L=2.5,the effect of interrupting inci-
     dent wave energy can not be expected,and the inner gap composed by
     breakwater was effective when the entrance gap G1 is wide.
   4.The numerical simulation results were larger than those of the experi-
     ment,but they coped well with complicated variation by themselves.
     From this characteristics of the numerical results,it is possible to
     predict the wave height in the harbor qualitatively.
   5.When the design of the harbor entrance gap is performed in the present
     models,G1/L=1.0 is considered effective if any certified ships can be
     navigated safely through the entrance gap.   In case of G1/L=1.0L,
     the inner gap G2/L=1.0 is most desirous on harbor calmness.

References

1.Harms,V.W.,"Diffraction of Water Waves by Isolated Structures,"J.Water
  way,Port,Coastal and Ocean Div.,ASCE,Vol.105,No.WW2,May,1979,pp.131-
  147
2.Hwang,L.S.,Tuck,E.O.,"On the Oscillations of Harbours of Arbitrary
  Shape,"J.Fluid Mechanics,Vol.42,part 3,1970,pp.447-464
3.Isaacson,M.St.Q.,"Vertical Cylinders of Arbitrary Section in Waves,"J.
  Waterway,Port,Coastal and Ocean Div.,ASCE,Vol.104,No.WW4,Aug.1978,pp.
  309-324
4.Lee,J.J.,"Wave-Induced Oscillations in Harbours of Arbitrary Geometry,
  "J.Fluid Mechanics,Vol.45,part 2,1971,pp.79-87
5.Lee,H.S.,"Numerical Simulation About Diffracted Waves in the Vicinity
  of Artificial Island,"International Symposium on Ocean Space Utization,
  Vol.1,1985,pp.205-212
6.Lee,H.S.,"Fundamental Study on the Planning of Double Entrances of
  Outer and Inner Harbors,"Report of the Research Institute of Science &
  Technology Nihon University(In Press)
7.Lee,H.S.,Kubo,M.,Takezawa,M.,"Oscillations in the Harbor and its Entrance Vicinity Interrupted by an Offshore Breakwater,(In Japanese)"Proc.
  40th Annual Conference of Japan Society of Civil Engineers,Vol.2,1985,
  pp.649-650
8.Lee,H.S.,Takezawa,M.,"Comparison of the Experimental Results with the
  Theoretical on Wave Height in the Harbor,(In Japanese)"Proc.35th Conference of Japan National Congress of Theoretical and Applied Mechanics,
  1985,pp.71-74

Simplified Prediction of Storm Surge on an Open Coast Using a Microcomputer

Nenad Duplancic[1], M. ASCE and Paul C. Rizzo[2], M. ASCE

Abstract

The manual calculation of wind fields and the processing of a wide variety of data associated with storm surge computations is costly, time consuming and often tedious. The inherent difficulties of the traditional process work suggests new organizational techniques and the potential for computer analysis. Computer-generated wind fields have a flexibility that is not available with standard manual procedure; i.e. different illustrative concepts can be given a trial run at low cost. A spreadsheet program has been developed for determination of overwater wind fields for the Standard Project Hurricane (SPH) and the Probable Maximum Hurricane (PMH). The output from the spreadsheet is used as an input to a storm surge program coded in FORTRAN and originally developed for a mainframe computer. Both programs output results in the tabular and graphical form. The programs have been tested on the site for a proposed nuclear power plant in the Far East.

Introduction

Many nuclear power plants have been sited along the coast line in different parts of the world. Some are vulnerable to hurricane or typhoon surge and associated surface waves. The public health and safety might be jeopardized if the plant is flooded by storm surge and surface waves associated with a Probable Maximum Hurricane (PMH). To determine the degree of protection required for a particular site, it has been the practice to select a hurricane with a given set of characteristics for the particular geographical location. Since the characteristics are specified, the postulate storm is called the hypothetical Hurricane or Hypo-Hurricane.

The emergence of new computer-based techniques, combined with improved capabilities in graphics and database management, and widespread availability of low-cost, powerful micro-computers, has opened the door to more comprehensive application of computers to the hurricane related problems. In this paper we will discuss a micro-computer-based methodology for predicting storm surge, including the current manual process of wind field computation. The methodology is demonstrated by calculating the storm surge for proposed coastal nuclear power plant site in the Far East. The names hurricane and typhoon are used with the same meaning in this article.

[1]Project Engineer, International Technology Corporation, 10 Duff Road, Pittsburgh, Pa. 15235

[2]President, Paul C. Rizzo Associates, 10 Duff Road, Pittsburgh, Pa. 15235

<u>Site Setting</u>

The site used for demonstration of the program is located on the coast of a large bay and the shore line runs almost due north. The bay has direct access to the ocean, but the mouth

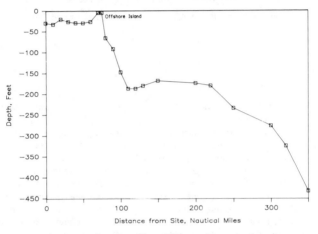

Figure 1: Depth profile -- Offshore demonstration site

of the bay is partially sheltered by offshore islands which tend to reduce the impact of typhoons on the site. The bathymetric setting is defined only in a limited sense. The available information indicates that the bay is shallow and that bathymetric levels offshore into the ocean are also shallow (i.e. the continental shelf is wide in the area of interest)--Figure 1.

<u>Wind Field Computation Using a Spreadsheet Program</u>

Although electronic spreadsheets were designed primarily for financial analysis, they are also applicable to many engineering computations. A spreadsheet is a two-dimensional matrix of cells where the value of each cell can be made to depend on any other cell. Hence the spreadsheet represents a quite general context for describing mathematical and logical relations.

Wind field computations may be conveniently organized in the form of a spreadsheet. When the empty work sheet is loaded on the screen, the program presents the user with a screen of organized information in the form of a wind field computation forms. The user must provide only that information necessary to calculate the results. To assist the analyst, input data is displayed in a different color from pre-defined cells which contain labels defining the form. The pre-defined parts of the form, computational formulae, etc., are protected so they cannot be inadvertently changed. The computational capabilities of the spreadsheet are used to automatically fill cells for results, eliminating much of the tedious and error prone work.

The program follows general criteria for determining wind fields for the most severe typhoons (hurricane) reasonably characteristic of a region, outlined in Reference 2. The spreadsheet program requires the input of the latitude in degrees, peripheral pressure (p_w).

central pressure (p_o), radius of maximum winds (R), forward storm speed (Γ), track direction, Coriolis parameter (f) and density coefficient (K). These parameters are all supplied from Reference 2. The rest of the calculation is performed by the spreadsheet automatically according to the procedure outlined in the following paragraphs.

Hurricane winds blow spirally inward and not along a circle concentric with the hurricane center. The angle between the true wind directions and a tangent to one of these circles is known as the inflow angle (Φ)--Figure 2.

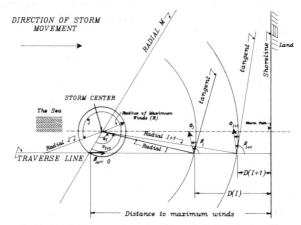

Figure 2: Radial distances and angles of the wind along traverse line

Maximum theoretical gradient wind is defined as a wind blowing under conditions of circular motion, parallel to the isobars, in which centripetal and Coriolis accelerations together exactly balance the horizontal pressure-gradient force per unit mass [2]. The maximum gradient wind speed (V_{gx}) in a hurricane is the maximum gradient wind at the radius of maximum winds. The gradient wind, independent of duration, is computed by solving equation:

$$V_{gx} = \sqrt{K(p_w - p_o)} - \frac{Rf}{2}$$

The larger the pressure drop $(p_w - p_o)$, the larger the gradient wind speed. Observed 10-meter (32.8-foot) 10-minute maximum winds (V_x) over open sea in hurricanes of above average intensity have been found to range from about 75 to slightly over 100 percent of V_{gx}. Two empirical equations for estimating V_x in a stationary hurricane are:

$$V_x = 0.90\, V_{gx}, \quad \text{for the SPH}$$

$$V_x = 0.95\, V_{gx}, \quad \text{for the PMH}$$

Knowing V_x and using the information on relative wind profiles 10-meter (32.8-foot), 10-minutes overwater winds at any distance from the hurricane center can be determined. Winds in a moving hurricane must be adjusted for asymmetry factor (A) which is given by formula:

$$A = 1.5 \ (T^{0.63}) \ (T_o^{0.37}) \cos \beta$$

where T_o is unity when the winds are in knots. β is the angle between track direction and the surface wind direction and it varies around the hurricane at any constant radial (r) and along a radial with varying distances from the hurricane center. "A" is added to the winds on the right of a storm and subtracted from those on the left.

V_x (maximum wind) occurs at the point along the circumference of maximum winds where the surface wind directions is parallel to track direction. Here $\beta = 0$ and $\cos\beta = 1$. The general equation for 10-meter (32.8-foot), 10-minutes overwater winds at any point other than where V_x occurs is:

$$V = V_s + 1.5 \ (T^{0.63}) \ (T_o^{0.37}) \cos \beta = V_s + A$$

where V is the wind speed at radius r and V_s is the wind speed in a stationary hurricane of radius r. The relative wind profiles (V_s/V_x) enable us to determine values of V_s at various r's given V_x $[V_x = f(V_{gx})]$.

For a radial through the point of maximum wind (radial M) the values of β are calculated using the following formula:

at $r \neq R$ $\beta = \Phi_r - \Phi_R$

at $r = R$ $\beta = \Phi_R - \Phi_r = 0$

where R is the radius of maximum winds (see Figure 2). The values for Φ can be obtained from the figures given in [2].

Once we have obtained the wind field along the radial M, the winds for other radials can be computed. First, the degree of rotation (α) (counterclockwise) between radial M and another radial is calculated. The values of α are added to the values of β_m values for corresponding distances. This gives values for the desired radial. The values of the coefficient A are then calculated for new values. The values of A are added to V_s values along radial M. This procedure is repeated for as many radials as required to adequately define the isotaches over all portions of the hurricane. The procedure is accomplished with a spreadsheet automatically. All formulae necessary for calculations are stored in the appropriate cells in the work sheet. Calculated results can be graphically presented and printed and/or plotted--(Figure 3).

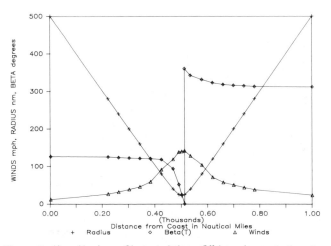

Figure 3: Hypo-Hurricane Characteristics -- Offshore demonstration site

Storm Surge Computer Program

The model used for storm surge calculations is based on the Bathystrophic Storm Tide Theory which can be described as a quasi-two-dimensional numerical scheme for predicting open-coast storm surge. The method is a steady state integration of the wind stress from the edge of the continental shelf, taking into account some of the effects of the alongshore flow caused by the earth's rotation.

The computer program was originally developed for mainframe computer in Reference (1). The program has been converted to run on microcomputer and improved to include the high quality graphical output of calculated surge. The program also accepts directly the input from spreadsheet overwater wind field computation program described above.

The line along which computations were carried - the traverse line - represents a line which, on the average, is about perpendicular to the sea floor contours. The actual path of the storm is taken parallel to and about 41 kilometers (22 nautical miles) south of the traverse line. Figure 1 shows the approximate bed profile along the traverse line from the demonstration site seaward to the 135-meter (450-foot) depth contour. Experience has shown that a point where the depth is 90 meters (300 feet) is usually sufficient for commencing the computations from the seaward position to the most landward location. Setup in regions deeper than this depth are generally negligible. The characteristics of the storm obtained by spreadsheet, as shown in Figure 3, are input directly to the program. The position of the storm is taken such that the maximum wind lies along the traverse line directly in line with the shore site and then the storm is postulated to move parallel to the traverse in discreet time increments. For each time increment, the surge is calculated at incremental points along the traverse until the maximum surge at the site is predicted. The complete time history of the resulting surge at the demonstration site is shown in Figure 4.

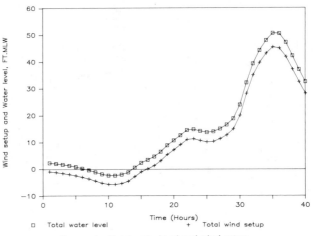

Figure 4: Total water level and wind setup

At the coast, onshore winds will significantly decrease as a result of change in surface friction characteristics. The adjustment of wind speed for these frictional effects have not been considered, nor have the "funneling" effects of the bay at the demonstration site. Consideration of these effects would require modifications to the criteria used in this study.

Summary and Conclusion

This paper discusses micro computers and standard software currently available to aid analysts in calculating, interpreting and presenting data associated with storm surge computations. The microcomputer based system provides improved capabilities in the storm surge calculations process. Data input is interactive, and the data processing sequence is selected by the user. The storm data calculated by a spreadsheet program are used as a direct input to a surge prediction program coded in FORTRAN. The procedure has been applied to a demonstration site located in a bay in the Far East for several different typhoon wind fields. The results of analysis show that the maximum range, considering several storms, is between 0.6 (2) and 15 (50) meters (feet) with a predominant figure of about 14 meters (45 feet).

REFERENCES

(1) Bodine, R. B., "Storm Surge on the Open Coast: Fundamentals and Simplified Prediction", Technical Memorandum No. 35., U.S. Army Corps of Engineers, Coastal Engineering Research Center, May 1971.

(2) Schwerdt, W. R., F. P. Ho and R. P. Watkins, "Meteorological Criteria for Standard Project Hurricane and Probable Maximum Hurricane Windfields, Gulf and East Coasts of the United States", NOAA Report No. NOAA-TR-NWS-23, Washington, DC., September 1979.

Corps of Engineers Automation of
Real-Time Water Control Management

Ming T. Tseng*, M.ASCE and Earl E. Eiker**, M.ASCE

Introduction

The U.S. Army Corps of Engineers has been one of the principle
water resources development agencies of the Federal government
since 1824, when Congress directed the Corps to perform clearing
and snagging operations for navigation improvement along the Ohio
and Upper Mississippi Rivers. Today, through its Civil Works
program, the Corps carries out a comprehensive water resources
planning, construction and operations effort in close cooperation
with government agencies at all levels and a wide variety of civic
and private interests. The Civil Works program is directed toward
the coordinated management of water resources in a manner that will
lead to the satisfaction of water-related requirements, both
immediate and long-range. These requirements include flood
control, navigation, power generation, water supply, water quality
control, recreation and fish and wildlife enhancement. The Corps
owns and operates some 558 water control projects with a total
active storage of approximately 198 million acre-feet. Of these,
129 have active storage greater than 250,000 acre-feet. In
addition to its own projects, the Corps is responsible for
prescribing flood control and navigation regulations for another 88
reservoir projects constructed and/or operated by other Federal,
non-Federal or private agencies. These responsibilities are set
forth in Section 7 of the 1944 Flood Control Act, the Federal Power
Act and other specific legislation. The annual cost for Corps
water control management activities is about $55 million, while
annual benefits from flood control alone have averaged about $10
billion per year over the past 10 years.

Organization

The Corps is organized into ten divisions throughout the
continental United States. Within each division, district offices
are generally responsible for day to day water control management,
while the division office provides oversight, technical support and
direction to the districts. The Office of the Chief of Engineers
is responsible for development of policy and technical guidance
and overall monitoring of water control management activities.

---

*Hydraulic Engineer, Office of the Chief of Engineers, U.S. Army
Corps of Engineers, Washington, DC 20314-1000.
**Chief, Water Control/Quality Branch, Office of the Chief of
Engineers, U.S. Army Corps of Engineers, Washington, DC 20314-1000.

Inherent to this organization is the need to maintain continuous coordination and communication, particularly during periods of flooding and other emergencies.

Water Control Management - A Growing Emphasis

Over the past fifteen years, construction of new projects has decreased dramatically, while public demands on our nation's water resources have continued to rise. Thus, increased emphasis has been placed on more efficient and effective operation of existing reservoirs and reservoir systems. Existing projects are now called upon to provide for additional flood control, increased water supplies, more water-based recreation and to be compatible with add-on hydropower. These demands have resulted in more and more pressure on an already strained resource. Faced with these additional demands, Corps water control managers had no choice but to improve their capabilities to collect and analyze data to support the increasingly difficult management decisions needed to minimize conflicts among project beneficaries.

Data Collection

Collection of a wide variety of real-time environmental and operational data is essential for effective water control management. Four major types of data are necessary. Project data are collected to monitor project performance and safety. Hydrologic data are collected to monitor basin hydrologic conditions and reservoir storage and effectiveness. Meteorologic data are collected to monitor climatic changes that may influence project operations. Water quality data are collected to assess environmental effects of project activities and to provide a basis for operations for water quality control.

There are presently about 6000 stations nationwide at which data are collected in support of Corps water control management. Some 10,000 observations are made daily at these stations under normal conditions. Generally, data are collected at intervals of from four to twenty-four hours, whereas during emergencies intervals as short as fifteen minutes may be required.

Until the mid-1970's, real-time data collection through the use of landlines was most common. While this method was cost effective, system vulnerability to failure under severe weather conditions, the time when data are needed the most, was a critical problem. Thus, in 1976 two Corps offices, the Huntington District and the New England Division, began testing the feasibility of employing satellite communications. This technology was proven to be extremely reliable during two separate severe storm events in the late 1970's. Based on these results, other Corps offices began to utilize this new technology. Today, the Corps has in place about 1600 automated stations to transmit data via the GOES satellite system and seven Corps-owned ground receive sites.

Master Plan Development

The complexity of Corps water control management activities requires the collection, processing, interpretation, display and dissemination of large volumes of information, a process ideally suited to automation. With the increase in ability to collect large amounts of data through implementation of new technology, there arose a parallel need to increase capability to manage the data. Accordingly, in 1978 the Office of the Chief of Engineers directed each division office to develop a Water Control Data System (WCDS) Master Plan which would fully integrate the data collection, data management and communication needs of the division office and its districts.

In developing the master plans, existing data collection and analysis systems were evaluated and total performance requirements were identified, considering appropriate water control management criteria. The difference between the total system requirements and the existing system capabilities defined the unmet needs. Viable alternatives were then identified and evaluated against three criteria: timeliness, reliability, and economics. Finally, a system was selected and recommended for implementation. The approved master plans provided the basis for the continued acquisition of data collection/transmission hardware and automatic data processing equipment, and also to define broad software development needs. The Master Plans are considered to be "living documents" and are updated annually to allow adjustments for continually changing requirements. Implementation of the Master Plans has been accomplished in two phases; hardware acquisition and software development.

Hardware Acquisition

Most division Master Plans clearly established a requirement for improved automatic data processing equipment (ADPE). Taken as a whole, seven of ten divisions recommended acquisition of new dedicated mini-computers as a vital component of their overall water control management capability. A total of 22 mini-computers were needed to satisfy Corps-wide requirements. With such a large number of computers identified, it was decided that procurement should be through one Corps-wide consolidated acquisition to obtain the cost savings associated with a large purchase. In addition, this approach would have two other important benefits. The identical equipment would ease the inherent difficulties in interoffice communication and transferability of software. Specifications were written to accommodate three sizes of equipment based on the complexities of water control management activities in each district and division office identified as needing ADPE in the Master Plans. Bids on the package were solicited in the fall of 1984 and the acquisition was completed, with all equipment installed and operational, by the fall of 1985.

Software Development

   As a result of the previously described hardware acquisition,
the Corps made great strides in improving its data collection and
processing capabilities. In order to make maximum use of these
capabilities however, it was necessary to establish an orderly plan
to provide for development of the software that was required to
fully realize this new potential.

   A considerable number of software development requirements were
identified in the division Master Plans. Some divisions estimated
that software development costs could be two or three times higher
than hardware acquisition costs. Recognizing this, the Southwestern Division (SWD) office in Dallas, following approval of
their Master Plan, began preparation of a Software Development
Manual to lay out in detail the division's software needs and a
schedule for development. Many of the needs described in the SWD
Manual coin- cided with those required by other divisions.
Therefore, using the SWD Manual as a basis, a more general working
document was prepared that has served as a guide for development of
software having Corps-wide application. Development of the
Corps-wide software has been carried out by several Corps offices
and private contractors, while development of software that is
division or district specific has remained the responsibility of
each local office. This process has allowed for a more effective
allocation of scarce research and development funds and has avoided
potential duplication of effort. Technical oversight and tracking
of development activities has been accomplished by the Corps
Hydrologic Engineering Center in Davis, California.

   The system applications software is divided into three distinct
groupings; data acquisition, database utility and analysis. In
addition, there is system support software that integrates all of
the components into a user friendly system. The system support
software includes routines for program and computer control, database interface and monitoring of system operations.

   The data acquisition group includes programs to receive data
from the GOES system, over landlines and radio networks, from the
National Weather Service River Forecast Centers and other computer
systems and through manual entry. All data received is processed
through a preliminary screening program prior to placement in the
database. Work is presently underway to develop the software to
accept satellite imagery data and radar imagery data.

   The database utility group includes programs to generate
reports, archive and retrieve data, compute summaries and
statistics, generate graphics, send data to other computer systems
and perform other routine tasks.

   The applications grouping includes streamflow forecasting models
and real-time reservoir systems operations models. Work is
presently underway to develop software to perform high level data
screening and validation prior to application or dissemination of

the data. Future developmental efforts are envisioned in the areas of economic analysis of flood related damages and damage prevented, water supply accounting, power demand evaluations, water surface profiles and sediment transport.

Interagency Coordination

The nature of Corps water control management activities requires that a significant amount of information be exchanged with other Federal and non-Federal agencies. The most important of these exchanges is between the Corps and the National Weather Service River Forecast Centers, particularly during periods of flooding. The quantity of information exchanged varies considerably from office to office, but some amount of data is exchanged among all offices. Until recently most of this information was exchanged through voice communications.

Similar to the Corps, during the 1970's, the National Weather Service (NWS) undertook the development of a nationwide automated data management system called Automation of Field Operational Services (AFOS) in order to improve communication among its field offices. The system became operational in October 1981. This change in NWS communications through implementation of a computerized system, resulted in a major evolution of the traditional techniques for data and information exchange between NWS and the Corps. After months of negotiations, the two agencies agreed on a program to pursue an experimental cooperative effort known as "Testing the Reliability of Automated Data Exchange" (TRADE). The program was established to develop and test improved means for data exchange between the NWS and Corps field offices.

As initially structured, the TRADE program consisted of four independent phases of development. However, due to resource constraints that surfaced during the course of the test, only Phases I and III were undertaken. Phase I involved development of a protocol to provide access to the NWS database by dial-in Corps users. This was accomplished through the RFC gateway computer systems by means of the NWS DATACOL software package. Phase III of the TRADE program prescribed that all data accessed through the RFC systems would be formatted in the Standard Hydrologic Exchange Format (SHEF). Work on Phases I and III was successfully completed in July 1985, and the capability for the automated access of NWS data by the Corps became operational in August 1985. Discussions between the NWS and the Corps to complete TRADE Phases II and IV were again initiated. These two phases of the original program have now been combined into a new expanded effort called "Program for Real-Time Interagency Data Exchange" (PRIDE). When completed, PRIDE will establish capabilities for two way data exchange between NWS and Corps computers and permit Corps offices to receive graphic products from the NWS AFOS system.

Summary

   Automation of real-time water control management activities has
enabled the Corps to keep pace with an ever increasing workload in
a time of fiscal constraint and reduced manpower. Where manual
procedures were only recently the norm the entire process is now
automated.   Data are collected automatically in the field,
transmitted through satellites to ground receive stations and
relayed to the office mini-computer to be processed. Once into the
computer, the data are analyzed and used for evaluation of
alternative management strategies to form a basis for water control
decisions. The processed data are then disseminated and ultimately
stored for future analyses.   The entire process permits more data
to be collected, more alternative operations to be evaluated and,
as final result, leads to better management decisions.

APPLICATION OF A STOCHASTIC HYDROLOGY MODEL

Sushil K. Arora, A.M. ASCE[1] and George W. Barnes, Jr., M. ASCE[2]

Abstract

This paper presents the development and application of a multi-site, multi-season stochastic hydrology model for the Sacramento Valley portion of the Central Valley of California. The model is autoregressive in approach and follows a disaggregation technique after Lane (3) for simultaneous generation of monthly streamflow data at several locations. The stochastic model is designed to generate synthetic inflows to be used as input in place of historic flows to the California Department of Water Resources Planning Simulation Model of the Central Valley Project (CVP) and State Water Project (SWP) system of reservoirs and conveyance facilities (2). Application of this model represents the successful use of a stochastic model applied to a large system simulation model for water resources planning in California. This will allow planners to not only analyze future projects and alternative operations criteria using historical data, but to also look at system performance using equally likely sequences of generated flows. Performance of the Stochastic Hydrology Model has been evaluated by investigating the statistics and other hydrologic features of streamflows. This paper also presents an application of the stochastic hydrologic model to the California State Water Project System to provide synthetic inflow data for development of optimal reservoir operations criteria. The procedure for development of such a policy consists of three main steps (i) application of a stochastic hydrology model to generate synthetic flows in the SWP system, (ii) use of the DWR Planning Simulation Model of the CVP-SWP system to study the system behavior for selected operations criteria, and (iii) statistical anaylsis of the results of the simulation model runs and identification of the optimal operations rules for SWP system storage reservoirs. Work on this project has not yet been completed and thus no attempt has been made to draw conclusions about results of this investigation.

I. STOCHASTIC STREAMFLOW MODEL DEVELOPMENT

In this section various steps in the development of a stochastic hydrology model for the Central Valley Project and the State Water Project portion of the Central Valley of California are presented.

Basic Structure of a Stochastic Model. The development of the model used in this study is derived from the basic equation of a Markovian generating scheme which can be written as:

[1] Operations Research Specialist, State of California, Department of Water Resources, P. O. Box 388, Sacramento, CA 95802. [2]Supervising Engineer, State of California, Department of Water Resources, P. O. Box 388, Sacramento, CA 95802.

$$Q_i = Q + r_1(Q_{i-1}-Q) + st_i(1- r_1^2)^{1/2} \quad \text{(Equation 1)}$$

where:

Q_i = flow during any time interval numbered serially from 1 to n.
Q = mean flow for the interval derived from historic data.
r_1 = serial correlation coefficient between successive flow values.
s = standard deviation of Q.
t_i = normally distributed random number with a mean of zero and a standard deviation of one.

In the development of a stochastic model using Equation 1, the mean Q and the standard deviations are determined from the historic data set. These annual values are then disaggregated into seasonal or monthly values as required by the particular problem. The value of the serial correlation coefficient r_1 is determined from successive values of historic flow. Where several inflow sites within a water resource system such as the CVP-SWP system of reservoirs are of concern, multi-site generation techniques are necessary. In these larger systems, the flows must be simultaneously generated and cross correlation between stations must be maintained.

The "LAST" Stochastic Hydrology Model. The computer model adopted for application is called Lanes' Applied Stochastic Techniques (LAST) and was developed by Dr. William L. Lane (1980) of U. S. Bureau of Reclamation, Denver, Colorado. The model is a package consisting of a set of computer programs. These programs were subjected to a number of changes in order to apply the model for use in CVP-SWP system. The essential attributes of the LAST modeling approach are: (1) Ability to preserve year-to-year serial correlations with a multi-lag linear autoregressive model in addition to seasonal serial correlations; (2) Ability to preserve cross correlations between "key" stations on an annual basis; (3) Ability to generate "key" stations and to disaggregate those values into component substations on an annual basis; and (4) Ability to likewise disaggregate annual values into seasonal values preserving both serial correlations and cross correlations between "key" stations on a seasonal basis.

Application of the "LAST" Model to the CVP-SWP System. In this development, the LAST model was used to generate synthetic inflows to be used as input to the DWR Planning Simulation Model (1). Streamflow or reservoir inflows were generated for the locations shown schematically in Figure 1, which shows the network representation of the CVP-SWP system for simulation purposes. Out of a total of twenty-two model streamflow locations, eight sites were defined as having stochastic inflows. Flows at the remaining fourteen model locations were determined through regression relationships with the neighboring sites where flows were generated stochastically.

Historic Streamflow Data Systemization: The first step in any stochastic generation scheme is the organization of the historic data. For chosen sites, a relatively long streamflow record was available (1922-1978) for a period of 57 years. Data at these locations was obtained from the Departments' hydrology depletion studies which represent the historic flow adjusted to the 1980 level of development. To check for errors or anomalies in the data, a serial plot of each station was made using program TERMPL (stands for TERMinal PLotting).

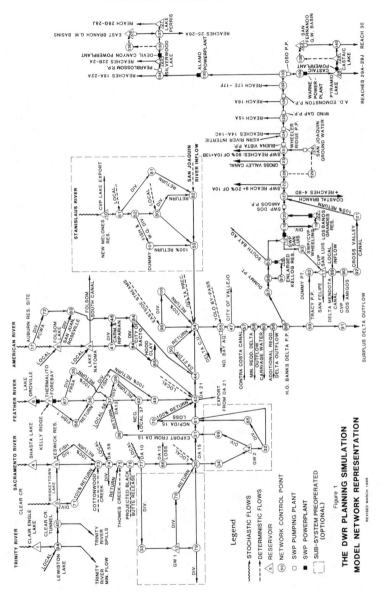

Legend

$\longrightarrow\!\!\!\sim$ STOCHASTIC FLOWS

- - - - DETERMINISTIC FLOWS

△ RESERVOIR

⑩ NETWORK CONTROL POINT

□ SWP PUMPING PLANT

■ SWP POWERPLANT

▢ SUB-SYSTEM PREOPERATED
  (OPTIONAL)

Figure 1

REVISED MARCH 1986

**THE DWR PLANNING SIMULATION
MODEL NETWORK REPRESENTATION**

The CORREL (stands for CORRELation) program was very useful in studying the cross-correlations between stations. This program was used to compute various correlation matrices between the stations for annual and monthly data. To reduce the complexity of the problem, the data file was trimmed to eight site studies.

Determination of the Stochastic Model Structure: The application of the LAST model requires that the problem be structured so as to identify key stations and substations. Key stations are identified and grouped for calculation purposes. Substation generation groups are also identified along with the groupings to be used in disaggregation of annual data into seasonal data. The main objective in the selection of generation groups is to preserve important correlations found in the historical data. The final model structure for the eight-site study was determined by the LAST programs and the physical location and similarity of climatic zones.

Normalization of Data: Through the use of appropriate transformations, it is necessary to change the basic data set into a set of data which follows a normal probability distribution. The reduction of the data to normally distributed data is a necessary stage to ensure that the generated data will adequately follow the observed distribution and will accurately reproduce the desired statistics. These transformations were performed both on the annual and the seasonal data. All the data, both annual and monthly were plotted on normal probability paper by using program TERMPL to determine how closely the data resembled a normal distribution with transformations. In order for the data for any period to be qualified, "normally distributed" it should fit a straight-line. The equations used to effect the transformations using the program TRNPAR (stands for TRaNsformation PARameters) for this study were:

$$T = (Q + a)^b \text{ (Equation 2) or } T = \log_e(Q + a) \qquad \text{(Equation 3)}$$

where: T = transformed data, Q = actual historic flow, a = a constant for the station and the period, and b = an exponent for the station and the period.

After a large number of trials, values for the parameters a and b in Equations (2) and (3) were determined so as to give the best possible straight-line fit.

Parameters for Stochastic Flow Generation: Three types of generation parameters need to be estimated for any typical stochastic flow generation problem. These parameters are key station generation parameters for annual data generation at a group of key stations, key substations generation parameters to generate substations annual flows by disaggregating already generated key station annual flows and finally, seasonal generation parameters which are needed to disaggregate generated annual data into the generated seasonal data. The program to estimate key generation parameters is KEYPAR (stands for KEY station PARameters). For the present investigation, the approach with lagged cross correlations ignored and with lag one serial correlations preserved was found to give satisfactory results. The program SEAPAR (stands for SEAsonal PARameters) estimates annual to seasonal parameters with no options available to the user. The use of transformations and model

inadequacies affect the exactness of the additive nature of seasonal
flows into annual flows. When generating synthetic data, program FLWGEN
(stands for FLOW GENeration) will automatically readjust the seasonal
data to preserve the additive nature after the inverse transformations
have been performed. Many cross-correlations and serial-correlations are
indirectly preserved through the annual correlations and the annual to
seasonal correlations. Since the problem was structured to have three
such groups, the program SEAPAR was run three times.

Generation of Synthetic Data: Once the necessary parameters to be
used in the key stations have been estimated or determined by programs
KEYPAR, DISPAR, SEAPAR, and TRNPAR and the results saved in a parameter
file, then the generation of synthetic flows may be performed using the
model. The program to be employed is FLWGEN. Generation of synthetic
flows is started using a "lead in" years approach, and remaining input
needed is the number of years to be generated and the random number
seed. Flows generated are stored in a data file and available to be used
and/or analyzed with other programs. The first step to generate
synthetic flows for the fourteen deterministic stations is the grouping
of these stations with stochastically generated stations. Program CORREL
is then run to get cross-correlation coefficients which aid in grouping
the stations into families. Regression equations for the annual data are
then determined. Stochastically generated data for any year is input to
the appropriate family regression equation and synthetic flows for a
station for the corresponding year are determined. Monthly flows for any
deterministic station for a year are given the same pattern as the
corresponding family seasonal pattern.

Assessment of Model Performance: The unimpaired Four River Index
(FRI) is often used as a measure of water conditions in California. The
Four River index is the total flow at four locations from four rivers:
Sacramento, Feather, American and Yuba. The model performance was
evaluated by comparing five stochastically generated sets of unimpaired
FRI flows to the historical FRI. The stochastic hydrology model per se
does not directly yield synthetic FRI flows. A regression equation was
developed for the historical FRI using historic modified annual inflows
to Shasta, Folsom, and Oroville Reservoirs. This regression equation was
used for determining the synthetic FRI by inputing stochastically
generated inflows (modified) to Shasta, Oroville, and Folsom Reservoirs
obtained from the stochastic model. The credibility of a stochastic
model, in general, is judged by its ability to match the statistical
characteristics of the historical record. A comparison of means,
standard deviations, skews, Hurst coefficient and correlations for the
historical and the synthetic data for the FRI are shown in Table 1. The
remaining trials from Set 1 through Set 5 are from five different
stochastic sequences each of 57 years length.

The ability of the stochastic model to reproduce "drought" conditions,
where "drought" is defined as an extended period of low flow, is
demonstrated by the similarity of the historic and generated flow-
duration curves presented in Figure 2. The Flow-duration curve of the
FRI for a duration of six years was obtained. For example, 5 percent of
the time in the 57-year sequence the flows were less than or equal to
71,000 TAF for Set 1 as compared to 68,000 TAF in case of historical
data.

TABLE 1

Historical and Synthetic Four River Index Statistics

Trial	Annual Mean (TAF)	Standard Deviation (TAF)	Coeff. of Skewness	Hurst Coefficient
Historical	17,126	7,059	0.4117	0.7166
Set 1	16,550	6,739	0.9590	0.5799
Set 2	17,310	7,365	0.9738	0.8065
Set 3	17,620	6,934	1.255	0.5183
Set 4	16,310	7,194	0.4725	0.7208
Set 5	17,260	7,456	0.7808	0.7091

(Note: 1 ac. ft. = 0.8107 deka m^3)

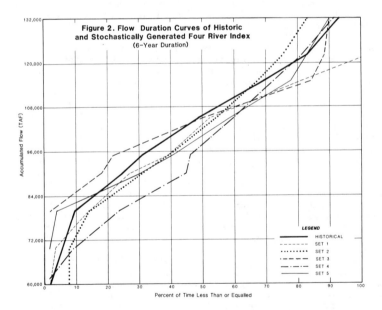

Figure 2. Flow Duration Curves of Historic and Stochastically Generated Four River Index (6-Year Duration)

II. DEVELOPMENT OF OPERATIONS RULES FOR THE
      STATE WATER PROJECT SYSTEM

This section describes a procedure which could possibly be used to
determine the optimum operations criteria for the State Water Project
(SWP). Each year the State Department of Water Resources must determine
how much water to deliver to contractors and how much to carry-over in
storage for future delivery, and at the same time, to provide protection
against a possible extended or severe dry period. Specifically, in this
study the objective is to demonstrate a methodology for determining the
annual SWP carry-over storage policy as shown by various performance
indices. The approach consists of three steps:

1. Applying the stochastic hydrology model to generate multiple
    sequences of stochastic flows in the system.
2. Select an operations policy and make repeated simulation runs by
    applying the mathematical model of the CVP-SWP system using the
    generated flows.
3. Investigate and statistically analyze the performance of the SWP
    system as obtained from simulation runs with selected policies.

After carefully iterating through these steps as many times as necessary
it is possible to analyze the effect of various operations policies and
to develop optimal strategies.

1) Generation of Stochastic Sequences: A decision was made to select
10 years as a planning horizon (longer than the longest historical dry
period of 1928-34) for development of SWP operations criteria. In other
words, it was assumed that 10 years was a long enough of a period over
which any significant long-term effects of an operations policy in the
first year would be permiated. It was also decided, that a total of 20
ten-year sequences, generated independently, was complete enough to
represent future uncertainties in hydrology, at least to test the
procedure. Obviously, the larger the number of sequences, the better the
statistical analysis one could perform.

2) Simulating the System for Selected Operations Rules: Simulation of
CVP-SWP system was carried out using DWR Planning Simulation model.
All the assumptions of the system were held constant for a given system
annual carryover storage rule. Each simulation run started with the
same initial conditions and system operation was simulated 20 times
using the 20 different stochastic sequences for each rule. Each
10-year sequence is time framed as if the first year of the sequence is
the present year and the simulation runs for a 10-year period. For
this project only three operation rules for SWP storage were tested.
These rules were indicative of two operational modes. Rule 1 was
established to deliver additional water when carryover storage in SWP
reservoirs was above 3,200 thousand acre-feet (TAF) and would
allow shortages if this storage fell below 2,900 TAF. Such a rule
would attempt to keep enough storage to protect pre-determined
dependable annual supplies of 2,300 TAF per year. Rule 2 on the other
hand would deliver surplus water more frequently while carrying over
to the following year only 2,700 TAF in storage. This rule has a lower
limit of 2,400 TAF. Such a rule should result in more frequent and more

severe shortages. Rule 3 was similar to Rule 1 with a small variation
in that carryover storage had a lower limit set at 2,400 TAF. While
these rules were quite simple, complex rules involving the entire
system could be easily developed and programmed into the model.

3) Analysis of Simulation Runs Output: As described, a total of 20
simulations were performed for each operation rule seleced. Each run
was 10 years long. The target deliveries for all the runs was assumed to
be of 2.3 MAF of dependable annual supply and a maximum of 870 TAF of
supplemental water for a total of 3.17 MAF.

Statistical investigations on results have not yet been completed.
Further refinements in the procedure are now envisioned and runs longer
than 20 years need to be conducted. In addition, the rules tested may be
more sophisticated. However, the feasibility of this procedure is now
demonstrated and it is felt these techniques may provide a useful tool
for analyzing SWP operations in the future.

Acknowledgments

The authors are grateful to their employer, the California Department of
Water Resources, for its permission to publish this paper. Special
thanks are due to Jerry Vayder for his guidance and support during this
investigation.

References

1. "A Stochastic Hydrology Model for Water Resources Planning for
    California," Department of Water Resources, State of California,
    Sacramento, CA, May, 1984.

2. Barnes, George W., Jr., and Francis I. Chung, "Operational Planning
    for California Water System", ASCE Journal of Water Resources
    Planning and Management, Vol. 112, No. 1, January 1986.

3. Lane, William L., "Applied Stochastic Techniques User Manual,"
    U. S. Bureau of Reclamation, Denver, Colorado, July, 1980.

Water Management of the Tenn-Tom Waterway

Edmund B. Burkett*

In December 1984 the final segments of the Tennessee-Tombigbee
Waterway were completed. The Waterway connects the Tennessee River to
the Gulf of Mexico at the City of Mobile. The project starts from the
existing Black Warrior-Tombigbee channel at Demopolis and generally
follows the Tombigbee River to its headwaters and cuts through the
basin divide to connect to the Pickwick Reservoir on the Tennessee
River. The total length of the project is 234 miles (377 km) with 10
locks and dams which raise the water surface a total of 340 feet (104
meters). The project can be divided into three distinct parts. The
first part, known as the river section, consists of 4 low-lift locks
and dams and channelization along the existing river alignment.
Upstream of this section a series of pools were created along the left
bank edge of the river valley. Five locks and dams raise the water
level 140 feet (43 meters) in a distance of 46 miles (74 km) along this
'Canal Section'. At the upstream end of the 'Canal Section' a high-
lift lock and dam (84 feet or 25.6 meters) raises the water surface to
the level of Pickwick Reservoir on the Tennessee River, 414 feet (126
meters) above sea level. A 39 mile (63 km) channel excavated through
the river basin divide completes the project to the Tennessee River.
These major features are shown on Figure 1.

The project is in a region of moderate rainfall - about 52 inches
(1321 mm) per year. A wet year may produce an annual rainfall of 70
inches (1780 mm) or greater and a dry year may have less than 40 inches
(1020 mm) of rainfall. Typically, the wet season is from December
through May and the dry season is September through November. The
wettest month, March produces an average rainfall of 6 inches (150 mm),
and the driest month is October with less than 3 inches (80 mm) of
rainfall. Frozen precipitation occurs but has insignificant impact on
the hydrology of the basin.

The project has greatly changed the appearance of the river
channel and valley and will have great impacts on land use and the
economy of the region. However, this paper will deal primarily with
several features involving the control of water in the project and the
impact the project has had on the flow regime and hydraulics of the
Tombigbee River basin.

The channelization has vastly changed the natural hydraulics of
the river. A channel 300 feet (90 meters) wide and 9 feet (3 meters)

* Chief, Water Management Section, Corps of Engineers, Mobile District,
P. O. Box 2288, Mobile, AL 36628-0001

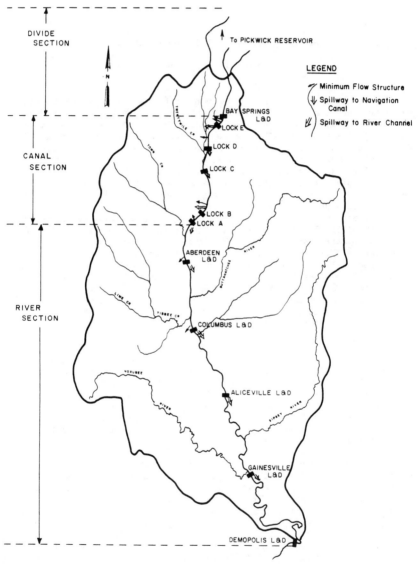

Figure 1 - General location of Tenn-Tom
water control structures

deep has been superimposed on a natural river 100 to 200 feet (30-60 meters) wide and a few feet deep. In addition the channelization has straightened the river so that water has less distance to flow. The natural river channel in the "river section" of the project traversed a distance of 200 miles (320 km) whereas the channel has shortened the distance of flow to 149 miles (240 km). Bank stabilization and snagging has reduced the hydraulic roughness. The result of these changes is a greatly more efficient hydraulic conveyance. Near the upper end of the channelization, five year to twenty year frequency flows are now accommodated by the channelization. Under natural conditions overbank floods would have occurred for the same discharge. Figure 2 illustrates the effect of the increased hydraulic efficiency resulting from the construction of the waterway.

Studies show that for larger floods the positive effects of the increased channel conveyance are diminished. This is a result of reduced overbank storage and flow area due to dredge disposal areas in the flood plains. The result is that stages for larger floods would not be as affected by the project.

Another change produced by the project is to the timing of the travel of the flood peak down the main stem of the river. At various tributary confluences with the main channel the tributaries peaked before or after the main river. With the project in place and the travel time reduced along the channelization, the coincidence or non-coincidence of the flood peaks has been changed. Locally this phenomena may have minor effects on flood heights, depending on the distribution and timing of the flood-producing rains.

A great impact on the flow regime of the Tombigbee River occurs in the upper basin along the portion of the river which parallels the Canal Section. In the Canal Section the navigation channel leaves the main stem of the river and is excavated in a series of pools along the east (left bank) side of the flood plain. The pools are created and separated from the main river channel by a levee constructed with material from the excavated channel. Five locks and dams raise the water level along this chain-of-lakes running parallel to the river. A number of changes in the flood plain result in a changed hydrologic environment in this section of the basin. Approximately one third of the flood plain has been diked and permanently flooded by the canal. This means that much of the valley storage capacity for storing and attenuating flood peaks has been removed. The result is higher flood elevations for the same discharge. An example of the expected result of this impact on stage frequencies is shown on Figure 3.

The points at which flows from east bank tributaries enter the river are modified by the project. Significant inflows into the Canal Section pools are discharged at two spillways from the Canal Section pools to the existing river channel. Between the spillway at Pool E discharging to Mackeys Creek and the spillway at Pool B discharging just downstream of the Tombigbee River's confluence with Bull Mountain Creek, runoff from about 200 square miles (518 sq km) of drainage area is collected by the canal and discharged at the Pool B spillway. This would tend to quicken the response of that part of the basin since

WATER FORUM '86

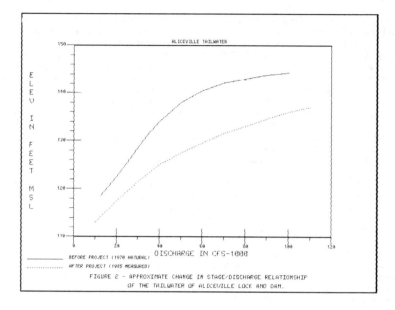

FIGURE 2 - APPROXIMATE CHANGE IN STAGE/DISCHARGE RELATIONSHIP
OF THE TAILWATER OF ALICEVILLE LOCK AND DAM.

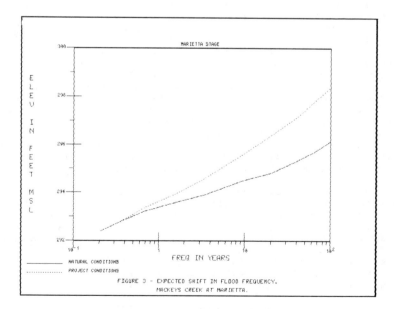

FIGURE 3 - EXPECTED SHIFT IN FLOOD FREQUENCY.
MACKEYS CREEK AT MARIETTA.

flows would be by-passing much of the old river channel and flood plain.

Another impact on the flow regime in the upper Tombigbee has been the use of the Canal Section by-pass structures at Lock B and the spillway at Lock A to carry flow - either excess lockage water or runoff from the eastern tributaries to the Canal Section - through the Canal Section. About 1,000 cubic feet per second (28.3 cubic meters per second) can be discharged through the Canal in this manner.

To provide sufficient low flow to the bottomland tributary channels cut off by the Canal, structures to pass flows from the Canal pools to several of these tributaries were included in the project. These structures generally were sized to continuously discharge twice the 7-Q-10 flow.

The purpose of these flows is to preserve the environment of the East Fork river channel and associated bottomland. These flows may be modified if it is found that different flows are more satisfactory for the environment. These structures have been troubled - as have the Columbus and Aberdeen minimum flow structures - by accumulated drift blocking the flow passages. The structures are now being cleared on a regular basis and such continuing maintenance should ensure that the structures work properly. Futhermore, trash racks or trash barriers that are being planned should reduce this problem.

The changes in flow regime described above are primarily a result of the structural modifications of the channel system and not the operation of flow control facilities. However, there are some water control features that should be mentioned. Water control of the Tenn-Tom project is fairly simple. It is a slackwater navigation system in which each of the projects hold constant pool levels by adjusting flow control structures. Certain continuous flows are maintained at various points for water quality or environmental reasons.

Maintaining minimum continuous flows with acceptable dissolved oxygen from the river section dams was a design criteria of the project. At the Gainesville and Aliceville projects weirs were incorporated into the spillways of the projects. The weirs pass a fairly small amount of flow. However, in the dry summer and fall when low dissolved oxygen is most likely to occur, the weirs may discharge a large proportion if not all of the flow. Special re-aeration features were incorporated into the downstream side of the weirs. At Gainesville a re-aeration ramp insures that the sheet flow passing over the spillway crest is entirely aspirated. At Aliceville a slightly different feature accomplishes the same aeration. An elevated flip bucket at the toe of the free-overflow spillway aerates the flow. These two devices assure that a continuous minimum flow is discharged and that such a discharge is fully aerated.

At the two upstream river section dams different low-flow situations occur. Both dams were built in bend-ways in such a way that segments of the old river channels were cut off from flow. To keep the water from being stagnant in these cut-off areas, minimum flow

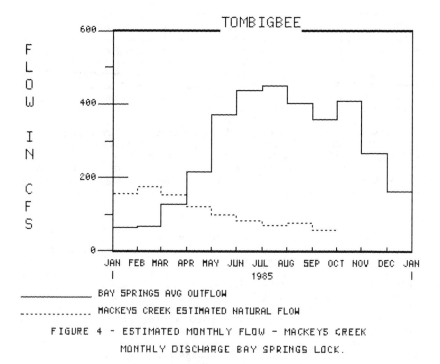

FIGURE 4 - ESTIMATED MONTHLY FLOW - MACKEYS CREEK
MONTHLY DISCHARGE BAY SPRINGS LOCK.

structures were constructed which pass about 200 cfs (5.5 cms) through the dams to the old channel.

The Bay Springs Reservoir and the Divide Cut portion of the Waterway create a unique water control situation. Bay Springs Dam impounded runoff from 66 square miles (171 sq km) drainage area of Mackeys Creek - a headwater tributary of the Tombigbee River. Natural average annual discharge of Mackeys Creek is about 100 cfs (3 cms). This flow is now diverted to the Tennessee River. However, countering this diversion of runoff is the discharge of lockage water to the Canal Section. Ultimately, this discharge may exceed ten times the flow diverted to the Tennessee River. Procedures have been established to account for the flow that Mackeys Creek would have carried as well as the volume of lockage water released from the project.

Even with the relatively low traffic on the Waterway during 1985, the net gain of the water to the Tombigbee River was significant. Figure 4 shows the monthly lockage release compared to the monthly Mackeys Creek diversion to the Tennessee River. For the first nine months of 1985 about 59,000 acre-feet (72.8 Mm^3) of Mackeys Creek runoff flowed to the Tennessee River. About 150,000 acre-feet (185 Mm^3) of water was used for lockages at Bay Springs. The net exchange of water was a gain of 91,000 acre-feet (112 Mm^3) of water for the Tombigbee River.

Much of the discussion above regarding the effects of the project derives from design information which is now ten to twenty years old. A data collection network has been maintained, and in some cases augmented, to be able to assess whether the expected changes in the flow regimes are correct. Post construction data will be analyzed with current available models and state-of-the-art techniques. It should be possible in a few years to confirm and refine the information on the impact of the Waterway on flow regimes.

Computational Enhancements to a
Multidimensional Dynamic Programming Algorithm

by Dennis Morrow,[1] M. ASCE and Bruce Loftis,[2] M. ASCE

ABSTRACT

This paper discusses ongoing work in investigating the vectorization potential (speedup) of multidimensional dynamic programming computer codes on the Control Data Corporation (CDC) CYBER 205 supercomputer at Florida State University. The conclusion to be drawn from the work performed to date is that, although dynamic programming is recursive over the stages, it is possible to achieve significant savings in computer cost by reordering and grouping the calculations which must be performed at each stage. A further benefit of using a supercomputer is that large, computationally intensive problems can now be tackled which were unmanageable only a few years ago without simplifying assumptions.

INTRODUCTION

Large-scale water resource operations problems with non-linear and discontinuous objectives and constraints have been solved by dynamic programming (DP) for a number of years [2]. The problem which is currently being solved by DP is the optimization of surface water reservoir releases over space and time. The objective is to control a system of reservoirs to maximize the benefits from any of a number of conflicting interests such as water supply, flood control, irrigation, recreation, fish and wildlife, and hydropower. This is an operational rather than a design problem—a dendritic (branching) system of reservoirs with deterministic inflows is to be operated on a month to month basis for a fixed period of time.

Several tools of systems analysis have typically been used to seek improvement in the traditional "rule curve" approach to reservoir operations. Among these are analytical calculus (which requires continuous, differentiable functions), linear programming (requires linear objectives and constraints), and dynamic programming which can often be formulated to take advantage of the time sequence of release decisions inherent in reservoir operations.

Dynamic programming seeks the best path through a discrete state-space of operational release policies. Non-linear and discontinuous objectives or constraints are readily accepted in tabulated form. Highly constrained problems require less work since the size of the feasible state space is reduced.

Solving a reservoir operations problem with DP requires that the overall problem be separated into a sequential decision process with stages identified in either space or time.

---

[1] Senior Consultant, Control Data Corp., Prof. Serv. Div.; Res. Assoc., Supercomputer Computations Research Inst., Florida State Univ., Tallahassee, FL 32306-4052

[2] Asst. Prof. of Civ. Engrg., Colorado State Univ., Ft. Collins, CO 80523

For a dendritic system it is both convenient and computationally advantageous to identify the stages in time, particularly if the period of record is long. Benefits for releases must be assigned separately for each time period (stage). Constraints on each stage may include upper and lower bounds on reservoir storage levels, upper and lower bounds on reservoir releases, and state equations (continuity) which link upstream reservoirs to downstream reservoirs.

MULTIDIMENSIONAL DP PROBLEMS

Real-world water resource problems typically consist of many operating variables and a highly constrained multidimensional solution state space. The difficulty in using DP to solve real-world operational problems is the so-called "curse of dimensionality" which states that the computational difficulty increases geometrically with the number of decisions at each stage (that is, the number of reservoirs at each time period for which a release is to be determined). A three reservoir system would have 27 decision points, corresponding to a state space of 27 points to be examined at each stage (Figure 1). A system of ten reservoirs would require the solution to a ten dimensional DP problem.

Multidimensional DP problems have been decomposed by several techniques including incremental DP [2], discrete differential DP [3], and successive approximations [4]. In both incremental and discrete differential DP approaches, a trial trajectory is selected and the optimal path computed through a limited set of discrete integer-valued lattice points surrounding the initial feasible trajectory of operating policies. This type of corridor approach limits the search for the optimal solution to a subdomain of the entire solution state space.[3] This in effect decomposes the large-scale multi-dimensional problem into a series of smaller one-dimensional problems limited by the size of the corridor. The method proceeds as follows:

1. An itital feasible trajectory is necessary. This may commonly be the vector of release policies for all reservoirs that results in no change in storage; i.e., releases equal inflows.

2. Improved operating policies are sought via a standard one-dimensional DP, limited to the range of policies defined by the corridor. This establishes a revised, improved trajectory of operating policies around which a new corridor is established.

3. This iterative optimization technique improves the operating policy vector for the reservoirs by successive optimizations within the moving corridor.

Computational experience with incremental DP and large systems of water reservoirs indicates that, for control problems of dimension five or higher, even these decomposition techniques require large computer memory and consume excessive execution time on strictly scalar machines[1,3].

SUPERCOMPUTERS

Supercomputers are new tools for water resources problems and offer larger memory, faster execution, and potential for dramatic speed-up of some codes through vectorization. The motivation behind vectorization on supercomputers for problems of large dimension is that with ten reservoirs there are 3^{10} or 59,049 possible combi-

DECISION POINTS AT EACH STAGE

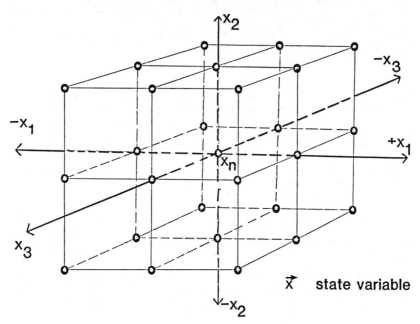

Figure 1.   Three Dimensional Problem

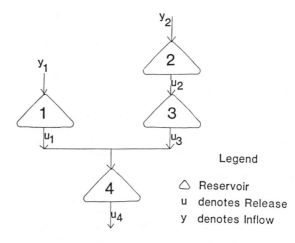

Figure 2.   Four Reservoir Problem

nations of state variables (reservoir storage) each of which must be compared with 59,049 possible combinations of control variables (reservoir release). This results in a potential total of 59049 * 59049 or almost 3.5 billion feasible reservoir simulations which must be tested for each stage (time period) for each corridor. Even assuming a relatively simple reservoir simulation model satisfying continuity only (no routing or time delay of flows between reservoirs) a considerable memory requirement and computational burden can be imposed on a scalar machine.

The CDC CYBER 205 is capable of rapidly performing calculations on contiguously stored sets of data (vectors) in special hardware units called vector pipes. An "automatic vectorizer" option is available on the compiler which converts ANSI standard FORTRAN code to vector hardware instructions. The compiler is unable, however, to redesign the numerical algorithm to make such changes as reordering and/or regrouping the calculations in order to allow the compiler to create the long vectors which can execute efficiently.

VECTORIZATION

New developments in supercomputer hardware now allow the solution of larger problems, but a re-working of numerical algorithms is necessary in order to take full advantage of the machines. Since dynamic programming is recursive over the stages, the greatest savings in computer execution time will result from vectorizing the calculations between stages. To vectorize the reservoir simulation (which is part of the inner-most FORTRAN "Do Loop" in the DP), one can write separate vector statements for both the beginning and ending states (storage levels) and the control variable (releases) for each reservoir. This effectively vectorizes all 59,049 reservoir simulation calculations. Also the feasibility check of the releases followed by the calculation of the penalty term as well as the maximization over the control variables can all be performed in vector mode. Performing these calculations in vector mode rather than scalar mode takes advantage of the special hardware and greatly reduces the overall computer cost for large problems.

The incremental DP algorithm has been implemented on the CDC CYBER 205 at Florida State University. The algorithm was modified to take advantage of the vector hardware capabilities and was initially verified, with moderate speedup, by solving the four reservoir problem shown in Figure 2. The next step is to solve an operational system of ten water reservoirs. A ten dimensional problem was presented in the literature by Murray and Yakowitz [5] and solved using a constrained differential DP algorithm, but with the assumption that the additive terms in the loss function and the law of motion had continuous second derivatives with respect to state (amount of water stored in the various reservoirs) and control (release levels for the reservoirs in the system). It is expected that the vectorized solution of the ten reservoir problem will yield considerably more relative speed-up than that of the four reservoir problem, even without the assumption of differentiability, because of the longer vectors (59,049 vs 81).

MULTITASKING

The value of multitasking is for those applications in real-time control where a quick solution is needed in order to provide lead time to activate valves, gates, or other reservoir or canal control devices. Future plans are to multitask the algorithm on the four-processor ETA-10 computer which is scheduled to become operational at

Florida State in early 1987. Multi-tasking the algorithm may yield a faster real-time
or wall-clock solution, especially for those problems with independent state equations which can be solved concurrently in the inner-most "do" loop. This can be
illustrated by the ten reservoir problem (Figure 3). The reservoirs furthest upstream
(numbers 1, 2, 3, 5, 6, and 8) could be solved concurrently on six separate processors.
The results from these six separate tasks would need to be complete prior to beginning the two separate tasks of solving reservoirs 4 and 9. Then reservoir 7 would
have to be solved prior to solving reservoir 10. Some additional computer overhead
would be necessary to ensure that the timing for completion of the individual tasks
is correct.

Evaluation of the outer loops could also be multi-tasked in a number of groups
equal to the number of independent processors available on a particular machine.
Another possibility is to use a separate processor for each of several different initial
trajectories which could be selected to increase the level of confidence in the final
solution, since incremental DP only guarantees a local rather than a global optimum.

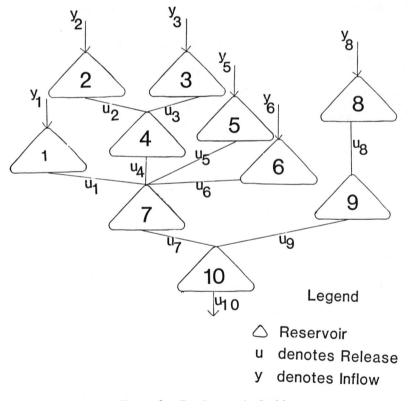

Figure 3.   Ten Reservoir Problem

SUMMARY

This paper presents tentative results from an investigation into the potential for vectorization of a multidimensional dynamic programming algorithm which can be used to solve water resource operations or allocation problems. Large-scale problems can now be more efficiently solved on supercomputers without the requirement of simplifying assumptions.

REFERENCES

1. Becker, L., W. W.-G. Yeh, D. Fults, and D. Sparks, "Operations Models For Central Valley Project." *J. Water Resour. Plann. Manage. Div. American Society of Civil Engineers*, **102(WR1)**, 101-115, 1976.

2. Hall, W.A. et al., "Optimum Firm Power Output from a Two-Reservoir System by Incremental Dynamic Programming", Cont. No. 130, Univ. of California, Los Angeles, Water Res. Ctr., Oct., 1969.

3. Heidari, M., V. Chow and P. Kokotovic, "Discrete Differential Dynamic Programming Approach to Water Resources Systems Optimization," *Water Resources Bulletin*, **Vol. 7**, No. 2, April 1971.

4. Larson, R., *State Increment Dynamic Programming*, Elsevier, New York, 1968.

5. Murray, D. and D. Yakowitz, "Constrained Differential Dynamic Programming and Its Application to Multireservoir Control", *Water Resources Research*, **Vol. 15**, 1017-1027, October 1979.

PROCEDURES IN A CHANGE OF WATER RIGHTS

Ronald K. Blatchley, F.ASCE*

The engineering required in a successful court suit to change the type, place, or time of use is varied and subject to the judgment of the professionals involved. Although state-of-the-art engineering technology is used in part to provide engineering facts for the change, many procedures must be used which may not meet rigors of a textbook procedure.

This paper is to complement the engineering-legal issues in the paper "Factual Issues in Water Rights Changes," by Leonard Rice in this same session. For clarity of this paper, it may be necessary to repeat principles stated in the Rice paper.

The procedures described herein were developed and are actively used in Colorado under the Colorado System of Appropriation. These techniques should be applicable in states that have adopted the "First in time, first in right" doctrine of appropriation.

The general procedures used in the water right analysis for a change in a water right must be applied to the historic use and then repeated for the proposed new use. After the historic and proposed use characteristics are determined, the two must be compared and analyzed to evaluate how the change affects any other water user. The applicant must show either noninjury or propose terms and conditions to be imposed to prevent injury for the changed conditions.

The required analysis includes consideration of legal-water rights impacts and administrative and physical effects. The administrative analysis includes water use practices such as how, when and where the water has been or will be used. The internal ditch or canal administration and legal structure is an important administrative issue in determining how, when and what quantity of water an individual water user has a right to when utilizing his water right. Such administrative procedures as assessment of canal losses, water run in sections, individual farm turnout measurements and cropping patterns may significantly affect the yield and should be included in the analysis.

*President, Blatchley Associates, Inc., 2525 South Wadsworth Blvd., Denver, Colorado 80227

The final step in the administrative picture is the river or stream administration of the water rights. Important questions are: How will the proposed change fit administratively into the river regime which has taken years to establish? What must be done to mitigate any injury that would result from a water right change?

Historic Use Analysis

The purpose of the water right historic use analysis is to determine the physical effects on the associate stream system which have occurred as a result of the appropriation. The analysis may involve disciplines such as soils, agronomy, agriculture, geology, hydrology, civil engineering and typically may be integrated by the water resource engineer. Each specialist must provide input to the overall analysis. Sometimes an experienced water resource engineer can wear all hats depending on the complexity of the change. Typically a pattern of depletions to the stream has occurred, requiring the following studies and/or actions:

Soils - The soils engineer should describe the ability of the soils to absorb applied irrigation water. Will the water applied infiltrate rapidly enough to saturate the root zone in accordance with the canal administration and water supply including times of brief water application and limited water supply? What is the effective depth of the root zone in the soil? What is the root zone soil moisture capacity?

Vegetation - The agronomist should describe the vegetation (crop) and how that vegetation reflects water use. The agronomist may be required to determine what effect the production of vegetation had on the consumptive use of irrigation water. By an analysis of the soil and cover, the agronomist may be able to reflect on the character of the irrigation practice and/or subirrigation. The source of subirrigation such as tail water from other irrigations, springs and alluvial water tables may be determined by others in the team described herein. The agricultural or civil engineer may provide certain special needs in the agricultural process of water use.

Geology - The hydrogeologist or hydrologist can help describe how the land forms relate to the water resources of the area involved. An understanding of how the soils were formed may give a better understanding of the soils. The hydrologist should also describe the ground water regime under the irrigated field and that portion of the subsurface hydrologic system affecting the flow of the nonconsumed portion of the historic water supply. The effect of continued subirrigation may substantially reduce the amount of water

transferable. The hydrologist must describe the ground
water flow of the deep percolation water in terms of
quantity and time distribution. The Glover Method (R.
E. Glover, April 1966) is widely accepted to analyze
the groundwater return flows. Drilling of observation
holes may be necessary to describe the ground water
aquifer. Water tables in the observation holes should
be monitored for several years to describe the effect
of irrigation on the water table aquifer. Especially
after irrigation is ceased, the ground water should be
observed to determine the nonirrigation characteristics
of the aquifer.

Area Hydrology - The hydrologist should describe and
quantify the effects of the climate on the historic
water supply and use. If climatic data are not
available locally, regional data may require adjustment
to reflect local conditions. Climatic records should
parallel the historic study period and available water
diversion records. Annual averages are not satisfactory for change proceedings, but monthly data generally
are.

Depletion Analysis - The water resource engineer is
generally the quarterback of the physical and administrative analysis because of his understanding of the
interrelationship of all the disciplines described
above. The engineer should integrate these technical
facts with the legal restraints of water rights
changes. The engineer will need to calculate, for the
study period, the effect of the diversions from the
river (either as surface or ground water or a combination of both), the applied irrigation water which
returns to the river as surface flows (called waste
water by some), the quantity of deep percolation
(beyond the crop root zone), the timing of the deep
percolation back to the river, and the consumptive use
of irrigation water applied. Estimating the time lag
of deep percolation back to the river will require
determination of transmissivity of the aquifer along
its entire pathway back to the river. A summary
equation of the depletion analysis of the historic use
of agricultural water may include:

Consumptive use of irrigation water = diversions
- canal system losses - deep percolation - surface
runoff - soil moisture.

A condition of this equation is that the consumptive
use of irrigation water cannot exceed the potential
consumptive use less effective precipitation at any
instant. This portion of the analysis is complete when

the historic use is defined within a time period sufficiently small to describe the depletive effect on the river system.

New Point of Use

The next phase of the analysis is to define how the water is proposed to be used. It is quite simple to evaluate the proposed use if it only adds additional water supply to an existing water use system, such as a municipality. It is relatively easy to define the character of use when adequate historic records of use exist. Most transfers and change of use in Colorado are from agricultural to municipal use and may involve a change to either direct flow or storage.

If the water right change is from direct flow to storage only, the consumptive use of irrigation water can be stored in the same timely fashion in which historic depletions occurred. It may be necessary to reduce the new diversion rate to protect the rights of others to the historic surface return flows. In this case, the diversion rate should be reduced to the historic depletion rate. Compensatory storage of unconsumed return flows and release of historic ground water return flows may be required in other circumstances. If the water is used on a direct flow basis, the municipality may have the opportunity to expand the use of the consumptive use of irrigation water provided it does not injure another vested water right.

In the instance of using the water right on a direct flow basis, the municipal users' characteristics must be defined, i.e., diversions, treatment and transmission losses, irrigation uses, and "in-house" uses returned to the river after treatment through a waste water treatment plant. The most difficult of the characteristics to define are the return flows from irrigation, principally lawn irrigation. Each municipality may exhibit different physical systems but the basic geologic system must be defined before the hydrologic method of analysis is chosen. The Glover Method may be appropriate in some circumstances while other circumstances may require different methods.

The analysis of balancing the historic and future or proposed depletions will determine what the terms and conditions of the transfer should be. The proposed use in most transfers must be adjusted to match the historic depletions to prevent injury to junior water rights. Any deviation from the historic depletion pattern of use may constitute an expanded use of an absolute water right which in fact should constitute a new and junior appropriation of water supplies.

General Rules and Conditions

Along the Front Range in Colorado, all easy transfers have been accomplished; only the more difficult are yet to be done. Generally, the more junior the irrigation water right, the more difficult it is to use it in a municipal system with year around water commitments. This is one of the reasons for frequent changes from direct flow to storage. This enables the municipality to utilize the water right at a more appropriate time than during the high spring runoff.

Several general rules must be followed when transferring a water right, either upstream or downstream, including the following:

· Limitations must be imposed on the transfer if the return flows may bypass a junior water right which historically diverted the return flows.

· Senior rights may be injured if the ground water return flows are not compensated during the river low flow seasons.

· Most municipal systems are more efficient than agricultural irrigation systems, requiring that some of the transferred water right be abandoned.

· Upstream transfers of water rights dependent on return flows may result in conditions imposed which would essentially abandon the entire water right.

· Points of zero flow on the river during the historic diversion season may eliminate upstream transfers.

Appendix 1 - References

Glover, R. E. "Ground Water Movement," Engineering Monograph No. 31, U. S. Department of the Interior, Bureau of Reclamation, April 1966.

Factual Issues in Water Rights Changes

Leonard Rice, F.ASCE[*]

When an appropriator of a water right desires to change the manner in which the right is exercised there are a number of factors that must be considered. These include the types of changes that are allowed, the procedures which must be followed to obtain the change, and the principles that govern the manner in which the changed water right may be exercised. The most important principle is that the exercise of the water right, after it has been changed, must not cause injury to any other water right, particularly junior water rights. The successful implementation of these principles depends heavily upon the extent and accuracy of the factual determinations that are made in support of the change.

Introduction

Under the Colorado System of Appropriation, water historically used for one purpose may be changed in the type, time and place of use and from direct flow diversion and use to storage and later use. To accomplish such a conversion, the applicant must demonstrate to the Water Court that the proposed new use and method of operation will not adversely impact the stream system or injure other vested water rights. Based on the evidence presented by both the applicant and objectors wishing to protect their rights, the Court may grant the application as filed or with certain conditions governing the future exercise of the water rights involved.

To assist the Court in evaluating applications and to inform objectors of the effect the change will have on the stream system, it is necessary to document the historic use of the water rights and define the proposed method of operation. While this is primarily an engineering task involving generally accepted procedures and analytic techniques, the results are not always (or usually) readily accepted by engineers representing objectors and state administrative officials. This is because although the procedures and techniques may be widely used and understood, their use involves areas of judgment that can lead to valid differences among qualified and experienced engineers and hydrologists.

[*]President, Leonard Rice Consulting Water Engineers, Inc., 2695 Alcott Street, Denver, Colorado 80211.

This paper discusses some of the factual issues involved
in changes of water rights and plans of augmentation and the
factors that must be considered and resolved in establishing
non-injury.

Determination of Injury

Traditionally, changes have been concerned with transfers
of the point of diversion of an irrigation right from one
place on the stream to another. As the demand for water
increases in magnitude and changes in the type of use required
occur in response to urbanization and industrial growth, the
need to convert water historically used for irrigation and
mining to other purposes, including municipal, manufacturing,
energy development and recreation, becomes more common.

Colorado law recognizes the need for flexibility in changing
water rights to maximize the beneficial use of the State's water
resources. The flexibility allowed in changing water rights
and implementing plans of augmentation is, however, limited
by the principle that injury to the rights of others must be
avoided. Injury can occur as an enlargement of use in either
time (period of diversion), quantity (greater amounts diverted
under the changed priority), or degradation of quality, by
the exercise of the changed water right as compared to its
historic use.

Once the potential for injury has been defined, terms and
conditions designed to eliminate possible injury can be
developed and incorporated in the application for the change
of water rights or plan of augmentation. These terms and
conditions become negotiable between the applicant seeking
the change and the objectors to the change and will be
included in the decree granting the change of water rights
or the plan of augmentation.

Table 1 summarizes the principal types of water right
changes encountered with examples and the corresponding
nature of potential injury and some commonly applied terms
and conditions for mitigation. In practice, a change of
water rights or plan of augmentation will most likely involve
one or more types of change and may require the imposition
of a combination of the terms and conditions listed in Table
1, plus other conditions limited only by the imagination of
the applicants and objectors.

The factual determination of potential injury and the
definition of appropriate terms and conditions should be
based on analysis of historic consumptive use under average
and dry year conditions. This includes determination of the
quantity, timing and location of return flows, the extent to
which the rights involved have historically been exercised in
priority and the degree to which junior rights have been
dependent upon the availability of return flow from the
rights to be changed or augmented. It is also necessary to

Table 1 - WATER RIGHTS CHANGES - SOURCES OF INJURY AND MITIGATING MEASURES

Type of Change/Example	Source of Injury	Terms & Conditions
1. Type of Use/Irrigation to municipal or industrial.	Extension of diversion period from seasonal to year-round.	Limit diversions to historic irrigation season.
	Elimination, reduction or alteration of return flow historically available to downstream junior appropriator.	Limit volume diverted to historic consumptive use.
		Return a portion of the water available to the changed right to the stream to maintain historic conditions.
		Abandon portion of right to stream.
2. Place of Use/Transfer point of diversion of ditch along river.	Increase in period and quantity of diversion due to greater availability of water at new or alternate point of diversion.	Limit diversions at new point of diversion to periods when water physically available and in priority at original point of diversion.
3. Time of Use/Irrigation to snowmaking.	Diversion for snowmaking is 100% depletion in fall with return in spring reduced by losses to evaporation and sublimination. Return of ground-water portion is delayed.	Provision of replacement water from other sources, such as non-tributary wells or imported water.
4. Direct flow to storage, usually accompanied by a change in type, place or time of use/Direct flow irrigation right changed to storage for municipal or industrial use.	Alteration of historic return flow available to downstream junior.	Limit amount stored to historic consumptive use.
		Require releases from storage to compensate for lost return flows.

consider the possibility that the change, if granted, will
increase the frequency of junior rights being called out by
the changed right.

Determination of Historic Consumptive Use

Historic beneficial consumptive use is the measure of a
water right and its determination is important in the appraisal
of the value of water rights and in establishing the basis for
developing terms and conditions to be imposed on water right
changes to prevent injury to other vested water rights.
Consumptive use is defined as diversions less returns, the
difference being the amount of water physically removed
(depleted) from the stream system through evapotranspiration
by irrigated crops or consumed by industrial processes,
manufacturing, power generation and municipal uses. Stream
depletions include both beneficial and non-beneficial
consumptive uses.

The determination of historic consumptive use involves
analysis of a number of factors, all of which are subject to
engineering judgment and legal interpretation. The first
factor to be established is usually the study period which is
selected to represent historic conditions. This is the
period of record to be analyzed and should be representative
of the conditions under which the water rights were exercised.
In selecting a study period, it is important that streamflow
and climatological records be available for analysis and that
the period contain at least one critically dry year. Recent
years are more likely to have better records available and
will also reflect current administrative practices. Older
periods, however, are often more representative of the extent
of past irrigation, which in recent times in many areas has
receded in the face of urbanization and other factors leading
to the decline of irrigated agriculture.

By far the most common need for determining historic
consumptive use involves an irrigation water right that is to
be changed to some other time, type or place of use. To do
this without allowing an enlarged use or causing injury to
others water rights means that both the quantity and timing
of the consumptive use under historic exercise of the right
must be determined. This involves defining the type of crops
irrigated, the diversions available under the right when in
priority and the potential and actual irrigation and consumptive
use occurring as a result of the irrigation.

The potential consumptive use is that which the crop would
consume if a full supply of water were available to meet plant
growth needs. The actual consumptive use is the amount the
plant consumed of the available irrigation water. Irrigation
consumptive use is the amount of consumptive use supplied by
irrigation water applied in addition to the natural
precipitation which is effectively available to the plant.
Irrigation consumptive use in some cases may be supplied by

natural sub-irrigation, which is generally not included in the amount of beneficial historic consumptive use available for transfer or conversion to other uses.

Figure 1 is a schematic representation of a stream and irrigation system showing the various components that must be analyzed and quantified in determining historic consumptive use.

When evaluating the historic operation of irrigation water rights it is useful to calculate the irrigation efficiency by dividing the consumptive use by the amount diverted. The result for normal flood irrigation practice will generally range between 40 to 60 percent, meaning that 60 to 40 percent of the water diverted at the stream headgate returns to the stream. Other methods of irrigation using center pivot or linear sprinklers and drip irrigation systems will have higher efficiencies on the order of 80 to 95 percent.

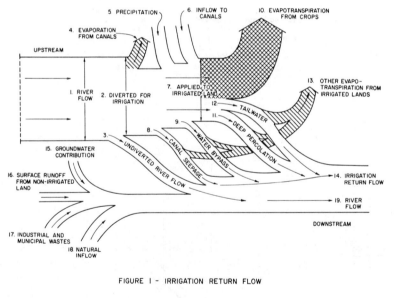

FIGURE I - IRRIGATION RETURN FLOW

LEGEND

River Inflow and Outflow

Beneficial Consumptive Use

Irrecoverable Losses

In the western United States, the most commonly used and recognized methods of computing consumptive use are the Blaney-Criddle and the Jensen-Haise formulas. The development and application of these two methods are described in detail in publications of the American Society of Civil Engineers and the Soil Conservation Service. Both methods have distinct advantages and limitations.

The problems most commonly encountered in using either method involve selection of an appropriate study period considered to represent historic conditions, the identification of the crops irrigated under historic operation and the determination of crop coefficients, all compounded by the lack of data needed for application of the method selected. The results obtained may vary significantly depending on the method of computation selected, even when identical parameters are used. This is illustrated by Figure 2.

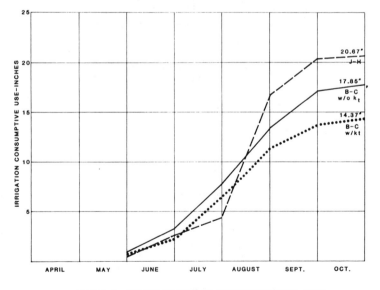

AVERAGE IRRIGATION CONSUMPTIVE USE
CORN AT CHERRY CREEK 1960-1975

TEMPERATURE AND PRECIPITATION: NOAA AT CHERRY CREEK DAM
GROWING SEASON: CORN 55° MEAN-32° FROST
                ALFALFA 50° MEAN-28° FROST
CROP COEFFICIENT: B-C TR21
                  J-H ASCE
R_s IN J-H USING S AT DENVER, R_{so} FOR LATITUDE 39 1/2°
B-C= BLANEY-CRIDDLE, TECHNICAL RELEASE NO. 21
J-H= JENSEN-HAISE, ASCE, 1973

FIGURE 2 - VARIATIONS IN CONSUMPTIVE USE

MEADOW ET IN THE BEAR RIVER BASIN OF UTAH, WYOMING AND IDAHO

by

R.W. Hill, L.N. Allen, R.D. Burman and C.E. Brockway

Abstract

Neither the SCS Blaney-Criddle or the Modified Penman ET equations can be used to predict irrigated meadow ET in the Upper Bear River Basin without calibration. A cooperative study involving Utah State University and the Universities of Idaho and Wyoming was begun in 1982 to assist the Bear River Commission in their statutory obligation of determining a duty of water under the Bear River compact. The study involved installing 7 non-weighing lysimeters in three states for the determination of meadow ET. At All study sites, climatic factors are measured by the use of Campbell Scientific CR21 automated wether stations. The study sites are located south of Evanston, Wyoming at an elevation of 7550 feet, near Randolph, Utah at an elevation of 6280 feet and near Bear Lake close to Montpelier, Idaho at an elevation of 5930 feet. The 1000 foot difference in elevation lead to marked differences in plant composition and other factors in the meadows. Most of the plants are grasses or grass like plants usually classified as sedges and rushes. In addition, many weeds and flowers also exist.

Introduction

In order to determine the duty of water on the Bear River, the Bear River Commission has contracted with Utah State University, University of Idaho and University of Wyoming to verify empirical methods used in estimating ET (evapotranspiration) in the Bear River Basin.

The Bear River Basin is located in the north east corner of Utah, the south east corner of Idaho and the south west corner of Wyoming. The Bear River Basin covers 19,330 square kilometers (7,465 square miles) of mountain and valley lands. It is composed of 5 major valleys ranging in elevation from 2,377 to 1,280 meters (7,800 to 4,200 feet). The climate in these valleys vary immensely from a growing season of about 30 frost free days in the higher valleys to over 150 days in the lowest valley. Within the basin there are about 190,280 hectares (470,000 acres) of agriculture crop land. The agriculture crops range from irrigated meadow in the higher valleys to vegetable crops in the lower valley.

A three state cooperative study sponsored by the Bear River Commission and the respective state Agricultural Experiment Stations.

Professor, Research Engineer, Ag. and Irr. Engr., Utah State Univ. Professor Ag. Engr., Univ. of Wyoming, Laramie, and Professor Ag. Engr., Univ. of Idaho, Moscow, respectively.

Objectives of Research

The main objectives of this research is to obtain the field data needed to determine crop water use in the Upper Bear River Basin and to determine which of the empirical ET equations can be best calibrated to reflect the measured water use. Although ET data has been collected on crops other than irrigated meadow, the paper deals only with meadow ET.

Procedure

In order to determine water use by crops and to calibrate empirical equations, it was necessary to build a data base of climatic and crop water use data.

Weather Stations were set up at selected sights along the Bear River in 1982; the sights are Montpelier, Idaho; Randolph, Utah and Hilliard Flat, Wyoming. The respective site elevations and north latitudes are 1806 meters (5928 feet), 42.2; 1914 meters (6280 feet), 41.75 and 2300 meters (7550 feet), 4.08. These weather stations measured daily maximum, minimum and average air and soil temperatures, precipitation, solar radiation wind speed and direction and relative minimum and maximum humidity and record the information on a Campbell Scientific CR21 Micrologger and to a cassette tape.

Seven non-weighing lysimeters were installed in the Upper Bear River area, three in Montpelier, Idaho, two at Randolph, Utah and two at Hilliard, Wyoming. The non-weighing lysimeters are one meter square (40 inches square) and 1.2 meters (4 feet) deep constructed of 4.76 mm (3/16 inch) flat steel welded to be water tight. The lysimeters were installed in meadows where the water table is quite shallow and in areas that are representative of the irrigated meadow. These lysimeters were replanted with sod removed during excavation. The sod vegetation is representative of the irrigated meadow at each of the sites and consists of mostly grass like plants usually classified as sedges and rushes.

Non-weighing lysimeters have an advantage over other methods of determining crop water in use in irrigated meadows because of the high water table. The non-weighing lysimeters prevent the water movement from the water table into the root zone of the meadow grass in the lysimeters. Without the separation of the water inside the lysimeter from the water table, it would be difficult to determine the amount of irrigation and drainage water added or removed from the root zone.

The meadow grass in the lysimeters were treated the same as the adjacent meadows. The meadows in the Upper Bear River are generally grazed until the first part of June, then they are allowed to grow until about the second week in August, at which time they are harvested for hay. The additional growth in the meadows after harvest is grazed in the fall.

During the growing season, the lysimeters were visited each week, at which time soil moisture measurements were made using a neutron probe. At each visit, measured irrigated water was added or measured drainage water was removed to maintain the water table in the lysimeter near to where it was outside the lysimeters. By measuring the soil water with a neutron probe and by keeping track of the total water added and removed from the lysimeters, it provided two methods to determine crop water use. With this information, consumptive use of the lysimeter vegetation could be measured using a simple water balance equation.

$$CU = -\Delta SW + IRR + RAIN - DRNG$$

where

CU   = Consumptive use
ΔSW   = Change in soil water
IRR   = Irrigation
RAIN = Rain
DRNG = Drainage water removed

With this information, consumptive use over a given time period can be calculated.

The weather data was used to calculate a predicted ET using the SCS Blaney-Criddle (2) and the Kimberly Modified Penman equations (1). The modified Penman equation calculations were done using the following coefficients: A = 1.22, B = -0.18, A1 = 0.325, B1 = -0.044, W1 = 0.75, W2 = 0.019 and a wind run limit of 161 kilometers/day (100 miles/day) at a height of 2 meters (78 inches).

Results

There are a couple of items to keep in mind as the results of this are studied. First, the weather patterns at the sites during 1983, 1984 and 1985 have been different each year, which has an effect on ET. For the months of April through October in 1983, the average precipitation at the three sites was 204 percent of normal, 147 percent of normal during 1984 and 104 percent of normal during 1985. From this information, it can be seen that there is only one normal growing season. Second, the lysimeters were planted during the first week of June in 1983, which made June 1983 a time for the sod to re-establish. The research will be carried on for at least two more years which will provide additional data which can be used in any conclusions that are reached.

Although weekly measurements water use were made at each lysimeter, only monthly data is presented in this paper because of the variability in the weekly data. The monthly meadow grass water use was averaged from the lysimeters at each site and is listed in Table 1. By comparing the meadow grass water use in June of 1983 with that of 1984 and 1985, it is apparent that the sod was re-establishing during the month of June and may have effected ET later into the season.

Table 1. Monthly Measured Meadow Grass Water Use From Lysimeters

		\multicolumn{8}{c}{Measured Monthly ET From Lysimeters}
		JUN		JUL		AUG		SEP	
		(MM)	(IN)	(MM)	(IN)	(MM)	(IN)	(MM)	(IN)
Montpelier	1983	42	1.65	68	2.69	113	4.44	83	3.27
ID	1984	104	4.10	163	6.42	85	3.35	39	1.55
	1985	147	5.79	162	6.38	130	5.12	38	1.48
Randolph	1983	78	3.06	139	5.49	116	4.58	89	3.50
UT	1984	107	4.21	177	6.96	95	3.75	81	3.18
	1985	179	7.06	156	6.14	135	5.30	77	3.04
Hilliard	1983	55	2.16	118	4.66	101	3.97	89	3.52
WY	1984	99	3.89	117	4.62	110	4.32	20	0.80
	1985	153	6.03	120	4.72	142	5.59	67	2.64

From the weather data, ET was calculated using the SCS TR21
Blaney-Criddle and the Modified Penman equations. This data is
presented in Table 2. By reviewing the data, it is apparent that these
equations cannot adequately predict ET without calibration. Crop
coefficients were also calculated for the various months and presented
in Table 3.

Table 2. Monthly Predicted ET Using SCS Blaney-Criddle Empirical
          Equation and Modified Penman Equation.

		\multicolumn{8}{c}{SCS Blaney-Criddle ET kc=1}
		JUN		JUL		AUG		SEP	
		(MM)	(IN)	(MM)	(IN)	(MM)	(IN)	(MM)	(IN)
Montpelier	1983	96	3.76	121	4.75	123	4.83	66	2.59
ID	1984	71	2.78	113	4.43	106	4.17	58	2.27
	1985	105	4.12	141	5.54	98	3.87	50	1.96
Randolph	1983	98	3.86	121	4.78	124	4.90	63	2.48
UT	1984	85	3.33	123	4.83	110	4.35	68	2.68
	1985	108	4.27	141	5.56	91	3.60	44	1.74
Hilliard	1983	96	3.76	121	4.75	123	4.83	66	2.59
WY	1984	71	2.78	113	4.43	106	4.17	58	2.27
	1985	88	3.45	121	4.75	99	3.89	47	1.84

		\multicolumn{8}{c}{Modified Penman ET Kc=1}
		JUN		JUL		AUG		SEP	
		(MM)	(IN)	(MM)	(IN)	(MM)	(IN)	(MM)	(IN)
Montpelier	1983	154	6.06	173	6.83	158	6.22	115	4.51
ID	1984	166	6.54	193	7.58	166	6.55	183	5.03
	1985	180	7.08	183	7.21	194	7.63	126	4.98

Table 2 continued

Randolph	1983	165	6.50	191	7.52	166	6.52	129	5.09
UT	1984	180	7.09	201	7.90	175	6.89	128	5.04
	1985	215	8.46	212	8.35	217	8.56	219	5.08
Hilliard	1983	154	6.06	170	6.70	151	5.94	124	4.88
WY	1984	166	6.53	184	7.25	169	6.65	129	5.09
	1985	192	7.56	200	7.86	198	7.80	115	4.53

Table 3. Calculated Monthly Coefficients Using the SCS Blaney-Criddle and Modified Penman Equations.

		SCS Blaney-Criddle kc				Modified Penman Kc			
		JUN	JUL	AUG	SEP	JUN	JUL	AUG	SEP
Montpelier	1983	0.44	0.57	0.92	1.26	0.27	0.39	0.71	0.73
ID	1984	1.47	1.45	0.80	0.68	0.63	0.85	0.51	0.31
	1985	1.41	1.15	1.32	0.76	0.82	0.88	0.67	0.30
Randolph	1983	0.79	1.15	0.93	1.41	0.47	0.73	0.70	0.69
UT	1984	1.26	1.44	0.86	1.19	0.59	0.88	0.54	0.63
	1985	1.65	1.10	1.47	1.75	0.83	0.74	0.62	0.60
Hilliard	1983	0.57	0.98	0.82	1.36	0.36	0.70	0.67	0.72
WY	1984	1.40	1.04	1.04	0.35	0.60	0.64	0.65	0.16
	1985	1.75	0.99	1.44	1.43	0.80	0.60	0.72	0.58

With this data, a stepwise regression analysis was run using the measured ET as the dependent or Y variable and the calculated or predicted ET independent or X variable. The results of these analyses are presented in Table 4. When all the monthly data was used in the

Table 4. Stepwise Regression Analysis of Measured ET (dependent or Y variable) with calculated or predicted ET using SCS Blaney-Criddle (kc=1) and Modified Penman ET (Kc=1) Equation.

Description			Number of observations	R (percent	
Site	Month	Years		SCS B-C	Penman
All Sites	All Months	All Years	36	39.4	63.4
All Sites	All Months	1984-85	24	60.7	76.2
All Sites	Less June 83	All Years	33	46.2	67.4
All Sites	June	All Years	9	5.3	87.2
All Sites	June	1984-85	6	78.2	83.2
All Sites	July	All Years	9	11.6	36.8
All Sites	July	1984-85	6	13.9	4.7

Table 4 Continued

All Sites	August	All Years	9	24.8	55.0
All Sites	August	1984-85	6	67.8	72.3
All Sites	September	All Years	9	13.2	7.7
All Sites	September	1984-85	6	.2	5.9
Montpelier	All Months	All Years	12	41.5	57.0
Montpelier	All Months	1984-85	8	75.0	88.2
Randolph	All Months	All Years	12	47.7	71.8
Randolph	All Months	1984-85	8	58.2	74.3
Hilliard	All Months	All Years	12	31.2	62.8
Hilliard	All Months	1984-85	8	47.2	76.2
All Sites	*Seasonal	All years	9	0.3	94.6
All Sites	*Seasonal	1984-85	6	0.6	93.5

*Seasonal May 15 - Oct 15 except for 1983 which is June 1 - Oct 15.

analysis, the Modified Penman equation does much better predicting ET than the SCS Blaney-Criddle equation. The ET equations do a better job of predicting ET when the 1983 months are not used in the analysis. The Modified Penman can be used to predict ET with much more confidence than the SCS Blaney-Criddle equation, but neither equation provides adequate predictions. The R^2 values when done by months among all the sites are very low but are better when done by sites among all the months. There could possibly be some ET measurement errors on a monthly basis that account for the poorer correlation on a monthly basis.

The seasonal (May 15 to October 15) measured meadow grass lysimeter water use data and calculated ET potential, using the SCS Blaney-Criddle and Modified Penman equations, is presented in Table 5

Table 5. Seasonal (May 15 - Oct. 15) Measured Lysimeter ET and Calculated Blaney-Criddle and Penman ET

		Lysimeter ET		Blaney-Criddle		Penman	
		(MM)	(IN)	(MM)	(IN)	(MM)	(IN)
Montpelier	1983	330	12.99	453	17.83	722	28.42
ID	1984	458	18.02	464	18.28	790	31.11
	1985	524	20.64	443	17.44	815	32.08
Randolph	1983	431	16.98	450	17.71	779	30.66
UT	1984	536	21.12	429	16.89	821	32.33
	1985	642	25.26	428	16.86	912	35.92
Hilliard	1983	376	14.82	398	15.66	713	28.07
WY	1984	415	16.33	398	15.66	775	30.51
	1985	527	20.76	399	15.70	834	32.85

*1983 Seasonal Water Use From June 1 - Oct. 15.

and Figure 1. On a seasonal basis, the ET data has less variability and comparisons can be made much easier. The measured ET and the Modified Penman calculated ET has increased each year while the SCS Blaney-Criddle calculated ET has remained almost constant. This indicates that the daily solar radiation, humidity and wind which are used in the Modified Penman equations have an effect on consumptive use. The only variable used in the SCS Blaney-Criddle equation that changes each year is the average monthly temperature. Although the weather patterns have been different, the temperatures have changed very little during this study, hence the ET potentials using the SCS Blaney-Criddle have remained almost constant. When a regression analysis is made using the seasonal measured water use and predicted water use, the SCS Blaney-Criddle equation shows no correlation. The Modified Penman equation has good correlation with an R of 94.6 percent, a t value of 11, a F value of 122 and a correlation factor of 97.2 percent.

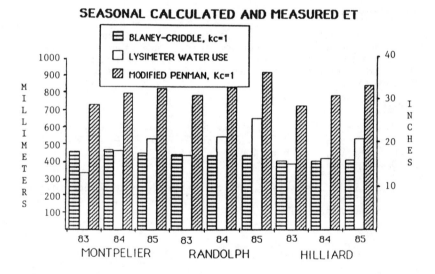

Figure 1. Seasonal (May 15 - Oct. 15) Measured Meadow Grass ET and Calculated Reference ET Potential Using the SCS Blaney-Criddle and Modified Penman Equations.

On a seasonal basis, the crop coefficient for the SCS Blaney-Criddle is 1.10 for all years and 1.21 using 1984 and 1985 data. When the SCS monthly crop coefficients from the Irrigation Water Requirement Technical Release Number 21 are used, the seasonal crop coefficient is .91, which underestimates the seasonal water use by 25 percent using the 1984 and 1985 data. The Modified Penman equation seasonal crop coefficient is .59 using all three years of data and .63 using 1984 and 1985 crop water use.

Conclusion

The results of this study show that neither the SCS Blaney-Criddle or the Modified Penman ET equation can be used to predict ET in irrigated meadows in the Upper Bear River Basin without calibration. The SCS Blaney-Criddle ET equation has poor correlation with the measured ET, and without additional data, it cannot be calibrated with any confidence. The Modified Penman equation can be calibrated to predict ET with a good correlation on a seasonal basis and moderately well on a monthly basis.

The additional two years of data planned for this study will be invaluable and will help in further calibration of the empirical ET equations.

Acknowledgements

We the authors wish to thank the following people for their assistance in the data collections: Garry Grabow, Mark Mulkay, Kelvin Andersen and Richard Humphreys. This research is supported by the Bear River Commission, which is funded equally by the states of Utah, Idaho and Wyoming.

References

1. Jensen, M.E. (Ed.), Consumptive Use of Water and Irrigation Water Requirements, Report by Technical Committee on Irrigation Water Requirements, American Society of Civil Engineers, Irrigation Drainage Division, 1974.

2. USDA, Soil Conservation Service, Irrigation Water Requirements, Engineering Division, Technical Release No. 21, U.S Government Printing Office, 1970.

MAXIMUM AND ACTUAL ET FROM GRASSES AND GRASS-LIKE PLANTS

R. D. Burman, M. ASCE, L. O. Pochop, M. ASCE*

Abstract

Two studies of mountain meadow water use were conducted along the Little Laramie River and in the Upper Green River Basin of Wyoming. Monthly and seasonal data from twelve non-weighing lysimeters are reported for 2 to 4 year periods. Water tables in the lysimeters were maintained at levels similar to the surrounding areas. During the latter portion of the growing season, water supplies often become limited and irrigation is infrequent or completely discontinued. Results show the variation in water use, from a relatively high rate in years when water supplies (thus, river flows) are high to low in years when water supplies are low and water tables are deep. A calibration of the Penman-Monteith model for the estimation of ET is given.

Introduction

A major portion of the irrigated land located in the high altitude areas of the Western U. S. is referred to as "mountain meadows." The vegetation on this land is usually harvested as hay or by grazing livestock. The vegetation may or may not represent seeded species, but almost always reflects the historical soil moisture and fertility levels (Siemer and Rumburg, 1975). The vegetation is extremely variable with many true grasses such as wheatgrass and timothy while due to high water table conditions, grass-like plants called sedges and rushes are often dominant. At other times, fertility and moisture conditions are suitable for the growth of forbs. Forbs may be common weeds, but often include plants commonly called flowers. A competent taxonomist can easily identify 20 or more species within a lysimeter of only 3.31 ft (1 m) square in surface area. It is difficult enough to estimate ET from monoculture crops while it is a formidable job to estimate ET from mountain meadows that are so variable in composition.

The irrigation of mountain meadows is also variable. Most land has not been leveled and water control structures are limited. In many cases, the water is merely spread around with an attempt being made to keep the entire soil profile in a saturated state. This kind of irrigation is known as "wild flooding." With limited water control, and often short supplies, much of the area is partially dry for at least part of the growing season.

---

*Professors, Agric. Engr. Dept., University of Wyoming, Laramie.

Irrigation water is usually removed from the fields to dry the fields for harvest or often when the natural stream flow becomes low and irrigation water right priorities are imposed. Still another reason for the removal of irrigation water is because the water right has been sold to more cost intensive downstream users such as municipalities. Any prolonged change in water or fertilizer regimes will lead to changes in vegetation type and density. However, most of the discussion here refers to modest changes in soil moisture within a season, not the profound changes found in the case of irrigation water right transfers.

The native hay or livestock grazing produced is very important to Western livestock operations although of modest monetary value. The water consumed is of very great hydrologic significance because of the area involved. Lewis (1957) estimated that there were about 14,000,000 acres (5,500,000 ha) of mountain meadows in the Western U.S.

Data Collection

Non-Weighing Lysimeter Methods. Non-weighing lysimeters are usually used to measure mountain meadow ET because of the remote locations involved, the numerous lysimeters required to study the highly variable vegetation involved and the high cost of weighing lysimeters. Simple square non-weighing lysimeters 3.28 ft (1 m) on a side and approximately 4.5 ft (1.37 m) deep were used to measure ET from mountain meadows at the two locations described later. Detailed drawings of the lysimeters appear in papers by Borrelli and Burman (1982) and Burman and Borrelli (1984). Climatic measurements were made to provide data needed for modeling. Changes in soil moisture were measured using a neutron probe. Water table depths both inside and outside the lysimeters were measured using piezometers. Water added or removed from the lysimeters was also measured. In most cases, the lysimeter water was managed so that the lysimeter water table was approximately that of the surrounding field. A water balance was used to estimate weekly ET from data collected. Details of the water balance and the method of calculation are described by Borrelli and Burman (1982).

Little Laramie River Study. A series of 9 lysimeters were located on a transect located across a typical mountain meadow approximately 23 miles west of Laramie, Wyoming and were operated during the summers of 1979 through 1981. Climatic data was measured at a central location using hygrothermographs and a cotton belt shelter. Rainfall was measured at each site using plastic rain gages. Calculations of changes of soil moisture inside each lysimeter due to fluctuations in the water table used specific yield data collected at each lysimeter (Borrelli and Burman, 1982).

Green River Study. Eight mountain meadow lysimeters were operated in the Upper Green River Basin of Wyoming during the summers of 1984 and 1985. The locations and other operational details are described by (Burman et al., 1983 and 1985, and Pochop and Burman, 1985). Climatic data was collected using Campbell-Scientific, CR-21 automated weather** stations from Campbell-Scientific in Logan, Utah. Estimates

**The use of a trade name does not imply endorsement.

of water contained in each lysimeter were more accurate because uncertainties involving specific yield were less due to more detailed measurements of the specific yield at each site. Estimates of ET were based on a water balance model as done in the Little Laramie River study.

Results and Discussion

Little Laramie River Study. The Little Laramie study was operated for four growing seasons. For three of the seasons, the winter snowpack was near normal, resulting in near normal streamflow. However, in 1981 when winter snow accumulations were low, the streamflow was only 29,900 acre feet (36.9×10^6 m^3), while streamflow during the other 3 years averaged over 81,000 acre feet (99.9×10^6 m^3) (Figure 1). Streamflow records were available from the Wyoming State Engineer's local hydrographer and represent streamflow approximately 4 miles (6.5 km) from the lysimeter sites. Summer rainfall was fairly constant throughout the period. The lysimeters were managed so that the lysimeter water tables were similar to those found in the nearby fields.

Four of the lysimeters represent conditions which are similar to those in nearby irrigated fields producing forage. Two of the fields have been leveled. Details concerning species and varieties of vegetation and management are given by (Borrelli and Burman, 1982, and Burman and Borrelli, 1984). ET measurements for the 4 years are shown in Table 1 and Figure 1. It is obvious that ET increases as available irrigation water increases. Relatively high water tables are associated with mountain meadow irrigation. When streamflow is high, water tables in the area are nearer to the surface. When streamflow is low, irrigation water is only available in the early summer. The results shown in Table 1 and Figure 1 are primarily due to an early loss of irrigation water and hence represent ET as a function of maximum ET. Figure 1 shows that ET in the irrigated areas is positively related to streamflow. In the Little Laramie River area, each additional 10,000 A.F. (12.3×10^6 m^3) of streamflow is associated with an increase of 1 in (25 mm) of additional ET.

Green River Study. Eight mountain meadow lysimeters were operated in the Upper Green River Basin of Wyoming in 1984 and 1985. Four of the eight lysimeters were managed so that water tables were maintained near the levels found in surrounding fields. This included allowing the lysimeters to dry out at the time irrigation water from surrounding fields was removed in preparation for haying operations. This treatment will be referred to as "actual."

Four of the eight lysimeters were operated so that regular weekly irrigations were applied until the end of the growing season. This is referred to as the "maximum" ET treatment. This should not be considered as being maximum in the sense all factors influencing ET were operating at a maximum level, but merely that a crop curve can be developed which relates actual ET to a reference ET, hopefully resulting in more accurate ET estimates.

The results of the paired Green River lysimeters are shown in Table 2 and in Figure 2. Seasonal and monthly data are shown in

Table 1. Seasonal ET, Little Laramie River - May 16 through September 15.

	Stream Flow ($10^6 m^3$)	TYPE OF SITE				Avg. of Four Sites
		Interm. Irrig. Saline	Irrig. Hay	Irrig. Hay & Pasture	Irrig. Pasture	
1979 ET	116	503	671	605	457	558
Rain		[135]	[140]	[147]	[135]	[140]
Water Table		(508)	(584)	(432)	(863)	(610)
1980 ET	93.3	546	485	544	485	516
Rain		[64]	[76]	[79]	[76]	[74]
Water Table		(660)	(660)	(457)	(1020)	(711)
1982 ET	91.9	358	465	579	437	460
Rain		[147]	[145]	[147]	[140]	[145]
Water Table		(584)	(660)	(559)	(711)	(635)
1981 ET	36.9	295	422	463	381	389
Rain		[178]	[160]	[163]	[168]	[168]
Water Table		(711)	(711)	(508)	(813)	(686)
ET Averages		470	541	577	460	510
ET Std. Dev.		119	109	61	43	56

ET equals rain + water added or removed + change in soil water. Rain is assumed to be 100% effective.
All ET units are mm.

Table 2. Seasonal ET for both "Actual" and "Maximum" conditions in the Green River Area, Wyoming.

	Lysimeter			Seasonal ET (mm)		Crop Resistance, 1984 (sec/m)				
No.	Location	Descrip.	Type	1984	1985	May	June	July	Aug	Sept
3A	Merna	MtnMeadow	M	600	531	89	46	105	107	774
3B	Merna	MtnMeadow	A	543	447	416	59	100	123	421
3C	HorseCr	ImprovedMdw	A	392	320	201	146	194	575	444
3D	HorseCr	MtnMeadow	M	508	401	364	150	171	225	195
3E	HorseCr	ImprovedMdw	A	422	411	259	130	177	284	669
3F	HorseCr	ImprovedMdw	M	518	533	168	141	150	252	131
4C	Daniel	MtnMeadow	M	683	541	95	77	128	146	113
4D	Daniel	MtnMeadow	A	516	444	105	82	99	224	397
Average Actual				467	406	245	104	142	301	482
Average Maximum				576	500	179	104	139	182	291
Reduction				109	94					

A means "Actual" ET
M means "Maximum" ET
Seasonal totals are from May 23 through October 18.

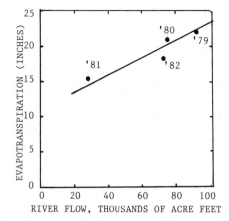

Fig. 1. Relationship between ET and summer
         stream flow in the Little Laramie River.

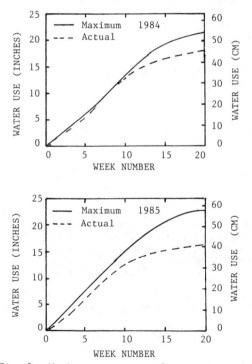

Fig. 2. Maximum versus actual mountain meadow
         accumulated water use, 1984 and 1985,
         in the Green River Basin.

Table 2, while cumulative ET data by weekly values are shown in Figure 2. In 1984, the average ET for both the maximum and actual agree very closely until week 10 which coincides with the end of July. Irrigation water had been curtailed two weeks prior to this time in the actual treatment. A distinct reduction in the rate of ET is noted as the lysimeters began to dry out. The majority of the reduction of 4.3 inches (109 mm) occurs after that time. In 1985, the water use rate in the lysimeters measuring the "actual" treatment was slightly less early in the season as well as later in the season. Siemer and Rumburg (1975) report that the vegetative composition of mountain meadows is the result of the fertility and moisture history of the field. It is quite possible that the previous year's dry conditions late in the season may have changed the vegetation from that found in 1984.

Various versions of the Penman method have been used to estimate reference crop or actual ET in many places. There is no way to introduce the resistance of a specific crop into the formula except by a calibration procedure. The Penman-Monteith extension has a term r_c representing a specific crop. As originally conceived, the term represented an individual leaf. At times, it was even applied to the resistance of an individual stomate. Since the introduction of the method in 1965, the use of the r_c has been used to numerically describe the resistance of an entire plant and to even include reductions in ET caused by limited soil moisture. If r_c values are available, the Penman-Monteith method is no more difficult to use than the Penman method. Monthly resistance values are presented in this paper for data from the Green River area.

The Penman-Monteith model (Monteith,1965) for the estimation of ET is shown below. The parameters such as R_n and Delta were calculated using methods described by (Burman and Jensen, 1974 and Burman et al., 1984).

$$ ET = \frac{\Delta(R_n-G) + \sigma C_p(e_s (T) - e)/r_a}{\Delta + \gamma (1 + (r_c/r_a))} \qquad (1) $$

Where R_n is net radiation in MJ day^{-1}, G is soil heat flow in MJ day^{-1}, σ is air density in kg m^{-3}, C_p is the specific heat capacity of air in KJ Kg^{-1} oC^{-1}, e is vapor pressure in KPa, T is temperature in oC, Δ is the slope of the saturation vapor pressure-temperature curve in KPa oC^{-1}, γ is the psychrometer constant in KPa oC^{-1}, r_a is the aerodynamic resistance in sm^{-1} and r_c is in sm^{-1} and is discussed below.

The aerodynamic resistance term may be determined by several procedures, but the function of Thom and Oliver (1977) was selected and is shown below.

$$ r_a = \frac{4.72 (\ln(2.0/Z_0))^2}{1 + 0.54U} \qquad (2) $$

where r_a is previously defined, z_0 is the roughness length in m, and U is wind velocity in m/s. The function is supposed to include a correction to reflect non-adiabatic conditions. This procedure was tested against a method of estimating r_a using the Richardson number and was found to result in only minor changes in r_a (Saad and Burman, 1983).

Results of calculations are shown in Table 2 and are intended for use with the Penman-Monteith method of estimating ET using the Thom-Oliver wind function. The r_c values are available for 1984 only. It is obvious that a large increase in r_c values occur in August and September when the lysimeters dry out.

Summary

Mountain meadow water use rates from two Basins in Wyoming show a tendency for actual water use to vary depending on available water supplies and irrigation practices. Thus, definition of historical water use must consider these factors. Estimation of maximum water use can be accomplished through use of any of the many ET models given in the literature, however, local calibration will be necessary. Methods for estimation of actual water use are not as readily apparent. One approach, investigated herein, is the Penman-Monteith model. Monthly resistance values are presented for data from the Green River Basin for 1984.

References

1. Borrelli, J. and R. D. Burman. 1982. Evapotranspiration from heterogeneous mountain meadows. Wyoming Water Resources Series No. 86, completion report to OWRT, Project A-026-Wyo. July. 31 pages mimeo.

2. Burman, R. D. and M. E. Jensen. 1974. Evaluation of estimation methods. Chapter VII in Consumptive Use of Water and Irrigation Water Requirements, a report of the Irrigation Water Requirements Committee of ASCE, New York, NY.

3. Burman, R. D., L. O. Pochop and J. Borrelli. 1983. Development of Evapotranspiration Crop Coefficients, Climatological Data and Evapotranspiration Models for the Upper Green River. Progress report to the Wyoming Water Development Commission.

4. Burman, R. D., R. H. Cuenca and Albert Weiss. 1984. Techniques for Estimating Irrigation Water Requirements, Advances in Irrigation, Vol. II. Daniel Hillel Editor, Academic Press, New York, pp, 335-394.

5. Burman, R. D. and J. R. Borrelli. 1984. Water Use Across a Mountain Meadow Valley. Proceedings 2nd Intermountain Meadow Symposium. Colorado State University Sp. Series 34, 123-131.

6. Burman, R. D., L. O. Pochop and J. Borrelli. 1985. Develop-
    ment of Evapotranspiration Crop Coefficients, Climatological
    Data and Evapotranspiration Models for the Upper Green River.
    Progress report to the Wyoming Water Development Commission.

7. Lewis, R. D. 1957. Mountain Meadow Improvement in Wyoming.
    Wyo. Agric. Exp. Station Bulletin 350.

8. Monteith, J. L. 1965. Evaporation and Environment Symp. Soc.
    Exp. Biol. pp. 205-234.

9. Pochop, L. O. and R. D. Burman. 1985. Water Requirements of
    Mountain Meadow Vegetation. Proceedings, Specialty Confer-
    ence, I & D Division, ASCE, San Antonio, TX, July 17-19.

10. Saad, A. and R. D. Burman. 1983. Evapotranspiration,
    elevation and combination theory. Winter meeting, ASAE,
    Chicago, Illinois. December 15.

11. Siemer, E. G. and C. B. Rumburg. 1975. Management Practices
    Determine Plant Species in Meadows. Colo. State Univ. Exp.
    Sta. Bull. No. 5645, 12 pgs.

12. Thom, A. S. and Oliver, H. R. 1977. On Penman's Equation for
    Estimating Regional Evaporation. Q.J.R. Meteorol. Soc.,
    103:345-357.

ACKNOWLEDGEMENTS

    Much of the research cited was sponsored in part by the Wyoming
Water Development Commission and the Water Research Center of the
University of Wyoming.

Water Requirements for Range Plant Establishment

Gary W. Frasier*

Abstract

A conceptual model was developed which describes a series of pathways or transition sequences which a seed or seedling may follow during the initial wet-dry-wet periods after planting. Associated with each pathway is an occurrence probability related to the plant's response to a wet or dry environment and the relative lengths of the initial wet and dry periods. In most instances, the most probable response pathway can be determined from the relative seedling counts at selected times during a set of short-term experiments, which include a wet-dry watering sequence and an everyday wet watering sequence. The model was validated using data collected in greenhouse and field studies evaluating seedling establishment characteristics of selected warm season range grasses. Preliminary model assessment showed that it was possible to delineate specific wet-dry watering sequences which could be critical to establishment of some warm season grass species.

Introduction

Plant establishment from seed in semiarid regions under natural rainfall regimes is difficult, because available soil moisture is favorable for seed germination and seedling establishment for only brief periods. Rainfall occurrences are highly variable, even in the 'rainy' season, and the dry periods between occurrences are usually longer than the wet periods.

Limited soil water availability during germination and seedling establishment was a factor in the survival of western wheatgrass (Agropyron smithii Rydb), alkali sacaton (Sporoblus airoides (Torr.) Torr.), galleta (Hilaria jamesii Torr.) Benth), blue grama (Bouteloua gracilis (Willd. ex. H.B.K.) Lag ex. Griffiths), mountain mahogany (Cercocarpus montanus Raf.), broom snakeweed (Gutierrezia sarothrae (Pursn) Butt. and Rusby), and mesquite (Prosopis juliflora (Sw.) DC) (Knipe 1968, 1973; Piatt 1976; Kruse 1970; Scifres and Brock 1969). A better understanding of the relationship between water availability, seed-germination and subsequent seedling-growth will improve the chances of successful plant establishment.

Germination, Seedling Emergence and Seedling Survival Model

Frasier et al. (1985) found two factors which significantly affect the number of warm season grass seedlings surviving the first wet-dry

*Research hydraulic engineer, United States Department of Agriculture, Agricultural Research Service, Aridland Watershed Management Research Unit, 2000 East Allen Road, Tucson, AZ 85719.

watering sequence following planting. These were: (1) the number of
seedlings produced in the first wet period with sufficient vigor to
survive the subsequent dry period, and (2) the number of ungerminated,
but viable, seeds which remain after the first wet-dry watering
sequence.   Frasier et al. (1984) showed how seedling emergence and
seedling survival probabilities, derived under various wet-dry watering
sequences, could be combined with estimates of the joint probability of
the lengths of the first wet and dry periods after planting to select
the optimum time for seeding.   It is hypothesized that these seed
germination, seedling emergence, and seedling survival probabilities can
be used to characterize the ability of a plant species to survive the
initial wet-dry periods following planting.

The response of a seed during the initial wet-dry watering sequence
depends, in part, upon the relative lengths of the wet and dry periods.
If the first wet period is short, the seed may not germinate, and may
survive the wet-dry period as viable seed.   If the wet period is of
sufficient duration to germinate most seeds, and is followed by a long
dry period, many, if not all, of the germinated seeds and seedlings will
die.   If the first wet period is long enough for the seedlings to
develop a root system with which the plant can survive a drought induced
quiescence, a high percentage of the plants might survive a long drought
period.

The seed and seedling responses to the wet-dry watering sequences can
be represented as possible pathways.   Possible response pathways for a
wet-dry-wet watering sequence are shown in Figure 1. Each box or circle
represents the 'state' of the seed or seedling.   The boxes indicate a
seed and the circles represent a seedling.   The transition from a seed
to seedling (germination and emergence) may occur during any of the
three moisture periods. The boxes or circles with an 'X' indicate the
seed or seedling dies before the end of the final watering sequence. The
solid lines connecting the points indicate pathways which are thought to
have the highest probability of occurrence.   The dashed lines are
pathways which are possible, but may have a low probability of
occurrence.

This approach assumes that the seeds are viable, and that any special
germination enhancement, such as scarification and ageing, has been
performed.   The durations of the 'initial wet' and 'dry' periods are
determined by the specific wet-dry watering combination under
consideration. The 'final wet' period is of sufficient duration so that
any ungerminated seed will have time to germinate and produce a viable
seedling.   The zone labeled 'wet-dry transition period' is the period
when the soil environment changes from a 'wet' to a 'dry' condition.
The length of this transition time depends upon the evaporative water
loss rate and the sensitivity of the seed or seedling to moisture.   In
most instances, the length of time during this change is not clearly
delineated.   The change from the dry period to the final wet period is
caused by the application of water, and is easily defined.

It is not expected that all seeds of a species in a given watering
sequence would follow the same pathway.   The model is concerned with
determining the pathway that the majority of the seeds might follow for
a given watering sequence.   Assuming that the indicated most probable

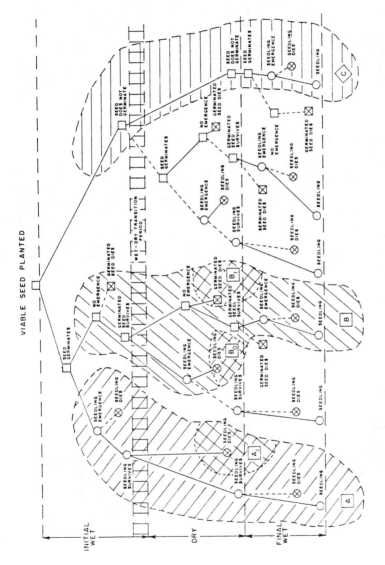

Figure 1. Possible pathways of a seed-to-seedling with an initial wet-dry watering sequence following seeding.

pathways are correct, there are 3 pathways which will result in a viable seedling (Figure 1). These pathways are: (A) In the first wet period, a seed germinates and a seedling emerges which survives the subsequent dry period; (B) the seed germinates in the first wet period, but does not produce a seedling until the final wet period; and (C) the seed does not germinate in the first wet and dry periods, but remains viable for a subsequent wet period. There are 3 pathway endings with a dead seed or seedling which have a high occurrence probability. These pathways are: (A_1) the seed germinates and produces a seedling in the initial wet period, but the seedling dies during the following dry period; (B_0) the seed germinates in the first wet period and forms a seedling which dies in the dry period; and (B_1) the seed germinates in the first wet period but dies in the dry period before producing a seedling.

To utilize this model, it is necessary to estimate transition probabilities from seedling counts at key points in time during the watering sequence. These relationships can be obtained from the seedling emergence counting process for a plant species subjected to a specific wet-dry watering sequence (Frasier et al. 1985). An example of a seedling emergence counting process for a specific wet-dry watering sequence of t_w wet days followed by a dry period of $t_d - t_w$ days where t_d is the end of the dry period as shown in Figure 2. The counting process represented by $N_{W:D}(t)$, t = 0, 1, 2,..., n, is the seedling emergence count on day(t) for a specific wet-dry watering sequence. The counting function $N_W(t)$ represents the number of seedlings on day(t) with an everyday wet watering regime. M is the number of viable seeds planted.

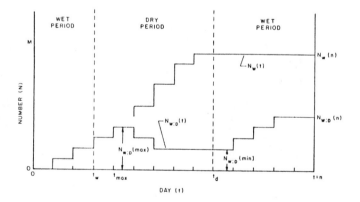

Figure 2.   Sketch of seedling emergence response counting process following planting for a given wet-dry-wet $\left(N_{W:D}(t)\right)$ watering sequence and an everyday wet $\left(N_W(t)\right)$ watering treatment

In most instances, the most probable response pathway for a species and a given watering sequence can be determined from the relative seedling counts at selected periods from a set of experiments of time t=n which include the specific wet-dry watering sequence and an everyday wet watering sequence. The specific seedling count data required are: (1) $N_{W:D}(max)$, the maximum number of emerged seedlings resulting from the first wet period, (2) $N_{W:D}(n)$, the number of live seedlings on day t=n, the end of the experiment, and (3) $N_W(n)$, the final seedling count for the simultaneous everyday wet watering regime.

With short dry periods, it may be difficult to distinguish between pathways 'B' and 'C'. A species tendency between these pathways can be separated by conducting simultaneous experiments with the same length of initial wet period t_w, but with different lengths of dry periods ($D_1 < D_2$). In pathway 'C', the final seedling counts will remain the same for the two experiments;

$$N_{W:D_1}(n) = N_{W:D_2}(n).$$ (1)

In pathway 'B', the final seedling count in the experiment with the shorter dry period (D_1) will be greater than the final seedling count with the longer dry period (D_2);

$$N_{W:D_1}(n) > N_{W:D_2}(n).$$ (2)

Model Verification

Procedure

The model has undergone preliminary evaluation with data collected from a series of greenhouse and small field plot experiments designed to examine the seedling emergence characteristics of five warm season perennial grass species with various wet-dry-wet watering sequences. The grasses used in the experiments were 'Premier' sideoats grama (Bouteloua curtipendula (Michx.) Torr.), 'Cochise' lovegrass (Eragrostis lehmanniana Nees X E. trichora Coss and Dur.), 'A-68' Lehmann lovegrass (E. lehmanniana Nees), 'Catalina' lovegrass (E. curvula var. conferta (Schrad.) Nees), and 'SDT' blue panicgrass (Panicum antidotale Retz).

Greenhouse studies: Tapered, plastic greenhouse container cones, 3.8-cm in diameter by 20-cm long, were filled with 210-g of dry 60 mesh sand. Ten cones were prepared for each grass within each watering sequence. Ten seeds were placed on the dry surface of each cone and covered with a 2-3 mm layer of dry sand. The watering sequences used in the studies were: (1) 2 days wet, 5 days dry; (2) 3 days wet, 5 days dry; (3) 5 days wet, 5 days dry; and (4) 14 days wet (everyday wet). Following the dry periods, the cones were wet everyday for a total experiment length of n=14 days. Water was applied to the cones on the predetermined wet-dry-wet watering sequence with an overhead reciprocating spray system. All cones were initially wetted to approximately field capacity with 20-g of water (10% moisture by weight). In the wet periods, cones were sprinkled daily with sufficient water to bring the average moisture content to the original 10% level. Cones in a dry-day period were covered during sprinkling. The number of live plants in each cone were counted and recorded daily.

Field studies: The study was conducted on a Laveen loam (thermic, Typic Calciorthids) on the Walnut Gulch Experimental Watershed near Tombstone, Arizona.   The study had the same watering sequences and grass species used in the greenhouse studies.   Each plot, 30.5 by 30.5 cm, was smoothed, and 100 small depressions (6-mm deep) were made 2.5-cm apart on a 10 by 10 grid.   Each plot was planted with 100 seeds of a single species, one seed in each depression, and covered with a 4-6 mm layer of soil.   Water was applied to the plots in the predetermined watering sequence with a reciprocating spray bar.   Ten to 12 mm of water was applied immediately following seeding.   The quantity of water applied on subsequent days was based on the pan evaporation loss which had occurred since the previous day or water application.   A moveable roof was used to protect the plots from precipitation.   The cover was pulled over the plots when rain was imminent, or at sundown, and removed at sunup the next morning.   Each morning, the number of live seedlings on each plot was counted and recorded.

Results and Discussion

Typical $N_{W:D}(t)$ and $N_W(t)$, counting functions of the mean daily seedling counts of Catalina lovegrass, sideoats grama and Lehmann lovegrass from 14-day greenhouse and field studies, are shown in Figures 3a, 3b, and 3c for initial wetting sequences of 2, 3 and 5 days wet, respectively.   Also shown are the 14 day wet sequences.   Figures 4a, 4b and 4c show the maximum plant count from the initial wet period ($N_{W:D}$ (max)) and the final plant count ($N_{W:D}(14)$) and ($N_W(14)$) for these same studies.   The predominant seedling emergence response pathways for the indicated wet-dry (W:D) water sequences are noted in each figure.

The probable pathway for the Catalina lovegrass (Figure 4a) is a 'C'. This is indicated by the relatively low plant count for the initial wet period ($N_{W:D}$(max)) of the wet-dry watering sequence and similar final plant counts, $N_{W:D}(14)$ and $N_W(14)$.

The sideoats grama generally followed the 'A' pathway.   This was indicated by a high initial plant count ($N_{W:D}$(max)).   In the field the final plant counts, $N_{W:D}(14)$ and $N_W(14)$ were similar.   In the greenhouse there was a decrease in plant count during the dry period, indicating an 'A_1' pathway.   The differences between the field and greenhouse studies are believed to be caused by a higher proportion of moisture loss from the sandy soil surface in the greenhouse during the dry period than from the finer textured soil surface in the field.   The species may also be susceptible to low soil moisture contents.

The most probable pathway for the Lehmann lovegrass is a combination of 'A' and 'B'.   The initial plant count, $N_{W:D}$(max), shows a significant number of seedling from the first wet period.   There are fewer seedlings at the end of the experiment with wet-dry watering sequence, $N_{W:D}(14)$, than with the everyday wet treatment, $N_W(14)$.   This indicates there were seeds which germinated but died before a seedling emerged.

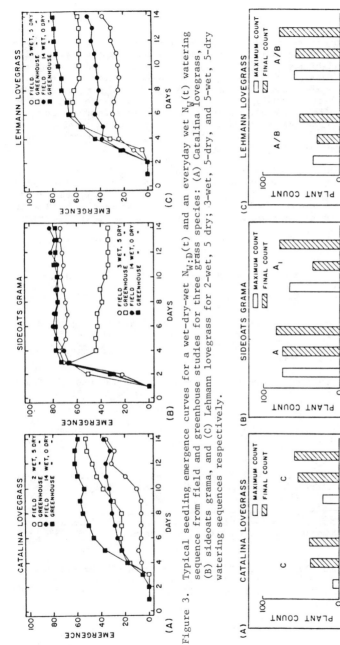

Figure 3. Typical seedling emergence curves for a wet-dry-wet $N_{W:D}(t)$ and an everyday wet $N_W(t)$ watering sequence from field and greenhouse studies for three grass species: (A) Catalina lovegrass, (B) sideoats grama, and (C) Lehmann lovegrass for 2-wet, 5 dry; 3-wet, 5-dry, and 5-wet, 5-dry watering sequences respectively.

Figure 4. Comparison of maximum initial seedling counts $N_W(max)$ and final seedling counts $N_{W:D}(14)$ and $N_W(14)$ from field and greenhouse studies for three grass species: (A) Catalina lovegrass, (B) sideoats grama, and (C) Lehmann lovegrass for 2-wet, 5-dry; 3-wet, 5-dry; and 5-wet, 5-dry watering sequences respectively.

Summary and Conclusions

This conceptual model of a seed to seedling response provides a means of comparing seedling establishment characteristics as related to water availability. Preliminary evaluation indicates that the model does describe probable pathways or responses to water availability as affected by the length of the initial wet and dry periods and differences between plant species. Similar results were obtained in greenhouse and field studies. It is believed that greenhouse data can be utilized to delineate specific combinations of initial wet-dry watering sequences, which could be critical to establishment of warm season grass species.

These studies were concerned with developing general trends. Further studies of other plant species are required to determine the full range of model applicability. It is believed that this approach can be combined with stochastic descriptions of daily weather variables to obtain estimates of the chances of successful field plantings for a given planting date.

Appendix-References

Frasier, G.W., Cox, J.R., and Woolhiser, D.A., "Emergence and Survival Response of Seven Grasses for Six Wet-Dry Sequences," Journal of Range Management, Vol. 38, No. 4, 1985, pp. 372-377.

Frasier, G.W., Woolhiser, D.A., and Cox, J.R., "Emergence and Seedling Survival of Two Warm-Season Grasses as Influenced by the Timing of Precipitation: A Greenhouse Study," Journal of Range Management, Vol. 37, No. 1, 1984, pp. 7-11.

Knipe, O.D., "Effects of Moisture Stress on Germination of Alkali Sacaton, Galleta, and Blue Grama," Journal of Range Management, Vol. 21, 1968, pp. 3-4.

Knipe, O.D., "Western Wheatgrass Germination as Related to Temperature, Light, and Moisture Stress," Journal of Range Management, Vol. 26, 1973, pp. 138-140.

Kruse, O.D., "Temperature and Moisture Stress Affect Germination of Gutierrezia Sarothrae (Broom Snakeweed)," Journal of Range Management, Vol. 23, 1970, pp.143-144.

Piatt, J.R., "Effects of Water Stress and Temperature on Germination of True Mountain Mahogany," Journal of Range Management, Vol. 29, 1976, pp. 138-140.

Scifres, C.J., and Brock, J.H., "Moisture-Temperature Interrelations in Germination and Early Seedling Development of Mesquite," Journal of Range Management, Vol. 22, 1969, pp.334-337.

PHREATOPHYTE WATER USE ESTIMATED BY EDDY-CORRELATION METHODS

H. L. Weaver[1], E. P. Weeks[1], G. S. Campbell[2],
D. I. Stannard[1] and B. D. Tanner[3]

Abstract

Water-use was estimated for three phreatophyte communities: a saltcedar community and an alkali-Sacaton grass community in New Mexico, and a greasewood rabbit-brush-saltgrass community in Colorado. These water-use estimates were calculated from eddy-correlation measurements using three different analyses, since the direct eddy-correlation measurements did not satisfy a surface energy balance. The analysis that seems to be most accurate indicated the saltcedar community used from 58 to 87 cm (23 to 34 in.) of water each year. The other two communities used about two-thirds this quantity.

Introduction

Water-use by plants is an important variable in the calculation of net aquifer recharge. Plants with roots systems that can reach the water table are termed phreatophytes, and are considered profligate in their use of water. The investigation herein designated the saltcedar study estimated water use by a phreatophyte, saltcedar (Tamarix chiniensis), on the Pecos River floodplain between Artesia and Acme, N. Mex. (Weeks et al., 1985). Water use in the same area by the vegetation that replaced saltcedar after rootplowing also was studied to help understand why the base flow of the Pecos River did not increase after the removal of saltcedar.

Another investigation, called the closed-basin study, estimated water use by phreatophytes growing in the closed-basin of the San Luis Valley in Colorado just prior to a large-scale pumping project that may lower the water table. The extent to which phreatophyte water-use may decrease as the water table declines is of particular interest.

Our water-use measurements were based on a micrometeorological method using eddy correlation. This is the most direct micrometeorological method in that it requires no assumptions about eddy diffusivity, but it requires faster-response instrumentation. The results of micrometeorological methods are accurate only to within 10 percent, at best. Gravimetric and volumetric lysimeters produce more accurate estimates of water-use, but these estimates represent water-use only from within the lysimeter tank. For diverse natural plant communities, several lysimeters would be required at a site to provide as representative estimate of water-use as is provided by micrometeorological methods. In most cases, such extensive lysimeter instrumentation is prohibitively expensive.

1/ Hydrologist, U.S. Geological Survey, MS 413, Denver, CO 80225
2/ Professor of Soils, Washington State University, Pullman, WA
3/ V. Pres. Marketing Campbell Scientific, Inc., Bx 551 Logan, UT

Theory and Instrumentation

Eddy-correlation techniques allow the direct measurement of water-vapor flux and of sensible-heat flux from a vegetation canopy. The eddy-correlation, water-vapor flux, E_{ec}, is given by the equation:

$$E_{ec} = \overline{w'q'} + \frac{\overline{q}}{\overline{T}} \, \overline{w'T'}. \qquad (1)$$

where $w' = w - \overline{w}$; $q' = q - \overline{q}$; and $T' = T - \overline{T}$. $\qquad (2)$

Here w is instantaneous vertical wind velocity; q is instantaneous water vapor density; and T is instantaneous absolute air temperature. Overbars denote averages. The first term on the right of eq. 1 represents the covariance between w and q. The second term on the right side of eq. 1 is a correction term to account for the effect of air density on measurements of w caused by a surface at a temperature different from that of the air (Webb and others, 1980). Sensible heat flux, H, is calculated from the covariance between w and T:

$$H = \rho C_p \, \overline{w'T'}. \qquad (3)$$

Here ρ is air density; C_p is the heat capacity of air at constant pressure. A correction term exists for this equation, as in eq. 1; but it is negligible (Webb and others, 1980).

The instrument used to measure w was a Campbell Scientific A 27-T sonic anemometer*. Water vapor density, q, was measured with a Campbell Scientific Lyman-α hygrometer (Tanner and others, 1985). A fine-wire thermocouple built into the sonic anemometer provided a fast-response air temperature sensor to measure T.

The water-vapor flux, E, may be converted to a latent energy flux by multiplying by the latent heat of vaporization for water, λ. The combined latent- and sensible-heat fluxes, as measured by the eddy-correlation system, should balance the surface energy budget equation:

$$H + \lambda E = R_n - G - S. \qquad (4)$$

Thus, measurement or estimation of the terms on the right side of eq. 8 provide a measure of the performance of the eddy-correlation system. Net radiation, R_n, was measured with a Fritschen (1965) net radiometer. Soil heat flux, G, was measured with either soil heat-flux plates (Tanner, 1963; Weaver and Campbell, 1985) or thermo-couples. S is the change in heat storage of the soil, air, and plant material between the location of the soil heat flux measurements and the eddy correlation instruments. The measured fluxes were integrated for 24 h in these studies: S was assumed to be zero.

During the saltcedar study, eddy-correlation instrument output was sampled at an effective rate of about 3 Hz and averaged for 5 min with a Campbell Scientific data logger, model CR-5 with special hardware modules. The same data logger also averaged the net
*Use of trade names is for identification purposes only and does not constitute endorsement by the U.S. Geological Survey.

radiometer and soil heat-flux outputs and then recorded 30-min averages of all fluxes. In the closed basin study, a Campbell Scientific 21X data logger with statistical hardware provided the same functions, except that the sampling rate for eddy correlation data was 5 Hz. The eddy-correlation instruments were mounted about 1 m (3.3 ft) above the plant canopy.

An energy-balance, Bowen-ratio instrument system (Stannard, 1986) was used in the closed basin study to provide an independent measure of water-vapor flux, E_{br}, using a rearranged surface energy balance:

$$E_{br} = \frac{R_n - G - S}{\lambda(1 + B)}.$$ (5)

The Bowen ratio, B, is:

$$B = \frac{\rho C_p \Delta T}{\lambda \Delta q},$$ (6)

where ΔT equals the average temperature difference measured across a vertical increment, and Δq equals the average vapor density difference across the same increment.

Eddy-correlation systems are subject to damage by rain, insects and birds; continuous unattended operation was not possible. Consequently, water use was measured periodically throughout the growing season to provide estimates from which water use could be estimated for the entire year. In the saltcedar study, measurements were obtained during approximately 5-d visits in June and October, 1980, and in May, June and September, 1981, and during 10-d visits in June and August, 1982. Additional measurements were attempted in August of both 1980 and 1981, but rain caused equipment failure. Data were collected using one to four eddy-correlation systems during each visit. Seven sites were sampled; four supported saltcedar, each with a different growth history; and three supported various communities of replacement vegetation. The first saltcedar site was a dry, old-growth thicket with a 3.6 m (12 ft) depth to water. The second saltcedar site, with a similar depth to water, had been mowed and had since regrown. The third saltcedar site, with a depth to water of about 2 m (6.6 ft) had been burned in 1974 and had fully recovered. A fourth was another old-growth thicket over a shallow water table 1 m (3.3 ft) deep. The first replacement vegetation site was relatively diverse, having some kochia (Kochia scoparia), alkali Sacaton grass (Sporobolus aeroides), desert seepweed (Suaeda spp.) and Russian thistle (Salsola kali) as dominant species. The second replacement-vegetation site was dominantly alkali Sacaton grass; the third replacement-vegetation site was dominantly kochia. Water table depths at all replacement-vegetation sites were about 1.5 to 2 meters (5.0 to 6.6 ft).

The closed-basin study was made in 1985 at the lysimeter site of stage 1 and 2 of the Closed Basin Project of the U.S. Bureau of Reclamation in the San Luis Valley. Continuous measurements were made during May 22-24, June 25-28, July 23-26, August 27-30, October 1-3, and November 7-8. Here the vegetation was diverse. Salt flats of about 0.5 ha (1.25 a.), on which grew saltgrass (Distichlis

stricta) and sedges (Carex spp.), were interspersed among sand
hummocks that rose about 1 m (3.3 ft) above the level of the salt
flats. Rabbit-brush (Chrysothamnus nauseosus) and greasewood
(Sarcobatus vermiculatus) were the dominant shrubs of the sand
hummocks. The water table depth varied from about 0.8 m (2.6 ft)
below the surface of the saltflats in late summer and autumn, to the
surface of the salt flats in the spring.

Results and Discussion
     The eddy-correlation measurements of water vapor and sensible-
heat fluxes generally did not satisfy the surface energy-balance.
The sum, λE_{ec} + H, usually was less than the energy available,
R_n - G, to drive these fluxes, assuming S = 0. Thus the direct
measurement of water-vapor flux is suspect as an estimate of water-
use. However, the eddy-correlation fluxes could be used with the
measured value of R_n - G to provide other estimates of water use.
     Consequently, three analyses were used to estimate water use
from eddy-correlation data. The first analysis used the direct eddy-
correlation measurement, E_{ec} (eq. 1), as a water-use estimate. The
second analysis subtracted the eddy-correlation measurement of
sensible heat, H, from the available energy to obtain water-use value
E_{re}:

$$E_{re} = \frac{R_n - G - H}{\lambda} . \tag{7}$$

The third analysis prorated the available energy into sensible and
latent heat to obtain water-use value, E_{ra}:

$$E_{ra} = \frac{R_n - G}{\lambda + \frac{H}{E_{ec}}} . \tag{8}$$

     As a matter of perspective, it is assumed in the first analysis
that the eddy-correlation, vapor-flux measurements are correct, and
that any failure to balance the energy budget results from errors in
measuring sensible heat flux and available energy, R_n - G. In the
second analysis, the eddy-correlation measured, sensible heat flux is
assumed to be correct, and all eddy-correlation errors arise from
the water-vapor flux measurements. The third analysis assumes
that eddy-correlation measurement errors for the sensible-heat and
water-vapor fluxes are proportionately distributed between the two
instruments.
     The averages of 24-h integrations of water-use values for the
various visits to the study site are shown in Tables 1 and 2. Usually
there were more sites to be sampled than available eddy-correlation
systems; the actual measurement period at each site is less than the
duration of the visit.
     E_{ec} often is only about one-half the value of E_{re}. However E_{ra}
always was intermediate between E_{ec} and E_{re}. The question of which
analysis is most reliable may have been clarified by comparison with
the results of the energy-balance, Bowen-ratio method, E_{br}. Bowen-
ratio results tend to agree best with the E_{ra} values, but were only
available in the closed basin study (Table 2).

Table 1. Average daily water use in the saltcedar study, Pecos River
floodplain, N. Mex. [The values are listed for each measurement
period by site. E_{ec} is the direct eddy correlation water use value.
E_{re} is water use determined from the surface energy balance using
eddy-correlation measurement of sensible heat, H. E_{ra} also is
determined from a surface energy balance using both H and E_{ec}. Data
from Weeks and others (1986). 1 cm = 0.39 in]

Site description	Date of measurement period	Water use (cm d^{-1})		
		E_{ec}	E_{re}	E_{ra}
Dry oldgrowth	6/25-26/80	0.12	0.19	0.13
Dry oldgrowth	10/22-23/80	.16	.18	.17
Dry oldgrowth	5/12/81	.31	.48	.41
Dry oldgrowth	6/24-25/81	.07	.12	.08
Dry oldgrowth	9/14-15/81	.40	.47	.46
Dry oldgrowth	6/24-25/82	.12	.27	.15
Dry oldgrowth	8/28-29/82	.13	.28	.18
Mowed regrowth	6/26/80	.18	--	--
Mowed regrowth	10/22-23/80	.14	.21	.17
Mowed regrowth	5/13/81	.22	.48	.35
Mowed regrowth	6/24-25/81	.35	.60	.56
Mowed regrowth	9/14-16/81	.26	.44	.38
Mowed regrowth	8/28-29/82	.22	.43	.35
Burned regrowth	6/26-27/82	.19	.41	.28
Burned regrowth	8/27-28/82	.28	.32	.30
Wet oldgrowth	6/28/82	.29	.50	.48
Wet oldgrowth	8/30-9/1/82	.22	.44	.37
Grass and forbs	6/24/80	.11	.15	.13
Grass and forbs	10/21/80	.10	.11	.10
Grass and forbs	5/11/81	.14	.29	.20
Grass and forbs	6/22-23/81	.05	.11	.06
Grass and forbs	9/16/81	.11	.22	.18
Grass and forbs	6/22-26/82	.14	.33	.22
Grass and forbs	8/24-28/82	.18	.27	.23
Grass	6/27/82	.06	.29	.10
Grass	8/30-9/1/82	.16	.31	.22
Forbs	8/31-9/1/82	.12	.29	.19

Annual estimates of water use were calculated by summing the
average daily water-use values of Tables 1 and 2 as a function of the
time of year. During the growing season, straight-line interpolation
between points was used; during the dormant season, water use was
assumed to equal 40 percent of potential evapotranspiration computed
by the Jensen-Haise method (Jensen, 1973, p. 73). An example using
E_{ra} is shown in Fig. 1. Three values for annual water use correspond
to those from the mowed saltcedar site (maximum), the dry oldgrowth
saltcedar site (minimum) and averages from all saltcedar sites
(median). The large differences between the maximum and minimum
values are the combined effects of lesser plant density at the dry
oldgrowth saltcedar site and greater depths to water.

Table 2. 1985 average daily water use in the closed basin study,
San Luis Valley, Colo. [The last column is water use estimated by
the energy-balance, Bowen-ratio method wherein available energy is
divided into latent-heat flux and sensible-heat flux in proportion to
the ratio of the vapor-density gradient to the temperature gradient.
E_{ec} is the direct, eddy-correlation, water-use value. E_{re} is water
use determined from the energy balance using eddy-correlation
measurement of sensible heat, H. E_{ra} also is determined from an
energy balance using both H and E_{ec}. 1 cm = 0.39 in.].

Date of measurement period	Water use (cm d^{-1})			
	E_{ec}	E_{re}	E_{ra}	E_{br}
5/22-5/24	0.12	0.34	0.19	0.19
6/25-6/28	.17	.44	.25	.21
7/23-7/26	.21	.33	.24	.26
8/27-8/30	.18	.25	.20	.22
10/1-10/3	.07	.08	.07	*
11/7-11/8	.07	.14	.08	*

*Freezing temperatures precluded reliable averages from energy-
balance Bowen ratio data.

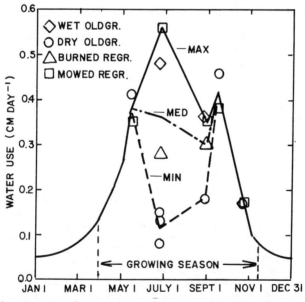

Figure 1.   Average of water-use value, E_{ra}, for saltcedar,
according to site and time of year.

Water use by replacement vegetation was more uniform. Thus
maximum, median, and minimum estimates used the same average for each
measurement period except in June. The June 1982 value at the grass
and forbs site provided the maximum annual estimate; the June 1981
value at the same site was used to define the curve of minimum annual
water use; a curve drawn through the mean of all June values gave the
median annual water use. In the closed basin study, no range of
annual water use values was computed because only one site was
monitored during one growing season.
Interpolation of periodic water use measurements as in Fig. 1
allowed annual water use projections. For saltcedar, these
projections ranged from 58 to 87 cm (23 to 34 in), depending on site,
using E_{ra} values. E_{re} values yielded a range of 77 to 107 cm (30 to
42 in). The water use by replacement vegetation varied more by time
of measurement than by site, with annual water use projected from 42
to 50 cm (16 to 20 in) from E_{ra} values, or 57 to 67 cm (22 to 26 in)
using E_{re} values. The greasewood-rabbit brush-saltgrass community in
Colorado had about the same annual water use as the replacement
vegetation in New Mexico.
These estimates of saltcedar water use are about the same as, or
less than, those from other micrometeorological studies. Gay (1980)
used Bowen-ratio methods in a saltcedar thicket, regrown from a burn,
on the Lake McMillan delta of the Pecos River floodplain. During 6
h, beginning at noon on a cloudy day in July, Gay (1980) reported
0.17 cm (0.07 in.) of water used. At the same time and place,
Fritschen et al. (1980) measured 0.23 cm (0.09 in.) of water used
during 8.5 h using eddy-correlation methods. An adjacent, oldgrowth
stand used 0.19 cm (0.07 in.) of water at the same time. During June
14-18, 1977, Gay and Fritschen (1979) reported an average of 0.74 cm
(0.29 in.), and 0.90 cm (0.35 in.) per day, for 2 locations 75 m (248
ft) apart in saltcedar near Bernardo, N.Mex., under more clear-sky
conditions, using a Bowen-ratio method. Leppanen (1981) also used
this method to obtain a 48 d average of 0.58 cm (0.23 in.) for daily
saltcedar water use, from August 17 to October 3, 1971, along the San
Carlos Reservoir in Arizona. Soil-water content was substantial,
despite a fluctuating water table level.
Micrometeorological measurements of water use by replacement
vegetation are few. Fritschen et al. (1980), using eddy-correlation
methods, and Gay (1980), using a Bowen-ratio method, indicated daily
water use of 0.3 cm (0.12 in.) in July 1979 at our forbs site. During
August 31 to September 1, 1982, we measured an average daily water
use at this site of 0.2 cm (0.08 in.) based on E_{ra} values.

Conclusions
    Water-use by three phreatophyte communities was estimated from
eddy-correlation measurements. Three different analyses were made of
the eddy-correlation data: one involving the direct, eddy-
correlation output and two involving energy balance constraints.
The analysis that used eddy-correlation measurements of both
water-vapor flux and sensible-heat flux in a surface energy balance
produced results in good agreement with energy-balance Bowen-ratio
measurements.

Within the study area of the Pecos River floodplain, saltcedar
used about 75 cm (30 in.) of water annually. The vegetation
replacing saltcedar after rootplowing uses about 2/3 as much water.
This is about the same as the annual water use by a
greasewood-rabbit-brush-saltgrass community that was studied in the
closed basin of San Luis Valley, Colorado.

Appendix A. References

Fritschen, L. J., 1965, Miniature net radiometer improvements:
    Journal Applied Meteorology, v. 2, p. 165-172.
Fritschen, L. J., Simpson, J. R., and Smith, M. O., 1980, Eddy-
    correlation measurements of evaporation from bare soil and of
    evapotranspiration from saltcedar groves in the Pecos River
    floodplain, New Mexico: Final Report to U.S. Geological Survey,
    Denver, 45 p.
Gay, L. W., 1980, Energy budget measurements of evaporation from bare
    ground and evapotranspiration from saltcedar groves in the Pecos
    River flood plain, New Mexico: Final Report to U.S. Geological
    Survey, Denver, 18 p.
Gay, L. W., and Fritschen, L. J., 1979, An energy balance budget
    analysis of water use by saltcedar: Water Resources Research,
    v. 15, p. 1589-1592.
Jensen, M. E., 1973, Consumptive use of water and irrigation water
    requirements: American Society Civil Engineers, Irrigation and
    Drainage Division, 215 p.
Leppanen, O. E., 1981, Water use by rapidly growing young saltcedar:
    U.S. Geological Survey Open-File Report 81-485, 17 p.
Stannard, D. I., 1986, Design and performance of a machine used in
    the calculation of Bowen ratios: National Water Well
    Association, Conference on Characterization and Monitoring of
    the Vadose Zone, December 1985, Proceedings, Denver, (in press).
Tanner, B. D., Tanner, M. S., Dugas, W. A., Campbell, E. C., and
    Bland, B. L., 1985, Evaluation of an operational eddy
    correlation system for evapotranspiration measurements:
    American Society Agricultural Engineers, Proceedings of the
    National Conference on Advances in Evapotranspiration, Chicago,
    p. 87-99.
Tanner, C. B., 1963, Basic instrumentation and measurements for plant
    environment and micrometeorology: Soils Bulletin no. 6,
    Department of Soil Science, College of Agriculture, University of
    Wisconsin, Madison, 216 p.
Weaver, H. L., and Campbell, G. S., 1985, Use of Peltier coolers as
    soil heat flux transducers: Soil Science Society of America
    v. 49, p. 1065-1067.
Webb, E. K., Pearman, G. I., and Leuning, R., 1980, Correction of flux
    measurements for density effects due to heat and water vapor
    transfer: Quarterly Journal of the Royal Meteorological Society,
    v. 106, p. 85-100.
Weeks, E. P., Weaver, H. L., Campbell, G. S., and Tanner, B. D., 1985,
    Water use by saltcedar and by replacement vegetation in the Pecos
    River floodplain between Acme and Artesia, New Mexico.
    U.S. Geological Survey Open-File Report 326, 107 p.

Water Use by Saltcedar in an Arid Environment

Lloyd W. Gay*

Abstract: Specialized instruments and measurement techniques developed at the University of Arizona facilitate precise estimation of evapotranspiration (ET) with the energy budget model. Use of the model is demonstrated in a study of ET from a dense stand of saltcedar (Tamarix chinensis Lour.) along the lower Colorado River. The measurements were carried out periodically with a portable, computerized Bowen ratio measurement system. Twenty-one days of good ET data were collected during two successive years on eight separate expeditions within the April to November growing season. Depth to water remained nearly constant at about 3.3 m during the study. Measured ET ranged from about 2 mm/day in the spring and fall up to 13 mm/day in midsummer. Water use at night was less than 0.6 mm/day. The ET totals for the growing season (233 days, March 23-November 11) were estimated as 1680 mm, including 42 mm of summer precipitation. Potential evapotranspiration (PET) estimates were developed from climatological data at nearby Blythe, California. PET estimates for the growing season ranged from 1160 mm with the Priestly Taylor net radiation model up to 2475 mm with the Penman model, with the Penman estimate being 113 percent greater than the smaller one. The PET estimates were converted to actual evapotranspiration (AET) with a calibration function that was developed by regressing daily totals of Bowen ratio ET against the corresponding daily totals of PET. The calibration function was then applied to each daily estimate of PET (n=233) to obtain growing season AET estimates that were within 1 percent of 1717 mm. The results demonstrate that excellent estimates of ET from well-watered vegetation can be obtained using climatological data if PET models are first calibrated against a relatively small set of Bowen ratio ET measurements.

Introduction

Phreatophytes transpire millions of acre feet of ground water from floodplains and water-course areas of the western United States each year. The water needs of arid states such as Arizona dictate that the available supplies be used in the most beneficial manner possible. Management programs in riparian communities might augment water supplies in the major rivers, thus reducing the need for groundwater pumpage. It is therefore surprising to find that many important questions are still unanswered. What, for example, are the water losses or savings associated with maintenance or removal of different species of phreatophytes? The research described here provides a method for obtaining results needed for future management decisions.

* Professor of Watershed Management, School of Renewable Natural Resources, University of Arizona, Tucson AZ 85716.

The difficulties in measuring ET have restricted the number of
suitable data that are available. The most widely used measurement
methods are based upon the water budget. This is a rather insensitive
method, however, because of problems in measuring changes in soil
moisture. This becomes especially difficult when plant roots reach the
water table, as in most stands of phreatophytes. With the recent
advent of microcomputers, the most promising method for measuring ET
now appears to be the Bowen ratio energy budget analysis.

This paper discusses Bowen ratio ET results from phreatophytes, and
demonstrates a new technique for extending ET measurements with the aid
of routine climatic data.

The Bowen Ratio Energy Budget Method

The Bowen ratio energy budget (Bowen, 1926) method has evolved
during the past decade from an experimental technique into a means for
operational measurements of ET. It is well known and described in many
texts, so details need not be repeated here. Webb (1965) thoroughly
reviews the theory of the method; Gay (1985a), Spittlehouse and Black
(1980) and Tanner (1960) discuss field applications.

The major energy flows at many evaporating surfaces are more
conveniently measured than are the flows of water and vapor. These
flows include net radiation (Q), change in stored energy in soil and
vegetation (G), sensible heat exchange between the surface and the air
(H), and latent heat which is used to evaporate water (LE). The Bowen
ratio model uses the ratio of the gradients in air temperature and
vapor concentration (dT/dZ, de/dZ) to partition available energy (Q+G)
into LE and H. Both gradients are measured in the air layer just over
the canopy over the same elevation difference dZ, which is typically
0.5 to 1.0 m. The gradients are typically rather small, so a high
degree of measurement precision is required for their evaluation.

Field Equipment

The energy budget measurement system used in this study is described
by Gay (1979). This system was generator powered; an upgraded version
using battery powered microcomputers and data systems has much greater
mobility (Gay and Greenberg, 1985). The field equipment includes a set
of specialized sensors, a data acquisition system and a microcomputer.

The key sensors in the Bowen ratio system are the unique
psychrometers which combine together a ceramic wetbulb element, high
output resistance thermometers and a new signal circuit to yield
exceptionally precise measurements of temperature and humidity (Hartman
and Gay, 1981). The psychrometers are used in pairs to measure the
vertical gradients of temperature and vapor concentration. The
excellent performance of the psychrometers is enhanced for gradient
measurements by an unusual exchange mechanism which interchanges
the pair of psychrometers between readings to eliminate small biases
that may exist between sensors (Gay and Fritschen, 1979).

The system uses recent advances in microcomputer technology. Data
is sampled with a high quality digital data system and is transmitted

to a microcomputer that transforms, analyzes and stores the data, and prints the results. The ET analysis is completed every 12 minutes and these values are combined to yield hourly and daily totals of ET. In this study, the system was operated with two separate sets of energy budget sensors simultaneously, and their agreement was monitored to insure proper operation. The generally accepted precision of water budget ET or energy budget ET measured elsewhere is about 15 or 20 percent. This system, however, could detect differences in the ET rates from two adjacent irrigated fields of as little as 0.5 percent (Osmolski and Gay, 1983).

Energy Budget Measurements

Details of the measurements have been given elsewhere , and the results summarized by Gay (1985b). The saltcedar study area was on the Cibola National Wildlife Refuge in the floodplain of the Colorado River, about 50 kilometers south of Blythe, CA. The elevation of the site was about 90 m. High water tables, dense vegetation, intense heat and low humidities combine to produce exceptionally high ET rates throughout this region.

The Bowen ratio measurements were made near the western edge of a vast saltcedar thicket of some 10 square kilometers in area. Fetch to the edge of the desert was about 1 kilometer to the west and north, and about 2 kilometers to the east and south. The floodplain soils were sandy and deep. The river flow was stable, and water table depth remained relatively constant at about 3.3 m during the measurements.

Bowen ratio ET measurements were obtained for periods of 2-4 days duration on each of 8 separate expeditions during the growing seasons of 1980 and 1981. Good data were obtained for 21 days (daytime periods of positive net radiation) and for 11 nights. The daytime water use ranged from about 2 mm/day in spring and fall, up to nearly 13 mm/day in midsummer. The ET rates at night were quite low, ranging from as little as 0.08 mm/day up to about 0.6 mm/day in midsummer. Night data were interpolated as needed to obtain 21 sets of 24-hour ET totals over the growing season. The mean daily ET totals for each expedition are summarized in Table 1.

The spring greenup and the fall dormancy dates were set at March 23 and November 11 after inspection of the sites and examination of the trends shown in Table 1. Integration of the data in Table 1 yields an estimate of saltcedar ET over the 233 day growing season of 1637 mm (1548 mm during daytime, and 89 mm at night). It is reasonable to assume that all of the scant precipitation at this site evaporates (42 mm during the growing season, and 90 mm for the year, based upon mean precipitation data from Ehrenberg, AZ, adjacent to Blythe and 50 km north of the measurement site). The mean saltcedar ET at this site is thus approximately 1680 mm for the growing season, and 1725 mm for the year.

----
1. Gay, L. W. 1984. The effects of vegetation conversion upon water use by riparian plant communities. USDI Proj. Compl. Rep. B-084-ARIZ. SRNR, University of Arizona, Tucson, AZ 85721.

Table 1. Mean daily ET totals (in mm). Means are for two masts
and for dates shown (Gay and Hartman, 1982).

day of yr	dates	day	night	24-hour
96	Apr 6,7	- 2.8	-0.1	- 2.9
118	Apr 28, 29	- 6.8	-0.3	- 7.1
149	May 28, 29, 30	- 8.2	-0.4	- 8.6
178	Jun 26, 27, 28	-10.5	-0.5	-11.0
210	Jul 28, 29	- 9.0	-0.6	- 9.6
229	Aug 15, 16, 17	- 8.4	-0.6	- 9.0
255	Sep 12, 13	- 6.9	-0.5	- 7.4
305	Oct 30-Nov 2	- 1.8	-0.1	- 1.9

Potential Evapotranspiration Estimates

Many scientists have worked on the problem of predicting potential
evapotranspiration (PET) from climatic data for use in estimating ET
from well-watered vegetation, such as phreatophyte stands or irrigated
crops. The methods that have evolved differ widely in complexity and
in consistency of PET estimates. The divergence between the various
prediction models increases in the extreme climatic conditions found in
arid and semi-arid zones. This section describes the results obtained
by application of a simple net radiation model and the more complex
Penman model to climatic data obtained from the FAA at the Blythe
Municipal Airport, approximately 50 km north of the saltcedar site.

The net radiation model (Priestly and Taylor, 1975) uses available
energy as the primary factor for predicting PET. Net radiation (Q) is
used as an estimate of available energy under the assumption that soil
heat flux (G) is small at any time, and negligible over a 24-hour
period. The model is:

$$PET \ (cm/day) = K*W*Q/L \qquad (1)$$

where K is an empirical constant (K=1.26), L is latent energy of
vaporization and W is a temperature dependent, dimensionless weighting
factor. $W = s/(s+g)$ where s is the slope of the saturation vapor
pressure curve at air temperature T , and g is the psychrometric
constant which varies with atmospheric pressure P (g=AP). The model
requires measurement or estimate of daily totals of net radiation and
mean daily air temperature. Calibration appears a necessity for this
simple model.

In comparison with the empirical net radiation model, the
fundamental basis of the more complex Penman model (Penman, 1948) gives
it some generality in application over a wide range of conditions.
There is a general concensus that the Penman model will provide a
reasonable estimate of PET when the needed climatic variables are
available (temperature, radiation, wind and humidity). The
applications here use Doorenbos and Pruitt's (1975) rearrangement of
the Penman equation

$$PET \ (cm/day) = W(Q+G)/L + (1-W)f(U)(es-e) \qquad (2)$$

where W, Q, G, and L are defined above, es-ea is the vapor pressure deficit of the atmosphere at 2 m height and f(U) is a wind function that approximates the diffusivity of the atmosphere near the surface. The wind function depends upon the units specified for the variables, as well as upon the length of the time period over which estimates are being made. Doorenbos and Pruitt (1975) used f(U) = 0.027(1+U/100) with U being in km/day at 2 m height and f(U) in cm/day/mb. Net radiation values were not measured directly at the FAA climatic station, so they were estimated from other climatic observations, using proceedures of Doorenbos and Pruitt (1975).

The two-year mean (1980, 1981) PET estimates from the two models are summarized in Table 2 for the growing season, based upon mean daily data from the FAA station at Blythe Municipal Airport. The climatological estimates of PET differ substantially. The Penman PET total (2475 mm) is 113 perecent larger than the Priestly Taylor total (1160 mm).

Table 2. ET estimates from climatic models (totals for the indicated period, in mm). PET columns are model predictions (Priestly-Taylor or Penman); AET columns have been adjusted by a calibration function. Data are means of 1980 and 1981.

period	day of yr	PET		AET	
		P-T	PM	P-T	PM
Mar 23-31	86	24	54	9	9
April	105	142	292	168	164
May	136	174	349	271	264
June	166	186	418	293	315
July	197	204	429	342	324
August	228	183	389	290	295
September	258	133	276	220	218
October	288	84	202	106	128
Nov 1-11	310	30	66	9	9
GROWING SEASON ET (mm):		1160	2475	1708	1726

Estimating Actual Evapotranspiration

The Bowen ratio ET data were used to calibrate the PET models to obtain a estimate of actual evaportranspiration (AET). The success of such an approach will depend upon the applicability of the function selected and upon the availability of data. It is assumed that the saltcedar stand is freely supplied with water so that variability between days results from differences in weather, rather than water stress. Further, the weather at the climatic station must represent that at the measurement site. The second assumption was probably not completely satisfied, since the FAA weather station was about 50 km north of the saltcedar site. Ideally, climatic data would have been collected with a remote weather station sited close to the ET measurement site.

The daily totals of PET were regressed against the Bowen ratio ET totals for those days with ET totals available. The best results were obtained with a 4th-order polynomial. After examination of the preliminary analyses, 3 of the 21 days were excluded, and the regression run with n=18. The function coefficients are tabulated in Table 3 along with the r-square and mean square error values. The r-square values of 0.88 and 0.92 for the Priestly Taylor and the Penman models are quite good, with mean square errors being 1.8 and 1.5. The function shapes are similar for both PET models: AET rises with leaf burst in the spring, plateaus in the late spring, and then increases sharply in the early summer as the demand for water intensifies.

Table 3. Regression analysis of the 4th order calibrating function. The model is Y = a + bX + cX**2 + dX**3 + eX**4, where Y is measured daily Bowen ratio ET, and X is estimated PET.   FAA data, Blythe.

model	regression coefficients					estimators	
	a	b	c	d	e	r-sq	MSE
Net rad.	23.86	-28.93	12.721	-2.1451	0.1266	0.88	1.80
Penman	41.57	-23.44	4.700	-0.3728	0.0104	0.92	1.46

The functions demonstrated unexpected instability when applied to daily climatological data. It became apparent that the 18 measurement days contained neither the maximum nor the minimum ET values that occured at the saltcedar measurement site. Large and erroneous vaues were generated when the 4th-order polynomials were extrapolated beyond the range of the observed data, particularly by low PET values that fell below the inflection point at about 2 mm/day. This problem was eliminated by restricting the function to the domain defined by the 18 days of PET (x) and ET (y). Values of PET that fell below this domain were handled by forcing predicted AET through zero, and high values were handled by linear interpolation of predicted AET to an assumed maximum of 14 mm/day. The largest measured ET was 12.8 mm/day.

Table 2 also summarizes the results of applying the calibration function to the climatological data for the growing season for 1980 and 1981. The calibrated AET totals became 1708 and 1726 mm. The Penman AET estimate is now only 1 percent greater than that of Priestly Taylor, instead of 113 percent greater as in the uncalibrated estimate. These values compare with 1677 mm estimated from the Bowen ratio measurements. The calibration function has removed most of the variability between methods, and also forced the seasonal totals to conform to measured Bowen ratio ET.

Conclusions

The Bowen ratio energy budget model appears to be an excellent method for evaluating the water use of phreatophyte stands. Measurements at approximately monthly intervals over a dense stand of phreatophytes on the floodplain of the lower Colorado River yielded an estimate of growing season ET of 1677 mm. The major difficulties experienced at this site were generally associated with the operation of the portable generator. However, the Bowen ratio method does require careful attention, and a considerable amount of data handling and processing, even though the measurements are obtained with a microcomputer.

This study showed that two common models used to estimate potential evapotranspiration performed poorly in the warm, arid conditions of southwestern Arizona. However, PET estimates can be transformed into estimates of actual evapotranspiration from well-watered vegetation by calibration against measured ET. The somewhat tedious and laborious Bowen ratio ET measurements can be extended over longer periods if local climatological data are available. Only a relatively small set of ET measurements appear necessary for the development of a calibration function. Once calibrated, the simple net radiation model performed as well as the more complex Penman model.

The improved methods described here for applying the energy budget to field estimates of ET have evolved from advances in data acquisition and processing. The basic techniques are similar to those used about 25 years ago by Tanner (1960). However, improved technology now makes it possible to visualize application of the energy budget method to problems of water management on an operational, rather than an experimental, basis.

Literature Cited

Bowen, I. S. 1926. The ratio of heat losses by conduction and evaporation from any water surfaces. Phys. Rev. 27:779-787.

Doorenbos, J., and W. O. Pruitt. 1975. Guidelines for predicting crop water requirements. Irrigation and Drainage Paper 24. 179 pp. FAO, Rome.

Gay, L. W. 1979. A simple system for real-time processing of energy budget data. Proceedings, WMO Symposium on Forest Meteorology, Ottawa. Pp. 81-83. WMO No. 527, Geneva.

Gay, L. W. 1985a. Bowen ratio estimates of wildland evapotranspiration. WMO Casebook on Operational Assessment of Areal Evaporation. Case Study No. 13, pp. 159-169. WMO No. 635, WMO, Geneva.

Gay, L. W. 1985b. Evapotranspiration from saltcedar along the lower Colorado River. Proc., 1st NA Riparian Conf., pp. 171-174. Gen. Tech. Rep. RM-120, USDA Forest Service, Rocky Mtn. Forest & Range Expt. Sta., Fort Collins, CO.

Gay, L. W., and L. J. Fritschen. 1979. An exchange system for precise measurements of temperature and humidity gradients in the air near the ground. Hydrol., Water Resources Ariz. and Southwest 9:37-42. Ariz. WRRC, Tucson.

Gay, L. W., and R. J. Greenberg. 1985. The AZET battery-powered Bowen ratio system. Proc., 17th Conf. Agric., Forest Meteor., pp. 181-182. Amer. Meteor. Soc., Boston.

Gay, L. W., and R. K. Hartman. 1982. ET measurements over riparian saltcedar on the Colorado River. Hydrol., Water Resources Ariz. and Southwest 12:9-15. Ariz. WRRC, Tucson.

Hartman, R. K., and L. W. Gay. 1981. Improvements in the design and calibration of temperature measurement systems. Proc., 15th Conf. Agric., Forest Meteor., pp. 150-151. Amer. Meteor. Soc., Boston.

Osmolski, Z., and L. W. Gay. 1983. Comparison of Bowen ratio estimates from two sets of sensors. Proc., 16th Conf. Agric., Forest Meteor., pp. 77-78. Amer. Meteor. Soc., Boston.

Penman, H. L. 1948. Natural evaporation from open water, soil and grass. Proc. Royal Soc. (London) Ser. A. 193:120-145.

Priestly, C. H. B., and R. J. Taylor. 1975. On the assessment of surface heat flux and evaporation using large-scale parameters. Monthly Wea. Review 100:81-92.

Spittlehouse, D. L., and T. A. Black. 1980. Evaluation of the Bowen ratio/energy balance method for determining forest evapotranspiration. Atmos. Ocean 18:98-116.

Tanner, C. B. 1960. Energy balance approach to evapotranspiration from crops. Soil Sci. Soc. Amer. Proc. 24:1-9.

Webb, E. K. 1965. Aerial microclimate. In: Waggoner, P. (Ed.), **Agricultural Meteorology**. Meteor. Monogr. 6:27-58.

Acknowledgements: The work reported here was supported in part by the Arizona Agricultural Experiment Station, and in part by federal funds provided by the U S Department of the Interior, as Authorized under the Water Research and Development Act of 1978 (P L 95-467). Approved for publication as Paper No. 579, Arizona Agricultural Experiment Station.

SEDIMENTATION PROBLEMS OF THE
CALIFORNIA AQUEDUCT

Jeanine Jones,* A.M. ASCE

ABSTRACT: The California Aqueduct crosses the alluvial fans
of many intermittent streams on the west side of the San
Joaquin Valley. At two sites where watershed sediment
yields were underestimated, sedimentation problems have been
experienced including: loss of floodwater storage capacity
due to sediment deposition, water quality concerns arising
from asbestos in the sediment, and the need to dredge
material from the aqueduct. These problems could have been
avoided during aqueduct design if geomorphic processes
occurring in the watersheds had been considered.

INTRODUCTION AND SETTING

The California Aqueduct was built in the late 1960's to link
northern California water supplies with agricultural and urban demands
in the southern part of the state. Part of the aqueduct's San Joaquin
Valley reach is located on gently sloping alluvial fan deposits
derived from the adjacent foothills of the Coast Range, and crosses
ephemeral streams draining the range's eastern flanks. Construction
of the aqueduct across the fan deposits blocked prior drainage
patterns; in some cases provisions were made to accept runoff from the
foothills into the canal. Excessive sedimentation in and adjacent to
the aqueduct has subsequently occurred. Problems experienced at two
of the most impacted sites, the Arroyo Pasajero and Cantua Creek
watersheds, are described below.

Figure 1 shows the location of the two drainage areas in western
Fresno County, near the City of Coalinga. The Arroyo Pasajero has
four main tributaries--Los Gatos Creek, Warthan Creek, Jacalitos
Creek, and Zapato-Chino Creek--which together drain an area of some
513 mi^2 (1330 km^2) to the east of the aqueduct. The watershed's chief
features are the hilly uplands of the Coast Range, the Pleasant Valley
trough on the edge of the Coast Range above the San Joaquin Valley
floor, and the alluvial fans of the valley floor. The Cantua Creek
watershed located immediately to the north covers an area of 55 mi^2
(143 km^2). This watershed is marked by an abrupt transition from the
hilly uplands to the alluvial fan deposits of the valley floor. Both
watersheds range in elevation from 5000 ft (1525 m) along the Coast
Range ridges to 300 ft (91 m) at the aqueduct.

*Senior Waste Management Engineer, California Department of Health
Services, 4250 Power Inn Road, Sacramento, CA 95826

The regional climate is semi-arid, with temperatures ranging from 32°F (0°C) in the winter to over 100°F (38°C) in the summer. Precipitation occurs mainly from December to March; average annual values range from 20 in (51 cm) at the highest elevations to 6 in (15 cm) on the valley floor.

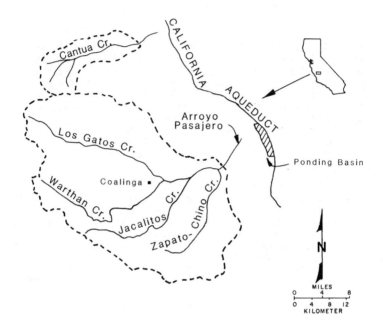

Figure 1.   Watershed Location

Geology.- Marine sedimentary deposits ranging in age from Jurassic to Tertiary dominate the upper watersheds.   Erodible shales are prominent features of the Warthan and Cantua drainages; a mixture of sandstones, siltstones, and shales cover the remainder of the area. An ultramafic mass covering some 48 mi^2 (125 km^2) has been intruded along the crests of ridges in the Los Gatos and Cantua Creek drainages.   The predominantly serpentinite intrusion is a highly sheared and pulverized mass of powdery asbestiform material.   The lower watershed consists of Quarternary sedimentary deposits, generally non-marine, including the alluvial fans which coalesce to form a piedmont along the edge of the San Joaquin Valley.   The fan deposits extend some 20 mi (32 km) eastward from the foothills, at an average east-west cross slope of 1 to 2%.

Both shallow and deep subsidence are commonly encountered on these alluvial fans, the former caused by application of irrigation water to loose, unconsolidated surficial soils, and the latter by compaction of the confined aquifer underlying the valley. Some 20 ft (6.1 m) of subsidence have occurred on these fans over the past 50 years (Ireland et al., 1982). Post-construction subsidence along the aqueduct's alignment across the fans has averaged about 4 ft (1.2 m).

Mud and debris flows were mapped on both the arroyo's and the creek's fans prior to agricultural development of the area. One mudflow on the Cantua Creek fan was estimated to extend 3 mi (4.8 km) in length (Bull, 1964), while another on the same fan was reported to contain an estimated 34 ac-ft (43,000 m³) of sediment (5). Bull noted that deposition on the subsiding fans was normally caused by mudflows, or by viscous flows of sediment-laden water, rather than by the transport of suspended solids in water. The relatively high clay content of both fans was another factor favoring the formation of mudflows.

Hydrology.- Original hydrology developed for aqueduct design was based on 20 years of streamflow records available for upper Los Gatos Creek in the Arroyo Pasajero watershed, and 7 years of records for the Cantua Creek watershed. The largest historic flood occurred one year after aqueduct construction, yielding a runoff volume equaling that originally estimated for the 100-year event. The maximum runoff measured to date at the aqueduct has been a 3-day volume of 24,000 ac-ft (29,607,000 m³) at Arroyo Pasajero, and 2,000 ac-ft (2,467,000 m³) at Cantua Creek. The estimated peak discharges for these events were 29,000 cfs (830 m³/sec) and 3,400 cfs (96 m³/sec), respectively.

Subsequent hydrologic reanalysis at Arroyo Pasajero yielded a revised 100-year, 5-day runoff volume of 56,000 ac-ft (69,083,000 m³), a value two to three times that which had been used in aqueduct design. Reanalysis of the Cantua Creek watershed has not yet been completed.

CROSS-DRAINAGE DESIGN

Arroyo Pasajero floodwaters were accommodated by providing a 6 mi (9.6 km) long ponding basin covering 2000 ac (8 km²) on the upslope side of the canal. A training dike directed flows into the basin, where they were confined by embankments on three sides, and on the fourth side by the natural slope of the alluvial fan. The basin was sized to contain runoff from the design flood along with 50 years of sediment deposition. Drainage of the basin was to be accomplished either by evaporation/percolation, or by releasing the floodwaters into the aqueduct through a set of gated drain inlets having a combined maximum capacity of 3400 cfs (96 m³/sec). A similar basin was provided at the aqueduct's crossing of the Cantua Creek fan. Floodwaters there were to enter the canal through an ungated inlet having a maximum capacity of 1,000 cfs (28 m³/sec). All water in the basin was to be handled by uncontrolled drainage into the canal.

PREDICTED AND OBSERVED SEDIMENTATION

Original design estimates of average annual sediment yields at the
aqueduct were 115 ac-ft/yr (141,900 m^3/yr) at Arroyo Pasajero and
8 ac-ft/yr (9,900 m^3/yr) at Cantua Creek. The Arroyo Pasajero
deposited an estimated 87 ac-ft (107,000 m^3) of sediment in the
aqueduct during the first major flood season one year after the
completion of canal construction. Another 5,145 ac-ft (6,347,000 m^3)
of material were deposited in the adjacent ponding basin, reducing its
capacity by 30% in a single season. Cantua Creek brought some 97
ac-ft (119,700 m^3) of sediment into the canal during the same time
period, completely filling the canal prism at the drain inlet.
Approximately 509 ac-ft (627,900 m^3) of sediment were concurrently
deposited in the creek's ponding basin, forcing the subsequent
abandonment of the basin and its drain inlet.

Surveys of the Arroyo Pasajero basin indicate that its average
annual sediment yield has been approximately 530 ac-ft/yr (653,800
m^3/yr), or over four times the predicted yield. At Cantua Creek, a
new ponding basin with a flume drain inlet over the top of the canal
lining was constructed roughly 1 mi (1.6 km) south of the abandoned
basin. Average annual sediment yield at the new basin has been some
150 ac-ft/yr (185,000 m^3/yr), or about nineteen times the predicted
value.

Sediment Sources.- Original studies at Arroyo Pasajero indicated
that 85% of the total sediment yield at the canal, or 98 ac-ft/yr
(120,900 m^3/yr), would be derived from the upper watershed above
Pleasant Valley. Subsequent studies indicated that only 40% of the
revised total yield, or 210 ac-ft/yr (259,000 m^3/yr), came from the
upper watershed (Munn, 1981). Over half of this upland sediment
production is generated by highly erodible shales in the Warthan Creek
drainage. Other major contributors are the serpentinite intrusion
area of upper Los Gatos Creek and the headwaters of Jacalitos Creek.

Channel erosion is the chief sediment source in Pleasant Valley and
on the alluvial fan. The lower watershed is estimated to yield the
remaining 60%, or 320 ac-ft/yr (394,800 m^3/yr), of the sediment
deposited at the canal. Original estimates assumed that only 80
ac-ft/yr (98,700 m^3/yr) of sediment would be derived from this area.
Channel degradation is a significant sediment source in the lower
watershed; Figure 2 shows the magnitude of channel downcutting which
has been experienced in this area. The date at which the current
degradation cycle began is unknown, but some 5 ft (1.5 m) of
degradation have been reported over the last 30 years (Munn, 1981).
Downcutting of the streambed causes bank caving, which provides
fine-grained alluvium for subsequent transport. Studies indicate that
bank erosion in the lower watershed yields about twice the volume of
material produced by bed erosion alone (Simons et al., 1985).

Detailed sedimentation studies have not yet been performed for the
Cantua Creek watershed. It appears that much of the creek's sediment
yield is also derived from channel erosion on the alluvial fan. The
high sediment-to-water ratio observed in the material entering the

ponding basin suggests that the viscous flow transport mechanism identified by Bull (Bull, 1964) prior to aqueduct construction is still occurring.

Figure 2. Channel Downcutting in Alluvium

CONSEQUENCES OF SEDIMENTATION

Sedimentation has reduced the floodwater storage capacity of the Arroyo Pasajero ponding basin by 65%. The aqueduct is now protected against overtopping only for flood events having a recurrence interval of less than 30 years. The reduced storage volumes available in both watersheds' ponding basins have also led to the payment of damage claims to adjacent landowners, where sediment deposition and flooding now occur outside of the basin's boundaries. Damage claims at the arroyo's basin can be triggered by a 6-year recurrence interval flood.

In 1981 high concentrations of the asbestiform mineral chrysotile, suspected by some researchers to be a carcinogen if ingested (4), were detected in the canal. Subsequent monitoring has identified concentrations as high as 25,500 million fibers per liter (MFL); average concentrations in the San Joaquin Valley portion of the aqueduct are on the order of 5,000 MFL. The U.S. Environmental Protection Agency recently established a recommended maximum contaminant level of 7.1 MFL for specified asbestos fiber sizes in potable water. The aqueduct's high asbestos levels are derived from sediment carried into the canal at Arroyo Pasajero and Cantua Creek.

Although the Coast Range serpentinite deposits constitute a small fraction of the two watersheds' drainages, the material's highly erodible nature and readily transportable size combine to yield a significant water quality impact. Sediment inflow has also created another water quality problem--aqueduct turbidity during the runoff season. Municipal water treatment plants which take aqueduct deliveries downstream of the drain inlets have been forced to shut down their operations when high turbidities cause filter plugging.

Sediment deposition in the canal requires the eventual removal of material to maintain hydraulic capacity. Since the aqueduct provides water deliveries on a continuous basis, it cannot be dewatered to facilitate sediment removal. Clamshell dredging has been periodically performed at the Cantua Creek inlet; the greatest amount of material removed at any one time has been 59 ac-ft (72,800 m^3). An estimated 465 ac-ft (573,600 m^3) of sediment has been deposited in the aqueduct by Arroyo Pasajero, in places reaching depths up to 5 ft (1.5 m). An estimated 165 ac-ft (206,500 m^3) of sediment were removed from a 10 mi (16 km) reach of canal near the drain inlets after the discovery of asbestos in the aqueduct. This work was performed with a self-propelled underwater dredge designed to limit resuspension of asbestos into the water column (Courtney and Jones, 1983).

REMEDIAL ACTIVITIES

Feasibility-level flood protection studies are now being performed on the Arroyo Pasajero cross-drainage problem, based on the criteria that the aqueduct will be protected against a 100-year flood, and that no floodwaters or sediment will be accepted into the canal. The remedial alternatives proposed have included items such as enclosing either the arroyo or the canal in a siphon, or constructing a floodway to drain the ponding basin. The most cost-effective alternatives identified to date have been a maximum enlargement of the basin, or combining a slightly enlarged basin with a dam on Warthan Creek. The estimated annualized cost over a 100-year project life would be approximately 6 million dollars per year for either alternative (1).

Several interim measures have been taken to lessen the impacts of sedimentation at the arroyo. Telemetering precipitation gages have been installed in the upper watershed to aid in predicting runoff at the canal, so that floodwater releases to the canal can be minimized. Some 620 ac-ft (764,600 m^3) of sediment were excavated from the ponding basin in 1983 to provide a temporary increase in storage capacity. A skimming weir was constructed in front of the basin's drain inlets to limit the transport of bedload material into the canal.

Reevaluation of watershed hydrology and sediment yield is just beginning at Cantua Creek. The major interim action taken to date has been the construction of a new flume drain inlet to the canal. The new inlet was sited south of the path taken by earlier mudflows, to reduce the amount of bedload material entering the aqueduct. The inlet was also provided with flashboards to control the amount of flow entering the canal and to allow for longer detention of floodwaters in the ponding basin.

SUMMARY AND CONCLUSIONS

Hindsight indicates that neither watershed should have been allowed to drain into the aqueduct, particularly considering the paucity of hydrologic and sediment yield data available at the time of aqueduct design. A major error in the predicted sediment yields was the determination that most of the yield would be derived from the upper watersheds. There was, however, geomorphic evidence such as active channel degradation, shallow and deep subsidence, and past history of mud or debris flows, to suggest the potential for high sediment yields from the alluvial fan deposits in the lower watershed.

Underestimating the sediment yields--by a factor of 4 to 5 at Arroyo Pasajero, and by a factor of 19 at Cantua Creek--has led to expensive consequences in terms of aqueduct operations and maintenance. The economic impacts of sediment accumulation in the canal extend to the domestic water systems which must modify their treatment plant operations to cope with high turbidity and asbestos levels caused by the sediment. A number of interim measures including dredging sediment from the canal, excavating material from the ponding basin, and modifying drain inlet facilities have been undertaken to mitigate the existing problems until a long-term solution to exclude floodwaters and sediment from the aqueduct can be implemented.

APPENDIX.- REFERENCES

1. "Arroyo Pasajero Alternatives", California Department of Water Resources, San Joaquin District Report, September 1984.
2. Bull, W. B., "Alluvial Fans and Near-Surface Subsidence in Western Fresno County, California", U.S. Geological Survey Professional Paper 437-A, 1964.
3. Courtney, W. A., and Jones, J. A., "Aqueduct Restoration", Proceedings, Eighth International Technical Conference on Slurry Transportation, San Francisco, California, March 1983.
4. "Drinking Water and Health. Vol. 5. Asbestos", Safe Drinking Water Committee, National Resources Council, National Academy Press, Washington, D.C., 1983.
5. "Engineering Geology of Debris Flows Along the Southwest Side of the San Joaquin Valley, California", California Department of Water Resources, Exploration Section Report No. E-3, April 1960.
6. Ireland, R. L., Poland, J. F., and Riley, F. S., "Land Subsidence in the San Joaquin Valley, California, as of 1980", U.S. Geological Survey Open-File Report 82-370, June 1982.
7. Munn, J. R., Jr., Busacca, A. J., and Trott, K. E., "California Aqueduct Sedimentation Study for the Arroyo Pasajero and Tributary Watersheds", Report prepared for the California Department of Conservation, September 1981.
8. Simons, Li, and Associates, Inc., "Stream Channel Erosion Study, Arroyo Pasajero Watershed", Report prepared for California Department of Water Resources, March 1985.

Sedimentation Processes in Hydrosystems, Numerical-Empirical Modeling

Sam S. Y. Wang and Sergio E. Adeff

This paper presents the results of a newly developed computer simulation model for studying the sedimentation processes in a variety of
hydrosystems. The most effective numerical methodology and the most
reliable empirical functions available are applied to attack this complex problem. The soil sediment transport in a hydrosystem is represented by a mixed dimensional, computational model, which contains one-
dimensional, two-dimensional and three-dimensional elements. Different
subdomains are represented by the appropriate elements to achieve the
best possible computational efficiency. This paper focuses on the newest part of the system, the three-dimensional domain. The test case
presented consists of a channel bend with relevant secondary flow.

Introduction

Soil sedimentation processes exist in all natural and manmade hydrosystems, which include watershed, river-stream systems, lake-reservoir
systems, irrigation-drainage networks, inland-coastal waterways, water
supply systems, etc. The sediment transport in these systems has profound effects on the welfare of mankind such as water resources and quality, navigation safety in waterways, flood control, environmental protection, among others. Therefore, the investigation to achieve better
understanding of the basic characteristics of soil sedimentation processes and transport has attracted great interest of researchers around the
world.

Due to the extreme complexity of the problem, it has been investigated traditionally by the empirical approaches up to the present. The
empirical studies are usually not only very costly and time-consuming,
but also site and time specific. It is desirable to improve the existing methodology and/or develop some new approaches to enhance the investigation of sediment transport and make it more cost-effective. The
numerical-empirical modeling is our contribution to achieve this objective.

With the rapid advancement of digital computer technology and numerical modeling methodology, the application of computational modeling and
simulation in hydrodynamic and sedimentation research has gained attention during the past few decades.

. Professor and Director, Center for Computational Hydroscience and
  Engineering, The University of Mississippi, University, MS 38677,
  Member, ASCE

. Research Assistant, Same institution, Member, ASCE

In the earlier stages, numerical models were mostly one-dimensional. They were based on the widely adopted Saint-Venant's model [1] to study unsteady river flows using first, the finite difference method [2], and only recently, the finite element method [3]. Most of those numerical simulation models were developed for investigating the hydrodynamics of river flows. About a decade ago, they were applied, in conjunction with the sediment transport equation, to the modeling of sedimentation processes. One-dimensional models are suitable to simulate long wave phenomena in long river reaches as well as the entire river system. Discharges and stages can be adequately predicted and utilized in design and optimization of flood control structures and other hydraulic engineering operations.

More recently, the two-dimensional models, or better known as the depth-integrated models, have been widely applied in the simulation of shallow water flows in estuaries and rivers. Again, the finite differences [4] were used first, but due to its versatility in handling irregular boundaries, the finite element method [5], [6] soon has gained attention by numerical modelers. The inclusion of sediment processes to depth-integrated models was a very recent breakthrough [7], [8], [9]. These models are restricted for technical and economical reasons to relatively short reaches of rivers in comparison with the 1D-models, but they provide greater details of flow conditions, in terms of mean velocities in depth and water levels, and they are capable of predicting large eddies, separation effects, transversal accelerations and other relevant effects.

Nevertheless, there are many important instances that call for a three-dimensional model (3D), such as secondary flows, countercurrents, three-dimensional eddies, etc. Early efforts in this direction were the so-called multilayered models, which, in essence, are developed based on the superposition of several depth-integrated models and the introduction of an interlayer friction with poor physical meaning [10], [11]. They were a logical extension to 2D models and filled the need for a period of time.

A second generation of 3D models are those based on the so-called wave-equation approach. It has produced some quite interesting solutions in cases which are not dominated by three-dimensional effects [12], [13]. Its ability to handle truly 3-D cases is still to be assessed, but this approach is promising. A more natural 3D formulation, based on the continuity and Navier-Stokes equations has been confronted with difficulties of either instability or numerical dissipation of waves simulated. Only very recently have these difficulties been successfully overcome by using the so-called Petrov-Galerkin method [14], [15].

A three-dimensional model for simulating river sedimentation processes has recently been presented by the authors [16] which incorporates the Petrov-Galerkin method to the complete Navier-Stokes equations.

Because the critical factor for an adequate simulation of transport of sediment in suspension is an adequate simulation of the flow pattern, the authors focus on the hydrodynamic model here. The case of a curved channel is chosen as an example.

Model Development

The complete set of governing equations are given below. It is suggested that readers refer to the authors previous paper [16] for details.

- the Navier-Stokes equation,

$$\frac{\partial \vec{u}}{\partial t} + \vec{u} \cdot \nabla \vec{u} + \frac{\nabla p}{\rho} - \epsilon_f \nabla^2 \vec{u} - \vec{B} = \vec{0} \tag{1}$$

- the flow continuity equation:

$$\nabla \cdot \vec{u} = 0 \tag{2}$$

- the kinetic condition of the free-surface:

$$\frac{\partial \eta}{\partial t} + u_\eta \frac{\partial \eta}{\partial x} + v_\eta \frac{\partial \eta}{\partial y} - w_\eta = 0 \tag{3}$$

- the convection-diffusion equation for sediments in suspension

$$\frac{\partial c}{\partial t} - \nabla \cdot (\epsilon_s \nabla c) + \nabla \cdot (c\vec{u}) - \frac{\partial}{\partial z} (w_s c) = 0 \tag{4}$$

- the continuity of sediments equation

$$(1 - p) \frac{\partial z_b}{\partial t} + \frac{\partial q_{ex}}{\partial x} + \frac{\partial q_{ey}}{\partial y} + \frac{\partial (h\bar{c})}{\partial t} = 0 \tag{5}$$

It is assumed that the reader is familiar with the notations. The three components of velocity and the water level are unknowns in a first submodel, the concentration of sediments in suspension is in the second one, and the bottom elevation is in the third. Pressure is assumed to be hydrostatic, and turbulent eddy viscosity distribution is assessed following empirical laws [17], [18]. Velocities at the bottom are null and friction forces at the bed are computed according to Von-Karman law, using the Prandtl's mixing length. Forces on the free surfaces are equated to the wind shear force and body forces are computed according to Coriolis theory. Sediment diffusion coefficient ϵ_s is computed as a function of the turbulent eddy viscosity ϵ_f through a well assessed empirical law [19].

The finite element model development and solution technique of the hydrodynamic model, including the refinements to overcome the difficulties of numerical instability and numerical dissipations, have been discussed in previous papers [15], [16]. The solution of the sediment transport model is highly dependent on an accurate solution of the hydrodynamic one. Therefore, the authors intend to use the remaining few pages to present important results upon the hydrodynamic problem, rather than the solution techniques.

Results of Test Case

Figure 1 shows a three-dimensional perspective view of the selected 90-degree curved channel section that contains several important features:

- The outer bend is chosen to be exactly a parabola, so that no boundary discontinuities are introduced by using nine nodes horizontal 2D elements.

- The width normal to the outer bank is constant along the channel. Thus, convective acceleration due to width changes are avoided. It should be noted that convective accelerations in both Cartesian directions are present elsewhere due to the bending.

- Cross-sections show a possible initial bed profile with a steep transversal slope, to introduce a strong convection.

- The channel chosen is simple enough to allow a clear physical interpretation of results, yet complex enough to demonstrate the capability of obtaining a stable solution of a difficult problem.

In figure 1, the mesh can be seen as a series of surfaces composed by two-dimensional nine nodes isoparametric elements in the 3D space, sharing common verticals through its nodes. The verticals (not shown) are high-order one-dimensional isoparametric elements. The product of the 2D and 1D elements produce the 3D finite element mesh. This scheme gives a very practical method of producing 3D meshes from easy-to-handle 2D meshes.

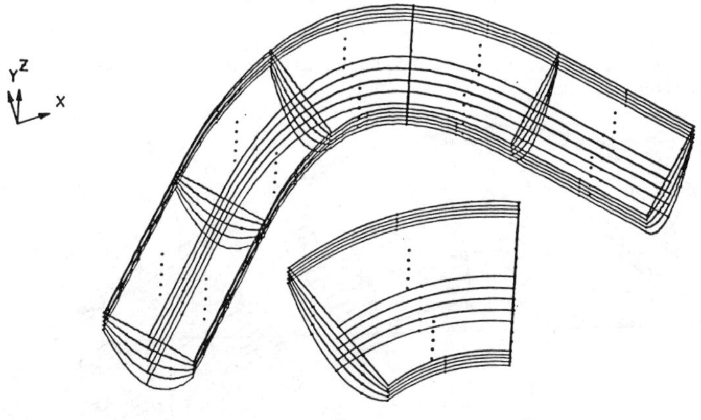

Figure 1: The three-dimensional mesh
    a) Complete channel, distortion 1.5
    b) The two central elements, with no distortion
    • Initial depth along banks: 0.32 ft (0.10 m)
                , along centerline: 1.64 ft (0.50 m)
    • Width: 3.28 ft (1 m), length 24.9 ft (7.6 m)
    • Slope along outer bend: 0.0001
    • Extreme elements are rectilinear shaped.

It is well known how the resulting flow field should be [20]: Velocities are to present an outward deviation at the surface and an inward
deviation at the bottom as well as an upward deviation at the inner bend
and an downward deviation at the outer bend. Transversal slopes at the
water surface should be maximum at the central section with the higher
elevation at the outer bend.

The model should be able to generate that condition even starting
from an inconsistent initial state. To accomplish that the selected
initial state had null transversal slopes, a symmetric horizontal distribution of velocities with respect to the channel axis and vertical
distributions had no deviation with respect to the channel mean deviation, conveying a purposedly wrong state. Results presented here were
obtained after 1.5 seconds (physical time). In such a short time for a
channel of more than 7 meters length, the model developed the cited flow
characteristics, as it can be seen in figure 2, which includes the central elements and lower reach (results in upper reach are quite similar
to lower reach although less deviated).

Figure 2 shows also the vertical distribution of horizontal component of velocities in each vertical. Being horizontal components, the
deviation with respect to the general direction of the channel is the
actual one in the horizontal plane. This deviation agrees with the previous description. Figure 3 shows more details (intermediate vectors
have been added to better show the deviation variation in depth).

Figure 4 shows the vertical components of velocities plotted over
the x direction. Vectors in the positive direction of x indicates
positive (upwards) vertical velocities and the opposite in the other
direction.

Figure 5 is a top view of horizontal components, demonstrating the
deviation effect.

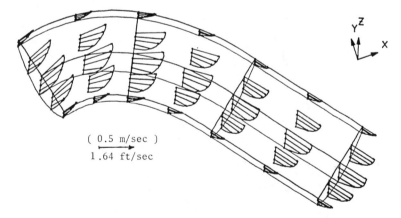

(0.5 m/sec)
1.64 ft/sec

Figure 2: **Vertical distributions of horizontal component of velocities**
observed shown from central to end elements (after 1.5 sec.).

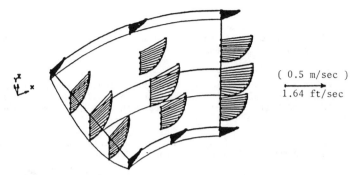

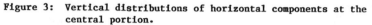

Figure 3: Vertical distributions of horizontal components at the central portion.

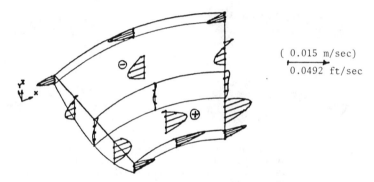

Figure 4: Vertical distributions of vertical components at the central portion (magnitudes exaggerated).

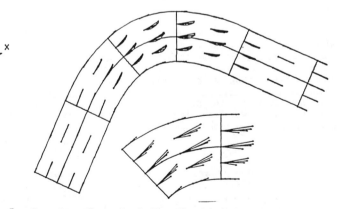

Figure 5: Top view of vertical distributions of horizontal velocities in the whole channel (after 1.5) sec.).

To illustrate the evolution of a bottom bed through a coupled system of equations for flow and sediment, the authors have selected an actual river bend to which a depth integrated model was applied to obtain the solution shown in figure 6a.

Figure 6b shows the erosion-deposition pattern developed in a curved channel in the presence of man-made structures, in this case a pair of groynes, transversal to the outer bed and occupying a third of the channel width. Solution was also obtained with a 2D model developed by Wang and Su [21].

Results of the latest sediment process three-dimensional model will be presented in greater detail at the Conference.

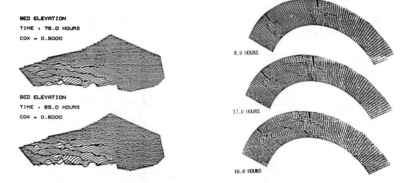

**Figure 6: a) Simulation of bed surface deformation due to the
sedimentation processes in selected river bend.
b) Simulation of scouring around man-made structures in a
curved channel.**

Conclusions

The simultaneous rapid advancement of both computer technology and numerical modeling methodology creates the possibility of cost-effective analysis of complex three-dimensional flow-sediment processes, that were out of reach a few years ago. Results being obtained promise a tremendous impact in engineering methodologies.

In this paper a successful simulation of secondary flow in a channel bend obtained with a few finite elements is shown to demonstrate the impressive potential of new techniques available.

Acknowledgements

This work is a result of research sponsored in part by the US Geological Survey, the Mississippi Water Resources Research Institute, under Grant # G-915-05, and The University of Mississippi. The utilization of the computing equipment of the Center for Computational Hydroscience and Engineering of the University, purchased with a Grant (CEE-8406286) from the National Science Foundation, is also acknowledged.

References

[1] Saint-Venant, Bare de, "Theorie du Movement Non-Permanent des
     eaux avec Application aux oues des riviere's et a l'Introduction
     des marees dans leur lit", Academy of Sciences Paris, Comptes
     rendus, Vol.73, pp.148-154, 237-240., 1871.
[2] Cunge, J.A.,"Applied Mathematical Modeling of Open Channel Flow",
     Ch.10 of Unsteady Flow in Open Channels, Fort Collins, 1975.
[3] Adeff, S.E. and Wang, S.Y.,"Hydrodynamic Model of River Flow on a
     Microcomputer", Proceedings, ASCE Conference on Hydraulics and
     Hydrology in the Small Computer Age", Orlando Florida, 1985.
[4] Lendertsee,J.J.,"Aspects of a Computational Model for Long-Period
     Water-Wave Propagation", Memo. RM-5294-PR, Rand Corp.,Calif.,1967
[5] Connor J.J. and Wang, J.D.,"Mathematical Modeling of Near Coastal
     Circulation. MIT Parsons Laboratory Report #200, 1975.
[6] Su, T.Y., Wang S.Y. and Alonso, C.V.,"Depth-Averaging Models of
     River Flows", Finite Elements in Water Resources, Vol.III, 1980
[7] Wang,S.Y., "Computer Simulation of Sedimentation Processes", Fi-
     nite Elements in Water Resources, Vol.IV, Springer Verlag, 1984.
[8] Adeff, S. E., "Simulation of Sedimentation Processes by Finite
     Element Method", Fifth Conference on Finite Elements in Water
     Resources, Burlington, Vermont , 1984.
[9] Galappatti, G. and Vreugdenhill, C. G. , "A Depth-Integrated
     Model for Suspended Sediment Transport", Journal of Hydraulic
     Research (IAHR), Vol. 23, No. 4., 1985.
[10] Kawahara, M., Kobayashi, M. and Nakata, K.,"Multiple Level Fini-
     te Element Analysis and Its Applications to Tidal Current Flow
     in Tokyo Bay", Applied Mathematic Modeling, Vol. 7, June, 1983.
[11] Kawahara, M., "Finite Element Method in Two-Layer and Multi-Level
     Flow Analysis", Finite Elements in Water Resources, Vol.III, 1980
[12] Laible, J. P., "Recent Developments in the Use of the Wave
     Equation for Finite Element Modelling Flow", 4th Interna-tional
     Conference on Applied Numerical Modeling, Tainan, Taiwan, 1984.
[13] Laible, J. P., "Finite Element Analysis of Depth Varying Flow in
     Lakes and Coastal Regions". Finite Elements in Water Resources,
     Vol.III, 1980.
[14] Katopodes, N.D., "A Dissipative Galerkin Scheme for Open-Channel
     Flow", Journal of Hydraulic Engineering, ASCE, Vol.11 , 1984.
[15] Wang, S. Y. and Adeff, S. E., "A Depth-Integrated Model for Sol-
     ving Navier-Stokes Equations Using Dissipative Galerkin Scheme",
     Proceedings, Second International Symposium on Refined Modeling
     of Flows, University of Iowa, 1985.
[16] Wang, S. Y. and Adeff, S. E., "Three-Dimensional Modeling of River
     Sedimentation Processes", River Sedimentation, Vol.III., 1986
[17] Coleman, N., "Flume Studies of the Sediment Transfer Coefficient"
     Water Resources Research, Vol. 6, No. 3., 1970.
[18] Van Rijn, L. C., "Sediment Transport, Part I; Bed Load Transport
     Journal of Hydraulic Eng., ASCE, Col. 110, No. 10., 1984a.
[19] Van Rijn, L. C., "Sediment Transport, Part II; Suspended Load
     Transport", Journal of Hydr. Eng., ASCE, Vol. 11, No.11., 1984b.
[20] Kalkwijk, J. P. and De Vriend, H. J., "Computation of the Flow In
     Shallow River Bends", J. of Hydr. Res. IAHR, Vol. 18, No.4., 1980
[21] Wang, S.Y., "Mathematical Models of Sediment Effects on Water Re-
     sources Systems", Interim Report No. 6915-05, Miss. Water Resour-
     ces Research Institute, Sept.,1985

Sedimentation in the All-American Canal
By J. P. Silva[1] and D. A. Twogood[2], M. ASCE

ABSTRACT

Imperial Irrigation District (District), receives its entire water
supply from the Colorado River. During the early part of the
century, sediment from the River flowed into and through the
District's irrigation system and continuous removal of sediment by
draglines and other equipment was necessary. The Ruth Dredge was
invented locally to keep the canals and laterals clean.

During the planning for the All-American Canal, by the U.S. Bureau of
Reclamation as part of the Boulder Canyon Project, works were
designed at the head of the canal to remove between 50 and 80 percent
of the sediment carried by the River water.

Since 1942, following completion of the All-American Canal, the
District has received its total water supply from the Colorado River
through the Canal.

The Desilting Works, operated and maintained by the District, remove
over 70 percent of the sediment each year from the River water before
it flows into the All-American Canal.

This paper describes the operating procedures for the Desilting Works
and maintenance practices for sediment removal from the All-American
Canal.

INTRODUCTION

Imperial Irrigation District, located in southeast California,
diverts water from the Colorado River at Imperial Dam, conveys it
through the All-American Canal for agricultural, domestic, and
industrial uses, this being the sole source of water for Imperial
Valley.

Imperial Valley produces a wide variety of field crops, and is one of
the leading areas in production of winter vegetables due to its
desert climate.

---

[1] Chief Civil Engineer, Imperial Irrigation District, Imperial,
California.
[2] Executive Officer to the Board of Directors, Imperial Irrigation
District, El Centro, California.

HISTORY

Development began in 1901, when water was diverted from the Colorado River into natural overflow channels traversing about 40 miles (64 km) through Mexico before entering the southern end of Imperial Valley (2). This early development was plagued by floods, droughts, and the continued problem of deposition of silt in the earth channels and lateral system. It was difficult to maintain water deliveries at times of maximum demand in spite of continuous dredging of the canals. In addition, silt was deposited on the farmlands making it necessary to relevel the fields every few years.

In 1908, a local blacksmith, Charles Ruth invented a machine to remove silt from canals. Ruth's dredge (see Figure 1) was widely used by the District for many years to maintain its canals.

Figure 1. Ruth Dredge.

IMPERIAL IRRIGATION DISTRICT

The District was formed in 1911 to acquire the rights and properties of the private developers. The District completed the irrigation and drainage systems during the next 20 years.

Today, the District diverts an average annual amount of 2.8 million acre feet (3.5 million dam^3) of water from the Colorado River into the 82-mile (132 km) long All-American Canal. This water, is delivered to about 500,000 acres (123,500 ha) of irrigated lands,

nine cities and towns, rural homes, and feed lots, this being the
sole source of water for Imperial Valley.

ALL-AMERICAN CANAL

The Bureau of Reclamation, in its planning for the All-American
Canal, a part of the Boulder Canyon Project, determined that,
although Hoover Dam would intercept sediment from the upstream river,
and other proposed dams would lessen the silt load in the Colorado
River arriving at Imperial Dam, it would be necessary to construct
works to prevent large volumes of silt from entering the All-American
Canal. The plan selected after careful study of alternatives was to
construct desilting basins described as follows (3):

> Three skewed basins, lying between intake channels and the head of
> the canal, are each divided in half by influent channels,
> vee-shaped in plan (see Figure 2). Each half-basin is 270 feet
> (82 km) by 770 feet (235 m) and contains twelve rotary scrapers.
> Each scraper sweeps a 125-foot (38 m) circular area, and consists
> of two diametrically opposed scraper arms revolving around a
> center pedestal on which a motor drive is mounted. Diagonal
> scraper blades move the silt toward the pedestal to which sludge
> pipes are connected, which extend lengthwise under the center of
> each half-basin and convey the sludge into the sluiceway in the
> river channel. River water enters the basins through streamlined
> slots designed to reduce turbulence, so that the velocity across
> the basins will closely approach 0.25 feet per second (.007 m/s),
> causing most of the sediment particles over .05 mm to settle. The
> design was based on 12,000 cfs (340 m^3/s) flow, carrying 90,000
> tons (81,600 Mg) dry weight per day of sediment load, allowing a
> 50 percent overload. The desilting system would remove 70,000
> tons (63,500 Mg) per day, about 78 percent of total sediments.

Figure 2. Desilting Basins at Imperial Dam.

OPERATION OF DESILTING BASINS

The untreated Colorado River water enters the basins from the
influent channel through vertical slots which help to distribute
the water evenly throughout the length of the channel. The
velocity of the water in the influent channel is approximately
7 ft/sec., (0.2 m/sec.) but once water enters each half-basin, the
velocity decreases to the design velocity, approximately 0.25 ft/sec.
(.007 m^3/s), as it travels the width of 270 feet (82 m). This
reduction in velocity causes most of the silt to settle and the
desilted water flows over the 770-foot (235 m) long skimming wier
into the All-American Canal.

The silt that is deposited on the bottom of the half-basin is scraped
toward the center of each of twelve rotary scrapers. Each scraper
sweeps a 125-foot (38 m) circular area revolving around the center
pier at a speed of 1/13th RPM.

The scrapers are driven by a 7.5 HP electric motor attached to a
reduction gear mechanism mounted on top of the center pier. The
center pier is a hollow, reinforced concrete cylinder 5 feet (1.5 m)
in diameter and 15'-9" (4.8 m) tall, with 8" thick walls. The
scraper arms push the silt into a trough at the base of the pier.
Silt and water then pass inside the pier through four 5" (162 cm)
diameter pipes placed at the bottom of the trough and extending
approximately 9 feet (2.7 m) high inside the pier. The driving
force is the approximately 6-foot (1.8 m) head differential between
the level of water in the basin and the top of silt-inlet pipes. The
silt and water travels approximately 50 feet (15.2 m) to a sludge
collector pipe through a silt discharge line. One collector sludge
pipe serves the twelve clarifiers in each half-basin. The collector
sludge pipes increase in size from 14-3/4" (37.5 cm) to 36" (91 cm)
in diameter, and are placed within a reinforced concrete gallery for
inspection and maintenance access.

The collected silt is discharged into a sluiceway in the river where
accumulated silt is sluiced down the Colorado River toward Laguna
Dam about five miles downstream, where dredges operated by the USBR
periodically remove the silt from the river bed.

The number of tons of dry silt removed from the water is calculated
by sampling the effluent on a monthly basis and measuring the
percentage of silt per unit of weight of water, and measured monthly
flow. The annual amounts of silt removed in recent years are shown
on Table 1, along with annual flows in the river and the All-American
Canal (1).

The record in the table shows that over 400,000 tons (363,000 metric
tons) of sediment have been removed in most years. The largest
annual amount occurred in 1980 for reasons given later. The peak
month was July of that year, when the average daily sediment removal
was about 43,000 tons (39,000 metric tons). District records (1)
show that removal during peak months - April through August - is

about 150,000 tons (136,000 metric tons) per month, whereas removal
during low flow fall and winter months averages less than 1,500 tons
(1,400 metric tons) per month.

TABLE 1.

TONS OF SEDIMENT REMOVED BY DESILTING BASINS AT IMPERIAL DAM

Year	Sediment (Tons)	Colorado River at Imperial Dam (1000 AF)	Diversions to All-American Canal (1000 AF)
1966	542 921	5 825	4 664
1967	318 777	5 595	4 510
1968	459 410	5 749	4 587
1969	467 052	5 609	4 477
1970	445 798	5 692	4 534
1971	441 146	5 832	4 656
1972	439 086	5 786	4 665
1973	481 774	5 849	4 728
1974	626 447	6 211	4 953
1975	470 161	6 184	4 922
1976	556 506	5 898	4 696
1977	530 026	5 698	4 535
1978	522 696	5 690	4 502
1979	646 766	6 124	5 186
1980	3 535 757	9 427	7 695
1981	455 671	6 260	5 051
1982	39 475	5 401	4 312
1983	1 104 265	16 923	7 794
1984	*	19 102	8 269
1985	1 652 685	14 952	8 367
Totals	13 736 419	153 807	107 103
Averages =	722 969	7 690	5 355

* Due to high water in Colorado River, the sediment pipes were submerged and no samples were taken July - December.

US Tons = 0.90718 Mg
1000 AF = 1233 dam^3

The basins are operated 24 hours a day approximately 10 months a year
by a crew of basin operators. Beginning in mid September of each
year when the flows decrease to about 8000 cfs (226 m^3/s), one basin
at a time is taken out of service for maintenance purposes. This
maintenance period continues until early March when the high flow
season begins. An amount of $320,000 is budgetted for operation of the
All-American Canal diversion and desilting works for calendar year
1986.

MAINTENANCE OF BASINS

During the two-month period each basin is not operating, the primary maintenance objective is to remove silt deposits in areas between the circular paths of the scraper arms, usually by hydraulic sluicing. Other routine maintenance is done at more frequent intervals as required.

During each maintenance period, the sludge collector pipes are inspected. The first signs of wear in the bottom invert of the sludge pipes was observed in 1965, 20 years after operations began. The pipes were rotated 180° and several worn sections replaced at that time. In 1969, a mortar coating was applied to the full inside diameter of the pipes. Since that time, an epoxy coating has been applied to the inverts where the mortar coating has been worn' off. In 1985, it was found that the many sections of silt discharge pipes were worn through at the invert. In February 1986, three 10" (25.4 cm) diameter pipes were replaced in the north half of Basin No. 2. The maintenance budget for the desilting works for calendar year 1986 is $245,000.

Beginning in the summer of 1980, and continuing intermittently to the present, higher than normal flows in the Colorado River caused by flood control releases from upstream storage, caused heavy debris and silt loads to occur at Imperial Dam. This abundance of water permitted higher flows to be introduced into the All-American Canal to run the District's hydroelectric power plant at Pilot Knob located 21 miles (34 km) downstream from Imperial Dam. The higher flows and higher concentration of silt caused accelerated wear to the desilting facilities.

In late May 1983, and continuing for 27 consecutive days, the USBR requested the District to divert up to 14,000 cfs (396 m³/s) in the All-American Canal to relieve the flooding and high watertable problems occurring downriver near Yuma, Arizona, and Winterhaven, California. This flow rate is 2,000 cfs (56.6 m³/s) greater than the design desilting capacity of the basins and, coupled with the already higher silt concentration, caused large amounts of silt to bypass the desilting basins and enter the canal. Flows higher than 12,000 cfs (340 m³/s) occurred again for 23 days in September 1983.

By November 1983, a wedge shaped wave of sediment six feet (1.8 m) deep at the head extended from the headworks of the All-American Canal for about six miles (9.6 km). In June 1984, it was found that the head of the sediment wave had moved about eleven miles (17.7 km), but the wedge shape was not as pronounced.

The bottom of the canal was then monitored on a monthly basis for the next four months, and it was observed that the wave moved down the canal at a relatively constant rate of approximately 4,750 feet (1448 m) per month, and the length of the wave stayed relatively constant at about 37,500 feet (8.3 km). During 1985, the sediment wave finally reached the Pilot Knob power plant near Winterhaven, where the majority of the silt was passed through the plant and back into the Colorado River.

The annual bottom profile taken during November 1985, showed that the bottom was back to normal.

CONCLUSIONS

The Desilting Basins have performed well in removing silt from Colorado River water, preventing desilting maintenance to be required along the All-American Canal. The operation and maintenance of the desilting works has been accomplished at a relatively low cost. For the years 1977 through 1979 inclusive, the cost was approximately $0.07 per acre-foot of water diverted into the All-American Canal.

BIBLIOGRAPHY

1. Imperial Irrigation District, 1986, 1985 Water Report, Imperial, California.

2. Imperial Irrigation District, 1982, Welcome to the Imperial Irrigation District, Imperial, California.

3. United States Bureau of Reclamation, 1949, Boulder Canyon Project, Final Reports Part IV - Design and Construction, Bulletin 6 Imperial Dam and Desilting Works, Denver, Colorado.

SEDIMENTATION AT CANAL IN-LINE STRUCTURES
by
Robert I. Strand*

Abstract

The addition of new structures or modifications to existing canal sections has resulted in sediment transport capacity reduction of some existing canals and the consequent deposition of sediment in localized sites. This paper describes the procedures used to compute the transport capabilities of existing canals and the process for predicting sediment deposition that will occur at or near the modified section. Two case studies are described in which the addition of moving screens has or will result in canal section changes and increased sediment deposition. The predicted versus experienced sedimentation is compared for both case studies. A computer model has been developed to aid in the prediction of canal sedimentation.

Introduction

Despite the best design efforts, it is not possible to eliminate troublesome sediment diversions at many canal intakes. It is in these instances that a combination of canal design to minimize deposition and isolation of the mechanical removal processes are employed to minimize operational costs. The techniques used to design stable canal sections capable of transporting the diverted sediment load have been well documented [1, 5, 6]. Of more concern in this discussion are those situations in which the diverted sediment load is greater than can be practically transported through the system or when subsequent modifications to the distribution system eliminate the formerly successful transport of sediment.

Sizing of settling basins

Einstein [2] developed a procedure for predicting the deposition rate of fine sediment particles flowing over a gravel bed. The results of these studies have been used to develop a technique for analyzing the operation of a settling basin or for deriving the dimensions of a settling basin which will accomplish the desired sediment removal. The original work provided three basic equations:

───────────────────────

*Head, Sedimentation and River Hydraulics Section, Engineering and Research Center, U.S. Bureau of Reclamation, Denver, Colorado.

885

$$T = 65.7 \frac{d}{\omega} \tag{1}$$

$$L_1 = VT \tag{2}$$

$$p_i = 1 - e^{-0.693\, L_2/L_1} \tag{3}$$

where T is time in seconds for sediment concentration to be reduced by one-half, d is water depth in m, ω is the settling velocity of a sediment particle in cm/s, L_1 is the length of channel (m) over which one-half the particles will be deposited, V is the average velocity in the settling basin (m/s), L_2 is the design basin length, and p_i is the fraction of material of size i deposited within the design basin. The coefficient, 65.7, was experimentally derived from flume studies. By combining the three equations, we obtain the predictive equation:

$$P_i = 1 - e^{-x} \tag{4}$$

$$\text{where } x = 0.01055 \frac{L_2 \omega}{Vd}$$

Equation 4 was used to develop a procedure to compute sediment deposition in a settling basin by Lara and Pemberton [3]. This procedure was subsequently converted to a computer model which has the capability of analyzing the quantity of sediment deposited in a settling basin or deriving the unknown dimension of a settling basin when the desired volume of sediment removal is known [4]. The required inputs to the model are the water and sediment concentration hydrographs for the diversion, the particle size distribution of the diverted suspended sediment and the dimensions of the basin.

The computer model may be operated for any time interval desired. The water and sediment parameters are constant for the time interval, but can be changed for each successive interval. The model proceeds by computing the particles deposited in the basin for the first time interval, distributing the deposition within the basin, and then updating the cross section dimensions. The next time interval is then analyzed. Because the model assumes uniform deposition, it is advisable to analyze particularly long basins in segments.

Case Study I

The Government Highline Canal serves 10,500 hectares with irrigation water from the Colorado River in western Colorado. The canal is 90 kilometers long and was originally constructed between 1908 and 1926. The original canal was unlined and was capable of transporting the diverted sediment load without major maintenance problems. The capacity of the canal is 10 m^3/s in the area of interest about 58 kilometers from the diversion. As a part of the Colorado River Salinity Control Project, 10.8 kilometers of the canal were rebuilt with a concrete lining in 1981. Subsequently (1983), a moss and debris removal structure was constructed at the entrance to the lined section of the canal (figure 1). To meet the design criteria for

Figure 1
Moss and debris removal structure - Government Highline Canal

the approach velocities to the traveling screens, the canal hydraulic
section had to be expanded. Whereas the normal canal section has a
bottom width of 2.4 m, a normal water depth of 2.15 m and side slopes
of 1.5:1; the forebay section to the screens has a 15.2 m bottom
width, a normal depth of 4.3 m and 2:1 side slopes. The expanded section is 67 m long and has a transition from the canal of another 24 m.
This forebay has therefore become a settling basin within the canal.

Suspended sediment samples had been collected from the canal in
previous years. The samples were spaced throughout the irrigation
season and were representative of the changing sediment concentrations
of the Colorado River during the runoff sequence. The mean monthly
concentrations are shown in table 1.

Table 1

Month	Sediment Concentration (mg/l)	Sediment Load (m³)
April	430	2,990
May	760	11,360
June	210	3,100
July	445	6,300
August	85	1,250
September	50	740
October	30	210
		25,950

The maximum observed concentration was 1,160 mg/l. The suspended sediment is predominantly silt size particles with particles greater than 0.062 mm generally being less than 10 percent of the sample.

The mass and debris structure forebay was analyzed using the above described model for a typical irrigation season in which the mean monthly discharges ranged between 8.8 and 9.8 m/s. The model indicated that of the 25,950 m^3 sediment load entering the forebay, approximately 3,920 m^3 would be deposited in the forebay. After the first season of operation the forebay was cleaned resulting in the removal of 2,830 m^3 and an estimated 610 m^3 remaining.

Case Study II

The Red Bluff Diversion Dam is located on the Sacramento River in the northern Central Valley of California. A large settling basin was incorporated into the construction of the dam and serves as the entrance to the Tehama-Colusa Canal and a forebay for the Corning Canal Pumping Plant. Although the diversion dam was built in 1964, it is only within recent years that the service area has reached a level of development that has required cleaning of the settling basin. The first dredging of the settling basin was accomplished in 1980.

The settling basin has a base width of 75.6 m, a normal water depth of 7.0 m, and side slopes of 2:1. The total basin length is 670 m excluding transitions. An analysis of the basin efficiency was made in 1983 to determine the anticipated cleaning frequency under present and future diversion requirements. The analysis was done on a monthly flow interval based on daily sediment discharge records for the Sacramento River for water years 1977-1980 inclusive. The model studies indicated a wide variation in volumes of sediment deposition dependent upon the type of runoff year on the Sacramento River and Red Bank Creek, a tributary which discharges immediately upstream of the canal headworks. The predicted sediment accumulations for the 4-year record are shown in table 2.

Table 2

	Deposition	
Water Year	Present Diversion (m^3)	Future Diversion (m3)
1977	3,850	4,510
1978	41,300	52,240
1979	9,230	11,400
1980	15,460	18,740

These volumes of sediment represent approximately 35 percent of the diverted sediment and all of the sand and gravel material. It was concluded that 14,800 m^3 would be an average volume of deposition per year.

The settling basin has been monitored twice a year since 1980. Annual accumulations of sediment have varied between 15,360 m^3 and

52,250 m^3 during the 1981-1984 period. Depths of deposits of up to
3.7 m have been recorded.

It is now proposed to install some mechanical drum screens in the
basin to aid in returning juvenile fish to the river. These screens
will be installed at the head of the basin at an angle of 22° with the
centerline. These screens are being designed to meet an approach
velocity criteria of 0.15 m/s in front of the screens at maximum
discharge, 90 m^3/s. Consequently, all discharges less than the design
will result in lesser velocities and greater sediment deposition. It
is of importance that the diversions are in the 20 m^3/s to 36 m^3/s
range when sediment concentrations are at the maximum.

Because of the potential impact of the deposition on the drum
screens, a more detailed modeling of the settling basin was undertaken. In this analysis daily time intervals were used and the
settling basin was divided into streamtubes of equal discharge in
order to predict the lateral deviations in deposition. It was found
that during periods of high river sediment concentrations, rates of
deposition in front of the screens of up to 0.2 m per day can be
anticipated for periods of up to 3 months. Obviously, provisions for
cleaning the settling basin on a more continuous basis will have to be
provided with the installation of the screens.

Conclusions

A model has been developed which is capable of predicting the
deposition rate of fine sediment particles in low velocity canal sections. The model predictions have proved reliable in the two case
studies presented. Recent modifications enable the prediction of
lateral variation in depths of deposits.

References

1. American Society of Civil Engineers, Sedimentation Engineering,
    1975, pp. 546-555.

2. Einstein, H. A., "Spawning Grounds - Final Report to U.S. Bureau
    of Reclamation," University of California - Berkeley, November
    1965.

3. Lara, J. M., and Pemberton, E. L., "A Procedure to Determine
    Sediment Deposition in a Settling Basin," U.S. Bureau of
    Reclamation, August, 1971.

4. Randle, T. J., "User's Guide to Computer Modeling of Settling
    Basins," U.S. Bureau of Reclamation, February, 1984.

5. U.S. Bureau of Reclamation, "Stable Channel Profiles," HYD 325,
    September, 1951.

6. U.S. Bureau of Reclamation, "Progress Report on Results of Studies
    on Design of Stable Channels," HYD 352, June, 1952.

Solving Stormwater Drainage Problems
Through an Area Drainage Master Study Program

Kebba Buckley*

Abstract: The Flood Control District of Maricopa County,
Arizona, is the floodplain and stormwater management agency
for the most densely populated county in the State. Located
in south-central Arizona, Maricopa County is home to the
Phoenix metropolitan area and a number of smaller cities and
towns. Stormwater management problems are both serious and
complex in the County, due to physical and
development-related factors. Storms are "flashy", sediment
loads are heavy, and many of the problem areas are on
alluvial fans, where wash paths may shift during any storm.
Many problem watersheds cross through two to four
jurisdictions, each with different development standards.
Numerous built-out areas developed in a time of little or no
drainage regulation, leaving zoning types far too dense for
street and culvert conveyance capacities. The District is in
a unique political and economic position for facilitating
multijurisdictional solutions. A major new tool being used
by the District is a program of Area Drainage Master Studies
(ADMSs). Each ADMS uses an approach individually tailored to
a specific watershed and produces a unique Area Drainage
Master Plan (ADMP). Each ADMP includes a surface conveyance
configuration together with development policies and
standards to be applied to that specific watershed. Each
ADMP, when adopted, will have the effect of regulation, and
all new development will conform to it. Because these
regulatory "umbrellas" are designed on a watershed by
watershed basis, each can be flexibly responsive to the
area it covers.

Introduction

     The Flood Control District of Maricopa County, Arizona, is the
floodplain and stormwater management agency for the most densely
populated County in the State. Located in south-central Arizona,
Maricopa County is home to the Phoenix metropolitan area and a number
of smaller cities and towns. The County covers 9,226 square miles
and has a population currently over 1.7 million. The Flood Control

*Project Engineer, Flood Control District of Maricopa County
 3335 W. Durango Street, Phoenix, AZ 85009

District has jurisdiction within the County and is funded by a
County-wide tax on real property.

Regional terrain varies from mountainous areas to nearly flat
agricultural lands. The climate is arid, and many of the
watercourses are naturally dry year-round, except during storm runoff
events. Typically, the County gets about seven inches of rain each
year. The greatest effects from these few inches are sometimes
produced by the intense convective thunderstorms prevalent during the
months of July to September. The runoff from these generally has
high peaks and low volumes, and while these storms tend to be very
localized, they can result in serious flash flooding.

Historically, agriculture has been a major industry in the Salt
River Valley, within which the metropolitan area has developed. As
desert lands were converted to farm fields, many of the washes were
filled and obliterated, and raised irrigation canals were built.
Flood flows then began to cause damage through breach of canals,
erosion and sedimentation.

Later, as development progressed, housing and commercial uses
began to replace the farm fields. Again depressions were smoothed
out, and many of the smaller irrigation canals were leveled. This
eliminated a great number of small, closely spaced features which had
been serving as drainage controls. This smoothing of the land
contours together with the increase in paved surfaces increased the
peak flows and decreased the lag times dramatically.

Many of the non-agricultural areas now being developed are on
pediments or alluvial fans. Here, wash paths may shift unpredictably
during any storm; washes split and rejoin in patterns that make
subwatershed delineation problematic at best. The normally dry
washes run with velocities sufficient to prevent road travel through
dip sections or even to carry vehicles well downstream. Sediment
loads are heavy, completely filling many culverts in a single flow
event.

Regulation and Stormwater Problems

These factors have lead to stormwater management problems that
are both serious and complex for a number of County watersheds. Some
neighborhoods experience street flooding and damage to yards and
homes every time there is a half inch of rainfall. Many of the
problem watersheds cross jurisdictional boundaries and some cross
through three or even four. Most have both incorporated and
unincorporated subareas.

Most formerly unincorporated areas developed in a time of little
or no regulation by the County. In areas of traditional Western
values, minimal government controls have been the norm. However,
growth is burgeoning throughout the County and skyrocketing in two
areas formerly thought of as small agricultural towns: the City of
Chandler and the Town of Gilbert together now comprise the

fastest growing area in Arizona. Easy regulations of the past have
left built-out areas with zoning types and densities in
helter-skelter juxtaposition to highly variable street and culvert
conveyance capacities.

Within older plats, stormwater easements, basins, and channels
are sometimes not maintained at all, even if they were originally
provided. Homeowners' associations may not have the expertise or
resources to keep facilities in proper repair, or the location and
functions of facilities may have been long forgotten.

In recent years, the municipalities have tried a range of more
effective requirements. Most of the jurisdictional agencies,
including the Flood Control District, now require review and approval
of drainage plans for virtually all new development. In the greater
Phoenix area, all governments now require at least detention of the
difference between pre-development and post-development onsite runoff
generation. Especially in the cities and towns with higher
requirements, the newer regulations are reducing significantly the
incidence of nuisance flooding within new developments.

Both criteria and standards are highly variable across the
County. In the older, fully-developed areas, stormwater still causes
serious problems, including transfer of high-velocity, short-lag
runoff flows to newer areas with surface conveyance systems built to
higher standards. Also, some towns still have minimal drainage
regulations. In one town, roads, homes and businesses must be built
to accomodate problematic rate of flow "belonging" to the town
upstream with the less stringent drainage criteria and standards.

Approaching the Problem

Resolution of these problems is not simple. Communities may
feel the need to keep regulation less stringent in order to attract
business and industry, and thus, economic growth. Smaller
municipalities often do not have the expertise to thoroughly
evaluate alternative solutions or the funding capability to implement
effective stormwater management plans. The communities differ widely
in a number of factors that must be taken into account in designing a
successful stormwater management plan. Some of these factors are:

-- Topography. The need for hillslope ordinances; the need to
    place required detention off-site for new developments in
    steeply sloping areas.

-- Predominant landscaping types. Irrigated grass lawn vs.
    "natural" desert vegetation, the balance of which affects local
    runoff characteristics. In some areas, most yards are graded
    to hold runoff, as they were designed for irrigated lawns.

-- Aesthetic preferences. Sometimes a sense that all channels are
    unattractive, that fences around public works are unattractive,
    or that either greenbelts or desertscapes are unattractive.

-- Convenience preferences. Some like to combine public works
   easements with park treatments, as long as athletic fields do
   not stay wet long.

-- History of success with different techniques. Some criteria
   have worked very well in some areas and failed in others. The
   City of Tempe, for example, has had consistent success with
   individual on-lot detention, whereas the other communities and
   the Flood Control District have experienced only failure with
   this.

Some communities experience needs and preferences which conflict
with those of an upstream or downstream neighboring community. The
Flood Control District is in a unique position to assist in
facilitating resolution of such problems. The District can not only
lend technical guidance, if needed, but can also assist with funding
mechanisms and cost-sharing. Such assistance can attenuate the
potential worsening of stormwater problems by partial solutions that
may prove ineffective.

The Area Drainage Master Study program was originally conceived
in 1983 as a potentially comprehensive tool for solving these
multifaceted stormwater problems. Areas throughout the County with a
history of stormwater problems were identified and mapped, as shown
in Figure 1. In order determined by the most pressing needs, the
District proposed to conduct an Area Drainage Master Study, or ADMS,
for each identified watershed or watershed cluster. Each ADMS would
have its unique Area Drainage Master Plan, or ADMP, as its outcome.
Each ADMP would be comprised of a surface conveyance configuration
together with development policies and standards to be applied to
that specific watershed. Each ADMP would have several advantages
beyond traditional uniform areawide regulation:

-- Its ADMS set up individually according to the needs and
   preferences of that study area, in study tasks, assessment
   techniques, and types of alternative solutions considered.

-- The provision of plans for the amicable sharing of facilities
   and right-of-way, where one town has no natural outlet except
   through another town.

-- Funding for the ADMP by a mechanism or combination of
   mechanisms best suited to that specific area.

-- The capability for updating of the ADMP whenever the need is
   perceived.

-- The participation, political, legal, technical, and financial,
   of the District.

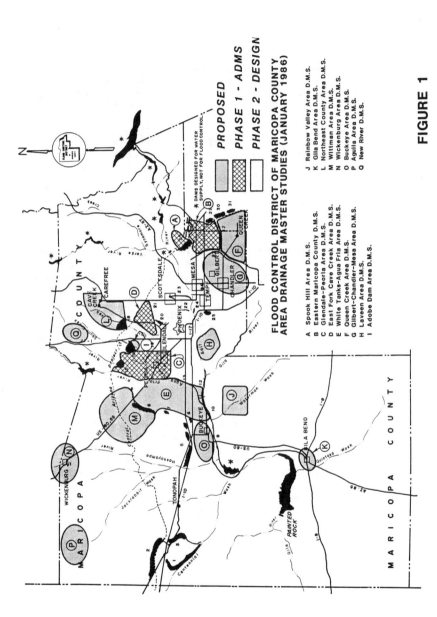

FLOOD CONTROL DISTRICT OF MARICOPA COUNTY
AREA DRAINAGE MASTER STUDIES (JANUARY 1986)

PROPOSED

PHASE 1 - ADMS

PHASE 2 - DESIGN

* DAMS DESIGNED FOR WATER
SUPPLY, NOT FOR FLOOD CONTROL.

A Spook Hill Area D.M.S.
B Eastern Maricopa County D.M.S.
C Glendale–Peoria Area D.M.S.
D East Fork Cave Creek Area D.M.S.
E White Tanks–Agua Fria Area D.M.S.
F Queen Creek Area D.M.S.
G Gilbert–Chandler–Mesa Area D.M.S.
H Laveen Area D.M.S.
I Adobe Dam Area D.M.S.

J Rainbow Valley Area D.M.S.
K Gila Bend Area D.M.S.
L Northeast County Area D.M.S.
M Wittman Area D.M.S.
N Wickenburg Area D.M.S.
O Buckeye Area D.M.S.
P Aguila Area D.M.S.
Q New River D.M.S.

FIGURE 1

Conclusions on the New Program

The first two ADMSs began in August 1984, in areas which had just experienced severe local flooding. By early 1985, the Flood Control District Board of Directors had approved the ADMSs for implementation as a complete program. Since that time, the District has learned some key lessons about the complexity of individualized studies and stormwater management plans.

1. Regardless of the care taken in researching the study area and writing the scope of work, there is always key information that comes to light during the study which changes the needed direction of the study or necessitates adding tasks. An allowance for contingency, of at least 10%, should be included in the contract whenever possible.

2. The study area boundaries must remain flexible until the engineering contract is underway, and sometimes later. Municipalities or other cooperators may decide to join or drop out, and the scope should be written to allow for this. In one case, a study area was extended further downstream and laterally, in stages, until it took in a dam and eventually another ADMS study area. Once the data acquisition began, it actually appeared impractical to separate the areas.

3. Floodplain delineations or redelineations are sometimes appropriate and important inclusions in the ADMSs. Rather than having two consultants gather and review data on the same area, one for drainage and one for floodplain analysis, a more comprehensive picture is achieved by wrapping both into the same study. In Maricopa County, there are a number of linear floodplains caused exclusively by storm drainage backwater effects along railroads, canals, and raised roads. Thus, the two aspects must be examined at the same time.

4. The financing and regulatory options have never been completely explored or defined. There is always something else to be considered, so look everywhere, including to the legislature and to the experiences of other areas around the country. More time should be allowed in the program schedule for this step than it could apparently take, because reaching the best option or group of options is not simple. Getting the County and the municipalities to adopt the ADMP can take a year easily, with adjustments to the ADMP. Any revision of drainage or development standards can take equally long. Also, a process that can last at least months is deciding which jurisdiction will pay for what items, what share, and when, together with who will be the lead agency for building what.

5. Public involvement, or at least public information, can be a key ingredient in achieving plan acceptance. The earlier in the ADMS this is begun, the greater the chances of being in step with the wishes of the public in that ADMS area, and the easier the adoption process.

Presently, the District has 5 ADMSs underway and several in research and scoping. The shortest implementation period now anticipated, for an adopted ADMP with structural options, is approximately 5 years. A total of 17 ADMSs are planned for initiation over the next ten years, and more may be needed as the population continues to rise rapidly. With the initiation of this new program for Maricopa County, a strongly improved approach to stormwater management is now underway.

FLOOD REDUCTION EFFICIENCY OF THE WATER-MANAGEMENT SYSTEM

IN DADE COUNTY (MIAMI), FLORIDA

By Bradley G. Waller*

ABSTRACT

Two tropical weather systems, Hurricane Donna (1960) and Tropical Storm Dennis (1981), produced nearly equivalent amounts of rainfall in a 48-hour period south of the Miami (Florida) area. These two systems caused extensive flooding over a 600-square mile (1,550 square kilometers), which is primarily agricultural and low density residential. Total rainfall for each of these events ranged from about 12 inches (305 millimeters) to more than 20 inches (508 millimeters); many stations recorded rainfall with a recurrence interval in excess of 100 years for the storm.

The 1960 and 1981 storms caused the highest water levels recorded in south Dade County since flood-control measures were initiated for south Florida in 1949. Ground-water levels during both storms rose 4 to 8 feet (1.2 to 2.4 meters) over most of the area causing widespread inundation. Operation of the water-management system in 1981 provided flood protection and rapid recession of ground-water levels thereby minimizing damage.

INTRODUCTION

Hurricanes, tropical storms, and tropical waves are climatic disturbances that can bring extensive rainfall and wind to south Florida. The last two major disturbances that brought extensive rainfall and widespread flooding in south Dade County (fig. 1) were Hurricane Donna in September 1960 and Tropical Storm Dennis in August 1981. Both disturbances were similar in duration, rainfall intensity, and location of the greatest amount of rainfall.

Implementation of the water-management system is the major difference in the effects of these two storm events. Flood-control practices in the area were ineffective in 1960 when Hurricane Donna hit. The impetus for installation and implementation of the water-management system in south Dade County was the 1960 flooding. Authorized by Congress in 1961, the flood-control and water-management system was designed and built by the U.S. Army Corps of Engineers in the early 1960's and operated by the South Florida Water Management District (SFWMD). The system consists of 6 primary canals with gated salinity-control structures, 20 secondary water-control structures, 3 divide

*Research Hydrologist, U.S. Geological Survey, Water Resources Division, P. O. Box 026052, Miami, FL 33102

structures, and about 50 miles (80 kilometers) of levees. These canals
and structures were designed to remove 40 percent of the standard
project flood or protection from a 10-year storm event.

This paper compares the flooding caused by Hurricane Donna in
September 1960 and Tropical Storm Dennis in August 1981 and analyzes
the rainfall, water levels, and runoff to determine the relative effectiveness of the south Dade County water-management system in removing
excess flood waters.

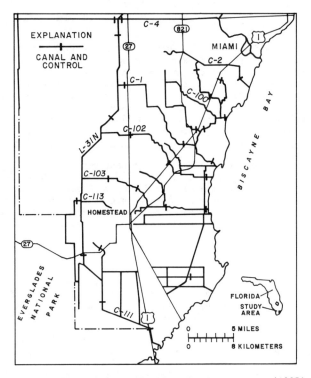

Figure 1.--South Dade County, Florida, showing current (1985) canals
and water-control structures.

HYDROLOGIC SETTING

South Dade County is underlain by the highly permeable Biscayne
aquifer. Parker and others (1955) state that the vertical permeability
greatly exceeds the horizontal permeability, thus, allowing rainfall to
percolate rapidly to the water table. The storage coefficient of the
surficial lithology in this portion of the county has been reported to
range from 0.15 to 0.20 by Parker and others (1955) and 0.18 to 0.23 by
Schneider and Waller (1980). This means that for a 2-inch (51-milli-
meter) rainfall, there will be a concurrent rise in the water table

of 1 foot (0.3 meter). There is virtually no soil cover over the developed portion of south Dade County so infiltration of rainfall is rapid, and temporary ponding occurs only after intense rainfall. In areas were there is marl or peat deposits, infiltration is much slower and ponding and surface runoff occurs.

The relief in south Dade County is extremely flat. In the western parts, the land-surface elevations generally range from 5 to 7 feet (1.5 to 2.1 meters). Along the coastal ridge where most urban and agricultural use occurs, land-surface elevations range from 8 to 15 feet (2.4 to 4.6 meters) with scattered areas where elevations are as high as 20 feet (6.1 meters). Cutting through the coastal ridge are the transverse glades where historic land-surface elevations ranged from 6 to 8 feet (1.8 to 2.4 meters).

Historically, during periods of high water, sheet flow occurred from the Everglades through the transverse glades and into Biscayne Bay. As development progressed, so did the need for improved flood control. Levees were built to contain the waters of the Everglades, and canals were constructed to drain the developed areas. Canals continued to be constructed into the 1950's as more land was developed for urban use in the low-lying areas. By 1960, most urban areas in south Florida had an adequate drainage network to handle a 10-year flood event. In contrast, south Dade County had few drainage canals (fig. 2), and most of the area south of Snapper Creek Canal (C-2) could not be drained by canals and control structures.

By 1981, a network of primary canals and control structures throughout south Dade County was complete (fig. 1). Most of these canals followed the transverse glades, the historic natural drainageways. Water levels in most areas in south Dade County could then be controlled, and flood waters could be more rapidly drained. The primary canals were constructed between 1960 and 1980 as part of the U.S. Army Corps of Engineers' south Dade project (U.S. Corps of Engineers, 1961).

Water-control structures were constructed on the downstream reaches of these canals to separate the saltwater from the freshwater. These primary controls are genrally operated in an automatic mode based on head between the freshwater and the saltwater. During flood conditions, these controls are operated manually and are generally open until the inland water levels recede. Secondary and tertiary control structures are located farther upstream to prevent overdrainage. In some canals, divide structures are present to separate the different canal basins.

EFFECTS OF THE TWO STORMS

Hurricane Donna began affecting the weather in peninsular Florida on September 9, 1960. The major effects in south Dade County occurred on September 10 and 11, as the center passed from the southwest coast and moved slowly in a northeasterly direction. Highest sustained winds in the Florida Keys and south Dade County were 140 miles per hour (225 kilometers per hour) with possible momentary gusts estimated at 175 to 180 miles per hour (280 to 290 kilometers per hour).

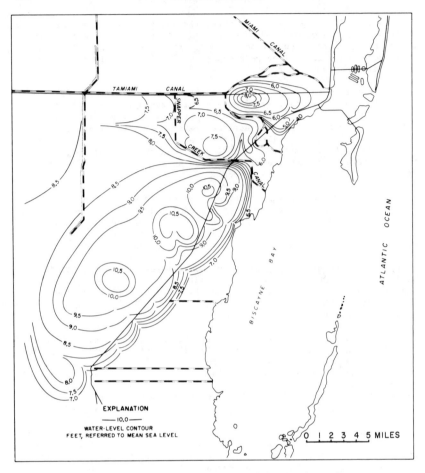

Figure 2.--High water levels caused by Hurricane Donna
in September 1960.

Damage from high water levels was extensive over much of south Dade
County. Storm tides of up to 8 feet (2.4 meters) caused coastal flooding, but the major flooding was caused by rising water-table levels
from the intense rainfall. More than 15 inches (380 millimeters) was
reported in the Black Creek Canal (C-1) area. Ground-water levels exceeded 10.5 feet (3.2 meters) above sea level in three areas (fig. 2).

On August 16, 1981, Tropical Storm Dennis moved abruptly north,
positioning itself over Florida, 110 miles (177 kilometers) south of
Miami. It then proceeded slowly north for 3 days and produced intense
rainfall over south Dade County between August 16 and 19. Total rainfall was more than 22 inches (560 millimeters) in some areas of south
Dade County. The greatest 1-day rainfall of 14.63 (371 millimeters)

was recorded at the Homestead General Aviation Airport on August 18.
The highest rate of rainfall, 6 inches per hour (152 millimeter per
hour), occurred in the early morning hours of August 18, north of
Homestead.

Flooding in south Dade County from storm tides did not occur because
relatively little wind was associated with the storm. Instead most
flooding was attributed to the rise in ground-water levels from the
intense rainfall. Peak water levels throughout most of the coastal
ridge area occurred on the morning of August 18. The highest water
level recorded (11.04 feet [3.37 meters]) above sea level was at monitor well G-614 near Newton Road (S.W. 157th Avenue) and Silver Palm
Drive (S.W. 232nd Street). Maximum recorded water levels for the
period of record at many stations were reached during Tropical Storm
Dennis.

DISCUSSION

The amount of surface water discharged by way of canals during
the 1981 storm was 29,000 acre-feet (36 cubic hectometers) within 24
hours, 54,00 acre-feet (67 cubic hectometers) within 48 hours, 158,000
acre-feet (195 cubic hectometers) within 7 days, and 220,000 acre-feet
(271 cubic hectometers) within 14 days. In contrast, the only direct
discharge of surface water after the 1960 hurricane was the short-term
sheet flow thorugh the low-lying transverse glades. Ground-water levels declined rapidly in 1981 as compared with 1960. At some stations,
water levels declined 2 feet (0.6 meter) more during the first 48 hours
in 1981 than in 1960 and 4 feet (1.2 meters) more after 14 days. After
Hurricane Donna (1960), however, ground-water levels receded at a lower
rate, causing prolonged inundation up to 30 days in the low-altitude
(5 to 10 feet [1.5 to 3.1 meters]) agricultural and residential areas.

Economic losses are greatest in this area when flood levels fail to
recede within 24 to 48 hours. Most losses occur in permanent groves
and nurseries. Seasonal crops are generally not grown during the
hurricane season, and residences are generally built at a high enough
elevation to prevent excessive damage; however, roads and yards are
subject to inundation.

The U.S. Army Corps of Engineers calculated cost to benefit ratio of
the water-management system in south Dade County was about 5:1 with an
estimated annual savings from flood damage of about 2 million dollars.
The SFWMD estimated savings from flood damage alone in the 1981
tropical storm probably exceeded 50 million dollars--more than twice
the construction cost of the intitial project.

ACKNOWLEDGMENTS

The author thanks the South Florida Water Management District, the
State of Florida Institute of Food and Agricultural Services, Dade
County Department of Environmental Resources Management, the National
Park Service, and the National Weather Service for providing historical
data for Hurricane Donna (1960) and Tropical Storm Dennis (1981).

REFERENCES CITED

Parker, G. G., Ferguson, G. E., Love, S. K., and others, 1955, Water
    resources of southeastern Florida with special reference to the
    geology and ground water of the Miami area: U.S. Geological Survey
    Water-Supply Paper 1255, 965 p.

U.S. Corps of Engineers, 1961, Survey review report on central and
    southern Florida project: South Dade County: U.S. Army Engineer
    District, Jacksonville, Florida.

EMERGENCY FLOOD MANAGEMENT

SALT LAKE CITY, UTAH

by

Charles H. Call, Jr.,* M. ASCE

ABSTRACT

This paper discusses Salt Lake City's response to the floods of 1983 and 1984. Peaks during these years were very high with historic records being set in both years. Management of flood fighting and cleanup is discussed. This includes clarifying roles and responsibilities in advance, establishing lines of communication, locating decision making close to field operations, fostering volunteer support, and establishing proper accounting and emergency contracting procedures. Salt Lake City's current emergency flood control plan is discussed.

Different and unique problems of controlling flood water were faced in each year. Some of the solutions included using City streets for rivers, (see Figure 1) diverting excess flow into local drain lines, and constructing levees, dikes and pump stations.

Figure 1. State Street River during 1983 Flood

*Drainage Engineer, Salt Lake City Corporation
Room 401 City and County Building
Salt Lake City, Utah 84111

INTRODUCTION

    Salt Lake City (SLC) experienced snowmelt floods during the springs of
1983 and 1984. The snowmelt peaks were larger than previous recorded peaks
for all streams in SLC except Emigration Creek. The location of these streams
and gaging stations are shown on Figure 2. Peak flow information for 1983 and
1984 has been summarized on Table 1.

    In 1983 the extreme flooding potential was not evident until a series of
snowstorms occurred the first few weeks of May. This delayed the snowmelt
runoff, increased low elevation snowpack and cooled off temperatures. The
weather warmed into the nineties just before the Memorial Day Weekend and very
high flood peaks resulted. The City was forced to react to flood emergencies
as they occurred. City streets - 1300 South, North Temple and State Street -
were diked mostly by volunteers to create rivers for the flood water. Flood
fight costs within SLC topped $ 5 million during 1983 with an additional $5
million being paid out for restoration.

    Similar heavy snowpack conditions existed in the spring of 1984 but
temperatures warmed more normally during May. This allowed for earlier and
more gradual melting. The flood fight and restoration costs within Salt Lake
City during 1984 were about $1.4 million.

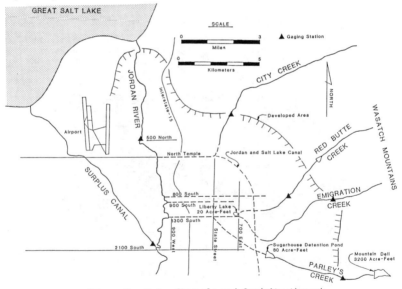

Figure 2. Major Channels and Conduits through
Salt Lake City, Utah.

TABLE 1

PEAK FLOW INFORMATION**

Stream (1)	Drainage Area in Square Kilometers (Sq. Miles) (2)	Date (3)	1983 Peak Flow in M^3/sec (ft³/sec) (4)	Date (5)	1984 Peak Flow in M^3/sec (ft³/sec) (6)	Previous Record Flow in M^3/sec (ft³/sec) (7)
City Creek	45.8 (17.7)	5/31/83	7.95 (281)	6/11/84	5.38 (190)	4.61 (163)
Red Butte	18.8 (7.25)	5/28/83	2.97 (105)	5/15/84	2.80 (99)	1.70 (60)
Emigration	46.6 (18.0)	5/28/83	4.19 (148)	5/13/84	3.96 (140)	4.41 (156)
Parley's	129.8 (50.1)	5/30/83	13.44 (475)	5/18/84	11.24 (397)	11.74 (415)
Surplus Canal at 1700 South	-	6/12/83	89.99 (3180)	6/01/84	124.8 (4410)	-
Jordan River at 500 North	-	6/01/83	26.38 (932)	6/01/84	23.55 (832)	-

**Information taken from Salt Lake City Public Utilities, Salt Lake County Flood Control, Linskov (1984) and Call (1979)

BACKGROUND ON CONVEYANCE SYSTEM

The major channels and conduits within Salt Lake City are shown on Figure 1. The largest system is the Jordan River which flows from Utah Lake on the south to the Great Salt Lake. It is approximately 50 kilometers (30 miles) long and has an elevation drop of about 90 meters (300 feet) between the two lakes. At 2100 South the flow is divided between the river channel and the Surplus Canal. The Surplus Canal diverts almost the entire flow at 2100 South and flows north-westerly to the Great Salt Lake. During 1983 the canal capacity, without spill-ing, was about 90 cubic meters per second (3200 cubic feet per second). The capacity was increased by channel dredging during the 1984 flood fight by the U.S. Army Corps of Engineers (COE) to over 125 cubic meters per second (4400 cubic feet per second).

Four streams enter Salt Lake City from the Wasatch Mountains, City Creek on the north, Red Butte, Emigration and Parley's Creek on the east. Red Butte and Emigration Creeks merge at Liberty Park and flow west in one underground conduit. This joins with Parley's Creek at State Street. The combined flow is in two parallel conduits under 1300 South Street for an additional 2.6 kilometers (1.6 miles) until it joins the Jordan River. The total capacity of these parallel conduits is about 12.74 cubic meters per second (450 cubic feet per second).

The flow from City Creek enters a closed conduit at Memory Grove just north of the SLC business district. It is then conveyed in this conduit along North Temple Street west about 3.2 kilometers (2 miles) to the Jordan River. The pressure capacity of this conduit is about 7.08 cubic meters per second (250 cubic feet per second).

There is one water storage reservoir and two storm water detention ponds on the system. These are Mountain Dell reservoir, and Sugarhouse and Liberty Park detention ponds. Their capacities are respectively, 4.0 (3200), 0.1 (80), 0.02 (20) cubic hectometers (acre-feet). None of these facilities are large enough to have much effect on the snowmelt runoff. However, Mountain Dell reservoir has been used successfully to provide some control to the Parley's Creek flows.

EMERGENCY FLOOD MANAGEMENT

A number of lessons were learned from the SLC flood experiences. Many of these lessons came from problems and obstacles which had to be overcome during the flooding. The lessons learned involved: responsibilities, communication, decision making, supervision and management of volunteers, and financial docu-mentation and intergovernmental relations. These are discussed below:

Responsibilities

Based on 1983 flood fight experiences, a detailed flood plan was developed by SLC. This plan established and assigned City department responsibilities and set forth policies and procedures. The various City department flood fight responsibilities were modeled after their normal duties within the City. Some examples of these are as follows (Call, 1985):

Mayor - Overall responsibility to control and direct flood control efforts.

Chief Administrative Officer (CAO) - Advise the Mayor on flood control programs and insure proper functioning of staff and operation center.

City Attorney - Prepare legal documents necessary for flood control operations. Process all claims for flood damage. Advise other departments on legal matters pertaining to flood fight operations.

Public Works Director - Responsible for the planning and preparation of flood control. Advise CAO and Mayor on all matters related to flood control. Control field operations.

Chief of Police - Maintain law and order. Provide necessary traffic control. Provide flood control documentation, video and still photos.

Director of Finance - Establish and maintain flood control cost accounting. Locate, purchase and lease necessary supplies and equipment.

Chief of Fire Department - Plan for and assist property owners in evacuation operations. Provide medical assistance.

Superintendent of Parks - Provide necessary personnel and equipment to the Public Works Department. Plan for and operate sandbag filling operation. Remove trees and debris from stream beds.

Director of Personnel - Plan for and provide health, food and drink comfort items to flood control personnel and volunteers. Prepare awards and recognition for outstanding service.

City Engineer - Administer necessary contracts for flood fighting. Plan for and supervise the construction of emergency sandbag berms as the situation dictates, using volunteer sandbaggers. Establish and operate the Public Works coordination duties.

Streets Superintendent - Monitor and clean streams and storm drains running through the City. Construction berms to control flood waters. Keep open ditches and bridges clear of debris.

Traffic Engineer - Operate and maintain normal traffic operations.
Coordinate barricading and signing of streets affected by flood
control operations.

Fleet Management - Set up and operate water pumps as necessary. Deliver
fuels and service to all stationary equipment. Maintain list of
site equipment.

Communication

Communication problem has two dimensions, equipment and personnel training.

Concerning equipment problems, the City discovered a number of "dead"
spots where communication was not possible. Also, radio batteries could not
always meet the demand of around-the-clock use on the hand-held radios.
Batteries could not be charged fast enough and extra batteries could not be
purchased fast enough.

As a result of the 1983 flood fight problems additional radios were
purchased and more independent telephone lines were established. Staff training of radio protocol was also implemented. As a result, communcation problems
were substantially reduced.

Decision Making

Two situations developed out of the flooding situation that raised questions
about the chain of command. Initially all major City departments were included
in the chain of command. This became too cumbersome. Effective communications were hampered because information was coming from too many sources. Everyone had somebody in the field. Second, as the emergency progressed there was
not a need for all City departments. Only certain departments were affected by
the current situation. Additional people in the chain of command slowed the
ability to react swiftly.

In the field, there was often no one person in charge with whom to coordinate. To remedy these problems in the chain of command, one site commander was
designated at each major problem area. This single commander was responsible for
decisions at the scene and communication with the command center. This individual directed all activities at the scene. Additionally, the levels of emergency and responsibilities were more clearly defined.

The command center was restructured to separate the decision makers and
technical support staff thus eliminating unnecessary confusion and expediting
information and decisions.

Supervision and Management of Volunteers

The logistics of obtaining flood fighting supplies, tools, equipment, food and then delivering it to the proper place in a timely manner were enormus. In 1983 there was no one department assigned to handle volunteers or feeding of volunteers. The demand on the purchasing division from the departments was never ending on a 24-hour basis. It was hard to direct supplies and food to the necessary places in the field because situations changed so rapidly. Food was brought to one location and attempts were made to distribute it. There was never enough food because the head accounts were never accurate or the crew sizes would increase or decrease according to the situations. The number of volunteers would also affect the number of meals needed. Additionally, most of the food or meals were donated and the amount varied greatly.

The majority of volunteers who reported to help out were gainfully employed. However, because the numbers were so great at times it was impossible to control all the volunteers' activities. Consequently some complained because they were not properly supervised and directed to areas where they might have been more beneficially used. Since there were, many times, no designated incident or site commanders, such complaints were often valid.

These problems were corrected in 1984 by establishing site commanders with responsibility for each major problem area. During 1983 and 1984 volunteers were very effective in assisting City personnel in managing the floods by constructing sandbag channels and other mitigation measures as shown on Figure 3.

Figure 3. Sandbag dikes and wood foot bridge
constructed by volunteers during
1983 flood.

Financial Documentation and Intergovernmental Relations

Two situations that went hand-in-hand were the need to document the cost of fighting the floods and providing to county, state and federal agencies the legitimacy of such flood fighting expenses. The normal day-to-day accounting system was unable to handle the volume and variety of expenses incurred during this emergency period. The second situation which required communication and coordination between the City and County, the City and the State, and the City and FEMA were difficult at times primarily because there were several people involved and procedures were all new and not well understood.

During 1984 documentation needs were better understood and as stated earlier in this paper the finance department was mobilized and charged with the responsibility of documenting costs and coordinating with other governmental groups.

CONCLUSIONS

To effectively respond to an emergency flood situation a community should:

(1) Establish department responsibilities similar to regular day-to-day responsibilities.

(2) Train staff in effective utilization of communication equipment and secure enough radios and telephone lines.

(3) Centralize major decision making but decentralize execution. Extra involvement of the decision makers in flood fight execution can be detrimental.

(4) Involve the community volunteers to free regular City staff to take care of more specialized and difficult flood fighting tasks.

(5) Document all flood fight and restoration costs so that reimbursement from other government agencies, if applicable, can be justified.

REFERENCES

Anderson, L.R., J.R. Keaton, T.F. Saarinen, and W.G. Wells, 1984. The Utah Landslides, Debris Flows and Floods of May and June 1983. Committee on Natural Disasters, Commission on Engineering and Technical Systems, National Research Council, National Academy Press Washington, D.C.

Call, C.H., February, 1979. Causes of flooding within Salt Lake Valley, Utah. Prepared for Federal Insurance Administration, Denver, Colorado

Call, C.H., L. Ritzman, and D. Fuller, 1985. Local Flood Fight and Cleanup Response. Proceedings of a Speciality Conference "Delineation of Landslide, Flash Flood, and Debris Flow Hazards in Utah" held at Utah State University, Logan, Utah on June 14 & 15, 1984.

Lindskov, K.L., 1984. Floods of May to June along the Northern Wasatch Front, Salt Lake City to North Ogden, Utah. U.S. Geological Survey, Open File Report 84-456.

PRECIPITATION ANALYSIS IN CLARK COUNTY, NEVADA

VIRGINIA E. BAX*, LES K. LAMPE**, AND LAURNAL GUBLER***

Introduction

The Clark County, Nevada Department of Public Works retained Black & Veatch in March 1985 to conduct a study of the Flamingo Wash and to recommend flood protection facilities, primarily detention basins. The Flamingo Wash, one of the major drainage courses through the Las Vegas Valley, has been the source of some of the valley's worst flood damage, including the 1975 flooding at Caesar's Palace. The study area included about 100 square miles of predominantly undeveloped watershed.

A rainfall runoff model was developed using the SCS TR-20 computer program. Precipitation data used in developing the model are based primarily on time and areal distribution. Selection of these parameters can have a considerable impact on the rainfall runoff relationships developed by using this model. To create the most representative model with the limited available data for calibration, a precipitation analysis was performed.

Depth-Area Ratios

Previous evaluations of peak flows in the Las Vegas area have been based on point-rainfall distributions given in NOAA Atlas 2[1]. These point-rainfall values have usually been modified to areal values using either Technical Paper 40[2], or HYDRO-40[3]. The depth-area curves of HYDRO-40 are based on data from Arizona and New

[1] National Oceanic and Atmospheric Administration (NOAA) Atlas 2, "Precipitation-Frequency Atlas of the Western United States, Volume VII-Nevada."

[2] Weather Bureau Technical Paper 40, "Rainfall Frequency Atlas of the United States for Durations from 30 minutes to 24 hours and Return Periods from 1 to 100 years."

[3] NOAA Technical Memorandum NWS HYDRO-40, "Depth-Area Ratios in the Semi-Arid Southwest United States."

* Project Engineer, Black & Veatch Engineers & Architects, Las Vegas, Nevada

** Director, Water Resources Division, Black & Veatch Engineers & Architects, Kansas City, Missouri

*** Assistant Director, Clark County, Nevada Department of Public Works

Mexico, and the curves of Technical Paper 40 are based on data for the eastern United States. Hence, HYDRO-40 must be considered more appropriate for the use in Clark County. The network of rain gages in Southern Nevada is not sufficiently dense to develop depth-area curves explicitly for this area.

A comparison of depth-area ratios from the two sources is given in Table 1. Because the study area for this project covers approximately 100 square miles, ratios for larger areas were not tabulated. The ratios are considered to be independent of the return period of the precipitation event.

TABLE 1
DEPTH-AREA RATIOS

Drainage Area		Precipitation Duration	From Tech. Paper 40	From HYDRO-40
sq. mi.	sq. km.	hours		
50	128	3	0.89	0.65
		6	0.93	0.71
		12	----	0.81
		24	0.95	0.88
100	256	3	0.85	0.59
		6	0.89	0.65
		12	----	0.77
		24	0.93	0.85

Point-Rainfall Distribution from the NOAA Atlas

A thorough review was made of point-rainfall distribution in the Las Vegas area. NOAA Atlas 2 gives curves of 6- and 24-hour maximum rainfall totals for recurrence intervals of 2, 5, 10, 25, 50, and 100 years. These curves were derived through analysis of substantial amounts of data and involved relating regional relationships to factors such as land slope, normal annual precipitation, orographic barriers to air flow, land elevation, distance to sources of moisture, location (latitude or longitude), and surface roughness. The Atlas also provides regression equations and nomographs to allow determination of 1-, 2-, and 3-hour maximum precipitation amounts. Since this reference was published in 1973, a significant number of major rainfall have occurred, which provide additional information for determining the rainfall intensity-frequency relationships.

Rain Gages

Hourly rainfall data were obtained for the first-order National Weather Service stations at McCarran Airport in Las Vegas, Searchlight, and Boulder City. Searchlight is approximately 40 miles south of the study area and Boulder City is about 20 miles east.

The periods of record for these stations were 1931 through 1983 for Boulder City, and 1948 through 1983 for both Searchlight and Las Vegas. Daily data were obtained for non-recording stations at Red Rock Summit, Roberts Ranch, North Las Vegas, Kyle Canyon, and Overton. Since the daily records for these five stations have considerable data gaps, they were excluded from the analysis. Daily precipitation totals for the Las Vegas, Searchlight, and Boulder City gages were analyzed to determine 24-hour precipitation frequencies. Hourly data for the Las Vegas gage were analyzed to determine 1-, 2-, and 3-hour precipitation frequency distributions. The analysis was completed by plotting the data points on Gumbel probability graph paper according to the Weibull plotting position $\frac{m}{n+1}$.

Lines of best fit were determined visually. The results of this analysis indicated that the 100-year daily rainfall at Boulder City was 2.97 inches, at Las Vegas the value was 2.62 inches, and at Searchlight the value was 5.09 inches. Some irregularities were noted in the data for the Searchlight gage. Therefore, the value for Searchlight is not as reliable as those for Las Vegas and Boulder City. These values were based on analysis of precipitation totals for individual calendar days and, since 24-hour precipitation events rarely coincide with separate calendar days, it was necessary to convert the daily precipitation values to equivalent 1440 minute values. This was done by multiplying the values determined by analysis of the daily data by 1.13, which is the conversion factor given in NOAA Atlas 2. This results in the following 100-year, 24-hour precipitation totals:

Las Vegas	2.96 inches	7.52 cm.
Boulder City	3.36 inches	8.53 cm.
Searchlight	5.75 inches	14.61 cm.

The corresponding values derived by using only the curves of NOAA Atlas 2 are 2.96 inches for Las Vegas, 2.98 inches for Boulder City, and 3.98 inches for Searchlight. Even though this analysis indicated that the 100-year, 24-hour precipitation totals for Boulder City and Searchlight should be increased by 13 and 44 percent, respectively, the values for Las Vegas are identical.

The hourly precipitation data for the Las Vegas gage were analyzed using the same procedure. The resultant 100-year precipitation amounts were 1.79 inches for 1 hour, 2.17 inches for 2 hours, and 2.34 inches for 3 hours. Since these values are based on clock hour precipitation totals, they had to be adjusted to reflect the fact that the maximum 60-minute rainfall probably spanned portions of two clock hours, the maximum 120-minute rainfall occurred during portions of three clock hours, and the maximum 180-minute rainfall in portions of four clock hours. NOAA Atlas 2 indicates that to convert a 6-hour precipitation total to a 360-minute amount, the 6-hour amount should be multiplied by 1.02. The factor used to convert a 24-hour value to a 1440-minute value is 1.01. Assuming that the factor to convert the 1-hour value to a 60-minute value is 1.13

(the same as for converting daily values to 1440-minute values), the
conversion factors for 2 and 3 hours were interpolated as 1.08 and
1.06, respectively. When these factors were applied to the values
mentioned previously, the resultant 100-year precipitation totals
for Las Vegas are 2.02 inches for 1 hour, 2.34 inches for 2 hours,
and 2.48 inches for 3 hours. The corresponding values derived by
using the procedures given in NOAA Atlas 2 are 1.44 inches for 1
hour, 1.61 inches for 2 hours, and 1.73 inches for 3 hours.

Previous investigations have indicated that the 3-hour design
storm is appropriate for use in hydrologic studies of the study
area. This is valid for estimating peak flows, but it is also valid
for detention basin sizing only if most of the 24-hour precipitation
total is contained in the 3-hour amount or if a high release rate
can be maintained from detention basins during a storm. The
significant discrepancy between the 100-year, 3-hour value of 1.73
inches from NOAA Atlas 2 and the 2.48 inches determined by analysis
of gaged data warranted further investigation, so a comparison was
made of the frequency distribution of the 3-hour precipitation for
the two approaches. This is shown in Figure 1. The difference
between the two data plots is significant, and supports the use of
larger 100-year, 3-hour design storm on the basis of local data.

As a check of the calculated rainfall versus the NOAA Atlas 2
data, a comparison of 3-hour maximum precipitation frequency
distributions was completed for the Searchlight gage. This
comparison, shown in Figure 2, also indicated additional
precipitation at the 100-year recurrence interval. The 100-year,
3-hour precipitation is 2.84 inches. This is an increase of 46
percent which is close to the 43 percent increase at the Las Vegas
gage. The point rainfall values determined by analysis of data from
the Las Vegas gage are as follows (values have been corrected to
180-minute totals):

Return Period Years	3-Hour Precipitation inches
10	1.39
25	1.82
50	2.15
100	2.48

Areal Distribution

The areal distributions of the major storms in 1975 and in 1983
were compared to the areal distribution presented in the NOAA Atlas
2. Isohyets of the 1975 and 1983 storms were compared to a NOAA
Atlas 2 type distribution using the 100-year, 3-hour storm and the
adjusted rainfall values. Although NOAA Atlas 2 indicates that
precipitation intensities are generally greatest at the upper end of
the Flamingo Wash watershed, which also conforms to observations of
experienced hydrologists in the region, both the 1975 and 1983
storms were centered over the lower part of the watershed. During

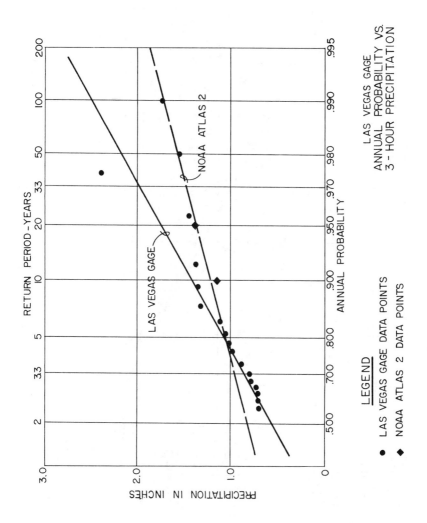

LAS VEGAS GAGE
ANNUAL PROBABILITY VS.
3 - HOUR PRECIPITATION

LEGEND

● LAS VEGAS GAGE DATA POINTS

◆ NOAA ATLAS 2 DATA POINTS

FIGURE I

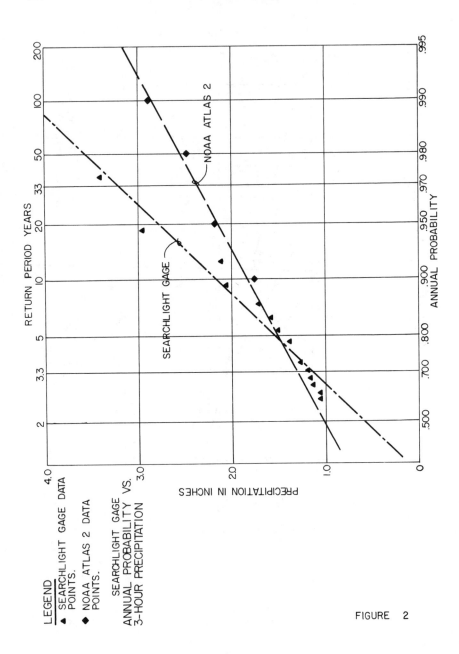

FIGURE   2

both storms, very little precipitation fell at either the upper end of the watershed or at the Las Vegas gage at McCarran Airport. This demonstrates that the adequacy of detention basins must be tested against design storms over both the entire watershed and the lower portion of the watershed.

Conclusions

Study of the historical storm data raises the question of how representative the NOAA Atlas 2 is for use in determining design storms. The NOAA distribution appears to be greatly influenced by average annual precipitation values. About two thirds of the average annual precipitation in the Las Vegas Valley comes from frontal storms. Flooding occurs primarily from thunderstorms. Some meteorologists have theorized, based on a limited amount of data, that thunderstorms rarely move higher in the valley than the surrounding foothills. In the Flamingo Wash study the NOAA Atlas 2 distribution was used for the design storm since it yielded slightly more conservative runoff values.

It also appears that although some historical storms have caused significant amounts of precipitation over the entire watershed, others such as the 1975 and 1983 storms have been concentrated in small areas. This may indicate that the areal reduction factors appropriate for use in the Las Vegas area may actually be smaller that those indicated in HYDRO-40. The available precipitation data for the area near Las Vegas are not adequate for determining local areal reduction factors. The appropriate factors can be determined only if a network of recording precipitation gages is installed in the region.

Depth-area ratios from HYDRO-40 appear to be more appropriate than those from Technical Paper 40. However, since HYDRO-40 was developed using data from Arizona and New Mexico, its application to other areas should be limited only to cases where local data are not available.

In the case of the Flamingo Wash Study, calculated point precipitation values derived by analysis of the entire period of record were found to be 43 percent higher than the NOAA values. In the relatively new areas of the Southwest, or in any areas for which maps have been developed on the basis of short period of record, point rainfall values should be checked using the most recent data available.

The peak runoff rates and volumes calculated using the higher values were critical in the design of detention basins on the Flamingo Wash. Because additional volume was created by raising the height of the detention dam, there was no significant increase in project cost but a higher level of flood protection will be provided.

Recommendations

The major flash flooding events correlated poorly with records
of significant precipitation at the McCarran Airport gage. However
since this gage is the only recording gage in the vicinity it has
been the single source of time distribution data used in modeling.
Therefore a dense network of rain gages with correspondening stream
gages in badly needed in the Las Vegas Valley. A new rain gage network would provide information on point rainfall values and areal
distribution of precipitation.

When selecting a design storm, every attempt should be made to
obtain all the available data. Recent flood events should be
evaluated with respect to the period of record. The periods of
record for the gages used by NOAA are listed in the front of the
atlases. NOAA should periodically update the atlases for areas
where the periods of record are short.

It is recommended that until the atlases are updated, local precipitation data be analyzed for comparison with the atlases'
results. The purpose of the comparison is to determine the atlases'
adequacy in characterizing a local precipitation. In summary, the
best information available should always be used.

STORMWATER MANAGEMENT IN KANSAS

Bruce M. McEnroe*, A.M. ASCE

ABSTRACT: This paper evaluates the current stormwater management practices of Kansas cities. This evaluation is based on a
survey of all Kansas cities with populations over 10,000. Issues
examined include stormwater problems, planning practices, detention policies, technical criteria and methodologies, and program
administration.

INTRODUCTION

In Kansas, as elsewhere, stormwater management practices have
changed substantially over the last decade. These changes reflect both
technical advances and a philosophical shift. Local stormwater ordinances in Kansas began to reflect this philosophical shift in the late
1970's. The 1980's microcomputer revolution has allowed smaller cities
and consulting firms to take advantage of advanced stormwater management technology. However, these changes have not occurred uniformly.
As a result, local stormwater management practices are perhaps more
diverse than ever.

The study described in this paper had two objectives: (1) to
evaluate the current stormwater management practices of Kansas municipalities and (2) to identify and address technology transfer needs in
Kansas within the stormwater management field. The study was designed
to lay the groundwork for an ongoing program of technology transfer and
applied research in stormwater management at Kansas State University
and the University of Kansas. Specific issues of concern were stormwater problems, planning practices, detention policies, technical
criteria and methodologies, and program administration.

To obtain an overview of stormwater problems, policies, and
practices across the state, an informal survey was conducted. Information was collected from all 34 cities with populations over 10,000.
Questionnaires were mailed to the most appropriate person in each city,
usually the city engineer. These city officials were also asked to
provide copies of any municipal ordinances, policy statements, regulations, and design standards relating to stormwater management. Respondents who indicated a major concern with any type of stormwater
problem were contacted by telephone to learn the specific nature of the
problem. City engineers were interviewed in person in eight of the
larger cities.

*Assistant Professor, Department of Civil Engineering, Seaton Hall,
Kansas State University, Manhattan, KS 66506.

The project report (McEnroe and Smith, 1985) not only presents the study findings, but also addresses some of the technology transfer needs identified in the study. The technology-transfer component of the report discusses the basic technical considerations encountered in stormwater management, with an emphasis on hydrologic methods.

PROBLEMS AND PRIORITIES

The average annual cost of urban flood damages in Kansas is over $10 million. Most of these damages result from flooding along stream channels; however, a significant fraction results from stormwater flooding in upland areas. Several cities experience frequent shallow flooding in floodplain areas protected by levees due to inadequate interior drainage.

Nearly one-half of the survey respondents expressed a major concern with stormwater flooding within their cities; all expressed at least a minor concern. Stream channel erosion is seen as a major concern in about one-quarter of the cities and at least a minor concern in more than three-quarters. More than half the respondents expressed no concern for water pollution from stormwater runoff, while the others expressed only minor concern. (This of course does not imply that stormwater pollution problems do not exist.)

About one-half of those contacted indicated that their cities assign stormwater management a low priority relative to other municipal issues. One-quarter indicated a high priority for stormwater issues. Total staff time spent on stormwater management obviously varies widely with city size. However, the respondents themselves (city engineers and public works directors) reported that they spend an average of 10 percent of their time on stormwater issues. As expected, funding problems were frequently cited. No city in Kansas currently funds its stormwater activities through a separate stormwater utility, despite the growing popularity of this funding mechanism nationwide.

PLANNING PRACTICES AND DETENTION POLICIES

Half the cities contacted reported having some type of stormwater management master-plan. Two-thirds of these plans were completed in the last 5 years. Most were performed by outside consultants; a few were performed in-house. Several of the larger cities conduct planning studies on individual drainage basins on a priority basis. The two most common master-planning objectives are to develop a capital improvements plan for upgrading existing facilities and to establish stormwater policies and design criteria for new developments.

The current trend in the larger cities is toward ongoing in-house stormwater planning using microcomputer-based stormwater models. In Overland Park, the city engineering staff does all such modelling in-house. Two other cities recently hired consulting engineers to set up stormwater modelling programs that will be used and updated as needed by city staff in their ongoing planning activities. There is a growing awareness of the need to calibrate these models using field data. Two cities have recently initiated data collection programs for model calibration.

City engineers were asked to comment on the effectiveness of their floodplain regulations in limiting flood damage potential. Floodplain regulations are generally perceived as effective for new developments in the controlled areas except where upstream development is expected to increase future flood levels. Two rapidly growing cities reported concerns regarding future flooding in unregulated areas just outside the flood boundaries shown on the National Flood Insurance Program maps.

About one-half of the cities contacted now require stormwater detention for new developments in at least some cases. Ten years ago none did so. Most Kansas detention ordinances state that detention is required for new developments that would otherwise cause or aggravate an existing or future flooding problem downstream. Such a determination is properly made on the basis of a stormwater planning study for the drainage basin. While some cities do base detention decisions on solid engineering planning, most do not. As a result, detention is often required where the benefits are marginal or nonexistent. At the same time, there is a growing awareness of the limitations of detention as a stormwater management tool. In Topeka, detention is used only to mitigate existing local stormwater problems. In Overland Park, detention is not required in watersheds that are still largely undeveloped. Enlightened drainage and floodplain management practices are expected to prevent future flooding problems in these watersheds.

In the Kansas City metropolitan area there is a trend toward standardization of stormwater policies and criteria. A committee of local officials has recently recommended that the model design criteria published in 1984 by the Kansas City Metropolitan Chapter of the American Public Works Association (KCMC/APWA, 1984) be adopted by local governments as a minimum standard. Several cities have already adopted the KCMC/APWA criteria; others expect to do so shortly.

DESIGN CRITERIA AND PROCEDURES

Only two-fifths of the cities surveyed any formal design criteria for stormwater facilities, although several others have unofficial or interim criteria or are currently developing formal criteria. Some of these criteria cover only storm drainage facilities, others cover detention facilities as well, and still others cover only detention facilities. These criteria range from simple statements of design return periods to comprehensive criteria that govern hydrologic, hydraulic, and structural design. Wichita, the largest city in the state, is among those without formal design criteria. The trend toward standardization of stormwater criteria in the Kansas City area has already been noted.

Design return periods for storm sewers range from 2 to 10 years in residential areas and from 2 to 25 years in commercial and industrial areas. A 10-year design is most common for residential areas. Design return periods for open drainage channels in residential areas range from 2 to 25 years, the latter being the most common requirement.

Manhattan further ties the design return periods of drainage system
components to the size of the contributing area upstream, requiring
higher return periods where this area exceeds 20 acres.

A small but growing number of Kansas cities now have policies
governing the major (overflow) drainage system. The recent KCMC/APWA
design criteria requiring a 50-year major system design is expected to
gain fairly widespread acceptance in the Kansas City area. In Overland
Park, major drainageways must be provided to convey storm sewer overflows for the 100-year event. Storm drainage easements are required
for all overflow drainageways. Low openings on structures adjacent to
these drainageways must be at least one foot above the 100-year flood
level.

Cities differ widely on detention design criteria. Design return
periods for the storage pool range from 10 to 100 years. The KCMC/APWA
criteria prescribe a 25-year design. Most cities require that the
maximum release rate not exceed the maximum outflow rate from the
controlled area prior to development. However. a few cities set flat
limits on release rates rather than tying these limits to pre-development runoff rates. The KCMC/APWA criteria. for example. specifies
maximum release rates of 1.2 cubic feet per second (cfs) per acre of
contributing area at the 2-year level. and 2.2 cfs per acre at the 50-
year level. Multiple-frequency design criteria such as this are still
the exception rather than the rule in Kansas. No city currently
requires that detention basins be designed to provide water quality
enhancement benefits.

Dams with more than 30 acre-feet of storage capacity. measured to
the top of the embankment. are regulated under state law by the Division of Water Resources of the State Board of Agriculture.
Smaller dams are subject only to local control. The state regulations
require dams in urban areas to have emergency spillways capable of
passing the runoff from a 6-hour rainfall equal to 40 percent of the
6-hour probable maximum precipitation. Local emergency spillway requirements range from nonexistent to the equivalent of the state requirements. The most common requirement is that an emergency spillway
be provided to protect the embankment during the 100-year event. A
structure designed according to this criterion theoretically has a 40
percent chance of failure over a 50-year design life. A risk of this
magnitude is intolerable in an urban setting. The KCMC/APWA criteria
contain a very inadequate requirement that allows additional freeboard
as an alternative to spillway capacity. The failure of most cities to
require adequate emergency spillways on small urban dams has attracted
concern at the state level. The working draft of the 1986 Kansas Water
Plan (Kansas Water Office. 1985) recommends that the Division of Water
Resources be given authority to regulate all dams over six feet high in
urban areas.

In Kansas, as elsewhere. cities have had problems with inadequate
maintenance of privately owned detention basins. Overland Park has
implemented a policy intended to insure that these basins perform as
designed. Upon completion and annually thereafter, the owner must
submit certification by a licensed professional engineer that the basin

has the required storage capacity and that the inlet and outlet structures are in working order.

Some cities either require or recommend the use of specific hydrologic methodologies for stormwater facilities design. Such requirements are intended to maintain some degree of design consistency, or to
simplify the design review process, or both. Despite its well known
theoretical shortcomings, the rational method is still the design
procedure most often required for storm sewers. For detention basins
the TR-55 hydrologic procedures of the U.S. Soil Conservation Service
(1975) are often specified. The TR-55 hydrologic procedures are recommended by the Kansas City Metropolitan Chapter of APWA and by several
of the larger cities.

The plethora of computer software for stormwater applications is
creating special problems for the city engineers who must review
stormwater designs. The assumptions incorporated in these programs
are often unknown to the user. let alone the reviewer. Overland Park
sidesteps the accuracy-vs.-consistency dilemma in its detention program
by developing all design hydrographs in-house. using the same hydrologic simulation procedure as is used in its stormwater planning program. The developer first submits certain preliminary site data to the
city engineer. Using this data, the city engineer develops design
inflow hydrographs for 5-year and 100-year return periods and sets the
maximum release rates for these return periods. The developer then
designs the facility for these inflow hydrographs and outflow limitations in accordance with city standards.

CONCLUSIONS

Among the diversity of local policies and practices. at least four
significant trends are apparent. First, the larger cities are increasingly conducting stormwater planning studies in-house using
microcomputer-based stormwater models. Second, recent ordinances and
design criteria reflect a growing awareness of the benefits of engineered overflow drainageways. Third, cities are increasingly recognizing the limitations of detention as a stormwater management tool, and
are exhibiting more flexibility in their detention policies. Fourth,
there is a trend toward formalization, and to a lesser extent toward
standardization of stormwater policies and design criteria.

Several concerns should also be noted. First, it is apparent that
many local policy-makers do not understand return-period concepts.
One-hundred-year flood boundaries are too often considered impenetra-
ble, and 100-year spillway designs are too often considered fail-safe.
The large uncertainties inherent in urban design hydrology and stormwater modelling are also not fully appreciated. Second, very little
attention is now being paid at the local and state levels to the
pollutional aspects of stormwater runoff. Finally, there is a widespread need to develop stable funding sources for local stormwater
activities.

ACKNOWLEDGMENTS

      This study was funded by the U.S. Geological Survey through the
Kansas Water Resources Research Institute (Project No. G907-23).

REFERENCES

1. Kansas City Metropolitan Chapter APWA, "Storm Drainage Systems,"
   Standard Specifications and Design Criteria, Division V, Section
   5600, Kansas City, MO. 1984.

2. Kansas Water Office. "Urban Flood Management Sub-Section," Kansas
   Water Plan (1986 Working Draft), Topeka, KS, Oct., 1985.

3. McEnroe, B. M., and Smith, R. L., "Stormwater Management in Kansas:
   An Evaluation of Current Practices." Contribution No. 248, Kansas
   Water Resources Research Institute, Manhattan. KS, Sept., 1985.

4. U.S. Soil Conservation Service. "Urban Hydrology for Small Watersheds," Technical Release No. 55, Washington. DC. Jan., 1975.

Design Storms for Urban Drainage

UWRRC Design Storm Task Committee*

The characteristics of design storms for urban drainage are reviewed. There are indications that, under certain conditions, design storms
produce runoff simulation results which are equivalent to those simulated for actual recorded precipitation.

Introduction

The subject of synthetic design storms for urban drainage has received much attention from both researchers and practitioners during the
last decade. Recognizing the importance of this issue to the engineering profession and the often controversial nature of reported findings
on design storms, the Urban Water Resources Research Council of ASCE
set up an ad hoc committee to study this issue. This committee produced
an annotated bibliography on the subject and is preparing a state-of-
the-art report. The paper that follows is another result of the committee's efforts.

Historical Perspective

The approach to urban drainage has evolved from the practice of fast
removal of surface runoff to complex drainage schemes that attempt to
solve local drainage problems, protect receiving waters against flooding and prevent deterioration of water quality. Such changes in design
philosophy spurred the development of a variety of design tools ranging
from simple empirical formulas for estimating peak discharge to complex
distributed urban runoff models. Block rainfall adequate for empirical
formulas was of no use as input for distributed routing models and,
consequently, design storms were developed. Finally, the use of historical rainfall records was introduced to satisfy the needs of continuous simulation. Table 1 presents a summary of current design practices
with reference to drainage problems, design tools and rainfall inputs.

It is apparent from Table 1 that urban drainage practice comprises
a whole spectrum of design problems and appropriate design tools. Considering uncertainties in all computational methods and their inputs,

*Jiri Marsalek, Res. Scientist, National Water Research Institute,
Burlington, Ontario, L7R 4A6, Canada
 Ronald Rossmiller, Prof. of Civil Engrg., Iowa State University, Ames,
Iowa 50011
 Ben Urbonas, Chief, Master Planning Program, Urban Drainage and Flood
Control District, Denver, CO 80211
 Harry Wenzel, Prof. of Civil Engrg., University of Illinois, Urbana,
IL 61801

advantages of more complex approaches over simple yet adequate ones are
questionable. Thus, the simplest method capable of meeting the design
requirements within some practical range of accuracies should be acceptable.

Table 1. Drainage Design Problems, Tools and Rainfall Inputs

Design Problem	Design Tool	Typical Design Rainfall
Sewer pipe sizing in small urban develop-ments(minor drainage)	Rational method	Block rainfall(Intensity -Duration-Frequency cur-ves)
Minor drainage design in small to interme-diate areas	Discrete event urban runoff models	Design storms, synthetic or historical
Minor and major drai-nage in large areas, systems with storage, water quality design	Continuous simulation models	Long-term rainfall re-cords

Examination of studies critical of design storms in late seventies
reveals that these studies addressed misuse of design storms or weaknesses of specific types of design storms. Recent work indicates, however, that properly structured design storms can produce results comparable to those obtained using continuous simulation with recorded
precipitation data(Voorhees and Wenzel, 1984). Instead of endorsing or
condemning the use of design storms, this paper attempts to objectively
evaluate their applicability.

Acceptance of Design Storms in Practice

Design storms are used widely in urban drainage practice partly because of the lack of proven alternatives and partly because they are
easy and inexpensive to use. Frequency analysis of synthetic runoff records obtained by continuous simulation is sometimes offered as an alternative to the use of design storms. However, the costs and complexity of this approach are hard to justify because the reliability of
simulated runoff is questionable due to the lack of calibration data.
On the other hand, perception of an uniform level of protection as a
design objective is widely accepted which leads to the specification
of a design event. Thus, for the design of a large portion of urban
drainage structures, the design storm concept has been and will continue to be used.

Ideally, the reliability of design storms should be assessed against
actual precipitation and runoff records. In the absence of such records, reliability analysis is reduced to the question whether design
storms can produce results comparable to those obtained by the best alternative methods, such as continuous simulation. Although conventional design storms are not particularly suitable for design of runoff

detention or quality control facilities, many designers use them because of the lack of other alternatives. In principle, the discussion in this paper is limited to the use of design storms in sewer sizing in catchments without runoff detention facilities.

Design Storm Characteristics

A design storm is generally defined as a synthesized rainfall event characterized by a certain return period, total rainfall depth , temporal rainfall distribution and other characteristics which may include spatial distribution, storm movement and development and decay. The relative importance of each of these factors varies with the type of application and catchment characteristics.

Ideally, the design return period, T, should be selected on the basis of economic efficiency, i.e. to minimize total costs defined as the investment plus damages, in order to optimize design. However, the concept of optimal design in urban drainage is conventionally replaced by a concept of a prescribed level of protection. This often is interpreted to apply to the exceedance probability of some rainfall event and not to the probability of exceedance of the peak flow.

The assignment of a return period is considered by some researchers among the weakest points of the design storm concept. Such criticism usually follows from the analysis of actual recorded storms which show widely varying characteristics and from the investigations of joint probabilities of factors affecting storm runoff peaks. In defence of design storms, it can be argued that the catchment acts as a filter which attenuates the effect of the variability in rainfall events. Pilgrim and Cordery(1975) noted that the actual relationship between the frequencies of rainfall events and produced floods is obscure, as each part of the overall design model introduces some joint probability. They argued that by adopting median or average values of all parameters other than rainfall, the effects of joint probabilities are minimized and the frequencies of design storms and generated runoff peaks will be similar.

The total rainfall depth, D, for a particular storm is a function of T and storm duration t_d. The total rainfall is then described by Intensity-Duration-Frequency(IDF) curves which are available from weather bureau offices, provided that both T and t_d were specified.

Storm duration is an important factor which defines D for a given T and affects the storm intensity and hence the resulting peak flow. The value of t_d selected in design depends on the catchment time constant t_k which has been traditionally defined as the time of concentration.

Variation of rainfall intensity over t_d is an important factor for determining the magnitude and timing of simulated peak flows. An estimate of this distribution is obtained by analysis of precipitation data from a recording rain gage network. Since the maximum intesities are reported for durations of 5 minutes or longer, it is practical to use the 5-minute interval as the minimum discretization interval.

Storm spatial characteristics arise from the geometry, movement and

development of storm cells. The present knowledge of these phenomena indicates their profound importance for large catchments, particularly
when dealing with operation or control of large drainage systems.

Design storms can be characterized by some antecedent precipitation
occurring within a certain time period before the storm. Such precipitation then controls catchment antecedent conditions which in turn may
affect the generation of runoff. In urban catchments, runoff is generated primarily on impervious surfaces and this reduces the sensitivity
of runoff peaks to antecedent precipitation.

Considering all the above storm characteristics, it would be almost
impossible to find an actual storm which would meet all the above conditions and had the stipulated return period. From the practical point
of view, this difficulty does not pose a serious problem because a synthetic design storm represents a certain convention developed for the
purpose of uniformity in drainage design. The attributes of the synthetic storm are then selected such as to produce calculated flows which
would have an approximately correct return period.

Design Storms Reported in the Literature

The earlier published annotated bibliography(UWRRC, 1983) lists details of 12 urban design storms. The basic characteristics of eight of
these storms, pertinent to Canadian and U.S. drainage studies, are listed in Table 2.

Table 2. Basic Characteristics of Eight Urban Design Storms

Design Storm	Recommended Storm Duration	Temporal Distri- bution	Primary Application
AES(Canada)	1 and 12h	tabulated	urban drainage design
Chicago	3h or t_c	from IDF curves	sewer sizing
Hydrotek (Canada)	1h	linear/exponen- tial functions	sewer sizing
ISWS	1h	tabulated	urban drainage design
SCS	1h - 48h	tabulated	design of small hy- draulic structures
Uniform	user specified	uniform	sewer sizing
Voorhees and Wenzel	three times the entry time	Beta function	urban drainage design
Yen and Chow	user specified	triangular	design of small drai- nage structures

Recommended Approach to Developing Design Storms

Conventional design storms are best applicable to design of minor drainage systems, without storage facilities, in relatively small areas (up to 100 ha). Applications to other cases increase the requirements on design storm characteristics. For storage design, frequencies of rainfall/runoff volumes need to be considered and, for larger areas, adjustments of catchment rainfall need to be done to account for spatial distribution. Both these aspects will require further study.

The return period of the design storm is usually given by design criteria produced by the client. For minor drainage design, such a period is typically selected in the range from two to ten years and applies strictly to the total rainfall depth. The total rainfall depth is determined from local IDF curves for a selected storm duration and return period.

The recommended storm durations vary substantially. Two approaches seem to be common - a fixed time duration which is convenient for data processing and relevant to the catchment response time(e.g. one hour) and durations related only to the catchment response. In the latter case, Voorhees and Wenzel(1984) recommended to select the storm duration as three times the entry(inlet) time. Difficulties with determining storm duration can be avoided by using several durations and adopting the value producing the maximum discharge for sewer sizing(Packman and Kidd, 1980). The above durations may not be suitable for storage design.

The literature survey suggests that the temporal intensity distributions are best determined by fitting a selected distribution model to rainfall data(UWRRC, 1983). For this purpose, local rainfall records are discretized into individual events and only severe storms are retained for distribution analysis. The selection criteria can be based on the total rainfall depth which would correspond to a particular return period(e.g. two years). The reduced set of events is then discretized using a certain interval and a selected distribution is fitted to these data. In the absence of comprehensive evaluations and comparisons of various distributions, it is recommended to use the simpler ones, such as the triangular or combined triangular/exponential distributions. The fitting of these distributions is done by the method of moments. The selected distribution is then applied to total rainfall and the storm hyetograph is produced.

In considerations of antecedent conditions, potential runoff contributions from pervious areas and their timing are analyzed. Such contributions decrease with an increasing soil infiltration capacity and decreasing storm return period(lower intensities). There are indications that in urban catchments the runoff from pervious parts is overshadowed by runoff from impervious surfaces and the catchment runoff peak is insensitive to antecedent conditions(Urbonas, 1979). In any case, design storms are best applicable to catchments with low sensitivity to antecedent moisture conditions.

Evaluation of Design Storms

Evaluation of properly developed design storms used within their applicability domain can be broken into two parts, depending on the catchment runoff peak generation sensitivity to antecedent conditions:

(A) Catchments with low sensitivity - can design storms produce runoff peak frequency curves comparable to those obtained from computations for recorded storms, and

(B) Catchments sensitive to antecedent conditions - can design storms produce runoff peak frequency curves comparable to those obtained from continuous simulation.

The first case is relatively simple and there is sufficient evidence that design storms derived from local historical storms produce results fully comparable to those obtained for historical storms(Hydrotek, 1985; Marsalek, 1978; Urbonas, 1979). Examples of such results for various design storms are shown in Fig.1.

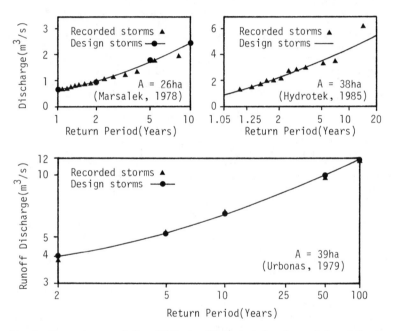

Fig.1. Comparisons of Runoff Peaks Simulated for Recorded and Design
Storms(after Hydrotek, 1985; Marsalek, 1978; Urbonas, 1979)

The second case is much more difficult because it has been rarely addressed in research studies. An approach based on the use of the expected value of antecedent moisture index was suggested by Voorhees and Wenzel(1984) and produced a good agreement between design storm and continuous simulation results,as shown in Fig.2. Another feasible approach is to select antecedent moisture conditions on the basis of sensitivity

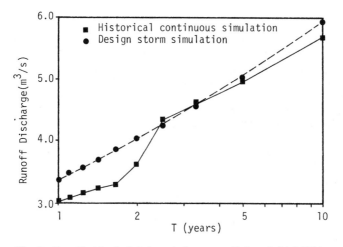

Fig.2. Hypothetical Catchment Response Using Reliability
Analysis(after Voorhees and Wenzel, 1984)

analyses(Packman and Kidd, 1980). Further research on these aspects is
needed.

Conclusions

A retrospective look at urban design storms indicates that their
concept which was developed in early days of runoff modeling for sewer
sizing may have been transposed to more recent design problems where it
may not be applicable. In particular, attempts to apply simple conventional design storms to catchments with high contributions of runoff
from pervious areas, large catchments with spatially nonuniform rainfall distribution, or even water quality considerations led to justified criticism of design storms. The other source of problems was the
lack of knowledge of rainfall patterns in urban areas.

It appears from the critical literature survey reported on here that
urban design storms are useful for and best applicable to a certain
class of urban drainage design problems. Such problems comprise the design of minor drainage, without storage, for sewer pipe sizing in catchments with small areas and low sensitivity of runoff peaks to antecedent moisture conditions. The design storms should be derived from recorded local severe storms and defined by storm duration(from one to
three hours, for catchments under consideration), total rainfall obtained from IDF curves for the selected duration, and temporal distribution derived from local recorded storms. As one departs from the above
conditions, the validity of the design storm concept may become questionable and should be tested.

References

Hydrotek, Inc., "Urban Design Storms for Canada," Report to the

Atmospheric Environment Service, Environment Canada, Toronto, March, 1985.

Marsalek, J., "Research on the Design Storm Concept," ASCE Urban Water Resources Research Program, Tech.Memo. No.33, September, 1978.

Packman, J.C., and Kidd, C.H.R., "A Logical Approach to the Design Storm Concept," Water Resources Research, Vol.16, No.6, 1980, pp.994 - 1000.

Pilgrim, D.H., and Cordery, I., "Rainfall Temporal Patterns for Design Floods," ASCE Journal of the Hydraulics Division, Vol.101, No.HY1, 1975, pp.81-95.

Urban Water Resources Research Council(UWRRC), "Annotated Bibliography on Urban Design Storms," ASCE, New York, N.Y., 1983.

Urbonas, B., "Reliability of Design Storms in Modeling," Proceedings of the International Symp. on Urban Storm Runoff, Lexington, Kentucky, July 23-26, 1979, pp.27-35.

Voorhees, M.L., and Wenzel, H.G., "Urban Design Storm Sensitivity and Reliability," Journal of Hydrology, Vol.68, 1984, pp.39-60.

CHARACTERISTICS OF INTENSE STORMS IN KANSAS

Bruce M. McEnroe*, A.M. ASCE

ABSTRACT: This paper examines point-rainfall characteristics of intense storms in Kansas. Hourly rainfall records were analyzed for 1006 intense storms selected from some 1800 station-years of data. Distributions were developed for seven parameters characterizing the hyetographs and antecedent conditions for these storms. Representative results are presented and design implications are discussed.

INTRODUCTION

In designing urban stormwater systems, engineers must estimate peak flowrates and develop design hydrographs for specified return periods. In practice this is normally accomplished by modelling the hydrologic response of the drainage basin to a design storm, despite the well known theoretical shortcomings of this approach. The required design inputs are a storm hyetograph and some indicator of antecedent soil wetness. Commonly used procedures can produce design storms with durations, depths, and temporal patterns quite uncharacteristic of actual intense storms. The rainfall intensity-duration-frequency relationships used to develop these design storms provide no information on the characteristics of storms within which extreme rainfalls occur. In design, the antecedent soil-wetness parameter is usually assigned a conservatively wet value which may be atypical of conditions that precede actual intense storms.

Considerable research has been conducted on design storms. An annotated bibliography compiled by the Urban Water Resources Research Council of ASCE (1983) identifies 65 publications on design storms and related topics. Much of the previous research has concentrated on determining appropriate nondimensional temporal patterns for design storms. The studies of Huff (1967) and Yen and Chow (1980) on the temporal patterns of actual storms have had major impacts on design-storm practice. Less attention has been devoted to the equally important problem of design antecedent conditions.

Frederick and Tracey (1977) investigated the conditional probabilities of intense rainfalls of different durations occurring within a single storm. Their study analyzed nearly 6000 station-years of hourly rainfall data for the southeastern United States. In general, their results show that an intense rainfall of a given duration and return period is unlikely to contain within it a shorter-duration rainfall of an equal or greater return period. The same intense rainfall is also

*Assistant Professor, Department of Civil Engineering, Seaton Hall, Kansas State University, Manhattan, KS 66506.

unlikely to occur within some longer-duration rainfall or an equal or greater return period. Their specific findings are useful for evaluating design hyetographs.

OBJECTIVE

The objective of this paper is to examine some important point-rainfall characteristics of intense storms in Kansas. A storm is defined herein as a continuous sequence of non-zero hourly rainfall amounts. A storm is considered intense if it contains a one-hour rainfall with a return period of 2 years or greater. These intense storms are most likely to govern the designs of urban stormwater systems.

Seven storm characteristics are examined: the nominal duration, the ratio of the maximum one-hour rainfall to the storm depth, two nondimensional parameters characterizing the hyetograph shape, and three indicators of antecedent conditions. The two nondimensional hyetograph parameters are the time to the centroid of the hyetograph and its radius of gyration about the centroidal axis, both expressed as fractions of the nominal storm duration. The three indicators of antecedent conditions are the 1-day (24-hour) and 5-day (120-hour) antecedent rainfall totals and the month of occurrence, an indicator of antecedent potential evapotranspiration.

PROCEDURE

The hourly precipitation records of 66 Kansas stations for the period 1949-1983 comprised the basic data set. These records were obtained on magnetic tape from the National Climatic Data Center. At least 15 complete, but not necessarily consecutive, years of record were available for each station. The average station record contained 27 complete years.

First, for each station, annual maximum one-hour rainfalls were determined for each complete year. A Type I asymptotic extreme-value distribution was fitted to the annual-maximum series. This annual-maximum probability distribution was then converted to an equivalent partial-duration distribution.

The next step was to assemble data on intense storms. For each station, all storms containing one-hour rainfalls with return periods of 2 years or greater were identified. A data base was created that contained the following data for each of these 1006 storms: the station number, the date of occurrence, the hourly rainfall amounts, the 1-day antecedent rainfall (AP1), and the 5-day antecedent rainfall (AP5). Finally, values of the four hyetograph parameters listed previously were computed for each storm.

These hyetograph parameters are defined as follows. Consider a storm record consisting of n discrete rainfall amounts of duration Δt. Let p_i represent the rainfall amount for period i. The nominal storm duration is $n\Delta t$, and the storm depth, D, is simply the sum of the incremental depths. The normalized time to the centroid of the hyetograph, $\bar{t}^{o}$, is defined as the time to the centroid divided by the nominal storm duration. It is given by the equation

$$\bar{t}^{o} = \frac{1}{nD} \sum_{i=1}^{n} (i - 1/2) \, p_i \tag{1}$$

A hyetograph is termed advanced if $\bar{t}^{o}$ is less than 0.5, and delayed if $\bar{t}^{o}$ is greater than 0.5. The nondimensional radius of gyration of the hyetograph, $\bar{k}^{o}$, is defined as the radius of gyration about the centroidal axis divided by the nominal storm duration. (The square of the radius of gyration about the centroidal axis equals the product of the storm depth and the hyetograph's moment of inertia about the centroidal axis.) The nondimensional radius of gyration is given by the equation

$$\bar{k}^{o} = \sqrt{ \frac{1}{3n^2 D} \left\{ \sum_{i=1}^{n} [i^3 - (i-1)^3] p_i \right\} - (\bar{t}^{o})^2 } \tag{2}$$

This parameter is an indicator of the peakedness of the hyetograph.

The storm data were analyzed by first dividing the state into the six geographic regions shown in Fig. 1. In each region, distributions were developed for the seven storm parameters based on data for all intense storms. Then the storms in each region were grouped by the return period of the maximum one-hour rainfall. The three return-period classes were 2 to 5 years, 5 to 10 years and greater than 10 years. An additional set of distributions was developed for the storms in each return-period class. The distributions for $\bar{t}^{o}$ and $\bar{k}^{o}$ do not include the storms of 1-hour duration, since a single data point does not provide any information on the rainfall temporal pattern.

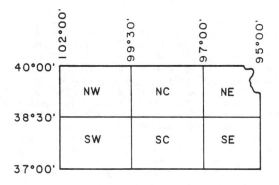

FIG. 1.--Map of Kansas Showing Six Geographic Regions

RESULTS

Representative results are presented in three forms. Table 1
shows the mean characteristics for all intense storms by geographic
region. Table 2 shows how these mean values vary with the return
period of the maximum one-hour rainfall in the northeast region.
Figures 2 through 4 show the distributions of three storm parameters
for all storms in the northeast region. The northeast region was
selected for illustrative purposes because it contains the largest
urban population as well as the most station-years of record. The
findings for each of the storm characteristics are discussed below.

Mean storm durations range from 4.6 hours in the north-central
region to 5.6 hours in the southeast. In general, mean duration is
about one-half hour longer in the southern half of the state than in
the northern half. Mean duration does not vary significantly with the
return period of the maximum hour. Figure 2 shows the distribution of
storm durations in the northeast region. Fifty-eight percent of all
storms have durations of 4 hours or less, and 70 percent have durations
of 5 hours or less. It is important to note that these nominal durations are based on clock-hour rainfall data. Actual storm durations
are somewhat shorter than nominal durations.

Mean values of P_{max}/D, the ratio of maximum clock-hour rainfall to
total storm depth, range from 0.76 in the southwest to 0.69 in the
east. The mean value of this ratio appears to be independent of the
return period of the maximum hour. In the northeast region, this ratio
has a nearly uniform distribution between the values 0.4 and 1.0, with
91 percent of the storms falling within this range. Again, it is important to note that these results are based on clock-hour rainfall data.
Hershfield (1961) found that actual annual-maximum one-hour rainfalls
are 13 percent greater, on average, than the values obtained from
clock-hour data.

Distributions of the nondimensional hyetograph parameters do not
vary significantly either with geographic region or with the return
period of the maximum hour. Statewide, t^o has a mean value of 0.38 and
a standard deviation of 0.15, while $\bar{k}^o$ has a mean value of 0.18 and a
standard deviation of 0.05. Comparisons with some common design-storm
shapes make these results more meaningful. A rectangular (uniform-
intensity) hyetograph has a $\bar{t}^o$ value of 0.50 and a $\bar{k}^o$ value of 0.29. A
triangular hyetograph with the peak at the midpoint of the duration has
a t^o value of 0.50 and a k^o value of 0.20. A triangular hyetograph
with a peak at the beginning of the storm has a $\bar{t}^o$ value of 0.33
and a $\bar{k}^o$ value of 0.24. The Type II intensity distribution of the U.S.
Soil Conservation Service (1964), a very peaked distribution that is
nearly symmetrical about the midpoint, has a $\bar{t}^o$ value of 0.50 and a $\bar{k}^o$
value of 0.17. Huff's first-quartile distribution for east-central
Illinois has a $\bar{t}^o$ value of 0.29 and a $\bar{k}^o$ value of 0.26. The nondimensional time to the controid is very short for this distribution because
it is derived from storm hyetographs for which the peak intensity
occurred in the first quarter of the duration.

TABLE 1.--Mean Characteristics for All Storms by Geographic Region

Storm Characteristic	Geographic Region					
	NW	SW	NC	SC	NE	SE
(1)	(2)	(3)	(4)	(5)	(6)	(7)
Number of storms	182	143	136	106	267	172
Mean duration (hours)	4.8	5.2	4.6	5.2	4.9	5.6
Mean P_{max}/D	0.75	0.76	0.72	0.69	0.69	0.69
Mean $\bar{t}^o$	0.36	0.38	0.40	0.39	0.38	0.39
Mean $\bar{k}^o$	0.18	0.18	0.18	0.19	0.19	0.18
Mean AP1 (mm)	3	3	5	4	6	10
Mean AP5 (mm)	14	11	17	13	19	25
Most common month	July	July	August	July	July	June

Table 2.--Mean Storm Characteristics by Return-Period Range, NE Region

Storm Characteristic	Return Period of Maximum 1-Hour Rainfall (years)		
	2-5	5-10	>10
(1)	(2)	(3)	(4)
Number of storms	163	54	50
Mean duration (hours)	4.8	5.1	5.0
Mean P_{max}/D	0.69	0.68	0.70
Mean $\bar{t}^o$	0.38	0.39	0.39
Mean $\bar{k}^o$	0.20	0.20	0.18
Mean AP1 (mm)	5	8	8
Mean AP5 (mm)	17	21	21
Most common month	July	July	July

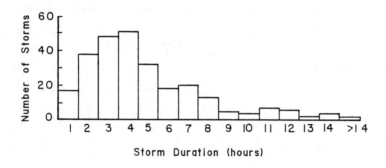

FIG. 2.--Distribution of Storm Durations, NE Region

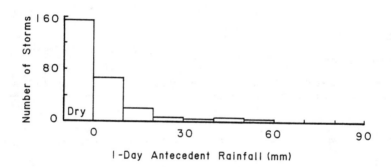

FIG. 3.--Distribution of 1-Day Antecedent Rainfalls, NE Region

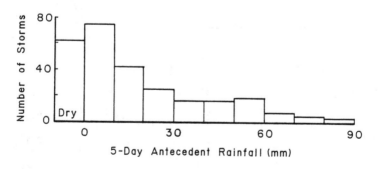

FIG. 4--Distribution of 5-Day Antecedent Rainfalls, NE Region

The mean $\bar{t}^o$ and $\bar{k}^o$ values of 0.38 and 0.18 for intense storms in Kansas indicate that the hyetographs of these storms are quite advanced and peaked, on average. For a triangular hyetograph with this same t^o value, the time to peak is only 14 percent of the storm duration. This same triangular hyetograph has a $\bar{k}^o$ value of 0.218. Yen and Chow (1980) found mean t^o values in the range of 0.47 to 0.50 for three stations in Illinois, Massachusetts, and North Carolina. However, most of the storms analyzed in this study had very low intensities. Their findings did indicate that the higher intensity storms tended to have more advanced hyetographs.

Mean antecedent rainfalls are quite small in comparison with mean storm depths. As expected, mean 1-day and 5-day antecedent rainfalls are lowest in the west and highest in the southeast. Overall, the data for the six regions show no apparent correlation between antecedent rainfall and storm intensity (as measured by the return period of the maximum one-hour rainfall). Figures 3 and 4 show the distributions of AP1 and AP5 for storms in the northeast region. AP1 is zero for 58 percent of these storms, less than 10 mm (0.4 in.) for 83 percent, and less than 20 mm (0.8 in.) for 91 percent. AP5 is zero for 23 percent of these storms, less than 10 mm for 51 percent, and less than 20 mm for 67 percent.

Intense storms occur most frequently in the summer months. The most common month of occurrence was August in the north-central region, June in the southeast, and July in the other four regions. In the northeast region, 73 percent of the storms occurred in the three summer months and 95 percent occurred between May 1 and September 30. Potential evapotranspiration rates are high during these months.

CONCLUSIONS

This study has examined some important characteristics of a particular set of storms. The storms in this set all produced one-hour rainfalls with return periods of 2 years or greater. It is these storms that are likely to control the designs of storm drainage systems and small detention basins in urban areas.

The results indicate that intense storms in Kansas are primarily convective-type summer storms. Although the nominal duration of these storms averages about 5 hours, most of the total rainfall typically occurs within a single hour. This intense rainfall usually occurs very near the beginning of the storm. Soils are likely to be rather dry initially except where irrigated. No rainfall is likely to have occurred in the previous 24 hours, and the median 5-day antecedent rainfall total is only 10 mm (0.4 in.). None of the mean storm characteristics examined varies significantly with storm intensity.

The results presented herein provide useful guidelines for constructing design hyetographs and selecting appropriate values of antecedent soil-wetness parameters. A reasonable approach would be to let the maximum hour contain the one-hour rainfall depth with the design return period. The mean characteristics of actual intense storms would

then provide a basis for constructing a complete design hyetograph
around this maximum hour.

It is important to note that the peak flowrate on a small urban
drainage basin can be quite sensitive to the time-distribution of rainfall within the maximum hour. The present study does not provide any
information on how this rainfall should be distributed. Future studies
of this type should focus on locations where long-term rainfall data is
available in shorter time increments.

Although the specific findings of this study are applicable only in
Kansas, the same type of analysis can be performed wherever long-term
rainfall data are available. It is hoped that practitioners will find
this a useful, practical approach to the design-input problem.

ACKNOWLEDGMENTS

This study was supported by the Department of Civil Engineering,
Kansas State University, and by the U. S. Geological Survey through the
Kansas Water Resources Research Institute (Project No. G907-23). Robert
Ward and Charles Bartlett assisted with the computer analysis.

REFERENCES

1. Frederick, R. H., and Tracey, R. J., "Conditional Probabilities of
   Intense Rains of Different Durations," Second Conference on Hydro-
   meteorology, Toronto, October 25-27, 1977, pp. 208-213.

2. Hershfield, D. M., "Rainfall Frequency Atlas of the United States
   for Durations from 30 Minutes to 24 Hours and Return Periods of 1 to
   100 Years," Technical Paper No. 40, U. S. Weather Bureau, Washington, D. C., May, 1961.

3. Huff, F. A., "Time Distribution of Rainfall in Heavy Storms," Water
   Resources Research, Vol. 3, No. 4, 1967, pp. 1007-1019.

4. U. S. Soil Conservation Service, "Watershed Planning," National
   Engineering Handbook, Sec. 4, Part 1, Washington, D. C., 1964.

5. Urban Water Resources Research Council, Annotated Bibliography on
   Urban Design Storms, American Society of Civil Engineers, New York,
   NY, 1983.

6. Yen, B. C., and Chow, V. T., "Design Hyetographs for Small Drainage
   Structures," Journal of the Hydraulics Division, ASCE, Vol. 106,
   No. HY6, June 1980, pp. 1055-1076.

Selecting a Stormwater Service Level for Urban Control

Richard D. Gibney* and Larry A. Roesner, Ph.D., P.E.**

Introduction

The use of service level solutions is certainly not new to the engineering field. Over the years, engineers concerned with water, wastewater, and solid waste have all used the concept of service level solutions. Historically, the service level solution for stormwater management has been to collect and remove the runoff as quickly as possible. For many jurisdictions, this service level solution is translated to a general rule of thumb such as: 1) no street flooding from the 5-year storm, 2) water below curb level for the 10-year storm, and 3) no flooding of the first floor of habitable structures for the 100-year storm. Recently, more and more emphasis is being placed on the maintenance of pre- and post-development runoff peaks from a specified design storm. The restriction is usually imposed at the point where a drainage system discharges to "waters of the state."

The limit on post-development flood peaks requires in most cases that some manner of storage be provided. For new development this requirement is met by setting aside the appropriate amount of land for detention facilities, but in older developments that require relief from flooding, the aquisition of land for storage is expensive or impossible. Thus, it becomes necessary to use streets and yards to provide some of this storage. The challange is to balance the degree of street and yard flooding against the cost of providing detention facilities that will eliminate this flooding to various degrees. The object of the study described herein was to establish the type of storage to be provided. Generally, the study focused on the acceptability of using streets and yards to provide a portion of the storage.

History of the Area

The Ybor City drainage basin is located just east of the Tampa Central Business District and contains approximately 1200 acres (see Figure 1). Ybor City had its beginning in the late 1800's when primarily Spanish, Cuban, and Italian immigrants developed a community founded on the cigar trade.

* Environmental Engineer, Camp Dresser & McKee Inc., One Tampa City Center, Suite 1750, Tampa, FL 33602.

** Vice President, Camp Dresser & McKee Inc., 555 Winderley Place, Maitland, FL 32751.

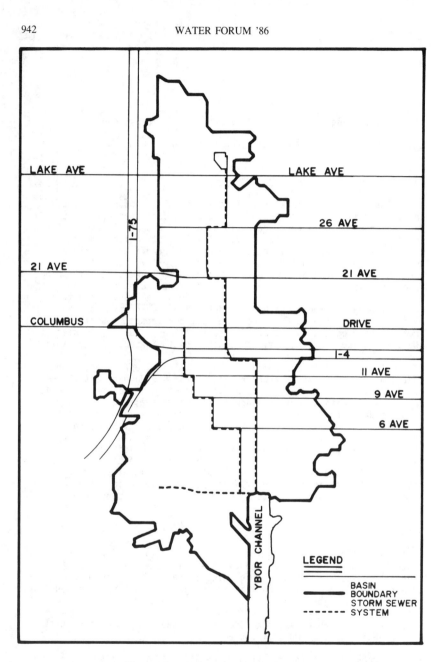

Figure 1.   Ybor City Study Area

A large portion of the southern half of the basin has been designated as Historic Preservation Area. The current City administration and other public and private entities have taken an active role in the revitalization of this area into a high quality, mixed use environment. Emphasis has been placed on retaining the existing cultural heritage of the area while stimulating private investment. The ongoing revitalization encourages the return of the residential population to the lower Ybor City area.

Definition of Performance Criteria and Service Levels

The objective of this Task (1) was to define the specific criteria and suitable hydraulic grade line relationships with respect to physical features and acceptable flooding conditions for three levels of stormwater service. The three levels of stormwater service were defined in terms of the extent of surface inundation (structure, yard and street flooding). Additionally, the stormwater management performance criteria for each service level were defined. The extent of acceptable flooding for each service level was defined in terms of location, extent, and severity of inundation. Criteria were defined which related the roadway segments and passability (as defined by depth of water) and the maximum permissible surface flow by street segment classification.

Basically, the service levels adopted for the various street segments can be described in generic terms as: Service Level A - no street flooding; B - some yard but no structure flooding; and C - some street and yard flooding, but no structure flooding.

SERVICE LEVEL A

Conceptually, Service Level A is the highest level of stormwater service and represents conditions where streets are not flooded. The citizen's perception of street flooding is somewhat different from the engineer's because the citizen is subjectively concerned with inconvenience while the engineer should be objectively evaluating vehicular passability.

An objective test of vehicular passability is the typical lower door and floor pan heights above pavement, as these measurements determine when ponded stormwater will enter the interior of a vehicle. At depths below this height, driving is slow and tedious, but roadways are passable. A second engineering concern is the rate at which vehicular traffic will travel on a flooded roadway segment.

A casual survey of a total of 121 passenger vehicles at two locations indicates that the typical pan and door heights are about 8 inches and 11 inches, respectively, above pavement.

The standard Florida Department of Transportation (FDOT) street design calls for the road to be round with a differential of less than 6 inches between the center line of the crown and the gutter. This criterion, along with the depth to floorpan, establishes the allowable level of flooding as follows:

o   Service Level A: This level represents the highest standard
     of stormwater service and features gutter flow during the
     5-year, 4-hour design storm which extends from the curb face
     to a maximum extent that is 5 feet from the roadway
     centerline. This provides for at least a 10-foot travel lane
     on arterial and collector thoroughfares.

SERVICE LEVEL B

Conditions in Service Level B can be described as street and some
yard flooding, without structure flooding, and represents an
intermediate level of stormwater service. When Service Level B
conditions exist on a street segment, the street may be passable with
difficulty by passenger vehicles, with some yard and right-of-way
flooding.

For the purposes of this study, Service Level B was defined as:

o   Service Level B: Allows street and yard flooding not to
     exceed 50 percent of the grassed area between the curb and
     structures as caused by the 5-year, 4-hour design storm.

SERVICE LEVEL C

The most severe surface ponding conditions are related to the
lowest level of service. Service Level C represents conditions which
exceed normal street flooding and approach structure flooding. Under
these conditions, passenger vehicle traffic may not be possible.

The City of Tampa has developed a criterion for establishing
minimum elevations for habitable structures that will, under
foreseeable design conditions, prevent structure flooding. The City
of Tampa Code, Section 42.28(i), requires that the minimum elevation
for all new construction be 18 inches above the roadway centerline.
This level can be used to establish a threshold structure flooding
level.

It must be noted that many of the first floor elevations in Ybor
City do not comply with this relatively recent criterion, and a
stormwater ponding condition of 18 inches above roadway centerlines
would cause structure flooding. Evaluation of four incidences of
flooding reported after the severe storm of September 6, 1982, (which
was greater than 5-year design event) indicated two examples of
variation from the "18 inch above centerline" criterion for structure
flooding.

With consideration of the potential for structure flooding at water
surface levels less than 18 inches above the centerline, Service Level
C was defined as follows:

o   Service Level C: This level represents a maximum ponding
     condition. It allows water levels resulting from 5-year,
     4-hour design storm which are greater than the depth

specified for Level B but not above the floor elevation of habitable structure.

The three service levels defined connote three distinct flood levels. Service Level A, the gold-plated solution, virtually eliminates all flooding, but at a great cost. Service Level C provides for the least flood protection. Service Level B, although not as stringent as Service Level A, provides for a great improvement over Service Level C's flood protection.

Development of Service Level Solutions

The objective of this task is to develop solutions to the stormwater management problems created by growth and development within the Ybor Basin. Computer simulations, using the EXTRAN block of the EPA Stormwater Management Model (2), were used to identify the most cost-effective solution based on the service levels identified and a 5-year, 4-hour design storm.

In the Ybor City Basin, the City of Tampa faces some unique and complex stormwater management problems. The current system is relatively old and in need of repair. In some cases, field inspection identified construction and other debris inside the pipes, as well as plugged pipes from systems no longer in use.

The southern portion of the Ybor Basin is within the Ybor City Historic Preservation District. To preserve the historic characteristics and features of the area, no detention facilities were considered as mitigation measures within the area. Thus, the service level solutions derived for the historic area rely primarily on an improved pipe network to carry the required stormwater runoff volume.

SERVICE LEVEL A

Service Level A has been identified as that level in which improvements to the existing system would provide for minimal street flooding with at least 10 feet of passable travel lane for local roads and at least 10 feet of traffic clearance in both directions for arterial and collector roads. If model-predicted flooding is found to exceed this level, improvements will be required which meet the City's current stormwater design criteria, i.e., the hydraulic grade line must be a minimum of 1 foot below the throat of the inlet and surface water flooding limited to gutter flow.

The first step in the determination of the requirements to provide Service Level A protection throughout the system was to identify locations for stormwater detention ponds. It was found that it is usually less expensive to construct detention areas than it is to construct new conveyance systems. Therefore, four probable sites for ponds were identified in the areas that currently experience flooding. The surface area associated with each of these locations was determined and an assumed working storage of 5 feet was used as input to the SWMM model.

Model simulation of the existing system using the detention areas showed that while the volume of flooding decreased, Service Level A was not attained. Therefore, in addition to the proposed detention areas, further conveyance system modifications proved necessary.

The second step in the service level solution determination regime was to increase the size and location of the conveyance system to provide for the required flow volume and velocity. The conveyance system was adjusted in a stair-step fashion whereby a pipe, unable to carry the required flow, is identified and its size adjusted until the hydraulic grade line (HGL) meets or exceeds the City's design requirements. This adjustment continues throughout the system, such that each pipe with insufficient capacity is adjusted until the Service Level A solution is obtained.

It was originally envisioned that the flooding in the Ybor City system was the result of several bottlenecks, and that resizing the bottlenecks plus creating detention storage at four sites, as mentioned above, would provide Level A protection. However, it was subsequently discovered that the system was undersized throughout its length. Each adjustment of pipe size eliminated the local surcharge problem, relieving flooding at the immediate upstream end of the pipe; however, the subsequent increase in flow caused problems elsewhere in the system.

The resulting costs to upgrade the entire system to a service Level A are substantial, requiring a large capital outlay estimated to be in the range of $7.5 to 9.0 million, excluding property and right-of-way costs.

SERVICE LEVEL B

Service Level B provides for street and yard flooding not to exceed 50 percent of the grassed area between the curb and structure. The same basic steps used to determine the Service Level A solution were applied to this system to determine a Service Level B solution. The adjustments to the existing system were small when compared to the Service Level A. This is due primarily to the requirement of Service Level A that the hydraulic grade line be a minimum of 1 foot below the inlet elevation. Under Service Level B, some areas within the basin will experience flooding above ground during the design storm. This flooding will be confined to the street surface and adjoining green space but will not, in general, present a threat to public health and safety or result in serious property damage. The estimated cost for a Service Level B solution ranged from $1.5 to 2.5 million, excluding property and right-of-way costs.

SERVICE LEVEL C

Service Level C allows significant yard and street flooding, but no water is permitted within a habitable structure. Surface flooding is allowed to exist to the extent that the yard space may be flooded to a depth of between 8 and 10 inches, depending on location. Because the existing stormwater retention and conveyance system generally provides

for Service Level C, no major modifications to the system were
required. However, it has been suggested that, as a minumum, a new
outfall to Ybor Channel, a new inlet to the existing retention pond,
and an increase in the size of the existing retention pond be
considered. These improvements will reduce the frequency of flooding
caused by insufficient hydraulic capacity in several flood prone
areas. The estimated costs for this solution ranged from $375,000 to
$425,000.

Selection of the Service Level to be Obtained

City staff were provided with the approximate areas, depths, and
duration of the flooding that was expected for the three service
levels. Because of the massive reconstruction that would have to take
place and the cost to provide Level A service, it was eliminated from
further consideration. Service Level C required little in the way of
improvements because the basin already exhibits this level of service,
which has been judged to be inadequate. Thus, of primary interest to
the City was further analysis of the flooding that would occur under
Service Level B.

For Service level B, approximately 240,300 cubic feet of water
would be ponding at some 10 different sites within the basin.
Additionally, some ground plane depressions located on private
property not connected to the stormwater conveyance system may also be
flooded. Generally, this flooding was determined to last a very short
time with the longest duration of flooding occurring near the outfall
at less than 2 hours.

The City was presented the approximate costs to correct flooding at
each location. City staff then compared corrective cost to the amount
of flooding that could be expected in each flooded area. The City
staff then recommended a "near B" solution and directed CDM to provide
four new "near B" solutions for their review. The four solutions
included:

Alternative 1 - Maintain the existing detention pond, and improve
the conveyance system as necessary.

Alternative 2 - Enlarge the existing pond, and improve the
conveyance system as necessary.

Alternative 3 - Maintain the existing detention pond, add a new
pond, and improve the conveyance system as necessary.

Alternative 4 - Enlarge the existing pond, add a new pond, and
improve the conveyance system as necessary.

As expected, the costs of the alternatives reflects the amount of
conveyance system modifications that have to be made to the system.
The alternatives that rely primarily on the increase in storage within
the basin cost much less than those which rely primarily on conveyance
system modifications.

The costs associated with the various alternatives were:

Alternative	Conveyance	Detention	Total
1	$6,993,000	$ 0	$6,993,000
2	$6,786,800	$142,800	$6,929,600
3	$4,020,050	$362,700	$4,382,750
4	$2,810,200	$505,500	$3,315,700

Alternative #4, the least costly, was selected for further study and the creation of an implementation schedule for a four-year capital improvements budget.

Summary

Thus, the selection of service level alternatives for this project was far from a simple task. Initially, the service levels have to be defined based on a perceived need. Solutions that will provide the levels of service are then derived. Finally, a service level is selected. This selection may not be an exact determination as illustrated by the "Near B" solution.

The methodology of service level solutions for stormwater management planning has proved itself with the City of Tampa, where the City was able to fund workable stormwater management plans to provide an acceptable level of flood control. Based on the successful completion of this study, the City of Tampa instituted a policy whereby all future stormwater planning studies will be required to provide various service level solutions.

References

(1) Camp Dresser & McKee Inc., Ybor City Stormwater Management Study, Phase II Final Report, October 1985, 75 pages.

(2) Roesner, L.A., Shubinski, R.P., and Aldrich, J.A. Stormwater Management Model User's Manual Version III, Addendum I EXTRAN, U.S. Environmental Protection Agency, Cincinnati Ohio, May 1981, 228 pages.

Use of Continuous Simulation
Versus The Design Storm Concept for Water Quality

Miguel A. Medina, Jr.*, M.ASCE

Introduction

For most hydrologic and water quality planning efforts, the probability of occurrence of events of various magnitudes and their duration is required. A model or methodology designed to simulate only discrete storm events cannot adequately provide this information. Although some regulatory agencies recognize the need for setting appropriate frequency and duration criteria to implement stormwater controls, proposed regulations are still based on the "design storm" concept. A precipitation event, either historical or artificial, is identified on the basis of an average return period or frequency. Once the return period is identified, it is usually assumed that the performance of the system that must accommodate such an event will retain that same frequency. In other words, it is assumed that the probability of the design capacity (e.g., storage volume, runoff) or the water quality standard being exceeded is equal to: the probability of the magnitude of the design storm being exceeded. The economic implications associated with design storm frequency decisions are seldom given any consideration. Traditional approaches to selection of design storms (depth-duration-frequency,intensity-duration-frequency) are deeply rooted in the pre-electronic-digital-computer era.

The assumptions regarding event return period or frequency can be shown to be theoretically false. The probability level attached to a particular flow event is not the same as that for the rainfall event from which it was generated, as noted by Linsley and Crawford (6) well over a decade ago. Even when a probability level can be established for a given rainfall rate at a specified duration, it is almost impossible to assign a probability level to a storm which consists of rainfall at various rates for various durations in several possible sequences. James and Drake (5) argue that design storms developed from statistical analysis of point rainfall records include all types of rainstorms, consequently, the resultant rainfall distributions are unlike any type of observed rain storm. When the synthetic temporal distribution of rainfall from a design storm is applied uniformly across the catchment, the runoff hydrographs are also unlike observed runoff hydrographs. Similarly, the event probability levels computed for a water quality constituent are not the same as those of its associated hydrographs and hyetographs.

*Associate Professor, Department of Civil and Environmental Engineering, Duke University, Durham, North Carolina 27706

Indeed, the return periods or frequencies among various water quality
variables generated by the same storm event time series may differ.
Non-linear aspects of the mechanics of the rainfall-runoff process,
including antecedent moisture conditions, and recognition of the
statistical heterogeneity of the rainfall, runoff and water quality
time series weigh heavily against use of the traditional approaches
for selection of design storms.

Recent advances in computer technology, and the availability of
powerful personal computers, have made obsolete the argument that
complex computer simulation models are impractical alternatives to the
design storm approach. By proposing stormwater quality control
criteria based on the design storm concept, regulatory agencies are
perpetuating a methodology which is inappropriate, lacks a sound
scientific basis, and may be quite costly in economic terms.

Evaluations of the Design Storm Concept and Alternatives

As noted above, the validity of the design storm concept has been
challenged by several investigators since the development of computer
simulation models. Of particular interest are the studies that
compare system performance (e.g., magnitudes and frequencies of peak
runoff, volumes, pollutant loads, pollutant concentrations) resulting
from choice of rainfall input data: either synthetic design storms or
historical storms. Continuous simulation involves the generation of
surface runoff quantity and quality time series with a physically-
based catchment model, from long-term historical precipitation data.
The simulated response of the system is described statistically, and
the proposed design is adjusted until an acceptable risk of violation
is obtained in terms of frequency or return period of the variable of
interest. Medina et al (9,10) and Nix (11) have extended this
methodology to evaluate the performance of urban stormwater detention
systems. An improved design storm can be obtained from: (1) detailed
analysis of historical rainfall data; (2) selection of several
discrete storm events (rather than the entire time series) for use
with a single event simulation model; and (3) determination, by trial
and error, of the combinations of hyetograph shape, duration, and
antecedent soil moisture conditions that yield accurate discharges for
a specified return period at a given location (13). This approach
would fail in the case of water quality variables, and is recognized
as an inappropriate approach by Wenzel and Voorhees (13) for such
purposes. For example, a sequence of smaller or less intense storm
events preceded by long dry-weather periods might result in greater
pollutant accumulation and washoff rates and place more stress on the
system.

Marsalek (7,8) compared simulated runoff peaks for historical
storms and two types of synthetic design storms, for a small catchment
(23 hectares) with fast response. For identical return periods, both
design storms produced higher runoff peaks than the historical storms.
Other aspects of urban drainage design besides runoff peaks were
considered: detention facilities, runoff volumes and runoff pollutant
loadings. The design storms produced runoff volumes widely varying
from those obtained for historical storms: detention storage changes

the return periods of outflow peaks. Simple design storms could not
approximate the volume, timing and multiple-peak nature of actual
hyetographs influencing the storage design. Geiger (2) used a 5-year
continuous data base for rainfall and runoff to demonstrate that
conclusions about runoff frequency could not be made from rainfall
analysis, and also found synthetic design storms unsafe for
dimensioning storage facilities: because they neglect the multi-
peaked rainfall shape encountered with the long duration historical
storms (resulting in large volumes). Huber (4) presents a ranking of
storm events by quantity (total rain, total flow, peak flow) and
quality (suspended solids load, BOD load, NO3 load) for a two-year
continuous simulation for an urban catchment in Minneapolis. The
rankings differ among all of the parameters.

     The large number of factors that affect the quality of surface
runoff (buildup between storms, washoff, transport, kinetic
interactions, etc.) prevents the use of any single event (either
synthetic or historical) for proper analysis and design. It is the
frequency response of the system which is significant, and also
duration (for receiving water violations). Thus, long-term historical
rainfall data are required. The reader is referred to an annotated
bibliography for an extensive summary and classification of
publications on urban design storms.(1)

Proposed Stormwater Quality Regulations

     State agencies are in the process of drafting and adopting
stormwater quality control criteria to comply with a Federal mandate.
An example is provided of a current regulation (12), and proposed
changes to implement stormwater controls, for North Carolina.
Organisms of the fecal coliform group are "not to exceed a median MF
of 14/100 ml and not more than 10 percent of the samples shall exceed
an MF count of 43/100 ml in those areas most probably exposed to fecal
contamination during the most unfavorable hydrographic and pollution
conditions" for SA waters. Best usage of these waters is shellfishing
for market purposes. In the proposed changes stormwater is defined as
"any waste discharged primarily in response to precipitation and
subsequent runoff which may impair the classified best usage of
surface waters." Several versions of stormwater control regulations
have been proposed over the past year, and public hearings have been
held. Interpretations of the "most unfavorable hydrographic and
pollution conditions" ranged up to the worst storm of record and the
100-year, 24-hour duration event (in terms of rainfall volume)! The
100-year storm was utilized since April 1985 as a guideline in
providing comments by Division of Environmental Management (DEM) staff
on major permits for development along the coast. The use of design
storms for water quality control was challenged at public hearings, as
well as other aspects (e.g., a 10 percent imperviousness limitation).
In the January 1986 draft two design storms were proposed to be used
in conjunction with the fecal coliform standard: a 10-year, 24-hour
duration event (return period for rainfall depth, volume) for areas
draining directly to SA waters and a 2-year, 24-hour storm for areas
draining to waters in proximity to SA waters. The fishery resource
agencies (Division of Marine Fisheries and Division of Health

Services) strongly supported the 10-year storm. It should be noted
that a 1/2 mile (0.8 kilometer) zone around SA waters is the boundary
within which the proposed stormwater controls apply.

The latest set of stormwater control proposals to date (February
1986) include specification of a 1-hour duration peak intensity:

  (i)   "Stormwater must not be discharged directly
        to class SA waters from precipitation events
        less severe than the 10-year, 24-hour event,
        including a 10-year, 1-hour intensity..."

  (ii) "Stormwater must not be discharged in close
        proximity to Class SA waters from precipitation
        events less severe than the 2-year, 24-hour
        event (including a 2-year, 1-hour peak
        intensity)..."

For other waters, the proposed regulations state that "appropriate
frequency/duration criteria for the design of stormwater controls...
shall be determined on a case-by-case basis..." New developments
within the stormwater control zone are imposed limits on effective
impervious cover: 10 percent effective impervious cover for areas
draining directly to SA waters and 30 percent for areas draining to
waters in close proximity.

As noted by the writer and other investigators, the design storm
is an inappropriate methodology for use with water quality standards.
This is demonstrated in the ensuing application. Unfortunately,
regulations such as these may perpetuate techniques made obsolete by
digital computers for the past 20 years.

Application

Ocean Isle Beach is an island off the southern tip of the North
Carolina coastline. A 35-year record of hourly precipitation data
recorded at nearby Wilmington, North Carolina (NOAA first-order
station) was analyzed in detail to obtain statistics on such storm
event variables as volume, intensity, duration and time between
events. An autocorrelation analysis of the hourly precipitation
record yielded a 12-hour minimum interevent time at 95 percent
confidence level, and was used subsequently to define storm event
independence. Frequencies and return periods were computed for all
the variables of interest: shown, respectively, for rainfall depth
(volume) in Figures 1 and 2. For example, a depth of 1.5 inches
(38 mm) was not exceeded 90 percent of the time, and had a return
period of 0.11 year (1.32 months). A depth of 5.0 inches (127 mm) was
not exceeded 99 percent of the time.

A sophisticated continuous urban stormwater model (3) was applied
to a 100-acre (40.5-hectare) catchment in Ocean Isle Beach, with both
residential and rural (open) land uses, to generate the runoff and
water quality time series. The results of a five-year simulation
(1978 to 1982) with hourly precipitation inputs are presented in

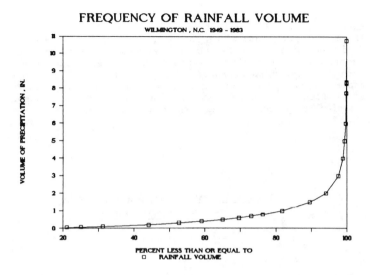

Figure 1. Frequency of Rainfall Depth (Volume)

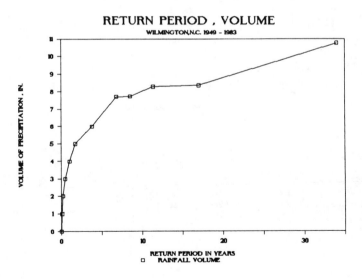

Figure 2. Return Periods of Rainfall Depth (Volume)

Figures 3 through 5, and Table 1. The simulation involved 397 storm
events. Figure 3 depicts frequency of runoff volume (total flow):
for example, a volume of 0.5 inch (12.7 mm) was not exceeded
93 percent of the time and 1.0 inch (25.4 mm) was not exceeded
99 percent of the time. Table 1 summarizes return periods and
frequencies for total runoff and flow-weighted average FCOLI
concentrations: major differences in the probability of occurrence of
event flows and concentrations are clearly demonstrated, shown
graphically for consecutively ranked events in Figure 5.

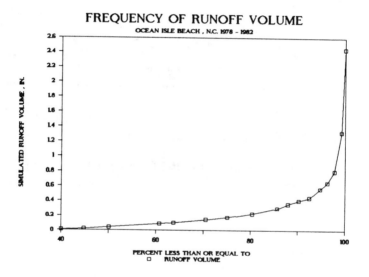

Figure 3. Frequency of Runoff Volume

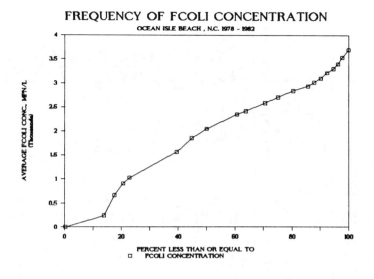

Figure 4. Frequency of FCOLI Concentration

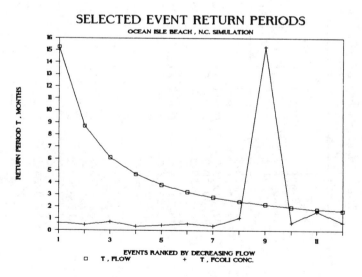

Figure 5. Return Periods for Flow and FCOLI Concentration, Rank-Ordered by Flow

Table 1.   Return Period and Frequency For Selected Events In Five-Year Simulation*, Ocean Isle Beach, N.C.

Event (YR/MO/DY/HR)	Total Runoff			Flow Weighted Average FCOLI Concentration		
	Magnitude in.(mm)	Return Period (months)	Percent < or Equal to	Magnitude MPN/L	Return Period (months)	Percent < or = to
79/09/03/08	2.44(62)	61.00	100.00	2153	0.326	53.15
78/12/24/08	1.33(34)	15.25	99.24	2725	0.642	76.32
82/01/03/09	0.95(24)	8.71	98.49	2500	0.469	67.51
82/09/20/13	0.80(20)	6.10	97.73	2804	0.718	78.84
78/11/29/11	0.72(18)	4.69	96.98	2268	0.351	56.42
81/05/06/23	0.65(17)	3.81	96.22	2431	0.442	65.49
78/01/19/14	0.62(16)	3.21	95.47	2677	0.575	73.55
80/07/26/18	0.56(14)	2.77	94.71	2338	0.379	59.70
78/01/25/07	0.52(13)	2.44	93.95	2935	1.052	85.64
79/04/13/19	0.48(12)	2.18	93.20	3678	15.25	99.24
78/08/11/11	0.44(11)	1.97	92.44	2737	0.656	76.83
82/02/02/09	0.42(10.7)	1.79	91.69	3137	1.605	90.68
79/12/06/10	0.414(10.5)	1.65	90.93	2761	0.670	77.33
78/06/23/21	0.405(10.3)	1.53	90.18	3694	61.00	100.00
80/09/13/14	0.225(5.7)	0.77	80.35	3311	3.05	95.21
81/03/02/01	0.143(3.6)	0.52	70.53	2632	0.545	72.04
82/03/06/05	0.087(2.2)	0.39	60.71	2354	0.389	60.71
78/11/27/14	0.042(1.1)	0.31	50.13	1923	0.285	46.35
81/10/24/20	0.011(0.28)	0.26	40.30	1427	0.229	33.25
81/11/30/19	0.004(0.1)	0.22	30.48	795	0.191	19.65
82/03/24/15	0.001(0.03)	0.19	20.65	1115	0.205	25.19
81/12/04/11	0.001(0.03)	0.178	13.85	373	0.179	14.61

*397 storms defined by 12-hour minimum interevent time, 1978-1982.

Acknowledgments

The writer wishes to thank engineers and planners of the Division of Environmental Management for their cooperation for the past year, in spite of opposing views on methodology.

References

1. ASCE, "Annotated Bibliography On Urban Design Storms," Urban Water Resources Research Council, 1983.
2. Geiger, W., "Use of Field Data In Urban Drainage Planning," in Urban Runoff Pollution, Torno, Marsalek and Desbordes (Eds.), Springer-Verlag, 1986 (in press).
3. Huber, W. C., et al, "Storm Water Management Model User's Manual, Version III," EPA-600/2-84-109a, November 1981.
4. Huber, W. C., "Deterministic Modeling of Urban Runoff Quality," in Urban Runoff Pollution, Torno, Marsalek and Desbordes (Eds.), Springer-Verlag, 1986 (in press).
5. James, W. and Drake, J. J., "Kinematic Design Storms Incorporating Spatial and Time Averaging," Proceedings of Stormwater Management Model Users Group Meeting of June 19-20, 1980, U.S. E.P.A., Athens, Ga., December 1980, pp. 133-149.
6. Linsley, R., and Crawford, N., "Continuous Simulation Models in Hydrology," Geophysical Research Letters, Vol. 1, No. 1, 1974, pp. 59-62.
7. Marsalek, J., "Synthesized and Historic Design Storms for Urban Drainage Design," Proceedings of the International Conference on Urban Storm Drainage, University of Southampton, England, April 1978, pp. 87-99.
8. Marsalek, J., "Research on the Design Storm Concept," ASCE Urban Water Resources Research Program, Technical Memorandum No. 33, September 1978.
9. Medina, M. A., et al, "Modeling Stormwater Storage/Treatment Transients: Applications," Journal of Environmental Engineering Division, ASCE, 107(EE4): pp 799-816, August 1981.
10. Medina, M. A., et al, "Modeling Stormwater Storage/Treatment Transients: Theory," Journal of Environmental Engineering Division, ASCE, 107(EE4): pp 781-797, August 1981.
11. Nix, Stephan J., "Integrated Design Methodology for Urban Stormwater Detention Facilities," Computer Applications in Water Resources, ASCE, N.Y., 1985, pp 835-844.
12. State of North Carolina, "Classifications and Water Quality Standards Applicable to Surface Waters of North Carolina," Environmental Management Commission, Raleigh, N. C., January 1, 1985.
13. Wenzel, Harry G. and Voorhees, Michael L., "An Evaluation of The Urban Design Storm Concept," WRC Research Report No. 164, University of Illinois, Urbana-Champaign, Illinois, August 1981.

Outlet Structure Hydraulics

Dr. Ronald L. Rossmiller, M ASCE*

Abstract

Current detention basin design procedure is to design the outlet structure for two or more return periods. This is sometimes done by combining weirs and/ or orifices of various sizes and shapes immediately in front of a pipe or box culvert. Tests on four plexiglas models have produced some preliminary equations which predict the calibrated flows within a reasonable range of accuracy. Recommendations are made where more research is needed.

Introduction

In the early 1970s, communities began to enact ordinances that required the peak rate of flow after development not to exceed the peak rate prior to development. These ordinances usually did not specify any particular return period storm for design. Thus, depending on the desires of the locality, the 2-, 10-, or 100-year storm would be used.

The most popular method of complying with these ordinances was to temporarily store the runoff in a detention basin and size the outlet pipe to discharge the predevelopment rate. After a few years' experience with these basins and outlet structures, the observation was made that they usually worked well for the design storm but not for others. Either the basin overtopped or the smaller flows would not be attenuated.

One solution was to require the outlet structure to reduce the outflow rate for several return periods, the 2- through 100-year events. This resulted in the use of multi-stage outlet structures consisting of weirs and orifices at various elevations. Some of these outlet structures consist of separate weirs or orifices through or over the downstream berms. Others consist of a single integral outlet structure made up of weirs and orifices in a headwall in front of the outlet pipe or box culvert.

The question is posed as to whether the existing weir, orifice, and culvert equations and coefficients are adequate to predict the flow through these latter types of structures. Historically, weirs were tested with straight, rectangular approach channels, had crest sections with well formed, often machined edges, and downstream channels with no obstructions. Outlet structures have no upstream channel, just the basin itself. The crest section is usually poured concrete. There is no downstream channel, only the outlet culvert which can obstruct the flow in some situations.

*Assoc. Prof. of Civ. Engrg., Iowa State University at Ames, Iowa.

Because of these differences between outlet structures and the weirs in the literature, the tables and figures used to estimate the coefficients in the equations may not be applicable when estimating the flow rates at various depths through these outlet structures.

To test this hypothesis, four plexiglas models were constructed. They were subjected to various flow depths, simulating storms of different magnitudes, and the results checked against a downstream calibrated V-notch weir. These four outlet structures incorporate V-notch and horizontal weirs, circular and rectangular orifices, and drop inlets in various combinations. These shapes were used because they illustrate the variety of outlet structures pictured and discussed in the journals and trade magazines.

This paper reports the results of these initial investigations and presents some preliminary equations which can predict the calibrated flows within a reasonable range of accuracy.

Test Facilities

All tests were made in a 9.15 m (30 ft) long plexiglas flume with a width and height of 0.61 m (2 ft) located in the basement laboratory. The flume's head tank has a height of 1.52 m (5 ft). Water is supplied from a constant head tank located on the second floor. Flows were measured at a calibrated ninety degree V-notch weir located at the flume's downstream end. The 1:13 scale models were positioned near the upstream end and consisted of a short outlet pipe and a headwall incorporating various weirs and/or orifices. The elevation of the model was set to ensure that the pipe operated in inlet control.

A Lory Type A point gage, with an accuracy of 0.0003 m (0.001 ft), was used to measure depth. It was mounted on a trolley that could be positioned both laterally and longitudinally. A 3.18 mm (1/8 in) diameter pitot tube was used to measure velocity head. Pressure differences could be read to within 0.003 m (0.01 ft).

Model Equations

The several equations for the four models are listed below. Some of the variables are shown in the figures for each model. Others are listed below each equation. Space limitations do not permit showing all the curves and tables necessary to display the range of values for each variable. This will be done in a paper to be submitted to the ASCE Hydraulics Division Journal.

The following preliminary equations are used to estimate the discharge through Model A which is depicted in Fig. 1.

For $O < H < P$

$$Qt = (C1 \tan O/2 \; H^{2.5}) \; RF2 \qquad\qquad (A-1)$$

Where Qt = total discharge, cfs
C1 = coefficient of discharge, dimensionless
O = total central angle of the V-notch weir, degrees
H = upstream depth, ft
RF2 = reduction factor for a V-notch weir, dimensionless

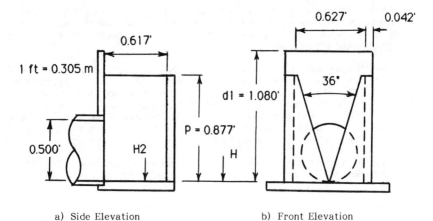

1 ft = 0.305 m

a) Side Elevation   b) Front Elevation

Figure 1. Dimensions of Model A - V-Notch Weir in a Headwall

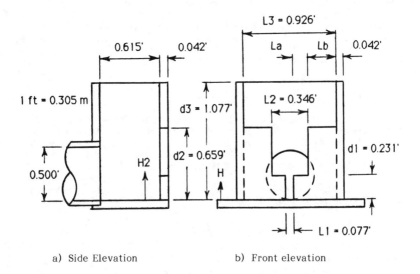

a) Side Elevation   b) Front elevation

Figure 2. Dimensions of Model B - Rectangular Weirs in a Headwall

For $P < H < d1$

$$Qt = \text{Equation A-1} + 2\ C^* \text{ Le } h1^{1.5} \tag{A-2}$$

where C^* = coefficient of discharge, dimensionless
Le = effective length, ft
h1 = $H - P$, effective head, ft

The following preliminary equations are used to estimate the discharge through Model B which is depicted in Fig. 2.

For $0 < H < d1$

$$Qt = C\ L1\ H\ (2\ g\ H1)^{0.5} \tag{B-1}$$

where C = coefficient of discharge, dimensionless
L1 = effective length (see Fig. 2), ft
g = 32.16 ft/sec/sec
H1 = $H - H2$, ft
H2 = depth within the headwall, ft

For $d1 < H < d2$ and $H < 0.45$ ft

$$Qt = \text{Equation B-1} + 2\ C^* \text{ La } h1^{1.5} \tag{B-2}$$

where La = effective length (see Fig. 2), ft
h1 = $H - d1$, effective head on the middle section, ft

For $d1 < H < d2$ and $H > 0.45$ ft

$$Qt = C\ L1\ d1\ (2\ g\ H1)^{0.5} + (C^*\ L2\ h1^{1.5})\ RF1 \tag{B-3}$$

where L2 = effective length (see Fig. 2), ft
RF1 = reduction factor for a horizontal weir, dimensionless

For $d2 < H < d3$ and $H < 0.80$ ft

$$Qt = C\ L1\ d1\ (2\ g\ H1)^{0.5} + (C^*\ L2\ h1^{1.5})\ RF1 +$$

$$2\ Ct\ Lb\ h2^{1.5} \tag{B-4}$$

where Lb = effective length (see Fig. 2), ft
h2 = $H - d2$, effective head on the upper section, ft

For $d2 < H < d3$ and $H > 0.80$ ft and $H2 < d2$

$$Qt = C\ L1\ d1\ (2\ g\ H1)^{0.5} + C\ L2\ (d2 - d1)\ (2\ g\ H3)^{0.5} +$$

$$C^*\ L3\ h2^{1.5} \tag{B-5}$$

where H3 = head on the circular orifice, ft = $H - H2$ or $H -$
(depth to center of orifice), whichever is less
L3 = effective length (see Fig. 2), ft

For d2 < H < d3 and H > 0.80 ft and h2 > d2

$$Qt = C \ L1 \ d1 \ (2 \ g \ H1)^{0.5} + C \ L2 \ (d2 - d1) \ (2 \ g \ H3)^{0.5} +$$

$$(C* \ L3 \ h2^{1.5}) \ RF1 \qquad (B-6)$$

The following preliminary equations are used to estimate the discharge through Model C which is depicted in Fig. 3.

For 0 < H < d1

$$Qt = 2 \ C^\wedge \ Af \ (2 \ g \ H)^{0.5} \qquad (C-1)$$

where $C^\wedge$ = coefficient of discharge, dimensionless
     Af = cross sectional area of flow, sq ft

For d1 < H < d2

$$Qt = 2 \ Co \ Ao \ (2 \ g \ Ho)^{0.5} \qquad (C-2)$$

where Co = coefficient of discharge, dimensionless
     Ao = area of the circular orifice, sq ft
     Ho = H - H2, head on the orifice, ft

For d2 < H < d3

$$Qt = \text{Equation C-2} + C* \ L1 \ Hr^{1.5} \qquad (C-3)$$

where L1 = effective length (see Fig. 3), ft
     Hr = H - d2, effective head on the rectangular weir, ft

For d3 < H < d4

$$Qt = \text{Equation C-2} + Co \ Ar \ (2 \ g \ hr)^{0.5} \qquad (C-4)$$

where Ar = area of the rectangular slot, sq ft
     hr = head on the rectangular orifice, ft = H - H2 or H - (depth to center of orifice), whichever is less

For d4 < H < d5 and H2 < d4

$$Qt = \text{Equation C-4} + C* \ L4 \ H4^{1.5} \qquad (C-5)$$

where L4 = 1.624 ft
     H4 = H - d4, head on the weir, ft

For d4 < H < d5 and H2 > d4

$$Qt = \text{Equation C-4} + (C* \ L4 \ H4^{1.5}) \ RF1 \qquad (C-6)$$

The following preliminary equations are used to estimate the discharge through Model D which is depicted in Fig. 4.

For 0 < H < d1

$$Qt = 2 \ C^\wedge \ Af \ (2 \ g \ H)^{0.5} \qquad (D-1)$$

For d1 < H < d2

$$Qt = Co \ Ao \ (2 \ g \ Ho)^{0.5} \qquad (D-2)$$

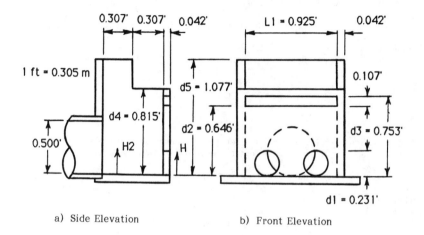

a) Side Elevation   b) Front Elevation

Figure 3. Dimensions of Model C - Orifices in a Headwall

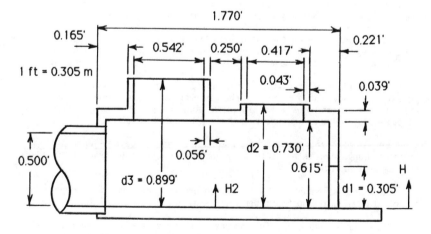

Figure 4. Dimensions of Model D - Multiple Outlet Structures

For d2 < H < d3

Use Equation D-3 or D-4, whichever yields the smaller discharge. Generally at lower depths of flow over the crest, the weir equation will govern.

$$Qt = \text{Equation D-2} + C^* \text{ Lw } h2^{1.5} \qquad\qquad (D\text{-}3)$$

where Lw = 2π R, ft
R = inner radius + 0.5 (thickness of wall), ft
h2 = H - d2, ft

$$Qt = \text{Equation D-2} + Co \text{ Ao } (2 \text{ g } h2)^{0.5} \qquad\qquad (D\text{-}4)$$

For d3 < H

Use Equation D-5 or D-6, whichever yields the smaller discharge. Generally at lower depths of flow over the crest, the weir equation will govern.

$$Qt = \text{Equation D-4} + C^* \text{ Lw } h3^{1.5} \qquad\qquad (D\text{-}5)$$

where h3 = H - d3, ft

$$Qt = \text{Equation D-4} + Co \text{ Ao } (2 \text{ g } h3)^{0.5} \qquad\qquad (D\text{-}6)$$

Recommendations

Based on the initial research, several recommendations are listed below for additional research to better define the actual conditions and equations applicable to these integral types of detention basin outlet structures. The ultimate payoff, of course, is that engineers will have better design tools and increased confidence that their detention basins, on which millions of dollars are spent each year, will actually perform as they have been designed.

The reduction factor for submerged flows in a headwall needs more investigation. Research should be conducted as to whether any changes will occur if the headwall length is increased or if other structure combinations are used.

The problem of predicting the depth of flow just upstream of the outlet pipe requires much more research. The research should use a pipe or other types of outlets to determine whether a general equation can be developed or, if possible, the flow calculations involving this depth could be avoided.

For stepped rectangular weirs, guidelines should be developed to assist in determining when three sections or one section should be used in the head-discharge calculations.

Research is needed to determine the proper flow equation through a circular orifice when the upstream depth is less than the diameter of the orifice.

Research is needed to define when the culvert charts can be used to predict the depth of flow just upstream of the outlet pipe or box culvert for various types of outlet structures.

Some outlet structures incorporate drop inlets with an outlet pipe. At high flows, the proper head to be used in the weir or orifice equation is difficult to determine. Research is needed to better define the proper heads to be used.

Some outlet structures use a narrow notch in the headwall upstream of the outlet pipe to control low flows. Research is needed to develop a methodology to determine the depth just upstream of the outlet pipe or to develop a flow equation dependent only on the depth just upstream of the notch.

Summary

The hypothesis was posed that flow through detention basin outlet devices, designed to reduce peak outflow rates to predevelopment levels for several return periods by incorporating weirs and orifices in the headwall of the outlet culvert, do not conform to the flows predicted by the normal weir, orifice, and culvert equations. Tests on four plexiglas models confirmed this hypothesis to the extent that the designer must be aware of the various flow patterns through these complex hydraulic structures in order to be able to properly evaluate the variables in the weir and orifice equations. Preliminary equations for each model at several depths of flow were developed and recommendations for additional research were made.

Uncertainties in Groundwater Transport Modeling

Eric. W. Strecker[1], Wen-sen Chu[2], Assoc. Members, ASCE
Dennis P. Lettenmaier[3], Member, ASCE

Abstract

Using synthetic data from a hypothetical aquifer, the effects of
data availability and data uncertainty were studied by the combined
use of a parameter identification (PI) algorithm and the United States
Geological Survey's contaminant transport code. The study results
found that the accuracy of transport modeling depends very much on the
estimates of transmissivity. It was also found that after the
installation of a critical number of observation wells, additional
data collected over time was more important to better prediction of
contaminant plume than adding more wells. The study results suggest
that with our present level of data availability, incorporation of
uncertainty analyses in groundwater contaminant transport modeling is
highly recommended.

Introduction

Contaminant transport modeling in groundwater has become an
increasingly used tool in groundwater restoration, and for evaluating
potential sites for underground hazardous waste repositories. Many
models have been developed for use in numerical simulations of
groundwater flow and transport (1,2,4,5,8).

There are two basic concerns associated with using models for
prediction of groundwater flow and contaminant transport phenomena.
The first is whether the model is capable of characterizing the flow
and transport in aquifers. The assumptions and approximations
introduced in the model formulation may not be appropriate for sites
with complex geological characteristics. Various solution schemes for
the models may also introduce errors into model predictions. The
second concern associated with using models as predictive tools is the
availability and quality of data used in model calibration. Groundwater flow and transport have a relatively large time scale, and
obtaining a good data set takes time, and is very expensive. For
these reasons, the amount of data available for model calibration and
validation in most investigations is very limited.

---

[1] Staff Engineer, Woodward-Clyde Consultants, One Walnut Creek
Center, 100 Pringle Ave., Walnut Creek, California 94596
[2] Assist. Prof., Department of Civil Engineering, FX-10, University
of Washington, Seattle, Washington 98195
[3] Research Professor, Department of Civil Engineering, FX-10,
University of Washington, Seattle, Washington 98195 (currently on
leave)

This paper summarizes the findings from a study which was designed to investigate the effects of data availability and data uncertainty on groundwater contaminant transport modeling. Since the technical details of the study have been reported elsewhere (6), only a brief description of the experimental procedures and the major findings of the study are presented here.

Description of the Study

Due to the geological complexity of any natural aquifer and the absence of extensive field data that could be assumed to accurately describe the true conditions of an aquifer, the use of data from an actual aquifer was not possible. Instead, the study was conducted using a hypothetical aquifer with geological and hydrological characteristics similar to selected actual sites.

The characteristics of the hypothetical aquifer were independently defined at the beginning of the study by a hydrogeologist who was not otherwise involved with the study. With the hypothetical aquifer characteristics, the hydrogeologist created a data set of monthly hydraulic heads and concentrations over a four year period using the United States Geological Survey's Method of Characteristics (USGS-MOC) code (3). With the exception of some limited point estimates at chosen observation wells, the pumping schedule, the source location and strength, and the boundary conditions, the aquifers parameters were kept from the investigators until the end of the study.

In order to reflect both the models' inability to completely characterize an aquifer (and its responses) and the sampling errors, fields of random noise (which were correlated in both space and time) were added to the model generated hydraulic heads and concentration fields as synthetic observations. Using these synthetic observations, the model parameters (transmissivity and dispersivity) were determined by combining a parameter identification (PI) technique (9) with the USGS-MOC model (7), The PI scheme (PI-MOC) was formulated as an ordinary least squares problem which minimizes the differences between model solutions and observations. In the PI-MOC scheme, transmissivities were first estimated by an objective function which minimized the difference between actual and observed heads. Then, with the estimated transmissivities fixed, dispersivities were found by minimizing the differences between the logarithms of observed and computed concentrations.

To assess the effects of data availability and uncertainty on parameter estimates and subsequently model predictive accuray, six sampling strategies were developed and tested. The strategies were defined by the length of observation record and the number and locations of observation wells.

All of the chosen sampling strategies were evaluated in the following manner. First, using each sampling strategy to reflect a particular data availability level, PI-MOC was used to determine the best possible model parameters (transmissivity and dispersivities) under different uncertainty conditions. Each uncertainty condition

was characterized by the level of random noise (uncertainties)
introduced into the data. To study the effects of data availability
and uncertainty, the PI-MOC estimated parameters were then used by the
USGS-MOC model to predict four years of monthly hydraulic heads and
concentrations. Finally, the predicted results were compared with the
exact aquifer response (generated by the hydrogeologist at the
beginning of the project) as well as the synthetic response.

To examine the effect of model simplification, the aquifer was
assumed to be characterized by one, three, and six transmissivity
zones. The effects of the proposed levels of simplification were
closely examined by the procedures described previously.

Major Findings of the Study

For the homogeneous (one zone transmissivity) cases, it was found
that the head and concentration predictions were generally poor. As
an example, Figure 1 shows the comparison of actual plume (generated)
with the predicted plume (using parameters determined from a
particular sampling strategy and medium noise levels). One can
observe that the assumed homogeneous aquifer does not describe the
shape of the plume as well as those represented by three and six zones
of transmissivity. In general, unless when transmissivity estimates
were accurately determined by PI-MOC, concentration predictions were
always poor.

As was expected, the most limiting data strategy produced model
parameters which gave the poorest prediction of contaminant plume.
Because of low transverse spreading of the plume, as observed in
Figure 2, concentration magnitudes in the comparison were close, but
the predicted plume shape was too narrow. It was found that after the
installation of a critical number of observation wells, additional
data collected over time was more important to better prediction of
contaminant plume than adding more wells.

In summary, our study results showed that getting the proper
transmissivity values was by far the most important task in contaminant transport modeling. Calibration of dispersivities in USGS-MOC
code for the designed aquifer was basically a fine tuning process.
When revealed, the actual transmissivity distribution in the hypothetical aquifer (created by the enlisted hydrogeologist) was quite
complex. It is found that the large variations of transmissivities in
adjacent nodes were what caused much of the dispersion of the pollutant, rather than the input dispersivities themselves. Having large
zones of constant transmissivity in calibration runs did not provide
the dispersion mechanism due to local velocity variations as found in
the actual data. The PI-MOC algorithm therefore attempted to make up
for the dispersion due to local velocity variations by enlarging the
dispersivity estimates. The large localized variation in transmissivities (as found in any aquifer) may not be properly represented even
by the more elaborate spatial interpolation techniques. One possible
alternative is to use stochastic representation of transmissivities
around a given mean transmissivity for a zone. The mean and standard

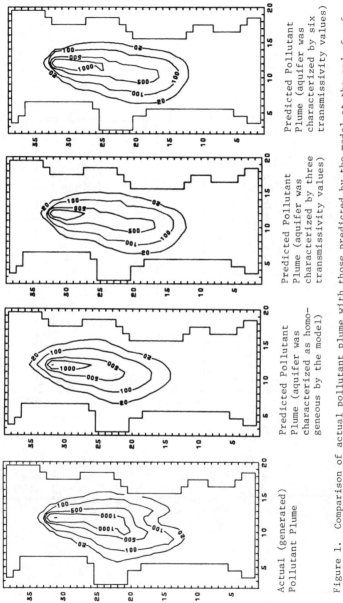

Actual (generated)
Pollutant Plume

Predicted Pollutant
Plume (aquifer was
characterized as homo-
geneous by the model)

Predicted Pollutant
Plume (aquifer was
characterized by three
transmissivity values)

Predicted Pollutant
Plume (aquifer was
characterized by six
transmissivity values)

Figure 1. Comparison of actual pollutant plume with those predicted by the model at the end of a four
year simulation. The parameters used in the prediction were obtained by PI-MOC.

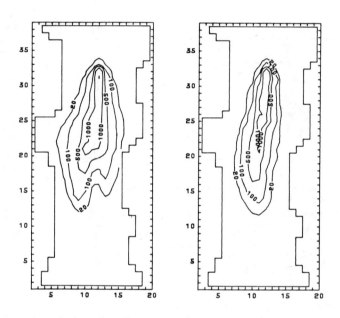

Actual (generated)   Predicted Pollutant
Pollutant Plume   Plume

Figure 2.   Comparison of actual and predicted pollutant plumes at
             the end of a four year simulation. The parameters used
             in the prediction were obtained by the most limiting
             sampling strategy tested (two years of monthly observa-
             tions in eight wells with high data uncertainty).

deviation for the transmissivity could both be determined by the PI-MOC algorithm.

Through the study, we have found that the predictive ability of a groundwater contaminant transport model is limited when the calibration data is scarce (as in most of the present cases), and the geological features of the aquifer are over-simplified. Using parameters determined from some hypothetical but realistic data set, our results showed significant prediction errors after only four years of simulation. With our present level of data availability, incorporation of uncertainty analyses in groundwater contaminant transport modeling is highly recommended.

Acknowledgements

We would like to thank Peg Michalek for the design of the hypothetical aquifer in the study, and Lori Nagle for the typing of the manuscript. The study is supported in part by funds provided by the U.S. Department of the Interior, Bureau of Reclamation, Office of Water Research, Under Bureau Grant No. 4-FG-93-00010, superseded by Geological Survey Grant No. 14-08-001-G-1059.

References

1. Bachmat, Y., Bredehoeft, J., Andrews, B., Holtz,ᐨD., and Sebastian S., Groundwater Management: The Use of Numerical Models, American Geophysical Union (AGU) Water Resources Monograph No. 5, AGU, Washington, D.C., 1980.

2. Javandel, I., Doughty, C., and Tsang, C.F., Groundwater Transport: Handbook of Mathematical Models, Water Resources Monograph 10, American Geophysical Union, Washington, D.C., 1984.

3. Konikow, L.F., and Bredehoeft, J.D., "Computer Model of Two-Dimensional Solute Transport and Dispersion in Ground Water", Chapter C2, Techniques of Water-Resources Investigations of the United States Geological Survey, U.S. Geological Survey, Reston, Virginia, 1978.

4. Pinder, G.F., and Gray, W., Finite Element Simulation in Surface and Subsurface Hydrology, Academic Press, New York, 1977.

5. Remson, I., Hornberger, G., and Molz, F., Numerical Methods in Subsurface Hydrology, Interscience, New York, 1971.

6. Strecker, E.W., Chu, W-S., and Lettenmaier, D.P., "Evaluation of Data Requirements for Groundwater Contaminant Transport Modeling", Water Resources Series Technical Report No. 94, Department of Civil Engineerng, University of Washington, 1985, 92 pp.

7. Strecker, E.W., and Chu, W-S., "Parameter Identification of Groundwater Contaminant Transport Model", Groundwater, Vol. 24, No. 1, 1986, pp. 56-62.

8. Wang, H., and Anderson, M., Introduction to Groundwater Modeling -
    Finite Difference and Finite Element Methods, W.H. Freeman and
    Co., San Francisco, California, 1982.

9. Yeh, W.W-G., "Review of Parameter Identification Procedures in
    Groundwater Hydrology: The Inverse Problem", Water Resources
    Research, Vol. 22, No. 2, 1986, pp. 95-108.

Estimation and Inference in the Inverse Problem

Hugo A. Loaiciga,[1] M. ASCE, and Miguel A. Mariño,[2] M. ASCE

ABSTRACT: The estimation of groundwater flow and mass transport parameters is approached via maximum likelihood. Confidence intervals and hypothesis tests as well as the asymptotic properties of estimators are presented. Two examples illustrate the methodology developed in this study.

INTRODUCTION

The estimation of groundwater flow parameters (i.e., transmissivity and storativity) and hydrodynamic dispersion coefficients in the convection-dispersion equation of miscible displacement is a research topic of main interest to hydrogeologists. Such parameters and coefficients are useful to simulate the response of subsurface formations to artificial and/or natural inputs. In the past two decades, a considerable effort has been devoted to the inverse problem for groundwater flow parameters. The estimation of dispersion-diffusion coefficients in the equation of miscible displacement has received substantial attention more recently, and it is an area of continuing debate nowadays (4).

The objectives of this study are: (1) To present a new approach for the solution of the inverse problem, for groundwater flow and mass transport; (2) to present the properties of estimators and some results concerning statistical inference relevant to such estimators; and (3) to illustrate the developed methodology with two applications. It is shown that the inverse problem for confined aquifer flow, and mass transport under saturated conditions, can be approached in a unique manner by maximum likelihood. Under mild statistical assumptions, estimated parameters are globally optimal, unique, and have all desirable (asymptotic) properties.

PROBLEM STATEMENT

It is assumed that two-dimensional confined aquifer flow, and miscible displacement of an ideal tracer in saturated flow, are correctly described by the following two equations:

---

[1] Postgraduate Research Engineer, Department of Land, Air and Water Resources, University of California, Davis, California 95616.
[2] Professor, Department of Land, Air and Water Resources, and Department of Civil Engineering, University of California, Davis, California 95616.

$$\frac{\partial}{\partial x}(T\frac{\partial \phi}{\partial x}) + \frac{\partial}{\partial y}(T\frac{\partial \phi}{\partial y}) - F = S\frac{\partial \phi}{\partial t} \quad \text{(groundwater flow)} \tag{1}$$

in which ϕ, $T(x,y)$, $S(x,y)$, and $F(x,y,t)$ denote piezometric head, transmissivity, storativity, and a sink/source, respectively.

$$\frac{\partial C}{\partial t} = \frac{\partial}{\partial x_i}(D_{hij}\frac{\partial C}{\partial x_j}) - V_i\frac{\partial C}{\partial x_i} \quad \text{(miscible displacement)} \tag{2}$$

in which C denotes solute concentration, V_i is the average flow velocity in the ith direction (i=1,2,3), and D_{hij} is a second-rank tensor, the coefficient of hydrodynamic dispersion (2).

Equations (1) and (2), which are associated with pertinent initial and boundary conditions, are discretized by the finite element method to obtain:

$$A_1 \underline{\phi}_t + A_2 \underline{\phi}_{t-1} + \underline{b}_t = \underline{e}_t \quad t = 1,2,\ldots,n \tag{3}$$

$$B_1 \underline{C}_t + B_2 \underline{C}_{t-1} + \underline{d}_t = \underline{u}_t \quad t = 1,2,\ldots,n \tag{4}$$

in which the subindex t indicates a value at time t; A_1 and A_2 are square matrices whose elements are functions of transmissivities and storativities according to the finite element discretization; $\underline{\phi}_t$ is the vector of (unknown) piezometric heads at time t; $\underline{b}_t$ is a vector function of known inputs (i.e., boundary and initial conditions), transmissivities and storativities; $\underline{e}_t$ is a white-noise Gaussian disturbance term that accounts for modeling and approximation errors in representing Eq. (1) by Eq. (3), and its covariance matrix Σ_1 is unknown; B_1 and B_2 are square matrices whose elements are functions of D_{hij} according to the finite element discretization; $\underline{d}_t$ is a vector function of known boundary and initial conditions as well as of D_{hij}; $\underline{u}_t$ is a white-noise Gaussian error term of unknown covariance Σ_2; and $\underline{C}_t$ is a vector of (unknown) concentrations at time t. It is convenient to express Eqs. (3) and (4) as follows:

$$\Psi_1 \underline{\phi}_t + \Gamma_1 \underline{x}_t = \underline{e}_t \tag{5a}$$

$$\Gamma_1 = [A_2, I] \tag{5b}$$

$$\underline{x}_t^T = [\underline{\phi}_{t-1}^T, \underline{b}_t^T] \tag{5c}$$

$$\Psi_2 \underline{C}_t + \Gamma_2 \underline{z}_t = \underline{u}_t \tag{6a}$$

$$\Gamma_2 = [B_2, I] \tag{6b}$$

$$\underline{z}_t^T = [\underline{C}_{t-1}^T, \underline{d}_t^T] \tag{6c}$$

in which I is a suitably dimensioned identity matrix in Eqs. (5b) and
(6b). It is implicit in Eqs. (5a) and (6a) that the realizations of
ϕ_t and C_t at time t are conditioned on the observed values of ϕ_{t-1}
and C_{t-1}, respectively. Since Eqs. (5a) and (6a) are mathematically
similar, we choose to express the field variable (either ϕ_t or C_t)
by y_t, and use the following general notation:

$$\Psi\ y_t + \Gamma\ w_t = v_t \qquad t = 1,2,\ldots,n \qquad (7)$$

Eq. (7) will represent the discretized formulation for the field
variable, with Ψ, Γ, w_t and v_t taking the proper connotation by
analogy with either Eq. (5a) or Eq. (6a). The developments to follow
are based on Eq. (7).

The estimation of parameters is approached via maximum likelihood. Under the (mild) Gaussian assumption on v_t (which has unknown
covariance Σ), the negative log-likelihood function is given by

$$L = K + \frac{n}{2}\ \ln\ |\hat{\Sigma}| - n\ \ln\ |\Psi| \qquad (8)$$

in which

$$K = \frac{nG}{2}\ \ln\ (2\pi) + \frac{n^2}{2} \qquad (9)$$

$$\hat{\Sigma} = \frac{1}{n}\ [\ \sum_{t=1}^{n}\ (\Psi\ y_t + \Gamma\ w_t)(\Psi\ y_t + \Gamma\ w_t)^T\ ] \qquad (10)$$

where G is the dimension of the vector y_t. Equation (10) is minimized
with respect to the unknown parameters (i.e., transmissivities and
storativities, or dispersion coefficients), to yield the maximum
likelihood estimators. The actual minimization of Eq. (10) is done
numerically via the Newton-Raphson technique (3). Using matrix
differentiation (Appendix I), the gradient and Hessian of L are
computed in closed-form, enhancing the convergence of the numerical
method and simplifying the assessment of statistical properties of
estimators.

PROPERTIES OF ESTIMATORS

Denote the vector of unknown parameters in Eq. (8) by θ (of
dimension $q \times 1$). The maximum likelihood estimator for θ is represented by $\hat{\theta}$, and it is obtained from applying the Newton-Raphson
method to Eq. (8). It is useful to derive expressions for confidence
ellipsoids as well as for testing hypotheses on the parameters.
Define

$$I(\theta) = E(L_{\theta\theta}) \qquad (11)$$

in which E denotes expectation with respect to the field variable y_t
and $L_{\theta\theta}$ denotes the second derivative (i.e., the Hessian) of L with
respect to θ. $I(\theta)$ is called the (Fisher) information matrix, and is
computable in closed-form for L as specified in Eq. (8). Let

$$i(\underline{\theta}) \equiv L_{\underline{\theta}\underline{\theta}} \tag{12}$$

in which $i(\underline{\theta})$ is the sample information matrix. Large-sample theory of maximum likelihood estimators leads to the following results:
(1) Confidence ellipsoids:

$$(\underline{\theta} - \hat{\underline{\theta}})^T I^{-1}(\hat{\underline{\theta}})(\underline{\theta} - \hat{\underline{\theta}}) \leq \chi_\alpha^2(q) \tag{13}$$

in which $\chi_\alpha^2(q)$ is a chi-squared variate such that

$$P(\chi^2(q) \geq \chi_\alpha^2(q)) = \alpha \tag{14}$$

Equation (13) determines an ellipsoid in the q-dimensional $\underline{\theta}$-space with center at $\hat{\underline{\theta}}$, and the probability that this random ellipsoid covers the true parameter point $\underline{\theta}^0$ is $1-\alpha$. The derivation of Eq. (13) is based on the fact that for sufficiently large sample sizes, the distribution of $\hat{\underline{\theta}}$ is multivariate normal, i.e., $\hat{\underline{\theta}} \sim N(\underline{\theta}^0, I^{-1}(\underline{\theta}^0))$ in which $\underline{\theta}^0$ is the true but unknown parameter vector.
(2) Test of hypothesis derived from confidence ellipsoids:
Suppose that the null hypothesis

$$H_0: \underline{\theta} = \underline{\theta}^* \tag{15}$$

is to be tested (against $H_1: \underline{\theta} \neq \underline{\theta}^*$) at a significance level α. Then, if

$$(\underline{\theta}^* - \hat{\underline{\theta}})^T I^{-1}(\underline{\theta}^*)(\underline{\theta}^* - \hat{\underline{\theta}}) > \chi_\alpha^2(q) \tag{16}$$

H_0 is rejected.
In Eqs. (13) and (16), $I(\ )$ can be replaced by $i(\ )$ (see Eq. (12)) when Eq. (11) is difficult to evaluate.

APPLICATIONS

Groundwater Flow.—We use the one-dimensional equation for con-fined aquifer flow with time-varying Dirichlet boundary conditions, and a point sink at $x = L/2$, i.e.,

$$T \frac{\partial^2 \phi}{\partial x^2} - S \frac{\partial \phi}{\partial t} = F \delta(x - L/2), \qquad 0 \leq x \leq L, \ t \geq 0 \tag{17}$$

subject to the boundary and initial conditions:

$$\phi_A(t) = H_A(t), \ x = 0, \ t \geq 0 \tag{18}$$

$$\phi_B(t) = H_B(t), \ x = L, \ t \geq 0 \tag{19}$$

$$\phi(0) = g(x), \ 0 \leq x \leq L, \ t = 0 \tag{20}$$

The analytical solution for Eqs. (17)-(20) under constant T and S is shown in Appendix II. Gaussian white-noise is superimposed to that solution to generate the desired field variable $\underline{\phi}_t$, $t=1,2,\ldots,n$, used in the estimation method. Table 1 contains the estimation results along with basic data and standard errors of estimators. It can be noticed the fast convergence of the Newton-Raphson search (in fact, a quadratic rate of convergence). The strict convexity of L follows from theoretical considerations related to the fact that the Gaussian distribution is an exponential density function. Global optimality of estimators was verified by a sensitivity analysis on the initial estimators in the Newton-Raphson search.

Table 1. Synopsis of Newton-Raphson's Search for T and S

Iteration	Transmissivity	Storativity	Negative log-likelihood function
	(m^2/day)		
(1)	(2)	(3)	(4)
0	350	0.0060	11.98
1	446	0.0080	7.98
2	445	0.0095	7.17
3	453	0.0105	6.77
4	455	0.0107	6.47
5	456	0.0108	5.97
	(47.7)	(0.00370)	

Notes: 1. 1 foot = 0.305 meter.
2. The standard errors of maximum likelihood estimators at the fifth iteration are within parentheses.
3. Data used to generate nodal head values: $T = 500$ m^2/day; $S = 0.012$; $L = 1000$ m; time step = 1 day; $F = 10$ m^2/day; $H_A(t) = 80 + t$; $H_B(t) = 100 - t$; $g(x) = H_A(t)+[H_B(t)-H_A(t)]x/L$.

Miscible Displacement.–The one-dimensional equation

$$\frac{\partial C}{\partial t} = D_{hxx} \frac{\partial^2 C}{\partial x^2} - \frac{q}{\eta} \frac{\partial C}{\partial x} , \qquad 0 \le x \le L, \ t \ge 0 \qquad (21)$$

subject to:

$$q(C_0 - C) = - \eta D_{hxx} \frac{\partial C}{\partial x} , \qquad x = 0, \ t \ge 0 \qquad (22)$$

$$\frac{\partial C}{\partial x} = 0 , \qquad x = L, \ t \ge 0 \qquad (23)$$

$$C = 0 , \qquad 0 \le x \le L, \ t = 0 \qquad (24)$$

describes the concentration of an ideal tracer in a homogeneous porous medium of constant porosity η, constant coefficient of dispersion D_{hxx}, and constant specific flow q in the positive x-direction. It is assumed that a constant concentration C_0 is maintained to $x = 0$ as $x \uparrow 0$. The analytical solution to Eqs. (21)-(24) is given in (1). A Gaussian white-noise is superimposed on the exact analytical solution to generate the field variable $\underline{C}_t$, t=1,2,...,n, used in the estimation methodology. Table 2 contains the results of the maximum likelihood estimation and basic data. It can be observed the fast rate of (quadratic) convergence to the maximum likelihood estimator, in only four iterations. As was the case for groundwater flow, the parameter estimator is a global minimum in the miscible displacement application.

Table 2.-Synopsis of Newton-Raphson's Search for D_{hxx}

Iteration	Hydrodynamic dispersion coefficient (m^2/day)	Negative log-likelihood function
(1)	(2)	(3)
0	0.500	-12.471
1	1.228	-15.846
2	1.097	-16.209
3	1.090	-16.207
4	1.076	-16.206
	(0.218)	

Notes: 1. 1 foot = 0.305 meter.
        2. Standard error of maximum likelihood estimator in iteration 4 is within parentheses.
        3. Data used to generate concentrations: $q/\eta = 1$ m/day; $L = 40$ m; time step = 1 day; $D_{hxx} = 1$ m^2/day; Equations (21)-(24) were normalized by dividing concentrations by C_0.

SUMMARY

     This paper has shown the applicability of maximum likelihood estimation to the inverse problem in groundwater flow and mass transport. A quadratic rate of convergence was observed in both cases to global minima. The maximum likelihood estimators have desirable large sample properties, that were used to obtain results concerning statistical inference on the estimators. The developed methodology is illustrated with one-dimensional processes. This allows the use of analytical solutions that serve as a test to the proposed estimation approach. Clearly, the theoretical developments given above on estimation and statistical inference are applicable to distributed parameter processes in two or three directions without modification.

APPENDIX I.-MATRIX DERIVATIVES

     The following matrix differentiation results are useful in obtaining the gradient and Hessian of the negative log-likelihood function, L, that are needed in implementing the Newton-Raphson algorithm. Let A be any nonsingular matrix, with a positive determinant, whose elements are a function of a set of parameters θ_i, $i = 1,2,...,q$. Then

$$\frac{\partial \ln|A|}{\partial \theta_i} = tr(A^{-1} \frac{\partial A}{\partial \theta_i})$$

$$\frac{\partial A^{-1}}{\partial \theta_i} = -A^{-1} \frac{\partial A}{\partial \theta_i} A^{-1}$$

$$\frac{\partial^2 \ln|A|}{\partial \theta_i^2} = tr(-A^{-1} \frac{\partial A}{\partial \theta_i} A^{-1} \frac{\partial A}{\partial \theta_i} + A^{-1} \frac{\partial^2 A}{\partial \theta_i^2})$$

APPENDIX II.—ANALYTICAL SOLUTION TO GROUNDWATER FLOW PROBLEM

By definig $X = \frac{x\pi}{L}$, $F^* = \frac{F}{S} \delta[\frac{L}{\pi}(X - \frac{\pi}{2})]$, and $c = \frac{T}{S}(\frac{\pi}{L})^2$, Eqs. (17)-(20) become

$$- c \frac{\partial^2 \phi}{\partial X^2} + \frac{\partial \phi}{\partial t} = - F^*$$

$$\phi_A(t) = H_A(t), \ X = 0, \ t \geq 0$$

$$\phi_B(t) = H_B(t), \ X = \pi, \ t \geq 0$$

$$\phi(0) = g(X), \ 0 \leq X \leq \pi, \ t = 0$$

whose solution is

$$\phi(X,t) = H_A(t)(1 - \frac{X}{\pi}) + H_B(t) \frac{X}{\pi}$$

$$+ \sum_{n=1}^{\infty} \sin(nX)\{\int_0^t [\exp(-cn^2(t-u))]F_n(u)du$$

$$+ b_n \exp(-cn^2)\}$$

in which

$$F_n(t) = \frac{2}{\pi}\{\int_0^{\pi} \sin(nX)[P(X,t) - F^*(X,t)]dX\}$$

$$b_n = \frac{2}{\pi}\{\int_0^{\pi} \sin(nX)[g(X) + f_1(X)]dX\}$$

$$P(X,t) = -H_A'(t)[1 - \frac{X}{\pi}] - H_B'(t)\frac{X}{\pi}$$

$$f_1(X) = -H_A(0)[1 - \frac{X}{\pi}] - H_B(0)\frac{X}{\pi}$$

APPENDIX III.—REFERENCES

1. Bastian, W. C., and Lapidus, L. (1956). "Longitudinal diffusion in ion exchange and chromatographic columns. Finite column." J. Phys. Chem., 60, 816-817.
2. Bear, J. (1972). Dynamics of fluids in porous media. American Elsevier, New York, N.Y.
3. Gill, P. E., Murray, W., and Wright, M. H. (1981). Practical optimization. Academic Press, London.
4. Sposito, G., Jury, W. A., and Gupta, V. K. (1986). "Fundamental problems in the stochastic convection-dispersion model of solute transport in aquifers and field soils." Water Resour. Res., 22(1):77-88.

APPENDIX IV.—NOTATION

A	= matrix in finite element discretization of groundwater flow equation,
B	= matrix in finite element discretization of miscible displacement equation,
b	= vector of inputs in discretized groundwater flow equation,
C	= concentration of ideal tracer,
D	= hydrodynamic dispersion coefficient,
d	= vector of inputs,
e	= Gaussian white-noise in discretized groundwater flow equation,
F	= sink in groundwater flow problem,
G	= dimension of field variable vector,
$g(x)$	= initial conditions in groundwater problem,
H	= Dirichlet boundary conditions in groundwater problem,
I	= identity matrix,
$I(\ )$	= Fisher information matrix,
i	= index for parameters and for coordinate directions,
$i(\ )$	= sample information matrix,
L	= negative log-likelihood function,
n	= number of observations in time,
q	= specific velocity,
S	= aquifer storativity,
T	= aquifer transmissivity,
t	= time index,
u	= Gaussian white-noise in discretized miscible displacement equation,
V	= average velocity,
v	= Gaussian white-noise in discretized field variable equation,
w	= vector of inputs in discretized field variable equation,
y	= field variable,
Γ	= matrix in discretized field variable equation,
η	= porosity,
θ	= parameter,
Σ	= covariance matrix,
ϕ	= piezometric head, and
Ψ	= matrix in discretized field variable equation.

MIXED SOLUTE INTERACTIONS IN GROUNDWATER SYSTEMS

by Christopher G. Uchrin[1], M. ASCE, Mary Gay Heagler[2], and Jack Katz[2]

ABSTRACT

Research results are presented from a study examining the competitive sorption effects of two organic chemicals, para-dichlorobenzene and 2,4-dichlorophenol, to solids from the Cohansey aquifer in the New Jersey coastal plain. It was found that the sorption of p-DCB onto solids previously sorbed with 2,4-DCP did not induce desorption of the 2,4-DCP while the sorption equilibrium characteristics of the p-DCB were not significantly different than that obtained for single solute systems. It was concluded that different sites may be involved in the sorption processes.

Introduction

Quantification of the sorptive characteristics of pollutants to soil particulates is essential to the prediction of their transport and fate in ground and surface water systems. Mathematical models of pollutant transport in subsurface water systems generally possess a reaction term for sorption kinetics as well as chemical and biochemical reactions and interactions (11). In some cases, the danger to an aquatic systems comes not from a pure substance spill or leak but from a mixture of various organic substances; an example being landfill leachate. Very little work, however, has been reported to date regarding the adsorption/desorption of mixtures of organic solutes to soils (2,10,12) as most of this type of effort has focused on single solutes, or sorbates. Most reported work on competitive, or multi-solute, adsorption has been focused on organic substance removal by activated carbon (3,4,15,16), and on the sorption of various inorganic ionic species on soils and clays, as reported by Murali and Aylmore (5,6,7). The study described in this paper focused on the adsorption of an organic substance, para-dichlorobenzene (p-DCB), to a soil to which another organic substance, 2,4-dichlorophenol (2,4-DCP), had been previously sorbed and the subsequent desorption of that substance.

---

[1]Assistant Professor, Department of Environmental Science, Cook College, New Jersey Agricultural Experiment Station, Rutgers University, New Brunswick, NJ 08903.

[2]Research Assistant, Department of Environmental Science, Cook College, New Jersey Agricultural Experiment Station, Rutgers University, New Brunswick, NJ 08903.

Procedure

Aquifer Solids. Solids from the Cohansey aquifer, located in the New Jersey coastal plain, were used in this study. This material was taken from an outcrop located at the Rutgers University Cranberry Culture Experiment Station near Chatsworth, NJ, and is a coarse to fine grain sand (90% sand, 8% silt, 2% clay) with an organic matter content of 4.4%. Organic matter content was determined by the Walkley and Black modification of the rapid dichromate oxidation technique (8), with the organic carbon content defined as 58 percent of the organic matter content.

Experimental Procedure. A 1.00 g mass of air-dried solids was introduced into a series of five 50-mL screw cap test tubes. Another five tubes were filled with 5.00 g of soil and another five tubes filled with 10.00 g of soil. The solids were then saturated with 2.5 mL of organic-free water. Each set of five tubes were then spiked with a 25.0 mL volume of five different concentrations of 2,4-DCP in water. A carrier solvent was not used. The tubes were immediately sealed by screwing on teflon-lined caps and agitated by a wrist shaker for 24 hours, by which time previous studies had shown equilibrium was reached (13,12). The tubes were then withdrawn and centrifuged for 10 minutes at 2000 rpm to separate the solids. A 5.0 mL volume aliquot was then withdrawn from each vial and extracted with 5.0 mL of hexane and the extract analyzed using a Hewlett-Packard 5840-A gas chromatograph. A 1.83 m (6 ft) x 2 mm-I.D. column packed with 20% SP2100 (100/120 mesh) was used together with an electron capture detector. Previous studies (12,13) showed losses to volatilization and to the glassware to be less than analytical error and thus, negligible.

The liquid centrifugate was then carefully drained from the test tubes and replaced with 25 mL of a 37.8 mg/L solution of p-DCB in organic free water. The tubes were then sealed with teflon-lined screw-tops and agitated for 24 hours. The tubes were then withdrawn, centrifuged, and the centrifugate analyzed as before. This procedure was reiterated to examine the dual effects of consecutive desorption and consecutive dosing.

All experiments were performed in a constant temperature room at $21\pm1^\circ$ C.

Results and Discussion

Figure 1 displays the results of the initial 2,4-DCP sorption experiment. A Freundlich isotherm was fitted to the data. This expression is given as:

$$q_e = KC_e^{1/n} \quad \dots\dots\dots\dots\dots\dots\dots\dots\dots\dots\dots\dots\dots\dots\dots(1)$$

where q_e is the solid phase equilibrium concentration [ug-organic substance/g-soil or ppm], C_e is the liquid phase equilibrium concentration [mg-organic substance/L-water or ppm], and n and K are

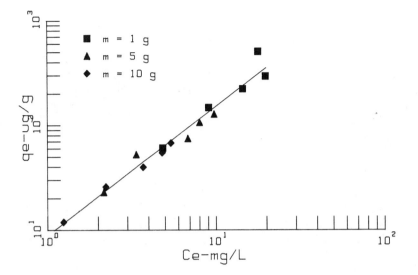

Figure 1. Fruendlich Adsorption Isotherm, 2,4-DCP on Cohansey Solids.

constants. An initial observation is that the dependency on the adsorber mass noted by other investigators (1,9,14) did not manifest itself for this system. Isotherm parameters are given in Table 1.

Figure 2 displays the results of the p-DCB dosing of the solids sorbed with the 2,4-DCP. These data show that virtually none of the 2,4-DCP desorbed from the soil. Previous studies (13) examining the desorption of 2,4-DCP showed similar results. The observation that the sorption of the p-DCB did not cause 2,4-DCP to be released suggests that different sorption sites may be involved.

Figure 3 displays the results of the successive p-DCB sorption together with the results of previous studies examining the sorption of p-DCB as a single solute and as a cosolvent with 2,4-DCP. In this case, a singular Freundlich isotherm can be regressed with good correlation to all the data, suggesting that the previously sorbed 2,4-

TABLE 2.—Freundlich Adsorption Isotherm Parameters.

Substance	K	1/n	r
2,4-DCP	8.87	1.23	0.983
p-DCB	37.2	0.538	0.905

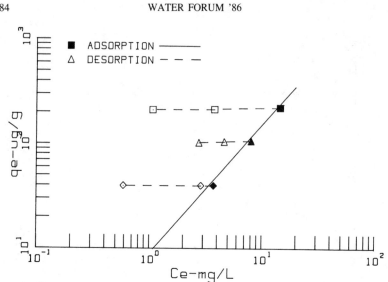

Figure 2.   Desorption of 2,4–DCP from Cohansey solids.

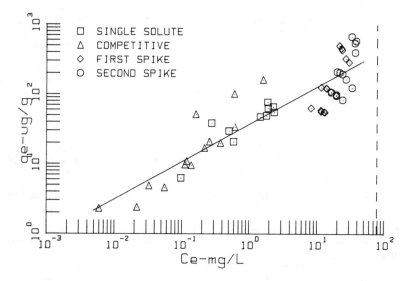

Figure 3.   Sorption of p–DCB to Cohansey solids, single solute data from (13), competitive data from (12).   Dashed line denotes liquid phase solubility of p–DCB in water.

DCP is not having an effect on the sorption equilibria of the p-DCB, thus lending further credence to the conclusion that different sorption sites may be involved. It is also of interest to note that the successive spike sorption data seems to be exhibiting a multi-layer adsorption effect due to its approaching the liquid phase solubility limit. Isotherm parameters are given in Table 1.

Acknowledgements

The research on which this report is based, was financed in part by the United States Department of the Interior as authorized by the Water Research and Development Act of 1978 (P.L. 95-467), the University/Industry Cooperative Research Center for Hazardous and Toxic Waste, New Jersey Institute of Technology and the New Jersey Agricultural Experiment Station, Publication No. J-27525-2-86, supported by State funds.

Contents of this publication do not necessarily reflect the views and policies of the U.S. Department of the Interior, nor does mention of trade names or commercial products constitute their endorsement or recommendation for use by the U.S. Government.

References

1. Carter, C.W., and I.H. Suffet, "Binding of DDT to Dissolved Humic Materials," Environmental Science and Technology, Vol. 16, 1982, pp. 735-740.

2. Chiou, D.T., P.E. Porter, and D.W. Schmedding, "Partition Equilibria of Nonionic Organic Compounds Between Soil Organic Matter and Water," Environmental Science and Technology, Vol. 17, No. 4, April, 1983, pp. 227-231.

3. Fritz, W., and E.U. Schlunder, "Competitive Adsorption of Two Dissolved Organics onto Activated Carbon-I: Adsorption Equilibria," Chem. Eng. Sci., Vol. 36, 1981, pp. 721-730.

4. Jain, J.S., and V.L. Snoeyink, "Adsorption from Bisolute Systems on Active Carbon", Journal Water Pollution Control Federation, Vol. 45, No. 12, Dec., 1973, pp. 2463-2479.

5. Murali, V. and L.A.G. Aylmore, "Competitive Adsorption During Solute Transport in Soils: Mathematical Models," Soil Science, Vol. 136, No. 3, Mar., 1983, pp. 143-150.

6. Murali, V., and L.A.G. Aylmore, "Competitive Adsorption During Solute Transport in Soils: Simulations of Competitive Adsorption," Soil Science, Vol. 136, No., 4, April, 1983, pp. 203-213.

7. Murali, V., and L.A.G. Aylmore, "Competitive Adsorption During Solute Transport in Soils: A Review of Experimental Evidence of Competitive Adsorption and an Evaluation of Simple Competition Models," Soil Science, Vol. 136, No., 5, Nov., 1983, pp. 279-290.

8. Nelson, D.W., and L.E. Sommers, in Methods of Soil Analysis, Part 2: Chemical and Microbiological Properties, 2nd ed., A.L. Page, R.H. Miller, and D.R. Keeney, Eds., Am. Soc. Agronomy, Inc. and Soil Sci. Soc. Am., Inc., Madison, Wis., 1982, pp. 565-571.

9. O'Connor, D.J., and J.P. Connolly, "The Effects of Concentration of Adsorbing Solids on the Partition Coefficient," Water Research, Vol. 14, 1980, pp. 1517-1523.

10. Rao, P.S.C., Hornsby, A.G., Kilcrease, D.P., and Nkedi-Kizza, P., "Sorption and Transport of Hydrophobic Organic Chemicals in Aqueous and Mixed Solvent Systems: Model Development and Preliminary Evaluation," Journal of Environmental Quality, Vol. 14, No. 3, 1985, pp. 376-383.

11. Uchrin, C.G., "Modeling Transport Processes and Differential Accumulation of Persistent Toxic Organic Substances in Groundwater Systems," Ecological Modeling, Vol. 22, 1984, pp. 135-143.

12. Uchrin, C.G., and J. Katz, "Sorption Kinetics of Competing Organic Substances on New Jersey Coastal Plain Aquifer Solids." Proceedings of the Third International Symposium on Management of Industrial and Hazardous Wastes, Alexandria, Egypt, June, 1985, pp. 351-364.

13. Uchrin, C.G., J.V. Hunter, J. Katz, and G. Mangels, "Characterization of Transport, Sorption and Degradation of Toxic and Hazardous Organic Substances in Groundwater Systems, Final Technical Completion Report, Center for Coastal and Environmental Studies, Rutgers University, 1986.

14. Voice, T.C., Rice, C.P., and Weber, W.J., Jr., "Effect of Solids Concentration on the Sorptive Partitioning of Hydrophobic Pollutants in Aquatic Systems," Environmental Science and Technology, Vol. 17, 1983, pp. 513-518.

15. Weber, W.J., Jr., and Morris, J.C., "Adsorption in Heterogeneous Aqueous Systems, Journal American Water Works Association, Vol. 56, No. 4, April, 1964, pp. 447-456.

16. Zogorski, J.S., "The Adsorption of Phenols onto Granular Activated Carbon from Aqueous Solution," Ph.D. Thesis, Rutgers University, New Brunswick, N.J., 1975.

DREDGED SPOIL STORAGE BASIN IN THE COASTAL WATERS NEAR ROTTERDAM
- environmental and coastal engineering aspects -
P. Vellinga*, J.P.J. Nijssen**, R.G.J. v. Orden**, M. de Rooij*

Abstract

The maintenance dredging for the Rotterdam harbour area amounts to 23 million m^3 per year, 10 million m^3 of which is polluted to such an extent that a controlled storage is required. To provide a sufficient storage capacity a large scale basin is being constructed in the shallow coastal waters. An Environmental Impact Statement (EIS) has been made for the decision on this project. The paper describes two important parts of an environmental impact study: the coastal engineering aspects of the design and the maintenance of the ring dike (fully constructed of sand) and the environmental aspects related to the long term behaviour and migration of the contaminants. The studies have been carried out by means of a numerical simulation of the hydraulic, the coastal morphologic and the chemical processes.

1. Introduction

To maintain the required depth of the port of Rotterdam it is necessary to dredge annually 23 million m^3 of silt from the river and the harbour basins. With the increasing awareness of the contamination of the dredged material and the possible effects of the contaminants upon humans, animals and plants it has become more and more difficult to find proper disposal sites, especially since the disposal at sea has recently been forbidden by the Government on the basis of an International Convention. As a result the continuity of the maintenance work in the harbours was threatened.

A real solution to the problem by reducing the production of pollutants cannot be reached before the year 2000, Van Leeuwen et al (1983). A solution for the next 15 years has been found by the construction of a large basin in the coastal waters near Rotterdam, see Fig. 1. The dimensions are such that the most polluted part of the dredged material, being 10 million m^3 per year, can be stored over a period of 15 years. Over an area of about 300 hectares the seabottom will be excavated to a depth of 21 m below mean sea level. The excavated material will be used to construct a ring dike with a top level of 23 m above mean sea level, see Fig. 2. Preliminary studies on consolidation have shown that the volume of the basin, 90 million m^3, corresponds with a storage capacity of 150 million m^3, Brassinga et al (1985). Four alternative locations for the basin have been developed with variable emphasis on economical, environmental and coastal engineering aspects. For the EIS a comprehensive study covering these aspects has been carried out. General conclusions from the EIS are:

*   Delft Hydraulics Laboratory, P.O. Box 152, 8300 AD Emmeloord,
    The Netherlands
** Municipality of Rotterdam, Department of Public Works, P.O. Box 5807,
    3002 AP Rotterdam, The Netherlands

1) The disposal of contaminated dredged material in the site can be accomplished for the next 15 years in an environmentally acceptable manner. Even after 3000 years most contaminants will stay within a few ten's of metres from the basin. There will be no effect on the groundwater of the dune coast on the mainland and no effect upon the bottom dwelling flora and fauna of the sea area. On this aspect there are no significant differences between the alternatives.

2) The interaction between the sea and the existing coastal dune area will change due to the sheltering effect of the basin. This will cause changes in the ecological communities in the coastal dune area. In general, the environmental impact increases as the distance between the basin and the coast decreases. Ultimately alternative IIIa has been chosen on the basis of the EIS. Alternative IIIa is an optimized version of alternative III. Construction has started in 1986. The basin will come into use in 1987, Van Orden (1986).

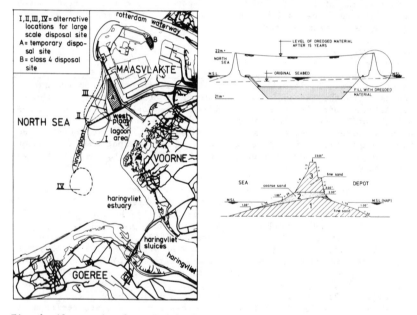

Fig. 1 Alternative location dredged spoil storage basin

Fig. 2 Cross-section of (sandy) ring dike

2. Coastal engineering aspects

Coastal morphology

The major part of the Netherlands' North Sea coast consists of sandy beaches and dunes. The tidal range is 1.5 m under normal conditions with extreme storm surge peak levels ranging from 3 m up to 5 m above mean sea level (occurrence frequency is 1/20 per year and 1/10,000 per year respectively). The average wave height is about 1 m. During storms the significant wave height may reach values ranging from 5 m up to 8 m.

The slope of the beaches is in the order of 1:20 to 1:50 above mean sea level and 1:75 to 1:150 below mean sea level. The foot of the coastal dunes is situated at a level of 3 m above mean sea level. The grain size ranges from 150 µm up to 300 µm.

The four alternatives are shown in Fig. 1. The present seabottom and shoreline developments in this area are strongly effected by the recent closure of some major branches of the estuary. Because of this closure the formerly east-west oriented system of tidal channels and headlands is changing into a mainly north-south oriented (continuous) coastline. The outer delta is eroding and the inner delta is accreting. Large shore parallel bars are formed in line with the coastline to the north. It looks as if a series of barrier islands will develop in the coming decades. Between the mainland and the barrier islands, shoaling will occur and tidal flats will develop.

Fig. 3 Storage basin location, the Hinderplaat with Rotterdam oil
         storage tanks on the background

The storage basin (alternative IV excluded) is for a large part situated on the most prominent example of a barrier island in the stage of development, the Hinderplaat, see Fig. 4. Consequently, the effect of the storage basin on the surrounding seabottom and shorelines is mainly an acceleration of the present developments. The rate of shoaling of the lagoon area increases as the wave action will be reduced to a large extent. As a result the sandy seabottom and the shore may be covered by silt. The rate of shoaling has been computed with the aid of numerical models for tidal flow and wave action. The rate of shoaling of the lagoon area has been found to increase from the present average rate of 0.05 m per year up to 0.15 m per year for alternative I. The effect of

the other alternatives ranges between these values. At present the
shoreline of the mainland is eroding at a rate of several metres per
year. The various alternative basins will cause a reduction of the
present rate of erosion.

Coastal erosion and maintenance of the dikes

The basin will effect the existing hydraulic and morphological system
and visa versa. The determination of the erosion of the sandy dikes
requires a detailed knowledge of the wave conditions, the (tidal) currents, the related sediment transport and the resulting seabottom and
shoreline changes. With this aim these processes have been simulated by
means of a system of numerical models, Boer et al (1984). The input, the
schematization and the output of the models is shown in Table 1.

measurements/input	schematization	computations/output
seabottom (from various bottom soundings)	initial situation	sediment transport, rate of seabottom changes and erosion/sedimentation locations and quantities after a certain time interval
waves (wave climate at the M.S.L.- 25 m depth contour)	5 wave directions with corresponding occurrence frequency	wave refraction, diffraction, shoaling and breaking, wave induced bottom shear stresses and wave induced currents in the zone of breaking waves
tide (tidal currents and water levels)	selection of a number of steady state conditions	tidal flow velocities flow pattern
sediment (type of sediment and grain size)	grain size and fall velocity	wave and tidal current induced sediment concentrations

Table 1   Input, schematization and output of the numerical models

An example of sediment transport induced by the combined action of waves
and currents is shown in Fig. 4. This shows one of the various steady
state conditions that have been simulated. The computations have been
carried out for the initial bottom configuration only. The result of
each run has been multiplied with the representative time interval. Next
the results have been superimposed and the total effect over a certain
time period is found in terms of coastline erosion and sedimentation and
seabottom changes.

The erosion of the dikes for the initial situation can be found from the
computations described above. For the present conditions this result can
also be used to determine the long term maintenance of the basin as a
deformation of the (artificial) coastline will not be accepted. The
computed erosion quantities for the various alternatives are shown in
Table 2.

The programme of beach nourishment should be such that a certain minimum
coastal profile will always be present to withstand an extreme storm
event. For the present basin a storm surge with a frequency of 1:5000
per year has been selected as a design storm surge. Under such conditions the sea level rises to 5 m above mean sea level and the significant wave height is 8 m. As a result a new beach profile will be formed
at a more elevated level, at the cost of sand from the dike. The erosion
to be expected during such a storm surge has been computed in accordance
with the governmental guidelines for the evaluation of the safety of the
dunes as a sea defence system by application of the dune erosion prediction model of Vellinga (1983). The results indicate a "dune" erosion
quantity of 600 m^3/m^1 (cubic metre per running metre). This quantity,

alternative	long term maintenance expressed in 1000 m³ per year (d$_{50}$ - μm)	accuracy range in 1000 m³ per year
I	270	180 - 450
II	340	225 - 510
III	500	330 - 750
IIIa	270	210 - 350
IV	800	530 - 1200

Table 2 Long term maintenance expressed in beach fill quantities per year

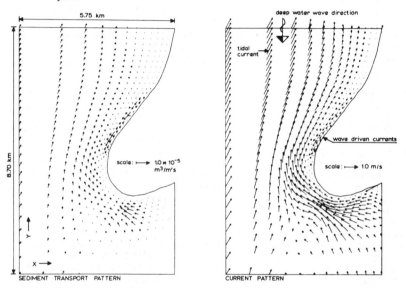

Fig. 4 Numerical simulation of tidal and wave induced currents and resulting sediment transport

increased by a certain spare volume to anticipate the normal rate of shoreline erosion has been the basis for the present design, see Fig. 2.

Finally, a slightly adjusted version of alternative 3 has been selected. The coastal alignment of alternative III has been optimized with respect to coastal erosion. The coastline has been straightened a little bit and the south western end has been reshaped as to anticipate the formation of a spit. Additional computations for the optimized basin layout have indicated a long term maintenance requirement of 270,000 m³ per year, see Table 1, alternative IIIa.

3. Long term behaviour and migration of contaminants

Problem definition

The dredged material is characterized by a high organic matter content (8%), as well as calcite (14%). About 40% is smaller than 16 micron. The material is contaminated with heavy metals and organic micro pollutants, (Cd 14 ppm, Cu 135 ppm, Zn 900 ppm, As 23 ppm, Cr 190 ppm, PCB 1.5 ppm).

As part of the environmental impact study, the behaviour of these pollutants has been studied to answer the question about the possible future
concentrations within the disposal site and the subsoil. The consolidation process expels the contaminated water which dissipates in the
surroundings, Brassinga et al (1985). Hydrological modelling of the dump
site itself and the surroundings was used to calculate the water movements. Diagnetic processes within the disposed dredged material, especially the decay of organic matter, determine the macro chemical conditions like pH, alkalinity, Eh and sulfide concentrations, which regulate
the dissolved concentrations of several heavy metals. The question about
the solubility controlling mechanism, sorption or mineral equilibria,
was one of the most important questions to be solved. A numerical chemical model was used to calculate the possible concentrations as a function of time and space. An extensive literature search, field measurements and experiments in the laboratory provided the information for the
model imput to perform the calculations.

Methodology

The numerical chemical model (CHARON) uses three modules, de Rooij
(1986):
● An equilibrium module for fast equilibrium processes.
  This module is based on the minimization of the Gibbs free energy and
  a mass balance for all chemical equilibrium components.
● A slow reaction module to calculate the progress of slow reactions.
  This module uses differential equations to calculate the amount of
  components to be transferred to or from the equilibrium system.
● A transport module where convective and dispersive transport between
  as homogeneous considered segments in the system is calculated.
An important aspect of this study was the question: what process does
and will control the solubility of the pollutants. About 99% of the
total mass of pollutants is present in the solid material. Changes in
solubility will cause changes in dissipation of pollutants from the
disposal site to the subsoil. The model calculations were used to calibrate parameters which could not be calibrated in the field, where time
and space parameters from the field were different from the actual
disposal site. Model calculations, combined with analysis of pore waters, were also used to give insight into the solubility mechanism. The
final (chemical) model calculations needed also the water flows and
dispersions within the sludge depot and the surroundings. These were
investigated with separate hydrological models which output was used as
an input for the chemical model calculations.

Contaminant behaviour in the disposal site

Solubility controlling mechanism

Chemical analysis and preliminary model calculations showed that in
anoxic environments the solubility controlling mechanism is mineral
formation for Cd, Cu and Zn, which will be present as sulfides. Cr will
be present as hydroxide while a substantial amount is adsorbed too and
As is adsorbed only, mostly to $Fe(OH)_3$ and partly to organic material.
An illustration is given in Fig. 5 which shows measurements of dissolved
and sediment concentrations against each other in anoxic systems. This
figure clearly demonstrates that no proportional relation is present,
which relation should exist in the case of adsorption behaviour. Adsorption experiments   under anoxic conditions also showed precipitation

behaviour. Adding Cd++ under anoxic conditions did not increase the dissolved concentration. The solubility products which were finally calibrated were within the literature range for these minerals. For the organic pollutants only adsorption behaviour was found.

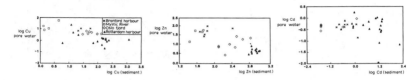

Figure 5   Measurements of dissolved and sediment concentrations

Macro chemical processes

The decay of organic matter is the driving force in the diagenetic process in the disposal site O2, NO3- and SO4= are consumed within a half year period. The main reaction from that moment on is:

$$4\ Fe(OH)3 + 7\ CH2O \rightarrow 4\ FeCO3 + 3\ CH4 + 7\ H2O \tag{1}$$

The pH will be around 7, depending on the solubility of Fe(OH)3, the amount of CO2 which will dissolve in the methane atmosphere and the carbonate chemistry. After depletion of Fe(OH)3 the process will be:

$$2\ CH2O \rightarrow CO2 + CH4 \tag{2}$$

Both CO2 and CH4 will be supersatured in the solution and gas bells are formed. As long as reaction (1) is taking place the amount of CO2 is still low. Reaction (2) will form an atmosphere with almost 50% CO2 and the concentration of dissolved CO2 will increase. As a consequence the pH will drop to lower values, depending on the carbonate buffer capacity. The high amount of CaCO3 (calcite) which is present in the sludge will keep the pH at a value between 6.2 and 6.5 depending on the depth and pressure in the system.

Micro chemistry

As long as the macro chemistry does not change, the concentration of the pollutants remains the same. However, when the pH drops, a shift occurs, thereby changing the speciation in solution and therefore the overall solubility of the heavy metals. The relation between the total solubility of some heavy metals and the pH and S-concentration is given in the three-dimensional figures 6 and 7. Cadmium concentrations are constant over a broad range of pH and sulfide concentrations, but Zinc concentrations increase regardless whether sulfide concentrations increase or decrease compared with present harbour sludge. The low pH also results in a higher solubility of Cr(OH)3, increasing the total dissolved chromium. The solubility of arsenic, which adsorbs to Fe(OH)3, increases dramatically when all Fe(OH)3 is reduced.

Migration of contaminants by groundwater flow

The migration is determined by the dispersion of the expelled water and the concentration in the water, Loxham (1985). The pore water flow to the subsoil is estimated at 20 mm/year, Brassinga (1985). This relatively low flow and the fact that the concentrations of the contaminants are not high, result in a low mass flow of contaminants to the subsoil. The concentrations of the sulfide controlled heavy metals are near to their natural background level (for anoxic systems), while the other contaminants show adsorption behaviour to the underground material (see

Table 3). As a consequence hardly any dissipation of contaminants to the surroundings is expected.

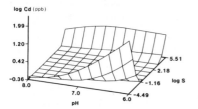

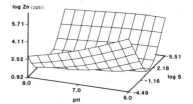
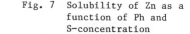

Fig. 6 Solubility of Cd as a function   Fig. 7 Solubility of Zn as a
of Ph and S-concentration   function of Ph and
                                                    S-concentration

Parameter	Background level (μgr/l)	Pore water concentration
Cd	0.12	0.43
Zn	17	29.5
Cr	2.6	96
As	0.3	126

Table 3 Background level and pore water concentrations

Discussion

An environmentally acceptable solution for the disposal of contaminated dredged material from the Rotterdam harbour area will be realised by using natural local materials in a well known civil-engineering way.
Nowadays suitable numerical models are available for accurate prediction of both the coastal morfophogical developments and the behaviour of contaminants in the site and moving outwards. These models are tested both by laboratory and field experiments.
It may be worthwhile to consider the possibilities of applying the basic concept of the Rotterdam disposal site and the calculation methods for similar situations where large quantities of contaminated dredged material or other hazardous waste should be disposed of.

REFERENCES

1. Boer, S., Vriend, H.J. de and Wind, H.G., 1984. A Mathematical Model for the Simulation of Morphological Processes in a Coastal Area.
   Abstracts 19th International Coastal Engineering Conference, Houston.
2. Brassinga, H.E., Elprama, R., Tol, A.F. van, Rijt, C. van, 1985. Consolidation of soft fine grained dredged material. Proceedings of the Eleventh Conference on Soil Mechanics and Foundation Engineering, San Fransisco, USA.
3. Leeuwen, P. van, Kleinbloesem, W.C.H., Groenewegen, H.J., 1983. A Policy Plan for the Disposal of Dredged Material from the Port of Rotterdam. Proceedings World Dredging Congress 1983, Singapore, Paper M2 part i pp. 499-508. Organised by BHRA Fluid Engineering, Cranfield, Bedford, England.
4. Loxham, M., Westrate, F.A., 1986. The Environmental Aspects of a large scale Disposal site for Dredging Spoil from the Rotterdam Harbour area. XIth World Dredging Congress, Brighton, U.K.
5. Orden, R.G.J. van, 1986. Environmental Impact Statement on a peninsula solution for the Disposal of Dredged Material. Proceedings of the XIth. World Dredging Congress, 1986, Brighton U.K. Organised by CEDA, Delft, The Netherlands.
6. Rooij, N.M. de, Mathematical Simulation of Bio-chemical Processes in Natural Waters by the Model CHARON, Delft Hydraulics Laboratory, Report on investigations, R1310-10, 1986 (in preparation).
7. Vellinga, P., 1983, "Predictive Computational Model for Beach and Dune Erosion during Storm Surges", Coastal Structures '83, printed by ASCE.

Land Renewal With Topsoil from Clyde Port Dredgings

George Fleming, John Riddell, and Paul Smith*

Abstract

The paper examines the potential of using sediment dredged from the
River Clyde estuary as a topsoil in land renewal. It presents results,
to date (1986) of a study sponsored by the Scottish Development Agency
and Clyde Port Authority into the physical characteristics of the Clyde
sediments, their quantity and quality and a comparison to naturally
occuring top soil. The economic implications of disposing of dredged
material are also considered.

Introduction

The rate of degradation of land worldwide is now between 50,000-70,000
square Kilometres per year every year (Lewis, 1980). The catalysts for
degradation include deforestation, acid rain, industrialisation,
intensive agriculture, waste disposal and construction. The effect is
to shift the natural balance of processes with a resultant change in
erosion and deposition rates, loss of fertile topsoil, change in
acidity, accumulation of heavy metals, alteration to soil structure,
and an imbalance in soil chemistry and biological activity. The
problem of soil and water resource management becomes increasingly
complex.

Against this background are the two separate problems common to many
ports with large industrial hinterlands, namely the dredging and
disposal of sediment accumulation in the navigable waterways and the
reclamation of derelict land as part of environmental improvement.
Although separate problems often considered by different statutory
authorities both are part of the Soil-Water system shown in Figure 1.

This paper examines this aspect of the soil-water system from an
engineering viewpoint by considering the potential of the dredged
material as a topsoil.

*All members of Staff at Department of Civil Engineering, University
of Strathclyde, 107 Rottenrow, Glasgow G4 0NG, Scotland, U.K.

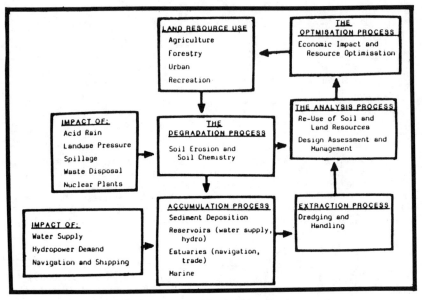

Figure 1.   The Soil-Water System

Topsoil

According to a descriptive definition (British Standard, 1965), top
soil "is the original surface layer of grassland or cultivated land.
It does not generally include soil from woodland, heathland, moorland
or bog or other special areas such as land impaired by industrial
activity". It is generally classified by texture, acid level, stone
content and the absence of weeds and roots. Given this definition
topsoil is a very limited resource and the supply of available topsoil
for land improvement is erratic in quantity, quality, location and
cost. There is a need to establish better guidelines and standards for
the use of natural soils and for the recycling of sediments originating
from the land surface. This paper proposes an urgent review of the
national and international guidelines.

Clyde Sediments: Quantity and Physical Type

The River Clyde system is shown on Figure 2. Its use as a waterway has
spanned several centuries (Riddell, 1979). The present study has shown
(Fleming et al 1986) that 12 million m^3 insitu volume of sediments are
present in the system between Broomlielaw and Greenock with 509,000 m^3
insitu volume between Broomlielaw and the River Cart.

Previous studies (Fleming, 1970) indicate the rate of inflow of
sediments at that time approximated to 200,000 tons/year (dry weight).
Table 1 shows a breakdown of the quantities of insitu material in the
upper half of the channel system. The navigational requirement involve
dredging in the order of 320,000 tons/year (1970). The cost of this

operation is approximately £1.2 million (1986).

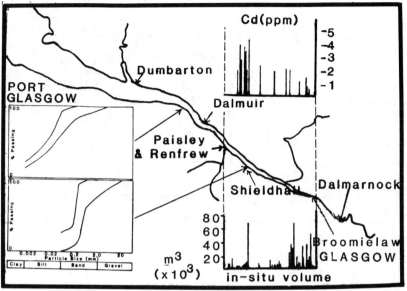

Figure 2. The Clyde System

The sediments vary in their physical characteristics depending on their
location within the System. Several parameters are considered important
including insitu bulk density, moisture content, particle size distribution, Atterberg Limits and dewatering characteristics.

Table 1: Insitu material in the Upper Clyde System

Location	Insitu Volume $m^3 \times 10^3$	Mean Insitu Bulk Density Mg/m^3	Mean Insitu Moisture Content (W)%	Mass Insitu Tonnes	Dry Wt.
0-3 km from Broomlielaw	223,421	1.347	116	300,946	128,203
3-11 to R. Cart	219,818	1.363	149	299,612	122,541

Particle size testing gives the range experienced in the channel as
shown in Figure 2. This is affected by the land use developments over
a long period of time. Samples taken 16 years ago (Fleming, 1970)
indicate a range from fine clay (0.003mm) at Broomlielaw (0 Kms) to
coarse sand (0.270 mm) at the River Leven (22 Kms). Recent sampling
(Fleming, et al (1986) reveals a change to the Broomlielaw sediments
with the increased presence of sands due to land use changes in the

River Clyde Basin.

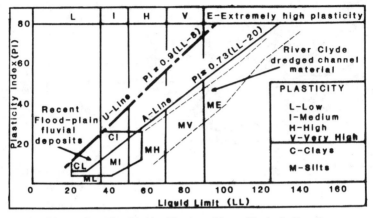

Figure 3. Plasticity Chart - River Clyde Sediments

The suitability of the sediments as topsoil depends on their workabil-
ity. This can be classified by reference to the Atterberg Limits.
Tests reveal two main types of dredged material as shown in Figure 3,
namely those at Broomlielaw (0 Km) and downstream of Bowling (16 Km)
which are non plastic and those lying between 0-16 Km which are highly
plastic. The highly plastic sediments are more difficult to handle
and dewater but mixing with coarser sediments improves handling and
dewatering and provides a suitable particle size distribution when
proposing the sediments for use as a topsoil. Shrinkage and dewatering
tests continue as part of the study in order to relate sediment
properties to their engineering use.

Clyde Sediments - Quality

The dredged Clyde sediments are very similar in mineralogy to the
topsoil found in the river basin. Furthermore, the clay composition is
identical. However, when proposing the use of the dredged sediment as a
topsoil, a major consideration must be the assessment of likely risk in
relation to contaminants. In the United Kingdom several Acts of
Parliament exist which classify waste material and control its disposal
(HMSO, 1974, 1977, 1980 and EEC, 1978, 1984). Few regulations exist in
relation to the use of the material for other purposes but interim
"guidelines" exist to provide some classification of chemical constituents in relation to risk (DOE, 1983). The principal constituents
present in dredged material of interest in relation to pollution are
the range in heavy metals, and the salinity levels. A summary of the
classifications and guidelines is shown on Table 2 together with data
on known concentrations of heavy metals in dredged sediments for different parts of the world.

From these results it is clear that sediment quality constituents vary
from one area to another and within the same system. The processes

involved in the migration of heavy metals within the hydro cycle are also extremely complex (Salomons, 1984). Generally speaking based on the trigger concentrations, most of the sediments are suitable for use in parks and recreational land use, and some are potentially suitable for other uses subject to analysis of specific metal problems such as cadmium in relation to health and zinc and copper in relation to the growth of a range of plant species. The results shown in Table 2 are for total metal concentrations in the dried soil. The availability of such metals to plants depends on the acidity of the soil and the soil water variation. More highly acid soils allow metals to leach out. The question of the availability of heavy metals to plants has been investigated and tests undertaken to determine the possible values. In Table 2, a set of results is included under the 1986 Clyde sediments which give the equivalent of average plant available heavy metal concentrations based on a number of samples. These figures are in parenthesis. A large difference exists between total concentration and average plant available. It is evident that a major difference in scientific opinion exists which requires clarification before guidelines can be established on the quantity of heavy metals taken up by plants, or leached to the water cycle.

Salinity of the dredged sediments, although present, is low and reduces further when the sediments were allowed to weather under natural rainfall conditions.

Handling and Drying Sediments, and Plant Growth Trials

The current methods used to dredge the Clyde system involve bucket and grab dredging techniques. As part of the study, bulk samples were obtained to conduct handling and drying trials. The dredged material was discharged by grab to the dock side and allowed to weather under natural conditions. The sandy material shows little variation, whereas the clay and silt samples dewatered by 60% in 50 days. The bulk samples were then mixed in equal parts and were readily handled by standard earth moving plant. The resulting soil mixture was then used in growth trials involving a standard grass seed mixture. Initial results show a satisfactory performance over one year with long term tests now underway. These tests include the reclamation and monitoring of a hectare of derelict land.

Economic considerations

The annual requirement of topsoil in Scotland amounts to approximately 1.2 million tonnes with 600,000 tonnes in the Glasgow/Clyde Valley. The average cost for topsoil is £4.5/tonne (delivered to site 1985). Dredging costs for approximately 225,000 tonnes (dried sediment) is approximately £1.2 million per year (1985). The cost of dredging the sediments and dumping them at sea equates approximately to the cost of supplying topsoil to a site. The major problem is then the supply and demand of topsoil from land sources, is highly variable, and quality control is difficult. The provision of top soil from the dredged sediments would account for between 20-40% of current local needs, at an associated cost in the same order as the current market range.

TABLE 2: SUMMARY OF HEAVY METAL CONCENTRATIONS IN DREDGED SEDIMENTS (Fleming, et al 1986)

CONSTITUENT	USES *	TRIGGER+ CONC mg/kg	CLYDE+ mg/kg 1974	1986	ROTTERDAM+ mg/kg	USA+ CAL/SAG	HAMBURG+	TOP SOIL
A. ARSENIC	a	10	6.0	-	-	-		0.1-50
	b	40						0.01-1
CADMIUM	a	3	14	0.27-3.72 (1.04)	10-27	3.7-18	9.1	
	b	15						
CHROMIUM	a	600	265	64-567 (2.8)	6-370	51-170	130	5-500
	b	1000						
LEAD	a	500	116	10-240 (6.75)	5-690	210-990	183	2-200
	b	2000						
MERCURY	a	1	1.4	0.8-16	0.01-6.47	.02-2.3	4.5	0.1-0.8
	b	20						
B. BORON all uses		3	-	-	-	-	3.4	-
COPPER all uses		50	350	7-201 (7.29)	2-250	68-180	149	2-100
NICKEL all uses		20	104	11.9-43 (5.5)	5-65	24-51	26	5-100
ZINC all uses		130	4500	217-801 (247)	21-1800	500-9400	260	10-300

Notes: + - All values total metals in dried soil, figures in brackets are acetate acid extraction

        * - a. Domestic Gardens   b. Parks and recreation

Conclusions

The study into the use of dredged sediments from the Clyde System has
revealed that the sediments are not grossly polluted, and would fall
within acceptable levels for use in land reclamation for recreational
purposes. Salinity was not present in high concentrations and reduced
quickly under natural rainfall. The dredged material shows good drying
characteristics when grab dredged and is workable with earth moving
plant within a few weeks of exposure to natural weathering. This can be
accelerated if the coarse sediments are mixed with the finer material
at the start of drying. The sediments support the growth of grass
without the addition of extra nutrients.

It is concluded that in the short term the Clyde Sediments can be
engineered to form a "topsoil" suitable for land reclamation within
existing guidelines. Further research is underway into the long term
implications of using this material for this purpose in order to
provide improved guidelines. The Commission of the European Communities
(EEC, 1985) has proposed that a maximum limit on the disposal to sea of
certain wastes be progressively reduced from 1990 onwards by 10% each
year for 5 years. This includes dredged material and sewage sludge and
adds impetus to the efforts required to find engineering solutions to
waste recycling and disposal.

Acknowledgements

The authors acknowledge the support given to this study by the Scottish
Development Agency and the Clyde Port Authority. The opinions expressed
in the paper are those of the authors.

References

BRITISH STANDARD (1965), "Topsoil" BS 3882, H.M. Stationery, London.
DOE - Inter-Departmental Committee on the Redevelopment of Contaminated Land, Guidance on the assessment and redevelopment of Contaminated Land ICRCL 59/1983. London.
EEC - Directive 781319 on Toxic and Dangerious Wastes 1978.
EEC - Directive 85/373 EC Commission proposal for the sea disposal of waste 1985. Brussels.
FLEMING, G. (1970), "Sediment Balance of Clyde Estuary", HY11, Paper 7676, Jnl. of Hydr. Proc. ASCE, Nov. 1970, pp.2219-2230.
FLEMING, G., RIDDELL, J., SMITH, P. "Feasibility Study on the Use of Dredged Material from the Clyde Estuary for Land Renewal". Report to Scottish Development Agency, by Strathclyde Univ., June 1985.
HMSO - Control of Pollution Act 1974. London.
HMSO - Dumping at Sea Act 1974.
HMSO - Control of Pollution (Licencing of Waste Disposal) (Scotland) Regulations 1977.
HMSO - Control of Pollution (Special Waste) Regulations 1980. London.
RIDDELL, J.R. (1979), "Clyde Navigation - A History of the Development and Deepending of the River Clyde". Published by John Donald, Edinburgh, Oct. 1979.
SALOMONS, W. and FORSTNER, U. "Metals in the Hydrocycle". Springer Varlag, MY 1984.
UNEP (1980) Working Papers : Lewis, J. "The Ecology of Natural Disaster".

Dredged Material Disposal in the Lower Great Lakes

Stephen M. Yaksich, John R. Adams, Richard P. Leonard*

Abstract

The Buffalo District Corps of Engineers is responsible for dredging the harbors in Lakes Erie and Ontario. Approximately 2,000,000 cubic yards (1,529,000 cubic meters) of material are dredged annually, of which 40 to 50 percent must be placed in confined disposal areas. In Toledo Harbor, open-lake disposal was recently approved with the provision an expanded monitoring program be started. Water quality in the disposal area was monitored during disposal operations. Results shown that the plume was confined in the disposal area and that water quality standards were not violated. Laboratory studies have shown that only a small percentage of the phosphorus contained in Toledo Harbor sediments becomes biologically available. At the Confined Disposal Facility in Times Beach in Buffalo, NY, contaminant mobility studies and surface and groundwater monitoring programs are being carried out. The Buffalo District has also developed a plan to contain toxic dredged materials at Ashtabula, OH.

Introduction

The Buffalo District Corps of Engineers is responsible for dredging the harbors in Lakes Erie and Ontario. In recent years, the annual amount of material which required confinement has been reduced by 600,000 cubic yards (459,000 cubic meters) resulting in annual savings of $1.5 million. This change in disposal methods is a result of an intensive District water quality and sediment sampling program. The District samples sediment from all its harbors on a 5-year cycle, with more frequent sampling when required. Nutrients, metals, and organics are measured. Bioassays are also used in harbors where open-lake disposal is considered. Buffalo District also performs special studies where necessary. A long-term research program is being undertaken in cooperation with Waterways Experiment Station at Times Beach in Buffalo, NY. At Ashtabula, OH, the District performed slurry classification and column leachate studies on toxic sediment from the Ashtabula River.

Open-Lake Disposal of Toledo Dredged Material

The disposal of dredged material in the open waters of Lake Erie during April and May 1985 marked the first open-lake disposal of Toledo Harbor sediments in 10 years. Sediments from the Maumee River and Lake Erie channel have been placed in a confined disposal facility

*U.S. Army Engineer District, Buffalo, 1776 Niagara Street, Buffalo, NY 14207

since they were declared to be heavily polluted in the early 1970's. Pollution control programs which have been implemented since that time have improved the quality of the sediments to a degree that permits unconfined open lake disposal of about half the material dredged from Toledo Harbor.

Table 1 compares chemical quality of sediments from the disposal areas and reference areas. For comparison, Column 1 of Table 1 gives chemical analyses of sediment proposed for open-lake disposal. In general, it is observed that sediments proposed for open-lake disposal are cleaner than sediments at Disposal Site 1 and associated reference area; the sediments at Disposal and Reference Sites II in general are cleaner than the sediments proposed for open-lake disposal.

The reinitiation of open lake disposal caused justifiable concern over impacts on water quality in Lake Erie, and the Corps of Engineers agreed as a condition of its Sec. 401 water quality certification to employ open-lake disposal to monitor the impacts of the operation on Lake Erie. The State of Ohio specifically requested that dissolved oxygen, phosphorus releases and turbidity plumes be monitored. A contractor was employed to perform the monitoring Measurements of dissolved oxygen, (D.O.), turbidity (by secchi disk), dissolved and total phosphorus, dissolved and suspended solids were made before, at the time of, and at intervals after dumping events and along a transect at 500-foot intervals up to 1500 feet away from the dumping site.

D.O. levels in the vicinity of the dumping operation were converted to percentage of oxygen saturation so that they could be compared to the results of other studies conducted in this same area. These other studies indicate that at this time of the year the D.O. saturation should be about 105 percent. Over the entire period of the dredged material disposal project the D.O. saturation averaged 87%. If the reduction in saturation can be attributed solely to disposal operations, then this activity resulted in a reduction of potential dissolved oxygen concentrations of about 20 percent. The minimum D.O. concentration observed during all of the monitoring was 6.8 mg/L. Since the temperature of the western basin of Lake Erie is a maximum of about 24°C in late August, corresponding to an oxygen solubility of 8.23 mg/L, a 20% reduction in D.O. saturation to 6.6 mg/L would not be likely to cause a violation of the Ohio Water Quality Standards.

A turbidity plume is a natural consequence of open lake disposal of dredged material. These materials consist of very fine particles (predominantly clay size), and even very small amounts remaining in suspension can give the appearance of a very heavy sediment plume. Even in this quite muddy looking water the suspended solids concentration was only about 15mg/L. Compared to previous studies the secchi depth was greater after 2 hours of settling (23 inches, 58 cm) than it had been in a nearby area (20 inches, 50 cm) without dredge material disposal in 1977.

A major concern in Lake Erie is phosphorus loads to the lake. Although dredged material can contain a considerable amount of

Table 1 - Comparative Quality of Dredge Sediments and
Sediments from Open-Lake Disposal Areas and Reference Areas

Parameter	Dredge (1) Sediments	Disposal Area I Reference (2)	Disposal (3)	Disposal Area II Reference (2)	Disposal (3)
Volatile Solids (Percent)	5.23	5.53	5.17	1.57	2.19
Oil and Grease (mg/g)	730	900	700	400	500
Chemical Oxygen Demand (mg/g)	79,062	78,400	63,600	20,400	29,700
Total Phosphorus (ug/g)	893	1,120	1,000	340	460
Kjeldahl Nitrogen (ug/g)	1,732	2,380	1,890	730	970
Ammonia Nitrogen (ug/g)	161	-	-	-	-
Cyanide (ug/g)	0.06	-	-	-	-
Arsenic (ug/g)	13	-	-	-	-
Cadmium (ug/g)	1.4	3.1	4.8	<0.1	2.5
Chromium (ug/g)	26	62	61	38	52
Copper (ug/g)	38	50	51	18	24
Lead (ug/g)	28	42	46	22	29
Mercury (ug/g)	0.20	0.46	0.27	0.34	0.46
Nickel (ug/g)	46	54	49	29	36
Zinc (ug/g)	132	174	191	71	105
Iron (ug/g)	27,200	33,200	33,700	11,700	14,200
Manganese (ug/g)	484	472	506	163	238

- No Data
(1) Average of 8 samples.
(2) Average of 10 samples.
(3) Average of 18 samples.

phosphorus, the crucial question is how much biologically available
material is released to the water column. The sampling was inconclu-
sive as to whether the dumping operations significantly increased
levels of dissolved reactive phosphorus within the dumpsite. Other
investigators have reported average dissolved phosphorus concentrations in this area of the lake to range from 0.02 mg/L to 0.04
mg/L. While the mean of the measurements within the mixing zone of
the dump site appear to be higher than the observations of others the
difference is not great. Mixing with lake water of presumably lower
concentration will rapidly dilute these levels to the ambient lake
concentration. Future monitoring of disposal operations will include
more measurements of phosphorus both within the disposal zone and at
reference locations far removed from it.

The District has funded a study to define the phosphorus availability
and settling velocities of the sediment disposed of in the open lake.
A mathematical model is then used with these data to determine how much

biologically available phosphorus is released to the water. The studies show the amount of available phosphorus in the dredged material
is similar to that which is available in lake sediment and that a
small amount (3.4 percent) of it will become available to algae during
disposal.

The influence of natural events e.g. rain, wind, and currents on the
resuspension and movement of sediments in the western basin of Lake
Erie were examined in comparison to the disposal operation. These
natural events cause turbidity far in excess of what can be expected
from open lake disposal. It was not possible, for example, to measure
any influence of the dredging operation on the turbidity of the water
intake at Toledo. Changes in turbidity at the intake were strongly
influenced by the discharge of suspended sediments from the Maumee
River and by winds blowing across Lake Erie.

Resuspension in the far 231 square miles (600 km^2) western basin of
Lake Erie in the vicinity of the Maumee is estimated as 21,497 tons/sq
mi. (50,800 mt/km^2) or 33,611,000 tons/yr (30,500,000 mt/yr) for the
area. The sediment from 500,000 yd^3 (382,000 m^3) of open-lake disposal is calculated as 338 tons/yr (307,000 mt/yr) or 1 percent of the
resuspension in the far western basin. Similar calculations of
resuspension in the total (1,190 mi^2) (3,100 km^2) western basin compared to open-lake disposal at Toledo shows that disposal constitutes
about 0.2 percent of natural wind induced resuspension. The quality
of the sediments discussed previously is about the same as in-lake
sediments. Thus, confined disposal as opposed to open-lake disposal
would account for approximately 0.4 percent of the nutrients and
metals present in this sector of the western basin.

The open-lake disposal operations in Lake Erie during the spring of
1985 did not cause any long term degradation of water quality.
Dissolved oxygen concentrations were reduced about 20 percent from
what they might have been at this time of year, but there were no
violations of Ohio water quality standards. Turbidity plumes were
created, but they did not contain much mass of sediment and always
were completely dissipated before they could have influenced any water
supplies. Dissolved phosphorus concentrations may have been increased
slightly within the mixing zone, but not so much that the operation
could influence the production of algae in the western basin of Lake
Erie. The open-lake disposal of dredged materials that are not
heavily contaminated and that are similar in chemical and physical
characteristics to the substrates over which they will eventually
become deposited may present a preferable alternative, both economically and environmentally, to the increasing occupation of productive
shallow-water habitat by CDF's.

Times Beach, Contaminant Mobility Studies

The Times Beach Disposal area is a 46-acre (18.6 hectare) confined dredge disposal area near the confluence of Lake Erie and the
Buffalo River. The site received approximately 550,000 yd^3 (420,500
m^3) of polluted dredge material from the Buffalo River and the Buffalo

Harbor from the period 1972 to 1976. While being filled, the area became intensively used by migratory waterfowl, songbirds, and other wildlife. At the request of local environmental groups, filling was stopped in 1976 because of the large numbers and varieties of birds using the site. The completely enclosed area now contains about 50 percent shallow open water, 25 percent marsh, and 25 percent scrub trees, mainly cottonwood.

Although the area is observed to foster lush vegetative growth and abundant wildlife, there is concern that contaminants from the sediment may accumulate and bioconcentrate in plant and animal food chains. Consequently, a long-term program has been initiated to study bioaccumulation by aquatic and terrestrial plants and animals and possible effects on organisms including growth, reproduction, vitality, and carcinogenicity. Initial work consisted of the chemical characterization of sediment and bioaccumulation by plants, earthworms, and fish. Principal contaminants found in the sediments include the heavy metals zinc, cadmium, copper, arsenic, mercury, chromium and lead, and organics including chlorobenzenes, PAH's, and aniline compounds.

The sedge, cyperus esculentus was planted at various locations in the dredge sediment, harvested after 45 days, and analyzed for heavy metals and organics. Uptake of organic pollutants was insignificant. The heavy metals cadmium, chromium, iron, and possibly arsenic were in higher concentrations than normally found in wetland plant communities of the Great Lakes. Earthworms incubated in Times Beach sediment for 28 days were found to have increased levels of cadmium, arsenic, mercury, PCB's, and PAH's. Native worms from the disposal area were also found to accumulate heavy metals PCB's and PAH's.

Fish samples collected from the open water at the Times Beach site did not accumulate elevated levels of heavy metals, but did have elevated levels of PCB's and PAH's. Mercury and PCB levels in fish did not exceed "Tolerance or Action" levels for edible fish (i.e., muscle). Accumulation of organics by fish livers was somewhat higher than by muscle.

Mammal, fish, and bird populations have been inventoried at the Times Beach CDF. Future study will be directed at sampling and analyzing key higher food chain species at the Times Beach for contaminant bioaccumulation and effects.

Surface and Groundwater Monitoring at Times Beach CDF

The 1984 report of the Niagara River Toxics Committee identified the Times Beach Confined Disposal Facility (CDF) as a possible source of contamination to the Niagara River. In addition, the Times Beach CDF was cited under the Comprehensive Environmental Response, Compensation and Liability Act of 1980 ("CERCLA") for the possible release of hazardous substances. These designations were based on a one-time sampling and analysis of pond water done by USGS in 1983. USGS also installed three monitoring wells in the dredged material at

Times Beach. These wells were sampled once in 1983. These four
samples showed high contaminant levels and resulting loading of 4,900
pounds (2,190 kilograms) of heavy metals to the Niagara River.

As a result of these studies, the Buffalo District started its own
surface and groundwater monitoring program. Three clusters of three
wells at different depths were installed in 1984. The clusters were
located in the wooded upland, the wetland, and in the shallow water
pond. Well screen placements were based on sediment and soil stratigraphy, and depths to bedrock as revealed by drilling investigations
prior to well placement.

Open water samples and monitoring well water samples were obtained and
analyzed by a contractor to the Buffalo District. Samples were
collected in December 1984 and April and September 1985. Samples from
the open water and pond wells could not be obtained in December, 1984.
Each well was evacuated a minimum of three well volumes with an Isco
well sampling pump and allowed to recharge before sample collection.
One set of samples from each well was filtered in the field through a
0.45 micron nucleopore pressure filter in order to provide filtered
and unfiltered samples for analyses. Temperature, ph, and conductivity were recorded before samples were drawn from the wells.

Table 2 compares the means of filtered and unfiltered well and surface
water samples analyzed in this study to national maximum allowable concentrations for drinking water and the USGS results. The means for
all parameters analyzed in this study are less than the national
drinking water standards. In all cases, the samples analyzed by USGS
were greater than those measured in this study, often by several
orders of magnitude. There appears to be two possible explanations
for the discrepancies. The first is that USGS wells were placed in
the dredge material, whereas the Corps wells were placed below the
dredged material. The other is that the unfiltered samples collected
by USGS may have had entrained particulates which greatly increased

Table 2 - Comparison of Times Beach Results

Parameter	:	Concentration (ug/l)								
	:	Wells		:	Pond		: Drinking	:	USGS	: USGS
	:	F	: U	: F	: U	:	Water	:	Well	: Pond
	:	:	:	:	:	:	:	:
Arsenic	:	11	: 28	:< 4	: < 4	:	50	:	67.3	: 115
Barium	:	150	: 196	:<100	: <100	:	1,000	:	929	: 331
Cadmium	:	<2.0	: 3.1	:<1.0	: <1.0	:	10	:	10.2	: 39
Chromium	:	19	: 27	: 22	: 17	:	50	:	223	: 758
Copper	:	40	: 97	: 17	: 20	:	1,000	:	472	: 912
Lead	:	12	: 17	:< 4	: 7	:	50	:	1,331	:2,020
Mercury	:	0.5	: .8	:<0.3	: <0.3	:	2	:	0.32	: ND
Nickel	:	50	: 57	:< 20	: 25	:	-	:	219	: 129
Thallium	:	5	: 3.4	:<4.5	: <4.5	:	-	:	ND	: 66
Zinc	:	72	: 91	: 23	: 15	:	5,000	:261,000	:3,340

ND - Not Detected

measured levels in the samples.   USGS evacuated their wells immediately before sampling.

Purgeable organics, nitrosomines, PAH's, napthalene, aniline, and
chloroaniline were analyzed in well water samples and in pond water
samples. Chlorobenzene was detected on one occassion each from three
wells. Concentrations in filtered and unfiltered samples ranged from
1.2 ug/l to 4.2 ug/l.   Toluene was measured at 60 ug/l for an
unfiltered sample from an open water well.   The filtered sample was
less than 1.0 ug/l.   No other organic contaminants were detected in
monitoring well samples.

The Buffalo District believes that the data collected to date indicates no substantial migration of pollutants from the dredge material
into groundwater, surface water of the pond, or Lake Erie water.   The
pollutant loads of heavy metals using data from this study is 133
pounds (59 kilograms) per year compared to 4,900 pounds (2,188
kilograms) per year calculated by USGS. The levels of metals found in
the open-water wells and to a lesser extent the wetland wells suggests
that continued monitoring should be done.   The District will sample
and analyze groundwater on two to three occassions in 1986.   The
District plans to filter all samples before analyses as a more correct
representation of soluble constituents that would be mobilized in
groundwater. In view of the 1985 sampling showing only chlorobenzene
above detection limits, 1986 organics analyses would be limited to
chlorobenzene.   The above steps will reduce unnecessary and costly
analytical expenses.

Toxic Waste Disposal at Ashtabula, Ohio

USEPA and the Buffalo District have been involved since 1971 in a
substantial amount of testing with regard to the pollutional characteristics of the Ashtabula Harbor and River sediments.   These sediments have been reclassified many times with varying degrees of
confinement required if the material is to be dredged.   The final
USEPA sediment classification classified the sediments in the project
area as toxic and heavily polluted.   The toxic material is subject to
TSCA (Toxic Substance Control Act) disposal requirements and the
heavily polluted material must be adequately confined.   Obtaining
approval from appropriate agencies for a disposal site has been the
major stumbling block over the past decade.

To date, the Buffalo District does not have an environmentally acceptable disposal facility for this material.   Consequently, the USEPA
restriction on the dredged material disposal has prevented the
District from maintaining adequate river navigation depths and, more
significantly, is expected to restrict the commercial operations in
the lower river and the outer harbor as the polluted sediments continue moving downstream.   To assure continued beneficial commercial
use of the lower river and outer harbor, plans have been formulated to
dredge and dispose all of the polluted Ashtabula River sediments in a
confined facility.

Slurry classification tests and column leachate studies were conducted on samples of polluted sediment from the Ashtabula River. The purpose of the clarification tests was to determine in vitro rates of clarification and to determine the removal of heavy metal and organic pollutants which would result from the deposition of slurry materials. The purpose of the column leachate studies was to ascertain the types and concentrations of metals and organic pollutants which might be leached from sediments if placed in a landfill. A 60-inch (152 cm) tall by 7-inch (17.8 cm) diameter column with sampling ports was used for clarification/ deposition settling tests. A 36-inch (91 cm) tall by 3.5-inch (8.9 cm) diameter column with leachate collection system was used for leachate studies. Results of clarification/deposition tests showed that toxic metal concentrations in the supernatant were lower than U.S. drinking water standards after 16 hours of settling. Traces of mono, di, and tri chlorobenzenes (<1 to 37 ug/l) remained in supernatant. Barium and chlorobenzene were consistently found in leachate collected from column leachate tests (Ba-700 to 1800 ug/l; chlorobenzenes - 6 to 33 ug/l).

The above tests demonstrated that receiving water quality standards should not be violated from clarified dredge supernatant discharge, and minor leaching of toxics from landfilled dredged material.

The Buffalo District recommends maintenance dredging of the Ashtabula River and confinement of the toxic and heavily polluted sediments for economical and environmental reasons. Dredging will be performed to the authorized project depths, in addition to a typical overdepth based on the accuracy of the dredged equipment used. The resulting depth will be at least equal to the historical maximum depth which is necessary because:

    a. USEPA believes that dredging to the historical maximum depth will expose sediments with less pollutant concentrations than sediments at a lesser depth.

    b. Based on economics of scale, it is best to remove and dispose of all the polluted sediments in one operation rather than on a continuing basis as the polluted sediments move downstream where they affect commercial navigation.

Confinement of the Ashtabula River dredged material is a one-time requirement. USEPA has agreed to prevent pollutants from existing Fields Brook (the major source of pollutants to the Ashtabula River) to the extent required.

All the dredged material will be disposed of in a privately-owned disposal facility. At present, this is the only identifiable environmentally and socially acceptable disposal plan for the toxic dredged material. In addition, it is the plan overwhelmingly preferred by all the appropriate agencies for containment of the heavily polluted dredged material.

A Robustness Constraint for the Analysis of Uncertainty

James G. Uber, Student Member ASCE,
E. Downey Brill, Jr., John T. Pfeffer, Members ASCE*

One definition of robustness is related to the performance of a
system given that actual parameter values are not the same as those
assumed for design. A sensitivity-based definition of system robustness
is presented that can be formulated as a constraint within an
optimization framework. The optimization framework permits the
tradeoffs between a measure of robustness and other objectives to be
quantified in a heuristic fashion. Significant insights can then be
obtained about how uncertainty in parameter values affects other
important design objectives. Results are presented for an application
to wastewater treatment plant design.

Introduction

Mathematical modeling is a convenient and cost effective tool for
the analysis of many large systems. A mathematical model can represent
the significant interactions that exist between system components, and
therefore can be used to obtain insights about how these complex
interactions influence system planning and design. The values of many
model parameters may be required, however, and uncertainty in these
values may also influence the planning and design process.
Unfortunately, the relationships between parameter uncertainty and other
important objectives may not be understood even by individuals with
expert knowledge of the system and of the mathematical model. One
problem, therefore, with the use of mathematical models is that the
values of model parameters are often uncertain and their probability
distributions are often difficult to obtain.

Quantitative methods are needed that can incorporate some of the
concerns about parameter uncertainty into the planning and design
process. A mathematical framework for the analysis of model parameter
uncertainty should yield, for many practical systems, significant
insights about the interactions between uncertainty in parameter values
and other important objectives. A mathematical framework has been
developed for generating alternative solutions that can be used to

*Graduate Research Assistant, Professor of Civil Engineering and
Environmental Studies, and Professor of Sanitary Engineering,
respectively, Department of Civil Engineering, University of Illinois at
Urbana-Champaign, 208 N. Romine St., Urbana, Illinois 61801.

ɔre these interactions quantitatively by joining optimization with a
.ion of system robustness.

The term "robustness" has been used in the statistical literature
since 1953, when G. E. P. Box introduced the concept of a robust
statistical procedure (5). A statistical procedure that is insensitive
to changes in its underlying assumptions is called robust (5), e.g. in
hypothesis testing robustness may be related to the sensitivity of the
sample size to the assumption of normally distributed populations. It
is interesting that explicit probabilistic measures are not used in this
application of the concept of robustness.

The literature on control of dynamic systems contains another
sensitivity-based definition of robustness. Verde and Frank (12)
state: "control systems that maintain their properties to a certain
degree despite variations in parameter values are called robust."
Although this definition is not precise, it reveals clearly a
relationship between sensitivity and robustness. In optimal control
theory the advantage of a "sub-optimal" design that is less sensitive to
variations in parameter values has been recognized for some time. A
design that is "minimally sensitive" may, by the definition of Verde and
Frank, be called relatively robust.

In both statistics and control theory, the notions of robust
procedures or systems are intimately linked to sensitivity. Matalas and
Fiering (6), and Hashimoto et al. (4), have introduced to the water
resources literature definitions of robustness that are
probability-based.

Matalas and Fiering consider the difficult question: If a
particular design D_i is chosen, what is the probability p that D_i is
truly optimal, given that the values of parameters are uncertain?
Robustness, as defined by Matalas and Fiering, is related to this
probability. Hashimoto et al. note, however, that a design may have a
very low probability of being optimal (i.e. low robustness) yet incur
very low economic opportunity costs if it is chosen in place of the true
optimal design. Thus Hashimoto et al. develop a probabilistic notion of
robustness that is allied with the concept of economic flexibility. The
robustness of a design D_i is defined as the probability that the total
costs associated with D_i are always within some percentage of the
minimum cost design.

The notions of robustness proposed by Matalas and Fiering and by
Hashimoto et al. are interesting concepts, but they are very broad and
hence their information requirements are very large. The definition of
Matalas and Fiering, for example, requires an estimate of the
probability that a design will be truly optimal, given uncertain
parameter values. Even if the values of design parameters are
deterministic, selection of the optimal design is a very complex
decision making task and may involve many social and political
objectives that are not easily quantified and possibly not even known.
Hashimoto et al. define the robustness of design D_i in terms of the
probability that the cost of D_i will be within some percentage of the
cost of the optimal design; the entire locus of optimal solutions,
corresponding to any feasible combination of parameter values, must be

known (i.e. the optimal value function must be specified). Given the
economic nature of their robustness definition, it might be difficult,
in general, even to specify the objective function since every concern
may not be expressed easily in economic units (a limitation of
traditional benefit-cost analysis).

Matalas and Fiering and Hashimoto et al. both construct notions of
robustness that rely on probability theory to model uncertainty in
parameter values. If the probability laws associated with the
parameters can be estimated with some confidence then a probabilistic
framework for the analysis of uncertainty may be desirable. Probability
information may be available to reflect the randomness in hydrologic
data, for example, but it may be difficult to determine probability
distributions for some of the other inputs to the planning and design
process. Thus for many water resources systems non-probabilistic
approaches to robustness and to the analysis of uncertainty in general
may also be desirable.

A non-probabilistic notion of system robustness is presented here.
Robustness is defined as the relative ability of a design to maintain a
level of system performance that meets the design criteria even if the
actual values of model parameters are not exactly the same as the values
assumed for design. This definition is based on the sensitivity of a
measure of system performance to changes in parameter values that are
uncertain, and is closely related to the sensitivity-based definitions
used in statistics and control theory. It is useful also to distinguish
between this definition, which is a definition of system robustness, and
other definitions of design robustness; in particular those presented by
Matalas and Fiering and by Hashimoto et al. In terms of sensitivity,
this definition is related to the sensitivity of the system while the
definitions of Matalas and Fiering and of Hashimoto et al. are more
related to the sensitivity of the design or decision process.

Another attribute of the robustness definition presented here is
that, because of its narrow scope, robustness can be expressed
mathematically as a constraint within a formal optimization framework
(see (11)). The mathematical optimization framework permits the
tradeoff between modeled objectives and a measure of system robustness
to be quantified in a heuristic fashion; for many complex systems the
nature of this tradeoff is not intuitive and is not practical to
determine by other methods. Thus it should be possible to obtain, for
many complex systems, new insights about the interactions between
parameter uncertainty and other important system planning and design
objectives.

Optimization models have been used recently in new and different
ways (1,2,3). These new techniques use heuristics and simple measures
in conjunction with optimization to generate a few attractive solutions
for further, detailed evaluation by decision-makers. The optimization
framework presented here for the analysis of parameter uncertainty uses
heuristic measures of robustness to generate alternative solutions and
thus is closely related in its use of optimization to these other new
techniques. The robustness constraint should be viewed as a tool for
gaining insights about the mathematical model and the corresponding
system by generating alternative solutions that contain some of the
concerns about uncertainty in model parameter values.

An Application to Wastewater Treatment Plant Design

The state of the art in optimal wastewater treatment plant design has progressed steadily over the past two decades. Relatively recent advances in nonlinear optimization algorithms and in the development of improved performance models of wastewater treatment unit processes has permitted the formulation of comprehensive, detailed optimization models that include many important process interactions. Two recent modeling efforts by Tyteca (10) and by Tang et al. (8,9) exemplify the current state of the art in least cost optimization models for wastewater treatment plant design. The solution from any least cost model is, however, rarely optimal since objectives other than cost are important. For example, least cost wastewater treatment plant designs typically use a sludge age of about two days, which is very short for a stable and reliable operation.

A robustness constraint has been included in the model by Tang et al. to examine the tradeoff between total system cost and robustness. Robustness is defined in this case as the sensitivity of a measure of effluent water quality, BOD_5, to changes in several parameter values that are uncertain. Preliminary results given in Uber et al. (11) indicate that a robustness constraint incorporated into least cost models for wastewater treatment plant design can generate solutions that are relatively cost effective, yet more representative of designs that are observed to work in practice. Table 1 presents a comparison between a least cost design and a robust design with respect to the values of several important design variables and the total system cost. The effect of a robustness constraint is to create designs that are more consistent with those recommended in a widely used design text (7).

Table 1 - Comparison of a Least Cost and a Robust Design

Design Variable	Least Cost	Robust	Recommended*
Sludge Age (days)	2.2	6.0+	5.0-15.0
Mixed Liquor Suspended Solids (g/m^3)	1520	3100	1500-3000
Recycle Ratio (%)	12.5	24.0	25.0-50.0
Overflow Rate of Final Settler (m/hr)	2.19	0.7	0.67-1.33
Total Cost ($/year)	500,000	600,000	—

*Metcalf and Eddy, Inc. (7)
+Variable is at upper bound

Summary

Complex system models typically contain a large number of parameters. Furthermore, the values of the parameters are often uncertain, and their probability distributions difficult to obtain. The interactions between parameter uncertainty and other important objectives are not generally understood even by experienced individuals, and thus quantitative methods are needed that incorporate some of the concerns related to parameter uncertainty into the planning and design process.

A non-probabilistic notion of system robustness that is based on the sensitivity of a performance measure can be formulated as a constraint in optimization models for planning and design. The optimization framework can be used to generate designs that are robust, and good with respect to other objectives, and permits the tradeoff between modeled objectives and a measure of system robustness to be quantified in a heuristic fashion. For many complex systems the nature of this tradeoff is not intuitive and is not practical to determine by other methods. Thus application of the method should make possible new insights, for many practical systems, about the interactions between parameter uncertainty and other planning and design objectives. Preliminary results for a wastewater treatment plant design problem indicate that the robustness constraint generates solutions that are compatible with recommended design practice, but very different from typical minimum cost designs.

Appendix — References

1. Brill, E. D., Jr., "The Use of Optimization Models in Public-Sector Planning," _Management Science_, Vol. 25, No. 5, May 1979.

2. Chang, S. Y., Brill, E. D., Jr., and Hopkins, L. D., "Use of Mathematical Models to Generate Alternative Solutions to Water Resources Planning Problems," _Water Resources Research_, Vol. 18, No. 1, pp. 58-64, Feb. 1982.

3. Chang, S. Y., and Liaw, S. L., "Generating Designs for Wastewater Systems," _Jour. of the Environmental Engineering Division, ASCE_, Vol. 111, No. 5, Oct. 1985.

4. Hashimoto, T., Loucks, D. P., and Stedinger, J. R., "Robustness of Water Resources Systems," _Water Resources Research_, Vol. 18, No. 1, pp. 21-26, Feb. 1982.

5. Kendall, M. and Stuart, A., _The Advanced Theory of Statistics_, Charles Griffin and Company Limited, Vol. 2, p. 492, 1979.

6. Matalas, N. C., and Fiering, M. B, "Water-Resource System Planning," _Climate, Climatic Change and Water supply_, National Academy of Sciences, Washington, D. C., 1977.

7. Metcalf and Eddy, Inc, _Wastewater Engineering Treatment, Disposal, Reuse_, McGraw-Hill, 1979.

8. Tang, C. C., Brill, E. D., Jr., and Pfeffer, J. T., "A Comprehensive Model of an Activated Sludge Waste Treatment System," Submitted for Publication, 1986a.

9. Tang, C. C., Brill, E. D., Jr., and Pfeffer, J. T., "Optimization Techniques for a Comprehensive Model of an Activated Sludge Secondary Wastewater Treatment System," Submitted for Publication, 1986b.

10. Tyteca, D., "Nonlinear Programming Model of Wastewater Treatment Plant," _Jour. of the Environmental Engineering Division, ASCE_, Vol. 107, No. EE4, pp. 747-766, Aug. 1981.

11. Uber, J. G., Brill, E. D., and Pfeffer, J. T., _A Nonlinear Programming Model of a Wastewater Treatment System: Sensitivity Analysis and a Robustness Constraint_, Water Resources Center Research Report 196, University of Illinois at Urbana-Champaign, June 1985.

12. Verde, C. and Frank, P. M., "A Design Procedure for Linear Suboptimal Regulators with Preassigned Trajectory Sensitivity," _Proceedings of the 21st Conf. on Decision and Control_, IEEE Control Systems Society, Vol 2, pp. 886-890, 1982.

An Optimization Approach For Locating Sediment Ponds
in Stripmined Areas

Mohammad Karamouz, M. ASCE

and

Reza M. Khanbilvardi , A.M. ASCE

Abstract

In this study, a mathematical model which can predict
erosion from a watershed and incorporated into an
optimization model has been investigated. The Erosion-
Deposition Model (EDM), which uses a two dimensional
analysis and single storm values of rainfall and runoff to
compute erosion and sediment transport for that storm, was
used in conjunction with a search technique to find near
optimal location of a sediment pond. With this new
approach, it will be possible to locate and size the
sedimentation ponds for controlling erosion.

INTRODUCTION

Effective planning to control erosion and sediment
yield from stripmined and reclaimed area depends on the
scientific tools available and on the abilities of the
operator or conservation planner. Watershed modeling has
been, recently, considered as one of the most useful tools
to simulate the effects of erosion control measures.
Modeling can explain the natural processes involved in
erosion phenomena and thus we can make predictions in a
deterministic or probabilistic sense. Accurate estimates
of sediment yield are required for planning, design,
successful operation of sediment control structures, and
for evaluating the effectiveness of management practices.

Soil loss from a watershed is the consequence of a
complex natural process involving soil detachment,
entrainment, transport, and deposition. Sediment yield is
only that portion of gross erosion (total detached soil
particles) that is transported away from a drainage basin.
Thus, the actual sediment yield is a function of detachment
and subsequent transport of the soil particles.

1. Assistant Professor, Polytechnic University, Brooklyn,
    N.Y. 11201
2. Assistant Professor, The City College of the City Uni-
    versity of New York, New York, N.Y. 10031

Detachment is the dislodging of soil particles by the erosive agents (rainfall and/or runoff), while transport is the entrainment and movement of detached soil particles. Either the rate of detachment or sediment transport capacity may limit the total amount of soil loss from a field. The primary factors involved in these processes are landscape topography, soil characteristics, amount of cover and rainfall, as well as infiltration and runoff rates, Onstad and Foster, 1975, Khanbilvardi et al., 1983a) These factors can change from season to season, from storm to storm, and even during a storm event.

In controlling the quality of surface runoff, the focus should be on suspended solids, partly because erosion and sedimentation are problems in surface mining areas. Furthermore, pollutants such as phosphorus, heavy metals, bacteria, and other pollutants are carried by soil particles (Whipple, 1979; Davis, 1979). Therefore, successful erosion and sediment control is also likely to lead to significant control of nonpoint source pollution.

To control erosion and the resulting sedimentation, and to minimize the nonpoint source pollution as the result of mining activity, federal and state agencies have imposed restrictions on earthmoving activities which create erosion or accelerated erosion. Implementation of effective soil conservation measures are thus, according to the Department of Environmental Resources, an essential part of protecting the natural resources.

According to Public Law 95-87, the Surface Mining Control and Reclamation Act of 1977, all runoff from a project area shall be collected and diverted to facilities for removal of sediment (US Congress, 1977). This requires that all runoff from mining areas should pass through a sedimentation pond before leaving the mining site. According to the Department of Environmental Resources regulations, Chapter 102, sedimentation ponds should have a capacity of 7000 cubic feet for each acre of project area. Also, regulations impose some contraints on the effluent discharge. The discharge of water from areas disturbed by mining activities is prohibited if the runoff does not meet effluent standards. The effluent standards specify a maximum of seventy milligrams per liter of total suspended solids, with a daily average of thirty-five milligrams per liter based on thirty days of consecutive discharge. If these effluent standards from reclaimed surface mined areas can not be met, even with normal control measures, treatment of the runoff water is then recommended.

The stripmining may increase sediment stormwater mixture. Although detention storage has been shown to be an effective way of control, random or unplanned placement can significantly reduce its effectiveness, and in some cases, can actually aggravate potential hazards. In addition, designs which fail to consider the long term performance of a basin can result in ineffective management for a wide range of runoff events.

The optimal design of sediment ponds involves two levels of optimization. The first level deals with the optimal location of the individual basins while the second level involves the optimal size of the ponds in a watershed. Abt and Grigg (1978) and Ormsbee et al. (1984) developed an approximate method for the sizing and placement of detention basins in series. Smith (1981) and Krapp (1982) and Ormsbee et al. (1984) considered the quality of runoff in addition to quantity of runoff in urban watersheds. Despite the growing use of stormwater management basins to control quality , little information is available as to the efficiency of these basins for removal of different kinds of pollutants.

Methodology

Khanbilvardi et al. (1983a, b) developed a hybrid lumped parameter-distributed model referred to as EDM (Erosion-Deposition Model). It was developed in response to a 1979 law intended to prevent or minimize pollution and to restore stripmined areas. The model provides services toward upholding the law by enabling mine operators to predict, based on scientific information, the post-mining conditon of the land. Therefore, operators will be more knowledgeable concerning ways to plan and design the erosion control measures.

In the model, a watershed, field or plot will be represented by a series of homogeneous square subareas (Figure 1). These can be as large or as small as need be. As a result, the site will be divided into a grid represented by a node point in the center. The parameters at each node are assumed to be constant for a given subarea. Normally the model plots, will be set up on a 100 by 100 m grid (1 ha) but on small plots grids as small as 0.6m have been used.

The model is based on the concept of dividing the erosion process into rill and interrill erosion. Rills are defined as the small channels where overland flows tend to concentrate. The areas between the rills are referred to as interrill areas. All the sediment detached from interrill areas is assumed to move laterally to the closest rills. Flows in rills transport this sediment as well as

the sediment detached in the rills themselves (rill scour).
The nature and extent of rill scour depends on factors such
as rill slope length, steepness, rate and amount of surface
runoff, as well as soil particle size distribution.

After delineating rill and interrill areas, the
model specifies the interrill contributing areas. The
interrill contributing areas are those portions of
interrill areas which according to partial area concept of
hydrology contribute detached soil material to rill areas.
Sediment load from the interrill erosion on a contributing
area is assumed to be transported into the closest rill and
the Universal Soil Loss Equation (USLE, Wischmeier and
Smith, 1978) is used to compute the soil detachment on
interrill areas.

Eroded soil contributed from the interrill areas
along with the rill erosion component (rill scour), are
then routed to the rill outlet. In order for detachment
(rill scour) to occur in the rill, the flow shear stress
must exceed the critical shear stress necessary for
sediment transport. This is believed to be the minimum
requirement for initiation of sediment movement off the
rill bed. This concept in its mathematical form can be
expressed as:

$$D_r = \beta\tau(\tau - \tau_{cr}) \qquad (1)$$

where:

D_r =   rill detachment capacity weight/length of
              flow width/sec).

β =   a sediment characteristic factor, which is
              a function of flow velocity, soil particle
              size, particle and fluid density.

τ =   actual shear stress (weight/length).

τ_{cr} =   critical shear stress from Shields' Diagram
              (Shields, 1936).

Once all the components have been computed, the
standard routing (Khanbilvardi et al, 1983a) is used to
balance the amount of available eroded soil against rill
flow transport capacity. At each node the eroded soil from
adjacent interrill areas plus the soil detached within the
rill (rill scour) are then compared with the rill flow
transport capacity to determine the net amount of soil
desposited or carried away from a given node.

Rill transport capacity will be computed from Yalin's (1963) transport equation.

$$T_r = 0.635 \cdot (\rho_s - \rho_w)m \cdot (ghB)^{\frac{1}{2}} \cdot g \cdot [\delta - \frac{1}{\alpha} \log (1 + \alpha \delta)] \tag{2}$$

where:

T_r = rill flow Transport Capacity (weight of sediment/time unit flow width), note that here the meaning of "weight" is that of mass acceleration,

ρ_s = mass density of the soil (weight/volume),

ρ_w = mass density of the fluid (weight/volume),

m   = soil particle diameter (length),

g   = gravity acceleration (Length/time),

h   = hydraulic radius of the rill (length),

B   = rill slope steepness,

$$\alpha = 2.45 (\frac{w}{s})^{0.40} (T)^{0.50} \quad \text{(dimensionless)}$$

$$T \text{ (force)} = \frac{\rho_w hB}{(\rho_s - \rho_w)m} = \frac{hB}{(\rho_s - 1)m} \quad \text{(dimensionless actual lift}$$

$$\frac{}{\frac{\rho_s}{\rho_w}}$$

T_{cr} = critical lift force from Shields' Diagram (Shields, 1936).

$$\delta = \frac{T - T_{cr}}{T_{cr}} \quad (\delta = 0, \text{ when } T < T_{cr}).$$

The model is able to predict the location and amount of erosion and deposition for individual storms over the entire watershed, as well as distribution of sediment load and potential stream inputs for any time after runoff has begun.

The output which is the magnitude of runoff and soil erosion and their flow path, has been incorporated into design formulation of sedimentation pond and diversion. Finally, the model estimates the size and location of an erosion control system.

Site Description

A site was selected to illustrate application of the model as explained in previous sections. The site is a 6.8

ha. stripmined area in central Pennsylvania with a Gilpin
silt loam as the dominant soil type.   Figure (1) shows the
pertinent features of the site and topography. A 1 yr - 24
hr design storm (5.84 cm type 1A) is used to demonstrate
model performance and selected outputs.   The site was
divided into a grid of relatively homogeneous subareas (7.6
x 7.6), excluding the active mining areas and any
contributions from a haul road.   The model was used to
evaluate the efficiency of five different control options
listed in Table 1.

Results and Discussion

        The model was first solved for option 1 in Table 1.
The simulated surface flow patters are generally parallel
and leave the site at the lower boundary.   Then, a system
of three diversions and one sedimentation pond (option 2 in
Table 1) were installed to control erosion.   These control
structures were believed to be adequate for control of
surface runoff and erosion at the site.   But, the result
shows that sediment yield and in particular the effluent
concentrations are more than the minimum set by Reclamation
Act 1977.   Therefore, to determine the best alternative
erosion control system options 3,4,5 (Table 1) were also
evaluated separately.

        Table 2 summarizes the total sediment yield from the
site and gives the effluent concentration for all five
options assuming d=30 mm (90 percent of soil particles by
weight are finer than 30 mm.) The results indicate the
efficiency of options (2 through 5) in controlling site
sediment yield and effluent concentration. The results
prove the fact that control structures in options 2 thru 5
change the overland flow patterns at the site and affect
total sediment yield.   It is also clear from the results
that the control system selected in option 5 (Figure 2) is
the optimal (among the options) control system because it
can reduce the sediment yield by as much as 92 percent over
no control system (option 1). Table 2 also indicates that
options 2, 3, and 4 also reduces the total sediment yield
by 40-70 percent over option 1. However, only option 5
(using d = 30 mm) can meet the requirement of 70 mg/l of
suspended solids in the effluent.

        The output indicates that the required storage for an
appropriate sedimentation pond would be about 220 cubic
meters.   Therefore, a storage rate of 33 cubic meters per
hectar should be sufficient to meet or exceed the effluent
standard established by law.   These results appear to
reflect the actual field conditions observed at the site.

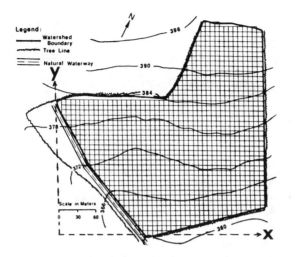

Figure 1. Square Grid Superimposed on the Topography of the Experimental Site.

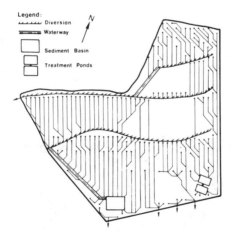

Figure 2. Rill Patterns and Flow Outlets Predicted by the Model (Option 5)

Table 1.   Erosion Control Systems

Option   Description   Pond Coordinates
                                           (x,y) in meters
----
1   no control structure   ------

2   3 diversions with one pond   (285,66)

3   "   "   "   "   "   (230,75)
                                           (285,66)*

4   "   "   "   "   "   (180,45)
                                           (285,66)*

5   "   "   "   "   "   (150,30)
                                           (285,66)*
----
* This pond is a treatment pond.

Table 2.   Sediment Yield Reduction and Soil Concentration
           in Effluent

Control Option   Sediment Yield   Effluent
                      reduction (%)   concentratin (mg/l)
----
     1   0   > 1000

     2   40   > 600

     3   50   323

     4   76   152

     5   92   40

References

Abt, S.R., and Gregg, N.S., 1978. "An Approximate Method
for Sizing Detention Reservoirs," Water Resources Bulletin,
Vol. 14, No. 4, pp. 956-961.

Davis, Ernest M, 1979, "Maximum Utilization of Water
Resources In A Planned Community - Bacterial
Characteristics of Stormwaters In Developing Areas", U.S.
Environmental Protection Agency, Environmental Protection
Technology Series EPA-600/2-79-050f.

Khanbilvardi, R.M., Rogowski, A.S., and Miller, A.C.,
1983a. "Modeling Upland Erosion", Water Resour. Bull,
19(1): 29-35.

Khanbilvardi, R.M., Rogowski, A.S., and Milelr, A.C., 1983b. "Predicting Erosion and Deposition On A Stripmined and Reclaimed Area", Water Resour. Bull., 19(4): 585-593. Krapp, 1982.

Krapp, R. 1982. "On The Computational Complexity of Combinational Problems, " Networked, Vol. 5, 1975, pp.45-68.

Mays, W.L. and Beident, P.B., "Model for Optimal Size and Location of Detention," Journal of the Water Resources Planning and Management Division ASCE, Vol. 108, No. WR3, Oct. 1982, pp. 270-285.

Onstad, C.A., and Foster, G.R., 1975. "Erosion Modeling On A Watershed", Transactions of the ASAE 18:288-292.

Ormsbee, L.E., Delleur, J.W., and Houck, M.H., 1984, "Development of General Manning Methodology for Storm Water Management In Urban Watersheds", Technical Report 163, Water Resources Research Center, Purdue University, W. Lafayette, IN, March.

Sheilds, A., 1936, ""Anwendung der Aehnlichkeitsmechanik Und Der Turbulenzforschung Auf Die Geschiebebewegung", Mitteilung der Preussischen Versuchsanstalt fuer Wasserbau und Schiffbau, Heft 26, Berlin.

Smith, W.G., 1982, "Water Quality Enhancement Through Stormwater Detention," Proceedings Engineering Foundation Conference on Stormwater detention ASCE, Hennicker, N.H., August 1-6.

United States Congress, "Surface Mining Control and Reclamation Act of 1977, 95th Congress, Washington, D.C., 1977.

Whipple, W., 1979, "Dual Purpose Detention Basins", American Society of Civil Engineers, Journal of Water Resources Planning and Management Division, 105(WR2): 403-412.

Winsdmeier, W. H., and Smith, D.D., 1978, "Predicting Rainfall Erosion Losses - A Guide to Conservation Planning", Science and Education Administration, USDA Handbook No. 537, pp. 1-58.

Yaline, Y.S., 1986, "An Expression for Bed-Load Transportation, "Journal of the Hydraulics Division, ASCE, Vol. 89, N. HY3, pp. 221-250.

Optimization, Simulation and Multiobjective
Analysis of Operating Rules for Reservoir Systems

Ricardo Harboe[*], M.A.S.C.E.

Abstract

   In this paper, three steps are proposed for establishing reservoir
operating rules which can be used in real-time without flow forecasting.
In the first step, optimization models are used to find optimal targets
for a standard operating rule for each reservoir. This is achieved via
a sequential application of dynamic programming models with physical
objective functions of the max-min type. In the second step, simulations
with historical and synthetic records are performed in order to improve
the simple standard operating rules and satisfy the decision-maker's
objectives more closely. In this step,targets are changed and a set of
critical storage levels as indicators for dry periods are introduced.
The third and last step includes a multiobjective analysis applied to
select the best operating rule among several alternatives developed in
the second step.

Introduction

Many of the mathematical models for reservoir operation developed so far
are for planning purposes (Yakowitz, 1982; Yeh, 1985) and do not deliver
an operating rule which can be used in future operation of the system.
It is the intention to present the development of such operating rules
which are simple in their structure (basically as a standard operating
rule), do not use flow forecasting (they could therefore be improved
with forecasting) and are fixed or established beforehand (no model
calculations in each time period during real time operations).

   Optimization models developed in the first step (Boehle et al,1981),
are basically standard dynamic programming models applied sequentially
to each reservoir. Here, the optimization of one reservoir uses the
results of the reservoirs previously optimized. Thus the operating
rules obtained should also be applied in a given sequence.

   The simulation model (Harboe, 1983) is a flexible computer program
which allows changing targets of the operating rules (for example reducing targets during dry periods), water transfers between reservoirs,
use of synthetic records generated with the Young-Pisano (1968) model.
This model calculates several indeces of performance such as securities
(% of months in which targets are achieved), minimum flows for the purpose of low-flow augmentation, one sided squared deviation from the

[*] Lehrstuhl für Wasserwirtschaft und Umwelttechnik I
   Ruhr-Universität Bochum, Postfach 102148, 4630 Bochum,
   Federal Republic of Germany

targets, etc. Since the simulation is a behavioural model, the decision as to which is the best operating rule must be taken outside the model, defining one or more objective functions.

In order to choose the best operating rule, several objectives (performance indeces) were defined on the basis of the evaluations of the simulation model. Among the many multiobjective analysis techniques available (Goicoechea, et al, 1982), four of them were applied in this case, namely: compromise programming, consensus, ELECTRE I and ELECTRE II. Different results are obtained and analysed for changing values of the parameters of the multiobjective method. These results make it difficult to make a final decision since subjective weighting of criteria and complex procedures are involved (for example in ELECTRE II). Nevertheless, a final solution with a single operating rule for the system of reservoirs is chosen.

System Description

A real world example was chosen for the development of the methodology, the Wupper-River System in Germany (see Figure 1). The main purpose of the system is low-flow augmentation for water quality improvement. For this purpose the flow at a control gage, downstream of all six reservoirs has to be kept as high as possible. Other purposes such as flood control, drinking water supply, mandatory releases for fish and wildlife and recreation are treated as fixed constraints of the models.

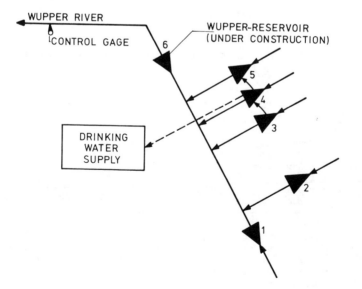

Figure 1: The Wupper-River System

Optimization models

Dynamic programming models were developed for each reservoir using a physical (low flow in m^3/s) and max-min (alternative) objective function. The recursive equation for a particular reservoir is:

$$f_n(S_n) = \max_{R_n} \left(\min \left[R_n + Q_n, f_{n-1}(S_{n-1}) \right] \right)$$

in which:

$f_n(S_n)$ = optimal return (target low-flow at control gage in m^3/s) when starting in month n with initial storage S_n (months are numbered backwards)

S_n = Initial storage in month n

R_n = Release during month n

Q_n = Flow to be augmented at control gage (i.e. the natural flow at the control gage plus optimal releases from reservoirs previously optimized).

With this recursive equation, an optimal low-flow augmentation target (T) can be obtained for each reservoir:

$$T = \max_{S_N} f_N(S_N)$$

T = low-flow augmentation target in m^3/s

N = Planning horizon in months

For the Wupper-River System the following targets were obtained (Table 1).

Table 1: Optimal low-flow augmentation targets

No.	Reservoir	Target[m^3/s]
5	Bever	2.45
4	Neye (Drinking Water only)	--
3	Schevelinger	2.46
2	Lingese	2.62
1	Brucher	2.80
6	Wupper	3.64

Neye-reservoir had only drinking water supply of $5.05 \cdot 10^6 m^3/a$. It should be noted that no forward run of the dynamic programming is performed (optimal releases are not used further), instead a forward simulation with the optimal targets is done to obtain the augmented flows for the next reservoir.

Simulation models

The simulation model includes standard operating rules with targets
as obtained in the optimization step. These rules are as presented in
Figure 2, where I_n = Inflow, E_n = evaporation, RMIN = mandatory re-

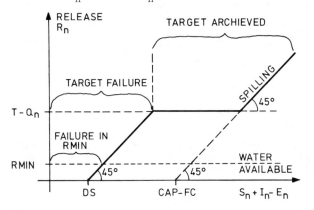

Figure 2: Standard operating rule for one reservoir

lease, CAP = capacity of the reservoir, FC = flood control storage and
DS = dead storage. As a result of the simulations, 100 % security is
obtained for the low-flow augmentation target of 3.64 m³/s for the
whole system when using the historical record. If simulations with
synthetic record are performed (10 records à 50 years), the security
is on the average 99.7 % but the smallest flow at the control gage is
3.05 m³/s. Since the decision-makers would accept a lower security
(< 99.7 %) for a higher low-flow augmentation target for the system
(T > 3.64 m³/s) several simulation runs with targets of 4.0, 4.5 and
5.0 m³/s were performed. These simulations showed very small values for
the lowest flow over the whole record which were not acceptable. It was
decided to define (on the basis of the failure years of the simulation)
some critical storage levels as indicators for dry period. The operating rule is then changed in order to reduce the target low-flow of
each reservoir for one period if its storage level falls below the
critical level. The main results for two switching factors (factor by
which the target is multiplied during dry periods), F = 0.8 and
F = 0.6, are presented in Table 2 (the target for the whole system was
5 m³/s).
As can be seen, the securities are lower than before but for a target
of 5 m³/s and the smallest flow at the control gage was acceptable.
It is interesting to notice that securities are higher and low-flow is
lower with synthetic records than with historical records. The results
for synthetic records are average values, i.e., individual series show
higher and lower values compared with historical record. Other simulations with different critical storage levels were performed and are
not shown here. A total of 5 different operating rules were developed
and simulation carried out. During the simulations 5 important per-

Table 2: Results of simulation with critical storage levels

| HYDROLOGIC | SWITCHING FACTOR | | | |
| TIME | F = 0.8 | | F = 0.6 | |
SERIES	SECURITY [%]	SMALLEST FLOW[m³/s]	SECURITY [%]	SMALLEST FLOW[m³/s]
HISTORICAL	83.8	1.23	85.7	2.21
10 SYNTHETIC RECORDS à 50 YEARS	86.3	1.15	88.1	1.67

formance indeces were calculated, namely:
security of achieving the target low-flow augmentation,
security of achieving the reduced target in dry periods,
smallest flow at control gage, percentage of time in which reservoir 5
was almost full during the summer (for recreation purposes) and one-
sided squared deviation from the target.

Multiobjective analysis

   The five alternative operating rules developed for the system have
different values of the five performance indeces (here considered as
objectives) and no one dominates the others. A multiobjective analysis
is necessary in order to choose among those five operating rules the
best rule (although not "optimal" since many more alternative operating
rules could be analysed). The results are shown in Table 3. The numbers
in the Table indicate the order of preference of the alternative operating rules indicated in column 1. As can be seen, the results of compromise programming and consensus (which is a special kind of compromise programming) differ from those of both ELECTRE methods. The
ELECTRE I results were discarded due to the following problems with the
algorithm: a complete ordering is not obtained and it is possible to
have one alternative in the preferred set of solutions while a better

Table 3: Ranking of alternative operating rules according to
          different multiobjective methods

ALTERNATIVE OPERATING RULE No.	COMPROMISE PROGRAMMING	CONSENSUS	ELECTRE I	ELECTRE II
1	1st	1st	2nd	2nd
2	3rd	3rd	1st	1st
3	4th	4th	2nd	4th
4	2nd	2nd	1st	3rd
5	5th	5th	2nd	5th

one is outside of this set. The ELECTRE II results seem not appropriate
since the algorithm is very complex and it is not possible to explain
every step without subjective interpretations of the attitude of the
decision maker. Under these circumstances, the operating rule No. 1

is recommended in the first place and rule No. 4 in the second place. Several security analyses showed that the subjective parameters (weights) included in each model could be changed without having effect on the priorities. Operating rule No. 1 has higher critical storage levels than rule No. 4 and they are both lower than in rule No. 2. Both rules No. 1 and No. 4 have a low switching factor of F = 0.6. These means that it is preferable to switch to a highly reduced target as soon as possible in a dry year (switch to 60 % of the target if storage level is below critical, whereby critical level is relatively high). The alternative 5, which corresponds to an operating rule without critical storages and no switching was the worst with all methods.

Conclusions

A methodology for defining operating rules for a system of reservoirs was developed and tested in a real world case. The basic steps were: optimization, simulation and multiobjective analysis. Through the optimization a standard operating rule for each reservoir is obtained. These rules are applied in a sequence as in a program like HEC-3 (Hydrologic Engineering Center, 1977). The simulation step introduced improvements of the operating rule and testing with synthetic records. Finally, multiobjective analysis was used to select the best operating rule.

Although the example application was for low-flow augmentation, the same approach can be used for irrigation, water supply and hydroelectric power production as main purpose (Harboe, 1985). For example, in hydropower production, the objective for one reservoir in particular is to augment the on-peak power production of the previous reservoirs (and power plants) while other purposes are considered as constraints.

Certainly many other alternative operating rules can be formulated for the simulation, one example would be to define two critical storage levels: below the lowest one targets are reduced, between both targets are satisfied and above the upper one targets are increased. One could also go on defining storage zones as in HEC-3. The main advantage would be that targets are found in a first step through optimization. The necessary sequential application of dynamic programming (one reservoir at-a-time) avoids the dimensionality problem (any number of reservoirs could be included with computer time increasing linearly).

The optimization step has up to now been applied to small watersheds (the Wupper basin has about 300 Km^2), where inflows to different reservoirs are crosscorrelated. Only for this case the local optimum obtained via sequential application of dynamic programming is very close to global optimum (Boehle et al., 1981). Future studies will be focused on application to large watersheds, where probably subsystems have to be optimized separately.

The computer programs developed for this approach, namely: optimization models, generation of synthetic streamflow data, simulation of the whole system and multiobjective analysis (4 methods) can be adapted to other systems and objectives.

References

Boehle, W., Harboe, R. & Schultz, G.A. (1981). Sequential
    Optimization for the Operation of Multipurpose Reservoir Systems.
    Proceedings, International Symposium on Real-Time Operations of
    Hydrosystems, Waterloo, Ontario, Canada, Vol. II, pp. 583-598.

Goicoechea, A., Hansen, D.R. & Duckstein, L. (1982).
    Multiobjective Decision Analysis with Engineering and Business
    Applications. John Wiley, New York.

Harboe, R. (1983). Use of Critical Storages in Operating Rules for
    Reservoir-System Simulation. Proceedings, XX IAHR Congress,
    Moscow, USSR, Vol. V, pp. 422-430.

Harboe, R. (1985). Use of Physical Objective Functions in Reservoir
    System Operation. Proceedings, Vth World Congress on Water
    Resources, IWRA, Brussels, Belgium, Vol. 1, pp. 337-346.

Hydrologic Engineering Center (1977). Reservoir System Analysis for
    Conservation. The Hydrologic Engineering Center, US Army,
    Corps of Engineers, Davis, California, Vol. 9.

Yakowitz, S. (1982). Dynamic Programming Applications in Water
    Resources. Water Resources Research, Vol. 18., No. 4, pp.673-693.

Yeh, W. W.-G. (1985). Reservoir Management and Operations Models:
    A State-of-the-Art Review. Water Resources Research., Vol. 21,
    No. 12, pp. 1797-1818.

Young, G.K. & Pisano, W.C. (1968). Operational Hydrology Using
    Residuals. Journal of the Hydraulics Division, ASCE, Vol. 94,
    No. HY 6.

Water Resources Systems Planning: Differential Dynamic Programming Models

LaDon Jones[*]
Robert Willis[*]
Brad A. Finney[*]

A Monte Carlo optimization methodology is presented for water resources systems. The planning model define the optimal storage and release policies for the reservoir system. The optimization models are solved using constrained differential dynamic programming. The repetitive optimization of the water resources system in conjunction with streamflow generating models will determine the statistical properties and the cumulative distribution functions for the reservoir releases and storages. The methodology is applied to the Mad River basin in northern California.

1. Introduction

Optimal planning and design policies for water resources systems are predicated on mathematical simulation and optimization models of the river basin system. As an outgrowth of mass diagram and sequent peak methods, the mathematical models can be used to determine the release and storage policies that maximize a given set of objectives reflecting hydropower generation, recreation, and flood control, while satisfying downstream water supply demands, and requirments for fishery resources or navigation. Variations of linear, nonlinear, and dynamic programming have been successfully used to optimally manage complex water resources systems (Biswas, 1976; Burus, 1972; Heidari et. al., 1971; Major and Lenton, 1979; Loucks, 1969).

The majority of water resources planning models are deterministic models and the reservoir release policies developed from these models do not reflect the hydrologic variability of the reservoir system. Determinisitc models, for example, are usually based on a mean hydrology, and the management decisions derived from these models tend to be optimistic in the sense that system benefits are over-estimated while costs and losses are underestimated (Loucks et. al., 1981) Nonlinear objectives, reflecting for example hydropower generation or capital costs, also introduce the problems of local optimality in the planning or design problem. Nonlinear optimization models are inherently more difficult to solve and for large water resources sysetms, many nonlinear algorithms require excessive core requirments or CPU time.

The objective of this paper is to address these problems via the development of a Monte-Carlo planning methodology. The methodology will be used to determine the statisical variation in optimal planning and design policies for complex water resources systems. In contrast to previous studies, differential dynamic programming (DDP) will be used for solution of the optimization model of the water resources systems. DDP has been shown to be superior to classical optimization methods for large-scale systems planning (see Jones et. al., 1986; Murray and Yakowitz, 1979). The paper will first review the DDP methodology and present preliminary optimization results for the Mad River Basin in Northern California.

2. The Management Model

Water resources systems planning and design models can be formulated as discrete time optimal control problems. The optimization model may be expressed as,

$$\min_{p_t} J = \sum_{t=1}^{N} L(x, p, t) \tag{1a}$$

subject to

$$x_{t+1} = T(x, p, t) \qquad t = 1, 2, ..., N-1 \tag{1b}$$
$$G(x, p, t) \leq \overline{G}(x, p, t) \qquad t = 1, 2, \cdots, N \tag{1c}$$
$$x \in R^n \tag{1d}$$
$$p \in R^m \tag{1e}$$

where x_t is the state vector of reservoir storages at the beginning of planning period t, p_t is the control vector defining the reservoir releases during planning period t, and x_{t+1} is the state at the end of planning period t. The term planning period denotes the length of time between x_t and x_{t+1}, during which a control p_t is active. There are N planning periods in the problem which correspond to the stages of the DDP model.

[*]Department of Environmental Resources Engineering, Humboldt State University, Arcata, Calif., 95521

Equation (1b) are the equations of motion of the control problem; these equations transform state z_t to state z_{t+1}, with control p_t. The objective function , L(x,p,t), is assumed to be a separable function for each planning period t. Equation (1c) represents constraints on the acceptable state and control vectors for planning period t to restrict reservoir storage volumes, releases, or water targets in the reservoir system.

The system dynamics, equation (1b), are the continuity equations for each reservoir in the water resources systems. The equations may be expressed for reservoir r as

$$S_{t+1}^r = S_t^r + I_t^r - R_t^{r'} - E_t^r, \quad t = 1, 2, \cdots N - 1 \tag{2}$$

where S_t^r is the storage in reservoir r time period t, R_t^r is the reservoir release, and I_t^r is the reservoir inflow during time period t. E_t^r represents the evaporation or seepage loss occurring from reservoir r. The optimal control model is a nonlinear programming problem.

3.1 Unconstrained Differential Dynamic Programming

The differential dynamic programming algorithm will be illustrated for the LQP optimal control problem. The objective functional will be assumed to be a positive definite, quadratic form; the system dynamics are described by linear difference equations.

The LQP problem can be expressed as,

$$\min_{p_t} Z = \sum_{t=1}^{N} L(x, p, t) \tag{3}$$

subject to,

$$z_{t+1} = F_t z_t + G_t p_t + I_t \quad t = 1, 2, ..., N - 1 \tag{4}$$

where z_t is an n vector, p_t is an m vector, F is an $n \times n$ matrix, G is an $n \times m$ matrix, I is an n vector, and

$$L(x, p, t) = x_t^T A_t x_t + p_t^T B_t z_t + p_t^T C_t p_t + D_t^T p_t + E_t^T z_t \tag{5}$$

A is an $n \times n$ symmetric matrix, B is an $m \times n$ matrix, C is an $m \times m$ symmetric matrix, D is an m vector, E is an n vector, and each L(x,p,t) is positive definite. All coefficient matrices and vectors may be functions of the stage t. Note also that all vectors are defined as row vectors.

Defining $f_t(z_t)$ as the optimal value function, that is, the optimal return with t stages remaining given the system is in state z_t, the recursive dynamic programming equation can be expressed as

$$f_t(z_t) = \min_{p_t} \{L(x, p, t) + f_{t+1}(z_{t+1})\} \tag{6}$$

subject to,

$$z_{t+1} = F_t z_t + G_t p_t + I_t \quad t = 1, 2, ..., N - 1$$

The recursive solution of the DP model can be obtained using a backward dynamic programming approach. For example, consider stage N. The recursive equation may be expressed as

$$f_N(z_N) = \min_{p_N} L(x, p, N) \tag{7}$$

where,

$$f_{N+1}(z_{N+1}) = 0.$$

We then have,

$$f_N(z_N) = \min_{p_N} \{z_N^T A_N z_N + p_N^T B_N z_N + p_N^T C_N p_N + D_N^T p_N + E_N^T z_N\}. \tag{8}$$

Since L(x,p,t) is a positive definite quadratic function, the optimal control vector, p_N^*, can be determined from the first-order necessary conditions,

$$\nabla_p L = 0 \tag{9}$$

or

$$B_N z_N + 2C_N p_N^* + D_N = 0 \tag{10}$$

which implies

$$p_N^* = -1/2 C_N^{-1} (B_N z_N + D_N) \tag{11}$$

The optimal control can be expressed as

$$p_N^* = H_N x_N + \alpha_N \tag{12}$$

where,

$$H_N = -1/2C_N^{-1}B_N \tag{12a}$$
$$\alpha_N = -1/2C_N^{-1}D. \tag{12b}$$

The m×m matrix H_N and the m vector α_N are functions of the stage and are stored in memory at each stage of the DP model. By substituting the optimal control p_N^* for p_N in the optimal value function (8), the optimal value function may be expressed as,

$$f_N(x_N) = x_N^T U_N x_N + V_N^T x_N \tag{13}$$

where,

$$U_N = A_N - 1/4B_N^T C_N^{-1}B_N \tag{13a}$$
$$V_N = E_N - 1/2B_N^T C_N^{-1}D_N, \tag{13b}$$

Note that the optimal value function is now expressed entirely in terms of the state at stage N, x_N. Proceeding by induction in the 'backward sweep', the optimal value function at stage n may be expressed as,

$$f_n(x_n) = \min_{p_n} \{L(x,p,n) + f_{n+1}(x_{n+1})\}. \tag{14}$$

Using the stage to stage transformation (4), equation (14) may be expressed

$$f_n(x_n) = \min_{p_n}\{L(x,p,n) + f_{n+1}(F_n x_n + G_n p_n + I_n)\} \tag{15}$$

Simplifying equation (15) we have,

$$f_n(x_n) = \min_{p_n}\{\tilde{L}(x,p,n)\} \tag{16}$$

where,

$$\tilde{L}(x,p,n) = x_n^T \tilde{A} x_n + p_n^T \tilde{B} x_n + p_n^T \tilde{C} p_n + \tilde{D}^T p_n + \tilde{E}^T x_n \tag{17}$$

and,

$$\tilde{A}_n = A_n + F_n^T U_{n+1} F_n \tag{17a}$$
$$\tilde{B}_n = B_n + 2G_n^T U_{n+1} F_n \tag{17b}$$
$$\tilde{C}_n = C_n + G_n^T U_{n+1} G_n \tag{17c}$$
$$\tilde{D}_n = D_n + 2G_n^T U_{n+1} I_n + G_n^T V_{n+1} \tag{17d}$$
$$\tilde{E}_n = E_n + 2F_n^T U_{n+1} I_n + F_n^T V_{n+1}. \tag{17e}$$

Since $\tilde{L}(x,p,n)$ is positive definite we may then proceed as before to find the minimizing control using the first order necessary conditions, or

$$p_n^* = -1/2\tilde{C}_n^{-1}(\tilde{B}_n x_n + \tilde{D}_n) \tag{18}$$

or

$$p_n^* = H_n x_n + \alpha_n \tag{19}$$

where,

$$H_n = -1/2\tilde{C}_n^{-1}\tilde{B}_n \tag{19a}$$
$$\alpha_n = -1/2\tilde{C}_n^{-1}\tilde{D}_n, \tag{19b}$$

Again H_n and α_n are stored in memory. Substituting p_n^* for p_n in the optimal value function for stage n (16) $f_n(x_n)$ can be expressed as,

$$f_n(x_n) = x_n^T U_n x_n + V_n^T x_n \tag{20}$$

where,

$$U_n = \tilde{A}_n - 1/4\tilde{B}_n^T \tilde{C}_n^{-1}\tilde{B}_n \tag{20a}$$
$$V_n = \tilde{E}_n - 1/2\tilde{B}_n^T \tilde{C}_n^{-1}\tilde{D}_n. \tag{20b}$$

This backward sweep continues until stage 1 is reached. The optimal control for stage 1 is

$$p_1^*(x_1) = H_1 x_1 + \alpha_1. \tag{21}$$

Assuming x_1 is given from the initial conditions of the problem we proceed in the "forward sweep" to determine the optimal control and resulting state for each stage. Denoting the initial state as x_1^* the optimal control for stage 1 is,

$$p_1^*(x_1^*) = H_1 x_1^* + \alpha_1 \tag{22}$$

The optimal control, p^*, and state vector, x^*, are determined for t=1,2,....,N-1 from the recursive equations,

$$x_{t+1}^* = F_t x_t^* + G_t p_t^* + I \tag{23}$$

$$p_{t+1}^* = H_{t+1} x_{t+1}^* + \alpha_{t+1} \tag{24}$$

Under the conditions stated for this problem DDP will identify the global minimum of the control model.

3.2 Nonlinear Objective Functionals

DDP can also be used in water resources managment problems characterized by nonlinear system dynamics and/or cost, loss, or benefit objective functionals. The DDP algorithm is essentially an iterative optimization method. The algorithm begins by selecting a nominal control vector, $\bar{p}$. The control vector is then used to determine the state vector $\bar{x}$ from the system dynamics, T(x,p,t), equation (1b). At each stage of the backward sweep a Taylor's series approximation of the optimal value function is found about the current nominal solution, $(\bar{p}, \bar{x})$, retaining quadratic and lower terms. The quadratic approximation of the optimal value function at stage n can be expressed as,

$$f_n(x_n) = \min_{p_n} \{(x_n - \bar{x}_n)^T \tilde{A}_n (x_n - \bar{x}_n) + (p_n - \bar{p}_n)^T \tilde{B}_n (x_n - \bar{x}_n) + (p_n - \bar{p}_n)^T \tilde{C}_n (p_n - \bar{p}_n)$$
$$+ \tilde{D}_n^T (p_n - \bar{p}_n) + \tilde{E}_n^T (x_n - \bar{x}_n)\}. \tag{25}$$

We may then compute the optimal control from the first order necessary conditions as,

$$p_n^* = H_n (x_n - \bar{x}_n) + \alpha_n + \bar{p}_n. \tag{26}$$

Proceeding in the same manner as for the LQP problem we determine a new nominal control and resulting nominal state. Iteration continues until a parameter or objective convergence criteria are satisfied.

3.3 Constrained Differential Dynamic Programming

Water resources systems optimization models typically have state and control variable constraints limiting reservoir releases or minimum storage volumes, or requiring that water targets are satisfied at various points throughout the reservoir system. DDP can also be applied to this class of water management problems. For illustration assume we have an otherwise LQP problem but with inequality constraints on the control vector. Consider an arbitrary stage of the backward sweep. The optimal return function may be expressed as,

$$f_n(x_n) = \min_{p_n} \{x_n^T A x_n + p_n^T B x_n + p_n^T C p_n + D^T p_n + E^T x_n\} \tag{27}$$

subject to,

$$p_n \leq \hat{p}_n. \tag{28}$$

The $\tilde{A}$ notation is neglected here for simplicity. Under these conditions the controls determined from the first order necessary conditions(9) may violate the constraints. If they do not, we may proceed as in the LQP problem described in Section 4.1. However if state or control variable constraints are violated, Kuhn-Tucker theory can be used to modify the DDP algorithm.

Consider the following nonlinear programming problem (NLP),

$$\min_x Z = f(x) \tag{29}$$

subject to,

$$g(x) \leq 0 \tag{30}$$

$$x \in X \tag{31}$$

where x is an n vector, $f(x)$ maps R^n into R^1, $g(x)$ is an m vector of constraints such that $g(x)$ maps R^n into R^m, and the set X is an opportunity set for x.

The Kuhn-Tucker necessary conditions characterizing a locally optimal solution $\hat{x} \in X$ can be expressed as (Mangasarian, 1969),

$$\nabla_x f(\hat{x}) - \hat{u}^T \nabla_x g(\hat{x}) = 0 \qquad (32)$$

$$\hat{u} g(\hat{x}) = 0 \qquad (33)$$

$$g(\hat{x}) \leq 0 \qquad (34)$$

$$\hat{u} \geq 0 \qquad (35)$$

where $\hat{u}$ is a m vector of Lagrange multipliers. For this problem the set X defines the set of states and controls that satisfy the dynamics of the system, $T(x,p,t)$.

Assume we have an estimate of $\hat{u}$ for each stage of the backward sweep, $\bar{u} \geq 0$. We append the inequality constraints(28) to the optimal value function(27) at stage n with the estimated Lagrange multipliers, or,

$$f_n(x_n) = \min_{p_n} \{x_n^T A x_n + p_n^T B x_n + p_n^T C p_n + D^T p_n + E^T x_n + \bar{u}^T(p_n - \hat{p}_n)\} \qquad (36)$$

and,

$$f_n(x_n) = \min_{p_n} \{x_n^T A x_n + p_n^T B x_n + p_n^T C p_n + \bar{D}^T p_n + E^T x_n\} \qquad (37)$$

where,

$$\bar{D} = D + \bar{u} \qquad (38)$$

The constant terms are ignored because they do not affect the optimization. The model now is essentially an LQP problem and we may proceed as described in section 4.1. However, the solution resulting from using the estimated Lagrange multipliers, $\hat{u}$, may not satisfy all of the Kuhn-Tucker necessary conditions. Generally, equations (32) and (35) will be satisfied, while conditions (33) and (34) will be violated. Our objective is to select a sequence of $\bar{u}$'s such that the Lagrange multiplier estimates converge to the $\hat{u}$ of the Kuhn-Tucker conditions.

The DDP algorithm can be modified using a procedure suggested by Murray and Yakowitz (1979). Quadratic programming is used at each backward sweep of the DDP algorithm. For illustration assume we we are at stage n of the backward sweep with the problem given by (27) and (28). Assume a nominal control has been chosen with a resulting nominal state, $\bar{x}$. Substituting the nominal state $\bar{x}_n$ for x_n in (27) gives,

$$f_n(\bar{x}_n) = \min_{p_n} \{\bar{x}_n^T A \bar{x}_n + p_n^T B \bar{x}_n + p_n^T C p_n + D^T p_n + E^T \bar{x}_n\} \qquad (39)$$

subject to,

$$p_n \leq \hat{p}. \qquad (40)$$

This is a quadratic programming problem that can be solved with an appropriate quadratic programming algorithm (see for example Gill et. al., 1984). The optimal Lagrange multipliers from the quadratic programming solution can be used as estimates for $\hat{u}$.

The inequality constraints of the control model are appended to the optimal value function, using the Lagrange multipliers from the quadratic programming problem. This occurs at each stage of the backward sweep as in (36). Note that the variability of the state vector has been reintroduced. The backward sweep then continues in the same manner as an LQP problem except that a quadratic programming problem is solved at each stage of the backward sweep. The forward sweep continues as in the LQP case yielding a new nominal control and resulting new nominal state variable vector.

Since the quadratic programming problem estimated the Lagrange multipliers based on the previous nominal state, the new nominal control and state may violate the inequality constraints. However, as the solution progresses the constraint violations are reduced. Convergence is can be assessed in the algorithm by examining the magnitude of the constraint violations; if the magnitude is less than a given tolerance, the algorithm has converged. This approach is similar to augmented Lagrangian penalty functions as described by Fletcher (1975). This method differs from that used by Murray and Yakowitz (1979), who constrained the forward sweep to maintain feasiblity at each iteration. This feasibility approach is less efficient than the algorithm described here.

4. Monte Carolo Optimization Methodology

The Monte Carlo optimization methodology is predicated on the DDP algorithm described in section 3 and a multi-site streamflow generating model for the water resources system. The optimization methodology is used to identify the effect of hydrologic uncertainity on the optimal planning policies for the water resources system. The methodology can be summarized by the following stages:

a. For each set of synthetic streamflow data solve the optimization model described by equations (1)-(2). DDP is generally the most efficient algorithm for complex water resources systems.

b. Store the optimal storages and releases obtained from step (a).

c. Return to step (a) if all synthetic data have not be used in the optimization analysis.

d. Statistically analyze the optimal storages and releases to determine the mean, variance, and culmulative and conditional distribution functions for the optimal reservoir storages and releases.

The following example problem illustrates the methodology for a simple reservoir system in northern California.

5. Model Application

The optimal planning model, equations 1-2, was applied to the Mad River basin in northern California. The reservoir system consists of a single water supply reservoir operated by the Humboldt Bay Municipal Water District. The objective of the optimization analysis is to determine the monthly release policy of the reservoir system that minimizes the total water deficit. The releases are used, in part, to satisfy domestic and industrial water demands at the Essex pump stations, approximately 70 miles downstream of Matthews Dam.

The hydrologic data base for the watershed was used to develop a streamflow generating model. The autoregressive moving average model was used to determine the probable streamflow inputs to the reservoir system (Willis and Chu, 1981). A total of 101 sets of 64 years of synthetic streamflow data were generated from the ARMA model.

In this preliminary planning study, the reservoir planning model was structured as a linear programming problem. The optimization model has 3073 decision variables defining the releases and storages occurring over the 64 year planning horizon, and 2305 constraints . These constraints include upper and lower bounds on the reservoir releases and storages, and the mass balance equations for the reservoir system.

DDP was used to solve the optimization model for each set of synthetic streamflow data. Execution time were approximately 30 seconds for each iteration of the Monte Carlo optimization. In contrast, the linear programming solution of the optimization model required approximately 8 minutes of CPU time on a CYBER 170/720.

The preliminary results of the optimization analysis are presented in Table 1 and Figure 1. Table 1 summarizes the statistics associated with the optimal monthly releases.

Statistics	Oct	Nov	Dec	Jan	Feb	March	April	May	June	July	Aug	Sept
Mean[1]	8.0	11.6	16.1	10.3	19.0	18.6	15.4	8.2	4.5	4.6	5.8	6.5
Variance[2]	5.5	10.5	8.6	6.1	4.6	4.0	5.1	3.7	2.4	1.8	1.3	2.1
Skewness[3]	1.2	-0.0	-0.9	-1.6	-1.8	-1.6	-0.5	0.8	2.3	2.0	3.6	2.8

[1] $\times 10^3$ Acre-feet/month
[2] $\times 10^7$ (Acre-feet/month)^2
[3] (Acre-feet)^3

TABLE 1

Statistics of The Optimal Monthly Release

The optimization data can also be used to infer a conditional release policy for the river basin. Figure 1 is a summary of the optimal release policy given a range of inflows and beginning of the period storages. The exceedance probability for the releases is 0.95. In conjunction with daily forecasting and operatinal models, the release policy could also be used for defining daily releases in the reservoir system. The daily releases could be selected in such a way as to minimize the deviations from the target storage volumes.

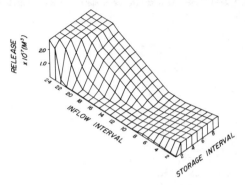

Figure 1 Optimal Release Policy

The optimization analysis also indicated that there were no system water deficits over the 64 year planning horizon. On a monthly basis, the optimization model provided operating policies that were capable of meeting all the water demands. This is to be contrasted with the current operating policies of the reservoir system which relies on a rule curve for setting release policies.

6. Final Comments

This study has demonstrated how Monte Carlo analysis in conjunction with DDP can be used to determine the statistical properties of reservoir storages and release policies. In contrast to previous studies, this information represents the variability in the optimal release or storage policies. The methodology described in this paper can also be applied to other more complex water resources systems to determine the culmulative distribution functions relating reservoir releases, storage volumes and streamflows.

7. References

Biswas, A.K., *Systems Approach to Water Management*, McGraw-Hill, New York, 1976.

Buras, N., *Scientific Allocation of Water Resources*, Elsevier, New York, 1972.

Fletcher, R., "An Ideal Penalty function for Constrained Optimization," *J. Inst. Math. App.*, 15:319-342, 1975.

Gill, P.E., Murray, W., Saunders, M.A. and M.H. Wright, User's Guide for QPSOL (Version 3.2), Department of Operations Research, Stanford University, 1984.

Heidari, M., Chow, V.T., Kokotovic, P.V. and D. Meredith, "Discrete Differential Dynamic Programming Approach to Water Resources Systems Optimization," *Water Resources Research*, 7:273-282, 1971.

Jones, L.C., Willis, R. and W. W-G. Yeh, "Optimal Control of Groundwater Hydraulics Using Differential Dynamic Programming," submitted to *Water Resources Research*, April 1986.

Loucks, D.P., "Stochastic Methods for Analyzing River Basin Systems," *Technical Report 16*, Water Resources Center, Cornell University, Ithaca, New York, 1969.

Loucks, D.P., Stedinger, J.R. and D.A. Haith, *Water Resources Systems Planning and Analysis*, Prentice-Hall, Englewood Cliffs, New Jersey, 1981.

Major, D.C. and R.L. Lenton, *Applied Water Resources Systems Planning*, Prentice-Hall, Englewood Cliffs, New Jersey, 1979.

Mangasarian, O.L., *Nonlinear Programming*, McGraw-Hill, New York, 1969.

Murray, D.M. and S.J. Yakowitz, "Constrained Differential Dynamic Programming and Its Application to Multireservoir Control," *Water Resources Research*, 15(5):1017-1027, 1979.

Willis, R. and W-S. Chu, "Water Resources Systems Investigation of the Mad River Basin," Final Report, Humboldt Bay Municipal Water District, Eureka, Calif., 1981.

Willis, R., Finney, B.A., and W. W-S. Chu, "Monte Carlo Optimization for Reservoir Operation," *Water Resources Research*, 20(9): 1177-1182, 1984.

8. Acknowledgments

The authors gratefully acknowledge the support of Arthur Bolli, General Manager of the Humboldt Bay Municipal Water District. Special thanks also to the Humboldt State University Computing Center.

Air-Water Oxygen Transfer at Spillways and Hydraulic Jumps

Alan J. Rindels[1] and John S. Gulliver,[2] M. ASCE

Dissolved oxygen measurements are reported for seven spillway structures in the vicinity of Minneapolis, Minnesota, corresponding to 27 individual surveys. The surveys are taken during the winter months to take advantage of large dissolved oxygen deficits due to upstream ice cover and the high saturation concentration of low water temperatures. Oxygen transfer is observed by measuring dissolved oxygen concentration at various locations upstream and downstream of a particular hydraulic structure. Samples were also taken on the spillway face where possible. These measurements indicate up to 50 percent of the total gas transfer can occur prior to the hydraulic jump on the spillway face, depending on the length of the air entrained flow.

Introduction

The oxygen transfer across the air-water interface at a spillway with a hydraulic jump is an important source or sink of dissolved oxygen in a river-reservoir system. Normally many river miles are required for a significant air-water transfer of oxygen to occur, but at a spillway this same oxygen transfer may occur in the short residence of the spillway/hydraulic jump. The primary reason for this accelerated oxygen transfer is that air is entrained into the flow, producing a large number of bubbles. These air bubbles greatly increase the surface area available for mass transfer. In addition, the bubbles are pulled to various depths downstream of the hydraulic jump, increasing gas transfer and the possibility of supersaturation because of an increased saturation concentration at the higher pressures. This is not a problem with oxygen, but in the case of dissolved nitrogen this supersaturation may cause fish mortality by nitrogen gas bubble disease. The results of this study will eventually be applicable to transfer of any chemical for which control of transport on the water side of the interface is important, but are herein limited to oxygen.

Because of the significant influence a hydraulic structure has on the downstream dissolved gas levels, engineers are being required to predict these levels for a particular mode of hydraulic structure operation. In particular some hydropower developments are being required to improve the downstream dissolved oxygen level, or show that development will not result in unacceptable dissolved oxygen concentrations. This is not currently possible with the predictive equations available in the literature. Usually the best technique is

---

[1] Graduate Research Assistant and [2] Assistant Professor, St. Anthony Falls Hydraulic Laboratory, Department of Civil & Mineral Engineering, University of Minnesota, Minneapolis, MN, USA 55414.

to measure the oxygen transfer; however, this is often not possible without employing relatively expensive tracers which require care in sampling and measurement.

This paper will present some measurements of oxygen transfer at low head spillways, and some conclusions that can be made as a result of those measurements. Eventually, it is hoped that these measurements will be useful in developing a theory for prediction of gas transfer at a spillway/hydraulic jump.

Review

Water-side controlled mass transfer across the air-water interface can be described by the equation

$$\frac{dC}{dt} = K_L \frac{A_s}{V} (C - C_s) \tag{1}$$

where K_L = liquid film coefficient (LT^{-1}), A_s = surface area (L^2), C_s = saturation concentration (ML^{-3}), C = instantaneous gas concentration (ML^{-3}) in water, and V = control volume in which C is measured (L^3). By following a control volume across a hydraulic structure and assuming $K_L A_s/V$ is a constant, this differential equation can be solved to yield:

$$\frac{1}{r} = \frac{C_s - C_d}{C_s - C_u} = \exp\left(- \frac{K_L A_s}{V} t\right) \tag{2}$$

where r = dimensionless deficit ratio, C_u = upstream dissolved gas concentration, C_d = downstream dissolved oxygen concentration, and t = time of passage.

Because of the complex fluid mechanics involved with two phase flow on spillways and hydraulic jumps, dimensional analysis has been used to describe spillway/hydraulic jump mass transfer. An overall dam equation developed by Gameson (1957) and revised by Notes on Water Pollution (1973) uses the following empirical relation:

$$r = 1 + 0.38 \; abh(1 - .11h)(1 + .046T) \tag{3}$$

where a = water quality factor, b = weir dam or spillway aeration coefficient, h = static headloss (m), and T = water temperature (°C). The Illinois State Water Survey has extensively fitted this equation to a number of low head dams to predict oxygen transfer (Butts and Evans, 1983) and concluded that the aeration coefficients varied widely due to subtle changes such as design or physical condition of the spillway. Furthermore, they noted the equations could not distinguish between the type of energy dissipator downstream from the spillway such as a hydraulic jump. Thus, Eq. 3 was not a good predictor of oxygen transfer. It was also noted, however, that for small changes in overall head this equation may give useful design information after measurements have been made at a given discharge.

Avery and Novak (1978) have developed an empirical equation using dimensional analysis to describe the aeration of a hydraulic jump in an experimental flume. Wilhelms et al. (1981) verified their results in another flume experiment with an insignificant difference between experimental results. Because the predominant mechanism for gas transfer at a hydraulic jump is the gas transfer which occurs across bubbles in the flow, however, scaling this experimental data to proto-type situations requires a separate investigation.

A more detailed approach is that developed by Roesner and Norton (1971). Assuming that gas transfer occurs in the hydraulic jump downstream of the spillway, they developed a computational model to describe the process. This concept has been extensively revised, most recently by Johnson (1984), using slot jet diffusion measurement to describe bubble path length in the hydraulic jump and a gas transfer coefficient which depends upon the ratio of velocity head and path length. The gas transfer coefficient is found from an empirical fit of field data from 24 structures. This technique appears to work well for nitrogen gas supersaturation, the emphasis of the field study, which would occur in the hydraulic jump of a deep plunge pool. The results may not be applicable to structures without deep plunge pools, however, because air entrainment and gas transfer which occur on the spillway are neglected. We will show that this gas transfer is significant, even for the low head spillways studied herein.

Gas transfer on the spillway face should also be incorporated into the analysis. Unfortunately, there are many aspects of the problem for which virtually no data are available, and thus no simplifications of the multiphase flow analysis are possible. Two key pieces of infor-mation are the bubble size distribution and the liquid film coef-ficient. To date, only measurements of air concentration and velocity distribution have been made in these flows (see Cain and Wood, 1981). The bubble size distribution is required to evaluate the available surface area for mass transfer from the air concentration profile. In addition, although the liquid film coefficient is fairly well known for bubbles rising through a quiescent body of water, the coefficient is different for a highly turbulent spillway flow. Currently, these two parameters can only be incorporated as coefficients to be fit to measurements of spillway gas transfer.

Measurements and Results

Oxygen transfer measurements have been performed on 15 hydraulic structures within the vicinity of Minneapolis, Minnesota, corresponding to 40 individual oxygen transfer surveys. Of these structures, seven can be defined as a spillway with a hydraulic jump, the topic of this paper. The measurements were taken during the winter months to take advantage of the ice formation upstream and downstream of a hydraulic structure. There are two important consequences produced by the ice formation: large upstream dissolved oxygen deficits and ease of sampling. Large upstream dissolved oxygen deficits occur because the ice cover minimizes photosynthesis and surface transfer while there is a net loss of dissolved oxygen due to respiration. There is usually no ice cover on the spillway, and the time of water passage across a hydraulic structure is very short. Thus, dissolved oxygen con-centration may be used directly to determine oxygen transfer. The ice formation also provided an excellent staging area from which dissolved oxygen measurements could be taken. This allowed sampling of D.O. immediately above, below, and at various locations across the crest of a spillway with relative safety.

The ice formation did have some detrimental effects on the measurements. In some cases the ice would form along the side of retaining walls and grow outward across the structure. This ice would then cap the spillway flow, influencing gas transfer. Another disadvantage is the continually changing ice thickness upstream and downstream of a dam, especially during a period of thawing. Continual ice thickness monitoring was required for safe sampling.

A Standard Methods type of D.O. sampler was used for all the measurements. Meters were not used because the measurements are not as accurate and cold weather greatly affects their calibration and operation. The azide modification of the Winkler titration method was used to determine D.O. concentration. To minimize sample degradation, the samples were typically titrated within 6 hours of collection. Overall, minimal error was found using this technique, with most upstream and downstream samples having an RMS error of less than 0.1 ppm. The results from these measurements are given in Table 1. The spillways with a deep plunge pool at Coon Rapids Dam, Elk River, and Shady Lake Dam are seen to have the greatest oxygen transfer.

TABLE 1. Measurements of Oxygen Transfer at Spillways.
1 ft = .3048 m. 1 cfs/ft - 0.093 cms/ft)

Dam	Type	Head on Crest	Head Difference	Specific Discharge	Upstream D.O. Conc.	Downstream D.O. Conc.	Deficit Ratio	Water Temp.
		(ft)	(ft)	(cfs/ft)	(ppm)	(ppm)	(1/r)	°C
St. Cloud	Ogee spillway with a baffle block stilling basin. Spillway jet impacted on blocks and dissipated before reaching lower pool. Effective plunge pool depth ≅ 1.0 ft.	1.72	17.44	7.27	9.30	11.65	.45	.7
		1.96	17.55	8.91	9.36	11.74	.41	1
		2.16	17.16	10.55	10.65	12.20	.66	.2
		2.34	16.34	11.82	10.83	12.27	.52	.1
Coon Rapids Dam	I. Non-aerated spillway flow w/uncontrolled hydraulic jump Plunge pool depth = 3.1 ft.	1.72	11.68	7.5	10.7	12.13	.50	.1
		2.55	12.43	14.0	11.15	12.41	.43	.1
	II. Non-Aerated spillway flow w/hydraulic jump run up against spillway Plunge pool depth = 13.6 ft.	1.72	11.68	7.5	10.7	12.36	.42	.1
		2.55	12.43	14.0	11.15	12.68	.36	.1
Shady Lake Dam	Aerated spillway flow w/hydraulic jump run up against spillway Plunge pool depth = 5.0 ft.	.60	16.62	*	11.75	13.24	.29	.1
		.60	16.62	*	9.97	12.56	.31	.1
Elk River	Aerated Spillway Flow w/submerged slotted flip bucket. U.S. BuRec Type VII Stilling Basin, jet dissipated by being director to surface at flip bucket. Plunge pool depth ≅ 5.2 ft.	.64	14.18	1.40	5.35	10.2	.41	.5
		.67	13.68	1.50	6.20	11.11	.35	.2
		.67	13.68	1.50	5.89	11.15	.31	.5
		.68	15.00	1.55	4.13	9.69	.39	.6
		.78	14.83	1.92	4.97	9.96	.44	.1
		.79	12.09	1.98	7.83	11.19	.40	1.5
		.86	14.66	2.22	6.42	10.59	.42	.5
Kost Dam	Aerated spillway flow w/ hydraulic jump maintained by a sloping stilling basin. Plunge pool depth = 1.2 ft.	.37	13.0	.60	7.40	10.18	.55	.5
		.45	12.95	.85	7.33	10.33	.51	.4
		.46	13.02	.90	7.95	10.53	.55	.1
		.51	13.00	1.05	9.21	11.03	.58	.15
		.63	13.14	1.45	10.49	11.61	.57	1.8
		.64	12.97	1.50	8.68	10.82	.58	.2
Faribault Woolen Mill Dam	Broad crested weir with sloping face and a small flip bucket spillway on bed rock Plunge pool depth = 1.4 ft.	.43	9.03	.87	8.91	10.94	.58	.2
		.45	9.07	.93	10.41	11.55	.61	.8
		.50	8.95	1.09	10.00	11.46	.61	.2
		.58	8.87	1.36	11.19	11.87	.63	1.7

*Not known at time of writing

Table 2

Water Sample	Theoretical/Measured Saturation Concentration	Difference	Initial Condition
	ppm	ppm	
Minneapolis Tap Water	7.41/7.11	0.30	Undersaturated
Minneapolis Tap Water	14.36/14.15	0.20	Supersaturated
Shady Lake River	10.30/9.75	0.55	Supersaturated
Kost Dam	11.05/10.54	0.51	Undersaturated
Miss. River at SAF	11.14/10.72	0.42	Supersaturated

A significant error can be promoted in the data by using the wrong saturation concentration. Butts and Evans (1984) observed that the saturation concentration varies with water quality, and proposed in situ saturation concentration measurements. Extreme care must be exercised in measuring the saturation concentration, however, because the BOD of the river water may limit the ability to reach saturation (Bennett and Rathbun, 1972). The saturation data given in Table 2 were collected using a jet aerator and a cold water bath with temperature control to ± 0.1 °C. The theoretical saturation values were taken from Standard Methods and adjusted for air pressure, which was measured by a mercury barometer. It is important to note the initial D.O. concentration (undersaturated or supersaturated). The difference between measured and theoretical saturation values for Minneapolis tap water is between 0.2 and 0.3, regardless of whether the initial D.O. concentration was supersaturated or undersaturated. The same is true for the three river samples, except that the difference is between 0.42 and 0.55 ppm. All river samples were taken in mid-winter, when the BOD is extremely low. We measured a three day BOD of 0.05 ppm for the Kost Dam. The Metropolitan Waste Control Commission for the region has said that the five day BOD was less than 0.1 ppm throughout the region. Thus, BOD would have insignificant effect on these saturation measurements. The error in saturation, though relatively small, can have a significant effect on the deficit ratio for a structure. The deficit ratios given in Table 1 assume a 0.50 ppm correction for saturation.

The data given in Table 1 are plotted versus head difference across the structure (headwater El. minus tailwater El.) in Fig. 1. There is little, if any, correlation with head difference, contrary to Eq. 3. Thus, head difference may not be a good indicator of oxygen transfer at a spillway.

The data given in Table 1 are also compared with Johnson's (1984) predictive theory in Fig. 2. They indicate that although the theory works well for gas supersaturation at structures with relatively deep plunge pools, as verified by Johnson's application to twenty-four structures, it does not apply to the reaeration of low D.O. concentrations at structures with shallow plunge pools. In addition, our measurements were taken at relatively low flows. Thus, the overemphasis on gas transfer in the hydraulic jump was more pronounced when compared to our data where oxygen transfer on the spillway would have a greater relative influence.

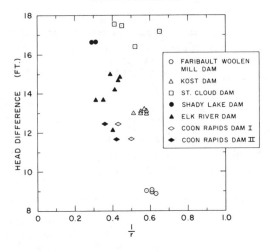

Fig. 1. Plot of deficit ratio versus head difference (headwater El.-Tailwater El.) for individual structures. (1 ft=.3048 m)

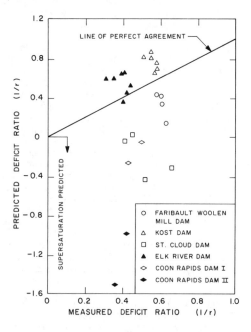

Fig. 2. Measured deficit ratio versus that predicted by Johnson's (1984) technique.

Where possible, spillway samples were taken to indicate the gas transfer which occurred on the spillway face. This was accomplished using a Pitot spillway sampler, fashioned from a U.S. Geological Survey wading rod, a current meter holder and 3/8-inch (9 mm) flexible tubing. The sampler was placed in the flow where stagnation pressure head drove the fluid through the tubing. The tubing was placed in the bottom of a 300 mℓ bottle and flushed at least three times. To account for the aeration due to the sampler, the device was placed at two locations, one upstream in non-aerated flow, and one downstream just prior to the hydraulic jump in the fully aerated flow. The difference between the non-aerated D.O. concentration and that above the spillway, measured with the D.O. sampler, was subtracted from the aerated value to give the spillway aeration deficit ratios. These ratios, shown in Fig. 3, indicate that gas transfer on the spillway face may be significant, even at low head structures. The measurements may be compared with the spillway/hydraulic jump deficit ratios in Table 1, indicating that up to half of the gas transfer occurs before the hydraulic jump with an aerated flow length of 12 ft (3.66 m). For large spillways, it is conceivable that the flow at the bottom of the spillway is close to fully saturated. Supersaturation, if observed, would typically occur in the hydraulic jump.

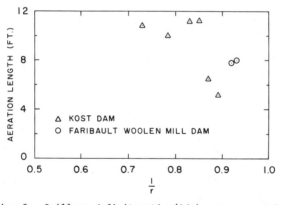

Fig. 3. Spillway deficit ratio (1/r) versus aeration length for two spillways. (1 ft = 0.3048 m)

Conclusions

Gas transfer in an air/water flow on a spillway and in a hydraulic jump is a complex problem, with a very limited data base for evaluation. Much of the data necessary for a proper analysis is unavailable. Each set of gas transfer measurements at hydraulic structures, therefore, results in one or more new questions to be addressed, and the measurements reported herein are no exception.

The stilling basin with a deep plunge pool is seen to be an excellent gas transfer mechanism. This set of data indicates that the gas transfer occurring on the face of the spillway is also important. After a 12 ft (3.66 m) aeration length, for example, approximately half

the oxygen transfer of one structure had already occurred. Gas transfer is not a simple function of spillway head either, since both the spillway flow and the hydraulic jump contribute.
Saturation D.O. concentration is difficult to predict accurately for natural streams. In Minnesota during mid-winter, however, the saturation concentration appears to be fairly consistently 0.50 ppm (± 0.08 ppm) below that given in Standard Methods.

Acknowledgements

This research is supported by the Legislative Commission on Minnesota Resources, Minnesota State Legislature, and by a doctoral dissertation fellowship, University of Minnesota Graduate School. Judson Woods and John Thene assisted in the field measurements.

References

1. Avery, S. and Novak, P., "Oxygen Transfer at Hydraulic Structures," Jour. of Hydraulics Div., ASCE, Vol. 104, No. HY11, Nov. 1978, pp. 1521-1540.
2. Bennett, J. P. and Rathbun, R. E., "Reaeration in Open Channel Flow," U.S. Geological Survey Professional Paper 737, 1972.
3. Butts, T. and Evans, R., "Small Stream Channel Dam Aeration Characteristics," Jour. Environmental Engineering Div., ASCE, Vol. 109, No. 3, June, 1983, pp. 555-573.
4. Butts, T. and Evans, R., Discussion Closure, Jour. Environmental Engineering Div., ASCE, Vol. 110, No. 3, June 1984, pp. 733-735.
5. Cain, P. and Wood, I. R., "Measurements of Self-Aerated Flow on a Spillway," Jour. of Hydraulics Div., ASCE, Vol. 107, No. HY11, Nov., 1981, pp. 1425-1444.
6. Gameson, A.L.H., "Weirs and the Aeration of Rivers," Jour. of the Institute of Water Engineers," Vol. 11, 1957, pp. 477-490.
7. Johnson, P., "Prediction of Dissolved Gas Transfer in Spillway and Outlet Works Stilling Basin Flows," Gas Transfer at Water Surfaces, W. Brutsart and G. Jirka, eds., Reidel Publishing Co., 1984, pp. 605-612.
8. Roesner, L. A. and Norton, W. R., "A Nitrogen Gas (N_2) Model for the Columbia River," Report No. 1-350, Water Resources Engineers, Inc., Jan., 1971.
9. Water Research Laboratory, Department of the Environment, Elder Way, Stevenage Herts, England. "Aeration at Weirs," Notes on Water Pollution, No. 61, June, 1973.
10. Wilhelms, S., Clark, L. and Wallace, J. R., "Gas Transfer in Hydraulic Jumps," Environmental and Water Quality Operational Studies, Tech. Report E-81-10, U.S. Army Waterways Experiment Station, March, 1981.

IMPROVING STREAMFLOW AND WATER QUALITY BELOW DAMS

R. J. Ruane, A.M., C. E. Bohac, J. L. Davis,
E. D. Harshbarger, R. M. Shane, and H. M. Goranflo*

Abstract

Progress by the Tennessee Valley Authority on improving dissolved
oxygen (DO) and flow conditions below hydropower projects is
discussed. New methods of turbine venting have resulted in DO
increases of up to 4.0 mg/L with efficiency losses of about 0.5%. A
reregulation weir made with gabions has provided a continuous minimum
streamflow of 200 cfs (5.7 m^3/s) below a hydropower project where
there previously was only leakage for extended periods. At a second
project comparisons between sluicing, adding a small hydroturbine to
the powerhouse, providing a reregulating weir, and pulsing of the
existing turbines, resulted in the selection of a small hydro addition
to provide a continuous minimum flow below the project.

Introduction

TVA has long recognized that water uses of many rivers below dams are
significantly influenced as a direct result of upstream dams and their
operation. These waters only marginally support fish and aquatic
life, and may also lack sufficient capability to assimilate pollutants
arising from downstream sources. Intermittent streamflows, low DO
concentrations, and occasionally high concentrations of materials such
as dissolved iron, dissolved manganese, and sulfide are responsible.
For the past six years the Tennessee Valley Authority (TVA) has
intensively investigated alternative methods to improve stream
conditions below its reservoirs. Progress on those efforts has been
periodically reported (TVA 1981, 1983, 1984; Davis et al 1983; Bohac
et al 1986). This paper is the most recent update on efforts to
improve DO and streamflow below reservoirs.

DO IMPROVEMENTS

Norris Dam

The two hydroturbines at Norris Dam have vertical Francis wheels which
are typically used at relatively high head locations. Francis units
are equipped with vacuum breaker systems which allow air to enter the
draft tube when excessive negative pressures occur below the turbine

---

* Air and Water Resources, Tennessee Valley Authority, 248 401 Bldg.,
  Chattanooga, Tennessee 37401.

wheel. These vacuum breaker systems usually vent through openings on the hub of the turbine and vent small amounts of air at wicket gate openings below about 50 to 60 percent. At Norris Dam the vacuum breaker system has been modified and used to aspirate enough air to oxygenate the turbine releases over a wide range of gate openings (Fox, 1980; Harshbarger, 1982 a, b, c, 1983).

To increase suction, baffles were placed over the vacuum breaker openings on the Norris turbine hub. Air flow was further enhanced by adding piping to bypass the existing vacuum breaker system and to supplement the existing venting system. Using wedge-shaped baffles, DO increases of 2.5 to 4 mg/L were observed in the releases; however, these increases were accompanied by hydro unit efficiency losses of about 2%.

Following laboratory hydraulic model studies, the baffles were modified into a more streamlined shape which aspirated significant amounts of air while causing much less energy loss. These baffles resulted in DO increases of 2.5 to 3.5 mg/L and unit efficiency losses of only about 0.5%.

Since the baffles have an associated energy loss, it was desired that they be installed only when needed to increase DO, usually from late August through October. Using a bolt-on design developed for this purpose, the baffles can be installed or removed in a 12-h period. Hub baffles have been in use on both units at Norris for the past three years and appear to be performing well with respect to aeration.

With the baffles in place, abnormally high amounts of cavitation damage were found on the turbine following a relatively short period of operation. This damage occurred in areas which had not previously been damaged, leading some to suspect that the baffles and/or air flow had altered the flow path of the water in the turbine. Cavitation damage is repaired by welding over the affected area with stainless steel. This not only repairs the damage, but because of the properties of the stainless steel, makes it less susceptible to future damage. It is hoped that once these new areas are covered, damage will not be as severe or as rapid. However, cavitation damage has recently appeared in some areas that are difficult to repair. It has been estimated that if cavitation damage continued in these same areas, it would be necessary every three or four years to disassemble the unit to make repairs. This would require a rather lengthy, expensive outage and could only be done a few times before unit replacement might be necessary. Agreement is not universal on the cause and seriousness of this new cavitation damage. Some experts within TVA and from outside the agency believe the more recent cavitation is related to other factors.

Tims Ford Dam

The 46 MW turbine at Tims Ford Dam is a diagonal-flow, fixed-blade unit that does not lend itself to aeration by aspiration because of the geometry of the runner and the location of the turbine venting ports (Harshbarger, 1984). Aeration of the discharges from this unit was accomplished by using a centrifugal blower to force air through the vacuum breaker system (Harshbarger, 1985). The blower itself was mounted on a concrete pad outside the powerhouse and connected to the headcover of the turbine via an 20-cm pipe. The existing vacuum-breaker port was used as access through the headcover. The air entered the draft tube through the open bottom of the runner cone. The vacuum-breaker valve which was originally located on the headcover was moved to a location on the 20-cm pipe, about 6.1 m downstream from the blower.

With the blower in operation and DO in the water entering the turbine at about 0.5 mg/L, DO in the tailrace was increased to about 4.5 mg/L. Admission of the air at waterflow conditions in which the unit is normally operated lowered unit efficiency by about 0.6% and lowered unit output less than 0.1 MW. The compressor is operated to sustain DO levels in releases at 4 mg/L. Under this arrangement proportionately more air is injected when incoming DO levels are 1 mg/L than at 3 mg/L. This procedure is directed at reducing cavitation damage.

Cherokee and Douglas Dams

Cherokee and Douglas Dams each have four Francis-type hydroturbines. These eight units are similar and it was hoped that aeration techniques suitable for one should be suitable for the others. Several attempts have been made to aerate the discharges from Cherokee and Douglas Dams using hub baffles or blowers (Harshbarger, 1981; 1982d, 1984b). Blowers were found to be undesireable because of space limitations, difficulties with routing piping in the existing plants, and high operating costs. Various hub baffles were tested over the existing vents which were located high on the hub and none were found to aspirate significant amounts of air at water flow rates where the units are normally run. Therefore, a new approach to hub baffle design was attempted.

Local flow patterns in the vicinity of baffles were expected to affect aspiration performance. One problem with hub baffles is that the flow around the turbine hub changes with wicket gate opening and is not well defined at any gate opening. To aid in the design of the Cherokee baffles, TVA contracted with the Allis-Chalmers Corporation to mathematically model the pressure and flow patterns through a Cherokee turbine. This information was then used to locate the hub baffles at an elevation on the hub where the pressure was a minimum. Model tests at the TVA Engineering Laboratory indicted that a cylindrical baffle would be less susceptible to changes in flow direction and still be relatively streamlined. From the model tests it was also determined that the baffle height relative to the thickness of the boundary layer of the flow was an important criteria. When installed on Unit 1 at Cherokee, the baffles enabled the turbine to aspirate air over its entire range of operation. However, the baffles only provided enough air to increase DO by about 0.5 to 1 mg/L rather than by 2 to 3 mg/L as had been desired.

Cost of DO Improvement

Alternatives for raising the DO at six TVA hydropower projects were evaluated by Lewis and Bohac (1984). Aeration using hub baffles, aeration using compressed air in the turbine system, and high-purity oxygen injection using small-pore diffusers in the reservoir in front of the penstock intakes were the alternatives compared. Hub baffles were found to be significantly more cost-effective than compressed air or oxygen systems. However, to date, hub baffles have been effective only at the Norris project. The costs of compressed air and oxygen systems appear comparable.

FLOW IMPROVEMENT

Norris Dam

In April 1984, construction of the Clinch River Reregulation Weir (CRRW) was completed and field testing of this new concept in flow reregulation was initiated. The CRRW project is a low-head, overflow storage structure located two miles (3.2 km) below Norris Dam, one of TVA's largest hydropower peaking projects. A free-flowing, cold-water fishery below Norris Dam extends about 13 miles (20.9 km) downstream to Melton Hill Lake and is stocked annually with rainbow and brown trout. The CRRW was placed in the tailwater to eliminate adverse fishery impacts due to inadequate streamflow when the Norris turbines were idle.

The rock weir was constructed of galvanized steel gabion baskets filled with 4- to 8-in. (10- to 20-cm) washed limestone rock. It is 5 ft (1.5 m) high, 21 ft (6.4 m) wide, 425 ft (29 m) long, and contains 54 12-in. (30-cm) diameter steel pipes for discharge control.

Field evaluations completed during 1984 and 1985 indicated that all design objectives were met as indicated by the following results.

The original design criteria called for a continuous minimum flow of 200 cfs (5.7 m^3/s) to be maintained downstream from the weir during off-peak load periods when the turbines were not being used. Flow measurements indicated that during the first 3 h after turbine shutdown, flow in the river gradually receded from generating levels far in excess of 200 cfs (5.7 m^3/s) to near 200 cfs as the stage dropped to the top of weir. For the next nine hours flow fluctuated between 210 cfs (5.9 m^3/s) and 160 cfs (4.5 m^3/s). It was concluded that during periods when the turbines would be idle for a period of more than 12 hours it would be necessary to operate with one turbine for 30 minutes every 12 hours.

The design criteria also specified that the weir should minimize the impact on operating head and flexibility of the Norris Dam power plant. Monitoring of Norris Dam turbine operation since completion of the weir has indicated that the weir has minimal impact. Examination of tailwater measurements before and after completion of the weir show an average tailwater increase of 0.26 ft (0.08 m) producing a loss of 0.016 MW/cfs (0.56 MW/m^3/s). Since normal values fall in the range of 0.8 to 1.2 MW/cfs (28 to 42 MW/m^3/s), the percentage reduction is less than 0.2%. Special pulses were required on 8 d during the last 6 mo of 1984 and 77 pulses were required during the first 6 mo. of 1985. The average cost of pulsing to date has been assessed at $48/pulse. The cost arises from shifting power from peak periods of power demand, when hydropower has a higher value, to off-peak periods when hydropower is valued less.

The safety of canoeists and fishermen was considered. During preliminary project planning, a physical model of the weir was constructed to study overflow conditions so that hazardous standing waves and rollers could be avoided below the weir. The final weir shape was selected based on these studies. Field evaluations indicated that the 21-ft (6.4-m) wide weir that drops in height in gradual steps from 5 ft (1.5 m) upstream to 3 ft (0.9 m) downstream reduces standing waves to acceptable levels and eliminates rollers. In addition, a canoe portage was added around the weir with signs on the river and at all access points instructing floaters to use the portage.

DO and temperature monitoring indicated that, as long as the Norris turbines are operated every 12 hours, good water quality control will be maintained. If extended periods without turbine operation occur, then warmer temperatures stressful to the fish could develop in some portions of the river. In addition, large algae die-offs could occur with the resulting decay of organic material and associated depletion of the DO. DO increases less than 0.5 mg/L have been measured as the water flows over the weir (Shane, 1985).

Tims Ford Dam

TVA's Tims Ford Project, located on the Elk River in Tennessee, was completed in 1972. Outlet works include an overflow chute spillway, 3 ft (0.9-m) diameter sluice pipe, and a 22 ft (6.7-m) diameter penstock which supplies water to a single 45 MW diagonal-flow, fixed-blade, generating unit. Both the sluice and the penstock draw water from the bottom of the reservoir, which due to thermal stratification provides cold water to the tailwater reaches varying from 5°C in the winter to 16°C in the fall.

Due to limited water availability, the generating unit is run only approximately 25% of the time, with heavier use in the wetter winter and early spring months than in the summer and early fall. Sluice releases are made in the summer time, primarily on weekends, to provide for water supply at downstream locations. This also aids in

maintaining a fishery and provides for recreational boating in the
tailwater reaches.

Alternatives for providing minimum flows for enhancing the cold
water fishery in a 40 mile (64-km) stretch of tailwater below the
dam were investigated (Tennessee Valley Authority, 1985; Bohac et
al, 1986). These alternatives included: using the existing sluice
at the dam to discharge 80 cfs (2.3 m^3/s) at all times during
which the 45 MW unit was not operating; installing a small hydro
unit on the sluice which would discharge 80 cfs (2.3 m^3/s) and
generate approximately 700 kW at all times during which the 45 MW
unit is not operating; constructing a rock gabion reregulating weir
approximately 2.5 miles (4 km) below the dam; and pulsing the 45 MW
unit at the dam. Each alternative was examined to determine its
impact on electrical power generation, recreation, reservoir
operations, safety, and other considerations.

It was decided to implement the small unit alternative. The unit
will be located on a platform on top of the draft tube. Water will
be supplied by a connection to the existing sluice pipe. A surplus
pump/motor unit from a deferred TVA nuclear plant is being converted
to a turbine/generator. Minor modifications to the shaft and
bearings will be required. A draft tube will be fabricated, and if
needed, aeration will be provided by the use of a small air
compressor. The capacitor bank and electrical switchgear will be
located in the existing switch-yard.

Several factors contributed to the selection of this alternative:
the relatively high head available for power generation (130- to
150-feet, or 40- to 46-m); the availability of a suitable water
conductor for water supply to the unit (no dam breach for penstock
is required); the projected usage of the unit (75% of the time); and
the availability of the hydraulic and electrical primary components
at reduced cost. Construction began July 1, 1985 with most civil
features completed during 1985. The facility will be completed in
late 1986 upon arrival of the auxiliary electrical equipment.

Summary

Although hub baffles have been used to provide significant increases
in DO, hub baffles are not generally applicable to all Francis
turbines. In cases where hub baffles have not been effective,
mathematical and physical models have not yet provided satisfactory
results when applied to a prototype turbine. Compressed air has
been used to significantly raise DO in cases when hub baffles could
not be used. Compressed air systems appear to be more expensive
than hub baffles but comparable in cost to high-purity oxygen
injection upstream from the turbine intakes.

Because of the differences in features and conditions associated
with each hydropower project, alternative methods of providing
minimum flows must be evaluated specifically for each project.

Gabion weir construction appears to be a viable approach. A small turbine through which minimum flows can be released is also expected to be satisfactory.

References

Bohac, C. E., R. M. Shane, E. D. Harshbarger, H. Morgan Goranflo. 1986. Recent progress on improving reservoir releases. Proceedings, Int. Symp. on Applied Lake and Watersheds Management. November 13-16, 1985. Lake Geneva, Wisconsin, North American Lake Management Society, Merrifield, Virginia.

Davis, J.L., C.E. Bohac, E.D. Harshbarger, and R.M. Shane. 1983. Experience with reservoir release aeration and flow improvement. Pages 1326-1335 in Proc. Waterpower '83, Am. Soc. Civ. Eng., New York, New York.

Fox, T.A. 1980. Vacuum breaker reaeration tests, turbine discharge oxygenation program, Norris Dam. WR28-1-2-100. Tennessee Valley Authority. Division of Air and Water Resources. Norris, Tennessee.

Harshbarger, E.D. 1981. Evaluation of hub baffles on Cherokee units 1 and 4. WR28-2-12-100. Tennessee Valley Authority. Division of Air and Water Resources. Norris, Tennessee.

Harshbarger, E.D. 1982a. Evaluation of turbine venting systems at Norris Dam, July 1979-November 1980. WR28-1-2-102. Tennessee Valley Authority. Division of Air and Water Resources. Norris, Tennessee.

Harshbarger, E.D. 1982b. Evaluation of vacuum breaker bypass, Norris unit 1. WR28 -2-101. Tennessee Valley Authority. Division of Air and Water Resources. Norris, Tennessee.

Harshbarger, E.D. 1982c. Streamlined hub baffles for aeration at Norris Dam. WR28-1-2-110. Tennessee Valley Authority. Division of Air and Water Resources. Norris, Tennessee.

Harshbarger, E.D. 1982d. Evaluation of hub baffles, Douglas unit 4. WR28-2-20-100. Tennessee Valley Authority. Division of Air and Water Resources. Norris, Tennessee.

Harshbarger, E.D., "Turbine Venting Tests, Vacuum Breaker Bypass, Norris unit 2," WR28-1-2-106, Tennessee Valley Authority, Division of Air and Water Resources, Norris, Tennessee, May 1983.

Harshbarger, E.D. 1984. Aeration tests at Tims Ford Dam. WR28-2-75-100. Tennessee Valley Authority. Division of Air and Water Resources. Norris, Tennessee.

Harshbarger, E.D. 1984b. Aeration tests using a draft tube
manifold, Douglas unit 2. WR28-2-20-101. Tennessee Valley
Authority. Division of Air and Water Resources. Norris,
Tennessee.

Harshbarger, E.D. 1985. Aeration tests at Tims Ford Dam using a
centrifugal blower. WR28-2-75-102. Tennessee Valley Authority.
Division of Air and Water Resources. Norris, Tennessee.

Lewis, A.R. and C.E. Bohac. 1984. Cost of reservoir releases
aeration. TVA/ONRED/AWR-85/7. Tennessee Valley Authority.
Division of Air and Water Resources. Chattanooga, Tennessee.

Shane, R. M. 1985. Experimental Clinch River flow reregulation
weir field evaluation interim report. WR28-4-590-118. Tennessee
Valley Authority. Division of Air and Water Resources. Norris,
Tennessee.

Tennessee Valley Authority 1985. Feasibility report, Tims Ford/Elk
River minimum flows. TVA/ONRED/AWR-85/22. Division of Air and
Water Resources. Knoxville, Tennessee.

Tennessee Valley Authority. 1981, 1983, 1984. Improving reservoir
releases. TVA/ONR/WR-82/6, TVA/ONR/WR-83/10,
TVA/ONRED/A&WR-84/27. Division of Air and Water Resources.
Knoxville, Tennessee

Gas Transfer and Secondary Currents in Open Channels

by John S. Gulliver, M. ASCE[1] and Martin J. Halverson[2]

Laboratory flume experiments on water-wide controlled gas transfer, such as reaeration, are described. The experiments indicate that gas transfer is a surface renewal process, well described by Dankwerts' (1951) model, as originally proposed by O'Connor and Dobbins (1958). The primary cause of surface renewal in flumes is proposed to be the upwelling of secondary currents and is documented by relating measurements of these currents to gas transfer measurements. A dimensionless liquid film coefficient is related to a shear Peclet number and a shear Reynolds number. The shear Reynolds number represents the effectiveness of secondary currents in penetrating the water surface.

Introduction

The flux of any dissolved chemical across the air-water interface is given by the equation,

$$F = K(C_a/H - C_w) \tag{1}$$

where F = flux/unit surface area, K = transfer coefficient, C_a = concentration in air, H = Henry's Law constant, an equilibrium constant, and C_w = concentration of the dissolved chemical in water. C_a/H is often called the saturation concentration. The transfer coefficient is given by the equation

$$\frac{1}{K} = \frac{1}{fK_L} + \frac{1}{HK_a} \tag{2}$$

where K_L = liquid film coefficient, representing transport in the water, = $K_2 h$, where K_2 is reaeration coefficient, and h is stream depth; K_a = gas film coefficient, representing transport in the air; and f = an enhancement factor for the reactivity of the gas in water, e.g. $SO_2 \rightarrow H_2SO_4$. The gas film coefficient depends upon the forced convention and natural convection of the air and is fairly well understood from studies on evaporation and heat transfer (Gulliver and Stefan, 1986). Henry's law coefficient (related to the saturation concentration) is a function of temperature, pressure, salinity, etc., and is well studied for the more common gases such as O_2, N_2, and CO_2 but has not been thoroughly studied for many compounds such as the wide variety of PCB's. The liquid film coefficient is influenced by the

[1] Assistant Professor and [2] Graduate Research Assistant, St. Anthony Falls Hydraulic Laboratory, Department of Civil & Mineral Engineering, University of Minnesota, Minneapolis, MN, 55414, USA.

ordering of the water molecules into a film on the surface, and very little is known about how the fluid motion acts to break down this film.

The liquid film coefficient is the topic of this presentation. It relates to low solubility and relatively unreactive gases such as O_2, N_2, CO_2, where transfer is controlled by the water phase and compounds where transfer is controlled by both phases such as DDT, Mercury, and several PCB's. The ability of existing equations to predict the liquid film coefficient has been reviewed by Brown (1974), Wilson and MacLeod (1974), and Rathbun (1977). In each of these three summaries the poor agreement between equations from the literature is pointed out. There are generally believed to be significant variables omitted from the analysis, and each predictive equation is reliably applicable only to the stream reaches from which the data were taken. Comprehensive and accurate sets of laboratory data which may be used to verify the theory behind a predictive equation simply does not exist. This paper descri- bes an attempt to identify one important omitted variable in flume and stream gas transfer, and to provide an accurate set of laboratory data which may be used to test predictive theories.

The Moving-Bed Flume

The primary restriction of standard laboratory flumes is their length; most flumes are 12 to 17 m long, and an extremely long flume is 30 m in length. The accuracy of a gas transfer experiment is severely hampered by this length restriction. For example, a typical change in concentration for oxygen with a deficit of 7 ppm over 30 m is 0.15 ppm. The accuracy of properly performed Winkler titrations is ± 0.05 ppm at best. Thus, the measurement uncertainty due to this one error alone is ± 30 percent.

The moving-bed flume, shown in Fig. 1, is designed to overcome the length restriction. The flume has a conveyor belt at the bottom of the test section that moves at a predesignated speed. There is no flow into or out of the flume except leakage across the endwalls. Thus, the cross-sectional mean velocity is virtually zero and the residence time is large. The result is "stationary flow," where the location of mean velocity in a fixed bed flume corresponds to a zero mean velocity point. The flume is described in more detail by Gulliver and Halverson (1985).

A number of mean velocity profiles were measured with an LDV system at three locations: one in the center of the flume and one on each end, within 25 cm of the guide vanes shown in Fig. 1. They were virtually indistinguishable and found to be well-described by the logarithmic law of the wall. It may therefore be assumed that the boundary layer was well developed within the middle 7.5 m of the test section. The shear velocity, $u*$, was determined to be 5.4 percent of the bed velocity at a flume depth of 15 cm, and calculated to be 5.9 percent of the bed velocity at a depth of 7.5 cm.

Measurements

The experiments were performed on air-water oxygen transfer because of the relatively accurate and simple Winkler titration proce- dures. The tank was initially filled with tap water to the desired

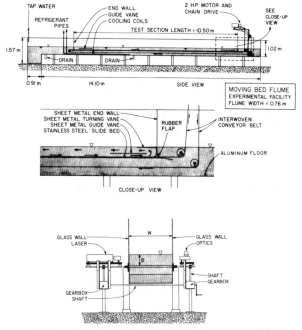

Fig. 1. Side and end sections of the moving bed flume.

level for the experiment, then chemically deoxygenated using sodium sulfite with cobaltous chloride as a catalyst. The reaction was relatively rapid. Samples taken during the experiment and preserved without fixing indicated that the sodium sulfite had reacted completely before initiation of the test. Both the test section and the outer section were deoxygenated because leaking across the end walls could otherwise mask the air-water transfer. An aerator pump was used in the outer section to keep the dissolved oxygen (D.O.) concentration as close as possible to that of the test section.

The experiments were run for approximately 90 minutes, with periodic sampling of D.O. along the test section and outside of the test section. The sampled water was flushed through the 305 mℓ BOD bottles five times before the sample was taken. A typical plot of D.O. concentration measurements is given in Figure 2.

Saturation D.O. concentration ($C_S = C_a/H$) as a function of temperature and chloride concentration is given in Standard Methods, and requires correction for air pressure. The molecular diffusivity of dissolved oxygen in water was determined from the Stokes-Einstein relation and measurements (Goldstock and Fatt, 1970).

Conductivity measurements were also taken to determine the leakage through the end walls. The volume flow through the end walls was determined and plotted versus belt speed. The leakage, although relatively small, was ± 25% around a mean value. This constituted the greatest possible error in the gas transfer experiments.

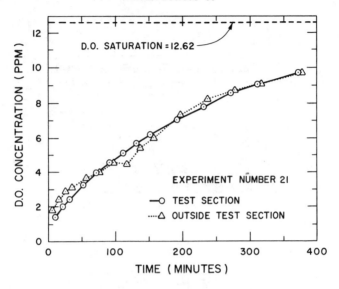

Fig. 2. Sample plot of dissolved oxygen measurements
taken during gas transfer experiment.

Results

Gas transfer experiments were undertaken at two depths over a range of shear velocity and temperature. The results are given in Fig. 3. These were determined from the D.O. measurements as follows:

1) The deficit, $D = C_S - C$, was plotted on semi-logarithmic paper versus time for the test section and the inflow (leakage) to the test section. C_S = saturation concentration.

2) If the slope of the graph deviated significantly from a straight line, the data were set aside for a more detailed analysis at a later date.

3) dC/dt was determined from the graph at the point where inflow and test section D.O. concentration were equal.

4) K_L was determined from the equation

$$K_L = \frac{h}{C_s - C} \frac{dC}{dt} \tag{3}$$

5) The K_L values reported are adjusted from the measurements because the gas transfer over the guide vanes is much less than over the belt. The reasoning used is as follows: a) there is a stagnant water surface over the vane at the downwelling end, as a result of water surface tension, which is bounded by a Reynolds ridge (Scott, 1982); b) a small portion of the water surface at the upstream end is covered by a turning vane; and c) the mean velocity over the guidevanes is approximately 5 percent of the bed velocity. It has been estimated

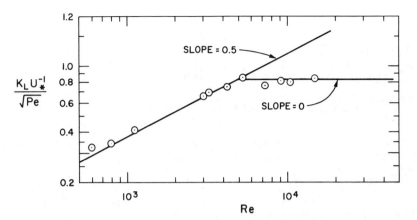

Fig. 3. Gas transfer data, plotted as dimensionless liquid film coefficient divided by the square root of the shear Peclet number, $u_* h/D_m$, versus shear Reynolds number, $u_* h/\nu$.

that the gas transfer over the vanes is less than or equal to 5 percent of that over the belt, specially when one considers points a and b, as well.

The K_L measurements were therefore adjusted to reflect the negligible gas transfer that occurred across the 2.2 m of test section with the vanes, etc. This adjustment is (assuming no gas transfer over the vanes) K_L (actual) = 1.27 K_L (measured). The maximum error which would occur due to this adjustment for the vanes is + 1.3%

An uncertainty analysis which incorporates all of the possible errors is currently being carried out on the data, including some not reported here. Based on preliminary estimates, the total uncertainty in K_L measurements caused by these possible errors is expected to be less than ± 10%.

Analysis

The experiments have proven to the authors satisfaction that gas transfer in streams and flumes is controlled by surface renewal. Fluid from below replaces the surface film periodically, creating a liquid film thickness which varies over time.

The surface renewal theory was first proposed by Higbie (1931) and is most easily fit to the equation developed by Dankwerts (1951),

$$K_L = \sqrt{D_m r} \tag{4}$$

where D_m = molecular diffusivity of the gas in water and r = average surface renewal rate. O'Connor and Dobbins (1958) originally proposed that Eq. 4 described the controlling processes in streams. They then related the surface renewal rate to turbulence properties in the flow. Numerous models have been proposed since based on some turbulent flow property, but none in the authors' opinions can match O'Connor and

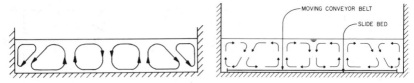

Fig. 4. Cross sectional view of secondary cells: (a) traditional
         laboratory flume and b) moving-bed flume.

Dobbins' model for its rational physical argument and pure simplicity.
The authors believe, however, that surface renewal is predominantly
caused by large scale coherent structures in the flow, i.e. the
upwelling due to secondary currents, rather than random turbulence.

The secondary current structure in the moving-bed flume and in a
traditional flume are illustrated in Fig. 4. The peak vertical secondary velocity (at the center of upwelling) has been measured in the
moving-bed flume by Halverson and Gulliver (1986) to be between 110 and
220 percent of the bed shear velocity. Let us propose that

$$r = \frac{K_1 \, v_s}{h} \, F \tag{5}$$

where v_s = peak secondary current velocity in a secondary cell, h =
flume depth, K_1 = a constant to reflect the fact that average surface
renewal would be some fraction of that caused by the peak secondary
velocity in a given cell, and F = a function which represents the portion of secondary cells which cause a surface upwelling event.

Halverson and Gulliver (1986) performed flow visualization experiments on the secondary currents of the moving-bed flume, and found that
the structure represented in Fig. 4 is simply a temporal mean, with the
secondary cells continually shifting from left to right. Two adjacent
cells which shift in opposite directions may not have sufficient
strength to cause a surface upwelling event. In addition, at low
values of v_s, adjacent cells shifting towards each other is required to
create a surface upwelling event. These conditions are represented by
the function F.

Let us assign the peak secondary velocity of a typical cell to be
the average of the measured values

$$v_s = \frac{1.1+2.2}{2} \, u_* = 1.65 \, u_* = K_2 u_* \tag{6}$$

where u_* = bed shear velocity. In addition, let us assume that F is
a function of a shear Reynolds number $u_* h/\nu$, where ν is the kinematic
viscosity of water. Then Eq. 4 becomes

$$\frac{K_L/u_*}{Pe^{1/2}} = \left[K_1 \, K_2 \, F \, (Re) \right]^{1/2} \tag{7}$$

where Pe = a shear Peclet number = $D_m/(u_* h)$, and Re = a shear Reynolds
number = $u_*/h/\nu$.

The data are plotted in a form represented by Eq. 7 in Fig. 3 and
indicate some interesting trends:

1. The data collapse onto a plot of the dimensionless grouping $K_L u_*^{-1} Pe^{-1/2}$. This indicates that surface renewal as originally proposed by Dankwerts (1951) does indeed control gas transfer. In addition, it proves some validity to the argument that secondary currents are the primary source of surface renewal.

2. The data increase with $Re^{1/2}$ below $Re = 4.5 \times 10^3$ and remain constant at greater values of Re. This may be interpreted in one of three manners: a) The hypothesis given herein is correct, and at high values of Re the upwelling due to secondary cells has reached a maximum value; b) The data at high Re were all taken at elevated temperatures, up to 50°C. It is also possible that the evaporation caused by the natural convection inhibited the gas transfer below what would occur without significant evaporation; and c) The function F may be correlated with a dimensionless parameter, which has u_* and h in the numerator and another fluid property in the denominator, such as a parameter which includes surface tension. The problem is that surface tension does not always represent surface ordering.

3. If we assume from Fig. 3 that the maximum attainable value of $K_L u_*^{-1} Pe^{-1/2}$ in the moving-bed flume is 0.83, the coefficient in Eq. 7 is $K_1 = 0.42$. This indicates that the average renewal rate is equal to 42 percent of the peak renewal rate (caused by peak secondary velocities) in a given cell. This is physically realistic, giving further credance to the secondary current-surface renewal argument.

Most laboratory flume data on the liquid film coefficient have Re values below 4.5×10^3, and indicate a Reynolds number dependence. Natural streams, however, mostly fall in the region with high Re because of an increase in depth. Therefore, F(Re) = 1, and Eq. 7, becomes very similar to that derived by O'Connor and Dobbins (1958).

$$\frac{K_L}{U_*} = 1.58 \sqrt{Pe} \qquad (8)$$

Wilson and MacLeod (1974) found the predictive capability of Eq. 10 to be comparable to many equations, even though it has no fitted coefficients. For the moving-bed flume $\sqrt{K_1 K_2} = 0.83$, which is 53 percent of 1.58. The value of K_2, however is probably different in natural streams than in the moving-bed flume.

Conclusions

The measurements indicate the following:

1) Water-side controlled gas transfer is a surface renewal process in flumes and streams, as first proposed by O'Connor and Dobbins (1958).

2) The rate of surface renewal in flumes is primarily controlled by the upwelling of secondary currents, i.e. secondary current velocity and the portion of the secondary cells which cause an upwelling event.

3) The maximum gas transfer may be related to an average renewal rate which is 42 percent of the peak renewal rate caused by peak secondary velocities. A dimensionless gas transfer parameter at this maximum value depends only upon shear Peclet number.

4)   Below this maximum value a dimensionless liquid film coefficient is found to be dependent upon both a shear Peclet number and a
shear Reynolds number.
5)   The resulting equations for liquid film coefficient are
amazingly similar to an equation developed by O'Connor and Dobbins
(1958), based upon turbulence properties. The reason is that the turbulence length scales proposed by O'Connor and Dobbins to be of importance are similar to those of secondary currents.
6)   Although the mechanism of surface renewal is identified herein
as secondary currents, extension of these results to natural streams
will be difficult because a) the relationship between secondary velocities and bottom shear is probably different for each stream and
b) there are other forms of upwelling in natural streams which must
also be considered such as expansions, contractions, and curvature.

Acknowledgements

     This work was supported by the Environmental Engineering Program
of the National Science Foundation, Contract No. CEE-8205078. Flume
construction was supported by a grant from the University of Minnesota
Graduate School.

References

1.   Brown, L. C., "Statistical Evaluation of Reaeration Prediction
     Equations," J. Environmental Engrg., ASCE, 100(EE5), 1974, pp.
     1051-1068.
2.   Dankwerts, P. V., "Significance of Liquid-Film Coefficients in Gas
     Absorption," Indust. & Eng. Chemistry, 43(6), 1951, pp. 1460-1467.
3.   Goldstock, T. K. and Fatt, I., "Diffusion of Oxygen in Solutions
     of Blood Proteins," Chem. Eng. Progress, Symposium Series 66,
     1970, pp. 101-113.
4.   Gulliver J. S. and Halverson, M. J., "Open Channel Flow
     Measurements in a Moving-Bed Flume," Proceedings of the 20th
     Congress, International Association for Hydraulic Research,
     Melbourne, Australia, August 19-22, 1985.
5.   Gulliver, J. S. and Stefan, H. G., "Wind Function for a Sheltered
     Stream," J. of Environmental Engrg., ASCE, 112(2), 1986, pp. 1-14.
6.   Halverson, M. J. and Gulliver, J. S., "Measurements of Secondary
     Flow in a Moving-Bed Flume," Advancements in Aerodynamics, Fluid
     Mechanics, and Hydraulics, ASCE, June 3-6, 1986.
7.   Higbie, R., "On the Adsorption of a Pure Gas into a Still Liquid
     During Short Periods of Exposure," American Inst. of Chem. Engrs.,
     Trans., 31, 1935, pp. 365-390.
8.   O'Connor D. J. and Dobbins, W. E., "Mechanism of Reaeration in
     Natural streams," Trans., ASCE, 123, 1958, pp. 641-666.
9.   Rathbun, R. E., "Reaeration Coefficients of Streams--State of the
     Art," J. Hydraulic Engrg., ASCE, 103(HY4), 1977, pp. 409-425.
10. Scott, J. C., "Flow Beneath a Stagnant Film on Water: The
     Reynold's Ridge," J. Fluid Mech., 116, 1982, pp. 283-296.
11. Wilson, G. T. and MacLeod, N., "A Critical Appraisal of Empirical
     Equations and Models for the Prediction of the Coefficient of
     Rearation of Deoxygenated Water," Water Research, 8(6), 1974,
     pp. 341-336.

OXYGENATION OF RELEASES FROM RICHARD B. RUSSELL DAM

By James W. Gallagher, Jr.[1] & Gary V. Mauldin[2]

INTRODUCTION

The Savannah District, U.S. Army Corps of Engineers, is currently completing construction and has begun operation of the Richard B. Russell Dam and Lake project on the Savannah River between Georgia and South Carolina. The Richard B. Russell Damsite is on the Savannah River 37 miles above Clarks Hill Dam and 30 miles below Hartwell Dam. Clarks Hill and Hartwell are both Corps of Engineers projects.

The Richard B. Russell Dam and Lake is a multi-purpose project designed to provide hydropower, some flood control, recreation, and has a potential for water supply. The dam consists of a 195-foot high, 1,900-foot long concrete gravity structure flanked by two earth embankments. The project is designed as a peaking powerplant with an installed capacity of 600 megawatts. The powerhouse will contain four 75-megawatt conventional units and four 75-megawatt pump units. This installation will make the project one of the largest Corps of Engineers' hydropower facilities in the nation. During periods of maximum generation the plant will release about 60,000 CFS. During maximum pumpback operation, 30,000 CFS will be pumped from Clarks Hill Lake back into Russell. The average daily release from the project is over 3,500 CFS. At maximum power pool the Russell Lake covers 26,650 acres and impounds 1,026,000 acre-feet of water.

The lake was impounded in 1984. Power-on-line for the first of the four conventional units occurred in December 1984, and the last conventional unit is scheduled to begin operation in August 1985. Power-on-line for the first of the four pump storage units is scheduled for February 1990. The current project cost estimate is 535 million dollars.

Like all deep lakes in the southeast, the Richard B. Russell Lake thermally stratifies in the warm summer months. During this time, the waters circulated by the wind are confined to the top 30 feet of the lake. With no means to replenish dissolved oxygen lost due to biological activity, the dissolved oxygen concentrations in the lower layer of the lake are gradually exhausted. Since the turbine intakes

[1]Hydraulic Engineer, U.S. Army Corps of Engineers, Savannah District, P.O. Box 889, Savannah, GA   31402-0889

[2]Hydraulic Engineer, U.S. Army Corps of Engineers, Savannah District, P.O. Box 889, Savannah, GA   31402-0889

are located in the lower layer of the lake, it is this water that is
released from the project for power generation, and during the summer
these waters have progressively reduced dissolved oxygen levels.

INTERAGENCY INVOLVEMENT

During the early planning stages of the Russell project, a major concern of the State and Federal agencies was that the project comply
with State water quality standards. The State of Georgia was particularly emphatic on this point, and as a result, the cost sharing agreement between the State of Georgia and the Federal Government for
development of the project's recreational areas includes the stipula-
tion that the operation of the project will meet State water quality
standards. Besides this commitment to Georgia, a commitment to
provide 6 parts per million (ppm) dissolved oxygen in the releases
from the reservoir is also explicitly stated in the Statement of
Findings for the project filed pursuant to Section 404 of the Federal
Water Pollution Control Act Amendments of 1972.

In July 1972, the Georgia Department of Natural Resources requested
the formation of a technical committee to analyze the water quality
matters relating to the Russell project. The objective of the committee was to evaluate the thermal and dissolved oxygen characteristics
of the Russell project as an integral part of the Hartwell-Clarks
Hill reservoir system including the following specifics:

   a. Maintenance of Federal and State water quality standards.

   b. Maintenance of a coldwater fishery in a 10-mile reach downstream from Hartwell Dam.

   c. Development of a warm and cold water fishery within Russell
Lake.

   d. Maintenance of a warm and cold water fishery within Clarks
Hill Lake.

With these objectives established, physical and mathematical modeling
were conducted to determine whether or not the objectives could be
met. The physical model determined travel time, level and thickness
of inflows, entrainment and pumpback currents which were then input
into a mathematical model which determined the dissolved oxygen and
temperature regimes in the lakes and in the hydropower releases.

In its final report, the committee observed that the water quality
objectives could be met with the artificial addition of oxygen.
Several methods of adding oxygen were then investigated including
surface aerators, diffused air injection, spillway aeration, penstock
air injection, multi-level penstock intakes, submerged weirs, oxygen
injection into the penstocks, side stream oxygenation, localized
destratification, pulsed oxygen injection through porous diffusers
into the lake at the face of the dam, and continuous oxygen injection
through porous diffusers into the lake at a point several days travel

time upstream of the dam. With the high oxygen and low temperature constraints, continuous oxygen injection with an on-site Government-owned cryogenic plant was identified as the most feasible alternative. Continuous oxygen injection is favored over pulsed oxygen injection because it avoids the high capital and operating costs associated with liquifying and storing gaseous oxygen.

FIELD TESTS

Between 1975 and 1980, the Savannah District, through contracts with Dr. Richard Speece of Drexel University, conducted field tests of an oxygen injection system at Clarks Hill Lake. As a first step, a small scale system capable of providing sufficient oxygen for the discharge of one turbine was installed adjacent to the dam face at Clarks Hill and operated in a pulsed mode by Speece, et al,[1] in the summer of 1975. This made it possible to rapidly monitor the oxygen level in the discharge and determine the oxygen absorption efficiency immediately.

It was concluded from these tests that it was technically feasible to dissolve oxygen in a pulsed mode that was matched to the water discharge rate. However, as mentioned earlier, the recommended method is continuous oxygen injection at an upstream point in the lake rather than pulsed oxygen injection at the face of the dam. Pulsed injection of oxygen to match the water discharge rate involves matching the peaking discharge pattern which normally occurs less than 12 hours each weekday and even less on weekends. With on-site cryogenic oxygen being produced in the gaseous state at a uniform rate, compression and storage would need to be provided to match the production with the usage rate. This would increase the capital costs of the oxygen production facility. Therefore, it was decided that field tests should be conducted to evaluate the feasibility of continuous injection into a diffuser system located approximately 1 mile upstream of the dam.

The field tests of the continuous injection system began the next summer[2]. The tests were divided into three phases. Phase I was an evaluation of the oxygen absorption efficiency of various diffusers. In this test, diffusers with a standard permeability of 0.5 to 2.0 feet per minute (fpm) were identified as the optimum diffusers. Phase II involved tests of racks of diffusers to determine the elevation in the water column at which the oxygenated water would come to equilibrium.

Phase III of the study involved installation of nine diffuser racks at a location approximately 1 mile upstream of the dam in water approximately 130 feet deep. The highest dissolved oxygen concentration recorded in the turbines was 4.1 ppm which occurred about 6 days after oxygen injection started. The background dissolved oxygen before oxygen injection commenced was 0.5 to 0.8 ppm. Only about 30 to 40 percent of the oxygen that was injected appeared to eventually reach the turbines. The low oxygen absorption efficiency was due to two factors. First, the diffusers on the rack were not the most

efficient as determined in Phase I of the study. Second, the close
semicircular spacing of the diffuser racks and high injection rates
per diffuser caused localized destratification in the vicinity of the
diffuser racks which resulted in the dissolved oxygen-rich water
coming to equilibrium in the upper level of the lake where it was
unavailable for dissolved oxygen enrichment of the turbine discharges.
It was determined that improvements in the performance of the oxygen
injection system could be realized by lowering the injection rate per
diffuser by quadrupling the number of diffusers per rack, equipping
the racks with the optimum 2 fpm diffusers, and spreading the racks
across the lake cross section.

These improvements were made to the system and field tests were
conducted in the summer of 1977[3]. The nine racks were fitted with
40 square feet of diffusers of 2 fpm standard permeability. The
racks were placed across the lake cross section 1 mile upstream from
the dam and spaced approximately 300 feet apart with the first rack
located approximately 1,200 feet from shore. Oxygen was injected
continuously for 30 days at a rate of 100 tons/day, and dissolved
oxygen and temperature were monitored in the lake and the turbines.
During this period of oxygen injection, dissolved oxygen concentrations of 4 to 5 ppm were maintained with an absorption efficiency of
50 percent. Although this represented an improvement over the
results from the previous year, the goal of 6 ppm dissolved oxygen
was still not achieved and the absorption efficiency was still
unacceptable. Although the lake did not destratify in the vicinity
of the racks, pumping of the oxygenated water occurred causing it to
reach the surface where it warmed and returned to an intermediate
layer generally above the turbine withdrawal zone. It was determined
that the pumping was due to the four-sided diffuser configuration of
the racks and that the pumping could be eliminated by employing a
linear diffuser configuration.

RICHARD B. RUSSELL OXYGEN INJECTION SYSTEM

The oxygen injection system at the Richard B. Russell project is
described in the Richard B. Russell Dam and Lake Design Memorandum 35
and Supplement No. 1 [4 and 5]. The system at Russell has a continuous injection system located 1 mile upstream of the Russell damsite
but also has supplemental injection capability at the face of the dam
to be used during periods of higher than normal releases and unusually high dissolved oxygen deficits. Gaseous oxygen is supplied from
a liquid oxygen storage facility on the lakeshore.

The continuous system consists of a distribution pipe from the oxygen
facility to two parallel diffuser pipes suspended 5 feet off the lake
bottom. The two diffuser pipes are over 1,600 feet long and are
spaced 100 feet apart. For the pulsed system, a main distribution
line extends from the oxygen supply site to the top of the dam.
Additionally, eight feeder pipes extend from the main distribution
line down the face of the dam and then connect to the diffuser lines
between each intake perpendicular to the face of the dam. Each
feeder pipe for the pulsed system is equipped with a motorized

control valve which allows operation of any combination of pulsed
diffuser lines. Power and telemetry for the motorized control valves
is provided from the oxygen supply facility by means of underground
cables.

A typical section of diffuser piping is shown on Figure 1. The
diffuser piping consists of an 8-inch center manifold pipe made of
fiberglass reinforced plastic. Flotation is attached to the manifold
pipe to provide a constant positive buoyancy to the system during
shutdown. Vertical and horizontal alignment of the system is secured
by guying the manifold pipe to concrete anchor blocks on the lake
bottom with stainless steel cables. Flanged to the manifold pipe are
20-feet sections of 4-inch schedule 80 PVC diffuser pipe. The
diffusers are spaced 1 foot apart along this pipe. A control orifice
is installed in each flanged connection between the manifold pipe and
the diffuser pipe to ensure proper flow distribution through this
system. The diffusers are 7 inches in diameter and are made of
silica glass bonded together with an organic binder. The diffusers
have a standard permeability of 2 fpm.

The cost of the oxygenation system is approximately 3.9 million
dollars: 1.0 million dollars for the oxygen storage facility and 2.9
million dollars for the distribution and diffusing system. The price
of liquid oxygen is currently $84/ton.

Based on the best estimates currently available on the expected
dissolved oxygen content of the reservoir releases, the expected
daily discharge from the project and the expected oxygen absorption
efficiency, approximately 5,500 tons of oxygen would have to be added
annually at a maximum rate of 150 tons/day to meet the downstream
dissolved oxygen objective of 6 ppm in the hydropower discharges that
would occur 90 percent of the time. For the first few years of operation, oxygen will be purchased from commercial suppliers, stored in
liquid oxygen storage tanks on the site, and then vaporized as needed.
Although ultimate plans are to install an on-site oxygen production
facility, purchased liquid oxygen will be used initially to gain
detailed data on project performance and oxygen requirements. After
this period, we will be in a better position to determine both the
desirability of an on-site production facility and the type of facility that will be most economical to operate.

The oxygen injection system began operation in April 1985 with the
onset of lake stratification. During the first year of operation,
the system has consistently maintained dissolved oxygen concentrations in the hydropower discharges in excess of 6 ppm. Over 90% of
the oxygen injected into the lake through the continuous injection
system is released through the hydropower discharges. Figure 2 shows
a dissolved oxygen profile just downstream of the system along with a
background dissolved oxygen profile taken 1-1/2 miles upstream of the
system. As the figure shows, the oxygenated water remains in the
lower layer of the lake where it is available for turbine discharge.

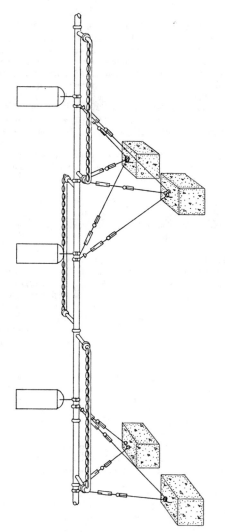

Figure 1. Typical section of diffuser piping.

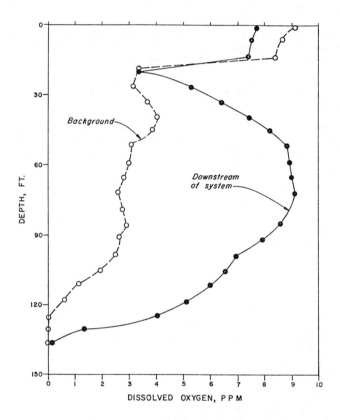

Figure 2. In-lake dissolved oxygen profiles upstream and downstream of continuous oxygen injection system.

REFERENCES

1. Speece, R. E., et al, "Final Report, Reservoir Discharge Oxygena-
    tion Demonstration of Clark Hill Lake," Contract No. DACW21-76-C-
    0003, for the U.S. Army Corps of Engineers, Savannah District,
    January 1976.

2. Speece, R. E., et al, "Final Report, Oxygenation Tests at Clark
    Hill Lake," Contract No. DACW21-76-C-0105 and 0011, for the U.S.
    Army Corps of Engineers, Savannah District, March 1977.

3. Speece, R. E., et al, "Final Report, 1977 Clark Hill Lake Oxygena-
    tion Study," Contract No. DACW21-77-C-0060, for the U.S. Army
    Corps of Engineers, Savannah District, May 1978.

4. U.S. Army Corps of Engineers, Savannah District, Design Memoran-
    dum 35, Richard B. Russell Dam and Lake, Oxygen Distribution and
    Diffusion System, November 1981.

5. U.S. Army Corps of Engineers, Savannah District, Design Memoran-
    dum 35 Supplement No. 1, Richard B. Russell Dam and Lake, Oxygen
    Production and Storage Facility, May 1982.

A Perspective on Performance Variability in Municipal Wastewater Treatment Facilities

Lewis A. Rossman*, M. ASCE
John J. Convery*

Excessive variability in effluent quality can cause wastewater treatment plants to fail to meet their discharge permit limits. This paper summarizes our understanding of the nature, causes, and control of this variability. It discusses studies made on the differences in performance variability observed among plants, the statistical characterization of this variability, and investigations into its causes. Methods of controlling and accomodating effluent variability are briefly reviewed. The results of an EPA workshop to develop research objectives related to these problems are discussed.

Introduction

Estimates indicate that a significant number of the Nation's 21,000 municipal wastewater treatment facilities do not consistently meet their discharge permit limits (U.S.Government Accounting Office, 1983; Water Pollution Control Federation, 1985). Surveys show that aside from gross design errors and chronic mismanagement, most noncompliance can be related to a lack of process control capability resulting in excessive variability of effluent quality (Gray, et al., 1982; Government Accounting Office, 1983). In addition to permit noncompliance, this variability can cause excessive periods of adverse impacts in receiving waters.

The purpose of this paper is to provide a perspective on our understanding of the characterization and causes of effluent variability, and on our ability to either control it operationally or to accomodate it through facility design. The paper also reports on the results of a structured group process used by US EPA's Water Engineering Research Laboratory to prioritize future research objectives in this area.

Characterization of Effluent Variability

Investigators have characterized wastewater treatment plant effluent variability in a number of different ways. The simplest and most common measures have been the standard deviation of effluent concentration measurements and its related statistic, the coefficient of variation (CV). The latter quantity is the standard deviation divided by the mean and offers a scale-free measure of variability. The time scale used to analyze effluent variability has ranged from

* U.S. Environmental Protection Agency, Water Engineering Research Laboratory, Cincinnati, Ohio 45268.

hourly measurements to monthly averages, depending on the purpose of
the analysis. The most commonly used time frame is based on daily
average values. Other measures of variability have included effluent concentration percentiles (the concentration not exceeded more
than a given percent of the time) and the frequency and duration
of "upsets" (periods where effluent quality is significantly worse
than some reference level).

Levels of variability differ significantly among treatment
facilities. Effluent CV's typically span a range of 0.2 to 1.2.
Figure 1 displays the variation in the means and CV's of daily
effluent BOD (Biochemical Oxygen Demand) from 37 well-operated
activated sludge plants (Niku, et al., 1979). Figure 2 plots the
medians of the mean and CV of daily effluent BOD from plants in eight
process categories based on a survey of 324 plants (U.S. EPA, 1984b).
The individual plants contained in any given category show considerable scatter about the median point plotted in Figure 2. There
appears be a trend towards higher levels of relative variability for
process categories that achieve lower mean levels of effluent BOD.

Numerous studies have been made that statistically characterize
the performance variability of individual plants. Histograms showing
the frequency with which effluent concentrations fall within specific intervals are typically skewed to the right, showing that "low"
values are more probable than "high" ones (Berthouex, 1974; Niku,
et al., 1979). Figure 4 shows such a histogram for the daily series
of effluent BOD values observed from an activated sludge plant in
Michigan as plotted in Figure 3. Various types of standard probability distribution functions have been fitted to such data. No single
distribution type has been found suitable for all plants. The log-
normal distribution is the one that provides an adequate fit most
often (Hann, et al., 1972; Dean and Forsythe, 1976; Niku, et al.,
1979). Figure 5 presents a lognormal probability plot for the data
of Figure 3. The straight line shape of this plot indicates that the
data do fit a lognormal distribution.

Strictly speaking, the use of probability plots and goodness of
fit tests for standard probability distributions is only valid for
data which are statistically independent and random. The sequence of
effluent quality levels found in continuous plant records are not
completely random. They can display considerable amounts of deterministic periodicities and autocorrelation (Thomann, 1970; Hann, et
al., 1972; Adams and Gemmell, 1973). Fourier Analysis (Bendat and
Piersol, 1966) can be used to represent systematic cyclic variations
as a weighted sum of sine and cosine terms of different time frequencies. For example, 31% of the variation in the BOD levels of
Figure 3 could be explained by weekly, monthly, bi-monthly, semiannual and annual periodicities.

The lag k autocorrelation coefficient of a time series measures
the degree of dependence of an observed value with one measured k
time units before it. The coefficient can vary from -1 to +1. Positive correlation implies that when one value is high (or low) relative to the mean, the other is also high (or low). Independent meas-

Figure 1. Mean and Coeff-
icient of Variation of
Effluent BOD From 37
Activated Sludge Plants

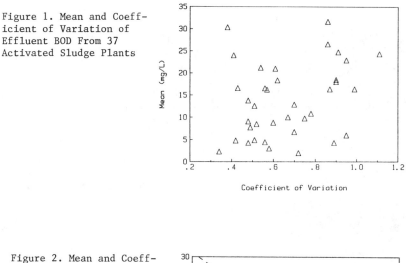

Figure 2. Mean and Coeff-
icient of Variation of
Effluent BOD for the
Median Plant From a
Survey of 324 Facilities

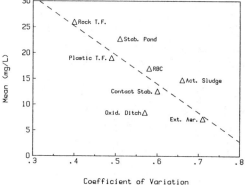

Figure 3. Time Series of
Daily Effluent BOD From
an Activated Sludge Plant
in Michigan

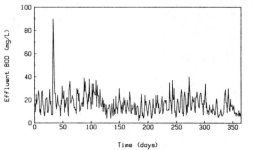

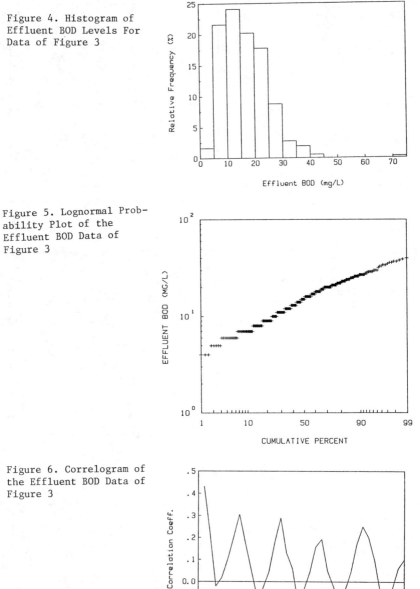

Figure 4. Histogram of
Effluent BOD Levels For
Data of Figure 3

Figure 5. Lognormal Prob-
ability Plot of the
Effluent BOD Data of
Figure 3

Figure 6. Correlogram of
the Effluent BOD Data of
Figure 3

urements have zero autocorrelation. First order (lag 1) autocorrelations for effluent BOD from activated sludge plants have been found to range between 0.3 and 0.55 (Adams and Gemmell, 1973). For trickling filters, coefficients between 0.36 and 0.85 have been reported (US EPA, 1984b). Figure 6 displays the correlogram (a plot of autocorrelation versus lag) of the data in Figure 3. The influence of a weekly periodicity is clearly evident from this plot.

Factors Affecting Effluent Variability

A number of investigators have attempted to establish statistically valid relationships between effluent variability and variations in such causative factors as influent pollutant loading, water temperature, and process operating conditions. The most ambitious effort of this kind found no consistent set of relations (Niku and Schroeder, 1981). In applying regression analysis to 21 different activated sludge plants, only 13-61% of the effluent BOD variability and 5-52% of the SS (suspended solids) variability could be explained by sets of such factors. For BOD, the factors appearing most frequently in the 21 regressions were temperature (6 times), time (4), and influent loading (4). For SS they were flow (6) and sludge volume index (5).

Similar results were obtained using more sophisticated time series transfer function modeling techniques at two other activated sludge plants (Bertheoux, et al., 1976; Debelak and Sims, 1981). These analyses showed that most of the variability in effluent BOD (or COD) could be explained by past values. Inclusion of causative factors in the models provided only a slight improvement in their explanatory power.

A systematic analysis of the factors causing "upset" conditions at 15 activated sludge plants has also been made (Bertheoux, et al., 1985). Upsets were subjectively identified as periods where performance was not typical of the recent past. Of 24,554 days of operation analyzed, 8.8% and 8.1% were characterized as BOD and SS upsets, respectively. Causes of the upset periods were determined by examining operating records and interviewing plant operators. The two most frequently assigned categories of causes were "operational problems" and "influent variables". Together they accounted for 61% of the BOD upsets and 60% of the SS upsets. A more specific listing of the most frequently observed causes is as follows:

Factor	Percentage of Upset Days Attributed to Factor	
	BOD	SS
High Flows	11	19
Solids Handling Problems	13	17
Low Mixed Liquor SS	13	9
Low Dissolved Oxygen	19	10

Mechanical failures accounted for only about 1% of the upset days. This confirms the mechanical component reliability data collected from 9 other plants (Shulz and Parr, 1982) indicating high availabilities for most components (e.g., > 98%). Availability is the percent of the time that a component is operational. Some exceptions to this finding were gas engines (93% availability), vacuum filters (93%), ball valves (87%), and incinerators (72%). The effect of mechanical component outages at these plants on effluent quality was not addressed.

The studies cited above suggest that on a day-to-day basis, the activated sludge process is relatively insensitive to variations in process parameters that remain within "acceptable" bounds. Only when these bounds are exceeded is the cause and effect relation readily identifiable. Under normal operation, the variations in process performance may be attributable to inherent process "noise" or to the effects of unobservable phenomena (e.g., parameter disturbances with durations shorter than the time scale used to measure effluent variability).

Approaches to Controlling Effluent Variability

Aside from the problems related to overloading, faulty design, and inadequately trained operators, a number of approaches can be suggested for either controlling or accomodating the effects of effluent variability. A brief sampling of these approaches is as follows:

Design redundancy and excess capacity (Niku, et al., 1979; US EPA, 1984a): accomodates effluent variability through a reduction in the design mean effluent concentration level.

Control charts and reference distributions (Fairall, 1973; Berthouex and Hunter, 1983): helps the operator know when a plant is "out of control" and special diagnoses or operational changes are called for.

Computer-assisted control (Stephenson, et al., 1983; Johnson, et al., 1984; Keck, et al., 1985): helps maintain dissolved oxygen, solids retention time, and clarifier solids loading within acceptable limits to avoid upset conditions.

Reliability evaluations (Waste & Water International, 1982): provides a comprehensive engineering study of all aspects of a plant's performance reliability and recommends remedial actions if needed.

No systematic study has been performed to assess the relative effectiveness or cost-efficiency of these various approaches. None of these methods allows a priori predictions to be made of the level of variability reduction that they can achieve.

Research Needs

The US EPA Water Engineering Research Laboratory held a workshop in December 1984 to identify and prioritize research objectives in

the area of municipal wastewater treatment plant performance reliability (Christakis and Keever, 1984). The highest ranking objectives
formulated at this workshop were as follows:

- Develop improved plant operational aids such as:
  computer-based expert systems,
  tools to help diagnose departures from normal performance,
  statistically valid control charts.

- Improve the ability of hybrid mechanistic-stochastic models to
  predict plant performance variability.

- Determine guidelines for designing plants to achieve specific
  levels of effluent variability.

- Determine how to incorporate uncertainty about plant performance
  prior to construction into the water quality planning and permit
  setting process.

The Water Engineering Research Laboratory is currently pursuing research projects directed at the first of these objectives, the development of improved plant operational aids.

Appendix - References

1. Adams, B.J. and Gemmell, R.S., "Performance of regionally related
   wastewater treatment plants", Jour. Water Pollut. Control Fed.,
   Vol. 45, No. 10, October, 1973.
2. Bendat, J.S. and Piersol, A.G., Measurement and Analysis of Random
   Data, J. Wiley and Sons, 1966.
3. Berthouex, P.M., "Some Historical Statistics Related to Future
   Standards", Jour. Envrion. Eng. Div., ASCE, Vol. 100, No. EE2,
   April, 1974.
4. Berthouex, P.M., et al., "The Use of Stochastic Models in the
   Interpretation of Historical Data From Sewage Treatment Plants",
   Water Research, Vol. 10, 1976, pp. 689-698.
5. Berthouex, P.M. and Hunter, W.G., "How to construct reference
   distributions to evaluate treatment plant effluent quality",
   Jour. Water Pollut. Control Fed., Vol. 55, No. 12, December, 1983.
6. Berthouex, P.M., et al., "Characterization of Treatment Plant
   Upsets" in Instrumentation and Control of Water and Wastewater
   Treatment and Transport Systems, R.A.R. Drake, ed., Pergamon
   Press, 1985.
7. Christakis, A.N. and Keever, D.B., "Report on the Objectives Identification and Structuring Session of the EPA's Seminar on Reliability Concepts in the Design of POTW's", The Interactive Management Corporation, Chantilly, VA, December 15, 1984.
8. Dean, R.B. and Forsythe, S.L., "Estimating the Reliability of
   Advanced Waste Treatment, Parts 1 and 2", Water and Sewage Works,
   June-July, 1976.
9. Debelak, K.A. and Sims, C.A., "Stochastic Modeling of an Industrial Activated Sludge Process", Water Research, Vol. 15, 1981,
   pp. 1173-1183.
10. Fairall, J.M., "Statistical Quality Control Charts for Wastewater

Evaluation", Proceedings of the 28th Industrial Waste Conference, Purdue University, Lafayette, IN, May 1-3, 1973.
11. Gray, A.C., et al., "Evaluation and Documentation of the Effects of Operation and Maintenance Practices on the Performance of Selected Biological Treatment Plants", EPA-600/2-82-050, U.S. Environmental Protection Agency, Municipal Environmental Research Laboratory, Cincinnati, OH, August, 1982.
12. Hann, R.W., et al., "Evaluation of Factors Affecting Discharge Quality Variation", Environmental Engineering Division, Civil Engineering Department, Texas A&M University, September 30, 1972.
13. Johnson, F.B., et al., "Operating experience with computer control of air nitrification", Jour. Water Pollut. Control Fed., Vol. 56, No. 12, December, 1984.
14. Keck, H.S., et al., "Computer Assist For Activated Sludge Process", WATER/Engineering & Management, Vol. 132, No. 10, September, 1985.
15. Niku, S., et al., "Performance of activated sludge processes and reliability-based design", Jour. Water Pollut. Control Fed., Vol. 51, No. 12, December, 1979.
16. Niku, S. and Schroeder, E.D., "Factors affecting effluent variability from activated sludge processes", Jour. Water Pollut. Control Fed., Vol. 53, No. 5, May, 1981.
17. Shultz, D.W. and Parr, V.B., "Evaluation and Documentation of Mechanical Reliability of Conventional Wastewater Treatment Plant Components", EPA-600/2-82-044, U.S. Environmental Protection Agency, Municipal Environmental Research Laboratory, Cincinnati, OH, March, 1982.
18. Stephenson, J.P., et al., "Pilot Scale Investigation of Computerized Control of the Activated Sludge Process", Report SCAT-12, Environmental Protection Service, Environment Canada, Ottowa, Ontario, 1983.
19. Thomann, R.V., "Variability of Waste Treatment Plant Performance", Jour. San. Eng. Div., ASCE, Vol. 96, No. SA3, June, 1970.
20. U.S. Environmental Protection Agency, "Construction Grants 1985 (CG-85)", EPA-430/9-84-004, Office of Water Program Operations, Washington, DC, July, 1984a.
21. U.S. Environmental Protection Agency, "Technical Support Document For Proposed Regulations Under Section 304(d)(4) of the Clean Water Act, as Amended", Faciltiy Requirements Division, Office of Water, Washington, DC, August, 1984b.
22. U.S. Government Accounting Office, "Wastewater Dischargers Are Not Complying With EPA Pollution Control Permits", GAO/RCED-84-53, Washington, DC, December 2, 1983.
23. Waste & Water International, "Reliability Evaluation", City of Palo Alto Water Quality Control Plant, January, 1982.
24. Water Pollution Control Federation, Highlights, Vol. 22, No. 12, December, 1985.

CHLORINATION OF WASTEWATER TREATED BY OVERLAND FLOW

T.J. Johnson[1] and E.D. Schroeder[2]

Abstract

Results are presented from an investigation of the efficiency of three chlorination schemes used for the disinfection of municipal wastewater treated by overland flow. In experimental studies conducted during the summer and fall of 1984 at the University of California, Davis Overland Flow Field Research Facility the levels of disinfection achieved by chlorinating primary effluent and oxidation pond effluent both before and after treatment by overland flow were compared. Additional studies monitored the performance of overland flow slopes treating primary effluent and oxidation pond effluent. Overland flow treatment of oxidation pond effluent prior to chlorination reduced the chlorine dosage necessary to meet effluent quality standards by as much as 50 percent. No statistically significant difference was observed between the chlorine dose required to disinfect primary effluent treated by overland flow and the dose required to disinfect pond effluent treated by overland flow. In addition, significantly higher removals of $CBOD_5$ and TSS were observed on the slopes treating primary effluent than were found on the slopes treating oxidation pond effluent. Based on these findings, overland flow treatment of primary effluent followed by chlorination is recommended as a reliable and efficient treatment process for municipal wastewaters.

Introduction

Since being introduced as an alternative method for the treatment of muncipal wastewaters, the overland flow process has attracted considerable attention. Limited operating and maintenance requirements coupled with the ability to produce high quality effluents have made overland flow an attractive alternative for small or rural communities seeking the means to improve their wastewater treatment capabilities. However, a lack of significant design and operating experience has hindered the development of successful full-scale systems. Updated information in the EPA Process Design Manual Supplement on Rapid Infiltration and Overland Flow (EPA, 1984) addresses a number of design, operating, and maintenance problems. Yet, additional work is needed to more clearly define the factors which govern the effective use of overland flow for full-scale treatment of municipal wastewater. In this

---

[1] T.J. Johnson, Environmental Engineer, Harza Engineering Co., 150 S. Wacker Drive, Chicago, IL 60606.

[2] E.D. Schroeder, Ph.D., Professor of Civil Engineering, University of California, Davis, Davis, CA 95616.

paper results are presented from a study conducted to address specific
performance and reliability problems associated with the operation of
the 19000 m^3/day (5.0 mgd) overland flow system at the Davis, CA Water
Pollution Control Plant.

Background

Added to an existing secondary treatment system in 1976, the Davis
overland flow facility was one of the earliest full-scale applications
of overland flow for the treatment of municipal wastewater in this
country. Currently, the Davis system remains the largest operating
municipal overland flow facility in the United States. Prior to 1976,
unit processes in the secondary treatment scheme included aeration,
grit removal, primary sedimentation, biological treatment in oxidation
ponds, and effluent chlorination. However, excessive concentrations of
algae in summertime effluents eventually forced the City to consider
alternatives for upgrading the treatment system. Following several
months of pilot studies, the overland flow process was selected to
provide algae removal, and approximately 81 hectares (200 acres) of
graded slopes were added to the end of the treatment train. Chlorination of pond effluent was continued prior to treatment by overland
flow to provide pre-application disinfection and to promote algae
die-off.

Since the installation of the overland flow slopes, plant operators have continued to struggle with reliability problems which have
resulted in poor effluent quality and high operating costs. Continued
high concentrations of algae in the plant effluent have resulted in
frequent violations of the 30 mg/L BOD$_5$ and 30 mg/L TSS effluent
standards. Prompted by the inconsistent performance of the treatment
system, the City of Davis, in conjunction with the University of
California, Davis and the Environmental Protection Agency initiated
this study to evaluate the performance and reliability of several
alternative configurations for the treatment of municipal wastewater
by overland flow.

Project Description

To meet the objectives of this study, experiments were planned to
compare both the general performance and the chlorination efficiency of
the existing Davis system and two alternative configurations. Alternative treatment-disinfection schemes selected for evaluation included:

- overland flow treatment of oxidation pond effluent followed
  by chlorination, and

- overland flow treatment of primary effluent followed by
  chlorination.

Process flowsheets for the existing treatment palnt and the two
alternatives are presented in Figure 1.

Experimental work associated with this study was conducted at the
University of California, Davis/City of Davis Overland Flow Field

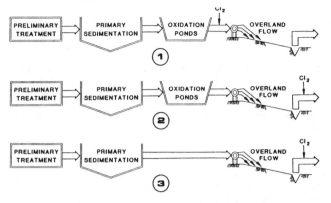

**Figure 1. Alternative Overland Flow
Treatment Schemes**

Research Facility located at the Davis Water Pollution Control Plant.
The research system consisted of 10 overland flow slopes, each 37 m
(121 ft) long, 2.5 m (8.2 ft) wide, and graded to a slope of 1.5%.
Vegetation covering the slopes was Kentucky 31 tall fescue. Piping to
the facility was constructed such that either screened raw wastewater,
primary treated wastewater, pond effluent, chlorinated pond effluent or
any combination of the above could be taken from the municipal treatment facility and applied to any slope. For the duration of the project
primary effluent was applied to slopes 2 and 3 of the pilot system
while oxidation pond effluent was applied to slopes 8 and 9. The
remaining slopes were utilized for research associated with another
overland flow study in progress. Slopes were operated 8 hours/day,
7 days/week, at an application rate of 0.25 m^3/hr-m (20 gal/hr-ft) giving the four slopes a cumulative treatment capacity of approximately
20 m^3/day (5300 gal/day).

Between June 1984 and November 1984 both a field monitoring study
and bench-scale chlorination experiments were conducted to evaluate
the performance and reliability of the alternatives being considered.
Influent/effluent monitoring was undertaken to characterize and compare
the performance of the pilot-scale slopes. Monitoring data also provided background water quality information for the chlorination study.
Eight hour composite influent and effluent samples taken once weekly
were tested for Five-day Carbonaceous Biochemical Oxygen Demand ($CBOD_5$),
Total Suspended Solids (TSS), Total Coliform Bacteria, Ammonia-nitrogen
(NH_3N), and Nitrate/Nitrite-nitrogen (NO_x-N). $CBOD_5$, TSS, and Total
Coliform measurements were made using procedures defined in Standard
Methods for the Examination of Water and Wastewater (1981). Nitrogen
concentrations were determined using a conductimetric procedure developed by Carlson (Carlson, 1974).

Bench-scale chlorination experiments performed on samples taken
from the field slopes examined the efficiency of the chlorination process as incorporated into the alternative schemes. Chlorine requirement

and chlorine demand tests as described in Standard Methods (1981) were
run once weekly on samples of pond effluent, pond effluent treated by
overland flow, and primary effluent treated by overland flow to determine the quantities of chlorine needed to achieve satisfactory disinfection of each. Direct comparisons of the bacterial kill achieved by
a predetermined dose of chlorine applied to each of the wastewaters
were also performed. In all of the disinfection experiments chlorine
was applied to samples as liquid sodium hypochlorite, and was reacted
with the wastewaters in 1-liter batch reactors for a contact time of
thirty minutes.

Experimental Results

    Results of the slope performance monitoring study concurred with
past studies which have defined the capabilities and the limitations of
the overland flow process (Overcash, 1976; Smith, 1982; Witherow and
Bledsoe, 1983). A summary of the monitoring study results is given in
Table 1.

Table 1. Slope Performance Monitoring Study Results

Test	Primary Slopes (Slopes 2 + 3)			Pond Slopes (Slopes 8 + 9)		
	Influent	Effluent	Removal	Influent	Effluent	Removal
$CBOD_5$ (mg/L)	98.9	12.9	86.8%	54.9	26.3	50.4%
TSS (mg/L)	108.9	8.9	91.8%	126.7	39.3	68.6%
Coliforms (MPN/100 mL)	2.5×10^7	1.3×10^6	94.0%	2.2×10^6	1.3×10^5	87.9%
NH_3-N (mg/L)	21.7	3.8	82.1%	7.6	0.8	93.3%
NO_x-N (mg/L)	0.2	2.7	*****	0.1	0.8	*****

    As expected, reductions of $CBOD_5$ and TSS on the slopes used to
treat primary effluent were significantly higher than those achieved on
the slopes treating oxidation pond effluent. In fact, while pond slope
effluent suspended solids concentrations frequently exceeded 30 mg/L,
effluent TSS concentrations from the primary slopes were consistently
in the 6 mg/L to 12 mg/L range. During the same period, ammonia-
nitrogen removals ranged from 70% to greater than 90% on both sets of
slopes. Although influent and effluent total coliform densities varied
widely, overland flow treatment of both wastewaters consistently resulted in significantly reduced levels of bacterial contamination. As
reported by others, however, coliform removals were not sufficient to
meet typical discharge requirements without further treatment (Hall,
et al, 1979; Peters, et al, 1981).

Throughout the various chlorination experiments high levels of bacterial kill were consistently observed. In the bench-scale tests greater than 99% of the coliform bacteria present in both the effluent from the slopes treating primary wastewater and the effluent from the slopes treating pond water were killed by chlorine doses of 2 mg/L at a contact time of thirty minutes. At similar contact times, chlorine doses of 4 mg/L applied to untreated oxidation pond effluent resulted in bacterial kills of greater than 98.5%.

Differences in the efficiency of the chlorination process in the three alternatives under consideration were evident in the results of the chlorine requirement test and the results of the comparative kill test. In the weekly chlorine requirement experiments, the lowest chemical dosages were consistently required to achieve the desired level of disinfection when chlorination was practiced following overland flow. Significantly higher dosages of chlorine were required to disinfect pond effluent prior to treatment by overland flow. No significant difference was observed between the chlorine dosage required to disinfect pond effluent following treatment by overland flow and the dosage required to disinfect primary effluent following treatment by overland flow. Results of the five week chlorine requirement study are given in Table 2 along with water quality data for the samples tested. A typical dose-response curve generated from chlorine requirement data is also presented as Figure 2.

Differences in the effectiveness of a 4 mg/L dose of chlorine applied to each of the wastewaters sampled are illustrated in Figure 3. In all of the samples of effluent from the overland flow slopes treating primary wastewater, and in 5 of 7 samples of effluent from the slopes treating pond water, 4 mg/L of chlorine provided sufficient disinfection to meet a 23 MPN/100 mL standard. However, the same dose was not sufficient to reduce the bacterial density in any of the samples of untreated oxidation pond effluent to the 23 MPN/100 mL level.

Despite significant differences in the quality of the wastewaters tested, little variation was observed in the chlorine demands exerted. In general, the demands observed throughout the testing period for all three wastewaters were similar in magnitude, ranging from 1-2 mg/L and increasing slightly with increasing chlorine dosage. Only on two occasions were significant differences in the chlorine demands exerted apparent. In both cases, the demand observed following chlorination of oxidation pond effluent treated by overland flow exceeded 7.5 mg/L at a chlorine dosage of 10 mg/L. Additional data collected indicated that these incidents of high demand coincided with sampling dates on which no ammonia-nitrogen was present in the pond slope effluent. Similar occurrences of high chlorine demand in the absence of ammonia-nitrogen have been described by White (White, 1974) and Dhaliwal and Baker (Dhaliwal and Baker, 1983).

Discussion

Based upon the results of both the slope performance monitoring study and the bench-scale disinfection study conducted during this project, a number of conclusions can be drawn concerning the overland flow

Table 2. Chlorine Requirement Results

Parameter	Effluent from Primary Slopes (Slopes 2 + 3)	Influent to Pond Slopes (Slopes 8 + 9)	Effluent from Pond Slopes (Slopes 8 + 9)
pH	7.5 - 8.1	8.0 - 8.7	8.0 - 8.3
$CBOD_5$ (mg/L)	12.9	54.9	26.3
TSS (mg/L)	8.9	126.7	39.3
NH_3-N (mg/L)	3.6	8.8	1.0
NO_x-N (mg/L)	2.7	0.1	0.8
TKN (mg/L)	6.5	20.8	7.3
Total Coliforms (MPN/100 mL)	1.3×10^6	2.2×10^6	1.3×10^5
Cl_2 Requirement Range (mg/L)	2.7 - 3.3	6.3 - 10.0	3.1 - 6.2
Mean (mg/L)	3.0	8.4	3.9

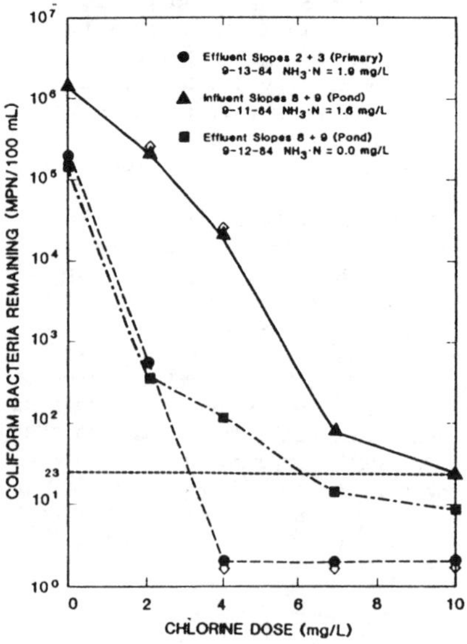

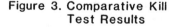

Figure 2. Chlorine Requirement Results: Week 2

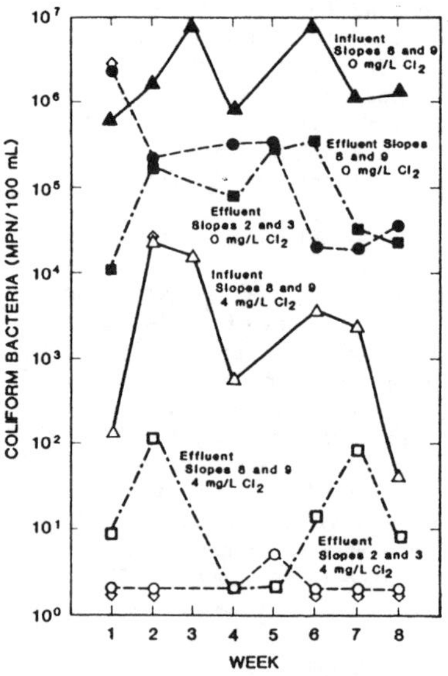

Figure 3. Comparative Kill Test Results

process and the chlorination of wastewaters treated by that process. For example, the excellent reductions of $CBOD_5$ and TSS accomplished during overland flow treatment of primary wastewater demonstrate the potential of the overland flow process as a reliable and effective form of secondary treatment for municipal wastewaters. In contrast, the reported inability of the process to effectively remove algae from pond effluent is further documented by the poor performance of the slopes treating oxidation pond effluent. Given these results, it is clear that the treatment capability of an overland flow system is not most effectively used when that system is operated for polishing rather than treatment of municipal wastewaters.

Also in this study, the efficiency of the chlorination process was found to depend heavily upon the performance of the treatment processes preceding disinfection. As is evident from a review of the chlorine requirement results, chlorination was most effective when practiced on high quality wastewaters. In particular, constituents such as organic matter (quantified in terms of $CBOD_5$), algal material, and Kjeldahl nitrogen appeared to interfere with the efficient action of the applied chlorine. When concentrations of these contaminants were reduced by overland flow treatment prior to chlorination, however, chemical dosages required to meet effluent bacterial standards were reduced by as much as 50%. Improving the quality of the wastewater to be disinfected prior to chlorination whould also allow for enhanced control of the chlorination process.

The implications of these findings with respect to performance and reliability for the Davis overland flow system and other similar facilities are significant. Clearly, the efficiency of overland flow systems depends not only on the design and construction of the physical facilities, but also on the manner in which those facilities are incorporated into the overall treatment scheme. At the Davis treatment plant, the unit processes required to economically and consistently produce high quality effluents are available. However, the system is not configured to take full advantage of the capabilities of the various processes. Given the ability of the overland flow process to efficiently treat primary effluent, use of the oxidation ponds for pre-application treatment is unnecessary. In fact, the algae produced in the ponds is currently the limiting factor with regard to the system's performance. Converting the ponds to off-line storage would effectively eliminate the algae problem in the system without reducing the plant's treatment capacity. At the same time, such a change in configuration would eliminate the need for application of chlorine prior to overland flow treatment for algae control. Having resolved the problems associated with algae removal, chlorination could be practiced with greater effectiveness following overland flow treatment.

In summary, although the modifications required to implement overland flow treatment of primary effluent followed by chlorination at the Davis Water Pollution Control Plant would be significant, the end result would be considerable improvement in the performance, the efficiency, and the reliability of the treatment system. New knowledge from research studies complemented by increasing experience with operating overland flow systems will continue to improve our understanding of the factors governing the performance of the process as well. In the future, consideration of these factors during the planning, design, and construction of treatment facilities will result in the successful application of overland flow for the treatment of municipal wastewater.

References

1. Carlson, Robert M. "Automated Separation and Conductimetric Determination of Ammonia and Dissolved Carbon Dioxide." Analytical Chemistry. 50, 1528 (Sept. 1978).

2. Dhaliwal, Bhupinder and Robert A. Baker, "Role of Ammonia-N in Secondary Effluent Chlorination." Journal of the Water Pollution Control Federation. 55, 454 (May 1983).

3. Hall, Dempsey H., et al. Municipal Wastewater Treatment by the Overland Flow Method of Land Application. EPA 600/2-79-178 Robert S. Kerr Environmental Research Laboratory (August 1979).

4. Overcash, Michael R., et al. Overland Flow Pretreatment of Wastewater. Water Resources Research Institute, University of North Carolina. (July 1976).

5. Peters, Robert E., et al. Field Investigations of Overland Flow Treatment of Municipal Lagoon Effluent. Technical Report EL-81-9. U.S. Army Engineer Waterways Experiment Station, Vicksburg, MS (Sept. 1981).

6. Smith, Robert G. "The Overland Flow Process." Environmental Progress. 1, 195 (August 1982).

7. Standard Methods for the Examination of Water and Wastewater. Fifteenth Edition. Published by the American Public Health Association, the American Water Works Association, and the Water Pollution Control Federation. (1981).

8. U.S. Environmental Protection Agency. Process Design Manual for Land Treatment of Municipal Wastewater - Supplement on Rapid Infiltration and Overland Flow. EPA 625/1-81-013a. (October 1984).

9. White, George C. "Disinfection Practices in the San Francisco Bay Area." Journal of the Water Pollution Control Federation. 46, 89 (January 1974).

10. Witherow, Jack L. and Bert E. Bledsoe, "Algae Removal by the Overland Flow Process." Journal of the Water Pollution Control Federation. 55, 1256 (October 1983).

The Reliability of Treatment Systems

Paul J. Ossenbruggen*
Kenneth Constantine**

Introduction

Questions of uncertainty in system performance are a major concern that must be addressed during design. In environmental engineering, performance uncertainty may be classified as (1) variability-in-demand and (2) treatment process noise. That is, the influent wastewater quality and flow vary over time, and there is an inherent variability with the treatment process itself. Probability based methodology (3,4,5,10) offers the designer a technique to explicitly evaluate variabilities-in-demand and treatment process noise. The purpose of this paper is to present the results of case studies of zero and first order reactor systems and an activated sludge treatment system consisting of a primary settling tank and a continuous flow stirred aeration tank reactor with recycle of cells from a secondary settling tank. The primary purpose is to demonstrate the use of probability based methods formulation for estimating process reliability for different treatment processes. Reliability is defined as the probability that the effluent wastewater quality, S, is less than or equal to a given effluent compliance standard, $\hat{s}$, i.e. $p_s = P[S \leq \hat{s}]$.

The same approach was used for each treatment process. Mass balance relationships were written to determine the interaction among variables. Unlike traditional design, random variables were introduced into the mass balance relationship and then substituted into the reliability function p_s. The new function consists of a set of random variables associated with the variabilities-in-demand and treatment process noise and a set of control variables. The control variables are assigned by the engineer during design and the plant operator to ensure effluent wastewater quality standards are met. The results of the analysis show the importance of considering uncertainty in design. The implications of using reliability based analysis for design and plant operation are compared to the margin of safety design approach.

Zero Order Reaction System

The solution to the zero order reaction system mass balance relationship, $ds/dt = -k$, is the linear function $s = s_o - kt$, where $s =$ effluent water quality, $s_o =$ influent water quality, $k =$ reaction rate and $t =$ treatment time. The influent water quality was assumed to vary

---

*Department of Civil Engineering, University of New Hampshire, Durham, NH.
**Department of Mathematics, University of New Hampshire, Durham, NH.

over time, thus, it may be classified as a variability-in-demand random
variable, S_o. The reaction rate was assumed to be an inherent random
variable, K. Introducing S_o and K into the mass balance equation gave
$S = S_o - Kt$, where t is assigned to be the control variable. The
random variables S_o and K were assumed to be independent normally
distributed random variables, $N(\mu_{S_o}, \sigma^2_{S_o})$ and $N(\mu_K, \sigma^2_K)$. The expected
value and variance of S are

$$\mu_S = E[S] = E[S_o - Kt] = \mu_{S_o} - \mu_K t$$

$$\sigma^2_s = V[S] = V[S_o - Kt] = \sigma^2_{S_o} + \sigma^2_K t^2$$

Since S is a linear function of S_o and K, $p_s = P[S \leq \hat{s}] = \phi(\dfrac{\hat{s} - \mu_s}{\sigma_s})$
where $\phi(\cdot)$ is cumulative unit normal distribution.

For a given value of t, p_s may be estimated. See Table 1. If the
design engineer determines that p_s is insufficient, t may be increased
and p_s increased to an acceptable level.

First Order Reaction System

The same approach was used for the first order reactor system.
The solution to the first order reaction system, $ds/dt = -ks$ is $s = s_o e^{-kt}$. Introducing the random variables, S_o and K, gives a nonlinear
function $S = S_o e^{-Kt}$. Since S is not a linear function, the assumptions
used for the zero order system are inapplicable. The first-order
second-moment formulation approach was employed.

The effluent compliance standard, $S \leq \hat{s}$, may be written as the
inequality or performance function, $G = \hat{s} - S = \hat{s} - S_o e^{-Kt}$. Since G is
a nonlinear function of two random variables, the first-order second-
moment formulation may be described with graphical means. The regions
of reliability, $G > 0$, and failure, $G < 0$, are bounded by the nonlinear
performance function $G = 0$ as shown in Figure 1.

Since S_o and K are assumed to be independent random variables, it
may be shown that joint distribution of S_o and K is a bivariate normal
probability distribution. The contour line of a bivariate normal
distribution is an ellipse. For the case when variances are equal as
shown in Figure 1, the contour line δ is a circle. Since $p_s + p_f = 1$,
$p_f = 1 - P[S \leq \hat{s}]$, the true probability of failure is the volume of the
bivariate normal distribution under $G < 0$, the failure region (i.e.,
the shaded region).

The first-order second-moment formulation gives an approximation

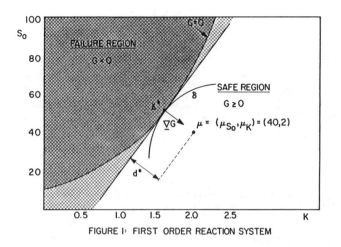

FIGURE I: FIRST ORDER REACTION SYSTEM

of the true probability of failure. It is the volume under the bivariate normal density surface and over the half plane (i.e., the cross-hatched region in Figure 1). The half plane is constructed by determining the tangent δ to $G = 0$ at the point $\underline{x}^*$ which is "closest" to the center $\underline{\mu}$ of the bivariate normal distribution. The point $\underline{X} = \underline{x}^* = (S_o = s_o^*, K = k^*)$ is called the "most probable failure point." The distance d^* may be written as

$$U = d^* = \frac{-\underline{\nabla G}^{*t}}{||\underline{\nabla G}^*||} (\underline{x}^* - \underline{\mu})$$

where $\underline{\nabla G}^*$ is gradient vector; here $-\partial G^*/\partial k = (S_o^* t) \exp(-K^* t)$ and $-\partial G^*/\partial S_o = -\exp(-K^* t)$, evaluated at $\underline{x}^*$ for a given t. The elements of the vector, of $-\underline{\nabla G}^*/||\underline{\nabla G}^*||$, are direction cosines. Consequently, U is a function of the random variables S_o and K, U is a random variable and shown to have a normal probability distribution. It may be shown that

$$p_s = P[U \le d^*] = \phi\left(\frac{-\underline{\nabla G}^* \ (\underline{x}^* - \underline{\mu})}{\{\underline{\nabla G}^{*t}[\underline{\sigma}^2] \ \underline{\nabla G}^*\}^{1/2}}\right) \tag{1}$$

where $[\underline{\sigma}^2]$ = variance matrix of K and S_o. See Table 1.

Numerical Results

A comparison of the two cases are shown in Table 1. It is assumed that for each case that the influent wastewater quality is the same. The mean and coefficient of variation were assumed to be 40 and 0.25, respectively. It should be evident from these results that the margin of safety and reliability give inconsistent results. In our opinion

Table 1

Reaction Order	μ_K	Coefficient of Variation	Margin of Safety	p_s = reliability
0	35.0	0.25	5.0	0.65
1	2.0	0.25	4.6	0.86

Margin of safety = $s - \mu_s$ where μ_s = expected effluent wastewater

quality. The treatment time was assigned to be equal to one

in each case, $t = 1$ and $\hat{s} = 5$.

the reliability is more representative because it accounts for both
variability-in-demand and process variability.

Activated Sludge System

The first-order second-moment approach was used for the activated
sludge system, a more complex problem. It was assumed to be a continuous flow system with sludge from the secondary settling tank
recycle. The analysis of the system was based on the following assumptions: (1) complete mixing was achieved in the aeration tank; (2)
no organic material was biodegraded in the primary or secondary settling
tanks; (3) steady state conditions prevailed throughout the system; and
(4) m_x, the net growth rate of cells, was based on the Monod equation

$$m_x = \frac{kys}{k_s + s} - k_d$$ where k = maximum rate of substrate utilization per mass

of microorganisms, k_d = endogeneous decay coefficient, k_s = half velocity constant, s = effluent wastewater quality, and y = maximum yield
coefficient.

The mass balance relationships for net change of cells and substrate in the aeration tank are

$$v\left(\frac{dx}{dt}\right) = q_r x_r - (q_r + q)x + vm_x x = 0 \tag{2}$$

and $$v\left(\frac{ds}{dt}\right) = qs_0' + q_r s - (q + q_r)s - \frac{(m_x + k_d)\,x}{y}\,v = 0 \tag{3}$$

where $$s_0' = s_0 - 0.923\,c\,ss_0, \tag{3a}$$

x = cell concentration, q_r = flow rate from secondary clarifier, q =
influent wastewater flow rate, v = aeration tank volume, and y =
maximum yield coefficient. The wastewater quality entering the aeration tank was assumed to be s_0' where the term, $0.923\,c\,ss_0$, is the BOD_5
equivalent to the biodegradable suspended solids removed in the primary

settling tank. It was assumed that 65 percent of the influent suspended solids are degradable (8). The coefficient 0.923 was derived from an assumed 1.42 mg BOD_L/mg ss times an assumed 0.65 mg BOD_5/BOD_L and is equivalent to the BOD_5 of the suspended solids in the wastewater.

Equations (2), (3) and (3a) were combined into a single equation and the random variables of Q, S_o, SS_o, C, K, K_a, K_s, Y and $\alpha = q_r/Q$, the recycle ratio, were introduced. The result was

$$S = S_o - 0.923 \ C \ SS_o - \frac{\alpha(M_x + K_d)}{(1 + \alpha - M_x \ v/Q)Y} \tag{4}$$

where

$$M_x = \frac{kYS}{K_s + S} - K_d$$

Substituting these expressions into $G = \hat{s} - S$ gave a performance function. The control variables are v and α.

The first-order second-moment formulation (6,7) was used to estimate the reliability. A computer algorithm was written to determine the most probable failure point $\underline{x}^*$ and equation (1) was employed to estimate p_s. The algorithm performed steps that are analogous to the ones used for solving the first and second order reaction system problems by graphical means.

Since first order estimates are used in reliability analysis, the mean and standard deviation of the random variables were used to characterize variability of each random variable. All random variables were assumed to be independent normally distributed random variables. The estimates given in Table 2 were calculated from a one year record (1982) of observations of daily influent flow and composite samples of influent BOD_5 and total suspended solids, SS, taken 3 times/week at a Concord, NH wastewater treatment plant. The coefficients of variation presented in Table 2 are consistent with the coefficients of variation presented by Niku and Schroeder (9) in their evaluation of 21 activated sludge treatment plants. The coeffecent of variation for the treatment noise random variables given in Table 3 were estimated from the ranges and typical values given by Metcalf and Eddy (8). The coefficient of variation was estimated with the following relationship: cov = (x_u - x_ℓ)/$4\bar{x}$. Where x_u and x_ℓ are the upper and lower bounds of the range, respectively, and $\bar{x}$ is the mean (1).

The required size of the aeration tank (2) was calculated with the following relationship:

$$v = \frac{q(s_o' - s_e')}{x(k/k_s)s_u}$$

for the mean values given in Tables 2 and 3, $s_e' = s_e - 0.692 \ ss_e$,

Table 2. Variabilities-in-Demand Random Variables

Symbol	Mean	Standard Deviation Monthly	Daily	Coef. of Variation Monthly	Daily
Q	3.45 Mgal/day	0.52	0.71	0.15	0.2
S_o	218. mg/L BOD_5	55.	108.	0.25	0.5
SS_o	248. mg/L TSS	87.	112.	0.35	0.6

Source: Concord, NH wastewater treatment plant

Table 3. Treatment Noise Random Variables

Symbol	Range	Typical Value or Mean	Coefficient of Variation
C	0.5-0.7	0.6	0.08
K	2.-10./day	5./day	0.4
K_d	0.04-0.075/day	0.06/day	0.15
K_s	25.-100./day	60 mg/L BOD_5	0.31
X_r	4000-12000 mg/L	8000. mg/L	0.25
Y	0.4-0.8 mg cells/mg BOD_5	0.6 mg cells/mg BOD_5	0.17

All values except X_r were taken from Metcalf and Eddy (8). X_r was estimated by experienced operators.

$s_u = s_e'/0.75$, the BOD_L, and x = 2000 mg/L SS, the cell concentration in the aeration tank. The design tank volume was calculated to be equal to 0.167 Mgal.

Results and Discussion

Since it is well known that the amount of recycle plays an important role in plant performance, p_s was determined for a range of recycle ratios from 0.1 to 2.0. The results for different cases are shown in Figures 2 through 5 where p_s is plotted as a function of α. The effects of different compliance standard limitations (Figure 2), influent flow rates (Figure 3), and influent variability-in-demand and no variability-in-demand for monthly and daily time averaging (Figures 4 and 5) were compared. As an overall observation, significant improvement in reliability was observed as the recycle ratio was increased.

ALL SYSTEMS ARE FOR THE ACTIVATED SLUDGE SYSTEM
WHERE P_S = RELIABILITY PROBABILITY AND α = RECYCLE RATIO

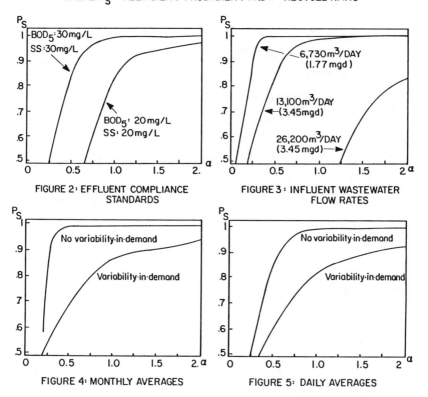

FIGURE 2: EFFLUENT COMPLIANCE
STANDARDS

FIGURE 3: INFLUENT WASTEWATER
FLOW RATES

FIGURE 4: MONTHLY AVERAGES

FIGURE 5: DAILY AVERAGES

Margin of Safety: When the means of the random variables are substituted into G, the result may be interpreted as a margin of safety. See Table 1. Margins of safety have been used in evaluating designs as well as incorporated into design codes. The greater the margin of safety, the less likely that a failure will be observed. For example, for α = 1.0 and the means given in Tables 2 and 3, G = 57.2 for the monthly effluent wastewater quality standard of 30 mg/L of BOD_5 and SS, respectively. For these conditions, $s_e' = 9.2$ and s = -48.0 making G a positive value and implying that there is sufficient capacity, an over capacity, to remove all influent wastewater contamination, when the plant is operating in the specified manner at average conditions. However, this value of G does not give the designer meaningful information about expected plant performance or process reliability.

In reliability analysis, the mean value as well as the variation in random variabilities are incorporated in p_s. The corresponding

value of p_s for $G = 57.2$ is 0.811 for the variabilities-in-demand case
(Figures 4). If an adequate design is specified to be one with a
minimum 95 percent reliability level, then the estimated reliability of
0.81 indicates that the design is inadequate. The designer will have
to make changes to meet the reliability criterion. The margin of
safety or G method does not alert the designer to a potential inadequacy
in design. It is a fundamentally inadequate design tool when performance
uncertainty is significant.

Further Work: The analyses presented in this paper make use of the
assumption that the random variables are uncorrelated and normally
distributed random variables. With the use of the first-order second-
moment formulation, it is possible to analyze nonlinear performance
functions with correlated nonnormally distributed random variables.
The analysis is more complex and was not deemed necessary for demonstrating the use of probability based design method for an activated
sludge treatment system.

For design, however, a slight change in p_s may lead to significant
design changes and to significant changes in construction and operation
costs. Before adapting the reliability based design method, more work
is needed in specifying probability distributions of influent characteristics, kinetic coefficients and secondary settling tank performance.
In addition, design specifications must be carefully drafted. For
example, averaging time is expected to be extremely important. Consider the implications of specifying daily and monthly (30 day) averages
in a design standard shown in Figures 4 and 5. From Table 2, the daily
and monthly averages of the Concord influent estimates are the same,
but the montly standard deviations of Q, S_o, and SS_o are less than the
corresponding daily standard deviation estimates. Using monthly time
averaging tends to smooth and to reduce perturbations of the time
series record. In specifying effluent compliance limits, the difference
in daily and monthly averaging is recognized. For daily observations,
the compliance standard is typically 50 mg/L BOD_5 and 50 mg/L SS, and
for monthly averages, the standard is 30 mg/L BOD_5 and 30 mg/L SS.

The specification of a daily or monthly time average has implications
on the outcome of the final design because time averaging effects the
probability distributions and correlation estimates used in the analysis.

An analysis of the daily observations of random variables in
equation (4) for the Concord record showed most variability pairs to be
weakly correlated. For daily averages, the introduction of ρ into the
second-moment formulation is not expected to significantly alter the
forecasts. For monthly averages, correlation between some variables
were greater than 0.5, consequently, the interaction among design
variables are expected to be significant factors in the reliability
analysis.

Incorporating this information into the analysis may significantly
change the reliability estimates, especially when evaluating design and
operation of a plant. Sensitivity analyses should be performed to
determine if the differences will significantly change the design,
i.e., the size of plants, or the manner in which the plant is operated.

References

1. Alfredo H-S. Ang and Wilson H. Tang, Probability Concepts in Engineering Planning and Design, Volume II Decision, Risk and Reliability, John Wiley and Sons, New York, 1984.

2. Benefield, L.D. and Randall, C.R., Biological Process Design for Wastewater Treatment, Prentice-Hall, Englewood Cliffs, NJ, 1980.

3. Bury, K.V., Statistical Models in Applied Science, John Wiley & Sons, New York, 1975.

4. Bury, K.V., "On Probabilistic Design", Journal of Engineering for Industry, ASME, Vol. 96, 1974, pp. 1291-1295.

5. Convery, J.J., "Reliability of Municipal Wastewater Treatment Facilities", November 1983 (unpublished manuscript).

6. Ditlevsen, O., "Generalized Second Moment Reliability Index", Journal of Structural Mechanics, Vol. 7, No. 4, 1979, pp. 435-451.

7. Hasofer, A.M. and Lind, N., "An Exact and Invariant First-Order Reliability Format", Journal of Engineering Mechanics, ASCE, Vol. 100, No. EM1, Feb. 1974, pp. 111-121.

8. Metcalf and Eddy, Inc., Wastewater Engineering: Treatment, Disposal Reuse, 2nd edition, McGraw-Hall, New York, 1979.

9. White, J.A., Agee, M.H., and Case, K.E., Principles of Engineering Economic Analysis, John Wiley & Sons, New York, 1977.

10. Niku, S. and Schroeder, E.D., "Factors Affecting Effluent Variability from Activated Sludge Processes", Journal WPCF, Vol. 53, No. 5, May 1981, pp. 546-689.

11. Niku, S., Schroeder, E.D., and Samaniego, "Performance of Activated Sludge Processes and Reliability - Based Design", Journal WPCF, Vol. 51, No. 12, Dec. 1979, pp. 2841-2857.

Acknowledgements

     The writers are grateful to John Bushold, Concord, N.H. Wastewater Treatment Plant, Wayne Kimball, New Hampshire Water Supply and Pollution Control Commission and Professor P.L. Bishop, University of New Hampshire for their helpful suggestions and assistance.

On-Site Microcomputer Control of a Combined
Sewer Overflow Diversion Structure

William James, Member ASCE and Mark Stirrup*

This paper describes the design of an inexpensive system for controlling combined sewer overflows using on-site equipment (raingauges, flow gauges, automatic gates, and microcomputers). The system is based on the Timex/Sinclair 1000 microcomputer. An interface was designed for the computer converting it into a real-time data acquisition system and controller.

Software for the controller was written in BASIC, and includes data acquisition and storage routines, data processing, runoff forecasting, and control routines. The forecasting and control software is based upon the results of continuous modelling using a PC version (PCSWMM3) of the U.S. EPA SWMM program at a five-minute time step. Both quantity and quality were modelled.

In order to evaluate the system's effectiveness in reducing the impacts of combined sewer overflows on local receiving waters, the control software was also incorporated in the PCSWMM3 model. Continuous modelling can then be used to estimate the benefits of various control programs at the diversion structure.

Introduction

The USEPA Storm and Combined Sewer Overflow Pollution Control Research and Development Program (SCSP) has supported research into the CSO pollution problem and the development of abatement techniques (Field and Struzeski, 1972; Lager and Smith, 1974; Field, 1982;1985). Their reports outline the state of the art in CSO pollution control. In Canada, similar research efforts were supported by the Inland Waters Branch of the Department of the Environment (Marsalek, 1972), and the Research Program for the Abatement of Municipal Pollution under Provisions of the Canada-Ontario Agreement on Great Lakes Quality (Environment Canada, 1980).

The construction of separate sanitary and storm sewer systems has been one of the most widely used remedies for CSO problems. However, recently it has become evident that separation of existing combined sewer systems is often an impractical and costly solution. An APWA study of combined sewer problems (1967) estimated the cost of complete separation in the United States at $90 billion (1967 US dollars). It was further estimated that the use of alternative control measures could reduce these costs by about 50 percent. Waller (1969) estimated $4.5 billion dollars would be required for complete separation in Canada. Sewer separation is also unacceptable from a water quality standpoint since it does not

*Computational Hydraulics Group, McMaster University, Hamilton, Ontario.

reduce the pollutional load contributed by the direct stormwater runoff. Direct runoff contributes at least 44 percent of the total annual pollution load in the United States (Lager and Smith, 1974).

Real-Time Control

One of the most promising approaches to the CSO pollution problem is real-time control of combined sewer regulator structures. RTC of a CSO network involves processing incoming hydrometeorological data to operate overflow regulators such that the performance of the system during overflow events is improved. Combined sewer systems are particularly suited for RTC since they are seldom fully utilized, carrying less than 10% of capacity for roughly 90% of the time (Schilling, 1985). During most storms there will be unused volume within some major conduits. In-line storage is provided by somehow restricting flow just downstream of the regulator. This creates additional storage by backing up the water in the sewers. In order to effectively implement this concept, these upstream conduits must have flat grades, the interceptor must be high capacity, and an extensive control and monitoring system must be in place. Easy, automatic control of the restriction is essential, in order to avoid upstream flooding as the backwater levels rise.

Off-line storage/treatment facilities can be used to retain the first flush of polluted water, until it can be handled by the treatment plant. The relatively clean remaining stormwater may be diverted to the receiving waters, preferably where the risk of infection is low because of low rates of population exposure.

The basic equipment needed for a RTC system is as follows :

a) sensors to detect flow, water level, rainfall, and/or pollutant concentration,

b) circuitry and software to transform the signals from the sensors into numerical quantities,

c) circuitry and software to drive the control mechanism (usually a gate),

d) streamflow forecasting and/or rainfall forecasting software running in real-time,

e) a (micro)computer acting as both data logger and controller,

f) for an integrated RTC system, telemetry equipment for the communication of data between the various regulators.

Data Acquisition

A study was undertaken to investigate the feasibility of implementing local RTC of the Royal Avenue CSO diversion structure in Hamilton, Ontario (Stirrup and James, 1984). This research involved the design, construction, and testing of a microcomputer based data acquisition and control system, based on the Timex/Sinclair 1000 (TS1000) microcomputer. A complete description of the development of this system can be found elsewhere (Stirrup, 1986).

Drop counter precipitation sensors (Haro, 1984) and tipping bucket raingauges were interfaced with the TS1000, creating a low-cost microcomputer-based system for acquiring rainfall data in real-time. In addition to data acquisition, the software for the TS1000, written in BASIC, performs tasks such as: data decoding, data processing, graphics, communications, and runoff forecasting (James and Stirrup, 1986).

Accurate measurement of depth and/or discharge in sewers and at overflow structures is essential for the implementation of RTC of CSO. Measurements can be used on their own as a decision variable for control purposes, or used to update or correct for errors in the performance of rainfall-runoff forecasting models, often used in RTC. A pressure transducer and analogue/digital converter (ADC) to measure head have not been completely tested. However, a design for an 8-channel, 8-bit ADC, suitable for the TS1000, has been published (Holmes, 1984). This could be added to the existing I/O interface.

Water quality sensors are used very little in RTC of combined sewer systems. Shelley and Kirkpatrick (1975) discussed many of the problems encountered by others in their experiences with combined sewer samplers, and suggested the need for further research and testing. Presently, automatic water quality sampling is used to a much greater extent in the monitoring of receiving waters and STP operations.

Streamflow Forecasting

The ability to predict the quantity of inflows to the interceptor sewer is essential if advantage is to be gained over normal independent regulator operation (McPherson, 1980). Large scale deterministic computer models such as SWMM3 cannot be run in real-time at such a fine timestep, on a machine such as the TS1000. In any case such models do not provide updates of forecasts in a computationally simple manner (O'Connell, 1980), although some methods have been suggested (O'Connell and Clarke, 1981). On the other hand, simple input-output methods, such as transfer function (TF) models, can provide accurate forecasts with very little computational effort.

A simple discrete linear transfer function model, based upon previous rainfall and runoff was developed for the Royal Avenue basin, using flow records computed using the RUNOFF and TRANSPORT modules of PCSWMM3, in continuous mode. The continuous model was run at a five-minute timestep to accurately determine the point at which overflows begin and end. Each continuous simulation covered a six-month period (May to October), and took over 30 hours. The model was calibrated and validated in continuous mode, using data collected over a two year period. The identification of a more detailed forecast model was beyond the scope of this study, but would have to be considered before attempting to implement real-time control at Royal Avenue. Control options at Royal Avenue are minimal. The best solution would probably involve the use of some type of on-site storage. The TS1000-based system (or equivalent design) would appear to be suitable for control of such a facility.

Since the usual objective of RTC is to reduce the pollutional load exerted on receiving waters by CSO, the prediction of water quality is also of major concern. Unfortunately, water quality forecasting presents a much more difficult problem than that of discharge prediction. Beck (1977) cited the inability to accurately measure the various important water quality indices, the difficulty involved in manipulating wastewater characteristics for control purposes, and a lack of clearly defined water quality management objectives and standards as reasons for the additional complications.

Control Strategies

Often, water quality problems are dealt with indirectly in urban stormwater management. Common design criterion include:

1) mean annual CSO volume,
2) mean annual CSO frequency,
3) mean annual CSO duration
4) mean annual CSO pollutant concentration (eg. BOD),
5) mean annual CSO pollutant load,

Once the objectives of the RTC system have been identified, a control strategy must be developed. This involves defining system constraints, choosing a control policy, and finally evaluating various schemes, in order to select the best system.

Trotta et al. (1977) summarized some of the constraints involved:

1) capacities of interceptor and trunk sewers, storage facilities, and STP,
2) rainfall-runoff forecast models,
3) data acquisition system,
4) computer hardware and software,
5) control timestep,
6) human error and equipment malfunction and breakdown.

Control policies are generally classified as either reactive or adaptive (Trotta et al., 1977). Reactive policies are generally developed off-line, and simply react to the current discharge and storage conditions. This type of control is also referred to as local or set point control. Adaptive policies comprise on-line forecasting and optimization. Control is based on continuous updating of runoff (and/or water quality) forecasts in real-time. Real-time data acquisition is a very important component of an adaptive control scheme. The observed data is needed to update forecast model parameters, thereby improving system performance.

A manual of practice was written by the APWA (1970) detailing design applications, operation, and maintenance of combined sewer overflow regulators. The manual also provides guidelines for the application of instrumentation and control, aimed at achieving optimum performance at each individual site, and the integrated management of the system as a whole. Automatic regulators, including motor operated gates and cylinder operated gates are fully adjustable and thus provide great potential for real-time control.

Our study considered local RTC of isolated CSO regulators. As such it did not address the problem of integrating the operation of several such sites. In an integrated system, there is need for communication of information between various regulators. Although the cost of

microcomputers has dropped significantly in the past few years, data
telemetry or long distance networking remains relatively expensive.

Evaluation of Real-Time Control Strategies

In order to accurately assess the relative impacts of DWF, separate
stormwater, and CSO, and to properly evaluate various CSO management
alternatives, continuous simulation models should be utilized (Linsley
and Crawford, 1974; Sullivan et al., 1977; Shapiro et al., 1980;
Berlamont and VanLangenhove, 1981; James and Robinson, 1982; Geiger,
1984; Verworn and Winter, 1984).

In order to evaluate the performance of the TS1000 as a real-time
controller, its operation must be simulated continuously. The benefits of
various control strategies can then be measured in terms of some
objective, in this case the reduction of the volume and/or frequency of
polluted CSO.

A framework was developed for evaluating the long-term effectiveness
of various control schemes, for the Royal Avenue diversion structure.
Simulations should include all of the elements of a RTC system,
including:

1) data acquisition,
2) adaptive runoff forecasting,
3) control strategy,
4) flow diversion.

A program was written by the authors to perform the first three
tasks; flow diversion is handled by the TRANSPORT module of PCSWMM3.
Several simulations were performed for program verification, but the
results are not quoted here. Without an accurate rainfall-runoff forecast
model, the simulations are only of academic interest, and of little value
in evaluating the effectiveness of any RTC strategies for Royal Avenue.
In any case, these simulations only cover a period of six months, and
consider only the Royal Avenue structure as a control point. Evaluation
of control strategies should be based on long-term simulations, and
should include all active diversion structures in the modelling.

A detailed investigation of control strategies, including coordinating the operation of several downstream diversion structures, was
beyond the scope of this study. It provides only a framework for
developing more sophisticated evaluation methods. There is a great need
for a means of continuously evaluating complicated RTC schemes,
especially a methodology which considers both environmental and economic
impacts.

Conclusions

A low-cost rainfall data acquisition system has been developed,
based on the TS1000 microcomputer. Communication between the computer and
the environment is handled by an input/output interface, designed, built,
and tested by the authors. Software, written in BASIC, performs various
tasks including: data acquisition, data decoding, data processing,
graphics, communications, and runoff forecasting. The new hardware and

software was successfully integrated into our previous data acquistion system, providing an efficient environment for hydrologic modelling, making much needed rainfall data available more quickly and easily than in the past.

The study investigated the feasibility of applying this system to local real-time control of combined sewer overflow diversion structures. A framework, based on continuous modelling with PCSWMM3, was developed for evaluating the performance of the system, and was applied to the a diversion structure in Hamilton. To this end, a detailed hydrologic study of the Chedoke Creek Basin, in Hamilton, was carried out.

Further work needs to be done before this system could be applied to real-time control of combined sewer overflows. The bulk of this research should be aimed at adaptive rainfall-runoff forecasting. With an accurate forecast model, a suitable control strategy could be developed. Also, a study which properly evaluates potential real-time control schemes is needed.

The TS1000 provided a workable basis for the development of a data acquisition and control system, which proved to be both reliable and inexpensive. Unfortunately, midway through the study, Timex/Sinclair discontinued production of the TS1000. Although still available for as little as $30, the concepts developed here should now be adapted to some other inexpensive microcomputer, or even a hand-held calculator. This would require some minor modifications to the current input/output interface. Although Sinclair BASIC is somewhat non-standard, few software changes would be necessary, provided the chosen controller runs BASIC in ROM.

Finally, as the price of more powerful (16-bit) microcomputers continues to drop, it becomes feasible to consider their application to local as well as co-ordinated real-time control. Their added speed and memory allow more sophisticated rainfall-runoff modelling, potentially even permitting deterministic modelling with a program such as PCSWMM3, in real-time. It might also be possible, in a co-ordinated real-time control system, to network PC's together, over short distances, with each communicating vital hydrometeorological data, forecast information, and respective regulator states to a central server, or to each other. As costs decrease and software performance improves, the potential number of underground regulators so controlled will likely increase.

References

American Public Works Association, (1967). Problems of Combined Sewer Facilities and Overflows, for the U.S. Department of the Interior, Federal Water Pollution Control Association, Publication WP-20-11.

American Public Works Association, (1970). Combined Sewer Regulation and Management: A Manual of Practice, for the Federal Water Quality Administration, U.S. Department of the Interior, Water Pollution Control Research Series, Program No. 11022 DMU, 133 pp.

Beck, M.B., (1977). Real-Time Control of Water Quantity and Quality, Proceedings of the 1st International Workshop on Real-Time Hydrological Forecasting and Control, Institute of Hydrology, Wallingford, Oxon, U.K., pp. 237-256.

Berlamont, J. and Van Langenhove, G., (1981). Diversion Frequency in Combined Sewer Systems, Proceedings of the Second International Conference on Urban Storm Drainage, Urbana, Illinois, pp. 295-303.

Environment Canada and the Ontario Ministry of the Environment, (1980). Manual of Practice for Urban Drainage, Research Program for the Abatement of Municipal Pollution under Provisions of the Canada-Ontario Agreement on Great Lakes Quality, Research Report No. 104, 326 pp.

Field, R., (1982). An Overview of the U.S. Environmental Protection Agency's Storm and Combined Sewer Program Collection System Research, Water Resources, Vol. 16, No. 6, pp. 859-870.

Field, R., (1985). Urban Runoff: Pollution Sources, Control, and Treatment, Water Resources Bulletin, Vol. 21, No. 2, pp. 197-206.

Field, R. and Struzeski, E.J., (1972). Management and Control of Combined Sewer Overflows, Journal of the Water Pollution Control Federation, Vol. 44, No. 7, pp. 1393-1415.

Geiger, W.F., (1984). Characteristics of Combined Sewer Runoff, Proceedings of the Third International Conference on Urban Storm Drainage, Goteborg, Sweden, Vol. 3, pp.851-860.

Haro, H., (1984). Instrumentation for Rainfall Sampling, Ph.D. Thesis, McMaster University, 222 pp.

Holmes, R., (1984). ZX Analogue-to-Digital Converter, Electronics Today International, January issue, pp. 20-23.

James, W. and Robinson, M.A., (1982). Continuous Models Essential for Detention Design, Conference on Stormwater Detention Facilities Planning Design Operation and Maintenance, co-sponsored by the Engineering Foundation and the Urban Water Resources Research Council of the ASCE, Henniker, New Hampshire, pp. 163-175.

James, W. and Stirrup, D.M., (1986). Microcomputer-Based Precipitation Instrumentation, to be presented at the International Symposium on Comparison of Urban Drainage Models with Real Catchment Data, Dubrovnik, Yugoslavia, 12 pp.

Lager, J.A. and Smith, W.G., (1974). Urban Stormwater Management and Technology: An Assessment, National Environmental Research Center, Office of Research and Development, USEPA, Report No. EPA/670/2-74-040, 471 pp.

Linsley, R. and Crawford, N., (1974). Continuous Simulation Models in Urban Hydrology, Geophysical Research Letters, Vol. 1, No. 1, pp. 59-62.

Marsalek, J., (1972). Abatement of Pollution Due to Combined Sewer Overflows, Inland Waters Directorate, Department of the Environment, Ottawa, Canada, Technical Bulletin No. 66, 67 pp.

McPherson, M.B., (1980). Integrated Control of Combined Sewer Regulators Using Weather Radar, Municipal Environmental Research Laboratory. Office of Research and Development, USEPA, 87 pp.

O'Connell, P.E., (1980). Real-time Hydrological Forecasting and Control, Proceedings of First International Workshop, July 1977, Institute of Hydrology, Wallingford, Oxon, U.K., 264 pp.

O'Connell, P.E. and Clarke, R.T., (1981). Adaptive Hydrological Forecasting - A Review, Hydrological Sciences Bulletin, Vol. 26, No. 2, pp. 179-205.

Schilling, W., (1985). Real Time Control of Combined Sewers, Proceedings of the Specialty Conference on Computer Applications in Water Resources, Water Resources Planning and Management Division, ASCE, Buffalo, New York. pp. 499-510.

Shapiro, H.M., Blenk, J.B. and Allen, M.P., (1980). CSO Impact Determination by Long Term Simulation, Proceedings of the Stormwater Management Model (SWMM) User's Group Meeting, USEPA, Gainesville, Florida, pp. 142-189.

Shelley P.E. and Kirkpatrick, G.A., (1975). An Assessment of Automatic Sewer Flow Samplers, Municipal Environmental Research Laboratory, Office of Research and Development, USEPA, Report No. EPA-600/2-75-065, 350 pp.

Stirrup, D.M., (1986). Use of Low-Cost Microcomputers for Distributed Data Acquisition and Real-Time Control of Combined Sewer Overflows, M.Eng. thesis, McMaster University, Hamilton, Ontario, 190 pp.

Stirrup, D.M. and James, W., (1984). Real Time Control of Combined Sewer Overflows Using On-Site Microcomputers, Proceedings of the Third International Conference on Urban Storm Drainage, Goteborg, Sweden, Vol. 4, pp. 1457-1464.

Sullivan, R.H., Manning, M.J., Heaney, J.P., Huber, W.C., Medina, M.A. Jr., Nix, S.J. and Hasan, S.M., (1977). Nationwide Evaluation of Combined Sewer Overflows and Urban Stormwater Discharges. Volume I: Executive Summary, Municipal Environmental Research Laboratory, Office of Research and Development, USEPA, Report No. EPA-600/2-77-064a, 107 pp.

Trotta, P.D., Labadie, J.W. and Grigg, N.S., (1977). Automated Control Strategies for Urban Stormwater, Journal of the Hydraulics Division, ASCE, Vol. 103, No. HY12, pp. 1443-1459.

Verworn, W. and Winter, J., (1984). Long-Term Simulation of Combined Sewer Overflows, Proceedings of the Third International Conference on Urban Storm Drainage, Goteborg, Sweden, Vol. 3, pp. 899-908.

Waller, D.H., (1969). Combined Sewers in Canada, Engineering Journal, Vol. 52, No. 6, pp. 22-30.

Computer-Aided Analyis of Treatment Plant Hydraulics

by Peter J. Kolsky, A.M. ASCE,[1]

and Gary Friedman[2]

ABSTRACT

This paper describes software for the hydraulic analysis of water and wastewater treatment works. HADES (the Hydraulic Analysis, Design, and Evaluation System,) provides interactive analysis of individual hydraulic components, computations of hydraulic profiles through a plant, and estimates of flow splits. This paper discusses the theory behind the package, with particular attention to flow distribution. The paper concludes with a practical example of its application at a large modern plant.

NEED FOR HADES MODEL DEVELOPMENT

In May 1985, the firm of James M. Montgomery, Consulting Engineers, Inc. was contracted by the County of Sacramento to perform a Capacity Evaluation for the Sacramento Regional Wastewater Treatment Plant. The scope of work called for the development of a plant hydraulic model capable of determining not only water surface profiles at varying flows, but also the flow distribution through various parallel units. Particular concern, rooted in plant personnel's operational experience, was focussed on flow distribution to the secondary clarifiers.

Software already existed for the computation of hydraulic profiles through treatment plants (Peterson, Van Dusen, and Davis, 1977), but not for flow distribution. While engineers have long understood the fundamental principles of flow distribution, (Camp 1961, Camp and Graber 1968), the lengthy computations involved have limited their application severely. Only recently has software been developed for the simple case of flow splits over free-flowing weirs in a single distribution channel (Chao and Trussell 1980). This program is relatively simple, as the presence of free flow at the weirs eliminates the need to consider the effect of any portion of the plant downstream of the weirs.

The Sacramento Regional Wastewater Treatment Plant, however, has no such free flowing condition in its various distribution channels. As a result, analysis of flow distribution at the existing plant must

---

1. Senior Engineer, James M. Montgomery, Consulting Engineers, Inc., Pasadena, California

2. Software Engineer, James M. Montgomery, Consulting Engineers, Inc., Pasadena, California

consider all energy losses between the point at which flow splits and the point at which it rejoins; downstream losses and flows, and not just those within the distribution channel, must be considered. The need to consider such effects led to the development of the HADES software package.

The HADES package assists the engineer in performing three types of analysis:

(1) Interactive analysis of the performance of individual hydraulic elements (weirs, channels, orifices, etc.).

(2) Computation of Hydraulic and Energy Grade Lines throughout a treatment works at varying flows.

(3) Determination of flow distribution between parallel systems.

A key to the analysis of all three problems is the concept of a hydraulic element (Peterson, VanDusen, and Davis, 1977). A hydraulic element is defined by a relationship between flow and energy loss determined from the physical characteristics of the element, as influenced by certain boundary conditions. Prismatic conduits, transitions, weirs, orifices, and sluice gates are examples of hydraulic elements. Roughness coefficients, discharge coefficients and element geometry are examples of physical characteristics which determine the energy-flow relation for an element. Downstream Hydraulic and Energy Grade Lines are boundary conditions on the element which influence the nature of the energy-flow relation. HADES analyzes hydraulic elements using the same methods used by environmental engineers in their analysis of such components in computing profiles through treatment works. These methods are described in detail in the program documentation (James M. Montgomery, Consulting Engineers Inc., 1986).

Single Element Analysis. HADES interactive single element analysis simply uses the computer to solve the flow-energy loss relation of a given element once the engineer specifies the known and unknown parts of the relation. In general, the engineer can specify the flow and HADES will compute the energy loss and change in water surface, or the engineer can specify an energy loss and obtain a capacity.

Hydraulic Profile Computation. Engineers can prepare data files to describe a series of hydraulic elements, and perform an analysis of the whole system to obtain a hydraulic profile. The program starts with the user-specified flow, Energy and Hydraulic Grade Lines at the downstream end of the plant, and then computes the loss across each upstream element in sequence. (The program proceeds upstream because flow is assumed to be subcritical throughout the plant, and is therefore subject to downstream control.)

The computation of a hydraulic profile along a single path by this method requires knowledge of the flow rate all along the path. In cases where the flow divides and recombines, (e.g., at the entrance and exit of parallel process units), most engineers prepare the hydraulic profile for a single path only, and assume that the flow is uniformly split through parallel units.

The error introduced by ignoring the effect of flow distribution upon such profiles is small, and a profile so prepared is generally adequate to answer most of the fundamental questions about the hydraulic capacity of a plant. Single path profiles can show whether the plant can pass the required flow, how much pumping head is required at the upstream end, and whether the proposed design can insure adequate hydraulic control with no submergence of control points. HADES permits the engineer to obtain such profiles rapidly and systematically, and to check the effects of units being out of service for repair, future expansions with identical units, and/or different flow rates in a fraction of the time required to do it by hand.

Flow Distribution Analysis. If, however, the engineer needs to determine the flow distribution through parallel units, a different analysis is required. Flow through a series of parallel units in a treatment plant will distribute itself in accordance with continuity and energy principles.

o   The continuity principle requires the sum of individual flows through each of the parallel units to equal the total flow.

o   The energy principle requires that the energy loss between the upstream and downstream ends of each of the parallel paths must be equal.

The application of these principles is explained most clearly in terms of an example, shown in Figure 1.

A distribution channel divides flow between three sedimentation tanks, which overflow into a common collection channel. The various hydraulic elements making up the system (numbered 1 through 9 in the diagram) have been defined by the designer. The downstream EGL E_d shown in the figure is known, as is the total flow Q. The designer wants to know (1) the flow distribution between the three sedimentation tanks (i.e., q_1, q_2, and q_3), and (2) the upstream EGL E_u.

The flow will distribute itself in such a way that it will satisfy both continuity and energy principles. Specifically, there is one continuity equation:

$$q_1 + q_2 + q_3 = Q \tag{1}$$

There are also three independent energy equations which describe the upstream energy E_u in terms of the downstream energy E_d and the energy losses incurred by each of the elements (EL_j) along each of the three flow paths:

$$E_u = E_d + EL_9(q_1+q_2+q_3) + EL_4(q_1) + EL_1(q_1+q_2+q_3) \tag{2}$$

$$E_u = E_d + EL_9(q_1+q_2+q_3) + EL_8(q_2+q_3) + EL_5(q_2) + EL_2(q_2+q_3) \tag{3}$$
$$+ EL_1(q_1+q_2+q_3)$$

and

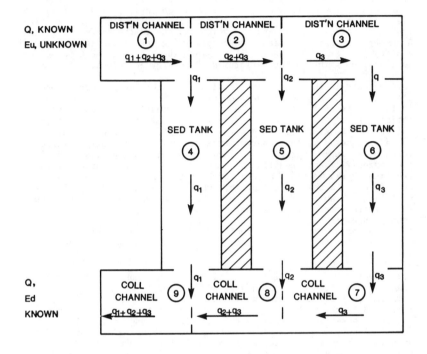

A TYPICAL FLOW DISTRIBUTION PROBLEM

FIGURE 1

$$E_u = E_d + EL_9(q_1+q_2+q_3) + EL_8(q_2+q_3) + EL_7(q_3) + EL_6(q_3) + EL_3(q_3)$$
$$+ EL_2(q_2+q_3) + EL_1(q_1+q_2+q_3) \tag{4}$$

Together, the continuity and energy principles yield four independent equations in four unknowns, $(E_u, q_1, q_2,$ and $q_3)$ and thus define the state of the system. HADES' flow distribution routines work to find the set of flows $q_1, q_2,$ and q_3 which (a) sum to the known total flow Q through the parallel paths (thus satisfying the continuity equation) and (b) provide consistent values for the upstream EGL over the various flow paths, (thus satisfying the energy equations).

The approach is in many ways similar to the Hardy-Cross method of iteration used in pipe network analysis. The idea is the same, which is to iterate on flows until a flow distribution is found that will satisfy both energy and continuity principles. A significant difference, however, lies in the nature of the energy "equations". For a pipe network, the energy relations are conveniently defined in terms of a simple hydraulics relationship between head loss and flow; the Hazen-Williams equation is the most commonly used. For a treatment works, a wide variety of head-flow relations exist, and the net effect of a change in flow through a single path made up of widely differing hydraulic elements cannot be found from a single equation. Furthermore, the presence of such discontinuous effects as weir submergence, critical depth and free fall energy losses complicate not only the computation of the individual head losses along a path, but also the response of the profile to small changes in independent variables.

The solution of simultaneous discontinuous non-linear algebraic equations is a topic of ongoing research in numerical analysis, and no fail-safe methods are currently known, or anticipated in the near future. Because of the complexity of the problem, computation times for such numerical methods are relatively long. HADES uses the numerical method known as BRENTM (More and Cosnard 1979, 1980) for the solution of simultaneous nonlinear algebraic equations which is relatively easy to implement and is reported to be relatively efficient.

LIMITATIONS AND ASSUMPTIONS

o <u>Subcritical Flow</u> is assumed throughout the plant, or at least "between" elements. Almost all treatment works actually operate in the subcritical flow regime, so this constraint is not in practice a severe one.

o <u>Momentum Effects</u> in flow distribution are not fully considered. Consider a distribution channel in which a single inflow is split over three outlet weirs to three sedimentation tanks. If the distribution channel inlet discharges directly opposite one of the weir outlets, then that outlet will receive more flow than the others. This is because the unchecked momentum of the flow from the inlet will tend to drive the flow over the directly opposite weir. HADES does not consider such momentum effects, but only the differences in energy. Momentum effects on discharge coefficients of orifices and side discharge weirs (Chao and Trussell, 1980) <u>are</u>

considered by the program.   In these cases, the discharge
coefficient is an explicit decreasing function of Froude number in
the distribution channel flow.

o Energy Losses in Distribution Channels   are neglected in the
analysis of flow distribution, although they will be considered in
any single path hydraulic profile.   This assumption is required to
keep the energy loss and flow accounting tractable.   In design of
treatment works, the losses along distribution channels are usually
kept deliberately low relative to other losses to improve the flow
distribution, so this assumption is a reasonable one.

More significant effects on flow distribution are (a) the increase
in head on weirs and orifices due to decreasing velocity head in
the downstream direction of a distribution channel, and (b) any
variation in orifice openings, weir elevations, etc. between
different paths.   The magnitude of frictional effects in the
distributional channel can easily be checked, but will usually be
found to be small.

o Distribution and Collection Channels must come in pairs. Each
collection channel is linked with a single upstream distribution
channel to define a single value of energy loss which is being
sought by the numerical method.   Similarly, each distribution
channel must be linked with a single downstream collection channel.
In addition, each distribution channel may only have one inflow,
and each collection conduit may only have one outflow.

o Assumptions within the Hydraulic Elements.   These are the commonly
used hydraulic assumptions required to make the problem of open
channel hydraulics tractable.   HADES in fact makes fewer of these
assumptions than design engineers do, and many effects are modelled
which the engineer usually neglects.

MODEL CALIBRATION

Preparation of input data files describing the physical
characteristics of the plant was the first step in applying the model.
Many of the physical characteristics required as input were readily
determined from a review of the construction drawings. Some, such as
discharge coefficients or minor loss coefficients, could only be
determined from a review of hydraulic test results. Such coefficients
were determined empirically, by adjusting their values until the
results predicted by the model corresponded to the observed results of
the hydraulic testing.   Calibration was performed using three
different flows was successful, predicting hydraulic performance well
within the margin of error of hydraulic measurements.

APPLICATION TO THE SECONDARY CLARIFIERS

Two early hypotheses to account for poor flow distribution to the
secondary clarifiers were that (a) momentum effects or (b) varying
head losses along the distribution channel could account for poor
distribution. (Momentum effects would be caused by the inertia of the
mixed liquor flowing by a clarifier entrance; if the velocity in the
channel were high, then the discharge to the clarifier would be

reduced, as the mixed liquor would continue to flow down the channel.) The momentum effect would predict higher clarifier discharges at the downstream end of the channel.   Variation in head losses along the distribution channel, however, would predict higher discharges at the upstream units, as these would have a higher energy at their inlets.
In April 1985 various preliminary hydraulic computations were performed to evaluate these hypotheses.   These revealed distribution channel velocities on the order of 0.5 ft/sec (0.1 m/sec), which were insufficient to generate either significant head loss differences between clarifiers, or a significant momentum effect. A later HADES analysis of a single battery of clarifiers confirmed this earlier analysis; if the clarifiers were identical, there was no basis for suspecting a poor flow distribution.

A third hypothesis was that slightly differing weir elevations could account for the problem. Given the extreme sensitivity of flow to the head on a v-notch weir, it was thought that a small variation in weir crest elevation among the clarifiers might result in a significant variation in the flow distribution.   HADES was used to examine this hypothesis.

HADES predicted that flow distribution to the secondary clarifier system is, in fact, relatively insensitive to variation in the weir crest elevations. Detailed examination of the output revealed that a change in weir crest elevation did not translate directly into a change in the head on the weir; on the contrary, the head on the weir (and consequently, the flow over it,) remained essentially the same, while the variation in energy was taken up in the orifice and inlet (feedwell) losses at the entrance to the clarifier. Halving the head on a v-notch reduces flow by more than a factor of 5; halving the head on an orifice only reduces the flow by a factor of 1.4. Thus if one weir crest is slightly higher than another, the reduced energy available to push flow through that clarifier is largely distributed over turbulent losses (e.g., orifice losses) which have a much less significant effect upon flow distribution.   In the test case run with a total effluent of 75 MGD split over 8 tanks, the effect of a 2" (0.05 m) variation in weir crest elevation was only on the order of 15%. A 2" variation is much greater than any detected in Sacramento. The normal energy loss across the entire clarifier from weir crest elevation to upstream channel was a total of 7.2" (0.18 m), of which only 1.2" (0.03 m) is head lost going over the weir. The assumed 2" (0.05 m) reduction in available energy thus primarily affects the upstream orifice losses, while the head on the weir remains relatively constant.   Tests with smaller variations in weir crest elevation confirmed this trend.

Field measurement of flow distribution to the secondary clarifiers was one of the principal objectives of the hydraulic testing program. These tests established that the second row of clarifiers received substantially less influent than did the other rows. Subsequent review of the construction drawings revealed the location of a diffused air sparger right at the entrance to the second row of clarifiers, which could create sufficient turbulence to impede entrance to these units. Experimentation with shut-off of these spargers improved the situation, although did not resolve it completely. This example is indicative of the importance of "real world" factors that cannot be modelled by a program such as HADES, and the need to temper mathematical prediction with field testing and engineering insight.

ACKNOWLEDGEMENTS

The authors gratefully acknowledge the assistance provided by the staff of the Sacramento Regional Wastewater Treatment Plant. In particular, the assistance of Bill Lewis and Mary Sanna in the planning and performance of the hydraulic testing program is greatly appreciated. Keith Conarroe, of JMM's Walnut Creek Office, played a key role in the hydraulic testing, the model calibration, and the overall development of the program from the user's perspective. Leadership and design of the software provided by Phil Naecker and Ali T. Diba are gratefully acknowledged, as are the effcrts of Bruce Sabin in the development of the screens interface and clear and readable output.

REFERENCES

1. Camp, T. R., "Applied Hydraulic Design of Treatment Plants, (Part 1)," in **Seminar Papers on Wastewater Treatment and Disposal,** edited by G. M. Reece, Boston Society of Civil Engineers, 231, Boston, Massachussetts. (cited in Benefield, L.D., Judkins, J.F., and Parr, A.D., **Treatment Plant Hydraulics for Environmental Engineers,** Prentice-Hall, Inc., Englewood Cliffs, NJ, 1984.)

2. Camp, T. R., and Graber, S. D., "Dispersion Corduits", **Journal of the Sanitary Engineering Division,** ASCE, 94, 169, 1968.

3. Chao, J. L., and Trussell, R. R., "Hydraulic Design of Flow Distribution Channels," **Journal of the Enviror.mental Engineering Division,** ASCE, 106, 321, 1980.

4. James M. Montgomery, Consulting Engineers, Inc., **User Manual for HADES Version 1.0,** Pasadena CA, 91101.

5. More, J. J., and Cosnard, M. Y., "Numerical Solution of Nonlinear Equations", **ACM Transactions on Mathematical Software,** Vol. 5, No. 1 (March, 1979), pp. 64-85.

6. More, J. J., and Cosnard, M. Y., "BRENTM, A Fortran Subroutine for the Numerical Solution of Systems of Nonlinear Equations." **ACM Transactions on Mathematical Software,** Vol. 6, No. 2, (June,1980), pp. 240-251.

7. Peterson, D.J., VanDusen K.W., and Davis, A.L., **Computer Analysis of Hydraulic Elements Commonly Encountered in Water and Wastewater Treatment Plants, (HYDRO Version 4, Mod 1),** CF2M Hill Engineers, Corvallis, Oregon, November 1977.

SUBJECT INDEX
Page number refers to first page of paper.

Accidents, 530
Activated carbon treatment, 1799
Activated sludge, 181, 1073, 1089
Administration, 1608
Advection, 1647, 1807
Aeration, 706, 738, 1057, 1630
Africa, 661
Aggradation, 1678
Agreements, 1516
Agricultural wastes, 358, 1751
Agriculture, 366, 1147, 1358, 1388, 1395, 1484, 1492, 1500, 1759, 1968
Air water interactions, 1057
Algae, 637
Algorithms, 195, 806, 966, 2017, 2025
Alluvial channels, 1928
Alluvial fans, 203, 863, 890, 1428
Alluvial streams, 1686, 1928
Alluvium, 2060
Ammonia, 1718
Analysis, 1743, 1872
Analytical techniques, 1, 427
Aquatic habitats, 1702, 1759, 1976, 2106
Aquatic plants, 1984
Aqueducts, 863
Aquifers, 97, 97, 105, 121, 251, 320, 336, 966, 973, 1374, 1382, 1407, 1413, 1516, 1544, 1783, 2060
Arid lands, 890, 1403
Arizona, 890, 2017, 2060
Artificial intelligence, 158, 174
Artificial recharge, 244, 310, 628, 1829
Assessments, 1615
Australia, 2120, 2128
Automation, 546, 785, 1202, 2017, 2025

Bank erosion, 1678
Barrier islands, 754
Basins, 59, 1544
Bays, 1556
Beaches, 1468
Benefit cost analysis, 2106
Biochemical oxygen demand, 1309
Biofilm, 1718
Biological treatment, 1718
Boating, 714
Boundary layer, 404, 420
Brazil, 1564
Breaking, 1225, 1726
Breakwaters, 771

Calibration, 443, 1823
California, 612, 791, 863, 1420, 1783
Canada, 1452, 2143, 2158, 2173
Canal linings, 1395
Canals, 97, 121, 858, 863, 878, 897, 2033, 2041
Cancer, 637
Case reports, 514, 858, 1256, 1351, 1853, 1912
Catchments, 1187
Cavitation, 706, 1049
Channel flow, 398
Channel improvements, 1179, 1476
Channel morphology, 1928
Channelization, 1686, 2000
Channels, waterways, 799, 1694
Chemical wastes, 738
Chemicals removal, 738
Chicago, 1860
China, People's Republic of, 690, 2136
Chlorides, 97
Chlorination, 1081
Classification, 420, 1694
Climatic changes, 35, 43, 51, 59
Climatology, 219, 1845
Cloud seeding, 2066
Coal mining, 81
Coastal engineering, 763, 779
Coastal morphology, 987
Cohesive sediment, 404
Colorado River, 546, 598, 855, 878
Columbia River, 557
Combined sewers, 1098, 1309
Community relations, 1374
Comparative studies, 675, 1598
Composting, 1639
Computer aided drafting (CAD), 1655
Computer analysis, 390, 484, 1106
Computer applications, 374, 785, 806, 1572, 1860
Computer models, 310, 459, 557, 858, 911, 1317, 1335, 1662, 1710, 1815, 1853
Computer programs, 552, 667, 675, 1194, 1435, 1452, 1710, 1968, 2009
Computer software, 390
Computerized control systems, 1098, 2017, 2025
Computerized simulation, 552, 870, 949, 1670, 1815

Conservation, 129
Consolidation, 121
Constraints, 1011
Construction, 66, 73, 134, 294, 738
Consultants, 2114
Consulting services, 1655
Contaminants, 966, 1003, 1301, 1799
Continental shelves, 1301
Control, 2033
Control systems, 546
Coral reefs, 1622
Cost effectiveness, 2049
Cost estimates, 475
Crop production, 129, 2206
Crops, 620, 1407
Cross sections, 675
Culverts, 958
Currents, 1057
Cutoffs, 1678, 1702

Dam breaches, 1
Dam safety, 27
Damage estimation, 754
Damage prevention, 244
Dams, 81, 653, 698, 706, 722, 1049,
    1065, 1187, 1435, 2025
Dams, earth, 1, 1837
Data acquisition, 382
Data collection, 785, 1098, 2049
Database management systems, 382,
    390, 398, 2009
Databases, 166
Debris, 10, 19, 203, 211, 219, 235
Decision making, 2082
Deposition, 1775
Design, 277, 435, 722, 738, 958, 1089,
    1403, 1598, 1872
Design standards, 763
Design storms, 925, 949
Detention basins, 958, 1179
Detention reservoirs, 919
Deterioration, 1726
Developing countries, 2082
Development, 73, 89, 1395
Dewatering, 995
Discharge, 682, 1582
Disinfection, 1081
Dispersion, 1647
Disposal, 1003
Dissolved oxygen, 1041, 1049, 1309,
    1630
Distributed processing, 166
Diversion, 2120
Diversion structures, 1098, 2025
Drainage, 35, 129, 143, 344, 358, 412,
    890, 919, 925, 933, 1179

Drainage systems, 134, 352, 1187,
    1853
Drains, 352, 722
Drawdown, 1524
Dredge spoil, 667, 987, 1003
Dredging, 645, 667, 863, 987, 995,
    1003
Drilling, 1743
Droughts, 661, 1615, 1896, 1904,
    1912, 1920, 2128, 2198
Dynamic models, 1823
Dynamic programming, 565, 806,
    1026, 1033, 1382
Dynamics, 1452

Earth fills, 1
Ecology, 1582, 1984, 1992
Economic analysis, 467, 1366, 1476,
    1536
Economic benefits, 1968
Economic feasibility, 105
Economics, 134, 1516
Ecosystems, 637, 2158
Education, 1240
Egypt, 661
Emergency services, 903, 1734
Energy budget, 855
Energy dissipation, 420, 2033
Energy dissipators, 698
Engineering firms, 2114
Engineers, 2114
Entrainment, 404
Environmental impacts, 89, 995,
    1544, 1630, 2098
Environmental Protection Agency,
    1710
Environmental quality, 1351, 1702,
    1890
Equipment, 484
Erosion, 1, 412, 1123, 2189
Erosion control, 1017, 1147, 1155
Estimation, 682, 847, 973
Estuaries, 1285, 1309, 1564, 1572
Europe, 1662
Evacuation, 903
Evaluation, 1500, 1880
Evapotranspiration, 823, 831, 847,
    855, 1528
Experimental data, 498
Experimentation, 771
Expert systems, 158, 174, 181, 187,
    195

Failures, 484
Feasibility studies, 1476
Federal project policy, 152

Federal role, 590, 1155, 1210
Fertilizers, 1751
Field investigations, 1590
Filtration, 612
Financing, 1210, 1218
Finite difference method, 1647
Fires, 1468
Fish habitats, 1959, 2000, 2089
Fish reproduction, 1968
Fisheries, 1992, 2098
Flocculation, 612
Flood, 27
Flood control, 158, 244, 492, 890,
    897, 903, 919, 933, 958, 1179, 1187,
    1194, 1460, 1476, 1860, 1943, 2151
Flood damage, 203
Flood damages, 1428, 1845
Flood drainage, 1468
Flood forecasting, 19, 203, 443, 1164,
    1172, 1202
Flood frequency, 2198
Flood irrigation, 320
Flood peaks, 897, 941
Flood plain studies, 19, 675
Flood routing, 10, 227, 443, 675, 903
Flooding, 890, 941, 1428, 1845, 2128
Floods, 682, 1920, 1951
Florida, 754
Flow characteristics, 10, 235
Flow profiles, 10
Fluid flow, 27, 227
Fluid mechanics, 10
Flumes, 1057
Flushing, 653, 1976
Fluvial hydraulics, 1686, 1928, 1959
Food supply, 637
Forecasting, 1662
Forests, 269
Forms, 134
Frequency analysis, 1710
Fresh water, 251, 1622
Furrow irrigation, 1131, 1139, 1147

Gates, 2017
Government policies, 129
Grade control structures, 714
Grains, crops, 1403
Grasses, 831
Gravel, 1935
Great Lakes, 1003, 1293, 1815, 2158
Greenhouse effect, 35
Groundwater, 97, 105, 121, 143, 310,
    320, 336, 1413, 1524, 1528, 1536,
    1544, 2049, 2057
Groundwater flow, 973
Groundwater management, 328,
    1407, 1516, 1670, 1783

Groundwater pollution, 195, 328,
    506, 514, 524, 738, 745, 966, 981,
    1500, 1751, 1783, 2060
Groundwater quality, 498, 506, 628,
    745, 1484, 1492, 1500, 1508, 1751,
    1791, 1880, 2060, 2206
Groundwater recharge, 261
Groundwater supply, 328
Guidelines, 763, 2000
Gullies, 412

Harbors, 771, 987
Hazardous waste, 506, 514, 1374,
    1783, 1791
Hazardous wastes, 1880
Hazards, 19
Heavy metals, 514, 995
Highway design, 2000
Humid areas, 1508
Hurricanes, 754, 779, 897
Hydraulic design, 730, 1106, 1403
Hydraulic gradients, 97, 2033
Hydraulic jump, 714, 1041
Hydraulic models, 390, 698, 730, 771,
    1106, 1582, 2009
Hydraulics, 27, 35, 443, 451, 958,
    1106, 1476, 1951, 1984
Hydrodynamics, 1, 1285, 1309, 1572,
    1590
Hydroelectric power, 81, 89, 302
Hydroelectric power generation, 66,
    73, 573, 1837, 2098
Hydroelectric powerplants, 66, 73,
    277, 284, 294, 552, 565, 730, 1049,
    1065, 1317
Hydrogeology, 105, 2049
Hydrographs, 682, 897, 1951
Hydrologic data, 2128, 2198
Hydrologic models, 166, 336, 382,
    451, 690, 791, 949, 1098, 1325
Hydrology, 35, 51, 59, 174, 219, 443,
    661, 785, 933, 995, 1382, 1468,
    1516, 1837, 1904, 2098, 2106, 2120

Identification, 195
Illinois, 682, 1444
Impoundment, 1065
Impoundments, 412
India, 1407
Indian reservations, 73, 1880
Industrial wastes, 524
Inflow, 2025
Information systems, 366
Infrastructure, 467, 475, 538, 1210,
    1218
Injection wells, 251, 628, 1528

Inorganic contaminants, 1935, 2057
Installation, 722
Institutions, 1598
Instream flow, 1358, 1976, 2089, 2098, 2106
Instrumentation, 404
Intakes, 858
Interactive graphics, 1670
International commissions, 2151, 2158
International treaties, 2143
International waters, 2143
Irrigation, 143, 284, 302, 336, 344, 598, 620, 812, 817, 823, 1123, 1388, 1395, 1484, 1492, 1500, 1508, 1528, 1536, 1896, 2098, 2120, 2151
Irrigation systems, 2041, 2206
Islands, 1351, 1622

Kansas, 919, 933
Kinematic wave theory, 451

Laboratory tests, 1951
Lakes, 43, 51, 244, 546, 667, 1065, 1556, 1590, 1823, 1845
Land application, 1639, 1751
Land reclamation, 995
Land treatment, 435, 1081, 2057
Land usage, 1388, 1759, 1890
Land usage planning, 754
Landslides, 27, 211, 219
Laws, 1890
Leaching, 1508
Legal factors, 812
Legislation, 1536, 2066, 2074
Levees, 1678
Liability, 235
Linear programming, 573
Litigation, 582, 1516
Local governments, 152
Louisiana, 1853
Lysimeters, 823

Maintenance, 475, 484, 1210, 1225, 1976
Maintenance costs, 492
Management, 187, 1544, 1662, 1702, 2158
Management methods, 1147
Management systems, 1508
Mapping, 19, 211
Markov chains, 1896
Mass transport, 973, 1285
Master plans, 1853
Mathematical models, 227, 390, 1011, 1017, 1301, 1343, 1366, 1524, 1630, 1647, 1815, 1860, 2120, 2128

Mathematical programming, 1011
Meandering streams, 1702, 1928
Meanders, 1694, 1702
Measurement, 1041, 1172, 1935
Meteorological data, 2128
Mexico, 66, 538, 1388
Microcomputers, 779, 1098, 1194, 1256, 1775
Migration, 1694
Mine wastes, 427
Mississippi River, 1694, 1984
Mixing, 1647
Model analysis, 398
Model studies, 251, 730, 1435, 1951
Models, 320, 427, 714, 839, 966, 1179, 1285, 1309, 1564, 1572, 1759
Monitoring, 745, 1172, 1202, 1767, 1880, 2060
Monte Carlo method, 1033
Mud, 19, 227, 235
Multiple purpose projects, 1343
Multiple regressions, 1420
Municipal wastes, 435, 1073
Municipal water, 812, 817

National Weather Service, 1164, 1202
Navigation, 799, 1564, 1686, 1943
Nebraska, 1358
Netherlands, 987
Network analysis, 2009
Network design, 1272, 1280, 1407, 1734
Networks, 166
New Jersey, 1615
Nile River, 661
Nitrates, 1492
Nitrification, 1718
Nitrogen, 1718, 1767
Nonpoint pollution, 152, 366, 1484, 1775, 1890
Numerical calculations, 1807
Numerical models, 27, 1943, 2049
Nutrient loading, 1767
Nutrients, 637, 1582

Objectives, 2151
Ocean disposal, 1301
Oil spills, 1815, 1880
Open channel flow, 1943, 1959
Open channels, 1057, 1686
Operating criteria, 1325
Operation, 552, 557, 565, 1026, 1912
Optimal design, 1280
Optimal use, 1343
Optimization, 310, 352, 1011, 1026
Optimization models, 181, 565, 573, 1017, 1033, 1280, 1872, 1912

Organic chemicals, 981, 2057
Organizational policies, 1598
Organizations, 2074
Overflow, 1098
Overland flow, 1081
Overseas assignments, 2114
Overtopping, 1476
Oxygenation, 1065

Parameters, 682
Percolation, 498
Performance, 451, 1073
Permeability, 97
Pesticides, 1492, 1508, 1751
Physical models, 27
Piers, 530
Pipelines, 2041, 2181
Pipes, 1225
Planning, 89, 187, 374, 492, 538, 791,
    1248, 1264, 1335, 1351, 1407, 1516,
    1536, 1608, 1670, 1829, 2009, 2082
Plumes, 427, 2060
Policies, 1382, 1890
Pollutants, 981, 1293, 1751, 1807
Ponds, 435
Pools, 1678
Ports, 538
Potable water, 1256, 1718, 1791
Precipitation, atmospheric, 459, 911,
    2066
Predictions, 779, 1420, 1428
Probabilistic models, 1225, 1726
Probability, 530, 1248
Problem solving, 1468, 1845, 2082
Productivity, 1131
Program evaluation, 66
Programming, 1335, 1366
Programs, 1164
Project evaluation, 277
Project management, 284, 294, 730
Project planning, 66, 294
Projects, 1374
Public works, 1218, 1240
Pumped storage, 81, 573
Pumping, 328, 336, 1413
Pumping stations, 546
Pumping tests, wells, 1524
Pumps, 1524

Rain gages, 911
Rainfall, 382, 839, 897, 933, 1164,
    1172, 1452, 1896, 2066
Rainfall-runoff relationships, 682,
    911
Rangeland, 839
Reclaimed water, 628

Reclamation, 412
Recreational facilities, 1468
Recycling, 358
Regional planning, 261, 1366
Regression analysis, 1444
Regulations, 1791
Rehabilitation, 467, 475, 524, 1225,
    1232, 1240, 1395, 1853, 2181
Reliability, 1225, 1256, 1726, 1734
Reliability analysis, 1264, 1272
Reliability resources, 1248
Remote sensing, 89, 174, 366, 690
Repairing, 284, 1210, 1726
Research, 1582, 1655
Research needs, 1240
Reservoir operation, 799, 1317, 1325,
    1343, 1662, 1904
Reservoir sedimentation, 645, 653,
    1435
Reservoir storage, 1413, 1622
Reservoir systems, 557, 653, 870,
    1026, 1335, 1343
Reservoirs, 187, 459, 552, 1366, 1823,
    1837, 1992
Responsibility, 235
Return flow, 2151
Reviews, 1608
Rheology, 10
Risk, 1734
Risk acceptance, 1791
Risk analysis, 203, 211
River basins, 310, 459, 557, 823,
    1662, 1670, 2074
River systems, 870, 1647, 1702
Rivers, 443, 714, 1358, 1476, 1572,
    1582, 1630, 1678, 1767, 1815, 2025,
    2120
Runoff, 690, 925, 941, 1194, 1759,
    1904
Runoff coefficient, 1460
Runoff forecasting, 113, 174, 366,
    459

Safety factors, 1089
Salinity, 143, 344, 1556
Salt water intrusion, 97, 97, 105, 328
Salt water-freshwater interfaces, 97
Salts, 344
Scheduling, 492, 565, 573
Scour, 690, 1435
Screening, 2041
Screens, 858, 2041
Sea level, 35
Sea walls, 763
Seasonal variations, 43
Secondary flow, 870, 1057

Sediment concentration, 667
Sediment control, 420, 1147, 1155
Sediment deposits, 645, 858, 1435,
  1935, 1984
Sediment load, 427, 645, 667, 1444,
  1992
Sediment production, 1123
Sediment transport, 404, 858, 870,
  1017, 1293, 1444, 1582, 1686, 1928,
  1959, 1992
Sediment yield, 398, 863, 1420, 1759,
  2189
Sedimentation, 858, 863, 870, 878,
  1123, 1139, 1943, 1984
Seepage, 1528
Selection, 1524
Selenium, 143
Sensitivity analysis, 2049
Sensors, 382
Settling velocity, 404
Sewage disposal, 2136
Sewage effluents, 1630
Sewage sludge, 1301
Sewage treatment plants, 484
Sewers, 1232
Shear effects, 1718
Shear stress, 1976
Ship bridge collisions, 530
Shore protection, 763
Silts, 645, 653, 878
Simulation, 771, 791, 925, 1026, 1285,
  1358, 2089
Simulation models, 565, 870, 1335,
  1775, 1896, 1912, 1959, 2082
Slope stability, 211
Sludge treatment, 181, 1639
Snowmelt, 174, 459
Soil conservation, 1155, 1968
Soil erosion, 1131, 1139, 1775
Soil loss, 1123
Soil mechanics, 211
Soil pollution, 506, 981, 2057
Soil properties, 1131
Soil water, 690
Soils, 498
Solar radiation, 1920
Sorption, 981
Spacing, 352
Spillways, 698, 706, 1041, 2025
Sprinkler irrigation, 1139, 2189
State government, 1155
State laws, 582, 607
Statistical analysis, 745
Statistical models, 1896
Steady state, 352
Stochastic models, 791, 1920
Stochastic processes, 435, 1904

Storage, 435, 987
Storm drains, 1187, 1460, 1468
Storm runoff, 451, 1460
Storm sewers, 919, 933
Storm surges, 779
Storm water, 1460
Storms, 933, 1293, 1452
Stormwater, 890
Stormwater management, 35, 158,
  919, 933, 941, 949, 1710
Stream channels, 1951, 1976
Stream erosion, 1710
Streambed armoring, 1928
Streamflow, 219, 269, 1049, 1325,
  2089, 2106
Streams, 1382, 1444, 1935, 1959, 2000
Strip mining, 1017
Subsidence, 121
Sunspots, 2198
Surface irrigation, 2189
Surface runoff, 1845
Surface waters, 1528
Surge, 1743
Surveys, 1743
Suspended sediments, 1147, 1590
Synthetic hydrology, 1026
System reliability, 1089
Systems engineering, 2136

Tailings, 427
Taiwan, 645, 653, 698, 706, 1608,
  1622
Teaching, 1880
Technology transfer, 2114
Tertiary treatment, 612, 620
Texas, 1172
Thermal power plants, 81
Three-dimensional models, 1943
Tidal energy, 1622
Tidel hydraulics, 1572
Time series analysis, 113, 1325, 1920
Topsoil, 1131
Toxic wastes, 358, 506, 1783, 1880
Transport phenomena, 966, 1807
Trees, 1639
Tributaries, 1293
Trickle irrigation, 1403
Tropical regions, 1992
Tunnels, 284, 706
Turbines, 1049
Two-dimensional, 1564
Two-dimensional models, 1943
Typhoons, 698, 779

Uncertainty principles, 1011
Underground storage, 251, 261, 1413,
  1622

United Kingdom, 1232
United States, 2143, 2158
Unsteady flow, 443
Urban areas, 925, 941
Urban studies, 1264
Urbanization, 1187, 1428, 1710
Utah, 903
Utilities, 1256, 1264

Variability, 1073
Vegetation, 831, 839, 847, 855
Vibration measurement, 484
Viscoplasticity, 10
Volume change, 43

Waste disposal, 412, 2136
Waste site cleanup, 514
Wastewater, 637
Wastewater disposal, 435, 498
Wastewater management, 1218
Wastewater treatment, 181, 524, 612,
 620, 1011, 1073, 1081, 1089, 1106,
 1351, 1639, 1872
Water allocation policy, 1608
Water conservation, 492, 598, 1187,
 1615, 1968, 2173
Water consumption, 831, 839, 847,
 855, 1615
Water costs, 1791
Water demand, 839, 1218, 1615, 2089
Water distribution, 467, 475, 546,
 1232, 1256, 1264, 1272, 1280, 1734,
 2009, 2017, 2181
Water law, 582, 590, 607, 812
Water level fluctuations, 43, 244,
 2206
Water levels, 97
Water loss, 113
Water management, 302, 785, 1492,
 1615, 2173
Water pipelines, 1225, 1726, 1743
Water plans, 2136
Water policy, 1358, 1799, 2173
Water pollution, 152, 366, 524, 1293,
 1301, 1484, 1807, 1935
Water pollution control, 158, 1351
Water pollution sources, 1799
Water quality, 344, 506, 949, 1003,
 1049, 1285, 1309, 1407, 1556, 1572,
 1590, 1670, 1767, 1823, 1860, 2000,
 2136
Water quality control, 374, 1791,
 1890
Water quality standards, 1799
Water reclamation, 620, 2074
Water resources, 59, 187, 261, 302,
 374, 785, 791, 1317, 1335, 1366,
 1413, 1544, 1655, 1670, 1904, 2082,
 2098, 2128, 2143
Water resources development, 785
Water resources management, 269, 590,
 607, 661, 799, 806, 812, 1033, 1382,
 1528, 1556, 1598, 1608, 1662, 1829,
 1860, 2066, 2074, 2089, 2151
Water reuse, 612, 620, 628
Water rights, 261, 582, 598, 812, 817,
 1528, 1536, 1837, 2143
Water sampling, 745, 2060
Water shortage, 1615, 1622
Water supply, 51, 97, 269, 467, 590,
 661, 817, 831, 878, 1210, 1218,
 1317, 1351, 1413, 1516, 1536, 1544,
 1783, 1837, 1860, 2074, 2106, 2136,
 2173
Water supply forecasting, 557
Water supply systems, 1240, 1248,
 1272, 1734, 1912
Water surface profiles, 1194
Water table, 2206
Water transfer, 582, 590, 598, 607,
 2120
Water transportation, 420
Water treatment, 358, 1799
Water treatment plants, 738, 1106
Water use, 310, 336, 817, 823, 831,
 847, 855, 1388, 1556, 1564, 1829
Water waves, 27
Water works, 1264
Water yield, 1759
Watershed, 398
Watershed management, 269, 1992
Watersheds, 113, 870, 1017, 1179,
 1420
Waterways, 530, 799, 1984
Waterworks, 1232, 1256
Wave forces, 763
Wave height, 771
Wave propagation, 1951
Weather forecasting, 1202
Weather modification, 2066
Weirs, 958, 2033
Wells, 498
Wetlands, 129

AUTHOR INDEX
Page number refers to first page of paper.

Abed, S. A. A., 328
Abraham, Charles E., 552
Abt, S. R., 1702
Abt, Steven R., 412
Adams, J. Rodger, 1984
Adams, John R., 1003
Adams, Rodger, 1444
Adeff, Sergio E., 870
Ahmad, Shahnawaz, 738
Ahmed, Nazeer, 81
Ainsworth, Bruce, 730
Allen, L N., 823
Alonso, C. V., 1959
Alvarez, Desi, 1428
Amar, Abnish C., 1420, 1435
Anderson, Loren R., 211
Anderson, M. Michael, 2181
Anderson Richard V., 1984
Andreou, Stefanos, 1225, 1726
Archer, Michael C., 1335
Arora, Sushil K., 791
Asano, Takashi, 612
Austin, Lloyd H., 1845

Bari, Muhammad F., 1366
Barnes, Geroge W., Jr., 791
Barrett, Curtis B., 1164
Bax, Virginia E., 911
Baxter-Potter, Wanada, 366
Bedford, Keith W., 404, 661, 1293
Beieler, Roger W., 2041
Beim, Gina K., 1248
Belville, James D., 1164
Berlandy, Richard, 1351
Berlien, Robert G., 738
Bhowmik, Nani G., 1444, 1582, 1984
Bird, John W., 607
Bird, Sandra, 1285
Bissell, Vernon C., 1202
Blatchley, Ronald K., 812
Blevins, Melvin L., 1544
Blumberg, Alan F., 1309
Bohac, C. E., 1049
Bonner, Vernon, 1194
Born, Robert H., 1837
Bradley, James C., 1476
Bradley, Jeffrey B., 1976
Branski, Joel M., 1564, 1807
Brill, E. Downey, Jr., 181, 1011, 1872
Brockway, C. E., 823, 1147
Brockway, Charles E., 2189
Brown, David L., 1179

Buchberger, Steven G., 435
Buckley, Kebba, 890
Bulkley, Jonathan W., 2136
Buras, Nathan, 1382
Burke, Christopher B., 1476
Burkett, Edmund B., 799
Burman, R. D., 823, 831
Buyalski, Clark P., 2025

Cada, Glenn F., 2098
Call, Charles H., Jr., 903, 2000
Campbell, G. S., 847
Carden, Richard S., 1743
Carter, D. L., 1131, 1147
Ceran, Turan, 1853
Chadwick, D. George, Jr., 1556
Chang, T. J., 1896
Chang, Tiao J., 113
Chantrill, Ralph L., 2198
Chaturvedi, Abinash C., 1407
Chen, Cheng-lung, 10
Chen, Kan, 2136
Cheng, Y., 698, 706
Chiang, Wen-Li, 27
Chow, Bruce M., 374
Christopher, J. N., 134
Chu, Wen-sen, 966
Chung, Francis I., 1335
Chung-Yue, Fung, 1608
Clark, Robert, 1225
Clemmens, A. J., 2033
Clyde, Calvin G., 244
Coe, James Q., 565
Cohen, Wendy L., 506
Colgan, Patrick, 730
Collins, John G., 1
Colston, Newton V., 2106
Constantine, Kenneth, 1089
Convery, John J., 1073
Cooper, Robert C., 620
Cotner, Don, 763
Coufal, Gene L., 1544
Cowan, M. S., 1904
Cox, William C., 590
Cox, William E., 1890
Crandell, Christopher M., 1743
Crouch, Craig E., 1317
Cullinane, M. John, Jr., 1264
Cummins, B. K., 134

Datta, Bithin, 195
Davis, D. A., 2143

Davis, J. L., 1049
Dawdy, David R., 1428
De Jesus, Jose A. O., 1564
de Rooij, M., 987
Deb, Arun K., 475
Debevec, Lewis, Jr., 484
DeCoursey, D. G., 1759
Dedrick, A. R., 2033
Delleur, J. W., 1896
Delwiche, Gregory K., 557
Demissie, Misganaw, 1582
Di Toro, Dominic M., 1309
Diaz, Henry F., 43
Dillon, Frank S., 1984
Dortch, Mark, 1285
Dresnack, Robert, 1615
Duan, Ning, 1272
Duffy, Christopher J., 244
Dunn, Alan, 158
Duplancic, Nenad, 779
Dworsky, Leonard B., 2158
Dzurik, Andrew A., 754

Easton, James L., 1187
Eichinger, Robert A., 1829
Eiker, Earl E., 785
El Zawahary, Alaa, 667
Ellis, Tracey J., 89
Engman, E. T., 174
Erlewine, Terry L., 336
Evans, W. A., Jr., 1172
Everest, William R., 1837
Everts, Craig H., 763

Falk, John A., 412
Fattah, Qais Nuri, 1630
Fattorelli, Sergio, 1662
Fead, Terri L., 451
Ferreira, Luis C. H., 1564
Fiddes, David, 1232
Finney, Brad A., 1033
Fitzgerald, Steven D., 1179
Fitzpatrick, James J., 1309
Fleming, George, 995, 1662
Frasier, Gary W., 839
Fread, D. L., 443
Freedman, Paul L., 2136
French, Richard H., 1655, 1823
Frevert, D. K., 1904
Friedman, Gary, 1106
Fukumori, E., 328

Gallagher, James W., Jr., 1065
Garbrecht, J., 1759, 1968
Garcia, Moseis, 1544
Gatwood, Elden J., 1420

Gay, Lloyd W., 855
Georgeson, Duane L., 1791
Geselbracht, James J., 181
Gibney, Richard D., 941
Gidley, James S., 1366
Gilbert, Jerome B., 1210
Gilliland, Martha W., 366, 1358, 1639
Glover, J. Ed, 1694
Goldman, C. R., 1992
Goldman, Jonathon C., 261
Golub, Eugene, 1615
Gooch, Robert S., 546
Goodrich, James A., 1256
Goranflo, H. M., 1049
Graves, Albert L., 546
Green, Sargeant J., 2057
Grigg, Neil S., 1240
Gubler, Laurnal, 911
Gulliver, John S., 1041, 1057

Hall, Brad R., 203
Hall, Ross, 1285
Hall, Stephen K., 143
Halliday, R. A., 2143
Halverson, Martin J., 1057
Hamilton, Douglas L., 227
Hanna, George P., Jr., 1799
Harboe, Ricardo, 1026
Hardt, Charles L., 451
Harleman, D. R. F., 1590
Harshbarger, E. D., 1049
Hartman, Robert K., 1202
Hasfurther, Victor R., 320, 1935
Hayes, Stanley J., 277
Heagler, Mary Gay, 981
Heefner, Scott, 203
Helweg, Otto J., 1403, 1524
Hill, R. W., 823
Hinks, Robert W., 1829
Hobbs, Benjamin F., 1248
Hofer, R. D., 2143
Hoffman, Robert E., 1639
Hoggan, Daniel H., 459
Holley, Edward R., 1807
Hosoi, Yoshihiko, 1718
Houck, Mark H., 1912
Howard, A. William, 1743
Howie, Barbara, 1751
Hsu, R. L., 698, 706
Hsu, Sheng-Chuan, 1928
Hubert, Wayne A., 1935
Humenik, F. J., 1492
Hutchinson, Harvey L., 284
Hwang, Jing-San, 653, 1622

Ishii, Audrey L., 682
Ivarson, W. R., 277

James, L. Douglas, 203
James, William, 158, 166, 382, 667, 1098, 1452, 1710
Jaques, Robert S., 612, 620
Jenks, James S., 105
Johnson, T. J., 1081
Johnson, T. L., 412
Johnston, William R., 358
Jones, Jeanine, 863
Jones, LaDon, 1033
Jourdan, Mark R., 1

Kabir, J., 352
Kabir, Nadira, 1951
Kaden, John C., 398
Kadivar, Steve, 2082
Kangari, Roozbeh, 187
Karamouz, Mohammad, 745, 1017, 1325
Katz, Jack, 981
Kavvas, M. L., 1896
Kay, Paul A., 43, 59
Keefer, Gary B., 1639
Keyes, Conrad G., Jr., 1536, 2066
Keyes, Deborah K., 1655
Khanbilvardi, Reza M., 498, 1017, 1775
King, L. G., 352
Kirkpatrick, William R., 612
Kishel, Jeff, 2017
Knisel, W. G., 1508, 2206
Kolsky, Peter J., 1106
Koluvek, Paul K., 1123
Koncsos, L., 1590
Krider, James N., 1500
Krull, Darrell L., 2151
Ku, Henry F. H., 628
Kubo, Masafumi, 771
Kumar, Sree, 19
Kuo, Chin Y., 35

Labadie, John W., 310
Lampe, Les K., 514, 911, 2106
Lane, W. L., 1904
Laursen, E. M., 328
Lawrence, John R., 2120, 2128
Lazaro, Roeglio C., 310
Lee, Deborah, 1293
Lee, Hong Sik, 771
Leonard, R. A., 1508
Leonard, Richard P., 1003
Lettenmaier, Dennis P., 966
Letter, Joseph V., 1943

Lewis, J. M., 443
Lindblom, Karen L. C., 730
Loaiciga, Hugo A., 973
Loar, James M., 2098
Loehlein, Werner, 459
Loftis, Bruce, 806
Long, Bruce W., 514
Loucks, Daniel P., 1670
Luettich, R. A., Jr., 1590

Macaitis, Bill, 1860
McAnally, William H., 1943
MacArthur, Robert C., 227
McEnroe, Bruce M., 919, 933
MacLare, James W., 2173
McLaughlin, Richard E., 714
McLellen, Floyd, 763
Maidment, David R., 435
Mancinelli, William F., 390
Mangelson, Kenneth A., 1528, 1880
Mariño, Miguel A., 973
Mark, David, 1293
Marks, David H., 1225, 1726
Martin, Edward H., 1694
Martinec, J., 174
Massey, Dean T., 582
Mauldin, Gary V., 1065
Mays, Larry W., 1272
Maza, José Antonio, 66
Medina, Miguel A., Jr., 949
Mendoza, C., 1959
Merkel, William H., 675
Merritt, Michael L., 251
Mifflin, Martin, 51
Milhous, Robert T., 1976, 2089
Miller, Jim, 763
Millner, Francis C., 302
Mizell, Steve A., 320
Mohammad, Faris Hammoudi, 1630
Morrow, Dennis, 806
Mossbarger, W. A., Jr., 1484
Murakami, Hitoshi, 1718
Myers, Carl F., 152

Nasseri, Iraj, 1468
Navin, Stephen J., 284
Neibling, W. H., 1139
Nelson, John D., 412
Nijssen, J. P. J., 987
Nimmrichter, Peter, 1452
Nocito, Jean A., 1301
Noyes, James A., 492
Nute, W. Edward, 1460

Oaksford, Edward T., 628
Ochs, Walter J., 129

Odgaard, A. Jacob, 1686, 1928
Orban, James E., 1374
Orsborn, John F., 1951
Ossenbruggen, Paul J., 1089
Ozbilgin, Melih M., 2049

Pack, Robert T., 211
Paleologos, Evangelos, 745
Paquin, Paul R., 1309
Park, Seok S., 1647
Patamatamkul, Sanguan, 310
Paul, John F., 1301
Paxman, Scott W., 203
Peck, Hilaire W., 320
Pederson, G. J., 1468
Peibo, Wang, 2136
Peralta, Richard C., 195
Peters, John C., 459
Petersen, M. S., 328
Peterson, Michael P., 366
Pfeffer, John T., 181, 1011, 1872
Pflaum, John M., 714
Pineda, Ricardo S., 573
Pitcher, David O., 203
Pochop, L. O., 831
Prokopovich, Nikola P., 121
Pugh, Clifford A., 27

Quade, Jay, 51

Rabalais, Gary P., 374
Ramos Valdez, Cesar O., 1388
Randall, Dean, 1912
Rango, A., 174
Rao, A. Ramachandra, 1920
Reeve, Donald Arthur David, 2074
Reiser, Dudley W., 1935
Replogle, J. A., 2033
Reuter, J. E., 1992
Rice, Leonard, 817
Richardson, Jerry R., 1678
Riddell, John, 995
Riley, J. Paul, 244, 1556, 1845
Riley, Paul, 1598
Rindels, Alan J., 1041
Ritter, W. F., 1492
Rizzo, Paul C., 779
Robinson, Mark, 1710
Robison, Clarence Wm., 2189
Robledo, Luis F., 538
Roche, W. Martin, 1413
Rodriguez, Alberto, 1343
Roesner, Larry A., 941
Rogowski, Andrew S., 1775
Rosquist, Arne E., Jr., 269
Rossman, Lewis A., 1073

Rossmiller, Ronald L., 958
Rouhani, Shahrokh, 187
Ruane, R. J., 1049
Ruiz, Darlene E., 1783
Ryan, Patrick J., 427

Sabet, M. Hossein, 565
Sale, Michael J., 2098
Salek, Franklin, 1615
Samad, Mohammed, 714
San Martin, Jose, 538
Scarlatos, Panagiotis, D., 1
Schaffranck, Raymond W., 1572
Schamber, David R., 227
Schmidt, Kenneth D., 2060
Schmidt, L. Stephen, 722, 1528
Schneider, Brian J., 628
Schroeder, E. D., 1081
Scott, Owen W., 73
Scott, Swayne F., 1155
Scott-Stevens, Susan, 2114
Sears, Stewart K., 89
Seierstad, Alberta J., 1556
Shane, R. M., 1049
Sheikh, Bahman, 620
Shen, Hsieh W., 1694
Shen, Hung Tao, 1815
Shields, F. D., Jr., 1702
Shirmohammadi, A., 2206
Shoji, Kuniaki, 530
Shovlin, Marjorie G., 1791
Shuirman, G., 235
Silva, J. P., 878
Singh, Udai P., 1374
Singh, Vijay P., 1
Skaggs, R. W., 1492
Skinner, Quentin D., 1935
Slocum, Dean, 1351
Slosson, J. E., 235
Smeal, Thomas, 484
Smith, Paul, 995
Smith, Scot E., 661
Smith, W. B., 294
Snow, Gerald E., 105
Somlyody, L., 1590
Sorensen, Darwin L., 1556
Souissi, A., 328
Spoljaric, Anita, 1686
Squires, Rodney C., 358
Stannard, D. I., 847
Stauffer, Norman E., Jr., 1556
Steele, William J., 1413
Stefan, Heinz G., 730
Stephantos, Basilis, 1582
Sterling, Jerry, 763
Stevens, Michael A., 1678

Stiftel, Bruce, 754
Stirrup, Mark, 382, 1098
Strachan, William M., 637
Strand, Robert I., 858
Strecker, Eric W., 966
Strong, Mark L., 1476
Su, Yu-Chun, 1272
Sullivan, John P., Jr., 1218
Summers, Paul C., 1845

Tabios, G. Q., III, 1959
Taggart, William C., 451, 714, 1743
Takezawa, Mitsuo, 771
Talbott, Michael D., 1179
Tallarico, Anita, 754
Tang, Chi-Chung, 1872
Tanji, K. K., 1147
Tanner, B. D., 847
Tanner, Terry L., 2009
Tao, Chen Jiang, 2136
Tavangar, Jahan, 514, 1598
Theurer, F. D., 1968
Thiessen, Jacob W., 1395
Thomas, William A., 1943
Thompson, Carol B., 1655
Trout, Thomas J., 1139
Tseng, Ming T., 785
Tung, Yeou-Koung, 1280
Tuor, Nancy R., 1374
Turjoman, Abdul-Mannan, 1403
Twogood, D. A., 598, 878

Uber, James G., 1011
Uchrin, Christopher G., 981, 1647
Unal, Ali, 166
UWRRC Design Storm Task Com-
    mittee, 925

v. Orden, R. G. J., 987
Vassilakis, Rita E., 1309
Vaux, P. D., 1992
Vellinga, P., 987
Velon, John P., 1734
Vershel, Amy R., 1544
Vinson, Michael D., 451
Voigt, Richard L., Jr., 730

Wagner, Philip L., 105
Wakao, Tomomi, 530
Walker, Henry A., 1301
Walker, William R., 1516
Waller, Bradley G., 97, 97, 897
Walski, Thomas M., 467
Wang, R. Y., 706
Wang, Sam S. Y., 870
Wang, Wen C., 1428

Wardwell, Robert, 1351
Warner, Curtis Q., 294
Weaver, H. L., 847
Weeks, E. P., 847
Wei, Wenqiu, 690
Wei-Min, Zheng, 2136
Weiss, Linda S., 682
Wesche, Thomas A., 1935
West, Mary H., 227
Weston, Aaron, 203
White, David B., 89
White, Sam C., 374
Wieczorek, Gerald F., 219
Willis, Robert, 1033
Wilson, George E., 344, 420
Wright, Jeff R., 1912
Wu, Chian Min, 645

Yaksich, Stephen M., 1003
Yapa, Poojitha D., 1815
Yen, C. L., 706
Yin, S. C. L., 1476
Yoakum, D., 235
Yost, R. W., 1484
Younkin, Larry M., 675
Yu, G. H., 1920
Yu, Yun-Sheng, 1343

Zavala, Anastasio Lopez, 524
Zeman, L. John, 1767
Zipparro, V. J., 277